Sears List of Subject Headings

Sears List

of

Subject

Headings

16th Edition

Edited by

JOSEPH MILLER

New York • Dublin

The H. W. Wilson Company

1997

Printed in the United States of America

00 99 98 97   5 4 3 2 1

ISBN 0-8242-0920-6

Contents

Preface

For over seven decades the *Sears List of Subject Headings* has served the needs of small and medium-sized libraries, suggesting headings appropriate for use in their collections and providing patterns and instructions for adding new headings as they are required. The successive editors of the List have faced the need to accommodate change while maintaining a sound continuity. The new and revised headings in each edition reflect developments in the world and in the use of the English language, while the changes in the form of the headings and in the structure and display of the List reflect shifts in the prevailing philosophy of subject cataloging.

A major revision in this sixteenth edition of the *Sears List* is in updating the suggested classification numbers to conform to the usage of the new thirteenth edition of the *Abridged Dewey Decimal Classification*. Even in a time when many libraries use centralized sources and vendors for their cataloging, it is clear that many librarians still depend upon the suggested numbers in *Sears* for direction in classifying parts of their collections. In the online environment the value of classification as a tool for retrieval has been greatly enhanced and complements rather than duplicates the function of subject headings. Both the *Abridged Dewey* and the *Sears List* are especially tailored to the cataloging needs of small libraries.

Also in this edition the suggested subdivisions found throughout the List have been carefully re-evaluated and revised according to the latest thinking on subdivisions and their application. These revisions are reflected in the List of Commonly Used Subdivisions found on p xli. For every commonly used subdivision there is now an entry point in the List and a general reference note with instructions on the application of that subdivision.

The headings in the field of religion have been extensively reviewed in this edition in an attempt to reduce their exclusively Christian application and make them more useful for cataloging materials on other religions. This was done more by revising the scope and reference structure of the headings than by changing the headings themselves. New headings and new subdivisions for the field of religion have also been added.

History and Scope

Minnie Earl Sears prepared the first edition of this work in response to demands for a list of subject headings that was better suited to the needs of the small library than the existing American Library Association and Library of Congress lists. Published in 1923, the *List of Subject Headings for Small Libraries* was based on the headings used by nine small libraries that were known to be well cataloged. Minnie Sears used only *See* and "refer from" references in the first edition. In the second edition (1926) she added *See also* references at the request of teachers of cataloging who were using the List as a textbook. To make the List more useful for that purpose, she wrote a chapter on "Practical Suggestions for the Beginner in Subject Heading Work" for the third edition (1933).

Isabel Stevenson Monro edited the fourth (1939) and fifth (1944) editions. A new feature of the fourth edition was the inclusion of Dewey Decimal Classification numbers as applied in the *Standard Catalog for Public Libraries*. The new subjects added to the List were based on those used in the Standard Catalog Series and on the catalog cards issued by The H.W. Wilson Company. Consequently, the original subtitle "Compiled from Lists used in Nine Representative Small Libraries" was dropped.

The sixth (1950), seventh (1954), and eighth (1959) editions were prepared by Bertha M. Frick. In recognition of the pioneering and fundamental contributions made by Minnie Sears the title was changed to *Sears List of Subject Headings* with the sixth edition. Since the List was being used by medium-sized libraries as well as small ones, the phrase "for Small Libraries" was deleted from the title. The symbols *x* and *xx* were substituted for the "Refer from (see ref.)" and "Refer from (see also ref.)" phrases to conform to the format adopted by the Library of Congress.

The ninth edition (1965), the first of four to be prepared by Barbara M. Westby, continued the policies of the earlier editions, with the one major exception that the Dewey Decimal Classification numbers were dropped. Many users of Sears had expressed the concern that the inclusion of numbers led to a misuse of the publication owing to a misunderstanding of the relationship between subject headings and classification. The tenth edition (1972) also omitted the Dewey numbers, but they were reintroduced in the eleventh edition (1977), largely in response to the needs of librarians in many small libraries who had been left with little or no assistance in the classification of their collections. Also with the eleventh edition, the "Practical Suggestions for the Beginner in Subject Heading Work" was retitled "Principles of the Sears List of Subject Headings" to emphasize "principles," and a section dealing with nonbook materials was added.

The thirteenth edition (1986), prepared by Carmen Rovira and Caroline Reyes, was the first to be created as an online database and to take advantage of computer validation capabilities. It also responded to changing theory in subject analysis occasioned by the development of online public access catalogs. This effort was taken further in the fourteenth edition (1991) under the editorship of Martha T. Mooney, who reduced the number of compound terms, simplified many subdivisions, and advanced the work of uninverting inverted headings.

In accord with a suggestion of the Cataloging of Children's Materials Committee of the American Library Association, many of the headings from *Subject Headings for Children's Literature* (Library of Congress) were incorporated into the Sears List with the thirteenth edition. Since the Sears List is intended for both adult and juvenile collections, wherever the Library of Congress has two different headings for adult and juvenile approaches to a single subject, a choice of a single term was made for Sears. In cases where the Sears List uses the adult form, the cataloger of children's materials may prefer to use the juvenile form found in *Subject Headings for Children's Literature.*

With the fifteenth edition (1994), edited by Joseph Miller, the interval between publication of editions was shortened to provide more timely updating of terminology. In keeping with prevailing thinking in the field of library and information science, all remaining inverted headings were canceled in favor of the uninverted form. Likewise, the display of the List on the page was changed to conform to the NISO standards for thesauri approved in 1993. While Sears remains a list of subject headings and not a true thesausus, it uses the labels BT, NT, RT, SA, and UF for broader terms, narrower terms, related terms, See Also, and Used for.

Other new features in the fifteenth edition were a list of canceled and replacement headings to facilitate the updating of catalogs; the use of the legend "[Former heading]" within the List to identify earlier forms of headings; and a new emphasis, in the "Principles of the Sears List" and in the rewording of the general reference notes, on the expandable nature of the List.

Also in the fifteenth edition many headings were added to enhance subject and genre access to individual works of fiction, poetry, drama, and other imaginative works, such as films and radio and television programs, based on the *Guidelines on Subject Access to Individual Works of Fiction, Drama, etc.* prepared by a subcommittee of the Subject Analysis Committee of the ALA.

Addition of New Headings

The new terms in the present edition represent developments in many different areas, especially computers, personal relations, politics, and popular culture. Among the new headings in the field of technology are **Computer simulation, Hypertext, HTML (Document markup language), Multimedia systems,** and **World Wide Web.** Among the new headings in other fields are **Big bang theory, Body image, Bombings, Forest conservation, Luminescence, Militia movements, Physical fitness centers, Sibling rivalry,** and **Stereotype (Psychology).**

Many of the headings new to this edition were suggested by librarians representing various sizes and types of libraries, by commercial vendors of bibliographic records, and by the catalogers and indexers at The H.W. Wilson Company who are responsible for the headings in the Standard Catalog Series, *Book Review Digest,* and such periodical indexes as *Readers' Guide to Periodical Literature.* In addition, *Library of Congress Subject Headings* was consulted.

No list can possibly provide a heading for every idea, object, process, or relationship. What Sears hopes to offer is a basic list that incorporates patterns and examples that will guide the cataloger in adding new headings as needed. Sources for establishing the wording of new headings are discussed in the Principles of the Sears List.

Revision of Headings

At the same time as new headings are added to the List, revision and updating of existing headings continues. Some terms have been changed to reflect current usage; for example, **Prehistoric peoples** replaces **Prehistoric man; Manic-depressive illness** replaces **Manic-depressive psychoses; Home schooling** replaces **Home instruction;** and **Mutual funds** replaces **Investment trusts.** In some cases a single heading has been split into two. For example, **Economic assistance** has been replaced by **Foreign aid** and **Domestic economic assistance,** and **Free trade and protection** is replaced by **Free trade** and **Protectionism.** In many instances subdivisions that were once used under geographic names are now established as headings that may be subdivided geographically. For example; **Civil defense, Constitutional law, Constitutional history, Executive departments, Occupations, Public buildings,** and **Public works** are now all subdivided geographically and are no longer used as subdivisions under geographic headings.

In the field of religion and theology an attempt was made to reduce the exclusively Christian application of certain headings without changing the form of the headings themselves. For example, **Doctrinal theology,** which previously stood for Christian doctrine, is now applicable to materials on any kind of doctrinal or systematic theology. New headings have been added for **Christianity—Doctrines** and **Judaism—Doctrines,** and further headings may be added as needed based on the same pattern. Libraries with religion collections devoted exclusively or almost exclusively to Christian materials still have the option of using the broader term **Doctrinal theology** for any or all doctrinal theology. In other cases the headings have been revised. **Fundamentalism,** for example, which formerly meant Christian fundamentalism, is now replaced by three headings: **Religious fundamentalism, Christian fundamentalism,** and **Islamic fundamentalism,** and further headings may be added as needed.

As in previous editions, certain headings of decreasing interest and some unnecessary examples have been deleted from the List, such as **Aeroponics, Cattle—Diseases,** and **Dominicans (Religious Order).** Such headings are not invalid and may be maintained in the catalog. Other headings that have been deleted are no longer valid and are now used as cross references to other headings. These references appear in Sears in the alphabetic listing and also in the List of Canceled and Replacement Headings on p xlvii.

Form of Headings

It was the policy of Minnie Earl Sears to use the Library of Congress form of subject headings with some modifications, chiefly the simplification of phrasing. The Sears List still reflects the usage of the Library of Congress unless there is some compelling reason to vary, but those instances of variation have become numerous over the years. A major variation is that in Sears the direct form of entry has replaced the inverted form, on the theory that most library users search for multiple-word terms in the order in which they occur naturally in the language. The only exceptions are the names of battles and massacres and **State, The,** which remain in the inverted form. In all cases cross references have been made from the inverted form and from the Library of Congress form where it otherwise varies.

Expandability of the List

It is only by being flexible and expandable that Sears has been able over the years to fill the needs of various kinds of libraries. The degree or level of specificity required for a collection depends on its size, its function, its nature, and the group of users it serves. Practicality rather than theory should determine the degree of specificity, and a balanced blend of theory and practice has been the philosophy of Sears. In a small collection the use of too many specific headings can result in the scattering of like materials. Over 500 places are indicated in the Sears List where headings of greater specificity may be added by the cataloger as needed.

The use of subdivisions also creates greater specificity. The Sears List has two ways of suggesting suitable subdivisions for terms. The first is a list of seven "Key" headings for which numerous subdivisions are provided. These are intended as patterns for subdividing similar terms whenever the quantity of materials warrants. The list of "Key" headings is found on p xl. The second is a "List of Commonly Used Subdivisions," found on p xli. All of the subdivisions that appear in the "List of Commonly Used Subdivisions" also appear in the alphabetical list as general references, with instructions and examples of how they can be applied to various subjects. The general references, which are attached both to subject headings and to the entries for free-floating subdivisions, increase considerably the coverage of the List and its usefulness. All the general reference notes now contain the words "to be added as needed" to emphasize the expandable nature of the List and to remind the cataloger that headings for types of things and examples of things can always be added to the List.

Scope Notes

The number of scope notes, which are intended either to clarify the use of a term or to distinguish between terms, has once more been increased in this edition. Scope notes have also been added to identify any headings that may be assigned to individual works of drama, fiction, poetry, etc.

Classification

The classification numbers in this edition of Sears are taken from the thirteenth edition of the *Abridged Dewey Decimal Classification*. The alphabetic notation of B for biographical materials is occasionally provided in addition to Dewey classification numbers for the benefit of libraries using such notation in shelving these materials. In most cases only one number is assigned to a subject heading. There are instances, however, when a given subject is susceptible to more than one point of view, and one number is consequently inadequate for the subject heading. In the example **Chemical industry 338.4; 660,** the numbers represent possible classification numbers for materials dealing with the chemical industry from the viewpoints of economics and technology respectively. Classification numbers are not assigned to some very general subject headings, such as **Charters, Exhibitions, Gifts, Hallmarks, Identification,** and **National characteristics,** which cannot be classified unless a specific application is identified.

Few of the Dewey numbers are carried out more than four places beyond the decimal point. Except for libraries with large collections, where more detailed numbers may be required, the numbers in this edition of Sears should be adequate. The need for more detailed classification can often be satisfied by the addition of form and geographic subdivisions, as given in the Dewey tables. To demonstrate the building of these numbers, the Dewey number has been carried out when an example of a form or geographic subdivision is provided in the List; for example, **Antiques—United States** is given the Dewey number **745.10973.** A library preferring broad classification might elect to use the number found at the unsubdivided **Antiques,** that is, **745.1.** Libraries for whom even relatively brief numbers are too long should consult the discussion of close and broad classification in the introduction to the Dewey volume.

Style, Filing, Etc.

For spelling and definition the editor consulted *Webster's Third New International Dictionary of the English Language, Unabridged* (1961) and *Webster's Tenth New Collegiate Dictionary* (1993). *Random House Unabridged Dictionary,* 2nd ed., newly revised and updated (1993), was used for technical terms and some other terms not present in either Webster's. Capitalization and the forms of corporate and geographic names used as examples are based on the *Anglo-American Cataloguing Rules,* 2nd ed., 1988 revision. The filing of entries follows the *ALA Filing Rules* (1980).

Every term in the List that may be used as a subject heading is printed in boldface type whether it is a main term; a term in a USE reference; a broader, narrower, or related term; or an example in a scope note or general reference. If a term is not printed in boldface type, it is not used as a heading. Earlier forms of revised headings and terms that were once subject headings and are no longer, are found after the UF (used for) label with the legend "[Former heading]."

Acknowledgments

The editor wishes to acknowledge with gratitude the contributions to this edition of the individual catalogers, reference librarians, and vendors of cataloging services who have offered suggestions for headings to be added to the List. The Cataloging of Children's Materials Committee of the American Library Association has also been an important source of advice.

Thanks are extended to the editors and catalogers of The H.W. Wilson Company; to Patricia Kuhr, Editor, Subject Authority Files, for her assistance in formulating subjects; to Martha T. Mooney, Editor of *Book Review Digest,* who edited the fourteenth edition of the Sears List, for her help and encouragement; and to Ann Case, Associate Director of Indexing Services.

The classification numbers have been reproduced from the *Abridged Dewey Decimal Classification Edition 13,* to be published in 1997, by permission of OCLC Forest Press, a division of OCLC Online Computer Library Center, owner of copyright. We extend special thanks to the editors of the *Dewey Decimal Classification* for providing information and advice on the application of Dewey numbers.

Every edition of the Sears List represents the work of many hands, especially those of the previous editors over the years. The contributions of the users of the List have also been invaluable. Every comment, suggestion, question, or request from a user represents an opportunity for improvement and is greatly valued.

J. Miller

Principles of the Sears List of Subject Headings

Certain principles and practices of subject cataloging should be understood before an attempt is made to assign subject headings to library materials. The discussion that follows makes reference to the Sears List of Subject Headings, but the principles are applicable to other lists of subject headings as well.

PURPOSE OF SUBJECT CATALOGING

The purpose of subject cataloging is to list under one uniform word or phrase all of the materials on a given subject that a library has in its collection. A subject is the topic treated in a book, videotape, or other work. A subject heading is the word or phrase used in the library catalog to express this topic. A subject entry is usually displayed at the top of the catalog record, above the main entry, regardless of the format of the catalog (card, book, microform, or online).

Library materials are given subject entries in the catalog in order to show what information the library has on a given subject, just as author entries are made to show the works that the library has by a given author. Properly made, the subject entry is a very important supplement to the reference tools in the library because it may enable the reader or librarian to identify rapidly and surely the material needed to provide information about a topic. Subject entries are sometimes also useful in locating a particular book. Ordinarily one consults the author entry for a specific work, but if there is uncertainty about the author's name, one may find the individual item more readily by searching under subject. Smith's *Basic Mathematics* would be difficult to find quickly if one did not know the author's first name and had to consult all the entries in the catalog under Smith. What if the author's name were really spelled Smyth? In either case, the book could be discovered under the subject **Mathematics.**

A printed list of subject headings, such as the Sears List, incorporates the thought and experience of many librarians in various types of libraries. By using the List as a basis for establishing headings, the cataloger has a standard on which to rely. Consistency in both the level of specificity and the form of subject headings is attained by working from an accepted list where the choice among possible wordings has been made and recorded. By following the patterns of heading printed in the List the cataloger will also be able to add new headings that will be compatible and to establish useful cross references.

DETERMINING THE SUBJECT OF THE WORK

The first step in subject cataloging is to ascertain the true subject of the material and the purpose for which it was produced. Sometimes this is readily determined. **Butterflies** is obviously the subject of the book titled *Butterfly Book.* In others cases, the subject is not so easy to discern because it may be a complex one or the author may not express it in a manner clear to someone unfamiliar with the subject. The subject of a work cannot always be determined from the title alone, which is often uninformative or misleading, and undue dependence on it can result in error. A book entitled *Great Masters in Art* immediately suggests the subject **Artists,** but closer examination reveals the book to be about painters specifically, not artists in general. Therefore, the more exact subject is **Painters,** not **Artists.** Another illustration is "Fundamentals of Instrumentation," part 1 of a *Manual of Instrumentation.* This title may suggest a treatise on musical instruments or music, but actually it is a book about engineering instruments.

The steps to follow in determining the subject of a work are the same whether one is considering its value for a reader, classifying it, or assigning subject headings to it. In the case of a book, after reading the title page, examine the table of contents and skim the preface and introduction. Then, if the subject is still not clear, examine the text carefully and read parts of it, if necessary. For nonbook materials examine the container, the label, any accompanying guides, etc., and view or listen to the contents if possible. The cataloger will be in a position to determine the subject of the item in hand only after this preliminary examination has been made. If the meaning of a subject is not clearly understood, one should consult reference sources, not only an unabridged dictionary and general encyclopedia, but specialized reference books as well. Only when the cataloger has decided on the subject content of the work and identified it with explicit words can the Sears List be used to advantage. The cataloger's own phrasing of the subject must next be adapted to the terminology of the List. The library catalog will be more useful if the cataloger considers materials from the reader's point of view. The reader's profile depends on age, background, education, occupation, and geographical location, and takes into account the type of library—school, public, university, or special—as well. When examining a work the cataloger should ask, "If I wanted material on this subject, under what words would I look in the catalog?" Then the List is consulted to insure uniformity in choice and form of the words. Local terminology may be used as references to the words in the List. In choosing these words, that is, in assigning the proper subject headings, there are certain principles that should be followed. These are considered in the next five sections: Specific and Direct Entry; Common Usage; Uniformity; Form Headings; and Classification and Subject Headings.

SPECIFIC AND DIRECT ENTRY

The principle of specific entry is fundamental both in using and in making a modern subject catalog. The rule of specific and direct entry is to enter a work directly under the most specific term (i.e., subject heading) that accurately and precisely represents its content. This term serves as a succinct abstract of the work.

The principle of specific entry holds that a work is entered under a specific term rather than under a broader heading. If a work is about penguins, it should be entered directly under the most specific heading available, that is, **Penguins.** It should not be listed under the heading **Birds** or even under **Water birds.** If it were, a reader would have to look through many entries to find information on penguins. The principle of direct entry holds that a topic is formulated as a specific term, rather than as a subdivision of a broader heading. If the reader wants information about bridges, the direct approach is to consult the catalog under the heading **Bridges,** not under the broader subject **Engineering** subdivided by the topic *Bridges.* In other words, make direct entry under **Bridges,** not indirectly under Engineering—Bridges or Engineering—Civil Engineering—Bridges. Note that **Penguins, Bridges,** Engineering—Bridges, and Engineering—Civil engineering—Bridges are all specific headings, but only **Penguins** and **Bridges** are both specific and direct.

Having found the most specific entry that will fit the item, the cataloger should not then make a duplicate entry under a general subject heading. A work with the title *Birds of the Ocean* should not be entered under both **Birds** and **Water birds** but only under **Water birds.** To eliminate this duplication, a network of "See also" references in the catalog directs the reader from the broader subject headings to the more specific ones, e.g., "**Birds.** See also **Water birds;** and names of specific birds. . . ." In many cases the most specific entry will be a general subject. *Birds of the World* would have the subject heading **Birds.** The specific term, as can be seen, refers to the exact word or phrase that comprehends the subject content of the work. The heading should be as specific as possible for the topic it is intended to cover.

If the name of a specific subject is not found in the List, the name of the larger group to which it belongs should be consulted. For example, in assigning subject headings to a work discussing elm and ash trees, the cataloger would find neither **Elm** nor **Ash** listed. However, under the broader subject, **Trees,** the following general reference is given: "SA [see also] names of trees, e.g., **Oak**; to be added as needed, in the singular form." The cataloger thus has the authority to use the two headings, **Elm** and **Ash.** (Further directions for adding headings can be found on p xliv.)

COMMON USAGE

The word or words used to express a subject must represent common usage. In American libraries this means current American spelling and terminology: **Labor** not Labour; **Color** not Colour; **Elevators** not Lifts. In British libraries these choices would be reversed. Foreign terms such as Laissez faire are not used unless they have been incorporated into the English language. By the same token contemporary words are to be used: **Home economics** not Domestic economy. Today a more current term might be Homemaking, or Household management, but changing a heading is not always simple. Terminology evolves slowly, and in the case of **Home economics,** the term is still being used and newer usage may not have stabilized.

A general rule is to use a popular or common rather than a scientific or technical term where there is a choice. Subject headings are chosen to fit the needs of the people who are likely to use the catalog. A reader in a small public library will look under **Birds,** not Ornithology. In a scientific library Ornithology might be more appropriate. After deciding on the common name as the heading, the cataloger should make a reference from the scientific name to the form used. Such references will be discussed later.

UNIFORMITY

Another very important factor to be considered is that of uniformity. One uniform term must be selected from several synonyms, and this term must be applied consistently to all works on the topic. Materials on China, Chinaware, and Porcelain are all entered under **Porcelain.** This example also illustrates the fact that the subject heading must be inclusive and cover the topic. The heading chosen must also be unambiguous. If several meanings attach to one word, that word must be qualified: for example, **Masks (Facial); Masks (Plays);** and **Masks (Sculpture).** When variant spellings are in use, one must be selected and uniformly applied: **Sulphur** not Sulfur. A decision also must be made whether the heading is to be in the singular or plural form. The choice of singular or plural will be further discussed under "Grammar of Subject Headings" below.

Some descriptive words also carry various connotations, as with Arab, Arabian, and Arabic. It may seem inconsistent to use all three forms, but they are used consistently in the following ways: Arab relating to the people; Arabian referring to the geographical area; and Arabic for the language, script, or literature. In subject headings such words should be used consistently, with distinctions being made among ethnic, geographical, and linguistic terms.

Materials should be considered in categories. The word or phrase chosen as a subject must fit not only the item being cataloged but also apply to a group of items on the same subject. The cataloger must consider not only the one item in hand but also the other book and nonbook materials that discuss the same subject, albeit under different titles, in order to select a subject heading that will serve the entire group with relation to other groups in the catalog. In cataloging *Everybody's Cook Book* the inexperienced cataloger might think first of Cookbooks as the term that will give the best description. But there are two other works that belong in the same group: *How's and Why's of Cooking* and *Cooking for Profit.* These contain not only recipes but also other material on cooking. **Cooking** fits the three closely related items better than Cookbooks, and it also fits well with the related subject **Cooking for the sick.** Terminology for a subject must be uniform to fit many similar works.

FORM HEADINGS

In addition to the subject headings that interpret the content of various materials, there are headings of another kind, usually known as form headings, or form subject headings, that have the same appearance as topical subject headings but refer to the literary or artistic form of a work and not to its subject matter. Headings for the major literary forms, such as **Fiction, Poetry, Drama,** and **Essays,** are usually used for collections only rather than for works of an individual. For example, the form heading **Essays** is used not for works of an individual author but for collections of essays by authors of various nationalities. If the collection includes essays only by American authors, then the more specific heading **American essays** would be used. While the use of form entries for works of individual authors might be helpful, the result in most libraries is not considered to be worth the effort. The proliferation of entries is an extra cost and increases the size of the catalog unnecessarily. Materials of this type are generally classified and arranged on the shelves according to their literary forms, and the reader often has access to the shelves or to the shelf list. Ordinarily individual works of literature are remembered in association with an author, and a reader consults the author or title entry in the catalog for such works.

In recent years, however, there has been a greatly increased demand for subject and genre access to individual works of literature as well as to individual nonbook materials, such as films, videos, and sound recordings. Subject access to individual works of fiction, poetry, and drama can be expressed with the subdivisions *Fiction, Poetry,* and *Drama* attached to any appropriate subject heading from the List, for example **Slavery—United States—Fiction.** Subject access to such materials is also available in reference sources such as *Short Story Index, Play Index,* etc. Unlike the major literary forms, minor literary forms and genres such as **Fantasy fiction; Pastoral poetry; Science fiction plays;** etc., are not identifiable by the classification numbers. Libraries that want to provide access to these kinds of materials may assign the appropriate form or genre headings to individual works as well as to collections and materials about the form or genre. The matter of subject and genre access to individual literary works will be further discussed under "Language and Literature" below.

Apart from literary works themselves there are also many kinds of library materials about literary forms that require subject headings. For a work about the essay as a literary form—for example, the appreciation of the essay or how to write it—the heading **Essay** represents a true subject and not a form heading. The distinction between form headings and topical subject headings can sometimes be made by using the singular form for the topical heading and the plural for the form heading, e.g., **Short story; Short stories.** But the peculiarities of language do not always permit this. For example, the heading **English poetry** is used for a book about English poetry, but in order to show that a book is a collection of poetry by several English authors, the subdivision *Collections* is added: **English poetry—Collections.** The headings for minor literary forms and genres may be used unsubdivided both for literary works and for materials about the form or genre, but if the amount of the latter material in a library warrants, subdivisions may be used to create such headings as **Fantasy fiction—History and criticism; Fantasy fiction—Bibliography;** etc.

In addition to the literary form headings there are some other useful form headings that are determined by the general format of the material and the purpose of the work, such as **Almanacs; Encyclopedias and dictionaries;** and **Gazetteers.** These headings are customarily assigned to individual works as well as to materials about such forms.

CLASSIFICATION AND SUBJECT HEADINGS

The cataloger should recognize a fundamental difference between classification and subject headings for the dictionary catalog. In a system of classification, which determines the arrangement of works on the shelves, a work can obviously have only one class number and stand in only one place, but in a catalog entries representing the work can appear, if necessary, under more than one subject. The cataloger does not have to decide on one subject to the exclusion of all others, but can make the work accessible with entries for as many different points of entry as there are distinct subjects in the work (usually, however, not more than three). Classification is used to gather in one numerical place on the shelf works that give similar treatment to a subject. Subject headings gather in one alphabetical place in a catalog all treatments of a subject regardless of shelf location.

Theoretically there is no limit to the number of subject entries that could be made for one work, but practically an excess of entries is not only expensive but also inefficient for the user of the catalog. For many works, a single subject heading will represent the contents accurately. A book such as *Guide to the Trees* is fully and specifically covered by the subject heading **Trees.** Frequently two headings are necessary; occasionally three are required to do justice to the work. More than three should be considered very carefully. The need for more than three may be due to the cataloger's inability to identify precisely the single broader heading that would cover all the topics in the work. Similarly, a subject heading should not be assigned for a topic that comprises less than one third of a work.

The commonest practice may be stated as follows: As many as three specific subject headings in a given area may be assigned, but if a work treats of more than three, then the next larger inclusive heading is adopted and the specific headings are omitted. A work about snakes and lizards would be entered under **Snakes** and **Lizards.** If the work also included material on turtles, a third entry with the heading **Turtles** would be made for the catalog. But if the work discussed alligators and crocodiles as well, the only subject heading assigned would be **Reptiles.** As mentioned above under the principle of specific entry, it is not advisable to assign both a general heading and one of its specific aspects to the same work. The work about reptiles in the example may have discussed the snakes in somewhat more detail than the other reptiles, but **Reptiles** and **Snakes** would not both be assigned.

The cataloger is now aware of another difference between classification and subject cataloging, and one particularly significant for small libraries: classification is frequently less precise than the subject entries for the catalog. Material on floriculture in general as well as on specific kinds of garden flowers are classed together in **635.9.** A book on flower gardening, one on perennial gardening, and one on rose gardening will all three be classified in one number in a library, while in the catalog each book will have its own specific subject heading: **Flower gardening; Perennials; Roses.**

It is well to remember that books are classified by discipline, not by subject. A single subject may be dealt with in many disciplines. The Dewey classification numbers given with a heading in the Sears List are intended only to direct the cataloger to the disciplines where that subject is most likely to be discussed. They are not meant to be absolute or cover all possibilities. The cataloger must examine the book at hand and determine the discipline in which the author is writing. On the basis of that decision the cataloger classifies the book, not the subject of the book.

Subject headings are used for materials that have definite, definable subjects. There are always, however, a few works in which the subject is so indefinite that it is better not to assign a heading. Such a work might be a collection of materials produced by several individuals on a variety of topics or one person's meandering thoughts and ideas. If a cataloger cannot determine a definite subject, the reader is unlikely to find the item under a makeshift or general heading. Vague terms are a disservice to the reader. The headings

Human behavior and **Happiness** are misleading when assigned to a book titled *Appreciation,* which is a personal account of the sources of the author's pleasure in life. The book has no specific subject.

Now that certain principles of assigning subject heading are understood, the cataloger should consider the structure of subject headings.

GRAMMAR OF SUBJECT HEADINGS

Single Noun

A single noun is the ideal type of subject heading when the language supplies it. Such terms are not only the simplest in form but often the easiest to comprehend. Most of the large fields of knowledge can be expressed by single words (**Art; Agriculture; Education; Religion**) as can many specific objects (**Apple; Chairs; Pottery; Trees; Violins**). Many words, however, have synonyms from which a choice has to be made. For others there is a choice in the spelling. A further consideration is the use of the singular or plural form. For example, in the case of **Pottery,** other words that might be used are Crockery, Dishes, Earthenware, Faience, and Stoneware. In the Sears List, the term chosen is **Pottery** and references are made from the other terms. On the other hand, there are many words that have two or more quite different meanings. The word Date may mean a fruit, an historical period, or a social engagement; File may refer to an arrangement of material, to a computer document, or to a tool; Forging may mean counterfeiting or metalwork. If possible these various meanings should be formulated into headings in ways that are not ambiguous and that bring out the specific meaning of each heading. Hence Depression can mean either an economic or a mental state, but one is formulated **Depressions** and the other **Depression (Psychology).** Stress can mean either stress on materials or stress of mind, and the two headings are **Strength of materials** and **Stress (Psychology).** Notice that the ambiguous word is qualified even when the other meaning is expressed in other words. Furthermore, an ambiguous term such as Feedback should be qualified, **Feedback (Psychology),** even when the other meaning, **Feedback (Electronics),** does not exist in the catalog. Whenever identical words with different meanings are used in the catalog, both require parenthetical qualifiers, usually either a broader term or discipline of study. Lime (the singular form, as Sears stipulates for all fruits and trees) is an ambiguous term; hence **Lime (Fruit)** is created to distinguish it from **Lime (Mineral).** Since **Seals (Animals)** and **Seals (Numismatics)** are already in the List, any subject that is added to the List but uses the same word must be qualified: **Seals (Christmas, etc.)** or **Seals (Law).**

A choice must be made between the singular and plural forms of a term. The plural is the more common, but in practice both are used. Abstract ideas are usually stated in the singular. A concept or action is singular (**Theater**), whereas objects and things are plural (**Theaters**). The names of trees are stated in the singular so that they can represent either the tree or the wood or the fruit of the tree. In this case, the singular is more inclusive than the plural. In other cases, the plural will have the broader coverage (**Art; Arts**).

Compound Headings

Two nouns joined by "and" usually group together under one heading closely related materials that cannot easily be separated in concept and are usually treated together (**Bow and arrow; Cities and towns; Publishers and publishing**), or two different subjects that are treated in their relation to each other (**Aeronautics and civilization; Religion and science; Television and children**), or two subjects that are opposites but are usually discussed together (**Belief and doubt; Good and evil; Joy and sorrow**).

A problem in forming such headings is word order. There is no rule to cover all situations, although catalogers have been prone to follow the alphabetic order when there is no common usage. Whichever order is chosen, reference must be made from the opposite order.

The current trend toward simplification of subject access, influenced by the development of electronic information retrieval systems, argues for limiting compound headings when possible. Subject headings that treat the relationship between two broad subjects from the perspective of each, as with **Religion and science,** are clear exceptions to this.

Adjective with Noun

Often a specific concept is best expressed by qualifying the noun with an adjective (**American literature; Electric engineering; Tropical fish**). In the past the expression was frequently inverted (**Psychology, Religious; Art, Municipal**). The reasons for inversion were two-fold: 1) an assumption was made that the searcher would think first of the noun; or 2) the noun was placed first in order to keep all aspects of a broad subject together. In recent years these arguments have been abandoned in favor of the direct order of natural language. (A few exceptions remain, such as the names of battles and massacres, and **State, The.**) When inverted headings have been uninverted, a reference from the older inverted form is usually added if it seems useful in sending the user to the uninverted form.

Phrase Headings

Some concepts that involve two areas of knowledge can be expressed only by more or less complex phrases. These are the least satisfactory headings as they offer the greatest variation in wording, are often the longest, and may not be thought of readily by either the maker or the user of the catalog, but for many topics the English language seems to offer no more compact terminology. Examples are **Bible as literature** and **Freedom of information.**

SUBDIVISIONS

The scope of the List can be enlarged far beyond the actual headings printed through the use of subdivisions. The principle of specific entry can be achieved in some cases only by subdividing a general subject:

Birds	**Food**	**Music**
Birds—Eggs	**Food—Analysis**	**Music—Acoustics and**
Birds—Migration	**Food—Fiber content**	**physics**
Birds—Protection	**Food—Sodium content**	**Music—Theory**

Under each of the subject headings **Birds; Food;** and **Music** above, the subdivisions used are appropriate to the one heading and are not applicable to the other two. The subdivision *Analysis,* however, would be applicable to a number of other topics besides **Food,** such as **Blood; Coal; Plants;** etc. Some terms or phrases used as subdivisions are applicable to so many different topics that the subdivisions are not printed in the List under all possible headings. Some are given in their alphabetic places in the List with instructions for their use. They vary in kind and in value to an individual library and should be used at the discretion of the cataloger or according to local policy.

Subdivisions by Physical Form

Some materials present a subject not in expository or narrative form but as lists, outlines, or tables; or, graphically as maps, pictures, or filmstrips. The work may be a directory of chemists, a bibliography of children's literature, a dictionary of psychology, a collection of geological maps, or a Bible picture book. In such cases, it is important to show the user of the catalog that these works are not expository treatises on chemists, or children's literature, or psychology, or geology, or the Bible, respectively. It is equally important to be able to locate a bibliography, a dictionary, maps, or pictures directly without having to read through all the entries under the main heading. Standard terms known as "form subdivisions" are the most common subdivisions and may be used whenever appropriate. Since they show what the material is, rather than what it is about, they are as necessary for a small library as for a large one. Following are examples of form subdivisions:

Bibliography	*Gazetteers*	*Pictorial works*
Catalogs	*Handbooks, manuals, etc.*	*Portraits*
Dictionaries	*Indexes*	*Registers*
Directories	*Maps*	*Statistics*

Most of these terms may also stand alone as actual subject headings, whenever there is material about the form. Each of these terms is listed in its alphabetic place in the List with directions for its use either as a topical subject or as a form subdivision. For example:

Bibliography
    SA [See also] subjects and names of persons and places with the subdivision
        Bibliography, e.g. **Agriculture—Bibliography; Shakespeare, William, 1564-1616—Bibliography; United States—Bibliography;** etc.,
        to be added as needed.

Dictionaries
    USE **Encyclopedias and dictionaries**
        and names of languages and subjects with the subdivision *Dictionaries*,
            e.g. **English language—Dictionaries; Biography—Dictionaries;** etc.,
            to be added as needed.

Comparable statements are included under each of the other form headings. Applying these directions to the types of materials mentioned above, the headings created would be these:

Chemists—Directories	**Geology—Maps**
Children's literature—Bibliography	**Bible—Pictorial works**
Psychology—Dictionaries	

These heading-subdivision combinations are not printed in the List except for isolated examples. As the references indicate, such subdivided headings are to be created as needed.

Form subdivisions are particularly valuable under headings for the large fields of knowledge that are represented by many entries in the catalog. The cataloger must be guided by the character of an item's content, not by the title. Many works whose titles begin with such expressions as "Outline of," "Handbook of," or "Manual of" are in fact comprehensive works. For example, H. G. Wells's *Outline of History* and H. J. Rose's *Handbook of Latin Literature* are comprehensive, lengthy treatises, and to use the form subdivisions that the titles suggest would be inaccurate. Other so-titled "Outlines" or "Manuals" or "Handbooks" may prove to be bibliographies, dictionaries, or statistics of the subject.

Subdivisions That Show Special Aspects or Topics

A subject may be presented from a particular point of view. The work may be a history of the subject (the most common of the special aspects) or it may deal with the philosophy of the subject, research in the field, the laws about it, or how to study and teach it. These concepts applied to general subjects are expressed by such headings as the following:

Education—History	**Radio—Law and legislation**
Religion—Philosophy	**Mathematics—Study and teaching**
Aeronautics—Research	

Subdivisions That Show Chronology

In any catalog, large or small, there will be many works on American history. If they are all entered under the general heading, the library user must look through many entries to find a specific era. However, with chronological subdivisions corresponding to generally accepted periods of a country's history or to the spans of time most frequently treated in materials, a search can be narrowed to **United States—History—1945-1953,** etc. If a chronological era has been given a specific name, this is included in the heading with dates. The current trend is to use dates rather than names. This facilitates filing both in the manual and machine modes. In fact, the computer needs very explicit instructions in order to create a chronological file if it must ignore a word or phrase preceding a date. Therefore, the Subject Analysis Committee of the American Library Association has recommended that dates precede phrases, as in **United States—History— 1775-1783, Revolution.** It has recommended further that century subdivisions be defined to insure correct numerical filing position, that 19th century, for example, be expressed as **1800-1899 (19th century);** and that indefinite subdivisions be written as filed, that To 1500, for example, be expressed as **0-1500.** These recommendations were adopted in the twelfth edition of Sears.

The List includes chronological subdivisions only for those countries about whose history a library is apt to acquire so many works (United States, Great Britain, France, Germany, Italy and a few others) that it is necessary to separate them into groups according to the period treated, or for contemporary events that have produced a considerable amount of literature, for example, **Lebanon—History—1982-1984, Israeli intervention.** Although some countries have a longer history than any of these, period subdivisions are not needed if the library acquires little material about them. In such cases all the materials, regardless of the period treated, would be assigned the general heading, e.g., **India—History.** Libraries that have larger than ordinary collections in the history of a particular country or region will want to establish period subdivisions and with them subdivide the material further than is spelled out in the Sears List.

Some of the topical and form subdivisions that are applicable to a considerable number of subjects are listed in their alphabetic places in the List and are also gathered together in the "List of Commonly Used Subdivisions" on p xli. Chronological subdivisions, however, are different for each country and so cannot be listed in one place. For these the cataloger may wish to consult *LC Period Subdivisions under Names of Places.*

Subdivisions That Show Place

Subdivision by names of places is discussed below under "Geographic Names: Subjects Subdivided by Place."

GEOGRAPHIC NAMES

Many works limit the discussion of an otherwise general subject to a specific country, state, city, or region. This is such a common practice that the List has provided directions for many subjects that may be so treated. Other subjects not so identified can be subdivided by the cataloger if this is needed or is desirable. Suggested reference sources to be used in researching and establishing geographic names are the most current editions of *The Columbia-Lippincott Gazetteer of the World, National Geographic Atlas of the World, Statesman's Year-book, Times Atlas of the World,* and *Merriam-Webster's Geographical Dictionary.*

Subjects Subdivided by Place

Various subject headings, especially in the fields of science, technology, and economics, are followed by a parenthetic statement giving permission to subdivide the heading geographically, such as **"Agriculture (May subdiv. geog.)."** In application this means that if the work in hand deals with agriculture in general, only the heading **Agriculture** is used;

but if it deals with agriculture in Iowa or in France, for example, then the cataloger may assign the heading **Agriculture—Iowa** or **Agriculture—France.** The unit used as a subdivision may be the name of a country, state, city, or other political or geographic area, depending on the nature of the subject and its treatment in the work.

Observe that the parenthetic note is permissive, not mandatory. If the library has only a few works on a subject for which geographic treatment is suggested, perhaps it would be easier for the user of the catalog to find these under the main heading without geographic subdivision. Some small libraries limit the use of geographic subdivision to countries other than the United States and to nationalities other than American since most of their material will be concerned with the United States. Furthermore, if a library prefers geographic subdivisions for subjects that are not so indicated in Sears, the library should feel free to add them.

Some subjects, such as art and music, have general references that read: "SA [See also] art of particular countries or regions, e.g. **French art.**" For these headings the geographic qualification is conveyed by a modifying adjective rather than by a subdivision. The Sears List historically has never distinguished between French art or Art in France (which is not necessarily French). Should a library have sufficient material to warrant such a distinction, **Art—France** could be established in addition to **French art,** which is suggested, and the art of particular countries could also be subdivided by other countries, e.g., **Italian art—Great Britain.** One of the fundamentals of cataloging is to use one's judgment based on the materials at hand and the purpose and needs of the library.

Geographic subdivisions can be either direct or indirect. The Sears List prefers direct subdivision as the most useful to the reader. In the direct form the name of the place discussed in the work is used as the subdivision, e.g., **Theater—Paris (France)** or **Hospitals—Chicago (Ill.).** The indirect form of subdivision interposes the name of the country or state (the larger geographic area) between the subject and the smaller area that is covered in the work, e.g., Theater—France—Paris and Hospitals—Illinois—Chicago.

Names of Places Subdivided by Subject

A different procedure is followed for most topics in the fields of history, geography, and politics, which are treated from a regional point of view. In works discussing the history of California, a census of Peru, the government of Italy, the boundaries of Bolivia, the population of Paris, or the climate of Alaska, the area treated is the unique factor and its name with the appropriate topical subdivision is the most specific heading for the work. Directions for formulating such headings are given under appropriate subjects, for example:

Census
> SA [See also] names of countries, cities, etc., with the subdivision *Census,* to be added as needed.

The SA label introduces a direction to the cataloger to formulate headings as needed for specific areas, and the example, which appears in the NT [narrower term] field under **Census,** is **United States—Census.** Similar directions appear under **Boundaries; Climate; Population;** etc., which, applied to the works cited above, would result in the following headings:

California—History	**Bolivia—Boundaries**
Peru—Census	**Paris (France)—Population**
Italy—Politics and government	**Alaska—Climate**

Some topical subdivisions may be used under the name of any country, state, city, or other area. Some topics are applicable to countries only (e.g., *Commercial policy*). Instructions for applications are explicit, for example, "Foreign relations. USE names of countries with the subdivision *Foreign relations,* e.g. **United States—Foreign relations;** to be added as needed."

A list of suggested subject subdivisions that may be used under the name of any city is given in the List under **Chicago (Ill.);** those that may be used under the name of any state are listed under **Ohio;** and those that may be used under the name of any country or region, except for chronological subdivisions, are given under **United States.** Since each country's history is unique, the period subdivisions for its history are also unique.

Local materials are an exception to these rules for establishing headings for geographic names. If the library wishes to keep community area materials together, then the discussion regarding subjects subdivided by place can be ignored, and all materials entered under the name of the locality with all aspects as subdivisions.

Note that there are no definite rules on whether to subdivide by place or by subject. In general, subject headings in the fields of science, technology, economics, education, and the arts are subdivided by place, while aspects of history, geography, and politics are subdivisions under place. In many of the social sciences, the aspect of the subject that is more important or has the primary focus is the criterion for decision. A work on social life and customs, for example, is likely to be about the social life and customs of a particular place, e.g., **United States—Social life and customs. Single parent family,** on the other hand, is a subject of general interest and is only secondarily about single parent families in a particular place. (Even though it is not subdivided by place in Sears, **Single parent family** may nonetheless be subdivided geographically if the material in a given library warrants.)

In summary, the cataloger should enter under place and subdivide by subject those topics whose predominant interest is focused on an area or political entity, such as history, geography, or government. One should enter under subject and subdivide by place those topics that are primarily of interest for the subject matter regardless of place. In the social sciences the decision must be made in each instance on the element of predominance, because no general rule applies.

Some headings in the subject areas of biography, language, and literature require subdivisions relevant to their areas, but others do not. Since knowing when not to subdivide is as important as when to use subdivisions, these areas are treated in some detail below.

BIOGRAPHY

Works in the field of biography fall into two categories: those in which biography as a form of writing is discussed, a relatively small class covered adequately by the subject heading **Biography as a literary form,** and lives of persons, a very large class that must be considered in two groups—individual biography and collective biography.

Individual Biography

Usually the only subject heading needed for the life of an individual is the name of the person, established in the same way as an author entry. If the work is an autobiography, some catalogers do not make a subject entry for it since the author and the subject are the same. However, since readers have been trained to look under subject entries it seems reasonable to make both an author and a subject heading, especially if there are many other entries as author, if there are subject entries by other authors, or if the library has a divided catalog.

Occasionally a biography will include so much material about the field in which the individual was working that a second subject heading is required in addition to the personal name. A life of Mary Baker Eddy, for example, may include a valuable account of the development of Christian Science that would require the subject heading, **Christian Science—History.** It must be emphasized that such additional subject headings should be used only when there is a substantial amount of material included in addition to the subject's personal life. They are not used simply because the biographee was prominent in the field. It is not customary practice to categorize an individual biographee by race, sex, occupation, etc. with the subdivision *Biography*. Headings such as **African American musicians—Biography** or **Women politicians—Biography** are ordinarily assigned only to collective biographies. Some libraries, however, may feel the need of this kind of access to individual biographies as well. Otherwise, a general reference to names of individuals could be made in the catalog under the heading for a class, for example: "Artists. See also names of individual artists." A third option is a specific reference to individual names.

There are a few individuals about whom a large amount of material exists that is other than biographical, such as works about their writings or other activities. In such cases, subdivisions are added to the person's name to specify various aspects treated, among them *Biography*. Two such examples are Jesus Christ and William Shakespeare. The List includes these names with subdivisions appropriate to material written about them. The subdivisions listed under Shakespeare may also be used, if needed, under the names of other individuals about whom there is a large amount of varied literature. Subdivisions listed under **Presidents—United States** are to be used where appropriate under the name of any president, or other ruler, if applicable. It must be noted that this represents the exceptional, not the usual, treatment. For most individual biographies only the name is needed.

Collective Biography

Collective biographies are works containing biographies of more than three persons. If there are no more than three, each subject is given a heading consisting of the person's name, as in individual biography. (Some catalogers will treat even larger collections as a group of individual biographies. If they do this, they are analyzing the work, i.e., they are making analytic entries.) There are several varieties of collective biography, each requiring a separate kind of treatment.

General. Collective biographies not limited to any area or to any class of persons are assigned the heading **Biography.** Sometimes the work includes many individuals, such as *International Who's Who;* sometimes a small group, such as *Biographies of Famous Men and Women.*

Local Biography. Very common are the biographies devoted to persons of a particular area, such as *Who's Who in Asia, Who's Who in the Arab World, Dictionary of American Biography, Eminent Californians, Leaders in London;* or to ethnic groups, such as *Who's Who among Hispanic Americans.* In such works the subject heading is the name of the area or ethnic group with the subdivision *Biography:*

Asia—Biography	**California—Biography**
Arab countries—Biography	**London (England)—Biography**
United States—Biography	**Hispanic Americans—Biography**

If there are many entries under any such heading, the literary works (i.e., those designed for continuous reading) may be separated from the reference works, which list a large number of names in alphabetical order, by adding to the heading for the latter the subdivision *Dictionaries.* The heading for such a work as *Who's Who in America* may be, therefore, **United States—Biography—Dictionaries.**

Classes of Persons. Collective biographies that are devoted to lives of persons of a particular occupation or profession are entered under the term applied to its members, such as **Artists; Authors; Engineers; Librarians; Musicians; Poets; Radiologists; Scientists;** etc., with the subdivision *Biography*. In a field where there is no adequate term to express its members, or when the name of the class or group refers to the subject in general, not to individuals, the heading used for the specific field is subdivided by the term *Biography:*

Catholic Church—Biography   **United States—History—1861-1865,**
Religions—Biography   **Civil War—Biography**
                                             Women—Biography

A subject is usually broader in scope than a single category of persons associated with that subject. For example, **Baseball—Biography** is broader than **Baseball players— Biography** and would be more suitable for a collective biography that includes managers, owners of teams, and other persons associated with the sport.

LANGUAGE AND LITERATURE

Language and literature are closely related, but they differ considerably in their treatment in the catalog. In both fields the major interest is not in the general treatment but in the national aspect, that is, French language, English literature, German grammar, or Italian drama, but the fields differ in the way particular aspects or forms are expressed.

Language

The subject heading for a general work about a specific language is the direct phrase: **English language; French language; German language.** If the work deals with a particular aspect or form of that language, a term representing the aspect or form is used as a subdivision of the name of the language:

English language—Etymology   **German language—Grammar**
French language—Dictionaries   **Spanish language—Terms and phrases**

Many of the general form and topical subdivisions discussed previously will also be needed under names of languages, for example, **Italian language—History.** Names of some languages are included in the List (and others are to be added as needed), but customarily no subdivisions are listed except under **English language.** This serves as a guide or "Key" to the subdivisions that may be used under the name of any language.

Literature

The field of literature includes two classes of material that must be distinguished carefully: (1) works about literature, a relatively small group; and (2) examples of literature, that is, the literature itself, a very large group. In the first we are dealing with actual subjects; in the second with literary forms, not subjects.

Works about Literature. The subject headings for works about the various literary forms are their specific names, e.g., **Drama; Essay; Fiction; Poetry.** Works about the major literary forms of national literatures are entered under the direct phrase, e.g., **Irish drama; Italian poetry; Russian fiction.** Specific aspects or forms are expressed by subdivisions, as for other subjects; e.g., **Drama—Technique; English literature— Dictionaries; Short story—Congresses; American literature—History and criticism.** It should be noted that the subdivision *History and criticism* is always used in its entirety and corresponds to the subdivision *History* used with subjects other than literature, motion pictures, or music.

Names of some national literatures are included in the List (and others are to be added as needed), but a suggested list of subdivisions appears only under **English literature,** which thus serves as the "Key" to subdivisions that may be used under the name of any national literature. Likewise, subject headings for works about the major literary forms may be formulated for any national literature by substituting its name for the word "English."

Examples of Literature, i.e., Belles Lettres. Items containing literary works themselves are of two types: those of individual authors and collections of several authors. These two types of items are treated differently in subject cataloging.

Individual Authors. In general, the literary works of individual authors receive no subject entry. Literature is best known by author and title, and readers usually want a specific novel or play, or poetry by a specific author—material that can be located in the catalog by author and title entries.

There are, however, many libraries where access by subject and genre to individual works of imaginative literature is thought desirable. Subject access is provided by using any applicable subject heading from the List with the subdivision *Fiction, Drama,* or *Poetry.* Hence a novel about the clergy could be assigned the heading **Clergy—Fiction;** a play in which Napoleon is a character could be assigned the heading **Napoleon I, Emperor of the French, 1769-1821—Drama;** and a single poem or volume of poems by a single author all on the theme of baseball could be assigned the heading **Baseball—Poetry.** This is the most common way of providing subject access to individual works. Personal and corporate names can always be added to the List in order to be used with the subdivisions *Fiction, Drama,* and *Poetry* to provide subject access to individual literary works that deal with real persons or corporate entities. Subjects can also be added to the List for this purpose, but it is not useful to devise very specific categories to describe the characters or situations of individual literary works. The purpose of subject headings is to draw similar works together rather than to describe each one individually.

Headings describing the major genres of literature, e.g., **Drama; Essays; Fiction;** and **Poetry;** and the headings describing the major genres of a national literature, e.g., **Irish drama; American essays; Russian fiction;** and **Italian poetry,** are never assigned to an individual work or to a collection by a single author. The genre and national origin of such a work are expressed in the classification. Headings for more specific forms and sub-genres, however, such as **Fantasy fiction; Epic poetry;** and **Science fiction plays,** which are not expressed in the classification, can be applied to individual works, to collections by one or several authors, or to materials about such works or about the form or sub-genre. In the Sears List these headings are identified in the scope notes as applicable to individual works as well as to material about the topic. If there is no scope note indicating that a literature heading can be applied to an individual work, it can be assumed that it is not intended to be so applied. This policy is in accordance with the *Guidelines on Subject Access to Individual Works of Fiction, Drama, etc.* prepared by the Subcommittee on Subject Access to Individual Works of Fiction, Drama, etc., of the ALA Subject Analysis Committee (ALA, 1990). It varies from the usage of the Library of Congress *Subject Cataloging Manual* in that it allows form and genre as well as subject access to certain kinds of literary works that are often requested in libraries.

Collections of Several Authors. Collections consisting of works of several authors are usually entered in the catalog under the title of the collection. Therefore, as an aid to their location in the catalog, these materials are given a heading that represents the form of literature included in the collection. Since such headings are used also for topical treatment of the subject, distinction must be made between the subject headings for works about a particular literary form and the form headings for collections of literature in a particular literary form. The singular form is used as a topical subject heading. If it has an acceptable plural, this can be used to represent the form heading for collections, but if there is no true plural then the subdivision *Collections* is added to the name of the literary form:

Topical Heading	*Form Heading for Collections*
Essay	**Essays; American essays; etc.**
Parody	**Parodies**
Short story	**Short stories**
Drama	**Drama—Collections**
French drama	**French drama—Collections**
Fiction	**Fiction—Collections**
Russian fiction	**Russian fiction—Collections**
Literature	**Literature—Collections**
German literature	**German literature—Collections**
Poetry	**Poetry—Collections**
Japanese poetry	**Japanese poetry—Collections**

Minor literary forms, such as ballads, fables, fairy tales, parodies, satire, sermons, and short stories, can also be given national adjectives, e.g., **American satire.** These headings are used not only for collections by several authors but also for works of individual authors and for works about such forms. Sub-genres, such as **Fantasy fiction** or **Epic poetry,** can likewise be used for individual works, collections, or works about the sub-genre, but they are not ordinarily given national adjectives. If the number of books for any of these form and genre headings is large, the heading may be subdivided to separate the works about them from the literature itself, e.g., **English satire—History and criticism.** They can also be subdivided as needed by any other subdivisions found under **English literature,** e.g., **Fantasy fiction—Bibliography.**

In concluding this discussion on subdivision, another fact should be noted: a subdivided subject can be further subdivided, more than once if necessary. As seen in an example above, **United States—Biography—Dictionaries** was the subject for *Who's Who in America.* For a bibliography of the history of education in the United States, the heading would be **Education—United States—History—Bibliography.** The general pattern of order for multiple subdivisions under topical headings is normally topic—place—chronology—form, although considerable variation exists. The use of multiple subdivisions is not the same thing as indirect entry, where the last element alone is the true subject. A subject heading and its subdivisions taken together constitute a single subject as specific as needed for the work being cataloged.

NONBOOK MATERIALS

The assignment of subject headings for audiovisual and special instructional materials should follow the same principles that are applied to books. The heading most specifically describing the contents of the material should be used, and the same headings should be applied to book and nonbook materials alike. This is especially important if the catalog integrates all media. An integrated catalog brings all materials on one subject together regardless of format. In the thirteenth edition of the List many of the subjects and subdivisions that included the word "book" were changed to make them applicable to all materials. Among the exceptions remaining are the subject **School yearbooks** and the subdivision *Handbooks, manuals, etc.*

Because nonbook materials often concentrate on very small aspects of larger subjects, the cataloger may not find in the List the specific heading that should be used. In such instances the cataloger should be generous in adding new subjects (see p xxxvi). There are many form and genre headings that apply equally to nonbook materials and to books about such materials, e.g., **Biographical films, Comedy television programs;** and **Science fiction comic books, strips, etc.**

Subject headings for nonbook materials should not include form subdivisions to describe physical format, i.e., motion pictures, slides, sound recordings, music, etc. Some libraries may choose to maintain a separate catalog for each format; others may choose to list all materials in an integrated or omnimedia catalog. For libraries using omnimedia catalogs, AACR2 provides the option of using general materials designations (GMD), which are placed at the end of the title proper and alert users to the general class to which an item belongs. The appropriate GMD is selected from either the North American list or the British list. Additional information on this aspect of descriptive cataloging can be found in the *Anglo-American Cataloguing Rules,* 2nd edition, 1988 revision, supplemented by *1993 Amendments,* and in the ALA's *Guidelines for Bibliographic Description of Interactive Multimedia.*

TERMINOLOGY

The subject headings for established fields of knowledge and for concrete objects are simple to comprehend, but terms for new or abstract ideas may offer some difficulty. By looking through the broader, narrower, and related terms under a given heading, or noting the UF [Used for] references to it, a cataloger may often determine how the term is used.

Sometimes two or more terms may seem to cover the same subject, unless the exact meaning and limitations of each is appreciated. Many headings in the List are accompanied by a scope note explaining their application as an aid to differentiating among related subjects. For example, the headings **Alcoholism; Drinking of alcoholic beverages; Liquor industry; Prohibition; Temperance** overlap to a certain degree, but because of distinctions in their definition one should not assign all of them for any one work. By means of the scope notes included with these terms, it is understood that **Alcoholism** is used for medical materials, including works on drunkenness; **Drinking of alcoholic beverages** for works on drinking in its social aspects and as a social problem; **Liquor industry** for works on the liquor industry and trade; **Prohibition** for works dealing with the legal prohibition of liquor traffic and liquor manufacture; and **Temperance** for general works on the virtue of temperance and on the temperance movement.

A cataloger must consult the library's own catalog in order to see how a subject heading has been used. Other available databases and catalogs such as the *Cumulative Book Index* and the "Standard Catalog Series" are also of value in determining what kind of works are included under a given subject. Other cataloging aids are the *American Book Publishing Record, Subject Guide to Books in Print,* and the *National Union Catalog: Books.* The *Readers' Guide to Periodical Literature* and other indexes are also useful. Aid in interpreting the scope and meaning of a subject heading may also be obtained by looking up its classification number in the *Dewey Decimal Classification.* There the topic can be studied in its relation to other topics, a development usually impossible to see directly in an alphabetic arrangement.

Each cataloger will have individual problems in the interpretation of subject headings. Whenever a decision has been made on the scope of a term about which there has been doubt, a definition or explanation should be recorded for future use. Such notes may be helpful to users of the catalog as well as to the cataloger. Whenever it is felt that such a note, either taken from the List or devised by the cataloger, would be of general value, it may be entered in the catalog preceding the entries under the subject heading.

REFERENCES

After an item has been assigned a subject heading, attention must be directed to insuring that the reader who is searching for this material will not fail to find it because of insufficient references to the proper heading. References direct the user from terms not used as headings to the term that is used, and from broader and related topics to the heading chosen to represent a given subject. The information needed to make these references is given in the List.

The Sears List uses the symbols found in most thesauri to label the terms associated with a heading. The List remains an alphabetical subject heading list and not a true thesaurus, but the thesaurus format is useful nonetheless in helping the cataloger to distinguish relationships among terms and to establish appropriate references in the public catalog based upon these relationships. Below is a sample heading from the List followed by an explanation of the labels and a summary of the types, methods of formulation, and use of references derived from the various terms listed under a heading.

Instrumental music   784
UF   Music, Instrumental
SA   Types of instrumental music, to be added as needed
BT   **Music**
NT   **Band music**
     Chamber music
     Guitar music
     Orchestral music
     Organ music
     Piano music
RT   **Musical instruments**

Specific "See" References

The UF label stands for "Used for" and designates those unpreferred terms or phrases for which the subject heading is used instead. Tracings from these unpreferred terms are absolutely essential to the success of a catalog. The reader must be directed from variant spellings and terminology to the one word or phrase that has been selected to represent the subject. Such unpreferred terms might include the following:

(1) synonyms or terms so nearly synonymous that they would cover the same material. For example, **Instructional materials centers** requires a reference from School media centers.

(2) the second part of compound headings. For example, **Desertion and nonsupport** requires a reference from Nonsupport.

(3) the inverted form of a heading, when the noun is preceded by an adjective. For example, **Adult education** requires a reference from Education, Adult.

(4) variant spellings. For example, **Color** requires a reference from Colour.

(5) the opposite of a term, when it is included in the meaning of a term without being specifically mentioned. For example, **Temperance** requires a reference from Intemperance.

(6) the singular of a plural term, when the two forms would not file together in the catalog. For example, **Mice** requires a reference from Mouse, and **Cats** requires a reference from Cat. (Note the long list of headings between Cat and **Cats.**)

The term following the UF label in the **Instrumental music** example above indicates that a reference exists in the "M" section of the List as follows:

Music, Instrumental
     USE   **Instrumental music**

In the public catalog this becomes a specific "See" reference, as follows:

Music, Instrumental
     See   **Instrumental music**

When the heading **Instrumental music** is assigned for the first time to a work in the collection, this See reference will be entered in the catalog. It will be entered only once, no matter how many times the heading **Instrumental music** is assigned, and the term "Music, Instrumental" is not to be assigned as a heading.

Specific "See also" references

Following the BT label is a term that is broader in application than the main heading term. As a rule, a term has only one broader term, unless the term is an example or aspect of two or more things. For example **Collies** has only one broader term **Dogs,** not **Dogs** and **Mammals. Dogs,** however, has two broader terms: **Mammals** and **Domestic animals.** Both terms are broader than **Dogs** by only one level of specificity.

The broader term serves two functions in the List. The first is to aid the cataloger in finding the best term to assign to a work. If the work being cataloged is about instrumental music but also about various other forms of music, the cataloger would realize that **Instrumental music** is too narrow and assign the broader term **Music** to the work.

The second function is to indicate where specific "See also" references should be made. In the public catalog a "See also" reference is made from a broader term to a narrower term, but not from a narrower term to a broader term. When the heading **Instrumental music** is assigned for the first time to a work in the collection, a reference is made at **Music** "See also **Instrumental music.**" If **Music** has never been assigned to a work in the collection, it is entered in the catalog and the reference "See also **Instrumental music**" is made.

Following the NT label are terms that are narrower than the main heading. If a work about **Instrumental music** is really about guitar and piano only, the cataloger will know to forgo the term **Instrumental music** in favor of the two more specific headings **Guitar music** and **Piano music.** As a rule, the narrower terms listed after the NT label are narrower than the main term by only one level of specificity. Hence, **Science** has the narrower term **Mathematics; Mathematics** has the narrower term **Arithmetic;** and **Arithmetic** has the narrower term **Mental arithmetic.**

In the public catalog "See also" references are made from a main term to its narrower terms only when the narrower term is assigned for the first time to a work in the collection. A reference at **Instrumental music** "See also **Chamber music**" would be considered a blind reference if there were no work in the collection assigned the heading **Chamber music.** Blind references are to be avoided.

Following the RT label are terms related to the main term, on similar or associated subjects. Related terms are of more or less equal specificity, neither broader nor narrower. The term **Instrumental music** is related to **Musical instruments.** Each term has the other as a related term in its listing because a cataloger or user may easily look first to one term only to realize that the other is the more precise term for the material being cataloged or being sought. In the public catalog references between related terms are reciprocal. When the term **Instrumental music** is assigned for the first time to a work in the collection, a reference is made at **Musical instruments** "See also **Instrumental music.**" If **Musical instruments** has never been assigned to a work in the collection, it is entered in the catalog with the reference to **Instrumental music.** If **Musical instruments** has been assigned to a work in the collection, and only if it has been assigned, is the reference made at **Instrumental music** "See also **Musical instruments.**"

In displaying references to related terms in the public catalog, only knowledge of the library's collection can determine what references should be made. For example, a work that discusses both wages and prices will be assigned the headings **Wages** and **Prices.** Because **Wages** and **Prices** are given as related terms, the List suggests the reference at **Wages** "See also **Prices,** " but this reference should not be made if the only material that is found in the catalog under **Prices** is the same work that is already listed under **Wages.**

General References

The SA stands for "See also" and introduces a "General Reference," not to a specific heading but to a general group or category of things that may be established as needed.

In the example of **Instrumental music** given above, the SA label introduces the general reference to "types of instrumental music, to be added as needed." This is a reminder to the cataloger not to be limited to the examples of types of instrumental music given in the List. In the List there happen to be six types of instrumental music which appear in the NT field under **Instrumental music,** but if the library acquires a work devoted to harpsichord music, which does not appear in the List, it only makes sense for the cataloger to establish a heading **Harpsichord music** and make references to and from it similar to those for the other kinds of instrumental music.

Following are the most common types of headings to which general references are made, along with an example of each:

(1) Common names of various members of a class

Flowers
SA types of flowers, e.g. **Roses;** to be added as needed

(2) Names of individual persons, etc.

Scientists
SA types of scientists and names of individual scientists, to be added as needed

(3) Names of particular institutions, buildings, societies, etc.

Church buildings
SA names of individual churches, e.g. **Westminster Abbey;** to be added as needed

Labor unions
SA types of unions and names of individual labor unions, to be added as needed

(4) Names of particular geographic features

Mountains
SA names of mountain ranges and of individual mountains, to be added as needed

(5) Names of places subdivided by subject

Population
SA names of countries, cities, etc., with the subdivision *Population,* to be added as needed

(6) Subjects followed by form subdivisions

Indexes
SA subjects with the subdivision *Indexes,* e.g. **Newspapers—Indexes; Short stories—Indexes; English literature—Indexes;** etc., to be added as needed

(7) Subjects with national adjectives

Historians
SA historians of particular countries, e.g. **American historians;** to be added as needed

There are two alternative ways of displaying general references in a public catalog. One way is to specify after "See also" only those narrower terms not covered by the general reference and follow these specific terms with a formulation of the general reference from the List (omitting, of course, the words "to be added as needed," which are addressed only to the cataloger). In the List the entry for **Planets** appears as follows:

> **Planets   523.4**
>> SA names of planets, e.g. **Saturn (Planet);** to be added as needed
>> BT **Astronomy**
>>   **Solar system**
>> NT **Earth**
>>   **Life on other planets**
>>   **Mars (Planet)**
>>   **Saturn (Planet)**
>> RT **Asteroids**

The display in the catalog would read as follows:

> **Planets**
>> *See also*
>>> **Asteroids**
>>> **Life on other planets**
>>> and names of planets

A second way of displaying the same information is to expand the general reference and specify after "See also" all the narrower and related terms that have been assigned to works in the collection, whether those terms were from the List or added as needed. For the example **Planets,** given that all the terms had been assigned to works in the collection, and that a heading had been added for **Venus (Planet),** an expanded general reference would read as follows:

> **Planets**
>> *See also*
>>> **Asteroids**
>>> **Earth**
>>> **Life on other planets**
>>> **Mars (Planet)**
>>> **Saturn (Planet)**
>>> **Venus (Planet)**

The directions and scope notes printed in the List for the guidance of the cataloger should be modified for the catalog if the cataloger feels that a note is needed for the public. Following is an example of a rewording:

As it appears in the List for the cataloger:

> **Skeleton   573.7;611**
>> Use for materials limited to the morphology or mechanics of the skeleton, human or animal. Comprehensive and systematic materials on the anatomy of bones are entered under **Bones.**

As it appears in the catalog for the reader:

> **Skeleton**
>> Here are listed materials limited to the morphology or mechanics of the skeleton, human or animal.
>>
>> Comprehensive and systematic materials on the anatomy of bones are entered under **Bones.**

NEW TERMINOLOGY FOR EXISTING SUBJECTS

The English language is evolving constantly so that from time to time new terms appear for subjects that are not new. As a result, many headings have had to be changed over the lifetime of the Sears List: **Child welfare** was formerly *Children—Charities, protection, etc.;* **Radio advertising** originated as *Radio broadcasting—Business applications;* and **Space shuttles** replaced *Space vehicles, Reusable.*

It is impossible for subject headings to reflect all the newest usage, particularly in fields whose terminology fluctuates frequently. A term that is current today may soon be superceded by another, or a term considered passé may return to favor. But at least new terms can be represented in the catalog by *See* references to the heading used.

If a heading is found to be incorrect or obsolete, or suddenly assumes a pejorative or biased connotation, action must be taken. New ideas in information science also prompt changes in the form of headings, as from inverted to direct word order. The adoption of a revised term means changing not only the various references to and from it but all the bibliographic records in which it appears as well. If replacement of a term is desirable but the number of bibliographic records to be revised is prohibitive, providing a history note can accomplish one's purpose. Using one of the aforementioned examples, the cataloger might make the following kind of entry, substituting the calendar year in which the change occurs for (date):

Space vehicles, Reusable

    For materials issued after (date) consult the following heading

Space shuttles

Space shuttles

    For materials issued before (date) consult the following heading

Space vehicles, Reusable

These references could also assume the following format for a card catalog. A guide card that protrudes above the other cards in the tray is more readily seen by the user.

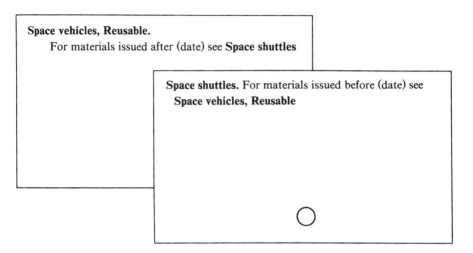

NEW SUBJECTS

No printed list of subject headings can be entirely up to date. There are constantly new ideas, new inventions, or new countries being created. The Sears List is not meant to be complete or final. New subjects, when it is determined that they are in fact new subjects and not just varying terminology for old subjects, should be added to the List by the cataloger as needed. New subject headings and the associated references should be constructed in the same way as other subject headings already in the List: with synonymous terms that the heading is used for; with broader, narrower, and related terms; and with *See* and *See also* references in the public catalog. Guides for the wording of new headings may be found in the works themselves as well as in periodical literature and indexes. Although daily newspaper terminology may be too colloquial for use as headings, it does provide a clue to the way in which a user may ask for materials, and also suggests terms to be used as cross references. Periodical indexes, such as *Readers' Guide to Periodical Literature, Applied Science & Technology Index,* etc., are especially helpful since their editors must assign subject headings to material as soon as it appears in the periodical literature. As the new subject develops and more periodical articles appear, some change in the heading may be made in succeeding issues of the index. By the time a book is written about the subject, the terminology may have stabilized. At this stage, bibliographies and review sources that suggest subject headings for the materials they cover are valuable aids. The Library of Congress issues *LC Subject Headings Weekly List* on its World Wide Web site and includes new "subject headings of current interest" in its quarterly *Cataloging Service Bulletin.* Library of Congress cataloging information, including subject headings, that emanates from the Cataloging in Publication (CIP) program is available in various online databases and is also printed in books whose publishers cooperate in the program.

It is not always possible to decide at once on the permanent form for a new subject heading, but the cataloger cannot wait for the subject to develop before giving headings to new material. Tentative headings can be assigned and used until the terminology becomes standardized. A list of these tentative headings should be kept (it will never be long) so that they can be reconsidered later and either adopted permanently or changed, as the case may be, and added to the List. One must be sure, of course, that the new term is not merely a new name or a colloquialism for a subject already in the catalog.

RECORDING HEADINGS AND REFERENCES

The cataloger should keep a record of subject headings used and references made for them. This may be kept on cards, as an electronic file, or by "checking" a copy of the Sears List. Additions to the List should be entered and references should be recorded as needed. Detailed directions for checking, adding, and canceling headings in a copy of the List and a sample page illustrating them will be found on pp xliv-xlv.

BIBLIOGRAPHY

The bibliography that follows lists those works that were the basis of the original version of the "Principles of the Sears List of Subject Headings" together with more recent scholarship in the field of subject cataloging.

Akers, Susan Grey. *Akers' Simple Library Cataloging.* 7th ed. Completely revised and rewritten by Arthur Curley and Jana Varlejs. Metuchen, N.J.: Scarecrow Press, 1984. (Chapter 2)

American Library Association. Filing Committee. *ALA Filing Rules.* Chicago: American Library Association, 1980.

Association for Library Collections and Technical Services. Subject Analysis Committee. *Guidelines on Subject Access to Individual Works of Fiction, Drama, etc.* Chicago: American Library Association, 1990.

Bakewell, K. G. B. *A Manual on Cataloging Practice.* New York: Pergamon Press, 1972. (Chapter 5)

Chan, Lois Mai. *Cataloging and Classification: an Introduction.* 2nd ed. New York: McGraw-Hill, 1994.

Chan, Lois Mai. *Library of Congress Subject Headings: Principles and Application.* 3rd ed. Littleton, Colo.: Libraries Unlimited, 1995.

Clack, Doris H. *Authority Control: Principles, Applications, and Instructions.* Chicago: American Library Association, 1990.

Coates, Eric. *Subject Catalogues: Headings and Structure.* repr. with new preface. London: Library Association, 1988.

Congress of Librarians (1991: St. John's University). *Cataloging Heresy: Challenging the Standard Bibliographic Product.* Edited by Bella Hass Weinberg. Medford, N.J.: Learned Information, 1992.

Dewey, Harry. *An Introduction to Library Cataloging and Classification.* 4th ed. rev. and enl. Madison, Wis.: Capital Press, 1957. (Chapters 10-13 and 15)

Dewey, Melvil. *Abridged Dewey Decimal Classification and Relative Index.* 13th ed. Edited by Joan S. Mitchell, et al. Albany, N.Y.: Forest Press, 1997. In press.

Dunkin, Paul S. *Cataloging U. S. A.* Chicago: American Library Association, 1969. (Chapter 5)

Eaton, Thelma. *Cataloging and Classification: an Introductory Manual.* 4th ed. Ann Arbor, Mich.: Edwards Brothers, 1967. (Chapters 5-6)

Ferl, Terry Ellen, and Larry Millsap. *Subject Cataloging: a How-to-do-it Workbook.* New York: Neal-Schuman, 1991.

Foskett, A. C. *The Subject Approach to Information.* 5th ed. London: Library Association Pub., 1996.

Haykin, David Judson. *Subject Headings: a Practical Guide.* Washington: U.S. Government Printing Office, 1951. Reprint. New York: Gordon Press, 1978.

Hennepin County Library (Minn.) *Unreal!: Hennepin County Library Subject Headings for Fictional Characters and Places.* 2nd ed. Jefferson, N.C.: McFarland & Co., 1992.

Interactive Multimedia Guidelines Review Task Force. *Guidelines for Bibliographic Description of Interactive Multimedia.* Chicago: American Library Association, 1994.

Intner, Sheila S., and Jean Riddle Weihs. *Standard Cataloging for School and Public Libraries.* 2nd ed. Englewood, Colo.: Libraries Unlimited, 1996.

Lancaster, F. W. *Vocabulary Control for Information Retrieval.* 2nd ed. Arlington, Va.: Information Resources Press, 1986.

Library Literature: an Index to Library and Information Science. New York: The H. W. Wilson Co., 1921-

Library of Congress. Office for Subject Cataloging Policy. *LC Period Subdivisions under Names of Places.* 5th ed. Washington, D.C.: Library of Congress, 1994.

Library of Congress. Cataloging Policy and Support Office. *Subject Cataloging Manual: Subject Headings.* 5th ed. Washington, D.C.: Library of Congress, 1996-

Lighthall, Lynne. *Sears List of Subject Headings: Canadian Companion.* 5th ed. New York: The H. W. Wilson Co., 1995.

Manheimer, Martha L. *Manheimer's Cataloging and Classification: a Workbook.* 3rd ed. Revised and expanded by Jerry D. Saye with Desretta V. McAllister-Harper. New York: Dekker, 1991.

Mann, Margaret. *Introduction to Cataloging and the Classification of Books.* 2nd ed. Chicago: American Library Association, 1943. (Chapters 9-10)

Miksa, Francis L. *The Subject in the Dictionary Catalog from Cutter to the Present.* Chicago: American Library Association, 1983.

Miller, Rosalind E., and Jane C. Terwillegar. *Commonsense Cataloging: a Cataloger's Manual.* 4th ed. rev. New York: The H. W. Wilson Co., 1990. (Chapters 7-9)

Milstead, Jessica L. *Subject Access Systems: Alternatives in Design.* San Diego: Academic Press, 1984.

Studwell, William E., and David V. Loertscher. *Cataloging Books. A Workbook of Examples.* Englewood, Colo.: Libraries Unlimited, 1989.

Tauber, Maurice Falcolm. *Technical Services in Libraries; Acquisitions, Cataloging, Classification, Binding, Photographic Reproduction, and Circulation Operations.* New York: Columbia University Press, 1954. (Chapters 10-11)

Taylor, Arlene G. *Cataloging with Copy: a Decision-Maker's Handbook.* 2nd ed. Englewood, Colo.: Libraries Unlimited, 1988. (pp. 135-169)

Theory of Subject Analysis: a Sourcebook. Edited by Lois Mai Chan, Phyllis A. Richmond, and Elaine Svenonius. Englewood, Colo.: Libraries Unlimited, 1985.

Wynar, Bohdan S. *Introduction to Cataloging and Classification.* 8th ed. by Arlene G. Taylor. Englewood, Colo.: Libraries Unlimited, 1992.

Headings to be Added by the Cataloger

It is neither possible nor necessary to enter all proper and common nouns in a subject heading list such as Sears. If a specific name is not included in the List, the cataloger must establish a heading for it, using available reference sources. Headings may be created for the kinds of names cited below. Note that wherever a term in the List has a general reference, the specific heading may be added even though the term in the List is not represented among the categories below. Furthermore, types of things and names of individual examples of things can always be added to the List even when there is no general reference in the List instructing the cataloger to do so. General references are given only for those terms considered most likely to represent many possible narrower terms or examples, but no attempt is made to cover all possibilities. New headings that are types or names of things are always entered as narrower terms in the NT field under the parent term.

A. PROPER NAMES
1. Names of persons
2. Names of families
3. Names of places
   a. Political units: countries, states, cities, provinces, counties, etc.
   b. Groups of states or countries: e.g. **Southern States; Baltic States;** etc.
   c. Geographic features: mountain ranges and individual mountains; island groups and individual islands; river valleys and individual rivers; regions; oceans; lakes; etc.
4. Names of nationalities
5. Names of national languages and literatures
6. Names of wars and battles
7. Names of treaties
8. Names of Indian peoples
9. Names of corporate bodies
   a. Names of associations, societies, clubs, etc.
   b. Names of institutions: colleges, libraries, hospitals, etc.
   c. Names of religious denominations
   d. Names of government bodies
   e. Names of hotels, retail stores, ships, etc.

B. COMMON NAMES
1. Names from such categories as:

animals	fruits	sports
birds	games	tools
fishes	musical	trees
flowers	instruments	vegetables
foods	nuts	

2. Names of diseases
3. Names of organs and regions of the body
4. Names of chemicals
5. Names of minerals

"Key" Headings

To enable the cataloger to see the full display of possible subdivisions that may be used with some of the most popular categories, the editor has provided certain headings in the List to serve as models or "keys." Note that the subdivisions under the "Keys" are illustrative, not exclusive.

Persons:

Presidents—United States (to illustrate subdivisions that may be used under presidents, prime ministers and other rulers)

Shakespeare, William, 1564-1616 (to illustrate subdivisions that may be used under any voluminous author)

Peoples:

Indians of North America (to illustrate subdivisions that may be used under names of peoples and linguistic families)

Places:

United States; Ohio; Chicago (Ill.) (to illustrate subdivisions—except for historical periods—under geographic names)

Languages and Literatures:

English language (to illustrate subdivisions that may be used with any language)

English literature (to illustrate subdivisions that may be used with any literature)

Wars:

World War, 1939-1945 (to illustrate subdivisions that may be used under any war or battle)

List of Commonly Used Subdivisions

To allow for a standardized formulation of many complex subjects, there are a large number of topical and form subdivisions that are generally applicable and may be used under a variety of subjects as needed. The most commonly used subdivisions are those listed under the **Key Headings** on the preceding page. The following is a list of the most common subdivisions apart from those listed under the **Key Headings,** which are not repeated here except when their application is more general than the pattern headings suggest. For each of the following subdivisions there is an alphabetical entry in the **List** describing the use of that subdivision. Other subdivisions of more limited application are provided for in the **List** at the appropriate places. Subdivisions not provided for in the **List** may also be established and used as needed.

Accidents
Accounting
Administration
Alcohol use
Analysis
Anatomy
Anecdotes
Anniversaries
Antiquities
Archives
Atlases
Attitudes
Audiovisual aids
Autographs
Automation
Awards
Behavior
Bibliography
Bio-bibliography
Biography
Books and reading
Buildings
Calendars
Care
Cartoons and caricatures
Case studies
Catalogs
Censorship
Chronology
Citizen participation
Civil rights
Claims
Classification
Collectibles

Collection and preservation
Collectors and collecting
Color
Comic books, strips, etc.
Communication systems
Competitions
Composition
Computer assisted instruction
Computer programs
Computer simulation
Concordances
Conduct of life
Congresses
Conservation and restoration
Control
Correspondence
Corrupt practices
Costs
Costume
Counseling of
Criticism
Curricula
Data processing
Death
Dental care
Description
Design
Design and construction
Designs and plans
Diaries
Dictionaries
Directories
Discography
Diseases

Diseases and pests
Documentation
Drama
Drug testing
Drug therapy
Drug use
Drying
Dwellings
Ecology
Economic aspects
Economic conditions
Editing
Education
Employees
Employment
Encyclopedias
Environmental aspects
Equipment and supplies
Estimates
Ethical aspects
Ethics
Evaluation
Evolution
Examinations
Exhibitions
Experiments
Exploration
Fiction
Filmography
Finance
Folklore
Food
Forecasting
Foreign influences
Gazetteers
Genealogy
Genetic aspects
Geographical distribution
Government policy
Growth
Guidebooks
Handbooks, manuals, etc.
Health and hygiene
Health aspects
Historiography
History
History and criticism
Housing
Humor
Identification
Indexes
Industrial applications
Influence

Information services
Intellectual life
International cooperation
Jargon
Juvenile literature
Kings and rulers
Labeling
Labor productivity
Laboratory manuals
Language
Law and legislation
Library resources
Life cycles
Life skills guides
Lighting
Literary collections
Maintenance and repair
Management
Manuscripts
Maps
Marketing
Materials
Mathematical models
Mathematics
Measurement
Medical care
Medical examinations
Mental health
Methodology
Miscellanea
Models
Monuments
Mortality
Museums
Names
Noise
Nutrition
Obituaries
Officials and employees
Origin
Outlines, syllabi, etc.
Parodies, imitations, etc.
Pensions
Periodicals
Personal finance
Personal narratives
Philosophy
Physiological aspects
Physiological effect
Physiology
Pictorial works
Planning
Poetry

Political activity
Political aspects
Portraits
Posters
Prayers
Preservation
Prevention
Prices
Problems, exercises, etc.
Production standards
Programmed instruction
Prophecies
Protection
Psychological aspects
Psychology
Public opinion
Quality control
Quotations
Rating
Rates
Recreation
Recycling
Registers
Rehabilitation
Religion
Religious aspects
Religious life
Remodeling
Repairing
Research
Reviews
Rites and ceremonies

Safety devices
Safety measures
Scholarships
Security measures
Sexual behavior
Social aspects
Social conditions
Social life and customs
Societies
Songs
Sources
Specifications
Statistics
Stories, plots, etc.
Study and teaching
Suffrage
Surgery
Tables
Taxation
Technique
Telephone directories
Terminology
Testing
Texts
Therapeutic use
Training
Transportation
Travel
Treatment
Vocational guidance
War use
Waste disposal
Wounds and injuries

Checking and Adding Headings

See Sample Page opposite

1. *Check the subject heading used.* When the subject heading **Birds** is used for the first time, the cataloger places a check mark in front of it.

2. *Make and check "See" references to the heading.* The UF terms under **Birds** are considered and the cataloger decides to make a reference from Bird and from Ornithology as suggested. Cards are made for the catalog reading: "Bird. See Birds" and "Ornithology. See Birds." The terms Bird and Ornithology are then checked in the List both in their alphabetic places and in the UF field under **Birds.**

3. *Make and check "See also" references to the heading.* The BT and RT headings given under **Birds** are examined to see whether they have been used in the catalog. The heading **Vertebrates** has a check mark beside it showing that it has been used. The cataloger decides to place a reference in the catalog reading: "Vertebrates. See also Birds." It is recorded in the List as follows:

   under **Birds,** in the BT field, **Vertebrates** is checked

   under **Vertebrates,** in the NT field, **Birds** is checked

   For purposes of this explanation, the assumption is made that **Zoology** has not yet been used.

4. *Adding headings to the List.* The library acquires material about ostriches. The term is not in the List, but the directions given in the note under **Birds** tell the cataloger that the names of specific birds may be added. **Ostriches** is written in the margin in its alphabetic place in the List and checked. If the practice is to trace all narrower terms, then the reference: "Birds. See also Ostriches" is added to the public catalog. It is recorded in the List as follows:

   under **Birds, Ostriches** is added to the NT field and checked

   under **Ostriches, Birds** is added in a BT field and checked

   The library acquires material on birds in Maine. Following the permission given with the heading **Birds,** "(May subdiv. geog.)," the cataloger uses the heading **Birds—Maine,** writing it in the margin in its alphabetic place and checking it. Since the library has very little material about this region, it is decided to make a reference for the catalog reading, "Maine—Birds. See Birds—Maine." This reference is also added in its alphabetical place in the List as "Maine—Birds. Use **Birds—Maine,**" and checked. The reference is traced under the new heading by writing "Maine—Birds" in a UF field under **Birds—Maine,** and checking it there.

5. *Canceled subjects* If all entries for a subject are withdrawn from the catalog, turn to the subject heading in the List and remove the check mark from that heading. Then examine the terms in the UF, BT, NT, and RT fields below that heading. Where those terms appear in the alphabetic list the check marks are removed unless those terms are also references to other active terms or are themselves assigned to materials contained in the library. For example, if the book on ostriches is lost or discarded, the heading **Ostriches** is canceled from the List and **Ostriches** is removed from the NT field under **Birds,** provided that there are no other books on ostriches in the library. The heading **Birds** remains checked, however, because there are other materials on birds.

Sample Page of Checking

Abbreviated entries taken from various pages of the Sears List. A check (√) indicates that the heading or reference has been used in the library's catalog. The marginal notes show how subjects may be added when needed.

√ Bird
    USE   **Birds**

√ **Birds** (May subdiv. geog.)   **598**
    UF √ Bird
         √ Ornithology
    SA   types of birds, e.g. **Birds of prey; Canaries;** etc., to be added as needed
    BT   **Animals**
        √ **Vertebrates**
    NT   **Birds of prey**
        Cage birds
        Canaries
        Ducks
        Eagles
        Game and game birds
        Geese   — √ *Ostriches*
        Peacocks
        Pheasants
        Poultry

Birds—Habits and behavior
    USE   **Birds—Behavior**

Birds in literature   **809**
    BT   **Animals in literature**
        Nature in literature

Birds—Marking   — √ *Birds—Maine*
    USE   **Birdbanding**   UF √ *Maine—Birds*

Birds—Migration   **598.156**
    UF   Migration of birds
    BT   **Animals—Migration**

Mail-order business   **658.8; 659.13**
    BT   **Business**
        Direct selling
        Selling   √ *Maine—Birds*

Mail service   USE *Birds—Maine*
    USE   **Postal service**

Mainstreaming in education   **371.9**
    BT   **Education**
        Exceptional children
        Handicapped children
    RT   **Special education**

Ornamental plants   **635.9; 715**
    UF   Plants, Ornamental *[Former heading]*
    BT   **Cultivated plants**
        Flower gardening
        Landscape gardening
    RT   **Shrubs**

√ Ornithology
    USE   **Birds**

Orphan drugs   **615**
    Use for materials on drugs that appear to be useful for the treatment of rare disorders but owing to their limited commercial value have difficulty in finding funding for research and marketing.
    UF   Drugs, Orphan
        Nonprofitable drugs
    BT   **Drugs**

Osteopathic medicine   **610; 615.5**
    Use for materials on the therapeutic system based on the theory that disease is caused by loss of a structural integrity that can be restored by manipulation of the bones and muscles.
    UF   Osteopathy *[Former heading]*
    BT   **Alternative medicine**
    NT   **Chiropractic**
    RT   **Massage**

Osteopathy
    USE   **Osteopathic medicine**

Ostrogoths   — √ *Ostriches*
    USE   **Goths**   BT √ *Birds*

√ **Vertebrates**   **596**
    BT   **Animals**
    NT   **Amphibians**
        √ **Birds**
        Fishes
        Mammals
        Reptiles

Vertical take off airplanes
    USE   **Vertically rising airplanes**

Vertically rising airplanes   **629.133**
    UF   Airplanes, Vertically rising
        V.T.O.L.'s

List of Canceled and Replacement Headings

CANCELED HEADINGS	REPLACEMENT HEADINGS
Abortion—Catholic Church	Abortion—Religious aspects—Catholic Church
Abortion—Moral and religious aspects	Abortion—Ethical aspects
	Abortion—Religious aspects
Aeronautics—Accidents	Aircraft accidents
African civilization	Africa—Civilization
Airways	Aeronautics
American civilization	America—Civilization
American economic assistance	American foreign aid
Animal food	Food of animal origin
Antarctic regions	Antarctica
Anthropogeography	Human geography
Aquanauts	Undersea research stations
	Underwater exploration
Asian civilization	Asia—Civilization
Astronautics—Accidents	Space vehicle accidents
Astronauts—Clothing	Space suits
Automobiles—Design	Automobiles—Design and construction
Automobiles—Restoration	Automobiles—Conservation and restoration
Baseball clubs	Baseball teams
Baseball stories	Baseball—Fiction
Bibliography—Editions	Editions
Bibliography—First editions	First editions
Bird houses	Birdhouses
Birds—Eggs and nests	Birds—Eggs
	Birds—Nests
Birth control—Moral and religious aspects	Birth control—Ethical aspects
	Birth control—Religious aspects
Birthrate	Birth rate
Body language	Nonverbal communication
Books and reading—Best books	Best books
Building—Contracts and specifications	Construction contracts
Carnivores	Carnivorous animals
Cataloging—Data processing	Automated cataloging
Cataloging—Music	Cataloging of music
Catholic religious orders for men	[no replacement]
Catholic religious orders for women	[no replacement]
CD-ROM	CD-ROMs
Ceramic materials	Ceramics
Challenger (Space shuttle)	Challenger (Spacecraft)
Cheese—Bacteriology	Cheese—Microbiology
Chicago (Ill.)—Civil defense	Civil defense—Chicago (Ill.)
Chicago (Ill.)—Industries	Industries—Chicago (Ill.)
Chicago (Ill.)—Manufactures	Industries—Chicago (Ill.)
Chicago (Ill.)—Occupations	Occupations—Chicago (Ill.)
Chicago (Ill.)—Public buildings	Public buildings—Chicago (Ill.)
Chicago (Ill.)—Public works	Public works—Chicago (Ill.)
Chicago (Ill.)—Suburbs and environs	Chicago Suburban Area (Ill.)
Chicago metropolitan area (Ill.)	Chicago Metropolitan Area (Ill.)
Children—Food	Children—Nutrition
Christianity—Biography	Christian biography
Christianity—Philosophy	Christian philosophy
Churches	Church buildings
Citrus fruit	Citrus fruits
Classification—Books	Books—Classification
Clones and cloning	Cloning
Compact automobiles	Compact cars
Cooking—Southern States	Southern cooking

CANCELED HEADINGS	REPLACEMENT HEADINGS
Copying processes and machines	Copying machines
	Copying processes
Cost of living	Cost and standard of living
Creation—Study and teaching	Creationism
	Evolution—Study and teaching
Crystallography	Crystals
Dancing	Dance
Down's syndrome	Down syndrome
Drug addiction	Drug abuse
Drugs and sports	Athletes—Drug use
Economic assistance	Foreign aid
	Domestic economic assistance
Economic depressions	Depressions
Education—Government policy	Education and state
Energy resources—Government policy	Energy policy
English language—Conversations and phrases	English language—Conversation and phrase books
Fertilizers and manures	Fertilizers
Firearms—Law and legislation	Gun control
Flower drying	Flowers—Drying
Flower painting and illustration	Botanical illustration
	Flowers in art
Foot—Care and hygiene	Foot—Care
Free trade and protection	Free trade
	Protectionism
French language—Conversations and phrases	French language—Conversation and phrase books
Fundamentalism	Christian fundamentalism
	Islamic fundamentalism
	Religious fundamentalism
Fundamentalism and education	Church and education
	Creationism
	Religion in the public schools
Genetic mapping	Gene mapping
Great Britain—Kings, queens, rulers, etc.	Great Britain—Kings and rulers
Greek civilization	Greece—Civilization
Home instruction	Home schooling
Human resources	Human capital
	Manpower
Human resources policy	Manpower policy
Indians of North America—Chronology	Indians of North America—History—Chronology
Indians of North America—Civilization and culture	Indians of North America
Indians of North America—Ethnology	Indians of North America
Indians of North America—Legends	Indians of North America—Folklore
Industrial insurance	Industrial life insurance
Industry	Industries
Industry—Government policy	Industrial policy
Instalment plan	Installment plan
Internet (Computer network)	Internet
Investment trusts	Mutual funds
Jewish-Christian relations	Christianity—Relations—Judaism
	Judaism—Relations—Christianity
Jewish holocaust (1933-1945)	Holocaust (1933-1945)
Jewish-Islamic relations	Islam—Relations—Judaism
	Judaism—Relations—Islam
Kings, queens, rulers, etc.	Kings and rulers
	Queens
Ku Klux Klan (1865-1876)	Ku Klux Klan
Ku Klux Klan (1915-)	Ku Klux Klan
Labor—Accidents	Industrial accidents
Left and right	Left and right (Direction)
Legal assistance to the poor	Legal aid
Librarians—Professional ethics	Librarians—Ethics

CANCELED HEADINGS	REPLACEMENT HEADINGS
Livestock	Domestic animals
	Livestock industry
Livestock—Breeding	Livestock breeding
Love (Theology)	Love—Religious aspects
Machinery in industry	Industrial equipment
	Machinery in the workplace
Man	Human beings
Manic-depressive psychoses	Manic-depressive illness
Manipulative materials	Manipulatives
Mars (Planet)—Photographs	Mars (Planet)—Pictorial works
Medicine and religion	Medicine—Religious aspects
Mental illness—Jurisprudence	Insanity defense
Mentally ill children	Emotionally disturbed children
Meteorology—Observatories	Meteorological observatories
Middle classes	Middle class
Millinery	Hats
Mineralogy	Minerals
Minicomputers	[no replacement]
Mobile home parks	Trailer parks
Modern languages—Conversations and phrases	Modern languages—Conversation and phrase books
Modernization	Modernization (Sociology)
Monasticism	Monasticism and religious orders
Moon—Photographs	Moon—Pictorial works
Mothers' pensions	Child welfare
Motion pictures—Moral and religious aspects	Motion pictures—Ethical aspects
	Motion pictures—Religious aspects
Nature study—United States	Natural history—United States
Nonliterate folk society	Primitive societies
Nonliterate man	Primitive societies
Ohio—Constitution	Constitutions—Ohio
Ohio—Constitutional history	Constitutional history—Ohio
Ohio—Executive departments	Executive departments—Ohio
Ohio—Executive departments—Reorganization	Administrative agencies—Reorganization—Ohio
Ohio—Industries	Industries—Ohio
Ohio—Occupations	Occupations—Ohio
Ohio—Public buildings	Public buildings—Ohio
Ohio—Public works	Public works—Ohio
Orange	Orange (Fruit)
Osteopathy	Osteopathic medicine
Parents' and teachers' associations	Parent-teacher associations
Pastoral work	Pastoral theology
Pearlfisheries	Pearl fisheries
Periodicity	Cycles
Pilots and pilotage	Navigation
	Ship pilots
Ping-pong	Table tennis
Pistols	Handguns
Plants—Ecology	Plant ecology
Poisonous gases—War use	Chemical warfare
Popes—Voyages and travels	Papal visits
Prehistoric man	Fossil hominids
	Prehistoric peoples
Presidents—United States—Spouses	Presidents' spouses—United States
Presidents—United States—Voyages and travels	Presidents—United States—Travel
Princes and princesses	Princes
	Princesses
Prophecies (Occultism)	Prophecies
Protests, demonstrations, etc.	Demonstrations
Railroads—Accidents	Railroad accidents
Railroads—Safety appliances	Railroads—Safety devices
Rapid reading	Speed reading

CANCELED HEADINGS	REPLACEMENT HEADINGS
Reducing	Weight loss
Regeneration (Theology)	Regeneration (Christianity)
Religions—Biography	Religious biography
Religious orders	Monasticism and religious orders
Religious orders for men	Monasticism and religious orders for men
Religious orders for women	Monasticism and religious orders for women
Robotics	Robots
Roman emperors	Emperors—Rome
Russia (Republic)	Russia (Federation)
Safety appliances	Safety devices
Salt free diet	Salt-free diet
Scholastic aptitude test	Scholastic Aptitude Test
Science—Government policy	Science and state
Sectionalism (United States)	Regionalism—United States
Shakespeare, William, 1564-1616—Criticism, interpretation, etc.	Shakespeare, William, 1564-1616—Criticism
Shakespeare, William, 1564-1616—Parodies, travesties, etc.	Shakespeare, William, 1564-1616—Parodies, imitations, etc.
Shakespeare, William, 1564-1616—Religion and ethics	Shakespeare, William, 1564-1616—Ethics
	Shakespeare, William, 1564-1616—Religion
Size and shape	Shape
	Size
Skin—Care and hygiene	Skin—Care
Soils—Bacteriology	Soil microbiology
Soils (Engineering)	Soil mechanics
Space ships	Space vehicles
Sports—Equipment and supplies	Sporting goods
Sports stories	Sports—Fiction
Standard of living	Cost and standard of living
State constitutions	Constitutions
Submarine diving	Deep diving
Substance abuse	Drug abuse
	Solvent abuse
Television in politics	Television and politics
Theory of structures	Structural analysis (Engineering)
Transplantation of organs, tissues, etc.—Moral and religious aspects	Transplantation of organs, tissues, etc.—Ethical aspects
	Transplantation of organs, tissues, etc.—Religious aspects
United States—Civil defense	Civil defense—United States
United States—Constitution	Constitutional history—United States
	Constitutional law—United States
	Constitutions—United States
United States—Constitutional history	Constitutional history—United States
United States—Constitutional law	Constitutional law—United States
United States—Diplomatic and consular service	American diplomatic and consular service
United States—Executive departments	Executive departments—United States
United States—Executive departments—Reorganization	Administrative agencies—Reorganization—United States
United States—Foreign population	Aliens—United States
	Immigrants—United States
United States—Industries	Industries—United States
United States—National security	National security—United States
United States—Neutrality	Neutrality—United States
United States—Occupations	Occupations—United States
United States—Public buildings	Public buildings—United States
United States—Public works	Public works—United States
Upper classes	Upper class
Victims of crime	Victims of crimes
Violinists, violoncellists, etc.	Violinists
	Violoncellists
Voluntarism	Volunteer work
War and religion	War—Religious aspects
Welfare work in industry	Industrial welfare

CANCELED HEADINGS	REPLACEMENT HEADINGS
World War, 1939-1945—Gas warfare	World War, 1939-1945—Chemical warfare
World War, 1939-1945—Human resources	World War, 1939-1945—Manpower
World War, 1939-1945—Moral and religious aspects	World War, 1939-1945—Ethical aspects
	World War, 1939-1945—Religious aspects
World War, 1939-1945—Protests, demonstrations, etc.	World War, 1939-1945—Protest movements
X rays	X-rays
Xerography	Photocopying
Young adults' literature	Young adult literature

Symbols Used

UF = Used for

SA = See also

BT = Broader term

NT = Narrower term

RT = Related term

[Former heading] = Term that was once used as a
   heading and is no longer

(May subdiv. geog.) = Heading that may be subdivided by name of place

See pp xxx-xxxiv for further explanation of how these symbols may be translated into cross references in the public catalog.

Sears List of Subject Headings

3-D photography
USE   **Three dimensional photogra-
       phy**
3 mile limit
USE   **Territorial waters**
3D photography
USE   **Three dimensional photogra-
       phy**
4-H clubs   630.6
UF   Boys' agricultural clubs
      Four-H clubs
      Girls' agricultural clubs
BT   **Agriculture—Societies**
      Boys' clubs
      Girls' clubs
4th of July
USE   **Fourth of July**
17 year locusts
USE   **Cicadas**
100 years' war
USE   **Hundred Years' War, 1339-
       1453**
200 mile limit
USE   **Territorial waters**
1200-1299 (13th century)
USE   **Thirteenth century**
1300-1399 (14th century)
USE   **Fourteenth century**
1400-1499 (15th century)
USE   **Fifteenth century**
1500-1599 (16th century)
USE   **Sixteenth century**
1600-1699 (17th century)
USE   **Seventeenth century**
1700-1799 (18th century)
USE   **Eighteenth century**
1800-1899 (19th century)
USE   **Nineteenth century**
1900-1999 (20th century)
USE   **Twentieth century**
2000-2099 (21st century)
USE   **Twenty-first century**

A.B.C.'s
USE   **Alphabet**
A.B.M.'s
USE   **Antimissile missiles**
A-bomb victims
USE   **Atomic bomb victims**
A.C.O.A.s
USE   **Adult children of alcoholics**
A.D.C.
USE   **Child welfare**
A.I.D.S. (Disease)
USE   **AIDS (Disease)**
A.T.V.'s
USE   **All terrain vehicles**
Abacus   513.028
BT   **Calculators**
Abandoned children   362.73
BT   **Child welfare**
      Children
RT   **Orphans**
Abandoned towns
USE   **Extinct cities**
       Ghost towns
Abandonment of family
USE   **Desertion and nonsupport**
Abbeys   271; 726
SA   names of individual abbeys, to
      be added as needed
BT   **Church architecture**
      Monasteries
NT   **Westminster Abbey**
RT   **Cathedrals**
**Abbreviations   411; 413; 421, etc.; 423,
      etc.**
UF   Contractions
      Symbols
BT   **Writing**
NT   **Acronyms**
      Code names
RT   **Ciphers**
      Shorthand
      Signs and symbols

BT = Broader Term   NT = Narrower Term   RT = Related Term   SA = See Also   UF = Used For

ABCs
USE   **Alphabet**
Abduction
USE   **Kidnapping**
Ability   153.9
    SA   types of ability, to be added as
            needed
    NT   **Creative ability**
            Executive ability
            Leadership
            Musical ability
    RT   **Success**
Ability grouping in education   371.2
    UF   Grouping by ability
    BT   **Grading and marking (Educa-
            tion)**
    NT   **Nongraded schools**
Ability—Testing   153.9; 371.26
    UF   Aptitude testing
    BT   **Educational tests and measure-
            ments**
            Intelligence tests
            Psychological tests
ABMs
USE   **Antimissile missiles**
Abnormal children
USE   **Exceptional children**
            Handicapped children
Abnormal growth
USE   **Growth disorders**
Abnormal psychology   616.89
    Use for systematic descriptions of mental
disorders. Materials on clinical aspects of
mental disorders, including therapy, are en-
tered under **Psychiatry.** Popular materials and
materials on regional or social aspects of
mental disorders are entered under **Mental ill-
ness.**
    UF   Diseases, Mental
            Mental diseases
            Pathological psychology
            Psychology, Abnormal
            Psychology, Medical
            Psychology, Pathological *[For-
                mer heading]*
            Psychopathology
            Psychopathy
    BT   **Mind and body**
            Nervous system
    NT   **Codependency**
            Compulsive behavior
            Depression (Psychology)

            Eating disorders
            Hallucinations and illusions
            Mental illness
            Mental retardation
            Multiple personality
            Neuroses
            Personality disorders
            Psychosomatic medicine
    RT   **Criminal psychology**
            Mental health
            Psychiatry
            Psychoanalysis
Abnormalities, Human
    USE   **Birth defects**
             Growth disorders
Abolition of capital punishment
    USE   **Capital punishment**
Abolition of slavery
    USE   **Abolitionists**
             Slavery
Abolitionists   326; 920
    UF   Abolition of slavery
            Antislavery
    BT   **Reformers**
    RT   **Slavery**
Abominable snowman
    USE   **Yeti**
Aborigines
    USE   **Native peoples**
Aborigines, Australian
    USE   **Australian aborigines**
Abortion   179.7; 344; 363.46; 618.8
    UF   Induced abortion
            Pregnancy, Termination of
            Termination of pregnancy
    BT   **Birth control**
Abortion—Catholic Church
    USE   **Abortion—Religious aspects—
             Catholic Church**
Abortion—Ethical aspects   179.7
    UF   Abortion—Moral and religious
               aspects *[Former heading]*
    BT   **Ethics**
    RT   **Pro-choice movement**
            Pro-life movement
Abortion—Moral and religious aspects
    USE   **Abortion—Ethical aspects**
             Abortion—Religious aspects
Abortion—Religious aspects   291.5
    May be further subdivided by religion or
sect.

BT = Broader Term   NT = Narrower Term   RT = Related Term   SA = See Also   UF = Used For

Abortion—Religious aspects—*Continued*
    UF   Abortion—Moral and religious
            aspects *[Former heading]*
    RT   **Pro-choice movement**
           Pro-life movement
Abortion—Religious aspects—Catholic
    Church   241
    UF   Abortion—Catholic Church *[For-*
            mer heading]
Abortion rights movement
    USE   **Pro-choice movement**
Abortion, Spontaneous
    USE   **Miscarriage**
Abrasives   553.6
    BT   **Ceramics**
Absence from school
    USE   **School attendance**
Absenteeism (Labor)   331.25; 658.3
    UF   Employee absenteeism
           Labor absenteeism
    BT   **Hours of labor**
           Personnel management
    RT   **Employee morale**
Absenteeism (School)
    USE   **School attendance**
Abstinence
    USE   **Fasting**
           Temperance
Abstinence, Sexual
    USE   **Sexual abstinence**
Abstract art   709.04
    UF   Art, Abstract *[Former heading]*
           Art, Geometric
           Art, Nonobjective
           Geometric art
           Nonobjective art
           Painting, Abstract
    BT   **Modern art—1900-1999 (20th**
           century)
    NT   **Cubism**
Abuse of animals
    USE   **Animal welfare**
Abuse of children
    USE   **Child abuse**
Abuse of husbands
    USE   **Husband abuse**
Abuse of medications
    USE   **Medication abuse**
Abuse of medicines
    USE   **Medication abuse**

Abuse of persons
    USE   **Offenses against the person**
Abuse of the elderly
    USE   **Elderly abuse**
Abuse of wives
    USE   **Wife abuse**
Abuse, Verbal
    USE   **Invective**
Abused aged
    USE   **Elderly abuse**
Abused children
    USE   **Child abuse**
Abused wives
    USE   **Abused women**
Abused women   362.82
    UF   Abused wives
           Battered wives
           Battered women
    BT   **Victims of crimes**
           Women
    RT   **Wife abuse**
Academic achievement   370.1; 371.2
    UF   Academic anxiety
           Academic failure
           Achievement, Academic
           Educational achievement
           Scholastic achievement
    BT   **Success**
Academic advising
    USE   **Educational counseling**
Academic anxiety
    USE   **Academic achievement**
Academic degrees   378.2
    UF   College degrees
           Degrees, Academic *[Former*
             heading]
           Doctors' degrees
           Honorary degrees
           University degrees
    BT   **Colleges and universities**
Academic dissertations
    USE   **Dissertations**
Academic failure
    USE   **Academic achievement**
Academic freedom (May subdiv. geog.)
    371.1; 378.1
    Use for materials on the freedom of teach-
    ers and students to teach, discuss, or investi-
    gate controversial subjects without penalty or
    restraint from officials, governments, or orga-
    nized groups.

BT = Broader Term   NT = Narrower Term   RT = Related Term   SA = See Also   UF = Used For

Academic freedom—*Continued*
  UF   Educational freedom
        Freedom, Academic
        Freedom of teaching
        Teaching, Freedom of
  BT   **Intellectual freedom**
        Toleration
Academic libraries   027.7
  UF   College and university libraries
        Libraries, College
        Libraries, University
        University libraries
  BT   **Libraries**
Accelerated reading
  USE   **Speed reading**
Accident insurance   368.38
  UF   Disability insurance
        Insurance, Accident *[Former
           heading]*
        Insurance, Disability
  BT   **Casualty insurance**
  NT   **Workers' compensation**
Accidents (May subdiv. geog.)   **363.1**
  UF   Emergencies
        Injuries
        Wrecks
  SA   types of accidents, e.g. **Railroad
           accidents;** subjects with the
           subdivision *Accidents,* e.g.
           **Chemical industry—Acci-
           dents; Nuclear power
           plants—Accidents;** etc.; and
           groups and classes of persons,
           animals, organs of the body,
           and plants and crops with the
           subdivision *Wounds and inju-
           ries,* e.g. **Horses—Wounds
           and injuries; Foot—Wounds
           and injuries;** to be added as
           needed
  NT   **Aircraft accidents**
        Explosions
        Fires
        Home accidents
        Industrial accidents
        Poisons and poisoning
        Railroad accidents
        Shipwrecks
        Space vehicle accidents
        Traffic accidents

        Wounds and injuries
  RT   **Disasters**
        First aid
Accidents—Prevention   363.1; 658.3
  UF   Prevention of accidents
        Safety measures
  SA   subjects with the subdivision
           Safety devices or *Safety mea-
           sures,* e.g. **Railroads—Safety
           devices; Radiation—Safety
           measures;** etc., to be added
           as needed
  NT   **Aeronautics—Safety measures**
        Radiation—Safety measures
        Railroads—Safety devices
        Safety education
        Water safety
  RT   **Safety devices**
Acclimatization
  USE   **Adaptation (Biology)**
        **Environmental influence on
           humans**
Accompaniment, Musical
  USE   **Musical accompaniment**
Accountability
  USE   **Liability (Law)**
Accountants   657.092; 920
  UF   Bookkeepers
        Certified public accountants
  RT   **Accounting**
Accounting   657
  UF   Financial accounting
  SA   types of industries, professions,
           etc., with the subdivision *Ac-
           counting,* to be added as
           needed
  BT   **Business**
        Business education
        Business mathematics
  NT   **Corporations—Accounting**
        Cost accounting
  RT   **Accountants**
        Auditing
        Bookkeeping
Accounting machines
  USE   **Calculators**
Accounts, Collecting of
  USE   **Collecting of accounts**
Accreditation (Education)   379.1
  UF   Educational accreditation

BT = Broader Term   NT = Narrower Term   RT = Related Term   SA = See Also   UF = Used For

Accreditation (Education)—*Continued*
    Schools—Accreditation
  SA   types of educational institutions
       and names of individual insti-
       tutions with the subdivision
       Accreditation, e.g. **Colleges**
       and universities—Accredita-
       tion; and subjects with the
       subdivision *Study and teach-*
       ing, for accreditation of pro-
       grams of study in those sub-
       jects, e.g. **Mathematics—**
       Study and teaching; to be
       added as needed
  BT   **Education**

Acculturation 303.48
  UF   Culture contact
  BT   **Anthropology**
       Civilization
       Culture
       Ethnology
  NT   **Ethnic relations**
       Multicultural education
       Race relations
       Socialization
  RT   **East and West**

Achievement, Academic
  USE   **Academic achievement**

Achievement tests
  USE   **Examinations**

Acid precipitation
  USE   **Acid rain**

Acid rain 363.738; 628.5
  UF   Acid precipitation
  BT   **Rain**
       Water pollution

Acids 546; 661
  SA   names of acids, to be added as
       needed
  BT   **Chemicals**
       Chemistry
  NT   **Carbolic acid**

Acne 616.5
  UF   Blackheads (Acne)
       Pimples (Acne)
  BT   **Skin—Diseases**

ACOAs
  USE   **Adult children of alcoholics**

Acoustics
  USE   **Architectural acoustics**
       Hearing
       Music—Acoustics and physics
       Sound

Acquaintance rape
  USE   **Date rape**

Acquired immune deficiency syndrome
  USE   **AIDS (Disease)**

Acquisition of corporations
  USE   **Corporate mergers and acqui-**
       sitions

Acquisitions (Libraries)
  USE   **Libraries—Acquisitions**

Acrobats and acrobatics 791.3; 796.47
  SA   types of acrobatic activities, e.g.
       Tumbling; to be added as
       needed
  BT   **Circus**
  NT   **Tumbling**
  RT   **Gymnastics**

Acronyms 411; 421, etc.
  UF   English language—Acronyms
       Initialisms
  BT   **Abbreviations**
       Code names

Acting 791.4; 792
    Use for materials on the art and technique
  of acting in any medium (stage, television,
  etc.) and on acting as a profession. Materials
  limited to the presentation of plays are entered
  under **Amateur theater** or **Theater—Produc-**
  tion and direction. Materials about members
  of the profession are entered under **Actors.**
  UF   Dramatic art
       Histrionics
       Stage
  BT   **Drama**
       Public speaking
  NT   **Mime**
       Pageants
       Pantomimes
  RT   **Actors**
       Amateur theater
       Drama in education
       Theater

Acting—Costume
  USE   **Costume**

Actions and defenses
  USE   **Litigation**

Activities curriculum
  USE   **Creative activities**

BT = Broader Term   NT = Narrower Term   RT = Related Term   SA = See Also   UF = Used For

Activity schools
USE Education—Experimental
methods
Actors   791.4; 792; 920

Use for materials on several persons of the acting profession, whether male or female. Materials on female actors that emphasize their identity as women are entered under **Actresses.** Materials on male actors that emphasize their identity as men are entered under **Men actors.**

UF Actors and actresses *[Former heading]*
Motion picture actors
Stage
Television actors
SA actors of particular countries, e.g. **American actors;** and names of individual actors, to be added as needed
BT **Celebrities**
Entertainers
NT **Actresses**
African American actors
American actors
Black actors
Comedians
Men actors
Stunt performers
RT **Acting**
Theater
Actors, African American
USE **African American actors**
Actors, American
USE **American actors**
Actors and actresses
USE **Actors**
Actors and actresses, American
USE **American actors**
Actors, Black
USE **Black actors**
Actors, Female
USE **Actresses**
Actors, Male
USE **Men actors**
Actresses   791.4; 792; 920

Use for materials on female actors that emphasize their identity as women. General materials on persons of the acting profession, whether male or female, are entered under **Actors.**

UF Actors, Female
Female actors

Women actors
BT **Actors**
Acupressure   615.8
UF Finger pressure therapy
Myotherapy
BT **Alternative medicine**
Massage
RT **Acupuncture**
Acupuncture   615.8
BT **Alternative medicine**
RT **Acupressure**
Adages
USE **Proverbs**
Adaptability (Psychology)
USE **Adjustment (Psychology)**
Adaptation (Biology)   578.4; 581.4; 591.4
UF Acclimatization
BT **Biology**
Ecology
Genetics
Variation (Biology)
NT **Environmental influence on humans**
Stress (Physiology)
Adaptation (Psychology)
USE **Adjustment (Psychology)**
Adaptations
USE **Film adaptations**
Television adaptations
and names of authors or titles of individual works entered under title with the subdivision *Adaptations* for individual works, collections, or criticism and interpretation of literary, cinematic, video, or television adaptations, e.g., **Shakespeare, William, 1564-1616—Adaptations; Beowulf—Adaptations;** etc., to be added as needed
Adaptations, Film
USE **Film adaptations**
Adaptations, Television
USE **Television adaptations**
Addiction
USE types of addiction, e.g. **Alcoholism; Drug abuse; Exercise**

Addiction—*Continued*

addiction; etc., to be added as needed

Addiction to alcohol
USE   **Alcoholism**

Addiction to drugs
USE   **Drug abuse**

Addiction to exercise
USE   **Exercise addiction**

Addiction to gambling
USE   **Compulsive gambling**

Addiction to nicotine
USE   **Tobacco habit**

Addiction to tobacco
USE   **Tobacco habit**

Addiction to work
USE   **Workaholism**

Addictive behavior
USE   **Compulsive behavior**

Addicts
USE   **Drug addicts**

Adding machines
USE   **Calculators**

Additives, Food
USE   **Food additives**

Addresses
USE   **Lectures and lecturing**
       Speeches

Adhesives   620.1; 668; 691
SA   types of adhesives, to be added as needed
BT   **Materials**
NT   **Cement**
       Glue
       Mortar

Adjustment (Psychology)   155.2
UF   Adaptability (Psychology)
       Adaptation (Psychology)
       Coping behavior
       Maladjustment (Psychology)
BT   **Psychology**

Adjustment, Social
USE   **Social adjustment**

Administration
USE   **Civil service**
       Management
       Political science
       Public administration
       State, The

and types of institutions and names of individual institutions with the subdivision *Administration,* e.g. **Libraries—Administration; Schools—Administration;** etc.; and names of countries, cities, etc., with the subdivision *Politics and government,* e.g. **United States—Politics and government;** to be added as needed

Administration of criminal justice 353.4
UF   Criminal justice, Administration of *[Former heading]*
BT   **Administration of justice**
       Criminal law
NT   **Amnesty**
       Corrections
       Crime
       Law enforcement
       Pardon
       Parole
       Police
       Prisons
       Punishment

Administration of justice   347
UF   Justice, Administration of *[Former heading]*
BT   **Law**
NT   **Administration of criminal justice**
       Due process of law
       Governmental investigations
       Impeachments
RT   **Courts**

Administrative ability
USE   **Executive ability**

Administrative agencies (May subdiv. geog.)   **351**
Use for materials on governmental bodies, such as boards, commissions, departments, etc., responsible for implementing and administering legislation.
UF   Administrative agencies—Law and legislation
       Executive agencies
       Government agencies
       Regulatory agencies

BT = Broader Term   NT = Narrower Term   RT = Related Term   SA = See Also   UF = Used For

Administrative agencies—*Continued*
    SA   names of administrative agen-
            cies, to be added as needed
    BT   **Administrative law**
            Public administration
    NT   **Executive departments**
Administrative agencies—Law and legisla-
    tion
    USE   **Administrative agencies**
Administrative agencies—Ohio—Reorgani-
    zation
    USE   **Administrative agencies—Reor-
            ganization—Ohio**
Administrative agencies—Reorganization
    (May subdiv. geog.)   **351**
    UF   Executive departments—Reorga-
            nization
            Executive reorganization
            Government reorganization
            Reorganization of administrative
            agencies
**Administrative agencies—Reorganiza-
    tion—Ohio   352.2**
    UF   Administrative agencies—Ohio—
            Reorganization
            Ohio—Executive departments—
            Reorganization *[Former head-
            ing]*
**Administrative agencies—Reorganiza-
    tion—United States   352.2**
    UF   Administrative agencies—United
            States—Reorganization
            United States—Executive depart-
            ments—Reorganization *[For-
            mer heading]*
Administrative agencies—United States—
    Reorganization
    USE   **Administrative agencies—Reor-
            ganization—United States**
Administrative law   342
    UF   Law, Administrative
    BT   **Law**
    NT   **Administrative agencies**
            Civil service
            Local government
            Ombudsman
    RT   **Constitutional law**
            Public administration
Administrators and executors
    USE   **Executors and administrators**

Admirals   359.0092; 920
    BT   **Military personnel**
            Navies
Admissions applications
    USE   **College applications**
Admissions essays
    USE   **College applications**
Adolescence   155.5; 305.235
    Use for materials on the process or the state
of growing to maturity. Materials on the time
of life between thirteen and twenty-five years,
and on people in this general age range, are
entered under **Youth.** Materials limited to teen
youth are entered under **Teenagers.** Materials
limited to people in the general age range of
eighteen through twenty-five years are entered
under **Young men** or **Young women.**
    UF   Teen age
            Teenagers—Development
    BT   **Age**
    RT   **Youth**
Adolescence—Psychology
    USE   **Adolescent psychology**
Adolescent fathers
    USE   **Teenage fathers**
Adolescent mothers
    USE   **Teenage mothers**
Adolescent pregnancy
    USE   **Teenage pregnancy**
Adolescent prostitution
    USE   **Juvenile prostitution**
Adolescent psychiatry   616.89
    UF   Psychiatry, Adolescent
            Teenagers, Psychiatry of
    BT   **Psychiatry**
Adolescent psychology   155.5
    UF   Adolescence—Psychology
            Psychology, Adolescent
            Teenagers—Psychology
    BT   **Psychology**
Adolescents
    USE   **Teenagers**
Adopted children   306.87; 362.82
    UF   Children, Adopted *[Former
            heading]*
    BT   **Adoptees**
            Children
    RT   **Adoption**
            Orphans
Adoptees   346.01; 362.73
    Use for materials on anyone formally adopt-
ed as a dependent.
    UF   Adult adoptees

Adoptees—*Continued*
    NT   **Adopted children**
    RT   **Adoption**
          Birthparents
Adoption   346.01; 362.73
    UF   Child placing
          Children—Adoption
          Children—Placing out
    BT   **Parent and child**
    NT   **Interracial adoption**
    RT   **Adopted children**
          Adoptees
          Foster home care
Adoption—Corrupt practices   364.1
    UF   Black market children
          Infants, Sale of
          Sale of infants
          Selling of infants
    BT   **Criminal law**
Adult adoptees
    USE   **Adoptees**
Adult child abuse victims   362.76
    UF   Adult survivors of child abuse
          Adults abused as children
          Child abuse survivors
          Grown-up abused children
    BT   **Victims of crimes**
    NT   **Adult child sexual abuse victims**
    RT   **Child abuse**
**Adult child sexual abuse victims
    362.76**
    UF   Adult survivors of child sexual
          abuse
          Adults sexually abused as children
    BT   **Adult child abuse victims**
    RT   **Child sexual abuse**
Adult children of alcoholics   362.292
    UF   A.C.O.A.s
          ACOAs
          Alcoholic parents
          Alcoholics' adult children
    BT   **Children of alcoholics**
          Parent and child
    RT   **Alcoholics**
          Alcoholism
Adult education   374
    UF   Education, Adult
          Education of adults

          Lifelong education
    BT   **Education**
          Higher education
          Secondary education
          University extension
    NT   **Agricultural extension work**
          Prisoners—Education
    RT   **Continuing education**
          **Evening and continuation
          schools**
Adult fiction
    USE   **Erotic fiction**
Adult films
    USE   **Erotic films**
Adult survivors of child abuse
    USE   **Adult child abuse victims**
Adult survivors of child sexual abuse
    USE   **Adult child sexual abuse vic-
          tims**
Adulteration of food
    USE   **Food adulteration and inspec-
          tion**
Adultery   176; 306.73; 363.4
    UF   Extramarital relationships
          Infidelity, Marital
          Marital infidelity
    BT   **Sexual ethics**
Adults abused as children
    USE   **Adult child abuse victims**
Adults and children
    USE   **Children and adults**
Adults, Runaway
    USE   **Runaway adults**
Adults sexually abused as children
    USE   **Adult child sexual abuse vic-
          tims**
**Adventure and adventurers   904;
          904.092; 910.4; 920**
    NT   **Escapes**
          Exploration
          Explorers
          Frontier and pioneer life
          Heroes and heroines
          Sea stories
          Seafaring life
          Shipwrecks
    RT   **Voyages and travels**
Adventure and adventurers—Fiction
    USE   **Adventure fiction**

BT = Broader Term   NT = Narrower Term   RT = Related Term   SA = See Also   UF = Used For

Adventure fiction   808.83; 813, etc.

May be used for individual works, collections, or materials about adventure fiction.

UF   Adventure and adventurers—Fiction *[Former heading]*

Adventure stories

Suspense novels

Swashbucklers

Thrillers

BT   Fiction

NT   Robinsonades

Romantic suspense novels

Science fiction

Sea stories

Spy stories

Western stories

Adventure films   791.43

May be used for individual works, collections, or materials about adventure films.

UF   Suspense films

Swashbucklers

Thrillers

BT   Motion pictures

NT   Superhero films

Western films

RT   Adventure television programs

Adventure radio programs   791.44

May be used for individual works, collections, or materials about adventure radio programs.

BT   Radio programs

NT   Superhero radio programs

Adventure stories

USE   **Adventure fiction**

Adventure television programs   791.45

May be used for individual works, collections, or materials about adventure television programs.

BT   Television programs

NT   Superhero television programs

RT   Adventure films

Advertisement writing

USE   **Advertising copy**

Advertising   659.1

May be subdivided by topic, e.g. **Advertising—Cosmetics**; to specify the thing advertised.

BT   Business

Retail trade

NT   Advertising and children

Advertising copy

Advertising layout and typography

Commercial art

Coupons (Retail trade)

Deceptive advertising

Electric signs

Fashion models

Market surveys

Newspaper advertising

Packaging

Posters

Printing—Specimens

Radio advertising

Show windows

Sign painting

Signs and signboards

Television advertising

RT   Marketing

Propaganda

Public relations

Publicity

Selling

Advertising and children   659.1

UF   Children and advertising

BT   **Advertising**

Children

Advertising art

USE   **Commercial art**

Advertising copy   659.13

UF   Advertisement writing

Copy writing

BT   **Advertising**

Authorship

Advertising—Cosmetics   659.1

UF   Cosmetics—Advertising

Advertising, Fraudulent

USE   **Deceptive advertising**

Advertising layout and typography   659.13

BT   **Advertising**

Printing

Typography

Advertising, Newspaper

USE   **Newspaper advertising**

Advertising—Newspapers   659.1

Use for materials on the advertising of newspapers. Materials on advertising in newspapers are entered under **Newspaper advertising**.

UF   Newspapers—Advertising

Advertising, Pictorial

USE   **Commercial art**

Posters

BT = Broader Term   NT = Narrower Term   RT = Related Term   SA = See Also   UF = Used For

Advertising, Radio
    USE   **Radio advertising**
Advertising, Television
    USE   **Television advertising**
Advisors
    USE   **Consultants**
Aerial bombs
    USE   **Bombs**
Aerial navigation
    USE   **Navigation (Aeronautics)**
Aerial photography   778.3
    UF   Photography, Aerial *[Former
        heading]*
    BT   **Photography**
    NT   **Remote sensing**
Aerial propellers   629.134
    UF   Airplanes—Propellers
        Propellers, Aerial *[Former head-
        ing]*
    BT   **Airplanes**
Aerial reconnaissance   355.4; 358.4
    UF   Reconnaissance, Aerial
    BT   **Military aeronautics**
        Remote sensing
Aerial rockets
    USE   **Rockets (Aeronautics)**
Aerial spraying and dusting
    USE   **Aeronautics in agriculture**
Aerobatic flying
    USE   **Stunt flying**
Aerobatics
    USE   **Stunt flying**
Aerobic dancing
    USE   **Aerobics**
Aerobic exercises
    USE   **Aerobics**
Aerobics   613.7
    UF   Aerobic dancing
        Aerobic exercises
    BT   **Exercise**
    RT   **Dance**
Aerobiology
    USE   **Air—Microbiology**
Aerodromes
    USE   **Airports**
Aerodynamics   533; 629.132
    UF   Streamlining
    BT   **Air**
        Dynamics
        Pneumatics

    NT   **Ground cushion phenomena**
        Supersonic aerodynamics
    RT   **Aeronautics**
Aerodynamics, Supersonic
    USE   **Supersonic aerodynamics**
Aeronautical instruments   629.135
    UF   Airplanes—Instruments
        Instruments, Aeronautical
    SA   types of instruments, e.g. **Gyro-
        scope;** to be added as needed
    BT   **Scientific apparatus and in-
        struments**
    NT   **Airplanes—Electric equipment**
        Gyroscope
        Instrument flying
Aeronautical sports   797.5
    SA   types of aeronautical sports, to
        be added as needed
    BT   **Aeronautics**
        Sports
    NT   **Airplane racing**
        Skydiving
Aeronautics   629.13
    Use for materials dealing collectively with various types of aircraft and for materials on the scientific or technical aspects of aircraft and their construction and operation. Materials on companies engaged in commercial aviation are entered under **Airlines.**
    UF   Air routes
        Airways *[Former heading]*
        Aviation
    SA   aeronautics in particular indus-
        tries or fields of endeavor,
        e.g. **Aeronautics in agricul-
        ture;** to be added as needed
    BT   **Engineering**
        Locomotion
    NT   **Aeronautical sports**
        Aeronautics and civilization
        Aeronautics in agriculture
        Air pilots
        Airplanes
        Airports
        Airships
        Astronautics
        Balloons
        Gliders (Aeronautics)
        Gliding and soaring
        Helicopters
        High speed aeronautics
        Kites

BT = Broader Term   NT = Narrower Term   RT = Related Term   SA = See Also   UF = Used For

Aeronautics—*Continued*

    Lasers in aeronautics
    Meteorology in aeronautics
    Military aeronautics
    Navigation (Aeronautics)
    Parachutes
    Radio in aeronautics
    Rocketry
    Rockets (Aeronautics)
    Unidentified flying objects
  RT   **Aerodynamics**
      Flight

Aeronautics—Accidents
  USE   **Aircraft accidents**

Aeronautics and civilization   306
  UF   Civilization and aeronautics
  BT   **Aeronautics**
      Civilization
  NT   **Astronautics and civilization**

Aeronautics, Commercial
  USE   **Commercial aeronautics**

Aeronautics, Commercial—Chartering
  USE   **Airlines—Chartering**

Aeronautics—Flights   387.7; 629.13
  UF   Aeronautics—Voyages
      Flights around the world
      Transatlantic flights
  BT   **Voyages and travels**
  NT   **Space flight**

Aeronautics, High speed
  USE   **High speed aeronautics**

Aeronautics in agriculture   631.3
  UF   Aerial spraying and dusting
      Airplanes in agriculture
      Crop dusting
      Crop spraying
  BT   **Aeronautics**
      Agriculture
      Spraying and dusting
  RT   **Agricultural pests**

Aeronautics—Medical aspects
  USE   **Aviation medicine**

Aeronautics, Meteorology in
  USE   **Meteorology in aeronautics**

Aeronautics, Military
  USE   **Military aeronautics**

Aeronautics, Naval
  USE   **Military aeronautics**

Aeronautics—Navigation
  USE   **Navigation (Aeronautics)**

Aeronautics—Piloting
  USE   **Airplanes—Piloting**

Aeronautics—Safety measures   387.7;
      629.134
  BT   **Accidents—Prevention**
  NT   **Air traffic control**

Aeronautics—Study and teaching
      629.1307
  UF   Flight training
  NT   **Airplanes—Piloting**

Aeronautics—Voyages
  USE   **Aeronautics—Flights**

Aeroplanes
  USE   **Airplanes**

Aerosol sniffing
  USE   **Solvent abuse**

Aerosols   541.3; 551.51; 660
  BT   **Air pollution**

Aerospace industries   338.4
  UF   Aircraft production
  BT   **Industries**
  NT   **Airplane industry**

Aerospace law
  USE   **Space law**

Aerospace medicine
  USE   **Aviation medicine**
      Space medicine

Aerothermodynamics   629.132; 629.4
  UF   Thermoaerodynamics
  BT   **Astronautics**
      High speed aeronautics
      Supersonic aerodynamics
      Thermodynamics

Aesthetics   111; 701; 801
  UF   Beauty
      Esthetics *[Former heading]*
      Taste (Aesthetics)
  SA   styles and movements in the
      arts, e.g. **Classicism; Post-**
      modernism; etc., to be added
      as needed
  BT   **Art**
      Arts
  NT   **Art appreciation**
      Classicism
      Color
      Criticism
      Modernism (Arts)
      Postmodernism
      Rhythm

BT = Broader Term   NT = Narrower Term   RT = Related Term   SA = See Also   UF = Used For

Aesthetics—*Continued*
        Romanticism
        Values
Affection
    USE   **Friendship**
               Love
Affirmative action programs   331.13;
        658.3
    BT   **Discrimination in employment**
            Personnel management
Affliction
    USE   **Joy and sorrow**
            Suffering
Affordable housing
    USE   **Housing**
Africa   960
    NT   **Africans**
            Central Africa
            East Africa
            North Africa
            Northeast Africa
            Northwest Africa
            Pan-Africanism
            South Africa
            Southern Africa
            Sub-Saharan Africa
            West Africa
Africa, Central
    USE   **Central Africa**
Africa—Civilization   306.096; 960
    UF   African civilization *[Former*
            heading]
            Civilization, African *[Former*
            heading]
    BT   **Civilization**
Africa, East
    USE   **East Africa**
Africa, Eastern
    USE   **East Africa**
Africa, French-speaking Equatorial
    USE   **French-speaking Equatorial Af-**
            rica
Africa, French-speaking West
    USE   **French-speaking West Africa**
Africa—History   960
Africa—History—1960-   960.3
Africa, North
    USE   **North Africa**
Africa, Northeast
    USE   **Northeast Africa**

Africa, Northwest
    USE   **Northwest Africa**
Africa, South
    USE   **South Africa**
Africa, Southern
    USE   **Southern Africa**
Africa—Study and teaching   960.07
    UF   African studies
    BT   **Area studies**
Africa, Sub-Saharan
    USE   **Sub-Saharan Africa**
Africa, West
    USE   **West Africa**
African American actors   791.4; 792;
        920
    UF   Actors, African American
            African American actors and ac-
            tresses
            Afro-American actors
    BT   **Actors**
            Black actors
African American actors and actresses
    USE   **African American actors**
African American art   704
    Use for materials on works of art by several
African American artists. Materials on African
Americans depicted in works of art are en-
tered under **African Americans in art.**
    UF   African Americans—Art
            Afro-American art
            Art, African American
    BT   **Art**
            Black art
    NT   **Harlem Renaissance**
    RT   **African American artists**
African American artists   709.2; 920
    Use for materials on several African Ameri-
cans artists.
    UF   Afro-American artists
            Artists, African American
    BT   **Artists**
            Black artists
    RT   **African American art**
African American athletes   796.092;
        920
    UF   Afro-American athletes
            Athletes, African American
    BT   **Athletes**
            Black athletes
African American authors   810.9; 920
    Use for materials on several African
American authors.

BT = Broader Term   NT = Narrower Term   RT = Related Term   SA = See Also   UF = Used For

African American authors—*Continued*
- UF   Afro-American authors
  - Authors, African American
- SA   particular forms of American literature with the subdivision *African American authors*, e.g. **American poetry—African American authors**; etc., to be added as needed
- BT   **Authors**
  - **Black authors**

African American business people   338.092; 658.0092; 920
- UF   Afro-American business people
  - Afro-Americans in business
  - Business people, African American
- BT   **African Americans—Employment**
  - **Black business people**
  - **Business people**

African American children   305.23
- UF   African Americans—Children
  - Afro-American children
  - Children, African American
- BT   **Black children**
  - **Children**

African American elderly   305.26
- BT   **Elderly**

African American folklore
- USE   **African Americans—Folklore**

African American librarians   020.92; 920
- UF   Afro-American librarians
  - Librarians, African American
- BT   **Black librarians**
  - **Librarians**

African American literature
- USE   **American literature—African American authors**

African American men   305.38
- UF   Afro-American men
  - Men, African American
- BT   **Men**

African American music (May subdiv. geog.)   780.089

Use for materials on the music of African Americans. Materials on the music of Blacks not limited to the United States are entered under **Black music.**
- UF   African American songs

African Americans—Music
- Afro-American music
- Afro-American songs
- Music, African American
- Songs, African American
- BT   **Black music**
  - **Music**
- NT   **Blues music**
  - **Gospel music**
  - **Harlem Renaissance**
  - **Rap music**
- RT   **African American musicians**
  - **Spirituals (Songs)**

African American musicians   780.92; 920
- UF   Afro-American musicians
  - Musicians, African American
- BT   **Black musicians**
  - **Musicians**
- RT   **African American music**

African American poetry
- USE   **American poetry—African American authors**

African American songs
- USE   **African American music**

African American suffrage
- USE   **African Americans—Suffrage**

African American women   305.48
- UF   Afro-American women
  - Women, African American
- BT   **Black women**
  - **Women**

African American youth   305.235
- BT   **Youth**

African Americans (May subdiv. geog. by cities, states, or regions of the U.S.)   305.896; 973

Use for materials dealing collectively with Blacks in the United States. General materials and materials on Blacks in places other than the United States are entered under **Blacks.**
- UF   Afro-Americans
  - Black Americans
  - Blacks—United States
  - Negroes
- SA   African Americans in various occupations and professions, e.g. **African American artists; African American librarians;** etc., to be added as needed

---

BT = Broader Term   NT = Narrower Term   RT = Related Term   SA = See Also   UF = Used For

African Americans—*Continued*
BT   Blacks
NT   Libraries and African Americans
      World War, 1939-1945—African Americans
RT   Slavery—United States
African Americans and libraries
USE   Libraries and African Americans
African Americans—Art
USE   African American art
African Americans—Biography   920
BT   Blacks—Biography
African Americans—Chicago (Ill.)   305.896; 977.3
UF   Chicago (Ill.)—African Americans
African Americans—Children
USE   African American children
African Americans—Civil rights   323.1; 342
BT   Blacks—Civil rights
      Civil rights
NT   African Americans—Suffrage
      Black power
African Americans—Economic conditions   330.973
BT   Blacks—Economic conditions
      Economic conditions
NT   Black power
African Americans—Education   370.89; 371.829
BT   Blacks—Education
      Education
African Americans—Employment   331.6
UF   African Americans—Occupations
BT   Blacks—Employment
      Employment
NT   African American business people
RT   Discrimination in employment
African Americans—Folklore   398
UF   African American folklore
      Folklore, African American
BT   Blacks—Folklore
      Folklore
African Americans—Housing   307.3; 363.5
UF   Housing, African American

BT   Blacks—Housing
      Housing
African Americans in art   704.9
Use for materials on African Americans depicted in works of art. Materials on the attainments of several African Americans in the area of art are entered under **African American artists.** Materials on works of art by several African American artists are entered under **African American art.**
UF   Afro-Americans in art
BT   Art
      Blacks in art
African Americans in literature   809
Use for materials on the theme of African Americans in works of literature. Materials on several African American authors are entered under **African American authors.** Materials on works of literature by several African American authors are entered under **American literature—African American authors** and the various forms of American literature with the subdivision *African American authors,* e.g. **American poetry—African American authors.**
UF   Afro-Americans in literature
BT   Blacks in literature
      Characters and characteristics in literature
African Americans in motion pictures   791.43
Use for materials on the depiction of African Americans in motion pictures. Materials on several African American actors are entered under **African American actors.** Materials discussing all aspects of African Americans' involvement in motion pictures are entered under **African Americans in the motion picture industry.**
BT   Blacks in motion pictures
      Motion pictures
African Americans in television   791.45
Use for materials on the portrayal of African Americans in television programs. Materials on all aspects of African Americans' involvement in the television industry are entered under **African Americans in television broadcasting.**
UF   African Americans on television
      Afro-Americans in television
BT   Television
African Americans in television broadcasting   791.45
Use for materials on all aspects of African Americans' involvement in the television industry. Materials on the portrayal of African Americans in television programs are entered under **African Americans in television.**
UF   African Americans in the television industry

BT = Broader Term   NT = Narrower Term   RT = Related Term   SA = See Also   UF = Used For

African Americans in television broad-
casting—*Continued*
      Afro-Americans in television
        broadcasting
  BT   **Television broadcasting**
**African Americans in the motion picture
    industry**   791.43092
    Use for materials on all aspects of African
    Americans' involvement in motion pictures.
    Materials on the depiction of African Ameri-
    cans in motion pictures are entered under
    African Americans in motion pictures.
  BT   **Blacks in the motion picture
       industry**
      Motion picture industry
African Americans in the television indus-
   try
  USE   **African Americans in television
      broadcasting**
African Americans—Intellectual life
    305.896
  BT   **Blacks—Intellectual life**
      Intellectual life
African Americans—Music
  USE   **African American music**
African Americans—Occupations
  USE   **African Americans—Employ-
      ment**
African Americans—Ohio   305.896;
    977.1
  UF   Ohio—African Americans
African Americans on television
  USE   **African Americans in television**
African Americans—Political activity
    322.4; 324
  BT   **Blacks—Political activity**
      Political participation
  NT   **Black nationalism**
      Black power
African Americans—Race identity
    305.896
  BT   **Blacks—Race identity**
      Race awareness
  NT   **Black nationalism**
African Americans—Religion   270.089;
    299
  BT   **Blacks—Religion**
      Religion
  NT   **Black Muslims**
African Americans—Segregation
    305.896
  BT   **Blacks—Segregation**

      Segregation
African Americans—Social conditions
    305.896
  BT   **Blacks—Social conditions**
      Social conditions
**African Americans—Social life and cus-
    toms**   305.896
  BT   **Blacks—Social life and cus-
      toms**
      Manners and customs
African Americans—Southern States
    305.896; 975
  UF   Southern States—African Ameri-
      cans
African Americans—Suffrage   324.6
  UF   African American suffrage
  BT   **African Americans—Civil
      rights**
      Blacks—Suffrage
      Suffrage
African civilization
  USE   **Africa—Civilization**
African literature (English)   820
  BT   **Literature**
African peoples
  USE   **Africans**
African relations
  USE   **Pan-Africanism**
African songs   782.42096
  UF   Songs, African *[Former head-
      ing]*
  BT   **Songs**
African studies
  USE   **Africa—Study and teaching**
Africans   305.896; 960
  UF   African peoples
  SA   names of African peoples, e.g.
      Yoruba (African people); to
      be added as needed
  BT   **Africa**
  NT   **Blacks—Africa**
      Yoruba (African people)
Afrikaaners
  USE   **Afrikaners**
Afrikaners   305.83; 968
  UF   Afrikaaners
      Boers
      South African Dutch
      South Africans, Afrikaans-
      speaking

BT = Broader Term   NT = Narrower Term   RT = Related Term   SA = See Also   UF = Used For

Afro-American actors
USE **African American actors**
Afro-American art
USE **African American art**
Afro-American artists
USE **African American artists**
Afro-American athletes
USE **African American athletes**
Afro-American authors
USE **African American authors**
Afro-American business people
USE **African American business people**
Afro-American children
USE **African American children**
Afro-American librarians
USE **African American librarians**
Afro-American men
USE **African American men**
Afro-American music
USE **African American music**
Afro-American musicians
USE **African American musicians**
Afro-American songs
USE **African American music**
Afro-American women
USE **African American women**
Afro-Americans
USE **African Americans**
Afro-Americans and libraries
USE **Libraries and African Americans**
Afro-Americans in art
USE **African Americans in art**
Afro-Americans in business
USE **African American business people**
Afro-Americans in literature
USE **African Americans in literature**
Afro-Americans in television
USE **African Americans in television**
Afro-Americans in television broadcasting
USE **African Americans in television broadcasting**
After dinner speeches   808.5; 808.85
BT **Speeches**
RT **Toasts**
After school day care
USE **After school programs**

After school programs   362.71; 372.12
UF After school day care
BT **Student activities**
Afterlife
USE **Future life**
Afternoon teas   642
Use for materials on the meal. Materials on the plant or on the beverage are entered under **Tea.**
UF Teas
BT **Cooking**
RT **Entertaining**
Tea
Age   305.2
UF Age groups
NT **Adolescence**
Age and employment
Aging
Children
Drinking age
Elderly
Longevity
Middle age
Middle aged persons
Old age
Teenagers
Youth
Age and employment   331.3
UF Employment and age
BT **Age**
Employment
NT **Career changes**
Children—Employment
Teenagers—Employment
Youth—Employment
RT **Age discrimination**
Discrimination in employment
Age discrimination   305.2
BT **Discrimination**
RT **Age and employment**
Age groups
USE **Age**
Age—Physiological effect
USE **Aging**
Aged
USE **Elderly**
Aged men
USE **Elderly men**
Aged parents
USE **Aging parents**

BT = Broader Term   NT = Narrower Term   RT = Related Term   SA = See Also   UF = Used For

Aged women
    USE   **Elderly women**
Ageing
    USE   **Aging**
Agent Orange   363.17; 615.9
    BT   **Herbicides**
Agents, Sales
    USE   **Sales personnel**
Aggregates
    USE   **Set theory**
Aggressive behavior
    USE   **Aggressiveness (Psychology)**
Aggressiveness (Psychology)   152.4;
      155.2
    UF   Aggressive behavior
    BT   **Human behavior**
          Psychology
    NT   **Assertiveness (Psychology)**
          Bullies
          Violence
Aging   571.8; 612.6
    UF   Age—Physiological effect
          Ageing
          Senescence
    BT   **Age**
          Elderly
          Gerontology
          Longevity
          Middle age
          Old age
    NT   **Male climacteric**
          Menopause
Aging parents   306.874
    UF   Aged parents
          Elderly parents
          Parents, Aging
    BT   **Elderly**
          Family life
Aging persons
    USE   **Elderly**
Agnosticism   149; 211
    BT   **Free thought**
          Religion
    RT   **Atheism**
          Belief and doubt
          Positivism
          Rationalism
          Skepticism
Agrarian question
    USE   **Agriculture—Economic aspects**

Agriculture—Government poli-
    cy
    Land tenure
Agrarian reform
    USE   **Land reform**
Agreements
    USE   **Contracts**
          Covenants
Agribusiness
    USE   **Agricultural industries**
Agricultural bacteriology   630.2
    UF   Bacteriology, Agricultural *[For-*
          mer heading]
          Diseases and pests
    SA   types of crops, plants, trees, etc.,
          with the subdivision *Diseases*
          and pests, e.g. **Fruit—Dis-**
          eases and pests; to be added
          as needed
    BT   **Bacteriology**
    RT   **Soil microbiology**
Agricultural botany
    USE   **Economic botany**
Agricultural chemicals   631.8; 668
    SA   types of agricultural chemicals
          and names of individual
          chemicals, to be added as
          needed
    BT   **Agricultural chemistry**
          Chemicals
    NT   **Fertilizers**
          Herbicides
          Insecticides
          Pesticides
Agricultural chemistry   630.2
    UF   Chemistry, Agricultural
    BT   **Chemistry**
    NT   **Agricultural chemicals**
    RT   **Soils**
Agricultural clubs
    USE   **Agriculture—Societies**
Agricultural cooperation
    USE   **Cooperative agriculture**
Agricultural credit   332.7
    UF   Credit, Agricultural
          Farm credit
          Rural credit
    BT   **Agriculture—Economic aspects**
          Banks and banking
          Credit

BT = Broader Term   NT = Narrower Term   RT = Related Term   SA = See Also   UF = Used For

Agricultural credit—*Continued*
      Mortgages
Agricultural economics
   USE   **Agriculture—Economic aspects**
Agricultural education
   USE   **Agriculture—Study and teach-
         ing**
Agricultural engineering   630
   UF   Agricultural mechanics
         Farm mechanics
   BT   **Engineering**
   NT   **Drainage**
         Electricity in agriculture
         Irrigation
   RT   **Agricultural machinery**
Agricultural experiment stations   630.7
   UF   Experimental farms
         Farms, Experimental
   BT   **Agriculture—Government poli-
         cy**
         Agriculture—Research
         **Agriculture—Study and teach-
         ing**
   NT   **Agricultural extension work**
Agricultural extension work (May subdiv.
   geog.)   **630.7**
   UF   Extension work, Agricultural
   BT   **Adult education**
         **Agricultural experiment sta-
         tions**
         **Agriculture—Government poli-
         cy**
   NT   **County agricultural agents**
   RT   **Agriculture—Study and teach-
         ing**
         Community development
Agricultural industries   338.1
   UF   Agribusiness
   BT   **Agriculture—Economic aspects**
Agricultural laborers   331.7
   UF   Farm laborers
   BT   **Labor**
   RT   **Migrant labor**
         Peasantry
Agricultural machinery   631.3
   UF   Agricultural tools
         Farm engines *[Former heading]*
         Farm equipment
         Farm implements
         Farm machinery

      Farm mechanics
      Implements, utensils, etc.
   SA   types of farm machinery, to be
         added as needed
   BT   **Machinery**
         Tools
   NT   **Electricity in agriculture**
         Harvesting machinery
         Plows
         Tractors
   RT   **Agricultural engineering**
Agricultural mechanics
   USE   **Agricultural engineering**
Agricultural pests   632
   UF   Diseases and pests
         Garden pests
   SA   types of crops, plants, trees, etc.,
         with the subdivision *Diseases
         and pests*, e.g. **Fruit—Dis-
         eases and pests;** to be added
         as needed
   BT   **Economic zoology**
         Pests
   NT   **Fruit—Diseases and pests**
         Fungi
         Pest control
         Plant diseases
         Spraying and dusting
         Weeds
   RT   **Aeronautics in agriculture**
         Insect pests
Agricultural policy
   USE   **Agriculture—Government poli-
         cy**
Agricultural products
   USE   **Farm produce**
Agricultural research
   USE   **Agriculture—Research**
Agricultural societies
   USE   **Agriculture—Societies**
Agricultural subsidies   338.9
   UF   Agriculture and state
         Farm subsidies
         State and agriculture
         Subsidies, Agricultural
         Subsidies, Farm
   BT   **Subsidies**
   RT   **Agriculture—Government poli-
         cy**

BT = Broader Term   NT = Narrower Term   RT = Related Term   SA = See Also   UF = Used For

Agricultural tools
USE **Agricultural machinery**
Agriculture (May subdiv. geog.)   **630**
   UF   Agronomy
         Farming
         Planting
   SA   types of agriculture, e.g. **Truck
         farming;** ethnic groups with
         the subdivision *Agriculture,*
         and names of agricultural
         products, e.g. **Corn;** to be
         added as needed
   BT   **Life sciences**
   NT   **Aeronautics in agriculture**
         Aquaculture
         Beekeeping
         Cooperative agriculture
         Crop rotation
         Cultivated plants
         Dairying
         Dry farming
         Economic botany
         Farmers
         Forests and forestry
         Fruit culture
         Gardening
         Horticulture
         Livestock industry
         Organic farming
         Pastures
         Plant breeding
         Reclamation of land
         Soils
         Truck farming
   RT   **Farms**
         Food supply
Agriculture and state
   USE **Agricultural subsidies**
        **Agriculture—Government poli-
        cy**
Agriculture—Bibliography   **016.63**
Agriculture, Cooperative
   USE **Cooperative agriculture**
Agriculture—Documentation   **025**
   BT   **Documentation**
Agriculture—Economic aspects   **338.1**
   UF   Agrarian question
         Agricultural economics
   BT   **Economics**
   NT   **Agricultural credit**

         Agricultural industries
         Land tenure
   RT   **Farm management**
         Farm produce—Marketing
Agriculture—Government policy   **338.9**
   UF   Agrarian question
         Agricultural policy
         Agriculture and state
         State and agriculture
   BT   **Industrial policy**
   NT   **Agricultural experiment sta-
        tions**
         Agricultural extension work
   RT   **Agricultural subsidies**
         Land reform
Agriculture—Research   **630.7**
   UF   Agricultural research
   BT   **Research**
   NT   **Agricultural experiment sta-
        tions**
Agriculture—Societies   **630.6**
   UF   Agricultural clubs
         Agricultural societies
         Boys' agricultural clubs
         Girls' agricultural clubs
   SA   names of agricultural societies,
         to be added as needed
   BT   **Associations**
         Country life
         Societies
   NT   **4-H clubs**
         Grange
Agriculture, Soilless
   USE **Hydroponics**
Agriculture—Statistics   **338.1; 630.2**
   UF   Crop reports
   BT   **Statistics**
Agriculture—Study and teaching   **630.7**
   UF   Agricultural education
   BT   **Vocational education**
   NT   **Agricultural experiment sta-
        tions**
         County agricultural agents
   RT   **Agricultural extension work**
Agriculture—Tenant farming
   USE **Farm tenancy**
Agriculture—Tropics   **630.913**
   BT   **Tropics**
Agriculture—United States   **630.973**
   UF   United States—Agriculture

BT = Broader Term   NT = Narrower Term   RT = Related Term   SA = See Also   UF = Used For

Agronomy
    USE   **Agriculture**
Ague
    USE   **Malaria**
AI (Artificial intelligence)
    USE   **Artificial intelligence**
Aid to dependent children
    USE   **Child welfare**
Aid to developing areas
    USE   **Foreign aid**
           Technical assistance
AIDS (Disease)   616.97
    UF   A.I.D.S. (Disease)
           Acquired immune deficiency
               syndrome
           HIV disease
    BT   **Communicable diseases**
           Diseases
AIDS (Disease)—Prevention   616.97
    NT   **Safe sex in AIDS prevention**
    RT   **Sexual hygiene**
AIDS (Disease)—Treatment   615.5
    BT   **Therapeutics**
Air   533; 546
        Use for materials dealing with air in general
    and with its chemical and physical properties.
    Materials on the body of air surrounding the
    earth are entered under **Atmosphere.**
    BT   **Meteorology**
    NT   **Aerodynamics**
           Atmosphere
           Ventilation
    RT   **Atmosphere**
Air bases   358.4
    UF   Air stations, Military
           Air stations, Naval
           Military air bases
           Naval air bases
    BT   **Airports**
           Military aeronautics
Air bearing lift
    USE   **Ground cushion phenomena**
Air bearing vehicles
    USE   **Ground effect machines**
Air cargo
    USE   **Commercial aeronautics**
Air carriers
    USE   **Airlines**
Air charters
    USE   **Airlines—Chartering**

Air conditioning   644; 697.9
    SA   subjects with the subdivision *Air
               conditioning,* to be added as
               needed
    NT   **Automobiles—Air conditioning**
    RT   **Refrigeration**
           Ventilation
Air crashes
    USE   **Aircraft accidents**
Air cushion vehicles
    USE   **Ground effect machines**
Air defenses (May subdiv. geog.)   **363.3**
        Use for materials on military defense
    against air attack. Materials on the protection
    of civilians from enemy attack are entered un-
    der **Civil defense.**
    UF   Air defenses, Civil
           Air defenses, Military
           Air raid defensive measures
    BT   **Military aeronautics**
    NT   **Ballistic missile early warning
               system**
           Radar defense networks
Air defenses, Civil
    USE   **Air defenses**
Air defenses, Military
    USE   **Air defenses**
Air freight
    USE   **Commercial aeronautics**
Air lines
    USE   **Airlines**
Air mail service   383
    BT   **Commercial aeronautics**
           Postal service
Air—Microbiology   579
    UF   Aerobiology
    BT   **Microbiology**
Air, Moisture of
    USE   **Humidity**
Air navigation
    USE   **Navigation (Aeronautics)**
Air pilots   629.13092; 920
    UF   Airplane pilots
           Aviators
           Pilots
           Test pilots
    BT   **Aeronautics**
    NT   **Astronauts**
           Women air pilots
Air piracy
    USE   **Hijacking of airplanes**

Air pollution (May subdiv. geog.)
363.739; 628.5
UF Atmosphere—Pollution
Pollution of air
BT **Environmental health**
Pollution
NT **Aerosols**
Air pollution—Measurement   363.739;
628.5
BT **Measurement**
Air pollution—United States   363.739;
628.5
UF United States—Air pollution
Air power   358.4
BT **Military aeronautics**
Air raid defensive measures
USE **Air defenses**
Military aeronautics
Air raid shelters   363.3
UF Blast shelters
Bomb shelters
Fallout shelters
Nuclear bomb shelters
Public shelters
Shelters, Air raid
BT **Civil defense**
Air rights law
USE **Airspace law**
Air routes
USE **Aeronautics**
Air-ships
USE **Airships**
Air space law
USE **Airspace law**
Air stations, Military
USE **Air bases**
Air stations, Naval
USE **Air bases**
Air surfing
USE **Gliding and soaring**
Air terminals
USE **Airports**
Air traffic control   387.7
UF Airports—Traffic control
BT **Aeronautics—Safety measures**
Air transport
USE **Commercial aeronautics**
Air warfare
USE **Military aeronautics**
Military airplanes

Aircraft
USE **Airplanes**
Airships
Balloons
Gliders (Aeronautics)
Helicopters
Aircraft accidents   363.12; 629.13
UF Aeronautics—Accidents [Former
heading]
Air crashes
Airplane accidents
Airplane crashes
Airplanes—Accidents
Aviation accidents
Plane crashes
BT **Accidents**
NT **Survival after airplane acci-**
dents, shipwrecks, etc.
Aircraft carriers   359.3; 623
UF Airplane carriers
Carriers, Aircraft
BT **Military aeronautics**
Warships
Aircraft production
USE **Aerospace industries**
Airplane industry
Airdromes
USE **Airports**
Airline hostesses
USE **Flight attendants**
Airline stewardesses
USE **Flight attendants**
Airline stewards
USE **Flight attendants**
Airlines   387.7
Use for materials on companies engaged in
commercial aviation. Materials on various
types of aircraft and on the scientific or tech-
nical aspects of aircraft and their construction
and operation are entered under **Aeronautics.**
UF Air carriers
Air lines
BT **Commercial aeronautics**
NT **Flight attendants**
Airlines—Chartering   387.7
UF Aeronautics, Commercial—Char-
tering [Former heading]
Air charters
Airplanes—Chartering
Charter flights

Airlines—Flight attendants
USE **Flight attendants**
Airlines—Hijacking
USE **Hijacking of airplanes**
Airplane accidents
USE **Aircraft accidents**
Airplane carriers
USE **Aircraft carriers**
Airplane crashes
USE **Aircraft accidents**
Airplane engines   629.134
UF Airplane motors
Airplanes—Engines *[Former heading]*
Airplanes—Motors
BT **Engines**
NT **Jet propulsion**
Airplane hijacking
USE **Hijacking of airplanes**
Airplane industry   338.4; 387.7
UF Aircraft production
BT **Aerospace industries**
Commercial aeronautics
Airplane motors
USE **Airplane engines**
Airplane pilots
USE **Air pilots**
Airplane racing   797.5
UF Airplanes—Racing
BT **Aeronautical sports**
Racing
Airplane spotting
USE **Airplanes—Identification**
Airplanes   387.7; 629.133
UF Aeroplanes
Aircraft
SA types of airplanes and specific makes of airplanes, to be added as needed
BT **Aeronautics**
NT **Aerial propellers**
Bombers
Gliders (Aeronautics)
Helicopters
Jet planes
Vertically rising airplanes
Airplanes—Accidents
USE **Aircraft accidents**
Airplanes—Chartering
USE **Airlines—Chartering**

Airplanes—Design and construction
629.134
Airplanes—Electric equipment   629.135
UF Airplanes—Instruments
BT **Aeronautical instruments**
Airplanes—Engines
USE **Airplane engines**
Airplanes—Flight testing
USE **Airplanes—Testing**
Airplanes—Hijacking
USE **Hijacking of airplanes**
Airplanes—Identification   623.7;
629.133
UF Airplane spotting
Airplanes—Recognition
BT **Identification**
Airplanes in agriculture
USE **Aeronautics in agriculture**
Airplanes—Inspection   387.7; 629.134
Airplanes—Instruments
USE **Aeronautical instruments**
Airplanes—Electric equipment
Airplanes, Jet propelled
USE **Jet planes**
Airplanes—Maintenance and repair
629.134
UF Airplanes—Repair
Airplanes—Materials   629.134
BT **Materials**
Airplanes, Military
USE **Military airplanes**
Airplanes—Models   629.133
UF Model airplanes
Paper airplanes
BT **Models and model making**
Airplanes—Motors
USE **Airplane engines**
Airplanes, Naval
USE **Military airplanes**
Airplanes—Noise   629.132
BT **Noise**
Noise pollution
Airplanes—Operation
USE **Airplanes—Piloting**
Airplanes—Piloting   629.132
UF Aeronautics—Piloting
Airplanes—Operation
Flight training

BT = Broader Term   NT = Narrower Term   RT = Related Term   SA = See Also   UF = Used For

Airplanes—Piloting—*Continued*
SA   types and names of airplanes
        with the subdivision *Piloting,*
        to be added as needed
BT   **Aeronautics—Study and teaching**
        Navigation (Aeronautics)
NT   **Helicopters—Piloting**
        Instrument flying
        Stunt flying
Airplanes—Propellers
USE   **Aerial propellers**
Airplanes—Racing
USE   **Airplane racing**
Airplanes—Recognition
USE   **Airplanes—Identification**
Airplanes—Repair
USE   **Airplanes—Maintenance and repair**
Airplanes, Rocket propelled
USE   **Rocket planes**
Airplanes—Testing   629.134
UF   Airplanes—Flight testing
        Test pilots
Airplanes, Vertically rising
USE   **Vertically rising airplanes**
Airports (May subdiv. geog.)   **387.7; 629.136**
UF   Aerodromes
        Air terminals
        Airdromes
SA   names of individual airports, to
        be added as needed
BT   **Aeronautics**
NT   **Air bases**
        Heliports
Airports—Traffic control
USE   **Air traffic control**
Airships   629.133
Use for materials on self-propelled aircraft that are lighter than air and steerable. Materials on aircraft held aloft by hot air or light gases that are nondirigible and propelled only by the wind are entered under **Balloons.**
UF   Air-ships
        Aircraft
        Balloons, Dirigible
        Blimps
        Dirigible balloons
        Zeppelins
BT   **Aeronautics**
RT   **Balloons**

Airspace law   341.4
UF   Air rights law
        Air space law
BT   **Property**
Airways
USE   **Aeronautics**
Alaska Highway (Alaska and Canada) 388.1; 979.8
BT   **Roads**
Alchemy   540.1
Use for materials on medieval attempts to change base metals into gold. Materials on the transmutation of metals in nuclear physics are entered under **Transmutation (Chemistry).**
UF   Hermetic art and philosophy
        Metals, Transmutation of
        Philosophers' stone
        Transmutation of metals
BT   **Chemistry**
        Occultism
        Superstition
RT   **Transmutation (Chemistry)**
Alcohol   547; 661
UF   Alcohol use
        Intoxicants
SA   classes of persons with the subdivision *Alcohol use,* e.g. **Employees—Alcohol use; Youth—Alcohol use;** etc., to be added as needed
BT   **Chemicals**
NT   **Alcohol as fuel**
        Alcoholic beverages
        Denatured alcohol
        Liquors
RT   **Alcoholism**
        Distillation
Alcohol and employees
USE   **Employees—Alcohol use**
Alcohol and teenagers
USE   **Teenagers—Alcohol use**
Alcohol and youth
USE   **Youth—Alcohol use**
Alcohol as fuel   662
UF   Alcohol fuel
        Ethanol
        Ethyl alcohol fuel
SA   types of alcohol fuels, e.g.
        Gasohol; to be added as needed
BT   **Alcohol**

BT = Broader Term   NT = Narrower Term   RT = Related Term   SA = See Also   UF = Used For

Alcohol as fuel—*Continued*
    Fuel
  NT   **Gasohol**
Alcohol consumption
  USE   **Drinking of alcoholic beverages**
Alcohol, Denatured
  USE   **Denatured alcohol**
Alcohol fuel
  USE   **Alcohol as fuel**
Alcohol in the workplace
  USE   **Employees—Alcohol use**
Alcohol, Industrial
  USE   **Denatured alcohol**
Alcohol—Physiological effect   615
Alcohol use
  USE   **Alcohol**
          Alcoholism
          and classes of persons with the
          subdivision *Alcohol use,* e.g.
          Employees—Alcohol use;
          Youth—Alcohol use; etc., to
          be added as needed
Alcoholic beverage consumption
  USE   **Drinking of alcoholic beverages**
Alcoholic beverages   641.2
  UF   Drinks
          Intoxicants
  BT   **Alcohol**
          Beverages
  NT   **Liquors**
          Wine and wine making
  RT   **Drinking of alcoholic beverages**
Alcoholic parents
  USE   **Adult children of alcoholics**
          Children of alcoholics
Alcoholics   362.292; 616.86
  UF   Drunkards
  NT   **Recovering alcoholics**
  RT   **Adult children of alcoholics**
          Alcoholism
          Children of alcoholics
Alcoholics' adult children
  USE   **Adult children of alcoholics**
Alcoholics' children
  USE   **Children of alcoholics**
Alcoholism   362.292; 616.86
  UF   Addiction to alcohol
          Alcohol use
          Drinking problem
          Drunkenness

          Intemperance
          Intoxication
          Liquor problem
          Problem drinking
  SA   classes of persons with the sub-
          division *Alcohol use,* e.g. **Em-**
          ployees—Alcohol use;
          Youth—Alcohol use; etc., to
          be added as needed
  BT   **Social problems**
  RT   **Adult children of alcoholics**
          Alcohol
          Alcoholics
          Children of alcoholics
          Drinking of alcoholic beverages
          Temperance
          Twelve-step programs
Alfalfa   583; 633.3
  BT   **Forage plants**
Algae   579.8
  UF   Sea mosses
          Seaweeds
  BT   **Marine plants**
Algebra   512
  BT   **Mathematical analysis**
          Mathematics
  NT   **Graph theory**
          Group theory
          Linear algebra
          Logarithms
          Number theory
          Probabilities
          Sequences (Mathematics)
Algebra, Boolean
  USE   **Boolean algebra**
Algebras, Linear
  USE   **Linear algebra**
Alienation (Social psychology)   302.5
  UF   Estrangement (Social psycholo-
          gy)
          Rebels (Social psychology)
          Social alienation
  BT   **Social psychology**
Aliens (May subdiv. geog.)   323.6
  UF   Foreign population
          Foreigners
          Noncitizens
          Nonnationals

BT = Broader Term   NT = Narrower Term   RT = Related Term   SA = See Also   UF = Used For

Aliens—*Continued*
- SA   national groups with the appropriate subdivision for the country of their residence, e.g. **Mexicans—United States;** to be added as needed
- BT   **Minorities**
- NT   **Illegal aliens**
         Refugees
- RT   **Citizenship**
         Immigrants
         Immigration and emigration
         Naturalization

Aliens from outer space
- USE   **Extraterrestrial beings**

Aliens, Illegal
- USE   **Illegal aliens**

Aliens—United States   325.73
- UF   United States—Foreign population *[Former heading]*
- NT   **Mexicans—United States**
- RT   **United States—Immigration and emigration**

Alkoran
- USE   **Koran**

All Fools' Day
- USE   **April Fools' Day**

All Hallows' Eve
- USE   **Halloween**

All terrain bicycles
- USE   **Mountain bikes**

All terrain vehicles   629.22
- UF   A.T.V.'s
         ATVs
- SA   types of vehicles, e.g. **Snowmobiles;** to be added as needed
- BT   **Vehicles**
- NT   **Mountain bikes**
         Snowmobiles

Allegories   808.88; 810.8, etc.

   May be used for individual works or for collections of allegories. Materials on allegory as a literary form or on allegory in the fine and decorative arts are entered under **Allegory.**
- BT   **Fiction**
- RT   **Fables**
         Parables

Allegory   704.9; 808

   Use for materials on allegory as a literary form as well as for allegory in the fine and decorative arts. Individual allegories and collections of allegories are entered under **Allegories.**
- BT   **Arts**
         Fiction
- RT   **Symbolism in literature**

Allergies
- USE   **Allergy**

Allergies, Food
- USE   **Food allergy**

Allergy   616.97
- UF   Allergies
- SA   types of allergies, to be added as needed
- BT   **Immunity**
- NT   **Food allergy**
         Hay fever

Allergy, Food
- USE   **Food allergy**

Alleys
- USE   **Streets**

Allied health personnel   610.69
- UF   Paramedical personnel
- SA   types of allied health personnel, to be added as needed
- NT   **Emergency medical technicians**
         Medical technologists
         Nurse practitioners

Alligators   597.98
- BT   **Reptiles**
- RT   **Crocodiles**

Allocation of time
- USE   **Time management**

Allowances, Children's
- USE   **Children's allowances**

Alloys   669
- SA   types of alloys, to be added as needed
- BT   **Industrial chemistry**
         Metals
- NT   **Aluminum alloys**
         Brass
         Pewter
- RT   **Metallurgy**

Allusions   031.02; 803
- SA   names of individual literary authors with the subdivision *Allusions,* e.g. **Shakespeare, William, 1564-1616—Allusions;** to be added as needed
- RT   **Terms and phrases**

BT = Broader Term   NT = Narrower Term   RT = Related Term   SA = See Also   UF = Used For

Almanacs   030
   UF   Annuals
   BT   **Serial publications**
   NT   **Nautical almanacs**
   RT   **Calendars**
        Chronology
Alphabet   411

Use for materials on the series of characters that form the elements of a written language and for materials to be used in teaching children the ABCs. Materials on the styles of alphabets used by artists, etc., are entered under **Alphabets.**

   UF   A.B.C.'s
        ABCs
        Alphabet books
        Letters of the alphabet
   SA   names of languages with the
        subdivision *Alphabet,* e.g.
        English language—Alphabet;
        to be added as needed
   BT   **Writing**
   NT   **Alphabets**
Alphabet books
   USE   **Alphabet**
Alphabetizing
   USE   **Files and filing**
Alphabets   745.6

Use for materials on the styles of alphabets used by artists, etc. Materials on the series of characters that form the elements of a written language and for materials to be used in teaching children the ABCs are entered under **Alphabet.**

   UF   Ornamental alphabets
   BT   **Alphabet**
        Sign painting
   NT   **Illumination of books and**
        manuscripts
        Monograms
   RT   **Initials**
        Lettering
Alpine animals
   USE   **Mountain animals**
Alpine fauna
   USE   **Mountain animals**
Alpine flora
   USE   **Mountain plants**
Alpine plants
   USE   **Mountain plants**
Alternate energy resources
   USE   **Renewable energy resources**

Alternate work sites
   USE   **Telecommuting**
Alternating current machinery
   USE   **Electric machinery—Alternat-**
          ing current
Alternating currents
   USE   **Alternating electric currents**
Alternating electric currents   621.31
   UF   Alternating currents
        Currents, Alternating
        Electric currents, Alternating
        [Former heading]
   BT   **Electric currents**
Alternative energy resources
   USE   **Renewable energy resources**
Alternative histories   808.3; 813, etc.

May be used for individual works, collections, or materials about imaginative works featuring key changes in historical facts.

   BT   **Fantasy fiction**
Alternative lifestyle
   USE   **Counter culture**
        Lifestyles
Alternative medicine   610; 613; 615.5
   UF   Therapeutic systems
   SA   types of alternative medicine, to
        be added as needed
   BT   **Medicine**
   NT   **Acupressure**
        Acupuncture
        Chiropractic
        Health self-care
        Holistic medicine
        Homeopathy
        Mental healing
        Naturopathy
        Osteopathic medicine
Alternative military service
   USE   **National service**
Alternative press (May subdiv. geog.)
        070.4; 071, etc.

Use for materials about publications issued clandestinely and contrary to government regulation and for materials about publications issued legally (and usually serially) and produced by radical, anti-establishment, or counter-culture groups.

   UF   Press, Alternative
        Press, Underground
        Underground literature *[Former*
        heading]

Alternative press—*Continued*
>Underground press *[Former heading]*

BT   **Press**

Alternative schools

USE   **Experimental schools**

Alternative universities

USE   **Free universities**

Alternative work schedules

USE   **Hours of labor**
>**Part-time employment**

Altitude, Influence of

USE   **Environmental influence on humans**

Altruists

USE   **Philanthropists**

Aluminum   669; 673

BT   **Metals**

NT   **Aluminum foil**

Aluminum alloys   669; 673

BT   **Alloys**

Aluminum foil   673

BT   **Aluminum**
>**Packaging**

Aluminum—Recycling   628.4; 673

BT   **Recycling**

Alzheimer's disease   616.8

BT   **Brain—Diseases**

Amateur films   778.5; 791.43
>May be used for individual works, collections, or materials about amateur films.

UF   Amateur motion pictures *[Former heading]*
>Films, Amateur
>Home movies
>Home video movies
>Motion pictures, Amateur
>Personal films

BT   **Motion pictures**

RT   **Camcorders**
>**Motion picture cameras**

Amateur motion pictures

USE   **Amateur films**

Amateur radio stations   384.54; 621.3841

UF   Ham radio stations
>Radio stations, Amateur

BT   **Shortwave radio**

Amateur theater   792

UF   Non-professional theater
>Play production
>Private theater

BT   **Amusements**
>**Theater**

NT   **Charades**
>**Children's plays**
>**College and school drama**
>**Little theater movement**
>**One act plays**
>**Pantomimes**
>**Readers' theater**
>**Shadow pantomimes and plays**

RT   **Acting**
>**Drama in education**

Ambassadors

USE   **Diplomats**

Amendments, Equal rights

USE   **Equal rights amendments**

America   970
>Use for general materials on the Western Hemisphere.

SA   names of individual countries of the Western Hemisphere, to be added as needed

NT   **Latin America**
>**North America**
>**South America**

America—Antiquities   970.01

BT   **Antiquities**

America—Civilization   970; 980
>Use for general materials on the civilization of the Western Hemisphere and on ancient American civilizations. Materials limited to the civilization of the United States are entered under **United States—Civilization.**

UF   American civilization *[Former heading]*
>Civilization, American *[Former heading]*

BT   **Civilization**

America—Discovery and exploration

USE   **America—Exploration**

America—Exploration   970.01

UF   America—Discovery and exploration

BT   **Exploration**

NT   **Northwest Passage**
>**United States—Exploration**

America—History   970

UF   American history

America—Politics and government   970

RT   **Pan-Americanism**

BT = Broader Term   NT = Narrower Term   RT = Related Term   SA = See Also   UF = Used For

American actors   791.4; 792; 920
UF   Actors, American *[Former head-*
      ing]
      Actors and actresses, American
      [Former heading]
      American actors and actresses
BT   **Actors**
American actors and actresses
USE   **American actors**
American architecture   720.973
UF   Architecture, American *[Former*
      heading]
BT   **Architecture**
American art   709.73
UF   Art, American *[Former heading]*
BT   **Art**
NT   **American folk art**
American artificial satellites   629.43;
      629.46
UF   Artificial satellites, American
      [Former heading]
BT   **Artificial satellites**
American artists   709.2; 920
UF   Artists, American *[Former head-*
      ing]
BT   **Artists**
American arts   700.973
UF   Arts, American *[Former head-*
      ing]
BT   **Arts**
American authors   810.9; 920
UF   Authors, American *[Former*
      heading]
BT   **Authors**
NT   **American dramatists**
      American novelists
      American poets
American ballads   811, etc.
UF   Ballads, American *[Former*
      heading]
BT   **American poetry**
American Bicentennial
USE   **American Revolution Bicenten-**
      nial, 1776-1976
American bison
USE   **Bison**
American characteristics
USE   **American national characteris-**
      tics

American Civil War
USE   **United States—History—1861-**
      1865, Civil War
American civilization
USE   **America—Civilization**
American colleges
USE   **Colleges and universities—**
      United States
American colonies
USE   **United States—History—1600-**
      1775, Colonial period
American color prints   769.973
UF   Color prints, American *[Former*
      heading]
BT   **Color prints**
American communism
USE   **Communism—United States**
American composers   780.92; 920
UF   Composers, American *[Former*
      heading]
BT   **Composers**
American Constitution
USE   **Constitutional history—United**
      States
      Constitutional law—United
      States
      Constitutions—United States
American cooking   641.5973
      Use for materials on cooking limited to
      American national and regional styles.
UF   Cookery, American
      Cooking—United States
SA   styles of regional American
      cooking, e.g. **Southern cook-**
      ing; to be added as needed
BT   **Cooking**
American decoration and ornament
      745.4
UF   Decoration and ornament,
      American *[Former heading]*
BT   **Decoration and ornament**
American diaries   809; 920
      Use for collections of American diaries and
      for materials about American diaries.
UF   American journals (Diaries)
      Diaries, American
BT   **Diaries**

American diplomatic and consular service (May subdiv. geog.) 327.73; 353.1

UF   Diplomatic and consular service, American

United States—Diplomatic and consular service *[Former heading]*

BT   Diplomatic and consular service

American drama 812

Use for general materials about American drama, not for individual works.

BT   American literature

Drama

American drama—Collections 812.008

American drama—History and criticism 812.009

American dramatists 812.009; 920

UF   Dramatists, American *[Former heading]*

BT   American authors

Dramatists

American drawing 741.973

UF   Drawing, American *[Former heading]*

BT   Drawing

American economic assistance

USE   American foreign aid

American engraving 760; 769

UF   Engraving, American *[Former heading]*

BT   Engraving

American environmental policy

USE   Environmental policy—United States

American espionage 327.1273; 355.3

UF   Espionage, American *[Former heading]*

BT   Espionage

American essays 814; 814.008

BT   American literature

Essays

American ethics 170.973

UF   Ethics, American *[Former heading]*

BT   Ethics

American exploring expeditions

USE   United States—Exploring expeditions

American fiction 813

May be used for collections or materials about American fiction, not for individual works.

BT   American literature

Fiction

American films

USE   Motion pictures—United States

American flag

USE   Flags—United States

American folk art 745.0973

UF   Folk art, American *[Former heading]*

BT   American art

Folk art

American folk dancing 793.3

UF   Folk dancing, American *[Former heading]*

BT   Dance—United States

Folk dancing

American folk music

USE   Folk music—United States

American folk songs

USE   Folk songs—United States

American foreign aid (May subdiv. geog.) 338.91; 361.6

UF   American economic assistance *[Former heading]*

Economic assistance, American *[Former heading]*

BT   Foreign aid

American furniture 684.100973; 749.213

UF   Furniture, American *[Former heading]*

SA   styles of American furniture, to be added as needed

BT   Furniture

American government

USE   United States—Politics and government

American graphic arts

USE   Graphic arts—United States

American historians 907; 920

UF   Historians, American *[Former heading]*

BT   Historians

American history

USE   America—History

United States—History

BT = Broader Term   NT = Narrower Term   RT = Related Term   SA = See Also   UF = Used For

American hostages (May subdiv. geog. except U.S.) 920
UF   Hostages, American *[Former heading]*
BT   Hostages
American hostages—Iran 920
NT   Iran hostage crisis, 1979-1981
American illustrators 741.6092; 920
UF   Illustrators, American *[Former heading]*
BT   Illustrators
American Indians
USE   Indians
      Indians of Central America
      Indians of Mexico
      Indians of North America
      Indians of South America
      Indians of the West Indies
American journals (Diaries)
USE   American diaries
American labor unions
USE   Labor unions—United States
American letters 816; 816.008
BT   American literature
      Letters
American literature (May subdiv. geog. by state or region) 810

May be subdivided by the topical subdivisions and literary forms used under **English literature;** or geographically by states or regions of the United States for works by or about several authors from a state or region or writing about a state or region, e.g. **American literature—Massachusetts; American literature—Southern States;** etc.

SA   various forms of American literature, e.g. **American poetry; American satire;** etc., to be added as needed
BT   Literature
NT   American drama
      American essays
      American fiction
      American letters
      American literature (Spanish)
      American poetry
      American prose literature
      American satire
      American speeches
      American wit and humor

American literature—African American authors 810.8; 810.9

May be used for collections or materials about American literature by several African American authors, not for individual works. Use same pattern for literatures and literary forms written by other ethnic groups or classes of authors.

UF   African American literature
      American literature—Afro-American authors
      American literature—Black authors *[Former heading]*
      Black literature (American)
SA   particular forms of American literature with the subdivision *African American authors;* e.g., **American poetry—African American authors;** to be added as needed
NT   **Harlem Renaissance**
American literature—Afro-American authors
USE   **American literature—African American authors**
American literature—American Indian authors 810.8; 810.9

May be used for collections or materials about American literature written in English by several American Indian authors, not for individual works. Collections or materials about literature written in Indian languages by several American Indian authors are entered under **Indians of North America—Literature.**

UF   Indian literature (American)
American literature—Black authors
USE   **American literature—African American authors**
American literature—Collections 810.8

Use for collections of both poetry and prose by several American authors. Collections consisting of prose only are entered under **American prose literature;** collections of poetry are entered under **American poetry—Collections.**

American literature—Hispanic American authors 810

Use for materials on American literature in English written by American authors of Spanish or Latin American origins. Materials on American literature written in Spanish are entered under **American literature (Spanish).**

UF   American literature—Latin American authors
      Hispanic American literature (English)

BT = Broader Term   NT = Narrower Term   RT = Related Term   SA = See Also   UF = Used For

American literature—Hispanic American
authors—*Continued*

SA genres of American literature
with the subdivision *Hispanic
American authors;* and
American literature and
genres of American literature
with subdivisions for specific
groups of Hispanic American
authors, e.g. **American literature—Mexican American au-
thors;** to be added as needed

NT **American literature—Mexican
American authors**

American literature—Latin American authors

USE **American literature—Hispanic
American authors**

American literature—Massachusetts
810

American literature—Mexican American
authors 810

Use for materials on American literature
written in English by American authors of
Mexican origins.

UF Chicano literature (English)
Mexican American literature
(English)

SA genres of American literature
with the subdivision *Mexican
American authors,* to be added as needed

BT **American literature—Hispanic
American authors**

American literature—Southern States
810

UF Southern literature

American literature (Spanish) 860

Use for materials on American literature
written in Spanish. Materials on American literature in English written by American authors of Spanish or Latin American origins
are entered under **American literature—Hispanic American authors.**

UF Hispanic American literature
(Spanish)
Spanish American literature

SA genres of American literature
with the qualifier (Spanish),
to be added as needed

BT **American literature**

American literature—Women authors
810.8; 810.9

May be used for collections or for materials
about several American women authors.

American Loyalists 973.3

UF Loyalists, American
Tories, American

BT **United States—History—1775-
1783, Revolution**

American military assistance 355

UF Military assistance, American
[Former heading]

BT **Military assistance**

NT **Iran-Contra Affair, 1985-1990**

American motion pictures

USE **Motion pictures—United States**

American music 780.973

UF Music, American *[Former head-
ing]*

BT **Music**

American musicians 780.92; 920

UF Musicians, American *[Former
heading]*

BT **Musicians**

American national characteristics
306.0973; 973

UF American characteristics
National characteristics,
American *[Former heading]*
United States—National charac-
teristics

BT **National characteristics**

American national songs

USE **National songs—United States**

American newspapers 071

BT **Newspapers**

American novelists 813.009; 920

UF Novelists, American *[Former
heading]*

BT **American authors
Novelists**

American orations

USE **American speeches**

American painters 759.13; 920

UF Painters, American *[Former
heading]*

BT **Painters**

American painting 759.13

UF Painting, American *[Former
heading]*

BT **Painting**

BT = Broader Term NT = Narrower Term RT = Related Term SA = See Also UF = Used For

American periodicals   051
    BT   **Periodicals**
American personal names
    USE   **Personal names—United States**
American philosophers   191; 920
    UF   Philosophers, American *[Former
            heading]*
    BT   **Philosophers**
American philosophy   191
    UF   Philosophy, American *[Former
            heading]*
    BT   **Philosophy**
American poetry   811
    Use for general materials about American
    poetry, not for individual works.
    BT   **American literature**
            Poetry
    NT   **American ballads**
American poetry—African American au-
    thors   811, etc.
    May be used for collections or materials
    about American poetry by several African
    American authors, not for individual works.
    UF   African American poetry
            American poetry—Afro-American
            authors
            American poetry—Black authors
            [Former heading]
            Black poetry (American)
American poetry—Afro-American authors
    USE   **American poetry—African
             American authors**
American poetry—Black authors
    USE   **American poetry—African
             American authors**
American poetry—Collections   811.008
American poetry—History and criticism
    811.009
American poets   811.009; 920
    UF   Poets, American *[Former head-
            ing]*
    BT   **American authors**
            Poets
American politicians
    USE   **Politicians—United States**
American politics
    USE   **United States—Politics and
            government**
American pottery   738.0973
    UF   Pottery, American *[Former
            heading]*

        United States—Pottery
    BT   **Pottery**
American prints   769.973
    UF   Prints, American *[Former head-
            ing]*
    BT   **Prints**
American prisoners of war   341.6;
    355.7
    UF   Prisoners of war, American
            [Former heading]
    BT   **Prisoners of war**
American propaganda   303.3; 327.1
    UF   Propaganda, American *[Former
            heading]*
    BT   **Propaganda**
American prose literature   818
    Use for collections of prose writings by
    several American authors that may include a
    variety of literary forms, such as essays, fic-
    tion, orations, etc. May also be used for gen-
    eral materials about such prose writings.
    UF   Prose literature, American
    BT   **American literature**
American Revolution
    USE   **United States—History—1775-
             1783, Revolution**
American Revolution Bicentennial, 1776-
    1976   973.3
    UF   American Bicentennial
            Bicentennial celebrations—United
            States—1976
            United States—Bicentennial cele-
            brations
            United States—History—1775-
            1783, Revolution—Centennial
            celebrations, etc.
    BT   **United States—Centennial cele-
            brations, etc.**
American Revolution Bicentennial, 1776-
    1976—Collectibles   973.3075
    BT   **Collectors and collecting**
American satire   817; 817.008
    UF   Satire, American *[Former head-
            ing]*
    BT   **American literature**
            Satire
American science
    USE   **Science—United States**
American sculptors   730.92; 920
    UF   Sculptors, American *[Former
            heading]*

BT = Broader Term   NT = Narrower Term   RT = Related Term   SA = See Also   UF = Used For

American sculptors—*Continued*
BT   Sculptors
American sculpture   730.973
  UF   Sculpture, American *[Former heading]*
  BT   Sculpture
American songs   782.420973
  UF   Songs, American *[Former heading]*
  BT   Songs
  NT   Folk songs—United States
      National songs—United States
      Spirituals (Songs)
American-Spanish War, 1898
  USE   **Spanish-American War, 1898**
American speeches   815; 815.008
  UF   American orations
      Speeches, addresses, etc.,
        American *[Former heading]*
  BT   American literature
      Speeches
American technical assistance (May
    subdiv. geog.)   338.91; 361.6
  UF   Technical assistance, American
      [Former heading]
  BT   Technical assistance
American teenagers
  USE   **Teenagers—United States**
American tourists
  USE   **American travelers**
American travelers   910.92; 920
  UF   American tourists
      Travelers, American *[Former heading]*
  BT   Travelers
American wit and humor   817;
    817.008; 817.009
    Use for collections by several authors or for materials about American wit and humor. Individual works by American humorists are entered under **Wit and humor.**
  BT   American literature
      Wit and humor
American youth
  USE   **Youth—United States**
Americana   069; 973
    Use for general materials about American objects of interest to collectors, such as historical documents, relics, etc., as well as items of little intrinsic value. Materials on old American objects that have aesthetic or historical importance and financial value are entered under **Antiques—United States.**

  BT   Collectors and collecting
      Popular culture—United States
      United States—Civilization
      United States—History
  RT   Antiques—United States
Americanisms   427
    Use for materials on words and expressions peculiar to the United States.
  UF   English language—Americanisms
  BT   **English language—Dialects**
Americanization   305.813; 306.0973
  BT   Socialization
  NT   United States—Immigration
      and emigration
  RT   **Immigration and emigration**
      Naturalization
Americans (May subdiv. geog. except
    U.S.)   305.813; 920; 973
    Use for materials on citizens of the United States.
  RT   **Ethnology—United States**
      United States
Americans—Greece   305.813
Amerindians
  USE   **Indians**
      Indians of Central America
      Indians of Mexico
      Indians of North America
      Indians of South America
      Indians of the West Indies
Amish   289.7
  BT   Christian sects
      Mennonites
Ammunition   623.4
  SA   types of ammunition, e.g.
      Bombs; to be added as needed
  BT   Explosives
      Ordnance
      Projectiles
  NT   Bombs
  RT   Firearms
      Gunpowder
Amnesty   364.6
  BT   Administration of criminal justice
      Executive power
  RT   Forgiveness
      Pardon
Amniocentesis   618.3
  BT   Prenatal diagnosis

BT = Broader Term   NT = Narrower Term   RT = Related Term   SA = See Also   UF = Used For

Amphetamines   615
    UF   Pep pills
    SA   types of amphetamines, e.g.
           Methamphetamine; to be
           added as needed
    BT   **Stimulants**
    NT   **Methamphetamine**
Amphibians   567; 597.8
    UF   Batrachia
    SA   names of amphibians, to be add-
           ed as needed
    BT   **Vertebrates**
    NT   **Frogs**
           Salamanders
Amplifiers (Electronics)   621.3815
    SA   types of amplifiers, to be added
           as needed
    BT   **Electronics**
    NT   **Masers**
           Transistor amplifiers
Amplifiers, Transistor
    USE   **Transistor amplifiers**
Amusement parks   791.06
    UF   Theme parks
    SA   names of specific parks, to be
           added as needed
    BT   **Parks**
    NT   **Walt Disney World (Fla.)**
    RT   **Carnivals**
Amusements (May subdiv. geog.)   790
    UF   Entertainments
           Pastimes
    SA   types of amusements, e.g. **Car-**
           nivals; to be added as needed
    NT   **Amateur theater**
           Carnivals
           Charades
           Children's parties
           Christmas entertainments
           Church entertainments
           Circus
           Concerts
           Creative activities
           Dance
           Fireworks
           Fortune telling
           Hobbies
           Juggling
           Literary recreations
           Magic tricks

           Mathematical recreations
           Motion pictures
           Puzzles
           Riddles
           Scientific recreations
           Shadow pictures
           Skits
           Theater
           Toys
           Tricks
           Vaudeville
           Ventriloquism
    RT   **Entertaining**
           Games
           Indoor games
           Play
           Recreation
           Sports
Anabolic steroids
    USE   **Steroids**
Anaesthetics
    USE   **Anesthetics**
Analysis
    USE   types of chemicals and sub-
           stances with the subdivision
           Analysis, e.g. **Water—Analy-**
           sis; Milk—Analysis; etc., for
           materials on methods of ana-
           lyzing those items, to be add-
           ed as needed
Analysis (Chemistry)
    USE   **Analytical chemistry**
Analysis (Mathematics)
    USE   **Calculus**
           Mathematical analysis
Analysis, Microscopic
    USE   **Metallography**
           Microscopes
Analysis of food
    USE   **Food adulteration and inspec-**
           tion
           Food—Analysis
Analysis situs
    USE   **Topology**
Analysis, Spectrum
    USE   **Spectrum analysis**
Analytic geometry   516.3
    UF   Geometry, Analytic *[Former*
           heading]
    BT   **Geometry**

BT = Broader Term   NT = Narrower Term   RT = Related Term   SA = See Also   UF = Used For

Analytical chemistry   543
UF   Analysis (Chemistry)
      Chemical analysis
      Chemistry, Analytic *[Former
         heading]*
      Qualitative analysis
      Quantitative analysis
SA   types of substances with the
         subdivision *Analysis,* e.g. **Wa-
         ter—Analysis;** to be added as
         needed
BT   **Chemistry**
NT   **Distillation**
      Food—Analysis
      Water—Analysis
Anarchism and anarchists   320.5; 335
BT   **Freedom**
      Political crimes and offenses
      Political science
RT   **Terrorism**
Anatomy   571.3; 611
UF   Morphology
SA   names of organs and regions of
         the body and subjects with
         the subdivision *Anatomy,* e.g.
         **Heart—Anatomy; Birds—
         Anatomy;** etc., to be added
         as needed
BT   **Biology**
      Medicine
NT   **Animals—Anatomy**
      Artistic anatomy
      Birds—Anatomy
      Cardiovascular system
      Comparative anatomy
      Foot
      Glands
      Head
      Heart—Anatomy
      Human anatomy
      Immune system
      Musculoskeletal system
      Nervous system
      Plants—Anatomy
      Reproductive system
      Respiratory system
      Skin
      Stomach
      Throat
RT   **Physiology**

Anatomy, Animal
USE   **Animals—Anatomy**
Anatomy, Artistic
USE   **Artistic anatomy**
Anatomy, Comparative
USE   **Comparative anatomy**
Anatomy, Dental
USE   **Teeth**
Anatomy, Human
USE   **Human anatomy**
Anatomy of animals
USE   **Animals—Anatomy**
Anatomy of plants
USE   **Plants—Anatomy**
Ancestor worship   291.2
UF   Worship of the dead
BT   **Religion**
RT   **Shinto**
Ancestry
USE   **Genealogy**
       Heredity
Ancient architecture   722
UF   Architecture, Ancient *[Former
         heading]*
BT   **Archeology**
      Architecture
NT   **Byzantine architecture**
      Greek architecture
      Pyramids
      Roman architecture
      Temples
Ancient art   709.01
UF   Art, Ancient *[Former heading]*
BT   **Art**
NT   **Byzantine art**
      Classical antiquities
      Greek art
      Roman art
Ancient civilization   306.093; 930
UF   Civilization, Ancient *[Former
         heading]*
BT   **Ancient history**
      Civilization
NT   **Classical civilization**
Ancient geography   913
   Use for materials on the geography of the
ancient world in general. Materials on the an-
cient geography of one country or region still
existing in modern times are entered under the
name of the place with the subdivision *Histor-
ical geography.* Materials on the geography of

BT = Broader Term   NT = Narrower Term   RT = Related Term   SA = See Also   UF = Used For

Ancient geography—*Continued*
regions or countries of antiquity that no longer exist as such in modern times are entered
under the name of the place with the subdivision *Geography.*
- UF   Classical geography
        Geography, Ancient *[Former
            heading]*
- SA   names of modern countries with
        the subdivision *Historical ge-
        ography,* e.g. **Greece—Histor-
        ical geography;** and names of
        places of antiquity with the
        subdivision *Geography,* e.g.
        Gaul—Geography; to be
        added as needed
- BT   **Ancient history**
        Historical geography
- NT   **Gaul—Geography**
        Greece—Historical geography
        Rome—Geography

Ancient Greece
- USE   **Greece—History—0-323**

Ancient Greece—Description
- USE   **Greece—Description—0-323**

Ancient history   930
- UF   History, Ancient *[Former head-
            ing]*
- SA   names of ancient peoples, e.g.
        Hittites; and names of coun-
        tries of antiquity, to be added
        as needed
- BT   **History**
        World history
- NT   **Ancient civilization**
        Ancient geography
        Bible
        Classical dictionaries
        Hittites
        Inscriptions
        Numismatics

Ancient philosophy   180
- UF   Greek philosophy
        Philosophy, Ancient *[Former
            heading]*
        Philosophy, Greek
        Philosophy, Roman
        Roman philosophy
- BT   **Philosophy**
- NT   **Stoics**

Androgyny   155.3; 305.3
- BT   **Sex differences (Psychology)**
        Sex role

Anecdotes   808.88; 818.008, etc.
    May be used for collections of anecdotes
    and for materials about anecdotes.
- UF   Facetiae
        Stories
- SA   subjects with the subdivision *An-
        ecdotes,* to be added as need-
        ed
- NT   **Music—Anecdotes**
- RT   **Wit and humor**

Anesthetics   615; 617.9
- UF   Anaesthetics
- BT   **Materia medica**
        Pain
        Surgery

Angels   235
- UF   Spirits
- BT   **Heaven**

Angina pectoris   616.1
- BT   **Heart diseases**

Anglican Church
- USE   **Church of England**

Angling
- USE   **Fishing**

Anglo-French intervention in Egypt, 1956
- USE   **Sinai Campaign, 1956**

Anglo-Saxon language   429
- UF   English language—0-1100
        English language—Old English
        Old English language
- BT   **Language and languages**
- RT   **English language**

Anglo-Saxon literature   829
- UF   English literature—0-1100
        English literature—Old English
        Old English literature
- BT   **Literature**
- RT   **English literature**

Anglo-Saxons   305.82; 941.01
- UF   Saxons
- BT   **Great Britain—History—0-1066**
        Teutonic peoples

Animal abuse
- USE   **Animal welfare**

Animal attacks   591.6
- UF   Attacks by animals
- BT   **Dangerous animals**

BT = Broader Term   NT = Narrower Term   RT = Related Term   SA = See Also   UF = Used For

Animal babies   591.3

    Use for materials on baby animals of several species. Baby animals of a particular species are entered under the name of the species.

UF   Animals—Infancy *[Former heading]*

        Baby animals

BT   **Animals**

Animal behavior   591.5

UF   Animals—Behavior *[Former heading]*

        Animals, Habits and behavior of

        Behavior

        Habits of animals

SA   types of specific behavior, e.g. **Animals—Migration; Hibernation; Sexual behavior in animals;** etc.; and types of animals with the subdivision *Behavior,* e.g. **Birds—Behavior;** to be added as needed

BT   **Animals**

        Zoology

NT   **Animal communication**

        Animal courtship

        Animal defenses

        Animal sounds

        Animals—Food

        Animals—Migration

        Hibernation

        Instinct

        Monkeys—Behavior

        Primates—Behavior

        Sexual behavior in animals

RT   **Animal intelligence**

        Tracking and trailing

Animal camouflage

USE **Camouflage (Biology)**

Animal communication   591.59

UF   Animal language

        Animals—Language

        Communication among animals

BT   **Animal behavior**

RT   **Animal sounds**

Animal courtship   591.56

UF   Animals—Courtship *[Former heading]*

        Courtship (Animal behavior)

        Courtship of animals

        Mate selection in animals

        Mating behavior

BT   **Animal behavior**

        Sexual behavior in animals

Animal defenses   591.47

UF   Defense mechanisms (Zoology)

        Self-defense in animals

        Self-protection in animals

BT   **Animal behavior**

NT   **Camouflage (Biology)**

Animal drawing

USE **Animal painting and illustration**

Animal embryos, Frozen

USE **Frozen embryos**

Animal experimentation   619

UF   Experimentation on animals

        Laboratory animal experimentation

BT   **Research**

NT   **Vivisection**

RT   **Animal welfare**

Animal exploitation

USE **Animal welfare**

Animal-facilitated therapy

USE **Pet therapy**

Animal flight   573.7

UF   Animal flying

        Animals—Flight

SA   types of animals with the subdivision *Flight,* e.g. **Birds—Flight;** to be added as needed

BT   **Animal locomotion**

        Flight

NT   **Birds—Flight**

Animal flying

USE **Animal flight**

Animal food

USE **Animals—Food**

        Food of animal origin

Animal habitations

USE **Animals—Habitations**

Animal homes

USE **Animals—Habitations**

Animal housing   636.08

    Use for materials on houses or habitations provided by humans for either wild or domestic animals. Materials on the natural shelters and homes animals build for themselves, such as burrows, dens, lairs, etc., are entered under **Animals—Habitations.**

UF   Animals—Housing

        Domestic animal dwellings

BT = Broader Term   NT = Narrower Term   RT = Related Term   SA = See Also   UF = Used For

Animal housing—*Continued*
>
> Domestic animals—Housing
>
> Habitations of domestic animals
>
> SA   types of animals with the subdivision *Housing,* e.g. **Pets—Housing;** to be added as needed
>
> BT   **Animals**
>
> NT   **Beehives**
>
> **Birdhouses**
>
> **Pets—Housing**
>
> RT   **Animals—Habitations**

Animal husbandry
>
> USE   **Livestock industry**

Animal industry
>
> USE   **Livestock industry**

Animal instinct
>
> USE   **Instinct**

Animal intelligence   591.5
>
> UF   Animal psychology
>
> Intelligence of animals
>
> SA   types of animals with the subdivision *Psychology,* to be added as needed
>
> BT   **Animals**
>
> NT   **Dogs—Psychology**
>
> **Psychology of learning**
>
> RT   **Animal behavior**
>
> **Comparative psychology**
>
> **Instinct**

Animal kingdom
>
> USE   **Zoology**

Animal language
>
> USE   **Animal communication**
>
> **Animal sounds**

Animal liberation movement
>
> USE   **Animal rights movements**

Animal light
>
> USE   **Bioluminescence**

Animal locomotion   573.7
>
> UF   Animals—Movements
>
> Movements of animals
>
> BT   **Animals**
>
> **Locomotion**
>
> NT   **Animal flight**

Animal lore
>
> USE   **Animals—Folklore**
>
> **Animals in literature**
>
> **Mythical animals**
>
> **Natural history**

Animal luminescence
>
> USE   **Bioluminescence**

Animal magnetism
>
> USE   **Hypnotism**

Animal migration
>
> USE   **Animals—Migration**

Animal oils
>
> USE   **Oils and fats**

Animal painting and illustration   704.9; 743.6; 758
>
> Use for materials on the art of painting or drawing animals. Materials on the depiction of animals in works of art are entered under **Animals in art.** Popular materials consisting chiefly of photographs or illustrations of animals are entered under **Animals—Pictorial works.**
>
> UF   Animal drawing
>
> BT   **Painting**
>
> RT   **Animals in art**
>
> **Animals—Pictorial works**
>
> **Photography of animals**

Animal parasites
>
> USE   **Parasites**

Animal photography
>
> USE   **Photography of animals**

Animal physiology
>
> USE   **Zoology**

Animal pictures
>
> USE   **Animals—Pictorial works**

Animal pounds
>
> USE   **Animal shelters**

Animal products   338.1; 338.4
>
> UF   Products, Animal
>
> SA   types of animal products, to be added as needed
>
> BT   **Commercial products**
>
> NT   **Dairy products**
>
> **Hides and skins**
>
> **Ivory**
>
> **Leather**
>
> **Wool**

Animal psychology
>
> USE   **Animal intelligence**
>
> **Comparative psychology**

Animal reproduction   571.8
>
> UF   Animals—Birth
>
> Animals—Reproduction
>
> BT   **Animals**
>
> **Reproduction**

BT = Broader Term   NT = Narrower Term   RT = Related Term   SA = See Also   UF = Used For

Animal rights   179

Use for materials on the inherent rights attributed to animals. Materials on the protection and treatment of animals are entered under **Animal welfare.**

UF   Animals' rights

Rights of animals

RT   **Animal rights movements**

Animal welfare

Animal rights movements   179

Use for materials on any of the politically diverse movements engaged in animal rights or animal welfare support activities.

UF   Animal liberation movement

Animal welfare movement

Antivivisection movement

BT   **Social movements**

RT   **Animal rights**

Animal welfare

Animal sexual behavior

USE   **Sexual behavior in animals**

Animal shelters   179; 636.08

UF   Animal pounds

Shelters, Animal

BT   **Animal welfare**

Animal signs

USE   **Animal tracks**

Animal sounds   573.9; 591.59

UF   Animal language

Animals—Sounds

BT   **Animal behavior**

NT   **Birdsongs**

RT   **Animal communication**

Animal stories

USE   **Animals—Fiction**

Animal tracks   590

UF   Animal signs

Tracks of animals

BT   **Tracking and trailing**

Animal training

USE   **Animals—Training**

Animal welfare   179

Use for materials on the protection and treatment of animals. Materials on the inherent rights attributed to animals are entered under **Animal rights.**

UF   Abuse of animals

Animal abuse *[Former heading]*

Animal exploitation

Animals, Cruelty to

Animals—Mistreatment

Animals—Protection

Animals—Treatment

Cruelty to animals

Humane treatment of animals

Laboratory animal welfare

Prevention of cruelty to animals

Protection of animals

NT   **Animal shelters**

RT   **Animal experimentation**

Animal rights

Animal rights movements

Animal welfare movement

USE   **Animal rights movements**

Animals (May subdiv. geog.)   590

Use for nonscientific materials. Materials on the science of animals are entered under **Zoology.** Subdivisions used under this heading may be used under the names of orders, classes, or individual species of animals.

UF   Beasts

Fauna

Wild animals

SA   names of orders and classes of the animal kingdom; kinds of animals characterized by their environments; and names of individual species, to be added as needed

NT   **Animal babies**

Animal behavior

Animal housing

Animal intelligence

Animal locomotion

Animal reproduction

Birds

Carnivorous animals

Dangerous animals

Desert animals

Domestic animals

Extinct animals

Forest animals

Freshwater animals

Furbearing animals

Game and game birds

Invertebrates

Jungle animals

Mammals

Marine animals

Mountain animals

Pets

Poisonous animals

Predatory animals

Prehistoric animals

BT = Broader Term   NT = Narrower Term   RT = Related Term   SA = See Also   UF = Used For

Animals—*Continued*
> Rare animals
> Stream animals
> Swamp animals
> Vertebrates
> Wildlife
> Working animals

RT Zoology
> Zoos

Animals—Anatomy 571.3

UF Anatomy, Animal
> Anatomy of animals
> Morphology
> Structural zoology
> Zoology—Anatomy

BT Anatomy
> Zoology

NT Fur

Animals and the handicapped 636.088

UF Handicapped and animals
> Pets and the handicapped
> Service dogs

BT Animals—Training

NT Guide dogs
> Hearing ear dogs
> Pet therapy

Animals as food
USE Food of animal origin

Animals—Behavior
USE Animal behavior

Animals—Birth
USE Animal reproduction

Animals—Camouflage
USE Camouflage (Biology)

Animals—Color 573.5; 591.47
BT Color

Animals—Courtship
USE Animal courtship

Animals, Cruelty to
USE Animal welfare

Animals—Diseases 571.9; 636.089

UF Diseases of animals
> Domestic animals—Diseases

SA types of animals with the subdivision *Diseases,* to be added as needed

BT Diseases

NT Horses—Diseases

RT Veterinary medicine

Animals, Domestic
USE Domestic animals

Animals, Edible
USE Food of animal origin

Animals, Extinct
USE Extinct animals

Animals—Fiction 808.83; 813, etc.

May be used for individual works, collections, or materials about animal stories. General materials about the portrayal of animals in literature are entered under **Animals in literature.**

UF Animal stories

SA types of animals with the subdivision *Fiction,* e.g. **Dogs—Fiction;** to be added as needed

RT Animals in literature
> Fables

Animals—Filmography 016.591

Animals—Flight
USE Animal flight

Animals—Folklore 398.24

UF Animal lore

BT Folklore

NT Dragons
> Monsters

RT Mythical animals

Animals—Food 591.5

Use for materials on the food and food habits of animals. Materials on human food of animal origin are entered under **Food of animal origin.**

UF Animal food
> Feeding behavior in animals

SA types of animals and species of animals with the subdivision *Food,* to be added as needed

BT Animal behavior
> Food

NT Feeds
> Food chains (Ecology)

Animals—Geographical distribution
USE Biogeography

Animals—Habitations 591.56

Use for materials on the natural shelters and homes animals build for themselves, such as burrows, dens, lairs, etc. Materials on houses or habitations provided by humans for either wild or domestic animals are entered under **Animal housing.**

UF Animal habitations
> Animal homes
> Habitations of wild animals

BT = Broader Term   NT = Narrower Term   RT = Related Term   SA = See Also   UF = Used For

Animals—Habitations—*Continued*
    Wild animal dwellings
NT   **Birds—Nests**
RT   **Animal housing**
Animals, Habits and behavior of
USE   **Animal behavior**
Animals—Hibernation
USE   **Hibernation**
Animals—Housing
USE   **Animal housing**
Animals, Imaginary
USE   **Mythical animals**
Animals in art   704.9

    Use for materials on the depiction of animals in works of art. Materials on the art of painting or drawing animals are entered under **Animal painting and illustration.** Materials consisting chiefly of photographs or illustrations of animals are entered under **Animals—Pictorial works.**

BT   **Art**
RT   **Animal painting and illustration**
        Animals—Pictorial works
Animals in literature   809

    Use for materials on the theme of animals in literature. Poems or stories about animals are entered under **Animals—Poetry** or **Animals—Fiction.**

UF   Animal lore
SA   phrase headings for specific animals in literature, e.g. **Dogs in literature;** to be added as needed
BT   **Literature**
        Nature in literature
NT   **Birds in literature**
        Dogs in literature
RT   **Animals—Fiction**
        Animals—Poetry
Animals in motion pictures   791.43
BT   **Motion pictures**
Animals in police work   363.2; 636.088
BT   **Police**
        Working animals
Animals—Infancy
USE   **Animal babies**
Animals—Language
USE   **Animal communication**
Animals—Migration   591.56
UF   Animal migration
        Migration of animals

SA   types of animals with the subdivision *Migration,* to be added as needed
BT   **Animal behavior**
NT   **Birds—Migration**
Animals—Mistreatment
USE   **Animal welfare**
Animals—Movements
USE   **Animal locomotion**
Animals, Mythical
USE   **Mythical animals**
Animals—Petting zoos
USE   **Petting zoos**
Animals—Photography
USE   **Photography of animals**
Animals—Pictorial works   590.22

    Use for popular materials consisting chiefly of photographs or illustrations of animals. Materials on the art of painting or drawing animals are entered under **Animal painting and illustration.** Materials on the depiction of animals in works of art are entered under **Animals in art.**

UF   Animal pictures
RT   **Animal painting and illustration**
        Animals in art
        Photography of animals
Animals—Poetry   808.81; 811, etc.; 811.008, etc.

    May be used for individual works or collections of poetry about animals. Materials on the theme of animals in literature are entered under **Animals in literature.**

BT   **Poetry**
RT   **Animals in literature**
Animals, Prehistoric
USE   **Prehistoric animals**
Animals—Protection
USE   **Animal welfare**
Animals, Rare
USE   **Rare animals**
Animals—Reproduction
USE   **Animal reproduction**
Animals' rights
USE   **Animal rights**
Animals—Sexual behavior
USE   **Sexual behavior in animals**
Animals—Sounds
USE   **Animal sounds**
Animals—Temperature
USE   **Body temperature**

BT = Broader Term   NT = Narrower Term   RT = Related Term   SA = See Also   UF = Used For

Animals—Training   636.088
  UF   Animal training
        Training of animals
  SA   types of animals with the subdi-
        vision *Training,* e.g. **Horses—
        Training;** to be added as
        needed
  NT   **Animals and the handicapped
        Dogs—Training**
Animals—Treatment
  USE   **Animal welfare**
Animals—United States   591.973
  UF   United States—Animals
        Zoology—United States *[Former
        heading]*
Animals, Useful and harmful
  USE   **Economic zoology**
Animals—War use   355.4
  UF   War use of animals
  BT   **Working animals**
  NT   **Dogs—War use**
Animals, Working
  USE   **Working animals**
Animated cartoons
  USE   **Animated films**
Animated films   741.5; 791.43
      May be used for individual works, collec-
      tions, or materials about animated films.
  UF   Animated cartoons
        Cartoons, Animated
        Motion picture cartoons *[Former
        heading]*
  BT   **Cartoons and caricatures
        Motion pictures**
  RT   **Animation (Cinematography)**
Animated television programs   791.45
      May be used for individual works, collec-
      tions, or materials about animated television
      programs.
  UF   Cartoons, Television
        Television cartoons
  BT   **Television programs**
Animation (Cinematography)   741.5;
        778.5
  BT   **Cinematography**
  RT   **Animated films**
Anniversaries
  USE   **Birthdays
        Holidays**

and ethnic groups, classes of
persons, individuals, coporate
bodies, places, religious denominations, or wars with the
subdivision *Anniversaries,* for
materials about anniversary
celebrations, e.g. **Shakespeare, William, 1564-1616—
Anniversaries;** to be added
as needed
Annual income guarantee
  USE   **Guaranteed annual income**
Annuals
  USE   **Almanacs
        Calendars
        Periodicals
        School yearbooks**
        and subjects and names of
        countries, cities, etc., individu-
        al persons, families, and cor-
        porate bodies with the subdi-
        vision *Periodicals,* e.g. **Engi-
        neering—Periodicals;** to be
        added as needed
Annuals (Plants)   582.1; 635.9
  BT   **Cultivated plants
        Flower gardening
        Flowers**
Annuities   368.3
  BT   **Investments
        Retirement income**
  NT   **Pensions**
  RT   **Life insurance**
Annulment of marriage
  USE   **Marriage—Annulment**
Anointing of the sick   265
  UF   Extreme unction
        Last rites (Sacraments)
        Last sacraments
        Unction, Extreme
  BT   **Sacraments**
Anonyms
  USE   **Pseudonyms**
Anorexia nervosa   616.85
  UF   Self-starvation
        Starvation, Self-imposed
  BT   **Eating disorders**
Answers to questions
  USE   **Questions and answers**

BT = Broader Term   NT = Narrower Term   RT = Related Term   SA = See Also   UF = Used For

Ant
   USE   **Ants**
Antarctic expeditions
   USE   **Antarctica—Exploration**
Antarctic regions
   USE   **Antarctica**
Antarctic regions—Exploration
   USE   **Antarctica—Exploration**
Antarctica   998
   Use for materials on the continent of Antarctica and the regions adjacent to it.
   UF   Antarctic regions *[Former heading]*
   BT   **Earth**
        Polar regions
   RT   **South Pole**
Antarctica—Exploration   919.8
   UF   Antarctic expeditions
        Antarctic regions—Exploration
        [Former heading]
        Polar expeditions
   SA   names of expeditions, e.g. **Byrd Antarctic Expedition;** to be added as needed
   BT   **Exploration**
        Scientific expeditions
   NT   **Byrd Antarctic Expedition**
Antenuptial contracts
   USE   **Marriage contracts**
Anthems, National
   USE   **National songs**
Anthologies   080; 808.8; 810.8, etc.
   Use for collections of general interest by more than one author not limited to a single literature or literary form or focused on a single subject.
   UF   Collected papers (Anthologies)
        Collected works
        Collections (Anthologies)
        Collections of literature
        Literary collections
        Papers, Collected (Anthologies)
        Readings (Anthologies)
   SA   names of literatures, e.g.
        American literature; and, for collections focused on a single subject by more than one author involving two or more literary forms, the subject with the subdivision *Literary collections,* e.g. **Cats—Liter-**

ary collections; to be added as needed
   BT   **Books**
Anthropogeography
   USE   **Human geography**
Anthropology   301; 599.9
   UF   Human race
   SA   names of races and peoples, e.g. **Navajo Indians;** to be added as needed
   BT   **Social sciences**
   NT   **Acculturation**
        Anthropometry
        Ethnopsychology
        Human geography
        Language and languages
        National characteristics
        Physical anthropology
        Social change
   RT   **Civilization**
        Culture
        Ethnology
        Human beings
Anthropology, Physical
   USE   **Physical anthropology**
Anthropometry   599.9
   UF   Skeletal remains
   BT   **Anthropology**
        Ethnology
        Human beings
   NT   **Fingerprints**
Anti-abortion movement
   USE   **Pro-life movement**
Anti-Americanism
   USE   **United States—Foreign opinion**
Anti-apartheid movement (May subdiv. geog.)   **172; 320.5; 323.1**
   BT   **Civil rights**
        Social movements
        South Africa—Race relations
   RT   **Apartheid**
Anti-fascist movements
   USE   **World War, 1939-1945—Underground movements**
Anti-Nazi movement
   USE   **World War, 1939-1945—Underground movements**
Anti-poverty programs
   USE   **Domestic economic assistance**

BT = Broader Term   NT = Narrower Term   RT = Related Term   SA = See Also   UF = Used For

Anti-Reformation
USE   Counter-Reformation
Anti-utopias
USE   Dystopias
Anti-war films
USE   War films
Anti-war poetry
USE   War poetry
Anti-war stories
USE   War stories
Antiabortion movement
USE   Pro-life movement
Antiamericanism
USE   United States—Foreign opinion
Antiballistic missiles
USE   Antimissile missiles
Antibiotics   615
SA   names of specific antibiotics, to
be added as needed
BT   Drug therapy
NT   Penicillin
Antibusing
USE   Busing (School integration)
Anticommunist movements   322.4
UF   Underground, Anticommunist
BT   Communism
Anticorrosive paint
USE   Corrosion and anticorrosives
Antimissile missiles   358.1; 623.4
UF   A.B.M.'s
ABMs
Antiballistic missiles
BT   Guided missiles
Antinuclear movement (May subdiv.
geog.)   303.48; 327.1; 363.17
UF   Nuclear freeze movement
BT   Arms control
Nuclear weapons
Social movements
RT   Nuclear power plants—Envi-
ronmental aspects
Antipathies
USE   Prejudices
Antipoverty programs
USE   Domestic economic assistance
Antiquarian books
USE   Rare books
Antiques (May subdiv. geog.)   745.1
BT   Antiquities
Decoration and ornament

Decorative arts
NT   Art objects
Collectors and collecting
Victoriana
Antiques—United States   745.10973
Use for materials about old American objects that have aesthetic or historical impor-
tance and financial value. General materials
about American objects of interest to collectors, such as historical documents, relics, etc.,
as well as items of little intrinsic value, are
entered under Americana.
UF   United States—Antiques
RT   Americana
Antiquities   930.1
Use for general materials on the relics or
monuments of ancient times. Materials on the
relics or monuments of an extinct city or town
are entered under the name of the city or
town.
UF   Archeological specimens
Ruins
SA   names of extinct cities, e.g. Del-
phi (Extinct city); and names
of groups of people extant in
modern times and names of
cities (except extinct cities),
countries, regions, etc., with
the subdivision Antiquities,
e.g. Indians of North Ameri-
ca—Antiquities; United
States—Antiquities; etc., to
be added as needed
NT   America—Antiquities
Antiques
Bible—Antiquities
Chicago (Ill.)—Antiquities
Christian antiquities
Classical antiquities
Egypt—Antiquities
Indians of North America—
Antiquities
Jews—Antiquities
Ohio—Antiquities
Prehistoric peoples
United States—Antiquities
RT   Archeology
Antiquities, Biblical
USE   Bible—Antiquities
Antiquities, Christian
USE   Christian antiquities
Antiquities, Classical
USE   Classical antiquities

BT = Broader Term   NT = Narrower Term   RT = Related Term   SA = See Also   UF = Used For

Antiquities—Collection and preservation
069
UF   Preservation of antiquities
BT   **Collectors and collecting**
Antiquities, Ecclesiastical
USE   **Christian antiquities**
Antiquity of man
USE   **Human origins**
Antisemitism   305.892
BT   **Prejudices**
NT   **Holocaust, 1933-1945**
      Jews—Persecutions
Antiseptics   614.4; 617.9
BT   **Surgery**
      Therapeutics
RT   **Disinfection and disinfectants**
Antislavery
USE   **Abolitionists**
      Slavery
Antitrust law   343.07
UF   Industrial trusts—Law and legislation
BT   **Commercial law**
      Industrial trusts
Antivivisection movement
USE   **Animal rights movements**
Antiwar movements
USE   **Peace movements**
Antonyms
USE   **Opposites**
      and names of languages with the subdivision *Synonyms and antonyms,* e.g. **English language—Synonyms and antonyms;** to be added as needed
Ants   595.79
UF   Ant
      Hymenoptera
BT   **Insects**
Anxieties
USE   **Anxiety**
Anxiety   152.4
UF   Anxieties
      Anxiousness
BT   **Emotions**
      Neuroses
      Stress (Psychology)
NT   **Post-traumatic stress disorder**
      Separation anxiety in children

RT   **Fear**
      Worry
Anxiousness
USE   **Anxiety**
Apartheid   320.5
    Use for materials on the economic, political, and social policies of the government of South Africa designed to segregate racial groups in South Africa and Namibia.
UF   Separate development (Race relations)
BT   **Segregation**
      South Africa—Race relations
RT   **Anti-apartheid movement**
Apartment houses (May subdiv. geog.)
647; 728
UF   Flats
BT   **Buildings**
      Domestic architecture
      Houses
      Housing
      Landlord and tenant
NT   **Condominiums**
      Tenement houses
Apiculture
USE   **Beekeeping**
Apocalyptic fantasies
USE   **Fantasy fiction**
      Fantasy films
      Fantasy television programs
      Robinsonades
      Science fiction
      War films
      War stories
Apollo project   629.45
UF   Project Apollo
BT   **Life support systems (Space environment)**
      Orbital rendezvous (Space flight)
      Space flight to the moon
Apologetic works
USE   **Apologetics**
      and religions and denominations with the subdivisions *Apologetic works* e.g. **Christianity—Apologetic works;** and religions, denominations, religious orders, and sacred works with the subdivision

---

BT = Broader Term   NT = Narrower Term   RT = Related Term   SA = See Also   UF = Used For

Apologetic works—*Continued*
    Controversial literature, e.g.
    Christianity—Controversial literature; to be added as needed
Apologetics   239; 291.2
  UF   Apologetic works
       Fundamental theology
  SA   religions and denominations with the subdivisions *Apologetic works* e.g. **Christianity—Apologetic works;** and religions, denominations, religious orders, and sacred works with the subdivision *Controversial literature,* e.g. **Christianity—Controversial literature;** to be added as needed
  BT   **Theology**
  NT   **Christianity—Apologetic works**
       Christianity—Controversial literature
       Natural theology
Apoplexy
  USE   **Stroke**
Apostles   225.92
  UF   Disciples, Twelve
  BT   **Christian saints**
       Church history—30-600, Early church
Apostles' Creed   238
  BT   **Creeds**
Apostolic Church
  USE   **Church history—30-600, Early church**
Apothecary shops
  USE   **Drugstores**
Apparatus, Chemical
  USE   **Chemical apparatus**
Apparatus, Electric
  USE   **Electric apparatus and appliances**
Apparatus, Electronic
  USE   **Electronic apparatus and appliances**
Apparatus, Scientific
  USE   **Scientific apparatus and instruments**
Apparitions   133.1
  UF   Phantoms

       Specters
       Spirits
  BT   **Parapsychology**
       Superstition
  RT   **Demonology**
       Ghosts
       Hallucinations and illusions
       Spiritualism
       Visions
Appearance, Personal
  USE   **Personal appearance**
Apperception   153.7
  BT   **Educational psychology**
       Psychology
  NT   **Attention**
       Consciousness
       Number concept
  RT   **Perception**
       Theory of knowledge
Apple   583; 634; 641.3
  UF   Apples
  BT   **Fruit**
       Trees
Apple Macintosh (Computer)
  USE   **Macintosh (Computer)**
Apples
  USE   **Apple**
Appliances, Electric
  USE   **Electric apparatus and appliances**
       Electric household appliances
Appliances, Electronic
  USE   **Electronic apparatus and appliances**
Applications for college
  USE   **College applications**
Applications for positions   331.12; 650.14
  UF   Employment applications
       Employment references
       Job applications
       Letters of recommendation
       Recommendations for positions
  BT   **Job hunting**
       Personnel management
  NT   **Interviewing**
       Résumés (Employment)
Applied arts
  USE   **Decorative arts**

BT = Broader Term   NT = Narrower Term   RT = Related Term   SA = See Also   UF = Used For

Applied mechanics   620.1

Use for materials on the application of the principles of mechanics to engineering structures other than machinery. Materials on the application of the principles of mechanics to the design, construction, and operation of machinery are entered under **Mechanical engineering.**

UF   Mechanics, Applied *[Former
       heading]*

BT   **Mechanics**

Applied psychology   158

UF   Industrial psychology

       Practical Psychology

       Psychology, Applied *[Former
       heading]*

       Psychology, Industrial

       Psychology, Practical

SA   subjects with the subdivision
       Psychological aspects, e.g.
       Drugs—Psychological aspects; to be added as needed

BT   **Psychology**

NT   **Behavior modification**

       Counseling

       Drugs—Psychological aspects

       Employee morale

       Human engineering

       Negotiation

       Pastoral psychology

       Psychological warfare

RT   **Educational psychology**

       Interviewing

       Social psychology

Applied science

USE   **Technology**

**Apportionment (Election law)   324;
328.3; 342**

UF   Legislative reapportionment

       Reapportionment (Election law)

BT   **Representative government and
       representation**

Appraisal

USE   **Tax assessment**

       Valuation

Appraisal of books

USE   **Books and reading**

       Books—Reviews

       Criticism

       Literature—History and criticism

Appreciation of art

USE   **Art appreciation**

Appreciation of music

USE   **Music appreciation**

Apprentices   331.5

BT   **Labor**

       Technical education

RT   **Employees—Training**

Apprenticeship novels

USE   **Bildungsromans**

Approximate computation   372.7; 513.2

UF   Arithmetic—Estimation

       Computation, Approximate

       Estimation (Mathematics)

BT   **Numerical analysis**

April First

USE   **April Fools' Day**

April Fools' Day   394.262

UF   All Fools' Day

       April First

BT   **Holidays**

Aptitude testing

USE   **Ability—Testing**

Aquaculture   639

UF   Aquiculture

       Freshwater aquaculture

       Mariculture

       Marine aquaculture

       Ocean farming

       Sea farming

BT   **Agriculture**

       Marine resources

NT   **Fish culture**

Aquanauts

USE   **Undersea research stations**

       Underwater exploration

Aquarian Age movement

USE   **New Age movement**

Aquariums   597.073; 639.34

SA   names of specific aquariums, to
       be added as needed

BT   **Freshwater biology**

       Natural history

NT   **Marine aquariums**

RT   **Fish culture**

       Fishes

Aquatic animals

USE   **Freshwater animals**

       Marine animals

Aquatic birds
USE   **Water birds**
Aquatic plants
USE   **Freshwater plants**
       Marine plants
Aquatic sports
USE   **Water sports**
Aquatic sports—Safety measures
USE   **Water safety**
Aqueducts   628.1
UF   Water conduits
BT   **Civil engineering**
       Hydraulic structures
       Water supply
Aquiculture
USE   **Aquaculture**
Arab architecture
USE   **Islamic architecture**
Arab civilization   306.0917; 909
UF   Civilization, Arab *[Former head-*
       ing]
BT   **Civilization**
Arab countries   956
   Use for materials on several Arabic-
   speaking countries. Materials on the region
   consisting of northeastern Africa and Asia
   west of Afghanistan are entered under **Middle**
   East.
BT   **Islamic countries**
       Middle East
Arab countries—Foreign relations—Israel
   956
UF   Arab-Israel relations
       Arab-Israeli relations
       Israel-Arab relations
       Israeli-Arab relations
NT   **Israel-Arab conflicts**
RT   **Israel—Foreign relations—**
       Arab countries
       Jewish-Arab relations
Arab countries—Politics and government
   956
BT   **Politics**
NT   **Pan-Arabism**
Arab-Israel conflicts
USE   **Israel-Arab conflicts**
Arab-Israel relations
USE   **Arab countries—Foreign rela-**
       tions—Israel
       Israel—Foreign relations—
       Arab countries

Arab-Israel War, 1948-1949
USE   **Israel-Arab War, 1948-1949**
Arab-Israel War, 1956
USE   **Sinai Campaign, 1956**
Arab-Israel War, 1967
USE   **Israel-Arab War, 1967**
Arab-Israel War, 1973
USE   **Israel-Arab War, 1973**
Arab-Israeli conflict, 1987-
USE   **Intifada, 1987-**
Arab-Israeli conflicts
USE   **Israel-Arab conflicts**
Arab-Israeli relations
USE   **Arab countries—Foreign rela-**
       tions—Israel
       Israel—Foreign relations—
       Arab countries
Arab-Jewish relations
USE   **Jewish-Arab relations**
Arab refugees (May subdiv. geog.)   **325**
UF   Refugees, Arab *[Former head-*
       ing]
BT   **Refugees**
Arabia
USE   **Arabian Peninsula**
Arabian Peninsula   953
UF   Arabia
BT   **Peninsulas**
Arabs   305.892; 909
SA   names of specific Arab peoples,
       to be added as needed
NT   **Bedouins**
       Jewish-Arab relations
       Moors
       Palestinian Arabs
Arabs—Palestine
USE   **Palestinian Arabs**
Arachnida
USE   **Spiders**
       Ticks
Arbitration and award   347
   Use for materials on the settlement of civil
   disputes by arbitration instead of a court trial.
UF   Awards (Law)
       Mediation
BT   **Commercial law**
       Courts
RT   **Litigation**
Arbitration, Industrial
USE   **Industrial arbitration**

BT = Broader Term   **NT** = Narrower Term   **RT** = Related Term   **SA** = See Also   **UF** = Used For

Arbitration, International
  USE   **International arbitration**
Arboriculture
  USE   **Forests and forestry**
             Fruit culture
             Trees
Arc light
  USE   **Electric lighting**
Arc welding
  USE   **Electric welding**
Archaeology
  USE   **Archeology**
Archeological specimens
  USE   **Antiquities**
Archeologists   920; 930.1092
  BT   **Historians**
Archeology (May subdiv. geog.)   **930.1**
    Use for materials on the discipline of arche-
    ology. General materials on the relics or mon-
    uments of ancient times are entered under **An-**
    tiquities. Materials on the relics or monu-
    ments of an extinct city or town are entered
    under the name of the city or town.
  UF   Archaeology
             Prehistory
  SA   names of extinct cities, e.g. **Del-**
             phi (Extinct city); to be add-
             ed as needed; and names of
             groups of people and of cities
             (except extinct cities), coun-
             tries, regions, etc., with the
             subdivision *Antiquities,* e.g.
             Indians of North America—
             Antiquities; United States—
             Antiquities; etc., to be added
             as needed
  BT   **Civilization**
             History
  NT   **Ancient architecture**
             Bible—Antiquities
             Brasses
             Bronzes
             Burial
             Buried treasure
             Christian antiquities
             Cliff dwellers and cliff dwell-
             ings
             Excavations (Archeology)
             Extinct cities
             Fossil hominids
             Gems
             Heraldry

             Historic sites
             Industrial archeology
             Inscriptions
             Mounds and mound builders
             Mummies
             Numismatics
             Obelisks
             Prehistoric peoples
             Pyramids
             Radiocarbon dating
             Rock drawings, paintings, and
               engravings
             Stone implements
             Temples
             Tombs
  RT   **Antiquities**
             Art
             Bronze Age
             Iron Age
             Stone Age
Archeology, Biblical
  USE   **Bible—Antiquities**
Archeology, Christian
  USE   **Christian antiquities**
Archeology, Classical
  USE   **Classical antiquities**
Archery   799.3
  BT   **Martial arts**
             Shooting
  RT   **Bow and arrow**
Architects   720.92; 920
  BT   **Artists**
Architectural acoustics   729; 690
  UF   Acoustics
  BT   **Sound**
  NT   **Soundproofing**
Architectural decoration and ornament
      729
  UF   Architecture—Decoration and or-
             nament
             Decoration and ornament, Archi-
             tectural *[Former heading]*
  BT   **Architecture**
             Decoration and ornament
Architectural design
  USE   **Architecture—Details**
Architectural designs
  USE   **Architecture—Designs and**
               plans

BT = Broader Term   NT = Narrower Term   RT = Related Term   SA = See Also   UF = Used For

Architectural details
  USE   Architecture—Details
Architectural drawing   720.28
  UF   Drawing, Architectural
         Plans
  BT   **Drawing**
         Mechanical drawing
  NT   **Architecture—Designs and**
            plans
         Architecture—Details
Architectural engineering
  USE   **Building**
         Strains and stresses
         Structural analysis (Engineer-
            ing)
Architectural features
  USE   **Architecture—Details**
Architectural metalwork   721
  UF   Metalwork, Architectural
  BT   **Metalwork**
Architectural perspective
  USE   **Perspective**
Architecture   720
     Use for materials on the design and style of
     structures. Materials on the process of con-
     struction are entered under **Building**. General
     materials on buildings and materials on build-
     ings in a particular place are entered under
     Buildings.
  SA   architecture of particular coun-
            tries, e.g. **American architec-**
            ture; styles of architecture,
            e.g. **Byzantine architecture**;
            and types of buildings, e.g.
            Farm buildings; to be added
            as needed
  BT   **Art**
  NT   **American architecture**
         Ancient architecture
         Architectural decoration and
            ornament
         Asian architecture
         Baroque architecture
         Byzantine architecture
         Church architecture
         Colonial architecture
         Domestic architecture
         Gothic architecture
         Greek architecture
         Indians of North America—
            Architecture
         Islamic architecture

         Landscape architecture
         Library architecture
         Lost architecture
         Medieval architecture
         Modern architecture
         Monuments
         Naval architecture
         Obelisks
         Renaissance architecture
         Roman architecture
         Romanesque architecture
         Spires
         Tombs
         Underground architecture
  RT   **Building**
         Buildings
Architecture, American
  USE   **American architecture**
Architecture, Ancient
  USE   **Ancient architecture**
Architecture and the handicapped   720
  UF   Barrier free design
         Handicapped and architecture
  BT   **Handicapped**
Architecture, Asian
  USE   **Asian architecture**
Architecture—Awards   720.79
Architecture, Baroque
  USE   **Baroque architecture**
Architecture, Byzantine
  USE   **Byzantine architecture**
Architecture, Colonial
  USE   **Colonial architecture**
Architecture—Composition, proportion,
    etc.   720; 729
  UF   Architecture—Proportion
         Proportion (Architecture)
  BT   **Composition (Art)**
Architecture—Conservation and restora-
    tion   690; 720.28
  UF   Architecture—Restoration
         Buildings, Restoration of
         Conservation of buildings
         Preservation of buildings
         Restoration of buildings
  RT   **Buildings—Maintenance and**
            repair
Architecture—Decoration and ornament
  USE   **Architectural decoration and**
            ornament

Architecture—Designs and plans
    720.28; 729
  UF   Architectural designs
        Architecture—Plans
        Designs, Architectural
  BT   **Architectural drawing**
  NT   **Domestic architecture—Designs and plans**

Architecture—Details   721; 729
  UF   Architectural design
        Architectural details
        Architectural features
  SA   types of architectural features, e.g. **Windows; Fireplaces;** etc., to be added as needed
  BT   **Architectural drawing**
  NT   **Chimneys**
        Doors
        Fireplaces
        Floors
        Foundations
        Roofs
        Windows
        Woodwork

Architecture, Domestic
  USE **Domestic architecture**

Architecture, Gothic
  USE **Gothic architecture**

Architecture, Greek
  USE **Greek architecture**

Architecture, Islamic
  USE **Islamic architecture**

Architecture, Medieval
  USE **Medieval architecture**

Architecture, Modern
  USE **Modern architecture**

Architecture, Modern—19th century
  USE **Modern architecture—1800-1899 (19th century)**

Architecture, Modern—20th century
  USE **Modern architecture—1900-1999 (20th century)**

Architecture, Naval
  USE **Naval architecture**
        Shipbuilding

Architecture—Plans
  USE **Architecture—Designs and plans**

Architecture—Proportion
  USE **Architecture—Composition, proportion, etc.**

Architecture, Renaissance
  USE **Renaissance architecture**

Architecture—Restoration
  USE **Architecture—Conservation and restoration**

Architecture, Roman
  USE **Roman architecture**

Architecture, Romanesque
  USE **Romanesque architecture**

Architecture, Rural
  USE **Domestic architecture**
        Farm buildings

Archives (May subdiv. geog.)   026; 027
  UF   Documents
        Government records—Preservation
        Historical records—Preservation
        Preservation of historical records
        Public records—Preservation
        Records—Preservation
  SA   subjects, ethnic groups, classes of persons, individuals, families, schools, and military services with the subdivision *Archives,* to be added as needed
  BT   **Bibliography**
        Documentation
        History—Sources
        Information services
  NT   **Manuscripts**
        Presidents—United States—Archives
  RT   **Charters**
        Libraries

Archives—United States   027.0973; 353.0071
  UF   United States—Archives

Arctic expeditions
  USE **Arctic regions—Exploration**

Arctic regions   919.8; 998
  UF   Far north
  BT   **Earth**
        Polar regions
  NT   **Northeast Passage**
        Northwest Passage
  RT   **North Pole**

BT = Broader Term   NT = Narrower Term   RT = Related Term   SA = See Also   UF = Used For

Arctic regions—Exploration   919.8
   UF   Arctic expeditions
           Polar expeditions
   SA   names of expeditions, to be add-
           ed as needed
   BT   **Exploration**
           Scientific expeditions
Ardennes, Battle of the, 1944-1945
    940.54
   UF   Bastogne, Battle of
           Battle of the Bulge
           Bulge, Battle of the
   BT   **World War, 1939-1945—Cam-**
           paigns
Area studies   940-999
    Use for general materials on area studies.
   UF   Foreign area studies
   SA   continents, countries, and geo-
           graphic regions with the sub-
           division *Study and teaching,*
           to be added as needed
   BT   **Education**
   NT   **Africa—Study and teaching**
Arena theater   725; 792
   UF   Round stage
           Theater-in-the-round
   BT   **Theater**
Argentine rummy
   USE   **Canasta (Game)**
Argumentation
   USE   **Debates and debating**
           Logic
Aristocracy   305.5
   BT   **Political science**
           Upper class
   RT   **Nobility**
Arithmetic   513
   UF   Computation (Mathematics)
   SA   types of arithmetic operations, to
           be added as needed
   BT   **Mathematics**
           Set theory
   NT   **Average**
           Calculators
           Cube root
           Fractions
           Mental arithmetic
           Metric system
           Multiplication
           Percentage

           Ratio and proportion
           Square root
           Subtraction
   RT   **Numbers**
Arithmetic, Commercial
   USE   **Business mathematics**
Arithmetic—Estimation
   USE   **Approximate computation**
Arithmetic, Mental
   USE   **Mental arithmetic**
Arithmetic—Study and teaching   372.7;
    513.07
   NT   **Counting**
           Mathematical readiness
           Number games
Arithmetical readiness
   USE   **Mathematical readiness**
Armada, 1588
   USE   **Spanish Armada, 1588**
Armaments
   USE   **Military readiness**
           Military weapons
Armaments industries
   USE   **Defense industries**
Armaments race
   USE   **Arms race**
Armed forces   343; 355
   UF   Armed services
           Military forces
   SA   specific branches of the armed
           forces under names of coun-
           tries, e.g. **United States.**
           Army; and names of coun-
           tries, regions, and internation-
           al organizations with the sub-
           division *Armed forces,* e.g.
           United States—Armed
           forces; United Nations—
           Armed forces; etc., to be
           added as needed
   BT   **Military art and science**
   NT   **Armies**
           Military personnel
           Navies
           Ohio—Militia
           Recruiting and enlistment
           United Nations—Armed forces
           United States—Armed forces
           United States—Militia
           Voluntary military service

BT = Broader Term   NT = Narrower Term   RT = Related Term   SA = See Also   UF = Used For

Armed forces—*Continued*
RT   **Military readiness**
      War
Armed forces—Recruiting, enlistment, etc.
USE   **Recruiting and enlistment**
Armed services
USE   **Armed forces**
Armies   355.3
UF   Army
      Military power
SA   names of countries with the sub-
      head *Army,* e.g. **United
      States. Army;** to be added as
      needed
BT   **Armed forces**
      Military personnel
NT   **Draft**
      Soldiers
      United States. Army
RT   **Military art and science**
Armies—Medical care   355.3
SA   names of wars with the subdivi-
      sion *Health aspects* or *Medi-
      cal care,* to be added as
      needed
BT   **Medical care**
      Military medicine
NT   **United States—History—1861-
      1865, Civil War—Medical
      care**
      **World War, 1939-1945—Health
      aspects**
      **World War, 1939-1945—Medi-
      cal care**
RT   **Military health**
Armistice Day
USE   **Veterans Day**
Armistices
USE   names of wars with the subdivi-
      sion *Armistices,* e.g. **World
      War, 1939-1945—Armistices;**
      to be added as needed
Armor   355.8; 623.4; 739.7
      Use for materials on protective covering
worn as a defense against weapons.
UF   Arms and armor *[Former head-
      ing]*
      Suits of armor
BT   **Art metalwork**
      Costume
      Military art and science

RT   **Weapons**
Armored cars (Tanks)
USE   **Military tanks**
Arms aid
USE   **Military assistance**
Arms and armor
USE   **Armor**
      Weapons
Arms, Coats of
USE   **Heraldry**
Arms control   327.1; 341.7
UF   Disarmament
      Limitation of armament
      Non-proliferation of nuclear
         weapons
      Nuclear non-proliferation
      Nuclear test ban
BT   **International relations**
      International security
      War
NT   **Antinuclear movement**
      Arms race
RT   **International arbitration**
      Military readiness
      Peace
Arms proliferation
USE   **Arms race**
Arms race   327.1; 355
      Use for materials on the competitive in-
crease in the military power of two or more
nations or blocs.
UF   Armaments race
      Arms proliferation
      Proliferation of arms
BT   **Arms control**
      International security
RT   **Military readiness**
      Military weapons
Arms sales
USE   **Defense industries**
      Military assistance
      Military weapons
Army
USE   **Armies**
      Military art and science
      and names of countries with the
         subhead *Army,* e.g. **United
         States. Army;** to be added as
         needed
Army bases
USE   **Military bases**

BT = Broader Term   NT = Narrower Term   RT = Related Term   SA = See Also   UF = Used For

Army desertion
  USE   **Military desertion**
Army life
  USE   **Soldiers**
         and names of armies with the
             subdivision *Military life,* e.g.
             United States. Army—Mili-
             tary life; to be added as
             needed
Army posts
  USE   **Military bases**
Army schools
  USE   **Military education**
Army tests
  USE   **United States. Army—Exami-**
             nations
Army vehicles
  USE   **Military vehicles**
Aromatic plant products
  USE   **Essences and essential oils**
Arrow
  USE   **Bow and arrow**
Art   700

   Use for materials on the visual arts only
(architecture, painting, etc.). Materials on the
arts in general, including the visual arts, literature, and the performing arts, are entered under **Arts.**

  UF   Iconography
  SA   types of art, e.g. **Commercial**
             art; movements in art, e.g.
             Surrealism; art and other
             subjects, e.g. **Art and my-**
             thology; subjects and themes
             in art, e.g. **Animals in art;**
             and art of particular countries
             or regions, e.g. **Greek art;** to
             be added as needed
  BT   **Arts**
         Humanities
  NT   **Aesthetics**
         African American art
         African Americans in art
         American art
         Ancient art
         Animals in art
         Architecture
         Art and mythology
         Art and religion
         Art and society
         Art forgeries

Art objects
Artistic anatomy
Artistic photography
Artists' models
Arts and crafts movement
Asian art
Baroque art
Black art
Blacks in art
Botanical illustration
Bronzes
Buddhist art
Byzantine art
Children in art
Christian art and symbolism
Collage
Collectors and collecting
Commercial art
Composition (Art)
Computer art
Copy art
Decoration and ornament
Drawing
Engraving
Erotic art
Etching
Folk art
Futurism (Art)
Gems
Graphic arts
Greek art
Illumination of books and
    manuscripts
Illustration of books
Indians of North America—
    Art
Interior design
Islamic art
Medieval art
Modern art
Modern art—1800-1899 (19th
    century)
Modern art—1900-1999 (20th
    century)
Municipal art
Nude in art
Painting
Pictures
Plants in art
Portraits

BT = Broader Term   NT = Narrower Term   RT = Related Term   SA = See Also   UF = Used For

Art—*Continued*
>> Prehistoric art
>> Realism in art
>> Religious art and symbolism
>> Renaissance art
>> Rock drawings, paintings, and engravings
>> Roman art
>> Sculpture
>> Surrealism
>> Symbolism
>> Women in art
>> World War, 1939-1945—Art and the war
> RT Archeology
>> Artists

Art, Abstract
> USE **Abstract art**

Art, African American
> USE **African American art**

Art, American
> USE **American art**

Art—Analysis, interpretation, appreciation
> USE **Art appreciation**
>> **Art criticism**
>> **Art—Study and teaching**

Art, Ancient
> USE **Ancient art**

Art and mythology 704.9
> UF Mythology in art
> BT **Art**
>> **Mythology**
> RT **Art and religion**

Art and religion 246; 291.1; 701
> UF Arts in the church
>> Religion and art
> BT **Art**
>> **Religion**
> RT **Art and mythology**
>> **Religious art and symbolism**

Art and society 701
> UF Art and sociology
>> Society and art
>> Sociology and art
> BT **Art**
> NT **Art patronage**
>> **Art—Political aspects**
>> **Folk art**

Art and sociology
> USE **Art and society**

Art, Applied
> USE **Industrial design**

Art appreciation 701
> UF Appreciation of art
>> Art—Analysis, interpretation, appreciation
> BT **Aesthetics**
>> **Art criticism**

Art, Asian
> USE **Asian art**

Art, Baroque
> USE **Baroque art**

Art, Black
> USE **Black art**

Art, Buddhist
> USE **Buddhist art**

Art, Byzantine
> USE **Byzantine art**

Art, Christian
> USE **Christian art and symbolism**

Art—Collections
> USE **Art collections**

Art collections (May subdiv. geog.) 708
> UF Art—Collections
>> Art—Private collections
>> Collections of art, painting, etc.
>> Private art collections
> SA names of collectors or of the original owners of private art collections with the subdivision *Art collections*, to be added as needed
> RT **Art museums**
>> **Collectors and collecting**

Art, Commercial
> USE **Commercial art**

Art—Composition
> USE **Composition (Art)**

Art criticism 701; 709
> UF Art—Analysis, interpretation, appreciation
> BT **Criticism**
> NT **Art appreciation**

Art, Decorative
> USE **Decoration and ornament**
>> **Decorative arts**

Art, Ecclesiastical
> USE **Christian art and symbolism**

Art education
> USE **Art—Study and teaching**

BT = Broader Term   NT = Narrower Term   RT = Related Term   SA = See Also   UF = Used For

Art, Electronic
USE   **Video art**
Art, Erotic
USE   **Erotic art**
Art—Exhibitions   707.4
BT   **Exhibitions**
Art—Federal aid
USE   **Federal aid to the arts**
Art forgeries   702.8; 751.5
UF   Art objects, Forgery of
       Forgery of works of art *[Former heading]*
BT   **Art**
       Counterfeits and counterfeiting
       Forgery
Art galleries
USE   **Art museums**
Art, Geometric
USE   **Abstract art**
Art, Gothic
USE   **Gothic art**
Art, Graphic
USE   **Graphic arts**
Art, Greek
USE   **Greek art**
Art—History   709
BT   **History**
Art in advertising
USE   **Commercial art**
Art in motion
USE   **Kinetic art**
Art, Indian
USE   **Indians of North America—Art**
Art industries and trade
USE   **Decorative arts**
Art, Islamic
USE   **Islamic art**
Art, Kinetic
USE   **Kinetic art**
Art, Medieval
USE   **Medieval art**
Art metalwork   739; 745.56
UF   Decorative metalwork
       Metalwork, Art
SA   types of art metalwork, to be added as needed
BT   **Decorative arts**
       Metalwork
NT   **Armor**

Brasses
Bronzes
Goldwork
Jewelry
Pewter
Silverwork
Art, Modern
USE   **Modern art**
       Modernism (Arts)
Art, Modern—19th century
USE   **Modern art—1800-1899 (19th century)**
Art, Modern—20th century
USE   **Modern art—1900-1999 (20th century)**
Art, Municipal
USE   **Municipal art**
Art—Museums
USE   **Art museums**
Art museums   708
UF   Art galleries
       Art—Museums *[Former heading]*
       Collections of art, painting, etc.
       Picture galleries
SA   names of individual art museums, to be added as needed
BT   **Museums**
RT   **Art collections**
Art, Nonobjective
USE   **Abstract art**
Art objects   700; 745
       Use for general materials about decorative articles of artistic merit such as snuff boxes, brasses, pottery, needlework, glassware, etc. Materials on old decorative objects having historical or financial value are entered under **Antiques.**
UF   Objets d'art
SA   types of art objects, e.g. **Furniture; Pottery;** etc., to be added as needed
BT   **Antiques**
       Art
       Decoration and ornament
       Decorative arts
NT   **Miniature objects**
Art objects, Forgery of
USE   **Art forgeries**
Art, Oriental
USE   **Asian art**

BT = Broader Term   NT = Narrower Term   RT = Related Term   SA = See Also   UF = Used For

Art patronage   700

Use for materials on patronage of the arts by individuals or corporations. Materials on government support of the arts are entered under **Arts—Government policy** or **Federal aid to the arts.**

UF   Art patrons

Business patronage of the arts

Corporate patronage of the arts

Corporations—Art patronage

Funding for the arts

Patronage of the arts

Private funding of the arts

BT   **Art and society**

RT   **Arts—Government policy**

Federal aid to the arts

Art patrons

USE   **Art patronage**

Art—Political aspects (May subdiv. geog.) **701**

BT   **Art and society**

Art, Prehistoric

USE   **Prehistoric art**

Art—Prices   707.5

BT   **Prices**

Art—Private collections

USE   **Art collections**

Art, Renaissance

USE   **Renaissance art**

Art robberies

USE   **Art thefts**

Art, Roman

USE   **Roman art**

Art, Romanesque

USE   **Romanesque art**

Art schools

USE   **Art—Study and teaching**

Art—Study and teaching   707

UF   Art—Analysis, interpretation, appreciation

Art education

Art schools

Art—Technique   702.8

Art thefts   364.16

UF   Art robberies

Thefts, Art

BT   **Crime**

Art, Video

USE   **Video art**

Artesian wells

USE   **Wells**

Arthritis   616.7

BT   **Diseases**

NT   **Gout**

Arthritis—Physical therapy   616.7

Arthur, King—Romances

USE   **Arthurian romances**

Arthurian romances   398.22; 808.8; 809

May be used for individual works, collections, or materials about Arthurian romances.

UF   Arthur, King—Romances

Knights of the Round Table

BT   **Romances**

RT   **Grail**

Articles of war

USE   **Military law**

Articulation (Education)   371.2

Use for materials that discuss the integration of various elements of the school system, between levels, between schools, between subjects, or between the school's programs and outside activities, aimed at promoting a continuous advancement by the student.

BT   **Education—Curricula**

Schools—Administration

Artificial flies   688.7; 799.1

UF   Fishing flies

Flies, Artificial *[Former heading]*

BT   **Fishing**

Fly casting

Artificial flowers   745.594

UF   Flowers, Artificial

BT   **Decoration and ornament**

Artificial foods   641.3; 664

UF   Food, Artificial *[Former heading]*

Synthetic foods

BT   **Food**

Synthetic products

Artificial fuels

USE   **Synthetic fuels**

Artificial heart   617.4

BT   **Artificial organs**

Heart

Artificial insemination   636.08

Use for general materials on artificial insemination and materials specifically on the artificial insemination of livestock and other animals. Materials limited to artificial insemination in humans are entered under **Human artificial insemination.**

UF   Impregnation, Artificial

Insemination, Artificial

BT   **Reproduction**

BT = Broader Term   NT = Narrower Term   RT = Related Term   SA = See Also   UF = Used For

Artificial insemination—*Continued*
NT   **Human artificial insemination**
Artificial insemination, Human
USE   **Human artificial insemination**
Artificial intelligence   006.3
UF   AI (Artificial intelligence)
      Electronic brains
      Intelligence, Artificial
      Machine intelligence
BT   **Bionics**
      Electronic data processing
NT   **Expert systems (Computer science)**
Artificial islands
USE   **Drilling platforms**
Artificial limbs   617.5
UF   Extremities, Artificial
      Limbs, Artificial
      Prosthesis
BT   **Orthopedics**
Artificial organs   617.9
UF   Organs, Artificial
      Prosthesis
SA   names of artificial organs, e.g.
      Artificial heart; to be added
      as needed
BT   **Surgery**
NT   **Artificial heart**
Artificial reality
USE   **Virtual reality**
Artificial respiration   617.1
UF   Pulmonary resuscitation
      Respiration, Artificial
      Resuscitation, Pulmonary
BT   **First aid**
Artificial satellites   629.43; 629.46
UF   Orbiting vehicles
      Satellites, Artificial
SA   satellites of particular countries,
      e.g. **American artificial satellites;** types of satellites; and
      names of specific satellites, to
      be added as needed
BT   **Astronautics**
NT   **American artificial satellites**
      Explorer (Artificial satellite)
      Meteorological satellites
      Soviet artificial satellites
      Space stations
RT   **Space vehicles**

Artificial satellites, American
USE   **American artificial satellites**
Artificial satellites—Control systems
      629.46
Artificial satellites in telecommunication
      384.5; 621.382
UF   Communication satellites
      Communications relay satellites
      Global satellite communications
        systems
      Satellite communication systems
SA   names of specific satellites or
      projects, to be added as needed
BT   **Telecommunication**
NT   **Telstar project**
Artificial satellites—Launching   629.43
UF   Launching of satellites
BT   **Rockets (Aeronautics)**
Artificial satellites—Law and legislation
USE   **Space law**
Artificial satellites—Orbits   629.4
BT   **Astrodynamics**
Artificial satellites, Soviet
USE   **Soviet artificial satellites**
Artificial satellites—Tracking   629.43
UF   Tracking of satellites
Artificial sweeteners
USE   **Sugar substitutes**
Artificial weather control
USE   **Weather control**
Artillery   355.8; 623.4
BT   **Military art and science**
RT   **Ordnance**
Artistic anatomy   704.9; 743.4
UF   Anatomy, Artistic *[Former heading]*
      Human anatomy in art
      Human figure in art
BT   **Anatomy**
      Art
      Drawing
      Nude in art
NT   **Figure drawing**
      Figure painting
Artistic photography   770; 779
UF   Photography—Aesthetics
      Photography, Artistic *[Former heading]*
BT   **Art**

BT = Broader Term   NT = Narrower Term   RT = Related Term   SA = See Also   UF = Used For

Artistic photography—*Continued*
          Photography
Artists   709.2; 920
    SA   artists of particular countries,
                e.g. **American artists;** and
                names of individual artists, to
                be added as needed
    NT   **African American artists**
            American artists
            Architects
            Black artists
            Child artists
            Engravers
            Etchers
            Illustrators
            Lithographers
            Painters
            Potters
            Sculptors
            Women artists
    RT   **Art**
            Arts
Artists, African American
    USE   **African American artists**
Artists, American
    USE   **American artists**
Artists, Black
    USE   **Black artists**
Artists' materials   741.2; 751.2
    UF   Drawing materials
            Painters' materials
    SA   types of artists' materials, to be
                added as needed
    BT   **Materials**
Artists' models   702.8
    UF   Models
            Models, Artists'
            Models (Persons)
    BT   **Art**
Arts   700
    Use for materials on the arts in general,
    including the visual arts, literature, and the
    performing arts. Materials on the visual arts
    only (architecture, painting, etc.) are entered
    under **Art.**
    UF   Arts, Fine
            Fine arts
    SA   arts of particular countries, e.g.
                American arts; to be added
                as needed
    BT   **Humanities**
    NT   **Aesthetics**

            Allegory
            American arts
            Art
            Decorative arts
            Handicraft
            Performing arts
            Visual literacy
    RT   **Artists**
Arts, American
    USE   **American arts**
Arts and crafts movement   745
    Use for materials on the movement originat-
    ing in England in the nineteenth century that
    promoted a return to craftsmanship in the ap-
    plied and decorative arts.
    UF   Crafts (Arts)
    BT   **Art**
            Decoration and ornament
            Decorative arts
            Industrial arts
    RT   **Folk art**
            Handicraft
Arts and state
    USE   **Arts—Government policy**
            Federal aid to the arts
Arts, Applied
    USE   **Decorative arts**
Arts, Decorative
    USE   **Decoration and ornament**
            Decorative arts
            Interior design
Arts—Federal aid
    USE   **Federal aid to the arts**
Arts, Fine
    USE   **Arts**
Arts—Government policy   353.7; 700
    UF   Arts and state
            Funding for the arts
            State and the arts
            State encouragement of the arts
    BT   **Social policy**
    RT   **Art patronage**
            Federal aid to the arts
Arts, Graphic
    USE   **Graphic arts**
Arts in the church
    USE   **Art and religion**
Arts, Minor
    USE   **Decorative arts**
Arts, Useful
    USE   **Industrial arts**

BT = Broader Term   NT = Narrower Term   RT = Related Term   SA = See Also   UF = Used For

Arts, Useful—*Continued*
      Technology
Asbestos   553.6; 620.1; 666; 691
  BT   **Minerals**
Asceticism   248.4; 291.4
    May be subdivided by religion or sect.
  BT   **Ethics**
        Religious life
  NT   **Fasting**
        Sexual abstinence
Asceticism—Catholic Church   248.4
Asia   950
  UF   East
        Orient
  SA   areas of Asia, to be added as
        needed
  NT   **Central Asia**
        East Asia
        Middle East
        Southeast Asia
Asia, Central
  USE   **Central Asia**
Asia—Civilization   306.095; 950
  UF   Asian civilization *[Former head-
        ing]*
        Civilization, Asian *[Former
        heading]*
        Civilization, Oriental
        Oriental civilization
  BT   **Civilization**
        East and West
Asia, East
  USE   **East Asia**
Asia—Politics and government   950
  BT   **Politics**
Asia, Southeast
  USE   **Southeast Asia**
Asian architecture   720.95
  UF   Architecture, Asian *[Former
        heading]*
        Oriental architecture
  BT   **Architecture**
  NT   **Temples**
  RT   **Mosques**
Asian art   709.5
  UF   Art, Asian *[Former heading]*
        Art, Oriental
        Oriental art
  BT   **Art**

Asian civilization
  USE   **Asia—Civilization**
Asphyxiating gases
  USE   **Poisonous gases**
Assassination   364.15
  SA   classes of persons and names of
        individuals with the subdivi-
        sion *Assassination,* to be add-
        ed as needed
  BT   **Crime**
        Homicide
        Political crimes and offenses
  NT   **Presidents—United States—As-
        sassination**
Assault, Criminal
  USE   **Offenses against the person**
Assault, Sexual
  USE   **Rape**
Assembly programs, School
  USE   **School assembly programs**
Assembly, Right of
  USE   **Freedom of assembly**
Assertive behavior
  USE   **Assertiveness (Psychology)**
Assertiveness (Psychology)   155.2; 158.2
  UF   Assertive behavior
  BT   **Aggressiveness (Psychology)**
        Psychology
  RT   **Self-confidence**
Assessment
  USE   **Tax assessment**
Assessment, Tax
  USE   **Tax assessment**
Assessments, Political
  USE   **Campaign funds**
Assistance in emergencies
  USE   **Helping behavior**
Assistance to developing areas
  USE   **Foreign aid**
        Technical assistance
Association, Freedom of
  USE   **Freedom of association**
Associations (May subdiv. geog.)   060;
        302.3; 366
  UF   Associations, institutions, etc.
        Networks (Associations, institu-
        tions, etc.)
        Organizations
        Voluntary associations
        Voluntary organizations

BT = Broader Term   NT = Narrower Term   RT = Related Term   SA = See Also   UF = Used For

Associations—*Continued*
    SA   types of associations; subjects,
              classes of persons, ethnic
              groups, and names of individ-
              ual persons, families, and cor-
              porate bodies, with the subdi-
              vision *Societies;* and names of
              specific associations, to be
              added as needed
    NT   **Agriculture—Societies**
              Charity organization
              Clubs
              Community life
              Cooperation
              Nonprofit organizations
              Societies
              **Trade and professional associa-
              tions**
Associations, institutions, etc.
    USE   **Associations**
Associations, International
    USE   **International agencies**
Asteroids   523.44
    UF   Minor planets
              Planetoids
              Planets, Minor
    BT   **Astronomy**
              Solar system
    RT   **Planets**
Astrobiology
    USE   **Life on other planets**
             Space biology
Astrodynamics   521; 629.4
    BT   **Dynamics**
    NT   **Artificial satellites—Orbits**
              Navigation (Astronautics)
    RT   **Astronautics**
              Space flight
Astrogeology   559.9
    SA   names of planets with the subdi-
              vision *Geology,* to be added
              as needed
    BT   **Geology**
    NT   **Lunar geology**
              Mars (Planet)—Geology
Astrology   133.5
    UF   Hermetic art and philosophy
    BT   **Astronomy**
              Divination
              Fortune telling

              Occultism
              Superstition
    NT   **Horoscopes**
              Zodiac
    RT   **Constellations**
Astronautical accidents
    USE   **Space vehicle accidents**
Astronautical communication systems
    USE   **Astronautics—Communication
              systems**
Astronautical instruments   629.4
    UF   Instruments, Astronautical
              Space vehicles—Instruments
    BT   **Navigation (Astronautics)**
              Space optics
    RT   **Astronautics—Communication
              systems**
Astronautics (May subdiv. geog.)   629.4
    BT   **Aeronautics**
    NT   **Aerothermodynamics**
              Artificial satellites
              Astronautics and civilization
              Interplanetary voyages
              Navigation (Astronautics)
              Outer space
              Rocketry
              Space flight
              Space flight to the moon
              Space stations
              Unidentified flying objects
    RT   **Astrodynamics**
              Space sciences
              Space vehicles
Astronautics—Accidents
    USE   **Space vehicle accidents**
Astronautics and civilization   306.4
    UF   Civilization and astronautics
              Outer space and civilization
              Space age
              Space power
    BT   **Aeronautics and civilization**
              Astronautics
              Civilization
    NT   **Space colonies**
              Space law
**Astronautics—Communication systems
629.47**
    UF   Astronautical communication sys-
              tems
              Space communication

Astronautics—Communication systems—
Continued
- BT   **Interstellar communication**
       Telecommunication
- NT   **Radio in astronautics**
       Television in astronautics
- RT   **Astronautical instruments**

Astronautics—International cooperation
    629.4
- UF   International space cooperation
- BT   **International cooperation**

Astronautics—Law and legislation
- USE   **Space law**

Astronautics, Photography in
- USE   **Space photography**

Astronautics—United States   629.40973
- UF   United States—Astronautics
- NT   **Project Voyager**

Astronauts   629.450092; 920
- UF   Cosmonauts
- BT   **Air pilots**
       Space flight
- NT   **Space vehicles—Piloting**

Astronauts—Clothing
- USE   **Space suits**

Astronauts—Nutrition   629.47
- UF   Space nutrition
- BT   **Nutrition**

Astronavigation
- USE   **Navigation (Astronautics)**

Astronomers   520.92; 920
- BT   **Scientists**

Astronomical instruments   522
- UF   Instruments, Astronomical
- SA   types of instruments, e.g. **Tele-
scopes;** to be added as need-
ed
- BT   **Scientific apparatus and in-
struments**
       Space optics
- NT   **Astronomical photography**
       Telescopes

Astronomical observatories   522
- UF   Observatories, Astronomical
- RT   **Astronomy**

Astronomical photography   522
- UF   Astrophotography
       Photography, Astronomical
- BT   **Astronomical instruments**
       Photography

Astronomical physics
- USE   **Astrophysics**

Astronomy   520
- BT   **Physical sciences**
       Science
       Universe
- NT   **Asteroids**
       Astrology
       Astrophysics
       Bible—Astronomy
       Black holes (Astronomy)
       Chronology
       Comets
       Galaxies
       Life on other planets
       Lunar eclipses
       Meteorites
       Meteors
       Moon
       Nautical astronomy
       Outer space
       Planetariums
       Planets
       Pulsars
       Quasars
       Radio astronomy
       Seasons
       Sky
       Solar eclipses
       Solar system
       Space environment
       Spectrum analysis
       Sun
       Tides
       Zodiac
- RT   **Astronomical observatories**
       Constellations
       Space sciences
       Stars

Astronomy—Atlases
- USE   **Stars—Atlases**

Astronomy—Mathematics   520.1
- BT   **Mathematics**

Astronomy, Nautical
- USE   **Nautical astronomy**

Astrophotography
- USE   **Astronomical photography**

Astrophysics   523.01
- UF   Astronomical physics
       Physics, Astronomical

BT = Broader Term   NT = Narrower Term   RT = Related Term   SA = See Also   UF = Used For

Astrophysics—*Continued*
  BT   Astronomy
        Physics
  NT   Black holes (Astronomy)
        Spectrum analysis
Astros (Baseball team)
  USE   Houston Astros (Baseball
        team)
Asylum   341.4
  UF   Asylum, Right of *[Former head-*
        ing]
        Political asylum
        Right of asylum
        Sanctuary (Law)
  BT   International law
  NT   Political refugees
        Sanctuary movement
Asylum, Right of
  USE   Asylum
Asylums
  USE   Institutional care
At-home employment
  USE   Home business
        Telecommuting
At risk students   371.93
    Use for materials on students considered
  prone to academic failure or other problems.
  UF   Disadvantaged students
        High risk students
        Students with problems
        Underprivileged students
  BT   Students
  RT   Dropouts
        Socially handicapped children
Atheism   211
  BT   Religion
        Secularism
        Theology
  RT   Agnosticism
        Deism
        Rationalism
        Theism
Athletes   796.092; 920
  SA   types of athletes, e.g. **Baseball
        players**; to be added as need-
        ed
  NT   African American athletes
        Baseball players
        Black athletes
  RT   Sports

Athletes, African American
  USE   African American athletes
Athletes, Black
  USE   Black athletes
Athletes—Drug use   362.29; 796
  UF   Drugs and sports *[Former head-*
        ing]
        Sports and drugs
  RT   Steroids
Athletic coaching
  USE   Coaching (Athletics)
Athletic medicine
  USE   Sports medicine
Athletics   796
  SA   types of athletic activities, to be
        added as needed
  NT   Boxing
        Coaching (Athletics)
        Gymnastics
        Martial arts
        Olympic games
        Rowing
        Track athletics
        Weight lifting
        Wrestling
  RT   Physical education
        Sports
Atlantic cable
  USE   Submarine cables
Atlantic Ocean   910.9163
  BT   Ocean
Atlantic States   974; 975
  UF   Eastern Seaboard
        Middle Atlantic States
        South Atlantic States
  BT   United States
Atlas (Missile)   623.4; 629.47
  BT   Ballistic missiles
        Intercontinental ballistic mis-
        siles
Atlases   912
    Use as a form heading for geographical at-
  lases of world coverage. General materials
  about maps and their history are entered under
  Maps.
  UF   Geographical atlases
  SA   scientific and technical subjects
        with the subdivision *Atlases,*
        for materials consisting of
        comprehensive, often system-

BT = Broader Term   NT = Narrower Term   RT = Related Term   SA = See Also   UF = Used For

Atlases—*Continued*

atically arranged, collections of illustrative plates, charts, etc., usually with explanatory captions, e.g. **Human anatomy—Atlases;** and names of countries, cities, etc., with the subdivision *Maps,* e.g. **United States—Maps;** to be added as needed

BT **Geography**
Maps

NT **Bible—Geography**
Historical atlases
Human anatomy—Atlases
Stars—Atlases
United States—Maps

Atlases, Astronomical
USE **Stars—Atlases**

Atlases, Historical
USE **Historical atlases**

Atmosphere   551.5

Use for materials on the body of air surrounding the earth. Materials on the chemical and physical properties of air are entered under **Air.**

BT **Air**
Earth

NT **Clouds**
Fog
Sky
Upper atmosphere

RT **Meteorology**

Atmosphere—Pollution
USE **Air pollution**

Atmosphere, Upper
USE **Upper atmosphere**

Atmospheric greenhouse effect
USE **Greenhouse effect**

Atmospheric humidity
USE **Humidity**

Atolls
USE **Coral reefs and islands**

Atom smashing
USE **Cyclotron**

Atomic bomb   355.8; 623.4

BT **Bombs**
Nuclear warfare
Nuclear weapons

NT **Radioactive fallout**

RT **Hydrogen bomb**

Atomic bomb—Physiological effect   616.9

RT **Radiation—Physiological effect**

Atomic bomb—Testing   623.4

Atomic bomb victims   940.54

UF A-bomb victims
Victims of atomic bombings

Atomic energy
USE **Nuclear energy**

Atomic industry
USE **Nuclear industry**

Atomic medicine
USE **Nuclear medicine**

Atomic nuclei
USE **Nuclear physics**

Atomic piles
USE **Nuclear reactors**

Atomic power
USE **Nuclear energy**

Atomic power plants
USE **Nuclear power plants**

Atomic powered vehicles
USE **Nuclear propulsion**

Atomic submarines
USE **Nuclear submarines**

Atomic theory   539.7; 541.2

BT **Physical chemistry**

RT **Quantum theory**

Atomic warfare
USE **Nuclear warfare**

Atomic weapons
USE **Nuclear weapons**

Atoms   539; 541.2

BT **Physical chemistry**

NT **Cyclotron**
Electrons
Isotopes
Neutrons
Protons
Transmutation (Chemistry)

Atonement—Christianity   232; 234

UF Jesus Christ—Atonement
Vicarious atonement

BT **Christianity**
Jesus Christ
Sacrifice
Salvation

Atonement, Day of
USE **Yom Kippur**

BT = Broader Term   NT = Narrower Term   RT = Related Term   SA = See Also   UF = Used For

Atonement—Judaism   296.3
    UF   Atonement (Judaism)
    BT   **Judaism**
Atonement (Judaism)
    USE   **Atonement—Judaism**
Atrocities (May subdiv. geog.)   909
    UF   Military atrocities
    SA   names of wars with the subdivision *Atrocities,* e.g. **World War, 1939-1945—Atrocities;** and names of specific atrocities, to be added as needed
    BT   **Crime**
          Cruelty
    NT   **Massacres**
          Persecution
          World War, 1939-1945—Atrocities
Attacks by animals
    USE   **Animal attacks**
Attendance, School
    USE   **School attendance**
Attention   153.1; 153.7
    UF   Concentration
    BT   **Apperception**
          Educational psychology
          Memory
          Psychology
          Thought and thinking
    NT   **Listening**
Attitude (Psychology)   152.4
    UF   Attitudes
    SA   ethnic groups and classes of persons with the subdivision *Attitudes,* e.g. **Teenagers—Attitudes;** to be added as needed
    BT   **Emotions**
          Psychology
    NT   **Conformity**
          Frustration
          Job satisfaction
          Prejudices
          Racism
          Sexism
          Stereotype (Psychology)
          Teenagers—Attitudes
    RT   **Public opinion**
Attitudes
    USE   **Attitude (Psychology)**

and ethnic groups and classes of persons with the subdivision *Attitudes,* e.g. **Teenagers—Attitudes;** to be added as needed
Attorneys
    USE   **Lawyers**
ATVs
    USE   **All terrain vehicles**
Auction bridge
    USE   **Bridge (Game)**
Auctions   658.8
    UF   Sales, Auction
    BT   **Selling**
Audio amplifiers, Transistor
    USE   **Transistor amplifiers**
Audio cassettes
    USE   **Sound recordings**
Audiodisc players
    USE   **Compact disc players**
Audiotapes
    USE   **Sound recordings**
Audiovisual aids
    USE   subjects with the subdivision *Audiovisual aids,* e.g. **Library education—Audiovisual aids;** and subjects with the subdivisions *Study and teaching—Audiovisual aids,* for the use of audiovisual aids in the teaching of those subjects, e.g. **Science—Study and teaching—Audiovisual aids;** to be added as needed
Audiovisual education   371.33
    UF   Visual instruction
    SA   subjects with the subdivision *Audiovisual aids,* to be added as needed
    BT   **Education**
    NT   **Audiovisual materials**
          Library education—Audiovisual aids
          Motion pictures in education
          Radio in education
          Television in education
Audiovisual materials   025.17; 371.33
    UF   Multimedia materials
          Nonbook materials
          Nonprint materials

BT = Broader Term   NT = Narrower Term   RT = Related Term   SA = See Also   UF = Used For

Audiovisual materials—*Continued*

    SA   subjects with the subdivision *Audiovisual aids;* and names of specific audiovisual materials, to be added as needed

    BT   **Audiovisual education**

           Teaching—Aids and devices

    NT   **Filmstrips**

           Library education—Audiovisual aids

           Manipulatives

           Motion pictures

           Sound recordings

           Videodiscs

           Videotapes

Audiovisual materials centers

    USE   **Instructional materials centers**

Auditing   657

    BT   **Bookkeeping**

    RT   **Accounting**

Auricular confession

    USE   **Confession**

Aurora australis

    USE   **Auroras**

Aurora borealis

    USE   **Auroras**

Auroras   538

    UF   Aurora australis

           Aurora borealis

           Northern lights

           Polar lights

           Southern lights

    BT   **Geophysics**

           Meteorology

Australia   994

    May be subdivided like United States except for *History.*

    NT   **Australians**

Australian aborigines   305.89

    UF   Aborigines, Australian

           Australians (Native people)

    BT   **Australians**

           Native peoples

Australians   305.82; 994

    BT   **Australia**

    NT   **Australian aborigines**

Australians (Native people)

    USE   **Australian aborigines**

Author and publisher

    USE   **Authors and publishers**

Authoring programs for computer assisted instruction

    USE   **Computer assisted instruction—Authoring programs**

Authoritarianism

    USE   **Fascism**

           Totalitarianism

Authors   809; 920

    UF   Writers

    SA   authors of particular countries, e.g. **American authors;** types of writers, e.g. **Poets;** names of national literatures with the subdivision for a particular kind of author, e.g. **American literature—Women authors; American literature—African American authors;** etc.; subjects and names of countries, cities, etc. with the subdivision *Bio-bibliography;* and names of individual authors, to be added as needed

    NT   **African American authors**

           American authors

           Black authors

           Child authors

           Dramatists

           English authors

           Historians

           Journalists

           Novelists

           Poets

           Women authors

    RT   **Books**

           Literature—Bio-bibliography

Authors, African American

    USE   **African American authors**

Authors, American

    USE   **American authors**

Authors and publishers   070.5

    Use for materials on the relations between author and publisher.

    UF   Author and publisher

           Publishers and authors

    BT   **Authorship**

           Contracts

           Publishers and publishing

    RT   **Copyright**

Authors, Black

    USE   **Black authors**

Authors—Correspondence   816, etc.;
    808.86; 809.6
BT   Letters
Authors, English
    USE   English authors
Authors—Homes and haunts
    USE   Literary landmarks
Authorship   808
    Use for general materials on being or be-
    coming an author. Materials concerning the
    composition of special types of literature are
    entered under more specific headings such as
    **Fiction—Technique; Biography as a liter-
    ary form; Short story;** etc.
    UF   Writing (Authorship)
    SA   individual writers, titles of liter-
          ary works, and sacred works
          with the subdivision *Author-
          ship;* e.g. **Shakespeare, Wil-
          liam, 1564-1616—Author-
          ship;** to be added as needed
    BT   Literature
    NT   Advertising copy
          Authors and publishers
          Biography as a literary form
          Copyright
          Creative writing
          Drama—Technique
          Editing
          Fiction—Technique
          Historiography
          Journalism
          Love stories—Technique
          Plots (Drama, fiction, etc.)
          Radio authorship
          Report writing
          Short story
          Technical writing
          Television authorship
          Versification
Authorship—Handbooks, manuals, etc.
    808
    RT   Printing—Style manuals
Autism   616.89; 618.92
    BT   Child psychiatry
Auto courts
    USE   Hotels and motels
Autobiographical fiction   808.83; 813,
    etc.
    May be used for individual works, collec-
    tions, or materials about autobiographical fic-
    tion.

    UF   Autobiographical novels
    BT   **Biographical fiction**
Autobiographical novels
    USE   **Autobiographical fiction**
Autobiographies   920
    Use for collections of autobiographies. Ma-
    terials about autobiography as a literary form
    are entered under **Autobiography.**
    UF   Memoirs
          Personal narratives
    SA   ethnic groups, classes of per-
          sons, and subjects with the
          subdivision *Biography* or *Cor-
          respondence,* e.g. **Women—
          Biography; Authors—Corre-
          spondence;** etc.; and names
          of diseases, events, and wars
          with the subdivision *Personal
          narratives,* to be added as
          needed
    BT   **Biography**
    NT   **Holocaust, 1933-1945—Personal
          narratives**
          **United States—History—1861-
          1865, Civil War—Personal
          narratives**
          **World War, 1939-1945—Per-
          sonal narratives**
    RT   **Diaries**
Autobiography   809
    Use for materials on autobiography as a lit-
    erary form. Collections of autobiographies are
    entered under **Autobiographies.**
    UF   Autobiography as a literary form
          Autobiography—History and crit-
          icism
          Autobiography—Technique
          Memoirs
    BT   **Biography as a literary form**
Autobiography as a literary form
    USE   **Autobiography**
Autobiography—History and criticism
    USE   **Autobiography**
Autobiography—Technique
    USE   **Autobiography**
Autocodes
    USE   **Programming languages (Com-
          puters)**
Autographs   929.8
    SA   ethnic groups, classes of per-
          sons, individuals, and wars

BT = Broader Term   NT = Narrower Term   RT = Related Term   SA = See Also   UF = Used For

Autographs—*Continued*

with the subdivision *Autographs*, to be added as needed

BT **Biography**
   Writing
RT **Manuscripts**

Automata
USE **Robots**

Automated cataloging   025.3
UF Cataloging—Data processing
   [Former heading]
BT **Cataloging**

Automated information networks
USE **Information networks**

Automatic bread machines
USE **Bread machines**

Automatic computers
USE **Computers**

Automatic control
USE **Automation**
   Cybernetics
   Electric controllers
   Servomechanisms

Automatic data processing
USE **Electronic data processing**

Automatic drafting
USE **Computer graphics**

Automatic drawing
USE **Computer graphics**

Automatic information retrieval
USE **Information systems**

Automatic machinery
USE **Automation**

Automatic programming languages
USE **Programming languages (Computers)**

Automatic speech recognition   006.4
UF Mechanical speech recognition
   Speech recognition, Automatic
BT **Speech processing systems**
   Voice

Automatic teaching
USE **Teaching machines**

Automation   629.8; 670.42
UF Automatic control
   Automatic machinery
   Computer control

SA subjects with the subdivision *Automation*, e.g. **Libraries—Automation;** to be added as needed
BT **Industrial equipment**
   Machinery in the workplace
NT **Feedback control systems**
   Industrial robots
   Libraries—Automation
   Servomechanisms
   Systems engineering
   Telecommuting

Automatons
USE **Robots**

Automobile accidents
USE **Traffic accidents**

Automobile design
USE **Automobiles—Design and construction**

Automobile driver education   629.28
UF Automobile drivers—Education
   [Former heading]
   Car driver education
   Driver education
BT **Education**

Automobile drivers   629.28
UF Automobile driving
   Automobiles—Driving
   Car drivers
   Drivers, Automobile

Automobile drivers—Education
USE **Automobile driver education**

Automobile driving
USE **Automobile drivers**

Automobile engines   629.25
UF Automobiles—Engines *[Former heading]*
   Automobiles—Motors
   Car engines
BT **Engines**
   Internal combustion engines
RT **Diesel automobiles**
   Electric automobiles

Automobile guides
USE **Automobile travel—Guidebooks**

Automobile industry   338.4; 388.3
UF Automotive industry
   Car industry
   Motor vehicle industry
BT **Industries**

BT = Broader Term   NT = Narrower Term   RT = Related Term   SA = See Also   UF = Used For

Automobile industry—*Continued*
    NT   Service stations
Automobile industry—Production standards   658.5
    BT   Production standards
Automobile insurance   368
    UF   Car insurance
          Insurance, Automobile *[Former heading]*
          No fault automobile insurance
    BT   Insurance
Automobile parts   629.28
    UF   Automobiles—Parts *[Former heading]*
          Car parts
    BT   Automobiles
Automobile pools
    USE   Car pools
Automobile racing   796.72
    UF   Automobiles—Racing
          Car racing
    SA   types of automobile racing and names of specific races, to be added as needed
    BT   Racing
    NT   Karts and karting
Automobile repairs
    USE   Automobiles—Maintenance and repair
Automobile service stations
    USE   Service stations
Automobile styling
    USE   Automobiles—Design and construction
Automobile touring
    USE   Automobile travel
Automobile transmission
    USE   Automobiles—Transmission devices
Automobile travel   796.7
    UF   Automobile touring
          Automobiles—Touring *[Former heading]*
          Car travel
          Motoring
    BT   Travel
Automobile travel—Guidebooks   912
    UF   Automobile guides
          Automobiles—Road guides *[Former heading]*

Car travel—Guidebooks
          Travel guides
    BT   Maps
    RT   Road maps
Automobile trucks
    USE   Trucks
Automobiles   388.3; 629.222
    UF   Cars (Automobiles)
          Motor cars
    SA   names of specific makes and models of automobiles, e.g. **Ford automobile;** to be added as needed
    BT   Highway transportation
          Vehicles
    NT   Automobile parts
          Buses
          Compact cars
          Diesel automobiles
          Electric automobiles
          Ford automobile
          Foreign automobiles
          Sports cars
          Trucks
Automobiles—Accidents
    USE   Traffic accidents
Automobiles—Air conditioning   629.2
    BT   Air conditioning
Automobiles—Brakes   629.2
    BT   Brakes
Automobiles, Compact
    USE   Compact cars
Automobiles—Conservation and restoration   629.28
    UF   Automobiles—Restoration *[Former heading]*
          Restoration of automobiles
Automobiles—Construction
    USE   Automobiles—Design and construction
Automobiles—Design
    USE   Automobiles—Design and construction
Automobiles—Design and construction   629.222
    UF   Automobile design
          Automobile styling
          Automobiles—Construction
          Automobiles—Design *[Former heading]*

BT = Broader Term   NT = Narrower Term   RT = Related Term   SA = See Also   UF = Used For

Automobiles—Design and construction—
Continued
    Automotive engineering
    Car design
  BT   **Industrial design**
Automobiles, Diesel
  USE   **Diesel automobiles**
Automobiles—Driving
  USE   **Automobile drivers**
Automobiles, Electric
  USE   **Electric automobiles**
Automobiles—Electric equipment
    629.25
  UF   Electric equipment of automo-
      biles
Automobiles—Engines
  USE   **Automobile engines**
Automobiles, Foreign
  USE   **Foreign automobiles**
Automobiles—Fuel consumption   629.28
  BT   **Energy consumption**
       Fuel
Automobiles—Gearing
  USE   **Automobiles—Transmission de-
      vices**
Automobiles—Law and legislation
    343.09
  BT   **Law**
       Legislation
  RT   **Traffic regulations**
Automobiles—Maintenance and repair
    629.28
  UF   Automobile repairs
      Automobiles—Repairing
      Car maintenance
      Car repair
Automobiles—Models   629.22
  UF   Model cars
  BT   **Models and model making**
Automobiles—Motors
  USE   **Automobile engines**
Automobiles—Parts
  USE   **Automobile parts**
Automobiles—Pollution control devices
    629.25
  UF   Pollution control devices (Motor
      vehicles)
  BT   **Pollution control industry**
Automobiles—Racing
  USE   **Automobile racing**

Automobiles—Repairing
  USE   **Automobiles—Maintenance and
      repair**
Automobiles—Restoration
  USE   **Automobiles—Conservation
      and restoration**
Automobiles—Road guides
  USE   **Automobile travel—Guidebooks**
Automobiles—Service stations
  USE   **Service stations**
Automobiles—Touring
  USE   **Automobile travel**
Automobiles—Trailers
  USE   **Travel trailers and campers**
Automobiles—Transmission devices
    629.2
  UF   Automobile transmission
      Automobiles—Gearing
      Car transmissions
      Transmissions, Automobile
  BT   **Gearing**
Automotive engineering
  USE   **Automobiles—Design and con-
      struction**
Automotive industry
  USE   **Automobile industry**
Autosuggestion
  USE   **Hypnotism**
      Mental suggestion
Autumn   508; 525
  UF   Fall
  BT   **Seasons**
Avant-garde churches
  USE   **Noninstitutional churches**
Avant-garde films
  USE   **Experimental films**
Avant-garde theater
  USE   **Experimental theater**
Avenues
  USE   **Streets**
Average   519.5
  BT   **Arithmetic**
      Probabilities
      Statistics
Aviation
  USE   **Aeronautics**
Aviation accidents
  USE   **Aircraft accidents**
Aviation medicine   616.9
  UF   Aeronautics—Medical aspects

BT = Broader Term   NT = Narrower Term   RT = Related Term   SA = See Also   UF = Used For

Aviation medicine—*Continued*
        Aerospace medicine
        Medicine, Aviation
  BT   **Medicine**
  NT   **Jet lag**
  RT   **Space medicine**
Aviators
  USE   **Air pilots**
Avocations
  USE   **Hobbies**
Awakening, Religious
  USE   **Religious awakening**
Awards   001.4
  UF   Competitions
        Prizes (Rewards)
        Rewards (Prizes, etc.) *[Former
          heading]*
  SA   types of awards and prizes; sub-
        jects, corporate entities, per-
        sons, and military services
        with the subdivision *Awards,*
        e.g. **Architecture—Awards;**
        and names of specific awards
        and prizes, e.g. **Nobel Prizes;**
        to be added as needed
  NT   **Literary prizes**
        Nobel Prizes
  RT   **Contests**
Awards (Law)   ʼ
  USE   **Arbitration and award**
Axiology
  USE   **Values**
Aztecs   972.004
  BT   **Indians of Mexico**
B-52 bomber   623.7
  BT   **Bombers**
B and B accommodations
  USE   **Bed and breakfast accommo-
         dations**
Babies
  USE   **Infants**
Baby animals
  USE   **Animal babies**
Baby care
  USE   **Infants—Care**
Baby sitters
  USE   **Babysitters**
Baby sitting
  USE   **Babysitting**

Babysitters   649
  UF   Baby sitters *[Former heading]*
        Sitters (Babysitters)
  RT   **Babysitting**
Babysitting   649
  UF   Baby sitting
  BT   **Child care**
        Infants—Care
  RT   **Babysitters**
Bacilli
  USE   **Bacteria**
        Germ theory of disease
Back packing
  USE   **Backpacking**
Backpack cycling
  USE   **Bicycle touring**
Backpacking   796.51
  UF   Back packing
        Pack transportation
  BT   **Camping**
        Hiking
Bacon-Shakespeare controversy
  USE   **Shakespeare, William, 1564-
         1616—Authorship**
Bacon's Rebellion, 1676   973.2
  BT   **United States—History—1600-
         1775, Colonial period**
Bacteria   579.3
    Use for general materials on bacteria. Mate-
    rials on the science of studying bacteria are
    entered under **Bacteriology.**
  UF   Bacilli
        Disease germs
        Germs
        Microbes
  BT   **Microorganisms**
        Parasites
  RT   **Bacteriology**
Bacterial warfare
  USE   **Biological warfare**
Bacteriology   579.3
    Use for materials on the science of studying
    bacteria. General materials on bacteria are en-
    tered under **Bacteria.**
  SA   types of bacteriology, e.g. **Agri-
        cultural bacteriology;** types
        of microbiology, e.g. **Soil mi-
        crobiology;** and subjects with
        the subdivision *Microbiology,*
        e.g. **Cheese—Microbiology;**
        to be added as needed

BT = Broader Term   NT = Narrower Term   RT = Related Term   SA = See Also   UF = Used For

Bacteriology—*Continued*
  BT   Microbiology
  NT   Agricultural bacteriology
  RT   Bacteria
Bacteriology, Agricultural
  USE   Agricultural bacteriology
Badges of honor
  USE   Decorations of honor
        Insignia
        Medals
Bahai Faith   297.9
  UF   Bahaism *[Former heading]*
  BT   Religions
Bahaism
  USE   Bahai Faith
Baking   641.7
  SA   types of baked products, to be
       added as needed
  BT   Cooking
  NT   Bread
       Cake
       Pastry
  RT   Bread machines
Balance of nature
  USE   Ecology
Balance of payments   382
  BT   International economic rela-
       tions
  RT   Balance of trade
Balance of power   327.1
  UF   Power politics
  BT   International relations
Balance of trade   382
  UF   Trade, Balance of
  BT   Commerce
       Economics
       Tariff
  RT   Balance of payments
Ball bearings
  USE   Bearings (Machinery)
Ball games   796.3
  SA   types of games, e.g. **Baseball;**
       and names of competitions, to
       be added as needed
  BT   Games
  NT   Baseball
       Basketball
       Bowling
       Football
       Soccer

        Softball
        Table tennis
        Volleyball
Ballads   808.1; 808.81; 811, etc.
      May be used for individual works, collec-
  tions, or materials about ballads. Materials on
  the folk tunes associated with these ballads
  and collections that include both words and
  music are entered under **Folk songs.**
  BT   Literature
       Poetry
       Songs
  RT   Folk songs
Ballads, American
  USE   American ballads
Ballet   792.8
      Use for musical works composed for the
  ballet and for materials about the ballet. Indi-
  vidual ballet plots or collections of ballet plots
  are entered under **Ballet—Stories, plots, etc.**
  UF   Ballets *[Former heading]*
  BT   Dance
       Drama
       Performing arts
       Theater
  RT   Pantomimes
Ballet dancers   792.8092; 920
  BT   Dancers
Ballet—Stories, plots, etc.   792.8
  RT   Literature—Stories, plots, etc.
Ballet, Water
  USE   Synchronized swimming
Ballets
  USE   Ballet
Ballistic missile early warning system
        358.1; 621.3848
  UF   BMEWS
       Early warning system, Ballistic
       missile
  BT   Air defenses
       Radar defense networks
Ballistic missiles   358.1; 623.4
      Use for materials on high-altitude, high-
  speed missiles that are self-propelled and
  guided in the first stage of flight only and lat-
  er have a natural and uncontrolled trajectory.
  UF   Missiles, Ballistic
  SA   types of ballistic missiles and
       names of specific missiles, to
       be added as needed
  BT   Guided missiles
       Nuclear weapons
       Rockets (Aeronautics)

BT = Broader Term   NT = Narrower Term   RT = Related Term   SA = See Also   UF = Used For

Ballistic missiles—*Continued*
  NT   Atlas (Missile)
        Intercontinental ballistic mis-
          siles
Balloons   629.133
    Use for materials on aircraft held aloft by
    hot air or light gases that are nondirigible and
    propelled only by the wind. Materials on self-
    propelled aircraft that are lighter than air and
    steerable are entered under **Airships.**
  UF   Aircraft
  BT   **Aeronautics**
  RT   **Airships**
Balloons, Dirigible
  USE   **Airships**
Ballot
  USE   **Elections**
Ballparks
  USE   **Stadiums**
Band music   784
  BT   **Instrumental music**
        Military music
Bandages   616.02
  UF   Bandages and bandaging *[For-*
          mer heading]
  BT   **First aid**
Bandages and bandaging
  USE   **Bandages**
Bandits
  USE   **Thieves**
Bandmasters
  USE   **Conductors (Music)**
Bands (Music)   784
  SA   types of bands and names of in-
          dividual bands, to be added
          as needed
  NT   **Drum majoring**
        Instrumentation and orchestra-
          tion
  RT   **Conducting**
        Orchestra
        Wind instruments
Bank credit cards
  USE   **Credit cards**
Bank debit cards
  USE   **Debit cards**
Bank failures   332.1
  UF   Failure of banks
  BT   **Bankruptcy**
        Banks and banking
        Business failures

Banking
  USE   **Banks and banking**
Bankruptcy   332.7; 336.3; 346.07
  UF   Business mortality
        Failure in business
        Insolvency
  BT   **Business failures**
        Commercial law
        Debtor and creditor
        Finance
  NT   **Bank failures**
Banks and banking (May subdiv. geog.)
        332.1
  UF   Banking
        Savings banks
  SA   names of individual banks, to be
          added as needed
  BT   **Business**
        Capital
        Commerce
        Finance
  NT   **Agricultural credit**
        Bank failures
        Consumer credit
        Cooperative banks
        Debit cards
        Federal Reserve banks
        Foreign exchange
        Interest (Economics)
        Investments
        Negotiable instruments
        Savings and loan associations
  RT   **Credit**
        Money
        Trust companies
Banks and banking, Cooperative
  USE   **Cooperative banks**
Banks and banking—Credit cards
  USE   **Credit cards**
Banks and banking—Data processing
        332.10285
  BT   **Electronic data processing**
Banks and banking—United States
        332.10973
  UF   United States—Banks and bank-
          ing
Banned books
  USE   **Books—Censorship**
Banners
  USE   **Flags**

BT = Broader Term   NT = Narrower Term   RT = Related Term   SA = See Also   UF = Used For

Banquets
USE **Dining**
Dinners
Baptism **234; 265**
UF **Christening**
BT **Sacraments**
Baptists **286**
BT **Christian sects**
Bar
USE **Lawyers**
Barbary corsairs
USE **Pirates**
Barbary States
USE **North Africa**
Barbecue cookery
USE **Barbecue cooking**
Barbecue cooking **641.7**
UF Barbecue cookery *[Former head-ing]*
Cooking, Barbecue
Grill cooking
BT **Outdoor cooking**
Barbering
USE **Hair**
Bargaining
USE **Negotiation**
Barns **631.2; 728**
BT **Farm buildings**
Barometer
USE **Barometers**
Barometers **551.5; 681**
UF Barometer *[Former heading]*
BT **Meteorological instruments**
Baronage
USE **Nobility**
Baroque architecture **724**
UF Architecture, Baroque *[Former heading]*
BT **Architecture**
Baroque art **709.03**
UF Art, Baroque *[Former heading]*
BT **Art**
Barrier free design
USE **Architecture and the handi-capped**
Barristers
USE **Lawyers**
Barrooms
USE **Bars**

Barrows
USE **Mounds and mound builders**
Bars (May subdiv. geog.) **647.95**
Use for materials on public drinking estab-lishments.
UF **Barrooms**
Pubs
Restaurants, bars, etc. *[Former heading]*
Saloons
Taverns
BT **Liquor industry**
RT **Restaurants**
Barter **332**
UF Exchange, Barter
BT **Commerce**
Economics
Money
Subsistence economy
Underground economy
Basal readers **372.41; 418**
Use for readers providing controlled vocab-ulary in a series of books intended to be read sequentially and for materials about such read-ers.
UF English language—Basal readers
BT **Reading materials**
Baseball **796.357**
BT **Ball games**
Sports
NT **Baseball teams**
Little League baseball
Softball
RT **Baseball players**
Baseball cards **769**
BT **Sports cards**
Baseball clubs
USE **Baseball teams**
Baseball—Fiction **808.83; 813, etc.**
May be used for individual works, collec-tions, or materials about baseball stories.
UF Baseball stories *[Former head-ing]*
Baseball players **796.357; 920**
BT **Athletes**
RT **Baseball**
Baseball stories
USE **Baseball—Fiction**
Baseball teams **796.35706**
UF Baseball clubs *[Former heading]*
SA names of individual baseball teams, to be added as needed

BT = Broader Term   NT = Narrower Term   RT = Related Term   SA = See Also   UF = Used For

Baseball teams—*Continued*
    BT   **Baseball**
    NT   **Houston Astros (Baseball**
           team)
Basements   **721**
    UF   Cellars
    BT   **Foundations**
           Underground architecture
Bases (Chemistry)   **546; 661**
    BT   **Chemistry**
Bashfulness
    USE   **Shyness**
Basic education   **370.11**
    UF   Basic skills education
           Fundamental education
    BT   **Education**
Basic life skills
    USE   **Life skills**
Basic rights
    USE   **Civil rights**
          Human rights
Basic skills education
    USE   **Basic education**
Basket making   **746.41**
    BT   **Weaving**
Basketball   **796.323**
    BT   **Ball games**
          Sports
Bastardy
    USE   **Illegitimacy**
Bastogne, Battle of
    USE   **Ardennes, Battle of the, 1944-**
           1945
Bat
    USE   **Bats**
Baths   **613; 615.8**
    BT   **Cleanliness**
          Hygiene
          Physical therapy
    RT   **Hydrotherapy**
Bathyscaphe   **387.2; 623.8**
    BT   **Oceanography—Research**
          Submersibles
Batik   **746.6**
    BT   **Dyes and dyeing**
Baton twirling   **791.6**
    RT   **Drum majoring**
Batrachia
    USE   **Amphibians**

Bats   **599.4**
    UF   Bat
    BT   **Mammals**
Battered children
    USE   **Child abuse**
Battered elderly
    USE   **Elderly abuse**
Battered husbands
    USE   **Husband abuse**
Battered men
    USE   **Husband abuse**
Battered wives
    USE   **Abused women**
Battered women
    USE   **Abused women**
Batteries, Electric
    USE   **Electric batteries**
          Storage batteries
Batteries, Solar
    USE   **Solar batteries**
Battering of wives
    USE   **Wife abuse**
Battle of the Bulge
    USE   **Ardennes, Battle of the, 1944-**
           1945
Battle ships
    USE   **Warships**
Battle songs
    USE   **War songs**
Battlefields (May subdiv. geog.)   **904**
    UF   Battlegrounds
    SA   names of wars with the subdivi-
          sion *Battlefields,* e.g. **World**
          War, 1939-1945—Battle-
          fields; and names of individu-
          al battlefields, to be added as
          needed
    BT   **Battles**
Battlegrounds
    USE   **Battlefields**
Battles   **355.4; 909; 930-990**
    UF   Fighting
          Sieges
    SA   names of wars with the subdivi-
          sion *Campaigns,* e.g. **United**
          States—History—1861-1865,
          Civil War—Campaigns; and
          names of individual battles,
          e.g. **Ardennes, Battle of the,**

BT = Broader Term   NT = Narrower Term   RT = Related Term   SA = See Also   UF = Used For

Battles—*Continued*
> 1944-1945; to be added as needed

- BT   Military art and science
       Military history
       War
- NT   Battlefields
- RT   Naval battles

Battleships
- USE   Warships

Bay of Pigs invasion
- USE   Cuba—History—1961, Invasion

Bazaars
- USE   Fairs

Beaches   551.45
- BT   Seashore

Beadwork   746.5
- BT   Crocheting
       Embroidery
       Weaving

Bearings (Machinery)   621.8
- UF   Ball bearings
- BT   Machinery
- RT   Lubrication and lubricants

Beasts
- USE   Animals

Beat generation
- USE   Bohemianism

Beatniks
- USE   Bohemianism

Beautification of landscape
- USE   Landscape protection

Beauty
- USE   Aesthetics

Beauty parlors
- USE   Beauty shops

Beauty, Personal
- USE   Personal appearance
        Personal grooming

Beauty salons
- USE   Beauty shops

Beauty shops   646.7
- UF   Beauty parlors
       Beauty salons
- BT   Business enterprises
- NT   Cosmetics

Beavers   599.37
- BT   Freshwater animals
       Furbearing animals
       Mammals

Bed and breakfast accommodations (May subdiv. geog.)   647.94
- UF   B and B accommodations
- BT   Hotels and motels

Bedouins   305.892; 909
- BT   Arabs

Bedspreads   643; 746.9
- UF   Coverlets
- BT   Interior design

Bedtime
- UF   Getting ready for bed
- BT   Night
       Sleep
- NT   Lullabies

Bee
- USE   Bees

Bee culture
- USE   Beekeeping

Bee hives
- USE   Beehives

Bee houses
- USE   Beehives

Beef   641.3; 664
- BT   Meat

Beef cattle   636.2
- UF   Steers
- SA   names of breeds of beef cattle, to be added as needed
- BT   Cattle
- NT   Hereford cattle

Beehives   638
- UF   Bee hives
       Bee houses
       Bees—Housing
- BT   Animal housing
- RT   Beekeeping

Beekeeping   638
- UF   Apiculture
       Bee culture
       Honeybee culture
- BT   Agriculture
- RT   Beehives
       Bees

Bees   595.79; 638
- UF   Bee
       Hymenoptera
- BT   Insects
- RT   Beekeeping
       Honey

BT = Broader Term   NT = Narrower Term   RT = Related Term   SA = See Also   UF = Used For

Bees—Housing
USE **Beehives**
Begging 362.5
UF Mendicancy
Panhandling
BT **Poor**
RT **Tramps**
Beginning reading materials
USE **Easy reading materials**
Behavior
USE **Animal behavior**
Human behavior
and types of specific behavior,
e.g. **Sexual behavior;** and
types of animals with the
subdivision *Behavior,* e.g.
Birds—Behavior; to be add-
ed as needed
Behavior genetics 155.7
UF Psychogenetics
BT **Genetics**
Psychology
Behavior, Helping
USE **Helping behavior**
Behavior modification 153.8
BT **Applied psychology**
Human behavior
Psychology of learning
NT **Brainwashing**
Twelve-step programs
Behavior problems (Children)
USE **Emotionally disturbed children**
Behavior, Sexual
USE **Sexual behavior**
Behaviorism 150.19
Use for materials on empirical psychology
dealing with the observable actions of organ-
isms rather than with mental phenomena.
UF Behavioristic psychology
Interbehaviorial psychology
BT **Human behavior**
Psychology
Psychophysiology
Behavioristic psychology
USE **Behaviorism**
Beijing Massacre, 1989
USE **China—History—1989, Tianan-**
men Square Incident
Belief and doubt 121
Use for materials on belief and doubt from
the philosophical standpoint. Materials on reli-

gious belief and doubt are entered under
Faith.
UF Certainty
Doubt
BT **Philosophy**
Theory of knowledge
NT **Truth**
RT **Agnosticism**
Faith
Rationalism
Skepticism
Bell System Telstar satellite
USE **Telstar project**
Belles lettres
USE **Literature**
Bells 786.8
UF Carillons
Chimes
Church bells
BT **Musical instruments**
Belts and belting 621.8
UF Chain belting
BT **Machinery**
RT **Power transmission**
Beneficial insects 591.6
UF Economic entomology
Entomology, Economic
Helpful insects
Insects, Injurious and beneficial
[Former heading]
Useful insects
SA types of beneficial insects, e.g.
Silkworms; to be added as
needed
BT **Economic zoology**
Insects
NT **Silkworms**
Benevolent institutions
USE **Institutional care**
Beowulf—Adaptations 829
Bequests
USE **Gifts**
Inheritance and succession
Wills
Bereavement 155.9; 248.8
Use for materials on the suffering of those
who have lost a loved one. Materials on men-
tal suffering or sorrow from other causes, es-
pecially loss or remorse, are entered under
Grief.
UF Mourning
Sorrow

BT = Broader Term   NT = Narrower Term   RT = Related Term   SA = See Also   UF = Used For

Bereavement—*Continued*
    Sympathy *[Former heading]*
BT   **Emotions**
RT   **Consolation**
    Grief
Bermuda Triangle   001.9
UF   Devil's Triangle
    Graveyard of the Atlantic
Berries   634
SA   types of berries, e.g. **Strawber-
    ries**; to be added as needed,
    in the plural form
BT   **Fruit**
    Fruit culture
NT   **Strawberries**
Best-book lists
USE   **Best books**
Best books   011
    Use for lists of recommended books and materials about recommended books. Materials on the principles of book selection for libraries are entered under **Book selection.**
UF   Best-book lists
    Bibliography—Best books
    Book lists
    Books and reading—Best books
    [Former heading]
    Choice of books
    Evaluation of literature
    Literature—Evaluation
BT   **Books**
RT   **Book selection**
Best sellers (Books)   028; 070.5
UF   Books—Best sellers
BT   **Book industries**
    Books and reading
Betting
USE   **Gambling**
Bevel gearing
USE   **Gearing**
Beverages   613; 641.2; 641.8; 663
UF   Drinks
SA   types of beverages and names of
    specific beverages, to be added as needed
BT   **Diet**
    Food
NT   **Alcoholic beverages**
    Cocoa
    Coffee
    Liquors

    Tea
Bias attacks
USE   **Hate crimes**
Bias crimes
USE   **Hate crimes**
Bias (Psychology)
USE   **Prejudices**
Bible   220
    The subdivisions provided under **Bible** may also be used with any part of the Bible, with single books of the Bible, and with groups of books, e.g. **Bible. O.T.—Biography; Bible. O.T. Pentateuch—Commentaries; Bible. O.T. Psalms—History; Bible. N.T. Gospels—Inspiration;** etc.
UF   Holy Scriptures
    Scriptures, Holy
BT   **Ancient history**
    Hebrew literature
    Jewish literature
    Sacred books
NT   **Bible stories**
Bible and science   220.8
UF   Bible—Science
    Science and the Bible
BT   **Religion and science**
    Science
RT   **Creationism**
Bible—Animals
USE   **Bible—Natural history**
Bible—Antiquities   220.9
UF   Antiquities, Biblical
    Archeology, Biblical
    Biblical archeology
BT   **Antiquities**
    Archeology
NT   **Christian antiquities**
Bible as literature   809
UF   Bible—Language, style, etc.
    Bible—Literary character
NT   **Bible—Criticism**
    Bible—Parables
RT   **Religious literature**
Bible—Astronomy   220.8
BT   **Astronomy**
Bible—Biography   220.92
UF   Biblical characters
BT   **Biography**
NT   **Women in the Bible**
Bible—Birds
USE   **Bible—Natural history**

BT = Broader Term   NT = Narrower Term   RT = Related Term   SA = See Also   UF = Used For

Bible—Botany
　　USE　**Bible—Natural history**
Bible—Catechisms, question books　220
　　UF　Bible—Question books
　　BT　**Bible—Study and teaching**
　　　　Catechisms
Bible—Chronology　220.9
　　Use for materials on the dates of events related in the Bible and their correlation with the dates of general history.
　　UF　Bible—History of biblical
　　　　　events—Chronology
　　　　Chronology, Biblical
　　BT　**Chronology**
Bible classes
　　USE　**Bible—Study and teaching**
　　　　Religious summer schools
　　　　Sunday schools
Bible—Commentaries　220.7
　　UF　Bible—Interpretation
　　　　Commentaries, Biblical
Bible—Concordances　220.3
　　Use for works that list the words of the Bible and give the passages where each word occurs. Works that list topics or names found in the Bible and give the passages where those topics or names rather than exact words are found are entered under **Bible—Indexes.**
Bible—Cosmology
　　USE　**Biblical cosmology**
Bible—Criticism　220.6
　　UF　Bible—Criticism, interpretation,
　　　　　etc. *[Former heading]*
　　　　Bible—Exegesis
　　　　Bible—Hermeneutics
　　　　Bible—Interpretation
　　　　Exegesis, Biblical
　　　　Hermeneutics, Biblical
　　　　Higher criticism
　　BT　**Bible as literature**
Bible—Criticism, interpretation, etc.
　　USE　**Bible—Criticism**
Bible—Dictionaries　220.3
　　BT　**Encyclopedias and dictionaries**
Bible—Drama
　　USE　**Bible plays**
Bible—Evidences, authority, etc.　220.1
　　Use for materials that attempt to establish the truth of statements in the Bible or the authority of its precepts. Materials on the divine inspiration of the Bible are entered under **Bible—Inspiration.**
　　UF　Evidences of the Bible
　　BT　**Bible—Inspiration**

Bible—Exegesis
　　USE　**Bible—Criticism**
Bible fiction　808.83; 813, etc.
　　May be used for individual works, collections, or materials about imaginative fiction in which characters and settings are taken from the Bible. Stories that are retold or adapted from the Bible while remaining faithful to the original are entered under **Bible stories.**
　　UF　Bible—History of biblical
　　　　　events—Fiction *[Former heading]*
　　SA　names of biblical characters with
　　　　the subdivision *Fiction,* to be
　　　　added as needed
　　BT　**Fiction**
　　RT　**Bible stories**
Bible films　791.43
　　May be used for individual works, collections, or materials about bible films.
　　UF　Biblical films
　　　　Films, Bible
　　BT　**Motion pictures**
　　RT　**Bible plays**
Bible—Flowers
　　USE　**Bible—Natural history**
Bible—Gardens
　　USE　**Bible—Natural history**
Bible—Geography　220.91
　　UF　Bible—Maps
　　　　Biblical geography
　　　　Geography, Biblical
　　BT　**Atlases**
　　　　Geography
Bible—Hermeneutics
　　USE　**Bible—Criticism**
Bible—History　220.9
　　Use for materials on the origin, authorship, and composition of the Bible as a book. Materials on historical events as described in the Bible are entered under **Bible—History of biblical events.**
Bible—History of biblical events　220.9
　　Use for materials on historical events as described in the Bible. Materials on the origin, authorship, and composition of the Bible as a book are entered under **Bible—History.**
　　UF　History, Biblical
Bible—History of biblical events—Chronology
　　USE　**Bible—Chronology**
Bible—History of biblical events—Fiction
　　USE　**Bible fiction**

BT = Broader Term　　　NT = Narrower Term　　　RT = Related Term　　　SA = See Also　　　UF = Used For

Bible—Illustrations
USE   **Bible—Pictorial works**

Bible in literature   809

Use for materials that discuss the Bible as a theme in literature.

BT   **Literature**

RT   **Religion in literature**

Bible in the schools
USE   **Religion in the public schools**

Bible—Indexes   220.3

Use for works that list topics or names found in the Bible and give the passages where those topics or names rather than exact words are found. Works that list the words of the Bible and give the passages where the exact word occurs are entered under **Bible—Concordances.**

Bible—Inspiration   220.1

Use for materials on the divine inspiration of the Bible. Materials that attempt to establish the truth of statements in the Bible or the authority of its precepts are entered under **Bible—Evidence, authority, etc.**

UF   Inspiration, Biblical

NT   **Bible—Evidences, authority, etc.**

Bible—Interpretation
USE   **Bible—Commentaries**
           Bible—Criticism

Bible—Introductions
USE   **Bible—Study and teaching**

Bible—Language, style, etc.
USE   **Bible as literature**

Bible—Literary character
USE   **Bible as literature**

Bible—Maps
USE   **Bible—Geography**

Bible—Miracles
USE   **Miracles**

Bible. N.T.   225

Use same subdivisions as those given under **Bible.** They may also be used for groups of books, e.g. **Bible. N.T. Gospels—Inspiration;** and for single books, e.g. **Bible. N.T. Matthew—Commentaries.**

UF   New Testament

Bible. N.T.—Miracles
USE   **Miracles—Christianity**

Bible—Natural history   220.8

UF   Bible—Animals
           Bible—Birds
           Bible—Botany
           Bible—Flowers
           Bible—Gardens
           Bible—Plants

Bible—Zoology
Botany of the Bible
Natural history, Biblical
Nature in the bible
Zoology of the Bible

BT   **Natural history**

Bible. O.T.   221

Use same subdivisions as those given under **Bible.** They may also be used for groups of books, e.g. **Bible. O.T. Pentateuch—Commentaries;** and for single books, e.g. **Bible. O.T. Psalms—History.**

UF   Old Testament

NT   **Ten commandments**

Bible—Parables   226.8

BT   **Bible as literature**
           Parables

NT   **Jesus Christ—Parables**

Bible—Pictorial works   220.022

UF   Bible—Illustrations

RT   **Christian art and symbolism**
           Jesus Christ—Art

Bible—Plants
USE   **Bible—Natural history**

Bible plays   808.82; 812, etc.

May be used for individual plays, collections, or materials about dramatizations of biblical events.

UF   Bible—Drama *[Former heading]*
           Biblical plays
           Plays, Bible

SA   names of biblical characters with the subdivision *Drama,* to be added as needed

BT   **Religious drama**

NT   **Mysteries and miracle plays**
           Passion plays

RT   **Bible films**

Bible—Prophecies   220.1

UF   Prophecies (Bible)

NT   **Jesus Christ—Prophecies**

Bible—Psychology   220.8

UF   Psychology, Biblical

BT   **Psychology**

Bible—Question books
USE   **Bible—Catechisms, question books**

Bible—Reading   220.5

BT   **Books and reading**

Bible—Science
USE   **Bible and science**

BT = Broader Term   NT = Narrower Term   RT = Related Term   SA = See Also   UF = Used For

Bible stories   220.9

May be used for individual works, collections, or materials about stories that are retold or adapted from the Bible while remaining faithful to the original. Imaginative fiction in which characters and settings are taken from the Bible is entered under **Bible fiction.**

UF   Stories

BT   **Bible**

RT   **Bible fiction**

Bible—Study

USE   **Bible—Study and teaching**

Bible—Study and teaching   220.07

UF   Bible classes

Bible—Introductions

Bible—Study [Former heading]

BT   **Christian education**

Sunday schools

NT   **Bible—Catechisms, question books**

Bible—Use   220.6

Use for materials that show how the Bible is used as a guide to living, to cultivation of a spiritual life, and to problems of doctrine.

Bible—Versions   220.4; 220.5

Use for materials on the various versions and translations of the Bible.

Bible—Women

USE   **Women in the Bible**

Bible—Zoology

USE   **Bible—Natural history**

Biblical archeology

USE   **Bible—Antiquities**

Biblical characters

USE   **Bible—Biography**

Biblical cosmology   231.7; 291.2; 296.3

UF   Bible—Cosmology

Cosmology, Biblical

BT   **Cosmology**

RT   **Creation**

Biblical films

USE   **Bible films**

Biblical geography

USE   **Bible—Geography**

Biblical plays

USE   **Bible plays**

Bibliographic control   025.3

UF   Universal bibliographic control

BT   **Documentation**

NT   **Cataloging**

Indexing

Information systems

MARC formats

Bibliographic data in machine readable form

USE   **Machine readable bibliographic data**

Bibliographic instruction   025.5

Use for materials on the instruction of readers in library use. Materials on the education of librarians are entered under **Library education.**

UF   Library instruction [Former heading]

Library orientation

Library skills

Library user orientation

BT   **Library services**

Bibliography   010

SA   subjects and names of persons and places with the subdivision Bibliography, e.g. **Agriculture—Bibliography; Shakespeare, William, 1564-1616—Bibliography; United States—Bibliography;** etc., to be added as needed

BT   **Documentation**

NT   **Archives**

Bookbinding

Books—Classification

Editions

Indexes

Indexing

Information systems

Manuscripts

Printing

Reference books

Serial publications

RT   **Books**

Cataloging

Library science

Bibliography—Best books

USE   **Best books**

Bibliography—Bilingual books

USE   **Bilingual books**

Bibliography—Editions

USE   **Editions**

Bibliography—First editions

USE   **First editions**

Bibliography—Reprints

USE   **Editions**

Bibliomania

USE   **Book collecting**

BT = Broader Term   NT = Narrower Term   RT = Related Term   SA = See Also   UF = Used For

Bibliophily
USE **Book collecting**

Bicameralism
USE **Legislative bodies**

Bicentennial celebrations—United States—
1976
USE **American Revolution Bicentennial, 1776-1976**

Biculturalism (May subdiv. geog.)
306.44

Use for materials on the presence of two distinct cultures within a single country or region. Materials on the preservation of various cultures or cultural identities within a unified society are entered under **Multiculturalism**

UF Pluralism (Social sciences)
BT **Civilization**
Culture
RT **Multiculturalism**

Biculturalism—United States 306.44
UF United States—Biculturalism

Bicycle camping
USE **Bicycle touring**

Bicycle racing 796.6
BT **Cycling**
Racing
RT **Bicycle touring**
Bicycles

Bicycle touring (May subdiv. geog.)
796.6
UF Backpack cycling
Bicycle camping
Touring, Bicycle
BT **Camping**
Cycling
Travel
RT **Bicycle racing**
Bicycles

Bicycles 629.227
UF Bicycles and bicycling *[Former heading]*
Bikes
BT **Vehicles**
NT **Minibikes**
Motorcycles
Mountain bikes
RT **Bicycle racing**
Bicycle touring
Cycling

Bicycles, All terrain
USE **Mountain bikes**

Bicycles and bicycling
USE **Bicycles**
Cycling

Bicycling
USE **Cycling**

Big bang cosmology
USE **Big bang theory**

Big bang theory 523.1
UF Big bang cosmology
BT **Cosmology**

Big books 372.41

Use for books produced in an oversize format and intended for use in shared-reading learning experiences or for materials about such books.

UF Enlarged texts for shared reading
Oversize books
Oversized books for shared reading
Shared reading books
BT **Children's literature**
Reading materials
RT **Large print books**

Big foot
USE **Sasquatch**

Bigfoot
USE **Sasquatch**

Bigotry
USE **Prejudices**
Toleration

Bigotry-motivated crimes
USE **Hate crimes**

Bikes
USE **Bicycles**

Bikes, Mountain
USE **Mountain bikes**

Biking
USE **Cycling**

Bildungsromans

May be used for individual works, collections, or materials about fiction in which the theme is the development of a character from youth to adulthood.

UF Apprenticeship novels
Coming of age stories
BT **Fiction**

Bilingual books 002; 011

Use for materials about bilingual books. As a form heading for the bilingual materials themselves, use this heading subdivided by the languages, e.g. **Bilingual books—English-Spanish.**

UF Bibliography—Bilingual books

BT = Broader Term   NT = Narrower Term   RT = Related Term   SA = See Also   UF = Used For

Bilingual books—*Continued*
    Books—Bilingual editions
  BT   **Books**
          Editions
Bilingual books—English-Spanish
    Use as a form heading for bilingual materials in English and Spanish.
  UF   Bilingual books—Spanish-English
Bilingual books—Spanish-English
  USE   **Bilingual books—English-Spanish**
Bilingual education   370.117
  UF   Education, Bilingual *[Former heading]*
  BT   **Bilingualism**
          Multicultural education
Bilingualism (May subdiv. geog.)
    306.44; 400
  BT   **Language and languages**
  NT   **Bilingual education**
Bilingualism—United States   306.44; 420
  UF   United States—Bilingualism
Billboards
  USE   **Signs and signboards**
Bills and notes
  USE   **Negotiable instruments**
Bills of credit
  USE   **Credit**
          Negotiable instruments
          Paper money
Bills of fare
  USE   **Menus**
Bimetallism
  USE   **Gold**
          Monetary policy
          Silver
Binary system (Mathematics)   513.5
  UF   Pair system
  BT   **Mathematics**
          Numbers
Binding of books
  USE   **Bookbinding**
Binge eating behavior
  USE   **Bulimia**
Binge-purge behavior
  USE   **Bulimia**
Bio-bibliography
  USE   subjects, groups and classes of persons, names of places, and

names of individual persons with the subdivision *Bio-bibliography*, e.g. **English literature—Bio-bibliography; United States—Bio-bibliography**; etc., to be added as needed
Bioastronautics
  USE   **Space biology**
          Space medicine
Biochemistry   572
  UF   Biological chemistry
          Chemistry, Biological
          Chemistry, Physiological
          Physiological chemistry *[Former heading]*
  BT   **Biology**
          Chemistry
          Medicine
  NT   **Clinical chemistry**
          Metabolism
          Molecular biology
          Nucleic acids
          Proteins
          Steroids
Bioconversion
  USE   **Biomass energy**
Biodiversity
  USE   **Biological diversity**
Bioethics   174
  UF   Biological ethics
          Biology—Ethics
          Biomedical ethics
          Ethics, Biological
          Life sciences ethics
  BT   **Social ethics**
  NT   **Medical ethics**
          Transplantation of organs, tissues, etc.—Ethical aspects
Biofeedback training   152.1
  UF   Visceral learning
  BT   **Feedback (Psychology)**
          Mind and body
          Psychology of learning
          Psychotherapy
Biogeography   578.09
    Use for materials on the geographical distribution of animals and plants collectively or of animals only. Materials on the geographical distribution of plants are entered under **Plants—Geographical distribution.**

Biogeography—*Continued*

UF   Animals—Geographical distribution

       Distribution of animals and plants

       Geographical distribution of animals and plants

       Paleobiogeography

       Zoogeography

SA   types of plants and animals with the subdivision *Geographical distribution,* e.g. **Fishes—Geographical distribution;** to be added as needed

BT   **Ecology**

       Geography

NT   **Fishes—Geographical distribution**

       Plants—Geographical distribution

RT   **Natural history**

Biographical dictionaries

USE   **Biography—Dictionaries**

Biographical fiction   808.83; 813, etc.

May be used for individual works, collections, or materials about fictionalized accounts of the lives of real persons.

UF   Biographical novels

SA   names of real persons with the subdivision *Fiction,* e.g. **Napoleon I, Emperor of the French, 1769-1821—Fiction;** or *In literature,* e.g. **Napoleon I, Emperor of the French, 1769-1821—In literature;,** to be added as needed

BT   **Fiction**

NT   **Autobiographical fiction**

RT   **Historical fiction**

Biographical films   791.43

May be used for individual works, collections, or materials about films depicting the lives of real persons.

BT   **Motion pictures**

Biographical novels

USE   **Biographical fiction**

Biographical radio programs   791.44

May be used for individual works, collections, or materials about radio programs recounting the lives of real persons.

BT   **Radio programs**

Biographical television programs 791.45

May be used for individual works, collections, or materials about television programs depicting the lives of real persons.

BT   **Television programs**

Biography   920

Use for collections of biographies not limited to one country or to one group or class of persons. Materials on the writing of biography are entered under **Biography as a literary form.**

UF   Life histories

       Memoirs

       Personal narratives

SA   subjects and names of places with the subdivision *Biography;* ethnic groups, classes of persons, and individual literary authors with the subdivision *Biography* or *Correspondence;* and names of diseases, events, and wars with the subdivision *Personal narratives,* to be added as needed

BT   **History**

NT   **Autobiographies**

       Autographs

       Bible—Biography

       Blacks—Biography

       Chicago (Ill.)—Biography

       Christian biography

       Epitaphs

       Greece—Biography

       Medicine—Biography

       Men—Biography

       Motion pictures—Biography

       Musicians—Biography

       Obituaries

       Ohio—Biography

       Portraits

       Religious biography

       Rome—Biography

       Shakespeare, William, 1564-1616—Biography

       Shakespeare, William, 1564-1616—Psychology

       United States. Army—Biography

       United States—Biography

       United States—History—1861-1865, Civil War—Biography

Biography—*Continued*
United States—History—1861-1865, Civil War—Personal narratives
United States. Navy—Biography
United States. Supreme Court—Biography
Women—Biography
World War, 1939-1945—Biography
World War, 1939-1945—Personal narratives
RT **Genealogy**
Biography (as a literary form)
USE **Biography as a literary form**
Biography as a literary form 809
Use for materials on the writing of biography.
UF Biography (as a literary form) *[Former heading]*
Biography—History and criticism
Biography—Technique
BT **Authorship**
Literature
NT **Autobiography**
Biography—Dictionaries 920.02
Use for collections of biographies in dictionary form not limited to one group or class of persons.
UF Biographical dictionaries
Dictionaries, Biographical
SA subjects, groups or classes of persons, and names of places with the subdivision *Biography—Dictionaries,* e.g. **Women—Biography—Dictionaries; United States—Biography—Dictionaries;** etc., to be added as needed
BT **Encyclopedias and dictionaries**
Biography—History and criticism
USE **Biography as a literary form**
Biography—Technique
USE **Biography as a literary form**
Biological anthropology
USE **Physical anthropology**
Biological chemistry
USE **Biochemistry**
Biological clocks
USE **Biological rhythms**

Biological diversification
USE **Biological diversity**
Biological diversity
Use for materials on the variety and variability among living organisms and the ecological complexes in which they occur, including ecosystem diversity, species diversity, and genetic diversity.
UF Biodiversity
Biological diversification
Diversity, Biological
BT **Biology**
RT **Ecology**
Biological ethics
USE **Bioethics**
Biological oceanography
USE **Marine biology**
Marine ecology
Biological parents
USE **Birthparents**
Biological physics
USE **Biophysics**
Biological rhythms 571.7
UF Biological clocks
Biology—Periodicity
Biorhythms
BT **Cycles**
NT **Jet lag**
Biological warfare 358; 623.4
UF Bacterial warfare
Germ warfare
BT **Military art and science**
Tactics
Biologists 570.92; 920
BT **Naturalists**
Scientists
Biology 570
UF Morphology
BT **Life sciences**
Science
NT **Adaptation (Biology)**
Anatomy
Biochemistry
Biological diversity
Biomathematics
Biophysics
Botany
Cells
Cryobiology
Death
Ecology

Biology—*Continued*
>> Embryology
>> Fossils
>> Freshwater biology
>> Gaia hypothesis
>> Genetics
>> Heredity
>> Life (Biology)
>> Life cycles (Biology)
>> Marine biology
>> Microbiology
>> Physiology
>> Protoplasm
>> Radiobiology
>> Reproduction
>> Sex (Biology)
>> Space biology
>> Symbiosis
>> Variation (Biology)
>> Zoology
> RT **Evolution**

Biology—Ecology
> USE **Ecology**

Biology—Ethics
> USE **Bioethics**

Biology, Marine
> USE **Marine biology**

Biology, Molecular
> USE **Molecular biology**

Biology—Periodicity
> USE **Biological rhythms**

Biology—Social aspects
> USE **Sociobiology**

Bioluminescence   572
> UF Animal light
>> Animal luminescence
>> Light production in animals
> BT **Luminescence**

Biomass energy   333.95
> Use for materials on organic matter that can be converted to fuel and is therefore regarded as a potential energy source.
> UF Bioconversion
>> Energy, Biomass
>> Energy conversion, Microbial
>> Microbial energy conversion
> SA types of matter as fuels, e.g. **Waste products as fuel;** to be added as needed
> BT **Energy resources**
>> **Fuel**

> RT **Waste products as fuel**

Biomass energy industries   338.2; 338.4
> BT **Energy resources**

Biomathematics   570.1
> BT **Biology**
>> **Mathematics**

Biomechanics
> USE **Human engineering**
>> **Human locomotion**

Biomedical ethics
> USE **Bioethics**

Bionics   003
> Use for materials on the science of technological systems that function in the manner of living systems.
> BT **Biophysics**
>> **Cybernetics**
>> **Systems engineering**
> NT **Artificial intelligence**
>> **Optical data processing**

Biophysics   571.4
> UF Biological physics
>> Molecular physiology
>> Physics, Biological
>> Physiology, Molecular
> BT **Biology**
>> **Physics**
> NT **Bionics**
>> **Molecular biology**
>> **Radiobiology**

Biorhythms
> USE **Biological rhythms**

Biosciences
> USE **Life sciences**

Biosociology
> USE **Sociobiology**

Biotechnology   620.8; 660.6
> Use for materials on the application of living organisms or their biological systems or processes to the manufacture of products.
> BT **Chemical engineering**
>> **Microbiology**
> RT **Genetic engineering**

Bipolar depression
> USE **Manic-depressive illness**

Bipolar disorder
> USE **Manic-depressive illness**

Bird
> USE **Birds**

Bird decoys (Hunting)
> USE **Decoys (Hunting)**

BT = Broader Term   NT = Narrower Term   RT = Related Term   SA = See Also   UF = Used For

Bird eggs
USE Birds—Eggs
Bird houses
USE Birdhouses
Bird photography
USE Photography of birds
Bird song
USE Birdsongs
Bird watching   598.07
BT Natural history
Birdbanding   598.07
UF Birds—Banding
Birds—Marking
BT **Wildlife conservation**
Birdhouses   690
UF Bird houses *[Former heading]*
BT **Animal housing**
Birds (May subdiv. geog.)   **598**
UF Bird
Ornithology
SA types of birds, e.g. **Birds of prey; Canaries;** etc., to be added as needed
BT **Animals**
Vertebrates
NT **Birds of prey**
Cage birds
Canaries
Ducks
Eagles
Game and game birds
Geese
Peacocks
Pheasants
Poultry
Robins
State birds
Terns
Turkeys
Water birds
Birds—Anatomy   598
BT **Anatomy**
Birds—Banding
USE **Birdbanding**
Birds—Behavior   598.15
UF Birds—Habits and behavior
[Former heading]

Birds—Collection and preservation   598.075
BT **Zoological specimens—Collection and preservation**
Birds—Color   598.147
BT **Color**
Birds—Eggs   598.14
UF Bird eggs
Birds' eggs
Birds—Eggs and nests *[Former heading]*
BT **Eggs**
Birds' eggs
USE **Birds—Eggs**
Birds—Eggs and nests
USE **Birds—Eggs**
Birds—Nests
Birds—Flight   591.5; 598.15
BT **Animal flight**
Birds—Habits and behavior
USE **Birds—Behavior**
Birds in literature   809
BT **Animals in literature**
Nature in literature
Birds—Marking
USE **Birdbanding**
Birds—Migration   598.156
UF Migration of birds
BT **Animals—Migration**
Birds—Nests   598.156
UF Birds—Eggs and nests *[Former heading]*
Birds' nests
BT **Animals—Habitations**
Birds' nests
USE **Birds—Nests**
Birds of prey   598.9
SA names of specific birds of prey, to be added as needed
BT **Birds**
Predatory animals
NT **Eagles**
Birds—Photography
USE **Photography of birds**
Birds—Protection   333.95; 639.9
UF Protection of birds
BT **Wildlife conservation**
RT **Game protection**
Birds—Song
USE **Birdsongs**

BT = Broader Term   NT = Narrower Term   RT = Related Term   SA = See Also   UF = Used For

Birds—United States   598.0973
  UF   United States—Birds
Birdsongs   598.159
  UF   Bird song *[Former heading]*
         Birds—Song
  BT   **Animal sounds**
Birth
  USE **Childbirth**
Birth attendants
  USE **Midwives**
Birth control   353.5; 363.9; 613.9
  UF   Conception—Prevention
         Contraception
         Family planning
         Fertility control
         Planned parenthood
  BT   **Population**
         Sexual hygiene
  NT   **Abortion**
         Sterilization (Birth control)
  RT   **Birth rate**
         Childlessness
         Family size
         Human fertility
         Infertility
         Sexual ethics
Birth control—Ethical aspects   176
  UF   Birth control—Moral and reli-
         gious aspects *[Former head-
         ing]*
  BT   **Ethics**
Birth control—Moral and religious aspects
  USE **Birth control—Ethical aspects**
        **Birth control—Religious as-
        pects**
Birth control—Religious aspects   248.4;
    291.5
  UF   Birth control—Moral and reli-
         gious aspects *[Former head-
         ing]*
Birth customs
  USE **Childbirth**
Birth defects   616
  UF   Abnormalities, Human
         Birth injuries
         Deformities
         Human abnormalities
         Infants—Birth defects
         Malformations, Congenital
  BT   **Medical genetics**

        Pathology
  RT   **Growth disorders**
Birth injuries
  USE **Birth defects**
Birth, Multiple
  USE **Multiple birth**
Birth order   306.87
  UF   Firstborn child
         Middle child
         Oldest child
         Sibling sequence
         Youngest child
  BT   **Children**
         Family
Birth rate   304.6
  UF   Birthrate *[Former heading]*
  BT   **Vital statistics**
  NT   **Human fertility**
  RT   **Birth control**
         Population
Birth records
  USE **Registers of births, etc.**
Birthday books
  USE **Birthdays**
Birthdays   394.2
  UF   Anniversaries
         Birthday books
  BT   **Days**
Birthparents   306.874
    Use for materials on natural, i.e. biological,
  parents who relinquished their children for
  adoption.
  UF   Biological parents
         Natural parents
         Parents, Biological
  BT   **Parent and child**
  RT   **Adoptees**
Birthrate
  USE **Birth rate**
Births, Registers of
  USE **Registers of births, etc.**
Bison   599.64; 636.2
  UF   American bison
         Buffalo, American
  BT   **Mammals**
Black actors   791.4; 792; 920
  UF   Actors, Black
         Black actors and actresses *[For-
         mer heading]*
  BT   **Actors**
  NT   **African American actors**

BT = Broader Term   NT = Narrower Term   RT = Related Term   SA = See Also   UF = Used For

Black actors and actresses
USE   **Black actors**
Black Africa
USE   **Sub-Saharan Africa**
Black Americans
USE   **African Americans**
Black art   704.03
   Use for materials on works of art by several
Black artists. Materials on Blacks depicted in
works of art are entered under **Blacks in art.**
   UF   Art, Black
          Blacks—Art
   BT   **Art**
   NT   **African American art**
   RT   **Black artists**
Black art (Magic)
   USE   **Magic**
          Witchcraft
Black artists   709.2; 920
   Use for materials on several Black artists.
   UF   Artists, Black
   BT   **Artists**
   NT   **African American artists**
   RT   **Black art**
Black athletes   796.092; 920
   UF   Athletes, Black
   BT   **Athletes**
   NT   **African American athletes**
Black authors   809; 920
   Use for collections and for materials on
several Black authors not limited to a single
national literature or literary form.
   UF   Authors, Black
   SA   names of national literatures oth-
          er than American literature
          and forms of literature with
          the subdivision *Black authors,*
          e.g. **French literature—Black
          authors; French poetry—
          Black authors;** etc., to be
          added as needed
   BT   **Authors**
   NT   **African American authors**
**Black business people   338.092;
          658.0092; 920**
   UF   Business people, Black
   BT   **Blacks—Employment
          Business people**
   NT   **African American business
          people**
Black children   305.23
   UF   Blacks—Children

Children, Black
   BT   **Children**
   NT   **African American children**
Black comedy (Literature)
   USE   **Black humor (Literature)**
Black death
   USE   **Plague**
Black folk songs
   USE   **Black music**
Black folklore
   USE   **Blacks—Folklore**
Black Hawk War, 1832   973.5
   BT   **Indians of North America—
          Wars
          United States—History—1815-
          1861**
Black holes (Astronomy)   523.8
   UF   Frozen stars
   BT   **Astronomy
          Astrophysics
          Stars**
**Black humor (Literature)   808.7;
          808.87; 813, etc.**
   May be used for individual works, collec-
tions, or materials about literary works charac-
terized by a desperate, sardonic humor intend-
ed to induce laughter as the appropriate re-
sponse to the apparent meaninglessness and
absurdity of existence.
   UF   Black comedy (Literature)
          Dark humor (Literature)
   BT   **Fiction
          Literature
          Wit and humor**
Black lead
   USE   **Graphite**
Black librarians   020.92; 920
   UF   Librarians, Black
   BT   **Librarians**
   NT   **African American librarians**
Black literature (American)
   USE   **American literature—African
          American authors**
Black literature (French)
   USE   **French literature—Black au-
          thors**
Black magic (Witchcraft)
   USE   **Magic
          Witchcraft**
Black market (May subdiv. geog.)   381
   Use for materials on illegal trade aimed at
avoiding government regulations, such as

Black market—*Continued*
fixed prices or rationing. Materials on goods and services that are produced and sold legally but not reported or taxed are entered under **Underground economy.**

UF   Grey market

BT   **Commerce**

RT   **Underground economy**

Black market children

USE   **Adoption—Corrupt practices**

Black music (May subdiv. geog.)
       780.089

Use for general materials and for materials on the music of Blacks not in the United States. Materials on the music of African Americans are entered under **African American music.**

UF   Black folk songs

       Black songs

       Blacks—Music

       Blacks—Songs and music *[Former heading]*

       Music, Black

BT   **Music**

NT   **African American music**

RT   **Black musicians**

Black musicians   780.92; 920

UF   Musicians, Black

BT   **Musicians**

NT   **African American musicians**

RT   **Black music**

Black Muslims   297.8

UF   Nation of Islam

BT   **African Americans—Religion**

       Black nationalism

       Muslims—United States

Black nationalism   320.5

UF   Black separatism

       Nationalism, Black

       Separatism, Black

BT   **African Americans—Political activity**

       African Americans—Race identity

       Blacks—Political activity

       Blacks—Race identity

NT   **Black Muslims**

Black poetry (American)

USE   **American poetry—African American authors**

Black poetry (French)

USE   **French poetry—Black authors**

Black power   322.4

BT   **African Americans—Civil rights**

       African Americans—Economic conditions

       African Americans—Political activity

       Blacks—Civil rights

       Blacks—Economic conditions

       Blacks—Political activity

Black separatism

USE   **Black nationalism**

Black songs

USE   **Black music**

Black suffrage

USE   **Blacks—Suffrage**

Black women   305.48

UF   Women, Black

BT   **Women**

NT   **African American women**

Blackboard drawing

USE   **Chalk talks**

       Crayon drawing

Blackheads (Acne)

USE   **Acne**

Blackouts, Electric power

USE   **Electric power failures**

Blacks (May subdiv. geog. except U.S.)
       305.896

Use for materials on the Black race in general or for materials on blacks as an element in the population, especially in countries where they are a minority. Works on black people in countries with a population predominantly black are assigned headings appropriate for the country without the use of the heading **Blacks,** except when the works discuss blacks as distinct from other groups in the country. Materials on blacks in the United States are entered under **African Americans.**

UF   Negroes

SA   Blacks in various occupations and professions, e.g. **Black artists; Black librarians;** etc., to be added as needed

NT   **African Americans**

Blacks—Africa   305.896; 960

BT   **Africans**

Blacks—Art

USE   **Black art**

Blacks—Biography   920

BT   **Biography**

NT   **African Americans—Biography**

BT = Broader Term   NT = Narrower Term   RT = Related Term   SA = See Also   UF = Used For

Blacks—Children
USE   **Black children**
Blacks—Civil rights   323.1; 342
BT   **Blacks—Political activity**
      Civil rights
NT   **African Americans—Civil**
      rights
      Black power
Blacks—Economic conditions   330.9
BT   **Economic conditions**
NT   **African Americans—Economic**
      conditions
      Black power
Blacks—Education   370.89; 371.829
BT   **Education**
NT   **African Americans—Education**
Blacks—Employment   331.6
UF   Blacks—Occupations
BT   **Employment**
NT   **African Americans—Employ-**
      ment
      Black business people
RT   **Discrimination in employment**
Blacks—Folklore   398
UF   Black folklore
      Folklore, Black
BT   **Folklore**
NT   **African Americans—Folklore**
Blacks—France   305.896; 944
UF   France—Blacks
Blacks—Housing   307.3; 363.5
UF   Housing, Black
BT   **Housing**
NT   **African Americans—Housing**
Blacks in art   704.9

Use for materials on Blacks depicted in works of art. Materials on African Americans depicted in works of art are entered under **African Americans in art.** Materials on the attainments of several Blacks in the area of art are entered under **Black artists.** Materials on the attainments of several African Americans in the area of art are entered under **African American artists.** Materials on works of art by several Black artists are entered under **Black art.** Materials on works of art by several African American artists are entered under **African American art.**

BT   **Art**
NT   **African Americans in art**
Blacks in literature   809

Use for materials on the theme of Blacks in works of literature. Materials on the attain-

ments of several Blacks in the area of literature are entered under **Black authors.** Materials on works of literature by several Black authors are entered under individual literatures and forms of literature with the subdivision *Black authors,* e.g. **French literature—Black authors; French poetry—Black authors;** etc. Materials on the theme of African Americans in works of literature are entered under **African Americans in literature.** Materials on the attainments of several African Americans in the area of literature are entered under **African American authors.** Materials on works of literature by several African American authors are entered under **American literature—African American authors** and the various forms of American literature with the subdivision *African American authors,* e.g. **American poetry—African American authors.**

BT   **Characters and characteristics**
      in literature
NT   **African Americans in litera-**
      ture
Blacks in motion pictures   791.43

Use for materials on the depiction of Blacks in motion pictures. Materials on several Black actors are entered under **Black actors.** Materials discussing all aspects of Blacks' involvement in motion pictures are entered under **Blacks in the motion picture industry.**

BT   **Motion pictures**
NT   **African Americans in motion**
      pictures
Blacks in the motion picture industry
      791.43092

Use for materials on all aspects of Blacks' involvement in motion pictures. Materials on the depiction of Blacks in motion pictures are entered under **Blacks in motion pictures.**

BT   **Motion picture industry**
NT   **African Americans in the mo-**
      tion picture industry
Blacks—Intellectual life   305.896
BT   **Intellectual life**
NT   **African Americans—Intellectu-**
      al life
Blacks—Music
USE   **Black music**
Blacks—Occupations
USE   **Blacks—Employment**
Blacks—Political activity   322.4; 324
BT   **Political participation**
NT   **African Americans—Political**
      activity
      Black nationalism
      Black power
      Blacks—Civil rights

Blacks—Race identity   305.896
   UF   Negritude
   BT   Race awareness
   NT   African Americans—Race iden-
        tity
        Black nationalism
Blacks—Religion   270.089; 299
   BT   Religion
   NT   African Americans—Religion
Blacks—Segregation   305.896
   BT   Segregation
   NT   African Americans—Segrega-
        tion
Blacks—Social conditions   305.896
   BT   Social conditions
   NT   African Americans—Social
        conditions
Blacks—Social life and customs
        305.896
   BT   Manners and customs
   NT   African Americans—Social life
        and customs
Blacks—Songs and music
   USE   Black music
Blacks—Suffrage   324.6
   UF   Black suffrage
   BT   Suffrage
   NT   African Americans—Suffrage
Blacks—United States
   USE   African Americans
Blacksmithing   682
   BT   Ironwork
   NT   Welding
   RT   Forging
Blast furnaces   669
   BT   Furnaces
        Smelting
Blast shelters
   USE   Air raid shelters
Bleaching   667
   BT   Cleaning
        Industrial chemistry
        Textile industry
   RT   Dyes and dyeing
Blended family
   USE   Stepfamily
Blessed Virgin Mary
   USE   Mary, Blessed Virgin, Saint
Blimps
   USE   Airships

Blind   362.4
   BT   Physically handicapped
        Vision disorders
Blind—Books and reading   011.63;
        027.6; 028
   UF   Books for the blind
        Braille books
   BT   Books and reading
   NT   Large print books
        Talking books
Blind—Education   371.91
   UF   Education of the blind
   BT   Education
Blind—Institutional care   362.4
   BT   Institutional care
Blizzards   551.55
   BT   Storms
   RT   Snow
Block grants
   USE   Grants-in-aid
Block printing
   USE   Color prints
        Linoleum block printing
        Textile printing
        Wood engraving
        Woodcuts
Block signal systems
   USE   Railroads—Signaling
Blood   573.1; 612.1
   BT   Physiology
   NT   Blood groups
        Blood pressure
Blood—Circulation   573.1; 612.1
   UF   Circulation of the blood
   RT   Blood pressure
        Cardiovascular system
Blood—Diseases   616.1
   UF   Diseases of the blood
   SA   types of blood diseases, e.g.
        Leukemia; to be added as
        needed
   BT   Diseases
   NT   Leukemia
Blood groups   612.1
   UF   Rh factor
   BT   Blood
   RT   Blood—Transfusion
Blood pressure   612.1
   BT   Blood
   NT   Hypertension

BT = Broader Term   NT = Narrower Term   RT = Related Term   SA = See Also   UF = Used For

Blood pressure—*Continued*
    RT   **Blood—Circulation**
Blood—Transfusion   615
    RT   **Blood groups**
Blowing the whistle
    USE   **Whistle blowing**
Blowouts, Oil well
    USE   **Oil wells—Blowouts**
Blue collar workers
    USE   **Labor**
           Working class
Blue prints
    USE   **Blueprints**
Blueprints   604.2; 692
    UF   Blue prints
    BT   **Mechanical drawing**
Blues music   781.643; 782.421643
    UF   Blues songs
    BT   **African American music**
           Folk music—United States
           Popular music
    RT   **Jazz music**
Blues songs
    USE   **Blues music**
BMEWS
    USE   **Ballistic missile early warning**
           system
Board sailing
    USE   **Windsurfing**
Boarding houses
    USE   **Hotels and motels**
Boarding schools
    USE   **Private schools**
Boards of education
    USE   **School boards**
Boards of health
    USE   **Health boards**
Boards of trade
    USE   **Chambers of commerce**
Boat building
    USE   **Boatbuilding**
Boat racing   797.1
    SA   types of boat racing and names
           of specific races, to be added
           as needed
    BT   **Boats and boating**
           Racing
Boatbuilding   623.8
    UF   Boat building
    BT   **Boats and boating**

           Naval architecture
    NT   **Yachts and yachting**
    RT   **Shipbuilding**
Boating
    USE   **Boats and boating**
Boats and boating   797.1
    UF   Boating
    BT   **Transportation**
           Water sports
    NT   **Boat racing**
           Boatbuilding
           Canoes and canoeing
           Catamarans
           Houseboats
           Hydrofoil boats
           Iceboats
           Marinas
           Motorboats
           Rowing
           Steamboats
           Tugboats
           Yachts and yachting
    RT   **Sailing**
           Ships
Boats, Submarine
    USE   **Submarines**
           Submersibles
Body
    USE   **Human body**
Body and mind
    USE   **Mind and body**
Body building
    USE   **Bodybuilding**
Body care
    USE   **Hygiene**
Body heat
    USE   **Body temperature**
Body image   128; 155.2
    Use for materials on the visual, mental, or memory image of one's own body or another's body, and one's attitude towards that image.
    BT   **Human body**
           Mind and body
           Personality
           Self-perception
Body language
    USE   **Nonverbal communication**
Body temperature   571.7; 612
    UF   Animals—Temperature
           Body heat

BT = Broader Term   **NT** = Narrower Term   **RT** = Related Term   **SA** = See Also   **UF** = Used For

Body temperature—*Continued*

Temperature, Animal and human

Temperature, Body

BT **Diagnosis**

Physiology

RT **Fever**

Body weight   613

BT **Human body**

Weights and measures

NT **Obesity**

Weight loss

Body weight control

USE **Weight loss**

Bodybuilding   646.7

UF Body building

Physique

BT **Exercise**

Physical fitness

RT **Weight lifting**

Boers

USE **Afrikaners**

Bogs

USE **Marshes**

Wetlands

Bohemianism   306

UF Beat generation

Beatniks

BT **Counter culture**

Manners and customs

NT **Hippies**

Bolshevism

USE **Communism**

Bomb attacks

USE **Bombings**

Bomb shelters

USE **Air raid shelters**

Bombers   358.4; 623.7

SA types of bombers, e.g. **B-52 bomber;** to be added as needed

BT **Airplanes**

Military airplanes

NT **B-52 bomber**

Bombings (May subdiv. geog.)   **364.1**

Use for materials on the use of explosive devices for the purposes of political terrorism or protest. Materials on bombs in general and on bombs launched from aircraft are entered under **Bombs.**

UF Bomb attacks

Terrorist bombings

SA names of individual bombings incidents, to be added as needed

BT **Offenses against public safety**

Political crimes and offenses

Terrorism

Bombs   355.8; 623.4

Use for materials on bombs in general and on bombs launched from aircraft. Materials on the use of explosive devices for the purposes of political terrorism or protest are entered under **Bombings.**

UF Aerial bombs

SA types of bombs, e.g. **Atomic bomb;** to be added as needed

BT **Ammunition**

Explosives

Ordnance

Projectiles

NT **Atomic bomb**

Guided missiles

Hydrogen bomb

Incendiary bombs

Neutron bomb

Bombs, Flying

USE **Guided missiles**

Bombs, Incendiary

USE **Incendiary bombs**

Bonds   332.63

BT **Finance**

Investments

Negotiable instruments

Securities

Stock exchange

NT **Junk bonds**

RT **Public debts**

Stocks

Bonds—Rating   332.63

BT **Performance standards**

Bones   573.7; 611; 612.7

Use for comprehensive and systematic materials on the anatomy of bones. Materials limited to the morphology or mechanics of the skeleton, human or animal, are entered under **Skeleton.**

UF Osteology

BT **Musculoskeletal system**

NT **Fractures**

RT **Skeleton**

Bonsai   635.9

UF Kamuti

BT **Dwarf trees**

BT = Broader Term   NT = Narrower Term   RT = Related Term   SA = See Also   UF = Used For

Book awards
  USE   **Literary prizes**
         and names of awards, e.g.
           Caldecott Medal; Newbery
           Medal; etc., to be added as
           needed
Book buying (Libraries)
  USE   **Libraries—Acquisitions**
Book catalogs   017; 025.3
    Use for materials on library catalogs in
    book form. Retail book catalogs and book
    auction catalogs and materials about such cat-
    alogs are entered under **Booksellers' catalogs.**
    Publishers' book catalogs and materials about
    such catalogs are entered under **Publishers'**
    catalogs.
  UF   Books—Catalogs
         Catalogs, Book *[Former head-*
           ing]
         Catalogs in book form
  BT   **Library catalogs**
Book collecting   002.075
  UF   Bibliomania
         Bibliophily
         Books—Collectors and collecting
  BT   **Book selection**
         Collectors and collecting
  RT   **Bookplates**
         Books
Book fairs
  USE   **Book industries—Exhibitions**
Book illustration
  USE   **Illustration of books**
Book industries   686
  UF   Book industries and trade *[For-*
           mer heading]
         Book trade
  BT   **Industries**
  NT   **Best sellers (Books)**
         Bookbinding
         Booksellers and bookselling
         Printing
  RT   **Paper industry**
         Publishers and publishing
Book industries and trade
  USE   **Book industries**
Book industries—Exhibitions   070.5074;
  686.074
  UF   Book fairs
         Book trade—Exhibitions
         Books—Exhibitions
  BT   **Exhibitions**

  RT   **Printing—Exhibitions**
Book lending
  USE   **Library circulation**
Book lists
  USE   **Best books**
Book numbers, Publishers' standard
  USE   **Publishers' standard book**
           numbers
Book plates
  USE   **Bookplates**
Book prices
  USE   **Books—Prices**
Book prizes
  USE   **Literary prizes**
         and names of prizes, e.g.
           Caldecott Medal; Newbery
           Medal; etc., to be added as
           needed
Book rarities
  USE   **Rare books**
Book reviews
  USE   **Books—Reviews**
Book sales
  USE   **Books—Prices**
Book selection   025.2
    Use for materials on the principles of book
    selection for libraries. Lists of recommended
    books and materials about recommended
    books are entered under **Best books.**
  UF   Books—Selection
         Choice of books
  BT   **Libraries—Acquisitions**
         Libraries—Collection develop-
           ment
  NT   **Book collecting**
  RT   **Best books**
Book talks   021.7; 028.1
  UF   Booktalking
         Booktalks
  BT   **Books—Reviews**
         Public relations—Libraries
         Public speaking
Book trade
  USE   **Book industries**
         Booksellers and bookselling
         Publishers and publishing
Book trade—Exhibitions
  USE   **Book industries—Exhibitions**
Book Week, National
  USE   **National Book Week**

BT = Broader Term   NT = Narrower Term   RT = Related Term   SA = See Also   UF = Used For

Bookbinding   025.7; 095; 686.3
  UF   Binding of books
  BT   **Bibliography**
        Book industries
        Industrial arts
        Leather industry
Bookkeepers
  USE   **Accountants**
Bookkeeping   657
  SA   types of industries, professions,
        and organizations, with the
        subdivision *Accounting,* to be
        added as needed
  BT   **Business**
        Business education
        Business mathematics
  NT   **Auditing**
        Corporations—Accounting
        Cost accounting
        Office equipment and supplies
  RT   **Accounting**
Bookmobiles   027.4
  BT   **Library extension**
Bookplates   025.7; 769.5
  UF   Book plates
        Ex libris
  BT   **Prints**
  RT   **Book collecting**
Books   002
  NT   **Anthologies**
        Best books
        Bilingual books
        Chapbooks
        Illumination of books and
          manuscripts
        Illustration of books
        Libraries
        Librettos
        Manuscripts
        Paperback books
        Rare books
        Reference books
        Textbooks
  RT   **Authors**
        Bibliography
        Book collecting
        Literature
        Printing
        Publishers and publishing

Books and reading   028
  Use for general materials on reading for in-
  formation and culture, advice to readers, and
  surveys of reading habits.
  UF   Appraisal of books
        Books—Appraisal
        Choice of books
        Evaluation of literature
        Literature—Evaluation
        Reading interests
  SA   names of individuals and classes
        of persons with the subdivi-
        sion *Books and reading,* e.g.
        Blind—Books and reading;
        to be added as needed
  BT   **Communication**
        Education
        Reading
  NT   **Best sellers (Books)**
        Bible—Reading
        Blind—Books and reading
        Books—Reviews
        Children—Books and reading
        Libraries
        National Book Week
        Reference books
        Teenagers—Books and reading
  RT   **Literature**
        Reading materials
Books and reading—Best books
  USE   **Best books**
Books and reading for children
  USE   **Children—Books and reading**
Books and reading for teenagers
  USE   **Teenagers—Books and reading**
Books and reading for young adults
  USE   **Teenagers—Books and reading**
Books—Appraisal
  USE   **Books and reading**
        Books—Reviews
        Criticism
        Literature—History and criti-
          cism
Books—Best sellers
  USE   **Best sellers (Books)**
Books—Bilingual editions
  USE   **Bilingual books**
Books—Catalogs
  USE   **Book catalogs**
        Booksellers' catalogs
        Publishers' catalogs

BT = Broader Term   NT = Narrower Term   RT = Related Term   SA = See Also   UF = Used For

Books—Censorship   025.2; 323.44
    UF   Banned books
          Index librorum prohibitorum
          Prohibited books
    BT   Censorship
Books—Classification   025.4
    May be further subdivided by the subject of
    the books classified.
    UF   Classification—Books [Former
              heading]
          Library classification
    BT   Bibliography
          Cataloging
          Classification
          Library technical processes
    NT   Dewey Decimal Classification
    RT   Classified catalogs
Books—Collectors and collecting
    USE   Book collecting
Books—Copyright
    USE   Copyright—Books
Books—Exhibitions
    USE   Book industries—Exhibitions
           Printing—Exhibitions
Books, Filmed
    USE   Film adaptations
Books—First editions
    USE   First editions
Books for children
    USE   Children's literature
Books for sight saving
    USE   Large print books
Books for teenagers
    USE   Young adult literature
Books for the blind
    USE   Blind—Books and reading
Books—Large print
    USE   Large print books
Books—Preservation
    USE   Library resources—Conserva-
           tion and restoration
Books—Prices   002.075
    UF   Book prices
          Book sales
    BT   Booksellers and bookselling
          Prices
Books—Reviews   028.1; 808
    UF   Appraisal of books
          Book reviews
          Books—Appraisal
          Evaluation of literature

          Literature—Evaluation
    BT   Books and reading
          Criticism
    NT   Book talks
Books, Sacred
    USE   Sacred books
Books—Selection
    USE   Book selection
Books, Talking
    USE   Talking books
Booksellers and bookselling   070.5; 381;
                658.8
    UF   Book trade
    BT   Book industries
          Sales personnel
          Selling
    NT   Books—Prices
          Booksellers' catalogs
    RT   Publishers and publishing
Booksellers' catalogs   017
    Use for retail book catalogs and book auc-
    tion catalogs and materials about such cata-
    logs. Materials on library catalogs in book
    form are entered under Book catalogs. Pub-
    lishers' book catalogs and materials about
    such catalogs are entered under Publishers'
    catalogs.
    UF   Books—Catalogs
          Catalogs
          Catalogs, Booksellers' [Former
              heading]
    BT   Booksellers and bookselling
Booktalking
    USE   Book talks
Booktalks
    USE   Book talks
Boolean algebra   511.3
    UF   Algebra, Boolean [Former head-
              ing]
    BT   Group theory
          Set theory
          Symbolic logic
Boots
    USE   Shoes
Border life
    USE   Frontier and pioneer life
Borders (Geography)
    USE   Boundaries
Boring   622
    Use for materials on the operation of cut-
    ting holes in earth or rock. Materials on work-
    shop operations in metal, wood, etc., are en-
    tered under Drilling and boring.

BT = Broader Term   NT = Narrower Term   RT = Related Term   SA = See Also   UF = Used For

Boring—*Continued*

    UF   Drilling and boring (Earth and
            rocks)

            Shaft sinking

            Well boring

    BT   **Hydraulic engineering**

            Mining engineering

            Tunnels

            Water supply engineering

    RT   **Wells**

Boring (Metal, wood, etc.)

    USE   **Drilling and boring**

Born again Christianity

    USE   **Regeneration (Christianity)**

Borrowing

    USE   **Loans**

Boss rule

    USE   **Political corruption**

Botanic gardens

    USE   **Botanical gardens**

Botanical chemistry   572

    UF   Chemistry, Botanical

            Plant chemistry

    BT   **Chemistry**

    NT   **Plants—Analysis**

Botanical classification

    USE   **Botany—Classification**

Botanical gardens (May subdiv. geog.)
    580.73

    UF   Botanic gardens

    SA   names of individual botanical
            gardens, to be added as need-
            ed

    BT   **Gardens**

            Parks

Botanical illustration   758

    UF   Flower painting and illustration
            [Former heading]

            Fruit painting and illustration

    BT   **Art**

            Illustration of books

    RT   **Botany**

            Plants in art

**Botanical specimens—Collection and pres-
    ervation**

    USE   **Plants—Collection and preser-
            vation**

Botanists   580.92; 920

    BT   **Naturalists**

Botany   580

    Use for materials on the science of plants.
Nonscientific materials on plants are entered
under **Plants.**

    UF   Flora

            Vegetable kingdom

    BT   **Biology**

            Science

    NT   **Economic botany**

            Medical botany

            Photosynthesis

            Plant physiology

            Plants—Anatomy

    RT   **Botanical illustration**

            Natural history

            Plants

Botany, Agricultural

    USE   **Economic botany**

Botany—Anatomy

    USE   **Plants—Anatomy**

Botany—Classification   580.1

    UF   Botanical classification

            Botany—Taxonomy

            Classification—Botany

            Classification—Plants

            Plant classification

            Plant taxonomy

            Plants—Classification

            Systematic botany

            Taxonomy (Botany)

    BT   **Classification**

Botany—Ecology

    USE   **Plant ecology**

Botany, Economic

    USE   **Economic botany**

Botany, Medical

    USE   **Medical botany**

Botany—Nomenclature

    USE   **Botany—Terminology**

            Popular plant names

Botany of the Bible

    USE   **Bible—Natural history**

Botany—Pathology

    USE   **Plant diseases**

Botany—Physiology

    USE   **Plant physiology**

Botany—Structure

    USE   **Plants—Anatomy**

Botany—Taxonomy

    USE   **Botany—Classification**

BT = Broader Term   NT = Narrower Term   RT = Related Term   SA = See Also   UF = Used For

Botany—Terminology   580.1

Use for materials on the scientific names of plants. Materials on the common or vernacular names are entered under **Popular plant names.**

UF   Botany—Nomenclature

         Plant names, Scientific

RT   **Popular plant names**

Botany—United States

USE   **Plants—United States**

Boulder Dam (Ariz. and Nev.)

USE   **Hoover Dam (Ariz. and Nev.)**

Boulevards

USE   **Streets**

Boundaries   320.1; 341.4

UF   Borders (Geography)

         Frontiers

         Geography, Political

         Political boundaries

         Political geography

SA   names of wars with the subdivision *Territorial questions,* and countries, cities, etc., with the subdivision *Boundaries,* to be added as needed

BT   **Geography**

         International law

         International relations

NT   **Chicago (Ill.)—Boundaries**

         Ohio—Boundaries

         United States—Boundaries

         World War, 1939-1945—Territorial questions

RT   **Geopolitics**

Bounties

USE   **Subsidies**

Bourgeoisie

USE   **Middle class**

Bow and arrow   799.2028

UF   Arrow

BT   **Weapons**

RT   **Archery**

Bowed instruments

USE   **Stringed instruments**

Bowling   794.6; 796.31

UF   Tenpins

BT   **Ball games**

Boxes   688.8; 745.593

UF   Boxes, Ornamental

         Boxes, Wooden

         Containers, Box

         Crates

BT   **Packaging**

Boxes—Collectors and collecting   745.593

BT   **Collectors and collecting**

Boxes, Ornamental

USE   **Boxes**

Boxes, Wooden

USE   **Boxes**

Boxing   796.83

UF   Fighting

         Prize fighting

         Pugilism

         Sparring

BT   **Athletics**

         Self-defense

Boy Scouts (May subdiv. geog.)   **369.43**

UF   Cub Scouts

BT   **Boys' clubs**

         Scouts and scouting

Boycott

USE   **Boycotts**

Boycotts   327.1; 331.89; 338.6; 341.5

UF   Boycott *[Former heading]*

         Consumer boycotts

BT   **Commerce**

         Consumers

         Passive resistance

RT   **Restraint of trade**

Boys   155.43; 305.23

BT   **Children**

NT   **Fathers and sons**

         Mothers and sons

RT   **Teenagers**

         Young men

Boys' agricultural clubs

USE   **4-H clubs**

         Agriculture—Societies

         Boys' clubs

Boys' clubs   369.42

UF   Boys' agricultural clubs

         Boys—Societies

BT   **Clubs**

         Men—Societies

         Social settlements

         Societies

NT   **4-H clubs**

         Boy Scouts

Boys—Employment

USE   **Children—Employment**

BT = Broader Term   NT = Narrower Term   RT = Related Term   SA = See Also   UF = Used For

Boys—Societies
USE   Boys' clubs
Boys, Teenage
USE   Teenagers
Boys' towns
USE   Children—Institutional care
Brahmanism   294.5
BT   Religions
RT   Hinduism
Braille books
USE   Blind—Books and reading
Brain   573.8; 611; 612.8
BT   Head
Nervous system
NT   Memory
Mind and body
Phrenology
Psychology
Sleep
Brain damaged children   618.92
BT   Exceptional children
Handicapped children
Brain death   616.07
UF   Irreversible coma
BT   Death
Brain—Diseases   616.8
BT   Diseases
NT   Alzheimer's disease
Cerebral palsy
Stroke
Brain opioids
USE   Endorphins
Brain storming
USE   Group problem solving
Brainwashing   153.8
Use for materials on the forcible indoctrination of an individual or group in order to alter basic political, social, religious, or moral beliefs.
UF   Deprogramming
Forced indoctrination
Indoctrination, Forced
Mind control
Thought control
Will
BT   Behavior modification
Mental suggestion
Psychological warfare
Psychology of learning

Brakes   625.2; 629.2
SA   types of vehicles with the subdivision *Brakes,* e.g. **Automobiles—Brakes;** to be added as needed
NT   **Automobiles—Brakes**
Branch stores
USE   Chain stores
Brand name products   380.1; 658.8
UF   Products, Brand name
BT   Commercial products
Manufactures
RT   Trademarks
Brass   669; 673
BT   Alloys
Metals
NT   Brasses
Brass instruments
USE   Wind instruments
Brasses   739.5
UF   Monumental brasses
Sepulchral brasses
BT   Archeology
Art metalwork
Brass
Inscriptions
Sculpture
Tombs
Bravery
USE   Courage
Brazilian literature   869
May use same subdivisions and names of literary forms as for **English literature.**
BT   Latin American literature
Literature
RT   Portuguese literature
Brazing
USE   Soldering
Bread   641.8; 664
BT   Baking
Cooking
Food
RT   Bread machines
Bread machines   641.7
UF   Automatic bread machines
BT   Kitchen utensils
RT   Baking
Bread
Breadstuffs
USE   Flour
Grain

BT = Broader Term   NT = Narrower Term   RT = Related Term   SA = See Also   UF = Used For

Breadstuffs—*Continued*
    Wheat
Break dancing   **793.3**
  BT   **Dance**
Breakers
  USE   **Ocean waves**
Breakfast cereals
  USE   **Prepared cereals**
Breakfasts   **642**
  BT   **Cooking**
       Menus
  NT   **Prepared cereals**
Breast—Cancer
  USE   **Breast cancer**
Breast cancer   **616.99**
  UF   Breast—Cancer
  BT   **Cancer**
       Women—Diseases
Breast feeding   **649**
  UF   Nursing (Infant feeding)
  BT   **Infants—Nutrition**
Breathing
  USE   **Respiration**
Breeder reactors
  USE   **Nuclear reactors**
Breeding   **631.5; 636.08**
  UF   Selection, Artificial
  SA   types of animals with the subdi-
       vision *Breeding,* to be added
       as needed
  BT   **Reproduction**
  NT   **Dogs—Breeding**
       Heredity
       Horses—Breeding
       Livestock breeding
       Mendel's law
       Plant breeding
  RT   **Genetics**
Breeding behavior
  USE   **Sexual behavior in animals**
Bricklaying   **693**
  BT   **Building**
  RT   **Bricks**
       Masonry
Bricks   **666; 691**
  BT   **Building materials**
       Clay industries
  NT   **Tiles**
  RT   **Bricklaying**

Bridal customs
  USE   **Marriage customs and rites**
Bridge (Game)   **795.41**
  UF   Auction bridge
       Contract bridge
       Duplicate bridge
  BT   **Card games**
Bridges (May subdiv. geog. by countries,
      states, cities, etc., and by rivers)
      624; 725
  UF   Suspension bridges
       Viaducts
  SA   names of individual bridges, to
       be added as needed
  BT   **Civil engineering**
       Transportation
  NT   **Golden Gate Bridge (San**
       Francisco, Calif.)
Bridges—Chicago (Ill.)   **624**
  UF   Chicago (Ill.)—Bridges
Bridges—Hudson River (N.Y. and N.J.)
      624
  UF   Hudson River (N.Y. and N.J.)—
       Bridges
Brigands
  USE   **Thieves**
Brigands and robbers
  USE   **Thieves**
Bright children
  USE   **Gifted children**
British Commonwealth countries
  USE   **Commonwealth countries**
British Commonwealth of Nations
  USE   **Commonwealth countries**
British Dominions
  USE   **Commonwealth countries**
British Empire
  USE   **Great Britain—Colonies**
Broadcast journalism   **070.4**
  UF   Radio journalism
       Television journalism
  BT   **Broadcasting**
       Journalism
       Press
  NT   **Radio broadcasting of sports**
       Television broadcasting of
        news
       Television broadcasting of
        sports

BT = Broader Term   NT = Narrower Term   RT = Related Term   SA = See Also   UF = Used For

Broadcasting   384.54
- BT   Telecommunication
- NT   Broadcast journalism
        Equal time rule (Broadcasting)
        Fairness doctrine (Broadcasting)
        Minorities in broadcasting
        Radio broadcasting
        Television broadcasting

Bronze Age   930.1
- RT   Archeology
        Iron Age

Bronzes   739.5
- BT   Archeology
        Art
        Art metalwork
        Decoration and ornament
        Metalwork
        Sculpture

Brothers and sisters   155.44; 306.875
- UF   Siblings
        Sisters and brothers
- BT   Family
- NT   Sibling rivalry
- RT   Twins

Brownies (Girl Scouts)
- USE   Girl Scouts

Brownouts
- USE   Electric power failures

Brutality
- USE   Cruelty

Bubonic plague
- USE   Plague

Buccaneers
- USE   Pirates

Bucolic poetry
- USE   Pastoral poetry

Buddhism   294.3
- BT   Religions
- NT   Zen Buddhism

Buddhism—Prayers   294.3
- UF   Buddhist prayers
- BT   Prayers

Buddhist art   294.3; 704.9
- UF   Art, Buddhist [Former heading]
- BT   Art

Buddhist prayers
- USE   Buddhism—Prayers

Budget (May subdiv. geog.)   352.4
Use for materials on government budgets or reports on governmental appropriations and expenditures. Materials on business budgets are entered under **Business budgets.** Materials on household budgets are entered under **Household budgets.** Materials on personal budgets are entered under **Personal finance.**
- UF   Government budgets
- SA   names of countries and names of individual government departments, agencies, etc., with the subdivision *Appropriations and expenditures,* e.g. **United States—Appropriations and expenditures;** to be added as needed
- BT   Public finance

Budget—United States   352.4
- UF   Federal budget
        United States—Budget
- NT   United States—Appropriations and expenditures

Budgets, Business
- USE   Business budgets

Budgets, Household
- USE   Household budgets

Budgets, Personal
- USE   Personal finance

Buffalo, American
- USE   Bison

Buffing
- USE   Grinding and polishing

Bugging, Electronic
- USE   Eavesdropping

Building   690
Use for materials on the process of constructing buildings and other structures. Materials on the design and style of structures are entered under **Architecture.** General materials on buildings and materials on buildings in a particular place are entered under **Buildings.**
- UF   Architectural engineering
        Construction
- SA   types of building features, e.g. **Roofs; Foundations;** etc., to be added as needed
- BT   Structural engineering
- NT   Bricklaying
        Carpentry
        Chimneys
        Concrete construction
        Doors
        Engineering
        Extraterrestrial bases
        Fireplaces

BT = Broader Term   NT = Narrower Term   RT = Related Term   SA = See Also   UF = Used For

Building—*Continued*
    Floors
    Foundations
    House construction
    Masonry
    Plumbing
    Roofs
    Steel construction
    Strength of materials
    Walls
    Windows
  RT Architecture
    Building materials
Building and earthquakes
  USE **Buildings—Earthquake effects**
Building and loan associations
  USE **Savings and loan associations**
Building, Concrete
  USE **Concrete construction**
Building contracts
  USE **Construction contracts**
Building—Contracts and specifications
  USE **Construction contracts**
Building—Estimates 692
Building failures 690
  BT **Structural failures**
Building, House
  USE **House construction**
Building, Iron and steel
  USE **Steel construction**
Building materials 691
  UF Structural materials
  SA types of building materials, e.g.
      Bricks; to be added as need-
      ed
  BT **Materials**
  NT **Bricks**
    Cement
    Concrete
    Glass construction
    Reinforced concrete
    Stone
    Structural steel
    Stucco
    Terra cotta
    Tiles
    Wood
  RT **Building**
    Strength of materials

Building repair
  USE **Buildings—Maintenance and
      repair**
Building—Repair and reconstruction
  USE **Buildings—Maintenance and
      repair**
Building security
  USE **Burglary protection**
Buildings (May subdiv. geog.) 690; 720
    Use for general materials on buildings and,
    with geographic subdivisions, for materials on
    buildings in a particular place. Materials on
    the design and style of structures are entered
    under **Architecture.** Materials on the process
    of constructing buildings and other structures
    are entered under **Building.**
  UF Edifices
    Structures
  SA types of building features, e.g.
      Doors; Windows; etc.; types
      of buildings and construction,
      e.g. **Farm buildings;** types of
      institutions and names of indi-
      vidual institutions and corpo-
      rate bodies with the subdivi-
      sion *Buildings,* e.g. **Colleges
      and universities—Buildings;**
      and names of specific build-
      ings, to be added as needed
  NT **Apartment houses**
    Castles
    Chimneys
    Church buildings
    **Colleges and universities—
      Buildings**
    Commercial buildings
    Doors
    Farm buildings
    Fireplaces
    Floors
    Foundations
    Historic buildings
    Houses
    Industrial buildings
    Office buildings
    Palaces
    Prefabricated buildings
    Public buildings
    Roofs
    Rooms
    School buildings
    Skyscrapers

BT = Broader Term   NT = Narrower Term   RT = Related Term   SA = See Also   UF = Used For

Buildings—*Continued*
  Synagogues
  Temples
  Theaters
  Windows
  RT   Architecture
Buildings, College
  USE   Colleges and universities—
    Buildings
Buildings—Earthquake effects   693.8
  Use for materials on the design and con-
  struction of buildings to withstand earth-
  quakes.
  UF   Building and earthquakes
    Earthquakes and building
  BT   Earthquakes
  NT   Skyscrapers—Earthquake ef-
    fects
Buildings, Farm
  USE   Farm buildings
Buildings, Industrial
  USE   Industrial buildings
Buildings, Library
  USE   Library architecture
Buildings—Maintenance and repair
  690
  UF   Building repair
    Building—Repair and reconstruc-
    tion
    Buildings—Remodeling *[Former
    heading]*
  SA   types of buildings with the sub-
    division *Maintenance and re-
    pair,* e.g. Houses—Mainte-
    nance and repair; and types
    of buildings and parts of
    buildings with the subdivision
    Remodeling, e.g. Houses—Re-
    modeling; Kitchens—Remod-
    eling; etc., to be added as
    needed
  RT   Architecture—Conservation
    and restoration
Buildings, Office
  USE   Office buildings
Buildings, Prefabricated
  USE   Prefabricated buildings
Buildings, Public
  USE   Public buildings

Buildings—Remodeling
  USE   Buildings—Maintenance and
    repair
Buildings, Restoration of
  USE   Architecture—Conservation
    and restoration
Buildings, School
  USE   School buildings
Buildings—Security
  USE   Burglary protection
Built-in furniture   645; 684.1; 749
  UF   Furniture, Built-in
  BT   Furniture
Bulbs   584; 635.9
  BT   Flower gardening
    Plants
Bulge, Battle of the
  USE   Ardennes, Battle of the, 1944-
    1945
Bulimarexia
  USE   Bulimia
Bulimia   616.85
  UF   Binge eating behavior
    Binge-purge behavior
    Bulimarexia
    Bulimia nervosa
    Gorge-purge syndrome
  BT   Eating disorders
Bulimia nervosa
  USE   Bulimia
Bulletin boards   371.33
  BT   Teaching—Aids and devices
  NT   Computer bulletin boards
Bullets
  USE   Projectiles
Bullfights   791.8
  UF   Fighting
  BT   Sports
Bullies   155.4; 302.3; 646.7
  UF   Bullying
    Bullyism
  BT   Aggressiveness (Psychology)
Bullion
  USE   Gold
    Precious metals
    Silver
Bullying
  USE   Bullies
Bullyism
  USE   Bullies

BT = Broader Term   NT = Narrower Term   RT = Related Term   SA = See Also   UF = Used For

Bunker Hill (Boston, Mass.), Battle of, 1775—Poetry 811

May be used for individual works, collections, or materials about poetry dealing with the Battle of Bunker Hill.

BT   **Historical poetry**
        War poetry

Bunnies
   USE   **Rabbits**

Bunny rabbits
   USE   **Rabbits**

Bunyan, Paul
   USE   **Bunyan, Paul (Legendary character)**

Bunyan, Paul (Legendary character) 398.22

UF   Bunyan, Paul
        Paul Bunyan

BT   **Folklore—United States**

Bureaucracy 302.3

BT   **Political science**
        Public administration

RT   **Civil service**
        Organizational sociology

Burglar alarms 621.389

BT   **Burglary protection**
        Electric apparatus and appliances

Burglars
   USE   **Thieves**

Burglary protection 621.389; 643

UF   Building security
        Buildings—Security
        Protection against burglary
        Residential security

SA   types of protective devices, e.g. **Burglar alarms;** and types of buildings with the subdivision *Security measures,* e.g. **Nuclear power plants—Security measures;** to be added as needed

BT   **Crime prevention**

NT   **Burglar alarms**
        Locks and keys

Burial 363.7; 393

UF   Burial customs
        Burying grounds
        Graves
        Interment

SA   names of individual persons and groups of notable persons with the subdivision *Death and burial,* e.g. **Presidents—United States—Death and burial;** to be added as needed

BT   **Archeology**
        Public health

NT   **Catacombs**
        Cemeteries
        Cryonics
        Mounds and mound builders
        Mummies
        Tombs

RT   **Cremation**
        Death
        Funeral rites and ceremonies

Burial customs
   USE   **Burial**

Burial statistics
   USE   **Mortality**
        Registers of births, etc.
        Vital statistics

Buried cities
   USE   **Extinct cities**

Buried treasure 622; 910.4

UF   Hidden treasure
        Sunken treasure
        Treasure trove

BT   **Archeology**
        Underwater exploration

Burn out (Psychology) 158.7

UF   Burnout syndrome

BT   **Job satisfaction**
        Job stress
        Mental health
        Motivation (Psychology)
        Occupational health and safety
        Stress (Psychology)

Burnout syndrome
   USE   **Burn out (Psychology)**

Burnt offering
   USE   **Sacrifice**

Bursaries
   USE   **Scholarships**

Burying grounds
   USE   **Burial**
        Cemeteries

Buses 388.4; 629.222

UF   Motor buses

BT = Broader Term   NT = Narrower Term   RT = Related Term   SA = See Also   UF = Used For

Buses—*Continued*
  BT   **Automobiles**
         Highway transportation
         Local transit
Bush survival
  USE   **Wilderness survival**
Business   650
  UF   Trade
  BT   **Commerce**
         Economics
  NT   **Accounting**
         Advertising
         Banks and banking
         Bookkeeping
         Business budgets
         Business enterprises
         Business failures
         Business people
         Commercial law
         Competition
         Customer relations
         Department stores
         Economic conditions
         Electronic spreadsheets
         Entrepreneurship
         Home business
         Industrial efficiency
         Installment plan
         Mail-order business
         Management
         Manufactures
         Marketing
         Markets
         Merchants
         Occupations
         Office management
         Profit
         Real estate business
         Selling
         Small business
         Trust companies
Business administration
  USE   **Management**
Business and government
  USE   **Industrial policy**
Business and politics   322
  UF   Business—Political activity
         Politics and business
  BT   **Politics**

Business arithmetic
  USE   **Business mathematics**
Business budgets   658.15
  UF   Budgets, Business *[Former*
         heading]
  BT   **Business**
Business colleges
  USE   **Business schools**
Business combinations
  USE   **Conglomerate corporations**
         Industrial trusts
Business correspondence
  USE   **Business letters**
Business cycles   338.5
  UF   Cycles, Business
         Economic cycles
         Stabilization in industry
  SA   types of business cycles, e.g.
         Depressions; to be added as
         needed
  BT   **Economic conditions**
  NT   **Depressions**
         Economic forecasting
         Recessions
  RT   **Financial crises**
Business depression, 1929-1939
  USE   **Great Depression, 1929-1939**
Business depressions
  USE   **Depressions**
         Economic conditions
Business education   650.07
  UF   Business—Study and teaching
         Clerical work—Training
         Commercial education
         Office work—Training
  BT   **Education**
  NT   **Accounting**
         Bookkeeping
         Commercial law
         Keyboarding (Electronics)
         Secretaries
         Shorthand
         Typewriting
Business English
  USE   **English language—Business**
         English
Business enterprises (May subdiv. geog.)
       338.7
      Use for materials on business concerns as
    legal entities, regardless of the form of organi-
    zation.

BT = Broader Term   NT = Narrower Term   RT = Related Term   SA = See Also   UF = Used For

Business enterprises—*Continued*
    UF   Business organizations
             Businesses
             Companies
             Enterprises
             Firms
             Organizations, Business
    SA   types of businesses, to be added
             as needed
    BT   **Business**
             Commercial law
             Industries
    NT   **Beauty shops**
             Corporations
             Minority business enterprises
             Multinational corporations
             New business enterprises
Business enterprises, International
    USE   **Multinational corporations**
Business enterprises, Minority
    USE   **Minority business enterprises**
Business enterprises, New
    USE   **New business enterprises**
Business entertaining   395.3; 658
    BT   **Entertaining**
             Public relations
Business ethics   174
    UF   Ethics, Business
    BT   **Ethics**
             Professional ethics
    NT   **Competition**
             Deceptive advertising
             Success
Business failures   338; 658
    UF   Business mortality
             Failure in business
    BT   **Business**
    NT   **Bank failures**
             Bankruptcy
Business forecasting   338.5
    BT   **Economic forecasting**
             Forecasting
Business—Information services   658.4
    BT   **Information services**
Business—International aspects
    USE   **Multinational corporations**
Business Japanese
    USE   **Japanese language—Business**
             Japanese

Business language
    USE   names of languages with unique
             language subdivisions, e.g.
             English language—Business
             English; Japanese lan-
             guage—Business Japanese;
             etc., to be added as needed
Business law
    USE   **Commercial law**
Business letters   651.7
    UF   Business correspondence
             Commercial correspondence
             Correspondence
    BT   **Letter writing**
Business libraries   026
    Use for materials on libraries with a subject
focus on business. Materials on libraries locat-
ed within companies, firms, or private busi-
nesses, covering any subject area, are entered
under **Corporate libraries.**
    UF   Libraries, Business
    BT   **Special libraries**
Business machines
    USE   **Office equipment and supplies**
Business management
    USE   **Management**
Business math
    USE   **Business mathematics**
Business mathematics   650.01
    UF   Arithmetic, Commercial
             Business arithmetic *[Former*
             heading]
             Business math
             Commercial arithmetic
             Commercial mathematics
             Finance—Mathematics
             Mathematics, Business
    BT   **Mathematics**
    NT   **Accounting**
             Bookkeeping
             Interest (Economics)
Business mortality
    USE   **Bankruptcy**
             Business failures
Business organizations
    USE   **Business enterprises**
Business patronage of the arts
    USE   **Art patronage**
Business people   338.092; 658.0092; 920
    UF   Businesspeople
    BT   **Business**

BT = Broader Term   NT = Narrower Term   RT = Related Term   SA = See Also   UF = Used For

Business people—*Continued*
  NT African American business
        people
      Black business people
      Businessmen
      Businesswomen
      Capitalists and financiers
      Entrepreneurs
      Merchants
      Self-employed
Business people, African American
  USE African American business
        people
Business people, Black
  USE Black business people
Business—Political activity
  USE Business and politics
Business recessions
  USE Recessions
Business schools   650.071
  UF Business colleges
      Colleges, Business
      Schools, Business
  BT Schools
Business secrets
  USE Trade secrets
Business, Small
  USE Small business
Business—Study and teaching
  USE Business education
Businesses
  USE Business enterprises
Businessmen   338.092; 658.0092; 920
  UF Men in business
  BT Business people
Businesspeople
  USE Business people
Businesswomen   338.092; 658.0092; 920
  UF Women in business
  BT Business people
      Women
Busing (School integration)   379.2
  UF Antibusing
      School busing
      Student busing
  BT School children—Transporta-
        tion
      School integration
Butter   637; 641.3
  BT Dairy products

  NT Margarine
Butter, Artificial
  USE Margarine
Butterflies   595.78
  UF Cocoons
      Lepidoptera
  BT Insects
  NT Caterpillars
  RT Moths
Buttons   646; 687
  BT Clothing and dress
Buy American policy
  USE Buy national policy—United
        States
Buy national policy (May subdiv. geog.)
        352.5
      Use for materials on the requirement that
    the government procure goods produced with-
    in the nation.
  BT Commercial policy
      Government purchasing
Buy national policy—United States
        352.5
  UF Buy American policy
Buyers' guides
  USE Consumer education
      Shopping
Buying   352.5; 658.7
      Use for materials on buying by government
    agencies and by commercial and industrial en-
    terprises. Materials on buying by the consum-
    er are entered under **Shopping.**
  UF Purchasing
  BT Management
  NT Government purchasing
      Installment plan
  RT Shopping
Buyouts, Corporate
  USE Corporate mergers and acqui-
        sitions
Buyouts, Leveraged
  USE Leveraged buyouts
By-products
  USE Waste products
Byrd Antarctic Expedition   919.8
  BT Antarctica—Exploration
Byzantine architecture   723
  UF Architecture, Byzantine [*Former
        heading*]
  BT Ancient architecture
      Architecture
      Medieval architecture

BT = Broader Term   NT = Narrower Term   RT = Related Term   SA = See Also   UF = Used For

Byzantine art   709.02
    UF   Art, Byzantine *[Former heading]*
    BT   Ancient art
          Art
          Medieval art
Byzantine Empire   949.5
    UF   Eastern Empire
C.A.D.
    USE   Computer aided design
C.A.I.
    USE   Computer assisted instruction
C.A.T.V.
    USE   Cable television
C.B. radio
    USE   Citizens band radio
C.I.S.
    USE   Commonwealth of Independent
           States
C.O.A.s
    USE   Children of alcoholics
C.R.T.'s
    USE   Cathode ray tubes
Cabala   135; 296.1
    UF   Cabbala
          Kabbala
    BT   Hebrew literature
          Jewish literature
          Judaism
          Mysticism
          Occultism
    RT   Symbolism of numbers
Cabbala
    USE   Cabala
Cabinet officers   352.24; 920
    UF   Ministers of state
    NT   Prime ministers
Cabinet work
    USE   Cabinetwork
Cabinetwork   684.1
    Use for materials on the making and finish-
    ing of fine woodwork, such as furniture or in-
    terior details. Materials on the construction of
    a wooden building or the wooden portion of
    any building are entered under **Carpentry.**
    UF   Cabinet work *[Former heading]*
    BT   Carpentry
    NT   Veneers and veneering
    RT   Furniture
          Woodwork
Cabins
    USE   Log cabins and houses

Cable codes
    USE   **Cipher and telegraph codes**
Cable railroads   385; 625.5
    UF   Funicular railroads
          Railroads, Cable
    BT   **Railroads**
    RT   **Street railroads**
Cable television   384.55
    UF   C.A.T.V.
          CATV
          Community antenna television
          Pay television, Cable
          Television, Cable
    BT   **Television broadcasting**
    NT   **Home Box Office**
Cables   384.6; 621.319; 624.1
    BT   **Power transmission**
          Rope
Cables, Submarine
    USE   **Submarine cables**
Cactus   583; 635.9
    BT   **Desert plants**
CAD
    USE   **Computer aided design**
Cage birds   636.6
    SA   types of cage birds, to be added
          as needed
    BT   **Birds**
    NT   **Canaries**
CAI
    USE   **Computer assisted instruction**
Cake   641.8; 664
    BT   **Baking**
          Confectionery
          Cooking
          Desserts
    RT   **Pastry**
Cake decorating   641.8
    BT   **Confectionery**
Calculating machines
    USE   **Calculators**
Calculators   510.28; 651.8; 681
    Use for materials on present-day calculators
    or on calculators and mechanical computers
    made before 1945. Materials on modern elec-
    tronic computers developed after 1945 are en-
    tered under **Computers.**
    UF   Accounting machines
          Adding machines
          Calculating machines
          Pocket calculators

BT = Broader Term   NT = Narrower Term   RT = Related Term   SA = See Also   UF = Used For

Calculators—*Continued*
  BT   **Arithmetic**
        Office equipment and supplies
  NT   **Abacus**
        Slide rule
  RT   **Computers**
Calculus   515
  UF   Analysis (Mathematics)
  BT   **Mathematical analysis**
        Mathematics
Caldecott Awards
  USE **Caldecott Medal**
Caldecott Medal   028.5
  UF   Caldecott Awards
        Caldecott Medal books *[Former heading]*
  BT   **Children's literature**
        Illustration of books
        Literary prizes
Caldecott Medal books
  USE **Caldecott Medal**
Calendars   529
  UF   Annuals
  SA   subjects, corporate bodies, and names of countries, cities, etc., with the subdivision *Calendars,* for works that list recurring, coming, or past events in those places or related to those topics or organizations, to be added as needed
  BT   **Time**
  NT   **Church year**
        Days
        Devotional calendars
        Months
        Week
  RT   **Almanacs**
California—Earthquakes
  USE **Earthquakes—California**
California—Gold discoveries   979.4
  UF   California gold rush
  BT   **Gold mines and mining**
California gold rush
  USE **California—Gold discoveries**
Calisthenics
  USE **Gymnastics**
        Physical education

Calligraphy   745.6
  BT   **Decorative arts**
        Handwriting
        Writing
Calvinism   284
  BT   **Reformation**
  RT   **Congregationalism**
        Puritans
Camcorders   621.388; 778.59
  UF   Home video cameras
        Video cameras, Home
  BT   **Cameras**
        Home video systems
        Video recording
  RT   **Amateur films**
Camels   599.63; 636.2
  UF   Dromedaries
  BT   **Desert animals**
        Mammals
Cameras   681; 771.3
  SA   types of cameras and names of individual makes of cameras, to be added as needed
  BT   **Photography**
        Photography—Equipment and supplies
  NT   **Camcorders**
        Kodak camera
        Motion picture cameras
Camouflage (Biology)   591.47
  UF   Animal camouflage
        Animals—Camouflage
  BT   **Animal defenses**
Camouflage (Military science)   355.4; 623
  BT   **Military art and science**
        Naval art and science
Camp cooking
  USE **Outdoor cooking**
Camp Fire Girls   369.47
  BT   **Girls' clubs**
Camp sites
  USE **Campgrounds**
Campaign funds (May subdiv. geog.)   **324.7**
  UF   Assessments, Political
        Elections—Finance
        Political assessments
        Political parties—Finance
  BT   **Elections**

BT = Broader Term   NT = Narrower Term   RT = Related Term   SA = See Also   UF = Used For

Campaign funds—*Continued*
    Politics
  RT   Political corruption
Campaign funds—United States   324.7
  UF   Elections—United States—Fi-
        nance
        United States—Campaign funds
Campaign literature (May subdiv. geog.)
    324.2
  UF   Political campaign literature
  BT   Literature
        Politics
Campaigns, Political
  USE   Politics
Campaigns, Presidential—United States
  USE   Presidents—United States—
        Election
Campers and trailers
  USE   Travel trailers and campers
Campgrounds   796.54
  UF   Camp sites
  NT   Trailer parks
  RT   Camping
Camping   796.54
    Use for materials on the technique of camp-
ing. Materials on camps with a definite pro-
gram of activities are entered under **Camps.**
  BT   Outdoor recreation
  NT   Backpacking
        Bicycle touring
        Outdoor cooking
        Tents
        Travel trailers and campers
        Wilderness survival
  RT   Campgrounds
        Outdoor life
Camps   796.54
    Use for materials on camps with a definite
program of activities. Materials on the tech-
nique of camping are entered under **Camping.**
  UF   Summer camps
  BT   Recreation
Camps (Military)
  USE   Military camps
Campus disorders
  USE   College students—Political ac-
        tivity
Canada   971
    May be subdivided like United States ex-
cept for *History.*

SA   names of individual provinces,
        territories, or regions, to be
        added as needed
Canada—English-French relations
    305.811; 306.44
  UF   Canada—French-English relations
  NT   Québec (Province)—History—
        Autonomy and independence
        movements
Canada—French-English relations
  USE   Canada—English-French rela-
        tions
Canada—History—0-1763 (New France)
    971.01
  UF   Canada—History—1755-1763
        New France—History
Canada—History—1755-1763
  USE   Canada—History—0-1763 (New
        France)
Canada—History—1763-1791
  USE   Canada—History—1763-1867
Canada—History—1763-1867   971.02
  UF   Canada—History—1763-1791
        [Former heading]
        Canada—History—1791-1841
        Canada—History—1841-1867
Canada—History—1791-1841
  USE   Canada—History—1763-1867
Canada—History—1800-1899 (19th
    century)   971.03
  UF   Canada—History—19th century
Canada—History—19th century
  USE   Canada—History—1800-1899
        (19th century)
Canada—History—1841-1867
  USE   Canada—History—1763-1867
Canada—History—1867-   971.05
Canada—History—1867-1914   971.05
Canada—History—1900-1999 (20th
    century)   971.06
Canada—History—1914-1945   971.06
Canada—History—1945-   971.06
Canadian Indians
  USE   Indians of North America—
        Canada
Canadian Invasion, 1775-1776   973.3
  BT   United States—History—1775-
        1783, Revolution

BT = Broader Term   NT = Narrower Term   RT = Related Term   SA = See Also   UF = Used For

Canadian literature (May subdiv. geog.)
810; C810

Use for general materials not limited to literature in a particular language or form. May use same subdivision and names of literary forms as for **English literature**; e.g. **Canadian poetry**; etc.

BT   Literature

NT   **Canadian literature (English)**

   Canadian literature (French)

   Canadian poetry

Canadian literature (English) (May subdiv. geog.)   810; C810

May use same subdivisions and names of literary forms as for **English literature**; e.g. **Canadian poetry (English)**; etc.

UF   English Canadian literature

BT   **Canadian literature**

NT   **Canadian poetry (English)**

Canadian literature (French) (May subdiv. geog.)   840; C840

May use same subdivisions and names of literary forms as for **English literature**; e.g. **Canadian poetry (French)**; etc.

UF   French Canadian literature *[Former heading]*

   French literature—Canada

BT   **Canadian literature**

NT   **Canadian poetry (French)**

Canadian poetry (May subdiv. geog.)
811; C811

Use for general materials about Canadian poetry not limited to a particular language, not for individual works.

BT   **Canadian literature**

NT   **Canadian poetry (English)**

   Canadian poetry (French)

Canadian poetry (English) (May subdiv. geog.)   811; C811

Use for general materials about Canadian poetry in English, not for individual works.

UF   English Canadian poetry

BT   **Canadian literature (English)**

   Canadian poetry

Canadian poetry (French) (May subdiv. geog.)   841; C841

Use for general materials about Canadian poetry in French, not for individual works.

UF   French Canadian poetry

BT   **Canadian literature (French)**

   Canadian poetry

Canadians   305.811; 971

NT   **French Canadians**

Canals (May subdiv. geog.)   386; 627

SA   names of individual canals, to be added as needed

BT   **Civil engineering**

   Hydraulic structures

   Transportation

   Waterways

NT   **Panama Canal**

RT   **Inland navigation**

Canaries   598.8; 636.6

BT   **Birds**

   Cage birds

Canasta (Game)   795.41

UF   Argentine rummy

BT   **Card games**

Cancer   616.99

UF   Carcinoma

   Malignant tumors

SA   types of cancer, to be added as needed

BT   **Diseases**

   Tumors

NT   **Breast cancer**

   Leukemia

   Lung cancer

Cancer—Chemotherapy   616.99

UF   Chemotherapy *[Former heading]*

BT   **Drug therapy**

Cancer—Diet therapy   616.99

BT   **Diet therapy**

Cancer—Genetic aspects   616.99

BT   **Medical genetics**

Cancer—Nursing   610.73

BT   **Nursing**

Cancer patients

USE   **Cancer—Patients**

Cancer—Patients   616.99

UF   Cancer patients

BT   **Patients**

Cancer—Surgery   616.99

BT   **Surgery**

Candles   621.32; 745.593

BT   **Lighting**

Candy

USE   **Confectionery**

Caning of chairs

USE   **Chair caning**

Cannabis

USE   **Marijuana**

BT = Broader Term   NT = Narrower Term   RT = Related Term   SA = See Also   UF = Used For

Canned goods
    USE   Canning and preserving
Cannibalism   291.3; 394
    BT   **Ethnology**
           Human behavior
Canning and preserving   641.4; 664
    UF   Canned goods
           Food, Canned
           Pickling
           Preserving
    SA   types of foods with the subdivi-
           sion *Preservation,* to be added
           as needed
    BT   **Cooking**
           Food—Preservation
           Industrial chemistry
    NT   **Fruit—Preservation**
           Vegetables—Preservation
Cannon
    USE   **Ordnance**
Canoes and canoeing   797.1
    BT   **Boats and boating**
           Water sports
Canon law
    USE   **Ecclesiastical law**
Canons, fugues, etc.
    USE   **Fugue**
Cantatas   782.2
    Use for musical scores and for materials on
    the cantata as a musical form.
    BT   **Choral music**
           Vocal music
Canvas embroidery
    USE   **Needlepoint**
Capital   332
    BT   **Economics**
           Finance
    NT   **Banks and banking**
           Human capital
           Industrial trusts
           Interest (Economics)
           Investments
           Profit
    RT   **Capitalism**
           Wealth
Capital and labor
    USE   **Industrial relations**
Capital equipment
    USE   **Industrial equipment**
Capital goods
    USE   **Industrial equipment**

Capital punishment (May subdiv. geog.)
    179.7; 364.6
    UF   Abolition of capital punishment
           Death penalty
           Executions
           Hanging
    BT   **Criminal law**
           Homicide
           Punishment
Capital punishment—United States
    364.6
    UF   United States—Capital punish-
           ment
Capitalism   330.12
    BT   **Economics**
           Labor
           Profit
    NT   **Entrepreneurship**
    RT   **Capital**
           Capitalists and financiers
           Free enterprise
Capitalists and financiers   332.092; 920
    UF   Financiers
    BT   **Business people**
    RT   **Capitalism**
           Millionaires
Capitalization (Finance)
    USE   **Corporations—Finance**
           Securities
           Valuation
Capitals (Cities)
    Use for materials on the capital cities of
    several countries or states.
    BT   **Cities and towns**
    NT   **Capitols**
Capitols   725
    BT   **Capitals (Cities)**
           Public buildings
Car accidents
    USE   **Traffic accidents**
Car design
    USE   **Automobiles—Design and con-
           struction**
Car driver education
    USE   **Automobile driver education**
Car drivers
    USE   **Automobile drivers**
Car engines
    USE   **Automobile engines**
Car industry
    USE   **Automobile industry**

BT = Broader Term   NT = Narrower Term   RT = Related Term   SA = See Also   UF = Used For

Car insurance
USE **Automobile insurance**
Car maintenance
USE **Automobiles—Maintenance and repair**
Car parts
USE **Automobile parts**
Car pools   388.4
UF Automobile pools
Carpools
Ride sharing
Van pools
BT **Traffic engineering**
Transportation
Car racing
USE **Automobile racing**
Car repair
USE **Automobiles—Maintenance and repair**
Car transmissions
USE **Automobiles—Transmission devices**
Car travel
USE **Automobile travel**
Car travel—Guidebooks
USE **Automobile travel—Guidebooks**
Car wheels
USE **Wheels**
Car wrecks
USE **Traffic accidents**
Carbines
USE **Rifles**
Carbolic acid   547; 661
BT **Acids**
Chemicals
Carbon   540; 660
BT **Chemical elements**
NT **Diamonds**
Graphite
Carbon 14 dating
USE **Radiocarbon dating**
Carbon dioxide greenhouse effect
USE **Greenhouse effect**
Carburetors   621.43
BT **Internal combustion engines**
Carcinoma
USE **Cancer**
Card catalogs   025.3
UF Catalogs, Card *[Former heading]*
BT **Library catalogs**

Card games   795.4
UF Cards, Playing
Playing cards
SA types of card games, to be added as needed
BT **Games**
NT **Bridge (Game)**
Canasta (Game)
Card tricks
Solitaire (Game)
Tarot
Card tricks   795.4
BT **Card games**
Magic tricks
Tricks
Cardiac diseases
USE **Heart diseases**
Cardiac resuscitation   616.02; 616.1
UF Heart resuscitation
Resuscitation, Heart
BT **First aid**
Cardinals   262
BT **Catholic Church—Clergy**
Cardiovascular system   612.1
UF Circulatory system
Vascular system
BT **Anatomy**
Physiology
NT **Heart**
RT **Blood—Circulation**
Cards, Debit
USE **Debit cards**
Cards, Greeting
USE **Greeting cards**
Cards, Playing
USE **Card games**
Cards, Sports
USE **Sports cards**
Care
USE parts of the body, classes of persons, and types of animals with the subdivision *Care,* e.g. Foot—Care; Infants—Care; Dogs—Care; etc.; classes of persons with the subdivisions *Medical care, Institutional care,* and *Home care,* e.g. Elderly—Medical care; Elderly—Institutional

---

BT = Broader Term   NT = Narrower Term   RT = Related Term   SA = See Also   UF = Used For

Care—*Continued*

> care; Elderly—Home care;
> etc.; ethnic groups and classes
> of persons with the subdivi-
> sion *Health and hygiene,* e.g.
> Infants—Health and hy-
> giene; and inanimate things
> with the subdivision *Mainte-*
> *nance and repair,* e.g. Auto-
> mobiles—Maintenance and
> repair; to be added as need-
> ed

Care givers

USE **Caregivers**

Care of children

USE **Child care**

Care of the dying

USE **Terminal care**

Career changes   650.14; 658.4

UF   Changing careers

Mid-career changes

SA   fields of knowledge, professions,
industries, and trades with the
subdivision *Vocational guid-*
ance, to be added as needed

BT   **Age and employment**

Vocational guidance

Career counseling

USE **Vocational guidance**

Career couples

USE **Dual career family**

Career development

USE **Personnel management**

Vocational guidance

Career education

USE **Vocational education**

Career guidance

USE **Vocational guidance**

Careers

USE **Occupations**

Professions

Vocational guidance

Caregivers   362; 649.8

Use for materials on family and friends
who on a voluntary basis provide personal
home care for the elderly, ill, or handicapped.

UF   Care givers

Family caregivers

BT   **Volunteer work**

RT   **Home care services**

Caricatures

USE **Cartoons and caricatures**

Caricatures and cartoons

USE **Cartoons and caricatures**

Carillons

USE **Bells**

Carnival (May subdiv. geog.)   394.25

Use for materials on festivals, merrymaking,
and revelry before Lent. Materials on traveling amusement enterprises, consisting of sideshows, games of chance, etc., are entered under **Carnivals.**

UF   Mardi Gras

Pre-Lenten festivities

BT   **Festivals**

Carnivals   394.25; 791

Use for materials on traveling amusement
enterprises, consisting of sideshows, games of
chance, merry-go-rounds, etc. Materials on
festivals, merrymaking, and revelry before
Lent are entered under **Carnival.**

UF   Traveling carnivals

BT   **Amusements**

Festivals

RT   **Amusement parks**

Circus

Fairs

Carnivora

USE **Carnivorous animals**

Carnivores

USE **Carnivorous animals**

Carnivorous animals   599.7

UF   Carnivora

Carnivores *[Former heading]*

Meat-eating animals

SA   types of carnivorous animals, to
be added as needed

BT   **Animals**

Carnivorous plants   583; 635.9

UF   Insect-eating plants

Insectivorous plants

BT   **Plants**

Carols   782.28

UF   Christmas carols

Easter carols

BT   **Christmas poetry**

Church music

Folk songs

Hymns

Songs

Vocal music

BT = Broader Term   NT = Narrower Term   RT = Related Term   SA = See Also   UF = Used For

Carpentry   694

Use for materials on the construction of a wooden building or the wooden portion of any building. Materials on the making and finishing of fine woodwork, such as furniture or interior details, are entered under **Cabinetwork.**

BT   **Building**
NT   **Cabinetwork**
      Turning
      Walls
RT   **Woodwork**

Carpentry—Tools
USE   **Carpentry tools**

Carpentry tools
NT   **Saws**

Carpentry tools   694

UF   Carpentry—Tools *[Former heading]*
SA   types of carpentry tools, to be added as needed
BT   **Carpentry tools**
      Tools

Carpentry tools
NT   **Carpentry tools**

Carpetbag rule
USE   **Reconstruction (1865-1876)**

Carpets   645; 677; 746.7

Use for materials on heavy woven or felted fabrics used as floor coverings, usually covering large areas. Materials on one-piece floor coverings, such as woven fabrics, animal skins, etc., are entered under **Rugs.**

BT   **Decoration and ornament**
      Interior design
      Textile industry
RT   **Rugs**
      Weaving

Carpools
USE   **Car pools**

Carriages and carts   388.3; 688.6

UF   Carts
      Stagecoaches
      Wagons
BT   **Vehicles**

Carriers, Aircraft
USE   **Aircraft carriers**

Cars, Armored (Tanks)
USE   **Military tanks**

Cars (Automobiles)
USE   **Automobiles**

Cartels
USE   **Industrial trusts**

Cartography
USE   **Charts**
      Map drawing
      Maps

Cartoons and caricatures   741.5

Use for collections of pictorial humor and for materials about caricatures and cartoons.

UF   Caricatures
      Caricatures and cartoons
      Humorous pictures
      Illustrations, Humorous
      Pictures, Humorous
SA   subjects, classes of persons, or names of individuals with the subdivision *Cartoons and caricatures,* to be added as needed
BT   **Pictures**
      Portraits
NT   **Animated films**
      Computers—Cartoons and caricatures
      World War, 1939-1945—Cartoons and caricatures
RT   **Comic books, strips, etc.**

Cartoons, Animated
USE   **Animated films**

Cartoons, Television
USE   **Animated television programs**

Carts
USE   **Carriages and carts**

Carts (Midget cars)
USE   **Karts and karting**

Carving (Art industries)
USE   **Carving (Decorative arts)**

Carving (Arts)
USE   **Carving (Decorative arts)**

Carving (Decorative arts)   731.4; 736

UF   Carving (Art industries)
      Carving (Arts)
SA   types of carving, e.g. **Wood carving;** to be added as needed
BT   **Decorative arts**
NT   **Wood carving**
RT   **Sculpture**

Carving (Meat, etc.)   642

BT   **Dining**
      Entertaining
      Meat

BT = Broader Term   NT = Narrower Term   RT = Related Term   SA = See Also   UF = Used For

Carving, Wood
USE **Wood carving**
Case studies
USE subjects with the subdivision
Case studies, e.g. **Juvenile
delinquency—Case studies;**
to be added as needed
Case work, Social
USE **Social case work**
Cassette books
USE **Talking books**
Cassette recorders and recording
USE **Magnetic recorders and re-
cording**
Cassette tapes, Audio
USE **Sound recordings**
Castaways
USE **Survival after airplane acci-
dents, shipwrecks, etc.**
Caste 305.5
BT **Manners and customs**
NT **Social classes**
Casting
USE **Founding**
Plaster casts
Castles (May subdiv. geog.) **728.8**
UF Chateaux
BT **Buildings**
RT **Medieval architecture**
Casts, Plaster
USE **Plaster casts**
Casualty insurance 368.5
UF Insurance, Casualty *[Former
heading]*
BT **Insurance**
NT **Accident insurance**
Cat
USE **Cats**
CAT scan
USE **Tomography**
Catacombs 393; 726
BT **Burial**
Cemeteries
Christian antiquities
Tombs
RT **Church history—30-600, Early
church**
Cataloging 025.3
UF Cataloguing
Libraries—Cataloging

Library cataloging
SA cataloging of particular subjects,
e.g., **Cataloging of music;** to
be added as needed
BT **Bibliographic control
Documentation
Library science
Library technical processes**
NT **Automated cataloging
Books—Classification
Cataloging of music
International Standard Biblio-
graphic Description
Machine readable bibliographic
data
Subject headings**
RT **Bibliography
Indexing
Library catalogs**
Cataloging data in machine readable form
USE **Machine readable bibliographic
data**
Cataloging—Data processing
USE **Automated cataloging**
Cataloging—Music
USE **Cataloging of music**
Cataloging of music 025.3
UF Cataloging—Music *[Former
heading]*
Music—Cataloging
BT **Cataloging**
Catalogs
USE **Booksellers' catalogs
Library catalogs
Publishers' catalogs**
and subjects with the subdivi-
sion *Catalogs,* e.g. **Motion
pictures—Catalogs;** to be
added as needed
Catalogs, Book
USE **Book catalogs**
Catalogs, Booksellers'
USE **Booksellers' catalogs**
Catalogs, Card
USE **Card catalogs**
Catalogs, Classified
USE **Classified catalogs**
Catalogs, Film
USE **Motion pictures—Catalogs**

BT = Broader Term   NT = Narrower Term   RT = Related Term   SA = See Also   UF = Used For

Catalogs in book form
    USE   **Book catalogs**
Catalogs, Library
    USE   **Library catalogs**
Catalogs on microfilm
    USE   **Library catalogs on microfilm**
Catalogs, Online
    USE   **Online catalogs**
Catalogs, Publishers'
    USE   **Publishers' catalogs**
Catalogs, Subject
    USE   **Subject catalogs**
Catalogs, Systematic
    USE   **Classified catalogs**
Cataloguing
    USE   **Cataloging**
Catalysis   541.3
    BT   **Physical chemistry**
    RT   **Catalytic RNA**
Catalytic ribonucleic acid
    USE   **Catalytic RNA**
Catalytic RNA   572.8
    UF   Catalytic ribonucleic acid
            Ribozymes
            RNA, Catalytic
    BT   **Enzymes**
            RNA
    RT   **Catalysis**
Catamarans   797.1
    BT   **Boats and boating**
Catastrophes
    USE   **Disasters**
Catechisms   238; 291.2
    SA   names of individual religions
            and sects with the subdivision
            Catechisms, to be added as
            needed
    BT   **Theology—Study and teaching**
    NT   **Bible—Catechisms, question**
            books
    RT   **Creeds**
Categories of persons
    USE   **Persons**
            and classes of persons, e.g. **El-**
            derly; Handicapped; Explor-
            ers; Drug addicts; etc., to be
            added as needed
Caterers and catering
    USE   **Catering**

Catering   642
    UF   Caterers and catering *[Former*
            heading]
    BT   **Cooking**
            Food service
    RT   **Menus**
Caterpillars   595.78
    UF   Cocoons
    BT   **Butterflies**
            Moths
Cathedrals (May subdiv. geog.)   726.6
    SA   names of individual cathedrals,
            to be added as needed
    BT   **Church buildings**
    RT   **Abbeys**
            Church architecture
            Gothic architecture
            Medieval architecture
Cathedrals—United States   726.60973
    UF   United States—Cathedrals
Cathode ray tubes   537.5; 621.3815
    UF   C.R.T.'s
            CRTs
    BT   **Vacuum tubes**
Catholic charismatic movement   282
    UF   Charismatic movement
            Charismatic renewal movement
    BT   **Catholic Church**
            Episcopal Church
    RT   **Pentecostalism**
            Spiritual gifts
Catholic Church (May subdiv. geog.)
    282
    UF   Roman Catholic Church
    SA   religious subjects with the subdi-
            vision *Catholic Church,* e.g.
            Asceticism—Catholic
            Church; Laity—Catholic
            Church; etc., and other sub-
            jects with the subdivisions
            Religious aspects—Catholic
            Church; e.g. **Abortion—Reli-**
            gious aspects—Catholic
            Church; to be added as
            needed
    BT   **Christian sects**
            Christianity
    NT   **Catholic charismatic movement**
            Inquisition
            Laity—Catholic Church

BT = Broader Term   NT = Narrower Term   RT = Related Term   SA = See Also   UF = Used For

Catholic Church—*Continued*
        Papacy
    RT   Catholics
Catholic Church—Charities   361.7
    BT   Charities
Catholic Church—Clergy   253
    BT   Clergy
        Priests
    NT   Cardinals
        Ex-priests
Catholic Church—Converts
    USE   Converts to Catholicism
Catholic Church—Foreign relations (May
        subdiv. geog.)   282; 327.456
    Use for materials on diplomatic relations
between the Catholic Church and various governments or political bodies. When this heading is subdivided geographically, an additional
entry is provided with the Catholic Church
and the place in reversed positions. Materials
on the relations between the Catholic Church
and other churches or religions are entered
under **Catholic Church—Relations.**
    UF   Catholic Church—Relations
        (Diplomatic) *[Former head-
        ing]*
        Vatican City—Foreign relations
    BT   **International relations**
Catholic Church—Liturgy   264
    Use for materials on the forms of prayers,
rituals, and ceremonies used in the official
public worship of the Catholic Church. Texts
of Catholic liturgies are entered under **Catholic Church—Liturgy—Texts.**
    UF   Catholic liturgies
    BT   **Liturgies**
        Rites and ceremonies
Catholic Church—Liturgy—Texts   264
Catholic Church—Missions   266
    BT   **Christian missions**
Catholic Church—Relations   282
    Use for materials on relations between the
Catholic Church and other churches or religions. This heading may be further subdivided
by church or religion, in which case an additional entry is provided with the two churches
or religions in reversed positions. Materials on
diplomatic relations between the Catholic
Church and various governments or political
bodies are entered under **Catholic Church—
Foreign relations.**
Catholic Church—Relations (Diplomatic)
    USE   **Catholic Church—Foreign rela-
        tions**
Catholic Church—United States   282
    UF   United States—Catholic Church

Catholic colleges and universities (May
        subdiv. geog.)   378
    UF   Catholic universities and colleges
    BT   **Colleges and universities**
Catholic converts
    USE   **Converts to Catholicism**
Catholic ex-nuns
    USE   **Ex-nuns**
Catholic ex-priests
    USE   **Ex-priests**
Catholic laity
    USE   **Laity—Catholic Church**
Catholic literature   282; 808; 809
    BT   **Christian literature**
        Literature
Catholic liturgies
    USE   **Catholic Church—Liturgy**
Catholic universities and colleges
    USE   **Catholic colleges and universi-
        ties**
Catholics (May subdiv. geog.)   282.092;
        305.6
    NT   **Converts to Catholicism**
    RT   **Catholic Church**
Catholics—United States   282.092;
        305.6
    UF   United States—Catholics
Cats   599.75; 636.8
    Use for materials on domestic cats. Materi-
als on non-domesticated species of cats or do-
mestic cats living in a wild state are entered
under **Wild cats.**
    UF   Cat
        Kittens
    SA   names of specific breeds of cat,
        to be added as needed
    BT   **Domestic animals**
        Mammals
    RT   **Wild cats**
Cats—Literary collections   808.8; 810.8,
        etc.
Cattle   599.64; 636.2
    UF   Cows
    BT   **Domestic animals**
        Mammals
    NT   **Beef cattle**
        Dairy cattle
    RT   **Dairying**
Cattle brands   636.2
CATV
    USE   **Cable television**

BT = Broader Term   NT = Narrower Term   RT = Related Term   SA = See Also   UF = Used For

Cautionary tales and verse
USE   **Fables**
       Parables
Cautionary tales and verses
USE   **Didactic fiction**
       Didactic poetry
Cave drawings   743; 759.01
BT   **Mural painting and decoration**
       Picture writing
RT   **Rock drawings, paintings, and**
       engravings
Cave dwellers   569.9; 930.1
BT   **Prehistoric peoples**
Caves   551.44
UF   Grottoes
       Speleology
CB radio
USE   **Citizens band radio**
CD-I technology   006.7
UF   CDI technology
       Compact disc interactive technol-
       ogy
       Interactive CD technology
BT   **Compact discs**
       Optical storage devices
CD players
USE   **Compact disc players**
CD-ROM
USE   **CD-ROMs**
CD-ROMs   004.5
UF   CD-ROM *[Former heading]*
       CDROM
       CDROMs
       Compact disc read-only memory
BT   **Compact discs**
       Optical storage devices
CDI technology
USE   **CD-I technology**
CDROM
USE   **CD-ROMs**
CDROMs
USE   **CD-ROMs**
CDs (Compact discs)
USE   **Compact discs**
Celebrities   920
UF   Famous people
       Public figures
SA   types of celebrities, e.g. **Actors;**
       and names of individual ce-

lebrities, to be added as need-
ed
BT   **Persons**
NT   **Actors**
Celery   635; 641.3
BT   **Vegetables**
Celibacy   248.4; 291.4
     Use for materials on the renunciation of
marriage for religious reasons. Materials on
the virtue that moderates and regulates the
sexual appetite in human beings are entered
under **Chastity**. Materials on abstinence from
sexual activity are entered under **Sexual absti-
nence**.
UF   Clerical celibacy
BT   **Clergy**
       Religious life
RT   **Chastity**
       Sexual abstinence
       Single people
Cellars
USE   **Basements**
Cellists
USE   **Violoncellists**
Cello
USE   **Violoncellos**
Cello players
USE   **Violoncellists**
Cells   571.6
UF   Cytology
BT   **Biology**
       Physiology
       Reproduction
NT   **DNA**
       Protozoa
RT   **Embryology**
       Protoplasm
Cells, Electric
USE   **Electric batteries**
Celtic legends   398.2
UF   Legends, Celtic *[Former head-
       ing]*
BT   **Legends**
Celtic mythology   299; 936
UF   Mythology, Celtic
BT   **Mythology**
Celts   305.891; 936.4
UF   Gaels
BT   **France—History—0-1328**
       Great Britain—History—0-1066
NT   **Druids and Druidism**

Cement   620.1; 666; 691
  UF   Hydraulic cement
  BT   **Adhesives**
       Building materials
       Ceramics
       Masonry
       Plaster and plastering
  RT   **Concrete**
       Lime (Mineral)
Cemeteries (May subdiv. geog.)   393;
       718
  UF   Burying grounds
       Churchyards
       Graves
       Graveyards
  SA   types of cemeteries and names
       of individual cemeteries, to be
       added as needed
  BT   **Burial**
       Public health
       Sanitation
  NT   **Catacombs**
       Epitaphs
  RT   **Tombs**
Censorship   303.3; 363.3
  Use for general materials on the limitation
  of freedom of expression in various fields.
  SA   subjects with the subdivision
       Censorship, e.g. **Books—Cen-**
       sorship; to be added as need-
       ed
  BT   **Intellectual freedom**
  NT   **Books—Censorship**
       Freedom of speech
       Libraries—Censorship
       Motion pictures—Censorship
       Television—Censorship
       World War, 1939-1945—Cen-
       sorship
  RT   **Freedom of information**
       Freedom of the press
Census   304.6; 310; 352.7
  SA   names of countries, cities, etc.,
       with the subdivision *Census,*
       to be added as needed
  BT   **Population**
       Statistics
       Vital statistics
  NT   **Chicago (Ill.)—Census**
       Ohio—Census
       United States—Census

Centennial celebrations, etc.
  USE   names of places, wars, and his-
        torical events with the subdi-
        vision *Centennial celebrations,*
        etc., e.g. **United States—His-**
        tory—1861-1864, Civil
        War—Centennial celebra-
        tions, etc.; to be added as
        needed
Centers for the performing arts   725;
       790.2
  SA   names of individual centers, to
       be added as needed
  BT   **Performing arts**
  NT   **Theaters**
Central Africa   967
  Use for materials dealing collectively with
  the region of Africa that includes what are
  now the Central African Republic, Equatorial
  Guinea, Gabon, Zaire, and the Congo.
  UF   Africa, Central *[Former head-*
       ing]
  BT   **Africa**
  NT   **French-speaking Equatorial Af-**
       rica
Central America   972.8
  BT   **North America**
Central American Indians
  USE   **Indians of Central America**
Central Asia   958
  UF   Asia, Central
  BT   **Asia**
Central Asia—History   958
Central Asia—History—1991-
  RT   **Former Soviet republics**
Central Europe   943
  Use for materials on the area included in
  the basins of the Danube, Elbe and Rhine riv-
  ers.
  UF   Europe, Central
Central planning
  USE   **Economic policy**
Central States
  USE   **Middle West**
Centralization of schools
  USE   **Schools—Centralization**
Centralized processing (Libraries)
  USE   **Library technical processes**
Ceramic industries   338.4
  SA   types of ceramic industries, e.g.
       Glass manufacture; to be
       added as needed

BT = Broader Term   NT = Narrower Term   RT = Related Term   SA = See Also   UF = Used For

Ceramic industries—*Continued*
    BT   **Industries**
    NT   **Clay industries**
           Glass manufacture
    RT   **Ceramics**
Ceramic materials
    USE   **Ceramics**
Ceramics   666
    Use for materials on the technology of fired earth products or on ceramic products intended for industrial use. Materials on ceramic products intended for the table or decorative use are entered under **Pottery** or **Porcelain.**
    UF   Ceramic materials *[Former heading]*
    BT   **Industrial chemistry**
           Materials
    NT   **Abrasives**
           Cement
           Clay
           Glass
           Glazes
           Pottery
           Tiles
    RT   **Ceramic industries**
Cereals
    USE   **Grain**
Cereals, Prepared
    USE   **Prepared cereals**
Cerebral palsy   616.8
    UF   Palsy, Cerebral
           Paralysis, Cerebral
           Paralysis, Spastic
           Spastic paralysis
    BT   **Brain—Diseases**
Cerebrovascular disease
    USE   **Stroke**
Ceremonies
    USE   **Etiquette**
          Manners and customs
          Rites and ceremonies
Certainty
    USE   **Belief and doubt**
          Probabilities
          Truth
Certified public accountants
    USE   **Accountants**
Chain belting
    USE   **Belts and belting**
Chain stores   658.8
    UF   Branch stores
    BT   **Retail trade**

          Stores
Chair caning   684.1
    UF   Caning of chairs
    BT   **Handicraft**
Chairs   645; 684.1; 749
    BT   **Furniture**
Chalk talks   741.2
    UF   Blackboard drawing
    BT   **Public speaking**
Challenger (Spacecraft)   629.44
    BT   **Space shuttles**
Chamber music   785
    BT   **Instrumental music**
           Music
    NT   **Quintets**
Chamber theater
    USE   **Readers' theater**
Chambers of commerce   380.106; 381.06
    UF   Boards of trade
           Trade, Boards of
    BT   **Commerce**
Change of life in men
    USE   **Male climacteric**
Change of life in women
    USE   **Menopause**
Change of sex
    USE   **Transsexuality**
Change, Organizational
    USE   **Organizational change**
Change, Social
    USE   **Social change**
Changing careers
    USE   **Career changes**
Chanties
    USE   **Sea songs**
Chants (Plain, Gregorian, etc.)   782.32
    Use for books of chants and for materials about chants.
    UF   Gregorian chant
           Plain chant
           Plainsong
    BT   **Church music**
Chanukah
    USE   **Hanukkah**
Chaos (Science)   003
    UF   Chaotic behavior in systems
    BT   **Dynamics**
           Science
           System theory

BT = Broader Term   NT = Narrower Term   RT = Related Term   SA = See Also   UF = Used For

Chaotic behavior in systems
  USE   Chaos (Science)
Chap-books
  USE   Chapbooks
Chapbooks   398
     May be used for individual works, collec-
     tions, or materials about chapbooks.
  UF   Chap-books
         Jestbooks
  BT   **Books**
         Folklore
         Literature
         Pamphlets
         Periodicals
         Wit and humor
  RT   **Comic books, strips, etc.**
Chaplains   253
  SA   corporate bodies and institutions
         with the subdivision *Chap-
         lains,* e.g. **United States.
         Army—Chaplains;** to be
         added as needed
  BT   **Clergy**
  NT   **United States. Army—Chap-
         lains**
Character   155.2
  BT   **Personality**
  NT   **Human behavior**
  RT   **Temperament**
Character assassination
  USE   **Libel and slander**
Character education
  USE   **Moral education**
Characteristics, National
  USE   **National characteristics**
**Characters and characteristics in litera-
     ture   809; 810.9, etc.**
  UF   Characters in literature
         Fictional characters
         Fictitious characters
         Literary characters
  SA   names of authors with the subdi-
         vision *Characters;* e.g.
         **Shakespeare, William, 1564-
         1616—Characters;** groups
         and classes of persons in lit-
         erature, e.g. **Children in lit-
         erature;** names of real per-
         sons with the subdivision *In
         literature,* e.g. **Napoleon I,**

**Emperor of the French,
     1769-1821—In literature;** and
     individual literary characters
     established in the inverted
     form with the qualifier (Ficti-
     tious character), e.g. **Holmes,
     Sherlock (Fictitious charac-
     ter);** to be added as needed
  BT   **Literature**
  NT   **African Americans in litera-
         ture**
         Blacks in literature
         Children in literature
         Plots (Drama, fiction, etc.)
         Women in literature
Characters in literature
  USE   **Characters and characteristics
         in literature**
Charades   793.2
  BT   **Amateur theater**
         Amusements
         Literary recreations
         Riddles
Charcoal   662
  BT   **Fuel**
Charismata
  USE   **Spiritual gifts**
Charismatic movement
  USE   **Catholic charismatic movement
         Pentecostalism**
Charismatic renewal movement
  USE   **Catholic charismatic movement
         Pentecostalism**
Charitable institutions
  USE   **Charities
         Institutional care
         Orphanages**
Charities (May subdiv. geog.)   **361.7;
         361.8**
     Use for materials on privately supported
     welfare activities. Materials on tax supported
     welfare activities are entered under **Public
     welfare.** Materials on the methods employed
     in welfare work, public or private, are entered
     under **Social work.**
  UF   Charitable institutions
         Endowed charities
         Homes (Institutions)
         Institutions, Charitable and phil-
         anthropic
         Philanthropy
         Poor relief

Charities—*Continued*
    Social welfare
    Welfare agencies
    Welfare work
SA   names of appropriate corporate
    bodies with the subdivision
    Charities, e.g. **Catholic
    Church—Charities;** and
    names of wars with the sub-
    division *Civilian relief,* e.g.
    **World War, 1939-1945—Ci-
    vilian relief;** to be added as
    needed
BT   **Social work**
NT   **Catholic Church—Charities**
    Child welfare
    Disaster relief
    Food relief
    Institutional care
    Medical charities
    Orphanages
    Social settlements
    **World War, 1939-1945—Civil-
    ian relief**
RT   **Charity organization**
    Endowments
    Public welfare
    Volunteer work
Charities, Medical
  USE   **Medical charities**
Charities, Public
  USE   **Public welfare**
Charity   177
  BT   **Ethics**
    Virtue
  RT   **Love—Religious aspects**
Charity organization   361
  UF   Philanthropy
  BT   **Associations**
  RT   **Charities**
Charlatans
  USE   **Impostors and imposture**
Charms   133.4
  UF   Spells
    Talismans
  BT   **Demonology**
    Folklore
    Superstition
    Witchcraft

Charter flights
  USE   **Airlines—Chartering**
Charters
  UF   Documents
  BT   **History—Sources**
  NT   **Magna Carta**
  RT   **Archives**
    Manuscripts
Chartography
  USE   **Charts**
    Map drawing
    Maps
Charts   912
  UF   Cartography
    Chartography
  RT   **Maps**
Chasidism
  USE   **Hasidism**
Chastity   176
    Use for materials on the virtue that moder-
ates and regulates the sexual appetite in hu-
man beings. Materials on the renunciation of
marriage for religious reasons are entered un-
der **Celibacy.** Materials on abstinence from
sexual activity are entered under **Sexual absti-
nence.**
  BT   **Ethics**
    Sexual ethics
    Virtue
  RT   **Celibacy**
    Sexual abstinence
Chateaux
  USE   **Castles**
Chattel mortgages
  USE   **Mortgages**
Cheating in sports
  USE   **Sports—Corrupt practices**
Checkers   794.2
  UF   Draughts
  BT   **Games**
    Indoor games
Cheerleaders
  USE   **Cheerleading**
Cheerleading   371.8; 791.6
  UF   Cheerleaders
    Cheers and cheerleading *[For-
    mer heading]*
  BT   **Student activities**
Cheers and cheerleading
  USE   **Cheerleading**
Cheese   637; 641.3
  BT   **Dairy products**

BT = Broader Term   NT = Narrower Term   RT = Related Term   SA = See Also   UF = Used For

Cheese—Bacteriology
  USE   Cheese—Microbiology
Cheese—Microbiology   637
  UF   Cheese—Bacteriology [Former
            heading]
  BT   Microbiology
Chemical analysis
  USE   Analytical chemistry
Chemical apparatus   542
  UF   Apparatus, Chemical
          Chemistry—Apparatus
  BT   Scientific apparatus and in-
            struments
Chemical elements   546
  UF   Elements, Chemical
  SA   names of chemical elements, to
            be added as needed
  BT   Chemistry
  NT   Carbon
          Gold
          Helium
          Hydrogen
          Iron
          Mercury
          Oxygen
          Radium
          Silver
          Sulphur
          Tin
          Uranium
          Zinc
  RT   Periodic law
Chemical engineering   660
  UF   Chemistry, Industrial
          Chemistry, Technical
  BT   Engineering
  NT   Biotechnology
          Fermentation
  RT   Industrial chemistry
          Metallurgy
Chemical equations   540
  UF   Equations, Chemical
  BT   Chemical reactions
Chemical geology
  USE   Geochemistry
Chemical industries
  USE   Chemical industry
Chemical industry   338.4; 660
    Use for materials about industries that pro-
    duce chemicals or are based on chemical pro-
cesses. General materials on chemicals,
including their manufacture, are entered under
Chemicals.
  UF   Chemical industries [Former
            heading]
          Chemistry, Industrial
          Chemistry, Technical
  SA   types of industries, e.g. Plastics
            industry; to be added as
            needed
  BT   Industries
  NT   Plastics industry
  RT   Chemicals
          Industrial chemistry
Chemical industry—Accidents   363.11
  BT   Industrial accidents
Chemical industry—Employees   331.11
  UF   Chemical workers
  BT   Employees
Chemical industry—Employees—Diseases
            616.9
  UF   Chemical workers' diseases
  BT   Occupational diseases
Chemical industry—Employees—Pensions
            331.25
Chemical industry—Law and legislation
        (May subdiv. geog.)   343
Chemical industry—Waste disposal
            363.72; 628.4
  BT   Refuse and refuse disposal
Chemical landfills
  USE   Hazardous waste sites
Chemical pollution
  USE   Pollution
Chemical reactions   541.3
  UF   Reactions, Chemical
  BT   Chemistry
  NT   Chemical equations
Chemical societies
  USE   Chemistry—Societies
Chemical technology
  USE   Industrial chemistry
Chemical warfare   358; 623.4
  UF   Gas warfare
          Poisonous gases—War use [For-
            mer heading]
  SA   names of wars with the subdivi-
            sion Chemical warfare, to be
            added as needed
  BT   Military art and science
          War

BT = Broader Term   NT = Narrower Term   RT = Related Term   SA = See Also   UF = Used For

Chemical warfare—*Continued*
   NT   Incendiary weapons
        World War, 1914-1918—Chemical warfare
        World War, 1939-1945—Chemical warfare
Chemical workers
   USE   **Chemical industry—Employees**
Chemical workers' diseases
   USE   **Chemical industry—Employees—Diseases**
Chemicals   540; 661
   Use for general materials on chemicals, including their manufacture. Materials about industries that produce chemicals or are based on chemical processes are entered under **Chemical industry.**
   SA   types of chemicals, e.g. **Acids; Agricultural chemicals;** etc.; and names of individual chemicals, to be added as needed
   NT   **Acids**
        Agricultural chemicals
        Alcohol
        Carbolic acid
        Deuterium oxide
        Petrochemicals
   RT   **Chemical industry**
        Industrial chemistry
Chemiculture
   USE   **Hydroponics**
Chemistry   540
   BT   **Physical sciences**
        Science
   NT   **Acids**
        Agricultural chemistry
        Alchemy
        Analytical chemistry
        Bases (Chemistry)
        Biochemistry
        Botanical chemistry
        Chemical elements
        Chemical reactions
        Color
        Combustion
        Explosives
        Fermentation
        Fire
        Geochemistry
        Industrial chemistry
        Inorganic chemistry

        Microchemistry
        Organic chemistry
        Pharmaceutical chemistry
        Pharmacy
        Photographic chemistry
        Physical chemistry
        Poisons and poisoning
        Space chemistry
        Spectrum analysis
Chemistry, Agricultural
   USE   **Agricultural chemistry**
Chemistry, Analytic
   USE   **Analytical chemistry**
Chemistry—Apparatus
   USE   **Chemical apparatus**
Chemistry, Biological
   USE   **Biochemistry**
Chemistry, Botanical
   USE   **Botanical chemistry**
Chemistry, Diagnostic
   USE   **Clinical chemistry**
Chemistry—Dictionaries   540.3
   BT   **Encyclopedias and dictionaries**
Chemistry—Experiments   540; 542
Chemistry, Industrial
   USE   **Chemical engineering**
        Chemical industry
        Industrial chemistry
Chemistry, Inorganic
   USE   **Inorganic chemistry**
Chemistry—Laboratory manuals 540.78
Chemistry, Medical
   USE   **Clinical chemistry**
Chemistry, Medical and pharmaceutical
   USE   **Pharmaceutical chemistry**
Chemistry of food
   USE   **Food—Analysis**
        Food—Composition
Chemistry, Organic
   USE   **Organic chemistry**
Chemistry, Pharmaceutical
   USE   **Pharmaceutical chemistry**
Chemistry, Photographic
   USE   **Photographic chemistry**
Chemistry, Physical and theoretical
   USE   **Physical chemistry**
Chemistry, Physiological
   USE   **Biochemistry**

BT = Broader Term   NT = Narrower Term   RT = Related Term   SA = See Also   UF = Used For

Chemistry—Problems, exercises, etc.
540.76
Chemistry—Societies   540.6
  UF   Chemical societies
  BT   Societies
Chemistry, Synthetic
  USE Organic chemistry—Synthesis
Chemistry, Technical
  USE Chemical engineering
        Chemical industry
        Industrial chemistry
Chemistry, Textile
  USE Textile chemistry
Chemists   540.92; 920
  BT   Scientists
Chemists' shops
  USE Drugstores
Chemotherapy
  USE Cancer—Chemotherapy
        Drug therapy
Chess   794.1
  BT   Games
        Indoor games
Chicago (Ill.)   917.73; 977.3

    The subdivisions under **Chicago (Ill.)** may be used under the name of any city. The subdivisions under **United States** may be further consulted as a guide for formulating other headings as needed.

Chicago (Ill.)—African Americans
  USE African Americans—Chicago
        (Ill.)
Chicago (Ill.)—Antiquities   977.3
  BT   Antiquities
Chicago (Ill.)—Bibliography   015.773;
016.9773
Chicago (Ill.)—Bio-bibliography   012
Chicago (Ill.)—Biography   920.0773
  BT   Biography
Chicago (Ill.)—Biography—Portraits
920.0773
Chicago (Ill.)—Boundaries   977.3
  BT   Boundaries
Chicago (Ill.)—Bridges
  USE Bridges—Chicago (Ill.)
Chicago (Ill.)—Census   317.73
  BT   Census
Chicago (Ill.)—City planning
  USE City planning—Chicago (Ill.)
Chicago (Ill.)—Civil defense
  USE Civil defense—Chicago (Ill.)

Chicago (Ill.)—Climate   551.69773
  BT   Climate
Chicago (Ill.)—Commerce   381
  BT   Commerce
Chicago (Ill.)—Demonstrations
  USE Demonstrations—Chicago (Ill.)
Chicago (Ill.)—Description   917.73
Chicago (Ill.)—Description—Guidebooks
  USE Chicago (Ill.)—Guidebooks
Chicago (Ill.)—Description—Views
  USE Chicago (Ill.)—Pictorial works
Chicago (Ill.)—Directories   917.73

    Use for lists of names and addresses. Lists of names without addresses are entered under **Chicago (Ill.)—Registers.**

  BT   Directories
  NT   Chicago (Ill.)—Telephone directories
  RT   Chicago (Ill.)—Registers
Chicago (Ill.)—Directories—Telephone
  USE Chicago (Ill.)—Telephone directories
Chicago (Ill.)—Economic conditions
330.9773
  BT   Economic conditions
Chicago (Ill.)—Employees
  USE Chicago (Ill.)—Officials and employees
Chicago (Ill.)—Government
  USE Chicago (Ill.)—Politics and government
Chicago (Ill.)—Government employees
  USE Chicago (Ill.)—Officials and employees
Chicago (Ill.)—Government publications
  USE Government publications—Chicago (Ill.)
Chicago (Ill.)—Guidebooks   917.73
  UF   Chicago (Ill.)—Description—
        Guidebooks *[Former heading]*
Chicago (Ill.)—Historic buildings
  USE Historic buildings—Chicago
        (Ill.)
Chicago (Ill.)—History   977.3
Chicago (Ill.)—History—Societies
977.3006
  BT   History—Societies
Chicago (Ill.)—Industries
  USE Industries—Chicago (Ill.)
Chicago (Ill.)—Intellectual life   977.3
  BT   Intellectual life

BT = Broader Term   NT = Narrower Term   RT = Related Term   SA = See Also   UF = Used For

Chicago (Ill.)—Manufactures
   USE   Industries—Chicago (Ill.)
Chicago (Ill.)—Maps   912.773
   BT   Maps
Chicago (Ill.)—Moral conditions   977.3
   BT   Moral conditions
Chicago (Ill.)—Occupations
   USE   Occupations—Chicago (Ill.)
Chicago (Ill.)—Officials and employees
    352.1773
   UF   Chicago (Ill.)—Employees
          Chicago (Ill.)—Government em-
          ployees
Chicago (Ill.)—Pictorial works   917.73
   UF   Chicago (Ill.)—Description—
          Views *[Former heading]*
Chicago (Ill.)—Poetry   811; 811.008,
   etc.
    May be used for individual works or collec-
   tions of poetry about Chicago, or for materials
   about such poetry.
   BT   Poetry
Chicago (Ill.)—Politics and government
    977.3
   UF   Chicago (Ill.)—Government
   BT   Municipal government
          Politics
Chicago (Ill.)—Popular culture
   USE   Popular culture—Chicago (Ill.)
Chicago (Ill.)—Population   304.609773
   BT   Population
Chicago (Ill.)—Public buildings
   USE   Public buildings—Chicago (Ill.)
Chicago (Ill.)—Public works
   USE   Public works—Chicago (Ill.)
Chicago (Ill.)—Race relations
    305.8009773
   BT   Race relations
Chicago (Ill.)—Registers   917.73
    Use for lists of names without addresses.
   Lists of names that include addresses are en-
   tered under **Chicago (Ill.)—Directories.**
   RT   Chicago (Ill.)—Directories
Chicago (Ill.)—Social conditions   977.3
   BT   Social conditions
Chicago (Ill.)—Social life and customs
    977.3
   BT   Manners and customs
Chicago (Ill.)—Social policy   361.6;
    977.3
   BT   Social policy

Chicago (Ill.)—Statistics   317.73
   BT   Statistics
Chicago (Ill.)—Streets
   USE   Streets—Chicago (Ill.)
Chicago (Ill.)—Suburbs and environs
   USE   Chicago Suburban Area (Ill.)
Chicago (Ill.)—Telephone directories
    917.73
   UF   Chicago (Ill.)—Directories—
          Telephone *[Former heading]*
   BT   Chicago (Ill.)—Directories
Chicago (Ill.)—Urban renewal
   USE   Urban renewal—Chicago (Ill.)
Chicago metropolitan area (Ill.)
   USE   Chicago Metropolitan Area
          (Ill.)
Chicago metropolitan area (Ill.)—Politics
   and government
   USE   Chicago Metropolitan Area
          (Ill.)—Politics and govern-
          ment
Chicago Metropolitan Area (Ill.)—Poli-
   tics and government   977.3
   UF   Chicago metropolitan area
          (Ill.)—Politics and government
          [Former heading]
   BT   Metropolitan government
Chicago Metropolitan Area (Ill.)   977.3
   UF   Chicago metropolitan area (Ill.)
          [Former heading]
   RT   Chicago Suburban Area (Ill.)
Chicago Suburban Area (Ill.)   977.3
   UF   Chicago (Ill.)—Suburbs and en-
          virons *[Former heading]*
   RT   Chicago Metropolitan Area
          (Ill.)
Chicanas
   USE   Mexican American women
Chicano literature (English)
   USE   American literature—Mexican
          American authors
Chicanos
   USE   Mexican Americans
Chicken pox
   USE   Chickenpox
Chickenpox   616.9
   UF   Chicken pox
   BT   Diseases
          Viruses

BT = Broader Term   NT = Narrower Term   RT = Related Term   SA = See Also   UF = Used For

Chief justices
USE   **Judges**
Child abuse   362.76; 364.15
    UF   Abuse of children
            Abused children
            Battered children
            Child battering
            Child neglect
            Children—Abuse
            Children, Cruelty to
            Cruelty to children
    BT   **Child welfare**
            Family violence
            Parent and child
    NT   **Child sexual abuse**
            Juvenile prostitution
    RT   **Adult child abuse victims**
Child abuse survivors
USE   **Adult child abuse victims**
Child and father
USE   **Father and child**
Child and grandparent
USE   **Grandparent and child**
Child and mother
USE   **Mother and child**
Child and parent
USE   **Parent and child**
Child artists   704; 709.2; 920
    Use for materials on children as artists and on works of art by children.
    UF   Children as artists
    BT   **Artists**
            Gifted children
    NT   **Finger painting**
Child authors   809; 920
    Use for materials on children as authors and discussions of literary works written by children. Individual literary works and collections of literary works written by children are entered under the form heading **Children's writings.**
    UF   Children as authors
    BT   **Authors**
            Gifted children
    RT   **Children's writings**
Child battering
USE   **Child abuse**
Child birth
USE   **Childbirth**
Child care   649
    UF   Care of children
            Children—Care

Children, Care of
    NT   **Babysitting**
            Child rearing
            Day care centers
            Infants—Care
Child care centers
USE   **Day care centers**
Child custody   306.89; 346.01; 362.7
    UF   Children—Custody
            Custody of children
            Joint custody of children
            Parental custody
            Shared custody
    BT   **Divorce mediation**
            Parent and child
    NT   **Parental kidnapping**
Child development   155.4; 305.231; 612.6
    UF   Child study
            Children—Development
    BT   **Children**
    NT   **Children—Growth**
    RT   **Child psychology**
            Child rearing
Child labor
USE   **Children—Employment**
            Teenagers—Employment
            Youth—Employment
Child molesting
USE   **Child sexual abuse**
Child neglect
USE   **Child abuse**
Child placing
USE   **Adoption**
            Foster home care
Child prostitution
USE   **Juvenile prostitution**
Child psychiatry   616.89; 618.92
    Use for materials on the clinical and therapeutic aspects of mental disorders in children. Materials on children suffering from mental or emotional illnesses are entered under **Emotionally distrubed children.**
    UF   Children—Mental health
            Pediatric psychiatry
    BT   **Psychiatry**
    NT   **Autism**
            Mentally handicapped children
    RT   **Child psychology**
            Emotionally disturbed children

BT = Broader Term   NT = Narrower Term   RT = Related Term   SA = See Also   UF = Used For

Child psychology   155.4
  UF Child study
        Children—Psychology
  BT **Psychology**
  NT **Children and adults**
        Emotions in children
        Intelligence tests
        Psychology of learning
        Separation anxiety in children
        Sibling rivalry
  RT **Child development**
        Child psychiatry
        Child rearing
        Educational psychology
Child raising
  USE **Child rearing**
Child rearing   392.1; 649
  Use for materials on the principles and techniques of rearing children. Materials on the psychological and social interaction between parents and their minor children are entered under **Parent and child.** Materials on the skills, attributes, and attitudes needed for parenthood are entered under **Parenting.**
  UF Child raising
        Children—Management
        Children—Training
        Discipline of children
        Training of children
  BT **Child care**
        Children and adults
        Parent and child
  NT **Children's allowances**
        Socialization
        Toilet training
  RT **Child development**
        Child psychology
        Parenting
Child sex abuse
  USE **Child sexual abuse**
Child sexual abuse   362.76; 364.15
  UF Child molesting *[Former heading]*
        Child sex abuse
        Children—Molesting
        Molesting of children
        Sexual abuse
        Sexually abused children
  BT **Child abuse**
        Incest
        Sex crimes

  RT **Adult child sexual abuse victims**
Child snatching by parents
  USE **Parental kidnapping**
Child study
  USE **Child development**
        Child psychology
Child support   346.01
  UF Support of children
  BT **Child welfare**
        Desertion and nonsupport
        Divorce mediation
Child welfare   362.7
  Use for materials on the aid, support, and protection of children, by the state or by private welfare organizations.
  UF A.D.C.
        Aid to dependent children
        Children—Charities, protection, etc.
        Mothers' pensions *[Former heading]*
        Protection of children
  BT **Charities**
        Public welfare
        Social work
  NT **Abandoned children**
        Child abuse
        Child support
        Children—Employment
        Children—Institutional care
        Day care centers
        Foster home care
        Unmarried fathers
        Unmarried mothers
  RT **Children's hospitals**
        Juvenile delinquency
        Orphanages
Childbirth   612.6; 618.2
  UF Birth
        Birth customs
        Child birth
        Labor (Childbirth)
        Obstetrics
  NT **Midwives**
        Multiple birth
        Natural childbirth
  RT **Pregnancy**
Childbirth, Natural
  USE **Natural childbirth**

BT = Broader Term   NT = Narrower Term   RT = Related Term   SA = See Also   UF = Used For

Childhood diseases
USE   Children—Diseases
Childlessness   306.85
BT   **Children**
     Family size
RT   **Birth control**
     Human fertility
     Infertility
Children (May subdiv. geog.)   **305.23**
  Use for materials on people from birth through age twelve. Materials limited to the first two years of a child's life are entered under **Infants.**
UF   Preschool children
SA   children of particular racial or ethnic groups, e.g. **African American children;** children and other subjects, e.g. **Children and war;** and names of wars with the subdivision *Children,* e.g. **World War, 1939-1945—Children;** to be added as needed
BT   **Age**
     Family
NT   **Abandoned children**
     Adopted children
     Advertising and children
     African American children
     Birth order
     Black children
     Boys
     Child development
     Childlessness
     Children and war
     Computers and children
     Exceptional children
     Foster children
     Girls
     Handicapped children
     Indians of North America—Children
     Infants
     Missing children
     Motion pictures and children
     Only child
     Orphans
     Runaway children
     School children
     Television and children

Children, Abnormal
USE   **Exceptional children**
      Handicapped children
Children—Abuse
USE   **Child abuse**
Children, Adopted
USE   **Adopted children**
Children—Adoption
USE   **Adoption**
Children, African American
USE   **African American children**
Children and adults   305.23; 362.7; 649
UF   Adults and children
BT   **Child psychology**
NT   **Child rearing**
     Children and strangers
     Conflict of generations
     Grandparent and child
     Parent and child
     Teacher-student relationships
Children and advertising
USE   **Advertising and children**
Children and grandparents
USE   **Grandparent and child**
Children and motion pictures
USE   **Motion pictures and children**
Children and prostitution
USE   **Juvenile prostitution**
Children and strangers   362.7
UF   Infants and strangers
     Strangers and children
BT   **Children and adults**
Children and television
USE   **Television and children**
Children and war (May subdiv. geog.)
      305.23
UF   War and children
SA   names of particular wars with the subdivision *Children,* e.g. **World War, 1939-1945—Children;** to be added as needed
BT   **Children**
     War
NT   **World War, 1939-1945—Children**
Children as artists
USE   **Child artists**
Children as authors
USE   **Child authors**

BT = Broader Term   NT = Narrower Term   RT = Related Term   SA = See Also   UF = Used For

Children as consumers
USE **Young consumers**
Children, Black
USE **Black children**
Children—Books and reading   011.62; 028.5

Use for materials on the reading interests of children and lists of books for children. Collections or materials about literature published for children are entered under **Children's literature.** Individual literary works and collections of literary works written by children are entered under **Children's writings.** Materials about works written by children and materials about children as authors are entered under **Child authors.**

UF   Books and reading for children
     Reading interests of children
BT   **Books and reading**
Children—Care
USE   **Child care**
Children, Care of
USE   **Child care**
Children—Charities, protection, etc.
USE   **Child welfare**
Children—Civil rights   323.3; 342
BT   **Civil rights**
Children—Clothing
USE   **Children's clothing**
Children—Costume   391

Use for descriptive and historical materials on children's costume among various nations or in the past. Materials on children's clothing from a practical standpoint are entered under **Children's clothing.**

BT   **Costume**
RT   **Children's clothing**
Children, Crippled
USE   **Physically handicapped children**
Children, Cruelty to
USE   **Child abuse**
Children—Custody
USE   **Child custody**
Children—Day care
USE   **Day care centers**
Children, Delinquent
USE   **Juvenile delinquency**
Children—Dental care   617.6
Children—Development
USE   **Child development**
Children—Diseases   618.92
UF   Childhood diseases
     Children's diseases
     Diseases of children
     Medicine, Pediatric
     Pediatrics
SA   types of diseases, e.g.
     Chickenpox; to be added as needed
BT   **Diseases**
RT   **Children—Health and hygiene**
Children—Education
USE   **Elementary education**
     Preschool education
Children—Employment (May subdiv. geog.) **331.3**
UF   Boys—Employment
     Child labor
     Employment of children
     Girls—Employment
     Working children
BT   **Age and employment**
     Child welfare
     Labor
     Labor supply
     Social problems
NT   **Moneymaking projects for children**
RT   **Hours of labor**
Children—Employment—United States 331.3
UF   United States—Children—Employment
Children, Exceptional
USE   **Exceptional children**
Children—Food
USE   **Children—Nutrition**
Children, Gifted
USE   **Gifted children**
Children—Growth   155.4; 612.6
BT   **Child development**
Children—Health and hygiene   613
UF   Children—Hygiene
     Pediatrics
BT   **Health**
     Hygiene
NT   **Children—Nutrition**
     School hygiene
RT   **Children—Diseases**
     Children's hospitals
     Health education
Children—Hospitals
USE   **Children's hospitals**

Children—Hygiene
USE **Children—Health and hygiene**
Children, Hyperactive
USE **Hyperactive children**
Children, Illegitimate
USE **Illegitimacy**
Children in art   704.9

Use for materials on children depicted in works of art. Materials on children as artists are entered under **Child artists.**

BT **Art**

Children in literature   809

Use for materials on the theme of children in works of literature. Individual literary works or collections of literary works written by children are entered under the form heading **Children's writings.** Materials about children as authors and about works written by children are entered under **Child authors.**

BT **Characters and characteristics in literature**

Children—Institutional care   362.73
UF Boys' towns
Children's homes
BT **Child welfare**
Institutional care
NT **Day care centers**
Orphanages
Reformatories
RT **Foster home care**

Children—Language   155.4
BT **Language and languages**
Children, Latchkey
USE **Latchkey children**
Children—Management
USE **Child rearing**
Children—Medical examinations   616.07
UF Medical inspection in schools
School children—Medical examinations
Children—Mental health
USE **Child psychiatry**
Children—Molesting
USE **Child sexual abuse**
Children—Nutrition   613.2083;
641.1083; 649
UF Children—Food *[Former heading]*
Children's food
BT **Children—Health and hygiene**
Nutrition
NT **School children—Food**

Children of alcoholics   362.292
UF Alcoholic parents
Alcoholics' children
C.O.A.s
COAs
BT **Parent and child**
NT **Adult children of alcoholics**
RT **Alcoholics**
Alcoholism
Children of divorced parents   306.874;
646.7
BT **Divorce**
Parent and child
Single parent family
RT **Part-time parenting**
Children of drug addicts   362.29
UF Children of narcotic addicts
Cocaine babies
Crack babies
Drug addicts' children
Drug addicts' infants
BT **Drug addicts**
Parent and child
Children of immigrants   305.23
UF First generation children
BT **Immigration and emigration**
Parent and child
Children of narcotic addicts
USE **Children of drug addicts**
Children of single parents
USE **Single parent family**
Children of working parents   306.874;
362.7
UF Working parents, Children of
BT **Parent and child**
NT **Latchkey children**
Children—Placing out
USE **Adoption**
Foster home care
Children—Psychology
USE **Child psychology**
Children, Retarded
USE **Mentally handicapped children**
Children—Socialization
USE **Socialization**
Children—Surgery   617
UF Pediatric surgery
Surgery, Pediatric
BT **Surgery**

BT = Broader Term   NT = Narrower Term   RT = Related Term   SA = See Also   UF = Used For

Children—Training
USE **Child rearing**
Children—United States   305.230973
UF United States—Children
Children's allowances   332.024; 649
UF Allowances, Children's
BT **Child rearing**
Money
Personal finance
RT **Moneymaking projects for children**
Children's books
USE **Children's literature**
Children's clothing   646.4; 649
Use for materials on children's clothing from a practical standpoint. Descriptive and historical materials on children's costume among various nations or in the past are entered under **Children—Costume.**
UF Children—Clothing
BT **Clothing and dress**
RT **Children—Costume**
Children's courts
USE **Juvenile courts**
Children's day care centers
USE **Day care centers**
Children's diseases
USE **Children—Diseases**
Children's food
USE **Children—Nutrition**
Children's homes
USE **Children—Institutional care**
Children's hospitals   362.1
UF Children—Hospitals
BT **Hospitals**
RT **Child welfare**
Children—Health and hygiene
Children's libraries   027.62
UF Libraries and children
Libraries, Children's
Library services to children
BT **School libraries**
RT **Children's literature**
Elementary school libraries
Libraries and schools
Young adults' library services
Children's literature   808.8; 810.8, etc.
Use for collections or materials about literature published for children. Materials on the reading interests of children and lists of books for children are entered under **Children—Books and reading.** Individual literary works

and collections of literary works written by children are entered under **Children's writings.** Materials about works written by children and materials about children as authors are entered under **Child authors.**
UF Books for children
Children's books
Children's stories
Juvenile literature
SA subjects with the subdivision *Juvenile literature,* e.g. **Computers—Juvenile literature;** to be added as needed
BT **Literature**
NT **Big books**
Caldecott Medal
Children's plays
Children's poetry
Easy reading materials
Fairy tales
Newbery Medal
Picture books for children
Plot-your-own stories
Reading materials
Storytelling
RT **Children's libraries**
Libraries and schools
Children's literature—History and criticism   809
Children's moneymaking projects
USE **Moneymaking projects for children**
Children's parties   395.3; 793.2
BT **Amusements**
Entertaining
Parties
Children's plays   808.82; 809.2; 812, etc.; 812.008, etc.; 812.009, etc.
May be used for individual works, collections, or materials about plays for children.
UF Plays for children
School plays
BT **Amateur theater**
Children's literature
Drama
Theater
Children's poetry   808.81; 809.1; 811, etc.; 811.008, etc.; 811.009, etc.
Use for individual poems, collections, or materials about poetry written for children. Individual works and collections of poetry written by children are entered under the form

---

BT = Broader Term   NT = Narrower Term   RT = Related Term   SA = See Also   UF = Used For

Children's poetry—*Continued*

heading **Children's writings.** Materials about poetry written by children are entered under **Child authors.**

UF   Poetry for children

BT   **Children's literature**

       Poetry

NT   **Children's songs**

       Lullabies

       Nonsense verses

       Nursery rhymes

       Tongue twisters

Children's reading

USE   **Reading**

Children's songs   782.42

Use for collections of songs that contain both words and music, and for materials about songs for children. Collections of songs without the music are entered under **Children's poetry.**

UF   Songs for children

BT   **Children's poetry**

       School songbooks

       Songs

NT   **Lullabies**

       Nursery rhymes

Children's stories

USE   **Children's literature**

         Fairy tales

Children's writings   808.8; 810.8, etc.

Use as a form heading for individual literary works or collections of literary works written by children. Materials on children as authors and discussions of literary works written by children are entered under **Child authors.** Collections of works published for children are entered under **Children's literature.**

UF   School prose

       School verse *[Former heading]*

RT   **Child authors**

       College and school journalism

Chimes

USE   **Bells**

Chimneys   697; 721

UF   Smoke stacks

BT   **Architecture—Details**

       Building

       Buildings

       Heating

       Ventilation

RT   **Fireplaces**

China   951

Use as a heading or as a geographic subdivision for materials dealing with mainland China, regardless of time period, or with the People's Republic of China, or for comprehensive materials on China including Taiwan. Materials dealing with the island of Taiwan, regardless of time period, or with the post-1948 Republic of China are entered under **Taiwan.** May be subdivided like United States except for *History.*

UF   China (People's Republic of China)

       People's Republic of China

China—History   951

China—History—1912-1949   951.04

China—History—1949-   951.05

China—History—1949-1976   951.05

China—History—1976-   951.05

China—History—1989, Tiananmen Square Incident   951.05

UF   Beijing Massacre, 1989

       Tiananmen Square Incident, China, 1989

       Tiananmen Square Massacre, China

China painting   738.1

UF   Porcelain painting

BT   **Decoration and ornament**

       Painting

       Porcelain

China (People's Republic of China)

USE   **China**

China (Porcelain)

USE   **Porcelain**

China (Republic of China, 1949-)

USE   **Taiwan**

Chinaware

USE   **Porcelain**

Chinese Americans   305.895; 973

Chinese satellite countries

USE   **Communist countries**

Chipmunks   599.36

BT   **Mammals**

       Squirrels

Chiropody

USE   **Podiatry**

Chiropractic   615.5

BT   **Alternative medicine**

       Massage

       Medicine

       Osteopathic medicine

RT   **Naturopathy**

Chivalry   394

BT   **Manners and customs**

BT = Broader Term   NT = Narrower Term   RT = Related Term   SA = See Also   UF = Used For

Chivalry—*Continued*
   RT   **Crusades**
        Feudalism
        Heraldry
        Knights and knighthood
        Medieval civilization
        Romances
Chivalry—Romances
   USE **Romances**
Chocolate   641.3
   BT   **Food**
   RT   **Cocoa**
        Desserts
Choice, Freedom of
   USE **Free will and determinism**
Choice of books
   USE **Best books**
        Book selection
        Books and reading
Choice of college
   USE **College choice**
Choice of profession, occupation, vocation,
   etc.
   USE **Vocational guidance**
Choice of school
   USE **School choice**
Choice (Psychology)   153.8
   BT   **Psychology**
   RT   **Decision making**
Choirs (Music)   782.5
   BT   **Church music**
   RT   **Choral conducting**
        Choral music
        Choral societies
        Singing
Cholesterol content of food
   USE **Food—Cholesterol content**
Choose-your-own story plots
   USE **Plot-your-own stories**
Choral conducting   782.5
   UF   Conducting, Choral *[Former
        heading]*
   BT   **Conducting**
   RT   **Choirs (Music)**
        Choral music
        Conductors (Music)
Choral music   782.5
   UF   Music, Choral
   BT   **Church music**
        Vocal music

   NT   **Cantatas**
   RT   **Choirs (Music)**
        Choral conducting
        Choral societies
Choral societies   782.506
   UF   Singing societies
   BT   **Societies**
   RT   **Choirs (Music)**
        Choral music
Choral speaking   808.5
   UF   Speaking choirs
        Unison speaking
   BT   **Drama**
        Recitations
Christ
   USE **Jesus Christ**
Christening
   USE **Baptism**
Christian antiquities   225.9; 270; 930.1
   UF   Antiquities, Christian
        Antiquities, Ecclesiastical
        Archeology, Christian
        Christian archeology
        Christians—Antiquities
        Church antiquities
        Ecclesiastical antiquities
   BT   **Antiquities**
        Archeology
        Bible—Antiquities
   NT   **Catacombs**
   RT   **Christian art and symbolism**
        Church architecture
        Gothic architecture
Christian archeology
   USE **Christian antiquities**
Christian art and symbolism   246;
      704.9
   UF   Art, Christian
        Art, Ecclesiastical
        Christian symbolism
        Ecclesiastical art
        Iconography
        Sacred art
   BT   **Art**
        Religious art and symbolism
        Symbolism
   NT   **Church architecture**
        Church furniture
        **Illumination of books and
          manuscripts**

BT = Broader Term   NT = Narrower Term   RT = Related Term   SA = See Also   UF = Used For

Christian art and symbolism—*Continued*
  Jesus Christ—Art
  Mary, Blessed Virgin, Saint—
   Art
  Symbolism of numbers
 RT Bible—Pictorial works
  Christian antiquities
  Gothic art
Christian biography 270.092; 920
 UF Christianity—Biography *[Former
   heading]*
  Christians—Biography
  Ecclesiastical biography
 BT **Biography**
  Religious biography
 NT **Fathers of the church**
Christian civilization 270; 909
 UF Civilization, Christian *[Former
   heading]*
 BT **Christianity**
  Civilization
Christian denominations
 USE **Christian sects**
Christian devotional calendars
 USE **Devotional calendars**
Christian doctrinal theology
 USE **Christianity—Doctrines**
Christian doctrine
 USE **Christianity—Doctrines**
Christian education 268
  Use for materials on the instruction of
 Christian religion in schools and private life.
 General materials on the instruction of reli-
 gion in schools and private life are entered
 under **Religious education.** Materials on the
 relation of the church to education and materi-
 als on the history of the part that the church
 has taken in secular education are entered un-
 der **Church and education.** Materials on
 church supported and controlled elementary
 and secondary schools are entered under
 Church schools.
 UF Education, Christian
 BT **Religious education**
 NT **Bible—Study and teaching**
 RT **Church and education**
Christian ethics 241
 UF Christian moral theology
  Ethics, Christian
  Moral theology, Christian
 BT **Ethics**
 NT **Conscience**
 RT **Christian life**

Christian fasts and feasts
 USE **Christian holidays**
Christian fiction 808.83; 813, etc.
  Use for individual works, collections, or
 materials about fiction that promotes Christian
 teachings or exemplifies a Christian way of
 life.
 BT **Fiction**
  Religious fiction
Christian fundamentalism 230; 270.8
  Use for materials on the modern conserva-
 tive movement in Protestantism emphasizing
 literal interpretation of the Bible, as opposed
 to religious liberalism, modernism, or evolu-
 tionism.
 UF Fundamentalism *[Former head-
   ing]*
  Modernist-fundamentalist contro-
   versy
 BT **Christianity—Doctrines**
  Religious fundamentalism
 RT **Modernism (Theology)**
Christian holidays 263; 394.266
 UF Christian fasts and feasts
  Christian holy days
  Fasts and feasts—Christianity
 SA names of Christian holidays, e.g.
   Christmas; to be added as
   needed
 BT **Church year**
  Religious holidays
 NT **Christmas**
  Easter
  Good Friday
Christian holy days
 USE **Christian holidays**
Christian-Jewish relations
 USE **Christianity—Relations—Juda-
   ism**
  **Judaism—Relations—Christian-
   ity**
Christian life 248.4
 UF Life, Christian
  Religious life (Christian)
 BT **Religious life**
 RT **Christian ethics**
Christian literature 230
 BT **Religious literature**
 NT **Catholic literature**
  Early Christian literature
  Papal encyclicals
  Sermons

BT = Broader Term NT = Narrower Term RT = Related Term SA = See Also UF = Used For

Christian literature—30-600, Early
    USE   **Early Christian literature**
Christian literature, Early
    USE   **Early Christian literature**
Christian ministry   253
    UF   Ministry, Christian *[Former
          heading]*
    BT   **Ministry**
Christian missionaries   266.0092; 920
    UF   Missionaries, Christian *[Former
          heading]*
    RT   **Christian missions**
Christian missions   266
    UF   Foreign missions, Christian
          Home missions, Christian
          Missions, Christian *[Former
          heading]*
    SA   names of Christian churches, de-
          nominations, religious orders,
          etc., with the subdivision *Mis-
          sions,* e.g. **Catholic Church—
          Missions;** and names of peo-
          ples evangelized with the sub-
          division *Christian missions,*
          e.g. **Indians of North Ameri-
          ca—Christian missions;** to
          be added as needed
    BT   **Christianity**
          Church history
          Church work
    NT   **Catholic Church—Missions**
          **Indians of North America—
          Christian missions**
          Salvation Army
    RT   **Christian missionaries**
          Evangelistic work
Christian moral theology
    USE   **Christian ethics**
Christian names
    USE   **Personal names**
Christian new birth
    USE   **Regeneration (Christianity)**
Christian philosophy   190; 230.01
    Use for materials on philosophy as prac-
ticed by Christian philosophers or on the na-
ture, origins, or validity of Christian beliefs
from a philosophical point of view.
    UF   Christianity—Philosophy *[Former
          heading]*
    BT   **Philosophy**

Christian regeneration
    USE   **Regeneration (Christianity)**
Christian saints   270.092; 920
    BT   **Saints**
    NT   **Apostles**
Christian Science   289.5
    UF   Church of Christ, Scientist
    BT   **Christian sects**
    RT   **Spiritual healing**
Christian sects   280
    UF   Christian denominations
          Church denominations
          Denominations, Christian
          Sects, Christian
    SA   names of Christian sects, e.g.
          Presbyterian Church; to be
          added as needed
    BT   **Christianity**
          Church history
          Sects
    NT   **Amish**
          Baptists
          Catholic Church
          Christian Science
          Church of England
          **Church of Jesus Christ of Lat-
          ter-day Saints**
          Community churches
          Congregationalism
          Eastern churches
          Episcopal Church
          Huguenots
          Mennonites
          Moravians
          Noninstitutional churches
          Orthodox Eastern Church
          Pentecostal churches
          Presbyterian Church
          Protestant churches
          Puritans
          Russian Orthodox Church
          Salvation Army
          Shakers
          Society of Friends
          Unitarianism
Christian sociology   261
    Use for materials on social theory from a
Christian point of view. Materials on religious
sociology in general are entered under **Religion and sociology.** Materials on the practical
treatment of social problems from the point of

BT = Broader Term   NT = Narrower Term   RT = Related Term   SA = See Also   UF = Used For

Christian sociology—*Continued*
> view of the church are entered under **Church and social problems.**

  UF   Sociology, Christian *[Former heading]*

  BT   **Religion and sociology**
          Sociology

  RT   **Christianity and economics**
          Church and social problems

Christian symbolism
  USE   **Christian art and symbolism**

Christian union
  USE   **Christian unity**

Christian unity   262.001; 280
> Use for materials on unity as a characteristic of the Christian Church and on movements aimed at bringing all Christian sects into cooperation and fellowship, with or without a single organization.

  UF   Christian union
          Church—Unity
          Ecumenical movement
          Ecumenism

  BT   **Church**
  NT   **Interfaith relations**

Christian year
  USE   **Church year**

Christianity   230
  SA   names of Christian churches and sects, e.g. **Catholic Church; Huguenots;** etc.; and Christianity and other subjects, e.g. **Christianity and economics;** to be added as needed

  BT   **Religions**
  NT   **Atonement—Christianity**
          Catholic Church
          Christian civilization
          Christian missions
          Christian sects
          Christianity and economics
          Councils and synods
          Counter-Reformation
          Eastern churches
          Miracles—Christianity
          Pentecostalism
          Protestantism
          Reformation
  RT   **Christians**
          Church
          Jesus Christ

Christianity and economics   261.8
  UF   Economics and Christianity
  BT   **Christianity**
          Economics
  RT   **Christian sociology**
          Church and labor

Christianity and evolution
  USE   **Creationism**

Christianity and other religions   261.2
> Use for materials on the relations between Christianity and several other religions. Materials on the relations between Christianity and one other religion are entered under **Christianity** subdivided by *Relations* further subdivided by the other religion, and also under the other religion subdivided by *Relations—Christianity,* e.g. **Christianity—Relations—Judaism** and **Judaism—Relations—Christianity.** The same pattern is followed for sects and denominations.

  UF   Christianity—Relations
          Comparative religion
  BT   **Religions**
  NT   **Christianity—Relations—Judaism**
          Judaism—Relations—Christianity
          Paganism

Christianity and other religions—Judaism
  USE   **Christianity—Relations—Judaism**
          Judaism—Relations—Christianity

Christianity and politics   261.7; 322
  UF   Christianity—Political aspects
          Politics and Christianity
  BT   **Church and state**
          Religion and politics

Christianity—Apologetic works   239
  BT   **Apologetics**

Christianity—Biography
  USE   **Christian biography**

Christianity—Controversial literature   239
  BT   **Apologetics**

Christianity—Doctrines   230
  UF   Christian doctrinal theology
          Christian doctrine
  BT   **Doctrinal theology**
  NT   **Christian fundamentalism**
          Creationism
          God—Christianity
          Liberation theology

BT = Broader Term   NT = Narrower Term   RT = Related Term   SA = See Also   UF = Used For

Christianity—Doctrines—*Continued*
    Modernism (Theology)
    Regeneration (Christianity)
    Trinity
Christianity—History
  USE **Church history**
Christianity—Origin
  USE **Church history—30-600, Early church**
Christianity—Philosophy
  USE **Christian philosophy**
Christianity—Political aspects
  USE **Christianity and politics**
Christianity—Psychology   **230.01; 253.5**
  BT **Psychology of religion**
Christianity—Relations
  USE **Christianity and other religions**
Christianity—Relations—Judaism
    261.2; 296.3
    Use for materials on the relations between Christianity and Judaism. When assigning this heading, provide an additional subject entry under **Judaism—Relations—Christianity.**
  UF Christian-Jewish relations
      Christianity and other religions—Judaism
      Jewish-Christian relations *[Former heading]*
  BT **Christianity and other religions**
      Judaism
Christians   **270.092**
  RT **Christianity**
Christians—Antiquities
  USE **Christian antiquities**
Christians—Biography
  USE **Christian biography**
Christians—Persecutions (May subdiv. geog.)   **272**
  BT **Church history**
      Persecution
Christmas (May subdiv. geog.)   **263; 394.2663**
  BT **Christian holidays**
      Holidays
  NT **Christmas entertainments**
      Santa Claus
  RT **Jesus Christ—Nativity**
Christmas cards   **741.6; 745.594**
  BT **Greeting cards**
Christmas carols
  USE **Carols**

Christmas decorations   **394.2663; 745.594**
  UF Christmas ornaments
  BT **Decoration and ornament**
  NT **Christmas trees**
Christmas—Drama
  USE **Christmas plays**
Christmas entertainments   **394.2663; 791**
  BT **Amusements**
      Christmas
  NT **Christmas plays**
Christmas ornaments
  USE **Christmas decorations**
Christmas plays   **394.2663; 792; 808.82; 812, etc.**
    May be used for individual works, collections, or materials about Christmas plays.
  UF Christmas—Drama *[Former heading]*
      Plays, Christmas
  BT **Christmas entertainments**
      Religious drama
Christmas—Poetry
  USE **Christmas poetry**
Christmas poetry   **808.81; 811, etc.; 811.008, etc.**
    May be used for individual works, collections, or materials about poetry about Christmas or associated with Christmas.
  UF Christmas—Poetry *[Former heading]*
  BT **Poetry**
  NT **Carols**
Christmas tree growing   **635.9**
  UF Growing of Christmas trees
  BT **Forests and forestry**
  RT **Christmas trees**
      Tree planting
Christmas trees   **394.2663; 745.594**
  BT **Christmas decorations**
      Trees
  RT **Christmas tree growing**
Christmas—United States   **394.2663**
  UF United States—Christmas
Christology
  USE **Jesus Christ**
Chromosome mapping
  USE **Gene mapping**
Chromosomes   **572.8**
  BT **Genetics**

BT = Broader Term   NT = Narrower Term   RT = Related Term   SA = See Also   UF = Used For

Chromosomes—*Continued*
      Heredity
  NT   Genetic recombination
Chronicle history (Drama)
  USE   Historical drama
Chronicle plays
  USE   Historical drama
Chronology   529
    Use for materials on the science that deals with measuring time by regular divisions and that assigns proper dates to events.
  SA   individual persons, wars, sacred works, topics that are inherently historical, and topics not subdivided by *History,* such as art, music, literature, etc., with the subdivision *Chronology,* e.g. **Bible—Chronology;** and ethnic groups, corporate bodies, military services, topics not inherently historical, and names of places with the subdivision *History—Chronology,* e.g. **Indians of North America—History—Chronology;** to be added as needed
  BT   Astronomy
      History
      Time
  NT   Bible—Chronology
      Day
      Historical chronology
      Months
      Night
      Week
  RT   Almanacs
Chronology, Biblical
  USE   Bible—Chronology
Chronology, Historical
  USE   Historical chronology
Church   260
  SA   church and other subjects, e.g. **Church and education;** to be added as needed
  BT   Theology
  NT   Christian unity
      Church and education
      Church and social problems
      Church and state
      Church work
      Clergy

      Ecclesiastical law
      Laity
      Sacraments
  RT   Christianity
Church and education   261
    Use for materials on the relation of the church to education in general, and for materials on the history of the part that the church has taken in secular education. Materials on church supported and controlled elementary and secondary schools are entered under **Church schools.** Materials on the instruction of religion in schools and private life are entered under **Religious education,** and of Christian religion under **Christian education.**
  UF   Education and church
      Education and religion
      Fundamentalism and education
        [Former heading]
      Religion and education
  BT   **Church**
      Education
  NT   **Religion in the public schools**
  RT   **Christian education**
Church and government
  USE   **Church and state**
Church and labor   261.8
  UF   Labor and the church
  BT   **Labor**
  RT   **Christianity and economics**
Church and race relations   261.8
  UF   Integrated churches
      Race relations and the church
  BT   **Church work**
Church and social problems   261.8
    Use for materials on the practical treatment of social problems from the point of view of the church. Materials on social theory from a Christian point of view are entered under **Christian sociology.** Materials on religious sociology in general are entered under **Religion and sociology.**
  UF   Religion and social problems
      Social problems and the church
  BT   **Church**
      Social problems
  NT   **Liberation theology**
      Sanctuary movement
  RT   **Christian sociology**
      Church work
Church and state (May subdiv. geog.)
      261.7; 291.1; 322
  UF   Church and government
      Church—Government policy
        [Former heading]

BT = Broader Term   NT = Narrower Term   RT = Related Term   SA = See Also   UF = Used For

Church and state—*Continued*
>> Government and church
>> Religion and state
>> Separation of church and state
>> State and church
>> State church
> BT Church
>> State, The
> NT Christianity and politics
>> Religion in the public schools
> RT Ecclesiastical law
>> Popes—Temporal power

Church and state—United States   322
> UF United States—Church—Govern-
>> ment policy

Church antiquities
> USE Christian antiquities

Church, Apostolic
> USE Church history—30-600, Early
>> church

Church architecture   726.5
> UF Ecclesiastical architecture
>> Religious art
> BT Architecture
>> Christian art and symbolism
> NT Abbeys
>> Monasteries
>> Mosques
>> Spires
>> Temples
> RT Cathedrals
>> Christian antiquities
>> Church buildings
>> Gothic architecture

Church attendance
> USE Public worship

Church bells
> USE Bells

Church buildings (May subdiv. geog.)
> 726.5
> Use for general descriptive and historical materials on church buildings that cannot be entered under **Church architecture.**
> UF Churches *[Former heading]*
> SA names of individual churches,
>> e.g. **Westminster Abbey;** to
>> be added as needed
> BT Buildings
> NT Cathedrals
>> Westminster Abbey
> RT Church architecture

Church buildings—United States
> 726.50973
> UF Churches—United States *[For-
>> mer heading]*
>> United States—Church buildings

Church councils
> USE Councils and synods

Church denominations
> USE Christian sects
>> Sects

Church entertainments   253.7
> UF Church sociables
>> Socials
> BT Amusements
>> Church work

Church fathers
> USE Fathers of the church

Church festivals
> USE Religious holidays

Church finance   254; 262.0068
> UF Finance, Church
> BT Finance
> NT Tithes

Church furniture   247
> UF Ecclesiastical furniture
> BT Christian art and symbolism
>> Furniture

Church—Government policy
> USE Church and state

Church history   270
> Use for materials dealing with the development of Christianity and church organization.
> UF Christianity—History
>> Ecclesiastical history
>> History, Church
>> Religious history
> SA names of countries, states, etc.
>> with the subdivision *Church
>> history,* e.g. **United States—
>> Church history;** and names
>> of individual denominations,
>> sects, churches, etc. to be
>> added as needed
> BT History
> NT Christian missions
>> Christian sects
>> Christians—Persecutions
>> Councils and synods
>> Martyrs
>> Miracles—Christianity
>> Monasteries

BT = Broader Term   NT = Narrower Term   RT = Related Term   SA = See Also   UF = Used For

Church history—*Continued*
    Ohio—Church history
    Papacy
    Popes
    Protestant churches
    Protestantism
    Sects
    United States—Church history
Church history—30-600, Early church
    270.1
  UF   Apostolic Church
       Christianity—Origin
       Church, Apostolic
       Church history—30(ca.)-600,
          Early church *[Former head-
          ing]*
       Early church history
       Primitive Christianity
  NT   **Apostles**
       Gnosticism
  RT   **Catacombs**
       Early Christian literature
Church history—30(ca.)-600, Early church
  USE **Church history—30-600, Early
       church**
Church history—600-1500, Middle Ages
    270.3
  UF   Medieval church history
  BT   **Middle Ages**
  NT   **Crusades**
       Popes—Temporal power
Church history—1500- , Modern period
    270.6
  UF   Modern church history
  RT   **Counter-Reformation**
       Reformation
Church history—1517-1648, Reformation
  USE **Reformation**
Church history—Ohio
  USE **Ohio—Church history**
Church history—United States
  USE **United States—Church history**
Church law
  USE **Ecclesiastical law**
Church libraries   027.6
  UF   Libraries, Church
       Parish libraries
  BT   **Libraries**
Church music   781.71
  UF   Religious music

       Sacred music
  SA   types of church music, e.g.
       Hymns; to be added as need-
       ed
  BT   **Music**
  NT   **Carols**
       Chants (Plain, Gregorian, etc.)
       Choirs (Music)
       Choral music
       Gospel music
       Hymnals
       Hymns
       Oratorio
       Organ music
  RT   **Liturgies**
Church of Christ, Scientist
  USE **Christian Science**
Church of England (May subdiv. geog.)
    283
  UF   Anglican Church
       England, Church of
  BT   **Christian sects**
Church of England—United States   283
    Use for materials on the Episcopal Church
  in the United States prior to 1789. Materials
  on the Episcopal Church in the United States
  after 1789 are entered under **Episcopal
  Church.**
  UF   United States—Church of Eng-
       land
  RT   **Episcopal Church**
       Puritans
Church of Jesus Christ of Latter-day
    Saints   289.3
  UF   Latter-day Saints
       Mormon Church
  BT   **Christian sects**
  RT   **Mormons**
Church schools   371.07
    Use for materials on church supported and
  controlled elementary and secondary schools.
  Materials on the relation of the church to edu-
  cation and on the history of the part that the
  church has taken in secular education are en-
  tered under **Church and education.** Materials
  on the instruction of religion in schools and
  private life are entered under **Religious education,** and of Christian religion under **Christian education.**
  UF   Denominational schools
       Nonpublic schools
       Parochial schools
       Schools, Parochial
  BT   **Private schools**

BT = Broader Term   NT = Narrower Term   RT = Related Term   SA = See Also   UF = Used For

Church schools—*Continued*
        Schools
Church service books
  USE   **Liturgies**
Church settlements
  USE   **Social settlements**
Church sociables
  USE   **Church entertainments**
Church—Unity
  USE   **Christian unity**
Church work   253; 291
  SA   church work with particular
          groups of persons, e.g.
          Church work with the sick;
          to be added as needed
  BT   **Church**
  NT   **Christian missions**
          Church and race relations
          Church entertainments
          Church work with the sick
          Church work with youth
          Evangelistic work
          Lay ministry
          Ministry
          Pastoral psychology
          Rural churches
          Sunday schools
  RT   **Church and social problems**
          Pastoral theology
Church work, Rural
  USE   **Rural churches**
Church work with the sick   259;
        362.1023
  BT   **Church work**
          Sick
Church work with youth   259
  BT   **Church work**
          Youth
Church year   263
    Use for materials on the seasons of obser-
vance and Christian festivals with their cycles,
as making up the Christian or church year.
Works on the origins of Christian festivals
and fasts are entered under **Christian holiday.**
  UF   Christian year
          Ecclesiastical year
          Liturgical year
  SA   festival seasons and seasons of
          the church year, e.g. **Lent;** to
          be added as needed
  BT   **Calendars**
          Religious holidays

          Worship
  NT   **Christian holidays**
          Holy Week
          Lent
Churches
  USE   **Church buildings**
Churches, Avant-garde
  USE   **Noninstitutional churches**
Churches, Community
  USE   **Community churches**
Churches, Country
  USE   **Rural churches**
Churches, Noninstitutional
  USE   **Noninstitutional churches**
Churches, Rural
  USE   **Rural churches**
Churches, Undenominational
  USE   **Community churches**
Churches—United States
  USE   **Church buildings—United**
          States
Churchyards
  USE   **Cemeteries**
Cicadas   595.7; 632
  UF   17 year locusts
          Locusts, Seventeen-year
          Seventeen-year locusts
  BT   **Insects**
Cigarettes   679
  BT   **Smoking**
          Tobacco
Cigars   679
  BT   **Smoking**
          Tobacco
Cinema
  USE   **Motion pictures**
Cinematography   778.5
    Use for materials on the technical aspects
of making motion pictures and their projection
onto a screen. General materials on motion
pictures, including motion pictures as an art
form, are entered under **Motion pictures.**
  UF   Motion picture photography
          [Former heading]
          Photography—Motion pictures
  BT   **Photography**
  NT   **Animation (Cinematography)**
          Motion picture cameras
Cinesiology
  USE   **Kinesiology**

BT = Broader Term   NT = Narrower Term   RT = Related Term   SA = See Also   UF = Used For

Cipher and telegraph codes 384.1
- UF Cable codes
  - Codes, Telegraph
  - Morse code
  - Telegraph codes
- BT **Ciphers**
  - **Telegraph**

Ciphers 652
- UF Codes
  - Contractions
- BT **Signs and symbols**
- NT **Cipher and telegraph codes**
- RT **Abbreviations**
  - **Cryptography**
  - **Writing**

Ciphers (Lettering)
- USE **Monograms**

Circuits, Electric
- USE **Electric circuits**

Circulation of library materials
- USE **Library circulation**

Circulation of the blood
- USE **Blood—Circulation**

Circulatory system
- USE **Cardiovascular system**

Circumnavigation
- USE **Voyages around the world**

Circus 791.3
- BT **Amusements**
- NT **Acrobats and acrobatics**
  - **Clowns**
- RT **Carnivals**

CIS
- USE **Commonwealth of Independent States**

Cities and towns (May subdiv. geog.)
  307.76

  Use for general materials on cities and towns. For materials on large cities and their surrounding areas use **Metropolitan areas.** General materials on the government of cities are entered under **Municipal government.** General materials on local government other than that of cities are entered under **Local government.**

- UF Municipalities
  - Towns
  - Urban areas
- SA names of individual cities and towns, to be added as needed
- BT **Local government**
  - **Municipal government**

   Sociology
- NT **Capitals (Cities)**
  - **City life**
  - **Extinct cities**
  - **Inner cities**
  - **Markets**
  - **Municipal art**
  - **Parks**
  - **Streets**
  - **Urbanization**
  - **Villages**
- RT **Urban sociology**

Cities and towns—Civic improvement 307.3; 354.3
- UF Civic improvement
  - Municipal improvements
- NT **City planning**
  - **Community centers**

Cities and towns—Growth 307.76
- UF Cities and towns, Movement to
  - Urban development
- BT **Internal migration**
  - **Population**
- NT **Metropolitan areas**
  - **Suburbs**
- RT **Urbanization**

Cities and towns—Lighting
- USE **Streets—Lighting**

Cities and towns, Movement to
- USE **Cities and towns—Growth**
  - **Urbanization**

Cities and towns—Planning
- USE **City planning**

Cities and towns, ruined, extinct, etc.
- USE **Extinct cities**

Cities and towns—United States 307.760973; 973
- UF United States—Cities and towns

Cities, Imaginary
- USE **Geographical myths**

Citizen participation
- USE **Political participation**
  - and subjects designating government activity with the subdivision *Citizen participation,* e.g. **City planning—Citizen participation;** to be added as needed

Citizens band radio 384.5; 621.3845
- UF C.B. radio

Citizens band radio—*Continued*
- CB radio
- Citizens radio service
- BT **Shortwave radio**

Citizen's defender
- USE **Ombudsman**

Citizens radio service
- USE **Citizens band radio**

Citizenship 172; 323.6
- UF Civics
- Franchise
- Nationality (Citizenship)
- BT **Constitutional law**
- **Political ethics**
- **Political science**
- **Social ethics**
- NT **Patriotism**
- **Suffrage**
- RT **Aliens**
- **Naturalization**

Citrus
- USE **Citrus fruits**

Citrus fruit
- USE **Citrus fruits**

Citrus fruits 634
- UF Citrus
- Citrus fruit *[Former heading]*
- SA types of citrus fruits, e.g. **Lemon**; to be added as needed, in the singular form
- BT **Fruit**
- NT **Lemon**
- **Lime (Fruit)**
- **Orange (Fruit)**

City and town life
- USE **City life**

City-federal relations
- USE **Federal-city relations**

City government
- USE **Municipal government**

City life 307.76
- UF City and town life
- Town life
- Urban life
- BT **Cities and towns**
- **Urban sociology**
- RT **Community life**

City manager
- USE **Municipal government by city manager**

City planning (May subdiv. geog.)
307.1; 354.3; 711

Use for materials on the architectural and engineering aspects of urban redevelopment. Materials on the economic, sociological, and political aspects are entered under **Urban renewal.**
- UF Cities and towns—Planning
- Municipal planning
- Slum clearance
- Town planning
- Urban development
- Urban planning
- BT **Cities and towns—Civic improvement**
- **Planning**
- NT **Suburbs**
- **Zoning**
- RT **Community development**
- **Housing**
- **Municipal art**
- **Public works**
- **Regional planning**
- **Urban renewal**

City planning—Chicago (Ill.) 307.1; 354.3; 711
- UF Chicago (Ill.)—City planning

City planning—Citizen participation (May subdiv. geog.) 307.1
- BT **Political participation**
- **Social action**

City planning—United States 307.1; 354.3; 711
- UF United States—City planning

City planning—Zone system
- USE **Zoning**

City-state relations
- USE **State-local relations**

City traffic 388.4
- UF Local traffic
- Street traffic
- Traffic, City
- Urban traffic
- BT **Streets**
- **Traffic engineering**

City transit
- USE **Local transit**

Civic art
- USE **Municipal art**

BT = Broader Term   NT = Narrower Term   RT = Related Term   SA = See Also   UF = Used For

Civic improvement
USE   Cities and towns—Civic improvement
Civic involvement
USE   **Political participation**
       and subjects with the subdivision *Citizen participation,* e.g. **City planning—United States—Citizen participation;** to be added as needed
Civics
USE   **Citizenship**
       Political science
       United States—Politics and government

Civil defense (May subdiv. geog.) **363.3**
Use for materials on the protection of civilians from enemy attack. Materials on military defenses against air attack are entered under **Air defenses.**
UF   Civilian defense
SA   names of wars with the subdivision *Evacuation of civilians,* to be added as needed
BT   **Military art and science**
NT   **Air raid shelters**
       Rescue work
       Survival skills
       World War, 1939-1945—Evacuation of civilians

Civil defense—Chicago (Ill.) **363.3**
UF   Chicago (Ill.)—Civil defense
       [Former heading]

Civil defense—United States **363.3**
UF   United States—Civil defense
       [Former heading]

Civil disobedience
USE   **Passive resistance**
       Resistance to government

Civil disorders
USE   **Riots**

Civil engineering **624**
BT   **Engineering**
NT   **Aqueducts**
       Bridges
       Canals
       Dams
       Drainage
       Dredging
       Excavation
       Extraterrestrial bases

       Foundations
       Harbors
       Highway engineering
       Hydraulic engineering
       Irrigation
       Lunar bases
       Marine engineering
       Masonry
       Mechanical engineering
       Military engineering
       Mining engineering
       Public works
       Railroad engineering
       Reclamation of land
       Roads
       Streets
       Strength of materials
       Structural engineering
       Structural steel
       Surveying
       Tunnels
       Walls
       Water supply
       Water supply engineering

Civil government
USE   **Political science**
       United States—Politics and government

Civil law suits
USE   **Litigation**

Civil liberty
USE   **Freedom**

Civil rights (May subdiv. geog.) **323; 342**
Use for materials on citizens' rights as established by law or protected by a constitution. Materials on the rights of persons regardless of their legal, socioeconomic, or cultural status and as recognized by the international community are entered under **Human rights.**
UF   Basic rights
       Constitutional rights
       Fundamental rights
       Rights, Civil
SA   ethnic groups and classes of persons with the subdivision *Civil rights,* to be added as needed
BT   **Constitutional law**
       Human rights
       Political science

BT = Broader Term   NT = Narrower Term   RT = Related Term   SA = See Also   UF = Used For

Civil rights—*Continued*

NT   African Americans—Civil
rights
Anti-apartheid movement
Blacks—Civil rights
Children—Civil rights
Due process of law
Fair trial
Freedom of assembly
Freedom of association
Freedom of information
Freedom of movement
Freedom of religion
Freedom of speech
Freedom of the press
Right of privacy
Women's rights

RT   Civil rights demonstrations
Discrimination
Freedom

Civil rights demonstrations (May subdiv.
geog.)   322.4

UF   Demonstrations for civil rights
Freedom marches for civil rights
Marches for civil rights
Sit-ins for civil rights

BT   Demonstrations

RT   Civil rights

Civil rights (International law)

USE   Human rights

Civil servants

USE   Civil service

Civil service (May subdiv. geog.)   342;
351; 352.6

Use for general materials on the history and
development of public service. Materials on
public personnel administration, including the
duties of civil service employees, their salaries, pensions, etc., are entered under the
name of the country, state, city, or corporate
body with the subdivision *Officials and employees.*

UF   Administration
Civil servants
Employees and officials
Government employees
Government service
Officials and employees
Tenure of office

SA   names of countries, states, cities,
etc., and corporate bodies
with the subdivision *Officials*
and employees, e.g. **United
States—Officials and em-
ployees; Ohio—Officials and
employees; Chicago (Ill.)—
Officials and employees;
United Nations—Officials
and employees;** etc., to be
added as needed

BT   **Administrative law**
Political science
Public administration

NT   **Municipal officials and employees**

RT   **Bureaucracy**

Civil service—Examinations   351.076

BT   **Examinations**

Civil service—United States   351.73

UF   United States—Civil service

RT   **United States—Officials and
employees**

Civil War—England

USE   **Great Britain—History—1642-
1660, Civil War and Com-
monwealth**

Civil War—United States

USE   **United States—History—1861-
1865, Civil War**

Civilian defense

USE   **Civil defense**

Civilian evacuation

USE   **World War, 1939-1945—Evacuation of civilians**

Civilization   306; 909

Use for materials on civilization in general
and on the development of social customs, art,
industry, religion, etc., of several countries or
peoples.

SA   names of continents, regions,
countries, states, etc., with the
subdivision *Civilization,* e.g.
United States—Civilization;
and the civilizations of peoples not confined to a single
place, e.g. **Arab civilization;**
Western civilization; etc., to
be added as needed

NT   **Acculturation**
Aeronautics and civilization
Africa—Civilization
America—Civilization
Ancient civilization

Civilization—*Continued*
> Arab civilization
> Archeology
> Asia—Civilization
> Astronautics and civilization
> Biculturalism
> Christian civilization
> Computers and civilization
> Education
> Inventions
> Jewish civilization
> Learning and scholarship
> Manners and customs
> Medieval civilization
> Modern civilization
> Ohio—Civilization
> Popular culture
> Primitive societies
> Progress
> Religions
> Science and civilization
> Social sciences
> Technology and civilization
> United States—Civilization
> War and civilization
> Western civilization

RT   Anthropology
> Culture
> Ethnology
> History
> Sociology

Civilization, African
USE   Africa—Civilization
Civilization, American
USE   America—Civilization
Civilization, Ancient
USE   Ancient civilization
Civilization and aeronautics
USE   Aeronautics and civilization
Civilization and astronautics
USE   Astronautics and civilization
Civilization and computers
USE   Computers and civilization
Civilization and science
USE   Science and civilization
Civilization and technology
USE   Technology and civilization
Civilization and war
USE   War and civilization

Civilization, Arab
USE   Arab civilization
Civilization, Asian
USE   Asia—Civilization
Civilization, Christian
USE   Christian civilization
Civilization, Classical
USE   Classical civilization
Civilization, Greek
USE   Greece—Civilization
Civilization, Jewish
USE   Jewish civilization
Civilization, Medieval
USE   Medieval civilization
Civilization, Modern
USE   Modern civilization
Civilization, Occidental
USE   Western civilization
Civilization, Oriental
USE   Asia—Civilization
Civilization, Western
USE   Western civilization
Claims
USE   ethnic groups, places, and wars
> with the subdivision *Claims*,
> e.g. **Indians of North America—Claims;** to be added as
> needed

Clairvoyance   133.8
BT   Extrasensory perception
> Occultism
> Parapsychology
> Spiritualism
RT   Divination
> Fortune telling
> Telepathy
Clans (May subdiv. geog.)   306.85;
> 941.1
SA   names of clans or of families, to
> be added as needed
BT   Family
NT   Tartans
RT   Kinship
Clans—Scotland   941.1
UF   Highland clans
> Scottish clans
Class conflict
USE   Social conflict
Class consciousness   305.5
BT   Social classes

Class consciousness—*Continued*
>> Social psychology
RT   **Marxism**
Class distinction
>> USE   **Social classes**
Class struggle
>> USE   **Social conflict**
Classed catalogs
>> USE   **Classified catalogs**
Classes (Mathematics)
>> USE   **Set theory**
Classes of persons
>> USE   **Persons**
>> and classes of persons, e.g. **Elderly; Handicapped; Explorers; Drug addicts;** etc., to be added as needed

Classical antiquities   937; 938
>> UF   Antiquities, Classical
>> Archeology, Classical
>> Classical archeology
>> Greek antiquities
>> Roman antiquities
>> SA   names of extinct cities of Greek and Roman antiquity e.g. **Delphi (Extinct city);** and names of groups of people extant in modern times and names of cities (except extinct cities), countries, regions, etc., with the subdivision *Antiquities,* to be added as needed
>> BT   **Ancient art**
>> **Antiquities**
>> NT   **Greece—Antiquities**
>> **Greek art**
>> **Roman art**
>> **Rome—Antiquities**
>> **Rome (Italy)—Antiquities**

Classical antiquities—Dictionaries
>> USE   **Classical dictionaries**
Classical archeology
>> USE   **Classical antiquities**
Classical art
>> USE   **Greek art**
>> **Roman art**
Classical biography
>> USE   **Greece—Biography**
>> **Rome—Biography**

Classical civilization (May subdiv. geog.)
>> **937**
>> Use for materials on both ancient Greek and Roman civilizations. Materials on the spread of Greek civilization throughout the ancient world following the conquests of Alexander the Great are entered under **Hellenism.**
>> UF   Civilization, Classical
>> BT   **Ancient civilization**
>> NT   **Greece—Civilization**
>> **Rome—Civilization**
>> RT   **Classicism**

Classical dictionaries   937.003; 938.003
>> UF   Classical antiquities—Dictionaries
>> Dictionaries, Classical
>> BT   **Ancient history**
>> **Encyclopedias and dictionaries**

Classical education   370.11
>> UF   Education, Classical
>> BT   **Education**
>> RT   **Humanism**
>> **Humanities**

Classical geography
>> USE   **Ancient geography**
>> **Greece—Historical geography**
>> **Rome—Geography**
Classical languages
>> USE   **Greek language**
>> **Latin language**

Classical literature   870; 880
>> UF   Literature, Classical
>> BT   **Literature**
>> RT   **Greek literature**
>> **Latin literature**

Classical music
>> USE   **Music**

Classical mythology   292.1
>> UF   Greek mythology
>> Mythology, Classical *[Former heading]*
>> Roman mythology
>> BT   **Mythology**

Classicism   709; 809
>> BT   **Aesthetics**
>> **Literature**
>> RT   **Classical civilization**

Classification   001
>> Use for materials on the organization of knowledge into a systematic arrangement of topics or categories. Materials on library classification are entered under the type of materi-

---

BT = Broader Term   **NT** = Narrower Term   **RT** = Related Term   **SA** = See Also   **UF** = Used For

Classification—*Continued*

als classified with the subdivision *Classifica-tion*, e.g. **Books—Classification**; which may be further subdivided by subject or discipline as needed.

UF   Classification of knowledge

SA   subjects with the subdivision *Classification*, e.g. **Botany—Classification**; to be added as needed

NT   **Books—Classification**
        Botany—Classification

Classification—Books
USE   **Books—Classification**

Classification—Botany
USE   **Botany—Classification**

Classification, Dewey Decimal
USE   **Dewey Decimal Classification**

Classification of knowledge
USE   **Classification**

Classification—Plants
USE   **Botany—Classification**

Classified catalogs   017; 025.3
UF   Catalogs, Classified *[Former heading]*
        Catalogs, Systematic
        Classed catalogs
BT   **Library catalogs**
RT   **Books—Classification**

Classroom management   371.102
BT   **School discipline**
        Teaching

Clay   553.6; 666; 738.1
BT   **Ceramics**
        Soils
NT   **Modeling**

Clay industries   338.4; 666
BT   **Ceramic industries**
NT   **Bricks**
        Pottery
        Tiles

Clay modeling
USE   **Modeling**

Cleaning   648; 667
BT   **Sanitation**
NT   **Bleaching**
        Cleaning compounds
        Dry cleaning
        House cleaning
        Laundry
        Street cleaning

Cleaning compounds   648; 667
BT   **Cleaning**
NT   **Detergents**
        Soap

Cleanliness   391.6; 613; 646.7
UF   Messiness
        Neatness
BT   **Hygiene**
        Sanitation
NT   **Baths**

Clearing of land
USE   **Reclamation of land**

Clearinghouses, Information
USE   **Information services**

Clergy   200.92; 270.092
UF   Curates
        Ministers of the gospel
        Pastors
        Preachers
        Rectors
SA   church denominations with the subdivision *Clergy*, e.g. **Catholic Church—Clergy**; to be added as needed
BT   **Church**
NT   **Catholic Church—Clergy**
        Celibacy
        Chaplains
        Priests
        Rabbis
        Women clergy
RT   **Ministry**
        Ordination
        Pastoral theology

Clergy—Office
USE   **Ministry**

Clergy—Political activity   261.7; 291.1
BT   **Political participation**

Clerical celibacy
USE   **Celibacy**

Clerical employees
USE   **Office workers**

Clerical psychology
USE   **Pastoral psychology**

Clerical work—Training
USE   **Business education**

Clerks
USE   **Office workers**

Clerks (Retail trade)
USE   **Sales personnel**

BT = Broader Term   NT = Narrower Term   RT = Related Term   SA = See Also   UF = Used For

Cliff dwellers and cliff dwellings 979
> BT Archeology
>   Indians of North America

Climacteric, Female
> USE Menopause

Climacteric, Male
> USE Male climacteric

Climate 551.6
> Use for materials on climate as it relates to humans and to plant and animal life, including the effects of changes of climate. Materials limited to the climate of a particular region are entered under the name of the place with the subdivision *Climate*. Materials on the state of the atmosphere at a given time and place with respect to heat or cold, wetness or dryness, calm or storm, are entered under **Weather.** Scientific materials on the atmosphere, especially weather factors, are entered under **Meteorology.**
> UF Climatology
> SA names of countries, cities, etc.,
>   with the subdivision *Climate*,
>   to be added as needed
> BT Earth sciences
> NT Chicago (Ill.)—Climate
>   Forest influences
>   Greenhouse effect
>   Ohio—Climate
>   Seasons
>   United States—Climate
> RT Meteorology
>   Weather

Climate and forests
> USE Forest influences

Climatology
> USE Climate

Climbing plants 582.1; 635.9
> UF Vines
> BT Gardening
>   Plants

Clinical chemistry 616.07
> Use for materials on the chemical diagnosis of disease and health monitoring.
> UF Chemistry, Diagnostic
>   Chemistry, Medical
>   Diagnostic chemistry
>   Medical chemistry
> BT Biochemistry
>   Diagnosis

Clinical drug trials
> USE Drugs—Testing

Clinical genetics
> USE Medical genetics

Clinical magnetic resonance imaging
> USE Magnetic resonance imaging

Clinical trials of drugs
> USE Drugs—Testing

Clinics
> USE Medical practice

Clip art 741.6
> Use for materials on clipping art work from published sources to use in creating documents, posters, newsletters, etc. Materials on the use of photocopying machines to create original works of art are entered under **Copy art.**
> BT Graphic arts

Clipper ships 387.2; 623.8
> BT Ships

Clippings (Books, newspapers, etc.)
>   025.17
> UF Newspaper clippings
>   Press clippings
> BT Newspapers

Clocks and watches 681.1; 739.3
> UF Horology
>   Watches
> BT Time
> NT Sundials

Clog dancing 793.3
> UF Clog-dancing
>   Clogging (Dance)
> BT Dance

Clog-dancing
> USE Clog dancing

Clogging (Dance)
> USE Clog dancing

Cloisters
> USE Convents
>   Monasteries

Clones and cloning
> USE Cloning

Cloning 174; 576.5; 660.6
> UF Clones and cloning *[Former heading]*
> BT Genetic engineering
> NT Molecular cloning

Cloning, Molecular
> USE Molecular cloning

Closed caption television 384.55
> BT Deaf
>   Television

Closed caption video recordings 384.55
> UF Video recordings, Closed caption

BT = Broader Term   NT = Narrower Term   RT = Related Term   SA = See Also   UF = Used For

Closed caption video recordings—*Continued*

    Video recordings for the hearing impaired

BT   **Deaf**

        Videodiscs

        Videotapes

Closed-circuit television   384.55

UF   Television, Closed-circuit

BT   **Intercommunication systems**

        Microwave communication systems

        Television

Closed shop

USE   **Open and closed shop**

Cloth

USE   **Fabrics**

Clothes

USE   **Clothing and dress**

Clothiers

USE   **Clothing industry**

Clothing and dress   646

    Use for materials on clothing from a practical standpoint including the art of dress. Descriptive and historical materials on the costume of various countries, peoples, or historical periods and materials on fancy dress and theatrical costumes are entered under **Costume.** Materials on the prevailing mode or style of dress are entered under **Fashion.**

UF   Clothes

        Dress

        Garments

SA   types of clothing articles and accessories, to be added as needed

BT   **Manners and customs**

NT   **Buttons**

        Children's clothing

        Clothing industry

        Dress accessories

        Dressmaking

        Fashion

        Hats

        Hosiery

        Infants—Clothing

        Leather garments

        Men's clothing

        Shoes

        Tailoring

        Women's clothing

RT   **Costume**

        Personal appearance

        Personal grooming

Clothing and dress—Dry cleaning

USE   **Dry cleaning**

Clothing and dress—Repairing   646.2

UF   Mending

Clothing industry   338.4; 687

UF   Clothiers

        Clothing trade *[Former heading]*

        Fashion industry

        Garment industry

BT   **Clothing and dress**

        Industries

NT   **Fashion design**

        Fashion models

        Shoe industry

        Tailoring

Clothing, Leather

USE   **Leather garments**

Clothing, Men's

USE   **Men's clothing**

Clothing trade

USE   **Clothing industry**

Cloud seeding

USE   **Weather control**

Clouds   551.57

BT   **Atmosphere**

        Meteorology

Clowns   791.3; 791.3092; 920

BT   **Circus**

        Entertainers

Clubs   367

BT   **Associations**

NT   **Boys' clubs**

        Girls' clubs

        Men—Societies

        Scouts and scouting

        Women—Societies

RT   **Societies**

Co-dependence

USE   **Codependency**

Co-dependency

USE   **Codependency**

Co-ops

USE   **Cooperative societies**

Co-parenting

USE   **Part-time parenting**

Coaching

USE   **Coaching (Athletics)**

        Horsemanship

BT = Broader Term   NT = Narrower Term   RT = Related Term   SA = See Also   UF = Used For

Coaching (Athletics)   796.07
    UF   Athletic coaching
          Coaching
          Sports coaching
    SA   types of sports with the subdivi-
          sion *Coaching*, to be added as
          needed
    BT   **Athletics**
          Physical education
          Sports
    NT   **Football—Coaching**
Coal   553.2
    BT   **Fuel**
    NT   **Coal gasification**
          Coal liquefaction
          Coal mines and mining
Coal gas
    USE **Gas**
Coal gasification   665.7
    UF   Gasification of coal
    BT   **Coal**
Coal liquefaction   622
    UF   Liquefaction of coal
    BT   **Coal**
Coal miners   622; 920
    BT   **Miners**
Coal mines and mining   622
    BT   **Coal**
          Mines and mineral resources
    NT   **Mining engineering**
Coal oil
    USE **Petroleum**
Coal tar products   547; 661
    BT   **Petroleum**
    RT   **Gas**
          Oils and fats
COAs
    USE **Children of alcoholics**
Coast pilot guides
    USE **Pilot guides**
Coastal landforms
    USE **Coasts**
Coastal signals
    USE **Signals and signaling**
Coasts (May subdiv. geog.)   **551.45**
    UF   Coastal landforms
    BT   **Landforms**
    RT   **Seashore**
Coats of arms
    USE **Heraldry**

Cocaine   362.29; 615
    BT   **Narcotics**
    NT   **Crack (Drug)**
Cocaine babies
    USE **Children of drug addicts**
Cocoa   633.7; 641.3
    BT   **Beverages**
    RT   **Chocolate**
Cocoons
    USE **Butterflies**
          Caterpillars
          Moths
          Silkworms
Code deciphering
    USE **Cryptography**
Code enciphering
    USE **Cryptography**
Code names   423
    BT   **Abbreviations**
          Names
    NT   **Acronyms**
Codependency   616.86
    UF   Co-dependence
          Co-dependency
          Codependent behavior
    BT   **Abnormal psychology**
Codependent behavior
    USE **Codependency**
Codes
    USE **Ciphers**
Codes, Penal
    USE **Criminal law**
Codes, Telegraph
    USE **Cipher and telegraph codes**
Coeducation   371.822
    BT   **Education**
    RT   **Girls—Education**
          Men—Education
          Women—Education
Coexistence
    USE **International relations**
Coffee   633.7; 641.8
    BT   **Beverages**
Coffee houses
    USE **Coffeehouses**
Coffee shops
    USE **Restaurants**
Coffeehouses   647.95
    Use for materials on public places that
serve coffee and sometimes provide informal

BT = Broader Term   NT = Narrower Term   RT = Related Term   SA = See Also   UF = Used For

Coffeehouses—*Continued*
entertainment or serve as a place where small groups meet. Materials on coffee shops, that is, small inexpensive restaurants, are entered under **Restaurants.**

    UF   Coffee houses *[Former heading]*

    BT   **Restaurants**

Cog wheels

    USE   **Gearing**

Cognition

    USE   **Theory of knowledge**

Cohabitation

    USE   **Unmarried couples**

Coiffure

    USE   **Hair**

Coin collecting

    USE   **Coins—Collectors and collecting**

Coinage   332.4
Use for materials on the processing and history of metal money. Lists of coins and general materials about coins are entered under **Coins.**

    BT   **Money**

    NT   **Counterfeits and counterfeiting**

    RT   **Gold**

            Mints

            Silver

Coinage of words

    USE   **New words**

Coins   737.4
Use for lists of coins and general materials about coins. Materials on coins from the point of view of art and archeology are entered under **Numismatics.** Materials on the processing of metal money are entered under **Coinage.**

    UF   Specie

    BT   **Money**

Coins—Collectors and collecting   737.4

    UF   Coin collecting

    RT   **Numismatics**

Cold   536; 551.5

    NT   **Cryobiology**

            Ice

    RT   **Low temperatures**

            Temperature

Cold (Disease)   616.2

    UF   Common cold

    BT   **Communicable diseases**

            Diseases

    NT   **Influenza**

Cold—Physiological effect   613

    BT   **Cryobiology**

Cold storage   641.4; 664

    BT   **Food—Preservation**

            Meat industry

    NT   **Compressed air**

    RT   **Refrigeration**

Cold—Therapeutic use   615.8

    UF   Cryotherapy

    BT   **Therapeutics**

    NT   **Cryosurgery**

Cold war   909.82
Use for materials on the rivalry between capitalist and communist nations following World War II.

    UF   Power politics

    BT   **World politics—1945-1991**

Collaborationists

    USE   **Treason**

Collage   702.8; 751.4

    BT   **Art**

            Handicraft

Collapse of structures

    USE   **Structural failures**

Collected papers (Anthologies)

    USE   **Anthologies**

Collected works

    USE   **Anthologies**

            Literature—Collections

            Storytelling—Collections

            and form headings that represent collections of works of several authors, e.g. **American essays; Essays; Parodies; Short stories;** etc.; and names of literatures and literary forms with the subdivision *Collections,* e.g. **English literature—Collections; Poetry—Collections;** etc., to be added as needed

Collectibles

    USE   subjects, classes of persons, ethnic groups, events, titles of works, and names of individual persons, corporate bodies, and fictitious and legendary characters with the subdivision *Collectibles,* e.g. **American Revolution Bicentennial, 1776-1976—Collectibles;** and types of objects

---

BT = Broader Term   NT = Narrower Term   RT = Related Term   SA = See Also   UF = Used For

Collectibles—*Continued*
collected, excluding antiquities
and natural objects, with the
subdivision *Collectors and
collecting*, e.g. **Boxes—Collectors and collecting;** to be
added as needed
Collecting
USE **Collectors and collecting**
Collecting of accounts   658.8
UF   Accounts, Collecting of
BT   **Commercial law**
Credit
Debt
Debtor and creditor
Collection and preservation
USE   antiquities and types of natural
objects, including animal
specimens and plant specimens, with the subdivision
Collection and preservation,
e.g. **Birds—Collection and
preservation;** for materials on
methods of collecting and
preserving those objects, to be
added as needed
Collection development (Libraries)
USE   **Libraries—Collection development**
Collections (Anthologies)
USE   **Anthologies**
Collections of art, painting, etc.
USE   **Art collections**
Art museums
Collections of literature
USE   **Anthologies**
Literature—Collections
Storytelling—Collections
and form headings that represent collections of works of
several authors, e.g.
**American essays; Essays;
Parodies; Short stories;** etc.;
and names of literatures and
literary forms with the subdivision *Collections*, e.g. **English literature—Collections;
Poetry—Collections;** etc., to
be added as needed

Collections of natural specimens
USE   **Plants—Collection and preservation**
Zoological specimens—Collection and preservation
and names of natural specimens
with the subdivision *Collection and preservation*, e.g.
Birds—Collection and preservation; to be added as
needed
Collections of objects
USE   **Collectors and collecting**
and names of events with the
subdivision *Collectibles*, e.g.
American Revolution Bicentennial, 1776-1976—Collectibles; and types of objects
collected, excluding antiquities
and natural objects, with the
subdivision *Collectors and
collecting*, e.g. **Boxes—Collectors and collecting;** to be
added as needed
Collective bargaining   331.89; 658.3
May be subdivided by groups of professional or nonprofessional workers, e.g. **Collective bargaining—Librarians.**
UF   Labor negotiations
BT   **Industrial relations**
Labor
Labor disputes
Negotiation
RT   **Industrial arbitration**
Labor contract
Labor unions
Participative management
Strikes
**Collective bargaining—Librarians
331.89**
UF   Librarians—Collective bargaining
Libraries—Collective bargaining
Collective farms
USE   **Collective settlements**
Cooperative agriculture
Collective labor agreements
USE   **Labor contract**
Collective security
USE   **International security**

BT = Broader Term   NT = Narrower Term   RT = Related Term   SA = See Also   UF = Used For

Collective settings (May subdiv. geog.)
  307.77; 335

  Use for materials on traditional, formally organized communal ventures, usually based on ideological, political, or religious affiliation. Materials on arrangements in voluntary cooperative living, usually informal, are entered under **Communal living.**

  UF Collective farms
      Communal settlements
      Communes
      Cooperative living
  SA names of individual collective
      settlements, to be added as
      needed
  BT **Communism**
      Cooperation
      Socialism
  RT **Communal living**
      Cooperative agriculture
      Counter culture
      Utopias

Collective settlements—Israel   307.77
  UF Israel—Collective settlements
      Kibbutz

Collective settlements—United States
  307.77
  UF United States—Collective settlements

Collectivism
  USE **Communism**
       Socialism

Collectors and collecting   790.1
  UF Collecting
      Collections of objects
  SA types of collecting, e.g. **Book**
      collecting; types of objects
      collected, excluding antiquities
      and natural objects, with the
      subdivision *Collectors and*
      collecting, e.g. **Postcards—**
      Collectors and collecting;
      names of original owners of
      private art collections with the
      subdivision *Art collections;*
      names of events with the subdivision *Collectibles,* e.g.
      American Revolution Bicentennial, 1776-1976—Collectibles; and antiquities and
      types of natural objects with

      the subdivision *Collection and*
      preservation, e.g. **Birds—Collection and preservation;** to
      be added as needed
  BT **Antiques**
      Art
      Hobbies
  NT **American Revolution Bicentennial, 1776-1976—Collectibles**
      Americana
      Antiquities—Collection and
      preservation
      Book collecting
      Boxes—Collectors and collecting
      Plants—Collection and preservation
      Stamp collecting
      Zoological specimens—Collection and preservation
  RT **Art collections**

Collects
  USE **Prayers**

College admissions essays
  USE **College applications**

College and school drama   371.8; 792

  Use for materials about college and school drama. Collections of plays for production in colleges and schools are entered under **College and school drama—Collections.**

  UF College drama
      School drama
      Theatricals, College
  BT **Amateur theater**
      Drama
      Student activities
  RT **Drama in education**

College and school drama—Collections
  808.82; 812.008, etc.
  UF College plays
      Plays, College
      School plays

College and school journalism   371.8
  UF College journalism
      College periodicals
      School journalism
      School newspapers
  BT **Journalism**
      Student activities
  RT **Children's writings**

BT = Broader Term   NT = Narrower Term   RT = Related Term   SA = See Also   UF = Used For

College and university libraries
    USE   **Academic libraries**
College applications   378.1
    UF   Admissions applications
            Admissions essays
            Applications for college
            College admissions essays
            Colleges and universities—Appli-
                cations
    RT   **Colleges and universities—En-
            trance requirements**
College athletics
    USE   **College sports**
College choice   378
    UF   Choice of college
            Colleges and universities—Selec-
                tion
    BT   **Colleges and universities**
            School choice
College costs   378.3
    UF   Tuition
    BT   **Colleges and universities—Fi-
            nance**
    NT   **Student aid**
            Student loan funds
College degrees
    USE   **Academic degrees**
College drama
    USE   **College and school drama**
College dropouts
    USE   **Dropouts**
College entrance examinations
    USE   **Colleges and universities—En-
            trance examinations**
College entrance requirements
    USE   **Colleges and universities—En-
            trance requirements**
College fraternities
    USE   **Fraternities and sororities**
College graduates   305.5; 378
    UF   Graduates, College
            University graduates
    BT   **Professions**
    RT   **College students**
College journalism
    USE   **College and school journalism**
College life
    USE   **College students**
College periodicals
    USE   **College and school journalism**

College plays
    USE   **College and school drama—
            Collections**
College songs
    USE   **Students' songs**
College sororities
    USE   **Fraternities and sororities**
College sports   371.8; 796
    UF   College athletics
            Intercollegiate athletics
            Varsity sports
    SA   types of sports, to be added as
                needed
    BT   **Sports**
            Student activities
    RT   **School sports**
College students   371.8; 378
    UF   College life
            Colleges and universities—Stu-
                dents
            Undergraduates
            University students
    BT   **Students**
    RT   **College graduates**
College students, Foreign
    USE   **Foreign students**
**College students—Political activity
            371.8; 378**
    UF   Campus disorders
    BT   **Political participation**
**College students—Sexual behavior
            371.8; 378**
    BT   **Sexual behavior**
College teachers
    USE   **Colleges and universities—Fac-
            ulty**
            Educators
            Teachers
College yearbooks
    USE   **School yearbooks**
Colleges and universities (May subdiv.
        geog.)   **378**
    UF   Universities
            Universities and colleges
    SA   types of colleges and universi-
                ties, e.g. **Catholic colleges
                and universities;** and names
                of individual colleges and
                universities, to be added as
                needed

BT = Broader Term   NT = Narrower Term   RT = Related Term   SA = See Also   UF = Used For

Colleges and universities—*Continued*
  BT Education
      Higher education
      Professional education
      Schools
  NT Academic degrees
      Catholic colleges and universities
      College choice
      Commencements
      Dissertations
      Fraternities and sororities
      Free universities
      Junior colleges
      Law schools
      Medical colleges
      Teachers colleges
      United States Military Academy
      University extension
Colleges and universities—Accreditation
      378; 379.1
Colleges and universities—Applications
  USE College applications
Colleges and universities—Buildings
      727
  UF Buildings, College
  BT Buildings
Colleges and universities—Curricula
      378.1
  UF Core curriculum
  SA types of education and schools
      with the subdivision *Curricula,* e.g. Library education—Curricula; to be added as needed
  BT Education—Curricula
Colleges and universities—Entrance examinations   378.1
  UF College entrance examinations
      Entrance examinations for colleges
  BT Educational tests and measurements
      Examinations
  NT Graduate Record Examination
      Scholastic Aptitude Test
Colleges and universities—Entrance requirements   378.1
  UF College entrance requirements

      Entrance requirements for colleges and universities
  SA names of individual colleges and universities with the subdivision *Entrance requirements,* to be added as needed
  BT Examinations
  RT College applications
Colleges and universities—Faculty
      378.1
  UF College teachers
      Faculty (Education)
  BT Teachers
Colleges and universities—Faculty—Pensions   331.25
Colleges and universities—Finance
      378.1
  UF Tuition
  BT Finance
  NT College costs
  RT Federal aid to education
Colleges and universities—Insignia
      378.2
  BT Insignia
Colleges and universities, Nonformal
  USE Free universities
Colleges and universities—Selection
  USE College choice
Colleges and universities—Students
  USE College students
Colleges and universities—United States
      378.73
  UF American colleges
      United States—Colleges and universities
      United States—Universities
Colleges, Business
  USE Business schools
Collies   636.737
  BT Dogs
Collisions, Railroad
  USE Railroad accidents
Colloids   541.3
  BT Physical chemistry
Colonial architecture   724
  UF Architecture, Colonial *[Former heading]*
  BT Architecture
  RT Historic buildings—United States

BT = Broader Term   NT = Narrower Term   RT = Related Term   SA = See Also   UF = Used For

Colonial history (U.S.)
USE   United States—History—1600-
          1775, Colonial period
Colonialism
USE   Colonies
        Imperialism
Colonies   321; 325

Use for materials on general colonial policy. Materials on the policy of settling immigrants or nationals abroad are entered under
Colonization. Materials on migration from
one country to another are entered under **Immigration and emigration.** Materials on the
movement of population within a country for
permanent settlement are entered under **Internal migration.**

UF   Colonialism
       Dependencies
SA   names of countries with the sub-
       divisions *Colonies,* or *Territo-
       ries and possessions,* e.g.
       **Great Britain—Colonies;
       United States—Territories
       and possessions;** etc., to be
       added as needed
BT   **Imperialism**
NT   **Great Britain—Colonies
       Land settlement
       Penal colonies**
RT   **Colonization**
Colonies, Space
USE   Space colonies
Colonization   325

Use for materials on the policy of settling
immigrants or nationals abroad. Materials on
general colonial policy are entered under **Colonies.** Materials on migration from one country to another are entered under **Immigration
and emigration.** Materials on the movement
of population within a country for permanent
settlement are entered under **Internal migration.**

SA   names of countries with the sub-
       division *Immigration and emi-
       gration,* to be added as need-
       ed
BT   **Imperialism
       Land settlement**
NT   **Internal migration
       Public lands
       United States—Immigration
       and emigration**
RT   **Colonies
       Immigration and emigration**

Color   535.6; 701; 752
UF   Colour
SA   subjects with the subdivision
       Color, and names of specific
       colors, to be added as needed
BT   **Aesthetics
       Chemistry
       Light
       Optics
       Painting
       Photometry**
NT   **Animals—Color
       Birds—Color
       Dyes and dyeing
       Red**
RT   **Pigments**
Color blindness   617.7
BT   **Color sense
       Vision disorders**
Color etchings
USE   Color prints
Color photography   778.6
UF   Color slides
       Photography, Color
BT   **Photography**
Color printing   686.2

Use for materials on practical printing in
color. Materials on hand-colored prints or on
pictures printed in color are entered under
Color prints.

SA   types of color printing processes,
       to be added as needed
BT   **Printing**
NT   **Illustration of books
       Lithography
       Silk screen printing**
RT   **Color prints**
Color prints   769

Use for materials on hand-colored prints or
on pictures printed in color. Materials on
practical printing in color are entered under
Color printing.

UF   Block printing
       Color etchings
       Painting—Color reproductions
SA   color prints of particular coun-
       tries, e.g. **American color
       prints;** to be added as needed
BT   **Prints**
NT   **American color prints
       Japanese color prints**
RT   **Color printing**

BT = Broader Term   NT = Narrower Term   RT = Related Term   SA = See Also   UF = Used For

Color prints, American
   USE   **American color prints**
Color prints, Japanese
   USE   **Japanese color prints**
Color—Psychological aspects   152.14
   UF   Psychology of color
   BT   **Color sense**
         Psychology
Color sense   152.14
   BT   **Psychophysiology**
         Senses and sensation
         Vision
   NT   **Color blindness**
         Color—Psychological aspects
Color slides
   USE   **Color photography**
         Slides (Photography)
Color television   621.388
   UF   Television, Color
   BT   **Television**
Colorado River—Hoover Dam
   USE   **Hoover Dam (Ariz. and Nev.)**
Coloring books   372.5
   UF   Painting books
   BT   **Picture books for children**
Colour
   USE   **Color**
Columnists
   USE   **Journalists**
COM catalogs
   USE   **Library catalogs on microfilm**
Combinations in restraint of trade
   USE   **Restraint of trade**
Combinations, Industrial
   USE   **Industrial trusts**
Combustion   541.3; 621.402
   BT   **Chemistry**
   NT   **Fuel**
   RT   **Fire**
         Heat
Comedians   791; 792.2; 920
   BT   **Actors**
         Entertainers
   NT   **Fools and jesters**
Comedies   808.82; 812, etc.
   May be used for individual works or for collections. Materials about comedy as a literary form are entered under **Comedy.**
   UF   Comic drama
         Comic plays
         Humorous plays

         Slapstick comedies
   BT   **Drama**
         Wit and humor
   NT   **Comedy films**
         Comedy television programs
         Farces
Comedy   792.2; 809.2
   Use for materials on comedy as a literary form. Individual works and collections of comedies are entered under **Comedies.**
   UF   Comic drama
         Comic literature
   BT   **Drama**
         Wit and humor
Comedy films   791.43
   May be used for individual works, collections, or materials about comedy films.
   UF   Comic films
         Humorous films
         Slapstick comedies
   SA   types of comedy films, e.g.
         Three Stooges films; to be added as needed
   BT   **Comedies**
         Motion pictures
   NT   **Three Stooges films**
   RT   **Comedy television programs**
Comedy radio programs   791.44
   May be used for individual works, collections, or materials about comedy radio programs.
   UF   Radio comedies
         Radio comedy programs
   BT   **Radio programs**
Comedy television programs   791.45
   May be used for individual works, collections, or materials about television comedies.
   UF   Comic television programs
         Sitcoms
         Situation comedies
         Slapstick comedies
         Television comedies
         Television comedy programs
   BT   **Comedies**
         Television programs
   RT   **Comedy films**
Comets   523.6
   BT   **Astronomy**
         Solar system
   NT   **Halley's comet**

BT = Broader Term   NT = Narrower Term   RT = Related Term   SA = See Also   UF = Used For

Comic books, strips, etc.   741.5

> May be used for individual works, collections, or materials about printed comic strips, i.e. groups of cartoons in narrative sequence, and books and magazines consisting of comic strips, etc.

UF   Comic strips

        Funnies

        Humorous pictures

SA   ethnic groups, classes of persons, corporate bodies, individual persons, literary authors, or sacred works with the subdivision *Comic books, strips, etc.;* and names of comic books, comic strips, and comic strip characters, to be added as needed

BT   **Wit and humor**

NT   **Mystery comic books, strips, etc.**

       Science fiction comic books, strips, etc.

       Superhero comic books, strips, etc.

       Western comic books, strips, etc.

RT   **Cartoons and caricatures**

       Chapbooks

Comic drama

USE **Comedies**

       Comedy

Comic epic literature

USE **Mock-heroic literature**

Comic films

USE **Comedy films**

Comic literature

USE **Comedy**

       Parody

       Satire

Comic novels

USE **Humorous fiction**

Comic opera

USE **Opera**

       Operetta

Comic plays

USE **Comedies**

Comic strips

USE **Comic books, strips, etc.**

Comic television programs

USE **Comedy television programs**

Comic verse

USE **Humorous poetry**

Coming of age stories

USE **Bildungsromans**

Commandments, Ten

USE **Ten commandments**

Commencements   394.2

UF   Graduation

BT   **Colleges and universities**

       High schools

       School assembly programs

Commentaries, Biblical

USE **Bible—Commentaries**

Commerce   380.1

> Use for general materials on foreign and domestic commerce. Materials limited to commerce between states are entered under **Interstate commerce.**

UF   Distribution (Economics)

        Trade

SA   names of countries, cities, etc., with the subdivision *Commerce,* e.g. **United States—Commerce;** and names of articles of commerce, e.g. **Cotton;** to be added as needed

BT   **Economics**

       Finance

NT   **Balance of trade**

       Banks and banking

       Barter

       Black market

       Boycotts

       Business

       Chambers of commerce

       Chicago (Ill.)—Commerce

       Commercial geography

       Commercial products

       Competition

       Contracts

       Cooperation

       Developing countries—Commerce

       Exchange

       Grocery trade

       Industrial trusts

       International trade

       Interstate commerce

       Marine insurance

       Markets

       Merchants

BT = Broader Term   NT = Narrower Term   RT = Related Term   SA = See Also   UF = Used For

Commerce—*Continued*
  Monopolies
  Multinational corporations
  Ohio—Commerce
  Prices
  Profit sharing
  Restraint of trade
  Retail trade
  Stock exchange
  Stocks
  Tourist trade
  Trade routes
  Trademarks
  United States—Commerce
 RT Transportation
Commerce, Interstate
 USE Interstate commerce
Commercial aeronautics 387.7
 UF Aeronautics, Commercial *[Former heading]*
   Air cargo
   Air freight
   Air transport
   Commercial aviation
 BT **Freight**
   Transportation
 NT **Air mail service**
   Airlines
   Airplane industry
Commercial aeronautics—Hijacking
 USE **Hijacking of airplanes**
Commercial arithmetic
 USE **Business mathematics**
Commercial art 741.6
 UF Advertising art
   Advertising, Pictorial
   Art, Commercial
   Art in advertising
 BT **Advertising**
   Art
   Drawing
 NT **Fashion design**
   Posters
   Textile design
Commercial aviation
 USE **Commercial aeronautics**
Commercial buildings (May subdiv. geog.) **333.33; 725**
 UF Mercantile buildings
   Store buildings

 BT **Buildings**
 NT **Shopping centers and malls**
   Stores
Commercial correspondence
 USE **Business letters**
Commercial education
 USE **Business education**
Commercial employees
 USE **Office workers**
Commercial endeavors in space
 USE **Space industrialization**
Commercial geography 330.9
 UF Economic geography
   Geography, Commercial *[Former heading]*
   Geography, Economic
   World economics
 BT **Commerce**
   Geography
 NT **Trade routes**
 RT **Economic conditions**
Commercial law 346.07
 UF Business law
   Law, Business
   Law, Commercial
   Mercantile law
 BT **Business**
   Business education
   Law
 NT **Antitrust law**
   Arbitration and award
   Bankruptcy
   Business enterprises
   Collecting of accounts
   Contracts
   Corporation law
   Debtor and creditor
   Fraud
   Insider trading
   Landlord and tenant
   Mortgages
   Negotiable instruments
   Restraint of trade
   Unfair competition
 RT **Maritime law**
Commercial mathematics
 USE **Business mathematics**
Commercial paper
 USE **Negotiable instruments**

Commercial photography 778
    UF   Photography, Commercial *[Former heading]*
    BT   **Photography**
    NT   **Photojournalism**
Commercial policy 380.1; 381.3; 382
    Use for general materials on the various regulations by which governments seek to protect and increase the commerce of a country, such as subsidies, tariffs, free ports, etc.
    UF   Government regulation of commerce
            Reciprocity
            Trade barriers
            World economics
    SA   names of countries with the subdivision *Commercial policy,* e.g. **United States—Commercial policy;** to be added as needed
    BT   **Economic policy**
            International economic relations
    NT   **Buy national policy**
            Commercial products
            Free trade
            Protectionism
            Tariff
            United States—Commercial policy
Commercial products 338; 380.1
    UF   Merchandise
            Products, Commercial
    SA   types of products and names of specific products, to be added as needed
    BT   **Commerce**
    NT   **Animal products**
            Brand name products
            Consumer goods
            Forest products
            Generic products
            Manufactures
            Marine resources
            Raw materials
            Substitute products
Commercial products recall
    USE   **Product recall**
Commercial products—Safety measures
    USE   **Product safety**

Commercial secrets
    USE   **Trade secrets**
Commercials, Radio
    USE   **Radio advertising**
Commercials, Television
    USE   **Television advertising**
Commission government
    USE   **Municipal government by commission**
Commission government with city manager
    USE   **Municipal government by city manager**
Common cold
    USE   **Cold (Disease)**
Common law marriage
    USE   **Unmarried couples**
Common market
    USE   **European Union**
Common schools
    USE   **Public schools**
Commonplaces
    USE   **Terms and phrases**
Commonwealth countries 909
    Use for materials dealing collectively with the member countries of the international organization that was founded in 1931 as the British Commonwealth of Nations, changed its name to the Commonwealth of Nations in 1950, and became known as the Commonwealth in 1969.
    UF   British Commonwealth countries
            British Commonwealth of Nations
            British Dominions
            Commonwealth of Nations *[Former heading]*
            Dominions, British
    RT   **Great Britain—Colonies**
Commonwealth of England
    USE   **Great Britain—History—1642-1660, Civil War and Commonwealth**
Commonwealth of Independent States 947.086
    Use for materials specifically on the federation of independent former Soviet republics that was established in December 1991 and does not include Georgia or the Baltic states. General materials on several or all of the countries that emerged from the dissolution of the Soviet Union in 1991 are entered under **Former Soviet republics.**
    UF   C.I.S.
            CIS

BT = Broader Term   NT = Narrower Term   RT = Related Term   SA = See Also   UF = Used For

Commonwealth of Independent States—
Continued
  RT   Former Soviet republics
        Russia (Federation)
        Soviet Union
Commonwealth of Nations
  USE   Commonwealth countries
Commonwealth, The
  USE   Political science
        Republics
        State, The
Communal living   307.77
   Use for materials on arrangements in volun-
tary cooperative living, usually informal. Ma-
terials on traditional, formally organized com-
munal ventures, usually based on ideological,
political, or religious affiliation are entered
under **Collective settlements.**
  UF   Communal settlements
        Communes
        Cooperative housing
        Cooperative living
        Group living
  RT   **Collective settlements**
        Counter culture
Communal settlements
  USE   **Collective settlements**
        Communal living
Communes
  USE   **Collective settlements**
        Communal living
Communicable diseases   614.4; 616.9
  UF   Contagion and contagious dis-
          eases
        Contagious diseases
        Diseases, Communicable
        Diseases, Contagious
        Diseases, Infectious
        Infection and infectious diseases
        Quarantine
  SA   names of communicable dis-
          eases, to be added as needed
  BT   **Diseases**
        Public health
  NT   **AIDS (Disease)**
        Cold (Disease)
        Fumigation
        Germ theory of disease
        Influenza
        Plague
        Rabies
        Sexually transmitted diseases

        Vaccination
  RT   **Epidemics**
        Immunity
        Insects as carriers of disease
**Communicable diseases—Prevention
      614.4**
  BT   **Preventive medicine**
Communication   302.2
   Use for general materials on communication
in its broadest sense, including the use of the
spoken and written word, signs, symbols, or
behavior.
  UF   Mass communication
  BT   **Sociology**
  NT   **Books and reading**
        Conversation
        Cybernetics
        **Deaf—Means of communica-
          tion**
        Information science
        Language and languages
        Language arts
        Mass media
        Nonverbal communication
        Popular culture
        Postal service
        Public speaking
        Signals and signaling
        Signs and symbols
        Telecommunication
        Writing
Communication among animals
  USE   **Animal communication**
Communication arts
  USE   **Language arts**
Communication satellites
  USE   **Artificial satellites in telecom-
          munication**
Communication systems
  USE   subjects with the subdivision
        Communication systems, e.g.
        **Astronautics—Communica-
          tion systems;** to be added as
          needed
Communications relay satellites
  USE   **Artificial satellites in telecom-
          munication**
Communion
  USE   **Lord's Supper**

BT = Broader Term   NT = Narrower Term   RT = Related Term   SA = See Also   UF = Used For

Communism (May subdiv. geog.) 320.5;
    321.9; 324.1; 335.43
  UF   Bolshevism
         Collectivism
  SA   communism and other subjects,
         e.g. **Communism and litera-
         ture;** to be added as needed
  BT   **Political science**
         Totalitarianism
  NT   **Anticommunist movements**
         Collective settlements
         Communism and literature
         Communism and religion
         Dialectical materialism
  RT   **Marxism**
         Socialism
Communism and literature 335.4; 809;
    810.9, etc.
  UF   Literature and communism
  BT   **Communism**
         Literature
Communism and religion 261.7; 335.4
  UF   Communism—Religious aspects
         Religion and communism
  BT   **Communism**
         Religion
Communism—Religious aspects
  USE   **Communism and religion**
Communism—Soviet Union 320.5;
    335.430947; 947.084
  UF   Russian communism
         Soviet communism
         Soviet Union—Communism
Communism—United States 320.5;
    335.43; 973
  UF   American communism
         United States—Communism
Communist countries 909
  UF   Chinese satellite countries
         Iron curtain countries
         People's democracies
         Russian satellite countries
         Soviet bloc
Communities, Space
  USE   **Space colonies**
Community action
  USE   **Political participation**
Community and libraries
  USE   **Libraries and community**

Community and school 371.19
    Use for materials on ways in which the
community at large, as distinct from govern-
ment, may aid the school program.
  UF   School and community
  BT   **Community life**
  NT   **Parent-teacher associations**
Community antenna television
  USE   **Cable television**
Community based residences
  USE   **Group homes**
Community centers 374; 790.06
  UF   Neighborhood centers
         Play centers
         Recreation centers
         School buildings as recreation
            centers
         Schools as social centers
  BT   **Cities and towns—Civic im-
         provement**
         Community life
         Community organization
         Recreation
         Social settlements
  NT   **Youth hostels**
  RT   **Playgrounds**
Community chests
  USE   **Fund raising**
Community churches 254
    Use for materials on local churches that
have no denominational affiliations.
  UF   Churches, Community
         Churches, Undenominational
         Nondenominational churches
         Undenominational churches
         Union churches
  BT   **Christian sects**
Community colleges
  USE   **Junior colleges**
Community councils
  USE   **Community organization**
Community development (May subdiv.
    geog.) 307.1; 361.6
  UF   Neighborhood development
  BT   **Domestic economic assistance**
         Social change
         Urban renewal
  RT   **Agricultural extension work**
         City planning
         Technical assistance

Community health services   362.1
  BT   Community services
        Public health
Community history
  USE Local history
Community life   307
  UF   Neighborhood
  BT   Associations
  NT   Community and school
        Community centers
        Community organization
        Scouts and scouting
  RT   City life
Community organization   307
  UF   Community councils
  BT   Community life
        Social work
  NT   Community centers
        Local government
  RT   Urban renewal
Community schools
  USE Public schools
Community services   361.7; 361.8
  SA   types of services, e.g. **Commu-
        nity health services;** to be
        added as needed
  BT   Social work
  NT   Community health services
Community songbooks
  USE Songbooks
Community surveys
  USE Social surveys
Community theater
  USE Little theater movement
Compact automobiles
  USE Compact cars
Compact cars   629.222
  UF   Automobiles, Compact *[Former
        heading]*
        Compact automobiles *[Former
        heading]*
        Compacts (Automobiles)
        Economy cars
        Small cars
  SA   names of specific makes and
        models of compact cars, to be
        added as needed
  BT   Automobiles
Compact disc interactive technology
  USE CD-I technology

Compact disc players   621.389
  UF   Audiodisc players
        CD players
        Digital audio disc players
  BT   Phonograph
        Sound—Recording and repro-
          ducing
Compact disc read-only memory
  USE CD-ROMs
Compact discs   621.389; 780.26
    Use for materials on small optical discs in
    general and on the compact disc format for
    sound recordings. Materials about sound
    recordings that emphasize the content of the
    recording rather than the format are entered
    under **Sound recordings.**
  UF   CDs (Compact discs)
        Compact disks
        Digital compact discs
        Discs, Compact
  BT   Optical storage devices
        Sound recordings
  NT   CD-I technology
        CD-ROMs
Compact disks
  USE Compact discs
Compacts (Automobiles)
  USE Compact cars
Companies
  USE Business enterprises
        Corporations
Companies, Trust
  USE Trust companies
Companion-animal partnership
  USE Pet therapy
Company libraries
  USE Corporate libraries
Company symbols
  USE Trademarks
Comparative anatomy   571.3
  UF   Anatomy, Comparative *[Former
        heading]*
        Morphology
  BT   Anatomy
        Zoology
Comparative government   320.3
  UF   Government, Comparative
  SA   names of countries, cities, etc.,
        with the subdivision *Politics
        and government,* e.g. **United
        States—Politics and govern-
        ment;** to be added as needed

BT = Broader Term   NT = Narrower Term   RT = Related Term   SA = See Also   UF = Used For

Comparative government—*Continued*
   BT   **Political science**
Comparative librarianship   020.9
   UF   Librarianship, Comparative
   BT   **International education**
        Library science
Comparative linguistics
   USE   **Linguistics**
Comparative literature   809
   UF   Literature, Comparative *[Former heading]*
   BT   **Literature**
Comparative philology
   USE   **Linguistics**
Comparative physiology   571.1
   UF   Physiology, Comparative *[Former heading]*
   BT   **Physiology**
Comparative psychology   156
   UF   Animal psychology
        Psychology, Comparative *[Former heading]*
   SA   types of animals with the subdivision *Psychology*, e.g. **Dogs—Psychology**; to be added as needed
   BT   **Zoology**
   NT   **Dogs—Psychology**
        Sociobiology
   RT   **Animal intelligence**
        Instinct
Comparative religion
   USE   **Christianity and other religions**
        Religions
Comparison (English grammar)
   USE   **English language—Comparison**
Comparison of cultures
   USE   **Cross cultural studies**
Compass   538; 623.8
   UF   Magnetic needle
        Mariner's compass
   BT   **Magnetism**
        Navigation
Compassion
   USE   **Consolation**
Compensation
   USE   **Pensions**
        Wages
        Workers' compensation

Compensatory spending
   USE   **Deficit financing**
Competition   338.6
   BT   **Business**
        Business ethics
        Commerce
   RT   **Industrial trusts**
        Monopolies
Competition, International
   USE   **International competition**
Competition, Unfair
   USE   **Unfair competition**
Competitions
   USE   **Awards**
        Contests
        and subjects with the subdivision *Competitions*, e.g. **Literature—Competitions**; to be added as needed
Composers   780.92; 920
   UF   Songwriters
   SA   composers of particular countries, e.g. **American composers**; to be added as needed
   BT   **Musicians**
   NT   **American composers**
Composers, American
   USE   **American composers**
Composition
   USE   natural substances of unfixed composition, including soils, plants and crops, animals, farm products, etc., with the subdivision *Composition*, for the results of analyses of those substances, e.g. **Food—Composition**; to be added as needed
Composition (Art)   701
   UF   Art—Composition
   BT   **Art**
   NT   **Architecture—Composition, proportion, etc.**
   RT   **Painting**
Composition (Music)   781.3
   UF   Music—Composition
        Musical composition
        Song writing
        Songwriting
   BT   **Music**

Composition (Music)—*Continued*
    Music—Theory
  NT **Counterpoint**
    Harmony
    Instrumentation and orchestration
    Musical accompaniment
    Musical form
    Popular music—Writing and publishing
Composition of natural substances
  USE natural substances of unfixed composition, including soils, plants and crops, animals, farm products, etc., with the subdivision *Composition* for the results of analyses of those substances, e.g. **Food— Composition;** to be added as needed
Composition (Printing)
  USE **Typesetting**
Composition (Rhetoric)
  USE **Rhetoric**
    and names of languages with the subdivision *Composition and exercises,* e.g. **English language—Composition and exercises;** to be added as needed
Compost 631.8
  BT **Fertilizers**
    Soils
  RT **Organic gardening**
Comprehensive health care organizations
  USE **Health maintenance organizations**
Compressed air 621.5
  UF Pneumatic transmission
  BT **Cold storage**
    Pneumatics
    Power (Mechanics)
Compressed work week
  USE **Hours of labor**
Compulsion (Psychology)
  USE **Compulsive behavior**
Compulsive behavior 616.85
  UF Addictive behavior
    Compulsion (Psychology)

  SA types of compulsive behavior, to be added as needed
  BT **Abnormal psychology**
    Human behavior
  NT **Compulsive gambling**
    Exercise addiction
    Workaholism
  RT **Twelve-step programs**
Compulsive exercising
  USE **Exercise addiction**
Compulsive gambling 616.85
  UF Addiction to gambling
    Gambling, Compulsive
  BT **Compulsive behavior**
    Gambling
Compulsive working
  USE **Workaholism**
Compulsory education 379.2
  UF Compulsory school attendance
    Education, Compulsory *[Former heading]*
  BT **Education and state**
  NT **Evening and continuation schools**
  RT **School attendance**
Compulsory labor
  USE **Convict labor**
    Peonage
    Slavery
Compulsory military service
  USE **Draft**
Compulsory school attendance
  USE **Compulsory education**
    School attendance
Computation, Approximate
  USE **Approximate computation**
Computation (Mathematics)
  USE **Arithmetic**
Computer aided design 620
  UF C.A.D.
    CAD
    Computer assisted design
    Computer drawing
    Drafting, Automatic
    Electronic drawing
  BT **Computers**
    Design
    Engineering
Computer art 700; 760
    Use for materials on works of art, mostly drawings and graphics, created or produced

---

BT = Broader Term   NT = Narrower Term   RT = Related Term   SA = See Also   UF = Used For

Computer art—*Continued*

with the aid of digital computing or plotting devices.

UF   Computer drawing

Drawing, Computer

Drawing, Electronic

Electronic art

Electronic drawing

BT   **Art**

Computer graphics

Computers

Modern art—1900-1999 (20th century)

Computer assisted design

USE   **Computer aided design**

Computer assisted instruction   371.33

Use for materials on automated instruction in which a student interacts directly with a computer.

UF   C.A.I.

CAI

Computer teaching

Computers—Educational use

Education—Automation

Education—Data processing

Teaching, Computer

Teaching—Data processing

SA   subjects with the subdivision

Computer assisted instruction,

to be added as needed

BT   **Electronic data processing**

Programmed instruction

NT   **Mathematics—Computer assisted instruction**

Computer assisted instruction—Authoring programs   005.3; 371.33

Use for materials on computer programs that allow the user with comparatively little expertise to design customized computer programs for educational purposes.

UF   Authoring programs for computer assisted instruction

Computer authoring programs

BT   **Computer software**

Computer authoring programs

USE   **Computer assisted instruction—Authoring programs**

Computer awareness

USE   **Computer literacy**

Computer-based information systems

USE   **Information systems**

Management information systems

Computer-based multimedia information systems

USE   **Multimedia systems**

Computer bulletin boards   004.693; 384.3

Use for works on computer services that function as a community bulletin board and allow a remote caller to dial a central calling place to enter and receive messages, or to read bulletins or notices.

UF   Electronic bulletin boards

BT   **Bulletin boards**

Computer networks

Electronic data processing

Electronic mail systems

Online data processing

Computer communication systems

USE   **Computer networks**

Computer control

USE   **Automation**

Computer crimes   364.16

UF   Computer fraud

Fraud, Computer

BT   **Crime**

NT   **Computer viruses**

RT   **Computer security**

Right of privacy

Computer drawing

USE   **Computer aided design**

Computer art

Computer fraud

USE   **Computer crimes**

Computer games   794.8

BT   **Computer software**

Electronic toys

Games

Computer graphics   006.6

Use for materials on the technique for producing line drawings, particularly engineering drawings, by the use of digital computing and plotting devices. Materials on the use of computer graphics to create artistic designs, drawings, or other works of art are entered under **Computer art.**

UF   Automatic drafting

Automatic drawing

Drafting, Automatic

Drawing, Automatic

Drawing, Electronic

Electronic drawing

Graphics, Computer

BT = Broader Term   NT = Narrower Term   RT = Related Term   SA = See Also   UF = Used For

Computer graphics—*Continued*
  BT   Electronic data processing
  NT   Computer art
Computer hardware
  USE   Computer peripherals
Computer industry (May subdiv. geog.)
        338.7
  BT   Industries
  RT   Computers
Computer input-output equipment
  USE   Computer peripherals
Computer interfaces   004.6; 621.39
        Use for materials on equipment and tech-
        niques linking computers to peripheral devices
        or to other computers.
  UF   Interfaces, Computer
  BT   Computer peripherals
Computer jargon
  USE   Computer science—Dictionaries
Computer keyboarding
  USE   Keyboarding (Electronics)
Computer keyboards
  USE   Keyboards (Electronics)
Computer literacy   004
        Use for materials on the basic knowledge of
        computers a person needs in order to function
        in a computer-based society.
  UF   Computer awareness
  BT   Computers
        Computers and civilization
Computer memory systems
  USE   Computer storage devices
Computer modeling
  USE   Computer simulation
Computer models
  USE   Computer simulation
Computer music   786.7
  UF   Music, Computer
  BT   Music
  RT   Computer sound processing
        Electronic music
Computer networks   004.6; 384.3
        Use for materials on systems consisting of
        two or more interconnected computers.
  UF   Computer communication sys-
          tems
        Networks, Computer
        Teleprocessing networks
  SA   types of computer networks and
          names of specific computer
          networks, to be added as
          needed

  BT   Data transmission systems
        Electronic data processing
        Information networks
        Telecommunication
  NT   Computer bulletin boards
        Internet
Computer operating systems   005.4
  UF   Computers—Operating systems
        Operating systems (Computers)
  BT   Computer systems
Computer peripherals   004.7; 621.39
  UF   Computer hardware
        Computer input-output equipment
        Input equipment (Computers)
        Output equipment (Computers)
  SA   types of computer peripherals, to
          be added as needed
  BT   Computer systems
  NT   Computer interfaces
        Computer storage devices
        Computer terminals
        Keyboards (Electronics)
        Video display terminals
Computer program languages
  USE   Programming languages (Com-
          puters)
Computer programming
  USE   Programming (Computers)
Computer programs
  USE   Computer software
          and subjects with the subdivi-
          sion *Computer programs,* e.g.
          Oceanography—Computer
          programs; to be added as
          needed
Computer science   004
        Use for materials discussing collectively the
        disciplines that deal with the general theory
        and application of computers.
  BT   Science
  RT   Computers
        Electronic data processing
Computer science—Dictionaries   004.03
  UF   Computer jargon
        Computer terms
        Computers—Dictionaries
        Computers—Jargon
        Jargon, Computer
  BT   Encyclopedias and dictionaries

Computer security   005.8

Use for materials on protecting computer hardware and software from accidental or malicious access, use, modification, disclosure, or destruction.

UF	Computers—Access control
	Computers—Security measures
BT	**Computers**
RT	**Computer crimes**
	Computer viruses

Computer simulation   003

UF	Computer modeling
	Computer models
	Simulation, computer
SA	subjects with the subdivision *Computer simulation,* e.g. **Psychology—Computer simulation;** to be added as needed
BT	**Mathematical models**
NT	**Psychology—Computer simulation**
	Virtual reality

Computer software   005.3

UF	Computer programs *[Former heading]*
	Programs, Computer
	Software, Computer
SA	types of computer software, e.g. **Computer games; Electronic spreadsheets;** etc.; subjects with the subdivision *Computer programs,* e.g. **Oceanography—Computer programs;** and names of individual computer programs, to be added as needed.
BT	**Computer systems**
NT	**Computer assisted instruction—Authoring programs**
	Computer games
	Computer software industry
	Computer viruses
	Database management—Computer programs
	Electronic spreadsheets
	Oceanography—Computer programs
	Programming languages (Computers)
	Utilities (Computer programs)
RT	**Computers**

Programming (Computers)

Computer software industry   338.4

BT	**Computer software**

Computer sound processing   006.5

UF	Sound processing, Computer
BT	**Computers**
	Sound
RT	**Computer music**
	Speech processing systems

Computer speech processing systems

USE	**Speech processing systems**

Computer storage devices   004.5; 621.39

UF	Computer memory systems
	Computers—Memory systems
	Computers—Storage devices
	Direct access storage devices (Data processing)
	Random access memories (Data processing)
	Random access storage devices (Data processing)
	Rotating memory devices (Data processing)
	Storage devices, Computer
BT	**Computer peripherals**
NT	**Optical storage devices**

Computer stored cataloging data

USE	**Machine readable bibliographic data**

Computer systems   004

Use for materials on computers, their peripheral devices, and their operating systems.

BT	**Electronic data processing**
NT	**Computer operating systems**
	Computer peripherals
	Computer software
	Computers

Computer teaching

USE	**Computer assisted instruction**

Computer terminals   004.7; 621.39

UF	Terminals, Computer
BT	**Computer peripherals**
NT	**Video display terminals**

Computer terms

USE	**Computer science—Dictionaries**

Computer utility programs

USE	**Utilities (Computer programs)**

Computer viruses   005.8

UF	Software viruses
	Viruses, Computer

BT = Broader Term   NT = Narrower Term   RT = Related Term   SA = See Also   UF = Used For

Computer viruses—*Continued*
  BT   Computer crimes
        Computer software
  RT   Computer security
Computerized tomography
  USE   Tomography
Computers   004; 621.39
  Use for materials on modern electronic computers developed after 1945. Materials on present-day calculators and on calculating machines and mechanical computers made before 1945 are entered under **Calculators.**
  UF   Automatic computers
        Computers, Electronic
        Computing machines (Electronic)
        Electronic calculating machines
        Electronic computers
        Mechanical brains
  SA   types of computers, e.g.
          Microcomputers; and names
          of specific computers, e.g.
          IBM 7090 (Computer); to be
          added as needed
  BT   Computer systems
        Cybernetics
        Electronic apparatus and appliances
  NT   Computer aided design
        Computer art
        Computer literacy
        Computer security
        Computer sound processing
        Computers and children
        Computers and civilization
        Electronic data processing
        IBM 7090 (Computer)
        Information systems
        Microcomputers
        Portable computers
        Supercomputers
  RT   Calculators
        Computer industry
        Computer science
        Computer software
Computers—Access control
  USE   Computer security
Computers and children   004
  BT   Children
        Computers
Computers and civilization   004; 303.48
  UF   Civilization and computers
  BT   Civilization

        Computers
        Technology and civilization
  NT   Computer literacy
**Computers—Cartoons and caricatures
        621.39; 741.5**
  BT   Cartoons and caricatures
Computers—Dictionaries
  USE   Computer science—Dictionaries
Computers—Educational use
  USE   Computer assisted instruction
Computers, Electronic
  USE   Computers
Computers—Jargon
  USE   Computer science—Dictionaries
Computers—Juvenile literature   004
Computers—Memory systems
  USE   Computer storage devices
Computers—Operating systems
  USE   Computer operating systems
Computers, Portable
  USE   Portable computers
Computers—Programming
  USE   Programming (Computers)
Computers—Security measures
  USE   Computer security
Computers—Storage devices
  USE   Computer storage devices
Computers—Utility programs
  USE   Utilities (Computer programs)
Computing machines (Electronic)
  USE   Computers
Con artists
  USE   Swindlers and swindling
Con game
  USE   Swindlers and swindling
Concentration
  USE   Attention
Concentration camps   365
  UF   Internment camps
  SA   names of wars with the subdivision *Prisoners and prisons;* and names of individual camps, to be added as needed
  BT   Military camps
        Political crimes and offenses
  NT   World War, 1939-1945—Prisoners and prisons
  RT   Prisoners of war
Concept formation
  USE   Concept learning

BT = Broader Term   NT = Narrower Term   RT = Related Term   SA = See Also   UF = Used For

174

Concept learning   153.2; 370.15

    Use for materials on the process of discovering the distinguishing features of particular concepts and the ensuing ability to use the concepts appropriately.

UF   Concept formation

        Learning, Concept

BT   **Concepts**

        Psychology of learning

Conception—Prevention

USE   **Birth control**

Concepts   153.2

SA   types of concepts and images,
            e.g. **Size; Shape;** etc., to be
            added as needed

BT   **Perception**

NT   **Concept learning**

        Opposites

        Shape

        Size

Concerto   784.18

    Use for musical scores and for materials on the concerto as a musical form.

UF   Concertos *[Former heading]*

BT   **Musical form**

        Orchestral music

Concertos

USE   **Concerto**

Concerts   780.78

BT   **Amusements**

        Music

RT   **Music festivals**

Conciliation, Industrial

USE   **Industrial arbitration**

Concordances   010

    Use for works that list words with references to passages in a text where the exact word occurs. Works that list topics or names with references to books, articles, or passages where those topics or name are to be found are entered under **Indexes.**

SA   names of individual authors, literary works, sacred works, literatures, and literary forms, with the subdivision *Concordances,* e.g. **Shakespeare, William, 1564-1616—Concordances; Bible—Concordances;** etc., to be added as needed

BT   **Indexes**

Concrete   691; 693

BT   **Building materials**

        Foundations

        Masonry

        Plaster and plastering

NT   **Reinforced concrete**

RT   **Cement**

        Concrete construction

Concrete construction   693

UF   Building, Concrete

        Construction, Concrete

BT   **Building**

RT   **Concrete**

Concrete—Testing   620.1

BT   **Strength of materials**

Condemnation of land

USE   **Eminent domain**

Condensers (Electricity)   621.31

UF   Electric condensers

BT   **Induction coils**

Condensers (Steam)   621.1

BT   **Steam engines**

Condominium timesharing

USE   **Timesharing (Real estate)**

Condominiums   346.04; 643

BT   **Apartment houses**

NT   **Timesharing (Real estate)**

Conduct of life   170

    Use for materials on standards of behavior and materials containing moral guidance and advice to the individual.

UF   Morals

        Personal conduct

SA   classes of persons with the subdivision *Conduct of life;* and names of vices and virtues, to be added as needed

BT   **Ethics**

        Human behavior

        Life skills

NT   **Vice**

        Virtue

Conducting   781.45

    Use for materials on orchestral conducting or a combination of orchestral and choral conducting. Materials limited to choral conducting are entered under **Choral conducting.**

BT   **Music**

NT   **Choral conducting**

RT   **Bands (Music)**

        Conductors (Music)

        Orchestra

Conducting, Choral

USE   **Choral conducting**

BT = Broader Term   NT = Narrower Term   RT = Related Term   SA = See Also   UF = Used For

Conductors, Electric
    USE   **Electric conductors**
Conductors (Music)   784.2092; 920
    UF   Bandmasters
            Music conductors
    BT   **Musicians**
            Orchestra
    RT   **Choral conducting**
            Conducting
Confectionery   641.8; 664
    UF   Candy
            Sweets
    BT   **Cooking**
    NT   **Cake**
            Cake decorating
Confederacies
    USE   **Federal government**
Confederate States of America   973.7
    BT   **United States—History—1861-**
            1865, Civil War
Confederation of American colonies
    USE   **United States—History—1783-**
            1809
Conference calls (Teleconferencing)
    USE   **Teleconferencing**
Conferences
    USE   **Congresses and conventions**
Conferences, Parent-teacher
    USE   **Parent-teacher conferences**
Confession   265
    UF   Auricular confession
            Forgiveness of sin
    RT   **Penance**
Confessions of faith
    USE   **Creeds**
Confidence game
    USE   **Swindlers and swindling**
Configuration (Psychology)
    USE   **Gestalt psychology**
Confirmation   265
    BT   **Sacraments**
Conflict of cultures
    USE   **Culture conflict**
Conflict of generations   306.874
    UF   Generation gap
    BT   **Children and adults**
            Human relations
            Social conflict
    RT   **Parent and child**

Conflict of interests   172; 353.4
    BT   **Political ethics**
    NT   **Misconduct in office**
            Political corruption
Conflict, Social
    USE   **Social conflict**
Conformity   153.8; 302.5; 303.3
    UF   Nonconformity
            Social conformity
    BT   **Attitude (Psychology)**
            Freedom
    RT   **Dissent**
            Individuality
Confucianism   181; 299
    BT   **Religions**
Congenital diseases
    USE   **Medical genetics**
Conglomerate corporations   338.8
    UF   Business combinations
            Corporations, Conglomerate
            Diversified corporations
    BT   **Corporate mergers and acqui-**
            sitions
            Corporations
Congregationalism   285.8
    BT   **Christian sects**
    NT   **Unitarianism**
    RT   **Calvinism**
            Puritans
Congress (U.S.)
    USE   **United States. Congress**
Congresses
    USE   **Congresses and conventions**
            and subjects with the subdivi-
            sion *Congresses,* e.g. **World**
            War, 1939-1945—Congress-
            es; Physics—Congresses; and
            names of specific congresses,
            to be added as needed
Congresses and conventions   060
    UF   Conferences
            Congresses
            Conventions
            International conferences
    SA   subjects with the subdivision
            Congresses, e.g. **World War,**
            1939-1945—Congresses;
            Physics—Congresses; and
            names of specific congresses,
            to be added as needed

BT = Broader Term   NT = Narrower Term   RT = Related Term   SA = See Also   UF = Used For

Congresses and conventions—*Continued*
  BT   **Intellectual cooperation**
          International cooperation
  NT   **International organization**
          Treaties
          World War, 1939-1945—Congresses
Congressional investigations
  USE   **Governmental investigations**
Conjuring
  USE   **Magic tricks**
Conscience   170; 241
  BT   **Christian ethics**
          Duty
          Ethics
  NT   **Freedom of conscience**
Conscientious objectors   343; 355.2
  SA   names of wars with the subdivision *Conscientious objectors,* to be added as needed
  BT   **Freedom of conscience**
          War—Religious aspects
  NT   **World War, 1939-1945—Conscientious objectors**
  RT   **Draft resisters**
          Pacifism
Consciousness   126; 153
  BT   **Apperception**
          Mind and body
          Perception
          Psychology
  NT   **Gestalt psychology**
          Individuality
          Personality
          Self
          Theory of knowledge
  RT   **Subconsciousness**
Consciousness expanding drugs
  USE   **Hallucinogens**
Conscription, Military
  USE   **Draft**
Conservation and restoration
  USE   types of art objects, library materials, architecture, and land vehicles with the subdivision *Conservation and restoration,* e.g. **Automobiles—Conservation and restoration;** to be added as needed

Conservation movement
  USE   **Environmental movement**
Conservation of buildings
  USE   **Architecture—Conservation and restoration**
Conservation of energy
  USE   **Energy conservation**
          Force and energy
Conservation of forests
  USE   **Forest conservation**
Conservation of natural resources
       333.7; 639.9
  UF   Preservation of natural resources
          Resource management
  BT   **Environmental protection**
          Natural resources
  NT   **Energy conservation**
          Forest conservation
          Nature conservation
          Plant conservation
          Soil conservation
          Water conservation
          Wildlife conservation
  RT   **Environmental policy**
          National parks and reserves
          Wilderness areas
Conservation of nature
  USE   **Nature conservation**
Conservation of plants
  USE   **Plant conservation**
Conservation of power resources
  USE   **Energy conservation**
Conservation of the soil
  USE   **Soil conservation**
Conservation of water
  USE   **Water conservation**
Conservation of wildlife
  USE   **Wildlife conservation**
Conservation of works of art, books, etc.
  USE   subjects with the subdivision *Conservation and restoration,* e.g. **Library resources—Conservation and restoration; Painting—Conservation and restoration;** etc., to be added as needed
Conservatism   320.5
  UF   Reaction (Political science)
          Right (Political science)
  BT   **Political science**

BT = Broader Term   NT = Narrower Term   RT = Related Term   SA = See Also   UF = Used For

Conservatism—*Continued*
        Social sciences
  RT   **Right and left (Political science)**
Conservatories, Home
  USE   **Garden rooms**
Consolation   152.4; 155.9
  UF   Compassion
       Solace
       Sympathy *[Former heading]*
  BT   **Emotions**
       Human behavior
  RT   **Bereavement**
       Grief
Consolidation and merger of corporations
  USE   **Corporate mergers and acquisitions**
Consolidation of schools
  USE   **Schools—Centralization**
Consortia, Library
  USE   **Library cooperation**
       Library information networks
Constellations   523.8
  SA   names of constellations, to be added as needed
  BT   **Sky**
  RT   **Astrology**
       Astronomy
       Stars
Constitution (U.S.)
  USE   **Constitutional history—United States**
       Constitutional law—United States
       Constitutions—United States
Constitutional history (May subdiv. geog.)
     342

Use for materials on the history of constitutions. Texts of constitutions are entered under **Constitutions.**
  UF   Constitutional law—History
  BT   **History**
  NT   **Democracy**
       Monarchy
       Representative government and representation
       Republics
  RT   **Constitutions**
       Political science

Constitutional history—Ohio   342.771
  UF   Ohio—Constitutional history *[Former heading]*
  BT   **Ohio—History**
Constitutional history—United States
     342.73
  UF   American Constitution
       Constitution (U.S.)
       United States—Constitution *[Former heading]*
       United States—Constitutional history *[Former heading]*
  BT   **United States—History**
  RT   **United States—History—1783-1809**
Constitutional law (May subdiv. geog.)
     342

Use for materials on constitutions or constitutional law. Texts of constitutions are entered under Constitutions.
  BT   **Law**
  NT   **Citizenship**
       Civil rights
       Democracy
       Eminent domain
       Executive power
       Federal government
       Injunctions
       Legislative bodies
       Magna Carta
       Monarchy
       Proportional representation
       Referendum
       Representative government and representation
       Republics
       Separation of powers
       Suffrage
       War and emergency powers
  RT   **Administrative law**
       Constitutions
       Political science
Constitutional law—History
  USE   **Constitutional history**
Constitutional law—Ohio   342.771
  UF   Ohio—Constitutional law
Constitutional law—United States
     342.73
  UF   American Constitution
       Constitution (U.S.)

BT = Broader Term   NT = Narrower Term   RT = Related Term   SA = See Also   UF = Used For

Constitutional law—United States—*Continued*

 United States—Constitution
  [Former heading]
 United States—Constitutional
  law *[Former heading]*

Constitutional rights
 USE **Civil rights**

Constitutions (May subdiv. geog.) **342**
 Use for texts of constitutions. Materials about constitutions are entered under either **Constitutional law** or **Constitutional history.**
 UF State constitutions *[Former heading]*
 BT **Law**
 NT **Equal rights amendments**
 RT **Constitutional history**
   Constitutional law

Constitutions—Ohio **342.771**
 UF Ohio—Constitution *[Former heading]*

Constitutions—United States **342.73; 973.3**
 Use for the individual texts or collections of texts of federal or state constitutions.
 UF American Constitution
   Constitution (U.S.)
   State constitutions *[Former heading]*
   United States—Constitution *[Former heading]*

Construction
 USE **Building**
   Engineering

Construction, Concrete
 USE **Concrete construction**

Construction contracts **692**
 UF Building contracts
   Building—Contracts and specifications *[Former heading]*
 BT **Contracts**

Construction, House
 USE **House construction**

Construction of roads
 USE **Roads**

Consular service
 USE **Diplomatic and consular service**

Consulates
 USE **Diplomatic and consular service**

Consuls
 USE **Diplomats**

Consultants
 UF Advisors
 SA types of consultants, to be added as needed
 BT **Counseling**
 NT **Educational consultants**

Consultative management
 USE **Participative management**

Consumer behavior
 USE **Consumers**

Consumer boycotts
 USE **Boycotts**

Consumer credit **332.7**
 BT **Banks and banking**
   Credit
   Personal finance
 NT **Credit cards**
   Installment plan
   Personal loans

Consumer education **640.73**
 Use for materials on the selection and efficient use of consumer goods and services and on methods of educating consumers. Materials on the decision-making processes, external factors, and individual characteristics of consumers that determine their purchasing behavior are entered under **Consumers.** Materials on the economic theory of consumption are entered under **Consumption (Economics).**
 UF Buyers' guides
   Consumers' guides
   Shoppers' guides
 BT **Education**
   Home economics
 RT **Consumers**
   Shopping

Consumer goods **338.4**
 Use for materials on products that are purchased for personal or household purposes.
 UF Consumer products
   Goods, Consumer
   Merchandise
 BT **Commercial products**
   Manufactures
 RT **Consumption (Economics)**

Consumer loans
 USE **Personal loans**

Consumer organizations
 USE **Cooperative societies**

Consumer price indexes **338.5**
 UF Cost of living indexes

BT = Broader Term NT = Narrower Term RT = Related Term SA = See Also UF = Used For

Consumer price indexes—*Continued*
>> Price indexes, Consumer
BT **Cost and standard of living**
>> **Prices**
Consumer products
USE **Consumer goods**
Consumer protection   343.07; 381.3
>> Use for materials on governmental and private activities that guard the consumer against dangers to his health, safety, or economic well-being.
UF **Consumerism**
BT **Industrial policy**
NT **Drugs—Testing**
>> **Food adulteration and inspection**
>> **Product recall**
>> **Product safety**
Consumerism
USE **Consumer protection**
Consumers   640.73; 658.8
>> Use for materials on the decision-making processes, external factors, and individual characteristics of consumers that determine their purchasing behavior. Materials on the selection and efficient use of consumer goods and services and on methods of educating consumers are entered under **Consumer education**. Materials on the economic theory of consumption are entered under **Consumption (Economics)**.
UF **Consumer behavior**
NT **Boycotts**
>> **Young consumers**
RT **Consumer education**
>> **Consumption (Economics)**
>> **Shopping**
Consumers' cooperative societies
USE **Cooperative societies**
Consumers' guides
USE **Consumer education**
Consumption (Economics)   339.4
>> Use for materials on the economic theory of consumption. Materials on the decision-making processes, external factors, and individual characteristics of consumers that determine their purchasing behavior are entered under **Consumers**. Materials on the selection and efficient use of consumer goods and services and on methods of educating consumers are entered under **Consumer education**.
BT **Economics**
NT **Prices**
RT **Consumer goods**
>> **Consumers**

Consumption of alcoholic beverages
USE **Drinking of alcoholic beverages**
Consumption of energy
USE **Energy consumption**
Contact lenses   617.7
BT **Eyeglasses**
>> **Lenses**
Contagion and contagious diseases
USE **Communicable diseases**
Contagious diseases
USE **Communicable diseases**
Container gardening   635.9
BT **Gardening**
RT **Flower gardening**
>> **House plants**
>> **Indoor gardening**
>> **Miniature gardens**
>> **Window gardening**
Containers, Box
USE **Boxes**
Contaminated food
USE **Food contamination**
Contamination of environment
USE **Pollution**
Contemporary art
USE **Modern art—1900-1999 (20th century)**
Contests   001.4; 790.1
UF Competitions
SA types of contests and names of specific contests, e.g. **Olympic games;** and subjects with the subdivision *Competitions* or *Tournaments*, e.g. **Literature—Competitions; Tennis—Tournaments;** to be added as needed
NT **Literature—Competitions**
>> **Olympic games**
>> **Tennis—Tournaments**
RT **Awards**
Continental drift   551.1
UF Drifting of continents
BT **Continents**
>> **Geology**
RT **Plate tectonics**
Continental shelf   551.41
BT **Geology**
RT **Territorial waters**

BT = Broader Term   NT = Narrower Term   RT = Related Term   SA = See Also   UF = Used For

Continents 551.41
    BT   **Earth**
    NT   **Continental drift**
Continuation schools
    USE   **Evening and continuation
            schools**
Continuing education 374
    UF   Education, Continuing
           Lifelong education
           Permanent education
           Recurrent education
    BT   **Education**
    NT   **Evening and continuation
            schools**
    RT   **Adult education**
Contra-Iran Affair, 1985-1990
    USE   **Iran-Contra Affair, 1985-1990**
Contraband trade
    USE   **Smuggling**
Contraception
    USE   **Birth control**
Contract bridge
    USE   **Bridge (Game)**
Contract labor 331.5
    UF   Indentured servants
    BT   **Labor**
    NT   **Convict labor**
    RT   **Peonage**
Contractions
    USE   **Abbreviations
            Ciphers**
Contracts 346.02
    UF   Agreements
    SA   types of contracts, e.g. **Con-
            struction contracts;** to be
            added as needed
    BT   **Commerce
            Commercial law**
    NT   **Authors and publishers
            Construction contracts
            Covenants
            Labor contract
            Liability (Law)
            Mortgages
            Negotiable instruments**
Contrition
    USE   **Penance**
Control
    USE   types of control, e.g. **Flood con-
            trol; Weather control;** etc.,

and animals, plants, or pro-
        cesses with the subdivision
        Control, e.g. **Mosquitoes—
        Control;** to be added as
        needed
Control of guns
    USE   **Gun control**
Control of self
    USE   **Self-control**
Controversial literature
    USE   religions, denominations, reli-
            gious orders, and sacred
            works with the subdivision
            Controversial literature, e.g.
            **Christianity—Controversial
            literature;** and religions and
            denominations with the subdi-
            visions *Apologetic works* e.g.
            **Christianity—Apologetic
            works;** to be added as needed
Conundrums
    USE   **Riddles**
Convenience cooking
    USE   **Quick and easy cooking**
Convenience foods 641.3; 664
       Use for materials on prepackaged foods that
       are easy to prepare for eating.
    UF   Fast foods
    BT   **Food**
Conventions
    USE   **Congresses and conventions**
            and subjects with the subdivi-
            sion *Congresses,* e.g. **World
            War, 1939-1945—Congress-
            es; Physics—Congresses;** and
            names of specific congresses,
            to be added as needed
Conventions, Political
    USE   **Political conventions**
Convents 271; 726
    UF   Cloisters
           Nunneries
    BT   **Monasteries**
    NT   **Monasticism and religious or-
            ders for women**
Conversation 808.56
    UF   Discussion
           Table talk
           Talking
    BT   **Communication
            Language and languages**

Conversation—*Continued*
  NT   **Discussion groups**
Conversation and phrase books
  USE   **Modern languages—Conversa-
        tion and phrase books**
Conversation in foreign languages
  USE   **Modern languages—Conversa-
        tion and phrase books**
Conversations and phrases
  USE   **Modern languages—Conversa-
        tion and phrase books**
Conversion   248.2; 291.4
  BT   **Evangelistic work**
       Salvation
       Spiritual life
  NT   **Converts**
  RT   **Regeneration (Christianity)**
Conversion of saline water
  USE   **Sea water conversion**
Conversion of waste products
  USE   **Recycling**
Converts   248.2; 291.4
    Use for materials on converts from one reli-
  gion or denomination to another.
  SA   converts to a particular religion
       or denomination, e.g. **Con-
       verts to Catholicism;** to be
       added as needed
  BT   **Conversion**
  NT   **Converts to Catholicism**
Converts, Catholic
  USE   **Converts to Catholicism**
Converts to Catholicism   282
  UF   Catholic Church—Converts
       Catholic converts *[Former head-
       ing]*
       Converts, Catholic *[Former
       heading]*
  BT   **Catholics**
       Converts
Conveying machinery   621.8
  UF   Conveyors
  BT   **Machinery**
       Materials handling
  RT   **Hoisting machinery**
Conveyors
  USE   **Conveying machinery**
Convict labor   331.5; 365
  UF   Compulsory labor
       Forced labor
       Prison labor

  BT   **Contract labor**
       Criminals
       Labor
  RT   **Peonage**
       Prisons
Convicts
  USE   **Criminals**
       Prisoners
Cook books
  USE **Cooking**
Cookbooks
  USE **Cooking**
Cookery
  USE **Cooking**
Cookery, American
  USE **American cooking**
Cookery for the sick
  USE **Cooking for the sick**
Cookery, French
  USE **French cooking**
Cooking   641.5
  UF   Cook books
       Cookbooks
       Cookery *[Former heading]*
       Food preparation
       Gastronomy
       Recipes
  SA   types of cooking, e.g. **Micro-
       wave cooking;** cooking of
       particular countries or regions,
       e.g. **French cooking;
       American Cooking; Southern
       cooking;** etc.; and, for materi-
       als on the cooking of specific
       foods or kinds of food, **Cook-
       ing** with a subdivision for the
       food, e.g. **Cooking—Vegeta-
       bles; Cooking—Natural
       foods;** etc., to be added as
       needed
  BT   **Home economics**
  NT   **Afternoon teas**
       American cooking
       Baking
       Bread
       Breakfasts
       Cake
       Canning and preserving
       Catering
       Confectionery

BT = Broader Term   NT = Narrower Term   RT = Related Term   SA = See Also   UF = Used For

Cooking—*Continued*
    Cooking for the sick
    Desserts
    Dinners
    Eggs
    Fish as food
    Flavoring essences
    French cooking
    Herbs
    Luncheons
    Meat
    Menus
    Microwave cooking
    Outdoor cooking
    Pastry
    Quantity cooking
    Quick and easy cooking
    Salads
    Sandwiches
    Sauces
    Shellfish
    Soups
    Southern cooking
    Vegetarian cooking
RT   Diet
    Food
Cooking, Barbecue
  USE **Barbecue cooking**
Cooking for institutions
  USE **Food service**
Cooking for large numbers
  USE **Quantity cooking**
Cooking for the sick   **641.5**
  UF Cookery for the sick *[Former heading]*
      Food for invalids
      Invalid cooking
  SA types of diets, e.g. **Salt-free diet;** to be added as needed
  BT **Cooking**
      Diet in disease
      Nursing
      Sick
  NT **Diet therapy**
      Salt-free diet
Cooking, French
  USE **French cooking**
Cooking, Microwave
  USE **Microwave cooking**

Cooking—Natural foods **641.5**
  UF Natural food cooking
  RT **Natural foods**
Cooking, Outdoor
  USE **Outdoor cooking**
Cooking—Southern States
  USE **Southern cooking**
Cooking—United States
  USE **American cooking**
Cooking utensils
  USE **Kitchen utensils**
Cooking—Vegetables   **641.6**
  BT **Vegetables**
  RT **Salads**
      Vegetarian cooking
Cooking, Vegetarian
  USE **Vegetarian cooking**
Cooling appliances
  USE **Refrigeration**
Cooperation   **334**
    Use for general materials on the theory and history of cooperation and the cooperative movement. Materials dealing specifically with cooperative enterprises are entered under **Cooperative societies.**
  UF Cooperative distribution
      Distribution, Cooperative
      Rochdale system
  BT **Associations**
      Commerce
      Economics
  NT **Collective settlements**
      Cooperative agriculture
      Cooperative banks
      Cooperative societies
      International cooperation
      Labor unions
      Savings and loan associations
  RT **Profit sharing**
Cooperation, Intellectual
  USE **Intellectual cooperation**
Cooperation, International
  USE **International cooperation**
Cooperation, Library
  USE **Library cooperation**
Cooperative agriculture   **334**
    Use for materials on cooperation in the production and disposal of agricultural products.
  UF Agricultural cooperation
      Agriculture, Cooperative *[Former heading]*
      Collective farms

BT = Broader Term   NT = Narrower Term   RT = Related Term   SA = See Also   UF = Used For

Cooperative agriculture—*Continued*
>Farmers' cooperatives
BT   **Agriculture**
>**Cooperation**
RT   **Collective settlements**
Cooperative banks   **334**
UF   Banks and banking, Cooperative
>*[Former heading]*
>People's banks
BT   **Banks and banking**
>**Cooperation**
>**Cooperative societies**
>**Personal loans**
NT   **Credit unions**
RT   **Savings and loan associations**
Cooperative building associations
USE   **Savings and loan associations**
Cooperative distribution
USE   **Cooperation**
>**Cooperative societies**
Cooperative housing
USE   **Communal living**
Cooperative learning   **371.3**
>Use for materials on the method of education that involves having students work together on projects in a structured manner.
UF   Group method in teaching
>Group teaching
>Group work in education
BT   **Education**
>**Teaching**
Cooperative living
USE   **Collective settlements**
>**Communal living**
Cooperative societies   **334; 658.8**
>Use for materials dealing specifically with cooperative enterprises. General materials on the theory and history of cooperation and the cooperative movement are entered under **Cooperation**.
UF   Co-ops
>Consumer organizations
>Consumers' cooperative societies
>Cooperative distribution
>Cooperative stores
SA   types of cooperative societies, e.g. **Credit unions;** to be added as needed
BT   **Cooperation**
>**Corporations**
>**Societies**
NT   **Cooperative banks**

>**Savings and loan associations**
Cooperative stores
USE   **Cooperative societies**
Copiers
USE   **Copying machines**
Coping behavior
USE   **Adjustment (Psychology)**
Coping skills
USE   **Life skills**
Copper engraving
USE   **Engraving**
Copperwork   **673; 739.5**
BT   **Metalwork**
Copy art   **760**
>Use for materials on the use of photocopying machines to create original works of art. Materials on clipping art work from published sources to use in creating documents, posters, newsletters, etc., are entered under **Clip art.**
UF   Copying machine art
>Reprographic art
>Xerographic art
BT   **Art**
RT   **Photocopying**
Copy writing
USE   **Advertising copy**
Copybooks
USE   **Handwriting**
Copying machine art
USE   **Copy art**
Copying machines   **681**
UF   Copiers
>Copying processes and machines
>*[Former heading]*
>Duplicating machines
>Photocopying machines
BT   **Office equipment and supplies**
RT   **Copying processes**
Copying processes   **686**
UF   Copying processes and machines
>*[Former heading]*
>Duplicating processes
>Reproduction processes
>Reprography
SA   names of specific processes, to be added as needed
BT   **Documentation**
NT   **Photocopying**
RT   **Copying machines**
Copying processes and machines
USE   **Copying machines**

BT = Broader Term   NT = Narrower Term   RT = Related Term   SA = See Also   UF = Used For

Copying processes and machines—*Continued*

Copying processes
Copyright   341.7; 346.04; 352.7
May be subdivided by topic, e.g. **Copyright—Books**; etc.
UF   Intellectual property
International copyright
Literary property
Property, Literary
BT   **Authorship**
NT   **Fair use (Copyright)**
RT   **Authors and publishers**
Publishers and publishing
Copyright—Books   341.7; 346.04
UF   Books—Copyright
Coral reefs and islands   551.42
UF   Atolls
BT   **Geology**
Islands
Corals   563; 593.6
BT   **Invertebrates**
Marine animals
Cordials (Liquor)
USE   **Liquors**
Core curriculum
USE   **Colleges and universities—Curricula**
Education—Curricula
Corn   633.1; 633.2
UF   Maize
BT   **Forage plants**
Grain
Coronary heart diseases
USE   **Heart diseases**
Corporate acquisitions
USE   **Corporate mergers and acquisitions**
Corporate downsizing
USE   **Downsizing of organizations**
Corporate libraries   027.6
Use for materials on libraries located within companies, firms, or private businesses, covering any subject areas. Materials on libraries with a subject focus on business are entered under **Business libraries.**
UF   Company libraries
Industrial libraries
Libraries, Company
Libraries, Corporate
Libraries, Industrial
BT   **Special libraries**

Corporate mergers
USE   **Corporate mergers and acquisitions**
Corporate mergers and acquisitions   338.8; 658.1
UF   Acquisition of corporations
Buyouts, Corporate
Consolidation and merger of corporations
Corporate acquisitions
Corporate mergers
Corporate takeovers
Industrial mergers
Merger of corporations
Takeovers, Corporate
BT   **Corporations**
NT   **Conglomerate corporations**
Leveraged buyouts
Corporate patronage of the arts
USE   **Art patronage**
Corporate symbols
USE   **Trademarks**
Corporate takeovers
USE   **Corporate mergers and acquisitions**
Corporation law   346
UF   Law, Corporation
BT   **Commercial law**
Corporations
Law
NT   **Public service commissions**
RT   **Industrial trusts**
Monopolies
Restraint of trade
Corporations   338.7; 658.1
UF   Companies
BT   **Business enterprises**
Stocks
NT   **Conglomerate corporations**
Cooperative societies
Corporate mergers and acquisitions
Corporation law
Government ownership
Multinational corporations
Municipal ownership
Public service commissions
Trust companies
RT   **Industrial trusts**
Public utilities

BT = Broader Term   NT = Narrower Term   RT = Related Term   SA = See Also   UF = Used For

Corporations—Accounting   657; 658.15
   BT   **Accounting**
          Bookkeeping
Corporations—Art patronage
   USE   **Art patronage**
Corporations, Conglomerate
   USE   **Conglomerate corporations**
Corporations—Finance   658.15
   UF   Capitalization (Finance)
   BT   **Finance**
Corporations, International
   USE   **Multinational corporations**
Corporations, Multinational
   USE   **Multinational corporations**
Corporations, Nonprofit
   USE   **Nonprofit organizations**
Corpulence
   USE   **Obesity**
Correctional institutions (May subdiv.
     geog.)   **365**
   UF   Penal institutions
   SA   types of correctional institutions,
          to be added as needed
   BT   **Punishment**
   NT   **Halfway houses**
          Penal colonies
          Prisons
          Reformatories
Correctional services
   USE   **Corrections**
Corrections   364.6
   Use for materials on the rehabilitation and
treatment of offenders through parole, penal
custody, and probation programs, and on the
administration of such programs.
   UF   Correctional services
          Criminals—Rehabilitation pro-
            grams
          Penology
   BT   **Administration of criminal jus-
            tice**
   NT   **Parole**
          Probation
          Punishment
Correctness, Political
   USE   **Political correctness**
Correspondence
   USE   **Business letters**
          Letter writing
          Letters

and ethnic groups, classes of
     persons, and names of indi-
     vidual persons and families
     with the subdivision *Corre-
     spondence,* e.g. **Authors—
     Correspondence;** to be added
     as needed
**Correspondence schools and courses
     374**
   UF   Home education
          Home study courses
   BT   **Distance education**
          Schools
          Technical education
          University extension
   RT   **Self-instruction**
Corrosion and anticorrosives   620.1
   UF   Anticorrosive paint
          Rust
          Rustless coatings
   BT   **Industrial chemistry**
   RT   **Paint**
Corrupt practices
   USE   subjects with the subdivision
          Corrupt practices, e.g. **Adop-
          tion—Corrupt practices;
          Sports—Corrupt practices;**
          etc., to be added as needed
Corruption in politics
   USE   **Political corruption**
Corruption in sports
   USE   **Sports—Corrupt practices**
Corruption, Police
   USE   **Police corruption**
Corsairs
   USE   **Pirates**
Cosmetic surgery
   USE   **Plastic surgery**
Cosmetics   646.7
   UF   Makeup (Cosmetics)
   SA   types of cosmetics, to be added
          as needed
   BT   **Beauty shops**
          Costume
          Personal grooming
   NT   **Perfumes**
          Theatrical makeup
   RT   **Toiletries**
Cosmetics—Advertising
   USE   **Advertising—Cosmetics**

BT = Broader Term   NT = Narrower Term   RT = Related Term   SA = See Also   UF = Used For

Cosmic chemistry
  USE   **Space chemistry**
Cosmic rays   539.7
  UF   Millikan rays
  BT   **Nuclear physics**
          Radiation
          Radioactivity
          Space environment
Cosmobiology
  USE   **Space biology**
Cosmochemistry
  USE   **Space chemistry**
Cosmogony
  USE   **Cosmology**
          Universe
Cosmography
  USE   **Cosmology**
          Universe
Cosmology   113; 523.1
    Use for general or theoretical materials on the science or philosophy of the universe. Materials limited to the physical description of the universe are entered under **Universe.**
  UF   Cosmogony
          Cosmography
  BT   **Universe**
  NT   **Biblical cosmology**
          Big bang theory
Cosmology, Biblical
  USE   **Biblical cosmology**
Cosmonauts
  USE   **Astronauts**
Cost accounting   657
  BT   **Accounting**
          Bookkeeping
Cost and standard of living (May subdiv. geog.)   **339.4**
  UF   Cost of living *[Former heading]*
          Food, Cost of
          Household finances
          Standard of living *[Former heading]*
  BT   **Economics**
          Home economics
          Quality of life
          Social conditions
          Wealth
  NT   **Consumer price indexes**
          Household budgets
          Subsistence economy
  RT   **Prices**

          Saving and thrift
          Wages
Cost of living
  USE   **Cost and standard of living**
Cost of living indexes
  USE   **Consumer price indexes**
Cost of medical care
  USE   **Medical care—Costs**
Costs
  USE   subjects with the subdivision *Costs,* e.g. **Medical care—Costs;** to be added as needed
Costume (May subdiv. geog.)   **391**
    Use for descriptive and historical materials on the costume of various countries, peoples, or historical periods and for materials on fancy dress and theatrical costumes. Materials on clothing from a practical standpoint, including the art of dress, are entered under **Clothing and dress.** Materials on the prevailing mode or style of dress are entered under **Fashion.**
  UF   Acting—Costume
          Fancy dress
          Style in dress
          Theatrical costume
  SA   ethnic groups and classes of persons with the subdivision *Costume,* e.g. **Indians of North America—Costume; Children—Costume;** etc., to be added as needed
  BT   **Decorative arts**
          Ethnology
          Manners and customs
  NT   **Armor**
          Children—Costume
          Cosmetics
          Fans
          Hats
          Indians of North America—Costume
          Jewelry
          Masks (Facial)
          Military uniforms
          Theatrical makeup
          Umbrellas and parasols
          Wigs
  RT   **Clothing and dress**
          Fashion
Costume jewelry
  USE   **Jewelry**

  BT = Broader Term   NT = Narrower Term   RT = Related Term   SA = See Also   UF = Used For

Costume, Military
 USE Military uniforms
Cot death
 USE Sudden infant death syndrome
Cottage industry
 USE Home business
Cotton 633.5; 677
 BT Economic botany
  Fabrics
  Fibers
  Yarn
Cotton manufacture 677
 BT Textile industry
Councils and synods 262
 UF Church councils
  Ecumenical councils
  Synods
 SA names of specific councils and
  synods, e.g. Vatican Council
  (2nd : 1962-1965); to be
  added as needed
 BT Christianity
  Church history
 NT Vatican Council (2nd : 1962-
  1965)
Counseling 361; 371.4
 UF Guidance
 SA types of counseling; and ethnic
  groups and classes of persons
  with the subdivision *Counsel-
  ing of*, e.g. Employees—
  Counseling of; to be added
  as needed
 BT Applied psychology
  Helping behavior
  Personnel management
 NT Consultants
  Crisis centers
  Drug abuse counseling
  Educational counseling
  Elderly—Counseling of
  Employees—Counseling of
  Family therapy
  Health counseling
  Hotlines (Telephone counseling)
  Marriage counseling
  Peer counseling
  School counseling
  Social group work
  Vocational guidance

 RT Interviewing
  Social case work
Counseling of the elderly
 USE Elderly—Counseling of
Counseling with the aged
 USE Elderly—Counseling of
Counter culture 306
 UF Alternative lifestyle
  Counterculture
  Nonconformity
  Subculture
 BT Lifestyles
  Social conditions
 NT Bohemianism
 RT Collective settlements
  Communal living
  Radicalism
Counter-Reformation 270.6
 UF Anti-Reformation
 BT Christianity
 RT Church history—1500- , Mod-
  ern period
  Reformation
Counterculture
 USE Counter culture
Counterespionage
 USE Intelligence service
Counterfeits and counterfeiting 332;
  364.1
 BT Coinage
  Crime
  Forgery
  Impostors and imposture
  Money
  Swindlers and swindling
 NT Art forgeries
  Credit card crimes
  Literary forgeries
Counterintelligence
 USE Intelligence service
Counterpoint 781.2
 BT Composition (Music)
  Music—Theory
 NT Fugue
Counting 513.2
 Use for materials on counting, including
 counting books. Materials on numbers, num-
 bering, and systems of numeration are entered
 under **Numbers**. Materials on the conceptual-
 ization of numbers are entered under **Number
 concept.**
 UF Counting books

BT = Broader Term NT = Narrower Term RT = Related Term SA = See Also UF = Used For

Counting—*Continued*
    BT   **Arithmetic—Study and teaching**
    NT   **Number games**
    RT   **Numbers**
Counting books
    USE   **Counting**
Country and western music
    USE   **Country music**
Country churches
    USE   **Rural churches**
Country life (May subdiv. geog.)
    307.72; 630
    Use for descriptive, popular, and literary materials on living in the country. Materials on social organization and conditions in rural communities are entered under **Rural sociology.**
    UF   Rural life
    BT   **Manners and customs**
    NT   **Agriculture—Societies**
             Farm life
             Mountain life
             Plantation life
    RT   **Outdoor life**
             Rural sociology
Country life—United States   **307.72; 630**
    UF   United States—Country life
Country music   **781.642**
    UF   Country and western music
             Hillbilly music
             Western and country music
    BT   **Folk music—United States**
             Popular music
    RT   **Cowhands—Songs**
Country schools
    USE   **Rural schools**
County agricultural agents   **630.7**
    BT   **Agricultural extension work**
             Agriculture—Study and teaching
County government   **320.8; 352.15**
    UF   County officers
    BT   **Local government**
County libraries   **027.4**
    UF   Libraries, County
    BT   **Library extension**
             Public libraries
             Regional libraries
County officers
    USE   **County government**

County planning
    USE   **Regional planning**
Couples, Married
    USE   **Married people**
Coupons (Retail trade)   **659**
    BT   **Advertising**
Coups d'état
    USE   **Revolutions**
Courage   **179**
    UF   Bravery
             Heroism
    BT   **Virtue**
    NT   **Morale**
    RT   **Heroes and heroines**
Courses of study
    USE   **Education—Curricula**
Court fools
    USE   **Fools and jesters**
Court life
    USE   **Courts and courtiers**
Court martial
    USE   **Courts martial and courts of inquiry**
Courtesy   **177; 395**
    UF   Manners
             Politeness
    BT   **Etiquette**
             Virtue
Courtiers
    USE   **Courts and courtiers**
Courting
    USE   **Dating (Social customs)**
Courtroom drama
    USE   **Legal drama (Films)**
             Legal drama (Radio programs)
             Legal drama (Television programs)
Courts (May subdiv. geog.)   **347**
    UF   Judiciary
    BT   **Law**
    NT   **Arbitration and award**
             Courts martial and courts of inquiry
             Criminal procedure
             Jury
             Juvenile courts
             United States. Supreme Court
    RT   **Administration of justice**
             Judges

BT = Broader Term   NT = Narrower Term   RT = Related Term   SA = See Also   UF = Used For

Courts and courtiers   394; 929.7
   UF   Court life
         Courtiers
   SA   names of countries, cities, etc.,
         with the subdivision *Courts*
         and courtiers, to be added as
         needed
   BT   **Manners and customs**
   NT   **Fools and jesters**
         Princes
         Princesses
   RT   **Kings and rulers**
         Queens
Courts martial and courts of inquiry
   343
   UF   Court martial
         Military courts
   BT   **Courts**
         Trials
   RT   **Military law**
Courts—United States   347.73
   UF   Federal courts
         United States—Courts
Courtship
   USE   **Dating (Social customs)**
Courtship (Animal behavior)
   USE   **Animal courtship**
Courtship of animals
   USE   **Animal courtship**
Covenants   231.7; 291.2
     Use for materials on religious covenants.
   May be subdivided by religion as needed. Ma-
   terials on non-religious covenants are entered
   under **Contracts.**
   UF   Agreements
   BT   **Contracts**
         Theology
Covens
   USE   **Witches**
Coverlets
   USE   **Bedspreads**
         Quilts
Cowboys
   USE   **Cowhands**
Cowgirls
   USE   **Cowhands**
Cowhands   636.2; 978
   UF   Cowboys
         Cowgirls
         Gauchos
   BT   **Frontier and pioneer life**

         Ranch life
   RT   **Rodeos**
Cowhands—Songs   782.42
   UF   Cowhands—Songs and music
         [Former heading]
   BT   **Music**
         Songs
   RT   **Country music**
Cowhands—Songs and music
   USE   **Cowhands—Songs**
Cows
   USE   **Cattle**
Crabs   565; 595.3
   BT   **Crustacea**
         Shellfish
Crack babies
   USE   **Children of drug addicts**
Crack cocaine
   USE   **Crack (Drug)**
Crack (Drug)   362.29; 615
   UF   Crack cocaine
   BT   **Cocaine**
Cradle songs
   USE   **Lullabies**
Craft festivals
   USE   **Craft shows**
Craft shows   745
   UF   Craft festivals
         Shows, Craft
   BT   **Exhibitions**
         Festivals
         Handicraft
Crafts (Arts)
   USE   **Arts and crafts movement**
         Handicraft
Cranes, derricks, etc.   621.8
   UF   Derricks
   BT   **Hoisting machinery**
Crank (Drug)
   USE   **Ice (Drug)**
Cranks
   USE   **Eccentrics and eccentricities**
Crashes (Finance)
   USE   **Financial crises**
Crates
   USE   **Boxes**
Crayon drawing   741.2
   UF   Blackboard drawing
   BT   **Drawing**
   RT   **Pastel drawing**

BT = Broader Term   NT = Narrower Term   RT = Related Term   SA = See Also   UF = Used For

Creation   213; 231.7
  BT   Natural theology
  RT   Biblical cosmology
       Creationism
       Evolution
       Universe
Creation (Literary, artistic, etc.)   153.3
  UF   Inspiration
  BT   Genius
       Imagination
       Intellect
       Inventions
  NT   Creative writing
       Planning
  RT   Creative ability
Creation—Study and teaching
  USE   Creationism
        Evolution—Study and teaching
Creationism   231.7
    Use for materials on the doctrine that the
  universe was created by God out of nothing in
  the initial seven days of time and that all bio-
  logical species were created rather than evolv-
  ing from pre-existing types through modifica-
  tions in successive generations.
  UF   Christianity and evolution
       Creation—Study and teaching
         [Former heading]
       Evolution and Christianity
       Fundamentalism and education
         [Former heading]
       Fundamentalism and evolution
       Scientific creationism
  BT   Christianity—Doctrines
  RT   Bible and science
       Creation
       Evolution
       Evolution—Study and teaching
       Religion and science
Creative ability   153.3; 701; 801
  UF   Creativity
  BT   Ability
  NT   Creative thinking
  RT   Creation (Literary, artistic,
         etc.)
Creative activities   372.5
    Use for materials on activities for children
  that result in some form of personal expres-
  sion such as painting, cooking, drama, etc.
  UF   Activities curriculum
  BT   Amusements
       Elementary education

       Kindergarten
  RT   Handicraft
Creative movement
  USE   Movement education
Creative thinking   153.4
  BT   Creative ability
Creative writing   808
  UF   Writing (Authorship)
  BT   Authorship
       Creation (Literary, artistic,
         etc.)
       Language arts
Creativity
  USE   Creative ability
Creature films
  USE   Horror films
Creatures, Imaginary
  USE   Mythical animals
Credibility
  USE   Truthfulness and falsehood
Credit   332.7
  UF   Bills of credit
       Letters of credit
  BT   Finance
       Money
  NT   Agricultural credit
       Collecting of accounts
       Consumer credit
       Installment plan
       Mortgages
       Negotiable instruments
  RT   Banks and banking
       Debtor and creditor
       Loans
Credit, Agricultural
  USE   Agricultural credit
Credit card crimes   364.16
  UF   Credit card fraud
       Fraud, Credit card
  BT   Counterfeits and counterfeiting
       Fraud
       Swindlers and swindling
Credit card fraud
  USE   Credit card crimes
Credit cards   332.7
  UF   Bank credit cards
       Banks and banking—Credit
         cards
  BT   Consumer credit

BT = Broader Term   NT = Narrower Term   RT = Related Term   SA = See Also   UF = Used For

Credit unions   334

Use for materials on cooperative associations that make small loans to its members at low interest rates.

BT Cooperative banks

Creditor

USE Debtor and creditor

Creeds   238; 291.2

UF Confessions of faith

BT Doctrinal theology

NT Apostles' Creed

Nicene Creed

RT Catechisms

Cremation   363.7; 393; 614

UF Incineration

Mortuary customs

BT Public health

Sanitation

RT Burial

Funeral rites and ceremonies

Creoles   305.84; 972.9; 976

Crests

USE Heraldry

Crewelwork   746.44

BT Embroidery

Crib death

USE Sudden infant death syndrome

Crime (May subdiv. geog.)   **364**

UF Crimes

Criminology

Felony

SA types of crimes, e.g. **Computer crimes;** to be added as needed

BT Administration of criminal justice

Social ethics

Social problems

NT Art thefts

Assassination

Atrocities

Computer crimes

Counterfeits and counterfeiting

Crime prevention

Crimes without victims

Criminals

Drugs and crime

Drunk driving

Forgery

Fraud

Hate crimes

Homicide

Impostors and imposture

Juvenile delinquency

Lynching

Offenses against the person

Organized crime

Racketeering

Riots

Sex crimes

Smuggling

Stealing

Swindlers and swindling

Treason

Victims of crimes

Vigilance committees

War crimes

White collar crimes

RT Criminal law

Police

Prisons

Punishment

Trials

Vice

Crime and drugs

USE Drugs and crime

Crime and narcotics

USE Drugs and crime

Crime comics

USE Mystery comic books, strips, etc.

Crime-drug relationship

USE Drugs and crime

Crime films

USE Film noir

Gangster films

Mystery films

Crime plays

USE Mystery and detective plays

Crime prevention (May subdiv. geog.)   **364.4**

UF Prevention of crime

BT Crime

NT Burglary protection

Criminal psychology

Crime prevention—Citizen participation (May subdiv. geog.)   **364.4**

BT Political participation

Crime programs

USE Mystery radio programs

Mystery television programs

BT = Broader Term   NT = Narrower Term   RT = Related Term   SA = See Also   UF = Used For

Crime stories
USE   **Mystery fiction**
Crime syndicates
USE   **Organized crime**
       Racketeering
Crime—United States   364.973
UF   United States—Crime
Crime victims
USE   **Victims of crimes**
Crimean War, 1853-1856   947
UF   Great Britain—History—1853-
       1856, Crimean War
       Russo-Turkish War, 1853-1856
Crimes
USE   **Crime**
Crimes against public safety
USE   **Offenses against public safety**
Crimes against the person
USE   **Offenses against the person**
Crimes, Military
USE   **Military offenses**
Crimes of hate
USE   **Hate crimes**
Crimes, Political
USE   **Political crimes and offenses**
Crimes, Sex
USE   **Sex crimes**
Crimes, White collar
USE   **White collar crimes**
Crimes without victims   364.1
UF   Non-victim crimes
       Nonvictim crimes
       Victimless crimes
BT   **Crime**
       Criminal law
Criminal assault
USE   **Offenses against the person**
Criminal investigation   363.25
BT   **Law enforcement**
NT   **Criminals—Identification**
       Eavesdropping
       Fingerprints
       Lie detectors and detection
       Missing children
       Missing persons
       Wiretapping
RT   **Detectives**
       Forensic sciences
       Police

Criminal justice, Administration of
USE   **Administration of criminal jus-
       tice**
Criminal law   345
UF   Codes, Penal
       Law, Criminal
       Misdemeanors (Law)
       Penal codes
       Penal law
SA   types of crimes, e.g. **Homicide;**
       to be added as needed
BT   **Law**
NT   **Administration of criminal jus-
       tice**
       Adoption—Corrupt practices
       Capital punishment
       Crimes without victims
       Homicide
       Insanity defense
       Jury
       Kidnapping
       Military offenses
       Misconduct in office
       Obscenity (Law)
       Offenses against public safety
       Offenses against the person
       Probation
       Prohibition
       Trials
       Vigilance committees
RT   **Crime**
       Criminal procedure
       Punishment
Criminal procedure   345
BT   **Courts**
NT   **Torture**
RT   **Criminal law**
Criminal psychology   364.3
UF   Psychology, Criminal
BT   **Crime prevention**
RT   **Abnormal psychology**
Criminalistics
USE   **Forensic sciences**
Criminals   364.3; 364.6
UF   Convicts
       Delinquents
       Outlaws
       Reform of criminals
BT   **Crime**
NT   **Convict labor**

BT = Broader Term   NT = Narrower Term   RT = Related Term   SA = See Also   UF = Used For

Criminals—*Continued*
> Gangs
> Impostors and imposture
> Pirates
> Prisoners
> Swindlers and swindling
> Thieves

Criminals and drugs
> USE **Criminals—Drug use**

Criminals and narcotics
> USE **Criminals—Drug use**

Criminals—Drug use   362.29; 364.3
> UF Criminals and drugs
> Criminals and narcotics
> Drugs and criminals
> Narcotics and criminals
> RT **Drugs and crime**

Criminals—Identification   363.25
> BT **Criminal investigation**
> **Identification**
> NT **Fingerprints**

Criminals—Rehabilitation programs
> USE **Corrections**

Criminology
> USE **Crime**

Crippled children
> USE **Physically handicapped children**

Crippled people
> USE **Physically handicapped**

Crisis centers   361.3; 362
> UF Crisis intervention centers
> SA types of crisis centers, e.g. **Hotlines (Telephone counseling)**; to be added as needed
> BT **Counseling**
> **Social work**
> RT **Hotlines (Telephone counseling)**

Crisis counseling
> USE **Hotlines (Telephone counseling)**

Crisis intervention centers
> USE **Crisis centers**

Crisis intervention telephone service
> USE **Hotlines (Telephone counseling)**

Crisis management   658.4
> BT **Management**
> **Problem solving**

Critical thinking   153.4; 160
> Use for materials on thinking that is based on sound logic and the careful evaluation of all pertinent evidence.

> BT **Decision making**
> **Logic**
> **Problem solving**
> **Reasoning**
> **Thought and thinking**

Criticism   801
> Use for materials on the history, principles, methods, etc., of criticism in general and of literary criticism in particular. Criticism of the work of an individual author, artist, composer, etc., is entered under that person's name as a subject; only in the case of voluminous authors is it necessary to add the subdivision *Criticism.* Criticism of a single work is entered under the name of the author, artist, or composer, followed by the title of the work.
> UF Appraisal of books
> Books—Appraisal
> Criticism and interpretation
> Criticism, interpretation, etc.
> Evaluation of literature
> Literary criticism
> Literature—Evaluation
> SA literature, film, and music subjects with the subdivision *History and criticism*, e.g. **English poetry—History and criticism;** and names of voluminous authors and of sacred works with the subdivision *Criticism,* e.g. **Shakespeare, William, 1564-1616—Criticism; Bible—Criticism;** etc., to be added as needed
> BT **Aesthetics**
> **Literature**
> **Rhetoric**
> NT **Art criticism**
> **Books—Reviews**
> **Dramatic criticism**
> **Feminist criticism**
> RT **Literary style**

Criticism and interpretation
> USE **Criticism**
> and names of voluminous authors and of sacred works with the subdivision *Criticism,* e.g. **Shakespeare, William, 1564-1616—Criticism; Bible—Criticism;** etc., to be added as needed

Criticism, Feminist
> USE **Feminist criticism**

BT = Broader Term   NT = Narrower Term   RT = Related Term   SA = See Also   UF = Used For

Criticism, interpretation, etc.
  USE   **Criticism**
        and names of voluminous au-
        thors and of sacred works
        with the subdivision *Criticism*,
        e.g. **Shakespeare, William,
        1564-1616—Criticism; Bi-
        ble—Criticism;** etc., to be
        added as needed
Cro-Magnons   569.9; 930.1
  UF   Cromagnons
  BT   **Prehistoric peoples**
Crocheting   746.43
  BT   **Needlework**
  NT   **Beadwork**
        Lace and lace making
Crockery
  USE   **Pottery**
Crocodiles   597.98
  BT   **Reptiles**
  RT   **Alligators**
Cromagnons
  USE   **Cro-Magnons**
Crop dusting
  USE   **Aeronautics in agriculture**
Crop reports
  USE   **Agriculture—Statistics**
Crop rotation   631.5
  UF   Crops, Rotation of
        Rotation of crops
  BT   **Agriculture**
Crop spraying
  USE   **Aeronautics in agriculture**
Crops
  USE   **Farm produce**
Crops, Rotation of
  USE   **Crop rotation**
Cross cultural conflict
  USE   **Culture conflict**
Cross cultural psychology
  USE   **Ethnopsychology**
Cross cultural studies   155.8; 306
  Use for materials on the systematic compar-
  ison of two or more cultural groups, either
  within the same country or in separate coun-
  tries.
  UF   Comparison of cultures
        Intercultural studies
        Transcultural studies
  BT   **Culture**
        Social sciences

Cross-examination
  USE   **Witnesses**
Crossword puzzles   793.73
  BT   **Puzzles**
        Word games
Crowds   302.3
  UF   Mobs
  NT   **Demonstrations**
        Riot control
  RT   **Riots**
        Social psychology
Crown lands
  USE   **Public lands**
CRT display terminals
  USE   **Video display terminals**
CRTs
  USE   **Cathode ray tubes**
Crucifixion of Christ
  USE   **Jesus Christ—Crucifixion**
Crude oil
  USE   **Petroleum**
Cruelty   179
  UF   Brutality
  BT   **Ethics**
  NT   **Atrocities**
        Torture
Cruelty to animals
  USE   **Animal welfare**
Cruelty to children
  USE   **Child abuse**
Cruises
  USE   **Ocean travel**
Crusades   909.07
  BT   **Church history—600-1500,
        Middle Ages**
        Middle Ages—History
  RT   **Chivalry**
Crustacea   565; 595.3
  SA   names of specific crustaceans,
        e.g. **Lobsters;** to be added as
        needed
  BT   **Invertebrates**
        Shellfish
  NT   **Crabs**
        Lobsters
Cryobiology   571.4
  UF   Freezing
        Low temperature biology
  BT   **Biology**
        Cold

BT = Broader Term   NT = Narrower Term   RT = Related Term   SA = See Also   UF = Used For

Cryobiology—*Continued*
    Low temperatures
  NT   **Cold—Physiological effect**
    Frozen embryos
Cryogenic interment
  USE **Cryonics**
Cryogenic surgery
  USE **Cryosurgery**
Cryogenics
  USE **Low temperatures**
Cryonics 621.5
  UF Cryogenic interment
    Freezing of human bodies
    Human cold storage
  BT **Burial**
Cryosurgery 617
  UF Cryogenic surgery
  BT **Cold—Therapeutic use**
    Surgery
Cryotherapy
  USE **Cold—Therapeutic use**
Cryptography 652
  UF Code deciphering
    Code enciphering
    Secret writing
  BT **Signs and symbols**
    Writing
  RT **Ciphers**
Crystal gazing
  USE **Divination**
Crystal meth (Drug)
  USE **Ice (Drug)**
Crystalline rocks
  USE **Rocks**
Crystallization
  USE **Crystals**
Crystallography
  USE **Crystals**
Crystals 548
  UF Crystallization
    Crystallography *[Former heading]*
  SA types of crystals, e.g. **Quartz;** to
    be added as needed
  BT **Physical chemistry**
    Solids
  NT **Quartz**
  RT **Minerals**
Cub Scouts
  USE **Boy Scouts**

Cuba 972.91
  May be subdivided like United States except for *History.*
  BT **Islands**
Cuba—History 972.91
**Cuba—History—1958-1959, Revolution
    972.9106**
Cuba—History—1959- 972.9106
**Cuba—History—1961, Invasion
    972.9106**
  UF Bay of Pigs invasion
    Cuban invasion, 1961
    Invasion of Cuba, 1961
Cuban invasion, 1961
  USE **Cuba—History—1961, Invasion**
Cube root 513.2
  BT **Arithmetic**
Cubic measurement
  USE **Volume (Cubic content)**
Cubism 709.04; 759.06
  BT **Abstract art**
    Painting
  RT **Postimpressionism (Art)**
Cultivated plants (May subdiv. geog.)
    581.6; 631.5
  UF Plants, Cultivated *[Former heading]*
  BT **Agriculture**
    Gardening
  NT **Annuals (Plants)**
    House plants
    Ornamental plants
    Perennials
**Cultivated plants—United States 581.6;
    631.5**
Cults 291.9; 306.6
  Use for materials on groups or movements whose beliefs or practices differ significantly from the traditional religions and are often focused upon a charismatic leader. Materials on the major world religions are entered under **Religions.** Materials on independent religious groups those teachings or practices fall within the normative bounds of the major world religions are entered under **Sects.**
  UF Religious cults
  BT **Religions**
  NT **New Age movement**
  RT **Sects**
Cultural anthropology
  USE **Ethnology**
Cultural change
  USE **Social change**

BT = Broader Term   NT = Narrower Term   RT = Related Term   SA = See Also   UF = Used For

Cultural exchange programs
    USE   **Exchange of persons programs**
Cultural life
    USE   **Intellectual life**
Cultural pluralism
    USE   **Multiculturalism**
Cultural relations   306; 341.7
    UF   Intercultural relations
    BT   **Intellectual cooperation**
           International cooperation
           International relations
    NT   **Exchange of persons programs**
Culturally deprived
    USE   **Socially handicapped**
Culturally deprived children
    USE   **Socially handicapped children**
Culturally handicapped
    USE   **Socially handicapped**
Culturally handicapped children
    USE   **Socially handicapped children**
Culture   306; 909
    Use for materials on the sum total of ways of living or thinking established by a group of human beings and transmitted from one generation to the next, including a concern for what is regarded as excellent in the arts, manners, scholarship, etc. Materials limited to the culture of individual nations are entered under names of countries with the subdivisions *Civilization; Intellectual life;* or *Social life and customs.*
    NT   **Acculturation**
           Biculturalism
           Cross cultural studies
           Humanism
           Intellectual life
           Popular culture
    RT   **Anthropology**
           Civilization
           Education
           Learning and scholarship
           Sociology
Culture conflict   155.8; 306; 155.8
    UF   Conflict of cultures
           Cross cultural conflict
           Culture shock
           Future shock
    BT   **Ethnic relations**
           Ethnopsychology
           Race relations
Culture contact
    USE   **Acculturation**

Culture, Popular
    USE   **Popular culture**
Culture shock
    USE   **Culture conflict**
Curates
    USE   **Clergy**
Curiosities and wonders   030
    UF   Enigmas
           Facts, Miscellaneous
           Miscellaneous facts
           Oddities
           Trivia
           Wonders
    SA   subjects with the subdivision *Miscellanea,* e.g. **Medicine—Miscellanea;** to be added as needed
    NT   **Eccentrics and eccentricities**
           Medicine—Miscellanea
           Monsters
           World records
Currency
    USE   **Money**
Currency devaluation
    USE   **Monetary policy**
Current events   909.82
    Use for materials on the study and teaching of current events. Periodicals and yearbooks devoted to the events themselves are entered under **History—Periodicals.**
    BT   **Modern history—Study and teaching**
Currents, Alternating
    USE   **Alternating electric currents**
Currents, Electric
    USE   **Electric currents**
Currents, Ocean
    USE   **Ocean currents**
Curricula (Courses of study)
    USE   **Education—Curricula**
Curriculum development
    USE   **Curriculum planning**
Curriculum materials centers
    USE   **Instructional materials centers**
Curriculum planning   375
    UF   Curriculum development
    BT   **Education—Curricula**
           Planning
    NT   **Interdisciplinary approach in education**

BT = Broader Term   NT = Narrower Term   RT = Related Term   SA = See Also   UF = Used For

Curtains
    USE   Drapery
Custody kidnapping
    USE   Parental kidnapping
Custody of children
    USE   Child custody
Custom duties
    USE   Tariff
Customer relations   658.8
    BT   Business
          Public relations
    NT   Customer service
Customer service   658.8
    UF   Service, Customer
          Service (in industry)
          Services, Customer
          Technical service
    BT   Customer relations
Customs and practices
    USE   religions, denominations, reli-
           gious orders, and religious
           holidays with the subdivision
           Customs and practices, e.g.
           **Judaism—Customs and
           practices;** to be added as
           needed
Customs, Social
    USE   Manners and customs
Customs (Tariff)
    USE   Tariff
Cybernetics   003
    UF   Automatic control
          Mechanical brains
    BT   Communication
          Electronics
          System theory
    NT   Bionics
          Computers
          System analysis
          Systems engineering
Cycles   115
    UF   Cyclic theory
          Natural cycles
          Periodicity *[Former heading]*
    NT   Biological rhythms
    RT   Rhythm
          Time
Cycles, Business
    USE   Business cycles

Cycles, Life (Biology)
    USE   Life cycles (Biology)
Cycles, Motor
    USE   Motorcycles
Cyclic theory
    USE   Cycles
Cycling   796.6
    UF   Bicycles and bicycling *[Former
          heading]*
          Bicycling
          Biking
    BT   Exercise
          Outdoor recreation
          Sports
    NT   Bicycle racing
          Bicycle touring
          Motorcycling
    RT   Bicycles
          Tricycles
Cyclones   551.55
    Use for materials on large-scale storms that
    involve high winds rotating around a center of
    low atmospheric pressure. Materials on the
    cyclones of the West Indies are entered under
    Hurricanes. Materials on the cyclones of the
    China Seas and the Philippines are entered
    under **Typhoons.**
    BT   Meteorology
          Storms
          Winds
    NT   Hurricanes
          Typhoons
Cyclopedias
    USE   Encyclopedias and dictionaries
Cyclotron   539.7
    UF   Atom smashing
          Magnetic resonance accelerator
    BT   Atoms
          Nuclear physics
          Transmutation (Chemistry)
Cytology
    USE   Cells
Czech Republic   943.71
    Use for materials on this part of the former
    country of Czechoslovakia since its becoming
    independent on January 1, 1993. May be sub-
    divided like United States except for *History.*
    RT   Czechoslovakia
Czechoslovakia   943.703
    Use for materials on the former country of
    Czechoslovakia through December 31, 1992.
    Materials on the two parts of the former coun-
    try of Czechoslovakia, which became indepen-

BT = Broader Term   NT = Narrower Term   RT = Related Term   SA = See Also   UF = Used For

Czechoslovakia—*Continued*
dent on January 1, 1993, are entered under
Czech Republic and **Slovakia.**
  RT **Czech Republic**
      Slovakia
Czechoslovakia—History—1918-1968
      943.703
Czechoslovakia—History—1968-1989
      943.704
  UF Czechoslovakia—History—1968- ,
      Intervention *[Former heading]*
      Russian intervention in Czecho-
      slovakia
      Soviet intervention in Czechoslo-
      vakia
Czechoslovakia—History—1968- , Interven-
  tion
  USE **Czechoslovakia—History—1968-1989**
Czechoslovakia—History—1989-
  USE **Czechoslovakia—History—1989-1992**
Czechoslovakia—History—1989-1992
      943.704
  UF Czechoslovakia—History—1989-
      [Former heading]
D.D.T. (Insecticide)   668
  UF DDT (Insecticide)
      Dichloro-diphenyl-trichloroethane
  BT **Insecticides**
D Day
  USE **Normandy (France), Attack on,**
       1944
D.N.A.
  USE **DNA**
Daily readings (Spiritual exercises)
  USE **Devotional calendars**
Dairies
  USE **Dairying**
Dairy cattle   636.2
  SA names of breeds of dairy cattle,
      to be added as needed
  BT **Cattle**
      Dairying
  NT **Holstein-Friesian cattle**
Dairy farming
  USE **Dairying**
Dairy products   637; 641.3
  UF Products, Dairy
  SA names of dairy products, to be
      added as needed
  BT **Animal products**
  NT **Butter**

      Cheese
      Milk
  RT **Dairying**
Dairying (May subdiv. geog.)   **636.2;**
      637
      Use for materials on the production and
  marketing of milk and milk products and for
  general materials on dairy farming.
  UF Dairies
      Dairy farming
  BT **Agriculture**
      Livestock industry
  NT **Dairy cattle**
      Milk
  RT **Cattle**
      Dairy products
Dams   627
  SA names of dams, e.g. **Hoover**
      Dam (Ariz. and Nev.); to be
      added as needed
  BT **Civil engineering**
      Flood control
      Hydraulic structures
      Irrigation
      Rivers
      Water power
      Water supply
  NT **Hoover Dam (Ariz. and Nev.)**
Dance (May subdiv. geog.)   **792.8; 793.3**
      Use for materials on recreational dancing as
  well as performance dance.
  UF Dances
      Dancing *[Former heading]*
  SA types of dances and dancing, to
      be added as needed
  BT **Amusements**
      Performing arts
  NT **Ballet**
      Break dancing
      Clog dancing
      Folk dancing
      Modern dance
      Tap dancing
  RT **Aerobics**
      Dance music
Dance music   781.5; 784.18
  BT **Music**
  RT **Dance**

BT = Broader Term   NT = Narrower Term   RT = Related Term   SA = See Also   UF = Used For

Dance—United States   792.80973;
      793.30973
   UF   Dancing—United States *[Former
            heading]*
         United States—Dance
   NT   American folk dancing
Dancers   792.8092; 793.3092; 920
   SA   types of dancers, e.g. **Ballet
            dancers;** to be added as
            needed
   BT   Entertainers
   NT   Ballet dancers
Dances
   USE   Dance
Dancing
   USE   Dance
Dancing—United States
   USE   Dance—United States
Dangerous animals   591.6
   BT   Animals
         Wildlife
   NT   Animal attacks
         Poisonous animals
Dangerous materials
   USE   Hazardous substances
Dangerous occupations
   USE   Hazardous occupations
Danish language   439.8
   May be subdivided like **English language.**
   BT   Language and languages
         Norwegian language
         Scandinavian languages
Danish literature   839.81
   May use same subdivisions and names of
   literary forms as for **English literature.**
   BT   Literature
         Scandinavian literature
Dark Ages
   USE   Middle Ages
Dark humor (Literature)
   USE   Black humor (Literature)
Dark night of the soul
   USE   Mysticism
Darkroom technique in photography
   USE   Photography—Processing
Darwinism
   USE   Evolution
Data base management
   USE   Database management
Data processing
   USE   Electronic data processing

Information systems
      and subjects with the subdivi-
      sion *Data processing,* e.g.
      **Banks and banking—Data
      processing;** to be added as
      needed
Data storage and retrieval systems
   USE   Information systems
Data transmission systems   004.6;
      621.38; 621.39
   UF   Transmission of data
   BT   Electronic data processing
         Telecommunication
   NT   Computer networks
         Electronic mail systems
         Facsimile transmission
         Information networks
         Library information networks
         Teletext systems
         Video telephone
         Videotex systems
Database management   005.74
   UF   Data base management
         Systems, Database management
   BT   Electronic data processing
         Information systems
Database management—Computer pro-
      grams   005.74
   BT   Computer software
Date etiquette
   USE   Dating (Social customs)
Date rape   362.883; 364.15
   UF   Acquaintance rape
         Dating violence
   BT   Dating (Social customs)
         Rape
Dates, Historical
   USE   Historical chronology
Dating, Radiocarbon
   USE   Radiocarbon dating
Dating (Social customs)   306.73; 392.4;
      646.7
   UF   Courting
         Courtship
         Date etiquette
   BT   Etiquette
         Manners and customs
   NT   Date rape
   RT   Love

BT = Broader Term   NT = Narrower Term   RT = Related Term   SA = See Also   UF = Used For

Dating violence
    USE   **Date rape**
Daughters and fathers
    USE   **Fathers and daughters**
Daughters and mothers
    USE   **Mothers and daughters**
Day   **529**
    BT   **Chronology**
           Time
    RT   **Night**
Day care centers   **362.71**
    UF   Child care centers *[Former*
           heading]
           Children—Day care
           Children's day care centers
           Day nurseries
           Nurseries, Day
    BT   **Child care**
           Child welfare
           Children—Institutional care
    RT   **Nursery schools**
Day dreams
    USE   **Fantasy**
Day nurseries
    USE   **Day care centers**
Day of Atonement
    USE   **Yom Kippur**
Days   **394.2**
    UF   Days of the week
    SA   types of days and names of par-
           ticular days, to be added as
           needed
    BT   **Calendars**
    NT   **Birthdays**
           Festivals
           Holidays
    RT   **Week**
Days of the week
    USE   **Days**
DDT (Insecticide)
    USE   **D.D.T. (Insecticide)**
Dead Sea scrolls   **221.4; 229; 296.1**
    UF   Qumran texts
Deaf   **362.4**
    BT   **Hearing impaired**
           Physically handicapped
    NT   **Closed caption television**
           Closed caption video record-
           ings

Deaf—Education   **371.91**
    UF   Education of the deaf
    BT   **Education**
Deaf—Institutional care   **362.4**
    BT   **Institutional care**
Deaf—Means of communication   **362.4;**
        419
    Use for general materials on communication
in the broadest sense by people who are deaf.
Materials on language systems based on hand
gestures are entered under **Sign language.**
    UF   Finger alphabet
           Lip reading
    BT   **Communication**
    NT   **Hearing ear dogs**
    RT   **Nonverbal communication**
           Sign language
Deaf—Sign language
    USE   **Sign language**
Deafness   **362.4; 617.8**
    BT   **Ear**
    NT   **Hearing aids**
    RT   **Hearing**
Death   **128; 236; 306.9; 571.9**
    SA   ethnic groups and classes of per-
           sons with the subdivision
           Death, e.g. **Infants—Death;**
           and names of individual per-
           sons and groups of notable
           persons with the subdivision
           Death and burial, e.g. **Presi-**
           dents—United States—Death
           and burial; to be added as
           needed
    BT   **Biology**
           Eschatology
           Life
    NT   **Brain death**
           Future life
           Infants—Death
           Near-death experiences
           Right to die
    RT   **Burial**
           Mortality
           Terminal care
           Terminally ill
Death, Apparent
    USE   **Near-death experiences**
Death masks
    USE   **Masks (Sculpture)**

BT = Broader Term   NT = Narrower Term   RT = Related Term   SA = See Also   UF = Used For

Death, Mercy
　USE　**Euthanasia**
Death notices
　USE　**Obituaries**
Death penalty
　USE　**Capital punishment**
Death rate
　USE　**Mortality**
　　　　Vital statistics
Deaths, Registers of
　USE　**Registers of births, etc.**
Debates and debating　808.53
　UF　Argumentation
　　　Discussion
　　　Speaking
　BT　**Public speaking**
　　　Rhetoric
　NT　**Parliamentary practice**
　　　Radio addresses, debates, etc.
　RT　**Discussion groups**
Debit cards　332.1
　UF　Bank debit cards
　　　Cards, Debit
　BT　**Banks and banking**
Debit insurance
　USE　**Industrial life insurance**
Debris, Space
　USE　**Space debris**
Debt　332.7
　　Use for economic and statistical materials
　on debt. Legal materials involving debtor and
　creditor are entered under **Debtor and credi-
　tor.**
　UF　Indebtedness
　BT　**Finance**
　NT　**Collecting of accounts**
　　　Public debts
　RT　**Debtor and creditor**
Debtor
　USE　**Debtor and creditor**
Debtor and creditor　346.07
　UF　Creditor
　　　Debtor
　BT　**Commercial law**
　NT　**Bankruptcy**
　　　Collecting of accounts
　RT　**Credit**
　　　Debt
Debts, Government
　USE　**Public debts**

Debts, Public
　USE　**Public debts**
Decalogue
　USE　**Ten commandments**
Deceit
　USE　**Fraud**
Decentralization of schools
　USE　**Schools—Decentralization**
Deceptive advertising　343.07
　UF　Advertising, Fraudulent *[Former
　　　　heading]*
　　　False advertising
　　　Fraudulent advertising
　　　Misleading advertising
　　　Misrepresentation in advertising
　　　Truth in advertising
　BT　**Advertising**
　　　Business ethics
Decimal system　513.5
　BT　**Numbers**
　RT　**Metric system**
Decision making　153.8; 302.3; 658.4
　BT　**Game theory**
　NT　**Critical thinking**
　RT　**Choice (Psychology)**
　　　Problem solving
Decks (Domestic architecture)
　USE　**Patios**
Declamations
　USE　**Monologues**
　　　Recitations
Declamations, Musical
　USE　**Monologues with music**
Declaration of independence (U.S.)
　USE　**United States—Declaration of
　　　　independence**
Decoration and ornament　745.4
　　Use for general materials on the forms and
　styles of decoration in various fields of fine
　arts or applied art and on the history of vari-
　ous styles of ornament. Materials limited to
　the decoration of houses are entered under **In-
　terior design.**
　UF　Art, Decorative
　　　Arts, Decorative
　　　Decorative art
　　　Decorative design
　　　Decorative painting
　　　Design, Decorative
　　　Ornament
　　　Painting, Decorative

Decoration and ornament—*Continued*
- SA decoration and ornament of particular countries, e.g. **American decoration and ornament;** and names of particular styles of decoration and ornament, e.g. **Renaissance decoration and ornament;** to be added as needed
- BT Art
  - Decorative arts
- NT American decoration and ornament
  - Antiques
  - Architectural decoration and ornament
  - Art objects
  - Artificial flowers
  - Arts and crafts movement
  - Bronzes
  - Carpets
  - China painting
  - Christmas decorations
  - Decoupage
  - Design
  - Egg decoration
  - Embroidery
  - Enamel and enameling
  - Flower arrangement
  - Furniture
  - Garden ornaments and furniture
  - Gems
  - Glass painting and staining
  - Holiday decorations
  - Illumination of books and manuscripts
  - Illustration of books
  - Interior design
  - Ironwork
  - Jewelry
  - Leather work
  - Lettering
  - Metalwork
  - Monograms
  - Mosaics
  - Mural painting and decoration
  - Needlework
  - Picture frames and framing
  - Plants in art
  - Pottery
  - Renaissance decoration and ornament
  - Sculpture
  - Show windows
  - Stencil work
  - Stucco
  - Table setting and decoration
  - Tapestry
  - Terra cotta
  - Textile design
  - Wood carving
- RT Handicraft
  - Painting

Decoration and ornament, American
- USE **American decoration and ornament**

Decoration and ornament, Architectural
- USE **Architectural decoration and ornament**

Decoration and ornament, Renaissance
- USE **Renaissance decoration and ornament**

Decoration Day
- USE **Memorial Day**

Decoration, Interior
- USE **Interior design**

Decorations, Holiday
- USE **Holiday decorations**

Decorations of honor   355.1; 929.8
- UF Badges of honor
  - Emblems
- SA names of medals, to be added as needed
- RT **Heraldry**
  - **Insignia**
  - **Medals**

Decorative art
- USE **Decoration and ornament**
  - **Decorative arts**

Decorative arts (May subdiv. geog.)
    745

Use for general materials on the various applied art forms having some utilitarian as well as decorative purpose, including furniture, silverware, the decoration of buildings, etc.
- UF Applied arts
  - Art, Decorative
  - Art industries and trade
  - Arts, Applied
  - Arts, Decorative

BT = Broader Term   NT = Narrower Term   RT = Related Term   SA = See Also   UF = Used For

Decorative arts—*Continued*
    Arts, Minor
    Decorative art
    Minor arts
SA   types of decorative arts, to be
      added as needed
BT   **Arts**
NT   **Antiques**
    Art metalwork
    Art objects
    Arts and crafts movement
    Calligraphy
    Carving (Decorative arts)
    Costume
    Decoration and ornament
    Decoupage
    Enamel and enameling
    Fabrics
    Furniture
    Glassware
    Interior design
    Jewelry
    Lacquer and lacquering
    Leather work
    Mosaics
    Needlework
    Porcelain
    Pottery
    Rugs
    Silverware
    Tapestry
    Victoriana
    Woodwork
RT   **Folk art**
    Handicraft
Decorative arts—United States
    745.0973
UF   United States—Decorative arts
Decorative design
USE   **Decoration and ornament**
Decorative metalwork
USE   **Art metalwork**
Decorative painting
USE   **Decoration and ornament**
Decoupage   745.54
BT   **Decoration and ornament**
    Decorative arts
    Paper crafts
Decoys (Hunting)   745.593; 799.2
UF   Bird decoys (Hunting)

BT   **Hunting**
    Shooting
Deduction (Logic)
USE   **Logic**
Deep diving   627
    Use for materials on underwater diving with
    equipment. Materials on diving from a board
    or platform are entered under **Diving.**
UF   Deep sea diving
    Diving, Submarine *[Former
      heading]*
    Submarine diving *[Former head-
      ing]*
    Underwater diving
BT   **Underwater exploration**
    Water sports
NT   **Scuba diving**
    Skin diving
RT   **Diving**
Deep diving vehicles
USE   **Submersibles**
Deep sea diving
USE   **Deep diving**
Deep sea drilling (Petroleum)
USE   **Offshore oil well drilling**
Deep sea engineering
USE   **Ocean engineering**
Deep sea mining
USE   **Ocean mining**
Deep-sea Photography
USE   **Underwater photography**
Deep sea technology
USE   **Oceanography**
Deep sea vehicles
USE   **Submersibles**
Deep submergence vehicles
USE   **Submersibles**
Deer   599.65
UF   Fawns
BT   **Game and game birds**
    Mammals
NT   **Reindeer**
Defamation
USE   **Libel and slander**
Defective speech
USE   **Speech disorders**
Defective vision
USE   **Vision disorders**
Defectors   325; 327.12
UF   Defectors, Political
    Political defectors

BT = Broader Term   NT = Narrower Term   RT = Related Term   SA = See Also   UF = Used For

Defectors—*Continued*
   Turncoats
 BT **Political refugees**
Defectors, Military
 USE **Military desertion**
Defectors, Political
 USE **Defectors**
Defense industries 338.4
  Use for materials on the industries produc-
  ing the implements of war. Materials on the
  implements of war themselves are entered un-
  der **Ordnance** or under **Military weapons.**
 UF Armaments industries
   Arms sales
   Military sales
   Military supplies industry
   Munitions *[Former heading]*
 BT **Industries**
 RT **Firearms industry**
   Military readiness
   Military weapons
   Ordnance
Defense (Law)
 USE **Litigation**
Defense mechanisms (Zoology)
 USE **Animal defenses**
Defense policy
 USE **Military policy**
Defense readiness
 USE **Military readiness**
Defenses
 USE types of defenses, e.g. **Air de-**
   fenses; and names of conti-
   nents, regions, countries, and
   individual colonies with the
   subdivision *Defenses,* e.g.
   United States—Defenses; to
   be added as needed
Defenses, National
 USE **Industrial mobilization**
Defenses, Radar
 USE **Radar defense networks**
Deficit financing (May subdiv. geog.)
  336.3
 UF Compensatory spending
   Deficit spending
 BT **Public finance**
 RT **Public debts**
Deficit spending
 USE **Deficit financing**

Defoliants
 USE **Herbicides**
Deformities
 USE **Birth defects**
Degrees, Academic
 USE **Academic degrees**
Degrees of latitude and longitude
 USE **Geodesy**
   Latitude
   Longitude
Dehydrated foods
 USE **Dried foods**
Dehydrated milk
 USE **Dried milk**
Deism 211
 BT **Religion**
   Theology
 RT **Atheism**
   Free thought
   Positivism
   Rationalism
   Theism
Deities
 USE **Gods and goddesses**
Dejection
 USE **Depression (Psychology)**
Delayed memory
 USE **Recovered memory**
Delinquency, Juvenile
 USE **Juvenile delinquency**
Delinquents
 USE **Criminals**
   Juvenile delinquency
Delivery of health care
 USE **Medical care**
Delivery of medical care
 USE **Medical care**
Delphi (Ancient city)
 USE **Delphi (Extinct city)**
Delphi (Extinct city) 938
 UF Delphi (Ancient city) *[Former*
   heading]
 BT **Extinct cities—Greece**
   Greece—Antiquities
Delusions
 USE **Hallucinations and illusions**
Demineralization of salt water
 USE **Sea water conversion**
Democracy 321.8
 UF Popular government

BT = Broader Term NT = Narrower Term RT = Related Term SA = See Also UF = Used For

205

Democracy—*Continued*

       Self-government

  BT   **Constitutional history**

       Constitutional law

       Political science

  NT   **Freedom**

       Referendum

       Suffrage

  RT   **Equality**

       Federal government

       Representative government and representation

       Republics

Democratic Party (U.S.)   324.2736

  BT   **Political parties**

Demography

  USE   **Population**

Demoniac possession   133.4

  BT   **Demonology**

  RT   **Devil**

       Exorcism

Demonology   133.4

  UF   Evil spirits

       Spirits

  BT   **Ghosts**

  NT   **Charms**

       Demoniac possession

  RT   **Apparitions**

       Devil

       Exorcism

       Occultism

       Superstition

       Witchcraft

Demonstrations (May subdiv. geog.)   322.4; 361.2

Use for materials on public gatherings, marches, etc., organized for nonviolent protest even though incidental disturbances or rioting may occur.

  UF   Demonstrations (Protest)

       Marches (Demonstrations)

       Protest marches and rallies

       Protest movements

       Protests, demonstrations, etc. *[Former heading]*

       Public demonstrations

       Rallies (Protest)

  SA   names of specific wars or other objects of protest with the subdivision *Protests move-*

ments, e.g. **World War, 1939-1945—Protest movements;** to be added as needed

  BT   **Crowds**

       Public meetings

  NT   **Civil rights demonstrations**

       Hunger strikes

  RT   **Peace movements**

       Riots

Demonstrations—Chicago (Ill.)   322.409773

  UF   Chicago (Ill.)—Demonstrations

       Protests, demonstrations, etc.—Chicago (Ill.) *[Former heading]*

Demonstrations for civil rights

  USE   **Civil rights demonstrations**

Demonstrations (Protest)

  USE   **Demonstrations**

Demonstrations—United States   322.40973; 361.2

  UF   Protests, demonstrations, etc.—United States *[Former heading]*

       United States—Demonstrations

Denationalization

  USE   **Privatization**

Denatured alcohol   661

  UF   Alcohol, Denatured *[Former heading]*

       Alcohol, Industrial

       Industrial alcohol

  BT   **Alcohol**

Denominational schools

  USE   **Church schools**

Denominations, Christian

  USE   **Christian sects**

Denominations, Protestant

  USE   **Protestant churches**

Denominations, Religious

  USE   **Sects**

Dental care (May subdiv. geog.)   617.6

Use for materials on the organization of services and facilities for dental care. Materials on the technical and medical aspects of dental care are entered under **Dentistry.**

  SA   ethnic groups, classes of persons, and military services with the subdivision *Dental care,* e.g. **Children—Dental care;** to be added as needed

---

BT = Broader Term   NT = Narrower Term   RT = Related Term   SA = See Also   UF = Used For

Dental care—*Continued*
> BT   Medical care
> RT   Dentistry

Dentistry   617.6
> Use for materials on the technical and medical aspects of dental care. Materials on the organization of services and facilities for dental care are entered under **Dental care.**
>
> UF   Medicine, Dental
> SA   ethnic groups, classes of persons, and military services with the subdivision *Dental care,* e.g. **Children—Dental care;** to be added as needed
> BT   **Medicine**
> RT   **Dental care**
>   **Teeth**

Deoxyribonucleic acid
> USE   **DNA**

Department stores   658.8
> BT   **Business**
>   **Retail trade**
>   **Stores**

Dependencies
> USE   **Colonies**

Depression, Mental
> USE   **Depression (Psychology)**

Depression (Psychology)   616.85
> UF   Dejection
>   Depression, Mental *[Former heading]*
>   Depressive psychoses
>   Melancholia
>   Mental depression
>   Mentally depressed
> BT   **Abnormal psychology**
>   **Neuroses**
> RT   **Manic-depressive illness**

Depressions (May subdiv. geog.)   338.5
> UF   Business depressions
>   Depressions, Economic *[Former heading]*
>   Economic depressions *[Former heading]*
> SA   names of countries, states, cities, etc., with the subdivision *Economic conditions,* to be added as needed
> BT   **Business cycles**
> NT   **Great Depression, 1929-1939**

Depressions—1929
> USE   **Great Depression, 1929-1939**

Depressions, Economic
> USE   **Depressions**

Depressive psychoses
> USE   **Depression (Psychology)**

Deprogramming
> USE   **Brainwashing**

Derailments
> USE   **Railroad accidents**

Dermatitis
> USE   **Skin—Diseases**

Derricks
> USE   **Cranes, derricks, etc.**

Desalination of water
> USE   **Sea water conversion**

Desalting of water
> USE   **Sea water conversion**

Descent
> USE   **Genealogy**
>   **Heredity**

Description
> USE   names of cities (except extinct cities), countries, states, and regions with the subdivision *Description,* e.g. **Chicago (Ill.)—Description; United States—Description;** etc., for descriptive materials and accounts of travel, including the history of travel, in those places; names of places with the subdivision *Geography* for broad geographical materials about a specific place, e.g. **United States—Geography;** and names of extinct cities or towns, without further subdivision, for general descriptive materials on those places, e.g. **Delphi (Extinct city);** to be added as needed

Description and travel
> USE   names of cities (except extinct cities), countries, states, etc., with the subdivision *Description,* e.g. **United States—Description;** and ethnic groups, classes of persons, and names

---

BT = Broader Term   NT = Narrower Term   RT = Related Term   SA = See Also   UF = Used For

Description and travel—*Continued*
  of individuals with the subdi-
  vision *Travel,* e.g. **Handi-
  capped—Travel;** to be added
  as needed
Descriptive geometry   516
  UF Geometry, Descriptive *[Former
    heading]*
  BT **Geometrical drawing
    Geometry**
  NT **Perspective**
Desegregated schools
  USE **School integration**
Desegregation
  USE **Segregation**
Desegregation in education
  USE **School integration**
Desert animals   578.754
  UF Desert fauna
  SA types of desert animals, e.g.
    Camels; to be added as need-
    ed
  BT **Animals
    Deserts
    Wildlife**
  NT **Camels**
Desert fauna
  USE **Desert animals**
Desert plants   581.7
  SA types of desert plants, e.g. **Cac-
    tus;** to be added as needed
  BT **Deserts
    Plant ecology
    Plants**
  NT **Cactus**
Desertion
  USE **Desertion and nonsupport
    Military desertion
    Runaway adults**
**Desertion and nonsupport   306.88;
  346.01**
  UF Abandonment of family
    Desertion
    Nonsupport
  BT **Divorce
    Domestic relations**
  NT **Child support
    Runaway adults**
Desertion, Military
  USE **Military desertion**

Deserts   551.41
  BT **Physical geography**
  NT **Desert animals
    Desert plants**
Design   745.4
  SA types of design, e.g. **Industrial
    design; Fashions design;** etc.;
    types of objects, structures,
    machines, equipment, etc., and
    types of educational tests and
    examinations with the subdivi-
    sion *Design and construction,*
    e.g. **Automobiles—Design
    and construction;** topical
    headings with which the sub-
    division *Design and construc-
    tion* would be inappropriate
    with the subdivision *Design,*
    e.g. **Quilts—Design; Pam-
    phlets—Design;** etc.; and
    types of architecture and land-
    scape with the form subdivi-
    sion *Designs and plans,* for
    materials containing designs
    and drawings, e.g. **Domestic
    architecture—Designs and
    plans;** to be added as needed
  BT **Decoration and ornament**
  NT **Computer aided design
    Fashion design
    Garden design
    Industrial design
    Interior design
    Machine design
    Quilts—Design
    Textile design**
  RT **Pattern making**
Design and construction
  USE types of objects, structures, ma-
    chines, equipment, etc., and
    types of educational tests and
    examinations with the subdivi-
    sion *Design and construction,*
    e.g. **Airplanes—Design and
    construction;** to be added as
    needed
Design, Decorative
  USE **Decoration and ornament**
Design, Industrial
  USE **Industrial design**

BT = Broader Term   NT = Narrower Term   RT = Related Term   SA = See Also   UF = Used For

Design, Interior
USE **Interior design**
Design, System
USE **System design**
Designed genetic change
USE **Genetic engineering**
Designer drugs 362.29; 615
Use for materials on illicit drugs manufac-
tured by altering the molecular structure of
existing drugs to mimic the effects of standard
narcotics, stimulants, or hallucinogens.
UF Drugs of abuse, Synthetic
Synthetic drugs of abuse
SA types of designer drugs, e.g. **Ice
(Drug);** to be added as need-
ed
BT **Drugs**
NT **Ice (Drug)**
Designs and plans
USE types of architecture and land-
scape with the form subdivi-
sion *Designs and plans,* for
materials containing designs
and drawings, e.g. **Domestic
architecture—Designs and
plans;** to be added as needed
Designs, Architectural
USE **Architecture—Designs and
plans**
Designs, Floral
USE **Flower arrangement**
Desktop computers
USE **Microcomputers**
Desktop publishing 070.5; 686.2
Use for materials on the use of a personal
computer with writing, graphics, and page lay-
out software to produce printed material for
publication. Materials on the process of pub-
lishing by which books and articles or any
kind of data are made available as an elec-
tronic product are entered under **Electronic
publishing.**
RT **Electronic publishing
Word processing**
Desoxyribonucleic acid
USE **DNA**
Desserts 641.8
SA types of desserts and names of
specific desserts, to be added
as needed
BT **Cooking**
NT **Cake
Ice cream, ices, etc.**

RT **Chocolate**
Destiny
USE **Fate and fatalism**
Destitution
USE **Poverty**
Destruction of Jews (1933-1945)
USE **Holocaust, 1933-1945**
Destructive insects
USE **Insect pests**
Detective and mystery comic books, strips,
etc.
USE **Mystery comic books, strips,
etc.**
Detective and mystery films
USE **Mystery films**
Detective and mystery plays
USE **Mystery and detective plays**
Detective and mystery radio programs
USE **Mystery radio programs**
Detective and mystery stories
USE **Mystery fiction**
Detective and mystery television programs
USE **Mystery television programs**
Detective comics
USE **Mystery comic books, strips,
etc.**
Detective fiction
USE **Mystery fiction**
Detective stories
USE **Mystery fiction**
Detectives 363.25; 920
BT **Police**
RT **Criminal investigation
Secret service**
Detergent pollution of rivers, lakes, etc.
USE **Water pollution**
Detergents 668
UF Detergents, Synthetic *[Former
heading]*
Synthetic detergents
BT **Cleaning compounds**
RT **Soap**
Detergents, Synthetic
USE **Detergents**
Determinism and indeterminism
USE **Free will and determinism**
Deuterium oxide 546
UF Heavy water
BT **Chemicals**

BT = Broader Term NT = Narrower Term RT = Related Term SA = See Also UF = Used For

Devaluation of currency
USE Monetary policy

Developing countries 330.9

Use for comprehensive materials on countries that are not fully modernized or industrialized. This heading may be subdivided by the topical subdivisions used under countries, regions, etc., and may be used as a geographic subdivision e.g. **Education—Developing countries.**

UF Fourth World
Less developed countries
Third World
Underdeveloped areas
BT **Economic conditions**
Industrialization
NT **New states**

Developing countries—Commerce
338.91; 382
BT **Commerce**

Developing countries—Education
USE **Education—Developing countries**

Development
USE **Embryology**
Evolution
Growth disorders
Modernization (Sociology)

Development, Economic
USE **Economic development**

Deviation, Sexual
USE **Sexual deviation**

Devices (Heraldry)
USE **Heraldry**
Insignia

Devil 235
UF Satan
RT **Demoniac possession**
Demonology

Devil's Triangle
USE **Bermuda Triangle**

Devotion
USE **Prayer**
Worship

Devotional calendars 242
UF Christian devotional calendars
Daily readings (Spiritual exercises)
Devotional exercises (Daily readings)
BT **Calendars**
Devotional literature

Devotional exercises 242; 248.3

Use for general materials on acts of private prayer and private worship and for materials on religious practices other than the corporate worship of a congregation. Materials on the religious literature used as aids in devotional exercises are entered under **Devotional literature.**

UF Devotional theology
Devotions
Family devotions
Family prayers
BT **Worship**
NT **Meditation**
RT **Prayer**

Devotional exercises (Daily readings)
USE **Devotional calendars**

Devotional literature 242

Use for materials on the religious literature used as aids in devotional exercises. General materials on acts of private prayer and private worship and materials on religious practices other than the corporate worship of a congregation are entered under **Devotional exercises.**

BT **Religious literature**
NT **Devotional calendars**
Meditations
Prayers

Devotional theology
USE **Devotional exercises**
Prayer

Devotions
USE **Devotional exercises**

Dewey Decimal Classification 025.4
UF Classification, Dewey Decimal
[Former heading]
BT **Books—Classification**

Diagnosis 616.07
UF Medical diagnosis
Symptoms
BT **Medicine**
NT **Body temperature**
Clinical chemistry
Magnetic resonance imaging
Pain
Prenatal diagnosis
RT **Pathology**

Diagnostic chemistry
USE **Clinical chemistry**

Diagnostic magnetic resonance imaging
USE **Magnetic resonance imaging**

Diagrams, Statistical
USE **Statistics—Graphic methods**

BT = Broader Term   NT = Narrower Term   RT = Related Term   SA = See Also   UF = Used For

Dialectical materialism   335.4
    UF   Historical materialism
    BT   **Communism**
          Socialism
    RT   **Marxism**
Dialectics
    USE **Logic**
Dialects
    USE names of languages with the
            subdivision *Dialects*, e.g.
            English language—Dialects;
            to be added as needed
Diamonds   553.8
    BT   **Carbon**
          Precious stones
Diaries   809; 920
    Use for collections of diaries from various countries and for materials about diaries in general.
    UF   Journals (Diaries)
    SA   diaries of particular countries,
          e.g. **American diaries;** and
          classes of persons, ethnic
          groups, and names of individ-
          ual persons and families with
          the subdivision *Diaries;* to be
          added as needed
    BT   **Literature**
    NT   **American diaries**
    RT   **Autobiographies**
Diaries, American
    USE **American diaries**
Dichloro-diphenyl-trichloroethane
    USE **D.D.T. (Insecticide)**
Dictators   321.9092; 920
    BT   **Heads of state**
          Totalitarianism
Dictionaries
    USE **Encyclopedias and dictionaries**
          and names of languages and
          subjects with the subdivision
          Dictionaries, e.g. **English lan-**
          guage—Dictionaries; Biogra-
          phy—Dictionaries; etc., to be
          added as needed
Dictionaries, Biographical
    USE **Biography—Dictionaries**
Dictionaries, Classical
    USE **Classical dictionaries**
Dictionaries, Machine readable
    USE **Machine readable dictionaries**

Dictionaries, Multilingual
    USE **Polyglot dictionaries**
Dictionaries, Picture
    USE **Picture dictionaries**
Dictionaries, Polyglot
    USE **Polyglot dictionaries**
Didactic drama   808.82; 812, etc.
    May be used for individual works, collections, or materials about didactic drama.
    BT   **Drama**
Didactic fiction   808.83; 813, etc.
    May be used for individual works, collections, or materials about didactic fiction.
    UF   Cautionary tales and verses
          Moral and philosophic stories
          Morality stories
    BT   **Fiction**
    RT   **Fables**
          Parables
Didactic poetry   808.81; 811, etc.
    May be used for individual works, collections, or materials about didactic poetry.
    UF   Cautionary tales and verses
    BT   **Poetry**
    RT   **Fables**
          Parables
Dies (Metalworking)   621.9; 671.2
    BT   **Metalwork**
Diesel automobiles   629.222
    UF   Automobiles, Diesel *[Former heading]*
          Diesel cars
    BT   **Automobiles**
    RT   **Automobile engines**
Diesel cars
    USE **Diesel automobiles**
Diesel engines   621.43
    BT   **Engines**
          Internal combustion engines
Diet   613.2
    UF   Dietetics
    SA   types of diets, e.g. **Salt-free diet;** to be added as needed
    BT   **Health**
          Hygiene
    NT   **Beverages**
          Dietetic foods
          Eating customs
          Fasting
          Menus
          Salt-free diet

BT = Broader Term   NT = Narrower Term   RT = Related Term   SA = See Also   UF = Used For

Diet—*Continued*
>> School children—Food
>> Vegetarianism
> RT Cooking
>> Digestion
>> Food
>> Nutrition
>> Weight loss

Diet in disease   613.2; 616.3
> UF Dieting
> SA types of diets, e.g. **Salt-free diet**; to be added as needed
> BT **Therapeutics**
> NT **Cooking for the sick**
>> **Diet therapy**
>> **Salt-free diet**

Diet—Therapeutic use
> USE **Diet therapy**

Diet therapy   615.8
> UF Diet—Therapeutic use
>> Invalid cooking
> SA names of diseases with the subdivision *Diet therapy,* and types of food with the subdivision *Therapeutic use,* to be added as needed
> BT **Cooking for the sick**
>> **Diet in disease**
>> **Therapeutics**
> NT **Cancer—Diet therapy**

Dietary fiber
> USE **Food—Fiber content**

Dietetic foods   641.3; 664
> UF Food, Dietetic *[Former heading]*
> BT **Diet**
>> **Food**

Dietetics
> USE **Diet**

Dieting
> USE **Diet in disease**
>> **Weight loss**

Diets, Reducing
> USE **Weight loss**

Digestion   573.3; 612.3
> BT **Physiology**
> NT **Food**
>> **Indigestion**
> RT **Diet**
>> **Nutrition**
>> **Stomach**

Digital audio disc players
> USE **Compact disc players**

Digital circuits
> USE **Digital electronics**

Digital compact discs
> USE **Compact discs**

Digital electronics   621.381
> UF Digital circuits
> BT **Electronics**

Dimension, Fourth
> USE **Fourth dimension**

Dining (May subdiv. geog.)   641.01
> Use for materials on dining customs and gastronomic travel. Materials on menus and recipes for dinners are entered under **Dinners.**
> UF Banquets
>> Dinners and dining *[Former heading]*
>> Eating
>> Gastronomy
> BT **Food**
> NT **Carving (Meat, etc.)**
> RT **Dinners**
>> **Eating customs**
>> **Entertaining**
>> **Table etiquette**

Dinners   642
> Use for materials on menus and recipes for dinners. Materials on dining customs and gastronomic travel are entered under **Dining.**
> UF Banquets
>> Dinners and dining *[Former heading]*
> BT **Cooking**
>> **Menus**
> RT **Dining**

Dinners and dining
> USE **Dining**
>> **Dinners**

Dinosaur eggs
> USE **Dinosaurs—Eggs**

Dinosaurs   567.9
> SA types of dinosaurs and names of specific dinosaurs, to be added as needed
> BT **Fossil reptiles**
>> **Prehistoric animals**

Dinosaurs—Eggs   567.9
> UF Dinosaur eggs
> BT **Eggs**

BT = Broader Term   NT = Narrower Term   RT = Related Term   SA = See Also   UF = Used For

Dioptrics
USE   Refraction
Diphtheria   616.9
BT   Diseases
Diplomacy   327.2; 341.3
SA   names of countries with the sub-
       division *Foreign relations,* to
       be added as needed
BT   **International relations**
NT   **Diplomats**
       Treaties
       **United States—Foreign rela-
       tions**
RT   **Diplomatic and consular ser-
       vice**
Diplomatic and consular service (May
       subdiv. geog.)   341.3
   Use for materials on diplomatic and consular service in general or on the diplomatic and
consular officials of various countries stationed abroad in various countries. Materials
on the diplomatic and consular officials of
various countries stationed in a specific country are entered under **Diplomatic and consular service** subdivided by the country where
they are stationed. Materials on the diplomatic
and consular officials of a specific country,
regardless of where they are stationed, are entered under the appropriately modified heading, e.g. **American diplomatic and consular
service.** Materials on the diplomatic and consular officials of a specific country stationed
in a specific country are entered under the appropriately modified heading subdivided by
the place where they are stationed.
UF   Consular service
       Consulates
       Embassies
       Foreign service
       Legations
SA   diplomatic and consular services
       of particular countries, e.g.
       **American diplomatic and
       consular service;** to be added
       as needed
BT   **International relations**
NT   **American diplomatic and con-
       sular service**
RT   **Diplomacy**
       Diplomats
Diplomatic and consular service, American
USE   **American diplomatic and con-
       sular service**
Diplomats   327.2092; 920
UF   Ambassadors

Consuls
Ministers (Diplomatic agents)
BT   **Diplomacy**
       International relations
       Statesmen
RT   **Diplomatic and consular ser-
       vice**
Direct access storage devices (Data pro-
       cessing)
USE   **Computer storage devices**
Direct current machinery
USE   **Electric machinery—Direct
       current**
Direct legislation
USE   **Referendum**
Direct primaries
USE   **Primaries**
Direct selling   658.8
BT   **Marketing**
       Retail trade
       Selling
NT   **Mail-order business**
       Peddlers and peddling
       Telemarketing
Direct taxation
USE   **Income tax**
       Taxation
Direction (Motion pictures)
USE   **Motion pictures—Production
       and direction**
Direction sense   152.1; 912
UF   Orientation
       Sense of direction
NT   **Left and right (Direction)**
RT   **Hiking**
       Navigation
       Orienteering
Direction (Theater)
USE   **Theater—Production and di-
       rection**
Directories   910.25
   Use for materials about directories and for
bibliographies of directories.
SA   subjects and names of countries,
       cities, etc., with the subdivi-
       sion *Directories,* for lists of
       persons, organizations, objects,
       etc., together with addresses
       or other identifying data, to
       be added as needed
NT   **Chicago (Ill.)—Directories**

BT = Broader Term   NT = Narrower Term   RT = Related Term   SA = See Also   UF = Used For

Directories—*Continued*
        Junior colleges—Directories
        Ohio—Directories
        Physicians—Directories
        United States—Directories
Directories—Telephone
  USE   names of cities with the subdivision *Telephone directories,* e.g. **Chicago (Ill.)—Telephone directories;** to be added as needed
Directors
  USE   producers and directors in specific media, e.g. **Motion picture producers and directors; Theatrical producers and directors;** etc., to be added as needed
Directory, French, 1795-1799
  USE   **France—History—1789-1799, Revolution**
Dirigible balloons
  USE   **Airships**
Disability insurance
  USE   **Accident insurance**
         Health insurance
Disability, Learning
  USE   **Learning disabilities**
Disability, Reading
  USE   **Reading disability**
Disabled
  USE   **Handicapped**
Disadvantaged
  USE   **Socially handicapped**
Disadvantaged children
  USE   **Socially handicapped children**
Disadvantaged students
  USE   **At risk students**
Disarmament
  USE   **Arms control**
Disaster preparedness
  USE   **Disaster relief**
Disaster relief (May subdiv. geog.)
      363.34
  UF   Disaster preparedness
         Emergency preparedness
         Emergency relief
  BT   **Charities**
         Public welfare
  NT   **Food relief**

Disasters 904
  UF   Catastrophes
         Emergencies
  SA   types of disasters, to be added as needed
  NT   **Fires**
         Natural disasters
         Railroad accidents
         Shipwrecks
  RT   **Accidents**
Disciples, Twelve
  USE   **Apostles**
Discipline
  USE   **Punishment**
Discipline of children
  USE   **Child rearing**
         School discipline
Discipline, Self
  USE   **Self-control**
Discography
  USE   **Sound recordings** and subjects and names of persons with the subdivision *Discography,* e.g. **Music—Discography; Shakespeare, William, 1564-1616—Discography;** etc., for lists or catalogs of sound recordings, to be added as needed
Discount stores   381; 658.8
  BT   **Retail trade**
         Stores
Discoverers
  USE   **Exploration**
         Explorers
Discoveries and exploration
  USE   **Exploration**
Discoveries in geography
  USE   **Exploration**
Discoveries in science
  USE   **Inventions**
         Patents
         Science
Discoveries, Maritime
  USE   **Exploration**
Discrimination   177; 305
    Use for general materials on discrimination by race, religion, sex, age, social status, or other factors, including reverse discrimination.
  BT   **Ethnic relations**
         Human relations

BT = Broader Term   NT = Narrower Term   RT = Related Term   SA = See Also   UF = Used For

Discrimination—*Continued*
    Prejudices
    Race relations
    Social problems
    Social psychology
  NT Age discrimination
    Discrimination in education
    Discrimination in employment
    Discrimination in housing
    Discrimination in public ac-
      commodations
    Hate crimes
    Race discrimination
    Sex discrimination
  RT Civil rights
    Minorities
    Segregation
    Toleration
Discrimination in education   379.2
  BT Discrimination
  RT Segregation in education
Discrimination in employment   331.13
  UF E.E.O.
    EEO
    Employment discrimination
    Equal employment opportunity
    Equal opportunity in employ-
      ment
    Fair employment practice
    Job discrimination
    Right to work
  SA national, racial, and ethnic
      groups and classes of persons
      with the subdivision *Employ-*
      ment, e.g. **African Ameri-**
      cans—Employment; to be
      added as needed
  BT Discrimination
  NT Affirmative action programs
    Equal pay for equal work
  RT African Americans—Employ-
      ment
    Age and employment
    Blacks—Employment
    Women—Employment
Discrimination in housing   363.5
  UF Fair housing
    Housing, Discrimination in
    Open housing
    Segregation in housing

  BT Discrimination
    Housing
Discrimination in public accommodations
    305
  UF Public accommodations, Discrim-
      ination in
    Segregation in public accommo-
      dations
  BT Discrimination
Discrimination, Racial
  USE Race discrimination
Discrimination, Sex
  USE Sex discrimination
Discs, Compact
  USE Compact discs
Discs, Optical
  USE Optical storage devices
Discs, Sound
  USE Sound recordings
Discussion
  USE Conversation
    Debates and debating
    Negotiation
Discussion groups   374
  UF Forums (Discussions)
    Great books program
    Group discussion
    Panel discussions
  BT Conversation
  RT Debates and debating
Disease germs
  USE Bacteria
    Germ theory of disease
Disease (Pathology)
  USE Pathology
Diseases   614.4; 616
  UF Illness
    Sickness
  SA names of animals, classes of
      persons, and parts of the body
      with the subdivision *Diseases,*
      types of diseases, and names
      of specific diseases, to be
      added as needed
  NT AIDS (Disease)
    Animals—Diseases
    Arthritis
    Blood—Diseases
    Brain—Diseases
    Cancer

BT = Broader Term   NT = Narrower Term   RT = Related Term   SA = See Also   UF = Used For

Diseases—*Continued*
> Chickenpox
> Children—Diseases
> Cold (Disease)
> Communicable diseases
> Diphtheria
> Elderly—Diseases
> Epidemics
> Heart diseases
> Hyperactivity
> Infants—Diseases
> Influenza
> Lungs—Diseases
> Lyme disease
> Men—Diseases
> Mental illness
> Nervous system—Diseases
> Occupational diseases
> Plant diseases
> Poliomyelitis
> Rheumatism
> Skin—Diseases
> Teeth—Diseases
> Typhoid fever
> Women—Diseases

RT Health
> Medicine
> Pathology
> Sick

Diseases and pests
USE Agricultural bacteriology
> Agricultural pests
> Fungi
> Household pests
> Insect pests
> Parasites
> Plant diseases
> and names of individual pests,
> e.g. **Locusts;** and types of
> crops, plants, trees, etc., with
> the subdivision *Diseases and
> pests,* e.g. **Fruit—Diseases
> and pests;** to be added as
> needed

Diseases, Communicable
USE **Communicable diseases**
Diseases, Contagious
USE **Communicable diseases**
Diseases, Industrial
USE **Occupational diseases**

Diseases, Infectious
USE **Communicable diseases**
Diseases, Mental
USE **Abnormal psychology
> Mental illness**
Diseases, Occupational
USE **Occupational diseases**
Diseases of animals
USE **Animals—Diseases**
Diseases of children
USE **Children—Diseases**
Diseases of occupation
USE **Occupational diseases**
Diseases of plants
USE **Plant diseases**
Diseases of the blood
USE **Blood—Diseases**
Diseases of women
USE **Women—Diseases**
Diseases—Prevention
USE **Preventive medicine**
Diseases—Treatment
USE **Therapeutics**
Diseases, Tropical
USE **Tropical medicine**
Dishes
USE **Glassware
> Porcelain
> Pottery
> Tableware**
Dishonesty
USE **Honesty**
Disinfection and disinfectants   614.4
UF Germicides
BT **Hygiene
> Pharmaceutical chemistry
> Public health
> Sanitation**
RT **Antiseptics
> Fumigation**
Disney World (Fla.)
USE **Walt Disney World (Fla.)**
Disobedience
USE **Obedience**
Displaced persons
USE **Political refugees
> Refugees**
Display terminals, Video
USE **Video display terminals**

BT = Broader Term   NT = Narrower Term   RT = Related Term   SA = See Also   UF = Used For

Disposal of medical waste
USE **Medical wastes**
Disposal of refuse
USE **Refuse and refuse disposal**
Disputes, Labor
USE **Labor disputes**
Dissent 303.48; 361.2
UF Nonconformity
Protest
BT **Freedom of conscience**
Freedom of religion
RT **Conformity**
Dissertations 378.2; 808
Use for materials about academic theses and dissertations.
UF Academic dissertations
Dissertations, Academic *[Former heading]*
Doctoral theses
Theses
BT **Colleges and universities**
Dissertations, Academic
USE **Dissertations**
Distance education 371.3
Use for materials on the various forms of long-distance instruction, usually in the field of adult education, made possible by written, audiovisual, or electronic communication between a student and a teacher.
UF Distance learning
BT **Education**
NT **Correspondence schools and courses**
University extension
Distance learning
USE **Distance education**
Distillation 641.2; 663
UF Stills
BT **Analytical chemistry**
Industrial chemistry
Technology
NT **Essences and essential oils**
RT **Alcohol**
Liquors
Distribution, Cooperative
USE **Cooperation**
Distribution (Economics)
USE **Commerce**
Marketing
Distribution of animals and plants
USE **Biogeography**

Distribution of wealth
USE **Economics**
Wealth
District libraries
USE **Regional libraries**
District nurses
USE **Nurses**
District schools
USE **Rural schools**
Districting (in city planning)
USE **Zoning**
Diversified corporations
USE **Conglomerate corporations**
Diversity, Biological
USE **Biological diversity**
Diversity movement
USE **Multiculturalism**
Dividends
USE **Securities**
Stocks
Divination 133.3
UF Crystal gazing
Necromancy
Soothsaying
BT **Occultism**
Supernatural
NT **Astrology**
Fortune telling
Palmistry
RT **Clairvoyance**
Oracles
Prophecies
Superstition
Divine healing
USE **Spiritual healing**
Diving 797.2
Use for materials on diving from a board or platform. Materials on underwater diving with equipment are entered under **Deep diving**.
BT **Swimming**
Water sports
RT **Deep diving**
Diving, Submarine
USE **Deep diving**
Divinity of Christ
USE **Jesus Christ—Divinity**
Division of powers
USE **Separation of powers**
Divorce 173; 306.89; 346.01
UF Separation (Law)
BT **Family**

BT = Broader Term   NT = Narrower Term   RT = Related Term   SA = See Also   UF = Used For

Divorce—*Continued*
NT   Children of divorced parents
       Desertion and nonsupport
       Divorce mediation
RT   Domestic relations
       Marriage
Divorce counseling
USE   Divorce mediation
Divorce mediation 362.82
UF   Divorce counseling
       Mediation, Divorce
BT   **Divorce**
NT   **Child custody**
       Child support
RT   **Marriage counseling**
DNA 572.8
UF   D.N.A.
       Deoxyribonucleic acid
       Desoxyribonucleic acid
BT   **Cells**
       Heredity
       Nucleic acids
NT   **Recombinant DNA**
DNA cloning
USE   **Molecular cloning**
DNA fingerprinting
USE   **DNA fingerprints**
DNA Fingerprints
USE   **DNA fingerprints**
DNA fingerprints 614
UF   DNA fingerprinting
       DNA Fingerprints *[Former*
       heading]
       DNA identification
       DNA profiling
       Genetic fingerprints
       Genetic profiling
BT   **Genetics**
       Identification
       Medical jurisprudence
DNA identification
USE   **DNA fingerprints**
DNA profiling
USE   **DNA fingerprints**
Docks 386; 387.1; 627
BT   **Hydraulic structures**
       Marinas
RT   **Harbors**
Doctor films
USE   **Medical drama (Films)**

Doctor novels
USE   **Medical novels**
Doctor radio programs
USE   **Medical drama (Radio pro-
       grams)**
Doctor television programs
USE   **Medical drama (Television
       programs)**
Doctoral theses
USE   **Dissertations**
Doctors
USE   **Physicians**
Doctors' degrees
USE   **Academic degrees**
Doctrinal theology 230; 291.2
UF   Dogmatic theology
       Dogmatics
       Fundamental theology
       Systematic theology
       Theology, Doctrinal *[Former
       heading]*
SA   names of religions or individual
       denominations with the subdi-
       vision *Doctrines,* e.g. **Chris-
       tianity—Doctrines; Juda-
       ism—Doctrines;** etc., to be
       added as needed
BT   **Theology**
NT   **Christianity—Doctrines**
       Creeds
       Grace (Theology)
       Judaism—Doctrines
       Man (Theology)
       Salvation
Doctrine of fairness (Broadcasting)
USE   **Fairness doctrine (Broadcast-
       ing)**
Documentaries (Motion pictures)
USE   **Documentary films**
Documentary films 070.1
UF   Documentaries (Motion pictures)
       Nonfiction films
BT   **Motion pictures**
Documentation 025
SA   subjects with the subdivision
       Documentation, e.g. **Agricul-
       ture—Documentation;** to be
       added as needed
BT   **Information science**
NT   **Agriculture—Documentation**

BT = Broader Term   NT = Narrower Term   RT = Related Term   SA = See Also   UF = Used For

Documentation—*Continued*

      Archives
      Bibliographic control
      Bibliography
      Cataloging
      Copying processes
      Information systems
      Libraries
      Library science
  RT   Information services

Documents
  USE   Archives
        Charters
        Government publications

Dog
  USE   Dogs

Dog breeding
  USE   Dogs—Breeding

Dog care
  USE   Dogs—Care

Dog guides
  USE   Guide dogs

Dogmatic theology
  USE   Doctrinal theology

Dogmatics
  USE   Doctrinal theology

Dogs   599.77; 636.7
  UF   Dog
        Puppies
  SA   types of dogs, e.g. **Guide dogs;**
        and names of specific breeds
        of dogs, to be added as need-
        ed
  BT   **Domestic animals**
        Mammals
  NT   **Collies**
        Guide dogs
        Hearing ear dogs

Dogs—Breeding   636.7
  UF   Dog breeding
  BT   **Breeding**

Dogs—Care   636.7
  UF   Dog care

Dogs—Fiction   808.83; 813, etc.
    May be used for individual works, collec-
tions, or materials about stories about dogs.
General materials about the portrayal of dogs
in literature are entered under **Dogs in literature.**

Dogs for the blind
  USE   Guide dogs

Dogs for the deaf
  USE   Hearing ear dogs

Dogs in literature   809
    Use for materials about poetry, fiction, and
plays about dogs. Individual dog stories and
collections of dog stories are entered under
Dogs—Fiction.
  BT   **Animals in literature**

Dogs—Psychology   636.7
  BT   **Animal intelligence**
        Comparative psychology
        Psychology

Dogs—Training   636.7
  BT   **Animals—Training**

Dogs—War use   355.4
  UF   War use of dogs
  BT   **Animals—War use**

Doll
  USE   Dolls

Dollhouses   688.7
  BT   **Miniature objects**
        Toys

Dolls   688.7
  UF   Doll
  BT   **Toys**

Domesday book   942.02
  UF   Doomsday book
  BT   **Great Britain—History—1066-
        1154, Norman period**

Domestic animal dwellings
  USE   **Animal housing**

Domestic animals   636
    Use for general materials on farm animals.
Materials limited to animals as pets are en-
tered under **Pets.** Materials on stock raising as
an industry are entered under **Livestock in-
dustry.**
  UF   Animals, Domestic
        Domestication
        Farm animals
        Livestock *[Former heading]*
  SA   types of domestic animals, e.g.
        Cattle; to be added as needed
  BT   **Animals**
  NT   **Cats**
        Cattle
        Dogs
        Pigs
        Poultry
        Reindeer
        Sheep
        Working animals

BT = Broader Term   NT = Narrower Term   RT = Related Term   SA = See Also   UF = Used For

Domestic animals—*Continued*
  RT **Livestock industry**
     Pets
Domestic animals—Diseases
  USE **Animals—Diseases**
Domestic animals—Housing
  USE **Animal housing**
Domestic appliances
  USE **Electric household appliances**
     **Household equipment and sup-
     plies**
Domestic architecture (May subdiv.
    geog.) **728**
    Use for materials on residential buildings
    from the standpoint of style and design. Gen-
    eral materials on buildings in which people
    live are entered under **Houses.**
  UF Architecture, Domestic *[Former
     heading]*
     Architecture, Rural
     Dwellings
     Habitations, Human
     Residences
     Rural architecture
  SA types of residential buildings,
     e.g. **Apartment houses;** to be
     added as needed
  BT **Architecture**
  NT **Apartment houses**
     House construction
     Prefabricated houses
     Solar homes
  RT **Houses**
**Domestic architecture—Designs and
   plans 728**
  UF Home designs
     House plans
  BT **Architecture—Designs and
     plans**
Domestic arts
  USE **Home economics**
Domestic economic assistance 338.9
  UF Anti-poverty programs
     Antipoverty programs
     Economic assistance *[Former
     heading]*
     Economic assistance, Domestic
     [Former heading]
     Poor relief
  BT **Economic policy**
  NT **Community development**

     Government lending
     Public works
     Subsidies
     Transfer payments
  RT **Grants-in-aid**
     Poverty
     Unemployed
Domestic finance
  USE **Household budgets**
     Personal finance
Domestic relations 346.01
  UF Family relations
  BT **Human relations**
  NT **Desertion and nonsupport**
     Grandparent and child
     Parent and child
     **Visitation rights (Domestic re-
     lations)**
  RT **Divorce**
     Family
     Family life education
     Marriage
Domestic violence
  USE **Family violence**
Domestic workers
  USE **Household employees**
Domestication
  USE **Domestic animals**
Dominion of the sea
  USE **Sea power**
Dominions, British
  USE **Commonwealth countries**
Donation of organs, tissues, etc. 362.1
  UF Organ donation
     Tissue donation
  BT **Gifts**
  RT **Transplantation of organs, tis-
     sues, etc.**
Donations
  USE **Gifts**
Doomsday book
  USE **Domesday book**
Door to door selling
  USE **Peddlers and peddling**
Doors 721
  BT **Architecture—Details**
     Building
     Buildings
Double consciousness
  USE **Multiple personality**

BT = Broader Term   NT = Narrower Term   RT = Related Term   SA = See Also   UF = Used For

Double employment
USE   Supplementary employment
Doubt
USE   Belief and doubt
Down syndrome   616.85
  UF   Down's syndrome *[Former
        heading]*
  BT   **Mental retardation**
Down's syndrome
USE   **Down syndrome**
Downsizing of organizations   658.1
  UF   Corporate downsizing
        Organizational downsizing
        Organizational retrenchment
        Retrenchment of organizations
  BT   **Organizational change**
  RT   **Employees—Dismissal**
Draft   355.2
  UF   Compulsory military service
        Conscription, Military
        Military draft
        Military service, Compulsory
        [Former heading]
        Military training, Universal
        Selective service
        Universal military training
  BT   **Armies**
        Military law
        Recruiting and enlistment
  RT   **Draft resisters**
Draft dodgers
USE   **Draft resisters**
Draft evaders
USE   **Draft resisters**
Draft resisters   355.2
  UF   Draft dodgers
        Draft evaders
  SA   names of wars with the subdivi-
        sion *Draft resisters,* to be
        added as needed
  NT   **World War, 1939-1945—Draft
        resisters**
  RT   **Conscientious objectors**
        Draft
        Military desertion
Drafting, Automatic
USE   **Computer aided design**
        Computer graphics
Drafting, Mechanical
USE   **Mechanical drawing**

Dragons   398.24
  BT   **Animals—Folklore**
        Folklore
        Monsters
        Mythical animals
Drainage   631.6
  Use for materials on land drainage. Materi-
  als on house drainage are entered under
  House drainage.
  UF   Land drainage
  BT   **Agricultural engineering**
        Civil engineering
        Hydraulic engineering
        Municipal engineering
        Reclamation of land
        Sanitary engineering
  RT   **Sewerage**
        Wetlands
Drainage, House
USE   **House drainage**
Drama   808.2; 808.82
  Use for general materials on drama, not for
  individual works. Materials on the history and
  criticism of drama as literature are entered un-
  der **Drama—History and criticism.** Materials
  on criticism of drama as presented on the
  stage are entered under **Dramatic criticism.**
  Materials on the presentation of plays are en-
  tered under **Acting; Amateur theater;** or
  Theater—Production and direction. Materials on how to write plays are entered under
  Drama—Technique. Collections of plays are
  entered   under   **Drama—Collections;
  American drama—Collections; English drama—Collections;** etc.
  UF   Stage
  SA   subjects, historical events, names
        of countries, cities, etc., eth-
        nic groups, classes of persons,
        and names of individual per-
        sons with the subdivision
        Drama, to express the theme
        or subject content of individu-
        al plays or collections of
        plays, e.g. **Easter—Drama;
        United States—History—
        1861-1865, Civil War—Dra-
        ma; Napoleon I, Emperor of
        the French, 1769-1821—Dra-
        ma;** etc., to be added as
        needed
  BT   **Literature**
  NT   **Acting**
        American drama
        Ballet

BT = Broader Term   NT = Narrower Term   RT = Related Term   SA = See Also   UF = Used For

Drama—*Continued*

  Children's plays
  Choral speaking
  College and school drama
  Comedies
  Comedy
  Didactic drama
  Drama in education
  Dramatists
  Easter—Drama
  English drama
  Folk drama
  Historical drama
  Horror plays
  Indians of North America—
   Drama
  Masks (Plays)
  Melodrama
  Morality plays
  Motion picture plays
  Mystery and detective plays
  One act plays
  Opera
  Pantomimes
  Pastoral drama
  Plots (Drama, fiction, etc.)
  Puppets and puppet plays
  Radio plays
  Religious drama
  Science fiction plays
  Television plays
  Tragedies
  Tragedy
 RT **Dramatic criticism**
  Theater

Drama—Collections 808.82; 812.008, etc.

Use for collections of plays by several authors.

 UF Plays

Drama—History and criticism 809.2

Use for materials on criticism of drama as a literary form. Materials on criticism of drama as presented on the stage are entered under **Dramatic criticism.**

 NT **English drama—History and criticism**
 RT **Dramatic criticism**

Drama in education 372.66

 BT **Drama**
 RT **Acting**
  Amateur theater

College and school drama
School assembly programs

Drama—Plots
 USE **Plots (Drama, fiction, etc.)**

Drama, Religious
 USE **Religious drama**

Drama—Technique 808.2
 UF Play writing
  Playwriting
 BT **Authorship**
 NT **Motion picture plays—Technique**
  Radio plays—Technique
  Television plays—Technique

Dramatic art
 USE **Acting**

Dramatic criticism 792.9

Use for materials on criticism of drama as presented on the stage. Materials on criticism of drama as a literary form are entered under **Drama—History and criticism; American drama—History and criticism;** etc.

 UF Theater criticism
 BT **Criticism**
 RT **Drama**
  Drama—History and criticism
  Theater

Dramatic music
 USE **Musicals**
  Opera
  Operetta

Dramatic plots
 USE **Plots (Drama, fiction, etc.)**

Dramatists 809.2; 920

Use for materials on the personal lives of several playwrights, not limited to a single national literature. Materials dealing with their literary work are entered under **Drama—History and criticism; English drama—History and criticism;** etc.

 UF Playwrights
 SA dramatists of particular countries, e.g. **American dramatists;** to be added as needed
 BT **Authors**
  Drama
 NT **American dramatists**

Dramatists, American
 USE **American dramatists**

Drapery 645; 684
 UF Curtains
 BT **Interior design**
  Upholstery

BT = Broader Term NT = Narrower Term RT = Related Term SA = See Also UF = Used For

222

Draughts
USE   Checkers
Drawing   741; 743
    UF   Drawings
            Sketching
    SA   drawing of particular countries,
            e.g. **American drawing;** to
            be added as needed
    BT   **Art**
            Graphic arts
    NT   **American drawing**
            Architectural drawing
            Artistic anatomy
            Commercial art
            Crayon drawing
            Figure drawing
            Geometrical drawing
            Graphic methods
            Landscape drawing
            Map drawing
            Mechanical drawing
            Pastel drawing
            Pen drawing
            Pencil drawing
            Shades and shadows
            Topographical drawing
    RT   **Illustration of books**
            Painting
            Perspective
Drawing, American
    USE   **American drawing**
Drawing, Architectural
    USE   **Architectural drawing**
Drawing, Automatic
    USE   **Computer graphics**
Drawing, Computer
    USE   **Computer art**
Drawing, Electronic
    USE   **Computer art**
            Computer graphics
Drawing materials
    USE   **Artists' materials**
Drawings
    USE   **Drawing**
Dream interpretation
    USE   **Dreams**
Dreaming
    USE   **Dreams**
Dreams   154.6
    UF   Dream interpretation

Dreaming
    BT   **Visions**
    NT   **Fantasy**
    RT   **Sleep**
            Subconsciousness
Dredging   627
    BT   **Civil engineering**
            Hydraulic engineering
Dress
    USE   **Clothing and dress**
Dress accessories   391.4; 646
    BT   **Clothing and dress**
Dressage
    USE   **Horsemanship**
Dressing of ores
    USE   **Ore dressing**
Dressmaking   646.4; 687
    UF   Garment making
    BT   **Clothing and dress**
            Fashion
    RT   **Needlework**
            Sewing
            Tailoring
Dressmaking—Patterns   646.4; 687
Dried flowers
    USE   **Flowers—Drying**
Dried foods   641.4; 664
    UF   Dehydrated foods
            Food, Dehydrated
            Food, Dried *[Former heading]*
    BT   **Food—Preservation**
    NT   **Dried milk**
            Freeze-dried foods
Dried milk   637
    UF   Dehydrated milk
            Powdered milk
    BT   **Dried foods**
            Milk
Drifting of continents
    USE   **Continental drift**
Drill and minor tactics   355.5
    UF   Military drill
            Minor tactics
    BT   **Tactics**
    RT   **Military art and science**
Drill (Nonmilitary)
    USE   **Marching drills**
Drilling and boring   621.9
        Use for materials on workshop operations in
        metal, wood, etc. Materials on the operation

BT = Broader Term   NT = Narrower Term   RT = Related Term   SA = See Also   UF = Used For

Drilling and boring—*Continued*
of cutting holes in earth or rock are entered
under **Boring.**
- UF   Boring (Metal, wood, etc.)
- BT   **Machine shop practice**
- RT   **Machine tools**

Drilling and boring (Earth and rocks)
- USE   **Boring**

Drilling, Oil well
- USE   **Oil well drilling**

Drilling platforms   627
- UF   Artificial islands
  Islands, Artificial
  Offshore structures
  Platforms, Drilling
  Structures, Offshore
- BT   **Ocean engineering**
  Offshore oil well drilling

Drills, Marching
- USE   **Marching drills**

Drinking age (May subdiv. geog.)   **344;**
    363.4
- UF   Minimum drinking age
- BT   **Age**
  Teenagers—Alcohol use
  Youth—Alcohol use

Drinking and employees
- USE   **Employees—Alcohol use**

Drinking and teenagers
- USE   **Teenagers—Alcohol use**

Drinking and youth
- USE   **Youth—Alcohol use**

Drinking in the workplace
- USE   **Employees—Alcohol use**

Drinking of alcoholic beverages (May
    subdiv. geog.)   **178; 363.4; 394.1;**
    613.81
Use for materials on drinking in its social
aspects and as a social problem.
- UF   Alcohol consumption
  Alcoholic beverage consumption
  Consumption of alcoholic beverages
  Drinking problem
  Liquor problem
  Social drinking
- SA   classes of persons and ethnic
  groups with the subdivision
  Alcohol use, e.g. **Employees—Alcohol use; Youth—**

Alcohol use; etc., to be added
    ed as needed
- NT   **Drunk driving**
- RT   **Alcoholic beverages**
  Alcoholism
  Temperance

Drinking problem
- USE   **Alcoholism**
  Drinking of alcoholic beverages

Drinking water   363.6; 628.1
- UF   Potable water
  Tap water
- BT   **Water**
  Water supply

Drinks
- USE   **Alcoholic beverages**
  Beverages
  Liquors

Driver education
- USE   **Automobile driver education**

Drivers, Automobile
- USE   **Automobile drivers**

Driving under the influence of alcohol
- USE   **Drunk driving**

Driving while intoxicated
- USE   **Drunk driving**

Dromedaries
- USE   **Camels**

Drop forging
- USE   **Forging**

Dropouts   371.2
- UF   College dropouts
  Elementary school dropouts
  High school dropouts
  School dropouts
  Student dropouts
  Teenage dropouts
- BT   **Students**
  Youth
- RT   **At risk students**
  Educational counseling
  School attendance

Droughts (May subdiv. geog.)   **551.57;**
    632
- BT   **Meteorology**
- NT   **Dust storms**
- RT   **Rain**

Drowning prevention
- USE   **Water safety**

BT = Broader Term   **NT = Narrower Term**   **RT = Related Term**   **SA = See Also**   **UF = Used For**

Drug abuse   362.29; 613.8; 616.86

Use for general materials on the misuse or abuse of drugs. Materials on the abuse of a particular drug or kind of drugs are entered under that drug or kind of drugs, e.g. **Cocaine; Hallucinogens;** etc., and also under **Drug abuse.**

UF	Addiction to drugs
	Drug addiction *[Former heading]*
	Drug habit
	Drug misuse
	Drug use
	Drugs—Abuse
	Drugs—Misuse
	Narcotic abuse
	Narcotic addiction
	Narcotic habit
	Substance abuse *[Former heading]*
SA	classes of persons with the subdivision *Drug use,* e.g. **Criminals—Drug use;** and types of drug abuse, e.g. **Medication abuse;** to be added as needed
BT	**Social problems**
NT	**Medication abuse**
RT	**Drug addicts**
	Drugs
	Solvent abuse
	Twelve-step programs

Drug abuse counseling   362.29; 613.8

UF	Drug addiction counseling
	Drug counseling
	Narcotic addiction counseling
BT	**Counseling**
NT	**Drug addicts—Rehabilitation**

Drug abuse education
USE   **Drug education**

Drug abuse—Physiological effect
USE   **Drugs—Physiological effect**

Drug abuse screening
USE   **Drug testing**

Drug abuse—Study and teaching
USE   **Drug education**

Drug abuse—Testing
USE   **Drug testing**

Drug abusing physicians
USE   **Physicians—Drug use**

Drug addicted physicians
USE   **Physicians—Drug use**

Drug addiction
USE   **Drug abuse**

Drug addiction counseling
USE   **Drug abuse counseling**

Drug addiction education
USE   **Drug education**

Drug addicts   362.29; 616.86

UF	Addicts
	Narcotic addicts
SA	classes of persons with the subdivision *Drug use,* e.g. **Criminals—Drug use;** to be added as needed
NT	**Children of drug addicts**
	Recovering addicts
RT	**Drug abuse**

Drug addicts' children
USE   **Children of drug addicts**

Drug addicts' infants
USE   **Children of drug addicts**

Drug addicts—Rehabilitation   362.29; 613.8; 616.86

BT	**Drug abuse counseling**

Drug counseling
USE   **Drug abuse counseling**

Drug-crime relationship
USE   **Drugs and crime**

Drug dealing
USE   **Drug traffic**

Drug education   362.29; 371.7; 613.8

Use for materials on the study of drugs, including their source, abuse, chemical composition, and social, physical, and personal effects.

UF	Drug abuse education
	Drug abuse—Study and teaching
	Drug addiction education
BT	**Health education**

Drug habit
USE   **Drug abuse**

Drug misuse
USE   **Drug abuse**

Drug plants
USE   **Medical botany**

Drug pushers
USE   **Drug traffic**

Drug stores
USE   **Drugstores**

Drug testing   344; 658.3

Use for materials on testing to identify personal use or misuse of drugs. Materials on the

---

BT = Broader Term   NT = Narrower Term   RT = Related Term   SA = See Also   UF = Used For

Drug testing—*Continued*
testing of drugs for safety or effectiveness are entered under **Drugs—Testing.**

UF   Drug abuse screening
Drug abuse—Testing
Screening for drug abuse
Testing for drug abuse

SA   classes of persons with the subdivision *Drug testing*, e.g. **Employees—Drug testing;** to be added as needed

NT   **Employees—Drug testing**

Drug testing in the workplace
USE   **Employees—Drug testing**

Drug therapy   615.5
UF   Chemotherapy *[Former heading]*
Pharmacotherapy

SA   names of diseases other than cancer with the subdivision *Drug therapy*, e.g. **Mental illness—Drug therapy;** to be added as needed

BT   **Therapeutics**
NT   **Antibiotics**
Cancer—Chemotherapy
Mental illness—Drug therapy
RT   **Drugs**
Pharmacology

Drug trade, Illicit
USE   **Drug traffic**

Drug traffic   363.45; 364.1
UF   Drug dealing
Drug pushers
Drug trade, Illicit
Narcotic traffic *[Former heading]*
Smuggling of drugs
Trafficking in drugs
Trafficking in narcotics

BT   **Drugs and crime**

Drug use
USE   **Drug abuse**
Drugs
and classes of persons with the subdivision *Drug use*, e.g. **Criminals—Drug use; Employees—Drug use; Teenagers—Drug use; Youth—Drug use;** etc., to be added as needed

Drugs   615
UF   Drug use
Pharmaceuticals

SA   classes of persons with the subdivision *Drug use*, e.g. **Criminals—Drug use;** types of drugs, e.g. **Amphetamines; Hallucinogens; Narcotics; Stimulants;** etc.; and names of individual drugs, e.g. **Crack (Drug); Marijuana;** etc., to be added as needed

BT   **Pharmacy**
Therapeutics

NT   **Designer drugs**
Drugs and crime
Generic drugs
Hallucinogens
Narcotics
Nonprescription drugs
Orphan drugs
Psychotropic drugs
Steroids
Stimulants
Sulfonamides

RT   **Drug abuse**
Drug therapy
Materia medica
Pharmacology

Drugs—Abuse
USE   **Drug abuse**

Drugs—Adulteration and analysis
USE   **Pharmacology**

Drugs and crime   364.1
Use for general materials on the relationship of drugs and crime. Materials on the illicit drug trade are entered under **Drug traffic.** Materials on the use of drugs by criminals are entered under **Criminals—Drug use.**

UF   Crime and drugs
Crime and narcotics
Crime-drug relationship
Drug-crime relationship
Narcotics and crime *[Former heading]*

BT   **Crime**
Drugs

NT   **Drug traffic**
RT   **Criminals—Drug use**

Drugs and criminals
USE   **Criminals—Drug use**

BT = Broader Term   NT = Narrower Term   RT = Related Term   SA = See Also   UF = Used For

Drugs and employees
USE **Employees—Drug use**
Drugs and sports
USE **Athletes—Drug use**
Drugs and teenagers
USE **Teenagers—Drug use**
Drugs and youth
USE **Youth—Drug use**
Drugs—Chemistry
USE **Pharmaceutical chemistry**
Drugs—Generic substitution
USE **Generic drugs**
Drugs in the workplace
USE **Employees—Drug use**
Drugs—Misuse
USE **Drug abuse**
Drugs, Nonprescription
USE **Nonprescription drugs**
Drugs of abuse, Synthetic
USE **Designer drugs**
Drugs, Orphan
USE **Orphan drugs**
Drugs—Physiological effect   615; 616.86
    Use for materials limited to the effect of drugs on the functions of living organisms.
    UF   Drug abuse—Physiological effect
    SA   names of drugs with the subdivision *Physiological effect*, to be added as needed
    BT   **Pharmacology**
    NT   **Opium—Physiological effect**
Drugs—Psychological aspects   615; 616.86
    BT   **Applied psychology**
Drugs, Psychotropic
USE **Psychotropic drugs**
Drugs—Testing   363.19
    Use for materials on the testing of drugs for safety or effectiveness. Materials on testing to identify the personal use or misuse or drugs are entered under **Drug testing.**
    UF   Clinical drug trials
           Clinical trials of drugs
    BT   **Consumer protection**
           Pharmacology
Drugstores   381
    Use for materials on business establishments that sell drugs. Materials on the art or practice of preparing, preserving, and dispensing drugs are entered under **Pharmacy.**
    UF   Apothecary shops
           Chemists' shops

           Drug stores
           Pharmacies
    BT   **Retail trade**
           Stores
Druids and Druidism   299
    BT   **Celts**
           Religions
Drum
USE **Drums**
Drum majoring   784.9; 791.6
    BT   **Bands (Music)**
    RT   **Baton twirling**
Drums   786.9
    UF   Drum *[Former heading]*
    BT   **Musical instruments**
           Percussion instruments
Drunk driving   363.12; 364.1
    UF   Driving under the influence of alcohol
           Driving while intoxicated
    BT   **Crime**
           Drinking of alcoholic beverages
Drunkards
USE **Alcoholics**
Drunkenness
USE **Alcoholism**
           Temperance
Dry cleaning   667
    UF   Clothing and dress—Dry cleaning
    BT   **Cleaning**
Dry farming   631.5
    UF   Farming, Dry
    BT   **Agriculture**
           Irrigation
Dry goods
USE **Fabrics**
Drying   660
    SA   materials, products, or objects dried with the subdivision *Drying*, e.g. **Flowers—Drying;** to be added as needed
    BT   **Industrial chemistry**
Dual career couples
USE **Dual career family**
Dual-career families
USE **Dual career family**
Dual career family   306.85; 646.7
    Use for materials on families in which both the husband and wife are pursuing careers.
    UF   Career couples

BT = Broader Term   NT = Narrower Term   RT = Related Term   SA = See Also   UF = Used For

Dual career family—*Continued*

    Dual career couples
    Dual-career families
    Dual career marriage
    Dual income couples
    Two-career couples
    Two-career families
    Two-career family
    Working couples
BT   **Family**
RT   **Work and family**

Dual career marriage
USE   **Dual career family**

Dual employment
USE   **Supplementary employment**

Dual income couples
USE   **Dual career family**

Ducks   598.4; 636.5
BT   **Birds**
    Poultry

Ductless glands
USE   **Endocrine glands**

Due process of law   347

Use for materials on the regular administration of the law, according to which citizens may not be denied their legal rights and all laws must conform to fundamental and accepted legal principles. Materials on legal hearings before an impartial and disinterested tribunal are entered under **Fair trial.**

UF   Procedural due process
    Substantive due process
BT   **Administration of justice**
    Civil rights
NT   **Fair trial**

Dueling   179.7; 394
UF   Fighting
BT   **Manners and customs**
    Martial arts

Dumps, Toxic
USE   **Hazardous waste sites**

Dunes
USE   **Sand dunes**

Dungeons
USE   **Prisons**

Duplicate bridge
USE   **Bridge (Game)**

Duplicating machines
USE   **Copying machines**

Duplicating processes
USE   **Copying processes**

Dust, Radioactive
USE   **Radioactive fallout**

Dust storms   551.55
BT   **Droughts**
    Erosion
    Storms

Dusting and spraying
USE   **Spraying and dusting**

Duties
USE   **Tariff**
    Taxation

Duty   170
BT   **Ethics**
    Human behavior
NT   **Conscience**

Dwarf trees   582.16; 635.9
SA   types of dwarf trees, e.g. **Bonsai**; to be added as needed
BT   **Trees**
NT   **Bonsai**

Dwarfism   616.4
UF   Growth retardation
BT   **Growth disorders**

Dwellings
USE   **Domestic architecture**
    Houses
    Housing
    and ethnic groups and classes of persons with the subdivision *Dwellings,* for materials on the residential buildings of a group from the standpoint of architecture, construction, or ethnology, e.g. **Indians of North America—Dwellings;** and ethnic groups and classes of persons with the subdivision *Housing,* for materials on the social and economic aspects of providing housing for the group, e.g. **Physically handicapped—Housing;** to be added as needed

Dwellings—Remodeling
USE   **Houses—Remodeling**

Dyes and dyeing   646.6; 667; 746.6
SA   types of dyes and types of dyeing, to be added as needed
BT   **Color**
    Pigments

BT = Broader Term   NT = Narrower Term   RT = Related Term   SA = See Also   UF = Used For

Dyes and dyeing—*Continued*
       Textile chemistry
       Textile industry
  NT Batik
       Tie dyeing
  RT Bleaching
Dying children
  USE Terminally ill children
Dying patients
  USE Terminally ill
Dynamics 531
  UF Kinetics
  BT **Mathematics**
       Mechanics
  NT **Aerodynamics**
       Astrodynamics
       Chaos (Science)
       Hydrodynamics
       Kinematics
       Matter
       Motion
       Quantum theory
       Thermodynamics
  RT **Force and energy**
       Physics
       Statics
Dynamite 662
  BT **Explosives**
Dynamos
  USE Electric generators
Dyslexia 371.91; 616.85
  BT **Reading disability**
Dyspepsia
  USE Indigestion
Dystopias 811, etc.; 813, etc.
  May be used for individual works, collections, or materials about dystopias.
  UF Anti-utopias
  BT **Fantasy fiction**
       Science fiction
  RT **Utopian fiction**
E.E.C.
  USE European Union
E.E.O.
  USE Discrimination in employment
E-mail
  USE Electronic mail systems
E.R.A.'s
  USE Equal rights amendments
E.S.P.
  USE Extrasensory perception

Eagles 598.9
  BT **Birds**
       Birds of prey
Ear 611; 612.8
  BT **Head**
  NT **Deafness**
  RT **Hearing**
Early Christian literature 270.1
  Use for individual works or collections of the writings of early Christian authors. Materials on the lives and thought of the leaders of the Christian church up to the time of Gregory the Great in the West and John of Damascus in the East are entered under **Fathers of the church.**
  UF Christian literature—30-600, Early
       Christian literature, Early
  BT **Christian literature**
       Literature
       Medieval literature
  RT **Church history—30-600, Early church**
       Fathers of the church
       Latin literature
Early church history
  USE Church history—30-600, Early church
Early printed books
  USE Rare books
Early warning system, Ballistic missile
  USE Ballistic missile early warning system
Earth 525; 550
  Use for general materials on the whole planet. Materials limited to the structure and composition of the earth and the physical changes it has undergone and is still undergoing are entered under **Geology.**
  UF World
  BT **Planets**
       Solar system
  NT **Antarctica**
       Arctic regions
       Atmosphere
       Continents
       Earthquakes
       Gaia hypothesis
       Geodesy
       Geography
       Ice age
       Latitude
       Longitude

BT = Broader Term   NT = Narrower Term   RT = Related Term   SA = See Also   UF = Used For

Earth—*Continued*
    Ocean
    Oceanography
    Tropics
  RT   Earth sciences
    Geology
    Physical geography
    Universe

Earth—Age 551.7

Earth—Chemical composition
  USE   **Geochemistry**

Earth—Crust 551.1
  BT   **Earth—Internal structure**
  NT   **Plate tectonics**
  RT   **Earth—Surface**

Earth, Effect of man on
  USE   **Human influence on nature**

Earth fills
  USE   **Landfills**

Earth—Internal structure 551.1
  NT   **Earth—Crust**

Earth sciences 550
  UF   Geoscience
  BT   **Physical sciences**
    Science
  NT   **Climate**
    Geochemistry
    Geography
    Geology
    Geophysics
    Meteorology
    Oceanography
    Water
  RT   **Earth**

Earth sheltered houses 690; 728
  UF   Houses, Earth sheltered
    Houses, Underground
    Underground houses
  BT   **House construction**
    Houses
    Underground architecture

Earth—Space attack and defense
  USE   **Space warfare**

Earth—Surface 551.1
  UF   Surface of the earth
  NT   **Landforms**
  RT   **Earth—Crust**

Earthenware
  USE   **Pottery**

Earthly paradise
  USE   **Paradise**

Earthquake sea waves
  USE   **Tsunamis**

Earthquakes (May subdiv. geog.)
    551.22
  UF   Seismography
    Seismology
  SA   types of structures subject to
    earthquake forces with the
    subdivision *Earthquake effects,*
    e.g. **Skyscrapers—Earth-**
    quake effects; to be added as
    needed
  BT   **Earth**
    Geology
    Natural disasters
    Physical geography
  NT   **Buildings—Earthquake effects**
    Skyscrapers—Earthquake ef-
    fects

Earthquakes and building
  USE   **Buildings—Earthquake effects**

Earthquakes—California 551.2209794
  UF   California—Earthquakes

Earthquakes—United States 551.220973
  UF   United States—Earthquakes

Earthwork
  USE   **Soil mechanics**

Earthworks (Archeology)
  USE   **Excavations (Archeology)**

Earthworks (Art) 709.04
  UF   Landscape sculpture
    Site oriented art
  BT   **Modern art—1900-1999 (20th**
    century)

East
  USE   **Asia**

East Africa 967.6
    Use for materials dealing collectively with
  the eastern region of the continent of Africa.
  Although used loosely, the term is usually
  used to include the areas now occupied by the
  countries of Burundi, Kenya, Rwanda, Tanzania, Uganda, and Somalia. Both the terms
  East Africa and Eastern Africa are sometimes
  used to cover the area extending from Sudan
  and Ethiopia in the north to the Zambizi River
  in the south, thereby including Malawi and
  Mozambique.
  UF   Africa, East *[Former heading]*
    Africa, Eastern
    Eastern Africa

BT = Broader Term   NT = Narrower Term   RT = Related Term   SA = See Also   UF = Used For

East Africa—*Continued*
BT   Africa
East and West   306; 909
> Use for materials on both acculturation and cultural conflict between Asian and Occidental civilizations.

BT   International relations
NT   Asia—Civilization
       Western civilization
RT   Acculturation
East Asia   950
> Use for materials on East Asia including China, Japan, Korea, Taiwan, Hong Kong and Macao.

UF   Asia, East
       East (Far East)
       Far East
       Orient
BT   Asia
RT   Pacific rim
East (Far East)
USE   East Asia
East Germany
USE   Germany (East)
East Goths
USE   Goths
East Indians   305.891; 954
UF   Indians (of India)
RT   Hindus
East (Near East)
USE   Middle East
Easter   263; 394.2667
BT   Christian holidays
       Holy Week
RT   Lent
Easter carols
USE   Carols
Easter—Drama   808.82; 812, etc.
> May be used for individual works, collections, or materials about Easter plays.

BT   Drama
       Religious drama
Easter egg decoration
USE   Egg decoration
Eastern Africa
USE   East Africa
Eastern churches   281
BT   Christian sects
       Christianity
NT   Orthodox Eastern Church
       Russian Orthodox Church

Eastern Empire
USE   Byzantine Empire
Eastern Europe   947
UF   Europe, Eastern
Eastern Europe—History   947
Eastern Europe—History—1989-
       947.085; 947.086
RT   Former Soviet republics
Eastern Seaboard
USE   Atlantic States
Easy and quick cooking
USE   Quick and easy cooking
Easy reading materials   372.41
UF   Beginning reading materials
       Preprimers
       Preschool reading materials
       Primers
BT   Children's literature
       Reading materials
Eating
USE   Dining
Eating customs   394.1
UF   Food customs
       Food habits
BT   Diet
       Human behavior
       Nutrition
NT   Table etiquette
RT   Dining
Eating disorders   616.85
SA   types of eating disorders, to be
       added as needed
BT   Abnormal psychology
NT   Anorexia nervosa
       Bulimia
Eavesdropping   363.25
UF   Bugging, Electronic
       Electronic bugging
       Electronic eavesdropping
       Electronic listening devices
       Listening devices
       Surveillance, Electronic
BT   Criminal investigation
       Right of privacy
RT   Wiretapping
Eccentrics and eccentricities   920
UF   Cranks
BT   Curiosities and wonders
       Personality
NT   Hermits

BT = Broader Term   NT = Narrower Term   RT = Related Term   SA = See Also   UF = Used For

Ecclesiastical antiquities
  USE   **Christian antiquities**
Ecclesiastical architecture
  USE   **Church architecture**
Ecclesiastical art
  USE   **Christian art and symbolism**
Ecclesiastical biography
  USE   **Christian biography**
Ecclesiastical fasts and feasts
  USE   **Religious holidays**
Ecclesiastical furniture
  USE   **Church furniture**
Ecclesiastical history
  USE   **Church history**
Ecclesiastical law   262.9
  UF   Canon law
        Church law
        Law, Ecclesiastical
  BT   **Church**
        Law
  NT   **Tithes**
  RT   **Church and state**
Ecclesiastical rites and ceremonies
  USE   **Rites and ceremonies**
Ecclesiastical year
  USE   **Church year**
Echo ranging
  USE   **Sonar**
Eclipses, Lunar
  USE   **Lunar eclipses**
Eclipses, Solar
  USE   **Solar eclipses**
Eclogues
  USE   **Pastoral poetry**
Eco-development
  USE   **Economic development—Environmental aspects**
Ecodevelopment
  USE   **Economic development—Environmental aspects**
Ecological agriculture
  USE   **Organic farming**
Ecological movement
  USE   **Environmental movement**
Ecology   577
  UF   Balance of nature
        Biology—Ecology
        Ecosystems

  SA   types of ecology, e.g. **Marine ecology**; and types of animals, plants, and crops with the subdivision *Ecology,* to be added as needed
  BT   **Biology**
        Environment
  NT   **Adaptation (Biology)**
        Biogeography
        Environmental protection
        Food chains (Ecology)
        Gaia hypothesis
        Marine ecology
        Plant ecology
        Symbiosis
  RT   **Biological diversity**
Ecology, Human
  USE   **Human ecology**
Ecology, Marine
  USE   **Marine ecology**
Ecology, Social
  USE   **Human ecology**
Economic aid
  USE   **Foreign aid**
Economic aspects
  USE   subjects with the subdivision *Economic aspects,* e.g. **Agriculture—Economic aspects;** to be added as needed
Economic assistance
  USE   **Domestic economic assistance**
        Foreign aid
Economic assistance, American
  USE   **American foreign aid**
Economic assistance, Domestic
  USE   **Domestic economic assistance**
Economic biology
  USE   **Economic botany**
        Economic zoology
Economic botany   581.6
  UF   Agricultural botany
        Botany, Agricultural
        Botany, Economic *[Former heading]*
        Economic biology
        Plants, Useful
  BT   **Agriculture**
        Botany
  NT   **Cotton**
        Edible plants

Economic botany—*Continued*
>> Forage plants
>> Forest products
>> Grain
>> Grasses
>> Plant conservation
>> Plant introduction
>> Poisonous plants
>> Weeds

Economic conditions   330.9

Use for general materials on some or all of the following: natural resources, business, commerce, industry, labor, manufactures, financial conditions. Materials on the history of the economic development of several countries are entered under **Economic development.**

UF Business depressions
>> Economic history
>> National resources
>> Stabilization in industry
>> World economics

SA racial and ethnic groups, classes of persons, and names of countries, cities, areas, etc., with the subdivision *Economic conditions,* e.g. **African Americans—Economic conditions; United States—Economic conditions;** etc., to be added as needed

BT **Business**
>> **Economics**
>> **Social conditions**
>> **Wealth**

NT **African Americans—Economic conditions**
>> **Blacks—Economic conditions**
>> **Business cycles**
>> **Chicago (Ill.)—Economic conditions**
>> **Developing countries**
>> **Economic policy**
>> **Great Depression, 1929-1939**
>> **Indians of North America—Economic conditions**
>> **Industrial revolution**
>> **Jews—Economic conditions**
>> **Labor supply**
>> **Natural resources**
>> **Ohio—Economic conditions**
>> **Poverty**
>> Quality of life
>> United States—Economic conditions

RT **Commercial geography**
>> **Economic development**

Economic cycles
USE **Business cycles**

Economic depressions
USE **Depressions**

Economic development   338.9

Use for materials on the theory and policy of economic development. Materials restricted to a particular place are entered under the name of the country, city, or area with the subdivisions *Economic conditions; Economic policy;* or *Industries.*

UF Development, Economic
>> Economic growth

BT **Economic policy**
>> **Economics**

NT **Sustainable development**

RT **Economic conditions**

Economic development—Environmental aspects   333.7; 338.9

Use for general materials on the environmental impact of economic development. Materials on economic development that satisfies the needs of the present generation without depleting natural resources for the future or having adverse environmental effects are entered under **Sustainable development.**

UF Eco-development
>> Ecodevelopment

Economic entomology
USE **Beneficial insects**
>> **Insect pests**

Economic forecasting   338.5

BT **Business cycles**
>> **Economics**
>> **Forecasting**

NT **Business forecasting**
>> **Employment forecasting**

Economic geography
USE **Commercial geography**

Economic geology   553

UF Geology, Economic *[Former heading]*

SA types of geological products, e.g. **Asbestos; Gypsum;** etc., to be added as needed

BT **Geology**

NT **Mines and mineral resources**
>> **Petroleum geology**

BT = Broader Term   NT = Narrower Term   RT = Related Term   SA = See Also   UF = Used For

Economic geology—*Continued*
       Quarries and quarrying
       Soils
       Stone
Economic growth
  USE   Economic development
Economic history
  USE   Economic conditions
Economic mobilization
  USE   Industrial mobilization
Economic planning
  USE   Economic policy
Economic policy   338.9
    Use for materials on the policy of government in economic affairs.
  UF   Central planning
       Economic planning
       National planning
       State planning
       World economics
  SA   names of countries or states
       with the subdivision *Economic policy* e.g. **United States— Economic policy;** subjects with the subdivision *Government policy,* e.g. **Agriculture—Government policy;** and types of activities, facilities, industries, services, and undertakings with the subdivision *Planning,* e.g. **Transportation—Planning;** to be added as needed
  BT   **Economic conditions**
       Economics
       Planning
  NT   **Commercial policy**
       Domestic economic assistance
       Economic development
       Energy policy
       Fiscal policy
       Foreign aid
       Free enterprise
       Government lending
       Government ownership
       Industrial mobilization
       Industrial policy
       Industrialization
       International economic relations
       Land reform

       Manpower policy
       Monetary policy
       Municipal ownership
       Ohio—Economic policy
       Privatization
       Sanctions (International law)
       Subsidies
       Tariff
       Transfer payments
       United States—Commercial policy
       United States—Economic policy
       Welfare state
  RT   **National security**
       Social policy
Economic recessions
  USE   **Recessions**
Economic relations, Foreign
  USE   **International economic relations**
Economic sanctions
  USE   **Sanctions (International law)**
Economic sustainability
  USE   **Sustainable development**
Economic zones (Maritime law)
  USE   **Territorial waters**
Economic zoology   591.6
    Use for general materials on animals injurious or beneficial to agriculture, and for materials on the extermination of wild animals, venomous snakes, etc.
  UF   Animals, Useful and harmful
       Economic biology
       Zoology, Economic *[Former heading]*
  BT   **Zoology**
  NT   **Agricultural pests**
       Beneficial insects
       Furbearing animals
       Insect pests
       Livestock industry
       Pest control
       Pests
       Poisonous animals
       Wildlife conservation
       Working animals
Economics   330
  UF   Distribution of wealth
       Political economy
       Production

BT = Broader Term   NT = Narrower Term   RT = Related Term   SA = See Also   UF = Used For

Economics—*Continued*
   SA   subjects with the subdivision
         Economic aspects, e.g. **Agri-**
         culture—Economic aspects;
         to be added as needed
   BT   Social sciences
   NT   Agriculture—Economic aspects
         Balance of trade
         Barter
         Business
         Capital
         Capitalism
         Christianity and economics
         Commerce
         Consumption (Economics)
         Cooperation
         Cost and standard of living
         Economic conditions
         Economic development
         Economic forecasting
         Economic policy
         Finance
         Government ownership
         Income
         Individualism
         Industrial trusts
         Industries
         Labor
         Land use
         Marxism
         Medical economics
         Money
         Monopolies
         Population
         Prices
         Profit
         Property
         Saving and thrift
         Socialism
         Statistics
         Underground economy
         Waste (Economics)
         Wealth
Economics and Christianity
   USE   Christianity and economics
Economics—History   330.09; 330.1
   Use for materials describing the development of economic theories. Materials on the
economic conditions and development of
countries are entered under **Economic condi-**
tions.

Economics, Medical
   USE   **Medical economics**
Economics of war
   USE   **War—Economic aspects**
Economy
   USE   **Saving and thrift**
Economy cars
   USE   **Compact cars**
Economy, Underground
   USE   **Underground economy**
Ecosystems
   USE   **Ecology**
Ectogenesis, Preimplantational
   USE   **Fertilization in vitro**
Ecumenical councils
   USE   **Councils and synods**
Ecumenical movement
   USE   **Christian unity**
Ecumenism
   USE   **Christian unity**
Eddas   839
   May be used for individual works, collec-
tions, or materials about eddas.
   BT   Old Norse literature
         Poetry
         Scandinavian literature
Eden
   USE   **Paradise**
Edible plants   581.6
   UF   Food plants
         Plants, Edible *[Former heading]*
         Plants, Useful
   BT   Economic botany
         Food
         Plants
Edifices
   USE   **Buildings**
Editing   070.5; 808
   Use for materials on the editing of books
and texts. Materials on the editing of newspa-
pers and periodicals are entered under **Jour-**
nalism—Editing.
   SA   subjects and types of literature
         with the subdivision *Editing,*
         e.g. **Poetry—Editing;** etc., to
         be added as needed
   BT   Authorship
         Publishers and publishing
   NT   Journalism—Editing
         Poetry—Editing

BT = Broader Term   NT = Narrower Term   RT = Related Term   SA = See Also   UF = Used For

Editions   016
  UF   Bibliography—Editions *[Former*
          heading]
         Bibliography—Reprints
         Reprints
  BT   **Bibliography**
  NT   **Bilingual books**
         First editions
         Paperback books
  RT   **Rare books**

Education (May subdiv. geog.)   370
    Subdivisions listed under this heading may
be used under other education headings where
applicable.
  UF   Instruction
         Pedagogy
         Study and teaching
  SA   types of education, to be added
         as needed, e.g. **Vocational**
         education; classes of persons
         and social and ethnic groups
         with the subdivision *Educa-*
         tion, e.g. **Deaf—Education;**
         African Americans—Educa-
         tion; etc.; and subjects with
         the subdivision *Study and*
         teaching, e.g. **Science—Study**
         and teaching; to be added as
         needed
  BT   **Civilization**
  NT   **Accreditation (Education)**
         Adult education
         African Americans—Education
         Area studies
         Audiovisual education
         Automobile driver education
         Basic education
         Blacks—Education
         Blind—Education
         Books and reading
         Business education
         Church and education
         Classical education
         Coeducation
         Colleges and universities
         Consumer education
         Continuing education
         Cooperative learning
         Deaf—Education
         Distance education
         Education and state

Educational evaluation
Educational games
Educational technology
Educational tests and measure-
    ments
Educators
Elementary education
Evening and continuation
    schools
Family life education
Foreign study
Girls—Education
Health education
Higher education
Home and school
Home schooling
Indians of North America—
    Education
International education
Labor—Education
Library education
Literacy
Mainstreaming in education
Men—Education
Mentally handicapped chil-
    dren—Education
Military education
Moral education
Multicultural education
Nature study
Naval education
Outdoor education
Physical education
Preschool education
Professional education
Psychology of learning
Religious education
Scholarships
School choice
Secondary education
Self-instruction
Simulation games in education
Socialization
Special education
Study skills
Teaching
Technical education
Veterans—Education
Vocational education
Women—Education

Education—*Continued*
    World War, 1939-1945—Education and the war
  RT   Culture
       Learning and scholarship
       Schools
Education, Adult
  USE Adult education
Education—Aims and objectives   370.11
Education and church
  USE Church and education
Education and radio
  USE Radio in education
Education and religion
  USE Church and education
Education and state   379
  UF   Education—Government policy
       [Former heading]
       Educational policy
       State and education
  BT   **Education**
       Social policy
       State, The
  NT   **Compulsory education**
       Federal aid to education
       State aid to education
Education and television
  USE Television in education
Education associations
  USE Educational associations
Education—Automation
  USE Computer assisted instruction
Education, Bilingual
  USE Bilingual education
Education, Character
  USE Moral education
Education, Christian
  USE Christian education
Education, Classical
  USE Classical education
Education, Compulsory
  USE Compulsory education
Education, Continuing
  USE Continuing education
Education—Curricula   375
  UF   Core curriculum
       Courses of study
       Curricula (Courses of study)
       Schools—Curricula

  SA   types of education and schools with the subdivision *Curricula,* e.g. **Library education—Curricula;** to be added as needed
  NT   **Articulation (Education)**
       Colleges and universities—Curricula
       Curriculum planning
       Library education—Curricula
Education—Data processing
  USE **Computer assisted instruction**
Education—Developing countries
       370.9172
  UF   Developing countries—Education
Education, Elementary
  USE **Elementary education**
Education, Ethical
  USE **Moral education**
Education—Experimental methods
       371.3
  UF   Activity schools
       Experimental methods in education
       Progressive education
       Teaching—Experimental methods
  SA   types of experimental methods, e.g. **Nongraded schools; Open plan schools;** etc., to be added as needed
  NT   **Experimental schools**
       Nongraded schools
       Open plan schools
       Whole language
Education—Federal aid
  USE **Federal aid to education**
Education—Finance   371.2; 379.1
  UF   School finance
       School taxes
       Tuition
  BT   **Finance**
  NT   **State aid to education**
  RT   **Federal aid to education**
Education for librarianship
  USE **Library education**
Education—Government policy
  USE **Education and state**
Education, Higher
  USE **Higher education**

BT = Broader Term   NT = Narrower Term   RT = Related Term   SA = See Also   UF = Used For

Education, Industrial
    USE   **Industrial arts education**
                    Technical education
Education—Integration
    USE   **School integration**
Education, International
    USE   **International education**
Education, Military
    USE   **Military education**
Education, Moral
    USE   **Moral education**
Education, Musical
    USE   **Music—Study and teaching**
Education, Naval
    USE   **Naval education**
Education, Nonformal
    USE   **Free universities**
Education of adults
    USE   **Adult education**
Education of children
    USE   **Elementary education**
Education of criminals
    USE   **Prisoners—Education**
Education of men
    USE   **Men—Education**
Education of prisoners
    USE   **Prisoners—Education**
Education of the blind
    USE   **Blind—Education**
Education of the deaf
    USE   **Deaf—Education**
Education of veterans
    USE   **Veterans—Education**
Education of women
    USE   **Women—Education**
Education of workers
    USE   **Labor—Education**
Education, Outdoor
    USE   **Outdoor education**
Education—Personnel service
    USE   **Educational counseling**
Education, Preschool
    USE   **Preschool education**
Education, Primary
    USE   **Elementary education**
Education, Secondary
    USE   **Secondary education**
Education, Segregation in
    USE   **Segregation in education**

Education, Special
    USE   **Special education**
Education—State aid
    USE   **State aid to education**
Education—Statistics   370
    BT   **Statistics**
Education—Study and teaching   370.7
    Use for materials on the study of education as a discipline. Materials on the history and methods of training teachers, including the educational functions of teachers colleges, are entered under **Teachers—Training.** Materials on the art of teaching and methods of teaching are entered under **Teaching.**
    UF   Pedagogy
    NT   **Teachers colleges**
                    Teachers—Training
Education, Technical
    USE   **Technical education**
Education, Theological
    USE   **Theology—Study and teaching**
Education—United States   370.973
    UF   United States—Education
Education, Vocational
    USE   **Vocational education**
Educational accreditation
    USE   **Accreditation (Education)**
Educational achievement
    USE   **Academic achievement**
Educational administration
    USE   **Schools—Administration**
Educational assessment
    USE   **Educational evaluation**
Educational associations   370.6
    UF   Education associations
    BT   **Societies**
                    Teachers
    NT   **Parent-teacher associations**
Educational consultants   370.7
    BT   **Consultants**
Educational counseling   371.4
    Use for materials on the assistance given to students by schools, colleges, or universities in the selection of a program of studies suited to their abilities, interests, future plans, and general circumstances. Materials on the assistance given to students in understanding and coping with adjustment problems are entered under **School counseling.** Materials on the activities and programs designed to help people plan, choose, and succeed in their careers are entered under **Vocational guidance.**
    UF   Academic advising
                    Education—Personnel service
                    Educational guidance

BT = Broader Term   NT = Narrower Term   RT = Related Term   SA = See Also   UF = Used For

Educational counseling—*Continued*
        Guidance counseling, Educational
        Personnel service in education
        Student guidance
        Students—Counseling
  BT   **Counseling**
  RT   **Dropouts**
       School counseling
       Vocational guidance
Educational evaluation   370.7; 379.1
  UF   Educational assessment
       Educational program evaluation
       Evaluation research in education
       Instructional systems analysis
       Program evaluation in education
       Self-evaluation in education
  SA   topics in education with the sub-
       division *Evaluation,* e.g. **Sci-**
       ence—Study and teaching—
       Evaluation; to be added as
       needed
  BT   **Education**
       Evaluation
Educational films
  USE **Libraries and motion pictures**
       Motion pictures in education
Educational freedom
  USE **Academic freedom**
Educational games   371.33
  UF   Instructional games
       Instructive games
  BT   **Education**
       Games
  NT   **Simulation games in education**
Educational gaming
  USE **Simulation games in education**
Educational guidance
  USE **Educational counseling**
Educational measurements
  USE **Educational tests and measure-**
       ments
Educational media
  USE **Teaching—Aids and devices**
Educational media centers
  USE **Instructional materials centers**
Educational policy
  USE **Education and state**
Educational program evaluation
  USE **Educational evaluation**

Educational psychology   370.15
  UF   Psychology, Educational
  BT   **Psychology**
       Teaching
  NT   **Apperception**
       Attention
       Imagination
       Intelligence tests
       Listening
       Memory
       Psychology of learning
       Thought and thinking
  RT   **Applied psychology**
       Child psychology
Educational reports
  USE **School reports**
Educational simulation games
  USE **Simulation games in education**
Educational sociology   306.43
  UF   Social problems in education
       Sociology, Educational
  BT   **Sociology**
Educational surveys (May subdiv. geog.)
       370
  UF   School surveys
  BT   **Surveys**
Educational technology   371.33
  UF   Instructional technology
  BT   **Education**
  RT   **Teaching—Aids and devices**
Educational television
  USE **Public television**
       Television in education
Educational tests and measurements
       371.26
  UF   Educational measurements
       Tests
  BT   **Education**
       Examinations
  NT   **Ability—Testing**
       Colleges and universities—En-
       trance examinations
       Examinations
       Grading and marking (Educa-
       tion)
  RT   **Intelligence tests**
       Psychological tests
Educators   370.92; 920
    Use for materials on people engaged profes-
sionally in the field of education in general.

Educators—*Continued*

Materials on educators engaged in classroom or other instruction are entered under **Teachers.**

UF   College teachers

       Faculty (Education)

       Professors

BT   **Education**

NT   **Teachers**

EEC

USE   **European Union**

EEO

USE   **Discrimination in employment**

Efficiency, Household

USE   **Home economics**

Efficiency, Industrial

USE   **Industrial efficiency**

Egg decoration   745.59

UF   Easter egg decoration

       Eggshell craft

BT   **Decoration and ornament**

       Handicraft

Eggs   636.5; 641

Use for materials on chicken eggs or on animal eggs in general.

SA   types of animals other than chickens with the subdivision *Eggs,* e.g. **Dinosaurs—Eggs;** to be added as needed

BT   **Cooking**

       Food

NT   **Birds—Eggs**

       Dinosaurs—Eggs

Eggshell craft

USE   **Egg decoration**

Egypt   962

May be subdivided like United States except for *History.*

Egypt—Antiquities   932

UF   Egyptology

BT   **Antiquities**

Egypt—History   932; 962

NT   **Sinai Campaign, 1956**

Egypt—History—1970-   962.05

Egyptology

USE   **Egypt—Antiquities**

Eight-hour day

USE   **Hours of labor**

Eighteenth century   909.7

Use for general materials covering progress and development during this period in one or in several countries.

UF   1700-1799 (18th century)

BT   **Modern history**

NT   **Enlightenment**

Elder abuse

USE   **Elderly abuse**

Elder care

USE   **Elderly—Care**

Elderly (May subdiv. geog.)   **155.67; 305.26**

UF   Aged

       Aging persons

       Elderly persons

       Older persons

       Senior citizens

SA   elderly of particular racial or ethnic groups, to be added as needed

BT   **Age**

       Gerontology

NT   **African American elderly**

       Aging

       Aging parents

       Elderly men

       Elderly women

       Libraries and the elderly

       Social work with the elderly

RT   **Old age**

       Retirees

Elderly abuse   362.6

UF   Abuse of the elderly

       Abused aged

       Battered elderly

       Elder abuse

       Elderly—Mistreatment

       Elderly neglect

       Parent abuse

BT   **Family violence**

Elderly and libraries

USE   **Libraries and the elderly**

Elderly—Care   362.6

Use for general materials on the care of the dependent elderly.

UF   Elder care

NT   **Elderly—Home care**

       Elderly—Institutional care

       Elderly—Medical care

       Nursing homes

Elderly—Counseling of   362.6

UF   Counseling of the elderly

       Counseling with the aged

BT   **Counseling**

BT = Broader Term   NT = Narrower Term   RT = Related Term   SA = See Also   UF = Used For

Elderly—Diseases   618.97
  UF   Geriatrics
  BT   **Diseases**
  RT   **Elderly—Health and hygiene**
Elderly—Health and hygiene   618.97
  UF   Geriatrics
  BT   **Health**
        Hygiene
  RT   **Elderly—Diseases**
Elderly—Home care   362.6
  BT   **Elderly—Care**
        Home care services
Elderly—Housing   362.6
  UF   Housing for the elderly
  BT   **Housing**
  NT   **Retirement communities**
Elderly—Institutional care   362.6
  UF   Homes for the elderly
        Old age homes
  BT   **Elderly—Care**
Elderly—Life skills guides   362.6; 646.7
  BT   **Life skills**
  RT   **Retirement**
Elderly—Medical care   362.1; 618.97
  UF   Medical care for the elderly
  BT   **Elderly—Care**
        Medical care
  NT   **Medicare**
Elderly men (May subdiv. geog.)   305.26
  UF   Aged men
  BT   **Elderly**
Elderly—Mistreatment
  USE   **Elderly abuse**
Elderly neglect
  USE   **Elderly abuse**
Elderly parents
  USE   **Aging parents**
Elderly persons
  USE   **Elderly**
Elderly—Recreation   790.084
  BT   **Recreation**
Elderly—Societies   367
  BT   **Societies**
Elderly—United States   305.260973
  UF   United States—Elderly
Elderly women (May subdiv. geog.)
        305.26
  UF   Aged women
  BT   **Elderly**

Election (Theology)
  USE   **Predestination**
Electioneering
  USE   **Politics**
Elections (May subdiv. geog.)   324
  UF   Ballot
        Franchise
        Polls, Election
        Voting
  BT   **Politics**
  NT   **Campaign funds**
        Presidents—United States—
          Election
        Primaries
        Referendum
        Suffrage
        Voter registration
  RT   **Proportional representation**
        Representative government and
          representation
Elections—Finance
  USE   **Campaign funds**
Elections, Primary
  USE   **Primaries**
Elections—United States   324.973
  UF   United States—Elections
Elections—United States—Finance
  USE   **Campaign funds—United**
          States
Electoral college
  USE   **Presidents—United States—**
          Election
Electric apparatus and appliances
        621.3028; 643
        Use for materials on small electrical ma-
        chines and appliances. Materials on large ma-
        chines powered by electricity are entered un-
        der **Electric machinery.**
  UF   Apparatus, Electric
        Appliances, Electric
        Electric appliances
  SA   types of electric apparatus and
        appliances, e.g. **Burglar**
        alarms; to be added as need-
        ed
  BT   **Electric engineering**
        Scientific apparatus and in-
          struments
  NT   **Burglar alarms**
        Electric batteries
        Electric generators

BT = Broader Term   NT = Narrower Term   RT = Related Term   SA = See Also   UF = Used For

Electric apparatus and appliances—*Continued*

    Electric household appliances
    Electric lamps
    Induction coils
    Storage batteries

Electric apparatus and appliances, Domestic
  USE   **Electric household appliances**

Electric appliances
  USE   **Electric apparatus and appliances**
    Electric household appliances

Electric automobiles 629.222
  UF   Automobiles, Electric *[Former heading]*
    Electric cars
  BT   **Automobiles**
  RT   **Automobile engines**

Electric batteries 621.31
  UF   Batteries, Electric
    Cells, Electric
  BT   **Electric apparatus and appliances**
    Electrochemistry
  NT   **Fuel cells**
    Solar batteries
  RT   **Storage batteries**

Electric cars
  USE   **Electric automobiles**

Electric circuits 621.319
  UF   Circuits, Electric
  BT   **Electric lines**
    Electricity
  NT   **Electronic circuits**

Electric communication
  USE   **Telecommunication**

Electric condensers
  USE   **Condensers (Electricity)**

Electric conductors 621.319
  UF   Conductors, Electric
  BT   **Electronics**
  NT   **Semiconductors**
    Superconductors

Electric controllers 629.8
  UF   Automatic control
  BT   **Electric machinery**

Electric currents 537.6; 621.31
  UF   Currents, Electric
  BT   **Electricity**
  NT   **Alternating electric currents**

    Electric measurements
    Electric transformers

Electric currents, Alternating
  USE   **Alternating electric currents**

Electric distribution
  USE   **Electric lines**
    Electric power distribution

Electric engineering 621.3
  UF   Electrical engineering
  BT   **Engineering**
    Mechanical engineering
  NT   **Electric apparatus and appliances**
    Electric lighting
    Electric machinery
    Electric power distribution
    Electric railroads
    Electricity in mining
    Radio
    Telegraph
    Telephone

Electric equipment of automobiles
  USE   **Automobiles—Electric equipment**

Electric eye
  USE   **Photoelectric cells**

Electric generators 621.31
  UF   Dynamos
    Generators, Electric
  BT   **Electric apparatus and appliances**
    Electric machinery

Electric heating 621.402; 644; 697
  UF   Electricity in the home
  BT   **Heating**

Electric household appliances 643
  UF   Appliances, Electric
    Domestic appliances
    Electric apparatus and appliances, Domestic
    Electric appliances
    Electricity in the home
    Household appliances, Electric *[Former heading]*
    Labor saving devices, Household
  SA   types of specific appliances, to be added as needed
  BT   **Electric apparatus and appliances**

BT = Broader Term   NT = Narrower Term   RT = Related Term   SA = See Also   UF = Used For

Electric household appliances—*Continued*
      Household equipment and supplies

Electric industries   338.4

Use for materials on industries producing products that contain electrical motors or otherwise employ electricity.

UF   Electric products industry
       Industries, Electric
BT   **Industries**

Electric lamps   621.32; 645

UF   Incandescent lamps
BT   **Electric apparatus and appliances**
       Lamps
RT   **Electric lighting**

Electric light
    USE   **Electric lighting**
          Photometry
          Phototherapy

Electric lighting   621.32

UF   Arc light
       Electric light
       Electricity in the home
       Light, Electric
BT   **Electric engineering**
       Electric wiring
       Lighting
NT   **Fluorescent lighting**
RT   **Electric lamps**

Electric lighting, Fluorescent
    USE   **Fluorescent lighting**

Electric lines   621.319

Use for materials on power transmission lines, their construction and properties.

UF   Electric distribution
       Electric power transmission
       Electric transmission
       Electricity—Distribution
       Power transmission, Electric
       Transmission of power
BT   **Electric power distribution**
NT   **Electric circuits**
       Electric switchgear
       Electric wiring

Electric machinery   621.31

Use for materials on large machines powered by electricity. Materials on smaller machines and appliances are entered under **Electric apparatus and appliances.**

BT   **Electric engineering**
       Machinery

NT   **Electric controllers**
       Electric generators
       Electric motors
       Electric transformers

Electric machinery—Alternating current   621.319

UF   Alternating current machinery

Electric machinery—Direct current   621.319

UF   Direct current machinery

Electric measurements   621.37

UF   Measurements, Electric
BT   **Electric currents**
       Weights and measures
NT   **Electric meters**
RT   **Electric testing**

Electric meters   621.37

UF   Meters, Electric
BT   **Electric measurements**

Electric motors   621.46

UF   Induction motors
       Motors
BT   **Electric machinery**
NT   **Electric transformers**

Electric power   621.31

BT   **Electricity**
       Energy resources
       Power (Mechanics)

Electric power distribution   621.319

UF   Electric distribution
       Electric power transmission
       Electric transmission
       Electricity—Distribution
       Power transmission, Electric
       Rural electrification
       Transmission of power
BT   **Electric engineering**
       Power transmission
NT   **Electric lines**
       Electric wiring

Electric power failures   621.319

UF   Blackouts, Electric power
       Brownouts
       Electric power interruptions
       Power blackouts
       Power failures

Electric power in mining
    USE   **Electricity in mining**

Electric power interruptions
    USE   **Electric power failures**

BT = Broader Term   NT = Narrower Term   RT = Related Term   SA = See Also   UF = Used For

Electric power plants   621.31
    UF   Electric utilities
           Power plants, Electric
    BT   **Power plants**
    NT   **Hydroelectric power plants**
Electric power transmission
    USE   **Electric lines**
           Electric power distribution
Electric products industry
    USE   **Electric industries**
Electric railroads   385; 621.33; 625.1
    UF   Interurban railroads
           Railroads, Electric
    BT   **Electric engineering**
           Public utilities
           Railroads
           Transportation
    RT   **Railroads—Electrification**
           Street railroads
Electric signs   621.32; 659.13
    UF   Signs (Advertising)
           Signs, Electric
    BT   **Advertising**
           Signs and signboards
    NT   **Neon tubes**
Electric smelting
    USE   **Electrometallurgy**
Electric switches
    USE   **Electric switchgear**
Electric switchgear   621.31
    UF   Electric switches
           Switches, Electric
    BT   **Electric lines**
Electric testing   621.37
    UF   Testing
    RT   **Electric measurements**
Electric toys   688.7
    BT   **Toys**
Electric transformers   621.31
    UF   Transformers, Electric
    BT   **Electric currents**
           Electric machinery
           Electric motors
Electric transmission
    USE   **Electric lines**
           Electric power distribution
Electric utilities
    USE   **Electric power plants**
           Public utilities

Electric waves   537; 621.381
    UF   Hertzian waves
           Radio waves
    BT   **Electricity**
           Waves
    NT   **Electromagnetic waves**
           Microwaves
Electric welding   671.5
    UF   Arc welding
           Resistance welding
           Spot welding
           Welding, Electric
    BT   **Welding**
Electric wiring   621.319
    UF   Wiring, Electric
    BT   **Electric lines**
           Electric power distribution
    NT   **Electric lighting**
Electrical engineering
    USE   **Electric engineering**
Electricity   537; 621.3
    SA   electricity in various endeavors,
           e.g. **Electricity in agricul-**
           ture; to be added as needed
    BT   **Physics**
    NT   **Electric circuits**
           Electric currents
           Electric power
           Electric waves
           Electricity in agriculture
           Electricity in mining
           Lightning
    RT   **Magnetism**
Electricity—Distribution
    USE   **Electric lines**
           Electric power distribution
Electricity in agriculture   333.79; 631.3
    UF   Electricity on the farm
           Rural electrification
    BT   **Agricultural engineering**
           Agricultural machinery
           Electricity
Electricity in medicine
    USE   **Electrotherapeutics**
Electricity in mining   622
    UF   Electric power in mining
           Mining, Electric
    BT   **Electric engineering**
           Electricity
    RT   **Mining engineering**

BT = Broader Term   NT = Narrower Term   RT = Related Term   SA = See Also   UF = Used For

Electricity in the home
    USE   **Electric heating**
               Electric household appliances
               Electric lighting
Electricity, Medical
    USE   **Electrotherapeutics**
Electricity on the farm
    USE   **Electricity in agriculture**
Electrification of railroads
    USE   **Railroads—Electrification**
Electrochemistry   541.3; 660
    BT   **Industrial chemistry**
            Physical chemistry
    NT   **Electric batteries**
            Electrometallurgy
            Electroplating
            Electrotyping
            Fuel cells
Electromagnetic waves   539.2
    UF   Waves, Electromagnetic
    BT   **Electric waves**
            Radiation
    NT   **Gamma rays**
            Heat
            Infrared radiation
            Light
            Microwaves
            Ultraviolet rays
            X-rays
Electromagnetism   621.34
    BT   **Magnetism**
    NT   **Masers**
Electromagnets   621.34
    UF   Magnet winding
    BT   **Magnetism**
            Magnets
Electrometallurgy   669.028
    UF   Electric smelting
    BT   **Electrochemistry**
            Metallurgy
            Smelting
    RT   **Electroplating**
            Electrotyping
Electron microscope and microscopy
    USE   **Electron microscopes**
Electron microscopes   502.8
    UF   Electron microscope and micros-
            copy *[Former heading]*
    BT   **Microscopes**

Electron tubes
    USE   **Vacuum tubes**
Electronic apparatus and appliances
            621.381
    UF   Apparatus, Electronic
            Appliances, Electronic
    SA   types of electronic apparatus and
            appliances, e.g. **Computers;**
            to be added as needed
    BT   **Electronics**
            Scientific apparatus and in-
            struments
    NT   **Computers**
            Electronic toys
            Intercommunication systems
Electronic art
    USE   **Computer art**
               Video art
Electronic brains
    USE   **Artificial intelligence**
Electronic bugging
    USE   **Eavesdropping**
Electronic bulletin boards
    USE   **Computer bulletin boards**
Electronic calculating machines
    USE   **Computers**
Electronic circuits   621.319; 621.3815
    BT   **Electric circuits**
            Electronics
Electronic computers
    USE   **Computers**
Electronic data processing   004
    UF   Automatic data processing
            Data processing
    SA   subjects with the subdivision
            Data processing, e.g. **Banks**
            and banking—Data process-
            ing; to be added as needed
    BT   **Computers**
            Information science
            Information systems
    NT   **Artificial intelligence**
            Banks and banking—Data pro-
            cessing
            Computer assisted instruction
            Computer bulletin boards
            Computer graphics
            Computer networks
            Computer systems
            Data transmission systems

BT = Broader Term   NT = Narrower Term   RT = Related Term   SA = See Also   UF = Used For

Electronic data processing—*Continued*
    Database management
    Expert systems (Computer science)
    HTML (Document markup language)
    Online data processing
    Optical data processing
    Programming (Computers)
    Programming languages (Computers)
    System design
  RT Computer science

Electronic data processing—Keyboarding
  USE Keyboarding (Electronics)

Electronic drawing
  USE Computer aided design
    Computer art
    Computer graphics

Electronic eavesdropping
  USE Eavesdropping

Electronic games
  USE Electronic toys
    Video games

Electronic listening devices
  USE Eavesdropping

Electronic mail systems   004.692; 384.3
    Use for materials on the electronic transmission of letters, messages, etc., primarily through the use of computers.
  UF E-mail
    Email
  BT Data transmission systems
    Telecommunication
  NT Computer bulletin boards

Electronic marketing
  USE Telemarketing

Electronic music   786.7
  UF Music, Electronic
    Synthesizer music
    Tape recorder music
  BT Music
  RT Computer music

Electronic musical instruments   786.7
  UF Musical instruments, Electronic
    [Former heading]
  SA types of instruments, e.g. Synthesizer (Musical instrument); to be added as needed
  BT Musical instruments

  NT Synthesizers (Musical instruments)

Electronic publishing   070.5; 686.2
    Use for materials on the process of publishing by which books and articles or any kind of data are made available as an electronic product. Materials on the use of a personal computer with writing, graphics, and page layout software to produce printed material for publication are entered under **Desktop publishing.**
  UF Online publishing
  BT Information services
    Publishers and publishing
  NT Teletext systems
  RT Desktop publishing

Electronic speech processing systems
  USE Speech processing systems

Electronic spread sheets
  USE Electronic spreadsheets

Electronic spreadsheets   005.3
  UF Electronic spread sheets
    Spread sheets, Electronic
    Spreadsheeting, Electronic
    Spreadsheets, Electronic
  BT Business
    Computer software

Electronic toys   688.7
  UF Electronic games
    Games, Electronic
  BT Electronic apparatus and appliances
    Toys
  NT Computer games
    Video games

Electronics   537.5; 621.381
  BT Engineering
    Physics
    Technology
  NT Amplifiers (Electronics)
    Cybernetics
    Digital electronics
    Electric conductors
    Electronic apparatus and appliances
    Electronic circuits
    Facsimile transmission
    High-fidelity sound systems
    Microelectronics
    Semiconductors
    Superconductors
    Transistors

BT = Broader Term   NT = Narrower Term   RT = Related Term   SA = See Also   UF = Used For

Electrons   539.7
  BT   Atoms
        Particles (Nuclear physics)
Electroplating   671.7
  BT   Electrochemistry
        Metalwork
  RT   Electrometallurgy
Electrotherapeutics   615.8
  UF   Electricity in medicine
        Electricity, Medical
        Medical electricity
  BT   Massage
        Physical therapy
        Therapeutics
  NT   Radiotherapy
Electrotyping   686.2
  BT   Electrochemistry
        Printing
  RT   Electrometallurgy
Elegiac poetry   808.81; 811, etc.
    May be used for individual works, collec-
    tions, or materials about elegiac poetry.
  UF   Elegies
        Lamentations
  BT   Poetry
Elegies
  USE   Elegiac poetry
Elementary education   372
    Use for general materials on education of
    children below the secondary school level.
  UF   Children—Education
        Education, Elementary [Former
          heading]
        Education of children
        Education, Primary
        Grammar schools
        Primary education
  BT   Education
  NT   Creative activities
        Exceptional children
        Kindergarten
        Montessori method of educa-
          tion
        Nursery schools
        Readiness for school
Elementary particles (Physics)
  USE   Particles (Nuclear physics)
Elementary school dropouts
  USE   Dropouts

Elementary school libraries   027.8
  UF   School libraries (Elementary
          school) [Former heading]
  BT   School libraries
  RT   Children's libraries
Elements, Chemical
  USE   Chemical elements
Elephants   599.67
  BT   Mammals
Elevators   621.8
  UF   Lifts
  BT   Hoisting machinery
Elite (Social sciences) (May subdiv. geog.)
        305.5
  BT   Leadership
        Power (Social sciences)
        Social classes
        Social groups
Elizabeth II, Queen of Great Britain,
        1926-   92; B
  BT   Queens—Great Britain
Elocution
  USE   Public speaking
Elves
  USE   Fairies
Email
  USE   Electronic mail systems
Emancipation
  USE   Freedom
Emancipation of slaves
  USE   Slavery
        Slavery—United States
Emancipation of women
  USE   Women's rights
Embarrassment
  USE   Self-consciousness
Embassies
  USE   Diplomatic and consular ser-
          vice
Emblems
  USE   Decorations of honor
        Heraldry
        Insignia
        Mottoes
        Seals (Numismatics)
        Signs and symbols
Emblems, National
  USE   National emblems
Emblems, State
  USE   State emblems

BT = Broader Term   NT = Narrower Term   RT = Related Term   SA = See Also   UF = Used For

Embracing
USE **Hugging**
Embroidery   746.44
SA types of embroidery, to be add-
ed as needed
BT **Decoration and ornament**
Needlework
Sewing
NT **Beadwork**
Crewelwork
Needlepoint
Samplers
Embryology   571.8; 612.6
UF Development
BT **Biology**
Zoology
NT **Fertilization in vitro**
Fetus
Frozen embryos
Genetics
RT **Cells**
Protoplasm
Reproduction
Embryos, Frozen
USE **Frozen embryos**
Emergencies
USE **Accidents**
Disasters
First aid
Emergency assistance
USE **Helping behavior**
Emergency medical technicians   610.69;
616.02
UF Emergency paramedics
EMTs (Medicine)
Paramedical personnel
Paramedics, Emergency
BT **Allied health personnel**
Emergency medicine   616.02
BT **Medicine**
Emergency paramedics
USE **Emergency medical technicians**
Emergency powers
USE **War and emergency powers**
Emergency preparedness
USE **Disaster relief**
Emergency relief
USE **Disaster relief**
Emergency survival
USE **Survival skills**

Emigrants
USE **Immigrants**
Emigration
USE **Immigration and emigration**
Eminent domain   333.1; 343
UF Condemnation of land
Expropriation
BT **Constitutional law**
Land use
Property
Emotional stress
USE **Stress (Psychology)**
Emotionally disturbed children   155.4;
362.2; 371.94; 618.92
Use for general materials on children suffer-
ing from mental or emotional illnesses. Mate-
rials on the clinical and therapeutic aspects of
mental disorders in children are entered under
Child psychiatry.
UF Behavior problems (Children)
Maladjusted children
Mentally ill children *[Former*
heading]
Neurotic children
Problem children
Psychotic children
BT **Exceptional children**
Mentally ill
RT **Child psychiatry**
Juvenile delinquency
Emotions   152.4
UF Feelings
Passions
SA types of emotions, to be added
as needed
BT **Psychology**
Psychophysiology
NT **Anxiety**
Attitude (Psychology)
Bereavement
Consolation
Emotions in children
Fanaticism
Fear
Frustration
Grief
Happiness
Hope
Horror
Joy and sorrow
Laughter

Emotions—*Continued*
>Loneliness
>Love
>Pain
>Pleasure
>Prejudices
>Self-confidence
>Shyness
>Worry

Emotions in children   155.4
>BT   Child psychology
>Emotions

Emperors (May subdiv. geog.)   920;
929.7
>UF   Rulers
>Sovereigns
>SA   names of emperors, e.g. **Nero,
Emperor of Rome, 37-68;** to
be added as needed
>BT   Kings and rulers

Emperors—Rome   920; 937
>UF   Roman emperors *[Former heading]*
>SA   names of Roman emperors, e.g.
Nero, Emperor of Rome, 37-68; to be added as needed
>NT   Nero, Emperor of Rome, 37-68

Empiricism   146
>UF   Experience
>BT   Philosophy
>Rationalism
>Theory of knowledge
>RT   Pragmatism

Employee absenteeism
>USE   Absenteeism (Labor)

Employee benefits
>USE   Nonwage payments

Employee counseling
>USE   Employees—Counseling of

Employee drinking
>USE   Employees—Alcohol use

Employee drug testing
>USE   Employees—Drug testing

Employee health services
>USE   Occupational health services

Employee morale   158.7; 658.3
>BT   Applied psychology
>Morale
>Personnel management
>Work

>NT   Job satisfaction
>RT   Absenteeism (Labor)

Employee sex in the workplace
>USE   Sex in the workplace

Employees   331.11; 920
>UF   Workers
>SA   types of employees, e.g. **Office
workers;** types of industries,
services, establishments, or institutions, with the subdivision
Employees; e.g. **Chemical industry—Employees; Railroads—Employees;** etc.; and
names of countries, states, cities, etc., and corporate bodies
with the subdivision *Officials
and employees,* e.g. **United
States—Officials and employees; Ohio—Officials and
employees; Chicago (Ill.)—
Officials and employees;
United Nations—Officials
and employees;** etc., to be
added as needed
>BT   Labor
>NT   **Chemical industry—Employees
Medical personnel
Migrant labor
Office workers
Railroads—Employees**
>RT   **Personnel management**

Employees—Accidents
>USE   Industrial accidents

Employees—Alcohol use   331.25; 658.3
>UF   Alcohol and employees
>Alcohol in the workplace
>Drinking and employees
>Drinking in the workplace
>Employee drinking
>Employees and alcohol

Employees and alcohol
>USE   Employees—Alcohol use

Employees and drugs
>USE   Employees—Drug use

Employees and narcotics
>USE   Employees—Drug use

Employees and officials
>USE   Civil service

Employees, Clerical
>USE   Office workers

Employees—Counseling of   658.3
    UF   Employee counseling
           Industrial counseling
    BT   **Counseling**
Employees—Dismissal   331.25; 658.3
    BT   **Job security**
           Personnel management
    RT   **Downsizing of organizations**
Employees—Drug testing   331.25; 344; 658.3
    UF   Drug testing in the workplace
           Employee drug testing
    BT   **Drug testing**
Employees—Drug use   331.25; 658.3
    UF   Drugs and employees
           Drugs in the workplace
           Employees and drugs
           Employees and narcotics
Employees—Rating   331.25; 658.3
    BT   **Performance standards**
Employees' representation in management
    USE   **Participative management**
Employees—Training   331.25; 658.3
    Use for materials discussing on-the-job training. Materials on teaching people a skill during the educational process are entered under **Vocational education.** Materials on teaching people a skill after formal education are entered under **Occupational training.** Materials on retraining are entered under **Occupational retraining.**
    UF   Factories—Training departments
           Factory schools
           In-service training
           Inservice training
           Training of employees
    SA   types of employees or personnel with the subdivision *Training,* e.g. **Teachers—Training;** or with the subdivision *In-service training,* e.g. **Librarians—In-service training;** to be added as needed
    BT   **Occupational training**
           Personnel management
           Vocational education
    NT   **Occupational retraining**
    RT   **Apprentices**
           Technical education
Employer-employee relations
    USE   **Industrial relations**

Employers' liability
    USE   **Workers' compensation**
Employment   331.1
    SA   racial and ethnic groups and classes of persons with the subdivision *Employment,* e.g. **African Americans—Employment; Veterans—Employment;** etc., to be added as needed
    BT   **Labor**
    NT   **African Americans—Employment**
           Age and employment
           Blacks—Employment
           Labor supply
           Part-time employment
           Summer employment
           Temporary employment
           Unemployment
           Veterans—Employment
           Women—Employment
           Youth—Employment
    RT   **Occupations**
           Vocational guidance
Employment agencies   331.12
    UF   Jobs
    BT   **Labor**
           Labor turnover
           Personnel management
           Recruiting of employees
           Unemployment
    NT   **Job hunting**
    RT   **Labor supply**
Employment and age
    USE   **Age and employment**
Employment applications
    USE   **Applications for positions**
Employment discrimination
    USE   **Discrimination in employment**
Employment forecasting   331.1
    UF   Occupational forecasting
    BT   **Economic forecasting**
    RT   **Labor supply**
Employment guidance
    USE   **Vocational guidance**
Employment management
    USE   **Personnel management**
Employment of children
    USE   **Children—Employment**

BT = Broader Term   NT = Narrower Term   RT = Related Term   SA = See Also   UF = Used For

Employment of teenagers
USE **Teenagers—Employment**
Employment of veterans
USE **Veterans—Employment**
Employment of women
USE **Women—Employment**
Employment of youth
USE **Youth—Employment**
Employment, Part-time
USE **Part-time employment**
Employment references
USE **Applications for positions**
Employment security
USE **Job security**
Employment, Supplementary
USE **Supplementary employment**
Employment, Temporary
USE **Temporary employment**
Empresses (May subdiv. geog.)   920
    SA   names of empresses; and countries, cities, etc., with the subdivision *Kings and rulers*, to be added as needed
    BT   **Monarchy**
    RT   **Queens**
EMTs (Medicine)
USE **Emergency medical technicians**
Enamel and enameling   738.4
    UF   Porcelain enamels
    BT   **Decoration and ornament**
           Decorative arts
Encounter groups
USE **Group relations training**
Encyclicals, Papal
USE **Papal encyclicals**
Encyclopedias
USE **Encyclopedias and dictionaries** and subjects, groups or classes of persons, and names of places with the subdivision *Encyclopedias,* e.g. **Philosophy—Encyclopedias; Jews—Encyclopedias;** etc., for materials that provide topical information usually in alphabetical order, to be added as needed
Encyclopedias and dictionaries   030; 031, etc.; 403; 413, etc.
    Use for general materials about encyclopedias and dictionaries.

    UF   Cyclopedias
           Dictionaries
           Encyclopedias
           Glossaries
           Subject dictionaries
    SA   subjects and names of languages with the subdivision *Dictionaries,* for materials in alphabetical order that define terms or identify things, e.g. **Chemistry—Dictionaries; English language—Dictionaries;** etc.; subjects, groups or classes of persons, and names of places with the subdivision *Biography—Dictionaries,* for biographical dictionaries, e.g. **Women—Biography—Dictionaries; Ohio—Biography—Dictionaries;** etc.; and subjects, groups or classes of persons, and names of places with the subdivision *Encyclopedias,* e.g. **Philosophy—Encyclopedias; Jews—Encyclopedias;** etc., for materials that provide topical information usually in alphabetical order, to be added as needed
    BT   **Reference books**
    NT   **Bible—Dictionaries**
           Biography—Dictionaries
           Chemistry—Dictionaries
           Classical dictionaries
           Computer science—Dictionaries
           English language—Dictionaries
           English language—Dictionaries—French
           French language—Dictionaries—English
           Geography—Dictionaries
           History—Dictionaries
           Jews—Encyclopedias
           Literature—Dictionaries
           Machine readable dictionaries
           Philosophy—Encyclopedias
           Picture dictionaries
           Polyglot dictionaries
           Shakespeare, William, 1564-1616—Dictionaries

BT = Broader Term   NT = Narrower Term   RT = Related Term   SA = See Also   UF = Used For

Encyclopedias and dictionaries—*Continued*

      Technology—Dictionaries

End of the earth
  USE   **End of the world**

End of the world   001.9; 236; 291.2; 523.1

Use for materials on the end of the world from an eschatological point of view (including Judgment Day, signs, fulfillments of prophecies, etc.) or from a scientific point of view.

  UF   End of the earth
         End of the world (Astronomy)
         World, End of the
  BT   **Eschatology**

End of the world (Astronomy)
  USE   **End of the world**

End-of-the-world fantasies
  USE   **Fantasy fiction**
         Fantasy films
         Fantasy television programs
         Robinsonades
         Science fiction
         War films
         War stories

Endangered species   333.95; 578.68
  UF   Threatened species
         Vanishing species
  BT   **Environmental protection**
         Nature conservation
  NT   **Plant conservation**
         Wildlife conservation
  RT   **Rare animals**
         Rare plants

Endocrine glands   616.4
  UF   Ductless glands
         Glands, Ductless
  BT   **Endocrinology**
  RT   **Hormones**

Endocrinology   616.4
  BT   **Medicine**
  NT   **Endocrine glands**
         Hormones

Endorphins   612.8; 615
  UF   Brain opioids
         Opioids, Brain
  BT   **Narcotics**

Endowed charities
  USE   **Charities**
         Endowments

Endowments   001.4; 361.6; 361.7
  UF   Endowed charities
         Foundations (Endowments)
         Philanthropy
  BT   **Finance**
  NT   **Scholarships**
  RT   **Charities**

Endurance, Physical
  USE   **Physical fitness**

Energy
  USE   **Energy resources**
         Force and energy

Energy and state
  USE   **Energy policy**

Energy, Biomass
  USE   **Biomass energy**

Energy conservation   333.791
  UF   Conservation of energy
         Conservation of power resources
         Power resources conservation
  SA   types of energy conservation, e.g. **Recycling**; to be added as needed
  BT   **Conservation of natural resources**
         Energy resources
  NT   **Recycling**
  RT   **Energy consumption**
         Energy policy

Energy consumption   333.79
  UF   Consumption of energy
  SA   subjects with the subdivision *Fuel consumption*, e.g. **Automobiles—Fuel consumption**; to be added as needed
  BT   **Energy resources**
  NT   **Automobiles—Fuel consumption**
  RT   **Energy conservation**

Energy consumption—Forecasting   333.79

Energy conversion from waste
  USE   **Waste products as fuel**

Energy conversion, Microbial
  USE   **Biomass energy**

Energy development   333.79
  UF   Energy resources development
         Power resources development
  BT   **Energy resources**
  NT   **Water resources development**

BT = Broader Term   NT = Narrower Term   RT = Related Term   SA = See Also   UF = Used For

Energy policy   333.79; 354.3
UF   Energy and state
     Energy resources—Government
        policy *[Former heading]*
     State and energy
BT   **Economic policy**
     Energy resources
RT   **Energy conservation**
Energy resources   333.79
   Use for materials on the available sources
of mechanical power in general. Materials on
the physics and engineering aspects of power
are entered under **Power (Mechanics)**.
UF   Energy
     Power resources
     Power supply
BT   **Natural resources**
     Power (Mechanics)
NT   **Biomass energy**
     Biomass energy industries
     Electric power
     Energy conservation
     Energy consumption
     Energy development
     Energy policy
     Fuel
     Ocean energy resources
     Renewable energy resources
     Solar energy
     Water power
     Wind power
Energy resources development
USE   **Energy development**
Energy resources—Government policy
USE   **Energy policy**
Energy resources, Ocean
USE   **Ocean energy resources**
Energy resources, Renewable
USE   **Renewable energy resources**
Energy technology
USE   **Power (Mechanics)**
Enforcement of law
USE   **Law enforcement**
Engineering   620
UF   Construction
SA   types of engineering, e.g. **Chem-
        ical engineering;** to be added
        as needed
BT   **Building**
     Industrial arts
     Technology

NT   **Aeronautics**
     Agricultural engineering
     Chemical engineering
     Civil engineering
     Computer aided design
     Electric engineering
     Electronics
     Genetic engineering
     Highway engineering
     Human engineering
     Hydraulic engineering
     Marine engineering
     Mechanical drawing
     Military engineering
     Mining engineering
     Minorities in engineering
     Municipal engineering
     Nuclear engineering
     Ocean engineering
     Railroad engineering
     Reliability (Engineering)
     Sanitary engineering
     Steam engineering
     Structural engineering
     Systems engineering
     Traffic engineering
     Water supply engineering
RT   **Engineers**
     Materials
     Mechanics
Engineering drawing
USE   **Mechanical drawing**
Engineering, Genetic
USE   **Genetic engineering**
Engineering instruments   620.0028
UF   Instruments, Engineering
BT   **Scientific apparatus and in-
        struments**
Engineering materials
USE   **Materials**
Engineering—Periodicals   620.005
Engineering, Structural
USE   **Structural engineering**
Engineering—Study and teaching
        620.007
BT   **Technical education**
Engineers   620.0092; 920
RT   **Engineering**
     Inventors

BT = Broader Term   NT = Narrower Term   RT = Related Term   SA = See Also   UF = Used For

Engines   621.4

UF   Motors

SA   types of engines, e.g. **Automobile engines;** to be added as needed

BT   **Machinery**

NT   **Airplane engines**

Automobile engines

Diesel engines

Fire engines

Fuel

Heat engines

Internal combustion engines

Marine engines

Pumping machinery

Solar engines

Steam engines

Turbines

England   942

May be subdivided like United States except for *History,* and *Politics and government,* or any subdivisions relating to history or politics and government. Such materials are entered instead under **Great Britain.**

BT   **Great Britain**

England, Church of

USE   **Church of England**

England—History

USE   **Great Britain—History**

English as a foreign language

USE   **English as a second language**

English as a second language   420.7; 428

UF   English as a foreign language

English for foreigners

English language as a second language

English language—Study and teaching, Foreign

English language—Texts for foreigners

BT   **English language—Study and teaching**

NT   **English language—Conversation and phrase books**

English authors   820.9; 920

UF   Authors, English *[Former heading]*

BT   **Authors**

English Canadian literature

USE   **Canadian literature (English)**

English Canadian poetry

USE   **Canadian poetry (English)**

English composition

USE   **English language—Composition and exercises**

English drama   822

Use for general materials about English drama, not for individual works.

BT   **Drama**

English literature

NT   **Morality plays**

Mysteries and miracle plays

English drama—Collections   822.008

English drama—History and criticism   822.009

BT   **Drama—History and criticism**

English essays   824; 824.008

Use for collections of literary essays by several authors.

BT   **English literature**

Essays

English fiction   823

May be used for collections or materials about English fiction, not for individual works.

BT   **English literature**

Fiction

English fiction—History and criticism   823.009

English for foreigners

USE   **English as a second language**

English language—Conversation and phrase books

English grammar

USE   **English language—Grammar**

English history

USE   **Great Britain—History**

English language   420

Subdivisions used under this heading may be used under other languages unless otherwise specified.

BT   **Language and languages**

RT   **Anglo-Saxon language**

English language—0-1100

USE   **Anglo-Saxon language**

English language—Acronyms

USE   **Acronyms**

English language—Alphabet   421

English language—Americanisms

USE   **Americanisms**

BT = Broader Term   NT = Narrower Term   RT = Related Term   SA = See Also   UF = Used For

English language—Antonyms
USE **English language—Synonyms and antonyms**

English language as a second language
USE **English as a second language**

English language—Basal readers
USE **Basal readers**

English language—Business English 428; 808

Business English is a unique subdivision for **English language.** Use same pattern with unique subdivisions for other languages, e.g. **Japanese language—Business Japanese;** etc.

UF Business English

English language—Comparison 425

UF Comparison (English grammar)
Grammatical comparison

English language—Composition and exercises 428; 808

UF English composition
RT **Rhetoric**

English language—Conversation and phrase books 428

UF English for foreigners
English language—Conversations and phrases *[Former heading]*
BT **English as a second language**

English language—Conversations and phrases
USE **English language—Conversation and phrase books**

English language—Dialects 427

NT **Americanisms**

English language—Dictionaries 423

Use for English language dictionaries. Dictionaries from English to another language are entered under this heading further subdivided by the other language, e.g. **English language—Dictionaries—French.** French-English dictionaries are entered under **French language—Dictionaries—English.** Combined English-French and French-English dictionaries are entered under both headings.

BT **Encyclopedias and dictionaries**
RT **English language—Terms and phrases**

English language—Dictionaries—French 443

Use for English-French dictionaries. French-English dictionaries are entered under **French language—Dictionaries—English.** Combined English-French and French-English dictionaries are entered under both headings.

UF Foreign language dictionaries
BT **Encyclopedias and dictionaries**

RT **French language—Dictionaries—English**

English language—Errors 428

English language—Etymology 422

BT **English language—History**

English language—Examinations 420.76

BT **Examinations**

English language—Foreign words and phrases 422

Use for materials on foreign words and phrases incorporated into the English language.

UF Foreign language phrases

English language—Grammar 425

UF English grammar
SA **English language** subdivided by topics in the study of grammar, e.g. **English language—Parts of speech; English language—Infinitive;** etc., to be added as needed
BT **Grammar**
NT **English language—Usage**

English language—History 420.9

NT **English language—Etymology**

English language—Homonyms 423

English language—Idioms 428

RT **English language—Provincialisms**

English language—Infinitive 425

English language—Jargon 427

English language—Old English
USE **Anglo-Saxon language**

English language—Orthography
USE **English language—Spelling**

English language—Parts of speech 425

English language—Phonetics
USE **English language—Pronunciation**

English language—Phrases and terms
USE **English language—Terms and phrases**

English language—Programmed instruction 420.7

BT **Programmed instruction**

English language—Pronunciation 421

UF English language—Phonetics
BT **Phonetics**
NT **Reading—Phonetic method**

English language—Provincialisms 427

RT **English language—Idioms**

English language—Punctuation
USE **Punctuation**
English language—Reading materials
USE **Reading materials**
English language—Rhetoric
USE **Rhetoric**
English language—Rhyme   808.1
BT **Rhyme**
English language—Slang   427
English language—Social aspects   420
English language—Spelling   421
UF English language—Orthography
NT **Spellers**
Spelling reform
RT **Word skills**
English language—Spelling reform
USE **Spelling reform**
**English language—Study and teaching
420.7**
NT **English as a second language**
English language—Study and teaching,
Foreign
USE **English as a second language**
**English language—Synonyms and ant-
onyms   423**
UF English language—Antonyms
RT **Opposites**
**English language—Terms and phrases
420**

Use for general lists of words and phrases
and for lists that are applicable to certain situations (collective nouns, curious expressions,
etc.) rather than to specific subjects. Lists of
words and phrases limited to specific subjects
are entered under the subject with the subdivision *Dictionaries*, e.g. **Chemistry—Dictionaries.**

UF English language—Phrases and
terms
RT **English language—Dictionaries**
English language—Texts for foreigners
USE **English as a second language**
English language—Usage   428
BT **English language—Grammar**
English language—Versification
USE **Versification**
English language—Vocabulary
USE **Vocabulary**
English letters   826; 826.008
BT **English literature
Letters**

English literature   820

Subdivisions used under this heading may
be used under other literatures.
BT **Literature**
NT **English drama
English essays
English fiction
English letters
English poetry
English prose literature
English satire
English speeches
English wit and humor**
RT **Anglo-Saxon literature**
English literature—0-1100
USE **Anglo-Saxon literature**
English literature—Bibliography   016.82
**English literature—Bio-bibliography
820.9**
English literature—Collections   820.8

Use for collections of English literature by
several authors in more than one genre. Collections of prose are entered under **English
prose literature.** Collections of poetry are entered under **English poetry—Collections.**
Collections of drama are entered under **English drama—Collections.**

English literature—Criticism
USE **English literature—History and
criticism**
English literature—Dictionaries   820.3
BT **Literature—Dictionaries**
**English literature—Examinations
820.76**
BT **English literature—Study and
teaching**
**English literature—History and criticism
820.9**
UF English literature—Criticism
English literature—Indexes   016.82
English literature—Old English
USE **Anglo-Saxon literature**
**English literature—Outlines, syllabi, etc.
820.2**
BT **Literature—Outlines, syllabi,
etc.**
RT **English literature—Study and
teaching**
**English literature—Study and teaching
820.7**
NT **English literature—Examina-
tions**

BT = Broader Term   NT = Narrower Term   RT = Related Term   SA = See Also   UF = Used For

256

English literature—Study and teaching—
Continued
- RT   English literature—Outlines,
  syllabi, etc.

English newspapers   072
- BT   Newspapers

English orations
- USE   **English speeches**

English periodicals   052
- BT   **Periodicals**

English poetry   821

Use for general materials about English po-
etry, not for individual works.
- BT   **English literature**
  Poetry

English poetry—Collections   821.008

English poetry—History and criticism
821.009

English prose literature   828

Use for collections of prose writings that
may include several literary forms, such as essays, fiction, orations, etc.
- UF   Prose literature, English
- BT   **English literature**

English public schools   373.2

Use for materials on British endowed sec-
ondary schools that are open to public admis-
sion but are not financed or administered by
any government body.
- UF   Public schools, Endowed (Great
  Britain) *[Former heading]*
  Public schools, English
- BT   **Private schools**

English satire   827; 827.008
- UF   Satire, English *[Former heading]*
- BT   **English literature**
  Satire

English speeches   825; 825.008
- UF   English orations
  Speeches, addresses, etc., Eng-
  lish *[Former heading]*
- BT   **English literature**
  Speeches

English wit and humor   827; 827.008;
827.009

Use for collections by several authors or for
materials about English wit and humor. Individual works by English humorists are entered
under **Wit and humor.**
- BT   **English literature**
  Wit and humor

Engravers   760.92; 920
- BT   **Artists**

- NT   **Etchers**
Engraving   760; 765
- UF   Copper engraving
  Engravings
  Line engraving
  Steel engraving
- SA   engraving of particular countries,
  e.g. **American engraving;** to
  be added as needed
- BT   **Art**
  Graphic arts
  Illustration of books
  Pictures
- NT   **American engraving**
  Gems
  Mezzotint engraving
  Photoengraving
  Wood engraving
- RT   **Etching**

Engraving, American
- USE   **American engraving**

Engravings
- USE   **Engraving**

Enhanced radiation weapons
- USE   **Neutron weapons**

Enigmas
- USE   **Curiosities and wonders**
  Riddles

Enlarged texts for shared reading
- USE   **Big books**

Enlarging (Photography)
- USE   **Photography—Enlarging**

Enlightenment   190; 909.7; 940.2

Use for materials on the philosophic movement of the 18th century marked by the ques-
tioning of traditional doctrines and values,
naturalistic and individualistic tendencies, and
an emphasis on the empirical method in science and the free use of reason.
- BT   **Eighteenth century**
  Modern philosophy
  Rationalism

Enlistment
- USE   **Recruiting and enlistment**

Ensemble playing
- USE   **Ensembles (Music)**

Ensembles (Mathematics)
- USE   **Set theory**

Ensembles (Music)   782; 784

Use for materials on small instrumental or
vocal groups and for the music written for
such groups.

BT = Broader Term   NT = Narrower Term   RT = Related Term   SA = See Also   UF = Used For

Ensembles (Music)—*Continued*
UF   Ensemble playing
         Instrumental ensembles
         Musical ensembles
         Vocal ensembles
SA   types of vocal or instrumental
         ensembles, e.g. **Jazz ensembles;** to be added as needed
BT   **Music**
         Musical form
         Musicians
NT   **Jazz ensembles**
RT   **Orchestra**
Ensigns
USE   **Flags**
Ensilage
USE   **Silage and silos**
Enteric fever
USE   **Typhoid fever**
Enterprises
USE   **Business enterprises**
Entertainers   791.092; 920
SA   types of entertainers and names
         of individual entertainers, to
         be added as needed
NT   **Actors**
         Clowns
         Comedians
         Dancers
         Fools and jesters
Entertaining   395.3; 642
Use for materials on hospitality and the art of entertaining guests.
UF   Guests
         Hospitality
BT   **Etiquette**
         Home economics
NT   **Business entertaining**
         Carving (Meat, etc.)
         Children's parties
         Games
         Parties
RT   **Afternoon teas**
         Amusements
         Dining
         Luncheons
Entertainments
USE   **Amusements**
Entomology
USE   **Insects**

Entomology, Economic
USE   **Beneficial insects**
Entomology, Medical
USE   **Insects as carriers of disease**
Entozoa
USE   **Parasites**
Entrance examinations for colleges
USE   **Colleges and universities—Entrance examinations**
Entrance requirements for colleges and universities
USE   **Colleges and universities—Entrance requirements**
Entrepreneurs (May subdiv. geog.)   **338; 920**
BT   **Business people**
         Self-employed
Entrepreneurship   338; 658.4
BT   **Business**
         Capitalism
         Small business
Environment   304.2; 333.7; 363.7
SA   subjects with the subdivision *Environmental aspects,* e.g. **Nuclear power plants—Environmental aspects;** to be added as needed
NT   **Ecology**
         Environmental movement
         Environmental policy
         Environmental protection
         Nuclear power plants—Environmental aspects
         Pesticides—Environmental aspects
         Work environment
Environment and pesticides
USE   **Pesticides—Environmental aspects**
Environment and state
USE   **Environmental policy**
Environment—Government policy
USE   **Environmental policy**
Environment, Space
USE   **Space environment**
Environmental aspects
USE   subjects with the subdivision *Environmental aspects,* e.g. **Nuclear power plants—Envi-**

BT = Broader Term   NT = Narrower Term   RT = Related Term   SA = See Also   UF = Used For

Environmental aspects—*Continued*
        ronmental aspects; Economic
        development—Environmental
        aspects; to be added as need-
        ed

Environmental health   616.9
  UF   Health—Environmental aspects
  SA   subjects with the subdivision *En-*
        vironmental aspects, e.g. **Nu-**
        clear power plants—Envi-
        ronmental aspects; to be
        added as needed
  BT   **Environmental influence on**
        humans
        Public health
  NT   **Air pollution**
        Nuclear power plants—Envi-
        ronmental aspects
        Occupational health and safety
        Pollution
        Water pollution

Environmental health engineering
  USE **Sanitary engineering**

Environmental influence on humans
        304.2; 599.9
  UF   Acclimatization
        Altitude, Influence of
        Man—Influence of environment
        [Former heading]
  BT   **Adaptation (Biology)**
        Human ecology
        Human geography
  NT   **Environmental health**
        Survival skills
        Weightlessness

Environmental lobby
  USE **Environmental movement**

Environmental movement   **322.4; 363.7**
  UF   Conservation movement
        Ecological movement
        Environmental lobby
        Environmentalism
        Green movement
  BT   **Environment**
        Social movements

Environmental policy (May subdiv. geog.)
        344; 354.3; 363.7
  UF   Environment and state
        Environment—Government poli-
        cy *[Former heading]*

        State and environment
  BT   **Environment**
  RT   **Conservation of natural re-**
        sources
        Human ecology
        Human influence on nature

Environmental policy—United States
        344; 354.30973; 363.7
  UF   American environmental policy
        United States—Environmental
        policy

Environmental pollution
  USE **Pollution**

Environmental protection   **344; 363.7**
  UF   Environmentalism
        Protection of environment
  BT   **Ecology**
        Environment
  NT   **Conservation of natural re-**
        sources
        Endangered species
        Landscape protection
        Soil conservation
        Wildlife conservation
  RT   **Pollution**

Environmental radioactivity
  USE **Radioactive pollution**

Environmentalism
  USE **Environmental movement**
        Environmental protection

Enzymes   **547; 572**
  BT   **Proteins**
  NT   **Catalytic RNA**

Eolithic period
  USE **Stone Age**

Epic films   **791.43**
    May be used for individual works, collec-
    tions, or materials about epic films.
  UF   Film epics
  BT   **Motion pictures**

Epic literature   **800**
    May be used for individual works, collec-
    tions, or materials about epic literature.
  BT   **Literature**
  NT   **Epic poetry**
  RT   **Mock-heroic literature**

Epic poetry   **808.81; 811, etc.**
    May be used for individual works, collec-
    tions, or materials about epic poetry.
  BT   **Epic literature**
        Narrative poetry

BT = Broader Term   **NT = Narrower Term**   **RT = Related Term**   **SA = See Also**   **UF = Used For**

Epic poetry—*Continued*
RT   Romances
Epidemics   614.4
UF   Pestilences
SA   names of contagious diseases,
e.g. **AIDS (Disease)**; to be
added as needed
BT   **Diseases**
Public health
NT   **Plague**
RT   **Communicable diseases**
Epigrams   808.88; 818, etc.
May be used for collections of epigrams
and for materials about epigrams.
UF   Sayings
BT   **Wit and humor**
NT   **Quotations**
Toasts
RT   **Proverbs**
Epigraphy
USE   **Inscriptions**
Epilepsy   616.8
BT   **Nervous system—Diseases**
Episcopal Church (May subdiv. geog.)
283
Use for materials on the Episcopal Church
in the United States after 1789. Materials on
the Episcopal Church in the United States pri-
or to 1789 are entered under **Church of Eng-
land—United States.**
UF   Protestant Episcopal Church in
the U.S.A.
BT   **Christian sects**
NT   **Catholic charismatic movement**
RT   **Church of England—United
States**
Epistemology
USE   **Theory of knowledge**
Epistolary fiction   813, etc.
May be used for individual works, collec-
tions, or materials about novels written in the
form of a series of letters.
UF   Epistolary novels
Novels in letters
BT   **Fiction**
Epistolary novels
USE   **Epistolary fiction**
Epistolary poetry   811, etc.
May be used for individual works, collec-
tions, or materials about epistolary verse.
UF   Verse epistles
BT   **Poetry**

Epitaphs   929
UF   Graves
BT   **Biography**
Cemeteries
Inscriptions
Tombs
Epithets
USE   **Names**
Nicknames
Epizoa
USE   **Parasites**
Equal employment opportunity
USE   **Discrimination in employment**
Equal opportunity in employment
USE   **Discrimination in employment**
Equal pay for equal work   331.2; 658.3
UF   Pay equity
BT   **Discrimination in employment**
Wages
Women—Employment
Equal rights amendments (May subdiv.
geog.)   305.42; 323.4; 342
UF   Amendments, Equal rights
E.R.A.'s
ERAs
BT   **Constitutions**
Sex discrimination
Equal time rule (Broadcasting)   324
Use for materials on the requirement that
all qualified candidates for public office be
granted equal broadcast time if one of one
such candidates is permitted to broadcast. Ma-
terials on the requirement that, if one side of
a controversial issue of public importance is
aired, the same opportunity must be given for
the presentation of contrasting views are en-
tered under **Fairness doctrine (Broadcast-
ing.)**
UF   Rule of equal time (Broadcast-
ing)
BT   **Broadcasting**
Television and politics
RT   **Fairness doctrine (Broadcast-
ing)**
Equality   323.42
UF   Inequality
Social equality
BT   **Political science**
Sociology
NT   **Individualism**
RT   **Democracy**
Freedom

BT = Broader Term   NT = Narrower Term   RT = Related Term   SA = See Also   UF = Used For

Equations, Chemical
USE **Chemical equations**
Equestrianism
USE **Horsemanship**
Equipment and supplies
USE subjects with the subdivision
Equipment and supplies, e.g.
**Television—Equipment and
supplies;** to be added as
needed
ERAs
USE **Equal rights amendments**
Ergonomics
USE **Human engineering**
Erosion   551.3
SA types of erosion, e.g. **Soil ero-
sion;** to be added as needed
BT **Geology**
NT **Dust storms**
Soil erosion
RT **Soil conservation**
Erotic art   704.9
UF Art, Erotic
Sex in art
BT **Art**
Erotica
Erotic fiction   808.83; 813, etc.
May be used for individual works, collec-
tions, or materials about erotic fiction.
UF Adult fiction
Erotic novels
Erotic stories
BT **Erotic literature**
Fiction
Erotic films   791.43
May be used for individual works, collec-
tions, or materials about erotic films.
UF Adult films
BT **Motion pictures**
Erotic literature   808.8; 809
UF Literature, Erotic
BT **Erotica**
Literature
NT **Erotic fiction**
Erotic poetry
Erotic novels
USE **Erotic fiction**
Erotic poetry   811, etc.
May be used for individual works, collec-
tions, or materials about erotic poetry.
BT **Erotic literature**

Poetry
RT **Love poetry**
Erotic stories
USE **Erotic fiction**
Erotica   704.9; 809
SA types of erotica, e.g. **Erotic art;
Erotic literature;** etc., to be
added as needed
NT **Erotic art
Erotic literature
Obscenity (Law)**
RT **Pornography**
Errors   001.9; 153.7; 165
Use for materials on errors of judgment, er-
rors of observation, scientific errors, popular
misconceptions, etc. Errors in language are
entered under names of languages with the
subdivision *Errors,* e.g. **English language—
Errors.**
UF Fallacies
Medical errors
Mistakes
Scientific errors
RT **Superstition**
Ersatz products
USE **Substitute products**
Erudition
USE **Learning and scholarship**
Eruptions
USE **Geysers
Volcanoes**
Escapes   365; 904
UF Hostage escapes
Prison escapes
BT **Adventure and adventurers
Prisons**
Eschatology   236; 291.2
UF Intermediate state
Last things (Theology)
BT **Theology**
NT **Death
End of the world
Future life
Heaven
Hell
Immortality
Millennium
Purgatory
Second Advent**
Eskimos
USE **Inuit**

BT = Broader Term   NT = Narrower Term   RT = Related Term   SA = See Also   UF = Used For

ESP
USE   Extrasensory perception
Esperanto   499
   BT   Universal language
Espionage   327.12
   UF   Spying
   SA   espionage practiced by particular
         countries, e.g. **American espi-**
         onage; to be added as needed
   BT   **Intelligence service**
         Secret service
         Subversive activities
   NT   **American espionage**
         Spies
Espionage, American
   USE   **American espionage**
Espionage films
   USE   **Spy films**
Espionage stories
   USE   **Spy stories**
Espionage television programs
   USE   **Spy television programs**
Esquimaux
   USE   **Inuit**
Essay   808.4

     Use for materials on the appreciation of the essay and on the technique of writing essays. Collections of essays are entered under **Essays; American essays;** etc.

   BT   **Literature**
Essays   808.84

     Use for collections of literary essays by authors of several nationalities. Collections of literary essays by American authors are entered under **American essays;** by English authors, under **English essays;** etc. Essays limited to a particular subject, by one or more authors, are entered under that subject. Materials on the appreciation of the essay and on the technique of writing essays are entered under **Essay.**

   BT   **Literature—Collections**
   NT   **American essays**
         English essays
Essences and essential oils   664; 668
   UF   Aromatic plant products
         Oils, Essential
         Vegetable oils
         Volatile oils
   BT   **Distillation**
         Oils and fats
   NT   **Flavoring essences**
         Perfumes

Estate planning   332.024; 343.05;
       346.05
   BT   **Personal finance**
         Planning
   NT   **Inheritance and transfer tax**
         Insurance
   RT   **Investments**
         Tax planning
Estate tax
   USE   **Inheritance and transfer tax**
Esthetics
   USE   **Aesthetics**
Estimates
   USE   types of engineering, technical
         processes, industries, etc.,
         with the subdivision *Esti-*
         mates, e.g. **Building—Esti-**
         mates; to be added as needed
Estimation (Mathematics)
   USE   **Approximate computation**
Estrangement (Social psychology)
   USE   **Alienation (Social psychology)**
Etchers   769.92; 920
   BT   **Artists**
         Engravers
Etching   767
   UF   Etchings
   BT   **Art**
         Pictures
   RT   **Engraving**
Etchings
   USE   **Etching**
Eternal life
   USE   **Eternity**
         Future life
         Immortality
Eternal punishment
   USE   **Hell**
Eternity   115

     Use for materials on the philosophical concept of eternity. Materials on the character and form of a future life are entered under **Future life.** Materials on the question of the endless existence of the soul are entered under **Immortality.**

   UF   Eternal life
   RT   **Future life**
Ethanol
   USE   **Alcohol as fuel**
Ethical aspects
   USE   subjects with the subdivision
         Ethical aspects, e.g. **Birth**

BT = Broader Term   NT = Narrower Term   RT = Related Term   SA = See Also   UF = Used For

Ethical aspects—*Continued*
            control—**Ethical aspects;** to
            be added as needed
Ethical education
  USE   **Moral education**
Ethics   170
  UF   Moral philosophy
        Morality
        Morals
        Philosophy, Moral
  SA   types of ethics, e.g. **Business**
        ethics; ethics of particular
        countries, e.g. **American eth-**
        ics; ethics of particular reli-
        gions, e.g. **Christian ethics;**
        names of individual persons,
        profess, and types of profes-
        sional personnel with the sub-
        division *Ethics,* e.g. **Librari-**
        ans—Ethics; and subjects
        with the subdivision *Ethical*
        aspects, e.g. **Birth control—**
        Ethical aspects; to be added
        as needed
  BT   **Philosophy**
  NT   **Abortion—Ethical aspects**
        American ethics
        Asceticism
        Birth control—Ethical aspects
        Business ethics
        Charity
        Chastity
        Christian ethics
        Conduct of life
        Conscience
        Cruelty
        Duty
        Good and evil
        Honesty
        Jewish ethics
        Joy and sorrow
        Justice
        Loyalty
        Moral education
        Motion pictures—Ethical as-
          pects
        Natural law
        Professional ethics
        Secularism

        Shakespeare, William, 1564-
          1616—Ethics
        Sin
        Social ethics
        Stoics
        Utilitarianism
        Values
        Vice
        Virtue
        Work ethic
        World War, 1939-1945—Ethi-
          cal aspects
  RT   **Human behavior**
Ethics, American
  USE   **American ethics**
Ethics, Biological
  USE   **Bioethics**
Ethics, Business
  USE   **Business ethics**
Ethics, Christian
  USE   **Christian ethics**
Ethics, Jewish
  USE   **Jewish ethics**
Ethics, Legal
  USE   **Legal ethics**
Ethics, Medical
  USE   **Medical ethics**
Ethics, Political
  USE   **Political ethics**
Ethics, Professional
  USE   **Professional ethics**
Ethics, Sexual
  USE   **Sexual ethics**
Ethics, Social
  USE   **Social ethics**
Ethics, Work
  USE   **Work ethic**
Ethiopian-Italian War, 1935-1936
  USE   **Italo-Ethiopian War, 1935-1936**
Ethnic conflict
  USE   **Ethnic relations**
Ethnic groups   305.8
      Use for materials on groups of people
  bound together by common ancestry and cul-
  ture. Materials on indigenous minorities are
  entered under **Native peoples.** Materials on
  the subjective sense of belonging to a particu-
  lar ethnic group are entered under **Ethnicity.**
  Materials on several ethnic groups in a particular region or country are entered under **Eth-**
  nology subdivided geographically. Materials
  on individual ethnic groups are entered under

BT = Broader Term   NT = Narrower Term   RT = Related Term   SA = See Also   UF = Used For

Ethnic groups—*Continued*
the name of the group, e.g. **Mexican Americans.**

UF   People
SA   names of individual ethnic
       groups, to be added as needed
BT   **Ethnology**
RT   **Ethnic relations**
       Ethnicity

Ethnic identity
USE   **Ethnicity**
       and ethnic groups with the subdivision *Ethnic identity,* e.g.
       Mexican Americans—Ethnic identity; to be added as needed

Ethnic psychology
USE   **Ethnopsychology**

Ethnic relations   305.8
UF   Ethnic conflict
       Relations among ethnic groups
SA   names of regions, countries, cities, etc., with the subdivision
       Ethnic relations; e.g. **United States—Ethnic relations;** to be added as needed
BT   **Acculturation**
       Ethnology
       Sociology
NT   **Culture conflict**
       Discrimination
       Multiculturalism
RT   **Ethnic groups**
       Minorities
       Race relations

**Ethnic relations—Political aspects
305.8**

**Ethnic relations—Religious aspects
305.8**

Ethnicity   305.8
Use for materials on the subjective sense of belonging to a particular ethnic group. Materials on groups of people bound together by a common ancestry or culture are entered under **Ethnic groups.** Materials on several ethnic groups in a particular region or country are entered under **Ethnology.**

UF   Ethnic identity
SA   ethnic groups with the subdivision *Ethnic identity,* e.g. **Mexican Americans—Ethnic identity;** and racial groups

with the subdivision *Race identity,* e.g. **African Americans—Race identity;** to be added as needed
BT   **Identity (Psychology)**
RT   **Ethnic groups**
       Multiculturalism

Ethnobotany (May subdiv. geog.)   **581.6**
SA   names of ethnic groups with the subdivision *Ethnobotany,* to be added as needed
BT   **Ethnology**
       Plants—Folklore

Ethnography
USE   **Ethnology**

Ethnology (May subdiv. geog.)   **305.8;
306; 599.97**
Use for materials on the disciplines of ethnology and cultural anthropology, and, with appropriate geographic subdivisions, for materials on the origin, distribution, and characteristics of the elements of the population of a particular region or country. General materials on groups of people who are bound together by common ties of ancestry and culture are entered under **Ethnic groups.** Materials on individual racial or ethnic groups are entered under the name of the group, e.g. **Australian aborigines.**

UF   Cultural anthropology
       Ethnography
       Geographical distribution of people
       Races of people
       Social anthropology
SA   names of countries with the subdivision *Social life and customs,* e.g. **United States—Social life and customs;** and names of individual ethnic groups, to be added as needed
BT   **Human beings**
NT   **Acculturation**
       Anthropometry
       Cannibalism
       Costume
       Ethnic groups
       Ethnic relations
       Ethnobotany
       Ethnopsychology
       Folklore
       Human geography
       Kinship

BT = Broader Term   NT = Narrower Term   RT = Related Term   SA = See Also   UF = Used For

Ethnology—*Continued*
      Language and languages
      Manners and customs
      Native peoples
      Physical anthropology
      Primitive societies
      Race
      Race relations
      Semitic peoples
      Totems and totemism
  RT   Anthropology
      Archeology
      Civilization
Ethnology—United States   305.813
  UF United States—Ethnology
      United States—Peoples
  SA names of individual ethnic
        groups, to be added as needed
  RT Americans
      Hispanic Americans
      Indians of North America
      Mexican Americans
Ethnopsychology   155.8
  UF Cross cultural psychology
      Ethnic psychology
      Folk psychology
      National psychology
      Psychology, Ethnic
      Psychology, National
      Psychology, Racial
      Race psychology
  SA names of racial or ethnic groups
        with the subdivision *Psycholo-*
        gy, to be added as needed
  BT Anthropology
      Ethnology
      Psychology
      Sociology
  NT Culture conflict
      Indians of North America—
        Psychology
  RT National characteristics
      Social psychology
Ethyl alcohol fuel
  USE Alcohol as fuel
Etiquette   395
  UF Ceremonies
      Manners
      Politeness
      Salutations

  SA types of etiquette, e.g. **Table et-**
        iquette; and names of coun-
        tries with the subdivision *So-*
        cial life and customs, e.g.
        United States—Social life
        and customs; to be added as
        needed
  BT Human behavior
  NT Courtesy
      Dating (Social customs)
      Entertaining
      Letter writing
      Table etiquette
  RT Manners and customs
Etymology
  USE names of languages with the
        subdivision *Etymology,* e.g.
        English language—Etymolo-
        gy; to be added as needed
Eucharist
  USE Lord's Supper
      Mass
Eugenics   363.9
  BT Genetics
      Population
  RT Heredity
Europe   940
  UF Europe, Western
      Western Europe
Europe, Central
  USE Central Europe
Europe, Eastern
  USE Eastern Europe
Europe—History   940
  NT Holy Roman Empire
Europe—History—0-476   936; 937
Europe—History—476-1492   940.1;
      940.2
  NT Hundred Years' War, 1339-
        1453
  RT Middle Ages—History
Europe—History—1492-1789   940.2
  NT Seven Years' War, 1756-1763
      Thirty Years' War, 1618-1648
Europe—History—1700-1799 (18th
    century)   940.2
  UF Europe—History—18th century
Europe—History—18th century
  USE Europe—History—1700-1799
      (18th century)

BT = Broader Term   **NT** = Narrower Term   **RT** = Related Term   **SA** = See Also   **UF** = Used For

Europe—History—1789-1815   940.2
  UF   Napoleonic Wars
  BT   Europe—History—1789-1900
Europe—History—1789-1900   940.2
  UF   Europe—History—1800-1899
        (19th century)
  NT   Europe—History—1789-1815
        Europe—History—1815-1848
        Europe—History—1848-1871
        Europe—History—1871-1918
Europe—History—1800-1899 (19th century)
  USE   Europe—History—1789-1900
Europe—History—1815-1848   940.2
  BT   Europe—History—1789-1900
Europe—History—1848-1871   940.2
  BT   Europe—History—1789-1900
Europe—History—1871-1918   940.2
  BT   Europe—History—1789-1900
        Europe—History—1900-1999
        (20th century)
  NT   World War, 1914-1918
Europe—History—1900-1999 (20th
  century)   940.5
  NT   Europe—History—1871-1918
Europe—History—1914-1945
  USE   Europe—History—1918-1945
Europe—History—1918-1945   940.5
  UF   Europe—History—1914-1945
        [Former heading]
  NT   Russo-Finnish War, 1939-1940
        World War, 1939-1945
Europe—History—1945-   940.55
Europe—Politics and government   940
        May be subdivided by period using the
     same subdivisions as under Europe—History,
     e.g. Europe—Politics and government—
     1789-1900.
  NT   European federation
Europe, Western
  USE   Europe
European Common Market
  USE   European Union
European Community
  USE   European Union
European Economic Community
  USE   European Union
European federation   321; 940
        Use for general materials on the political or
     economic union of European countries. Mate-
     rials on the corporate body formerly known as
     the European Economic Community and the

European Community, which became known
as the European Union upon ratification of the
Treaty of European Union on October 29,
1993, are entered under European Union.
  UF   Federation of Europe
        Paneuropean federation
        United States of Europe (pro-
           posed)
  BT   Europe—Politics and govern-
           ment
        Federal government
        International organization
  NT   European Union
European Union   341.242; 382
        Use for materials on the corporate body for-
     merly known as the European Economic
     Community and the European Community,
     which became known as the European Union
     upon ratification of the Treaty on European
     Union on October 29, 1993. General materials
     on the political or economic union of Europe-
     an countries are entered under European fed-
     eration.
  UF   Common market
        E.E.C.
        EEC
        European Common Market
        European Community
        European Economic Community
           [Former heading]
  BT   European federation
European War, 1914-1918
  USE   World War, 1914-1918
European War, 1939-1945
  USE   World War, 1939-1945
Euthanasia   179.7
  UF   Death, Mercy
        Killing, Mercy
        Mercy killing
  BT   Homicide
        Medical ethics
  RT   Right to die
Evacuation of civilians
  USE   names of wars with the subdivi-
           sion Evacuation of civilians,
           e.g. World War, 1939-
           1945—Evacuation of civil-
           ians; to be added as needed
Evaluation   001.4
  SA   names of corporate bodies and
           types of institutions, products,
           services, equipment, activities,
           projects, and programs with

BT = Broader Term   NT = Narrower Term   RT = Related Term   SA = See Also   UF = Used For

Evaluation—*Continued*

    the subdivision *Evaluation,*
e.g. **Public health—Evaluation; Science—Study and teaching—Evaluation;** etc., to be added as needed

  BT   **Research**
  NT   **Educational evaluation**

Evaluation of literature
  USE **Best books**
        Books and reading
        Books—Reviews
        Criticism
        Literature—History and criticism

Evaluation research in education
  USE **Educational evaluation**

Evangelism
  USE **Evangelistic work**

Evangelism and politics
  USE **Religion and politics**

Evangelistic healing
  USE **Spiritual healing**

Evangelistic work   253; 269
  UF   Evangelism
        Revival (Religion)
  BT   **Church work**
  NT   **Conversion**
        Revivals
  RT   **Christian missions**

Evening and continuation schools   374
  UF   Continuation schools
        Evening schools
        Night schools
  BT   **Compulsory education**
        Continuing education
        Education
        Public schools
        Schools
        Secondary education
        Technical education
  RT   **Adult education**

Evening schools
  USE **Evening and continuation schools**

Evergreens   582.1; 635.9
  BT   **Landscape gardening**
        Shrubs
        Trees

Evidences of the Bible
  USE **Bible—Evidences, authority, etc.**

Evil
  USE **Good and evil**

Evil spirits
  USE **Demonology**

Evolution   576.8
  UF   Darwinism
        Development
        Mutation (Biology)
        Origin of species
  SA   types of animals, plants, crops, chemicals, and organs of the body with the subdivision *Evolution,* to be added as needed
  BT   **Philosophy**
  NT   **Life—Origin**
  RT   **Biology**
        Creation
        Creationism
        Human origins
        Natural selection
        Religion and science
        Variation (Biology)

Evolution and Christianity
  USE **Creationism**

Evolution—Study and teaching   576.807
  UF   Creation—Study and teaching *[Former heading]*
  RT   **Creationism**

Ex libris
  USE **Bookplates**

Ex-nuns   305.48
  UF   Catholic ex-nuns
        Former nuns
  BT   **Nuns**

Ex-priests   305.33; 920
  UF   Catholic ex-priests
        Former priests
  BT   **Catholic Church—Clergy**
        Priests

Ex-service men
  USE **Veterans**

Ex-Soviet republics
  USE **Former Soviet republics**

Ex-Soviet states
  USE **Former Soviet republics**

BT = Broader Term   NT = Narrower Term   RT = Related Term   SA = See Also   UF = Used For

Examinations   371.26

Use for general materials on examinations. Materials discussing the requirements for examinations in particular branches of study, or compilations of questions and answers for such examinations, are entered under the subject with the subdivision *Examinations.*

UF   Achievement tests

Objective tests

Tests

SA   branches of study with the subdivision *Examinations,* e.g. **English language—Examinations;** and names of individual examinations, to be added as needed

BT   **Educational tests and measurements**

Questions and answers

Teaching

NT   **Civil service—Examinations**

Colleges and universities—Entrance examinations

Colleges and universities—Entrance requirements

Educational tests and measurements

English language—Examinations

Graduate Record Examination

Music—Examinations

Scholastic Aptitude Test

United States. Army—Examinations

Examinations—Design and construction 371.26

Excavation   624.1

BT   **Civil engineering**

Tunnels

Excavations (Archeology) (May subdiv. geog.)   930.1

UF   Earthworks (Archeology)

Ruins

BT   **Archeology**

RT   **Extinct cities**

Mounds and mound builders

Excavations (Archeology)—United States 973

UF   United States—Excavations (Archeology)

Exceptional children   155.45

UF   Abnormal children

Children, Abnormal

Children, Exceptional

BT   **Children**

Elementary education

NT   **Brain damaged children**

Emotionally disturbed children

Gifted children

Handicapped children

Mainstreaming in education

Slow learning children

Wild children

Excess government property

USE   **Surplus government property**

Exchange   332.4; 332.64

BT   **Commerce**

NT   **Foreign exchange**

Money

Stock exchange

Exchange, Barter

USE   **Barter**

Exchange, Foreign

USE   **Foreign exchange**

Exchange of persons programs   327.1; 370.116

UF   Cultural exchange programs

Interchange of visitors

Specialists exchange programs

Visitors' exchange programs

SA   types of exchange programs for particular classes of persons, e.g. **Teacher exchange;** to be added as needed

BT   **Cultural relations**

International cooperation

NT   **Teacher exchange**

Exchange of prisoners of war

USE   **Prisoners of war**

Exchange of teachers

USE   **Teacher exchange**

Exchange rates

USE   **Foreign exchange**

Executions

USE   **Capital punishment**

Executive ability   658.4

UF   Administrative ability

BT   **Ability**

NT   **Leadership**

Planning

RT   **Industrial efficiency**

Executive agencies
USE **Administrative agencies**
Executive departments (May subdiv. geog.) **351**

Use for materials on major administrative divisions of the executive branch of government, usually headed by an officer of cabinet rank.

UF   Government departments
      Government ministries
      State ministries
SA   names of executive departments, to be added as needed
BT   **Administrative agencies**
Executive departments—Ohio   **352.2**
UF   Ohio—Executive departments
      [Former heading]
SA   names of executive departments, to be added as needed
Executive departments—Reorganization
USE   **Administrative agencies—Reorganization**
Executive departments—United States   **352.2**
UF   United States—Executive departments *[Former heading]*
SA   names of executive departments, to be added as needed
NT   **Presidents—United States—Staff**
Executive investigations
USE   **Governmental investigations**
Executive power (May subdiv. geog.)   **351**

Use for materials on the powers of the executive or administrative branch of government.

UF   Presidents—Powers
BT   **Constitutional law**
      Political science
NT   **Amnesty**
      Heads of state
      Monarchy
      Pardon
      Prime ministers
      Separation of powers
      War and emergency powers
RT   **Presidents**
Executive power—United States   **352.230973**
UF   Presidents—United States—Power

      United States—Executive power
Executive reorganization
USE   **Administrative agencies—Reorganization**
Executors and administrators   **346.05**
UF   Administrators and executors
BT   **Inheritance and succession**
RT   **Wills**
Exegesis, Biblical
USE   **Bible—Criticism**
Exercise   **613.7**
SA   types of exercises and physical activities, to be added as needed
BT   **Health**
      Hygiene
NT   **Aerobics**
      Bodybuilding
      Cycling
      Gymnastics
      Hatha yoga
      Physical fitness
      Rowing
      Weight lifting
RT   **Physical education**
      Weight loss
Exercise addiction   **616.85**
UF   Addiction to exercise
      Compulsive exercising
BT   **Compulsive behavior**
Exercises, problems, etc.
USE   subjects with the subdivision *Problems, exercises, etc.,* for compilations of practice problems or exercises for use in the study of a topic, e.g. **Chemistry—Problems, exercises, etc.;** to be added as needed
Exhaustion
USE   **Fatigue**
Exhibitions
UF   Exhibits
      Expositions
      Industrial exhibitions
      International exhibitions
      Trade shows
      World's fairs

BT = Broader Term   **NT** = Narrower Term   **RT** = Related Term   **SA** = See Also   **UF** = Used For

Exhibitions—*Continued*

SA   types of exhibitions, e.g. **Flower shows;** subjects and names of individual persons with the subdivision *Exhibitions,* e.g. **Printing—Exhibitions;** and names of particular exhibitions, e.g. **Expo 92 (Seville, Spain);** to be added as needed

NT   **Art—Exhibitions**
       Book industries—Exhibitions
       Craft shows
       Expo 92 (Seville, Spain)
       Fashion shows
       Flower shows
       Printing—Exhibitions
       Science—Exhibitions

RT   **Fairs**

Exhibits
USE   **Exhibitions**

Exiles
USE   **Refugees**

Existentialism   142
BT   **Metaphysics**
       Modern philosophy
       Phenomenology

Exobiology
USE   **Life on other planets**
       Space biology

Exorcism   133.4; 291.3
BT   **Superstition**
RT   **Demoniac possession**
       Demonology
       Witchcraft

Expansion (United States politics)
USE   **United States—Territorial expansion**

Expeditions, Scientific
USE   **Scientific expeditions**

Experience
USE   **Empiricism**

Experiences, Near-death
USE   **Near-death experiences**

Experimental farms
USE   **Agricultural experiment stations**

Experimental films   791.43
   May be used for individual works, collections, or materials about experimental films.
UF   Avant-garde films

       Motion pictures, Experimental
       Personal films
       Underground films
BT   **Motion pictures**

Experimental methods in education
USE   **Education—Experimental methods**

Experimental psychology
USE   **Psychophysiology**

Experimental schools   371.04
   Use for materials on schools in which new teaching methods, organizations of subject matter, educational theories, personnel practices, etc., are tested.
UF   Alternative schools
       Free schools
       Nonformal schools
       Project schools
       Schools, Nonformal
BT   **Education—Experimental methods**
       Schools
RT   **Open plan schools**

Experimental theater   792
UF   Avant-garde theater
BT   **Theater**

Experimental universities
USE   **Free universities**

Experimentation on animals
USE   **Animal experimentation**

Experimentation on humans, Medical
USE   **Human experimentation in medicine**

Experiments
USE   scientific subjects with the subdivision *Experiments,* e.g. **Chemistry—Experiments;** to be added as needed

Experiments, Scientific
USE   **Science—Experiments**

Expert systems (Computer science)   006.3
UF   Knowledge-based systems (Computer science)
       Systems, Expert (Computer science)
BT   **Artificial intelligence**
       Electronic data processing
       Information systems

BT = Broader Term   NT = Narrower Term   RT = Related Term   SA = See Also   UF = Used For

Exploration   910.9

Use for materials on voyages and explorations that have advanced geographic knowledge.

UF   Discoverers
Discoveries and exploration
Discoveries in geography
Discoveries, Maritime
Explorations
Maritime discoveries
Navigators

SA   names of celestial bodies, continents, regions, countries, states, etc., with the subdivision *Exploration* for materials on the exploration of those areas when they were unsettled or sparsely settled and largely unknown to the world at large, e.g. **America—Exploration;** or with the subdivision *Description* for materials on later and recent travels is those areas, e.g. **United States—Description;** and names of countries, states, etc., with the subdivision *Exploring expeditions* for materials on explorations sponsored by those governments, e.g. **United States—Exploring expeditions;** to be added as needed

BT   **Adventure and adventurers**
Geography
History

NT   **America—Exploration**
Antarctica—Exploration
Arctic regions—Exploration
Northeast Passage
Outer space—Exploration
Underwater exploration
United States—Exploration

RT   **Explorers**
Scientific expeditions
Voyages and travels

Exploration, Space
USE   **Outer space—Exploration**

Exploration, Submarine
USE   **Underwater exploration**

Exploration, Underwater
USE   **Underwater exploration**

Exploration—United States
USE   **United States—Exploration**

Explorations
USE   **Exploration**
Explorers

Explorer (Artificial satellite)   629.46
BT   **Artificial satellites**

Explorers   910.92; 920
UF   Discoverers
Explorations
Navigators
Voyagers

SA   names of places explored with the subdivision *Exploration,* e.g. **America—Exploration;** names of countries with the subdivisions *Description* and *Exploring expeditions;* and names of individual explorers, to be added as needed

BT   **Adventure and adventurers**
Heroes and heroines

NT   **United States—Exploring expeditions**

RT   **Exploration**
Travelers
Voyages and travels

Exploring expeditions
USE   names of countries sponsoring exploring expeditions with the subdivision *Exploring expeditions,* e.g. **United States—Exploring expeditions;** etc.; and names of expeditions, e.g. **Lewis and Clark Expedition (1804-1806);** to be added as needed

Explosions   904
BT   **Accidents**

Explosives   363.17; 363.3; 623.4; 662
SA   types of explosives and explosive devices, to be added as needed

BT   **Chemistry**
NT   **Ammunition**
Bombs
Dynamite
Gunpowder

BT = Broader Term   NT = Narrower Term   RT = Related Term   SA = See Also   UF = Used For

Explosives—*Continued*
    Torpedoes
Expo 92 (Seville, Spain)   **909.82**
    UF   Seville (Spain). World's Fair,
            1992
            World's Fair (1992 : Seville,
            Spain)
    BT   **Exhibitions**
            Fairs
Exports (May subdiv. geog.)   **382**
    BT   **International trade**
Expositions
    USE   **Exhibitions**
Express highways   **388.1; 625.7**
    UF   Freeways
            Interstate highways
            Limited access highways
            Motorways
            Parkways
            Superhighways
            Toll roads
            Turnpikes (Modern)
    BT   **Roads**
            Traffic engineering
Express service   **388**
    BT   **Railroads**
            Transportation
    NT   **Pony express**
Expressionism (Art)   **759.06**
    BT   **Painting**
    RT   **Postimpressionism (Art)**
Expropriation
    USE   **Eminent domain**
Expulsion
    USE   **Penal colonies**
Extended care facilities
    USE   **Long-term care facilities**
Extension work, Agricultural
    USE   **Agricultural extension work**
Extermination of Jews (1933-1945)
    USE   **Holocaust, 1933-1945**
Extermination of pests
    USE   **Pest control**
External trade
    USE   **International trade**
Extinct animals   **560**
    UF   Animals, Extinct
    SA   types of extinct animals, to be
            added as needed
    BT   **Animals**

    NT   **Mastodon**
    RT   **Fossils**
            Prehistoric animals
            Rare animals
Extinct cities (May subdiv. geog.)   **930**
    UF   Abandoned towns
            Buried cities
            Cities and towns, ruined, extinct,
              etc. *[Former heading]*
            Ruins
            Sunken cities
    SA   names of extinct cities and
            towns, e.g. **Delphi (Extinct**
            city); to be added as needed
    BT   **Archeology**
            Cities and towns
    NT   **Ghost towns**
    RT   **Excavations (Archeology)**
Extinct cities—Greece   **938**
    NT   **Delphi (Extinct city)**
Extinct plants
    USE   **Fossil plants**
Extracurricular activities
    USE   **Student activities**
Extragalactic nebulae
    USE   **Galaxies**
Extramarital relationships
    USE   **Adultery**
Extrasensory perception   **133.8**
    UF   E.S.P.
            ESP
    BT   **Parapsychology**
    NT   **Clairvoyance**
            Telepathy
Extraterrestrial bases   **629.44**
    Use for materials on bases established on natural extraterrestrial bodies for specific functions other than colonization. Materials on communities established in space or on natural extraterrestrial bodies are entered under **Space colonies.** Materials on manned installations orbiting in space for specific functions, such as servicing space ships, are entered under **Space stations.**
    BT   **Building**
            Civil engineering
    RT   **Space colonies**
Extraterrestrial beings   **576.8**
    UF   Aliens from outer space
            Interplanetary visitors
    BT   **Life on other planets**
Extraterrestrial communication
    USE   **Interstellar communication**

BT = Broader Term   NT = Narrower Term   RT = Related Term   SA = See Also   UF = Used For

Extraterrestrial environment
USE **Space environment**
Extraterrestrial life
USE **Life on other planets**
Extravehicular activity (Space flight)
629.45
UF Space vehicles—Extravehicular
activity
Space walk
Walking in space
BT **Space flight**
Extreme unction
USE **Anointing of the sick**
Extremism (Political science)
USE **Radicalism**
Extremities, Artificial
USE **Artificial limbs**
Eye   611; 612.8
BT **Face**
Head
RT **Optometry**
Vision
Eyeglasses   617.7; 681
UF Spectacles
SA types of eyeglasses, e.g. **Contact**
lenses; to be added as needed
NT **Contact lenses**
F.M. radio
USE **Radio frequency modulation**
Fables   398.2; 808.8; 811, etc.; 813, etc.
May be used for individual works, collec-
tions, or materials about short tales intended
to teach moral lessons, often with animals or
inanimate objects speaking and acting like hu-
man beings, and usually with the lesson stated
briefly at the end.
UF Cautionary tales and verse
Moral and philosophic stories
Tales
BT **Fiction**
Literature
RT **Allegories**
Animals—Fiction
Didactic fiction
Didactic poetry
Folklore
Legends
Parables
Romances
Fabric design
USE **Textile design**

Fabrics   677
UF Cloth
Dry goods
Textiles
SA types of fabrics, to be added as
needed
BT **Decorative arts**
NT **Cotton**
Linen
Silk
Synthetic fabrics
Wool
Fabrics, Synthetic
USE **Synthetic fabrics**
Face   611; 612
BT **Head**
NT **Eye**
Nose
RT **Physiognomy**
Facetiae
USE **Anecdotes**
Wit and humor
Facsimile transmission   384.1; 621.382
UF Fax
Telefax
BT **Data transmission systems**
Electronics
Telecommunication
Factories   338.6; 670; 725
UF Industrial plants
Mill and factory buildings
Plants, Industrial
SA types of factories, to be added
as needed
BT **Industrial buildings**
RT **Factory management**
Mills
Factories—Management
USE **Factory management**
Factories—Training departments
USE **Employees—Training**
Factory and trade waste
USE **Industrial wastes**
Factory management   658.5
Use for materials on the technical aspects
of manufacturing processes. Materials on gen-
eral principles of management of industries
are entered under **Management.**
UF Factories—Management
Production engineering
Shop management

BT = Broader Term   NT = Narrower Term   RT = Related Term   SA = See Also   UF = Used For

Factory management—*Continued*

BT   **Management**

NT   **Job analysis**

       Motion study

       Office management

       Participative management

       Supervisors

       Time study

RT   **Factories**

       Industrial efficiency

       Industrial revolution

       Personnel management

Factory schools

USE   **Employees—Training**

Factory waste

USE   **Industrial wastes**

Factory workers

USE   **Labor**

       Working class

Facts, Miscellaneous

USE   **Curiosities and wonders**

Faculty

USE   types of educational institutions and names of individual educational institutions with the subdivision *Faculty,* e.g. **Colleges and universities—Faculty;** to be added as needed

Faculty (Education)

USE   **Colleges and universities—Faculty**

       Educators

       Teachers

Faience

USE   **Pottery**

Failure in business

USE   **Bankruptcy**

       Business failures

Failure of banks

USE   **Bank failures**

Failure to thrive syndrome

USE   **Growth disorders**

Failures, Structural

USE   **Structural failures**

Fair employment practice

USE   **Discrimination in employment**

Fair housing

USE   **Discrimination in housing**

Fair trade

USE   **Unfair competition**

Fair trade (Tariff)

USE   **Free trade**

Fair trial   345

Use for materials on legal hearings before an impartial and disinterested tribunal. Materials on the regular administration of the law, according to which citizens may not be denied their legal rights and all laws must conform to fundamental and accepted legal principles, are entered under **Due Process of law.**

UF   Right to a fair trial

BT   **Civil rights**

       Due process of law

NT   **Freedom of the press and fair trial**

Fair trial and free press

USE   **Freedom of the press and fair trial**

Fair use (Copyright)   341.7; 346.04

BT   **Copyright**

Fairies   398.21

UF   Elves

       Gnomes

       Goblins

BT   **Folklore**

       Superstition

Fairness doctrine (Broadcasting)   343.09

Use for materials on the requirement that, if one side of a controversial issue of public importance is aired, the same opportunity must be given for the presentation of contrasting views. Materials on the requirement that all qualified candidates for public office be granted equal broadcast time if any one such candidate is permitted to broadcast are entered under **Equal time rule (Broadcasting).**

UF   Doctrine of fairness (Broadcasting)

BT   **Broadcasting**

       Television and politics

RT   **Equal time rule (Broadcasting)**

Fairs   381; 394; 607; 907.4

Use for general materials on public showings that suggest a variety of kinds of display and entertainment, usually in an outdoor setting, sometimes for the promotion of sales and sometimes in competition for prizes of excellence.

UF   Bazaars

       Trade fairs

       World's fairs

SA   names of fairs, e.g. **Expo 92 (Seville, Spain);** to be added as needed

NT   **Expo 92 (Seville, Spain)**

RT   **Carnivals**

BT = Broader Term   NT = Narrower Term   RT = Related Term   SA = See Also   UF = Used For

Fairs—*Continued*
>   Exhibitions
>   Markets

Fairy tales   398.2; 808.83; 813, etc.;
>   813.008, etc.

>   May be used for individual works, collections, or materials about short, simple narratives, often of folk origin and usually intended for children, involving fantastic forces and magical beings such as dragons, elves, fairies, goblins, witches, and wizards.

>   UF   Children's stories
>   Stories
>   Tales
>   BT   **Children's literature**
>   **Fiction**
>   **Legends**
>   **Literature**
>   RT   **Fantasy fiction**
>   **Folklore**

Faith   121; 234; 291.1

>   Use for materials on religious belief and doubt. Materials on belief and doubt from the philosophical standpoint are entered under Belief and doubt.

>   UF   Religious belief
>   BT   **Religion**
>   **Salvation**
>   **Spiritual life**
>   **Theology**
>   **Virtue**
>   RT   **Belief and doubt**

Faith cure
>   USE   **Spiritual healing**

Faith healing
>   USE   **Spiritual healing**

Faith—Psychology   200.1; 248; 253.5
>   BT   **Psychology of religion**

Faithfulness
>   USE   **Loyalty**

Falconry   799.2
>   UF   Hawking
>   BT   **Game and game birds**
>   **Hunting**

Fall
>   USE   **Autumn**

Fallacies
>   USE   **Errors**
>   **Logic**

Falling stars
>   USE   **Meteors**

Fallout, Radioactive
>   USE   **Radioactive fallout**

Fallout shelters
>   USE   **Air raid shelters**

False advertising
>   USE   **Deceptive advertising**

False memories
>   USE   **False memory syndrome**

False memory syndrome   616.85
>   UF   False memories
>   BT   **Memory**
>   RT   **Recovered memory**

Falsehood
>   USE   **Truthfulness and falsehood**

Family (May subdiv. geog.)   306.85

>   Use for materials stressing the sociological concept and structure of the family. Materials stressing the everyday life, interaction, and relationships of family members are entered under **Family life.**

>   SA   types of family members, e.g.
>   **Children; Fathers; Mothers;**
>   etc., and names of individual persons with the subdivision *Family*, to be added as needed
>   BT   **Human relations**
>   **Sociology**
>   NT   **Birth order**
>   **Brothers and sisters**
>   **Children**
>   **Clans**
>   **Divorce**
>   **Dual career family**
>   **Family life**
>   **Family size**
>   **Farm family**
>   **Fathers**
>   **Grandparent and child**
>   **Husbands**
>   **Kinship**
>   **Married people**
>   **Mothers**
>   **Parent and child**
>   **Single parent family**
>   **Stepfamily**
>   **Teenage parents**
>   **Widowers**
>   **Widows**
>   **Wives**
>   **Work and family**
>   RT   **Domestic relations**
>   **Family reunions**

BT = Broader Term   NT = Narrower Term   RT = Related Term   SA = See Also   UF = Used For

Family—*Continued*
    Home
    Marriage
Family and work
  USE   **Work and family**
Family budget
  USE   **Household budgets**
Family caregivers
  USE   **Caregivers**
Family counseling
  USE   **Family therapy**
Family—Counseling of
  USE   **Family therapy**
Family devotions
  USE   **Devotional exercises**
           Family—Religious life
Family farms   338.1; 630
  BT   **Farms**
  RT   **Farm family**
           Farm life
Family finance
  USE   **Personal finance**
Family group therapy
  USE   **Family therapy**
Family histories
  USE   **Genealogy**
Family life   306.85; 392.3; 646.7
    Use for materials stressing the everyday
life, interaction, and relationships of family
members. Materials on the sociological con-
cept and structure of the family are entered
under **Family.**
  UF   Family relations
           Home life
  BT   **Family**
  NT   **Aging parents**
Family life education   306.85; 362.82;
       372.82
  BT   **Education**
  NT   **Home economics**
           Marriage counseling
           Sex education
  RT   **Domestic relations**
Family names
  USE   **Personal names**
Family planning
  USE   **Birth control**
Family prayers
  USE   **Devotional exercises**
           Family—Religious life
Family psychotherapy
  USE   **Family therapy**

Family relations
  USE   **Domestic relations**
           Family life
Family—Religious life   248.4; 249;
       291.4
  UF   Family devotions
           Family prayers
           Family worship
  BT   **Religious life**
Family reunions   394.2
  UF   Reunions, Family
  RT   **Family**
Family size   304.6
  BT   **Family**
  NT   **Childlessness**
           Only child
  RT   **Birth control**
Family social work
  USE   **Social case work**
Family therapy   616.89
  UF   Family counseling
           Family—Counseling of
           Family group therapy
           Family psychotherapy
           Problem families—Counseling of
  BT   **Counseling**
           Psychotherapy
Family trees
  USE   **Genealogy**
Family—United States   306.850973
Family violence   362.82
  UF   Domestic violence
           Household violence
  BT   **Violence**
  NT   **Child abuse**
           Elderly abuse
           Husband abuse
           Wife abuse
Family worship
  USE   **Family—Religious life**
Famines (May subdiv. geog.)   904
  BT   **Food supply**
           Starvation
Famines—United States   363.80973; 973
  UF   United States—Famines
Famous people
  USE   **Celebrities**
Fanaticism   152.4; 200.1; 303
  UF   Intolerance
  BT   **Emotions**

Fancy dress
USE　Costume
Fans　**391.4**
BT　**Costume**
Fantastic fiction
USE　**Fantasy fiction**
Fantastic films
USE　**Fantasy films**
Fantastic poetry
USE　**Fantasy poetry**
Fantastic radio programs
USE　**Fantasy radio programs**
Fantastic television programs
USE　**Fantasy television programs**
Fantasy　**154.3**
Use for materials on fantasy as an aspect of psychology. Literary fantasies are entered under **Fantasy fiction.**
UF　Day dreams
BT　**Dreams**
　　　Imagination
RT　**Hallucinations and illusions**
Fantasy fiction　**808.83; 809.3; 813, etc.**
May be used for individual works, collections, or materials about imaginative fiction with strange settings, grotesque or fanciful characters, and supernatural or impossible events or forces.
UF　Apocalyptic fantasies
　　　End-of-the-world fantasies
　　　Fantastic fiction *[Former heading]*
　　　Time travel (Fiction)
BT　**Fiction**
NT　**Alternative histories**
　　　Dystopias
　　　Ghost stories
　　　Imaginary voyages
　　　Utopian fiction
RT　**Fairy tales**
　　　Horror fiction
　　　Interplanetary voyages
　　　Occult fiction
　　　Science fiction
Fantasy films　**791.43**
May be used for individual works, collections, or materials about fantasy films.
UF　Apocalyptic fantasies
　　　End-of-the-world fantasies
　　　Fantastic films
　　　Time travel (Fiction)
BT　**Motion pictures**

RT　**Horror films**
　　　Science fiction films
Fantasy poetry　**808.81; 811, etc.**
May be used for individual works, collections, or materials about fantasy poetry.
UF　Fantastic poetry
BT　**Poetry**
Fantasy radio programs　**791.44**
May be used for individual works, collections, or materials about fantasy radio programs.
UF　Fantastic radio programs
BT　**Radio programs**
Fantasy television programs　**791.45**
May be used for individual works, collections, or materials about fantasy television programs.
UF　Apocalyptic fantasies
　　　End-of-the-world fantasies
　　　Fantastic television programs
　　　Time travel (Fiction)
BT　**Television programs**
RT　**Horror television programs**
　　　Science fiction television programs
Far East
USE　**East Asia**
Far north
USE　**Arctic regions**
Farces　**808.82; 812, etc.**
May be used for individual works, collections, or materials about farces.
BT　**Comedies**
Farm animals
USE　**Domestic animals**
Farm buildings　**631.2; 728**
UF　Architecture, Rural
　　　Buildings, Farm
　　　Rural architecture
SA　types of farm buildings, to be added as needed
BT　**Buildings**
NT　**Barns**
Farm credit
USE　**Agricultural credit**
Farm crops
USE　**Farm produce**
Farm engines
USE　**Agricultural machinery**
Farm equipment
USE　**Agricultural machinery**

BT = Broader Term　　NT = Narrower Term　　RT = Related Term　　SA = See Also　　UF = Used For

Farm family 306.85
  BT   **Family**
  RT   **Family farms**
        Farm life
        Rural sociology
Farm implements
  USE **Agricultural machinery**
Farm laborers
  USE **Agricultural laborers**
Farm life (May subdiv. geog.) 306.3;
     630
  UF   Rural life
  BT   **Country life**
        Farmers
  NT   **Ranch life**
  RT   **Family farms**
        Farm family
        Rural sociology
Farm life—United States 306.3; 630
  UF   United States—Farm life
Farm machinery
  USE **Agricultural machinery**
Farm management 630
  BT   **Farms**
        Management
  RT   **Agriculture—Economic aspects**
Farm mechanics
  USE **Agricultural engineering**
       Agricultural machinery
Farm produce 338.1; 630; 631.5
  UF   Agricultural products
       Crops
       Farm crops
  SA   types of farm products, to be
       added as needed
  BT   **Food**
        Raw materials
  NT   **Hay**
Farm produce—Marketing 338.1
  UF   Marketing of farm produce
  BT   **Marketing**
        Prices
  RT   **Agriculture—Economic aspects**
Farm subsidies
  USE **Agricultural subsidies**
Farm tenancy 333.5
    Use for materials on the economic and so-
  cial aspects of farm tenancy. Materials on the
  legal aspects are entered under **Landlord and
  tenant.**
  UF   Agriculture—Tenant farming

Farming on shares
       Sharecropping
       Tenant farming
  BT   **Farms**
        Land tenure
  RT   **Landlord and tenant**
Farmers 630.92; 920
  BT   **Agriculture**
  NT   **Farm life**
Farmers' cooperatives
  USE **Cooperative agriculture**
Farming
  USE **Agriculture**
Farming, Dry
  USE **Dry farming**
Farming on shares
  USE **Farm tenancy**
Farming, Organic
  USE **Organic farming**
Farms 333.76; 630; 636
  BT   **Land use**
        Real estate
  NT   **Family farms**
        Farm management
        Farm tenancy
        Vineyards
  RT   **Agriculture**
Farms, Experimental
  USE **Agricultural experiment sta-
       tions**
Fascism (May subdiv. geog.) 320.53;
     321.9; 335.6
    Use for materials on the political philoso-
  phy, movements, or regimes that advocate a
  centralized autocratic government, severe eco-
  nomic and social regimentation, and the exal-
  tation of nation and race over the individual.
  Materials on fascism in Germany during the
  Nazi regime are entered under **National so-
  cialism.**
  UF   Authoritarianism
       Neo-fascism
  BT   **Totalitarianism**
  NT   **National socialism**
        Neo-Nazis
Fascism—United States 320.5; 973.9
  UF   United States—Fascism
Fashion 391
    Use for materials on the prevailing mode or
  style of dress. Descriptive and historical mate-
  rials on the costume of particular countries,
  periods, or peoples and materials on fancy
  dress and theatrical costumes are entered un-

Fashion—*Continued*
der **Costume.** Materials on clothing from a practical standpoint, including the art of dress, are entered under **Clothing and dress.**

UF Style in dress
BT **Clothing and dress**
NT **Dressmaking**
   Tailoring
RT **Costume**
   Fashion design

Fashion design   746.9
BT **Clothing industry**
   Commercial art
   Design
RT **Fashion**

Fashion industry
USE **Clothing industry**

Fashion models   659.1; 746.9
UF Manikins (Fashion models)
   Mannequins (Fashion models)
   Models
   Models, Fashion *[Former head-ing]*
   Models (Persons)
   Style manikins
BT **Advertising**
   Clothing industry

Fashion shows   391; 659.1
BT **Exhibitions**

Fashionable society
USE **Upper class**

Fast breeder reactors
USE **Nuclear reactors**

Fast foods
USE **Convenience foods**

Faster reading
USE **Speed reading**

Fasting   178; 248.4; 291.4; 296.7
UF Abstinence
BT **Asceticism**
   Diet
NT **Hunger strikes**
RT **Hunger**
   Religious holidays
   Starvation

Fasts and feasts
USE **Religious holidays**

Fasts and feasts—Christianity
USE **Christian holidays**

Fasts and feasts—Judaism
USE **Jewish holidays**

Fat
USE **Oils and fats**

Fatally ill children
USE **Terminally ill children**

Fatally ill patients
USE **Terminally ill**

Fate and fatalism   149
UF Destiny
   Fortune
BT **Philosophy**
RT **Free will and determinism**
   Predestination

Father and child   306.874
UF Child and father
   Father-child relationship
BT **Parent and child**
NT **Fathers and daughters**
   Fathers and sons

Father-child relationship
USE **Father and child**

Fathers   306.8
BT **Family**
   Homemakers
   Men
NT **Teenage fathers**
   Unmarried fathers

Fathers and daughters   306.874
UF Daughters and fathers
BT **Father and child**
   Girls

Fathers and sons   306.874
UF Sons and fathers
BT **Boys**
   Father and child

Fathers of the church   270.1; 920
Use for materials on the lives and thought of the leaders of the Christian church up to the time of Gregory the Great in the West and John of Damascus in the East. Individual works or collections of the writings of early Christian authors are entered under **Early Christian literature.**
UF Church fathers
   Patristic philosophy
   Patristics
BT **Christian biography**
RT **Early Christian literature**

Fathers, Single parent
USE **Single parent family**

Fatigue   152.1; 612; 613.7
UF Exhaustion
   Weariness

BT = Broader Term   NT = Narrower Term   RT = Related Term   SA = See Also   UF = Used For

Fatigue—*Continued*
  BT   Physiology
  NT   Jet lag
  RT   Rest
Fatness
  USE   Obesity
Fats
  USE   Oils and fats
Fauna
  USE   Animals
        Zoology
Fawns
  USE   Deer
Fax
  USE   Facsimile transmission
Fear   152.4
  BT   Emotions
  NT   Horror
        Phobias
  RT   Anxiety
Feast of Dedication
  USE   Hanukkah
Feast of Lights
  USE   Hanukkah
Feasts
  USE   Religious holidays
Fecundity
  USE   Fertility
Federal aid
  USE   Subsidies
Federal aid to education   379.1
    Use same pattern for federal aid to other
    subjects.
  UF   Education—Federal aid
  BT   Education and state
        Grants-in-aid
        Subsidies
  RT   Colleges and universities—Fi-
          nance
        Education—Finance
Federal aid to libraries   021.8
  UF   Libraries—Federal aid
  BT   Grants-in-aid
        Libraries—Government policy
        Subsidies
  RT   Library finance
Federal aid to minority business enter-
        prises   338.6
  UF   Minority business enterprises—
          Federal aid
  BT   Grants-in-aid

        Minority business enterprises
        Subsidies
Federal aid to the arts   353.7; 700
  UF   Art—Federal aid
        Arts and state
        Arts—Federal aid
        Funding for the arts
        State and the arts
        State encouragement of the arts
  BT   Grants-in-aid
        Subsidies
  RT   Art patronage
        Arts—Government policy
Federal budget
  USE   Budget—United States
Federal-city relations   351.09
  UF   City-federal relations
        Federal-municipal relations
        Municipal-federal relations
        Urban-federal relations
  BT   Federal government
        Municipal government
Federal courts
  USE   Courts—United States
Federal debt
  USE   Public debts
Federal government   321.02; 351
  UF   Confederacies
        Federalism
  BT   Constitutional law
        Political science
        Republics
  NT   European federation
        Federal-city relations
        Federal-state relations
  RT   Democracy
        State governments
Federal grants
  USE   Grants-in-aid
Federal-Indian relations
  USE   Indians of North America—
          Government relations
Federal libraries
  USE   Government libraries
Federal-municipal relations
  USE   Federal-city relations
Federal Republic of Germany
  USE   Germany
        Germany (West)

BT = Broader Term   NT = Narrower Term   RT = Related Term   SA = See Also   UF = Used For

Federal Reserve banks   332.1
   BT   **Banks and banking**
Federal revenue sharing
   USE   **Revenue sharing**
Federal spending policy
   USE   **United States—Appropriations
           and expenditures**
Federal-state relations   321.02
   UF   State-federal relations
   BT   **Federal government
         State governments**
Federal-state tax relations
   USE   **Intergovernmental tax relations**
Federalism
   USE   **Federal government**
Federation, International
   USE   **International organization**
Federation of Europe
   USE   **European federation**
Feedback control systems   629.8
   BT   **Automation**
   NT   **Servomechanisms**
Feedback (Psychology)   153.1
   BT   **Psychology of learning**
   NT   **Biofeedback training**
Feeding behavior in animals
   USE   **Animals—Food**
Feeds   633.2; 633.3
   UF   Fodder
   SA   types of feeds, e.g. **Oats;** to be
         added as needed
   BT   **Animals—Food**
   NT   **Forage plants
         Oats
         Silage and silos**
   RT   **Grasses
         Hay
         Root crops**
Feeling
   USE   **Perception
          Touch**
Feelings
   USE   **Emotions**
Feet
   USE   **Foot**
Felidae
   USE   **Wild cats**
Fellowships
   USE   **Scholarships**

Felony
   USE   **Crime**
Female actors
   USE   **Actresses**
Female climacteric
   USE   **Menopause**
Female identity
   USE   **Women—Identity**
Female role
   USE   **Sex role**
Feminine identity
   USE   **Women—Identity**
Feminine psychology
   USE   **Women—Psychology**
Femininity of God   212; 231
   UF   God—Femininity
   BT   **God**
   RT   **Goddess religion**
Feminism   305.42; 323.3
     Use for materials on the theory of the polit-
     ical and social equality of the sexes and wom-
     en's perspectives on various subjects. Materi-
     als on activities aimed at obtaining equal
     rights and opportunities for women are en-
     tered under **Women's movement.**
   UF   Feminist theory
   SA   types of feminist endeavors, e.g.
         **Feminist criticism; Feminist
         theology;** etc., to be added as
         needed
   NT   **Women—History**
   RT   **Suffragists
         Women's movement
         Women's rights**
Feminist criticism   801
   UF   Criticism, Feminist
   BT   **Criticism**
Feminist theology   230
     Use for materials on the feminist critique of
     traditional theology and on alternative theolo-
     gy from a feminist perspective.
   UF   Theology, Feminist
   BT   **Theology**
Feminist theory
   USE   **Feminism**
Fencing   796.86
   UF   Fighting
   BT   **Physical education**
Feral animals
   USE   **Wildlife**
Feral cats
   USE   **Wild cats**

BT = Broader Term   NT = Narrower Term   RT = Related Term   SA = See Also   UF = Used For

Feral children
USE **Wild children**
Fermentation   547; 660; 663
UF   Ferments
BT   **Chemical engineering**
       Chemistry
       Microbiology
NT   **Yeast**
RT   **Wine and wine making**
Ferments
USE   **Fermentation**
Ferns   587; 635.9
BT   **Plants**
Fertility   573.6; 591.1

Use for general materials on fertility in animals, including humans. Materials limited to fertility in humans are entered under **Human fertility.**

UF   Fecundity
BT   **Reproduction**
NT   **Human fertility**
RT   **Infertility**
Fertility control
USE   **Birth control**
Fertility, Human
USE   **Human fertility**
**Fertilization in vitro   176; 618.1;
        636.089**
UF   Ectogenesis, Preimplantational
       Fertilization in vitro, Human
         [Former heading]
       Fertilization, Laboratory
       Fertilization, Test tube
       In vitro fertilization
       Laboratory fertilization
       Preimplantational ectogenesis
       Test tube babies
       Test tube fertilization
BT   **Embryology**
       Genetic engineering
       Reproduction
Fertilization in vitro, Human
USE   **Fertilization in vitro**
Fertilization, Laboratory
USE   **Fertilization in vitro**
Fertilization of plants   575.6
UF   Plants—Fertilization
       Pollination
BT   **Flowers**
       Plant breeding
       Plant physiology

Plants
RT   **Insects**
Fertilization, Test tube
USE   **Fertilization in vitro**
Fertilizers   631.8; 668
UF   Fertilizers and manures *[Former
         heading]*
       Manures
BT   **Agricultural chemicals**
       Soils
NT   **Compost**
       Lime (Mineral)
       Nitrates
       Phosphates
       Potash
Fertilizers and manures
USE   **Fertilizers**
Festivals (May subdiv. geog.)   **394.26**

Use for materials on occasions other than holidays devoted to festive community observances or to programs of cultural events. Materials on days of general exemption from work or days publicly dedicated to the commemoration of some person, event, or principle are entered under **Holidays.** Materials on religious fasts and feasts are entered under **Religious holidays.**

UF   Fiestas
SA   types of festivals and names of
         specific festivals, e.g. **Carni-
         val;** to be added as needed
BT   **Days**
       Manners and customs
NT   **Carnival**
       Carnivals
       Craft shows
       Film festivals
       Music festivals
       Parades
       Powwows
RT   **Holidays**
       Pageants
       Religious holidays
Festivals—Jews
USE   **Jewish holidays**
Festivals—United States   394.260973
UF   United States—Festivals
Fetal death
USE   **Miscarriage**
Fetus   571.8; 612.6
UF   Unborn child
BT   **Embryology**
       Reproduction

BT = Broader Term   NT = Narrower Term   RT = Related Term   SA = See Also   UF = Used For

Feudalism   321
    UF   Fiefs
            Vassals
    BT   **Land tenure**
            Medieval civilization
    NT   **Peasantry**
    RT   **Chivalry**
            Middle Ages

Fever   616
    SA   types of fevers, e.g. **Malaria;** to
            be added as needed
    BT   **Pathology**
    NT   **Malaria**
            Typhoid fever
    RT   **Body temperature**

Fiat money
    USE   **Paper money**

Fiber content of food
    USE   **Food—Fiber content**

Fiber glass
    USE   **Glass fibers**

Fiberglass
    USE   **Glass fibers**

Fibers   677
    UF   Textile fibers
    NT   **Cotton**
            Flax
            Glass fibers
            Hemp
            Linen
            Paper
            Silk
            Wool

Fibers, Glass
    USE   **Glass fibers**

Fiction   808.3
    Use for collections and materials about fiction from several countries and for materials on fiction as a literary form, not for individual works.
    UF   Novels
            Stories
    SA   fiction of particular national literatures, e.g. **American fiction;** genres of fiction, e.g. **Fantasy fiction;** and, to express the themes or subject content of collections or individual works, subjects, names of places, and personal and corporate names with the subdivision *Fiction,* e.g. **Slavery—United States—Fiction; United States—History—1861-1865, Civil War—Fiction; Ohio—Fiction; Napoleon I, Emperor of the French, 1769-1821—Fiction;** etc., to be added as needed
    BT   **Literature**
    NT   **Adventure fiction**
            Allegories
            Allegory
            American fiction
            Bible fiction
            Bildungsromans
            Biographical fiction
            Black humor (Literature)
            Christian fiction
            Didactic fiction
            English fiction
            Epistolary fiction
            Erotic fiction
            Fables
            Fairy tales
            Fantasy fiction
            Folklore
            Historical fiction
            Horror fiction
            Humorous fiction
            Interplanetary voyages
            Jewish religious fiction
            Legal stories
            Legends
            Love stories
            Medical novels
            Movie novels
            Mystery fiction
            Occult fiction
            Pastoral fiction
            Picaresque literature
            Plot-your-own stories
            Plots (Drama, fiction, etc.)
            Radio and television novels
            Religious fiction
            Romances
            Romans à clef
            School stories
            Science fiction
            Sea stories

BT = Broader Term   NT = Narrower Term   RT = Related Term   SA = See Also   UF = Used For

Fiction—*Continued*
    Short stories
    Short story
    War stories
    Western stories
Fiction—History and criticism   809.3
Fiction—Plots
  USE   **Plots (Drama, fiction, etc.)**
Fiction—Technique   808.3
  BT   **Authorship**
Fictional characters
  USE   **Characters and characteristics**
        in literature
Fictitious characters
  USE   **Characters and characteristics**
        in literature
Fictitious names
  USE   **Pseudonyms**
Fictitious places
  USE   **Geographical myths**
Fiddle
  USE   **Violins**
Fiefs
  USE   **Feudalism**
        Land tenure
Field athletics
  USE   **Track athletics**
Field hockey   796.35
  BT   **Sports**
Field hospitals
  USE   **Military hospitals**
        Military medicine
Field photography
  USE   **Outdoor photography**
Field trips   069; 371.3
  UF   School excursions
        School trips
  BT   **Student activities**
Fiestas
  USE   **Festivals**
        Religious holidays
Fifteenth century   909
    Use for general materials covering progress and development during this period in one or in several countries.
  UF   1400-1499 (15th century)
  BT   **Middle Ages**
        Renaissance
Fifth column
  USE   **Subversive activities**

        World War, 1939-1945—Collaborationists
Fighting
  USE   **Battles**
        Boxing
        Bullfights
        Dueling
        Fencing
        Gladiators
        Military art and science
        Naval art and science
        Self-defense
        Self-defense for women
        War
Figure drawing   743.4
  UF   Human figure in art
  BT   **Artistic anatomy**
        Drawing
  RT   **Figure painting**
Figure painting   757
  UF   Human figure in art
  BT   **Artistic anatomy**
        Painting
  RT   **Figure drawing**
        Portrait painting
Figure skating
  USE   **Ice skating**
        Roller skating
Files and filing   005.74; 025.3; 651.5
  UF   Alphabetizing
        Filing systems
  BT   **Office management**
  RT   **Indexing**
Filing systems
  USE   **Files and filing**
Filling stations
  USE   **Service stations**
Fills (Earthwork)
  USE   **Landfills**
Film adaptations   791.43
    May be used for individual works, collections, or materials about film adaptations of material from other media.
  UF   Adaptations
        Adaptations, Film
        Books, Filmed
        Filmed books
        Films from books
        Literature—Film and video adaptations
        Motion picture adaptations

BT = Broader Term   NT = Narrower Term   RT = Related Term   SA = See Also   UF = Used For

Film adaptations—*Continued*
SA national literatures and names of
   literary authors with the sub-
   division *Film and video adap-*
   tations, to be added as needed
BT **Motion pictures**
Film catalogs
USE **Motion pictures—Catalogs**
Film direction
USE **Motion pictures—Production**
   and direction
Film directors
USE **Motion picture producers and**
   directors
Film epics
USE **Epic films**
Film festivals 791.43
UF Motion picture festivals
   Movie festivals
BT **Festivals**
Film industry (Motion pictures)
USE **Motion picture industry**
Film noir 791.43
 May be used for individual works, collec-
 tions, or materials about films of crime and
 detection photographed in somber tones and
 permeated by a feeling of disillusionment and
 pessimism.
UF Crime films
   Films noirs
BT **Motion pictures**
RT **Mystery films**
Film posters 741.6; 791.43
UF Motion picture posters
   Motion pictures—Posters
   Movie posters
   Playbills
   Posters, Film
BT **Posters**
Film producers
USE **Motion picture producers and**
   directors
Film production
USE **Motion pictures—Production**
   and direction
Film projectors
USE **Projectors**
Film scripts
USE **Motion picture plays**
Filmed books
USE **Film adaptations**

Filmmaking
USE **Motion pictures—Production**
   and direction
Filmography
USE **Motion pictures—Catalogs**
   and types of motion pictures
   with the subdivision *Catalogs,*
   e.g. **Science fiction films—**
   Catalogs; and subjects, class-
   es of persons, corporate enti-
   ties, and names of individual
   persons with the subdivision
   Filmography, e.g. **Animals—**
   Filmography; Shakespeare,
   William, 1564-1616—Filmog-
   raphy; etc., to be added as
   needed
Films
USE **Filmstrips**
   Microfilms
   Motion pictures
Films, Amateur
USE **Amateur films**
Films, Bible
USE **Bible films**
Films from books
USE **Film adaptations**
Films noirs
USE **Film noir**
Filmscripts
USE **Motion picture plays**
Filmstrips 371.33; 778.2
UF Films
   Strip films
BT **Audiovisual materials**
   Photography
RT **Slides (Photography)**
Finance (May subdiv. geog.) **332**
 Use for general materials on the manage-
 ment of money and credit. Materials on the
 raising and expenditure of funds in the public
 sector are entered under **Public finance.**
UF Funding
   Funds
SA subjects with the subdivision *Fi-*
   nance, e.g. **Education—Fi-**
   nance; to be added as needed
BT **Economics**
NT **Bankruptcy**
   Banks and banking
   Bonds

BT = Broader Term NT = Narrower Term RT = Related Term SA = See Also UF = Used For

Finance—*Continued*
    Capital
    Church finance
    Colleges and universities—Finance
    Commerce
    Corporations—Finance
    Credit
    Debt
    Education—Finance
    Endowments
    Financial crises
    Foreign exchange
    Fund raising
    Income
    Inflation (Finance)
    Insurance
    Interest (Economics)
    Investments
    Library finance
    Loans
    Money
    Personal finance
    Prices
    Public finance
    Railroads—Finance
    Securities
    Speculation
    Stock exchange
    United Nations—Finance
    Wealth
  RT   Monetary policy
Finance, Church
  USE   Church finance
Finance, Household
  USE   Household budgets
Finance—Mathematics
  USE   Business mathematics
Finance, Municipal
  USE   Municipal finance
Finance, Personal
  USE   Personal finance
Finance, Public
  USE   Public finance
Finance—United States   332.0973;
    336.73
  UF   United States—Finance
Financial accounting
  USE   Accounting

Financial aid, Student
  USE   Student aid
Financial aid to students
  USE   Student aid
Financial crashes
  USE   Financial crises
Financial crises (May subdiv. geog.)
    338 5
  UF   Crashes (Finance)
      Financial crashes
      Financial panics
      Panics (Finance)
      Stock exchange crashes
      Stock market panics
  BT   Finance
  RT   Business cycles
Financial panics
  USE   Financial crises
Financial planning, Personal
  USE   Personal finance
Financiers
  USE   Capitalists and financiers
Finding things
  USE   Lost and found possessions
Fine arts
  USE   Arts
Finger alphabet
  USE   Deaf—Means of communication
Finger games
  USE   Finger play
Finger marks
  USE   Fingerprints
Finger painting   751.4
  UF   Painting, Finger
  BT   Child artists
      Painting
Finger play   793.4
  UF   Finger games
  BT   Play
Finger pressure therapy
  USE   Acupressure
Finger prints
  USE   Fingerprints
Fingerprints   363.25
  UF   Finger marks
      Finger prints
  BT   Anthropometry
      Criminal investigation
      Criminals—Identification

BT = Broader Term   NT = Narrower Term   RT = Related Term   SA = See Also   UF = Used For

Fingerprints—*Continued*
    Identification
Finishes and finishing
  USE   **House painting**
          Industrial painting
          Lacquer and lacquering
          Paint
          Varnish and varnishing
          Wood finishing
Finno-Russian War, 1939-1940
  USE   **Russo-Finnish War, 1939-1940**
Fire   536; 541.3
  BT   **Chemistry**
  NT   **Fires**
          Fuel
  RT   **Combustion**
          Heat
Fire balls
  USE   **Meteors**
Fire bombs
  USE   **Incendiary bombs**
Fire departments   628.9
  UF   Fire stations
  RT   **Fire fighters**
Fire engines   628.9
  BT   **Engines**
          Fire fighting
Fire fighters   363.37092; 920
  UF   Firemen and firewomen
  RT   **Fire departments**
Fire fighting   628.9
  BT   **Fire prevention**
          Fires
  NT   **Fire engines**
Fire insurance   368.1
  UF   Insurance, Fire *[Former heading]*
  BT   **Insurance**
  NT   **Fireproofing**
Fire prevention (May subdiv. geog.)
          363.37; 628.9
  UF   Prevention of fire
  SA   types of institutions, buildings,
          industries, and vehicles with
          the subdivision *Fires and fire*
          prevention, e.g. **Nuclear pow-**
          er plants—Fires and fire
          prevention; to be added as
          needed
  BT   **Fires**

  NT   **Fire fighting**
          Fireproofing
          Nuclear power plants—Fires
          and fire prevention
Fire stations
  USE   **Fire departments**
Firearms   623.4; 739.7
  UF   Guns
          Small arms
  SA   types of firearms, to be added
          as needed
  BT   **Weapons**
  NT   **Gunpowder**
          Handguns
          Rifles
          Shotguns
  RT   **Ammunition**
          Shooting
Firearms control
  USE   **Gun control**
Firearms industry   338.4; 683.4
      Use for materials on the small arms indus-
      try. Materials on heavy firearms are entered
      under **Ordnance.**
  UF   Firearms industry and trade
          [Former heading]
          Firearms trade
          Gunsmithing
  BT   **Weapons**
  RT   **Defense industries**
Firearms industry and trade
  USE   **Firearms industry**
Firearms—Law and legislation
  USE   **Gun control**
Firearms trade
  USE   **Firearms industry**
Firemen and firewomen
  USE   **Fire fighters**
Fireplaces   697; 749
  BT   **Architecture—Details**
          Building
          Buildings
          Heating
          Space heaters
  RT   **Chimneys**
Fireproofing   628.9; 693.8
  BT   **Fire insurance**
          Fire prevention
Fires (May subdiv. geog.)   **363.37; 904**
  SA   types of institutions, buildings,
          industries, and vehicles with

BT = Broader Term   NT = Narrower Term   RT = Related Term   SA = See Also   UF = Used For

Fires—*Continued*
>the subdivision *Fires and fire prevention,* e.g. **Nuclear power plants—Fires and fire prevention;** to be added as needed

BT **Accidents**
  Disasters
  Fire
NT **Fire fighting**
  Fire prevention
  Forest fires
  Nuclear power plants—Fires and fire prevention

Fireworks 662
BT **Amusements**
Firms
USE **Business enterprises**
First aid 362.1; 616.02
UF Emergencies
  Injuries
  Wounded, First aid to
BT **Health self-care**
  Home accidents
  Medicine
  Nursing
  Rescue work
  Sick
NT **Artificial respiration**
  Bandages
  Cardiac resuscitation
RT **Accidents**
  Lifesaving
First editions 016
UF Bibliography—First editions
  [Former heading]
  Books—First editions
BT **Editions**
RT **Rare books**
First generation children
USE **Children of immigrants**
First ladies—United States
USE **Presidents' spouses—United States**
Firstborn child
USE **Birth order**
Fiscal policy (May subdiv. geog.) **336.3**
BT **Economic policy**
  Public finance
RT **Monetary policy**

Fiscal policy—United States 336.73
UF United States—Fiscal policy
Fish
USE **Fish as food**
  Fishes
Fish as food 641.3
UF Fish
BT **Cooking**
  Fishes
  Food
RT **Seafood**
Fish culture 639.3
>Use for materials on the cultivation of fish in captivity. Materials on the fishing industry are entered under **Fisheries.**

UF Fish farming
  Fish hatcheries
BT **Aquaculture**
  Fishes
RT **Aquariums**
  Fisheries
Fish farming
USE **Fish culture**
Fish hatcheries
USE **Fish culture**
Fisheries (May subdiv. geog.) **338.3; 639.2**
>Use for materials on the fishing industry. Materials on the cultivation of fish in captivity are entered under **Fish culture.** Materials on fishing as a sport are entered under **Fishing.**

UF Fishing industry
  Sea fisheries
BT **Fishes**
  Marine resources
  Natural resources
NT **Pearl fisheries**
  Whaling
RT **Fish culture**
Fisheries—United States 338.3; 639.2
UF United States—Fisheries
Fishes (May subdiv. geog.) **597**
UF Fish
  Ichthyology
SA types of fishes, e.g. **Salmon;** to be added as needed
BT **Freshwater animals**
  Marine animals
  Vertebrates
NT **Fish as food**
  Fish culture

BT = Broader Term NT = Narrower Term RT = Related Term SA = See Also UF = Used For

Fishes—*Continued*
      Fisheries
      Fishing
      Goldfish
      Salmon
      Tropical fish
  RT   Aquariums
Fishes—Geographical distribution
    597.09
  BT   Biogeography
Fishes—Photography
  USE   Photography of fishes
Fishes—United States   597.0973 ⸍
  UF   United States—Fishes
Fishing (May subdiv. geog.)   799.1
    Use for materials on fishing as a sport. Materials on fishing as an industry are entered under **Fisheries.**
  UF   Angling
  SA   types of fishing, to be added as
        needed
  BT   **Fishes**
        Water sports
  NT   **Artificial flies**
        Fly casting
        Spear fishing
        Trout fishing
Fishing—Equipment and supplies   799.1
  UF   Fishing tackle
Fishing flies
  USE   **Artificial flies**
Fishing industry
  USE   **Fisheries**
Fishing tackle
  USE   **Fishing—Equipment and supplies**
Fishing—United States   799.10973
  UF   United States—Fishing
Fitness
  USE   **Physical fitness**
Five-day work week
  USE   **Hours of labor**
Fixing
  USE   **Repairing**
Flags (May subdiv. geog.)   929.9
  UF   Banners
        Ensigns
  BT   **Heraldry**
  RT   **National emblems**
        Signals and signaling

Flags—United States   929.9
  UF   American flag
        United States—Flags
Flats
  USE   **Apartment houses**
Flatware, Silver
  USE   **Silverware**
Flavoring essences   664
  BT   **Cooking**
        Essences and essential oils
        Food
Flax   633.5; 677
  BT   **Fibers**
        Yarn
  RT   **Linen**
Flexible hours of labor
  USE   **Hours of labor**
Flexitime
  USE   **Hours of labor**
Flies   595.77
  UF   Fly
        House flies
  SA   types of flies, to be added as
        needed
  BT   **Household pests**
        Insects
        Pests
  NT   **Fruit flies**
Flies, Artificial
  USE   **Artificial flies**
Flight   629.13
  UF   Flying
  BT   **Locomotion**
  NT   **Animal flight**
  RT   **Aeronautics**
Flight attendants   387.7
  UF   Airline hostesses
        Airline stewardesses
        Airline stewards
        Airlines—Flight attendants *[Former heading]*
        Stewardesses, Airline
        Stewards, Airline
  BT   **Airlines**
Flight to the moon
  USE   **Space flight to the moon**
Flight training
  USE   **Aeronautics—Study and teaching**
        Airplanes—Piloting

BT = Broader Term   NT = Narrower Term   RT = Related Term   SA = See Also   UF = Used For

Flights around the world
    USE   **Aeronautics—Flights**
Flint implements
    USE   **Stone implements**
Floating hospitals
    USE   **Hospital ships**
Floats (Parades)
    USE   **Parades**
Flood control   627
    UF   Flood prevention
           Floods—Control *[Former heading]*
    BT   **Hydraulic engineering**
    NT   **Dams**
    RT   **Forest influences**
Flood prevention
    USE   **Flood control**
Floods (May subdiv. geog. by countries, states, cities, etc. and by rivers) **363.34; 551.48; 904**
    BT   **Meteorology**
           Natural disasters
           Rain
           Water
    RT   **Rivers**
Floods and forests
    USE   **Forest influences**
Floods—Control
    USE   **Flood control**
Floors   690; 721
    BT   **Architecture—Details**
           Building
           Buildings
Flora
    USE   **Botany**
           Plants
Floral decoration
    USE   **Flower arrangement**
Floriculture
    USE   **Flower gardening**
Florists' designs
    USE   **Flower arrangement**
Flour   641.3; 664
    UF   Breadstuffs
    NT   **Grain**
    RT   **Wheat**
Flour mills   664
    UF   Grist mills
           Milling (Flour)
    BT   **Mills**

Flow charts
    USE   **Graphic methods**
           System analysis
Flow charts (Computer science)
    USE   **Programming (Computers)**
Flowcharting
    USE   **Graphic methods**
           System analysis
Flowcharting (Computer science)
    USE   **Programming (Computers)**
Flower arrangement   745.92
    Use for materials on the artistic arrangement of flowers, including decoration of houses, churches, etc., with flowers.
    UF   Designs, Floral
           Floral decoration
           Florists' designs
           Flowers—Arrangement
    BT   **Decoration and ornament**
           Flowers
           Table setting and decoration
Flower drying
    USE   **Flowers—Drying**
Flower gardening   635.9
    Use for practical materials on the cultivation of flowering plants for either commercial or private purposes.
    UF   Floriculture
    SA   types of flowers, e.g. **Roses;** to be added as needed
    BT   **Gardening**
           Horticulture
    NT   **Annuals (Plants)**
           Bulbs
           Greenhouses
           House plants
           Ornamental plants
           Perennials
    RT   **Container gardening**
           Flowers
           Window gardening
Flower painting and illustration
    USE   **Botanical illustration**
           Flowers in art
Flower prints
    USE   **Flowers in art**
Flower shows   635.9074
    UF   Flowers—Exhibitions
    BT   **Exhibitions**

BT = Broader Term   NT = Narrower Term   RT = Related Term   SA = See Also   UF = Used For

Flowers (May subdiv. geog.)   **575.6; 582.13**

    Use for general materials on flowers. Materials limited to the cultivation of flowers are entered under **Flower gardening.**

  SA   types of flowers, e.g. **Roses;** to be added as needed
  BT   **Plants**
  NT   **Annuals (Plants)**
        Fertilization of plants
        Flower arrangement
        Perennials
        Roses
        State flowers
        Wild flowers
  RT   **Flower gardening**
        Flowers in art

Flowers—Arrangement
  USE   **Flower arrangement**

Flowers, Artificial
  USE   **Artificial flowers**

Flowers, Drying
  USE   **Flowers—Drying**

Flowers—Drying   **745.92**
  UF   Dried flowers
        Flower drying *[Former heading]*
        Flowers, Drying *[Former heading]*
  BT   **Plants—Collection and preservation**

Flowers—Exhibitions
  USE   **Flower shows**

Flowers in art   **758**
  UF   Flower painting and illustration *[Former heading]*
        Flower prints
  BT   **Plants in art**
  RT   **Flowers**

Flowers, State
  USE   **State flowers**

Flowers—United States   **582.130973**
  UF   United States—Flowers

Flowers, Wild
  USE   **Wild flowers**

Flu
  USE   **Influenza**

Fluid mechanics   **532; 620.1**

    Use for materials on the branch of mechanics dealing with the properties of liquids or gases, either at rest or in motion.

  UF   Hydromechanics

  BT   **Mechanics**
  NT   **Gases**
        Hydraulic engineering
        Hydraulics
        Hydrodynamics
        Hydrostatics
        Liquids

Fluorescent lighting   **621.32**
  UF   Electric lighting, Fluorescent
  BT   **Electric lighting**

Fluoridation of water
  USE   **Water fluoridation**

Flute
  USE   **Flutes**

Flutes   **788.3**
  UF   Flute *[Former heading]*
  BT   **Wind instruments**

Fly
  USE   **Flies**

Fly casting   **799.1**
  UF   Fly fishing
  BT   **Fishing**
  NT   **Artificial flies**

Fly fishing
  USE   **Fly casting**

Flying
  USE   **Flight**

Flying bombs
  USE   **Guided missiles**

Flying saucers
  USE   **Unidentified flying objects**

FM radio
  USE   **Radio frequency modulation**

Foals
  USE   **Horses**
        Ponies

Fodder
  USE   **Feeds**

Fog   **551.57**
  BT   **Atmosphere**
        Meteorology

Fog signals
  USE   **Signals and signaling**

Foliage
  USE   **Leaves**

Folk art   **745**

    Use for materials on objects of fine or decorative art produced in a peasant, popular, or naive style, often in cultural isolation and by unschooled artists or artisans.

  UF   Peasant art

BT = Broader Term   **NT = Narrower Term**   **RT = Related Term**   **SA = See Also**   **UF = Used For**

Folk art—*Continued*

SA   folk art of particular countries or ethnic groups, e.g. **American folk art;** to be added as needed

BT   **Art**
           Art and society

NT   **American folk art**

RT   **Arts and crafts movement**
           Decorative arts
           Handicraft

Folk art, American
    USE   **American folk art**

Folk dances
    USE   **Folk dancing**

Folk dancing   793.3

UF   Folk dances
           National dances

SA   folk dancing of particular countries or ethnic groups, e.g. **American folk dancing;** to be added as needed

BT   **Dance**

NT   **American folk dancing**
           Indians of North America— Dances
           Square dancing

Folk dancing, American
    USE   **American folk dancing**

Folk drama   808.82; 812, etc.; 812.008, etc.

May be used for collections or materials about folk drama, not for individual works.

UF   Folk plays

BT   **Drama**

NT   **Puppets and puppet plays**

Folk lore
    USE   **Folklore**

Folk medicine
    USE   **Traditional medicine**

Folk music (May subdiv. geog.)   781.62

BT   **Music**

Folk music—United States   781.6200973

UF   American folk music
           United States—Folk music

NT   **Blues music**
           Country music

Folk plays
    USE   **Folk drama**

Folk psychology
    USE   **Ethnopsychology**

Folk songs (May subdiv. geog. for the U.S. and Canada or for states, provinces, or regions of the U.S. and Canada)   782.42162

Use for materials about folk songs and collections of folk songs that include both words and music. Materials about ballads and collections of ballads without music are entered under **Ballads.**

SA   folk songs of particular ethnic or language groups, e.g. **French folk songs;** to be added as needed

BT   **Folklore**
           Songs
           Vocal music

NT   **Carols**
           French folk songs

RT   **Ballads**
           National songs

Folk songs, American
    USE   **Folk songs—United States**

Folk songs—France
    USE   **French folk songs**

Folk songs, French
    USE   **French folk songs**

Folk songs—Ohio   782.42162009771

UF   Ohio—Folk songs

Folk songs—United States   782.4216200973

UF   American folk songs
           Folk songs, American
           United States—Folk songs

BT   **American songs**

NT   **Spirituals (Songs)**

Folk tales
    USE   **Folklore**
                 Legends

Folklore (May subdiv. geog.)   398

Use for general materials on folklore. May also be used for individual works, collections, and materials about stories based on spoken rather than written traditions.

UF   Folk lore
           Folk tales
           Tales
           Traditions

SA   topics as themes in folklore with the subdivision *Folklore,* e.g. **Plants—Folklore;** names of ethnic or occupational groups

---

Folklore—*Continued*
        with the subdivision *Folklore,*
        e.g. **Inuit—Folklore;** and
        names of individual legendary
        characters, e.g. **Bunyan, Paul
        (Legendary character);** to be
        added as needed
  BT   Ethnology
       Fiction
       Manners and customs
  NT   African Americans—Folklore
       Animals—Folklore
       Blacks—Folklore
       Chapbooks
       Charms
       Dragons
       Fairies
       Folk songs
       Ghosts
       Giants
       Graffiti
       Grail
       Indians of North America—
         Folklore
       Inuit—Folklore
       Jews—Folklore
       Monsters
       Nursery rhymes
       Plants—Folklore
       Proverbs
       Sagas
       Superstition
       Tall tales
       Tongue twisters
       Weather—Folklore
       Wicca
       Witchcraft
  RT   Fables
       Fairy tales
       Legends
       Mythology
       Storytelling
Folklore, African American
  USE   **African Americans—Folklore**
Folklore, Black
  USE   **Blacks—Folklore**
Folklore, Inuit
  USE   **Inuit—Folklore**
Folklore, Jewish
  USE   **Jews—Folklore**

Folklore, Medical
  USE   **Traditional medicine**
Folklore—United States   398.0973
  UF   United States—Folklore
  NT   **Bunyan, Paul (Legendary char-
        acter)**
Folkways
  USE   **Manners and customs**
Food   641; 641.3; 664
  UF   Gastronomy
  SA   types of foods, names of specif-
       ic foods, and subjects with
       the subdivision *Food,* to be
       added as needed
  BT   **Digestion**
       Home economics
  NT   **Animals—Food**
       Artificial foods
       Beverages
       Bread
       Chocolate
       Convenience foods
       Dietetic foods
       Dining
       Edible plants
       Eggs
       Farm produce
       Fish as food
       Flavoring essences
       Food of animal origin
       Fruit
       Grain
       Honey
       Meat
       Milk
       Natural foods
       Nuts
       Prepared cereals
       School children—Food
       Seafood
       Shellfish
       Spices
       Sugar
       Vegetables
       Vitamins
  RT   **Cooking**
       Diet
       Grocery trade
       Nutrition

BT = Broader Term   NT = Narrower Term   RT = Related Term   SA = See Also   UF = Used For

Food additives   641.3; 664
  UF   Additives, Food
  BT   Food—Analysis
        Food—Preservation
Food adulteration and inspection
      363.19
  UF   Adulteration of food
        Analysis of food
        Food inspection
        Inspection of food
        Pure food
  BT   Consumer protection
        Public health
  NT   Food contamination
        Meat inspection
        Milk supply
  RT   Food—Law and legislation
Food allergies
  USE   Food allergy
Food allergy   616.97
  UF   Allergies, Food
        Allergy, Food
        Food allergies
  SA   types of food allergies, to be
        added as needed
  BT   Allergy
Food—Analysis   664
    Use for materials on methods of analyzing
    foods. Materials presenting the results of the
    analysis of foods are entered under Food—
    Composition.
  UF   Analysis of food
        Chemistry of food
        Food chemistry
  SA   types of foods with the subdivi-
        sion *Analysis,* e.g. Milk—
        Analysis; to be added as
        needed
  BT   Analytical chemistry
        Industrial chemistry
  NT   Food additives
  RT   Food—Composition
Food, Artificial
  USE   Artificial foods
Food assistance programs
  USE   Food relief
Food buying
  USE   Grocery shopping
Food, Canned
  USE   Canning and preserving

Food chains (Ecology)   577
  BT   Animals—Food
        Ecology
Food chemistry
  USE   Food—Analysis
        Food—Composition
Food—Cholesterol content   613.2
  UF   Cholesterol content of food
  BT   Food—Composition
Food—Composition   641; 664
    Use for materials presenting the results of
    the analysis of foods. Materials on methods of
    analyzing foods are entered under Food—
    Analysis.
  UF   Chemistry of food
        Food chemistry
  SA   food and types of food with
        subdivisions to indicate the
        particular content being ana-
        lyzed, e.g. Food—Cholesterol
        content; to be added as need-
        ed
  NT   Food—Cholesterol content
        Food—Fiber content
        Food—Sodium content
  RT   Food—Analysis
Food contamination   363.19
  UF   Contaminated food
  BT   Food adulteration and inspec-
        tion
Food control
  USE   Food supply
Food, Cost of
  USE   Cost and standard of living
Food customs
  USE   Eating customs
Food, Dehydrated
  USE   Dried foods
Food, Dietetic
  USE   Dietetic foods
Food, Dried
  USE   Dried foods
Food—Fiber content   613.2
  UF   Dietary fiber
        Fiber content of food
        Roughage
  BT   Food—Composition
Food for invalids
  USE   Cooking for the sick
Food for school children
  USE   School children—Food

BT = Broader Term   NT = Narrower Term   RT = Related Term   SA = See Also   UF = Used For

Food, Freeze dried
USE   **Freeze-dried foods**
Food, Frozen
USE   **Frozen foods**
Food habits
USE   **Eating customs**
Food inspection
USE   **Food adulteration and inspec-
tion**
Food—Labeling   363.19; 641
UF   Food labels
Food labels
USE   **Food—Labeling**
Food—Law and legislation   344
UF   Food laws
BT   **Law
Legislation**
RT   **Food adulteration and inspec-
tion**
Food laws
USE   **Food—Law and legislation**
Food, Natural
USE   **Natural foods**
Food of animal origin   641.3
Use for materials on human food of animal
origin. Materials on the food and food habits
of animals are entered under **Animals—Food.**
UF   Animal food [*Former heading*]
Animals as food
Animals, Edible
BT   **Food**
Food plants
USE   **Edible plants**
Food poisoning   615.9
BT   **Poisons and poisoning**
Food preparation
USE   **Cooking**
Food—Preservation   641.4; 664
UF   Preservation of food
SA   types of foods with the subdivi-
sion *Preservation,* to be added
as needed
NT   **Canning and preserving
Cold storage
Dried foods
Food additives
Frozen foods
Fruit—Preservation**
Food—Purchasing
USE   **Grocery shopping**

Food relief (May subdiv. geog.)   **363.8**
UF   Food assistance programs
SA   types of food relief, e.g. **Meals
on wheels programs;** and
names of wars with the sub-
division *Civilian relief* or
Food supply, to be added as
needed
BT   **Charities
Disaster relief
Public welfare
Unemployed**
NT   **Meals on wheels programs
World War, 1939-1945—Civil-
ian relief
World War, 1939-1945—Food
supply**
Food service   642; 647.95
Use for materials on the preparation, deliv-
ery, and serving of ready-to-eat foods in large
quantities outside of the home. Materials sole-
ly on the preparation of food in large quanti-
ties are entered under **Quantity cooking.**
UF   Cooking for institutions
Mass feeding
Volume feeding
BT   **Service industries**
NT   **Catering
Restaurants
Waiters and waitresses**
RT   **Quantity cooking**
Food—Sodium content   613.2
UF   Sodium content of food
BT   **Food—Composition**
Food supply   363.8
Use for economic materials on the availabil-
ity of food. Materials on the conservation of
food in wartime are entered under the name
of the war with the subdivision *Food supply,*
e.g. **World War, 1939-1945—Food supply.**
UF   Food control
NT   **Famines
Meat industry**
RT   **Agriculture**
Fools and jesters   791.092; 920
UF   Court fools
Jesters
BT   **Comedians
Courts and courtiers
Entertainers**
Foot   611; 612
UF   Feet
BT   **Anatomy**

BT = Broader Term   NT = Narrower Term   RT = Related Term   SA = See Also   UF = Used For

Foot—Care   617.5
    UF   Foot—Care and hygiene *[For-
        mer heading]*
    BT   **Podiatry**
Foot—Care and hygiene
    USE   **Foot—Care**
Foot injuries
    USE   **Foot—Wounds and injuries**
Foot—Wounds and injuries   617.5
    UF   Foot injuries
    RT   **Podiatry**
Football   796.332
    BT   **Ball games**
        Sports
    NT   **Soccer**
Football—Coaching   796.33207
    BT   **Coaching (Athletics)**
Footwear
    USE   **Shoes**
Forage plants   633.2
    SA   names of forage plants, to be
        added as needed
    BT   **Economic botany**
        Feeds
        Plants
    NT   **Alfalfa**
        Corn
        Hay
        Silage and silos
        Soybean
    RT   **Grasses**
Force and energy   531
    UF   Conservation of energy
        Energy
    BT   **Power (Mechanics)**
    RT   **Dynamics**
        Mechanics
        Motion
        Quantum theory
Force pumps
    USE   **Pumping machinery**
Forced indoctrination
    USE   **Brainwashing**
Forced labor
    USE   **Convict labor**
        Peonage
        Slavery
Ford automobile   629.222
    BT   **Automobiles**

Forecasting   003
    UF   Forecasts
        Futurology
        Predictions
    SA   types of forecasting, e.g. **Weath-
        er forecasting;** and subjects
        and names of countries, cities,
        etc., with the subdivision
        Forecasting, e.g. **Energy con-
        sumption—Forecasting;** to be
        added as needed
    NT   **Business forecasting**
        Economic forecasting
        Weather forecasting
Forecasts
    USE   **Forecasting**
Foreign affairs
    USE   **International relations**
Foreign aid (May subdiv. geog.)   338.91
    Use for general materials on international
economic aid given in the form of gifts, loans,
relief grants, etc. Materials limited to foreign
aid in the form of technical expertise are entered under **Technical assistance.**
    UF   Aid to developing areas
        Assistance to developing areas
        Economic aid
        Economic assistance *[Former
        heading]*
        Foreign aid program
        Foreign assistance
    SA   foreign aid from particular coun-
        tries, e.g. **American foreign
        aid;** to be added as needed
    BT   **Economic policy**
        International cooperation
        **International economic rela-
        tions**
    NT   **American foreign aid**
        Technical assistance
        **World War, 1939-1945—Civil-
        ian relief**
    RT   **Reconstruction (1914-1939)**
        Reconstruction (1939-1951)
Foreign aid program
    USE   **Foreign aid**
        Military assistance
        Technical assistance
Foreign area studies
    USE   **Area studies**

BT = Broader Term   NT = Narrower Term   RT = Related Term   SA = See Also   UF = Used For

Foreign assistance
  USE **Foreign aid**
Foreign automobiles 629.222
  UF Automobiles, Foreign *[Former heading]*
      Foreign cars
  SA names of specific makes and models, to be added as needed
  BT **Automobiles**
Foreign cars
  USE **Foreign automobiles**
Foreign commerce
  USE **International trade**
Foreign economic relations
  USE **International economic relations**
Foreign economic relations—United States
  USE **United States—Foreign economic relations**
Foreign exchange 332.4
  UF Exchange, Foreign
      Exchange rates
      International exchange
  BT **Banks and banking**
      Exchange
      Finance
      Money
      Stock exchange
Foreign influences
  USE subjects, ethnic groups, and literatures with the subdivision *Foreign influences,* e.g. **United States—Civilization—Foreign influences;** to be added as needed
Foreign investments 332.6
  UF International investment
      Investments, Foreign *[Former heading]*
  BT **Investments**
      Multinational corporations
Foreign language dictionaries
  USE **English language—Dictionaries—French**
      French language—Dictionaries—English
Foreign language laboratories
  USE **Language laboratories**

Foreign language phrases
  USE **English language—Foreign words and phrases**
      Modern languages—Conversation and phrase books
Foreign missions, Christian
  USE **Christian missions**
Foreign opinion
  USE names of countries with the subdivision *Foreign opinion,* which may be further subdivided by the country holding the opinion, e.g. **United States—Foreign opinion; United States—Foreign opinion—France;** etc., to be added as needed
Foreign policy
  USE **International relations**
Foreign population
  USE **Aliens**
      Immigrants
      Immigration and emigration
      Minorities
      Population
      and names of countries with the subdivision *Population,* e.g. **United States—Population;** or with the subdivision *Immigration and emigration,* e.g. **United States—Immigration and emigration;** to be added as needed
Foreign public opinion
  USE names of countries with the subdivision *Foreign opinion,* which may be further subdivided by the country holding the opinion, e.g. **United States—Foreign opinion; United States—Foreign opinion—France;** etc., to be added as needed
Foreign relations
  USE **International relations**
      and names of countries with the subdivision *Foreign relations,* e.g. **United States—Foreign relations;** to be added as needed

---

BT = Broader Term   NT = Narrower Term   RT = Related Term   SA = See Also   UF = Used For

Foreign service
USE   Diplomatic and consular service
Foreign students   370.116
UF   College students, Foreign
Students, Foreign [Former heading]
BT   Students
Foreign study   370.116
UF   Overseas study
Study abroad
Study, Foreign
Study overseas
BT   Education
Foreign trade
USE   International trade
Foreigners
USE   Aliens
Immigrants
Foremen
USE   Supervisors
Forenames
USE   Personal names
Forensic medicine
USE   Medical jurisprudence
Forensic science
USE   Forensic sciences
Forensic sciences   363.25
Use for materials on science as applied in courts of law or in criminal investigations.
UF   Criminalistics
Forensic science
BT   Science
NT   Medical jurisprudence
RT   Criminal investigation
Foreordination
USE   Predestination
Forest animals   578.73
UF   Forest fauna
BT   Animals
Wildlife
NT   Jungle animals
Forest conservation   333.75
UF   Conservation of forests
Forest preservation
Preservation of forests
BT   Conservation of natural resources
RT   Forest reserves
Forests and forestry

Forest fauna
USE   Forest animals
Forest fires   634.9
BT   Fires
Forest influences   577.3
UF   Climate and forests
Floods and forests
Forests and climate
Forests and floods
Forests and rainfall
Forests and water supply
Rainfall and forests
BT   Climate
Water supply
RT   Flood control
Forests and forestry
Plant ecology
Rain
Forest plants   581.7
BT   Forests and forestry
Plant ecology
Plants
Forest preservation
USE   Forest conservation
Forest products   634.9; 674
BT   Commercial products
Economic botany
Raw materials
NT   Gums and resins
Lumber and lumbering
Rubber
Wood
Forest reserves   333.75; 719
UF   National forests
BT   Public lands
NT   Wilderness areas
RT   Forest conservation
Forests and forestry
National parks and reserves
Forestry
USE   Forests and forestry
Forests and climate
USE   Forest influences
Forests and floods
USE   Forest influences
Forests and forestry (May subdiv. geog.)
577.3; 578.73; 634.9
UF   Arboriculture
Forestry
Timber

BT = Broader Term   NT = Narrower Term   RT = Related Term   SA = See Also   UF = Used For

Forests and forestry—*Continued*
       Woods
  BT   **Agriculture**
       Natural resources
  NT   **Christmas tree growing**
       Forest plants
       Jungles
       Lumber and lumbering
       Pruning
       Rain forests
       Reforestation
       Tree planting
  RT   **Forest conservation**
       Forest influences
       Forest reserves
       Trees
       Wood
Forests and forestry—**United States**
       577.30973; 634.90973
  UF   United States—Forests and for-
       estry
Forests and rainfall
  USE **Forest influences**
Forests and water supply
  USE **Forest influences**
Forgery   332; 364.16
  BT   **Crime**
       Fraud
       Impostors and imposture
  NT   **Art forgeries**
       Counterfeits and counterfeiting
       Literary forgeries
Forgery of works of art
  USE **Art forgeries**
Forging   671.3; 682
  UF   Drop forging
  BT   **Metalwork**
  NT   **Welding**
  RT   **Blacksmithing**
       Ironwork
Forgiveness   179
  BT   **Virtue**
  RT   **Amnesty**
       Pardon
Forgiveness of sin
  USE **Confession**
       Penance
Form, Musical
  USE **Musical form**

Formal gardens
  USE **Gardens**
Former nuns
  USE **Ex-nuns**
Former priests
  USE **Ex-priests**
Former Soviet republics   947.086
      Use for general materials on several or all
    of the countries that emerged from the disso-
    lution of the Soviet Union in 1991. Materials
    specifically on the federation of independent
    former Soviet republics that was established in
    1991 and does not include Georgia or the Bal-
    tic states are entered under **Commonwealth**
    of Independent States.
  UF   Ex-Soviet republics
       Ex-Soviet states
       Former Soviet states
  RT   **Central Asia—History—1991-**
       Commonwealth of Independent
       States
       Eastern Europe—History—
       1989-
       Soviet Union
Former Soviet states
  USE **Former Soviet republics**
Formosa
  USE **Taiwan**
Formula translation (Computer language)
  USE **FORTRAN (Computer lan-**
       guage)
Fortification   623
  UF   Forts
  SA   names of countries with the sub-
       division *Defenses,* to be added
       as needed
  BT   **Military art and science**
  RT   **Military engineering**
FORTRAN (Computer language)
       005.13
  UF   Formula translation (Computer
       language)
       FORTRAN (Computer program
       language) *[Former heading]*
  BT   **Programming languages (Com-**
       puters)
FORTRAN (Computer program language)
  USE **FORTRAN (Computer lan-**
       guage)
Forts
  USE **Fortification**

BT = Broader Term   NT = Narrower Term   RT = Related Term   SA = See Also   UF = Used For

Fortune
USE   Fate and fatalism
       Probabilities
       Success
       Wealth
Fortune telling   133.3
    BT   **Amusements**
          Divination
          Occultism
          Prophecies
          Superstition
    NT   **Astrology**
          Palmistry
          Tarot
    RT   **Clairvoyance**
Fortunes
    USE   Income
           Wealth
Forums (Discussions)
    USE   Discussion groups
Fossil botany
    USE   Fossil plants
Fossil hominids   569.9
    UF   Hominids, Fossil
          Human fossils
          Human paleontology
          Man, Prehistoric *[Former head-
          ing]*
          Prehistoric man *[Former head-
          ing]*
          Prehistory
    BT   **Archeology**
    RT   **Human origins**
Fossil mammals   569
    UF   Mammals, Fossil *[Former head-
          ing]*
    SA   types of extinct mammals, to be
          added as needed
    BT   **Fossils**
          Mammals
    NT   **Mastodon**
Fossil plants   561
    UF   Extinct plants
          Fossil botany
          Paleobotany
          Plants, Extinct
          Plants, Fossil *[Former heading]*
    BT   **Fossils**
          Plants

Fossil reptiles   567.9
    UF   Reptiles, Fossil *[Former head-
          ing]*
    SA   types of fossil reptiles, e.g. **Di-
          nosaurs;** to be added as
          needed
    BT   **Fossils**
          Reptiles
    NT   **Dinosaurs**
Fossils   560
    UF   Paleontology
    BT   **Biology**
          Natural history
          Science
          Stratigraphic geology
    NT   **Fossil mammals**
          Fossil plants
          Fossil reptiles
          Prehistoric animals
    RT   **Extinct animals**
Foster children   306.874
    BT   **Children**
    RT   **Foster home care**
Foster grandparents   362.73
    BT   **Volunteer work**
Foster home care   362.73
    UF   Child placing
          Children—Placing out
    BT   **Child welfare**
    RT   **Adoption**
          Children—Institutional care
          Foster children
          Group homes
Foundations   624.1; 721
    BT   **Architecture—Details**
          Building
          Buildings
          Civil engineering
          Structural engineering
    NT   **Basements**
          Concrete
    RT   **Masonry**
          Soil mechanics
          Walls
Foundations (Endowments)
    USE   **Endowments**
Founding   671.2
        Use for materials on the melting and cast-
    ing of metals.
    UF   Casting
          Foundry practice

BT = Broader Term   NT = Narrower Term   RT = Related Term   SA = See Also   UF = Used For

Founding—*Continued*

        Molding (Metal)

        Moulding (Metal)

  BT   **Metalwork**

  NT   **Type and type founding**

  RT   **Pattern making**

Foundlings

  USE   **Orphans**

Foundry practice

  USE   **Founding**

Four-day work week

  USE   **Hours of labor**

Four-H clubs

  USE   **4-H clubs**

Fourteenth century   909

    Use for general materials covering progress and development during this period in one or in several countries.

  UF   1300-1399 (14th century)

  BT   **Middle Ages**

Fourth dimension   530.11

  UF   Dimension, Fourth

        Hyperspace

        Time travel

  BT   **Mathematics**

  NT   **Space and time**

Fourth of July   394.2634

  UF   4th of July

        Independence Day (United

          States)

        July Fourth

  BT   **Holidays**

        United States—History—1775-

        1783, Revolution

Fourth World

  USE   **Developing countries**

Fractal geometry

  USE   **Fractals**

Fractals   514

    Use for materials on shapes or mathematical sets that have fractional, i.e. irregular, dimensions as opposed to the regular dimensions of Euclidean geometry.

  UF   Fractal geometry

        Sets, Fractal

        Sets of fractional dimension

  BT   **Geometry**

        Mathematical models

        Set theory

        Topology

Fractions   513.2

  BT   **Arithmetic**

        Mathematics

Fractures   617.1

  BT   **Bones**

        Wounds and injuries

Framing of pictures

  USE   **Picture frames and framing**

France   944

    May be subdivided like United States except for *History*.

France—Blacks

  USE   **Blacks—France**

France—Folk songs

  USE   **French folk songs**

France—History   944

France—History—0-1328   944

  NT   **Celts**

France—History—1328-1589, House of

    Valois   944

  NT   **Hundred Years' War, 1339-**

        1453

        Saint Bartholomew's Day,

        Massacre of, 1572

France—History—1589-1789, Bourbons

    944

France—History—1789-1799, Revolution

    944.04

  UF   Directory, French, 1795-1799

        French Revolution

        Napoleonic Wars

        Reign of Terror

        Revolution, French

        Terror, Reign of

  BT   **Revolutions**

France—History—1799-1815   944.05

  UF   Napoleonic wars

France—History—1815-1914   944.06-

    944.08

France—History—1914-1940   944.081

France—History—1940-1945, German occupation   944.081

  UF   German occupation of France,

        1940-1945

France—History—1945-1958   944.082

France—History—1958-1969   944.083

France—History—1969-   944.083

Franchise

  USE   **Citizenship**

        Elections

        Suffrage

Franciscans   271

  UF   Friars Minor

BT = Broader Term   NT = Narrower Term   RT = Related Term   SA = See Also   UF = Used For

Franciscans—*Continued*
>Gray Friars
>Grey Friars
>Mendicant orders
>Minorites
>Saint Francis, Order of
>St. Francis, Order of

>BT   **Monasticism and religious orders**

Fraternities and sororities   **371.8**
>UF   College fraternities
>College sororities
>Greek letter societies
>Sororities

>BT   **Colleges and universities**
>**Students—Societies**

>RT   **Secret societies**

Fraud   **364.16**
>UF   Deceit
>Ripoffs

>BT   **Commercial law**
>**Crime**
>**White collar crimes**

>NT   **Credit card crimes**
>**Forgery**

>RT   **Impostors and imposture**
>**Swindlers and swindling**

Fraud, Computer
>USE   **Computer crimes**

Fraud, Credit card
>USE   **Credit card crimes**

Frauds, Literary
>USE   **Literary forgeries**

Fraudulent advertising
>USE   **Deceptive advertising**

Free agency
>USE   **Free will and determinism**

Free coinage
>USE   **Monetary policy**

Free diving
>USE   **Scuba diving**
>**Skin diving**

Free enterprise (May subdiv. geog.)
>**330.12**
>UF   Free markets
>Laissez-faire
>Private enterprise

>BT   **Economic policy**

>RT   **Capitalism**

Free fall
>USE   **Weightlessness**

Free love   **176; 306.7**
>BT   **Sexual ethics**

Free markets
>USE   **Free enterprise**

Free material
>UF   Freebies
>Giveaways

>BT   **Gifts**

Free press
>USE   **Freedom of the press**

Free press and fair trial
>USE   **Freedom of the press and fair trial**

Free schools
>USE   **Experimental schools**

Free speech
>USE   **Freedom of speech**

Free thought   **211**
>BT   **Freedom of conscience**

>NT   **Agnosticism**
>**Skepticism**

>RT   **Deism**
>**Rationalism**

Free time (Leisure)
>USE   **Leisure**

Free trade (May subdiv. geog.)   **382**
>UF   Fair trade (Tariff)
>Free trade and protection *[Former heading]*
>Tariff question—Free trade and protection

>BT   **Commercial policy**
>**International trade**

>RT   **Protectionism**
>**Tariff**

Free trade and protection
>USE   **Free trade**
>**Protectionism**

Free universities   **378**
>UF   Alternative universities
>Colleges and universities, Nonformal
>Education, Nonformal
>Experimental universities
>Nonformal colleges and universities
>Open universities

>BT   **Colleges and universities**

BT = Broader Term   NT = Narrower Term   RT = Related Term   SA = See Also   UF = Used For

Free verse 808.1

May be used for collections or materials about free verse, not for individual works.

UF   Vers libre

BT   **Poetry**

Free will and determinism 123

UF   Choice, Freedom of

Determinism and indeterminism

Free agency

Freedom of choice

Freedom of the will

Indeterminism

Liberty of the will

Will

BT   **Philosophy**

RT   **Fate and fatalism**

Predestination

Freebies

USE   **Free material**

Freebooters

USE   **Pirates**

Freedom 323.4

UF   Civil liberty

Emancipation

Liberty

Personal freedom

BT   **Democracy**

Political science

NT   **Anarchism and anarchists**

Conformity

Freedom of assembly

Freedom of association

Freedom of conscience

Freedom of movement

Freedom of religion

Freedom of speech

Freedom of the press

Intellectual freedom

RT   **Civil rights**

Equality

Freedom, Academic

USE   **Academic freedom**

Freedom marches for civil rights

USE   **Civil rights demonstrations**

Freedom of assembly 323.4

UF   Assembly, Right of

Right of assembly

BT   **Civil rights**

Freedom

NT   **Public meetings**

Riots

RT   **Freedom of association**

Freedom of speech

Freedom of association 323.4

UF   Association, Freedom of

Right of association

BT   **Civil rights**

Freedom

RT   **Freedom of assembly**

Freedom of choice

USE   **Free will and determinism**

Freedom of choice movement

USE   **Pro-choice movement**

Freedom of conscience 323.44

UF   Liberty of conscience

BT   **Conscience**

Freedom

Toleration

NT   **Conscientious objectors**

Dissent

Free thought

Public opinion

RT   **Freedom of religion**

Freedom of information 323.44

UF   Information, Freedom of

Right to know

BT   **Civil rights**

Intellectual freedom

NT   **Press—Government policy**

RT   **Censorship**

Freedom of speech

Freedom of the press

Freedom of movement 323.4

UF   Movement, Freedom of

BT   **Civil rights**

Freedom

Freedom of religion 261.7; 291.1; 323.44

UF   Freedom of worship

Religious freedom *[Former heading]*

Religious liberty

BT   **Civil rights**

Freedom

Toleration

NT   **Dissent**

RT   **Freedom of conscience**

Persecution

Freedom of speech 323.44

UF   Free speech *[Former heading]*

Liberty of speech

Freedom of speech—*Continued*
    Speech, Freedom of
  BT Censorship
    Civil rights
    Freedom
    Intellectual freedom
  RT Freedom of assembly
    Freedom of information
    Libel and slander
Freedom of teaching
  USE Academic freedom
Freedom of the press   323.44
  UF Free press
    Liberty of the press
    Press censorship
  BT Civil rights
    Freedom
    Intellectual freedom
    Press
  NT Freedom of the press and fair
      trial
  RT Censorship
    Freedom of information
    Libel and slander
Freedom of the press and fair trial
    323.42; 323.44; 342
  UF Fair trial and free press
    Free press and fair trial
    Prejudicial publicity
    Trial by publicity
  BT Fair trial
    Freedom of the press
    Press
Freedom of the will
  USE Free will and determinism
Freedom of worship
  USE Freedom of religion
Freelancers
  USE Self-employed
Freemasons   366
  UF Masonic orders
    Masons (Secret order)
  BT Secret societies
Freeways
  USE Express highways
Freeze-dried foods   641.4; 664
  UF Food, Freeze dried *[Former
      heading]*
  BT Dried foods

Freezing
  USE Cryobiology
    Frost
    Ice
    Refrigeration
Freezing of human bodies
  USE Cryonics
Freight   388
  UF Freight and freightage *[Former
      heading]*
  BT Maritime law
    Materials handling
    Railroads
    Transportation
  NT Commercial aeronautics
    Trucking
  RT Railroads—Rates
Freight and freightage
  USE Freight
French and Indian War
  USE United States—History—1755-
      1763, French and Indian
      War
French Canadian literature
  USE Canadian literature (French)
French Canadian poetry
  USE Canadian poetry (French)
French Canadians   305.811; 971
  BT Canadians
French cookery
  USE French cooking
French cooking   641.5944
  UF Cookery, French *[Former head-
      ing]*
    Cooking, French
    French cookery
  BT Cooking
French Equatorial Africa
  USE French-speaking Equatorial Af-
      rica
French folk songs   782.4216200944
  UF Folk songs—France
    Folk songs, French *[Former
      heading]*
    France—Folk songs
  BT Folk songs
French foreign opinion—United States
  USE United States—Foreign opin-
      ion—France

BT = Broader Term   NT = Narrower Term   RT = Related Term   SA = See Also   UF = Used For

French language   440

May be subdivided like **English language.**

BT   **Language and languages**

  Romance languages

French language—Conversation and phrase books   448

UF   French language—Conversations and phrases [Former heading]

French language—Conversations and phrases

USE   **French language—Conversation and phrase books**

French language—Dictionaries—English 443

Use for French-English dictionaries. English-French dictionaries are entered under **English language—Dictionaries—French.** Combined French-English and English-French dictionaries are entered under both headings.

UF   Foreign language dictionaries

BT   **Encyclopedias and dictionaries**

RT   **English language—Dictionaries—French**

French language—Reading materials 448.6

French literature   840

May use same subdivisions and names of literary forms as for **English literature.**

BT   **Literature**

  Romance literature

NT   **French poetry**

French literature—Black authors 840.8; 840.9

May be used for collections or materials about French literature by several Black authors, not for individual works.

UF   Black literature (French)

French literature—Canada

USE   **Canadian literature (French)**

French poetry   841

BT   **French literature**

  Poetry

NT   **Troubadours**

French poetry—Black authors   841, etc.

May be used for collections or materials about French poetry by several Black authors, not for individual works.

UF   Black poetry (French)

French Revolution

USE   **France—History—1789-1799, Revolution**

French-speaking Equatorial Africa   967

Use for materials dealing collectively with the Central African Republic, Chad, Congo, and Gabon. The former name for the region was French Equatorial Africa.

UF   Africa, French-speaking Equatorial [Former heading]

  French Equatorial Africa

BT   **Central Africa**

French-speaking West Africa   966

Use for materials dealing collectively with Benin, Burkina Faso, Guinea, Ivory Coast, Mali, Mauritania, Niger, Senegal, and Togo.

UF   Africa, French-speaking West [Former heading]

  French West Africa

BT   **West Africa**

French West Africa

USE   **French-speaking West Africa**

Frequency modulation, Radio

USE   **Radio frequency modulation**

Fresco painting

USE   **Mural painting and decoration**

Freshwater animals   591.76

UF   Aquatic animals

  Freshwater fauna

  Water animals

SA   types of fresh water animals, e.g. **Beavers;** to be added as needed

BT   **Animals**

  Freshwater biology

  Wildlife

NT   **Beavers**

  Fishes

Freshwater aquaculture

USE   **Aquaculture**

Freshwater biology   578.76

BT   **Biology**

NT   **Aquariums**

  Freshwater animals

  Freshwater plants

RT   **Marine biology**

Freshwater fauna

USE   **Freshwater animals**

Freshwater plants   581.7

UF   Aquatic plants

  Water plants

BT   **Freshwater biology**

  Plants

RT   **Marine plants**

BT = Broader Term   NT = Narrower Term   RT = Related Term   SA = See Also   UF = Used For

Friars Minor
    USE   **Franciscans**
Friends
    USE   **Friendship**
Friends, Imaginary
    USE   **Imaginary playmates**
Friends, Society of
    USE   **Society of Friends**
Friendship   177
    UF   Affection
           Friends
    BT   **Human behavior**
           Social ethics
    NT   **Imaginary playmates**
    RT   **Love**
Friesian cattle
    USE   **Holstein-Friesian cattle**
Fringe benefits
    USE   **Nonwage payments**
Frogs   597.8
    UF   Tadpoles
    BT   **Amphibians**
Frontier and pioneer life (May subdiv.
    geog.)   **978**
    UF   Border life
           Pioneer life
    BT   **Adventure and adventurers**
    NT   **Cowhands**
           Indians of North America—
             Captivities
           Overland journeys to the Pa-
             cific
           Ranch life
Frontiers
    USE   **Boundaries**
Frost   551.57
    UF   Freezing
    BT   **Meteorology**
           Water
    NT   **Ice**
           Refrigeration
Frozen animal embryos
    USE   **Frozen embryos**
Frozen embryos   176; 571.8; 612.6
    UF   Animal embryos, Frozen
           Embryos, Frozen
           Frozen animal embryos
           Frozen human embryos
           Human embryos, Frozen
    BT   **Cryobiology**

           Embryology
Frozen foods   641.4; 664
    UF   Food, Frozen *[Former heading]*
    BT   **Food—Preservation**
    NT   **Ice cream, ices, etc.**
Frozen human embryos
    USE   **Frozen embryos**
Frozen stars
    USE   **Black holes (Astronomy)**
Fruit   634; 641.3
    Use the names of tree fruits, expressed in
    the singular form, for materials on the fruit or
    the tree or both.
    SA   types of fruit, e.g. **Berries; Cit-**
           rus fruits; etc.; and names of
           fruits, e.g. **Apple;** to be add-
           ed as needed, in the singular
           form for tree fruits
    BT   **Food**
           Plants
    NT   **Apple**
           Berries
           Citrus fruits
           Fruit culture
           Grapes
Fruit—Canning
    USE   **Fruit—Preservation**
Fruit culture   634
    UF   Arboriculture
           Orchards
    BT   **Agriculture**
           Fruit
           Gardening
           Horticulture
           Trees
    NT   **Berries**
           Nurseries (Horticulture)
           Plant propagation
           Pruning
Fruit—Diseases and pests   634
    BT   **Agricultural pests**
           Insect pests
           Pests
           Plant diseases
    NT   **Spraying and dusting**
Fruit flies   595.77
    BT   **Flies**
Fruit painting and illustration
    USE   **Botanical illustration**
Fruit—Preservation   641.4; 664
    UF   Fruit—Canning

BT = Broader Term   NT = Narrower Term   RT = Related Term   SA = See Also   UF = Used For

Fruit—Preservation—*Continued*
    BT   Canning and preserving
           Food—Preservation
Frustration   152.4
    UF   Futility
    BT   **Attitude (Psychology)**
           Emotions
Fuel   333.8; 662
    SA   types of fuel; and subjects with
           the subdivision *Fuel consump-*
           tion, to be added as needed
    BT   **Combustion**
           Energy resources
           Engines
           Fire
           Home economics
    NT   **Alcohol as fuel**
           Automobiles—Fuel consump-
           tion
           Biomass energy
           Charcoal
           Coal
           Gas
           Gasoline
           Natural gas
           Petroleum as fuel
           Synthetic fuels
           Wood
    RT   **Heating**
Fuel cells   621.31
    BT   **Electric batteries**
           Electrochemistry
Fuel consumption
    USE   subjects with the subdivision
           Fuel consumption, e.g. **Auto-**
           mobiles—Fuel consumption;
           to be added as needed
Fuel, Liquid
    USE   **Petroleum as fuel**
Fuel oil
    USE   **Petroleum as fuel**
Fugue   784.18
    Use for musical scores and for materials on
the fugue as a musical form.
    UF   Canons, fugues, etc.
           Fugues
           Prelude and fugue
           Preludes and fugues
    BT   **Counterpoint**
           Musical form

Fugues
    USE   **Fugue**
Fulfillment, Self
    USE   **Self-realization**
Fumigation   614.4; 648
    BT   **Communicable diseases**
           Insecticides
    RT   **Disinfection and disinfectants**
Functional competencies
    USE   **Life skills**
Functional literacy   302.2; 374
    UF   Occupational literacy
    BT   **Literacy**
Fund raising   361.7068; 658.15
    UF   Community chests
           Money raising
    BT   **Finance**
    RT   **Gifts**
Fundamental education
    USE   **Basic education**
Fundamental life skills
    USE   **Life skills**
Fundamental rights
    USE   **Civil rights**
           Human rights
Fundamental theology
    USE   **Apologetics**
           Doctrinal theology
Fundamentalism
    USE   **Christian fundamentalism**
           Islamic fundamentalism
           Religious fundamentalism
Fundamentalism and education
    USE   **Church and education**
           Creationism
           Religion in the public schools
Fundamentalism and evolution
    USE   **Creationism**
Fundamentalisms
    USE   **Religious fundamentalism**
Fundamentalist movements
    USE   **Religious fundamentalism**
Funding
    USE   **Finance**
Funding for the arts
    USE   **Art patronage**
           Arts—Government policy
           Federal aid to the arts
Funds
    USE   **Finance**

BT = Broader Term   NT = Narrower Term   RT = Related Term   SA = See Also   UF = Used For

Funds, Scholarship
USE **Scholarships**
Funeral directors
USE **Undertakers and undertaking**
Funeral rites and ceremonies   393
UF   Graves
Mortuary customs
Mourning customs
SA   ethnic groups and native peoples
with the subdivision *Funeral
customs and rites;* to be add-
ed as needed
BT   **Manners and customs**
Rites and ceremonies
RT   **Burial**
Cremation
Fungi   579.5
UF   Diseases and pests
Mycology
BT   **Agricultural pests**
Pests
Plants
NT   **Molds (Fungi)**
Plant diseases
Yeast
RT   **Mushrooms**
Fungicides   632; 668
UF   Germicides
BT   **Pesticides**
RT   **Spraying and dusting**
Funicular railroads
USE **Cable railroads**
Funnies
USE **Comic books, strips, etc.**
Fur   675; 685
BT   **Animals—Anatomy**
RT   **Hides and skins**
Fur-bearing animals
USE **Furbearing animals**
Fur seals
USE **Seals (Animals)**
Fur trade   338.3
BT   **Trapping**
Furbearing animals   599.7; 636.97
UF   Fur-bearing animals
SA   types of furbearing animals, e.g.
Beavers; to be added as
needed
BT   **Animals**
Economic zoology

Wildlife
NT   **Beavers**
Furnaces   697
BT   **Heating**
NT   **Blast furnaces**
Smelting
Furniture   645; 684.1; 749
SA   furniture of particular countries,
e.g. **American furniture;**
types of furniture, and names
of specific articles of furni-
ture, to be added as needed
BT   **Decoration and ornament**
Decorative arts
Interior design
NT   **American furniture**
Built-in furniture
Chairs
Church furniture
Furniture making
**Garden ornaments and furni-
ture**
**Libraries—Equipment and
supplies**
Mirrors
**Schools—Equipment and sup-
plies**
Veneers and veneering
RT   **Cabinetwork**
Upholstery
Furniture, American
USE **American furniture**
Furniture building
USE **Furniture making**
Furniture, Built-in
USE **Built-in furniture**
Furniture—Conservation and restoration
USE **Furniture finishing**
Furniture—Repairing
Furniture finishing   684.1; 749
UF   Furniture—Conservation and res-
toration
Furniture—Refinishing
Furniture—Restoration
Refinishing furniture
Restoration of furniture
BT   **Furniture making**
Handicraft
Wood finishing
RT   **Furniture—Repairing**

BT = Broader Term   NT = Narrower Term   RT = Related Term   SA = See Also   UF = Used For

Furniture making 684.1; 749
UF   Furniture building
BT   **Furniture**
     Woodwork
NT   **Furniture finishing**
     Furniture—Repairing
Furniture—Refinishing
USE   **Furniture finishing**
Furniture—Repairing 684.1; 749
UF   Furniture—Conservation and res-
     toration
     Furniture—Restoration
     Restoration of furniture
BT   **Furniture making**
RT   **Furniture finishing**
Furniture—Restoration
USE   **Furniture finishing**
     Furniture—Repairing
Futility
USE   **Frustration**
Future life 129; 236
     Use for materials on the character and form
     of a future existence. Materials on the ques-
     tion of the endless existence of the soul are
     entered under **Immortality.** Materials on the
     philosophical concept of eternity are entered
     under **Eternity.**
UF   Afterlife
     Eternal life
     Intermediate state
     Life after death
     Life, Future
     Resurrection
     Retribution
BT   **Death**
     Eschatology
NT   **Heaven**
     Hell
     Paradise
     Soul
     Spiritualism
RT   **Eternity**
     Immortality
Future shock
USE   **Culture conflict**
Futurism (Art) 759.06
BT   **Art**
     Painting
NT   **Kinetic sculpture**
RT   **Postimpressionism (Art)**
Futurology
USE   **Forecasting**

Fuzzy logic
USE   **Fuzzy systems**
Fuzzy systems 629.8
UF   Fuzzy logic
     Systems, Fuzzy
BT   **System analysis**
G.I.'s
USE   **Soldiers—United States**
     Veterans—United States
G.R.E.
USE   **Graduate Record Examination**
Gaels
USE   **Celts**
Gaia concept
USE   **Gaia hypothesis**
Gaia hypothesis 550.1; 570.1
     Use for materials on the theory formulated
     by James Lovelock that various terrestrial life
     forms can act as a unified organism regulating
     earth's temperature, atmospheric conditions,
     and other physical characteristics.
UF   Gaia concept
     Gaia principle
     Gaia theory
     Living earth theory
BT   **Biology**
     Earth
     Ecology
     Life (Biology)
Gaia principle
USE   **Gaia hypothesis**
Gaia theory
USE   **Gaia hypothesis**
Galaxies 523.1
UF   Extragalactic nebulae
     Nebulae, Extragalactic
BT   **Astronomy**
     Stars
Gales
USE   **Winds**
Gambling 175; 795
UF   Betting
     Gaming
SA   types of gambling, e.g. **Lot-**
     teries; to be added as needed
BT   **Games**
NT   **Compulsive gambling**
     Lotteries
RT   **Horse racing**
Gambling, Compulsive
USE   **Compulsive gambling**

Game and game birds   636.6
  UF   Wild fowl
  SA   types of animals and birds, e.g.
       Deer; Pheasants; etc., to be
       added as needed
  BT   **Animals**
       Birds
       Wildlife
  NT   **Deer**
       Falconry
       Game protection
       Pheasants
  RT   **Hunting**
       Trapping
Game preserves
  USE **Game reserves**
Game protection   333.95; 636.9
  UF   Game wardens
       Protection of game
  BT   **Game and game birds**
       Hunting
       Wildlife conservation
  RT   **Birds—Protection**
Game reserves   333.95
  UF   Game preserves *[Former head-
       ing]*
  BT   **Hunting**
       Wildlife conservation
Game theory   519.3
  UF   Games, Theory of
       Theory of games
  BT   **Mathematical models**
       Mathematics
       Probabilities
  NT   **Decision making**
       Simulation games in education
Game wardens
  USE **Game protection**
Games   790
  UF   Pastimes
  SA   types of games and names of
       individual games, to be added
       as needed
  BT   **Entertaining**
       Physical education
       Recreation
  NT   **Ball games**
       Card games
       Checkers
       Chess

       Computer games
       Educational games
       Gambling
       **Indians of North America—
         Games**
       Indoor games
       Olympic games
       Singing games
       Video games
       Word games
  RT   **Amusements**
       Play
       Sports
Games, Electronic
  USE **Electronic toys**
       Video games
Games, Theory of
  USE **Game theory**
Gaming
  USE **Gambling**
Gaming, Educational
  USE **Simulation games in education**
Gamma rays   537.5; 539.7
  BT   **Electromagnetic waves**
       Radiation
       X-rays
Gangs (May subdiv. geog.)   302.3;
       364.106
  UF   Gangsters
       Street gangs
       Teenage gangs
  BT   **Criminals**
       Juvenile delinquency
       Organized crime
Gangster films   791.43
      May be used for individual works, collec-
    tions, or materials about gangster films.
  UF   Crime films
  BT   **Motion pictures**
  RT   **Mystery films**
Gangsters
  USE **Gangs**
Garage sales   381
  UF   Yard sales
  BT   **Secondhand trade**
Garbage
  USE **Refuse and refuse disposal**
Garbage disposal
  USE **Refuse and refuse disposal**

Garden design 712
- UF   Gardens—Design *[Former heading]*
- BT   **Design**
         Gardening
- RT   **Landscape gardening**

Garden farming
- USE   **Truck farming**

Garden furniture
- USE   **Garden ornaments and furniture**

Garden of Eden
- USE   **Paradise**

Garden ornaments and furniture 717
- UF   Garden furniture
- BT   **Decoration and ornament**
         Furniture
         Gardens
         Landscape architecture
- NT   **Sundials**

Garden pests
- USE   **Agricultural pests**
         Insect pests
         Plant diseases

Garden rooms 643
- UF   Conservatories, Home
         Home conservatories
- BT   **Houses**
         Rooms
- RT   **Greenhouses**

Gardening 635

Use for materials on the practical aspects of creating gardens and cultivating flowers, fruits, vegetables, etc. Materials on the design or rearrangement of extensive gardens or estates are entered under **Landscape gardening.** Materials on the scientific and economic aspects of the cultivation of plants are entered under **Horticulture.** General materials about gardens, the history of gardens, various types of gardens, etc., are entered under **Gardens.**

- UF   Planting
- BT   **Agriculture**
- NT   **Climbing plants**
         Container gardening
         Cultivated plants
         Flower gardening
         Fruit culture
         Garden design
         Gardening in the shade
         Greenhouses
         Grounds maintenance
         Indoor gardening
         Landscape gardening
         Nurseries (Horticulture)
         Organic gardening
         Plant propagation
         Pruning
         Truck farming
         Vegetable gardening
         Weeds
         Window gardening
- RT   **Gardens**
         Horticulture
         Plants

Gardening in the shade 635
- UF   Gardens, Shade
         Shade gardens
         Shady gardens
- BT   **Gardening**

Gardening, Organic
- USE   **Organic gardening**

Gardens (May subdiv. geog.) 635; 712

Use for general materials about gardens, the history of gardens, various types of gardens, etc. Materials on the design or rearrangement of extensive gardens or estates are entered under **Landscape gardening.** Materials on the practical aspects of creating gardens and cultivating flowers, fruits, vegetables, etc., are entered under **Gardening.**

- UF   Formal gardens
- SA   types of gardens, e.g. **Botanical gardens;** and names of individual gardens, to be added as needed
- NT   **Botanical gardens**
         Garden ornaments and furniture
         Miniature gardens
         Rock gardens
- RT   **Gardening**

Gardens—Design
- USE   **Garden design**

Gardens, Miniature
- USE   **Miniature gardens**

Gardens, Shade
- USE   **Gardening in the shade**

Garment industry
- USE   **Clothing industry**

Garment making
- USE   **Dressmaking**
         Tailoring

Garments
- USE   **Clothing and dress**

BT = Broader Term   NT = Narrower Term   RT = Related Term   SA = See Also   UF = Used For

Garments, Leather
USE   **Leather garments**
Gas   **665.7**
   UF   Coal gas
           Illuminating gas
   BT   **Fuel**
           Public utilities
   RT   **Coal tar products**
Gas and oil engines
USE   **Internal combustion engines**
Gas companies
USE   **Public utilities**
Gas engines
USE   **Internal combustion engines**
Gas, Natural
USE   **Natural gas**
Gas stations
USE   **Service stations**
Gas turbines   **621.43**
   BT   **Turbines**
Gas warfare
USE   **Chemical warfare**
Gases   **530.4; 533**
   SA   types of gases, e.g. **Nitrogen;** to
           be added as needed
   BT   **Fluid mechanics**
           Hydrostatics
           Physics
   NT   **Helium**
           Natural gas
           Nitrogen
           Oxygen
           Poisonous gases
   RT   **Pneumatics**
Gases, Asphyxiating and poisonous
USE   **Poisonous gases**
Gases, Poisonous
USE   **Poisonous gases**
Gasification of coal
USE   **Coal gasification**
Gasohol   **662**
   BT   **Alcohol as fuel**
Gasoline   **665.5**
   BT   **Fuel**
           Petroleum
Gasoline engines
USE   **Internal combustion engines**
Gastronomy
USE   **Cooking**
         Dining

Food
Menus
Gauchos
USE   **Cowhands**
Gaul—Geography   **914.4**
   BT   **Ancient geography**
           Historical geography
Gay liberation movement   **305.9**
   BT   **Homosexuality**
Gay lifestyle
USE   **Homosexuality**
Gay men   **305.38; 306.76**
   UF   Gays, Male
           Homosexuals, Male
   BT   **Men**
   NT   **Gays and lesbians in the mili-**
           tary
   RT   **Gay men's writings**
           Homosexuality
Gay men's writings   **808.8; 810.8, etc.**
     Use for collections of gay men's writings
     by more than one author and for materials
     about such writings.
   UF   Writings of gay men
   BT   **Literature**
   RT   **Gay men**
Gay women
USE   **Lesbians**
Gay women's writings
USE   **Lesbians' writings**
Gays and lesbians in the military
           355.008
   UF   Gays in the military
           Lesbians and gays in the mili-
           tary
           Lesbians in the military
           United States—Armed forces—
           Gays
   BT   **Gay men**
           Lesbians
           Military personnel
Gays, Female
USE   **Lesbians**
Gays in the military
USE   **Gays and lesbians in the mili-**
           tary
Gays, Male
USE   **Gay men**
Gazetteers   **910.3**
   SA   names of countries, states, etc.,
           with the subdivision *Gazet-*

BT = Broader Term   NT = Narrower Term   RT = Related Term   SA = See Also   UF = Used For

Gazetteers—*Continued*
      teers, e.g. **United States—Gazetteers;** to be added as needed
- BT   **Geography**
- NT   **Ohio—Gazetteers**
      United States—Gazetteers
- RT   **Geographic names**

Gearing   621.8
- UF   Bevel gearing
      Cog wheels
      Gears
      Spiral gearing
- BT   **Machinery**
      Power transmission
      Wheels
- NT   **Automobiles—Transmission devices**
- RT   **Mechanical movements**

Gears
- USE   **Gearing**

Geese   598.4; 636.5
- UF   Goose
- BT   **Birds**
      Poultry
      Water birds

Gemini project   629.45
- UF   Project Gemini
- BT   **Orbital rendezvous (Space flight)**
      Space flight

Gems   736
    Use for materials on cut and polished precious stones treated from the point of view of art or antiquity. Materials on gem stones treated from a mineralogical or technological point of view are entered under **Precious stones.** Materials on gems in which the emphasis is on the setting are entered under **Jewelry.**
- UF   Jewels
- BT   **Archeology**
      Art
      Decoration and ornament
      Engraving
      Minerals
- RT   **Jewelry**
      Precious stones

Gemstones
- USE   **Precious stones**

Gender identity
- USE   **Sex role**

Gene mapping   572.8
- UF   Chromosome mapping
      Genetic mapping *[Former heading]*
      Genome mapping
- BT   **Genetics**

Gene splicing
- USE   **Genetic engineering**
      Recombinant DNA

Gene therapy   616
    Use for materials on therapeutic efforts involving the replacement or supplementation of genes in order to cure diseases caused by genetic defects.
- UF   Therapy, Gene
- BT   **Genetic engineering**
      Therapeutics

Gene transfer
- USE   **Genetic engineering**

Genealogy   929
- UF   Ancestry
      Descent
      Family histories
      Family trees
      Pedigrees
- SA   countries, cities, etc., corporate bodies, ethnic groups, and classes of persons with the subdivision *Genealogy;* names of individual persons with the subdivision *Family;* and names of families, e.g. **Lincoln family;** to be added as needed
- BT   **History**
- NT   **Registers of births, etc.**
      Wills
- RT   **Biography**
      Heraldry

Generals   355.0092; 920
- BT   **Military personnel**

Generation
- USE   **Reproduction**

Generation gap
- USE   **Conflict of generations**

Generative organs
- USE   **Reproductive system**

Generators, Electric
- USE   **Electric generators**

BT = Broader Term   NT = Narrower Term   RT = Related Term   SA = See Also   UF = Used For

Generic drugs   615
    UF   Drugs—Generic substitution
          [Former heading]
    BT   **Drugs**
          Generic products
Generic products   658.8
    UF   Products, Generic
    BT   **Commercial products**
          Manufactures
    NT   **Generic drugs**
Genes
    USE   **Heredity**
Genetic aspects
    USE   types of diseases with the subdivision *Genetic aspects,* e.g. **Cancer—Genetic aspects;** to be added as needed
Genetic code   572.8
    BT   **Molecular biology**
Genetic counseling   616; 618
    BT   **Medical genetics**
          Prenatal diagnosis
Genetic engineering   660.6
    UF   Designed genetic change
          Engineering, Genetic
          Gene splicing
          Gene transfer
          Genetic intervention
          Genetic surgery
          Splicing of genes
          Transgenics
    BT   **Engineering**
          Genetic recombination
    NT   **Cloning**
          Fertilization in vitro
          Gene therapy
          Molecular cloning
          Recombinant DNA
    RT   **Biotechnology**
Genetic engineering—Government policy
    353.7; 660.6
Genetic engineering—Social aspects
    306.4
Genetic fingerprints
    USE   **DNA fingerprints**
Genetic intervention
    USE   **Genetic engineering**
Genetic mapping
    USE   **Gene mapping**

Genetic profiling
    USE   **DNA fingerprints**
Genetic recombination   572.8
    UF   Recombination, Genetic
    BT   **Chromosomes**
    NT   **Genetic engineering**
          Genetic transformation
          Recombinant DNA
Genetic surgery
    USE   **Genetic engineering**
Genetic transformation   576.5
    UF   Transformation (Genetics)
    BT   **Genetic recombination**
Genetics   576.5
    SA   types of diseases with the subdivision *Genetic aspects,* e.g. **Cancer—Genetic aspects;** to be added as needed
    BT   **Biology**
          Embryology
          Life (Biology)
          Mendel's law
          Reproduction
    NT   **Adaptation (Biology)**
          Behavior genetics
          Chromosomes
          DNA fingerprints
          Eugenics
          Gene mapping
          Medical genetics
          Natural selection
          Variation (Biology)
    RT   **Breeding**
          Heredity
Genitalia
    USE   **Reproductive system**
Genius   153.9
    UF   Talent
    BT   **Psychology**
    NT   **Creation (Literary, artistic, etc.)**
          Gifted children
Genome mapping
    USE   **Gene mapping**
Geochemistry   551.9
    UF   Chemical geology
          Earth—Chemical composition
          Geological chemistry
    BT   **Chemistry**
          Earth sciences

BT = Broader Term   NT = Narrower Term   RT = Related Term   SA = See Also   UF = Used For

Geochemistry—*Continued*
      Petrology
NT   **Geothermal resources**
Geodesy 526
  UF   Degrees of latitude and longitude
  BT   **Earth**
          Measurement
  NT   **Latitude**
          Longitude
  RT   **Surveying**
Geographic names (May subdiv. geog.)
      910
  UF   Names, Geographical *[Former heading]*
          Place names
  BT   **Names**
  RT   **Gazetteers**
Geographic names—United States
      917.3
  UF   United States—Geographic names
Geographical atlases
  USE   **Atlases**
Geographical distribution
  USE   types of plants and animals with the subdivision *Geographical distribution,* e.g. **Fishes—Geographical distribution;** to be added as needed
Geographical distribution of animals and plants
  USE   **Biogeography**
Geographical distribution of people
  USE   **Ethnology**
          Human geography
Geographical distribution of plants
  USE   **Plants—Geographical distribution**
Geographical myths 398.23
  UF   Cities, Imaginary
          Fictitious places
          Imaginary places
          Islands, Imaginary
          Places, Imaginary
  BT   **Mythology**
Geography 910
  Use for general materials, frequently school materials, that describe the surface of the earth and its interrelationship with various peoples, animals, natural products, and industries. Materials limited to a particular place are entered under the name of the place with the subdivision *Geography.* General descriptive materials and travel materials limited to a particular place are entered under the name of the place (except extinct cities) with the subdivision *Description.* Materials on the physical features of the earth's surface and its atmosphere are entered under **Physical geography.**
  UF   Social studies
  SA   names of countries, states, etc., with the subdivisions *Description* and *Geography;* and sacred works with the subdivision *Geography,* e.g. **Bible—Geography;** to be added as needed
  BT   **Earth**
          Earth sciences
          World history
  NT   **Atlases**
          Bible—Geography
          Biogeography
          Boundaries
          Commercial geography
          Exploration
          Gazetteers
          Greece—Geography
          Historical geography
          Human geography
          Maps
          Military geography
          Physical geography
          Regionalism
          Surveying
          United States—Description
          United States—Geography
          Voyages and travels
Geography, Ancient
  USE   **Ancient geography**
Geography, Biblical
  USE   **Bible—Geography**
Geography, Commercial
  USE   **Commercial geography**
Geography—Dictionaries 910.3
  Use for dictionaries of geographic terms. Materials listing names and descriptions of places are entered under **Gazetteers.**
  BT   **Encyclopedias and dictionaries**
Geography, Economic
  USE   **Commercial geography**
Geography, Historical
  USE   **Historical geography**

BT = Broader Term   NT = Narrower Term   RT = Related Term   SA = See Also   UF = Used For

Geography, Military
    USE   **Military geography**
Geography, Physical
    USE   **Physical geography**
Geography, Political
    USE   **Boundaries**
               Geopolitics
Geography, Social
    USE   **Human geography**
Geological chemistry
    USE   **Geochemistry**
Geological physics
    USE   **Geophysics**
Geologists   551.092; 920
    BT   **Scientists**
Geology (May subdiv. geog.)   **550**
      Use for materials limited to the structure
    and composition of the earth and the physical
    changes it has undergone and is still undergo-
    ing. General materials on the whole planet are
    entered under **Earth.**
    UF   Geoscience
    SA   names of planets and types of
               ore with the subdivision *Geol-*
               ogy, to be added as needed
    BT   **Earth sciences**
               Science
    NT   **Astrogeology**
               Continental drift
               Continental shelf
               Coral reefs and islands
               Earthquakes
               Economic geology
               Erosion
               Geysers
               Glaciers
               Landforms
               Minerals
               Oceanography
               Ore deposits
               Physical geography
               Stratigraphic geology
               Submarine geology
               Volcanoes
    RT   **Earth**
               Petrology
               Rocks
Geology, Dynamic
    USE   **Geophysics**
Geology, Economic
    USE   **Economic geology**

Geology, Historical
    USE   **Stratigraphic geology**
Geology, Lunar
    USE   **Lunar geology**
Geology—Maps   550.22
    BT   **Maps**
Geology—Moon
    USE   **Lunar geology**
Geology, Petroleum
    USE   **Petroleum geology**
Geology, Stratigraphic
    USE   **Stratigraphic geology**
Geology, Submarine
    USE   **Submarine geology**
Geology—United States   557.3
    UF   United States—Geology
Geometric art
    USE   **Abstract art**
Geometric patterns
    USE   **Patterns (Mathematics)**
Geometrical drawing   516; 604.2
    UF   Mathematical drawing
               Plans
    BT   **Drawing**
               Geometry
    NT   **Descriptive geometry**
               Graphic methods
               Perspective
    RT   **Mechanical drawing**
Geometry   516
    UF   Geometry, Plane
               Geometry, Solid
               Plane geometry
               Solid geometry
    BT   **Mathematics**
    NT   **Analytic geometry**
               Descriptive geometry
               Fractals
               Geometrical drawing
               Projective geometry
               Ratio and proportion
               Shape
               Square
               Topology
               Trigonometry
               Volume (Cubic content)
Geometry, Analytic
    USE   **Analytic geometry**
Geometry, Descriptive
    USE   **Descriptive geometry**

BT = Broader Term   NT = Narrower Term   RT = Related Term   SA = See Also   UF = Used For

Geometry, Plane
  USE   **Geometry**
Geometry, Projective
  USE   **Projective geometry**
Geometry, Solid
  USE   **Geometry**
Geophysics 550
  UF   Geological physics
       Geology, Dynamic
       Physics, Terrestrial
       Terrestrial physics
  BT   **Earth sciences**
       Physics
  NT   **Auroras**
       Oceanography
       Plate tectonics
Geopolitics 320.1; 327.101
  UF   Geography, Political
       Political geography
  BT   **International relations**
       Political science
  RT   **Boundaries**
       Human geography
       World politics
Geoscience
  USE   **Earth sciences**
       Geology
Geotechnique
  USE   **Soil mechanics**
Geothermal resources 333.8
  UF   Natural steam energy
       Thermal waters
  SA   types of geothermal resources,
         e.g. **Geysers;** to be added as
         needed
  BT   **Geochemistry**
       Ocean energy resources
       Renewable energy resources
  NT   **Geysers**
Geriatrics
  USE   **Elderly—Diseases**
       Elderly—Health and hygiene
Germ theory
  USE   **Life—Origin**
Germ theory of disease 616
  UF   Bacilli
       Disease germs
       Germs
       Microbes
  BT   **Communicable diseases**

Germ warfare
  USE   **Biological warfare**
German Democratic Republic
  USE   **Germany (East)**
German Federal Republic
  USE   **Germany (West)**
German Hebrew
  USE   **Yiddish language**
German language 430
     May be subdivided like **English language.**
  BT   **Language and languages**
German literature 830
     May use same subdivisions and names of literary forms as for **English literature.**
  BT   **Literature**
German occupation of France, 1940-1945
  USE   **France—History—1940-1945,**
         German occupation
German occupation of Netherlands, 1940-1945
  USE   **Netherlands—History—1940-**
         1945, German occupation
Germany 943
     Use for materials on Germany before or after the division of the country following World War II and for materials on East and West Germany discussed collectively as occupied zones or countries. Materials limited to the eastern part of Germany from 1945 to 1990, the Russian occupation zone, or the German Democratic Republic, are entered under **Germany (East).** Materials limited to the western part of Germany from 1945 to 1990, the American, British, and French occupation zones, or the German Federal Republic, are entered under **Germany (West).** May be subdivided like United States except for *History.*
  UF   Federal Republic of Germany
  NT   **Germany (East)**
       Germany (West)
Germany (Democratic Republic)
  USE   **Germany (East)**
Germany (East) 943
     Use for materials limited to the eastern part of Germany from 1945 to 1990, the Russian occupation zone, or the German Democratic Republic. Materials on Germany before or after the division of the country following World War II and materials on East and West Germany discussed collectively as occupied zones or countries are entered under **Germany.**
  UF   East Germany
       German Democratic Republic
       Germany (Democratic Republic)
  BT   **Germany**

BT = Broader Term   NT = Narrower Term   RT = Related Term   SA = See Also   UF = Used For

Germany (Federal Republic)
USE   Germany (West)
Germany—History   943
Germany—History—0-1517   943
Germany—History—1517-1740   943
   NT   Thirty Years' War, 1618-1648
Germany—History—1740-1815   943
Germany—History—1815-1866   943
Germany—History—1848-1849, Revolution   943
Germany—History—1866-1918   943.08
Germany—History—1918-1933   943.085
Germany—History—1933-1945   943.086
Germany—History—1945-1990   943.087
Germany—History—1990-   943.087
   UF   Germany—History—Unification, 1990
Germany—History—Unification, 1990
USE   Germany—History—1990-
Germany (West)   943.087
   Use for materials limited to the western part of Germany from 1945 to 1990, the American, British, and French occupation zones, or the German Federal Republic. Materials on Germany before or after the division of the country following World War II and materials on East and West Germany discussed collectively as occupied zones or countries are entered under **Germany.**
   UF   Federal Republic of Germany
           German Federal Republic
           Germany (Federal Republic)
           West Germany
   BT   **Germany**
Germicides
USE   **Disinfection and disinfectants**
           Fungicides
Germination   571.8
   UF   Seeds—Germination
   BT   **Plant physiology**
Germs
USE   **Bacteria**
           Germ theory of disease
           Microorganisms
Gerontology   305.26; 362.6; 612.6
   BT   **Social sciences**
   NT   **Aging**
           Elderly
   RT   **Old age**
Gestalt psychology   150.19
   UF   Configuration (Psychology)
           Psychology, Structural
           Structural psychology

   BT   **Consciousness**
           Perception
           Psychology
           Senses and sensation
           Theory of knowledge
Getting ready for bed
   USE   **Bedtime**
Gettysburg (Pa.), Battle of, 1863   973.7
   BT   **United States—History—1861-1865, Civil War—Campaigns**
Geysers   551.2
   UF   Eruptions
           Thermal waters
   BT   **Geology**
           Geothermal resources
           Physical geography
           Water
Ghettoes, Inner city
   USE   **Inner cities**
Ghost stories   808.83; 813, etc.
   May be used for individual works, collections, or materials about ghost stories.
   UF   Ghosts—Fiction *[Former heading]*
           Terror tales
   BT   **Fantasy fiction**
           Horror fiction
           Occult fiction
   RT   **Gothic novels**
           Mystery fiction
Ghost towns
   UF   Abandoned towns
           Towns, abandoned
   BT   **Extinct cities**
Ghosts   133.1
   UF   Haunted houses
           Phantoms
           Poltergeists
           Specters
           Spirits
   BT   **Folklore**
   NT   **Demonology**
   RT   **Apparitions**
           Hallucinations and illusions
           Parapsychology
           Spiritualism
           Superstition
Ghosts—Fiction
   USE   **Ghost stories**

BT = Broader Term   NT = Narrower Term   RT = Related Term   SA = See Also   UF = Used For

Giantism 616.4

Use for materials on excessive growth in humans. Materials on beings with a human form but with superhuman size or strength in folklore or imaginative literature are entered under **Giants.**

UF Gigantism

BT **Growth disorders**

Giants 398.21

Use for materials on beings with a human form but with superhuman size or strength in folklore or imaginative literature. Materials on excessive growth in humans are entered under **Giantism.**

BT **Folklore**

   Monsters

Gift of tongues

USE **Glossolalia**

Gift wrapping 745.54

UF Wrapping of gifts

BT **Packaging**

   Paper crafts

Gifted children 155.45

UF Bright children

   Children, Gifted

   Precocious children

   Superior children

   Talent

BT **Exceptional children**

   Genius

NT **Child artists**

   Child authors

Gifts

UF Bequests

   Donations

   Philanthropy

   Presents

BT **Manners and customs**

NT **Donation of organs, tissues, etc.**

   Free material

RT **Fund raising**

Gifts of grace

USE **Spiritual gifts**

Gifts of the Holy Spirit

USE **Spiritual gifts**

Gifts, Spiritual

USE **Spiritual gifts**

Gigantism

USE **Giantism**

Gipsies

USE **Gypsies**

Girl Scouts (May subdiv. geog.)
   369.463

UF Brownies (Girl Scouts)

BT **Girls' clubs**

   Scouts and scouting

Girls 155.43; 305.23

BT **Children**

NT **Fathers and daughters**

   Mothers and daughters

RT **Teenagers**

   Young women

Girls' agricultural clubs

USE **4-H clubs**

   Agriculture—Societies

   Girls' clubs

Girls' clubs 369.46

UF Girls' agricultural clubs

   Girls—Societies and clubs

BT **Clubs**

   Social settlements

   Societies

   Women—Societies

NT **4-H clubs**

   Camp Fire Girls

   Girl Scouts

Girls—Education 371.822

BT **Education**

RT **Coeducation**

Girls—Employment

USE **Children—Employment**

   Women—Employment

Girls—Societies and clubs

USE **Girls' clubs**

Girls, Teenage

USE **Teenagers**

GIs

USE **Soldiers—United States**

   Veterans—United States

Giveaways

USE **Free material**

Glacial epoch

USE **Ice age**

Glaciers 551.3

BT **Geology**

   Ice

   Physical geography

Gladiators 796.8092; 920

UF Fighting

Gladness

USE **Happiness**

BT = Broader Term   NT = Narrower Term   RT = Related Term   SA = See Also   UF = Used For

Glands   571.7; 573.4; 611; 612.4
  BT   Anatomy
        Physiology
Glands, Ductless
  USE Endocrine glands
Glass   666
  BT   Ceramics
  NT   Glass fibers
  RT   Windows
Glass construction   693
  BT   Building materials
Glass fibers   666
  UF   Fiber glass
        Fiberglass
        Fibers, Glass
        Glass, Spun
        Spun glass
  BT   Fibers
        Glass
Glass industry
  USE Glass manufacture
Glass manufacture   666
  UF   Glass industry
  BT   Ceramic industries
Glass painting and staining   748.5
  UF   Glass, Stained
        Painted glass
        Stained glass
        Windows, Stained glass
  BT   Decoration and ornament
        Painting
Glass, Spun
  USE Glass fibers
Glass, Stained
  USE Glass painting and staining
Glassware   642; 748.2
  UF   Dishes
  BT   Decorative arts
        Tableware
  RT   Vases
Glazes   666; 738.1
  BT   Ceramics
        Pottery
Gliders (Aeronautics)   629.133
  UF   Aircraft
        Sailplanes (Aeronautics)
  BT   Aeronautics
        Airplanes
Gliding and soaring   797.5
  UF   Air surfing

Hang gliding
        Soaring flight
  BT   Aeronautics
Global satellite communications systems
  USE Artificial satellites in telecom-
        munication
Global warming
  USE Greenhouse effect
Globes   912
  BT   Maps
Glossaries
  USE Encyclopedias and dictionaries
Glossolalia   234
  UF   Gift of tongues
        Speaking in tongues
        Speaking with tongues
  BT   Spiritual gifts
  RT   Pentecostalism
Glow-in-the-dark books
  UF   Luminescent books
        Luminous books
  BT   Picture books for children
        Toy and movable books
Glue   668
  BT   Adhesives
Glue sniffing
  USE Solvent abuse
Gnomes
  USE Fairies
Gnosticism   273; 299
  BT   Church history—30-600, Early
        church
        Philosophy
        Religions
Go karts
  USE Karts and karting
Goblins
  USE Fairies
God   211; 212; 231
  May subdivide by religion as needed, e.g.
  God—Christianity.
  NT   Femininity of God
        Providence and government of
        God
        Revelation
  RT   Metaphysics
        Religion
        Theism
        Theology
God—Christianity   231
  BT   Christianity—Doctrines

BT = Broader Term   NT = Narrower Term   RT = Related Term   SA = See Also   UF = Used For

God—Christianity—*Continued*
   NT   Holy Spirit
          Jesus Christ
          Trinity
God—Femininity
   USE   **Femininity of God**
God—Providence and government
   USE   **Providence and government of God**
God—Sovereignty
   USE   **Providence and government of God**
Goddess movement
   USE   **Goddess religion**
Goddess religion   291.2
   UF   Goddess movement
         Mother Goddess religion
   BT   **Paganism**
         Witchcraft
   RT   **Femininity of God**
         Gods and goddesses
         New Age movement
         Women—Religious life
Goddesses
   USE   **Gods and goddesses**
Gods
   USE   **Gods and goddesses**
Gods and goddesses   291.2
   UF   Deities
         Goddesses
         Gods
   SA   names of gods and goddesses, e.g. **Zeus (Greek deity); Vesta (Roman deity);** etc., to be added as needed
   NT   **Vesta (Roman deity)**
         Zeus (Greek deity)
   RT   **Goddess religion**
         Mythology
         Religions
Gold   332.4; 553.4; 669
   UF   Bimetallism
         Bullion
   BT   **Chemical elements**
         Precious metals
   NT   **Goldwork**
   RT   **Coinage**
         Gold mines and mining
         Money

Gold articles
   USE   **Goldwork**
Gold fish
   USE   **Goldfish**
Gold mines and mining   622
   UF   Gold rush
         Gold rushes
   SA   names of places with the subdivision *Gold discoveries,* to be added as needed
   BT   **Mines and mineral resources**
   NT   **California—Gold discoveries**
         Prospecting
   RT   **Gold**
Gold plate
   USE   **Plate**
Gold rush
   USE   **Gold mines and mining**
Gold rushes
   USE   **Gold mines and mining**
Gold work
   USE   **Goldwork**
Golden Gate Bridge (San Francisco, Calif.)   624; 979.4
   BT   **Bridges**
Goldfish   597.5
   UF   Gold fish
   BT   **Fishes**
Goldsmithing
   USE   **Goldwork**
Goldwork   739.2
   UF   Gold articles
         Gold work
         Goldsmithing
   BT   **Art metalwork**
         Gold
         Metalwork
   NT   **Plate**
   RT   **Jewelry**
Golf courses   796.352
   BT   **Grounds maintenance**
Good and evil   170; 214; 241
   UF   Evil
         Wickedness
   BT   **Ethics**
         Philosophy
         Theology
   NT   **Sin**
Good Friday   263
   BT   **Christian holidays**

BT = Broader Term   NT = Narrower Term   RT = Related Term   SA = See Also   UF = Used For

Good Friday—*Continued*
> Holy Week
> Lent
> RT   Jesus Christ—Crucifixion

Good grooming
> USE   Personal grooming

Goods, Consumer
> USE   Consumer goods

Goose
> USE   Geese

Gorge-purge syndrome
> USE   Bulimia

Gospel music   781.71; 782.25
> UF   Music, Gospel
>   Revivals—Music
> BT   African American music
>   Church music
>   Popular music
> RT   Spirituals (Songs)

Gossip   070.4; 177; 302.2
> BT   Journalism
>   Libel and slander

Gothic architecture   723
> UF   Architecture, Gothic *[Former
>   heading]*
> BT   Architecture
> RT   Cathedrals
>   Christian antiquities
>   Church architecture
>   Gothic art

Gothic art   709.02
> UF   Art, Gothic
> BT   Medieval art
> RT   Christian art and symbolism
>   Gothic architecture

Gothic fiction
> USE   Gothic novels

Gothic novels   813, etc.
> May be used for individual works, collections, or materials about novels that have a medieval setting and usually include castles and ghosts.
> UF   Gothic fiction *[Former heading]*
> BT   Historical fiction
>   Horror fiction
>   Occult fiction
> RT   Ghost stories
>   Love stories
>   Romantic suspense novels

Goths   305.83
> UF   East Goths

> Ostrogoths
> BT   Teutonic peoples

Gout   616.3
> BT   Arthritis
>   Rheumatism

Government
> USE   Political science
>   and names of countries, cities,
>   etc., with the subdivision *Politics and government,* e.g.
>   United States—Politics and
>   government; to be added as
>   needed

Government agencies
> USE   Administrative agencies

Government and business
> USE   Industrial policy

Government and church
> USE   Church and state

Government and the press
> USE   Press—Government policy

Government budgets
> USE   Budget

Government buildings
> USE   Public buildings

Government by commission
> USE   Municipal government by commission

Government, Comparative
> USE   Comparative government

Government debts
> USE   Public debts

Government departments
> USE   Executive departments

Government documents
> USE   Government publications

Government employees
> USE   Civil service

Government health insurance
> USE   National health insurance

Government housing
> USE   Public housing

Government investigations
> USE   Governmental investigations

Government lending (May subdiv. geog.)
>   332.7; 354.8
> BT   Domestic economic assistance
>   Economic policy
>   Loans
>   Public finance

BT = Broader Term   NT = Narrower Term   RT = Related Term   SA = See Also   UF = Used For

Government libraries   027.5

Use for materials on special libraries maintained by government funds.

UF	Federal libraries
	Libraries, Governmental
BT	**Special libraries**
NT	**National libraries**
	State libraries

Government, Local

USE   **Local government**

Government, Mandatory

USE   **Mandates**

Government, Military

USE   **Military government**

Government ministries

USE   **Executive departments**

Government, Municipal

USE   **Municipal government**

Government ownership   333.1; 338.9

UF	Nationalization
	Public ownership
	Socialization of industry
	State ownership
BT	**Corporations**
	Economic policy
	Economics
	Industrial policy
	Political science
	Socialism
NT	**Municipal ownership**
	Railroads—Government policy
RT	**Privatization**

Government ownership of railroads

USE   **Railroads—Government policy**

Government policy

USE   ethnic groups, classes of persons, and subjects not inherently governmental with the subdivision *Government policy,* e.g. **Homeless persons— Government policy; Agriculture—Government policy;** etc., to be added as needed

Government procurement

USE   **Government purchasing**

Government property, Surplus

USE   **Surplus government property**

Government publications (May subdiv. geog.)   **011; 015; 025.17**

UF	Documents
	Government documents
	Official publications
	Public documents
BT	**Library resources**

Government publications—Chicago (Ill.) 015.773

UF	Chicago (Ill.)—Government publications *[Former heading]*

Government publications—Ohio 015.771

UF	Ohio—Government publications *[Former heading]*

Government publications—United States 015.73; 025.17

UF	United States—Government publications *[Former heading]*

Government purchasing (May subdiv. geog.)   **352.5**

UF	Government procurement
	Procurement, Government
	Public procurement
	Purchasing, Government
BT	**Buying**
NT	**Buy national policy**

Government records—Preservation

USE   **Archives**

Government regulation of commerce

USE	**Commercial policy**
	Industrial laws and legislation
	Interstate commerce
	Tariff

Government regulation of industry

USE   **Industrial policy**

Government regulation of railroads

USE   **Railroads—Government policy**

Government reorganization

USE   **Administrative agencies—Reorganization**

Government, Resistance to

USE   **Resistance to government**

Government service

USE   **Civil service**

Government spending policy

USE   **United States—Appropriations and expenditures**

Government surveys

USE   **Surveys**

Government transfer payments

USE   **Transfer payments**

BT = Broader Term   NT = Narrower Term   RT = Related Term   SA = See Also   UF = Used For

Governmental investigations (May subdiv. geog.)   328.3; 353.4

   Use for materials on investigations initiated by the legislative, executive, or judicial branches of the government, usually of some particular problem of public interest.

   UF   Congressional investigations
         Executive investigations
         Government investigations
         Judicial investigations
         Legislative investigations
   BT   **Administration of justice**
Governmental investigations—United States   328.3; 353.4
   UF   United States—Governmental investigations
Governments in exile
   USE   **World War, 1939-1945—Governments in exile**
Governors (May subdiv. geog.)   352.23; 920
   BT   **State governments**
Graal
   USE   **Grail**
Grace (Theology)   234; 291.2
   BT   **Doctrinal theology**
         Salvation
   NT   **Sacraments**
         Spiritual gifts
Grade repetition
   USE   **Promotion (School)**
Grade retention
   USE   **Promotion (School)**
Grading and marking (Education)   371.27
   UF   Grading and marking (Students)
         [Former heading]
         Marking (Students)
         Students—Grading and marking
   BT   **Educational tests and measurements**
   NT   **Ability grouping in education**
         Promotion (School)
   RT   **School reports**
Grading and marking (Students)
   USE   **Grading and marking (Education)**
Graduate record examination
   USE   **Graduate Record Examination**
Graduate Record Examination   378.1
   UF   G.R.E.

Graduate record examination
   [Former heading]
   GRE
   BT   **Colleges and universities—Entrance examinations**
         Examinations
Graduates, College
   USE   **College graduates**
Graduation
   USE   **Commencements**
Graffiti   080; 808.88
   BT   **Folklore**
         Inscriptions
Graft in politics
   USE   **Political corruption**
Grafting   631.5
   BT   **Plant propagation**
Grail   398.22
   UF   Graal
         Holy Grail
   BT   **Folklore**
         Legends
   RT   **Arthurian romances**
Grain   633.1
   UF   Breadstuffs
         Cereals
   SA   types of cereal plants, e.g. **Corn**; **Wheat**; etc., to be added as needed
   BT   **Economic botany**
         Flour
         Food
   NT   **Corn**
         Wheat
Grammar   415
   SA   names of languages with the subdivision *Grammar*, to be added as needed
   BT   **Language and languages**
         Linguistics
   NT   **English language—Grammar**
Grammar schools
   USE   **Elementary education**
         Public schools
Grammatical comparison
   USE   **English language—Comparison**
Gramophone
   USE   **Phonograph**
Grandchild and grandparent
   USE   **Grandparent and child**

BT = Broader Term   NT = Narrower Term   RT = Related Term   SA = See Also   UF = Used For

Grandparent and child   306.874

Use for materials on the interaction between grandparents and their grandchildren. Materials restricted to the legal right of grandparents to visit their grandchildren are entered under **Visitation rights (Domestic relations)**.

UF   Child and grandparent
      Children and grandparents
      Grandchild and grandparent
      Grandparent and grandchild
      Grandparenting
BT   **Children and adults**
      Domestic relations
      Family
      Human relations

Grandparent and grandchild
USE   **Grandparent and child**

Grandparenting
USE   **Grandparent and child**

Grange   334
BT   **Agriculture—Societies**

Granite   552; 553.5
BT   **Rocks**
      Stone

Grants
USE   **Subsidies**

Grants-in-aid   336.1; 352.73

Use for materials on grants of money made from a central government to a local government.

UF   Block grants
      Federal grants
SA   federal aid to particular endeavors, e.g. **Federal aid to education;** to be added as needed
BT   **Public finance**
NT   **Federal aid to education**
      Federal aid to libraries
      Federal aid to minority business enterprises
      Federal aid to the arts
RT   **Domestic economic assistance**

Grapes   634.8; 641.3
UF   Viticulture
BT   **Fruit**
RT   **Vineyards**
      Wine and wine making

Graph theory   511
UF   Graphs, Theory of
      Theory of graphs
BT   **Algebra**
      Mathematical analysis

      Topology

Graphic arts (May subdiv. geog.)   760
UF   Art, Graphic
      Arts, Graphic
SA   types of graphic arts, to be added as needed
BT   **Art**
NT   **Clip art**
      Drawing
      Engraving
      Painting
      Photography
      Printing
      Prints
      Typography

Graphic arts, American
USE   **Graphic arts—United States**

Graphic arts—United States   760.0973
UF   American graphic arts
      Graphic arts, American *[Former heading]*
      United States—Graphic arts

Graphic methods   001.4; 511
UF   Flow charts
      Flowcharting
      Graphs
BT   **Drawing**
      Geometrical drawing
      Mechanical drawing
NT   **Statistics—Graphic methods**

Graphics, Computer
USE   **Computer graphics**

Graphite   553.2
UF   Black lead
BT   **Carbon**

Graphology   137; 155.2

Use for materials on handwriting as an expression of the writer's character. General materials on the history and art of writing are entered under **Writing**. Materials on writing with a pen or pencil and practical or prescriptive guides to penmanship are entered under **Handwriting**.

BT   **Handwriting**
      Writing

Graphs
USE   **Graphic methods**

Graphs, Theory of
USE   **Graph theory**

Grass (Drug)
USE   **Marijuana**

BT = Broader Term   NT = Narrower Term   RT = Related Term   SA = See Also   UF = Used For

Grasses   584; 633.2
   UF   Herbage
   BT   Economic botany
        Plants
   RT   Feeds
        Forage plants
        Hay
        Lawns
Grasslands (May subdiv. geog.)   577.4;
   578.74
   BT   Land use
   NT   Prairies
Graves
   USE   Burial
         Cemeteries
         Epitaphs
         Funeral rites and ceremonies
         Mounds and mound builders
         Tombs
Graveyard of the Atlantic
   USE   Bermuda Triangle
Graveyards
   USE   Cemeteries
Gravitation   521; 531
   UF   Gravity
   BT   Physics
   RT   Relativity (Physics)
Gravity
   USE   Gravitation
Gravity free state
   USE   Weightlessness
Gray Friars
   USE   Franciscans
GRE
   USE   Graduate Record Examination
Grease
   USE   Lubrication and lubricants
         Oils and fats
Great books program
   USE   Discussion groups
Great Britain   941
     Use for materials on the United Kingdom
   of Great Britain and Northern Ireland, which
   comprises England, Scotland, Wales, and
   Northern Ireland, as well as for materials on
   the island of Great Britain. May be subdivided
   like United States except for *History*. Materi-
   als limited to one of the constituent parts of
   the United Kingdom, apart from materials relating to history or politics and government,
   are entered under that part, e.g. **England.**
   NT   England

Great Britain—Colonies   325
   UF   British Empire
   BT   Colonies
   RT   Commonwealth countries
Great Britain—History   941
   UF   England—History
         English history
Great Britain—History—0-1066   941.01
   NT   Anglo-Saxons
         Celts
Great Britain—History—1066-1154, Nor-
   man period   941.02
   NT   Domesday book
         Hastings (East Sussex, Eng-
         land), Battle of, 1066
         Normans
Great Britain—History—1154-1399, Plan-
   tagenets   941.03
   NT   Magna Carta
Great Britain—History—1399-1485, Lan-
   caster and York   941.04
   NT   Hundred Years' War, 1339-
         1453
Great Britain—History—1455-1485, War
   of the Roses   941.04
   UF   Wars of the Roses, 1455-1485
Great Britain—History—1485-1603, Tu-
   dors   941.05
   NT   Spanish Armada, 1588
Great Britain—History—1603-1714, Stu-
   arts   941.06
Great Britain—History—1642-1660, Civil
   War and Commonwealth   941.06
   UF   Civil War—England
         Commonwealth of England
Great Britain—History—1714-1837
   941.07
Great Britain—History—1800-1899 (19th
   century)   941.081
   UF   Great Britain—History—19th
         century
   RT   Industrial revolution
Great Britain—History—19th century
   USE   Great Britain—History—1800-
         1899 (19th century)
Great Britain—History—1853-1856, Crime-
   an War
   USE   Crimean War, 1853-1856

BT = Broader Term   NT = Narrower Term   RT = Related Term   SA = See Also   UF = Used For

Great Britain—History—1900-1999 (20th century)   941.082
  UF   Great Britain—History—20th century
Great Britain—History—20th century
  USE   **Great Britain—History—1900-1999 (20th century)**
Great Britain—History—1945-1952   941.085
Great Britain—History—1952-   941.085
Great Britain—Kings and rulers   920; 941.092
  UF   Great Britain—Kings, queens, rulers, etc. *[Former heading]*
  BT   **Kings and rulers**
Great Britain—Kings, queens, rulers, etc.
  USE   **Great Britain—Kings and rulers**
Great Britain—Prime ministers
  USE   **Prime ministers—Great Britain**
Great Britain—Queens
  USE   **Queens—Great Britain**
Great Depression
  USE   **Great Depression, 1929-1939**
Great Depression, 1929-1939 (May subdiv. geog.)   338.5; 909.82
  UF   Business depression, 1929-1939
      Depressions—1929
      Great Depression
  BT   **Depressions**
      Economic conditions
Greece   938; 949.5
  May be subdivided like United States except for *History.*
Greece, Ancient
  USE   **Greece—History—0-323**
Greece—Antiquities   938
  BT   **Classical antiquities**
  NT   **Delphi (Extinct city)**
Greece—Biography   920.038; 920.0495
  UF   Classical biography
  BT   **Biography**
Greece—Civilization   938
  Use for materials on the civilization of Greece, ancient and modern. Materials on the spread of Greek civilization throughout the ancient world following the conquests of Alexander the Great are entered under **Hellenism.** Materials on both ancient Greek and Roman civilizations are entered under **Classical civilization.**
  UF   Civilization, Greek *[Former heading]*

Greek civilization *[Former heading]*
  BT   **Classical civilization**
  NT   **Hellenism**
Greece—Description   914.95
  Use for descriptive materials on modern Greece, including materials for travelers. Descriptive materials on ancient Greece, including accounts by travelers in ancient times, are entered under **Greece—Description—0-323.**
  UF   Greece—Description and travel *[Former heading]*
Greece—Description—0-323   913.8
  Use for descriptive materials on ancient Greece including accounts by travelers of ancient times.
  UF   Ancient Greece—Description
      Greece—Description and geography *[Former heading]*
Greece—Description and geography
  USE   **Greece—Description—0-323**
      Greece—Historical geography
Greece—Description and travel
  USE   **Greece—Description**
Greece—Geography   914.95
  Use for materials on the geography of modern Greece. Materials on the geography of ancient Greece are entered under **Greece—Historical geography.**
  BT   **Geography**
  NT   **Greece—Historical geography**
Greece—Historical geography   911; 913.8
  UF   Classical geography
      Greece—Description and geography *[Former heading]*
  BT   **Ancient geography**
      Greece—Geography
      Historical geography
Greece—History   938; 949.5
Greece—History—0-323   938
  UF   Ancient Greece
      Greece, Ancient
Greece—History—323-1453   949.5
  UF   Greece, Medieval
Greece—History—1453-   949.5
  UF   Greece, Modern
Greece—History—1967-1974   949.507
Greece—History—1974-   949.507
Greece, Medieval
  USE   **Greece—History—323-1453**
Greece, Modern
  USE   **Greece—History—1453-**

BT = Broader Term   NT = Narrower Term   RT = Related Term   SA = See Also   UF = Used For

Greek antiquities
　　USE　　**Classical antiquities**
Greek architecture　722
　　UF　　Architecture, Greek *[Former
　　　　　　heading]*
　　BT　　**Ancient architecture**
　　　　　　Architecture
Greek art　709.38; 709.495
　　UF　　Art, Greek *[Former heading]*
　　　　　　Classical art
　　BT　　**Ancient art**
　　　　　　Art
　　　　　　Classical antiquities
Greek Church
　　USE　　**Orthodox Eastern Church**
Greek civilization
　　USE　　**Greece—Civilization**
Greek language　480
　　　　Use for classical Greek. Modern Greek is
　　entered under **Modern Greek language.** May
　　be subdivided like **English language.**
　　UF　　Classical languages
　　BT　　**Language and languages**
　　RT　　**Modern Greek language**
Greek language, Modern
　　USE　　**Modern Greek language**
Greek letter societies
　　USE　　**Fraternities and sororities**
Greek literature　880
　　　　May use same subdivisions and names of
　　literary forms as for **English literature.**
　　BT　　**Literature**
　　RT　　**Classical literature**
Greek literature, Modern
　　USE　　**Modern Greek literature**
Greek mythology
　　USE　　**Classical mythology**
Greek philosophy
　　USE　　**Ancient philosophy**
Greek sculpture　730.938; 730.9495
　　UF　　Sculpture, Greek *[Former head-
　　　　　　ing]*
　　BT　　**Sculpture**
Green movement
　　USE　　**Environmental movement**
**Greenhouse effect　363.738; 551.5;
　　　　　551.6**
　　UF　　Atmospheric greenhouse effect
　　　　　　Carbon dioxide greenhouse ef-
　　　　　　　fect
　　　　　　Global warming

Greenhouse effect, Atmospheric
　　BT　　**Climate**
　　　　　　Solar radiation
Greenhouse effect, Atmospheric
　　USE　　**Greenhouse effect**
Greenhouses　631.5
　　UF　　Hothouses
　　BT　　**Flower gardening**
　　　　　　Gardening
　　　　　　Horticulture
　　RT　　**Garden rooms**
Greenhouses, Window
　　USE　　**Window gardening**
Greeting cards　741.6; 745.594
　　UF　　Cards, Greeting
　　SA　　types of greeting cards, to be
　　　　　　added as needed
　　NT　　**Christmas cards**
Gregorian chant
　　USE　　**Chants (Plain, Gregorian, etc.)**
Grey Friars
　　USE　　**Franciscans**
Grey market
　　USE　　**Black market**
Grief　152.4; 155.9
　　　　Use for materials on mental suffering or
　　sorrow from causes such as loss or remorse
　　other than the loss of a loved one. Materials
　　on the suffering of those who have lost a
　　loved one are entered under **Bereavement.**
　　UF　　Sorrow
　　BT　　**Emotions**
　　RT　　**Bereavement**
　　　　　　Consolation
　　　　　　Joy and sorrow
Grievance procedures (Public administra-
　　　tion)
　　USE　　**Ombudsman**
Grill cooking
　　USE　　**Barbecue cooking**
Grinding and polishing　621.9
　　UF　　Buffing
　　　　　　Polishing
　　BT　　**Machine shop practice**
　　RT　　**Machine tools**
Grippe
　　USE　　**Influenza**
Grist mills
　　USE　　**Flour mills**
Groceries—Purchasing
　　USE　　**Grocery shopping**

BT = Broader Term　　NT = Narrower Term　　RT = Related Term　　SA = See Also　　UF = Used For

Grocery shopping   641.3

Use for materials on food buying. Materials on the principles and methods involved in the transfer of merchandise from producer to consumer are entered under **Marketing.**

UF   Food buying

Food—Purchasing

Groceries—Purchasing

Marketing (Home economics)

Supermarket shopping

BT   **Home economics**

Shopping

Grocery trade   338.4

BT   **Commerce**

NT   **Supermarkets**

RT   **Food**

Grooming

USE   **Personal grooming**

and types of animals with the subdivision *Grooming,* to be added as needed

Grooming for men

USE   **Personal grooming**

Grooming for women

USE   **Personal grooming**

Grooming, Personal

USE   **Personal grooming**

Grottoes

USE   **Caves**

Ground cushion phenomena   629.3

UF   Air bearing lift

BT   **Aerodynamics**

Pneumatics

NT   **Ground effect machines**

Ground effect machines   629.3

UF   Air bearing vehicles

Air cushion vehicles

Ground proximity machines

Hovercraft

Surface effect machines

BT   **Ground cushion phenomena**

NT   **Helicopters**

Vertically rising airplanes

Ground proximity machines

USE   **Ground effect machines**

Grounds maintenance   712

Use for materials on maintenance of public, industrial, and institutional grounds and large estates.

BT   **Gardening**

NT   **Golf courses**

Roadside improvement

Group discussion

USE   **Discussion groups**

Group dynamics

USE   **Social groups**

Group health

USE   **Health insurance**

Group homes   362; 363.5

Use for materials on planned housing for groups of unrelated people needing supervision.

UF   Community based residences

Group residences

Residential treatment centers

BT   **Institutional care**

Social work

NT   **Halfway houses**

RT   **Foster home care**

Group hospitalization

USE   **Hospitalization insurance**

Group insurance   368.3

Use for materials on group life insurance. Materials on group insurance in other fields are entered under the specific kind of insurance, e.g. **Health insurance.**

UF   Insurance, Group *[Former heading]*

BT   **Life insurance**

Group living

USE   **Communal living**

Group medical practice

USE   **Medical practice**

Group medical practice, Prepaid

USE   **Health maintenance organizations**

Group medical service

USE   **Health insurance**

Group method in teaching

USE   **Cooperative learning**

Group problem solving   153.4

UF   Brain storming

Problem solving, Group *[Former heading]*

Team problem solving

Think tanks

BT   **Problem solving**

Group relations training   302

UF   Encounter groups

Sensitivity training

T groups

BT   **Human relations**

Group residences

USE   **Group homes**

BT = Broader Term   NT = Narrower Term   RT = Related Term   SA = See Also   UF = Used For

Group social work
USE **Social group work**
Group teaching
USE **Cooperative learning**
Group theory 512
UF Groups, Theory of
BT **Algebra**
Mathematics
Number theory
NT **Boolean algebra**
Group travel
USE **Travel**
Group values
USE **Social values**
Group work in education
USE **Cooperative learning**
Group work, Social
USE **Social group work**
Grouping by ability
USE **Ability grouping in education**
Groups of persons
USE **Persons**
Groups, Social
USE **Social groups**
Groups, Theory of
USE **Group theory**
Growing of Christmas trees
USE **Christmas tree growing**
Grown-up abused children
USE **Adult child abuse victims**
Growth 155; 571.8; 612.6
SA subjects with the subdivision
Growth, e.g. **Children—**
Growth; Cities and towns—
Growth; Plants—Growth;
etc., to be added as needed
BT **Physiology**
Growth disorders 616.4
UF Abnormal growth
Abnormalities, Human
Development
Failure to thrive syndrome
Human abnormalities
BT **Metabolism**
NT **Dwarfism**
Giantism
RT **Birth defects**
Growth retardation
USE **Dwarfism**

Guaranteed annual income
Use for materials on compensation provided
by a government to anyone whose annual in-
come falls below a specified level.
UF Annual income guarantee
Guaranteed income
BT **Income**
Guaranteed income
USE **Guaranteed annual income**
Guerillas
USE **Guerrillas**
Guerrilla warfare 355.02; 355.4
Use for materials on the military aspects of
irregular warfare. General and historical mate-
rials are entered under **Guerrillas.**
UF Unconventional warfare
BT **Insurgency**
Military art and science
Tactics
War
Guerrillas (May subdiv. geog.) **356**
Use for general and historical materials.
Materials on the military aspects of irregular
warfare are entered under **Guerrilla warfare.**
UF Guerillas
Partisans
SA individual wars with the subdivi-
sion *Underground movements,*
e.g. **World War, 1939-**
1945—Underground move-
ments; to be added as needed
BT **National liberation movements**
Guests
USE **Entertaining**
Guidance
USE **Counseling**
Guidance counseling, Educational
USE **Educational counseling**
Guidance counseling, School
USE **School counseling**
Guidance, Vocational
USE **Vocational guidance**
Guide dogs 636.7
UF Dog guides
Dogs for the blind
Seeing eye dogs
BT **Animals and the handicapped**
Dogs
Working animals
Guide posts
USE **Signs and signboards**

BT = Broader Term   NT = Narrower Term   RT = Related Term   SA = See Also   UF = Used For

Guidebooks
    USE   names of cities (except ancient cities), countries, states, etc., with the subdivision *Guidebooks,* e.g. **Chicago (Ill.)— Guidebooks; United States— Guidebooks;** etc., to be added as needed

Guided missiles   358.1; 623.4
    UF   Bombs, Flying
            Flying bombs
            Missiles, Guided
    SA   types of missiles and names of specific missiles, to be added as needed
    BT   **Bombs**
            Projectiles
            Rocketry
            Rockets (Aeronautics)
    NT   **Antimissile missiles**
            Ballistic missiles
            Nike rocket

Guitar
    USE   **Guitars**

Guitar music   787.87
    BT   **Instrumental music**

Guitars   787.87
    UF   Guitar *[Former heading]*
    BT   **Stringed instruments**

Gulf States (U.S.)   976
    BT   **United States**

Gulf War, 1991
    USE   **Persian Gulf War, 1991**

Gums and resins   547; 668
    UF   Resins
            Rosin
    BT   **Forest products**
            Industrial chemistry
            Plastics

Gun control   323.4; 344; 363.3
    Use for materials about existing laws governing the purchase and use of firearms and for materials about the political controversy over limiting legal access to firearms and stopping the traffic in illegal firearms.
    UF   Control of guns
            Firearms control
            Firearms—Law and legislation *[Former heading]*
            Guns—Control
            Handgun control

            Right to bear arms
    BT   **Law**
            Legislation

Gunning
    USE   **Hunting**
              Shooting

Gunpowder   623.4
    UF   Powder, Smokeless
            Smokeless powder
    BT   **Explosives**
            Firearms
    RT   **Ammunition**

Guns
    USE   **Firearms**
              Ordnance
              Rifles
              Shotguns

Guns—Control
    USE   **Gun control**

Gunsmithing
    USE   **Firearms industry**

Gymnastics   613.7; 796.44
    UF   Calisthenics
    BT   **Athletics**
            Exercise
            Sports
    RT   **Acrobats and acrobatics**
            Physical education

Gynecology
    USE   **Women—Diseases**
              Women—Health and hygiene

Gypsies   305.891
    UF   Gipsies
            Romanies

Gypsum   553.6
    BT   **Minerals**

Gyroscope   629.135; 681
    BT   **Aeronautical instruments**

H.B.O.
    USE   **Home Box Office**

H bomb
    USE   **Hydrogen bomb**

H.M.O.'s
    USE   **Health maintenance organizations**

Habit   152.3
    BT   **Human behavior**
            Psychology
    NT   **Tobacco habit**
    RT   **Instinct**

BT = Broader Term   NT = Narrower Term   RT = Related Term   SA = See Also   UF = Used For

Habitations
  USE   types of animals with the subdi-
         vision *Habitations,* for materi-
         als on the natural shelters and
         homes animals build for
         themselves, such as burrows,
         dens, lairs, etc., to be added
         as needed
Habitations, Human
  USE   **Domestic architecture**
         Housing
Habitations of domestic animals
  USE   **Animal housing**
Habitations of wild animals
  USE   **Animals—Habitations**
Habits of animals
  USE   **Animal behavior**
Hades
  USE   **Hell**
Haiku   808.1; 808.81; 811, etc.
    May be used for collections of haiku by
  one or several authors or for materials about
  haiku.
  BT   **Poetry**
Hair   612.7; 646.7
    Use for general materials on hair as well
  for as materials on hairdressing and haircut-
  ting.
  UF   Barbering
         Coiffure
         Hair and hairdressing *[Former
           heading]*
         Haircutting
         Hairdressing
         Hairstyles
         Hairstyling
  BT   **Head**
         Personal grooming
  NT   **Wigs**
Hair and hairdressing
  USE   **Hair**
Haircutting
  USE   **Hair**
Hairdressing
  USE   **Hair**
Hairstyles
  USE   **Hair**
Hairstyling
  USE   **Hair**
Halftone process
  USE   **Photoengraving**

Halfway houses   362; 365
    Use for materials on centers for formerly
  institutionalized individuals, such as mental
  patients or drug addicts, that are designed to
  facilitate their readjustment to private life.
  BT   **Correctional institutions**
         Group homes
Halley's comet   523.6
  BT   **Comets**
Hallmarks
  UF   Marks
         Marks on plate
  SA   types of things with identifying
         marks, other than plate, with
         the subdivision *Marks,* e.g.
         Pottery—Marks; to be added
         as needed
  BT   **Plate**
Halloween   394.2646
  UF   All Hallows' Eve
  BT   **Holidays**
Hallucinations and illusions   616.85;
         616.89
  UF   Delusions
         Illusions
  BT   **Abnormal psychology**
         Parapsychology
         Subconsciousness
         Visions
  NT   **Optical illusions**
  RT   **Apparitions**
         Fantasy
         Ghosts
         Magic
         Magic tricks
         Personality disorders
Hallucinogenic drugs
  USE   **Hallucinogens**
Hallucinogenic plants
  USE   **Hallucinogens**
Hallucinogens   615
  UF   Consciousness expanding drugs
         Hallucinogenic drugs
         Hallucinogenic plants
  SA   types of hallucinogens, to be
         added as needed
  BT   **Drugs**
         Psychotropic drugs
         Stimulants
  NT   **Marijuana**

BT = Broader Term   NT = Narrower Term   RT = Related Term   SA = See Also   UF = Used For

Ham radio stations
USE   **Amateur radio stations**
Hand shadows
USE   **Shadow pictures**
Hand weaving
USE   **Weaving**
Handbooks, manuals, etc.
USE   subjects with the subdivision
      Handbooks, manuals, etc., e.g.
      Photography—Handbooks,
      manuals, etc.; to be added as
      needed
Handedness
USE   **Left- and right-handedness**
Handgun control
USE   **Gun control**
Handguns   683.4
UF   Pistols *[Former heading]*
     Revolvers
BT   **Firearms**
Handheld computers
USE   **Portable computers**
Handicapped   305.9; 362.4
UF   Disabled
NT   **Architecture and the handi-**
     capped
     Handicapped children
     Mentally handicapped
     Physically handicapped
     Sick
     Socially handicapped
     Sports for the handicapped
     Vocational guidance for the
     handicapped
Handicapped and animals
USE   **Animals and the handicapped**
Handicapped and architecture
USE   **Architecture and the handi-**
      capped
Handicapped children   362.7
UF   Abnormal children
     Children, Abnormal
BT   **Children**
     Exceptional children
     Handicapped
NT   **Brain damaged children**
     Hyperactive children
     Mainstreaming in education
     Mentally handicapped children

Physically handicapped chil-
dren
Socially handicapped children
Handicapped—Travel   910.2
BT   **Travel**
Handicraft   745.5; 746
   Use for materials on creative work done by
hand, sometimes with the aid of simple tools
or machines.
UF   Crafts (Arts)
SA   types of handicrafts, to be added
     as needed
BT   **Arts**
NT   **Chair caning**
     Collage
     Craft shows
     Egg decoration
     Furniture finishing
     Hooked rugs
     Industrial arts
     Leather work
     Models and model making
     Nature craft
     Paper crafts
     Picture frames and framing
     Quilting
     Weaving
RT   **Arts and crafts movement**
     Creative activities
     Decoration and ornament
     Decorative arts
     Folk art
     Hobbies
     Occupational therapy
Handling of materials
USE   **Materials handling**
Handwriting   652
   Use for materials on writing with a pen or
pencil and for practical or prescriptive guides
to penmanship. General materials on the his-
tory and art of writing are entered under
Writing. Materials on handwriting as an ex-
pression of the writer's character are entered
under **Graphology.**
UF   Copybooks
     Legibility of handwriting
     Penmanship
     Writing—Study and teaching
BT   **Writing**
NT   **Calligraphy**
     Graphology
     Writing of numerals

Hang gliding
    USE   Gliding and soaring
Hanging
    USE   Capital punishment
Hanukkah   296.4; 394.267
    UF   Chanukah
            Feast of Dedication
            Feast of Lights
            Lights, Feast of
            Maccabbees, Feast of the
    BT   Jewish holidays
Happening (Art)
    USE   Performance art
Happiness   158
    UF   Gladness
    BT   Emotions
    NT   Mental health
    RT   Joy and sorrow
            Pleasure
Harassment, Sexual
    USE   Sexual harassment
Harbors (May subdiv. geog.)   386;
        387.1; 627
    UF   Ports
    BT   Civil engineering
            Hydraulic structures
            Merchant marine
            Navigation
            Shipping
            Transportation
    NT   Marinas
    RT   Docks
Hard-of-hearing
    USE   Hearing impaired
Hares
    USE   Rabbits
Harlem Renaissance   810.9; 974.7
    UF   New Negro Movement
            Renaissance, Harlem
    BT   African American art
            African American music
            American literature—African
            American authors
Harmful insects
    USE   Insect pests
Harmony   781.2
    BT   Composition (Music)
            Music
            Music—Theory

Harry S. Truman Library   026
    BT   Presidents—United States—Ar-
            chives
Harvesting machinery   631.3
    UF   Reapers
    BT   Agricultural machinery
Hashish
    USE   Marijuana
Hasidism   296.8
    UF   Chasidism
            Hassidism
    BT   Judaism
Hassidism
    USE   Hasidism
Hastings (East Sussex, England), Battle
        of, 1066   941.02
    BT   Great Britain—History—1066-
            1154, Norman period
Hate crimes   364
    UF   Bias attacks
            Bias crimes
            Bigotry-motivated crimes
            Crimes of hate
            Prejudice-motivated crimes
    BT   Crime
            Discrimination
            Violence
Hatha yoga   613.7
    UF   Yoga exercises
            Yoga, Hatha
    BT   Exercise
            Yoga
Hats   391.4; 646.5; 687
    UF   Millinery [Former heading]
    BT   Clothing and dress
            Costume
Haunted houses
    USE   Ghosts
Hawking
    USE   Falconry
Hay   633.2
    SA   types of hay crops, e.g. Alfalfa;
            to be added as needed
    BT   Farm produce
            Forage plants
    RT   Feeds
            Grasses
Hay fever   616.2
    BT   Allergy

BT = Broader Term   NT = Narrower Term   RT = Related Term   SA = See Also   UF = Used For

Hazardous materials
   USE   **Hazardous substances**

Hazardous occupations   331.7
   UF   Dangerous occupations
          Injurious occupations
          Occupations, Dangerous *[Former heading]*
   BT   **Occupations**
   RT   **Industrial accidents**
          Occupational diseases
          Occupational health and safety

Hazardous substances   363.17; 604.7
   UF   Dangerous materials
          Hazardous materials
          Inflammable substances
          Toxic substances
   BT   **Materials**
   NT   **Hazardous wastes**
          Poisons and poisoning

Hazardous substances—Transportation
       363.17; 604.7
   BT   **Transportation**

Hazardous waste disposal
   USE   **Hazardous wastes**

Hazardous waste sites   363.72; 628.4
   UF   Chemical landfills
          Dumps, Toxic
          Toxic dumps
   BT   **Landfills**
   NT   **Love Canal Chemical Waste Landfill (Niagara Falls, N.Y.)**

Hazardous wastes   363.72
   UF   Hazardous waste disposal
          Toxic wastes
          Wastes, Hazardous
   BT   **Hazardous substances**
          Industrial wastes
          Refuse and refuse disposal
   RT   **Medical wastes**
          Pollution

HBO
   USE   **Home Box Office**

HDTV (Television)
   USE   **High definition television**

Head   611; 612
   BT   **Anatomy**
   NT   **Brain**
          Ear
          Eye

          Face
          Hair
          Nose
          Phrenology
          Teeth

Heads of state (May subdiv. geog.)
       352.23; 920
   UF   Rulers
          State, Heads of
   SA   names of individual heads of state, to be added as needed
   BT   **Executive power**
          Statesmen
   NT   **Dictators**
          Kings and rulers
          Presidents

Healing, Mental
   USE   **Mental healing**

Healing, Spiritual
   USE   **Spiritual healing**

Health   613
      Use for materials on physical, mental, and social well-being. Materials on personal body care are entered under **Hygiene.**
   UF   Personal health
   SA   parts of the body with the subdivision *Care,* e.g. **Foot—Care;** classes of persons and ethnic groups with the subdivision *Health and hygiene,* e.g. **Women—Health and hygiene;** and subjects and names of wars with the subdivision *Health aspects,* e.g. **World War, 1939-1945—Health aspects;** to be added as needed
   BT   **Medicine**
          Physiology
          Preventive medicine
   NT   **Children—Health and hygiene**
          Diet
          Elderly—Health and hygiene
          Exercise
          Health education
          Health self-care
          Infants—Health and hygiene
          Mental health
          Physical fitness
          Public health
          Rest

BT = Broader Term   NT = Narrower Term   RT = Related Term   SA = See Also   UF = Used For

Health—*Continued*
    Sleep
    Women—Health and hygiene
  RT   **Diseases**
    Holistic medicine
    Hygiene
Health and hygiene
  USE   classes of persons and ethnic
      groups with the subdivision
      Health and hygiene, e.g.
      Women—Health and hy-
      giene; and parts of the body
      with the subdivision *Care,*
      e.g. **Foot—Care; Skin—**
      Care; etc., to be added as
      needed
Health aspects
  USE   subjects, industries, and wars
      with the subdivision *Health*
      aspects, e.g. **World War,**
      1939-1945—Health aspects;
      to be added as needed
Health boards   614.06
  UF   Boards of health
    Public health boards
  BT   **Public health**
Health care
  USE   **Medical care**
Health care delivery
  USE   **Medical care**
Health care personnel
  USE   **Medical personnel**
Health care reform (May subdiv. geog.)
    362.1
  UF   Health reform
    Health system reform
    Medical care reform
    Reform of health care delivery
    Reform of medical care delivery
  RT   **Health insurance**
    Medical care
Health care, Self
  USE   **Health self-care**
Health clubs
  USE   **Physical fitness centers**
Health counseling   362.1; 613
  BT   **Counseling**
    Health education
Health education   372.3; 613.07
  UF   Health—Study and teaching

Hygiene—Study and teaching
  BT   **Education**
    Health
  NT   **Drug education**
    Health counseling
    School hygiene
  RT   **Children—Health and hygiene**
    School nurses
Health—Environmental aspects
  USE   **Environmental health**
Health examinations
  USE   **Periodic health examinations**
Health foods
  USE   **Natural foods**
Health, Industrial
  USE   **Occupational health and safety**
Health insurance   368.38
  UF   Disability insurance
    Group health
    Group medical service
    Health plans, Prepaid
    Insurance, Disability
    Insurance, Health *[Former head-*
      ing]
    Insurance, Sickness
    Medical care, Prepaid
    Medical insurance
    Medical service, Prepaid
    Prepaid health plans
    Prepaid medical care
    Sickness insurance
  BT   **Insurance**
  NT   **Health maintenance organiza-**
      tions
    Hospitalization insurance
    National health insurance
    Workers' compensation
  RT   **Health care reform**
Health insurance, Government
  USE   **National health insurance**
Health insurance, National
  USE   **National health insurance**
Health maintenance organizations
    368.38; 610.6
  UF   Comprehensive health care orga-
      nizations
    Group medical practice, Prepaid
    H.M.O.'s
    HMOs
    Prepaid group medical practice

BT = Broader Term   NT = Narrower Term   RT = Related Term   SA = See Also   UF = Used For

Health maintenance organizations—*Continued*
  BT   **Health insurance**
          Medical care
Health manpower
  USE   **Medical personnel**
Health personnel
  USE   **Medical personnel**
Health plans, Prepaid
  USE   **Health insurance**
Health professions
  USE   **Medical personnel**
Health program evaluation
  USE   **Public health—Evaluation**
Health, Public
  USE   **Public health**
Health reform
  USE   **Health care reform**
Health resorts (May subdiv. geog.)   613
  UF   Health resorts, spas, etc. *[Former heading]*
          Health spas
          Sanatoriums
          Spas
          Watering places
  BT   **Resorts**
  RT   **Hydrotherapy**
Health resorts, spas, etc.
  USE   **Health resorts**
         Physical fitness centers
Health sciences personnel
  USE   **Medical personnel**
Health self-care   613; 616
  UF   Health care, Self
          Medical self-care
          Self-care, Health *[Former heading]*
          Self-care, Medical
          Self-examination, Medical
          Self health care
          Self-help medical care
          Self-medication
  BT   **Alternative medicine**
          Health
          Medical care
  NT   **First aid**
          Nutrition
          Physical fitness
  RT   **Holistic medicine**
          Popular medicine

Health services personnel
  USE   **Medical personnel**
Health spas
  USE   **Health resorts**
         Physical fitness centers
Health—Study and teaching
  USE   **Health education**
Health system reform
  USE   **Health care reform**
Healths, Drinking of
  USE   **Toasts**
Hearing   152.1; 612.8
  UF   Acoustics
  BT   **Senses and sensation**
          Sound
  RT   **Deafness**
          Ear
          Listening
Hearing aids   617.8
  BT   **Deafness**
Hearing ear dogs   636.7
  UF   Dogs for the deaf
  BT   **Animals and the handicapped**
          Deaf—Means of communication
          Dogs
Hearing impaired   362.4; 617.8
  UF   Hard-of-hearing
          Partial hearing
          Partially hearing
  BT   **Physically handicapped**
  NT   **Deaf**
Heart   573.1; 611; 612.1
  BT   **Cardiovascular system**
  NT   **Artificial heart**
Heart—Anatomy   573.1; 611
  BT   **Anatomy**
Heart attack   616.1
  UF   Heart—Infarction
          Myocardial infarction
  BT   **Heart diseases**
Heart disease
  USE   **Heart diseases**
Heart—Diseases
  USE   **Heart diseases**
Heart diseases   616.1
  UF   Cardiac diseases
          Coronary heart diseases
          Heart disease

BT = Broader Term   NT = Narrower Term   RT = Related Term   SA = See Also   UF = Used For

Heart diseases—*Continued*
      Heart—Diseases *[Former head-ing]*
  BT   **Diseases**
  NT   **Angina pectoris**
        Heart attack
Heart diseases—Prevention   616.1
  BT   **Preventive medicine**
Heart—Infarction
  USE **Heart attack**
Heart—Physiology   612.1
  BT   **Physiology**
Heart resuscitation
  USE **Cardiac resuscitation**
Heart—Surgery   617.4
  UF   Open heart surgery
  BT   **Surgery**
Heart—Surgery—Nursing   610.73;
      617.4
  BT   **Nursing**
Heart—Transplantation   617.4
  BT   **Transplantation of organs, tis-sues, etc.**
Heat   536
  BT   **Electromagnetic waves**
  NT   **Steam**
        Thermometers
  RT   **Combustion**
        Fire
        Temperature
        Thermodynamics
Heat—Conduction   536
Heat engines   621.4
  UF   Hot air engines
  BT   **Engines**
        Thermodynamics
  NT   **Steam engines**
Heat insulating materials
  USE **Insulation (Heat)**
Heat pumps   621.4
  BT   **Pumping machinery**
        Thermodynamics
Heat—Transmission   536
Heathenism
  USE **Paganism**
Heating   644; 697
  SA   subjects with the subdivision
      Heating and ventilation, e.g.
      Houses—Heating and venti-lation; to be added as needed

  BT   **Home economics**
  NT   **Chimneys**
        Electric heating
        Fireplaces
        Furnaces
        Hot air heating
        Hot water heating
        Houses—Heating and ventila-tion
        Insulation (Heat)
        Oil burners
        Radiant heating
        Solar heating
        Space heaters
        Steam heating
        Stoves
  RT   **Fuel**
        Ventilation
Heaven   236; 291.2
  BT   **Eschatology**
        Future life
  NT   **Angels**
  RT   **Paradise**
Heavy water
  USE **Deuterium oxide**
Hebrew language   492.4
      May be subdivided like **English language.**
  UF   Jewish language
        Jews—Language
  BT   **Language and languages**
Hebrew literature   892.4
      May use same subdivisions and names of literary forms as for **English literature.**
  UF   Jews—Literature
  BT   **Literature**
  NT   **Bible**
        Cabala
        Talmud
  RT   **Jewish literature**
Hebrews
  USE **Jews**
Heirs
  USE **Inheritance and succession**
Helicopters   387.7; 629.133
  UF   Aircraft
  BT   **Aeronautics**
        Airplanes
        Ground effect machines
Helicopters—Piloting   629.132
  BT   **Airplanes—Piloting**

BT = Broader Term   NT = Narrower Term   RT = Related Term   SA = See Also   UF = Used For

Heliports 387.7
BT Airports
Helium 546
BT Chemical elements
Gases
Hell 236; 291.2
UF Eternal punishment
Hades
Retribution
BT Eschatology
Future life
Hellenism 938
Use for materials on the spread of Greek civilization throughout the ancient world following the conquests of Alexander the Great. Materials limited to the civilization of Greece, ancient and modern, are entered under **Greece—Civilization**. Materials on both ancient Greek and Roman civilizations are entered under **Classical civilization.**
BT Greece—Civilization
Helpful insects
USE **Beneficial insects**
Helpfulness
USE **Helping behavior**
Helping behavior 158
UF Assistance in emergencies
Behavior, Helping
Emergency assistance
Helpfulness
BT **Human behavior**
Human relations
NT **Counseling**
Hemp 633.5; 677
BT **Fibers**
RT **Rope**
Heraldry 929.6
UF Arms, Coats of
Coats of arms
Crests
Devices (Heraldry)
Emblems
Pedigrees
BT **Archeology**
Signs and symbols
Symbolism
NT **Flags**
Insignia
Mottoes
Seals (Numismatics)
RT **Chivalry**
Decorations of honor

Genealogy
Knights and knighthood
National emblems
Nobility
Herbage
USE **Grasses**
Herbal medicine
USE **Medical botany**
Herbals
USE **Herbs**
Materia medica
Medical botany
Herbaria
USE **Plants—Collection and preservation**
Herbicides 632; 668
UF Defoliants
Plants—Effect of poisons on *[Former heading]*
Weed killers
SA types of herbicides, e.g. **Agent Orange;** to be added as needed
BT **Agricultural chemicals**
Pesticides
NT **Agent Orange**
RT **Plants**
Spraying and dusting
Herbs 581.6; 635
UF Herbals
BT **Cooking**
Plants
Herbs, Medical
USE **Medical botany**
Hereditary diseases
USE **Medical genetics**
Hereditary succession
USE **Inheritance and succession**
Heredity 576.5
UF Ancestry
Descent
Genes
Inheritance (Biology)
BT **Biology**
Breeding
NT **Chromosomes**
DNA
Variation (Biology)
RT **Eugenics**
Genetics

BT = Broader Term   NT = Narrower Term   RT = Related Term   SA = See Also   UF = Used For

339

Heredity—*Continued*
    Mendel's law
    Natural selection
Heredity of diseases
  USE   **Medical genetics**
Hereford cattle   636.2
  BT   **Beef cattle**
Hermeneutics, Biblical
  USE   **Bible—Criticism**
Hermetic art and philosophy
  USE   **Alchemy**
        Astrology
        Occultism
Hermits   920
  UF   Recluses
  BT   **Eccentrics and eccentricities**
  RT   **Monasticism and religious or-
        ders**
        Saints
Heroes and heroines   920
  UF   Heroines
        Heroism
  BT   **Adventure and adventurers**
  NT   **Explorers**
        Martyrs
        Saints
  RT   **Courage**
        Mythology
Heroin   362.29; 615
  BT   **Morphine**
        Narcotics
Heroines
  USE   **Heroes and heroines**
Heroism
  USE   **Courage**
        Heroes and heroines
Hertzian waves
  USE   **Electric waves**
Hi-fi systems
  USE   **High-fidelity sound systems**
Hibernation   591.56
  UF   Animals—Hibernation *[Former
        heading]*
        Hibernation of animals
  BT   **Animal behavior**
Hibernation of animals
  USE   **Hibernation**
Hidden economy
  USE   **Underground economy**

Hidden treasure
  USE   **Buried treasure**
Hides and skins   636.088; 675
  UF   Pelts
        Skins
  BT   **Animal products**
  RT   **Fur**
        Leather
        Tanning
Hieroglyphics   411
  BT   **Inscriptions**
        Writing
  NT   **Rosetta stone inscription**
  RT   **Picture writing**
High blood pressure
  USE   **Hypertension**
High definition television   621.388
  UF   HDTV (Television)
  BT   **Television**
High-fidelity sound systems   621.389
  UF   Hi-fi systems
  BT   **Electronics**
        **Sound—Recording and repro-
        ducing**
  NT   **Stereophonic sound systems**
  RT   **Phonograph**
High-frequency radio
  USE   **Shortwave radio**
High rise buildings
  USE   **Skyscrapers**
High risk students
  USE   **At risk students**
High school dropouts
  USE   **Dropouts**
High school education
  USE   **Secondary education**
High school libraries   027.8
  UF   Junior high school libraries
        School libraries (High school)
        [Former heading]
        Secondary school libraries
  BT   **School libraries**
  RT   **Young adults' library services**
High school life
  USE   **High school students**
High school students   373
  UF   High school life
        High schools—Students
  BT   **Students**

BT = Broader Term   NT = Narrower Term   RT = Related Term   SA = See Also   UF = Used For

High school yearbooks
    USE   **School yearbooks**

High schools (May subdiv. geog.)   **373**
    UF   Secondary schools
    BT   **Public schools**
           Schools
    NT   **Commencements**
           Junior high schools
    RT   **Secondary education**

High schools, Junior
    USE   **Junior high schools**

High schools, Rural
    USE   **Rural schools**

High schools—Students
    USE   **High school students**

High society
    USE   **Upper class**

High speed aerodynamics
    USE   **Supersonic aerodynamics**

High speed aeronautics   **629.132**
    UF   Aeronautics, High speed
    BT   **Aeronautics**
    NT   **Aerothermodynamics**
           Rocket planes
           Rockets (Aeronautics)
           Supersonic aerodynamics

High tech
    USE   **Technology**

High technology
    USE   **Technology**

High treason
    USE   **Treason**

High-yield junk bonds
    USE   **Junk bonds**

Higher criticism
    USE   **Bible—Criticism**

Higher education   **378**
    Use for general materials on education
above the secondary level.
    UF   Education, Higher *[Former*
           heading]
    BT   **Education**
    NT   **Adult education**
           Colleges and universities
           Junior colleges
           Professional education
           Technical education
           University extension

Highjacking of airplanes
    USE   **Hijacking of airplanes**

Highland clans
    USE   **Clans—Scotland**

Highland costume
    USE   **Tartans**

Highway accidents
    USE   **Traffic accidents**

Highway beautification
    USE   **Roadside improvement**

Highway construction
    USE   **Roads**

Highway engineering   **625.7**
    UF   Road engineering
    BT   **Civil engineering**
           Engineering
    NT   **Traffic engineering**
    RT   **Roads**

Highway transportation   **388.3**
    UF   Transportation, Highway *[For-*
           mer heading]
    BT   **Transportation**
    NT   **Automobiles**
           Buses
           Trucks

Highwaymen
    USE   **Thieves**

Highways
    USE   **Roads**

Hijacking of airplanes   **364.15**
    Use same form for the hijacking of other
modes of transportation.
    UF   Air piracy
           Airlines—Hijacking
           Airplane hijacking
           Airplanes—Hijacking
           Commercial aeronautics—Hijack-
             ing
           Highjacking of airplanes
           Sky hijacking
           Skyjacking
    BT   **Offenses against public safety**

Hiking   **796.51**
    SA   types of hiking, e.g.
           Backpacking; to be added as
           needed
    BT   **Outdoor life**
    NT   **Backpacking**
           Orienteering
    RT   **Direction sense**
           Walking

Hillbilly music
    USE   **Country music**

BT = Broader Term   NT = Narrower Term   RT = Related Term   SA = See Also   UF = Used For

Hindoos
USE   Hindus
Hindu philosophy   181
    UF   Philosophy, Hindu *[Former
            heading]*
    BT   **Philosophy**
    NT   **Yoga**
Hinduism   294.5
    BT   **Religions**
    NT   **Vedas**
            Yoga
    RT   **Brahmanism**
Hindus   294.5092
    UF   Hindoos
    RT   **East Indians**
Hippies (May subdiv. geog.)   **306**
    UF   Yippies
    BT   **Bohemianism**
Hippies—United States   306
    UF   United States—Hippies
Hire-purchase plan
    USE   **Installment plan**
Hispanic American literature (English)
    USE   **American literature—Hispanic
            American authors**
Hispanic American literature (Spanish)
    USE   **American literature (Spanish)**
Hispanic Americans   305.868; 973
        Use for materials on United States citizens
    of Latin American descent. Materials on citi-
    zens of Latin American countries are entered
    under **Latin Americans.**
    UF   Latinos (U.S.)
    SA   names of groups of United
            States citizens from specific
            countries, e.g. **Mexican
            Americans;** to be added as
            needed
    NT   **Mexican Americans**
    RT   **Ethnology—United States**
Hispano-American War, 1898
    USE   **Spanish-American War, 1898**
Historians   907; 920
    UF   Historiographers
    SA   historians of particular countries,
            e.g. **American historians;** to
            be added as needed
    BT   **Authors**
    NT   **American historians**
            Archeologists
    RT   **Historiography**

History
Historians, American
    USE   **American historians**
Historic buildings (May subdiv. geog.)
            363.6; 720.9
    UF   Historic houses
    SA   types of historic buildings, e.g.
            **Castles; Church buildings;
            Temples; Theaters;** etc., to
            be added as needed
    BT   **Buildings**
            Historic sites
            Monuments
    NT   **Literary landmarks**
**Historic buildings—Chicago (Ill.)
            720.9773; 977.3**
    UF   Chicago (Ill.)—Historic buildings
**Historic buildings—Ohio   720.9771;
            977.1**
    UF   Ohio—Historic buildings *[For-
            mer heading]*
**Historic buildings—United States
            720.973; 973**
    UF   United States—Historic buildings
    RT   **Colonial architecture**
Historic houses
    USE   **Historic buildings**
Historic sites (May subdiv. geog.)   **363.6**
    UF   Historical sites
    BT   **Archeology**
            History
    NT   **Historic buildings**
    RT   **National monuments**
Historical atlases   911
    UF   Atlases, Historical *[Former
            heading]*
            Historical geography—Maps
            History—Atlases
            Maps, Historical
    BT   **Atlases**
    RT   **Historical geography**
Historical chronology   902
        Use for materials in which historical events
    are arranged by date.
    UF   Chronology, Historical *[Former
            heading]*
            Dates, Historical
            History—Chronology
    SA   ethnic groups, corporate bodies,
            military services, topics not

BT = Broader Term   NT = Narrower Term   RT = Related Term   SA = See Also   UF = Used For

Historical chronology—*Continued*
inherently historical, and names of places with the subdivision *History—Chronology,* e.g. **Indians of North America—History—Chronology; United States—History—Chronology;** and names of individual persons, wars, sacred works, topics that are inherently historical, and topics not subdivided by *History,* such as art, music, literture, etc., with the subdivision *Chronology,* e.g. **Bible—Chronology;** to be added as needed

BT   **Chronology**
      History
NT   **Indians of North America—History—Chronology**
      United States—History—Chronology

Historical dictionaries
USE   **History—Dictionaries**

Historical drama   **808.82; 812, etc.**
May be used for individual works, collections, or materials about historical drama.

UF   Chronicle history (Drama)
      Chronicle plays
      History plays
SA   historical topics, events, or personages with the subdivision *Drama,* e.g. **United States—History—1861-1865, Civil War—Drama; Napoleon I, Emperor of the French, 1769-1821—Drama;** to be added as needed
BT   **Drama**
NT   **United States—History—1861-1865, Civil War—Drama**
      United States—History—Drama
      War films
      Western films

Historical fiction   **808.83; 813, etc**
May be used for individual works, collections, or materials about fiction set during a time significantly prior to the time in which it was written.

UF   Historical novels
      Historical romances

SA   historical topics, events, or personages with the subdivision *Fiction,* e.g. **Slavery—United States—Fiction; United States—History—1861-1865, Civil War—Fiction; Napoleon I, Emperor of the French, 1769-1821—Fiction;** etc., to be added as needed
BT   **Fiction**
NT   **Gothic novels**
      Regency novels
      War stories
      Western stories
RT   **Biographical fiction**
      History

Historical geography   **911**
Use for materials that discuss the extent of territory held by the states or nations at a given period of history. Materials limited to one country or region still existing in modern times are entered under the name of the place with the subdivision *Historical geography.* Materials on the geography of regions or countries of antiquity that no longer exist as such in modern times are entered under the name of the place with the subdivision *Geography.*

UF   Geography, Historical *[Former heading]*
SA   names of modern countries or regions with the subdivision *Historical geography,* e.g. **Greece—Historical geography; United States—Historical geography;** etc.; and names of places of antiquity with the subdivision *Geography,* e.g. **Gaul—Geography;** to be added as needed
BT   **Geography**
      History
NT   **Ancient geography**
      Gaul—Geography
      Greece—Historical geography
      Rome—Geography
      United States—Historical geography
RT   **Historical atlases**

Historical geography—Maps
USE   **Historical atlases**

Historical geology
USE   **Stratigraphic geology**

BT = Broader Term   NT = Narrower Term   RT = Related Term   SA = See Also   UF = Used For

Historical materialism
    USE   **Dialectical materialism**
Historical novels
    USE   **Historical fiction**
Historical poetry   808.81; 811, etc.
    May be used for individual works, collections, or materials about historical poetry.
    UF   Poetry, Historical
    BT   **Narrative poetry**
    NT   **Bunker Hill (Boston, Mass.),
            Battle of, 1775—Poetry
            United States—History—Poetry
            World War, 1939-1945—Poetry**
Historical records—Preservation
    USE   **Archives**
Historical romances
    USE   **Historical fiction**
Historical sites
    USE   **Historic sites**
Historical societies
    USE   **History—Societies**
Historiographers
    USE   **Historians**
Historiography   907
    Use for materials limited to the study and criticism of sources of history, methods of historical research, and the writing of history. General materials on history as a science, including the principles of history, the influence of various factors on history, and the relation of the science of history to other subjects, are entered under **History.** Materials on the interpretation and meaning of history and on the course of events and their resulting consequences are entered under **History—Philosophy.**
    UF   History—Criticism
            History—Historiography
    SA   subjects, wars, historical events, and names of countries, cities, etc., with the subdivision *Historiography,* to be added as needed
    BT   **Authorship
            History**
    NT   **History—Sources
            Local history
            Philosophy—Historiography
            United States—Historiography
            United States—History—1861-
            1865, Civil War—Historiography**
    RT   **Historians**

History   900
    Use for general materials on history as a science. This includes the principles of history, the influence of various factors on history, and the relation of the science of history to other subjects. Materials on the interpretation and meaning of history and on the course of events and their resulting consequences are entered under **History—Philosophy.** Materials limited to the study and criticism of sources of history, methods of historical research, and the writing of history are entered under **Historiography.**
    UF   Social studies
    SA   countries, states, etc., with the subdivisions *Antiquities; Foreign relations; History; Politics and government;* and subjects with the subdivision *History,* or, for literature, film, and music headings, *History and criticism,* e.g. **Art—History; English literature—History and criticism;** to be added as needed
    BT   **Humanities
            Social sciences**
    NT   **Ancient history
            Archeology
            Art—History
            Biography
            Chronology
            Church history
            Constitutional history
            Exploration
            Genealogy
            Historic sites
            Historical chronology
            Historical geography
            Historiography
            Indians of North America—
            History
            Local history
            Massacres
            Military history
            Modern history
            Naval history
            Numismatics
            Oral history
            Seals (Numismatics)
            Women—History
            World history**
    RT   **Civilization**

BT = Broader Term   NT = Narrower Term   RT = Related Term   SA = See Also   UF = Used For

History—*Continued*
    Historians
    Historical fiction
History, Ancient
    USE   **Ancient history**
History—Atlases
    USE   **Historical atlases**
History, Biblical
    USE   **Bible—History of biblical**
            events
History—Chronology
    USE   **Historical chronology**
History, Church
    USE   **Church history**
History—Criticism
    USE   **Historiography**
History—Dictionaries   903
    UF   Historical dictionaries
    BT   **Encyclopedias and dictionaries**
    NT   **United States—History—Dic-**
           tionaries
History—Historiography
    USE   **Historiography**
History, Local
    USE   **Local history**
History, Medieval
    USE   **Middle Ages—History**
History, Military
    USE   **Military history**
History, Modern
    USE   **Modern history**
History, Modern—19th century
    USE   **Modern history—1800-1899**
            (19th century)
History, Modern—20th century
    USE   **Modern history—1900-1999**
            (20th century)
History, Naval
    USE   **Naval history**
History, Oral
    USE   **Oral history**
History—Periodicals   905
History—Philosophy   901

    Use for materials on the interpretation and meaning of history and on the course of events and their resulting consequences. General materials on history as a science, including the principles of history, the influences of various factors on history, and the relation of the science of history to other subjects, are entered under **History**. Materials limited to the study and criticism of the sources of his-

tory, methods of historical research, and the writing of history are entered under **Historiography**.
    UF   Philosophy of history
    BT   **Philosophy**
History plays
    USE   **Historical drama**
History—Societies   906
    UF   Historical societies
    BT   **Societies**
    NT   **Chicago (Ill.)—History—**
            Societies
            Ohio—History—Societies
            United States—History—
            Societies
History—Sources   900
    Use for collections of documents, records, and other source materials upon which narrative history is based and for materials about such sources.
    SA   historical subjects, periods of history, individual literary and sacred works, and names of wars with the subdivision *Sources,* e.g. **World War, 1939-1945—Sources;** and subjects, ethnic groups, classes of persons, coporate bodies, and names of countries, states, etc., with the subdivision *History—Sources;* e.g. **United States—History—Sources;** to be added as needed
    BT   **Historiography**
    NT   **Archives**
            Charters
            Ohio—History—Sources
            United States—History—1861-
            1865, Civil War—Sources
            United States—History—
            Sources
            World War, 1939-1945—
            Sources
History, Universal
    USE   **World history**
Histrionics
    USE   **Acting**
            Theater
Hittites   939
    BT   **Ancient history**

BT = Broader Term   NT = Narrower Term   RT = Related Term   SA = See Also   UF = Used For

HIV disease
    USE   AIDS (Disease)
HMOs
    USE   Health maintenance organiza-
               tions
Hoaxes
    USE   Impostors and imposture
Hobbies   790.1
    UF   Avocations
              Recreations
    SA   types of hobbies, to be added as
              needed
    BT   **Amusements**
              Leisure
              Recreation
    NT   **Collectors and collecting**
    RT   **Handicraft**
Hoboes
    USE   **Tramps**
Hockey   796.962
    UF   Ice hockey *[Former heading]*
    BT   **Winter sports**
Hogs
    USE   **Pigs**
Hoisting machinery   621.8
    UF   Lifts
    SA   types of hoisting machinery, to
              be added as needed
    BT   **Machinery**
    NT   **Cranes, derricks, etc.**
              Elevators
    RT   **Conveying machinery**
Holiday decorations   394.26; 745.5
    UF   Decorations, Holiday
    BT   **Decoration and ornament**
Holidays (May subdiv. geog.)   **394.26**
    Use for materials on days of general ex-
emption from work or days publicly dedicated
to the commemoration of some person, event,
or principle. Materials on occasions other than
holidays devoted to festive community observances or to programs of cultural events are
entered under **Festivals.**
    UF   Anniversaries
              Legal holidays
              National holidays
    SA   names of holidays, to be added
              as needed
    BT   **Days**
              Manners and customs
    NT   **April Fools' Day**
              Christmas

              Fourth of July
              Halloween
              Lincoln's Birthday
              Martin Luther King Day
              Memorial Day
              Religious holidays
              Thanksgiving Day
              Valentine's Day
              Veterans Day
    RT   **Festivals**
              Vacations
Holidays, Jewish
    USE   **Jewish holidays**
Holistic health
    USE   **Holistic medicine**
Holistic medicine   610; 615.5
    UF   Holistic health
              Humanistic medicine
              Wholistic medicine
    BT   **Alternative medicine**
              Medicine
    RT   **Health**
              Health self-care
              Mind and body
Holland
    USE   **Netherlands**
Holmes, Sherlock (Fictitious character)
        823
    UF   Sherlock Holmes (Fictitious
              character)
Holocaust, 1933-1945   940.53
    UF   Destruction of Jews (1933-1945)
              Extermination of Jews (1933-
              1945)
              Holocaust, Jewish (1933-1945)
              [Former heading]
              Holocaust, Jewish (1939-1945)
              Jewish Holocaust (1933-1945)
              [Former heading]
    SA   names of concentration camps,
              to be added as needed
    BT   **Antisemitism**
              Jews—Persecutions
    NT   **Holocaust survivors**
    RT   **World War, 1939-1945—Jews**
Holocaust, 1933-1945—Personal narra-
        tives   920
    BT   **Autobiographies**
Holocaust, Jewish (1933-1945)
    USE   **Holocaust, 1933-1945**

BT = Broader Term   NT = Narrower Term   RT = Related Term   SA = See Also   UF = Used For

Holocaust, Jewish (1939-1945)
　USE　**Holocaust, 1933-1945**
Holocaust survivors　940.53
　　Use for materials on Jews who survived persecution or imprisonment under the Nazis. Accounts by Holocaust survivors are entered under **Holocaust, 1933-1945—Personal narratives.**
　BT　**Holocaust, 1933-1945**
Holography　774
　UF　Laser photography
　　　Lensless photography
　　　Photography, Laser
　　　Photography, Lensless
　BT　**Laser recording**
　　　Photography
　RT　**Three dimensional photography**
Holstein-Friesian cattle　636.2
　UF　Friesian cattle
　BT　**Dairy cattle**
Holy communion
　USE　**Lord's Supper**
Holy days
　USE　**Religious holidays**
Holy Ghost
　USE　**Holy Spirit**
Holy Grail
　USE　**Grail**
Holy Office
　USE　**Inquisition**
Holy Roman Empire　943
　BT　**Europe—History**
　　　Middle Ages—History
Holy Scriptures
　USE　**Bible**
Holy See
　USE　**Papacy**
　　　Popes
Holy Spirit　231
　UF　Holy Ghost
　BT　**God—Christianity**
　　　Trinity
　RT　**Spiritual gifts**
Holy Week　263
　BT　**Church year**
　　　Lent
　NT　**Easter**
　　　Good Friday
Home　306.8; 640
　RT　**Family**

Home economics
Home accidents　363.13
　BT　**Accidents**
　NT　**First aid**
Home and school　371.19
　UF　School and home
　BT　**Education**
　RT　**Parent-teacher associations**
　　　Parent-teacher relationships
Home-based education
　USE　**Home schooling**
Home Box Office　384.55
　UF　H.B.O.
　　　HBO
　BT　**Cable television**
　　　Subscription television
Home business　338.6; 658
　UF　At-home employment
　　　Cottage industry
　　　Home labor
　　　Work at home
　　　Working at home
　BT　**Business**
　　　Self-employed
　　　Small business
　NT　**Telecommuting**
Home buying
　USE　**Houses—Buying and selling**
Home care
　USE　**Home care services**
　　　and classes of persons with the subdivision *Home care,* e.g. **Elderly—Home care;** to be added as needed
Home care services　362.1
　UF　Home care
　　　Home health care
　　　Home medical care
　　　Respite care
　SA　classes of persons with the subdivision *Home care,* e.g. **Elderly—Home care;** to be added as needed
　BT　**Medical care**
　NT　**Elderly—Home care**
　　　Home nursing
Home computers
　USE　**Microcomputers**
Home conservatories
　USE　**Garden rooms**

BT = Broader Term　　NT = Narrower Term　　RT = Related Term　　SA = See Also　　UF = Used For

Home construction
USE House construction
Home decoration
USE Interior design
Home delivered meals programs
USE Meals on wheels programs
Home designs
USE Domestic architecture—Designs and plans
Home economics   640
UF Domestic arts
Efficiency, Household
Homemaking
Household management
Housekeeping
BT Family life education
NT Consumer education
Cooking
Cost and standard of living
Entertaining
Food
Fuel
Grocery shopping
Heating
House cleaning
Household employees
Household equipment and supplies
Household pests
Interior design
Laundry
Mobile home living
Moving
Sewing
Shopping
Storage in the home
Ventilation
RT Home
Homemakers
Home economics—Accounting
USE Household budgets
Home education
USE Correspondence schools and courses
Home schooling
Self-instruction
Home health care
USE Home care services
Home instruction
USE Home schooling

Home labor
USE Home business
Telecommuting
Home life
USE Family life
Home loans
USE Mortgages
Home medical care
USE Home care services
Home missions, Christian
USE Christian missions
Home movies
USE Amateur films
Home nursing   649.8
BT Home care services
Nursing
RT Sick
Home purchase
USE Houses—Buying and selling
Home remodeling
USE Houses—Remodeling
Home repairing
USE Houses—Maintenance and repair
Home repairs
USE Houses—Maintenance and repair
Home schooling   371.04
Use for materials on the provision of compulsory education in the home as an alternative to traditional public or private schooling. General materials on the instruction of children in the home are entered under **Child rearing.**
UF Home-based education
Home education
Home instruction [Former heading]
Home teaching by parents
Homeschooling
BT Education
Home service insurance
USE Industrial life insurance
Home sharing
USE Shared housing
Home storage
USE Storage in the home
Home study courses
USE Correspondence schools and courses
Self-instruction

BT = Broader Term   NT = Narrower Term   RT = Related Term   SA = See Also   UF = Used For

Home teaching by parents
  USE   **Home schooling**
Home video cameras
  USE   **Camcorders**
Home video movies
  USE   **Amateur films**
Home video systems   384.55; 621.388;
     778.59
  BT   **Television**
  NT   **Camcorders**
        Videotapes
  RT   **Video recording**
Homeless
  USE   **Homeless persons**
        Homelessness
Homeless people
  USE   **Homeless persons**
Homeless persons   305.5; 362.5
  UF   Homeless
        Homeless people *[Former head-*
          ing]
        Street people
  BT   **Poor**
  NT   **Refugees**
        Runaway adults
        Runaway children
        Runaway teenagers
        Tramps
  RT   **Homelessness**
Homeless persons—Government policy
   362.5
  BT   **Social policy**
Homelessness   305.5; 362.5
  UF   Homeless
  BT   **Housing**
        Poverty
        Social problems
  RT   **Homeless persons**
Homemakers   306.85; 640
  UF   Househusbands
        Housewives
  NT   **Fathers**
        Mothers
  RT   **Home economics**
Homemaking
  USE   **Home economics**
Homeopathy   615.5
  BT   **Alternative medicine**
        Pharmacy

Homes
  USE   **Houses**
Homes for the elderly
  USE   **Elderly—Institutional care**
Homes (Institutions)
  USE   **Charities**
        Institutional care
        Orphanages
Homes, Mobile
  USE   **Mobile homes**
Homeschooling
  USE   **Home schooling**
Homework   371.3028
  BT   **Study skills**
Homicide   364.15
  UF   Manslaughter
        Murder *[Former heading]*
  BT   **Crime**
        Criminal law
        Offenses against the person
  NT   **Assassination**
        Capital punishment
        Euthanasia
        Poisons and poisoning
        Trials (Homicide)
  RT   **Suicide**
Homicide trials
  USE   **Trials (Homicide)**
Hominids
  USE   **Human origins**
Hominids, Fossil
  USE   **Fossil hominids**
Homo sapiens
  USE   **Human beings**
Homonyms
  USE   names of languages with the
          subdivision *Homonyms,* e.g.
          English language—Hom-
          onyms; to be added as need-
          ed
Homosexuality   306.76
  UF   Gay lifestyle
  BT   **Sexual behavior**
  NT   **Gay liberation movement**
        Lesbianism
  RT   **Gay men**
        Lesbians
Homosexuals, Female
  USE   **Lesbians**

BT = Broader Term   NT = Narrower Term   RT = Related Term   SA = See Also   UF = Used For

Homosexuals, Male
　USE　**Gay men**
Honesty　**179**
　UF　Dishonesty
　BT　**Ethics**
　　　Human behavior
　RT　**Truthfulness and falsehood**
Honey　**638; 641.3**
　BT　**Food**
　RT　**Bees**
Honeybee culture
　USE　**Beekeeping**
Honor system
　USE　**Student government**
Honorary degrees
　USE　**Academic degrees**
Hooked rugs　**746.7**
　UF　Rugs, Hooked *[Former heading]*
　BT　**Handicraft**
　　　Rugs
Hoover Dam (Ariz. and Nev.)　**627**
　UF　Boulder Dam (Ariz. and Nev.)
　　　Colorado River—Hoover Dam
　BT　**Dams**
Hope　**152.4; 179; 234**
　BT　**Emotions**
　　　Spiritual life
　　　Virtue
Hormones　**571.7; 573.4; 612.4**
　BT　**Endocrinology**
　RT　**Endocrine glands**
　　　Steroids
Hornbooks　**028.5; 096; 372.41**
　BT　**Reading materials**
Horology
　USE　**Clocks and watches**
　　　Sundials
　　　Time
Horoscopes　**133.5**
　BT　**Astrology**
Horror　**152.4**
　BT　**Emotions**
　　　Fear
Horror—Fiction
　USE　**Horror fiction**
Horror fiction　**808.83; 809.3; 813, etc.**
　May be used for individual works, collections, or materials about horror fiction.
　UF　Horror—Fiction *[Former heading]*
　　　Horror novels

Horror stories
Horror tales
Terror tales
　BT　**Fiction**
　NT　**Ghost stories**
　　　Gothic novels
　RT　**Fantasy fiction**
　　　Occult fiction
Horror films　**791.43**
　May be used for individual works, collections, or materials about horror films.
　UF　Creature films
　　　Horror movies
　　　Monster films
　SA　types of horror films, e.g. **Vampire films**; to be added as needed
　BT　**Motion pictures**
　NT　**Vampire films**
　RT　**Fantasy films**
Horror movies
　USE　**Horror films**
Horror novels
　USE　**Horror fiction**
Horror plays　**808.82; 812, etc.**
　May be used for individual works, collections, or materials about horror plays.
　BT　**Drama**
Horror radio programs　**791.44**
　May be used for individual works, collections, or materials about horror radio programs.
　BT　**Radio programs**
Horror stories
　USE　**Horror fiction**
Horror tales
　USE　**Horror fiction**
Horror television programs　**791.45**
　May be used for individual works, collections, or materials about horror television programs.
　BT　**Television programs**
　RT　**Fantasy television programs**
Horse
　USE　**Horses**
Horse breeding
　USE　**Horses—Breeding**
Horse racing　**798.4**
　BT　**Racing**
　RT　**Gambling**
　　　Horsemanship

BT = Broader Term　　NT = Narrower Term　　RT = Related Term　　SA = See Also　　UF = Used For

Horse riding
USE   **Horsemanship**
Horseback riding
USE   **Horsemanship**
Horsebreaking
USE   **Horses—Training**
Horsemanship   798.2
UF   Coaching
       Dressage
       Equestrianism
       Horse riding
       Horseback riding *[Former heading]*
       Riding
BT   **Locomotion**
NT   **Horses—Breeding**
       Horses—Training
RT   **Horse racing**
       Rodeos
Horses   599.665; 636.1
UF   Foals
       Horse
BT   **Mammals**
NT   **Ponies**
Horses—Breeding   636.1
UF   Horse breeding
BT   **Breeding**
       Horsemanship
Horses—Diseases   636.089
BT   **Animals—Diseases**
Horses—Training   636.1
UF   Horsebreaking
BT   **Horsemanship**
Horses—Wounds and injuries   636.1
Horticulture   635

> Use for materials on the scientific and economic aspects of the cultivation of flowers, fruits, vegetables, etc. Materials on the practical aspects of creating gardens and cultivating plants are entered under **Gardening**. General materials about gardens, the history of gardens, various types of gardens, etc., are entered under **Gardens**.

BT   **Agriculture**
       Plants
NT   **Flower gardening**
       Fruit culture
       Greenhouses
       Hydroponics
       Landscape gardening
       Organic gardening
       Plant breeding

       Truck farming
       Vegetable gardening
RT   **Gardening**
Hosiery   391.4; 687
UF   Stockings
BT   **Clothing and dress**
       Textile industry
Hospices   362.1
BT   **Hospitals**
       Social medicine
       Terminal care
Hospital libraries   027.6
UF   Libraries, Hospital
BT   **Libraries**
Hospital ships   362.1; 623.8
UF   Floating hospitals
BT   **Hospitals**
       Ships
Hospital wastes
USE   **Medical wastes**
Hospitality
USE   **Entertaining**
Hospitalization insurance   368.38
UF   Group hospitalization
       Insurance, Hospitalization *[Former heading]*
BT   **Health insurance**
Hospitals (May subdiv. geog.)   **362.1**
UF   Infirmaries
       Sanatoriums
SA   types of hospitals and names of individual hospitals, to be added as needed
BT   **Institutional care**
       Public health
NT   **Children's hospitals**
       Hospices
       Hospital ships
       Life support systems (Medical environment)
       Long-term care facilities
       Military hospitals
       Nursing homes
       Psychiatric hospitals
RT   **Medical centers**
       Medical charities
Hospitals, Military
USE   **Military hospitals**
Hospitals—United States   362.1
UF   United States—Hospitals

BT = Broader Term   NT = Narrower Term   RT = Related Term   SA = See Also   UF = Used For

Hostage escapes
USE   Escapes
Hostage negotiation
   BT   **Hostages**
         Negotiation
Hostages (May subdiv. geog.)   **920**
   SA   hostages from a particular coun-
         try, e.g. **American hostages;**
         to be added as needed
   BT   **Terrorism**
   NT   **American hostages**
         Hostage negotiation
Hostages, American
   USE   **American hostages**
Hostels, Youth
   USE   **Youth hostels**
Hot air engines
   USE   **Heat engines**
Hot air heating   697
   UF   Warm air heating
   BT   **Heating**
Hot water heating   697
   BT   **Heating**
Hotels and motels (May subdiv. geog.)
         647.94; 728
   Use for materials on public accommoda-
tions, including inns and guest houses.
   UF   Auto courts
         Boarding houses
         Hotels, motels, etc. *[Former*
            heading]
         Inns
         Lodging houses
         Motels
         Motor courts
         Rooming houses
         Tourist accommodations
   BT   **Service industries**
   NT   **Bed and breakfast accommo-**
         dations
         Youth hostels
Hotels and motels—United States
         647.9473; 728
   UF   United States—Hotels and mo-
         tels
Hotels, motels, etc.
   USE   **Hotels and motels**
Hothouses
   USE   **Greenhouses**

Hotlines (Telephone counseling)   361;
         362.2
   UF   Crisis counseling
         Crisis intervention telephone ser-
            vice
         Switchboard hotlines
         Telephone counseling
   BT   **Counseling**
         Human relations
         Information services
         Social work
   RT   **Crisis centers**
Hours of labor   331.25
   UF   Alternative work schedules
         Compressed work week
         Eight-hour day
         Five-day work week
         Flexible hours of labor
         Flexitime
         Four-day work week
         Labor, Hours of
         Overtime
         Working day
         Working hours
   BT   **Labor**
   NT   **Absenteeism (Labor)**
         Part-time employment
   RT   **Children—Employment**
House boats
   USE   **Houseboats**
House buying
   USE   **Houses—Buying and selling**
House cleaning   648
   BT   **Cleaning**
         Home economics
         Household sanitation
House construction   690
   UF   Building, House
         Construction, House
         Home construction
         Residential construction
   SA   types of house construction and
            special kinds of houses, to be
            added as needed
   BT   **Building**
         Domestic architecture
   NT   **Earth sheltered houses**
         Houses—Remodeling
         Log cabins and houses
         Prefabricated houses

BT = Broader Term   NT = Narrower Term   RT = Related Term   SA = See Also   UF = Used For

House construction—*Continued*
    RT   **Houses**

House decoration
    USE   **Interior design**

House drainage   690

        Use for materials on house drainage. Materials on land drainage are entered under **Drainage.**

    UF   Drainage, House *[Former heading]*
    BT   **Household sanitation**
    NT   **Sewerage**
    RT   **Plumbing**

House flies
    USE   **Flies**

House furnishing
    USE   **Interior design**

House of Representatives (U.S.)
    USE   **United States. Congress. House**

House painting   698
    UF   Finishes and finishing
    BT   **Painting**
    NT   **Paint**

House plans
    USE   **Domestic architecture—Designs and plans**

House plants   635.9
    BT   **Cultivated plants**
          Flower gardening
          Plants
          Window gardening
    RT   **Container gardening**
          Indoor gardening

House purchase
    USE   **Houses—Buying and selling**

House repairing
    USE   **Houses—Maintenance and repair**

House repairs
    USE   **Houses—Maintenance and repair**

House sanitation
    USE   **Household sanitation**

House selling
    USE   **Houses—Buying and selling**

House sharing
    USE   **Shared housing**

House trailers
    USE   **Mobile homes**
          Travel trailers and campers

Houseboats   728.7
    UF   House boats
    BT   **Boats and boating**

Household appliances
    USE   **Household equipment and supplies**

Household appliances, Electric
    USE   **Electric household appliances**

Household budgets   640
    UF   Budgets, Household *[Former heading]*
          Domestic finance
          Family budget
          Finance, Household
          Home economics—Accounting
          Household finances
    BT   **Cost and standard of living**
          Personal finance

Household employees   640
    UF   Domestic workers
          Housemaids
          Servants
    BT   **Home economics**
          Labor

Household equipment and supplies   643; 683
    UF   Domestic appliances
          Household appliances
          Implements, utensils, etc.
          Labor saving devices, Household
    BT   **Home economics**
    NT   **Electric household appliances**
          Kitchen utensils

Household finances
    USE   **Cost and standard of living**
          Household budgets

Household management
    USE   **Home economics**

Household moving
    USE   **Moving**

Household pests   648
    UF   Diseases and pests
          Vermin
    SA   types of pests, e.g. **Flies;** to be added as needed
    BT   **Home economics**
          Household sanitation
          Pests
    NT   **Flies**
    RT   **Insect pests**

BT = Broader Term   NT = Narrower Term   RT = Related Term   SA = See Also   UF = Used For

Household repairs
USE **Houses—Maintenance and re-**
pair
Household sanitation   648
UF House sanitation
Sanitation, Household *[Former*
heading]
BT **Sanitation**
NT **House cleaning**
House drainage
Household pests
Laundry
Ventilation
RT **Plumbing**
Household utensils
USE **Kitchen utensils**
Household violence
USE **Family violence**
Househusbands
USE **Homemakers**
Housekeeping
USE **Home economics**
Housemaids
USE **Household employees**
Houses (May subdiv. geog.)   **643; 728**
Use for general materials on buildings in
which people live. Materials on residential
buildings from the standpoint of style and de-
sign are entered under **Domestic architecture.**
UF Dwellings
Homes
Residences
SA types of houses, e.g. **Earth shel-**
tered houses; types of archi-
tectural features, e.g. **Win-**
dows; Fireplaces; etc.; and
rooms and parts of the house,
e.g. **Kitchens;** to be added as
needed
BT **Buildings**
NT **Apartment houses**
Earth sheltered houses
Garden rooms
Housing
Kitchens
Log cabins and houses
Prefabricated houses
Rooms
Solar homes
RT **Domestic architecture**
House construction

Houses—Buying and selling   333.33
UF Home buying
Home purchase
House buying
House purchase
House selling
BT **Real estate business**
NT **Urban homesteading**
Houses, Earth sheltered
USE **Earth sheltered houses**
Houses—Heating and ventilation   644;
697
BT **Heating**
Houses, Log
USE **Log cabins and houses**
Houses—Maintenance and repair   643
UF Home repairing
Home repairs
House repairing
House repairs
Household repairs
Houses, Prefabricated
USE **Prefabricated houses**
Houses—Remodeling   643
UF Dwellings—Remodeling
Home remodeling
Remodeling (Architecture)
Remodeling of dwellings
Remodeling of houses
SA types of houses and parts of
houses with the subdivision
Remodeling, e.g. **Kitchens—**
Remodeling; to be added as
needed
BT **House construction**
NT **Kitchens—Remodeling**
Houses, Underground
USE **Earth sheltered houses**
Housewives
USE **Homemakers**
Housing (May subdiv. geog.)   **307.3;**
363.5
Use for materials on the social and econom-
ic aspects of housing. Materials on the social
and economic aspects of housing as it pertains
to specific ethnic groups or classes of persons
are entered under that group or class of persons with the subdivision *Housing.* Materials
on the residential buildings of ethnic groups
or classes of persons from the standpoint of
architecture, construction, or ethnology are entered under the name of the ethnic group or

---

BT = Broader Term   NT = Narrower Term   RT = Related Term   SA = See Also   UF = Used For

Housing—*Continued*
class of persons with the subdivision *Dwell-ings.*
 UF Affordable housing
 Dwellings
 Habitations, Human
 Housing needs
 Slum clearance
 Urban housing
 SA ethnic groups, classes of per-
 sons, and domestic animals
 with the subdivision *Housing,*
 to be added as needed
 BT **Houses**
 Landlord and tenant
 NT **African Americans—Housing**
 Apartment houses
 Blacks—Housing
 Discrimination in housing
 Elderly—Housing
 Homelessness
 Labor—Housing
 Mobile homes
 **Physically handicapped—Hous-
 ing**
 Public housing
 Shared housing
 Timesharing (Real estate)
 Urban homesteading
 RT **City planning**
Housing, African American
 USE **African Americans—Housing**
Housing, Black
 USE **Blacks—Housing**
Housing, Discrimination in
 USE **Discrimination in housing**
Housing for the elderly
 USE **Elderly—Housing**
Housing for the physically handicapped
 USE **Physically handicapped—Hous-
 ing**
Housing loans
 USE **Mortgages**
Housing needs
 USE **Housing**
Housing projects, Government
 USE **Public housing**
Houston Astros (Baseball team)
 796.357
 UF Astros (Baseball team)

 Houston (Tex.). Baseball Club
 (National League)
 BT **Baseball teams**
Houston (Tex.). Baseball Club (National
 League)
 USE **Houston Astros (Baseball
 team)**
Hovercraft
 USE **Ground effect machines**
How to start a business
 USE **New business enterprises**
How-to-stop-smoking programs
 USE **Smoking cessation programs**
HTML (Document markup language)
 005.7
 UF HyperText Markup Language
 (Document markup language)
 BT **Electronic data processing**
Hudson River (N.Y. and N.J.)—Bridges
 USE **Bridges—Hudson River (N.Y.
 and N.J.)**
Hugging 158; 302.2; 395
 UF Embracing
 Hugs
 BT **Manners and customs**
 Nonverbal communication
 Touch
Hugs
 USE **Hugging**
Huguenots 284
 BT **Christian sects**
 Reformation
 NT **Saint Bartholomew's Day,
 Massacre of, 1572**
Hull House
 USE **Hull House (Chicago, Ill.)**
Hull House (Chicago, Ill.) 361.4
 UF Hull House *[Former heading]*
 BT **Social settlements**
Human abnormalities
 USE **Birth defects**
 Growth disorders
Human anatomy 611
 UF Anatomy, Human *[Former head-
 ing]*
 SA parts of the body, e.g. **Foot;** and
 names of organs and regions
 of the body with the subdivi-
 sion **Anatomy,** e.g. **Heart**—

BT = Broader Term NT = Narrower Term RT = Related Term SA = See Also UF = Used For

Human anatomy—*Continued*
    Anatomy; to be added as
    needed
  BT   Anatomy
  RT   Human body
Human anatomy—Atlases   611
  BT   Atlases
Human anatomy in art
  USE   Artistic anatomy
        Nude in art
Human artificial insemination   176;
    346.01; 618.1
  UF   Artificial insemination, Human
        [Former heading]
  BT   Artificial insemination
        Reproduction
  RT   Sexual ethics
Human assets
  USE   Human capital
Human behavior   150; 302
  UF   Behavior
        Morals
        Social behavior
  BT   Character
        Psychology
        Social sciences
  NT   Aggressiveness (Psychology)
        Behavior modification
        Behaviorism
        Cannibalism
        Compulsive behavior
        Conduct of life
        Consolation
        Duty
        Eating customs
        Etiquette
        Friendship
        Habit
        Helping behavior
        Honesty
        Lifestyles
        Love
        Patience
        Patriotism
        Sexual behavior
        Social adjustment
        Sportsmanship
        Truthfulness and falsehood
        Vice
        Virtue

  RT   Ethics
        Human relations
        Life skills
Human beings (May subdiv. geog.)
    128; 599.9
    Use for materials on the human species
    from the point of view of biology or anthro-
    pology. Materials on human beings as individ-
    uals are entered under **Persons.**
  UF   Homo sapiens
        Human race
        Man *[Former heading]*
  BT   Primates
  NT   Anthropometry
        Ethnology
        Human body
        Persons
        Prehistoric peoples
  RT   Anthropology
Human body   612
    Use for materials on the human body not
    limited to anatomy or physiology.
  UF   Body
  SA   parts of the body, e.g. **Foot;** to
        be added as needed
  BT   Human beings
        Self
  NT   Body image
        Body weight
  RT   Human anatomy
        Mind and body
        Physiology
Human capital (May subdiv. geog.)
    Use for materials on investments of capital
    in training and educating employees to im-
    prove their productivity. Materials on the
    strength of a country in terms of available
    personnel, both military and industrial, are en-
    tered under **Manpower.**
  UF   Human assets
        Human Resources *[Former
            heading]*
  BT   Capital
  RT   Labor supply
Human cold storage
  USE   Cryonics
Human ecology   304.2
  UF   Ecology, Human
        Ecology, Social
        Social ecology
  BT   Sociology
  NT   Environmental influence on
            humans

BT = Broader Term   NT = Narrower Term   RT = Related Term   SA = See Also   UF = Used For

Human ecology—*Continued*
      Human geography
      Human influence on nature
      Population
      Social psychology
      Survival skills
  RT   Environmental policy
Human embryos, Frozen
  USE Frozen embryos
Human engineering   620.8
    Use for materials on engineering design as related to human anatomical, physiological, and psychological capabilities and limitations.
  UF   Biomechanics
       Ergonomics
  BT   Applied psychology
       Engineering
       Industrial design
       Psychophysiology
  NT   Life support systems (Space environment)
       Life support systems (Submarine environment)
  RT   Machine design
Human experimentation in medicine   174
  UF   Experimentation on humans, Medical
       Medical experimentation on humans
  BT   Medical ethics
       Medicine—Research
Human fertility   304.6; 612.6; 616.6
    Use for materials on fertility in humans. General materials on fertility in animals, including humans, are entered under **Fertility**.
  UF   Fertility, Human *[Former heading]*
  BT   Birth rate
       Fertility
       Population
  RT   Birth control
       Childlessness
Human figure in art
  USE Artistic anatomy
       Figure drawing
       Figure painting
       Nude in art
Human fossils
  USE Fossil hominids

Human geography   304.2
  UF   Anthropogeography *[Former heading]*
       Geographical distribution of people
       Geography, Social
  BT   Anthropology
       Ethnology
       Geography
       Human ecology
       Immigration and emigration
  NT   Environmental influence on humans
  RT   Geopolitics
Human influence on nature   304.2; 363.7
  UF   Earth, Effect of man on
       Man—Influence on nature *[Former heading]*
       Nature, Effect of man on
  BT   Human ecology
  NT   Pollution
  RT   Environmental policy
Human life education
  USE Sex education
Human locomotion   152.3; 612.7
  UF   Biomechanics
       Human mechanics
       Human movement
  BT   Locomotion
       Physiology
  NT   Kinesiology
  RT   Musculoskeletal system
Human mechanics
  USE Human locomotion
Human movement
  USE Human locomotion
Human origins   599.9
  UF   Antiquity of man
       Hominids
       Man—Antiquity
       Man—Origin *[Former heading]*
       Origin of man
  BT   Physical anthropology
  RT   Evolution
       Fossil hominids
       Prehistoric peoples
Human paleontology
  USE Fossil hominids

BT = Broader Term   NT = Narrower Term   RT = Related Term   SA = See Also   UF = Used For

Human physiology
  USE   Physiology
Human race
  USE   Anthropology
         Human beings
Human records
  USE   World records
Human relations   158; 302
    Use for materials on group behavior, social relations between persons, and problems arising from organizational and interpersonal relations.
  UF   Interpersonal relations
  SA   interpersonal relations between groups of persons or individuals, e.g. **Jewish-Arab relations; Landlord and tenant; Parent and child;** etc., to be added as needed
  BT   **Social psychology**
  NT   **Conflict of generations**
         Discrimination
         Domestic relations
         Family
         Grandparent and child
         Group relations training
         Helping behavior
         Hotlines (Telephone counseling)
         Interfaith relations
         Landlord and tenant
         Loneliness
         Parent and child
         Personal space
         Personnel management
         Prejudices
         Social adjustment
         Social values
         Teacher-student relationships
         Toleration
         Transactional analysis
  RT   **Human behavior**
         Life skills
Human resource management
  USE   **Personnel management**
Human Resources
  USE   **Human capital**
         Manpower
Human resources development
  USE   **Manpower policy**
Human resources policy
  USE   **Manpower policy**

Human rights   323; 341.4
    Use for materials on the rights of persons regardless of their legal, socioeconomic, or cultural status, as recognized by the international community. Materials on citizens' rights as established by law or protected by a constitution are entered under **Civil rights.**
  UF   Basic rights
         Civil rights (International law)
         Fundamental rights
         Rights, Human
         Rights of man
  NT   **Civil rights**
Human survival skills
  USE   **Survival skills**
Human values
  USE   **Values**
Humane treatment of animals
  USE   **Animal welfare**
Humanism   001.2; 880
    Use for materials on culture founded on the study of the classics, or more narrowly on Greek and Roman scholarship. Materials on any intellectual or philosophical movement or set of beliefs that promotes human values as separate and distinct from religious doctrines are entered under **Secularism.**
  BT   **Culture**
         Literature
         Philosophy
  NT   **Humanities**
  RT   **Classical education**
         Learning and scholarship
         Renaissance
         Secularism
Humanism—1900-1999 (20th century)
  USE   **Secularism**
Humanism, Secular
  USE   **Secularism**
Humanistic medicine
  USE   **Holistic medicine**
Humanitarians
  USE   **Philanthropists**
Humanities   001.3
  BT   **Humanism**
         Learning and scholarship
  NT   **Art**
         Arts
         History
         Literature
         Music
         Philosophy
         Science and the humanities

BT = Broader Term   NT = Narrower Term   RT = Related Term   SA = See Also   UF = Used For

Humanities—*Continued*
   RT   **Classical education**
Humanities and science
   USE   **Science and the humanities**
Humans in space
   USE   **Space flight**
Humidity   551.57
   UF   Air, Moisture of
         Atmospheric humidity
         Relative humidity
   BT   **Meteorology**
         Weather
Humor
   USE   **Wit and humor**
         and subjects with the subdivision *Humor,* e.g. **World War, 1939-1945—Humor;** to be added as needed
Humorists   809.7; 920
   BT   **Wit and humor**
Humorous fiction   808.83; 813, etc.
     May be used for individual works, collections, or materials about humorous fiction.
   UF   Comic novels
         Humorous stories *[Former heading]*
   BT   **Fiction**
         Wit and humor
   RT   **Mock-heroic literature**
Humorous films
   USE   **Comedy films**
Humorous pictures
   USE   **Cartoons and caricatures**
         Comic books, strips, etc.
Humorous plays
   USE   **Comedies**
Humorous poetry   808.81; 811, etc.; 811.008, etc.
     May be used for individual works, collections, or materials about humorous poetry.
   UF   Comic verse
         Humorous verse
         Light verse
   BT   **Poetry**
         Wit and humor
   NT   **Limericks**
         Nonsense verses
Humorous stories
   USE   **Humorous fiction**
Humorous verse
   USE   **Humorous poetry**

Hundred Years' War, 1339-1453   944
   UF   100 years' war
   BT   **Europe—History—476-1492**
         France—History—1328-1589, House of Valois
         Great Britain—History—1399-1485, Lancaster and York
Hungary—History   943.9
Hungary—History—1956, Revolution   943.905
   BT   **Revolutions**
Hunger   363.8
   RT   **Fasting**
         Starvation
Hunger strikes   303.6
   BT   **Demonstrations**
         Fasting
         Nonviolence
         Passive resistance
         Resistance to government
Hunting (May subdiv. geog.)   799.2
   UF   Gunning
   SA   types of hunting, to be added as needed
   NT   **Decoys (Hunting)**
         Falconry
         Game protection
         Game reserves
         Tracking and trailing
         Whaling
   RT   **Game and game birds**
         Shooting
         Trapping
Hunting, Job
   USE   **Job hunting**
Hunting—United States   799.2973
   UF   United States—Hunting
Hurricanes (May subdiv. geog.)   551.55
     Use for cyclonic storms originating in the region of the West Indies.
   BT   **Cyclones**
         Storms
         Winds
   RT   **Typhoons**
Husband abuse   362.82
   UF   Abuse of husbands
         Battered husbands
         Battered men
         Husband battering
         Husband beating
   BT   **Family violence**

BT = Broader Term   NT = Narrower Term   RT = Related Term   SA = See Also   UF = Used For

Husband battering
USE   Husband abuse
Husband beating
USE   Husband abuse
Husbands   306.872
    UF   Married men
           Spouses
    BT   Family
           Marriage
           Married people
           Men
    NT   Widowers
Husbands, Runaway
    USE   Runaway adults
Hybridization
    USE   Plant breeding
Hydraulic cement
    USE   Cement
Hydraulic engineering   627
    BT   Civil engineering
           Engineering
           Fluid mechanics
           Water power
    NT   Boring
           Drainage
           Dredging
           Flood control
           Hydraulic structures
           Hydrodynamics
           Hydrostatics
           Irrigation
           Pumping machinery
           Reclamation of land
           Wells
    RT   Hydraulics
           Rivers
           Water
           Water supply engineering
Hydraulic machinery   621.2
    BT   Machinery
           Water power
    NT   Turbines
Hydraulic structures   627
    SA   types of hydraulic structures, to
           be added as needed
    BT   Hydraulic engineering
           Structural engineering
    NT   Aqueducts
           Canals
           Dams

           Docks
           Harbors
           Pipelines
           Reservoirs
Hydraulics   621.2; 627
    Use for materials on technical applications
of the theory of hydrodynamics.
    UF   Water flow
    BT   Fluid mechanics
           Liquids
           Mechanics
           Physics
    NT   Hydrodynamics
           Hydrostatics
           Water
           Water power
    RT   Hydraulic engineering
Hydrodynamics   532
    Use for materials on the theory of the mo-
tion and action of fluids. Materials on the experimental investigation and technical application of this theory are entered under **Hydraulics.**
    BT   Dynamics
           Fluid mechanics
           Hydraulic engineering
           Hydraulics
           Liquids
           Mechanics
    NT   Hydrostatics
           Viscosity
           Waves
Hydroelectric power
    USE   Water power
Hydroelectric power plants   621.31
    UF   Power plants, Hydroelectric
    BT   Electric power plants
           Water power
           Water resources development
Hydrofoil boats   623.8
    BT   Boats and boating
Hydrogen   546
    BT   Chemical elements
Hydrogen bomb   623.4
    UF   H bomb
           Thermonuclear bomb
    BT   Bombs
           Nuclear warfare
           Nuclear weapons
    NT   Radioactive fallout
    RT   Atomic bomb

BT = Broader Term   NT = Narrower Term   RT = Related Term   SA = See Also   UF = Used For

Hydrogen nucleus
USE Protons
Hydrology
USE Water
Hydromechanics
USE Fluid mechanics
Hydropathy
USE Hydrotherapy
Hydrophobia
USE Rabies
Hydroponics 631.5; 635
UF Agriculture, Soilless
Chemiculture
Plants—Soilless culture
Soilless agriculture
Water farming
BT **Horticulture**
Hydrostatics 532
BT **Fluid mechanics**
Hydraulic engineering
Hydraulics
Hydrodynamics
Liquids
Mechanics
Physics
Statics
NT **Gases**
Hydrotherapy 615.8
UF Hydropathy
Water cure
BT **Physical therapy**
Therapeutics
Water
RT **Baths**
Health resorts
Hygiene 613
UF Body care
Personal cleanliness
Personal hygiene
SA parts of the body with the sub-division *Care*, e.g. **Foot—Care**; and classes of persons and ethnic groups with the subdivision *Health and hygiene*, e.g. **Women—Health and hygiene**; to be added as needed
BT **Medicine**
Preventive medicine
NT **Baths**

Children—Health and hygiene
Cleanliness
Diet
Disinfection and disinfectants
Elderly—Health and hygiene
Exercise
Infants—Health and hygiene
Military health
Personal grooming
Rest
School hygiene
Sexual hygiene
Sleep
Ventilation
Women—Health and hygiene
RT **Health**
Sanitation
Hygiene, Industrial
USE **Occupational health and safety**
Hygiene, Military
USE **Military health**
Hygiene, School
USE **School hygiene**
Hygiene, Sexual
USE **Sexual hygiene**
Hygiene, Social
USE **Public health**
Hygiene—Study and teaching
USE **Health education**
Hygiene, Tropical
USE **Tropical medicine**
Hymenoptera
USE **Ants**
Bees
Wasps
Hymn books
USE **Hymnals**
Hymnals 782.27
Use for collections of sacred songs that contain both words and music. Materials about hymns are entered under **Hymns**.
UF Hymn books
Hymnbooks
BT **Church music**
Hymns
Songbooks
Hymnbooks
USE **Hymnals**
Hymnology
USE **Hymns**

BT = Broader Term   NT = Narrower Term   RT = Related Term   SA = See Also   UF = Used For

Hymns 264; 782.27

> Use for materials about hymns. Collections of hymns that contain both words and music are entered under **Hymnals.**

  UF   Hymnology
  BT   **Church music**
        Liturgies
        Songs
        Vocal music
  NT   **Carols**
        Hymnals
        Spirituals (Songs)
  RT   **Religious poetry**

Hyperactive children 155.4; 618.92

  UF   Children, Hyperactive
        Hyperkinetic children
        Overactive children
  BT   **Handicapped children**
  RT   **Hyperactivity**

Hyperactivity 616.85; 616.92

  UF   Hyperkinesia
        Overactivity
  BT   **Diseases**
  RT   **Hyperactive children**

Hyperkinesia
  USE   **Hyperactivity**

Hyperkinetic children
  USE   **Hyperactive children**

Hyperspace
  USE   **Fourth dimension**

Hypertension 616.1

  UF   High blood pressure
  BT   **Blood pressure**

Hypertext 005.75

> Use for materials on document retrieval networks having text files and dynamic indexes for links among documents.

  UF   Hypertext systems
  BT   **Multimedia systems**

HyperText Markup Language (Document markup language)
  USE   **HTML (Document markup language)**

Hypertext systems
  USE   **Hypertext**

Hypnosis
  USE   **Hypnotism**

Hypnotism 154.7

  UF   Animal magnetism
        Autosuggestion
        Hypnosis

        Mesmerism
  BT   **Mental healing**
        Psychophysiology
  RT   **Mental suggestion**
        Mind and body
        Psychoanalysis
        Subconsciousness
        Suggestive therapeutics

I.B.M. 7090 (Computer)
  USE   **IBM 7090 (Computer)**

I.C.B.M.
  USE   **Intercontinental ballistic missiles**

I. Q. tests
  USE   **Intelligence tests**

I.R.A.'s (Pensions)
  USE   **Individual retirement accounts**

I.S.B.D
  USE   **International Standard Bibliographic Description**

I.S.B.N.
  USE   **International Standard Book Numbers**

I.S.S.N.
  USE   **International Standard Serial Numbers**

IBM 7090 (Computer) 621.39

  UF   I.B.M. 7090 (Computer)
  BT   **Computers**

ICBM
  USE   **Intercontinental ballistic missiles**

Ice 551.3

  UF   Freezing
  BT   **Cold**
        Frost
        Physical geography
        Water
  NT   **Glaciers**
        Icebergs

Ice age 551.7

  UF   Glacial epoch
  BT   **Earth**

Ice boats
  USE   **Iceboats**

Ice cream, ices, etc. 637; 641.8

  UF   Ices
  BT   **Desserts**
        Frozen foods

BT = Broader Term   NT = Narrower Term   RT = Related Term   SA = See Also   UF = Used For

Ice (Drug) 362.29; 615
    UF Crank (Drug)
        Crystal meth (Drug)
    BT Designer drugs
        Methamphetamine
Ice hockey
    USE Hockey
Ice manufacture
    USE Refrigeration
Ice skating 796.91
    UF Figure skating
        Skating
    BT Winter sports
Ice sports
    USE Winter sports
Icebergs 551.3
    BT Ice
        Ocean
        Physical geography
Iceboats 623.8
    UF Ice boats
    BT Boats and boating
Icelandic language 439
    BT Language and languages
        Scandinavian languages
Icelandic language—0-1500
    USE Old Norse language
Icelandic literature 839
    UF Icelandic literature, Modern
    BT Literature
        Scandinavian literature
    RT Old Norse literature
Icelandic literature, Modern
    USE Icelandic literature
Ices
    USE Ice cream, ices, etc.
Ichthyology
    USE Fishes
Iconography
    USE Art
        Christian art and symbolism
        Portraits
        Religious art and symbolism
Ideal states
    USE Utopian fiction
        Utopias
Idealism 141
    BT Philosophy
    RT Materialism
        Realism

Transcendentalism
Identification
    SA subjects with the subdivision
        Identification, to be added as
        needed
    NT Airplanes—Identification
        Criminals—Identification
        DNA fingerprints
        Fingerprints
Identity
    USE Identity (Psychology)
        Individuality
        Personality
Identity (Psychology) 126
    UF Identity
    SA classes of persons with the sub-
        division *Identity*, e.g. Wom-
        en—Identity; ethnic groups
        with the subdivision *Ethnic
        identity*, e.g. Mexican Ameri-
        cans—Ethnic identity; and
        racial groups with the subdi-
        vision *Race identity*, e.g.
        African Americans—Race
        identity; to be added as
        needed
    BT Personality
        Psychology
        Self
    NT Ethnicity
        Women—Identity
Ideology 140
    BT Philosophy
        Political science
        Psychology
        Theory of knowledge
        Thought and thinking
    NT Political correctness
Idioms
    USE names of languages with the
        subdivision *Idioms*, e.g. Eng-
        lish language—Idioms; to be
        added as needed
Idyllic poetry
    USE Pastoral poetry
Illegal aliens 323.6; 325; 342
    UF Aliens, Illegal *[Former heading]*
        Underground aliens
        Undocumented aliens
    BT Aliens

BT = Broader Term   NT = Narrower Term   RT = Related Term   SA = See Also   UF = Used For

Illegal aliens—*Continued*
      Immigration and emigration
      Underground economy
  RT   Sanctuary movement
Illegitimacy   306.874; 346.01
  UF   Bastardy
      Children, Illegitimate
      Legitimacy (Law)
  BT   **Social problems**
  NT   **Unmarried fathers**
      Unmarried mothers
Illiteracy
  USE   **Literacy**
Illness
  USE   **Diseases**
Illuminated manuscripts
  USE   **Illumination of books and**
          manuscripts
Illuminating gas
  USE   **Gas**
Illumination
  USE   **Lighting**
Illumination of books and manuscripts
    096; 745.6
  UF   Illuminated manuscripts
      Manuscripts, Illuminated
      Miniatures (Illumination of
        books and manuscripts)
      Ornamental alphabets
  BT   **Alphabets**
      Art
      Books
      Christian art and symbolism
      Decoration and ornament
      Illustration of books
      Manuscripts
      Medieval art
  RT   **Initials**
Illusions
  USE   **Hallucinations and illusions**
      Optical illusions
Illustration of books   741.6
  UF   Book illustration
  SA   types of illustration, e.g. **Botani-**
      cal illustration; to be added
      as needed
  BT   **Art**
      Books
      Color printing
      Decoration and ornament

  NT   **Botanical illustration**
      Caldecott Medal
      Engraving
      Illumination of books and
          manuscripts
      Photomechanical processes
  RT   **Drawing**
      Picture books for children
Illustrations
  USE   subjects with the subdivision
      Pictorial works, e.g. **Ani-**
      mals—Pictorial works; Unit-
      ed States—History—1861-
      1865, Civil War—Pictorial
      works; etc., to be added as
      needed
Illustrations, Humorous
  USE   **Cartoons and caricatures**
Illustrators   741.6092; 920
  SA   illustrators of particular coun-
      tries, e.g. **American illustra-**
      tors; to be added as needed
  BT   **Artists**
  NT   **American illustrators**
Illustrators, American
  USE   **American illustrators**
Images, National
  USE   **National characteristics**
Imaginary animals
  USE   **Mythical animals**
Imaginary friends
  USE   **Imaginary playmates**
Imaginary places
  USE   **Geographical myths**
Imaginary playmates   155.4
  UF   Friends, Imaginary
      Imaginary friends
      Invisible playmates
      Make-believe playmates
      Playmates, Imaginary
  BT   **Friendship**
      Imagination
      Play
Imaginary voyages   808.83; 813, etc.
    May be used for individual works, collec-
  tions, or materials about imaginary voyages.
  UF   Space flight (Fiction)
      Subterranean voyages
      Time travel (Fiction)
      Voyages, Imaginary
      Voyages to the moon

BT = Broader Term   NT = Narrower Term   RT = Related Term   SA = See Also   UF = Used For

Imaginary voyages—*Continued*
  BT Fantasy fiction
      Science fiction
  NT Robinsonades
  RT Interplanetary voyages
Imagination 153.3
  BT Educational psychology
      Intellect
      Psychology
  NT Creation (Literary, artistic,
        etc.)
      Fantasy
      Imaginary playmates
Imaging, Magnetic resonance
  USE **Magnetic resonance imaging**
Imitations
  USE types of literature and names of
        prominent authors with the
        subdivision *Parodies, imita-*
        tions, etc., e.g. **Shakespeare,**
        William, 1564-1616—Paro-
        dies, imitations, etc.; to be
        added as needed
Immigrants (May subdiv. geog.) **304.8**
  Use for materials on foreign-born persons
  who enter a country intending to become per-
  manent residents or citizens. This heading
  may be locally subdivided by the names of
  places where immigrants have settled.
  UF Emigrants
      Foreign population
      Foreigners
  SA names of immigrant ethnic
        groups, e.g. **Mexican Ameri-**
        cans; and, for immigrants
        who are not citizens, the
        names of national groups with
        the appropriate subdivision for
        the country of their residence,
        e.g. **Mexicans—United**
        States; to be added as needed
  BT **Minorities**
  RT **Aliens**
      Immigration and emigration
Immigrants—United States **325.73**
  UF United States—Foreign popula-
        tion *[Former heading]*
  NT **Mexican Americans**
  RT **United States—Immigration**
        and emigration

Immigration and emigration 304.8; 325
  Use for materials on migration from one
  country to another. Materials on the movement of population within a country for per-
  manent settlement are entered under **Internal**
  migration.
  UF Emigration
      Foreign population
      Migration
  SA names of countries with the sub-
        division *Immigration and emi-*
        gration, e.g. **United States—**
        Immigration and emigration;
        and names of nationality
        groups, e.g. **Mexican Ameri-**
        cans; Mexicans—United
        States; etc., to be added as
        needed
  BT **Population**
  NT **Children of immigrants**
      Human geography
      Illegal aliens
      Naturalization
      Refugees
      United States—Immigration
        and emigration
  RT **Aliens**
      Americanization
      Colonization
      Immigrants
      Internal migration
Immoral literature
  USE **Pornography**
Immortality **129**
  Use for materials on the question of the
  endless existence of the soul. Materials on the
  character and form of a future existence are
  entered under **Future life.** Materials on the
  philosophical concept of eternity are entered
  under **Eternity.**
  UF Eternal life
      Life after death
  BT **Eschatology**
      Soul
      Theology
  RT **Future life**
Immune system **616.07**
  UF Immunological system
  BT **Anatomy**
      Physiology
  RT **Immunity**
Immunity **571.9; 616.07**
  BT **Pathology**

BT = Broader Term   NT = Narrower Term   RT = Related Term   SA = See Also   UF = Used For

Immunity—*Continued*
    Preventive medicine
  NT   Allergy
  RT   Immune system
        Vaccination
Immunization
  USE   Vaccination
Immunological system
  USE   Immune system
Impaired vision
  USE   Vision disorders
Impeachments   342
  BT   **Administration of justice**
  NT   **Recall (Political science)**
Imperialism   325
  UF   Colonialism
  SA   names of countries with the sub-
        division *Foreign relations* or
        Colonies, to be added as
        needed
  BT   **Political science**
  NT   **Colonies**
        Colonization
Implements, utensils, etc.
  USE   **Agricultural machinery**
        **Household equipment and sup-
        plies**
        Stone implements
        Tools
Imports (May subdiv. geog.)   382
  BT   **International trade**
Impostors and imposture   364.1
  UF   Charlatans
        Hoaxes
        Pretenders
  BT   **Crime**
        Criminals
  NT   **Counterfeits and counterfeiting**
        Forgery
        Quacks and quackery
  RT   **Fraud**
        Swindlers and swindling
Impregnation, Artificial
  USE   **Artificial insemination**
Impressionism (Art)   709.03; 759.05
  UF   Neo-impressionism (Art)
  BT   **Modern art—1800-1899 (19th
        century)**
        Painting
  RT   **Postimpressionism (Art)**

Imprisonment
  USE   **Prisons**
In-line skating   796.2
  UF   Rollerblading
  BT   **Roller skating**
In-service training
  USE   **Employees—Training**
        and types of employees or per-
        sonnel with the subdivision
        In-service training, e.g. **Li-
        brarians—In-service train-
        ing;** to be added as needed
In vitro fertilization
  USE   **Fertilization in vitro**
Inaudible sound
  USE   **Ultrasonics**
Incandescent lamps
  USE   **Electric lamps**
Incas   985
  BT   **Indians of South America**
Incendiary bombs   623.4
  UF   Bombs, Incendiary
        Fire bombs
  BT   **Bombs**
        Incendiary weapons
Incendiary weapons   623.4
  BT   **Chemical warfare**
  NT   **Incendiary bombs**
Incentive (Psychology)
  USE   **Motivation (Psychology)**
Incest   306.877; 616.85
  BT   **Sex crimes**
  NT   **Child sexual abuse**
Incineration
  USE   **Cremation**
        Refuse and refuse disposal
Income   331.2; 339.3
  UF   Fortunes
  BT   **Economics**
        Finance
        Property
        Wealth
  NT   **Guaranteed annual income**
        Retirement income
        Wages
  RT   **Profit**
Income tax   336.24
  UF   Direct taxation
        Payroll taxes
        Taxation of income

BT = Broader Term   NT = Narrower Term   RT = Related Term   SA = See Also   UF = Used For

Income tax—*Continued*
    BT   **Internal revenue**
           Taxation
    NT   **Tax credits**
Income, Untaxed
    USE   **Underground economy**
Indebtedness
    USE   **Debt**
Indentured servants
    USE   **Contract labor**
Independence Day (United States)
    USE   **Fourth of July**
Independent schools
    USE   **Private schools**
Independent study   371.39

    Use for materials on individual study that may be directed or assisted by instructional staff through periodic consultations.

    BT   **Study skills**
           Tutors and tutoring
Indeterminism
    USE   **Free will and determinism**
Index librorum prohibitorum
    USE   **Books—Censorship**
Indexes   016

    Use for works that list topics or names with references to books, articles, or passages where those topics or names are to be found. Works that list words with references to passages in a text where the exact word occurs are entered under **Concordances.**

    SA   subjects with the subdivision *Indexes,* e.g. **Newspapers—Indexes; Short stories—Indexes; English literature—Indexes;** etc., to be added as needed
    BT   **Bibliography**
    NT   **Concordances**
           Subject headings
Indexing   025.3
    BT   **Bibliographic control**
           Bibliography
    RT   **Cataloging**
           Files and filing
India rubber
    USE   **Rubber**
Indian art (North American)
    USE   **Indians of North America—Art**

Indian languages (North American)
    USE   **Indians of North America—Languages**
Indian literature (American)
    USE   **American literature—American Indian authors**
Indian literature (East Indian)
    USE   **Indic literature**
Indian literature (North American Indian)
    USE   **Indians of North America—Literature**
Indian missions
    USE   **Indians of North America—Christian missions**
Indian mythology
    USE   **Indians of North America—Folklore**
Indian reservations
    USE   **Indians of North America—Reservations**
Indian women (North American)
    USE   **Indians of North America—Women**
Indians   970.004

    Use for general materials on the Indians of the Western Hemisphere. May be subdivided topically like **Indians of North America.**

    UF   American Indians
           Amerindians
    SA   names of Indian peoples and linguistic families, e.g. **Indians of Mexico; Aztecs;** etc., to be added as needed
    NT   **Indians of Central America**
           Indians of Mexico
           Indians of North America
           Indians of South America
           Indians of the West Indies
Indians of Canada
    USE   **Indians of North America—Canada**
Indians of Central America (May subdiv. geog.)   972.8004

    May be subdivided topically like **Indians of North America.**

    UF   American Indians
           Amerindians
           Central American Indians
           Indians of North America—Central America
    BT   **Indians**

BT = Broader Term   NT = Narrower Term   RT = Related Term   SA = See Also   UF = Used For

Indians of Central America—*Continued*
NT   Mayas
Indians of Central America—Guatemala
976.81004
Indians (of India)
USE   East Indians
Indians of Mexico (May subdiv. geog.)
972.004

May be subdivided topically like **Indians of North America.**

UF   American Indians
Amerindians
Indians of North America—Mexico
Mexico, Indians of
BT   Indians
NT   Aztecs
Mayas
Indians of North America (May subdiv.
geog. except U.S.)   970.004

Use for materials on the Indians of the United States and Canada collectively or on the Indians of the United States. Topical subdivisions used under this heading may also be used under the names of specific American Indian peoples and linguistic families.

UF   American Indians
Amerindians
Indians of North America—Civilization and culture *[Former heading]*
Indians of North America—Ethnology *[Former heading]*
Indians of North America—United States
Native Americans
North American Indians
Pre-Columbian Americans
Precolumbian Americans
SA   names of Indian peoples and linguistic families, e.g. **Navajo Indians;** to be added as needed
BT   Indians
Native peoples
NT   Cliff dwellers and cliff dwellings
Mounds and mound builders
Navajo Indians
RT   Ethnology—United States

Indians of North America—Amusements
USE   Indians of North America—Games
Indians of North America—Social life and customs
Indians of North America—Antiquities
970.004
BT   Antiquities
United States—Antiquities
NT   Mounds and mound builders
Indians of North America—Architecture
720.97; 970.004
BT   Architecture
NT   Indians of North America—Dwellings
Indians of North America—Art   704;
709.01
UF   Art, Indian
Indian art (North American)
BT   Art
Indians of North America—Canada
971.004
UF   Canadian Indians
Indians of Canada
Indians of North America—Captivities
970.004
BT   Frontier and pioneer life
Indians of North America—Central America
USE   Indians of Central America
Indians of North America—Children
305.23; 970.004
BT   Children
Indians of North America—Christian missions   266
UF   Indian missions
Indians of North America—Missions, Christian *[Former heading]*
Missions, Indian
BT   Christian missions
Indians of North America—Chronology
USE   Indians of North America—History—Chronology
Indians of North America—Civilization and culture
USE   Indians of North America

Indians of North America—Claims
323.1; 970.004
UF   Indians of North America—Land
claims
Indians of North America—Le-
gal status, laws, etc.
Indians of North America—Costume
970.004
UF   Indians of North America—Cos-
tume and adornment [Former
heading]
BT   Costume
Indians of North America—Costume and
adornment
USE   Indians of North America—
Costume
Indians of North America—Customs
USE   Indians of North America—So-
cial life and customs
Indians of North America—Dances
793.3; 970.004
BT   Folk dancing
Indians of North America—Drama
812, etc.
May be used for individual works, collec-
tions, or materials about plays about the Indi-
ans of North America.
BT   Drama
Indians of North America—Dwellings
728
UF   Teepees
Tepees
Tipis
Wigwams
BT   Indians of North America—
Architecture
Indians of North America—Economic
conditions   970.004
BT   Economic conditions
Indians of North America—Education
371.829; 970.004
UF   Indians of North America—
Schools
BT   Education
Indians of North America—Ethnology
USE   Indians of North America
Indians of North America—Fiction
808.83; 813, etc.
May be used for individual works, collec-
tions, or materials about fiction about the In-
dians of North America.

Indians of North America—First contact
with Europeans   970.004
BT   Indians of North America—
History
RT   Indians of North America—
Relations with early settlers
Indians of North America—Folklore
398
Use for collections of North American Indi-
an legends, myths, tales, etc., and for materi-
als about the folklore and mythology of North
American Indians.
UF   Indian mythology
Indians of North America—Leg-
ends [Former heading]
Indians of North America—My-
thology
BT   Folklore
Indians of North America—Games
790.1; 970.004
UF   Indians of North America—
Amusements
Indians of North America—Rec-
reations
Indians of North America—
Sports
BT   Games
Indians of North America—So-
cial life and customs
Indians of North America—Government
policy
USE   Indians of North America—
Government relations
Indians of North America—Government
relations   323.1; 970.004
Use for materials on the Indian policy of
the United States government and on relations
between North American governments and the
Indians of North America.
UF   Federal-Indian relations
Indians of North America—Gov-
ernment policy [Former head-
ing]
Indians of North America—Le-
gal status, laws, etc.
RT   Indians of North America—
Relations with early settlers
Indians of North America—History
970.004
BT   History

BT = Broader Term   NT = Narrower Term   RT = Related Term   SA = See Also   UF = Used For

Indians of North America—History—*Continued*

NT   Indians of North America—
       First contact with Europe-
       ans
       Indians of North America—
       Relations with early settlers
       Indians of North America—
       Wars

Indians of North America—History—
    Chronology   970.004

    Use for materials that list events and dates
in the history of the Indians of North America
in the order of their occurrence.

UF   Indians of North America—
       Chronology *[Former heading]*

BT   **Historical chronology**

Indians of North America—Industries
    338.4; 680; 970.004

BT   **Industries**

Indians of North America—Land claims

USE   **Indians of North America—**
       Claims

Indians of North America—Languages
    497

    Use for materials on the several languages
of North American Indians.

UF   Indian languages (North
       American)

SA   names of individual languages,
       e.g. **Navajo language;** to be
       added as needed

BT   **Language and languages**

NT   **Indians of North America—**
       Sign language
       Navajo language

Indians of North America—Legal status,
    laws, etc.

USE   **Indians of North America—**
       Claims
       Indians of North America—
       Government relations

Indians of North America—Legends

USE   **Indians of North America—**
       Folklore

Indians of North America—Literature
    897

    Use for collections or materials about litera-
ture written in Indian languages by several
American Indian authors. Collections or materials about literature written in English by
several American Indian authors are entered

under **American literature—American Indian authors.**

UF   Indian literature (North
       American Indian)

BT   **Literature**

Indians of North America—Medicine
    615.8

BT   **Medicine**

Indians of North America—Mexico

USE   **Indians of Mexico**

Indians of North America—Missions,
    Christian

USE   **Indians of North America—**
       Christian missions

Indians of North America—Music
    780.89

    Use for musical transcriptions or for materi-
als about the music of the North American Indians.

UF   Indians of North America—
       Songs and music *[Former
       heading]*
       Music, Indian

BT   **Music**

Indians of North America—Mythology

USE   **Indians of North America—**
       Folklore

Indians of North America—Names
    929.4

BT   **Names**

Indians of North America—Origin
    970.004

Indians of North America—Poetry
    811, etc.

    May be used for individual works, collec-
tions, or materials about poetry about the Indians of North America.

BT   **Poetry**

**Indians of North America—Politics and
    government   970.004**

UF   Indians of North America—Trib-
       al government

BT   **Politics**

Indians of North America—Psychology
    155.8

BT   **Ethnopsychology**
       Psychology

Indians of North America—Recreations

USE   **Indians of North America—**
       Games

BT = Broader Term   **NT** = Narrower Term   **RT** = Related Term   **SA** = See Also   **UF** = Used For

Indians of North America—Relations
with early settlers 970.004
BT Indians of North America—
History
RT Indians of North America—
First contact with Europe-
ans
Indians of North America—
Government relations
Indians of North America—Religion
270.089; 299
BT Religion
Indians of North America—Reservations
333.1
UF Indian reservations
Reservations, Indian
Indians of North America—Rites and
ceremonies 970.004
BT Rites and ceremonies
NT Powwows
Indians of North America—Schools
USE Indians of North America—
Education
Indians of North America—Sign lan-
guage 419
BT Indians of North America—
Languages
Sign language
Indians of North America—Silverwork
739.2
BT Silverwork
Indians of North America—Social condi-
tions 970.004
BT Social conditions
Indians of North America—Social life
and customs 970.004
UF Indians of North America—
Amusements
Indians of North America—Cus-
toms
BT Manners and customs
NT Indians of North America—
Games
Powwows
Indians of North America—Songs and mu-
sic
USE Indians of North America—
Music

Indians of North America—Sports
USE Indians of North America—
Games
Indians of North America—Tribal govern-
ment
USE Indians of North America—
Politics and government
Indians of North America—United States
USE Indians of North America
Indians of North America—Wars
970.004
BT Indians of North America—
History
NT Black Hawk War, 1832
King Philip's War, 1675-1676
Pontiac's Conspiracy, 1763-
1765
United States—History—1689-
1697, King William's War
United States—History—1755-
1763, French and Indian
War
Indians of North America—Women
305.4; 970.004
UF Indian women (North American)
Native American women
Women, Indian
BT Women
Indians of South America (May subdiv.
geog.) 980
May be subdivided topically like Indians of
North America.
UF American Indians
Amerindians
South American Indians
BT Indians
NT Incas
Indians of South America—Peru 985
Indians of the West Indies (May subdiv.
geog.) 972.9004
May be subdivided topically like Indians of
North America.
UF American Indians
Amerindians
West Indies, Indians of the
BT Indians
Indic literature 891.4
UF Indian literature (East Indian)
BT Literature
Indigenous peoples
USE Native peoples

BT = Broader Term   NT = Narrower Term   RT = Related Term   SA = See Also   UF = Used For

Indigestion   616.3
    UF   Dyspepsia
    BT   **Digestion**
Individual retirement accounts   332.024
    UF   I.R.A.'s (Pensions)
            IRAs (Pensions)
    BT   **Pensions**
            Retirement income
Individualism   141; 302.5; 330.1
    BT   **Economics**
            Equality
            Political science
            Sociology
    RT   **Persons**
Individuality   155.2
    UF   Identity
    BT   **Consciousness**
            Psychology
    NT   **Self**
    RT   **Conformity**
            Personality
Individualized instruction   371.39
    Use for materials on the adaptation of instruction to meet individual needs within a group. Materials on individual one-on-one instruction are entered under **Tutors and tutoring.**
    BT   **Open plan schools**
    RT   **Tutors and tutoring**
Indochina   959
    Use for the area comprising Laos, Cambodia, and Vietnam.
    BT   **Southeast Asia**
Indoctrination, Forced
    USE   **Brainwashing**
Indoor games   793
    BT   **Games**
    NT   **Checkers**
            Chess
    RT   **Amusements**
Indoor gardening   635.9
    BT   **Gardening**
    NT   **Terrariums**
            Window gardening
    RT   **Container gardening**
            House plants
            Miniature gardens
Induced abortion
    USE   **Abortion**
Induction coils   537.6; 621.319
    BT   **Electric apparatus and appliances**

    NT   **Condensers (Electricity)**
Induction (Logic)
    USE   **Logic**
Induction motors
    USE   **Electric motors**
Industrial accidents   363.11; 658.3
    UF   Employees—Accidents
            Industrial disasters
            Industrial injuries
            Labor—Accidents *[Former heading]*
            Occupational accidents
            Occupational injuries
    SA   industries with the subdivision *Accidents*, e.g. **Chemical industry—Accidents;** to be added as needed
    BT   **Accidents**
    NT   **Chemical industry—Accidents**
    RT   **Hazardous occupations**
Industrial alcohol
    USE   **Denatured alcohol**
Industrial antiquities
    USE   **Industrial archeology**
Industrial applications
    USE   scientific phenomena, chemicals, plants, and crops with the subdivision *Industrial applications*, e.g. **Ultrasonic waves—Industrial applications;** to be added as needed
Industrial arbitration   331.89
    UF   Arbitration, Industrial *[Former heading]*
            Conciliation, Industrial
            Industrial conciliation
            Labor arbitration
            Labor courts
            Labor negotiations
            Mediation, Industrial
            Trade agreements (Labor)
    BT   **Industrial relations**
            Labor
            Labor disputes
            Labor unions
            Negotiation
    RT   **Collective bargaining**
            Strikes
Industrial archaeology
    USE   **Industrial archeology**

BT = Broader Term   NT = Narrower Term   RT = Related Term   SA = See Also   UF = Used For

Industrial archeology (May subdiv. geog.)
609

Use for materials on the study of the physical remains of industries from the eighteenth and nineteenth centuries, including buildings, machinery, and tools.
- UF Industrial antiquities
  - Industrial archaeology
- BT **Archeology**
  - **Industries—History**

Industrial arts   600
- UF Arts, Useful
  - Mechanic arts
  - Trades
  - Useful arts
- SA types of industries, arts, and trades; and names of countries, cities, etc., with the subdivision *Industries,* to be added as needed
- BT **Handicraft**
- NT **Arts and crafts movement**
  - **Bookbinding**
  - **Engineering**
  - **Industrial arts education**
  - **Printing**
  - **Shipbuilding**
- RT **Technology**

Industrial arts education   607
- UF Education, Industrial
  - Industrial education
  - Industrial schools
  - Manual training
- BT **Industrial arts**
  - **Vocational education**
- RT **Technical education**

Industrial arts shops
- USE **School shops**

Industrial buildings   725
- UF Buildings, Industrial
- BT **Buildings**
- NT **Factories**

Industrial chemistry   660
- UF Chemical technology
  - Chemistry, Industrial
  - Chemistry, Technical *[Former heading]*
  - Technical chemistry
- SA types of industries and products, e.g. **Clay industries; Dyes**

and dyeing; etc., to be added as needed
- BT **Chemistry**
  - **Technology**
- NT **Alloys**
  - **Bleaching**
  - **Canning and preserving**
  - **Ceramics**
  - **Corrosion and anticorrosives**
  - **Distillation**
  - **Drying**
  - **Electrochemistry**
  - **Food—Analysis**
  - **Gums and resins**
  - **Synthetic products**
  - **Tanning**
  - **Textile chemistry**
  - **Waste products**
- RT **Chemical engineering**
  - **Chemical industry**
  - **Chemicals**
  - **Metallurgy**

Industrial combinations
- USE **Industrial trusts**

Industrial conciliation
- USE **Industrial arbitration**

Industrial councils
- USE **Participative management**

Industrial counseling
- USE **Employees—Counseling of**

Industrial design   745.2
- UF Art, Applied
  - Design, Industrial *[Former heading]*
- BT **Design**
- NT **Automobiles—Design and construction**
  - **Human engineering**
  - **Systems engineering**

Industrial disasters
- USE **Industrial accidents**

Industrial diseases
- USE **Occupational diseases**

Industrial disputes
- USE **Labor disputes**

Industrial drawing
- USE **Mechanical drawing**

Industrial education
- USE **Industrial arts education**
  - **Technical education**

BT = Broader Term   NT = Narrower Term   RT = Related Term   SA = See Also   UF = Used For

Industrial efficiency   658

    Use for materials on the various means of increasing efficiency and output in business and industries, including time and motion studies and materials on the application of psychological principles to industrial production.

    UF   Efficiency, Industrial *[Former heading]*

    BT   **Business**

          Industries

          Management

    NT   **Job analysis**

          Labor productivity

          Motion study

          Office management

          Time study

    RT   **Executive ability**

          Factory management

          Personnel management

Industrial equipment   621.8

    UF   Capital equipment

          Capital goods

          Industries—Equipment and supplies

          Industry—Equipment and supplies

          Machinery in industry *[Former heading]*

    SA   types of industries with the subdivision *Equipment and supplies,* to be addes as needed

    BT   **Machinery**

    NT   **Automation**

          Industrial robots

Industrial exhibitions

    USE   **Exhibitions**

Industrial health

    USE   **Occupational health and safety**

Industrial injuries

    USE   **Industrial accidents**

Industrial insurance

    USE   **Industrial life insurance**

Industrial laws and legislation (May subdiv. geog.)   **343**

    UF   Government regulation of commerce

          Industry—Law and legislation

    SA   types of industries with the subdivision *Law and legislation,* e.g. **Chemical industry—Law and legislation;** to be added as needed

Industrial libraries

    USE   **Corporate libraries**

Industrial life insurance   368.36

    Use for materials on low-valued life insurance, the premiums of which are collected from policy holders in small weekly or monthly payments.

    UF   Debit insurance

          Home service insurance

          Industrial insurance *[Former heading]*

          Insurance, Industrial *[Former heading]*

          Weekly premium insurance

    BT   **Life insurance**

Industrial management

    USE   **Management**

Industrial materials

    USE   **Materials**

Industrial mergers

    USE   **Corporate mergers and acquisitions**

          Industrial trusts

          Railroads—Consolidation

Industrial mobilization   355.2

    Use for materials on industrial and labor policies and programs for defense mobilization.

    UF   Defenses, National

          Economic mobilization

          Industry and war

          Mobilization, Industrial

          National defenses

    BT   **Economic policy**

          Military art and science

          War—Economic aspects

    RT   **Military readiness**

          Military weapons

Industrial organization

    USE   **Management**

Industrial painting   698

    UF   Finishes and finishing

          Mechanical painting

          Painting, Industrial *[Former heading]*

          Painting, Mechanical

    BT   **Painting**

    NT   **Lettering**

          Paint

          Sign painting

BT = Broader Term   NT = Narrower Term   RT = Related Term   SA = See Also   UF = Used For

Industrial painting—*Continued*
    Varnish and varnishing
    Wood finishing
Industrial plants
    USE   Factories
Industrial policy (May subdiv. geog.)
    338.9; 354
    UF   Business and government
          Government and business
          Government regulation of indus-
             try
          Industry and state
          Industry—Government policy
             [Former heading]
          Industry—Organization, control,
             etc.
          Laissez faire
          Socialization of industry
          State and industry
          State regulation of industry
    BT   Economic policy
    NT   Agriculture—Government poli-
             cy
          Consumer protection
          Government ownership
          Privatization
          Public service commissions
          Railroads—Government policy
          Subsidies
Industrial policy—United States
    338.973; 354
    UF   Industry—Government policy—
             United States *[Former head-
             ing]*
          United States—Industries—Gov-
             ernment policy
Industrial psychology
    USE   Applied psychology
Industrial relations   331
    Use for general materials on employer-
    employee relations. Materials on problems of
    personnel and relations from the employer's
    point of view are entered under **Personnel
    management.**
    UF   Capital and labor
          Employer-employee relations
          Labor and capital
          Labor-management relations
          Labor relations
    BT   Labor
          Management
    NT   Collective bargaining

Industrial arbitration
    Labor contract
    Labor disputes
    Labor unions
    Participative management
    Personnel management
    Strikes
Industrial revolution (May subdiv. geog.)
    330.9; 909.81
    Use for materials on the historical shift
    from home-based industries to large-scale fac-
    tory production. Materials on the development
    of organized productions as industries, espe-
    cially factory-based industries, are entered un-
    der **Industrialization.**
    SA   names of countries with the sub-
             division *Economic conditions,*
             to be added as needed
    BT   Economic conditions
          Industries—History
    RT   Factory management
          Great Britain—History—1800-
             1899 (19th century)
          Industrialization
          Technology and civilization
Industrial robots   629.8
    UF   Robots, Industrial *[Former head-
             ing]*
          Working robots
    BT   Automation
          Industrial equipment
          Robots
Industrial safety
    USE   Occupational health and safety
Industrial schools
    USE   Industrial arts education
           Technical education
Industrial secrets
    USE   Trade secrets
Industrial trusts   338.8; 658
    Use for materials on combinations in re-
    straint of trade in which stock ownership is
    transferred to trustees, who in turn issue trust
    certificates and dividends and who attempt to
    achieve monopolistic control over output,
    prices, or markets.
    UF   Business combinations
          Cartels
          Combinations, Industrial
          Industrial combinations
          Industrial mergers
          Mergers, Industrial

BT = Broader Term   NT = Narrower Term   RT = Related Term   SA = See Also   UF = Used For

Industrial trusts—*Continued*

      Trusts, Industrial *[Former heading]*

  BT   **Capital**

       Commerce

       Economics

  NT   **Antitrust law**

       Railroads—Consolidation

  RT   **Competition**

       Corporation law

       Corporations

       Monopolies

       Restraint of trade

Industrial trusts—Law and legislation

  USE **Antitrust law**

Industrial uses of space

  USE **Space industrialization**

Industrial wastes   363.72; 628.4

  UF   Factory and trade waste

       Factory waste

       Trade waste

       Wastes, Industrial

  BT   **Refuse and refuse disposal**

       Waste products

  NT   **Hazardous wastes**

  RT   **Pollution**

       Water pollution

Industrial welfare   658.3

  UF   Welfare work in industry *[Former heading]*

  BT   **Labor**

       Management

       Social work

  NT   **Social settlements**

Industrial workers

  USE **Labor**

       Working class

Industrialization (May subdiv. geog.)
   338

  Use for materials on the development of organized productions as industries, especially factory-based industries. Materials on the historical shift from home-based industries to large-scale factory production are entered under **Industrial revolution.**

  BT   **Economic policy**

       Industries

  NT   **Developing countries**

       Space industrialization

  RT   **Industrial revolution**

       Modernization (Sociology)

Industries (May subdiv. geog.)   **338**

  UF   Industry *[Former heading]*

       Production

  SA   types of industries, e.g. **Steel industry;** and ethnic groups with the subdivision *Industries,* e.g. **Indians of North America—Industries;** to be added as needed

  BT   **Economics**

  NT   **Aerospace industries**

       Automobile industry

       Book industries

       Business enterprises

       Ceramic industries

       Chemical industry

       Clothing industry

       Computer industry

       Defense industries

       Electric industries

       Indians of North America—Industries

       Industrial efficiency

       Industrialization

       Iron industry

       Leather industry

       Liquor industry

       Management

       Manufactures

       Motion picture industry

       Paper industry

       Petroleum industry

       Service industries

       Steel industry

       Textile industry

Industries—Chicago (Ill.)   338.09773

  UF   Chicago (Ill.)—Industries *[Former heading]*

       Chicago (Ill.)—Manufactures

Industries, Electric

  USE **Electric industries**

Industries—Equipment and supplies

  USE **Industrial equipment**

Industries—History (May subdiv. geog.)
   338.09

  UF   Industry—History *[Former heading]*

  NT   **Industrial archeology**

       Industrial revolution

BT = Broader Term   NT = Narrower Term   RT = Related Term   SA = See Also   UF = Used For

Industries—Ohio   338.09771
   UF   Ohio—Industries *[Former head-*
           ing]
           Ohio—Manufactures
Industries, Service
   USE   **Service industries**
Industries—United States   338.0973;
        658; 670
   UF   United States—Industries *[For-*
           mer heading]
           United States—Manufactures
Industry
   USE   **Industries**
Industry and state
   USE   **Industrial policy**
Industry and war
   USE   **Industrial mobilization**
          War—Economic aspects
Industry—Equipment and supplies
   USE   **Industrial equipment**
Industry—Government policy
   USE   **Industrial policy**
Industry—Government policy—United
   States
   USE   **Industrial policy—United**
          States
Industry—History
   USE   **Industries—History**
Industry—Law and legislation
   USE   **Industrial laws and legislation**
Industry—Organization, control, etc.
   USE   **Industrial policy**
Inequality
   USE   **Equality**
Infallibility of the Pope
   USE   **Popes—Infallibility**
Infant care
   USE   **Infants—Care**
Infant mortality
   USE   **Infants—Mortality**
Infant sudden death
   USE   **Sudden infant death syndrome**
Infantile paralysis
   USE   **Poliomyelitis**
Infants   155.42; 305.232; 362.7; 618.92
   Use for materials about children in the ear-
   liest period of life, usually the first two years
   only.
   UF   Babies
   BT   **Children**

Infants and strangers
   USE   **Children and strangers**
Infants—Birth defects
   USE   **Birth defects**
Infants—Care   649
   UF   Baby care
           Infant care
   BT   **Child care**
   NT   **Babysitting**
Infants—Clothing   646; 649
   BT   **Clothing and dress**
Infants—Death   306.9; 618.92
   Use for general materials on the death of
   infants. Materials on infant death rates and
   causes are entered under **Infants—Mortality.**
   BT   **Death**
   NT   **Sudden infant death syndrome**
Infants—Diseases   618.92
   UF   Pediatrics
   BT   **Diseases**
   RT   **Infants—Health and hygiene**
Infants—Education
   USE   **Preschool education**
Infants—Health and hygiene   613;
        618.92
   UF   Infants—Hygiene
           Pediatrics
   BT   **Health**
          Hygiene
   RT   **Infants—Diseases**
Infants—Hygiene
   USE   **Infants—Health and hygiene**
Infants—Mortality (May subdiv. geog.)
        304.6
   Use for materials on infant death rates and
   causes. General materials on the death of in-
   fants are entered under **Infants—Death.**
   UF   Infant mortality
   BT   **Mortality**
Infants—Nutrition   613.2; 649
   BT   **Nutrition**
   NT   **Breast feeding**
Infants, Sale of
   USE   **Adoption—Corrupt practices**
Infection and infectious diseases
   USE   **Communicable diseases**
Infectious wastes
   USE   **Medical wastes**
Infertility   616.6
   Use for materials on infertility in humans
   and in animals.
   UF   Sterility in animals

BT = Broader Term   NT = Narrower Term   RT = Related Term   SA = See Also   UF = Used For

Infertility—*Continued*
  Sterility in humans
  BT **Reproduction**
  RT **Birth control**
      Childlessness
      Fertility
      Human fertility
Infidelity, Marital
  USE **Adultery**
Infirmaries
  USE **Hospitals**
Inflammable substances
  USE **Hazardous substances**
Inflation (Finance) (May subdiv. geog.)
  332.4
  BT **Finance**
  NT **Wage-price policy**
  RT **Monetary policy**
      Paper money
Influence
  USE subjects, corporate bodies, indi-
       vidual persons, literary au-
       thors, religions, denomina-
       tions, sacred works, and wars
       with the subdivision *Influence,*
       e.g. **World War, 1939-**
       1945—Influence; Shake-
       speare, William, 1564-1616—
       Influence; to be added as
       needed
Influenza   616.2
  UF Flu
      Grippe
  BT **Cold (Disease)**
      Communicable diseases
      Diseases
Informal sector (Economics)
  USE **Underground economy**
Information centers
  USE **Information services**
Information clearinghouses
  USE **Information services**
Information, Freedom of
  USE **Freedom of information**
Information networks   004.6
  UF Automated information networks
      Networks, Information
      Telereference

  SA types of information networks
      and names of specific net-
      works, to be added as needed
  BT **Data transmission systems**
      Information services
      Information systems
  NT **Computer networks**
      Internet
      Library information networks
Information science   020
  BT **Communication**
  NT **Documentation**
      Electronic data processing
      Information services
      Information systems
      Library science
Information services   025.5
  UF Clearinghouses, Information
      Information centers
      Information clearinghouses
  SA subjects, ethnic groups, classes
      of persons, individual persons,
      coporate bodies, industries,
      and names of countries, cities,
      etc., with the subdivision *In-*
      formation services, e.g. **Busi-**
      ness—Information services;
      United Nations—Information
      services; etc., to be added as
      needed
  BT **Information science**
  NT **Archives**
      Business—Information services
      Electronic publishing
      Hotlines (Telephone counseling)
      Information networks
      Information systems
      Machine readable bibliographic
      data
      Reference services (Libraries)
      United Nations—Information
      services
  RT **Documentation**
      Libraries
      Research
Information storage and retrieval systems
  USE **Information systems**
Information systems   025.04
  UF Automatic information retrieval

BT = Broader Term   NT = Narrower Term   RT = Related Term   SA = See Also   UF = Used For

Information systems—*Continued*
Computer-based information systems
Data processing
Data storage and retrieval systems
Information storage and retrieval systems *[Former heading]*
Punched card systems
BT   **Bibliographic control**
Bibliography
Computers
Documentation
Information science
Information services
NT   **Database management**
Electronic data processing
Expert systems (Computer science)
Information networks
Machine readable bibliographic data
Management information systems
Multimedia systems
Teletext systems
Videotex systems
RT   **Libraries—Automation**
Information systems—Management 025.04
Use for materials on the management of information systems.
BT   **Management**
Infrared radiation   535.01; 621.36
BT   **Electromagnetic waves**
Radiation
Inhalant abuse
USE   **Solvent abuse**
Inhalation abuse of solvents
USE   **Solvent abuse**
Inheritance and succession   346.05
UF   Bequests
Heirs
Hereditary succession
Intestacy
Legacies
Succession, Intestate
BT   **Parent and child**
Wealth
NT   **Executors and administrators**
Inheritance and transfer tax

RT   **Wills**
Inheritance and transfer tax   343.05
UF   Estate tax
Taxation of legacies
Transfer tax
BT   **Estate planning**
Inheritance and succession
Internal revenue
Taxation
Inheritance (Biology)
USE   **Heredity**
Initialisms
USE   **Acronyms**
Initials   745.6
NT   **Printing—Specimens**
RT   **Alphabets**
Illumination of books and manuscripts
Lettering
Monograms
Type and type founding
Initiative and referendum
USE   **Referendum**
Injunctions   331.89
BT   **Constitutional law**
Labor unions
RT   **Strikes**
Injuries
USE   **Accidents**
First aid
Wounds and injuries
Injurious insects
USE   **Insect pests**
Injurious occupations
USE   **Hazardous occupations**
Ink drawing
USE   **Pen drawing**
Inland navigation   386
UF   Navigation, Inland
BT   **Navigation**
Shipping
Transportation
Water resources development
RT   **Canals**
Lakes
Rivers
Waterways
Inner cities   307.76
Use for materials on the densely populated, economically depressed, central areas of large cities.

BT = Broader Term   NT = Narrower Term   RT = Related Term   SA = See Also   UF = Used For

Inner cities—*Continued*
    UF   Ghettoes, Inner city
             Inner city ghettoes
             Inner city problems
    BT   **Cities and towns**
Inner city ghettoes
    USE **Inner cities**
Inner city problems
    USE **Inner cities**
Inns
    USE **Hotels and motels**
Innuit
    USE **Inuit**
Inoculation
    USE **Vaccination**
Inorganic chemistry   546
    UF   Chemistry, Inorganic *[Former heading]*
    BT   **Chemistry**
    NT   **Metals**
Input equipment (Computers)
    USE **Computer peripherals**
Inquisition (May subdiv. geog.)   272
    UF   Holy Office
    BT   **Catholic Church**
Insane
    USE **Mentally ill**
Insanity defense   345
    UF   Insanity—Jurisprudence
             Insanity plea
             Mental illness—Jurisprudence *[Former heading]*
    BT   **Criminal law**
Insanity—Jurisprudence
    USE **Insanity defense**
Insanity plea
    USE **Insanity defense**
Inscriptions   411
    UF   Epigraphy
    BT   **Ancient history**
          Archeology
    NT   **Brasses**
          Epitaphs
          Graffiti
          Hieroglyphics
          Seals (Numismatics)
Insect-eating plants
    USE **Carnivorous plants**
Insect pests   632
    UF   Destructive insects

             Diseases and pests
             Economic entomology
             Garden pests
             Harmful insects
             Injurious insects
             Insects, Injurious and beneficial *[Former heading]*
    SA   types of insect pests, e.g. **Locusts;** etc.; and types of crops, plants, trees, etc., with the subdivision *Diseases and pests,* e.g. **Fruit—Diseases and pests;** to be added as needed
    BT   **Economic zoology**
          Insects
          Pests
    NT   **Fruit—Diseases and pests**
          Insects as carriers of disease
          Locusts
    RT   **Agricultural pests**
          Household pests
          Parasites
Insecticides   632; 668
    SA   types of insecticides, to be added as needed
    BT   **Agricultural chemicals**
          Pesticides
    NT   **D.D.T. (Insecticide)**
          Fumigation
    RT   **Spraying and dusting**
Insecticides—Toxicology   615.9
    BT   **Poisons and poisoning**
Insectivorous plants
    USE **Carnivorous plants**
Insects   595.7
    UF   Entomology
    SA   types of insects, to be added as needed
    BT   **Invertebrates**
    NT   **Ants**
          Bees
          Beneficial insects
          Butterflies
          Cicadas
          Flies
          Insect pests
          Locusts
          Mosquitoes
          Moths

BT = Broader Term   **NT** = Narrower Term   **RT** = Related Term   **SA** = See Also   **UF** = Used For

Insects—*Continued*
    Silkworms
    Wasps
  RT   **Fertilization of plants**
Insects as carriers of disease   614.4
  UF   Entomology, Medical
       Medical entomology
  BT   **Insect pests**
  RT   **Communicable diseases**
       Lyme disease
Insects, Injurious and beneficial
  USE **Beneficial insects**
      Insect pests
Insemination, Artificial
  USE **Artificial insemination**
Inservice training
  USE **Employees—Training**
Insider trading   346.07; 364.16
  UF   Securities trading, Insider
       Stocks—Insider trading
  BT   **Commercial law**
      Securities
      Stock exchange
Insignia   929.9
  UF   Badges of honor
       Devices (Heraldry)
       Emblems
  SA   armies, navies, and other appro-
       priate subjects with the subdi-
       vision *Insignia* or *Medals,*
       badges, decorations, etc., to
       be added as needed
  BT   **Heraldry**
  NT   **Colleges and universities—In-
       signia**
      United States. Army—Insignia
      **United States. Army—Medals,
      badges, decorations, etc.**
      United States. Navy—Insignia
      **United States. Navy—Medals,
      badges, decorations, etc.**
  RT   **Decorations of honor**
      Medals
      National emblems
Insolvency
  USE **Bankruptcy**
Insomnia   616.8
  UF   Sleeplessness
       Wakefulness
  RT   **Sleep**

Inspection of food
  USE **Food adulteration and inspec-
      tion**
Inspection of meat
  USE **Meat inspection**
Inspection of schools
  USE **School supervision**
      Schools—Administration
Inspiration
  USE **Creation (Literary, artistic,
      etc.)**
Inspiration, Biblical
  USE **Bible—Inspiration**
Installment plan   658.8
  UF   Hire-purchase plan
       Instalment plan *[Former head-
       ing]*
  BT   **Business**
      Buying
      Consumer credit
      Credit
Instalment plan
  USE **Installment plan**
Instinct   152.3; 156
  UF   Animal instinct
  BT   **Animal behavior**
      Psychology
  RT   **Animal intelligence**
      Comparative psychology
      Habit
Institutional care   361
  UF   Asylums
       Benevolent institutions
       Charitable institutions
       Homes (Institutions)
  SA   classes of persons with the sub-
       division *Institutional care,* to
       be added as needed
  BT   **Charities**
      Medical charities
      Public welfare
  NT   **Blind—Institutional care**
      Children—Institutional care
      Deaf—Institutional care
      Group homes
      Hospitals
      Mentally ill—Institutional care
      Nursing homes
Institutions, Charitable and philanthropic
  USE **Charities**

BT = Broader Term   NT = Narrower Term   RT = Related Term   SA = See Also   UF = Used For

Instruction
    USE   **Education**
                Teaching
Instructional games
    USE   **Educational games**
Instructional materials
    USE   **Teaching—Aids and devices**
Instructional materials centers   027.7
    UF   Audiovisual materials centers
             Curriculum materials centers
             Educational media centers
             Learning resource centers
             Media centers (Education)
             Multimedia centers
             School media centers
    BT   **Libraries**
    NT   **School libraries**
Instructional supervision
    USE   **School supervision**
Instructional systems analysis
    USE   **Educational evaluation**
Instructional technology
    USE   **Educational technology**
Instructive games
    USE   **Educational games**
Instrument flying   629.132
    BT   **Aeronautical instruments**
             Airplanes—Piloting
Instrumental ensembles
    USE   **Ensembles (Music)**
Instrumental music   784
    UF   Music, Instrumental
    SA   types of instrumental music, to
             be added as needed
    BT   **Music**
    NT   **Band music**
             Chamber music
             Guitar music
             Orchestral music
             Organ music
             Piano music
    RT   **Musical instruments**
Instrumentalists   784
    SA   types of instrumentalists, e.g. **Vi-**
             olinists; to be added as need-
             ed
    BT   **Musicians**
    NT   **Organists**
             Pianists
             Violinists

             Violoncellists
Instrumentation and orchestration
             781.3; 784.13
    UF   Orchestration
    BT   **Bands (Music)**
             Composition (Music)
             Music
             Orchestra
    RT   **Musical instruments**
Instruments, Aeronautical
    USE   **Aeronautical instruments**
Instruments, Astronautical
    USE   **Astronautical instruments**
Instruments, Astronomical
    USE   **Astronomical instruments**
Instruments, Engineering
    USE   **Engineering instruments**
Instruments, Measuring
    USE   **Measuring instruments**
Instruments, Meteorological
    USE   **Meteorological instruments**
Instruments, Musical
    USE   **Musical instruments**
Instruments, Negotiable
    USE   **Negotiable instruments**
Instruments, Optical
    USE   **Optical instruments**
Instruments, Scientific
    USE   **Scientific apparatus and in-**
             struments
Insulation (Heat)   691; 693.8
    UF   Heat insulating materials
             Thermal insulation
    BT   **Heating**
Insulation (Sound)
    USE   **Soundproofing**
Insults
    USE   **Invective**
Insurance   368
    UF   Underwriting
    SA   types of insurance, e.g. **Automo-**
             bile insurance; to be added
             as needed
    BT   **Estate planning**
             Finance
             Personal finance
    NT   **Automobile insurance**
             Casualty insurance
             Fire insurance
             Health insurance

BT = Broader Term   NT = Narrower Term   RT = Related Term   SA = See Also   UF = Used For

Insurance—*Continued*
      Life insurance
      Malpractice insurance
      Marine insurance
      Saving and thrift
      Unemployment insurance
Insurance, Accident
  USE   Accident insurance
Insurance, Automobile
  USE   Automobile insurance
Insurance, Casualty
  USE   Casualty insurance
Insurance, Disability
  USE   Accident insurance
         Health insurance
Insurance, Fire
  USE   Fire insurance
Insurance, Group
  USE   Group insurance
Insurance, Health
  USE   Health insurance
Insurance, Hospitalization
  USE   Hospitalization insurance
Insurance, Industrial
  USE   Industrial life insurance
Insurance, Life
  USE   Life insurance
Insurance, Malpractice
  USE   Malpractice insurance
Insurance, Marine
  USE   Marine insurance
Insurance, Old age
  USE   Old age pensions
Insurance, Professional liability
  USE   Malpractice insurance
Insurance, Sickness
  USE   Health insurance
Insurance, Social
  USE   Social security
Insurance, State and compulsory
  USE   Social security
Insurance, Unemployment
  USE   Unemployment insurance
Insurance, Workers'
  USE   Social security
Insurance, Workers' compensation
  USE   Workers' compensation
Insurgency (May subdiv. geog.) 322.4;
    355.02
  UF   Rebellions

  BT   Revolutions
  NT   Guerrilla warfare
         Subversive activities
         Terrorism
  RT   Internal security
         Resistance to government
Integrated churches
  USE   Church and race relations
Integrated curriculum
  USE   Interdisciplinary approach in
         education
Integrated language arts (Holistic)
  USE   Whole language
Integrated schools
  USE   School integration
Integration in education
  USE   School integration
         Segregation in education
Integration, Racial
  USE   Race relations
Intellect 153.4
  UF   Intelligence
         Mind
         Understanding
  BT   Psychology
  NT   Creation (Literary, artistic,
         etc.)
         Imagination
         Logic
         Memory
         Perception
         Reason
         Senses and sensation
  RT   Reasoning
         Theory of knowledge
         Thought and thinking
Intellectual cooperation   327.1; 370.116
  UF   Cooperation, Intellectual
  BT   International cooperation
  NT   Congresses and conventions
         Cultural relations
  RT   International education
Intellectual freedom   323.44
  BT   Freedom
  NT   Academic freedom
         Censorship
         Freedom of information
         Freedom of speech
         Freedom of the press

BT = Broader Term   NT = Narrower Term   RT = Related Term   SA = See Also   UF = Used For

Intellectual life   001.1

Use for general materials on learning and scholarship, literature, the arts, etc. Materials on literature, art, music, motion pictures, etc. produced for a mass audience are entered under **Popular culture.**

UF   Cultural life

SA   classes of persons, ethnic groups, and names of countries, cities, etc., with the subdivision *Intellectual life,* to be added as needed

BT   **Culture**

NT   **African Americans—Intellectual life**

       Blacks—Intellectual life

       Chicago (Ill.)—Intellectual life

       Learning and scholarship

       Ohio—Intellectual life

       Popular culture

       United States—Intellectual life

Intellectual property

USE   **Copyright**

       Inventions

       Patents

Intellectuals (May subdiv. geog.)   **305.5**

UF   Intelligentsia

SA   ethnic groups, classes of persons, and names of countries, cities, etc., with the subdivision *Intellectual life,* e.g. **African Americans—Intellectual life; United States—Intellectual life;** etc., to be added as needed

BT   **Persons**

       Social classes

Intelligence

USE   **Intellect**

Intelligence agents

USE   **Spies**

Intelligence, Artificial

USE   **Artificial intelligence**

Intelligence of animals

USE   **Animal intelligence**

Intelligence service (May subdiv. geog.)   **327.12; 355.3**

Use for materials on a government agency that is engaged in obtaining information, usually about an enemy but sometimes about an ally or a neutral country, and also in blocking the attempts by foreign agents to obtain information about one's own national secrets.

UF   Counterespionage

       Counterintelligence

BT   **Public administration**

       Research

NT   **Espionage**

RT   **Secret service**

Intelligence service—United States   327.1273; 355.3

UF   United States—Intelligence service

Intelligence testing

USE   **Intelligence tests**

Intelligence tests

UF   I. Q. tests

       Intelligence testing

       IQ tests

       Mental tests *[Former heading]*

BT   **Child psychology**

       Educational psychology

NT   **Ability—Testing**

RT   **Educational tests and measurements**

Intelligentsia

USE   **Intellectuals**

Intemperance

USE   **Alcoholism**

       Temperance

Inter-American relations

USE   **Pan-Americanism**

Interactive CD technology

USE   **CD-I technology**

Interactive multimedia

USE   **Multimedia systems**

Interactive videotex

USE   **Videotex systems**

Interbehaviorial psychology

USE   **Behaviorism**

Interchange of teachers

USE   **Teacher exchange**

Interchange of visitors

USE   **Exchange of persons programs**

Intercollegiate athletics

USE   **College sports**

Intercommunication systems   621.38; 651.7

UF   Interoffice communication systems

BT   **Electronic apparatus and appliances**

       Telecommunication

BT = Broader Term   NT = Narrower Term   RT = Related Term   SA = See Also   UF = Used For

Intercommunication systems—*Continued*
NT   Closed-circuit television
       Microwave communication systems
Intercontinental ballistic missiles   623.4
UF   I.C.B.M.
       ICBM
SA   names of specific ICBM missiles, e.g. **Atlas (Missile)**; to be added as needed
BT   **Ballistic missiles**
NT   **Atlas (Missile)**
Intercultural education
USE   **Multicultural education**
Intercultural literature
USE   **Multicultural literature**
Intercultural relations
USE   **Cultural relations**
Intercultural studies
USE   **Cross cultural studies**
Interdependence of nations
USE   **International relations**
Interdisciplinarity in education
USE   **Interdisciplinary approach in education**
Interdisciplinary approach in education   375
UF   Integrated curriculum
       Interdisciplinarity in education
       Interdisciplinary studies
BT   **Curriculum planning**
Interdisciplinary studies
USE   **Interdisciplinary approach in education**
Interest centers approach to teaching
USE   **Open plan schools**
Interest (Economics)   332.8
BT   **Banks and banking**
       Business mathematics
       Capital
       Finance
       Loans
Interest groups
USE   **Lobbying**
       Political action committees
Interfaces, Computer
USE   **Computer interfaces**

Interfaith marriage   261.8; 291.1; 306.84
UF   Intermarriage, Religious *[Former heading]*
       Marriage, Mixed
       Mixed marriage
BT   **Intermarriage**
Interfaith relations   261.2; 291.1
BT   **Christian unity**
       Human relations
Intergovernmental tax relations   336.2
UF   Federal-state tax relations
       State-local tax relations
       Tax relations, Intergovernmental
       Tax sharing
BT   **Taxation**
NT   **Revenue sharing**
Interior decoration
USE   **Interior design**
Interior design   729; 747
    Use for materials on the art and techniques of planning and supervising the design and execution of architectural interiors and their furnishings.
UF   Arts, Decorative
       Decoration, Interior
       Design, Interior
       Home decoration
       House decoration
       House furnishing
       Interior decoration
BT   **Art**
       Decoration and ornament
       Decorative arts
       Design
       Home economics
NT   **Bedspreads**
       Carpets
       Drapery
       Furniture
       Lighting
       Mural painting and decoration
       Paperhanging
       Quilts
       Rugs
       Tapestry
       Upholstery
       Wallpaper
RT   **Rooms**
Interlibrary loans   025.6
BT   **Library circulation**

BT = Broader Term   NT = Narrower Term   RT = Related Term   SA = See Also   UF = Used For

Interlibrary loans—*Continued*
        Library cooperation
Interlocking signals
    USE   Railroads—Signaling
Intermarriage   306.84
       Use for materials that discuss collectively marriage between persons of different religions, religious denominations, races, and ethnic groups.
    UF   Marriage, Mixed
           Mixed marriage
    BT   **Marriage**
    NT   **Interfaith marriage**
           Interracial marriage
Intermarriage, Racial
    USE   **Interracial marriage**
Intermarriage, Religious
    USE   **Interfaith marriage**
Intermediate state
    USE   **Eschatology**
           Future life
Interment
    USE   **Burial**
Internal combustion engines   621.43
    UF   Gas and oil engines *[Former heading]*
           Gas engines
           Gasoline engines
           Oil engines
           Petroleum engines
    BT   **Engines**
    NT   **Automobile engines**
           Carburetors
           Diesel engines
Internal migration   304.8
       Use for materials on the movement of population within a country for permanent settlement. Materials on casual or seasonal workers who move from place to place in search of employment are entered under **Migrant labor.** Materials on migration from one country to another are entered under **Immigration and emigration.**
    UF   Migration, Internal *[Former heading]*
           Rural-urban migration
           Urban-rural migration
    BT   **Colonization**
           Population
    NT   **Cities and towns—Growth**
    RT   **Immigration and emigration**
           Land settlement
           Migrant labor

Internal revenue   336.2
    UF   Revenue, Internal
    BT   **Taxation**
    NT   **Income tax**
           Inheritance and transfer tax
Internal revenue law   343.04
    UF   Law, Internal revenue
    BT   **Law**
Internal security (May subdiv. geog.)   353.3; 363.2
    UF   Loyalty oaths
           Security, Internal
    RT   **Insurgency**
           Subversive activities
Internal security—United States   353.3; 363.2
    UF   United States—Internal security
International agencies   060
    UF   Associations, International
           International associations
           International organizations
    SA   names of individual agencies, to be added as needed
    BT   **International cooperation**
International arbitration   341.5
    UF   Arbitration, International *[Former heading]*
           International mediation
           Mediation, International
    BT   **International cooperation**
           International law
           International relations
           International security
           Treaties
    NT   **League of Nations**
           United Nations
    RT   **Arms control**
           Peace
International associations
    USE   **International agencies**
International business enterprises
    USE   **Multinational corporations**
International competition   337; 382; 658
    UF   Competition, International
           World economics
    BT   **International relations**
           International trade
    RT   **War—Economic aspects**

BT = Broader Term   NT = Narrower Term   RT = Related Term   SA = See Also   UF = Used For

International conferences
USE **Congresses and conventions**
International cooperation   327.1; 341.7

Use for general materials on international cooperative activities, with or without the participation of governments.

UF   Cooperation, International
SA   subjects with the subdivision *International cooperation,* e.g.
Astronautics—International cooperation; to be added as needed
BT   **Cooperation**
International law
International relations
NT   **Astronautics—International cooperation**
Congresses and conventions
Cultural relations
Exchange of persons programs
Foreign aid
Intellectual cooperation
International agencies
International arbitration
International police
League of Nations
Space sciences—International cooperation
United Nations
RT   **International education**
International organization
Reconstruction (1914-1939)
Reconstruction (1939-1951)
Technology transfer
International copyright
USE **Copyright**
International economic relations   382
UF   Economic relations, Foreign
Foreign economic relations
BT   **Economic policy**
International relations
NT   **Balance of payments**
Commercial policy
Foreign aid
International trade
Multinational corporations
Sanctions (International law)
Technical assistance
United States—Foreign economic relations

International education   370.116

Use for materials on education for international understanding, world citizenship, etc.

UF   Education, International
BT   **Education**
NT   **Comparative librarianship**
Teacher exchange
RT   **Intellectual cooperation**
International cooperation
Multicultural education
International exchange
USE **Foreign exchange**
International exhibitions
USE **Exhibitions**
International federation
USE **International organization**
International investment
USE **Foreign investments**
International language
USE **Universal language**
International law   341
UF   Law of nations
BT   **Law**
NT   **Asylum**
Boundaries
International arbitration
International cooperation
Intervention (International law)
Mandates
Marine salvage
Maritime law
Military law
Naturalization
Neutrality
Pirates
Political refugees
Privateering
Sanctions (International law)
Slave trade
Space law
Treaties
War crimes
RT   **International organization**
International relations
Natural law
War
International mediation
USE **International arbitration**
International organization   341.2

Use for materials on plans leading towards political organization of nations.

BT = Broader Term   NT = Narrower Term   RT = Related Term   SA = See Also   UF = Used For

International organization—*Continued*
 UF Federation, International
   International federation
   Organization, International
   World government
   World organization
 SA names of specific organizations,
    e.g. **United Nations;** to be
    added as needed
 BT **Congresses and conventions**
   International relations
   International security
 NT **European federation**
   International police
   League of Nations
   Mandates
   North Atlantic Treaty Organi-
    zation
   United Nations
 RT **International cooperation**
   International law
   World politics
International organizations
 USE **International agencies**
International police 341.7
 UF Interpol
   Police, International
 BT **International cooperation**
   International organization
   International relations
   International security
International politics
 USE **World politics**
International relations 327; 341.3
  Use for materials on the theory of interna-
 tional relations. Historical accounts are en-
 tered under **World politics; Europe—Politics**
 and government; etc. Materials on the for-
 eign relations of an individual country are en-
 tered under the name of the country with the
 subdivison *Foreign relations.* Materials limited to diplomatic relations between two countries are entered under the name of each country with the subdivision *Foreign relations* further subdivided by the name of the other
 country, e.g. **United States—Foreign rela-**
 tions—Iran and also **Iran—Foreign rela-**
 tions—United States.
 UF Coexistence
   Foreign affairs
   Foreign policy
   Foreign relations
   Interdependence of nations
   Peaceful coexistence

   World order
 SA names of countries with the sub-
   division *Foreign relations,*
   e.g. **United States—Foreign**
   relations; to be added as
   needed
 NT **Arms control**
   Balance of power
   Boundaries
   Catholic Church—Foreign rela-
   tions
   Cultural relations
   Diplomacy
   Diplomatic and consular ser-
   vice
   Diplomats
   East and West
   Geopolitics
   International arbitration
   International competition
   International cooperation
   International economic rela-
   tions
   International organization
   International police
   International security
   Mandates
   Monroe Doctrine
   Nationalism
   Neutrality
   Peace
   Political refugees
   Treaties
   United States—Foreign rela-
   tions
 RT **International law**
   National security
   Technology transfer
   World politics
International security 327.1; 341.7
 UF Collective security
   Security, International *[Former*
    heading]
 BT **International relations**
 NT **Arms control**
   Arms race
   International arbitration
   International organization
   International police
   Neutrality

BT = Broader Term NT = Narrower Term RT = Related Term SA = See Also UF = Used For

International security—*Continued*
    RT   Peace
International space cooperation
    USE   Astronautics—International co-
            operation
International Standard Bibliographic De-
        scription   025.3
    UF   I.S.B.D
            ISBD
    BT   Cataloging
International Standard Book Numbers
        070.5
    UF   I.S.B.N.
            ISBN
    BT   Publishers' standard book
            numbers
International Standard Serial Numbers
        070.5
    UF   I.S.S.N.
            ISSN
    RT   Serial publications
International trade (May subdiv. geog.)
        382
        Use for general materials about trade among
    nations. Materials on foreign trade of specific
    countries, cities, etc., are entered under the
    name of the place with the subdivision *Com-
    merce*. Materials limited to trade between two
    countries are entered under the name of each
    country with the subdivision *Commerce* fur-
    ther subdivided by the name of the other
    country, i.e. **United States—Commerce—Ja-
    pan** and also **Japan—Commerce—United
    States.**
    UF   External trade
            Foreign commerce
            Foreign trade
            Trade, International
    BT   Commerce
            International economic rela-
            tions
    NT   Exports
            Free trade
            Imports
            International competition
Internationalism
    USE   Nationalism
Internet   004.67
    UF   Internet (Computer network)
            [Former heading]
    BT   Computer networks
            Information networks
    NT   World Wide Web

Internet (Computer network)
    USE   Internet
Internment camps
    USE   Concentration camps
Interoffice communication systems
    USE   Intercommunication systems
Interpersonal relations
    USE   Human relations
Interplanetary communication
    USE   Interstellar communication
Interplanetary visitors
    USE   Extraterrestrial beings
Interplanetary voyages   808.83; 813,
        etc.; 919.904
        Use for general materials about travel to
    other planets and for individual works, collec-
    tions, or materials about imaginary accounts
    of such travels. Materials on the physics and
    technical details of flight beyond the earth's
    atmosphere are entered under **Space flight.**
    UF   Interstellar travel
            Outer space travel
            People in space
            Space travel
    BT   Astronautics
            Fiction
    NT   Outer space—Exploration
    RT   Fantasy fiction
            Imaginary voyages
            Rockets (Aeronautics)
            Science fiction
            Space flight
Interplanetary warfare
    USE   Space warfare
Interpol
    USE   International police
Interpreting and translating
    USE   Translating and interpreting
Interpretive dance
    USE   Modern dance
Interracial adoption   362.73
    BT   Adoption
            Race relations
Interracial marriage   306.84
    UF   Intermarriage, Racial
            Marriage, Interracial
            Mixed marriage
            Racial intermarriage
    BT   Intermarriage
Interracial relations
    USE   Race relations

BT = Broader Term   NT = Narrower Term   RT = Related Term   SA = See Also   UF = Used For

Interscholastic sports
USE   School sports
Interstate commerce   381
    Use for materials limited to commerce be-
tween states. General materials on foreign and
domestic commerce are entered under **Com-
merce.**
  UF   Commerce, Interstate
       Government regulation of com-
       merce
  BT   **Commerce**
Interstate highways
USE   **Express highways**
Interstellar communication   621.382
  UF   Extraterrestrial communication
       Interplanetary communication
       Outer space—Communication
       Space communication
       Space telecommunication
  BT   **Life on other planets**
       Telecommunication
  NT   **Astronautics—Communication
       systems**
       Radio astronomy
Interstellar travel
USE   **Interplanetary voyages**
Interstellar warfare
USE   **Space warfare**
Interurban railroads
USE   **Electric railroads**
       Street railroads
Intervention (International law)   341.5
  UF   Military intervention
  BT   **International law**
       War
  NT   **Monroe Doctrine**
  RT   **Neutrality**
Interviewing   158
  BT   **Applications for positions**
       Social psychology
  NT   **Talk shows**
  RT   **Applied psychology**
       Counseling
Interviewing (Journalism)
USE   **Reporters and reporting**
Interviews, Parent-teacher
USE   **Parent-teacher conferences**
Intestacy
USE   **Inheritance and succession**
Intifada, 1987-   956.9405
  UF   Arab-Israeli conflict, 1987-

       Israeli-Arab conflict, 1987-
       Palestinian-Israeli conflict, 1987-
       Palestinian uprising, 1987-
  BT   **Israel-Arab conflicts**
Intolerance
USE   **Fanaticism**
       Toleration
Intoxicants
USE   **Alcohol**
       Alcoholic beverages
       Liquors
Intoxication
USE   **Alcoholism**
       Temperance
Intuition   153.4
  BT   **Philosophy**
       Psychology
       Rationalism
       Theory of knowledge
  RT   **Perception**
Inuit   970.004
    Use for materials on the native peoples of
the arctic regions of Alaska, Canada, and
Greenland. If local usage dictates, libraries
may establish **Eskimos** as a broader term than
Inuit; and the names of other groups of Arc-
tic peoples may be added as needed.
  UF   Eskimos
       Esquimaux
       Innuit
  BT   **Native peoples**
Inuit—Folklore   398
  UF   Folklore, Inuit
  BT   **Folklore**
Invalid cooking
USE   **Cooking for the sick**
       Diet therapy
Invalids
USE   **Physically handicapped**
       Sick
Invasion of Cuba, 1961
USE   **Cuba—History—1961, Invasion**
Invasion of privacy
USE   **Right of privacy**
Invective   808.88
  UF   Abuse, Verbal
       Insults
       Verbal abuse
  BT   **Satire**
Inventions   608
  UF   Discoveries in science
       Intellectual property

BT = Broader Term   NT = Narrower Term   RT = Related Term   SA = See Also   UF = Used For

Inventions—*Continued*
  BT   **Civilization**
          Technology
  NT   **Creation (Literary, artistic,**
          etc.)
          Technology transfer
  RT   **Inventors**
          Patents
Inventors   609.2; 920
  RT   **Engineers**
          Inventions
Inventory control   658.7
  UF   Stock control
  BT   **Management**
          Retail trade
Invertebrates   592
  BT   **Animals**
  NT   **Corals**
          Crustacea
          Insects
          Mollusks
          Protozoa
          Shellfish
          Spiders
          Sponges
          Worms
Investment companies
  USE   **Mutual funds**
Investment in real estate
  USE   **Real estate investment**
Investment trusts
  USE   **Mutual funds**
Investments   332.6
  BT   **Banks and banking**
          Capital
          Finance
  NT   **Annuities**
          Bonds
          Foreign investments
          Mortgages
          Mutual funds
          Real estate investment
          Savings and loan associations
          Securities
  RT   **Estate planning**
          Loans
          Saving and thrift
          Speculation
          Stock exchange
          Stocks

Investments, Foreign
  USE   **Foreign investments**
Invincible Armada
  USE   **Spanish Armada, 1588**
Invisible playmates
  USE   **Imaginary playmates**
IQ tests
  USE   **Intelligence tests**
Iran   935; 955
> May be subdivided like United States ex-
> cept for *History.*

  UF   Persia
Iran-Contra Affair, 1985-1990   973.927
  UF   Contra-Iran Affair, 1985-1990
          Iran-Contra Arms Scandal, 1985-
          1990
  BT   **American military assistance**
          Political corruption
          United States—History—1974-
          1989
          United States—History—1989-
Iran-Contra Arms Scandal, 1985-1990
  USE   **Iran-Contra Affair, 1985-1990**
Iran—Foreign relations—United States
      327.55073
  NT   **Iran hostage crisis, 1979-1981**
Iran—History—1941-1979   955.05
Iran—History—1979-   955.05
Iran hostage crisis, 1979-1981
      327.55073; 327.73055; 955
  UF   Iranian seizure of American em-
          bassy
  BT   **American hostages—Iran**
          Iran—Foreign relations—Unit-
          ed States
          United States—Foreign rela-
          tions—Iran
Iranian seizure of American embassy
  USE   **Iran hostage crisis, 1979-1981**
IRAs (Pensions)
  USE   **Individual retirement accounts**
Iron   669; 672
  BT   **Chemical elements**
          Metals
  NT   **Iron ores**
          Ironwork
          Steel
Iron Age   930.1
  RT   **Archeology**
          Bronze Age

BT = Broader Term   NT = Narrower Term   RT = Related Term   SA = See Also   UF = Used For

Iron and steel building
    USE   **Steel construction**
Iron curtain countries
    USE   **Communist countries**
Iron industry   338.2
    UF   Iron industry and trade *[Former heading]*
          Iron trade
    BT   **Industries**
    NT   **Ironwork**
    RT   **Steel industry**
Iron industry and trade
    USE   **Iron industry**
Iron ores   553.3
    BT   **Iron**
          Ore deposits
          Ores
Iron trade
    USE   **Iron industry**
Ironing
    USE   **Laundry**
Ironwork   672; 682; 739.4
    UF   Wrought iron work
    BT   **Decoration and ornament**
          Iron
          Iron industry
          Metalwork
    NT   **Blacksmithing**
          Welding
    RT   **Forging**
Irreversible coma
    USE   **Brain death**
Irrigation (May subdiv. geog.)   **333.91; 627; 631.5**
    BT   **Agricultural engineering**
          Civil engineering
          Hydraulic engineering
          Reservoirs
          Water resources development
          Water supply
    NT   **Dams**
          Dry farming
          Windmills
    RT   **Reclamation of land**
Irrigation—United States   333.91; 627; 631.5
    UF   United States—Irrigation
ISBD
    USE   **International Standard Bibliographic Description**

ISBN
    USE   **International Standard Book Numbers**
Islam   297
    Use for materials on the religion. Materials on the believers in this religion are entered under **Muslims.**
    UF   Islamism
          Mohammedanism
          Moslemism
          Muhammedanism
          Muslimism
    BT   **Religions**
    NT   **Islam—Relations—Judaism**
          Islamic fundamentalism
          Judaism—Relations—Islam
          Koran
    RT   **Islamic law**
          Muslims
Islam—Relations—Judaism   297
    Use for materials on the relations between Islam and Judaism. When assigning this heading, provide an additional subject entry under **Judaism—Relations—Islam.** Materials on the conflicts between the Arab countries and Israel are entered under **Israel-Arab conflicts.** Materials that discuss collectively the relations between Arabs and Jews, including religious, ethnic, and ideological relations, are entered under **Jewish-Arab relations.**
    UF   Islamic-Jewish relations
          Jewish-Islamic relations
    BT   **Islam**
          Judaism
    RT   **Jewish-Arab relations**
Islamic architecture   720.917
    UF   Arab architecture
          Architecture, Islamic
          Moorish architecture
          Muslim architecture
          Saracenic architecture
    BT   **Architecture**
    NT   **Mosques**
Islamic art   709.1
    UF   Art, Islamic *[Former heading]*
          Mohammedan art
          Muslim art
          Saracenic art
    BT   **Art**
Islamic countries   956
    UF   Moslem countries
          Muslim countries
    NT   **Arab countries**

BT = Broader Term   NT = Narrower Term   RT = Related Term   SA = See Also   UF = Used For

Islamic fundamentalism (May subdiv. geog.) **297.09**
   UF   Fundamentalism *[Former heading]*
   BT   **Islam**
         Religious fundamentalism
Islamic-Jewish relations
   USE **Islam—Relations—Judaism**
         Judaism—Relations—Islam
Islamic law (May subdiv. geog.) **340.5**
   UF   Law, Islamic
         Law, Muslim
         Muslim law
   BT   **Law**
   RT   **Islam**
Islamism
   USE **Islam**
Islands   **551.42**
   SA   names of islands and groups of islands, to be added as needed
   NT   **Coral reefs and islands**
         Cuba
         Islands of the Pacific
Islands, Artificial
   USE **Drilling platforms**
Islands, Imaginary
   USE **Geographical myths**
Islands of the Pacific   **990**
   Use for comprehensive materials on all the islands of the Pacific Ocean. Materials restricted to comprehensive treatment of the island groups of Melanesia, Micronesia, and Polynesia are entered under **Oceania**.
   UF   Pacific Islands
         Pacific Ocean Islands
   BT   **Islands**
   NT   **Oceania**
   RT   **Pacific rim**
Isotopes   **539.7; 541.3**
   BT   **Atoms**
   NT   **Radioisotopes**
Israel   **956.94**
   May be subdivided like United States except for *History*.
   BT   **Middle East**
Israel-Arab conflicts   **965.04; 956.05**
   Use for materials on the conflicts between the Arab countries and Israel. Materials that discuss collectively the relations between Arabs and Jews, including religious, ethnic, and ideological relations, are entered under

Jewish-Arab relations. Materials on relations between the religions of Judaism and Islam are entered under **Judaism—Relations—Islam** and under **Islam—Relations—Judaism**.
   UF   Arab-Israel conflicts
         Arab-Israeli conflicts
         Israeli-Arab conflicts
         Palestine problem, 1917-
   BT   **Arab countries—Foreign relations—Israel**
         Israel—Foreign relations—Arab countries
   NT   **Intifada, 1987-**
         Israel-Arab War, 1948-1949
         Israel-Arab War, 1967
         Israel-Arab War, 1973
         Lebanon—History—1982-1984, Israeli intervention
         Sinai Campaign, 1956
   RT   **Jewish-Arab relations**
Israel-Arab relations
   USE **Arab countries—Foreign relations—Israel**
         Israel—Foreign relations—Arab countries
Israel-Arab War, 1948-1949   **956.04**
   UF   Arab-Israel War, 1948-1949
   BT   **Israel-Arab conflicts**
Israel-Arab War, 1956
   USE **Sinai Campaign, 1956**
Israel-Arab War, 1967   **956.04**
   UF   Arab-Israel War, 1967
         Six Day War, 1967
   BT   **Israel-Arab conflicts**
Israel-Arab War, 1973   **956.04**
   UF   Arab-Israel War, 1973
         Yom Kippur War, 1973
   BT   **Israel-Arab conflicts**
Israel—Collective settlements
   USE **Collective settlements—Israel**
Israel—Foreign relations—Arab countries 956
   UF   Arab-Israel relations
         Arab-Israeli relations
         Israel-Arab relations
         Israeli-Arab relations
   NT   **Israel-Arab conflicts**
   RT   **Arab countries—Foreign relations—Israel**
         Jewish-Arab relations

BT = Broader Term   NT = Narrower Term   RT = Related Term   SA = See Also   UF = Used For

Israeli-Arab conflict, 1987-
  USE   **Intifada, 1987-**
Israeli-Arab conflicts
  USE   **Israel-Arab conflicts**
Israeli-Arab relations
  USE   **Arab countries—Foreign rela-
          tions—Israel
          Israel—Foreign relations—
          Arab countries**
Israeli intervention in Lebanon, 1982-1984
  USE   **Lebanon—History—1982-1984,
          Israeli intervention**
Israelis 305.892; 920; 956.94
  BT   **Jews**
Israelites
  USE   **Jews**
ISSN
  USE   **International Standard Serial
          Numbers**
Italo-Ethiopian War, 1935-1936   963
  UF   Ethiopian-Italian War, 1935-1936
  BT   **Modern history—1900-1999
          (20th century)**
Italy 945
    May be subdivided like United States ex-
    cept for *History*.
Italy—History 945
Italy—History—0-1559 945
Italy—History—1559-1789 945
Italy—History—1789-1815 945
Italy—History—1815-1914 945; 945.09
Italy—History—1914-1945 945.091
Italy—History—1945-1976 945.092
Italy—History—1976- 945.092
Ivory   679
  BT   **Animal products**
Jails
  USE   **Prisons**
Japan   952
    May be subdivided like United States ex-
    cept for *History*.
Japan—Commerce—United States   382
Japan—History 952
Japan—History—0-1868   952
Japan—History—1868-1945   952.03
**Japan—History—1945-1952, Allied occu-
      pation   952.04**
  BT   **Military occupation
          World War, 1939-1945—Occu-
          pied territories**
Japan—History—1952-   952.04

Japanese color prints   769.952
  UF   Color prints, Japanese *[Former
          heading]*
  BT   **Color prints**
Japanese language   495.6
    May be subdivided like **English language**.
  BT   **Language and languages**
**Japanese language—Business Japanese
    495.6**
    Business Japanese is a unique subdivision
    for **Japanese language**.
  UF   Business Japanese
Japanese paper folding
  USE   **Origami**
Jargon
  USE   subjects and names of languages
          with the subdivision *Jargon*,
          e.g. **English language—Jar-
          gon;** to be added as needed
Jargon, Computer
  USE   **Computer science—Dictionaries**
Jazz ensembles   784.4
  BT   **Ensembles (Music)**
Jazz music   781.65; 782.42165
  BT   **Music**
  RT   **Blues music**
Jestbooks
  USE   **Chapbooks**
Jesters
  USE   **Fools and jesters**
Jesus Christ   232
  UF   Christ
          Christology
  BT   **God—Christianity**
  NT   **Atonement—Christianity
          Lord's Supper
          Second Advent**
  RT   **Christianity**
Jesus Christ—Art   704.9
  UF   Jesus Christ—Iconography
          Jesus Christ in art
  BT   **Christian art and symbolism**
  RT   **Bible—Pictorial works
          Mary, Blessed Virgin, Saint—
          Art**
Jesus Christ—Atonement
  USE   **Atonement—Christianity**
Jesus Christ—Biography   232.9
  NT   **Jesus Christ—Crucifixion
          Jesus Christ—Historicity
          Jesus Christ—Nativity**

BT = Broader Term   NT = Narrower Term   RT = Related Term   SA = See Also   UF = Used For

Jesus Christ—Birth
  USE   **Jesus Christ—Nativity**
Jesus Christ—Crucifixion 232.96
  UF   Crucifixion of Christ
  BT   **Jesus Christ—Biography**
  RT   **Good Friday**
Jesus Christ—Divinity 232
  UF   Divinity of Christ
  RT   **Trinity**
Jesus Christ—Drama 808.82; 812, etc.
    May be used for individual works, collections, or materials about plays about Jesus Christ.
  BT   **Religious drama**
  NT   **Passion plays**
Jesus Christ—Historicity 232.9
  BT   **Jesus Christ—Biography**
Jesus Christ—Iconography
  USE   **Jesus Christ—Art**
Jesus Christ in art
  USE   **Jesus Christ—Art**
Jesus Christ—Last Supper
  USE   **Lord's Supper**
Jesus Christ—Messiahship 232
Jesus Christ—Nativity 232.92
  UF   Jesus Christ—Birth
        Nativity of Christ
  BT   **Jesus Christ—Biography**
  RT   **Christmas**
Jesus Christ—Parables 226.8; 232.9
  BT   **Bible—Parables**
        Parables
Jesus Christ—Prayers 232.9
  NT   **Lord's prayer**
Jesus Christ—Prophecies 232
  BT   **Bible—Prophecies**
Jesus Christ—Resurrection 232.9
  UF   Resurrection
        Resurrection of Jesus Christ
Jesus Christ—Second Advent
  USE   **Second Advent**
Jesus Christ—Sermon on the mount
  USE   **Sermon on the mount**
Jesus Christ—Teachings 232.9
  UF   Teachings of Jesus
Jet airplanes
  USE   **Jet planes**
Jet lag 616.9
  BT   **Aviation medicine**
        Biological rhythms
        Fatigue

Jet planes 629.133
  UF   Airplanes, Jet propelled
        Jet airplanes
        Jets (Airplanes)
  BT   **Airplanes**
  NT   **Short take off and landing aircraft**
        Supersonic transport planes
Jet propulsion 621.43
  BT   **Airplane engines**
  RT   **Rockets (Aeronautics)**
Jets (Airplanes)
  USE   **Jet planes**
Jewelry 391.7; 739.27
    Use for general materials on jewelry and for materials on gems in which the emphasis is on the setting. Materials on cut and polished precious stones treated from the point of view of art or antiquity are entered under **Gems.** Materials on gem stones treated from the mineralogical or technological point of view are entered under **Precious stones.**
  UF   Costume jewelry
        Jewels
  SA   styles of jewelry and types of jewelry items, to be added as needed
  BT   **Art metalwork**
        Costume
        Decoration and ornament
        Decorative arts
        Metalwork
  RT   **Gems**
        Goldwork
        Silverwork
Jewels
  USE   **Gems**
        Jewelry
        Precious stones
Jewish-Arab relations 956
    Use for materials that discuss collectively the relations between Arabs and Jews, including religious, ethnic, and ideological relations. Materials on the conflicts between the Arab countries and Israel are entered under **Israel-Arab conflicts.** Materials on relations between the religions of Judaism and Islam are entered under **Judaism—Relations—Islam;** and **Islam—Relations—Judaism.**
  UF   Arab-Jewish relations
  BT   **Arabs**
        Judaism
  RT   **Arab countries—Foreign relations—Israel**
        Islam—Relations—Judaism

BT = Broader Term   NT = Narrower Term   RT = Related Term   SA = See Also   UF = Used For

Jewish-Arab relations—*Continued*
        Israel-Arab conflicts
        Israel—Foreign relations—
          Arab countries
        Judaism—Relations—Islam
        Palestinian Arabs
Jewish-Christian relations
  USE   **Christianity—Relations—Juda-
          ism**
          **Judaism—Relations—Christian-
          ity**
Jewish civilization   909
  UF   Civilization, Jewish
         Jews—Civilization *[Former
          heading]*
  BT   **Civilization**
Jewish customs
  USE   **Jews—Social life and customs
          Judaism—Customs and prac-
          tices**
Jewish doctrines
  USE   **Judaism—Doctrines**
Jewish ethics   296.3
  UF   Ethics, Jewish
  BT   **Ethics**
Jewish folklore
  USE   **Jews—Folklore**
Jewish holidays   296.4; 394.267
  UF   Fasts and feasts—Judaism *[For-
         mer heading]*
         Festivals—Jews
         Holidays, Jewish
         Jews—Festivals
  SA   names of individual holidays,
         e.g. **Hanukkah;** to be added
         as needed
  BT   **Judaism
         Religious holidays**
  NT   **Hanukkah
         Passover
         Yom Kippur**
Jewish Holocaust (1933-1945)
  USE   **Holocaust, 1933-1945**
Jewish-Islamic relations
  USE   **Islam—Relations—Judaism
          Judaism—Relations—Islam**
Jewish language
  USE   **Hebrew language
          Yiddish language**

Jewish legends   296.1; 398.2
    May be used for individual works, collec-
  tions, or materials about Jewish legends.
  UF   Jews—Legends
         Legends, Jewish *[Former head-
          ing]*
  BT   **Legends**
Jewish life
  USE   **Jews—Social life and customs
          Judaism—Customs and prac-
          tices**
Jewish literature   296; 808.8
  UF   Jews—Literature
  BT   **Literature
         Religious literature**
  NT   **Bible
         Cabala
         Jewish religious fiction
         Talmud
         Yiddish literature**
  RT   **Hebrew literature**
Jewish liturgies
  USE   **Judaism—Liturgy**
Jewish religion
  USE   **Judaism**
**Jewish religious fiction   808.83; 813,
    etc.**
    Use for individual works, collections, or
  materials about fiction that promotes Jewish
  teachings or exemplifies a Jewish religious
  way of life.
  BT   **Fiction
         Jewish literature
         Religious fiction**
Jewish theology
  USE   **Judaism—Doctrines**
Jews (May subdiv. geog.)   **296.092;
    305.892; 909**
  UF   Hebrews
         Israelites
  BT   **Judaism**
  NT   **Israelis**
Jews—Antiquities   933
  BT   **Antiquities**
Jews—Civilization
  USE   **Jewish civilization**
Jews—Customs
  USE   **Jews—Social life and customs
          Judaism—Customs and prac-
          tices**

BT = Broader Term   NT = Narrower Term   RT = Related Term   SA = See Also   UF = Used For

Jews—Economic conditions 305.892; 330.9
   BT   Economic conditions
Jews—Encyclopedias 909
   BT   Encyclopedias and dictionaries
Jews—Festivals
   USE   Jewish holidays
Jews—Folklore 398
   UF   Folklore, Jewish
         Jewish folklore
   BT   Folklore
Jews—Language
   USE   Hebrew language
         Yiddish language
Jews—Legends
   USE   Jewish legends
Jews—Literature
   USE   Hebrew literature
         Jewish literature
Jews—Persecutions (May subdiv. geog.) 909; 933
   BT   Antisemitism
         Persecution
   NT   Holocaust, 1933-1945
         World War, 1939-1945—
           Jews—Rescue
Jews—Political activity 909; 956.94
   BT   Political participation
Jews—Religion
   USE   Judaism
Jews—Restoration 956.94
   Use for materials on the belief that the Jews, in fulfillment of Biblical prophecy, would some day return to Palestine.
   RT   Zionism
Jews—Rites and ceremonies
   USE   Judaism—Customs and practices
Jews—Ritual
   USE   Judaism—Customs and practices
         Judaism—Liturgy
Jews—Social conditions 305.892; 909
   BT   Social conditions
Jews—Social life and customs 305.892
   Use for materials on Jewish social customs. General materials on Jewish religious practices are entered under **Judaism—Customs and practices**. Materials on the forms of public worship in Judaism are entered under **Judaism—Liturgy.**
   UF   Jewish customs

         Jewish life
         Jews—Customs
   BT   Manners and customs
Job analysis 658.3
   UF   Personnel classification
   BT   Factory management
         Industrial efficiency
         Management
         Occupations
         Personnel management
         Wages
   NT   Motion study
         Time study
Job applications
   USE   Applications for positions
Job discrimination
   USE   Discrimination in employment
Job hunting 650.14
   UF   Hunting, Job
         Job searching
   SA   fields of knowledge, professions, industries, and trades with the subdivision *Vocational guidance,* to be added as needed
   BT   Employment agencies
         Vocational guidance
   NT   Applications for positions
         Résumés (Employment)
Job performance standards
   USE   Performance standards
Job placement guidance
   USE   Vocational guidance
Job résumés
   USE   Résumés (Employment)
Job retraining
   USE   Occupational retraining
Job satisfaction 650.1; 658.3
   UF   Satisfaction in work
         Work satisfaction
   BT   Attitude (Psychology)
         Employee morale
         Personnel management
         Work
   NT   Burn out (Psychology)
Job searching
   USE   Job hunting
Job security 331.25; 650.1; 658.3
   UF   Employment security
         Security, Job
   BT   Personnel management

BT = Broader Term   NT = Narrower Term   RT = Related Term   SA = See Also   UF = Used For

Job security—*Continued*
  NT   Employees—Dismissal
Job sharing   331.2; 658.3
  UF   Sharing of jobs
  BT   **Part-time employment**
Job stress   158.7; 658.3
  UF   Occupational stress
        On the job stress
        Organizational stress
        Work stress
  BT   **Stress (Physiology)**
        Stress (Psychology)
  NT   **Burn out (Psychology)**
Job training
  USE   **Occupational training**
Jobless people
  USE   **Unemployed**
Joblessness
  USE   **Unemployment**
Jobs
  USE   **Employment agencies**
        Occupations
        Professions
Jogging   613.7
  BT   **Running**
Joint custody of children
  USE   **Child custody**
        Part-time parenting
Joke books
  USE   **Jokes**
Jokes   808.7; 808.88; 818, etc.
    May be used for collections of jokes and
    for materials about jokes.
  UF   Joke books
  BT   **Wit and humor**
  NT   **Practical jokes**
Journalism (May subdiv. geog.)   070.4
    Use for materials on writing for the periodi-
    cal press or on journalism as an occupation.
    Materials limited to the history, organization,
    and management of newspapers are entered
    under **Newspapers.**
  SA   types of journalism, e.g. **Scien-**
        tific journalism; to be added
        as needed
  BT   **Authorship**
        Literature
  NT   **Broadcast journalism**
        College and school journalism
        Gossip
        Libel and slander
        Photojournalism

        Press
        Reporters and reporting
        Scientific journalism
  RT   **Journalists**
        Newspapers
        Periodicals
Journalism—Editing   070.4
  UF   Magazine editing
        News editing
        Newspapers—Editing
        Periodicals—Editing
  BT   **Editing**
Journalism—Objectivity   070.4
  UF   Slanted journalism
  BT   **Professional ethics**
Journalism, Scientific
  USE   **Scientific journalism**
Journalistic photography
  USE   **Photojournalism**
Journalists   070.92; 920
  UF   Columnists
  BT   **Authors**
  NT   **World War, 1939-1945—Jour-**
        nalists
  RT   **Journalism**
Journals
  USE   **Periodicals**
Journals (Diaries)
  USE   **Diaries**
Journeys
  USE   **Travel**
        Voyages and travels
Joy and sorrow   152.4
  UF   Affliction
        Sorrow
  BT   **Emotions**
        Ethics
  NT   **Pleasure**
  RT   **Grief**
        Happiness
        Suffering
Judaeo-German
  USE   **Yiddish language**
Judaism   296
  UF   Jewish religion
        Jews—Religion
  SA   names of Jewish sects, e.g. **Has-**
        idism; to be added as needed
  BT   **Religions**
  NT   **Atonement—Judaism**

BT = Broader Term   NT = Narrower Term   RT = Related Term   SA = See Also   UF = Used For

Judaism—*Continued*

    Cabala

    Christianity—Relations—Judaism

    Hasidism

    Islam—Relations—Judaism

    Jewish-Arab relations

    Jewish holidays

    Jews

    Judaism—Relations—Christianity

    Judaism—Relations—Islam

    Rabbis

    Sabbath

    Talmud

  RT   **Synagogues**

Judaism—Customs and practices   **296.4**

    Use for materials on Jewish religious practices in general. Materials on the forms of public worship in Judaism are entered under **Judaism—Liturgy.** Materials on Jewish social customs are entered under **Jews—Social life and customs.**

  UF   Jewish customs

          Jewish life

          Jews—Customs

          Jews—Rites and ceremonies

          Jews—Ritual

  BT   **Rites and ceremonies**

  RT   **Judaism—Liturgy**

Judaism—Doctrines   **296.3**

  UF   Jewish doctrines

          Jewish theology

  BT   **Doctrinal theology**

Judaism—Liturgy   **296.4**

    Use for materials on the forms of public worship in Judaism and for texts of Jewish liturgies. Materials on Jewish religious practices in general are entered under **Judaism—Customs and practices.** Materials on Jewish social customs are entered under **Jews—Social life and customs.**

  UF   Jewish liturgies

          Jews—Ritual

  BT   **Liturgies**

  RT   **Judaism—Customs and practices**

Judaism—Relations—Christianity
   261.2; 296.3

    Use for materials on the relations between Judaism and Christianity. When assigning this heading, provide an additional subject entry under **Christianity—Relations—Judaism.**

  UF   Christian-Jewish relations

          Christianity and other religions—Judaism

          Jewish-Christian relations *[Former heading]*

  BT   **Christianity and other religions**

         Judaism

Judaism—Relations—Islam   **296.3**

    Use for materials on the relations between Judaism and Islam. When assigning this heading, provide an additional subject entry under **Islam—Relations—Judaism.** Materials on the conflicts between the Arab countries and Israel are entered under **Israel-Arab conflicts.** Materials that discuss collectively the relations between Arabs and Jews, including religious, ethnic, and ideological relations, are entered under **Jewish-Arab relations.**

  UF   Islamic-Jewish relations

          Jewish-Islamic relations *[Former heading]*

  BT   **Islam**

         Judaism

  RT   **Jewish-Arab relations**

Judges   **347; 920**

  UF   Chief justices

  BT   **Lawyers**

  NT   **Women judges**

  RT   **Courts**

Judicial investigations

  USE   **Governmental investigations**

Judiciary

  USE   **Courts**

Judo   **796.815**

  BT   **Physical education**

         Self-defense

         Wrestling

  NT   **Karate**

Juggling   **793.8**

  UF   Legerdemain

          Sleight of hand

  BT   **Amusements**

         Tricks

July Fourth

  USE   **Fourth of July**

Jungle animals   **578.734**

  UF   Jungle fauna

  BT   **Animals**

         Forest animals

         Wildlife

Jungle fauna

  USE   **Jungle animals**

BT = Broader Term   NT = Narrower Term   RT = Related Term   SA = See Also   UF = Used For

Jungles   634.9

Use for materials on impenetrable thickets of second-growth vegetation replacing tropical rain forests that have been disturbed or degraded. Materials on forests of broad-leaved, mainly evergreen trees found in moist climates in the tropics, subtropics, and some parts of the temperate zones, are entered under **Rain forests.**

    UF   Tropical jungles

    BT   **Forests and forestry**

    RT   **Rain forests**

Junior colleges   378.1

    UF   Community colleges

    BT   **Colleges and universities**

            Higher education

Junior colleges—Directories   378.1

    BT   **Directories**

Junior high school libraries

    USE   **High school libraries**

Junior high schools   373.236

    UF   High schools, Junior

            Secondary schools

    BT   **High schools**

            Public schools

            Schools

    RT   **Secondary education**

Junk

    USE   **Waste products**

Junk bonds   332.63

    UF   High-yield junk bonds

    BT   **Bonds**

Junk in space

    USE   **Space debris**

Jurisprudence

    USE   **Law**

Jurisprudence, Medical

    USE   **Medical jurisprudence**

Jurists

    USE   **Lawyers**

Jury   345; 347

    UF   Trial by jury

    BT   **Courts**

            Criminal law

Justice   340

    BT   **Ethics**

            Law

            Virtue

Justice, Administration of

    USE   **Administration of justice**

Juvenile courts   345

    UF   Children's courts

    BT   **Courts**

    RT   **Juvenile delinquency**

            Probation

Juvenile delinquency   364.3

    UF   Children, Delinquent

            Delinquency, Juvenile

            Delinquents

    BT   **Crime**

            Social problems

    NT   **Gangs**

            Juvenile prostitution

            School violence

    RT   **Child welfare**

            Emotionally disturbed children

            Juvenile courts

            Reformatories

            Teenagers—Drug use

            Youth—Drug use

Juvenile delinquency—Case studies   364.3

Juvenile literature

    USE   **Children's literature**

            and subjects with the subdivision *Juvenile literature*, e.g. **Computers—Juvenile literature**; to be added as needed

Juvenile prostitution   176; 306.74; 362.7; 363.4; 364.1

    UF   Adolescent prostitution

            Child prostitution

            Children and prostitution

            Prostitution, Juvenile *[Former heading]*

            Teenage prostitution

    BT   **Child abuse**

            Juvenile delinquency

            Prostitution

K.K.K.

    USE   **Ku Klux Klan**

Kabbala

    USE   **Cabala**

Kamuti

    USE   **Bonsai**

Karate   796.815

    BT   **Judo**

            Self-defense

Kart racing

    USE   **Karts and karting**

Karting

    USE   **Karts and karting**

BT = Broader Term   NT = Narrower Term   RT = Related Term   SA = See Also   UF = Used For

Karts and karting   796.7

Use for materials on miniature, lightweight, low-slung, four-wheeled racing or recreational motorcars that can be driven at speeds of up to 60 mph.

UF   Carts (Midget cars)

       Go karts

       Kart racing

       Karting

       Karts (Midget cars)

       Midget cars

BT   **Automobile racing**

Karts (Midget cars)

USE   **Karts and karting**

Keyboarding (Electronics)   004.7; 652.5

UF   Computer keyboarding

       Electronic data processing—Keyboarding

       Word processor keyboarding

BT   **Business education**

       Office practice

RT   **Typewriting**

Keyboards (Electronics)   004.7

UF   Computer keyboards

       Word processor keyboards

BT   **Computer peripherals**

       Office equipment and supplies

Keyboards (Musical instruments)   786

BT   **Organs (Musical instruments)**

       Pianos

Keys

USE   **Locks and keys**

Kibbutz

USE   **Collective settlements—Israel**

Kidnapping   364.15

UF   Abduction

BT   **Criminal law**

       Offenses against the person

Kidnapping, Parental

USE   **Parental kidnapping**

Killing, Mercy

USE   **Euthanasia**

Kin recognition

USE   **Kinship**

Kindergarten   372.21

BT   **Elementary education**

       Schools

NT   **Creative activities**

       Montessori method of education

RT   **Nursery schools**

       Preschool education

Kinematics   531

BT   **Dynamics**

NT   **Mechanical movements**

RT   **Mechanics**

       Motion

Kinesiology   613.7

UF   Cinesiology

BT   **Human locomotion**

       Physical fitness

Kinetic art   701; 709.04

UF   Art in motion

       Art, Kinetic

BT   **Modern art—1900-1999 (20th century)**

NT   **Kinetic sculpture**

Kinetic sculpture   731; 735

UF   Sculpture in motion

       Sculpture, Kinetic

BT   **Futurism (Art)**

       Kinetic art

       Sculpture

NT   **Mobiles (Sculpture)**

Kinetics

USE   **Dynamics**

       Motion

King, Martin Luther, holiday

USE   **Martin Luther King Day**

King Philip's War, 1675-1676   973.2

UF   United States—History—1675-1676, King Philip's War

BT   **Indians of North America—Wars**

       United States—History—1600-1775, Colonial period

King William's War, 1689-1697

USE   **United States—History—1689-1697, King William's War**

Kings and rulers   920; 929.7

Use for materials on monarchs and other heads of state not democratically elected.

UF   Kings, queens, rulers, etc. *[Former heading]*

       Monarchs

       Royal houses

       Royalty

       Rulers

       Sovereigns

SA   names of places with the subdivision *Kings and rulers*, e.g.

BT = Broader Term   NT = Narrower Term   RT = Related Term   SA = See Also   UF = Used For

Kings and rulers—*Continued*

> Great Britain—Kings and rulers; and names of individual monarchs or rulers, to be added as needed

  BT   Heads of state

  NT   Emperors

          Great Britain—Kings and rulers

  RT   Courts and courtiers

          Monarchy

          Queens

Kings, queens, rulers, etc.

  USE   **Kings and rulers**

Kinship (May subdiv. geog.)   **306.83**

  UF   Kin recognition

  SA   ethnic groups with the subdivision *Kinship,* to be added as needed

  BT   Ethnology

          Family

  RT   Clans

Kitchen gardens

  USE   **Vegetable gardening**

Kitchen remodeling

  USE   **Kitchens—Remodeling**

Kitchen renovation

  USE   **Kitchens—Remodeling**

Kitchen utensils   **643; 683**

  UF   Cooking utensils

          Household utensils

          Kitchenware

          Utensils, Kitchen

  SA   types of kitchen utensils, e.g. **Bread machines;** to be added as needed

  BT   **Household equipment and supplies**

  NT   **Bread machines**

Kitchens   **643**

  BT   **Houses**

          Rooms

Kitchens—Remodeling   **643**

  UF   Kitchen remodeling

          Kitchen renovation

          Remodeling of kitchens

  BT   **Houses—Remodeling**

Kitchenware

  USE   **Kitchen utensils**

Kites   **629.133; 796.1**

  BT   **Aeronautics**

Kittens

  USE   **Cats**

Knighthood

  USE   **Knights and knighthood**

Knights and knighthood   **394; 940.1**

  UF   Knighthood

  BT   **Middle Ages**

          Nobility

  RT   **Chivalry**

          Heraldry

Knights of the Round Table

  USE   **Arthurian romances**

Knitting   **677; 746.43**

  BT   **Needlework**

Knots and splices   **623.88**

  UF   Splicing

  BT   **Navigation**

          Rope

Knowledge-based systems (Computer science)

  USE   **Expert systems (Computer science)**

Knowledge, Theory of

  USE   **Theory of knowledge**

Kodak camera   **771.3**

  BT   **Cameras**

Koran   **297.1**

  UF   Alkoran

          Qur'an

  BT   **Islam**

          Sacred books

Korea   **951.9**

> Use for comprehensive materials on all of Korea and for materials on Korea before it was divided in 1948 into two separate republics.

  NT   **Korea (North)**

          Korea (South)

Korea (Democratic People's Republic)

  USE   **Korea (North)**

Korea (North)   **951.93**

> Use for materials on the Democratic People's Republic of Korea, established in 1948. May be subdivided like United States except for *History.*

  UF   Korea (Democratic People's Republic)

          North Korea

  BT   **Korea**

Korea (Republic)
USE   Korea (South)
Korea (South)   951.95
Use for materials on the Republic of Korea, established in 1948. May be subdivided like United States except for *History.*
UF   Korea (Republic)
South Korea
BT   Korea
Korean War, 1950-1953   951.904
BT   Modern history—1900-1999
(20th century)
Ku Klux Klan   322.4
UF   K.K.K.
Ku Klux Klan (1865-1876)
[Former heading]
Ku-Klux Klan (1866-1869)
Ku Klux Klan (1915-) *[Former heading]*
BT   Secret societies
RT   Reconstruction (1865-1876)
Ku Klux Klan (1865-1876)
USE   Ku Klux Klan
Ku-Klux Klan (1866-1869)
USE   Ku Klux Klan
Ku Klux Klan (1915-)
USE   Ku Klux Klan
Labeling
USE   subjects with the subdivision *Labeling,* e.g. Food—Labeling; to be added as needed
Labor (May subdiv. geog.)   331
Use for materials on the collective human activities involved in the production and distribution of goods and services in an economy, especially activities performed by workers for wages as distinguished from those performed by entrepreneurs for profits. Also use for general materials on workers. Materials on laborers as a social class are entered under Working class. Materials on the physical or mental exertion of individuals to produce or accomplish something are entered under Work.
UF   Blue collar workers
Factory workers
Industrial workers
Labor and laboring classes *[Former heading]*
Laborers
Manual workers
Skilled workers
Unskilled workers
Workers

SA   types of laborers, e.g. Agricultural laborers; Miners; etc., to be added as needed
BT   Economics
Social conditions
Sociology
NT   Agricultural laborers
Apprentices
Capitalism
Children—Employment
Church and labor
Collective bargaining
Contract labor
Convict labor
Employees
Employment
Employment agencies
Hours of labor
Household employees
Industrial arbitration
Industrial relations
Industrial welfare
Labor supply
Labor unions
Libraries and labor
Men—Employment
Migrant labor
Miners
Occupations
Open and closed shop
Part-time employment
Peasantry
Peonage
Proletariat
Slavery
Supplementary employment
Teenagers—Employment
Wages
Work ethic
Youth—Employment
RT   Labor movement
Work
Working class
Labor absenteeism
USE   Absenteeism (Labor)
Labor—Accidents
USE   Industrial accidents
Labor and capital
USE   Industrial relations

BT = Broader Term   NT = Narrower Term   RT = Related Term   SA = See Also   UF = Used For

Labor and laboring classes
    USE   **Labor**
              Labor movement
              Working class
Labor and libraries
    USE   **Libraries and labor**
Labor and the church
    USE   **Church and labor**
Labor arbitration
    USE   **Industrial arbitration**
Labor (Childbirth)
    USE   **Childbirth**
Labor contract   331.1; 331.89

> Use for materials on agreements between employer and employee in which the latter agrees to perform work in return for compensation from the former.

    UF   Collective labor agreements
              Trade agreements (Labor)
    BT   **Contracts**
              Industrial relations
    NT   **Open and closed shop**
              Wages
    RT   **Collective bargaining**
Labor courts
    USE   **Industrial arbitration**
Labor disputes   331.89
    UF   Disputes, Labor
              Industrial disputes
    BT   **Industrial relations**
    NT   **Collective bargaining**
              Industrial arbitration
              Strikes
Labor—Education   331.25
    UF   Education of workers
    BT   **Education**
Labor force
    USE   **Labor supply**
Labor, Hours of
    USE   **Hours of labor**
Labor—Housing   363.5
    BT   **Housing**
Labor—Insurance
    USE   **Old age pensions**
              Social security
              Unemployment insurance
Labor-management relations
    USE   **Industrial relations**
Labor market
    USE   **Labor supply**

Labor, Migratory
    USE   **Migrant labor**
Labor movement   331.8

> Use for materials on the efforts of organizations and individuals to improve conditions for labor.

    UF   Labor and laboring classes *[Former heading]*
    BT   **Social movements**
    RT   **Labor**
              Labor unions
Labor negotiations
    USE   **Collective bargaining**
              Industrial arbitration
Labor organizations
    USE   **Labor unions**
Labor output
    USE   **Labor productivity**
Labor participation in management
    USE   **Participative management**
Labor productivity   331.11
    UF   Labor output
              Productivity of labor
    SA   types of industries, occupations, and processes with the subdivision *Labor productivity,* e.g. **Steel industry—Labor productivity;** to be added as needed
    BT   **Industrial efficiency**
    NT   **Production standards**
              Steel industry—Labor productivity
Labor relations
    USE   **Industrial relations**
Labor saving devices, Household
    USE   **Electric household appliances**
              Household equipment and supplies
Labor supply (May subdiv. geog.)
              331.11
    UF   Labor force
              Labor market
    BT   **Economic conditions**
              Employment
              Labor
    NT   **Children—Employment**
              Men—Employment
              Occupational retraining
              Teenagers—Employment
              Unemployed

BT = Broader Term   NT = Narrower Term   RT = Related Term   SA = See Also   UF = Used For

Labor supply—*Continued*
    Unemployment
    Women—Employment
    Youth—Employment
  RT Employment agencies
    Employment forecasting
    Human capital
    Manpower
    Manpower policy
Labor turnover   331.12
  BT Personnel management
  NT Employment agencies
Labor unions (May subdiv. geog.)
    331.88
  UF Labor organizations
    Organized labor
    Trade unions
    Unions, Labor
  SA types of unions and names of
    individual labor unions, to be
    added as needed
  BT Cooperation
    Industrial relations
    Labor
    Socialism
    Societies
  NT Industrial arbitration
    Injunctions
    Librarians' unions
    Open and closed shop
    United Steelworkers of America
  RT Collective bargaining
    Labor movement
    Strikes
Labor unions—United States
    331.880973
  UF American labor unions
    United States—Labor unions
Labor—United States   331.0973
  UF United States—Labor
Laboratories, Language
  USE Language laboratories
Laboratories, Space
  USE Space stations
Laboratory animal experimentation
  USE Animal experimentation
Laboratory animal welfare
  USE Animal welfare

Laboratory fertilization
  USE Fertilization in vitro
Laboratory manuals
  USE scientific and technical subjects
    with the subdivision *Labora-*
    tory manuals, e.g. **Chemis-**
    try—Laboratory manuals; to
    be added as needed
Laborers
  USE Labor
    Working class
    and types of laborers, e.g. **Ag-**
    ricultural laborers; Miners;
    etc., to be added as needed
Laboring class
  USE Working class
Laboring classes
  USE Working class
Lace and lace making   677; 746.2
  BT Crocheting
    Needlework
    Weaving
Lacquer and lacquering   667; 745.7
  UF Finishes and finishing
  BT Decorative arts
    Wood finishing
  RT Varnish and varnishing
Laissez-faire
  USE Free enterprise
    Industrial policy
Laity   262
    May be subdivided by religion or sect.
  UF Laymen
  BT Church
  RT Lay ministry
Laity—Catholic Church   262
  UF Catholic laity
  BT Catholic Church
Lakes (May subdiv. geog.)   551.48
  SA names of lakes, to be added as
    needed
  BT Physical geography
    Water
    Waterways
  RT Inland navigation
Lakes—United States   551.48
  UF United States—Lakes
Lamaze method of childbirth
  USE Natural childbirth

BT = Broader Term   NT = Narrower Term   RT = Related Term   SA = See Also   UF = Used For

Lambs
USE   Sheep
Lamentations
USE   Elegiac poetry
Lamps   621.32; 749
   BT   **Lighting**
   NT   **Electric lamps**
Land
USE   **Land use**
          Wetlands
Land drainage
USE   **Drainage**
Land forms
USE   **Landforms**
Land question
USE   **Land tenure**
Land, Reclamation of
USE   **Reclamation of land**
Land reform (May subdiv. geog.)   333.3
   UF   Agrarian reform
          Reform, Agrarian
   BT   **Economic policy**
          Land use
          Social policy
   NT   **Land tenure**
   RT   **Agriculture—Government poli-**
          cy
Land settlement (May subdiv. geog.)
          304.8; 325
   UF   Resettlement
          Settlement of land
   BT   **Colonies**
   NT   **Colonization**
   RT   **Internal migration**
Land settlement—United States   304.8;
          325.73
   UF   United States—Land settlement
          Westward movement
Land surveying
USE   **Surveying**
Land surveys
USE   **Surveying**
Land tenure   333.3
   Use for general and historical materials on
   systems of holding land. Materials on the le-
   gal relationships between landlord and tenant
   are entered under **Landlord and tenant.**
   UF   Agrarian question
          Fiefs
          Land question
          Tenure of land

   BT   **Agriculture—Economic aspects**
          Land reform
          Land use
   NT   **Farm tenancy**
          Feudalism
          Landlord and tenant
   RT   **Peasantry**
          Real estate
Land use   333.73
   Use for general materials that cover such
   topics as types of land; the utilization, distri-
   bution, and development of land; and the eco-
   nomic factors affecting the value of land. Ma-
   terials dealing only with ownership of land
   are entered under **Real estate.**
   UF   Land
   BT   **Economics**
   NT   **Eminent domain**
          Farms
          Grasslands
          Land reform
          Land tenure
          Landfills
          Lawns
          Pastures
          Public lands
          Real estate
          Reclamation of land
          Regional planning
          Wetlands
Landfills   363.72; 628.3; 628.4
   Use for materials on places for waste dis-
   posal in which waste is buried in layers of
   earth in low ground.
   UF   Earth fills
          Fills (Earthwork)
          Sanitary landfills
   SA   names of landfills, to be added
          as needed
   BT   **Land use**
   NT   **Hazardous waste sites**
          Love Canal Chemical Waste
          Landfill (Niagara Falls,
          N.Y.)
Landforms   551.41
   UF   Land forms
   SA   types of landforms, e.g. **Moun-**
          tains; Coasts; etc., to be add-
          ed as needed
   BT   **Earth—Surface**
          Geology
   NT   **Coasts**

BT = Broader Term   NT = Narrower Term   RT = Related Term   SA = See Also   UF = Used For

Landforms—*Continued*
  Mountains
  Seashore
Landlord and tenant   333.5; 346.04
  Use for materials on the legal relationships
  between landlord and tenant. General and his-
  torical materials on systems of holding land
  are entered under **Land tenure.**
  UF   Tenant and landlord
  BT   **Commercial law**
       Human relations
       Land tenure
       Real estate
  NT   **Apartment houses**
       Housing
  RT   **Farm tenancy**
Landmarks, Literary
  USE   **Literary landmarks**
Landmarks, Preservation of
  USE   **National monuments**
        Natural monuments
Landscape architecture   712
  Use for materials on modifying or arranging
  the features of a landscape, urban area, etc.,
  for aesthetic or pragmatic purposes.
  UF   Landscape design
  BT   **Architecture**
  NT   **Garden ornaments and furni-**
       ture
       Parks
       Patios
       Roadside improvement
  RT   **Landscape gardening**
       Landscape protection
Landscape design
  USE   **Landscape architecture**
Landscape drawing   743
  BT   **Drawing**
  RT   **Landscape painting**
Landscape gardening   712
  Use for materials on the design or rear-
  rangement of extensive gardens or estates.
  UF   Planting
  BT   **Gardening**
       Horticulture
  NT   **Evergreens**
       Lawns
       Ornamental plants
  RT   **Garden design**
       Landscape architecture
       Shrubs
       Trees

Landscape painting   758
  BT   **Painting**
  RT   **Landscape drawing**
Landscape protection   333.73
  UF   Beautification of landscape
       Natural beauty conservation
       Preservation of natural scenery
       Protection of natural scenery
       Scenery
  BT   **Environmental protection**
       Nature conservation
  NT   **Natural monuments**
  RT   **Landscape architecture**
       Regional planning
Landscape sculpture
  USE   **Earthworks (Art)**
Language
  USE   disciplines, classes of persons,
        types of newspapers, and
        names of individual persons,
        corporate bodies, and literary
        works entered under title with
        the subdivision *Language,* e.g.
        Technology—Language;
        Children—Language; etc., to
        be added as needed
Language and languages   400
  Use for general materials on the history,
  philosophy, origin, etc., of language. Materials
  on the scientific study of speech and compara-
  tive studies of language are entered under
  Linguistics.
  UF   Languages
       Philology
  SA   names of languages or groups of
       languages, e.g. **English lan-**
       guage; Scandinavian lan-
       guages; disciplines, classes of
       persons, types of newspapers,
       and names of individual per-
       sons, corporate bodies, and
       literary works entered under
       title with the subdivison *Lan-*
       guage, e.g. **Technology—**
       Language; Children—Lan-
       guage; etc., and names of
       ethnic groups or native peo-
       ples and countries, cities, etc.,
       with the subdivison *Lan-*
       guages, for materials on the
       several languages spoken by a

BT = Broader Term   NT = Narrower Term   RT = Related Term   SA = See Also   UF = Used For

Language and languages—*Continued*
        group or in a place, e.g. **Indians of North America—Languages; United States—Languages;** etc., to be added as needed
BT   Anthropology
       Communication
       Ethnology
NT   Anglo-Saxon language
       Bilingualism
       Children—Language
       Conversation
       Danish language
       English language
       French language
       German language
       Grammar
       Greek language
       Hebrew language
       Icelandic language
       Indians of North America—Languages
       Japanese language
       Latin language
       Linguistics
       Modern Greek language
       Modern languages
       Norwegian language
       Old Norse language
       Phonetics
       Programming languages (Computers)
       Rhetoric
       Romance languages
       Russian language
       Scandinavian languages
       Semantics
       Sign language
       Sociolinguistics
       Spanish language
       Swedish language
       Translating and interpreting
       Universal language
       Verbal learning
       Vocabulary
       Voice
       Writing
       Yiddish language
RT   Speech

Language and languages—Business language
USE   names of languages with unique language subdivisions, e.g. **English language—Business English; Japanese language—Business Japanese;** etc., to be added as needed
Language and languages—Comparative philology
USE   **Linguistics**
Language and languages—Political aspects   400
    Use for general materials on the political aspects of languages.
SA   names of countries, cities, etc., with the subdivision *Languages,* e.g. **United States—Languages;** or with the two subdivisions *Languages—Political aspects;* and names of individual languages and groups of languages with the subdivision *Political aspects,* to be added as needed
Language and society
USE   **Sociolinguistics**
Language arts   372.6; 400
UF   Communication arts
BT   **Communication**
NT   **Creative writing**
       Literature
       Reading
       Speech
       Whole language
       Writing
Language arts (Holistic)
USE   **Whole language**
Language arts—Patterning   372.6
UF   Patterns (Language arts)
       Reading—Patterning
       Writing—Patterning
Language experience approach in education
USE   **Whole language**
Language games
USE   **Literary recreations**
Language, International
USE   **Universal language**
Language laboratories   407
UF   Foreign language laboratories
       Laboratories, Language

BT = Broader Term   NT = Narrower Term   RT = Related Term   SA = See Also   UF = Used For

Language laboratories—*Continued*
    RT   **Modern languages—Study and teaching**

Language, Universal
    USE   **Universal language**

Languages
    USE   **Language and languages**
          and names of ethnic groups or native peoples and countries, cities, etc., with the subdivision *Languages*, for materials on the several languages spoken by a group or in a place, e.g. **Indians of North America—Languages; United States—Languages;** etc., to be added as needed

Languages, Modern
    USE   **Modern languages**

Languages—Vocabulary
    USE   **Vocabulary**

Lantern projection
    USE   **Projectors**

Lantern slides
    USE   **Slides (Photography)**

Laptop computers
    USE   **Portable computers**

Larceny
    USE   **Stealing**

Large and small
    USE   **Size**

Large print books   028
    UF   Books for sight saving
          Books—Large print
          Large type books
          Sight saving books
    BT   **Blind—Books and reading**
    RT   **Big books**

Large type books
    USE   **Large print books**

Laser-beam recording
    USE   **Laser recording**

Laser photography
    USE   **Holography**

Laser recording   621.36; 621.38
    UF   Laser-beam recording
          Recording, Laser
    BT   **Lasers**
    NT   **Holography**
    RT   **Optical storage devices**

Lasers   621.36
    UF   Light amplification by stimulated emission of radiation
          Masers, Optical
          Optical masers
    SA   lasers in particular subjects or fields of endeavor, e.g. **Lasers in aeronautics;** to be added as needed
    BT   **Light**
    NT   **Laser recording**
          Lasers in aeronautics

Lasers in aeronautics   629.13
    BT   **Aeronautics**
          Lasers

Last rites (Sacraments)
    USE   **Anointing of the sick**

Last sacraments
    USE   **Anointing of the sick**

Last Supper
    USE   **Lord's Supper**

Last things (Theology)
    USE   **Eschatology**

Latchkey children   306.874; 362.7; 640
          Use for materials on children who carry keys to let themselves into the house on returning from school because their parents are at work.
    UF   Children, Latchkey
    BT   **Children of working parents**

Lateness
    USE   **Punctuality**

Lathe work
    USE   **Lathes**
          Turning

Lathes   621.9
    UF   Lathe work
    BT   **Woodworking machinery**
    RT   **Turning**

Latin America   980
          Use for materials on several or all of the countries of the Western Hemisphere south of the United States in which Spanish, Portuguese, or French is the principal language.
    UF   Spanish America
    SA   names of individual Latin American countries, to be added as needed
    BT   **America**
    NT   **Pan-Americanism**

BT = Broader Term   NT = Narrower Term   RT = Related Term   SA = See Also   UF = Used For

Latin America—Politics and government
 980
 BT Politics
Latin American literature 860
   Use for materials on the French, Portu-
   guese, or Spanish literature of several Latin
   American countries. May use same subdivi-
   sions and names of literary forms as for Eng-
   lish literature.
 UF South American literature
    Spanish American literature
 SA names of individual Latin
     American literatures, to be
     added as needed
 BT Literature
 NT Brazilian literature
    Mexican literature
 RT Spanish literature
Latin Americans 920; 980
   Use for materials on citizens of Latin
   American countries. Materials on United
   States citizens of Latin American descent are
   entered under Hispanic Americans.
Latin civilization
 USE Rome—Civilization
Latin language 470
   May be subdivided like English language.
 UF Classical languages
 BT Language and languages
 RT Romance languages
Latin literature 870
   May use same subdivisions and names of
   literary forms as for English literature.
 UF Roman literature
 BT Literature
 RT Classical literature
    Early Christian literature
Latinos (U.S.)
 USE Hispanic Americans
Latitude 526; 527
 UF Degrees of latitude and longi-
     tude
 BT Earth
    Geodesy
    Nautical astronomy
Latter-day Saints
 USE Church of Jesus Christ of Lat-
     ter-day Saints
Laughter 152.4
 BT Emotions
Launching of satellites
 USE Artificial satellites—Launching

Laundry 648
 UF Ironing
    Washing
 BT Cleaning
    Home economics
    Household sanitation
Law (May subdiv. geog.) 340
 UF Jurisprudence
    Laws
    Statutes
 SA names of particular legal sys-
     tems, e.g. Islamic law; spe-
     cial branches of law, e.g.
     Criminal law; and subjects
     with the subdivision Law and
     legislation, e.g. Automo-
     biles—Law and legislation;
     to be added as needed
 BT Political science
 NT Administration of justice
    Administrative law
    Automobiles—Law and legisla-
     tion
    Commercial law
    Constitutional law
    Constitutions
    Corporation law
    Courts
    Criminal law
    Ecclesiastical law
    Food—Law and legislation
    Gun control
    Internal revenue law
    International law
    Islamic law
    Justice
    Law reform
    Lawyers
    Libraries—Law and legislation
    Litigation
    Maritime law
    Medicine—Law and legislation
    Military law
    Natural law
    Space law
    Water rights
 RT Legislation
Law, Administrative
 USE Administrative law

Law and legislation
   USE   subjects with the subdivision
          Law and legislation, e.g. **Au-**
          tomobiles—Law and legisla-
          tion; to be added as needed
Law, Business
   USE   **Commercial law**
Law, Commercial
   USE   **Commercial law**
Law, Corporation
   USE   **Corporation law**
Law, Criminal
   USE   **Criminal law**
Law, Ecclesiastical
   USE   **Ecclesiastical law**
Law enforcement   363.2
   UF   Enforcement of law
   BT   **Administration of criminal jus-**
        tice
   NT   **Criminal investigation**
        Police
Law—Fiction
   USE   **Legal stories**
Law, Internal revenue
   USE   **Internal revenue law**
Law, Islamic
   USE   **Islamic law**
Law, Maritime
   USE   **Maritime law**
Law, Muslim
   USE   **Islamic law**
Law of nations
   USE   **International law**
Law of nature
   USE   **Natural law**
Law of the sea
   USE   **Maritime law**
Law reform   340
   UF   Legal reform
   BT   **Law**
Law schools (May subdiv. geog.)
        340.071
   BT   **Colleges and universities**
Law, Space
   USE   **Space law**
Law suits
   USE   **Litigation**
Law—United States   349.73
   UF   United States—Law

Law—Vocational guidance   340.023
   BT   **Professions**
        Vocational guidance
Lawn tennis
   USE   **Tennis**
Lawns   635.9; 712
   BT   **Land use**
        Landscape gardening
   RT   **Grasses**
Laws
   USE   **Law**
        Legislation
Lawsuits
   USE   **Litigation**
Lawyers   340.092; 920
   UF   Attorneys
        Bar
        Barristers
        Jurists
        Legal profession
        Solicitors
   BT   **Law**
   NT   **Judges**
   RT   **Legal ethics**
Lawyers—Fiction
   USE   **Legal stories**
Lay ministry   253
   UF   Volunteers in church work
   BT   **Church work**
   RT   **Laity**
Laymen
   USE   **Laity**
LBOs (Corporations)
   USE   **Leveraged buyouts**
Lead poisoning   615.9
   UF   Lead—Toxicology
   BT   **Occupational diseases**
        Poisons and poisoning
Lead—Toxicology
   USE   **Lead poisoning**
Leadership   158; 303.3
   BT   **Ability**
        Executive ability
        Social groups
        Success
   NT   **Elite (Social sciences)**
League of Nations   341.22
   BT   **International arbitration**
        International cooperation
        International organization

BT = Broader Term   NT = Narrower Term   RT = Related Term   SA = See Also   UF = Used For

League of Nations—*Continued*
           World War, 1914-1918—Peace
League of Nations—Mandatory system
  USE   **Mandates**
Learned institutions and societies
  USE   **Learning and scholarship**
Learned societies
  USE   **Societies**
Learning and scholarship   001.2
  UF   Erudition
         Learned institutions and societies
         Scholarship
  BT   **Civilization**
         Intellectual life
  NT   **Humanities**
         Professional education
  RT   **Culture**
         Education
         Humanism
         Research
Learning, Art of
  USE   **Study skills**
Learning center approach to teaching
  USE   **Open plan schools**
Learning, Concept
  USE   **Concept learning**
Learning disabilities   153.1; 371.9;
         616.85
  UF   Disability, Learning
         Learning disorders
  SA   types of learning disabilities, to
         be added as needed
  BT   **Psychology of learning**
         Slow learning children
  NT   **Reading disability**
Learning disorders
  USE   **Learning disabilities**
Learning, Psychology of
  USE   **Psychology of learning**
Learning resource centers
  USE   **Instructional materials centers**
Learning, Verbal
  USE   **Verbal learning**
Lease and rental services   333.5
  UF   Lease services
         Rental services
  BT   **Service industries**
Lease services
  USE   **Lease and rental services**

Leather   675
  BT   **Animal products**
  RT   **Hides and skins**
         Tanning
Leather clothing
  USE   **Leather garments**
Leather garments   391; 685
  UF   Clothing, Leather
         Garments, Leather
         Leather clothing
         Skin garments
  BT   **Clothing and dress**
         Leather work
Leather industry   338.4
  UF   Leather industry and trade *[For-
           mer heading]*
         Leather trade
  BT   **Industries**
  NT   **Bookbinding**
         Shoe industry
Leather industry and trade
  USE   **Leather industry**
Leather trade
  USE   **Leather industry**
Leather work   745.53
  BT   **Decoration and ornament**
         Decorative arts
         Handicraft
  NT   **Leather garments**
Leaves   575.5; 581.4
  UF   Foliage
  BT   **Plants**
Lebanon   956.92
    May be subdivided like United States ex-
  cept for *History.*
Lebanon—History   956.92
Lebanon—History—1975-1976, Civil War
         956.9204
Lebanon—History—1982-1984, Israeli in-
         tervention   956.05
  UF   Israeli intervention in Lebanon,
           1982-1984
  BT   **Israel-Arab conflicts**
Lectures and lecturing   808.5
    Use for general materials on lectures and
  the art of delivering speeches on academic
  subjects. Collections of speeches on several
  subjects and materials about non-academic
  speeches are entered under **Speeches.** Collections of lectures on a single subject are entered under that subject.
  UF   Addresses

BT = Broader Term   NT = Narrower Term   RT = Related Term   SA = See Also   UF = Used For

412

Lectures and lecturing—*Continued*
      Speaking
  BT   **Public speaking**
      Rhetoric
      Teaching
  NT   **Radio addresses, debates, etc.**
  RT   **Speeches**

Left and right
  USE   **Left and right (Direction)**
      Right and left (Political science)

Left and right (Direction)   152.1

Use for children's materials on left and right as indications of location or direction. Materials on political views or attitudes are entered under **Right and left (Political science)**. Materials on the physical characteristics of favoring one hand or the other are entered under **Left- and right-handedness.**

  UF   Left and right *[Former heading]*
      Right and left
  BT   **Direction sense**

Left- and right-handedness   152.3
  UF   Handedness
      Right- and left-handedness
  BT   **Psychophysiology**

Left (Political science)
  USE   **Liberalism**
      Right and left (Political science)

Legacies
  USE   **Inheritance and succession**
      Wills

Legal aid   362.5

Use for materials on legal services to the poor, usually provided under the sponsorship of local bar associations or governmental units.

  UF   Legal assistance to the poor
      [Former heading]
      Legal representation of the poor
      Legal services for the poor
  BT   **Public welfare**

Legal assistance to the poor
  USE   **Legal aid**

Legal drama (Films)   791.43

May be used for individual works, collections, or materials about motion pictures dealing with trials or litigations.

  UF   Courtroom drama
  BT   **Motion pictures**

Legal drama (Radio programs)   791.44

May be used for individual works, collections, or materials about radio programs dealing with trials or litigations.

  UF   Courtroom drama
  BT   **Radio programs**

Legal drama (Television programs)   791.45

May be used for individual works, collections, or materials about television programs dealing with trials or litigations.

  UF   Courtroom drama
  BT   **Television programs**

Legal ethics   174; 340
  UF   Ethics, Legal
  BT   **Professional ethics**
  RT   **Lawyers**

Legal fiction
  USE   **Legal stories**

Legal holidays
  USE   **Holidays**

Legal medicine
  USE   **Medical jurisprudence**

Legal novels
  USE   **Legal stories**

Legal profession
  USE   **Lawyers**

Legal reform
  USE   **Law reform**

Legal representation of the poor
  USE   **Legal aid**

Legal responsibility
  USE   **Liability (Law)**

Legal services for the poor
  USE   **Legal aid**

Legal stories   808.83; 813, etc.

May be used for individual works, collections, or materials about fiction dealing with trials or litigations.

  UF   Law—Fiction
      Lawyers—Fiction
      Legal fiction
      Legal novels
  BT   **Fiction**

Legal tender
  USE   **Paper money**

Legations
  USE   **Diplomatic and consular service**

Legendary characters
  USE   names of individual legendary characters, e.g. **Bunyan, Paul**

Legendary characters—*Continued*
    (Legendary character); to be added as needed

Legends (May subdiv. geog.) **398.2**

May be used for individual works, collections, or materials about tales coming down from the past, especially those relating to actual events or persons. Collections of tales written between the eleventh and fourteenth centuries and dealing with the age of chivalry or the supernatural are entered under **Romances.**

UF	Folk tales
	Stories
	Tales
	Traditions
SA	names of individual persons or sacred works with the subdivision *Legends;* legends of particular ethnic or religious groups, e.g. **Jewish legends;** and names of individual legendary characters, e.g. **Bunyan, Paul (Legendary character);** to be added as needed
BT	**Fiction**
	Literature
NT	**Celtic legends**
	Fairy tales
	Grail
	Jewish legends
	Mythology
	Norse legends
	Tall tales
RT	**Fables**
	Folklore
	Romances
	Saints

Legends, Celtic
    USE **Celtic legends**
Legends, Jewish
    USE **Jewish legends**
Legends, Norse
    USE **Norse legends**
Legends—United States **398.20973; 973**
    UF United States—Legends
Legerdemain
    USE **Juggling**
          Magic tricks
Legibility of handwriting
    USE **Handwriting**

Legislation **328**

Use for materials on the theory of lawmaking and descriptions of the preparation and enactment of laws.

UF	Laws
SA	subjects with the subdivision *Law and legislation,* to be added as needed
BT	**Political science**
NT	**Automobiles—Law and legislation**
	Food—Law and legislation
	Gun control
	Legislative bodies
	Libraries—Law and legislation
	Medicine—Law and legislation
	Parliamentary practice
RT	**Law**

Legislation, Direct
    USE **Referendum**
Legislative bodies **328.3**

Use for descriptions and histories of law making bodies, discussions of one-house legislatures, etc.

UF	Bicameralism
	Legislatures
	Parliaments
	Unicameral legislatures
SA	names of individual legislative bodies, e.g. **United States. Congress;** to be added as needed
BT	**Constitutional law**
	Legislation
	Representative government and representation
NT	**Parliamentary practice**
	United States. Congress
	War and emergency powers

Legislative investigations
    USE **Governmental investigations**
Legislative reapportionment
    USE **Apportionment (Election law)**
Legislatures
    USE **Legislative bodies**
Legitimacy (Law)
    USE **Illegitimacy**
Leisure **790.01**
    UF Free time (Leisure)
         Leisure time
    BT **Recreation**

BT = Broader Term   NT = Narrower Term   RT = Related Term   SA = See Also   UF = Used For

Leisure—*Continued*
NT   **Hobbies**
        Recreation
        Retirement
Leisure time
USE   **Leisure**
LEM
USE   **Lunar excursion module**
Lemon   634; 641.3
UF   Lemons
BT   **Citrus fruits**
        Trees
Lemons
USE   **Lemon**
Lending
USE   **Loans**
Lending of library materials
USE   **Library circulation**
Lenses   535
SA   types of lenses, e.g. **Contact lenses**; etc.
BT   **Optical instruments**
NT   **Contact lenses**
Lensless photography
USE   **Holography**
Lent   263
BT   **Church year**
NT   **Good Friday**
        Holy Week
RT   **Easter**
Lepidoptera
USE   **Butterflies**
        Moths
Lesbianism   306.76
BT   **Homosexuality**
RT   **Lesbians**
Lesbians   305.48; 306.76
UF   Gay women *[Former heading]*
        Gays, Female
        Homosexuals, Female
BT   **Women**
NT   **Gays and lesbians in the military**
RT   **Homosexuality**
        Lesbianism
        Lesbians' writings
Lesbians and gays in the military
USE   **Gays and lesbians in the military**

Lesbians in the military
USE   **Gays and lesbians in the military**
Lesbians' writings   808.8; 810.8, etc.
Use for collections of lesbians' writings by more than one author and for materials about such writings.
UF   Gay women's writings
        Writings of lesbians
BT   **Literature**
RT   **Lesbians**
Less developed countries
USE   **Developing countries**
Letter-sound association
USE   **Reading—Phonetic method**
Letter writing   383; 808.6
Use for materials on composition, forms, and etiquette of correspondence. Materials limited to business correspondence are entered under **Business letters**. Collections of literary letters are entered under **Letters**.
UF   Correspondence
        Salutations
BT   **Etiquette**
        Literary style
        Rhetoric
NT   **Business letters**
Lettering   745.6
UF   Ornamental alphabets
BT   **Decoration and ornament**
        Industrial painting
        Mechanical drawing
NT   **Monograms**
RT   **Alphabets**
        Initials
        Sign painting
Letters   808.86
Use for collections of literary letters. Materials on the composition, forms, and etiquette of correspondence are entered under **Letter writing**. Materials limited to business correspondence are entered under **Business letters**.
UF   Correspondence
SA   ethnic groups, classes of persons, and names of individual persons and families with the subdivision *Correspondence,* e.g. **Authors—Correspondence;** to be added as needed
BT   **Literature—Collections**
NT   **American letters**
        Authors—Correspondence
        English letters

BT = Broader Term   NT = Narrower Term   RT = Related Term   SA = See Also   UF = Used For

Letters of credit
USE **Credit**
Negotiable instruments
Letters of marque
USE **Privateering**
Letters of recommendation
USE **Applications for positions**
Letters of the alphabet
USE **Alphabet**
Leukemia 616.99
BT **Blood—Diseases**
Cancer
Levant
USE **Middle East**
Leveraged buyouts 338.8; 658.1
UF Buyouts, Leveraged
LBOs (Corporations)
Management buyouts
BT **Corporate mergers and acqui-sitions**
**Lewis and Clark Expedition (1804-1806)
973.4**
BT **United States—Exploring expe-ditions**
United States—History—1783-1809
Liability (Law) 346.02
UF Accountability
Legal responsibility
Responsibility, Legal
BT **Contracts**
NT **Malpractice**
Liability, Professional
USE **Malpractice**
Libel and slander 346.03
UF Character assassination
Defamation
Slander (Law)
BT **Journalism**
NT **Gossip**
RT **Freedom of speech**
Freedom of the press
Right of privacy
Liberalism 148; 320.5
UF Left (Political science)
BT **Political science**
Social sciences
RT **Right and left (Political sci-ence)**

Liberation movements, National
USE **National liberation movements**
Liberation theology 261.8
UF Theology of liberation
BT **Christianity—Doctrines**
Church and social problems
Liberty
USE **Freedom**
Liberty of conscience
USE **Freedom of conscience**
Liberty of speech
USE **Freedom of speech**
Liberty of the press
USE **Freedom of the press**
Liberty of the will
USE **Free will and determinism**
Librarians 020.92; 920
NT **African American librarians**
Black librarians
Library technicians
RT **Libraries**
Librarians, African American
USE **African American librarians**
Librarians, Black
USE **Black librarians**
Librarians—Collective bargaining
USE **Collective bargaining—Librari-ans**
Librarians—Education
USE **Library education**
Librarians—Ethics 174
UF Librarians—Professional ethics
[Former heading]
BT **Professional ethics**
Librarians—In-service training 023
BT **Library education**
Librarians—Professional ethics
USE **Librarians—Ethics**
Librarians—Rating 023
BT **Performance standards**
Librarians—Recruiting 023
BT **Recruiting of employees**
Librarians—Training
USE **Library education**
Librarians' unions 331.88
UF Library unions
BT **Labor unions**
Librarianship
USE **Library science**

BT = Broader Term   NT = Narrower Term   RT = Related Term   SA = See Also   UF = Used For

Librarianship, Comparative
USE **Comparative librarianship**
Libraries (May subdiv. geog.)   027
SA   types of libraries, e.g. **Academic
      libraries;** names of individual
      libraries, e.g. **Library of
      Congress;** libraries and partic-
      ular groups of people, e.g. **Li-
      braries and African Ameri-
      cans;** and libraries and other
      subjects, e.g. **Libraries and
      motion pictures;** to be added
      as needed
BT   **Books
      Books and reading
      Documentation**
NT   **Academic libraries
      Church libraries
      Hospital libraries
      Instructional materials centers
      Libraries and community
      Libraries and motion pictures
      Libraries and pictures
      Library architecture
      Library catalogs
      Library cooperation
      Library of Congress
      Library resources
      Library services
      Library technical processes
      Public libraries
      School libraries
      Special libraries**
RT   **Archives
      Information services
      Librarians**
Libraries—Acquisitions   025.2
UF   Acquisitions (Libraries)
      Book buying (Libraries)
      Libraries—Order department
      Library acquisitions
BT   **Libraries—Collection develop-
      ment
      Library technical processes**
NT   **Book selection**
Libraries—Administration   025.1
UF   Library administration
      Library policies
NT   **Libraries—Trustees
      Library finance**

Libraries and African Americans   027.6
UF   African Americans and libraries
      Afro-Americans and libraries
      Library services to African
          Americans
BT   **African Americans
      Library services**
Libraries and children
USE **Children's libraries**
Libraries and community   021.2
UF   Community and libraries
BT   **Libraries**
NT   **Public relations—Libraries**
Libraries and labor   027.6
UF   Labor and libraries
      Library services to labor
BT   **Labor
      Library services**
Libraries and motion pictures   021
UF   Educational films
      Motion pictures and libraries
BT   **Libraries
      Motion pictures
      Motion pictures in education**
Libraries and pictures   021
BT   **Libraries
      Pictures**
Libraries and readers
USE **Library services**
Libraries and schools   021
UF   Schools and libraries
BT   **Schools**
NT   **Libraries and students**
RT   **Children's libraries
      Children's literature
      School libraries**
Libraries and state
USE **Libraries—Government policy**
Libraries and students   027.62
UF   Students and libraries
BT   **Libraries and schools
      Library services
      School libraries**
Libraries and the elderly   027.6
UF   Elderly and libraries
      Library services to the elderly
BT   **Elderly
      Library services**
Libraries and young adults
USE **Young adults' library services**

BT = Broader Term   NT = Narrower Term   RT = Related Term   SA = See Also   UF = Used For

Libraries—Automation   025.04
   UF   Library automation
   SA   names of projects, formats, and
            systems, e.g. **MARC formats;**
            to be added as needed
   BT   **Automation**
   NT   **Machine readable bibliographic**
            data
            MARC formats
   RT   **Information systems**
            Online catalogs
Libraries—Boards of trustees
   USE   **Libraries—Trustees**
Libraries, Business
   USE   **Business libraries**
Libraries—Cataloging
   USE   **Cataloging**
Libraries—Catalogs
   USE   **Library catalogs**
Libraries—Censorship   025.2
   BT   **Censorship**
Libraries—Centralization   021.6
   UF   Library systems
Libraries, Children's
   USE   **Children's libraries**
Libraries, Church
   USE   **Church libraries**
Libraries—Circulation, loans
   USE   **Library circulation**
Libraries—Collection development
       025.2
   UF   Collection development (Librar-
            ies)
   BT   **Library technical processes**
   NT   **Book selection**
            Libraries—Acquisitions
Libraries—Collective bargaining
   USE   **Collective bargaining—Librari-**
           ans
Libraries, College
   USE   **Academic libraries**
Libraries, Company
   USE   **Corporate libraries**
Libraries—Cooperation
   USE   **Library cooperation**
Libraries, Corporate
   USE   **Corporate libraries**
Libraries, County
   USE   **County libraries**

Libraries—Equipment and supplies
       022
   UF   Library equipment and supplies
            Library supplies
   BT   **Furniture**
Libraries—Federal aid
   USE   **Federal aid to libraries**
Libraries—Finance
   USE   **Library finance**
Libraries—Government policy   021.8
   UF   Libraries and state
   BT   **Social policy**
   NT   **Federal aid to libraries**
            State aid to libraries
Libraries, Governmental
   USE   **Government libraries**
Libraries, Hospital
   USE   **Hospital libraries**
Libraries, Industrial
   USE   **Corporate libraries**
Libraries—Law and legislation   344
   UF   Library laws
            Library legislation
   BT   **Law**
            Legislation
Libraries—Lighting   022
   BT   **Lighting**
Libraries, Music
   USE   **Music libraries**
Libraries, National
   USE   **National libraries**
Libraries—Order department
   USE   **Libraries—Acquisitions**
Libraries, Presidential
   USE   **Presidents—United States—Ar-**
           chives
Libraries, Public
   USE   **Public libraries**
Libraries—Public relations
   USE   **Public relations—Libraries**
Libraries, Regional
   USE   **Regional libraries**
Libraries, School
   USE   **School libraries**
Libraries, Special
   USE   **Special libraries**
Libraries—Special collections   026
      May be subdivided by subject or form, e.g.
      Libraries—Special collections—Science fic-
      tion; Libraries—Special collections—Video-
      tapes; etc.

BT = Broader Term   NT = Narrower Term   RT = Related Term   SA = See Also   UF = Used For

Libraries—Special collections—*Continued*
UF   Special collections in libraries
Libraries—Standards   020
Libraries—State aid
    USE   **State aid to libraries**
Libraries—Statistics   020
    BT   **Statistics**
Libraries—Technical services
    USE   **Library technical processes**
Libraries—Trustees   021.8
    UF   Libraries—Boards of trustees
           Library boards
           Library trustees
    BT   **Libraries—Administration**
Libraries—United States   027.073
    UF   United States—Libraries
Libraries, University
    USE   **Academic libraries**
Libraries, Young adults'
    USE   **Young adults' library services**
Library acquisitions
    USE   **Libraries—Acquisitions**
Library administration
    USE   **Libraries—Administration**
Library architecture   727
    UF   Buildings, Library
           Library buildings
    BT   **Architecture**
           Libraries
Library assistants
    USE   **Library technicians**
Library automation
    USE   **Libraries—Automation**
Library boards
    USE   **Libraries—Trustees**
Library buildings
    USE   **Library architecture**
Library cataloging
    USE   **Cataloging**
Library catalogs   017; 025.3
    UF   Catalogs
           Catalogs, Library
           Libraries—Catalogs
    SA   types of library catalogs, e.g.
           Online catalogs; to be added
           as needed
    BT   **Libraries**
    NT   **Book catalogs**
           Card catalogs
           Classified catalogs

           Library catalogs on microfilm
           Online catalogs
           Subject catalogs
    RT   **Cataloging**
Library catalogs on microfilm   025.3
    UF   Catalogs on microfilm
           COM catalogs
    BT   **Library catalogs**
           Microfilms
Library circulation   025.6
    UF   Book lending
           Circulation of library materials
           Lending of library materials
           Libraries—Circulation, loans
    BT   **Library services**
    NT   **Interlibrary loans**
Library classification
    USE   **Books—Classification**
Library clerks
    USE   **Library technicians**
Library consortia
    USE   **Library cooperation**
           Library information networks
Library cooperation   021.6
    UF   Consortia, Library
           Cooperation, Library
           Libraries—Cooperation
           Library consortia
    BT   **Libraries**
    NT   **Interlibrary loans**
           Library information networks
Library education   020.71
    Use for materials on the education of librarians. Materials on the instruction of readers in library use are entered under **Bibliographic instruction.**
    UF   Education for librarianship
           Librarians—Education
           Librarians—Training
           Library science—Study and
              teaching
    BT   **Education**
           Professional education
    NT   **Librarians—In-service training**
           Library schools
Library education—Audiovisual aids   020.71
    BT   **Audiovisual education**
           Audiovisual materials
Library education—Curricula   020.71
    BT   **Education—Curricula**

BT = Broader Term   NT = Narrower Term   RT = Related Term   SA = See Also   UF = Used For

Library equipment and supplies
USE **Libraries—Equipment and supplies**
Library extension 021.6
BT **Library services**
NT **Bookmobiles**
County libraries
Library finance 025.1
UF Libraries—Finance
BT **Finance**
Libraries—Administration
NT **State aid to libraries**
RT **Federal aid to libraries**
Library information networks 021.6
UF Consortia, Library
Library consortia
Library networks
Library systems
Networks, Library
BT **Data transmission systems**
Information networks
Library cooperation
Library instruction
USE **Bibliographic instruction**
Library laws
USE **Libraries—Law and legislation**
Library legislation
USE **Libraries—Law and legislation**
Library materials
USE **Library resources**
Library networks
USE **Library information networks**
Library of Congress 027.573
UF United States. Library of Congress
BT **Libraries**
Library orientation
USE **Bibliographic instruction**
Library policies
USE **Libraries—Administration**
Library processing
USE **Library technical processes**
Library reference services
USE **Reference services (Libraries)**
Library resources (May subdiv. geog.)
025
Use for general materials on the resources and collections available in libraries for research. Materials on the library resources and collections available in a particular field or on a particular subject are entered under that field or subject with the subdivision *Library resources.*
UF Library materials
SA subjects, ethnic groups, classes of persons, corporate bodies, individual persons, literary authors, and names of countries, cities, etc., with the subdivision *Library resources,* e.g. **United States—History—Library resources;** to be added as needed
BT **Libraries**
NT **Government publications**
Library resources—Conservation and restoration 025.8
UF Books—Preservation
Library resources—Preservation
Preservation of library resources
Library resources—Preservation
USE **Library resources—Conservation and restoration**
Library schools 020.71
BT **Library education**
Library science 020
Use for general materials on the knowledge and skill necessary for the organization and administration of libraries. Materials on services offered by libraries to patrons are entered under **Library services.**
UF Librarianship
BT **Documentation**
Information science
NT **Cataloging**
Comparative librarianship
Library surveys
Library technical processes
RT **Bibliography**
Library services
Library science—Study and teaching
USE **Library education**
Library services 025.5
Use for materials on services offered by libraries to patrons. General materials on the knowledge and skill necessary for the organization and administration of libraries are entered under **Library science.**
UF Libraries and readers
Library services to readers
Reader services (Libraries) *[Former heading]*
Readers and libraries

BT = Broader Term   NT = Narrower Term   RT = Related Term   SA = See Also   UF = Used For

Library services—*Continued*
  SA   libraries and specific types of
        users or specific activities for
        which services are provided,
        e.g. **Libraries and the elder-
        ly;** to be added as needed
  BT   **Libraries**
  NT   **Bibliographic instruction**
        **Libraries and African Ameri-
        cans**
        Libraries and labor
        Libraries and students
        Libraries and the elderly
        Library circulation
        Library extension
        Reference services (Libraries)
        Young adults' library services
  RT   **Library science**
Library services to African Americans
  USE   **Libraries and African Ameri-
        cans**
Library services to children
  USE   **Children's libraries**
Library services to labor
  USE   **Libraries and labor**
Library services to readers
  USE   **Library services**
Library services to teenagers
  USE   **Young adults' library services**
Library services to the elderly
  USE   **Libraries and the elderly**
Library services to young adults
  USE   **Young adults' library services**
Library skills
  USE   **Bibliographic instruction**
Library supplies
  USE   **Libraries—Equipment and
        supplies**
Library surveys   020
  BT   **Library science**
        Surveys
Library systems
  USE   **Libraries—Centralization**
        Library information networks
Library technical processes   025
    Use for materials on the activities and pro-
    cesses concerned with the acquisition, organi-
    zation, and preparation of library materials for
    use.
  UF   Centralized processing (Libraries)
        Libraries—Technical services

        Library processing
        Processing (Libraries)
        Technical services (Libraries)
  BT   **Libraries**
        Library science
  NT   **Books—Classification**
        Cataloging
        Libraries—Acquisitions
        **Libraries—Collection develop-
        ment**
Library technicians   020.92
  UF   Library assistants
        Library clerks
        Paraprofessional librarians
  BT   **Librarians**
        Paraprofessionals
Library trustees
  USE   **Libraries—Trustees**
Library unions
  USE   **Librarians' unions**
Library user orientation
  USE   **Bibliographic instruction**
Librettos   780; 780.26
    Use for collections of miscellaneous libret-
    tos and for materials on the history and criti-
    cism of librettos and on writing librettos. Indi-
    vidual librettos and collections of librettos of
    a specific type are entered under the specific
    type of libretto.
  SA   types of librettos, e.g. **Opera li-
        brettos;** to be added as need-
        ed
  BT   **Books**
  NT   **Opera librettos**
Lie detectors and detection   363.2
  UF   Polygraph
  BT   **Criminal investigation**
        Medical jurisprudence
        Truthfulness and falsehood
Life   128
    Use for materials on philosophical or reli-
    gious considerations of life. Materials on life
    from a scientific point of view are entered un-
    der **Life (Biology)**.
  NT   **Death**
        Longevity
  RT   **Life (Biology)**
Life after death
  USE   **Future life**
        Immortality
Life (Biology)   570.1
    Use for materials on life from a scientific
    point of view. Materials on philosophical or

Life (Biology)—*Continued*
religious considerations of life are entered under **Life.**

    BT   **Biology**
    NT   **Gaia hypothesis**
            Genetics
            Life cycles (Biology)
            Middle age
            Protoplasm
            Reproduction
    RT   **Life**
Life care communities
    USE   **Retirement communities**
Life, Christian
    USE   **Christian life**
Life cycles
    USE   **Life cycles (Biology)**
            and types of plants or animals with the subdivision *Life cycles,* to be added as needed

Life cycles (Biology)   571.8
    UF   Cycles, Life (Biology)
            Life cycles
    SA   types of plants or animals with the subdivision *Life cycles,* to be added as needed
    BT   **Biology**
            Life (Biology)
Life expectancy
    USE   **Longevity**
Life, Future
    USE   **Future life**
Life histories
    USE   **Biography**
Life insurance   368.32
    UF   Insurance, Life *[Former heading]*
    BT   **Insurance**
    NT   **Group insurance**
            Industrial life insurance
    RT   **Annuities**
Life on other planets   576.8
    Use for materials on the possibility of indigenous life in outer space. Materials on the biology of humans or other earth creatures while in outer space are entered under **Space biology.**
    UF   Astrobiology
            Exobiology
            Extraterrestrial life
            Planets, Life on other
    BT   **Astronomy**

            Planets
            Space biology
            Universe
    NT   **Extraterrestrial beings**
            Interstellar communication
Life—Origin   113
    UF   Germ theory
            Origin of life
    BT   **Evolution**
Life quality
    USE   **Quality of life**
Life saving
    USE   **Lifesaving**
Life sciences   570
    UF   Biosciences
    BT   **Science**
    NT   **Agriculture**
            Biology
            Medicine
Life sciences ethics
    USE   **Bioethics**
Life skills   158; 640
    Use for materials on skills needed by an individual to exist in modern society, including skills related to education, employment, finance, etc.
    UF   Basic life skills
            Coping skills
            Functional competencies
            Fundamental life skills
            Life skills guides
            Living skills
            Personal life skills
    SA   groups and classes of persons with the subdivision *Life skills guides,* e.g. **Elderly— Life skills guides;** to be added as needed
    BT   **Success**
    NT   **Conduct of life**
            Elderly—Life skills guides
            Self-improvement
            Survival skills
    RT   **Human behavior**
            Human relations
Life skills guides
    USE   **Life skills**
            and groups and classes of persons with the subdivision *Life skills guides,* e.g. **Elderly—**

BT = Broader Term   NT = Narrower Term   RT = Related Term   SA = See Also   UF = Used For

Life skills guides—*Continued*
>   **Life skills guides;** to be added as needed
Life span prolongation
>   USE   **Longevity**
Life styles
>   USE   **Lifestyles**
Life support systems (Medical environment)   362.1
>   BT   **Hospitals**
>   **Terminal care**
Life support systems (Space environment)   629.47
>   BT   **Human engineering**
>   **Space medicine**
>   NT   **Apollo project**
>   **Lunar bases**
>   **Space suits**
Life support systems (Submarine environment)   627
>   BT   **Human engineering**
Lifelong education
>   USE   **Adult education**
>   **Continuing education**
Lifesaving   363.1
>   UF   Life saving
>   BT   **Rescue work**
>   RT   **First aid**
Lifestyles   306
>   Use for materials on the distinctive way of life or manner of living characteristic of individuals or groups of people.
>   UF   Alternative lifestyle
>   Life styles
>   SA   types of lifestyles, to be added as needed
>   BT   **Human behavior**
>   **Quality of life**
>   NT   **Counter culture**
>   **Unmarried couples**
Lifts
>   USE   **Elevators**
>   **Hoisting machinery**
Light   535
>   BT   **Electromagnetic waves**
>   **Physics**
>   NT   **Color**
>   **Lasers**
>   **Lighting**
>   **Luminescence**
>   **Refraction**

>   RT   **Optics**
>   **Photometry**
>   **Radiation**
>   **Spectrum analysis**
Light amplification by stimulated emission of radiation
>   USE   **Lasers**
Light and shade
>   USE   **Shades and shadows**
Light, Electric
>   USE   **Electric lighting**
Light production in animals
>   USE   **Bioluminescence**
Light ships
>   USE   **Lightships**
Light—Therapeutic use
>   USE   **Phototherapy**
Light verse
>   USE   **Humorous poetry**
Lighthouses   387.1; 623.89; 627
>   BT   **Navigation**
>   NT   **Lightships**
Lighting (May subdiv. geog.)   **621.32**
>   UF   Illumination
>   SA   subjects with the subdivision *Lighting*, to be added as needed
>   BT   **Interior design**
>   **Light**
>   NT   **Candles**
>   **Electric lighting**
>   **Lamps**
>   **Libraries—Lighting**
>   **Photography—Lighting**
>   **Stage lighting**
>   **Streets—Lighting**
Lightning   551.56
>   BT   **Electricity**
>   **Meteorology**
>   **Thunderstorms**
Lights, Feast of
>   USE   **Hanukkah**
Lightships   623.89; 627
>   UF   Light ships
>   BT   **Lighthouses**
>   **Ships**
Limbs, Artificial
>   USE   **Artificial limbs**
Lime
>   USE   **Lime (Fruit)**

BT = Broader Term   NT = Narrower Term   RT = Related Term   SA = See Also   UF = Used For

Lime—*Continued*
> Lime (Mineral)

Lime (Fruit)   634
- UF   Lime
-       Limes
- BT   **Citrus fruits**
-       **Trees**

Lime (Mineral)   631.8; 666
- UF   Lime *[Former heading]*
- BT   **Fertilizers**
- RT   **Cement**

Limericks   808.81; 811, etc.; 811.008, etc.

May be used for collections of limericks by one or several authors or for materials about limericks.
- UF   Rhymes
- BT   **Humorous poetry**
- RT   **Nonsense verses**

Limes
- USE   **Lime (Fruit)**

Limitation of armament
- USE   **Arms control**

Limited access highways
- USE   **Express highways**

Lincoln, Abraham, 1809-1865   92; B
- BT   **Presidents—United States**

Lincoln Day
- USE   **Lincoln's Birthday**

Lincoln family   920; 929

Lincoln's Birthday   394.261
- UF   Lincoln Day
- BT   **Holidays**

Line engraving
- USE   **Engraving**

Linear algebra   512
- UF   Algebras, Linear *[Former heading]*
- BT   **Algebra**
-       **Mathematical analysis**
- RT   **Topology**

Linear system theory
- USE   **System analysis**

Linen   677
- BT   **Fabrics**
-       **Fibers**
- RT   **Flax**

Linguistic science
- USE   **Linguistics**

Linguistics   410

Use for materials on the scientific study of speech and for comparative studies of languages. General materials on the history, philosophy, origin, etc., of languages are entered under **Language and languages.**
- UF   Comparative linguistics
-       Comparative philology
-       Language and languages—Comparative philology
-       Linguistic science
-       Linguistics, Comparative
-       Philology
-       Philology, Comparative *[Former heading]*
- BT   **Language and languages**
- NT   **Grammar**
-       **Semantics**
-       **Universal language**

Linguistics, Comparative
- USE   **Linguistics**

Linoleum block printing   761
- UF   Block printing
- BT   **Printing**
-       **Prints**

Linotype   686.2
- BT   **Printing**
-       **Type and type founding**
-       **Typesetting**

Lip reading
- USE   **Deaf—Means of communication**

Liquefaction of coal
- USE   **Coal liquefaction**

Liqueurs
- USE   **Liquors**

Liquid fuel
- USE   **Petroleum as fuel**

Liquids   532
- BT   **Fluid mechanics**
-       **Physics**
- NT   **Hydraulics**
-       **Hydrodynamics**
-       **Hydrostatics**

Liquor industry   338.4
- BT   **Industries**
-       **Liquors**
- NT   **Bars**

Liquor problem
- USE   **Alcoholism**
-       **Drinking of alcoholic beverages**

BT = Broader Term   NT = Narrower Term   RT = Related Term   SA = See Also   UF = Used For

Liquors 663; 641.2
UF   Cordials (Liquor)
       Drinks
       Intoxicants
       Liqueurs
       Liquors and liqueurs *[Former heading]*
       Spirits, Alcoholic
SA   types of liquors and liqueurs, to be added as needed
BT   **Alcohol**
       Alcoholic beverages
       Beverages
NT   **Liquor industry**
RT   **Distillation**
Liquors and liqueurs
USE   **Liquors**
Listening 153.6; 153.7
BT   **Attention**
       Educational psychology
RT   **Hearing**
Listening devices
USE   **Eavesdropping**
Literacy (May subdiv. geog.) 302.2; 379.2
UF   Illiteracy
BT   **Education**
NT   **Functional literacy**
       Visual literacy
Literacy, Visual
USE   **Visual literacy**
Literary awards
USE   **Literary prizes**
Literary characters
USE   **Characters and characteristics in literature**
Literary collections
USE   **Anthologies**
       Literature—Collections
       and names of literatures, e.g. **American literature;** and, for collections focused on a single subject by more than one author involving two or more literary forms, the subject with the subdivision *Literary collections,* e.g. **Cats—Literary collections;** to be added as needed

Literary criticism
USE   **Criticism**
       Literature—History and criticism
Literary forgeries 098
UF   Frauds, Literary
BT   **Counterfeits and counterfeiting**
       Forgery
Literary landmarks (May subdiv. geog.) 809; 810.9, etc.
UF   Authors—Homes and haunts
       Landmarks, Literary
BT   **Historic buildings**
       Literature—History and criticism
Literary landmarks—United States 810.9
UF   United States—Literary landmarks
Literary prizes 807.9
UF   Book awards
       Book prizes
       Literary awards
       Literature—Prizes
SA   names of awards, e.g. **Caldecott Medal;** to be added as needed
BT   **Awards**
NT   **Caldecott Medal**
       Literature—Competitions
       Newbery Medal
Literary property
USE   **Copyright**
Literary recreations 793.73
UF   Language games
       Recreations, Literary
BT   **Amusements**
NT   **Charades**
       Plot-your-own stories
       Riddles
       Word games
Literary style 808; 809
UF   Style, Literary *[Former heading]*
BT   **Literature**
NT   **Letter writing**
RT   **Criticism**
       Rhetoric
Literature 800
    Literatures are described by countries or geographic regions. In countries or regions

---

BT = Broader Term   NT = Narrower Term   RT = Related Term   SA = See Also   UF = Used For

Literature—*Continued*

with more than one major language the literature may be further qualified by the language in parentheses, e.g. **Canadian literature (French)**. There is no distinction made in subject headings between literary works in their original languages and in translations.

UF   Belles lettres

SA   names of national literatures, e.g.
        English literature; French literature; etc.; national literatures qualified if needed by the language in which the literature was originally written or subdivided by a sub-set of authors within the literature, e.g. **African literature (English); American literature— African American authors;** and subjects and themes in literature, e.g. **Bible in literature; Children in literature; Characters and characteristics in literature; Symbolism in literature;** etc., to be added as needed

BT   Humanities
      Language arts

NT   African literature (English)
      American literature
      Anglo-Saxon literature
      Animals in literature
      Authorship
      Ballads
      Bible in literature
      Biography as a literary form
      Black humor (Literature)
      Brazilian literature
      Campaign literature
      Canadian literature
      Catholic literature
      Chapbooks
      Characters and characteristics in literature
      Children's literature
      Classical literature
      Classicism
      Communism and literature
      Comparative literature
      Criticism
      Danish literature
      Diaries

Drama
Early Christian literature
English literature
Epic literature
Erotic literature
Essay
Fables
Fairy tales
Fiction
French literature
Gay men's writings
German literature
Greek literature
Hebrew literature
Humanism
Icelandic literature
Indians of North America—
  Literature
Indic literature
Jewish literature
Journalism
Latin American literature
Latin literature
Legends
Lesbians' writings
Literary style
Medieval literature
Mexican literature
Mock-heroic literature
Modern Greek literature
Multicultural literature
Music and literature
Nature in literature
Norwegian literature
Old Norse literature
Parody
Picaresque literature
Plots (Drama, fiction, etc.)
Poetry
Portuguese literature
Realism in literature
Religion in literature
Religious literature
Romance literature
Romances
Russian literature
Sagas
Satire
Scandinavian literature
Short story

BT = Broader Term   NT = Narrower Term   RT = Related Term   SA = See Also   UF = Used For

Literature—*Continued*
    Soviet literature
    Spanish literature
    Speeches
    Swedish literature
    Symbolism in literature
    Travel in literature
    West Indian literature
      (French)
    Wit and humor
    World War, 1939-1945—Literature and the war
    Young adult literature
  RT   **Books**
      Books and reading
      Modernism (Arts)
      Romanticism
Literature and communism
  USE   **Communism and literature**
Literature and music
  USE   **Music and literature**
Literature—Bio-bibliography   809
  RT   **Authors**
Literature, Classical
  USE   **Classical literature**
Literature—Collections   808.8
  UF   Collected works
      Collections of literature
      Literary collections
      Literature—Selections
  SA   literary forms and national literatures with the subdivision *Collections,* e.g. **Poetry—Collections; English literature—Collections;** etc., to be added as needed
  NT   **Essays**
      Letters
      Parodies
      Quotations
      Short stories
Literature, Comparative
  USE   **Comparative literature**
Literature—Competitions   807.9
  BT   **Contests**
      Literary prizes
Literature—Criticism
  USE   **Literature—History and criticism**

Literature—Dictionaries   803
  BT   **Encyclopedias and dictionaries**
  NT   **English literature—Dictionaries**
Literature, Erotic
  USE   **Erotic literature**
Literature—Evaluation
  USE   **Best books**
      Books and reading
      Books—Reviews
      Criticism
      Literature—History and criticism
Literature—Film and video adaptations
  USE   **Film adaptations**
      Television adaptations
Literature—History and criticism   809
  UF   Appraisal of books
      Books—Appraisal
      Evaluation of literature
      Literary criticism
      Literature—Criticism
      Literature—Evaluation
  NT   **Literary landmarks**
Literature—Indexes   016.8
Literature, Intercultural
  USE   **Multicultural literature**
Literature, Medieval
  USE   **Medieval literature**
Literature, Multicultural
  USE   **Multicultural literature**
Literature—Outlines, syllabi, etc.   802
  NT   **English literature—Outlines, syllabi, etc.**
Literature—Prizes
  USE   **Literary prizes**
Literature—Selections
  USE   **Literature—Collections**
Literature—Stories, plots, etc.   802
    Use for collections of literary plots. Materials that analyze plots or discuss the technique of constructing plots are entered under **Plots (Drama, fiction, etc.).**
  UF   Stories, plots, etc.
  SA   types of literature and specific genres with the subdivision *Stories, plots, etc.;* to be added as needed
  RT   **Ballet—Stories, plots, etc.**
      Opera—Stories, plots, etc.
Literatures of the Soviet Union
  USE   **Soviet literature**

BT = Broader Term   NT = Narrower Term   RT = Related Term   SA = See Also   UF = Used For

Lithographers   763.092; 920
  BT   Artists
Lithography   686.2; 763; 764
  UF   Lithoprinting
  BT   Color printing
       Printing
       Prints
  NT   Offset printing
Lithoprinting
  USE Lithography
       Offset printing
Litigation   347
  UF   Actions and defenses *[Former heading]*
       Civil law suits
       Defense (Law)
       Law suits
       Lawsuits
       Personal actions (Law)
       Suing (Law)
       Suits (Law)
  BT   Law
  NT   Witnesses
  RT   Arbitration and award
Littering
  USE Refuse and refuse disposal
Little league baseball
  USE Little League baseball
Little League baseball   796.357
  UF   Little league baseball *[Former heading]*
  BT   Baseball
Little theater movement   792
  UF   Community theater
       Theater—Little theater movement
  BT   Amateur theater
       Theater
Liturgical year
  USE Church year
Liturgics
  USE Liturgies
Liturgies   264; 291.3
  Use for general materials on the forms of prayers, rituals, and ceremonies used in public worship, including the theological and historical study of liturgies, and for texts of liturgies from more than one religion.
  UF   Church service books
       Liturgics
       Liturgy
       Ritual

       Service books (Liturgy)
  SA   names of individual religions and denominations with the subdivision *Liturgy,* to be added as needed
  BT   Religion
       Rites and ceremonies
  NT   Catholic Church—Liturgy
       Hymns
       Judaism—Liturgy
       Lord's Supper
       Mass
  RT   Church music
Liturgy
  USE Liturgies
Live poliovirus vaccine
  USE Poliomyelitis vaccine
Livestock
  USE Domestic animals
       Livestock industry
Livestock breeding   636.08
  UF   Livestock—Breeding *[Former heading]*
  BT   Breeding
       Livestock industry
Livestock—Breeding
  USE Livestock breeding
Livestock industry   636
  Use for materials on stock raising as an industry. General materials on farm and other domestic animals are entered under **Domestic animals.**
  UF   Animal husbandry
       Animal industry
       Livestock *[Former heading]*
       Stock and stock breeding
       Stock raising
  BT   Agriculture
       Economic zoology
  NT   Dairying
       Livestock breeding
       Livestock judging
  RT   Domestic animals
Livestock judging   636
  UF   Stock judging
  BT   Livestock industry
Living earth theory
  USE Gaia hypothesis
Living skills
  USE Life skills

BT = Broader Term   NT = Narrower Term   RT = Related Term   SA = See Also   UF = Used For

Living together
    USE   Unmarried couples
Living wills   344
    BT   **Wills**
    RT   **Right to die**
          Terminal care
Livres à clef
    USE   **Romans à clef**
Lizards   597.95
    BT   **Reptiles**
Loan associations
    USE   **Savings and loan associations**
Loan funds, Student
    USE   **Student loan funds**
Loans   332.7
    UF   Borrowing
          Lending
    BT   **Finance**
    NT   **Government lending**
          Interest (Economics)
          Mortgages
          Personal loans
          Public debts
          Savings and loan associations
          Student aid
    RT   **Credit**
          Investments
Loans, Personal
    USE   **Personal loans**
Lobbying   328.3
    Use for materials on groups that promote
    their own interests with public officials. Mate-
    rials on special interest groups that support
    sympathetic candidates for public office
    through campaign contributions are entered
    under **Political action committees.**
    UF   Interest groups
          Lobbying and lobbyists *[Former
              heading]*
          Lobbyists
          Pressure groups
    SA   names of specific lobbying and
              pressure groups, to be added
              as needed
    BT   **Politics**
          Propaganda
    RT   **Political action committees**
Lobbying and lobbyists
    USE   **Lobbying**
Lobbyists
    USE   **Lobbying**

Lobsters   595.3
    BT   **Crustacea**
          Shellfish
Local government   320.8; 352.14
    Use for materials on the government of dis-
    tricts, counties, townships, etc. Materials limit-
    ed to county government only are entered un-
    der **County government.** Materials limited to
    the government of cities and towns are en-
    tered under **Municipal government.**
    UF   Government, Local
          Town meeting
          Township government
    BT   **Administrative law**
          Community organization
          Political science
    NT   **Cities and towns**
          County government
          Metropolitan government
          Municipal government
          Public administration
          State-local relations
Local history   907
    Use for materials on the writing and com-
    piling of local histories. Collective histories of
    several localities are entered under the coun-
    tries, states, etc., with the subdivision *Local
    history,* e.g. **United States—Local history;
    Ohio—Local history;** etc. Individual local
    histories are entered under the place with the
    subdivision *History,* e.g. **Chicago (Ill.)—His-
    tory.**
    UF   Community history
          History, Local
          Regional history
    SA   names of countries, states, etc.,
              with the subdivision *Local
              history,* and names of cities,
              counties, or other localities
              with the subdivision *History,*
              to be added as needed
    BT   **Historiography**
          History
    NT   **Ohio—Local history**
          United States—Local history
Local-state relations
    USE   **State-local relations**
Local traffic
    USE   **City traffic**
Local transit (May subdiv. geog.)   **388.4**
    Use for materials on the various modes of
    local public transportation.
    UF   City transit
          Mass transit

BT = Broader Term   NT = Narrower Term   RT = Related Term   SA = See Also   UF = Used For

Local transit—*Continued*

       Municipal transit
       Public transit
       Rapid transit
       Transit systems
       Urban transportation
  BT   **Traffic engineering**
      Transportation
  NT   **Buses**
      Street railroads
      Subways

Localism
  USE   **Regionalism**

Localisms
  USE   names of languages with the
      subdivision *Provincialisms*,
      e.g. **English language—Pro-**
      vincialisms; to be added as
      needed

Lockouts
  USE   **Strikes**

Locks and keys   683
  UF   Keys
  BT   **Burglary protection**

Locomotion   152.3; 388
  NT   **Aeronautics**
      Animal locomotion
      Flight
      Horsemanship
      Human locomotion
      Navigation
      Transportation
      Walking

Locomotives   625.26
  BT   **Machinery**
      Steam engines

Locomotives—Models   625.1
  UF   Model trains
  BT   **Models and model making**

Locusts   595.7; 632
  BT   **Insect pests**
      Insects

Locusts, Seventeen-year
  USE   **Cicadas**

Lodging houses
  USE   **Hotels and motels**

Log cabins and houses   728
  UF   Cabins
      Houses, Log
  BT   **House construction**

      Houses

Logarithms   513.2
  BT   **Algebra**
      Mathematics—Tables
      Trigonometry—Tables
  NT   **Slide rule**

Logging
  USE   **Lumber and lumbering**

Logic   160
  UF   Argumentation
      Deduction (Logic)
      Dialectics
      Fallacies
      Induction (Logic)
  BT   **Intellect**
      Philosophy
      Science—Methodology
  NT   **Critical thinking**
      Probabilities
      Symbolic logic
      Theory of knowledge
  RT   **Reasoning**
      Thought and thinking

Logic, Symbolic and mathematical
  USE   **Symbolic logic**

Lone Ranger films   791.43
    May be used for individual works, collections, or materials about Lone Ranger films.
  BT   **Western films**

Loneliness   155.9; 158
  UF   Social isolation
      Solitude
  BT   **Emotions**
      Human relations

Long distance running
  USE   **Marathon running**

Long distance swimming
  USE   **Marathon swimming**

Long life
  USE   **Longevity**

Long-term care facilities   362.1
  UF   Extended care facilities
  BT   **Hospitals**
      Medical care
  NT   **Nursing homes**

Longevity   612.6; 613
  UF   Life expectancy
      Life span prolongation
      Long life
  BT   **Age**
      Life

BT = Broader Term   NT = Narrower Term   RT = Related Term   SA = See Also   UF = Used For

Longevity—*Continued*
NT Aging
RT Middle age
    Old age
Longitude   526; 527
UF Degrees of latitude and longitude
BT Earth
    Geodesy
    Nautical astronomy
Looking glasses
USE Mirrors
Looms   677; 746.1
BT Weaving
Loran   621.384
BT Navigation
Lord's Day
USE Sabbath
Lord's prayer   226.9; 242
BT Jesus Christ—Prayers
Lord's Supper   232.9; 264
UF Communion
    Eucharist
    Holy communion
    Jesus Christ—Last Supper
    Last Supper
BT Jesus Christ
    Liturgies
    Rites and ceremonies
    Sacraments
RT Mass
Losing things
USE Lost and found possessions
Lost and found possessions   330.1
UF Finding things
    Losing things
    Lost possessions
    Lost things
    Possessions, Lost and found
BT Property
Lost architectural heritage
USE Lost architecture
Lost architecture (May subdiv. geog.)
    720
    Use for materials on buildings and structures that have been destroyed or demolished.
UF Lost architectural heritage
    Lost buildings
BT Architecture
Lost buildings
USE Lost architecture

Lost children
USE Missing children
Lost possessions
USE Lost and found possessions
Lost things
USE Lost and found possessions
Lotteries   336.1
BT Gambling
Louisiana Purchase   973.4; 976.3
BT United States—History—1783-1809
Love   152.4; 177; 306.7
UF Affection
BT Emotions
    Human behavior
NT Marriage
RT Dating (Social customs)
    Friendship
Love Canal Chemical Waste Landfill
    (Niagara Falls, N.Y.)   363.72
BT Hazardous waste sites
    Landfills
Love poetry   808.81; 811, etc.
    May be used for individual works, collections, or materials about love poetry.
BT Poetry
RT Erotic poetry
Love—Religious aspects   231 ; 291.2
UF Love (Theology) *[Former heading]*
RT Charity
Love stories   808.83; 813, etc.
    May be used for individual works, collections, or materials about love stories.
UF Romance novels
    Romances (Love stories)
    Romantic fiction
    Romantic stories
BT Fiction
RT Erotic fiction
    Gothic novels
    Romantic suspense novels
Love stories—Technique   808.3
BT Authorship
Love (Theology)
USE Love—Religious aspects
Low income housing
USE Public housing
Low sodium diet
USE Salt-free diet

BT = Broader Term   NT = Narrower Term   RT = Related Term   SA = See Also   UF = Used For

Low temperature biology
USE **Cryobiology**
Low temperatures   536; 621.5
UF Cryogenics
Temperatures, Low
BT **Temperature**
NT **Cryobiology**
RT **Cold**
Refrigeration
Loyalists, American
USE **American Loyalists**
Loyalty   172
UF Faithfulness
BT **Ethics**
Virtue
NT **Patriotism**
Loyalty oaths
USE **Internal security**
Lubrication and lubricants   621.8
UF Grease
BT **Machinery**
RT **Bearings (Machinery)**
Oils and fats
Lullabies   782.42
UF Cradle songs
Slumber songs
BT **Bedtime**
Children's poetry
Children's songs
Songs
Lumber and lumbering   634.9; 674
Use for general materials on lumber and for
materials on the felling of trees and the prepa-
ration of lumber.
UF Logging
Timber
Woods
BT **Forest products**
Forests and forestry
Trees
Wood
Luminescence   535
BT **Light**
Radiation
NT **Bioluminescence**
Phosphorescence
Luminescent books
USE **Glow-in-the-dark books**
Luminous books
USE **Glow-in-the-dark books**

Lunar bases   629.45
UF Moon bases
BT **Civil engineering**
Life support systems (Space
environment)
Lunar cars
USE **Moon cars**
Lunar eclipses   523.3
UF Eclipses, Lunar *[Former head-*
ing]
Moon—Eclipses
BT **Astronomy**
Lunar excursion module   629.45
UF LEM
Lunar module
BT **Space vehicles**
Lunar expeditions
USE **Space flight to the moon**
Lunar exploration
USE **Moon—Exploration**
Lunar geology   559.9
UF Geology, Lunar
Geology—Moon
Moon—Geology
BT **Astrogeology**
NT **Lunar petrology**
Lunar soil
Lunar module
USE **Lunar excursion module**
Lunar petrology   552; 552.0999
UF Lunar rocks
Moon rocks
Rocks, Moon
BT **Lunar geology**
Petrology
Lunar probes   629.43
UF Moon probes
SA names of specific lunar probe
projects, to be added as need-
ed
BT **Space probes**
NT **Project Ranger**
Lunar rocks
USE **Lunar petrology**
Lunar rover vehicles
USE **Moon cars**
Lunar soil   523.3; 552.0999; 631.4
UF Moon soil
Soils, Lunar
BT **Lunar geology**

BT = Broader Term   NT = Narrower Term   RT = Related Term   SA = See Also   UF = Used For

Lunar soil—*Continued*
   RT   **Moon—Surface**
Lunar surface
   USE   **Moon—Surface**
Lunar surface radio communication
   USE   **Radio in astronautics**
Lunar surface vehicles
   USE   **Moon cars**
Luncheons   **642**
   BT   **Cooking**
          Menus
   RT   **Entertaining**
Lunchrooms
   USE   **Restaurants**
Lung cancer   **616.99**
   UF   Lungs—Cancer
   BT   **Cancer**
          Lungs—Diseases
Lungs   **611; 612.2**
   BT   **Respiratory system**
Lungs—Cancer
   USE   **Lung cancer**
Lungs—Diseases   **616.2**
   SA   types of lung diseases, to be
          added as needed
   BT   **Diseases**
   NT   **Lung cancer**
          Pneumonia
          Tuberculosis
Lying
   USE   **Truthfulness and falsehood**
Lyme disease   **616.9**
   BT   **Diseases**
   RT   **Insects as carriers of disease**
          Ticks
Lymphatic system   **573.1; 612.4; 616.4**
   BT   **Physiology**
Lynching   **364.1**
   BT   **Crime**
   RT   **Vigilance committees**
Lyric drama
   USE   **Opera**
Lyricists   **782.0092; 920**
   UF   Songwriters
   BT   **Poets**
Lyrics
   USE   **Popular music—Texts**
M.I.A.'s
   USE   **Missing in action**

Maccabbees, Feast of the
   USE   **Hanukkah**
Machine design   **621.8**
   UF   Machinery—Construction
          Machinery—Design and con-
          struction *[Former heading]*
   SA   types of machines, equipment,
          etc., with the subdivision *De-*
          sign and construction, e.g.
          Airplanes—Design and con-
          struction; to be added as
          needed
   BT   **Design**
          Machinery
   NT   **Machinery—Models**
Machine intelligence
   USE   **Artificial intelligence**
Machine language
   USE   **Programming languages (Com-**
          puters)
Machine readable bibliographic data
   025.3
   UF   Bibliographic data in machine
          readable form
          Cataloging data in machine read-
          able form
          Computer stored cataloging data
   SA   names of projects, formats, and
          systems, e.g. **MARC formats;**
          to be added as needed
   BT   **Cataloging**
          Information services
          Information systems
          Libraries—Automation
   NT   **MARC formats**
Machine readable catalog system
   USE   **MARC formats**
Machine readable dictionaries   **423, etc.**
   UF   Dictionaries, Machine readable
   BT   **Encyclopedias and dictionaries**
Machine shop practice   **670.42**
   UF   Shop practice
   NT   **Drilling and boring**
          Grinding and polishing
   RT   **Machine shops**
Machine shops   **670.42**
   RT   **Machine shop practice**
Machine tools   **621.9**
   SA   types of machine tools, to be
          added as needed

BT = Broader Term   NT = Narrower Term   RT = Related Term   SA = See Also   UF = Used For

Machine tools—*Continued*
 BT Machinery
  Tools
 NT Planing machines
 RT Drilling and boring
  Grinding and polishing
Machinery 621.8
 UF Machines
 BT Manufactures
  Mechanical engineering
  Power (Mechanics)
  Technology
  Tools
 NT Agricultural machinery
  Bearings (Machinery)
  Belts and belting
  Conveying machinery
  Electric machinery
  Engines
  Gearing
  Hoisting machinery
  Hydraulic machinery
  Industrial equipment
  Locomotives
  Lubrication and lubricants
  Machine design
  Machine tools
  Mechanical drawing
  Metalworking machinery
  Robots
  Simple machines
  Steam engines
  Woodworking machinery
 RT Mechanics
  Mills
  Power transmission
Machinery—Construction
 USE Machine design
Machinery—Design and construction
 USE Machine design
Machinery—Drawing
 USE Mechanical drawing
Machinery in industry
 USE Industrial equipment
  Machinery in the workplace
Machinery in the workplace 338
 Use for materials on the social and econom-
 ic aspects of mechanization in the area of
 work.
 UF Machinery in industry *[Former
  heading]*

Technology in the workplace
 BT Work environment
 NT Automation
Machinery—Models 621.8
 UF Mechanical models
  Models, Mechanical
 BT Machine design
  Models and model making
Machines
 USE Machinery
Machines, Simple
 USE Simple machines
Macintosh (Computer) 004.165
 UF Apple Macintosh (Computer)
 BT Microcomputers
Made-for-TV movies
 USE Television movies
Madonna
 USE Mary, Blessed Virgin, Saint
Magazine editing
 USE Journalism—Editing
Magazines
 USE Periodicals
Maghreb
 USE North Africa
Magic 133.4
 Use for materials on charms, spells, etc.,
 believed to have supernatural power. Materials
 on types of entertainment involving
 illusionistic tricks are entered under **Magic
 tricks.**
 UF Black art (Magic)
  Black magic (Witchcraft)
  Necromancy
  Sorcery
  Spells
 BT Occultism
 RT Hallucinations and illusions
  Magic tricks
  Witchcraft
Magic tricks 793.8
 UF Conjuring
  Legerdemain
  Prestidigitation
  Sleight of hand
 BT Amusements
  Tricks
 NT Card tricks
 RT Hallucinations and illusions
  Magic

BT = Broader Term NT = Narrower Term RT = Related Term SA = See Also UF = Used For

Magna Carta   342; 942.03
  BT   Charters
        Constitutional law
        Great Britain—History—1154-
        1399, Plantagenets
Magnet schools   373.24
    Use for materials on schools offering spe-
    cial courses not available in the regular school
    curriculum and designed to attract students
    without reference to the usual attendance zone
    rules, often as an aid to voluntary school de-
    segregation.
  UF   Schools, Magnet
  BT   Public schools
        School integration
        Schools
Magnet winding
  USE   Electromagnets
Magnetic needle
  USE   Compass
Magnetic recorders and recording
        621.382
    Use for general materials on audio, comput-
    er, and video recording on a magnetizable me-
    dium.
  UF   Cassette recorders and recording
        Recorders, Tape
        Tape recorders
  RT   Optical storage devices
        Sound—Recording and repro-
            ducing
        Video recording
Magnetic resonance accelerator
  USE   Cyclotron
Magnetic resonance imaging   616.07
  UF   Clinical magnetic resonance im-
            aging
        Diagnostic magnetic resonance
            imaging
        Imaging, Magnetic resonance
        NMR imaging
        Nuclear magnetic resonance im-
            aging
  BT   Diagnosis
Magnetism   538
  BT   Physics
  NT   Compass
        Electromagnetism
        Electromagnets
        Magnets
  RT   Electricity

Magnets   538; 621.34
  BT   Magnetism
  NT   Electromagnets
Mail-order business   658.8; 659.13
  BT   Business
        Direct selling
        Selling
Mail service
  USE   Postal service
Mainstreaming in education   371.9
  BT   Education
        Exceptional children
        Handicapped children
  RT   Special education
Maintenance and repair
  USE   Repairing
        and types of things that require
            maintenance with the subdivi-
            sion *Maintenance and repair,*
            e.g. **Automobiles—Mainte-
            nance and repair; Build-
            ings—Maintenance and re-
            pair;** etc., and types of things
            that require no maintenance
            with the subdivision *Repair-
            ing,* e.g. **Radio—Repairing;**
            to be added as needed
Maize
  USE   Corn
Make-believe playmates
  USE   Imaginary playmates
Makeup (Cosmetics)
  USE   Cosmetics
Makeup, Theatrical
  USE   Theatrical makeup
Making-choices stories
  USE   Plot-your-own stories
Maladjusted children
  USE   Emotionally disturbed children
Maladjustment (Psychology)
  USE   Adjustment (Psychology)
Malaria   616.9
  UF   Ague
  BT   Fever
Male actors
  USE   Men actors
Male change of life
  USE   Male climacteric
Male climacteric   612.6
  UF   Change of life in men

BT = Broader Term   NT = Narrower Term   RT = Related Term   SA = See Also   UF = Used For

Male climacteric—*Continued*
>Climacteric, Male *[Former heading]*
>Male change of life
>Male menopause
>Menopause, Male

BT   **Aging**

Male menopause
USE   **Male climacteric**

Male role
USE   **Sex role**

Malfeasance in office
USE   **Misconduct in office**

Malformations, Congenital
USE   **Birth defects**

Malignant tumors
USE   **Cancer**

Malls, Shopping
USE   **Shopping centers and malls**

Malnutrition   362.1; 616.3
BT   **Nutrition**
RT   **Starvation**

Malpractice   346.03
UF   Liability, Professional
>Professional liability
>Professions—Tort liability
>Tort liability of professions

SA   types of professional personnel with the subdivision *Malpractice,* to be added as needed
BT   **Liability (Law)**
NT   **Medical personnel—Malpractice**
>**Physicians—Malpractice**

Malpractice insurance   368.5
UF   Insurance, Malpractice *[Former heading]*
>Insurance, Professional liability
>Professional liability insurance

BT   **Insurance**

Mammals   599
SA   types of mammals, e.g. **Marine mammals; Primates; Bats;** etc., to be added as needed
BT   **Animals**
>**Vertebrates**

NT   **Bats**
>**Beavers**
>**Bison**
>**Camels**
>**Cats**
>**Cattle**
>**Chipmunks**
>**Deer**
>**Dogs**
>**Elephants**
>**Fossil mammals**
>**Horses**
>**Marine mammals**
>**Mice**
>**Pigs**
>**Primates**
>**Rabbits**
>**Reindeer**
>**Seals (Animals)**
>**Sheep**
>**Squirrels**
>**Whales**
>**Wild cats**

Mammals, Fossil
USE   **Fossil mammals**

Mammals, Marine
USE   **Marine mammals**

Man
USE   **Human beings**

Man—Antiquity
USE   **Human origins**

Man in space
USE   **Space flight**

Man—Influence of environment
USE   **Environmental influence on humans**

Man—Influence on nature
USE   **Human influence on nature**

Man—Origin
USE   **Human origins**

Man power
USE   **Manpower**

Man, Prehistoric
USE   **Fossil hominids**
>**Prehistoric peoples**

Man, Primitive
USE   **Primitive societies**

Man (Theology)   218; 233; 291.2
BT   **Doctrinal theology**
NT   **Soul**

Management   658
>Use for materials on the theory of management and on the application of management principles to business and industry.

UF   Administration

BT = Broader Term   NT = Narrower Term   RT = Related Term   SA = See Also   UF = Used For

Management—*Continued*
    Business administration
    Business management
    Industrial management *[Former heading]*
    Industrial organization
    Management science
    Management, Scientific
    Organization and management
    Scientific management
SA   types of management, e.g. **Office management;** types of businesses and industries, types of industrial plants and processes, and names of individual corporate bodies, with the subdivision *Management,* e.g. **Information systems— Management;** and types of government agencies and special activities, types of institutions, and names of individual institutions with the subdivision *Administration,* e.g. **Libraries—Administration; Schools—Administration;** etc., to be added as needed
BT   **Business**
    Industries
NT   **Buying**
    Crisis management
    Factory management
    Farm management
    Industrial efficiency
    Industrial relations
    Industrial welfare
    Information systems—Management
    Inventory control
    Job analysis
    Marketing
    Materials handling
    Natural resources—Management
    Occupational health and safety
    Office management
    Organizational change
    Personnel management
    Planning
    Production standards

    Sales management
    Time management
RT   **Operations research**
Management buyouts
USE   **Leveraged buyouts**
Management—Employee participation
USE   **Participative management**
Management information systems   658.4
UF   Computer-based information systems
    MIS (Information systems)
BT   **Information systems**
Management, Sales
USE   **Sales management**
Management science
USE   **Management**
Management, Scientific
USE   **Management**
Managers
USE   **Supervisors**
Mandates   321
UF   Government, Mandatory
    League of Nations—Mandatory system
BT   **International law**
    International organization
    International relations
    World War, 1914-1918—Territorial questions
Mania
USE   **Manic-depressive illness**
Manic depression
USE   **Manic-depressive illness**
Manic-depressive illness   616.89
UF   Bipolar depression
    Bipolar disorder
    Mania
    Manic depression
    Manic-depressive psychoses
    [Former heading]
    Manic-depressive psychosis
    Melancholia
BT   **Mental illness**
RT   **Depression (Psychology)**
Manic-depressive psychoses
USE   **Manic-depressive illness**
Manic-depressive psychosis
USE   **Manic-depressive illness**

BT = Broader Term   NT = Narrower Term   RT = Related Term   SA = See Also   UF = Used For

Manifest destiny (United States)
    USE   **United States—Territorial expansion**
Manikins (Fashion models)
    USE   **Fashion models**
Manipulative materials
    USE   **Manipulatives**
Manipulatives   **371.33**
    Use for works on educational materials designed to be handled or touched by students in learning mathematical concepts.
    UF   Manipulative materials *[Former heading]*
           Manipulatives (Education)
    BT   **Audiovisual materials**
           Mathematics—Study and teaching
           Teaching—Aids and devices
Manipulatives (Education)
    USE   **Manipulatives**
Manned space flight
    USE   **Space flight**
Manned undersea research stations
    USE   **Undersea research stations**
Mannequins (Fashion models)
    USE   **Fashion models**
Manners
    USE   **Courtesy**
           Etiquette
Manners and customs   **390**
    UF   Ceremonies
           Customs, Social
           Folkways
           Social customs
           Social life and customs
           Traditions
    SA   ethnic groups and names of countries, cities, etc., with the subdivision *Social life and customs,* to be added as needed
    BT   **Civilization**
           Ethnology
    NT   **African Americans—Social life and customs**
           Blacks—Social life and customs
           Bohemianism
           Caste
           Chicago (Ill.)—Social life and customs

           Chivalry
           Clothing and dress
           Costume
           Country life
           Courts and courtiers
           Dating (Social customs)
           Dueling
           Festivals
           Folklore
           Funeral rites and ceremonies
           Gifts
           Holidays
           Hugging
           Indians of North America—Social life and customs
           Jews—Social life and customs
           Marriage customs and rites
           Ohio—Social life and customs
           Popular culture
           Seafaring life
           Tattooing
           Travel
           United States—Social life and customs
    RT   **Etiquette**
           Rites and ceremonies
Manpower (May subdiv. geog.)   **331.11**
    Use for materials on the strength of a country in terms of available personnel, both military and industrial. Materials on personnel in specific fields are entered under kinds of workers, e.g. **Agricultural laborers; Nurses;** etc. Materials on investments of capital in training and educating employees to improve their productivity are entered under **Human capital.**
    UF   Human resources *[Former heading]*
           Man power
    SA   names of wars with the subdivision *Manpower;* e.g. **World War, 1939-1945—Manpower;** to be added as needed
    RT   **Labor supply**
           Military readiness
Manpower policy (May subdiv. geog.)
    331.11
    UF   Human resources development
           Human resources policy *[Former heading]*
    BT   **Economic policy**
    NT   **Occupational retraining**
           Occupational training

BT = Broader Term   NT = Narrower Term   RT = Related Term   SA = See Also   UF = Used For

Manpower policy—*Continued*
    Unemployment
    Vocational education
  RT   Labor supply
Manslaughter
  USE   Homicide
Manual training
  USE   Industrial arts education
Manual workers
  USE   Labor
    Working class
Manufactures   338.4; 670
  SA   types of industries and names of
      manufactured articles, to be
      added as needed
  BT   **Business**
    Commercial products
    Industries
    Technology
  NT   **Brand name products**
    Consumer goods
    Generic products
    Machinery
    Mills
    Papermaking
    Patents
    Prices
    Trademarks
    Waste products
Manufactures—Defects
  USE   **Product recall**
Manufactures recall
  USE   **Product recall**
Manufacturing in space
  USE   **Space industrialization**
Manures
  USE   **Fertilizers**
Manuscripts   091
  SA   subjects, literatures, groups of
      authors, individual literary au-
      thors, literary works entered
      under title, and sacred works
      with the subdivision *Manu-
      scripts,* to be added as needed
  BT   **Archives**
    Bibliography
    Books
  NT   **Illumination of books and
      manuscripts**
  RT   **Autographs**

    Charters
Manuscripts, Illuminated
  USE   **Illumination of books and
      manuscripts**
Map drawing   526.022
  UF   Cartography
    Chartography
    Plans
  BT   **Drawing**
  RT   **Topographical drawing**
Maple sugar   641.3; 664
  BT   **Sugar**
Maps   912
    Use for general materials about maps and
    their history. Materials on the methods of map
    making and the mapping of areas are entered
    under **Map drawing.** Geographical atlases of
    world coverage are entered under **Atlases.**
  UF   Cartography
    Chartography
    Plans
  SA   types of maps, e.g. **Road maps;**
      subjects with the subdivision
      Maps, e.g. **Geology—Maps;**
      and names of countries, cities,
      etc., with the subdivision
      Maps, to be added as needed
  BT   **Geography**
  NT   **Atlases**
    Automobile travel—Guidebooks
    Chicago (Ill.)—Maps
    Geology—Maps
    Globes
    Moon—Maps
    Ohio—Maps
    Road maps
    United States—Maps
    World War, 1939-1945—Maps
  RT   **Charts**
Maps, Historical
  USE   **Historical atlases**
Maps, Military
  USE   **Military geography**
Maps, Road
  USE   **Road maps**
Marathon running   796.42
  UF   Long distance running
  BT   **Running**
Marathon swimming   797.2
  UF   Long distance swimming
  BT   **Swimming**

BT = Broader Term   NT = Narrower Term   RT = Related Term   SA = See Also   UF = Used For

Marble   552; 553.5
　BT　**Rocks**
　　　Stone
MARC formats   025.3
　UF　Machine readable catalog system
　　　MARC system *[Former head-
　　　　ing]*
　BT　**Bibliographic control**
　　　Libraries—Automation
　　　**Machine readable bibliographic
　　　　data**
MARC system
　USE　**MARC formats**
Marches (Demonstrations)
　USE　**Demonstrations**
Marches (Exercises)
　USE　**Marching drills**
Marches for civil rights
　USE　**Civil rights demonstrations**
Marches (Music)   783.18
　BT　**Military music**
Marching
　USE　**Marching drills**
Marching drills   613.7
　UF　Drill (Nonmilitary) *[Former
　　　　heading]*
　　　Drills, Marching
　　　Marches (Exercises)
　　　Marching
　BT　**Physical education**
Mardi Gras
　USE　**Carnival**
Margarine   641.3; 664
　UF　Butter, Artificial
　　　Oleomargarine
　BT　**Butter**
Mariculture
　USE　**Aquaculture**
Marihuana
　USE　**Marijuana**
Marijuana   362.29; 613.8; 615; 633.7
　UF　Cannabis
　　　Grass (Drug)
　　　Hashish
　　　Marihuana
　　　Pot (Drug)
　BT　**Hallucinogens**
　　　Narcotics
Marinas   387.1
　UF　Yacht basins

　BT　**Boats and boating**
　　　Harbors
　　　Yachts and yachting
　NT　**Docks**
Marine animals   591.77
　UF　Aquatic animals
　　　Marine fauna
　　　Marine zoology
　　　Sea animals
　　　Water animals
　BT　**Animals**
　　　Marine biology
　　　Wildlife
　NT　**Corals**
　　　Fishes
　　　Marine mammals
Marine aquaculture
　USE　**Aquaculture**
Marine aquariums   597.073; 639.34
　UF　Oceanariums
　　　Salt water aquariums
　　　Sea water aquariums
　SA　names of specific marine aquari-
　　　　ums, to be added as needed
　BT　**Aquariums**
　NT　**Marineland (Fla.)**
Marine architecture
　USE　**Naval architecture**
　　　Shipbuilding
Marine biology   578.77
　UF　Biological oceanography
　　　Biology, Marine
　　　Ocean life
　　　Sea life
　BT　**Biology**
　　　Oceanography
　　　Underwater exploration
　NT　**Marine animals**
　　　Marine ecology
　　　Marine plants
　　　Marine resources
　RT　**Freshwater biology**
Marine disasters
　USE　**Shipwrecks**
Marine ecology   578.77
　UF　Biological oceanography
　　　Ecology, Marine
　BT　**Ecology**
　　　Marine biology

BT = Broader Term　　NT = Narrower Term　　RT = Related Term　　SA = See Also　　UF = Used For

Marine engineering   623.8
   Use for materials on engineering as applied
   to ships and their machinery.
   UF   Naval engineering
   BT   **Civil engineering**
         Engineering
         Mechanical engineering
         Naval architecture
         Naval art and science
         Steam navigation
Marine engines   623.8
   BT   **Engines**
         Shipbuilding
         Steam engines
Marine fauna
   USE   **Marine animals**
Marine flora
   USE   **Marine plants**
Marine geology
   USE   **Submarine geology**
Marine insurance   368.2
   UF   Insurance, Marine *[Former head-
         ing]*
   BT   **Commerce**
         Insurance
         Maritime law
         Merchant marine
         Shipping
Marine law
   USE   **Maritime law**
Marine mammals   599.5
   UF   Mammals, Marine *[Former
         heading]*
   SA   types of marine mammals, to be
         added as needed
   BT   **Mammals**
         Marine animals
   NT   **Seals (Animals)**
         Whales
Marine mineral resources   333.8; 553
   UF   Mineral resources, Marine
         Ocean mineral resources
   BT   **Marine resources**
         Mines and mineral resources
         Ocean bottom
         Ocean engineering
   NT   **Ocean mining**
   RT   **Ocean energy resources**
Marine painting   758
   UF   Sea in art
         Seascapes

Ships in art
   BT   **Painting**
Marine plants   579
   UF   Aquatic plants
         Marine flora
         Water plants
   BT   **Marine biology**
         Plants
   NT   **Algae**
   RT   **Freshwater plants**
Marine pollution   363.739
   UF   Ocean pollution
         Offshore water pollution
         Sea pollution
   BT   **Oceanography**
         Water pollution
   RT   **Oil pollution of water**
Marine resources   333.91; 591.77
   UF   Ocean—Economic aspects
         Ocean resources
         Resources, Marine
         Sea resources
   BT   **Commercial products**
         Marine biology
         Natural resources
         Oceanography
   NT   **Aquaculture**
         Fisheries
         Marine mineral resources
         Ocean energy resources
         Ocean engineering
         Seafood
Marine salvage   387.5; 627
   UF   Salvage, Marine
         Ship salvage
   BT   **International law**
         Maritime law
         Salvage
   RT   **Shipwrecks**
Marine transportation
   USE   **Shipping**
Marine zoology
   USE   **Marine animals**
Marineland (Fla.)   597.073; 639.34
   BT   **Marine aquariums**
Mariners
   USE   **Sailors**
Mariner's compass
   USE   **Compass**

BT = Broader Term   NT = Narrower Term   RT = Related Term   SA = See Also   UF = Used For

Marionettes
USE **Puppets and puppet plays**
Marital counseling
USE **Marriage counseling**
Marital infidelity
USE **Adultery**
Maritime discoveries
USE **Exploration**
Maritime law **341.7; 343.09**
UF Law, Maritime
Law of the sea
Marine law
Merchant marine—Law and leg-
islation
Naval law
Navigation—Law and legislation
Sea laws
BT **International law**
Law
Shipping
NT **Freight**
Marine insurance
Marine salvage
Merchant marine
Pirates
RT **Commercial law**
Territorial waters
Market gardening
USE **Truck farming**
Market surveys (May subdiv. geog.)
658.8
BT **Advertising**
Surveys
RT **Public opinion polls**
Marketing **380.1; 658.8**
Use for materials on the principles and
methods involved in the transfer of merchan-
dise from producer to consumer. Materials on
food buying are entered under **Grocery shop-
ping.**
UF Distribution (Economics)
Merchandising
SA subjects with the subdivision
Marketing, e.g. **Farm pro-
duce—Marketing;** to be add-
ed as needed
BT **Business**
Management
NT **Direct selling**
Farm produce—Marketing
Sales management

Telemarketing
RT **Advertising**
Selling
Marketing (Home economics)
USE **Grocery shopping**
Shopping
Marketing of farm produce
USE **Farm produce—Marketing**
Markets (May subdiv. geog.) **381; 658.8**
Use for materials on places where many
buyers and sellers are brought into contract
with one another in order to exhange goods
and services.
BT **Business**
Cities and towns
Commerce
RT **Fairs**
Marking (Students)
USE **Grading and marking (Educa-
tion)**
Marks
USE **Hallmarks**
and types of things with identi-
fying marks, other than plate,
with the subdivision *Marks,*
e.g. **Pottery—Marks;** to be
added as needed
Marks on plate
USE **Hallmarks**
Marriage **173; 306.81; 346.01**
UF Matrimony
BT **Love**
Sacraments
NT **Husbands**
Intermarriage
Marriage contracts
Marriage counseling
Marriage customs and rites
Married people
Remarriage
Weddings
Wives
RT **Divorce**
Domestic relations
Family
Marriage—Annulment **262.9; 346.01**
UF Annulment of marriage
Marriage contracts **306.81; 346.01**
UF Antenuptial contracts
Premarital contracts
Prenuptial contracts

Marriage contracts—*Continued*
   BT   **Marriage**
Marriage counseling   362.82
   UF   Marital counseling
         Premarital counseling
   BT   **Counseling**
         Family life education
         Marriage
   RT   **Divorce mediation**
Marriage customs and rites   392.5
   UF   Bridal customs
   BT   **Manners and customs**
         Marriage
         Rites and ceremonies
         Weddings
Marriage, Interracial
   USE   **Interracial marriage**
Marriage, Mixed
   USE   **Interfaith marriage**
         Intermarriage
Marriage registers
   USE   **Registers of births, etc.**
Marriage statistics
   USE   **Vital statistics**
Married men
   USE   **Husbands**
Married people   306.872
   UF   Couples, Married
         Married persons
   BT   **Family**
         Marriage
   NT   **Husbands**
         Wives
Married persons
   USE   **Married people**
Married women
   USE   **Wives**
Mars (Planet)   523.43
   BT   **Planets**
   NT   **Mars probes**
Mars (Planet)—Exploration   629.43
   BT   **Planets—Exploration**
Mars (Planet)—Geology   559.9
   BT   **Astrogeology**
Mars (Planet)—Photographs
   USE   **Mars (Planet)—Pictorial works**
Mars (Planet)—Pictorial works   523.43;
     778.3
   UF   Mars (Planet)—Photographs
         [Former heading]

   BT   **Space photography**
Mars (Planet)—Satellites   523.9
   UF   Satellites—Mars
   BT   **Satellites**
Mars probes   629.43
   UF   Martian probes
   BT   **Mars (Planet)**
         Space probes
Marshall Plan
   USE   **Reconstruction (1939-1951)**
Marshes   333.91; 577.68
   UF   Bogs
         Swamps
   BT   **Wetlands**
   NT   **Swamp animals**
Martial arts   796.8
   BT   **Athletics**
   NT   **Archery**
         Dueling
   RT   **Self-defense**
         Self-defense for women
Martian probes
   USE   **Mars probes**
Martin Luther King Day   394.261
   UF   King, Martin Luther, holiday
   BT   **Holidays**
Martyrs   200.92; 272.092
   BT   **Church history**
         Heroes and heroines
   RT   **Persecution**
         Saints
Marxian theory
   USE   **Marxism**
Marxism   335.4
      Use for materials on the system of econom-
     ic and political thought developed by Karl
     Marx, Friedrich Engels, or their followers.
   UF   Marxian theory
         Marxist theory
   BT   **Economics**
         Philosophy
         Political science
         Sociology
   RT   **Class consciousness**
         Communism
         Dialectical materialism
         Socialism
Marxist theory
   USE   **Marxism**
Mary, Blessed Virgin, Saint   232.91
   UF   Blessed Virgin Mary

BT = Broader Term   NT = Narrower Term   RT = Related Term   SA = See Also   UF = Used For

Mary, Blessed Virgin, Saint—*Continued*
      Madonna
      Virgin Mary
  BT   **Saints**
Mary, Blessed Virgin, Saint—Art   704.9
  BT   **Christian art and symbolism**
  RT   **Jesus Christ—Art**
Mary, Blessed Virgin, Saint—Prayers
      242
  BT   **Prayers**
Masculine psychology
  USE   **Men—Psychology**
Masers   621.381
  UF   Microwave amplification by
        stimulated emission of radia-
        tion
  BT   **Amplifiers (Electronics)**
      Electromagnetism
      Microwaves
Masers, Optical
  USE   **Lasers**
Masks (Facial)   391.4
  BT   **Costume**
Masks (Plays)   808.82; 812, etc.
    May be used for individual works, collec-
  tions, or materials about masks.
  UF   Masques (Plays)
  BT   **Drama**
      Pageants
      Theater
Masks (Sculpture)   731
  UF   Death masks
  BT   **Sculpture**
Masonic orders
  USE   **Freemasons**
Masonry   693
  BT   **Building**
      Civil engineering
      Stone
  NT   **Cement**
      Concrete
      Plaster and plastering
      Stonecutting
  RT   **Bricklaying**
      Foundations
      Walls
Masons (Secret order)
  USE   **Freemasons**
Masques (Plays)
  USE   **Masks (Plays)**

Mass   264
  UF   Eucharist
  BT   **Liturgies**
  RT   **Lord's Supper**
Mass communication
  USE   **Communication**
      Mass media
      Telecommunication
Mass culture
  USE   **Popular culture**
Mass feeding
  USE   **Food service**
Mass media   302.23
  UF   Mass communication
      Media
  BT   **Communication**
  NT   **Motion pictures**
      Newspapers
      Periodicals
      Radio broadcasting
      Television broadcasting
  RT   **Popular culture**
Mass political behavior
  USE   **Political participation**
Mass psychology
  USE   **Social psychology**
Mass spectra
  USE   **Mass spectrometry**
Mass spectrometry   543; 547
  UF   Mass spectra
      Mass spectrum analysis
  BT   **Spectrum analysis**
Mass spectrum analysis
  USE   **Mass spectrometry**
Mass transit
  USE   **Local transit**
Massacres (May subdiv. geog.)   179.7;
      904
  SA   names of individual massacres,
        e.g. **Saint Bartholomew's**
        Day, Massacre of, 1572; to
        be added as needed
  BT   **Atrocities**
      History
      Persecution
  NT   **Saint Bartholomew's Day,**
      Massacre of, 1572
Massage   615.8; 646.7
  BT   **Physical therapy**
  NT   **Acupressure**

BT = Broader Term   NT = Narrower Term   RT = Related Term   SA = See Also   UF = Used For

Massage—*Continued*
    Chiropractic
    Electrotherapeutics
  RT   **Osteopathic medicine**
Mastodon   569
  BT   **Extinct animals**
    Fossil mammals
Mate selection in animals
  USE **Animal courtship**
Materia medica   615
  UF   Herbals
    Pharmacopoeias
  SA   types of drugs, to be added as
    needed
  BT   **Medicine**
    Therapeutics
  NT   **Anesthetics**
    Narcotics
    Pharmacology
  RT   **Drugs**
    Pharmacy
Materialism   146
  BT   **Philosophy**
    Positivism
  RT   **Idealism**
    Realism
Materials   620.1

Use for comprehensive works on the basic processed materials used in engineering and industry. Works on unprocessed minerals and unprocessed animal and vegetable products are entered under **Raw materials.**

  UF   Engineering materials
    Industrial materials
    Strategic materials
  SA   types of materials, e.g. **Building materials; Hazardous substances;** etc.; and scientific and technical disciplines and types of equipment and construction with the subdivision *Materials*, to be added as needed
  NT   **Adhesives**
    Airplanes—Materials
    Artists' materials
    Building materials
    Ceramics
    Hazardous substances
    Strength of materials
  RT   **Engineering**

Materials handling   388; 658.7
  UF   Handling of materials
    Mechanical handling
  BT   **Management**
  NT   **Conveying machinery**
    Freight
  RT   **Trucks**
Materials, Strength of
  USE **Strength of materials**
Maternity
  USE **Mothers**
Mathematical analysis   515
  UF   Analysis (Mathematics)
  BT   **Mathematics**
  NT   **Algebra**
    Calculus
    Graph theory
    Linear algebra
    Numerical analysis
    Programming (Computers)
Mathematical drawing
  USE **Geometrical drawing**
    Mechanical drawing
Mathematical logic
  USE **Symbolic logic**
Mathematical models   511
  UF   Models
    Models, Mathematical
  SA   subjects with the subdivision *Mathematical models,* e.g. **Pollution—Mathematical models;** to be added as needed
  BT   **Mathematics**
  NT   **Computer simulation**
    Fractals
    Game theory
    Pollution—Mathematical models
    Programming (Computers)
    System analysis
Mathematical notation   510

Use for materials on the system of graphic symbols used in mathematics as well as for materials on the process or method of setting these down.

  UF   Mathematical symbols
    Mathematics—Notation
    Mathematics—Symbols
    Notation, Mathematical
    Symbols, Mathematical

BT = Broader Term   NT = Narrower Term   RT = Related Term   SA = See Also   UF = Used For

Mathematical notation—*Continued*
    RT   **Mathematics**
Mathematical readiness   372.7
    UF   Arithmetical readiness
           Mathematics readiness
           Number readiness
           Readiness for mathematics
    BT   **Arithmetic—Study and teach-
           ing**
           **Mathematics—Study and
           teaching**
Mathematical recreations   793.7
    UF   Recreations, Mathematical
    BT   **Amusements**
           Puzzles
           Scientific recreations
    NT   **Number games**
Mathematical sequences
    USE   **Sequences (Mathematics)**
Mathematical sets
    USE   **Set theory**
Mathematical symbols
    USE   **Mathematical notation**
Mathematicians   510.92; 920
    BT   **Scientists**
Mathematics   510
    SA   subjects with the subdivision
           Mathematics, e.g. **Astrono-
           my—Mathematics;** to be
           added as needed
    BT   **Science**
    NT   **Algebra**
           Arithmetic
           Astronomy—Mathematics
           Binary system (Mathematics)
           Biomathematics
           Business mathematics
           Calculus
           Dynamics
           Fourth dimension
           Fractions
           Game theory
           Geometry
           Group theory
           Mathematical analysis
           Mathematical models
           Measurement
           Metric system
           Number theory
           Patterns (Mathematics)

           Probabilities
           Sequences (Mathematics)
           Set theory
           Symbolic logic
           Trigonometry
    RT   **Mathematical notation**
Mathematics, Business
    USE   **Business mathematics**
**Mathematics—Computer assisted instruc-
    tion   372.7; 510.78**
    BT   **Computer assisted instruction**
Mathematics—Notation
    USE   **Mathematical notation**
Mathematics readiness
    USE   **Mathematical readiness**
**Mathematics—Study and teaching
    372.7; 510.7**
    NT   **Manipulatives**
           Mathematical readiness
Mathematics—Symbols
    USE   **Mathematical notation**
Mathematics—Tables   510
    UF   Ready reckoners
    NT   **Logarithms**
           Trigonometry—Tables
Mating behavior
    USE   **Animal courtship**
           Sexual behavior in animals
Matrimony
    USE   **Marriage**
Matter   117; 530
    BT   **Dynamics**
           Physics
Mausoleums
    USE   **Tombs**
Maxims
    USE   **Proverbs**
Mayas   972.004
    BT   **Indians of Central America**
           Indians of Mexico
Meal planning
    USE   **Menus**
           Nutrition
Meals
    USE   types of meals, e.g. **Breakfasts;
           Dinners;** etc., to be added as
           needed
Meals for school children
    USE   **School children—Food**

BT = Broader Term   NT = Narrower Term   RT = Related Term   SA = See Also   UF = Used For

Meals on wheels programs   362
 Use for materials on programs that deliver meals to the homebound.
 UF   Home delivered meals programs
 BT   Food relief

Measurement   389; 530.8
 UF   Mensuration
   Metrology
 SA   subjects with the subdivision *Measurement,* e.g. **Air pollution—Measurement;** to be added as needed
 BT   **Mathematics**
 NT   **Air pollution—Measurement**
   Geodesy
   Measuring instruments
   Photometry
   Surveying
   Volume (Cubic content)
 RT   **Weights and measures**

Measurements, Electric
 USE   **Electric measurements**

Measures
 USE   **Weights and measures**

Measuring instruments   389; 681
 UF   Instruments, Measuring
 BT   **Measurement**
   Weights and measures

Meat   641.3; 664
 SA   types of meat, to be added as needed
 BT   **Cooking**
   Food
 NT   **Beef**
   Carving (Meat, etc.)

Meat-eating animals
 USE   **Carnivorous animals**

Meat industry   338.1
 UF   Meat industry and trade *[Former heading]*
   Meat packing industry
   Meat trade
   Packing industry
   Stockyards
 BT   **Food supply**
 NT   **Cold storage**
   Meat inspection

Meat industry and trade
 USE   **Meat industry**

Meat inspection   363.19
 UF   Inspection of meat

 BT   **Food adulteration and inspection**
   Meat industry
   Public health

Meat packing industry
 USE   **Meat industry**

Meat trade
 USE   **Meat industry**

Mechanic arts
 USE   **Industrial arts**

Mechanical brains
 USE   **Computers**
   Cybernetics

Mechanical drawing   604.2
 UF   Drafting, Mechanical
   Engineering drawing
   Industrial drawing
   Machinery—Drawing
   Mathematical drawing
   Plans
   Structural drafting
 BT   **Drawing**
   Engineering
   Machinery
   Pattern making
 NT   **Architectural drawing**
   Blueprints
   Graphic methods
   Lettering
 RT   **Geometrical drawing**

Mechanical engineering   621
 Use for materials on the application of the principles of mechanics to the design, construction, and operation of machnery. Materials on the application of the principles of mechanics to engineering structures other than machinery are entered under **Applied mechanics.**
 BT   **Civil engineering**
 NT   **Electric engineering**
   Machinery
   Marine engineering
   Mechanical movements
   Power (Mechanics)
   Power transmission
 RT   **Steam engineering**

Mechanical handling
 USE   **Materials handling**

Mechanical models
 USE   **Machinery—Models**

Mechanical movements   531
 UF   Mechanisms (Machinery)

BT = Broader Term   NT = Narrower Term   RT = Related Term   SA = See Also   UF = Used For

Mechanical movements—*Continued*
- BT   Kinematics
         Mechanical engineering
         Mechanics
         Motion
- NT   Robots
         Simple machines
- RT   Gearing

Mechanical musical instruments   786.6
- UF   Musical instruments, Mechanical
         [Former heading]
- SA   types of instruments, e.g. **Music boxes;** to be added as needed
- BT   **Musical instruments**
- NT   **Music boxes**

Mechanical painting
- USE   **Industrial painting**

Mechanical speech recognition
- USE   **Automatic speech recognition**

Mechanics   530; 531
- BT   Physics
- NT   Applied mechanics
         Dynamics
         Fluid mechanics
         Hydraulics
         Hydrodynamics
         Hydrostatics
         Mechanical movements
         Power (Mechanics)
         Simple machines
         Soil mechanics
         Statics
         Steam engines
         Strains and stresses
         Strength of materials
         Vibration
         Viscosity
         Wave mechanics
- RT   Engineering
         Force and energy
         Kinematics
         Machinery
         Motion

Mechanics, Applied
- USE   **Applied mechanics**

Mechanics (Persons)   920

Mechanisms (Machinery)
- USE   **Mechanical movements**

Medallions
- USE   **Medals**

Medals   355.1; 737
- UF   Badges of honor
         Medallions
- SA   names of military services and other appropriate subjects with the subdivision *Medals, badges, decorations, etc.,* to be added as needed
- NT   **United States. Army—Medals, badges, decorations, etc.**
         United States. Navy—Medals, badges, decorations, etc.
- RT   **Decorations of honor**
         Insignia
         Numismatics

Media
- USE   **Mass media**

Media centers (Education)
- USE   **Instructional materials centers**

Mediation
- USE   **Arbitration and award**

Mediation, Divorce
- USE   **Divorce mediation**

Mediation, Industrial
- USE   **Industrial arbitration**

Mediation, International
- USE   **International arbitration**

Medicaid   368.4
- UF   Medical care for the poor
- BT   **National health insurance**
         Poor—Medical care
         State medicine
- RT   **Medicare**

Medical appointments and schedules
- USE   **Medical practice**

Medical botany   581.6
- UF   Botany, Medical *[Former heading]*
         Drug plants
         Herbal medicine
         Herbals
         Herbs, Medical
         Medicinal plants
         Plants, Medicinal
- BT   **Botany**
         Medicine
         Pharmacy

Medical care (May subdiv. geog.)   **362.1**
   Use for materials on the organization of services and facilities for medical care. Mate-

---

BT = Broader Term   NT = Narrower Term   RT = Related Term   SA = See Also   UF = Used For

Medical care—*Continued*
rials on the technical and scientific aspects of medical care are entered under **Medicine.**

UF   Delivery of health care
      Delivery of medical care
      Health care
      Health care delivery
      Medical services
      Personal health services

SA   classes of people with the subdivision *Medical care,* e.g. **Elderly—Medical care;** to be added as needed

BT   **Public health**

NT   **Armies—Medical care**
      Dental care
      Elderly—Medical care
      Health maintenance organizations
      Health self-care
      Home care services
      Long-term care facilities
      Medical charities
      Occupational health services
      Poor—Medical care
      Sports medicine
      Terminal care

RT   **Health care reform**
      Medicine

Medical care—Costs   362.1

UF   Cost of medical care
      Medical service, Cost of
      Medicine—Cost of medical care

BT   **Medical economics**

Medical care—Ethical aspects
USE   **Medical ethics**

Medical care for the elderly
USE   **Elderly—Medical care**
      Medicare

Medical care for the poor
USE   **Medicaid**
      Poor—Medical care

Medical care, Prepaid
USE   **Health insurance**

Medical care reform
USE   **Health care reform**

Medical care—Social aspects
USE   **Social medicine**

Medical centers   362.1
RT   **Hospitals**

Medical charities   362.1

UF   Charities, Medical *[Former heading]*
      Socialized medicine

BT   **Charities**
      Medical care
      Public health

NT   **Institutional care**

RT   **Hospitals**

Medical chemistry
USE   **Clinical chemistry**

Medical colleges (May subdiv. geog.)   610.71

UF   Medical schools

BT   **Colleges and universities**

RT   **Medicine—Study and teaching**

Medical consultation
USE   **Medical practice**

Medical diagnosis
USE   **Diagnosis**

Medical drama (Films)   791.43
May be used for individual works, collections, or materials about medical films.

UF   Doctor films

BT   **Motion pictures**

Medical drama (Radio programs)   791.44
May be used for individual works, collections, or materials about medical radio programs.

UF   Doctor radio programs

BT   **Radio programs**

Medical drama (Television programs)   791.45
May be used for individual works, collections, or materials about medical television programs.

UF   Doctor television programs

BT   **Television programs**

Medical economics   338.4
Use for comprehensive materials on the economic aspects of medical service from the point of view of both the practitioner and the public. Materials on special aspects of medical economics are entered under specific headings, e.g. **Medical care—Costs;** etc.

UF   Economics, Medical

BT   **Economics**

NT   **Medical care—Costs**

Medical education
USE   **Medicine—Study and teaching**

Medical electricity
USE   **Electrotherapeutics**

Medical entomology
USE   **Insects as carriers of disease**
Medical errors
USE   **Errors**
       Medical personnel—Malpractice
       Physicians—Malpractice
Medical ethics   174
UF   Ethics, Medical
       Medical care—Ethical aspects
       Medicine—Ethical aspects
BT   **Bioethics**
       Professional ethics
NT   **Euthanasia**
       Human experimentation in medicine
       Medical personnel—Malpractice
       Physicians—Malpractice
       Right to die
RT   **Social medicine**
Medical examinations
USE   **Periodic health examinations**
       and subjects, classes of persons, ethnic groups, and military services with the subdivision *Medical examinations,* e.g. **Children—Medical examinations;** to be added as needed
Medical experimentation on humans
USE   **Human experimentation in medicine**
Medical folklore
USE   **Traditional medicine**
Medical genetics   616
UF   Clinical genetics
       Congenital diseases
       Hereditary diseases
       Heredity of diseases
SA   names of diseases with the subdivision *Genetic aspects,* to be added as needed
BT   **Genetics**
       Pathology
NT   **Birth defects**
       Cancer—Genetic aspects
       Genetic counseling
Medical inspection in schools
USE   **Children—Medical examinations**

Medical insurance
USE   **Health insurance**
Medical insurance, National
USE   **National health insurance**
Medical jurisprudence   614
       Use for materials on the application of medical knowledge to questions of law. Materials on the law as it affects medicine and the medical profession are entered under **Medicine—Law and legislation.**
UF   Forensic medicine
       Jurisprudence, Medical
       Legal medicine
BT   **Forensic sciences**
NT   **DNA fingerprints**
       Lie detectors and detection
       Poisons and poisoning
       Suicide
RT   **Medicine—Law and legislation**
Medical law and legislation
USE   **Medicine—Law and legislation**
Medical malpractice
USE   **Medical personnel—Malpractice**
Medical manpower
USE   **Medical personnel**
Medical missions   362.1
UF   Missions, Medical *[Former heading]*
BT   **Medicine**
Medical novels   813, etc.
       May be used for individual works, collections, or materials about novels with a medical setting.
UF   Doctor novels
BT   **Fiction**
Medical offices
USE   **Medical practice**
Medical partnership
USE   **Medical practice**
Medical personnel   610.69
UF   Health care personnel
       Health manpower
       Health personnel
       Health professions
       Health sciences personnel
       Health services personnel
       Medical manpower
       Medical profession
BT   **Employees**
RT   **Medicine**

BT = Broader Term   NT = Narrower Term   RT = Related Term   SA = See Also   UF = Used For

Medical personnel—Malpractice   346.03
    UF   Medical errors
          Medical malpractice
    SA   classes of persons in the medical
          field with the subdivision
          Malpractice; e.g. **Physi-**
          cians—Malpractice; to be
          added as needed
    BT   **Malpractice**
          Medical ethics
          Medicine—Law and legislation

Medical photography   621.36; 778.3
    UF   Photography, Medical *[Former*
          heading]
    BT   **Photography**
          Photography—Scientific appli-
          cations

Medical practice   610.6
    Use for materials on the organization and management of medicine as a profession. Scientific materials on the practice of medicine are entered under **Medicine.**
    UF   Clinics
          Group medical practice
          Medical appointments and schedules
          Medical consultation
          Medical offices
          Medical partnership
          Medical profession
          Medicine—Practice *[Former heading]*
    SA   types of medicine with the subdivision *Practice,* e.g. **Nuclear medicine—Practice;** to be added as needed
    BT   **Medicine**
    NT   **Nuclear medicine—Practice**

Medical profession
    USE **Medical personnel**
           Medical practice
           Medicine
           Physicians
           Surgeons

Medical research
    USE **Medicine—Research**

Medical schools
    USE **Medical colleges**

Medical self-care
    USE **Health self-care**

Medical service, Cost of
    USE **Medical care—Costs**

Medical service, Prepaid
    USE **Health insurance**

Medical services
    USE **Medical care**

Medical sociology
    USE **Social medicine**

Medical technologists   610.69
    BT   **Allied health personnel**

Medical technology   610.28
    BT   **Medicine**

Medical transplantation
    USE **Transplantation of organs, tissues, etc.**

Medical waste disposal
    USE **Medical wastes**

Medical wastes   363.72
    UF   Disposal of medical waste
          Hospital wastes
          Infectious wastes
          Medical waste disposal
          Wastes, Medical
    BT   **Refuse and refuse disposal**
    RT   **Hazardous wastes**

Medicare   368.4
    UF   Medical care for the elderly
    BT   **Elderly—Medical care**
          National health insurance
          State medicine
    RT   **Medicaid**

Medication abuse   362.29; 613.8; 616.86
    Use for materials on the abuse or misuse of therapeutic or medicinal drugs, either prescription or non-prescription.
    UF   Abuse of medications
          Abuse of medicines
          Misuse of therapeutic drugs
          Pharmaceutical abuse
          Prescription drug abuse
    BT   **Drug abuse**

Medicinal chemistry
    USE **Pharmaceutical chemistry**

Medicinal plants
    USE **Medical botany**

Medicine (May subdiv. geog.)   610
    Use for materials on the technical and scientific aspects of medical care. Materials on the organization of services and facilities for medical care are entered under **Medical Care.** Materials on the organization and management of medicine as a profession are entered under **Medical practice.**

Medicine—*Continued*

UF   Medical profession

SA   types of medicine, e.g. **Sports medicine;** and names of diseases and groups of diseases, e.g. **AIDS (Disease); Fever; Nervous system—Diseases;** etc., to be added as needed

BT   **Life sciences**
        Therapeutics

NT   **Alternative medicine**
        Anatomy
        Aviation medicine
        Biochemistry
        Chiropractic
        Dentistry
        Diagnosis
        Emergency medicine
        Endocrinology
        First aid
        Health
        Holistic medicine
        Hygiene
        Indians of North America—Medicine
        Materia medica
        Medical botany
        Medical missions
        Medical practice
        Medical technology
        Military medicine
        Mind and body
        Nuclear medicine
        Nursing
        Orthopedics
        Pathology
        Periodic health examinations
        Pharmacology
        Pharmacy
        Physiology
        Podiatry
        Popular medicine
        Preventive medicine
        Psychiatry
        Psychosomatic medicine
        Quacks and quackery
        Social medicine
        Space medicine
        Sports medicine
        State medicine

        Submarine medicine
        Surgery
        Therapeutics
        Traditional medicine
        Tropical medicine
        Veterinary medicine

RT   **Diseases**
        Medical care
        Medical personnel
        Physicians

Medicine and religion

    USE   **Medicine—Religious aspects**

Medicine, Atomic

    USE   **Nuclear medicine**

Medicine, Aviation

    USE   **Aviation medicine**

Medicine—Biography   610.92; 920

    BT   **Biography**

Medicine—Cost of medical care

    USE   **Medical care—Costs**

Medicine, Dental

    USE   **Dentistry**
                Teeth—Diseases

Medicine—Ethical aspects

    USE   **Medical ethics**

Medicine—Law and legislation   344

      Use for materials on the law as it affects medicine and the medical profession. Materials on the application of medical knowledge to questions of law are entered under **Medical jurisprudence.**

    UF   Medical law and legislation

    BT   **Law**
            Legislation

    NT   **Medical personnel—Malpractice**
            Physicians—Malpractice
            Right to die

    RT   **Medical jurisprudence**

Medicine, Military

    USE   **Military medicine**

Medicine—Miscellanea   610.2

    BT   **Curiosities and wonders**

Medicine, Nuclear

    USE   **Nuclear medicine**

Medicine, Pediatric

    USE   **Children—Diseases**

Medicine—Physiological effect

    USE   **Pharmacology**

Medicine, Popular

    USE   **Popular medicine**

Medicine—Practice
  USE   **Medical practice**
Medicine, Preventive
  USE   **Preventive medicine**
Medicine, Psychosomatic
  USE   **Psychosomatic medicine**
Medicine—Religious aspects 261.5;
      291.1; 615.8
  UF   Medicine and religion *[Former*
       heading]
      Religion and medicine
  NT   **Spiritual healing**
Medicine—Research 610.7
  UF   Medical research
  BT   **Research**
  NT   **Human experimentation in**
       medicine
Medicine, Social
  USE   **Social medicine**
Medicine—Social aspects
  USE   **Social medicine**
Medicine, State
  USE   **State medicine**
Medicine—Study and teaching 610.7
  UF   Medical education
  RT   **Medical colleges**
Medicine, Submarine
  USE   **Submarine medicine**
Medicine, Tropical
  USE   **Tropical medicine**
Medicine—United States 610.973
  UF   United States—Medicine
Medieval architecture 723
  UF   Architecture, Medieval *[Former*
       heading]
  BT   **Architecture**
      Medieval civilization
  NT   **Byzantine architecture**
      Romanesque architecture
  RT   **Castles**
      Cathedrals
Medieval art 709.02
  UF   Art, Medieval *[Former heading]*
  BT   **Art**
      Medieval civilization
  NT   **Byzantine art**
      Gothic art
      Illumination of books and
        manuscripts
      Romanesque art

Medieval church history
  USE   **Church history—600-1500,**
       Middle Ages
Medieval civilization 909.07
  UF   Civilization, Medieval *[Former*
       heading]
  BT   **Civilization**
  NT   **Feudalism**
      Medieval architecture
      Medieval art
      Medieval literature
      Medieval philosophy
  RT   **Chivalry**
      Middle Ages
Medieval history
  USE   **Middle Ages—History**
Medieval literature 809
    May use same subdivisions as for **Litera-**
ture.
  UF   Literature, Medieval *[Former*
       heading]
  BT   **Literature**
      Medieval civilization
  NT   **Early Christian literature**
      Old Norse literature
Medieval philosophy 189
  UF   Philosophy, Medieval *[Former*
       heading]
  BT   **Medieval civilization**
      Philosophy
Meditation 158; 248.3; 291.4; 296.7
    Use for materials on spiritual contemplation
or mental prayer. Collections of personal re-
flections or thoughts for use in meditation are
entered under **Meditations.**
  BT   **Devotional exercises**
      Spiritual life
  NT   **Transcendental meditation**
  RT   **Meditations**
Meditations 242; 291.4
    Use for collections of personal reflections
or thoughts for use in meditation. Materials on
spiritual contemplation or mental prayer are
entered under **Meditation.**
  BT   **Devotional literature**
      Prayers
  RT   **Meditation**
Meetings, Public
  USE   **Public meetings**
Melancholia
  USE   **Depression (Psychology)**
      Manic-depressive illness

BT = Broader Term   NT = Narrower Term   RT = Related Term   SA = See Also   UF = Used For

Melodrama 808.82; 812, etc.

    May be used for individual works, collections, or materials about melodrama.

  BT   **Drama**

Memoirs

  USE   **Autobiographies**

           Autobiography

           Biography

Memorial Day 394.262

  UF   Decoration Day

  BT   **Holidays**

Memory 153.1

  UF   Mnemonics

  BT   **Brain**

           Educational psychology

           Intellect

           Psychology

           Psychophysiology

           Thought and thinking

  NT   **Attention**

           False memory syndrome

           Psychology of learning

           Recovered memory

Men (May subdiv. geog.) 305.31

  NT   **African American men**

           Fathers

           Gay men

           Husbands

           Single men

           Widowers

           Young men

Men actors 791.4; 792; 920

    Use for materials on male actors that emphasize their identity as men. General materials on persons of the acting profession, whether male or female, are entered under **Actors.**

  UF   Actors, Male

           Male actors

  BT   **Actors**

Men, African American

  USE   **African American men**

Men—Biography 920

  BT   **Biography**

Men—Clothing

  USE   **Men's clothing**

Men—Clubs

  USE   **Men—Societies**

Men—Diseases 616.0081

  BT   **Diseases**

Men—Education 370.81

  UF   Education of men

  BT   **Education**

  RT   **Coeducation**

Men—Employment 331.11

  BT   **Labor**

           Labor supply

Men in business

  USE   **Businessmen**

Men—Psychology 155.3

  UF   Masculine psychology

  BT   **Psychology**

Men, Single

  USE   **Single men**

Men—Social conditions 305.32

  BT   **Social conditions**

  NT   **Men's movement**

Men—Societies 367

  UF   Men—Clubs

           Men's clubs

           Men's organizations

  BT   **Clubs**

           Societies

  NT   **Boys' clubs**

Mendel's law 576.5

  BT   **Breeding**

           Variation (Biology)

  NT   **Genetics**

  RT   **Heredity**

Mendicancy

  USE   **Begging**

Mendicant orders

  USE   **Franciscans**

Mending

  USE   **Clothing and dress—Repairing**

           Repairing

Mennonites 289.7

  BT   **Christian sects**

  NT   **Amish**

Menopause 612.6; 618.1

  UF   Change of life in women

           Climacteric, Female

           Female climacteric

  BT   **Aging**

Menopause, Male

  USE   **Male climacteric**

Men's clothing 646; 687

  UF   Clothing, Men's

           Men—Clothing

  BT   **Clothing and dress**

Men's clubs

  USE   **Men—Societies**

BT = Broader Term   NT = Narrower Term   RT = Related Term   SA = See Also   UF = Used For

Men's liberation movement
   USE   **Men's movement**
Men's movement   305.32
   UF   Men's liberation movement
         [Former heading]
   BT   **Men—Social conditions**
Men's organizations
   USE   **Men—Societies**
Menstruation   612.6
   BT   **Reproduction**
   NT   **Premenstrual syndrome**
Mensuration
   USE   **Measurement**
Mental arithmetic   513
   UF   Arithmetic, Mental *[Former
         heading]*
         Oral arithmetic
   BT   **Arithmetic**
Mental deficiency
   USE   **Mental retardation**
Mental depression
   USE   **Depression (Psychology)**
Mental diseases
   USE   **Abnormal psychology**
         Mental illness
Mental healing   615.8
   Use for materials on psychic or psychologi-
   cal means to treat illness. Materials on the use
   of faith, prayer, or religious means to treat ill-
   ness are entered under **Spiritual healing.**
   UF   Healing, Mental
         Mind cure
         Psychic healing
   BT   **Alternative medicine**
   NT   **Hypnotism**
   RT   **Mental suggestion**
         Mind and body
         Psychotherapy
         Spiritual healing
         Subconsciousness
         Suggestive therapeutics
Mental health   362.2
   UF   Mental hygiene
   SA   ethnic groups, classes of per-
         sons, and individual persons
         with the subdivision *Mental
         health,* e.g. **Women—Mental
         health;** to be added as need-
         ed
   BT   **Happiness**
         Health

   NT   **Burn out (Psychology)**
         Occupational therapy
         Stress (Psychology)
         Women—Mental health
   RT   **Abnormal psychology**
         Mental illness
         Mind and body
         Psychiatry
         Psychology
Mental hospitals
   USE   **Psychiatric hospitals**
Mental hygiene
   USE   **Mental health**
Mental illness   362.2; 616.89
   Use for popular materials and materials on
   regional or social aspects of mental disorders.
   Materials on clinical aspects of mental disor-
   ders, including therapy, are entered under **Psy-
   chiatry.** Systematic descriptions of mental
   disorders are entered under **Abnormal psy-
   chology.**
   UF   Diseases, Mental
         Mental diseases
         Nervous breakdown
         Psychoses
   SA   names of specific illnesses, e.g.
         Manic-depressive illness; to
         be added as needed
   BT   **Abnormal psychology**
         Diseases
   NT   **Manic-depressive illness**
         Multiple personality
   RT   **Mental health**
         Mentally ill
         Personality disorders
         Psychiatry
Mental illness—Drug therapy   616.89
   BT   **Drug therapy**
Mental illness—Jurisprudence
   USE   **Insanity defense**
**Mental illness—Physiological aspects
         616.89**
   BT   **Physiology**
Mental institutions
   USE   **Mentally ill—Institutional care**
Mental patients
   USE   **Mentally ill**
Mental retardation   362.3; 616.85
   UF   Mental deficiency
   BT   **Abnormal psychology**
   NT   **Down syndrome**
   RT   **Mentally handicapped**

BT = Broader Term   NT = Narrower Term   RT = Related Term   SA = See Also   UF = Used For

Mental stereotype
  USE   Stereotype (Psychology)
Mental stress
  USE   Stress (Psychology)
Mental suggestion   131; 154.7; 615.8
  UF   Autosuggestion
         Suggestion, Mental
  BT   **Mind and body**
         Parapsychology
         Subconsciousness
  NT   **Brainwashing**
  RT   **Hypnotism**
         Mental healing
         Suggestive therapeutics
Mental telepathy
  USE   **Telepathy**
Mental tests
  USE   **Intelligence tests**
         Psychological tests
Mentally depressed
  USE   **Depression (Psychology)**
Mentally deranged
  USE   **Mentally ill**
Mentally handicapped   305.9; 362.2;
         362.3
  UF   Mentally retarded
  BT   **Handicapped**
  NT   **Mentally handicapped children**
  RT   **Mental retardation**
Mentally handicapped children   155.45;
         362.2; 362.3
  UF   Children, Retarded
         Mentally retarded children
         Retarded children
  BT   **Child psychiatry**
         Handicapped children
         Mentally handicapped
  RT   **Slow learning children**
Mentally handicapped children—Educa-
         tion   371.92
  BT   **Education**
         Special education
Mentally ill   362.2; 616.89
  UF   Insane
         Mental patients
         Mentally deranged
         Psychotics
  BT   **Sick**
  NT   **Emotionally disturbed children**
  RT   **Mental illness**

Mentally ill children
  USE   **Emotionally disturbed children**
Mentally ill—Institutional care   362.2
  UF   Mental institutions
  BT   **Institutional care**
  RT   **Psychiatric hospitals**
Mentally retarded
  USE   **Mentally handicapped**
Mentally retarded children
  USE   **Mentally handicapped children**
Menus   642
  UF   Bills of fare
         Gastronomy
         Meal planning
  BT   **Cooking**
         Diet
  NT   **Breakfasts**
         Dinners
         Luncheons
  RT   **Catering**
Mercantile buildings
  USE   **Commercial buildings**
Mercantile law
  USE   **Commercial law**
Mercantile marine
  USE   **Merchant marine**
Mercenary soldiers   355.3
  UF   Mercenary troops
         Soldiers of fortune
  BT   **Military personnel**
         Soldiers
Mercenary troops
  USE   **Mercenary soldiers**
Merchandise
  USE   **Commercial products**
         Consumer goods
Merchandising
  USE   **Marketing**
         Retail trade
Merchant marine (May subdiv. geog.)
         387.5
  UF   Mercantile marine
  BT   **Maritime law**
         Sailors
         Ships
         Transportation
  NT   **Harbors**
         Marine insurance
  RT   **Shipping**

BT = Broader Term   NT = Narrower Term   RT = Related Term   SA = See Also   UF = Used For

Merchant marine—Law and legislation
 USE **Maritime law**
Merchant marine—United States
  387.50973
 UF United States—Merchant marine
Merchants   380.1092; 920
 BT **Business**
   Business people
   Commerce
Mercury   546; 669
 UF Quicksilver
 BT **Chemical elements**
   Metals
Mercy killing
 USE **Euthanasia**
Merger of corporations
 USE **Corporate mergers and acqui-**
   sitions
Mergers, Industrial
 USE **Industrial trusts**
   Railroads—Consolidation
Mermaids and mermen   398.21
 BT **Mythical animals**
Mesmerism
 USE **Hypnotism**
Messages to Congress
 USE **Presidents—United States—**
   Messages
Messiness
 USE **Cleanliness**
Metabolism   572
 BT **Biochemistry**
 NT **Growth disorders**
 RT **Nutrition**
Metal work
 USE **Metalwork**
Metallography   669
  Use for materials on the science of metal
  structures and alloys, especially the study of
  such structures with the microscope. Materials
  on the process of extracting metals from their
  ores, refining them, and preparing them for
  use, are entered under **Metallurgy.**
 UF Analysis, Microscopic
   Micrographic analysis
   Microscopic analysis
 BT **Metals**
Metallurgy   669
  Use for materials on the process of extract-
  ing metals from their ores, refining them, and
  preparing them for use. Materials on the science of metal structures and alloys, especially

the study of such structures with the micro-
scope, are entered under **Metallography.**
 NT **Electrometallurgy**
 RT **Alloys**
   Chemical engineering
   Industrial chemistry
   Metals
   Ores
   Smelting
Metals   669
 SA types of metals, to be added as
   needed
 BT **Inorganic chemistry**
   Ores
 NT **Alloys**
   Aluminum
   Brass
   Iron
   Mercury
   Metallography
   Pewter
   Precious metals
   Soldering
   Tin
   Zinc
 RT **Metallurgy**
   Metalwork
Metals, Transmutation of
 USE **Alchemy**
   Transmutation (Chemistry)
Metalwork   671; 739
 UF Metal work
 BT **Decoration and ornament**
 NT **Architectural metalwork**
   Art metalwork
   Bronzes
   Copperwork
   Dies (Metalworking)
   Electroplating
   Forging
   Founding
   Goldwork
   Ironwork
   Jewelry
   Plate metalwork
   Sheet metalwork
   Silverwork
   Soldering
   Steel
   Tinwork
   Welding

BT = Broader Term   NT = Narrower Term   RT = Related Term   SA = See Also   UF = Used For

Metalwork—*Continued*
  RT Metals
      Metalworking machinery
Metalwork, Architectural
  USE Architectural metalwork
Metalwork, Art
  USE Art metalwork
Metalworking machinery   621.9
  BT Machinery
  RT Metalwork
Metamorphic rocks
  USE Rocks
Metaphysics   110
  BT Philosophy
  NT Existentialism
      Space and time
      Theory of knowledge
  RT God
Meteorites   523.5
  BT Astronomy
      Meteors
Meteorological instruments   551.5028
  UF Instruments, Meteorological
  SA types of meteorological instru-
      ments, to be added as needed
  BT Scientific apparatus and in-
      struments
  NT Barometers
      Thermometers
Meteorological observatories   551.5028
  UF Meteorology—Observatories
      [Former heading]
      Observatories, Meteorological
      Weather stations
  RT Meteorology
Meteorological satellites   551.63
  UF Weather satellites
  SA names of satellites, e.g. **Tiros
      (Meteorological satellite);** etc.
  BT Artificial satellites
  NT Tiros (Meteorological satellite)
Meteorology   551.5
    Use for scientific materials on the atmo-
  sphere, especially weather factors. Materials
  on climate as it relates to humans and to plant
  and animal life, including the effects of
  changes of climate, are entered under **Cli-
  mate.** Materials on the state of the atmosphere
  at a given time and place with respect to heat
  or cold, wetness or dryness, calm or storm,
  are entered under **Weather.**
  BT Earth sciences
  NT Air

      Auroras
      Clouds
      Cyclones
      Droughts
      Floods
      Fog
      Frost
      Humidity
      Lightning
      Rain
      Rainbow
      Seasons
      Snow
      Solar radiation
      Storms
      Sunspots
      Thunderstorms
      Tornadoes
      Weather control
      Weather—Folklore
      Weather forecasting
      Winds
  RT Atmosphere
      Climate
      Meteorological observatories
      Weather
Meteorology in aeronautics   629.132
  UF Aeronautics, Meteorology in
  BT Aeronautics
      Weather forecasting
Meteorology—Observatories
  USE Meteorological observatories
Meteorology—Tables   551.5
Meteors   523.5
  UF Falling stars
      Fire balls
      Shooting stars
      Stars, Falling
  BT Astronomy
      Solar system
      Stars
  NT Meteorites
Meter
  USE Musical meter and rhythm
      Versification
Meters, Electric
  USE Electric meters
Meth (Drug)
  USE Methamphetamine

BT = Broader Term   NT = Narrower Term   RT = Related Term   SA = See Also   UF = Used For

Methamphetamine   362.29; 615
   UF   Meth (Drug)
          Speed (Drug)
   BT   **Amphetamines**
   NT   **Ice (Drug)**
Method of study
   USE   **Study skills**
Methodology
   USE   subjects with the subdivision
          Methodology, e.g. **Science—**
          Methodology; to be added as
          needed
Metric system   389; 530.8
   BT   **Arithmetic**
          Mathematics
   RT   **Decimal system**
          Weights and measures
Metrical romances
   USE   **Romances**
Metrology
   USE   **Measurement**
          Weights and measures
Metropolitan areas   307.76
   UF   Urban areas
   SA   names of metropolitan areas, e.g.
          Chicago Metropolitan Area
          (Ill.); to be added as needed
   BT   **Cities and towns—Growth**
   NT   **Suburbs**
          Urban renewal
Metropolitan finance   336
   Use for general materials on the public finance of metropolitan areas. Materials on the finance of a particular metropolitan area are entered under **Public finance** with a geographic subdivision.
   BT   **Municipal finance**
          Public finance
Metropolitan government   320.8; 352.16
   SA   names of metropolitan areas
          with the subdivision *Politics
          and government,* to be added
          as needed
   BT   **Local government**
   NT   **Chicago Metropolitan Area
          (Ill.)—Politics and government**
   RT   **Municipal government**
Metropolitan planning
   USE   **Regional planning**

Mexican American literature (English)
   USE   **American literature—Mexican
          American authors**
Mexican American women   305.868
   UF   Chicanas
          Mexican Americans—Women
          Women, Mexican American
   BT   **Mexican Americans
          Women**
Mexican Americans   305.868; 973
   Use for materials on American citizens of Mexican descent. Materials on noncitizens from Mexico are entered under **Mexicans—United States.** Use these same patterns for other ethnic groups in the U.S. and other countries.
   UF   Chicanos
   BT   **Hispanic Americans
          Immigrants—United States
          Minorities**
   NT   **Mexican American women**
   RT   **Ethnology—United States
          Mexicans—United States**
Mexican Americans—Ethnic identity
   305.868
Mexican Americans—Women
   USE   **Mexican American women**
Mexican literature   860; M860
   May use same subdivisions and names of literary forms as for **English literature.**
   BT   **Latin American literature
          Literature**
Mexican War, 1846-1848   973.6
   UF   United States—History—1845-
          1848, War with Mexico *[For-
          mer heading]*
   BT   **United States—History—1815-
          1861**
Mexicans (May subdiv. geog.)   305.868;
   920; 972
Mexicans—United States   305.868
   Use for materials on noncitizens from Mexico. Materials on American citizens of Mexican descent are entered under **Mexican Americans.** Use these same patterns for other ethnic groups in the U.S. and other countries.
   BT   **Aliens—United States
          Minorities**
   RT   **Mexican Americans**
Mexico, Indians of
   USE   **Indians of Mexico**
Mexico—Presidents
   USE   **Presidents—Mexico**

Mezzotint engraving   766
   BT   **Engraving**
MIA's
   USE   **Missing in action**
Mice   599.35; 636.088
   UF   Mouse
   BT   **Mammals**
Microbes
   USE   **Bacteria**
          Germ theory of disease
          Microorganisms
          Viruses
Microbial energy conversion
   USE   **Biomass energy**
Microbiology   579
   SA   subjects with the subdivision *Mi-*
          crobiology, to be added as
          needed
   BT   **Biology**
   NT   **Air—Microbiology**
          Bacteriology
          Biotechnology
          Cheese—Microbiology
          Fermentation
          Soil microbiology
   RT   **Microorganisms**
Microchemistry   540
   BT   **Chemistry**
Microcomputers   004.16; 621.39
   Use for materials on small, usually desktop-sized computers that have a self-contained central processing unit.
   UF   Desktop computers
          Home computers *[Former head-*
          ing]
          PC computers
          PC's
          Personal computers
   SA   types of personal computers, e.g.
          Macintosh (Computer); to be
          added an needed
   BT   **Computers**
   NT   **Macintosh (Computer)**
          Microprocessors
          Portable computers
Microelectronics   621.381
   UF   Microminiature electronic equip-
          ment
          Microminiaturization (Electron-
          ics)
   BT   **Electronics**

          Semiconductors
Microfilming
   USE   **Microphotography**
Microfilms   302.23; 686.4
   UF   Films
   BT   **Microforms**
   NT   **Library catalogs on microfilm**
Microforms   302.23; 686.4
   UF   Micropublications
   SA   types of microforms, to be add-
          ed as needed
   NT   **Microfilms**
   RT   **Microphotography**
Micrographic analysis
   USE   **Metallography**
          Microscopes
Microminiature electronic equipment
   USE   **Microelectronics**
Microminiaturization (Electronics)
   USE   **Microelectronics**
Microorganisms   579
   UF   Germs
          Microbes
          Microscopic organisms
   NT   **Bacteria**
          Protozoa
          Viruses
   RT   **Microbiology**
Microphotography   686.4
   Use for materials on the photographing of objects of any size to produce minute images. Materials on the photographing of minute objects through a microscope are entered under **Photomicrography.**
   UF   Microfilming
   BT   **Photography**
   RT   **Microforms**
Microprocessors   004.16
   Use for materials on the central processing units of microcomputers.
   BT   **Microcomputers**
Micropublications
   USE   **Microforms**
Microscope and microscopy
   USE   **Microscopes**
Microscopes   502.8
   UF   Analysis, Microscopic
          Micrographic analysis
          Microscope and microscopy
          [Former heading]
          Microscopic analysis
   BT   **Optical instruments**

Microscopes—*Continued*
   NT   Electron microscopes
   RT   Photomicrography
Microscopic analysis
   USE   Metallography
          Microscopes
Microscopic organisms
   USE   Microorganisms
Microwave amplification by stimulated
    emission of radiation
   USE   Masers
Microwave communication systems
       621.381
   BT   Intercommunication systems
          Shortwave radio
          Telecommunication
   NT   Closed-circuit television
Microwave cookery
   USE   Microwave cooking
Microwave cooking   641.5
   UF   Cooking, Microwave
          Microwave cookery *[Former
            heading]*
   BT   Cooking
Microwaves   537.5
   BT   Electric waves
          Electromagnetic waves
          Shortwave radio
   NT   Masers
Mid-career changes
   USE   Career changes
Middle age   305.24
   BT   Age
          Life (Biology)
   NT   Aging
   RT   Longevity
          Middle aged persons
Middle aged men (May subdiv. geog.)
       305.24
   BT   Middle aged persons
Middle aged persons (May subdiv. geog.)
       305.24
   BT   Age
   NT   Middle aged men
          Middle aged women
   RT   Middle age
Middle aged women (May subdiv. geog.)
   BT   Middle aged persons
Middle Ages   909.07; 940.1
   UF   Dark Ages

   BT   World history
   NT   Church history—600-1500,
            Middle Ages
          Fifteenth century
          Fourteenth century
          Knights and knighthood
          Thirteenth century
   RT   Feudalism
          Medieval civilization
          Renaissance
Middle Ages—History   909.07; 940.1
   UF   History, Medieval
          Medieval history
   BT   World history
   NT   Crusades
          Holy Roman Empire
   RT   Europe—History—476-1492
Middle Atlantic States
   USE   Atlantic States
Middle child
   USE   Birth order
Middle class   305.5
   UF   Bourgeoisie
          Middle classes *[Former heading]*
          Middle-income class
   BT   Social classes
Middle classes
   USE   Middle class
Middle East   956
      Use for materials on the region consisting
   of northeastern Africa and Asia west of Af-
   ghanistan. Materials on several Arab-speaking
   countries are entered under **Arab countries.**
   UF   East (Near East)
          Levant
          Near East
          Orient
   BT   Asia
   NT   Arab countries
          Israel
Middle East—Strategic aspects   956
   BT   Military geography
          Strategy
Middle East War, 1991
   USE   Persian Gulf War, 1991
Middle-income class
   USE   Middle class
Middle West   977
   UF   Central States
          Midwest
          North Central States

BT = Broader Term   **NT** = Narrower Term   **RT** = Related Term   **SA** = See Also   **UF** = Used For

Middle West—*Continued*
  BT   **Mississippi River Valley**
        United States
  RT   **Old Northwest**
Midget cars
  USE   **Karts and karting**
Midwest
  USE   **Middle West**
Midwifery
  USE   **Midwives**
Midwives   618.2
  UF   Birth attendants
        Midwifery
        Nurse widwives
        Traditional birth attendants
  BT   **Childbirth**
        Natural childbirth
        Nurses
Migrant labor   331.5; 362.85
    Use for materials on casual or seasonal
  workers who move from place to place in
  search of employment. Materials on the move-
  ment of population within a country for per-
  manent settlement are entered under **Internal
  migration.**
  UF   Labor, Migratory
        Migratory workers
  BT   **Employees**
        Labor
  RT   **Agricultural laborers**
        Internal migration
Migration
  USE   **Immigration and emigration**
Migration, Internal
  USE   **Internal migration**
Migration of animals
  USE   **Animals—Migration**
Migration of birds
  USE   **Birds—Migration**
Migratory workers
  USE   **Migrant labor**
Military aeronautics   358.4
  UF   Aeronautics, Military *[Former
          heading]*
        Aeronautics, Naval
        Air raid defensive measures
        Air warfare
        Naval aeronautics
  SA   names of wars with the subdivi-
          sion *Aerial operations,* e.g.
          World War, 1939-1945—Ae-

rial operations; to be added
          as needed
  BT   **Aeronautics**
        Military art and science
        War
  NT   **Aerial reconnaissance**
        Air bases
        Air defenses
        Air power
        Aircraft carriers
        Military airplanes
        Parachute troops
        **World War, 1939-1945—Aerial
          operations**
Military aid
  USE   **Military assistance**
Military air bases
  USE   **Air bases**
Military airplanes   623.7
  UF   Air warfare
        Airplanes, Military *[Former
          heading]*
        Airplanes, Naval
        Naval airplanes
  SA   types of military airplanes, to be
          added as needed
  BT   **Military aeronautics**
  NT   **Bombers**
Military art and science   355
  UF   Army
        Fighting
        Military power
        Military science
  NT   **Armed forces**
        Armor
        Artillery
        Battles
        Biological warfare
        Camouflage (Military science)
        Chemical warfare
        Civil defense
        Fortification
        Guerrilla warfare
        Industrial mobilization
        Military aeronautics
        Military camps
        Military hospitals
        Military transportation
        Ordnance
        Psychological warfare

BT = Broader Term   NT = Narrower Term   RT = Related Term   SA = See Also   UF = Used For

Military art and science—*Continued*
     Signals and signaling
     Tactics
     Veterans
  RT   Armies
     Drill and minor tactics
     Military personnel
     Naval art and science
     Strategy
     War
     Weapons
Military art and science—Study and teaching
  USE   **Military education**
Military assistance   355
  UF   Arms aid
     Arms sales
     Foreign aid program
     Military aid
     Military sales
     Mutual defense assistance program
  SA   military assistance from particular countries, e.g. **American military assistance;** to be added as needed
  BT   **Military policy**
  NT   **American military assistance**
Military assistance, American
  USE   **American military assistance**
Military atrocities
  USE   **Atrocities**
     War crimes
Military bases   355.7
  UF   Army bases
     Army posts
     Military facilities
     Military installations
     Military posts *[Former heading]*
     Military stations
Military biography
  USE   names of armies and navies with the subdivision *Biography,* e.g. **United States. Army—Biography; United States. Navy—Biography;** etc., to be added as needed
Military camps   355.7
  UF   Camps (Military) *[Former heading]*

  BT   **Military art and science**
  NT   **Concentration camps**
Military costume
  USE   **Military uniforms**
Military courts
  USE   **Courts martial and courts of inquiry**
Military crimes
  USE   **Military offenses**
Military desertion (May subdiv. geog.)
     343; 355.1
  UF   Army desertion
     Defectors, Military
     Desertion
     Desertion, Military *[Former heading]*
  SA   names of wars with the subdivision *Desertions,* to be added as needed
  BT   **Military offenses**
  NT   **World War, 1939-1945—Desertions**
  RT   **Draft resisters**
Military desertion—United States   343
  UF   United States. Army—Desertions
Military draft
  USE   **Draft**
Military drill
  USE   **Drill and minor tactics**
Military education   355.007; 355.5
  UF   Army schools
     Education, Military
     Military art and science—Study and teaching
     Military training
     Schools, Military
  SA   names of military schools, e.g. **United States Military Academy;** to be added as needed
  BT   **Education**
  NT   **Military training camps**
Military engineering   623
  SA   names of wars with the subdivision *Engineering and construction,* to be added as needed
  BT   **Civil engineering**
     Engineering
  NT   **World War, 1939-1945—Engineering and construction**

BT = Broader Term   NT = Narrower Term   RT = Related Term   SA = See Also   UF = Used For

Military engineering—*Continued*
RT   **Fortification**
Military facilities
USE   **Military bases**
Military forces
USE   **Armed forces**
Military geography   355.4
UF   Geography, Military
       Maps, Military
       Military maps
SA   areas of the world with the sub-
       division *Strategic aspects,* to
       be added as needed
BT   **Geography**
NT   **Middle East—Strategic aspects**
Military government   341.6; 355.4
    Use for general materials on governments
under military regimes. Materials on govern-
ments of particular countries under military
rule are entered under the name of the country
with the subdivision *Politics and government,*
or *History,* with appropriate dates as needed.
Materials on military governments of occupa-
tion are entered under the name of the country
occupied with the appropriate subdivision un-
der *History,* e.g., *History—1940-1945, Ger-
man occupation;* or *History—1945- , Allied
Occupation.*
UF   Government, Military
BT   **Public administration**
RT   **Military occupation**
Military health   613.6
UF   Hygiene, Military
       Soldiers—Hygiene
SA   names of wars with the subdivi-
       sion *Health aspects* or *Medi-
       cal care,* to be added as
       needed
BT   **Hygiene**
       Sanitation
NT   **World War, 1939-1945—Health
       aspects**
       **World War, 1939-1945—Medi-
       cal care**
RT   **Armies—Medical care**
       Military medicine
Military history   355.009
UF   History, Military
       Wars
SA   names of countries with the sub-
       head *Army* or the subdivision
       Military history, e.g. **United
       States. Army; United**

States—Military history; and
    names of wars, battles, sieges,
    etc., to be added as needed
BT   **History**
NT   **Battles**
       Military policy
       United States. Army
       United States—Military history
RT   **Naval history**
Military hospitals   355.7
UF   Field hospitals
       Hospitals, Military *[Former
       heading]*
       Veterans—Hospitals
SA   names of wars with the subdivi-
       sion *Medical care,* to be add-
       ed as needed
BT   **Hospitals**
       Military art and science
       Military medicine
NT   **World War, 1939-1945—Medi-
       cal care**
RT   **Veterans**
Military installations
USE   **Military bases**
Military intervention
USE   **Intervention (International law)**
Military law   343
UF   Articles of war
       War, Articles of
BT   **International law**
       Law
NT   **Draft**
       Military offenses
       **Veterans—Legal status, laws,
       etc.**
RT   **Courts martial and courts of
       inquiry**
       War
Military life
USE   **Military personnel**
       and names of countries with the
       subdivision *Armed forces* or
       the subheads *Army* or *Navy;*
       etc., with the subdivision *Mil-
       itary life,* e.g. **United
       States—Armed forces—Mili-
       tary life; United States.
       Army—Military life;** etc., to
       be added as needed

BT = Broader Term   NT = Narrower Term   RT = Related Term   SA = See Also   UF = Used For

Military maps
  USE **Military geography**
Military medicine   616.9
  UF Field hospitals
      Medicine, Military *[Former*
        heading]
  SA names of wars with the subdivi-
      sion *Medical care,* to be add-
      ed as needed
  BT **Medicine**
  NT **Armies—Medical care**
      Military hospitals
      World War, 1939-1945—Medi-
        cal care
  RT **Military health**
Military motorization
  USE **Military transportation**
Military music   781.5
  UF Music, Military
  SA names of wars with the subdivi-
      sion *Songs,* to be added as
      needed
  BT **Music**
  NT **Band music**
      Marches (Music)
      World War, 1939-1945—Songs
Military occupation   341.6; 355.4
  UF Occupation, Military
      Occupied territory
  SA names of occupied countries
      with the appropriate subdivi-
      sion under *History,* e.g., *His-*
      tory—1940-1945, German oc-
      cupation; or *History—1945- ,*
      Allied occupation, to be added
      as needed
  BT **War**
  NT **Japan—History—1945-1952,**
      Allied occupation
      Netherlands—History—1940-
      1945, German occupation
      World War, 1939-1945—Occu-
      pied territories
  RT **Military government**
Military offenses (May subdiv. geog.)
      343; 355.1
  UF Crimes, Military
      Military crimes
      Naval offenses
      Offenses, Military

  SA types of military offenses, e.g.
      Military desertion; to be
      added as needed
  BT **Criminal law**
      Military law
  NT **Military desertion**
Military offenses—United States   343;
    355.1
  UF United States. Army—Crimes
      and misdemeanors
      United States—Military offenses
Military pensions   331.25
  UF Naval pensions
      Pensions, Military *[Former*
        heading]
      Pensions, Naval
      War pensions
  BT **Pensions**
  RT **Veterans**
Military personnel (May subdiv. geog.)
    355.3
  UF Military life
      Servicemen
      Servicewomen
  SA names of countries with the sub-
      division *Armed forces* or the
      subheads *Army* or *Navy,* etc.,
      with the subdivision *Military*
      life, e.g. **United States—**
      Armed forces—Military life;
      United States. Army—Mili-
      tary life; etc., to be added as
      needed
  BT **Armed forces**
      War
  NT **Admirals**
      Armies
      Gays and lesbians in the mili-
      tary
      Generals
      Mercenary soldiers
      Navies
      Recruiting and enlistment
      Sailors
      Soldiers
      United States—Armed forces—
      Military life
      United States. Army—Military
      life
      United States. Army—Officers

Military personnel—*Continued*
        United States. Navy—Officers
  RT   Military art and science
        Veterans
Military personnel missing in action
  USE   Missing in action
Military personnel—United States
        355.30973
  UF   United States—Military person-
          nel
Military policy   355
  UF   Defense policy
  SA   names of countries with the sub-
          division *Military policy,* e.g.
          United States—Military poli-
          cy; etc.
  BT   Military history
  NT   Military assistance
        Military readiness
        United States—Military policy
  RT   National security
Military posts
  USE   Military bases
Military power
  USE   Armies
        Military art and science
        Navies
        Sea power
Military preparedness
  USE   Military readiness
Military readiness   355
    Use for materials on military strength,
including military personnel, munitions, natu-
ral resources, and industrial war potential. Ma-
terials on the implements of war are entered
under **Ordnance** or **Military weapons.** Mate-
rials on the industries producing them are en-
tered under **Defense industries.** Materials on
the armaments of a particular country are entered under the name of the country with the
subdivision *Defenses,* e.g. **United States—Defenses;** etc.
  UF   Armaments *[Former heading]*
        Defense readiness
        Military preparedness
        National defenses
  BT   Military policy
  NT   United States—Defenses
  RT   Armed forces
        Arms control
        Arms race
        Defense industries
        Industrial mobilization

        Manpower
Military sales
  USE   Defense industries
        Military assistance
Military science
  USE   Military art and science
Military service, Compulsory
  USE   Draft
Military service, Voluntary
  USE   Voluntary military service
Military signaling
  USE   Signals and signaling
Military stations
  USE   Military bases
Military strategy
  USE   Strategy
Military supplies industry
  USE   Defense industries
Military tactics
  USE   Tactics
Military tanks   358; 623.7
  UF   Armored cars (Tanks)
        Cars, Armored (Tanks)
        Tanks (Military science) *[For-
          mer heading]*
  BT   Military vehicles
Military training
  USE   Military education
Military training camps   355.7
  UF   Students' military training camps
        Training camps, Military
  BT   Military education
Military training, Universal
  USE   Draft
Military transportation   358
  UF   Military motorization
        Motorization, Military
        Transportation, Military *[Former
          heading]*
  SA   names of wars with the subdivi-
          sion *Transportation,* e.g.
          World War, 1939-1945—
          Transportation; to be added
          as needed
  BT   Military art and science
        Transportation
  NT   Military vehicles
Military uniforms   355.1; 355.8
  UF   Costume, Military
        Military costume

Military uniforms—*Continued*
    Naval uniforms
    Uniforms, Military *[Former heading]*
    Uniforms, Naval
  BT Costume
    Tailoring
Military vehicles 355.8
  UF Army vehicles
    Vehicles, Military *[Former heading]*
  BT **Military transportation**
    Vehicles
  NT **Military tanks**
Military weapons 355.8; 623.4
  UF Armaments *[Former heading]*
    Arms sales
    Munitions *[Former heading]*
  SA names of wars with the subdivision *Equipment and supplies,* to be added as needed
  BT **War**
    Weapons
  NT **Nuclear weapons**
    Space weapons
    World War, 1939-1945—Equipment and supplies
  RT **Arms race**
    Defense industries
    Industrial mobilization
    Ordnance
Militia
  USE names of countries and states with the subdivision *Militia,* e.g. **United States—Militia;** to be added as needed
Militia movements (May subdiv. geog.) 303.48
  Use for materials on anti-government paramilitary social movements.
  UF Militias
    Paramilitary militia movements
  BT **Radicalism**
    Social movements
Militias
  USE **Militia movements**
Milk 637; 641.3
  BT **Dairy products**
    Dairying
    Food
  NT **Dried milk**

Milk—Analysis 637; 641.3
Milk supply 338.1
  BT **Food adulteration and inspection**
    Public health
Mill and factory buildings
  USE **Factories**
Millenarianism
  USE **Millennium**
Millennialism
  USE **Millennium**
Millennium 236
  UF Millenarianism
    Millennialism
  BT **Eschatology**
  RT **Second Advent**
Millikan rays
  USE **Cosmic rays**
Millinery
  USE **Hats**
Milling (Flour)
  USE **Flour mills**
Millionaires 920
  BT **Wealth**
  RT **Capitalists and financiers**
Mills 670.42
  UF Mills and millwork *[Former heading]*
  SA types of mills, to be added as needed
  BT **Manufactures**
    Technology
  NT **Flour mills**
  RT **Factories**
    Machinery
Mills and millwork
  USE **Mills**
Mime 792.3
  BT **Acting**
  RT **Pantomimes**
Mind
  USE **Intellect**
    Psychology
Mind and body 128; 150
  UF Body and mind
  BT **Brain**
    Medicine
    Parapsychology
    Philosophy
  NT **Abnormal psychology**

BT = Broader Term   NT = Narrower Term   RT = Related Term   SA = See Also   UF = Used For

Mind and body—*Continued*
>> Biofeedback training
>> Body image
>> Consciousness
>> Mental suggestion
>> Psychosomatic medicine
>> Sleep
>> Temperament
> RT Holistic medicine
>> Human body
>> Hypnotism
>> Mental healing
>> Mental health
>> Phrenology
>> Psychoanalysis
>> Psychophysiology
>> Spiritual healing
>> Subconsciousness

Mind control
> USE **Brainwashing**

Mind cure
> USE **Mental healing**

Mind reading
> USE **Telepathy**

Mine surveying   622.028
> BT **Mining engineering**
>> **Prospecting**
>> **Surveying**

Mineral lands
> USE **Mines and mineral resources**

Mineral resources
> USE **Mines and mineral resources**

Mineral resources, Marine
> USE **Marine mineral resources**

Mineralogy
> USE **Minerals**
>> **Natural history**

Minerals   549

Use for materials on the chemical and geological aspects of natural compounds extracted from the earth. Materials on mines and mining and the potential economic value of minerals are entered under **Mines and mineral resources.**

> UF Mineralogy [*Former heading*]
> SA names of minerals, e.g. **Quartz;** to be added as needed
> BT **Geology**
> NT **Asbestos**
>> **Gems**
>> **Gypsum**
>> **Ores**

>> **Precious stones**
>> **Quartz**
> RT **Crystals**
>> **Mines and mineral resources**
>> **Natural history**
>> **Petrology**

Miners   622.092; 920
> SA types of miners, to be added as needed
> BT **Labor**
> NT **Coal miners**

Miners—Diseases   616.9
> UF Miners' diseases
> BT **Occupational diseases**

Miners' diseases
> USE **Miners—Diseases**

Mines and mineral resources (May subdiv. geog.)   333.8; 338.2

Use for materials on mines and mining and the potential economic value of minerals. Materials on the chemical or geological aspects of natural compounds extracted from the earth are entered under **Minerals.**

> UF Mineral lands
>> Mineral resources
>> Mining
> SA types of mines and mining, e.g. **Coal mines and mining;** to be added as needed
> BT **Economic geology**
>> **Natural resources**
>> **Raw materials**
> NT **Coal mines and mining**
>> **Gold mines and mining**
>> **Marine mineral resources**
>> **Mining engineering**
>> **Precious metals**
>> **Prospecting**
>> **Silver mines and mining**
> RT **Minerals**

Mines and mineral resources—United States   333.8; 338.2
> UF United States—Mines and mineral resources

Miniature gardens   635.9
> UF Gardens, Miniature [*Former heading*]
>> Tray gardens
> BT **Gardens**
>> **Miniature objects**
> RT **Container gardening**

BT = Broader Term   NT = Narrower Term   RT = Related Term   SA = See Also   UF = Used For

Miniature gardens—*Continued*
> Indoor gardening
> Terrariums

Miniature objects   688; 745.592
> UF   Miniatures
> Tiny objects
> SA   types of objects with the subdivision *Models,* to be added as needed
> BT   Art objects
> NT   Dollhouses
> Miniature gardens
> Miniature painting
> Models and model making
> RT   Toys

Miniature painting   751.7; 757
> UF   Miniatures (Portraits)
> Portrait miniatures
> BT   Miniature objects
> Painting
> RT   Portrait painting

Miniatures
> USE   Miniature objects

Miniatures (Illumination of books and manuscripts)
> USE   Illumination of books and manuscripts

Miniatures (Portraits)
> USE   Miniature painting

Minibikes   629.227
> BT   Bicycles
> Motorcycles

Minimum drinking age
> USE   Drinking age

Minimum wage   331.2
> UF   Wages—Minimum wage *[Former heading]*
> BT   Wages

Mining
> USE   Mines and mineral resources
> Mining engineering

Mining, Electric
> USE   Electricity in mining

Mining engineering   622
> UF   Mining
> BT   Civil engineering
> Coal mines and mining
> Engineering
> Mines and mineral resources
> NT   Boring

Mine*surveying
> Ocean mining
> RT   Electricity in mining

Mining, Ocean
> USE   Ocean mining

Ministers (Diplomatic agents)
> USE   Diplomats

Ministers of state
> USE   Cabinet officers

Ministers of the gospel
> USE   Clergy

Ministry   253; 291.6
> UF   Clergy—Office
> SA   ministries of particular religions, e.g. **Christian ministry;** to be added as needed
> BT   Church work
> Pastoral theology
> NT   Christian ministry
> RT   Clergy

Ministry, Christian
> USE   Christian ministry

Minor arts
> USE   Decorative arts

Minor planets
> USE   Asteroids

Minor tactics
> USE   Drill and minor tactics

Minorites
> USE   Franciscans

Minorities (May subdiv. geog.)   305.8; 323.1
> UF   Foreign population
> Minority groups
> SA   names of particular ethnic and racial minorities and of national groups in a foreign country, e.g. **African Americans; Mexican Americans; Mexicans—United States;** etc.; names of places with the subdivision *Race relations,* e.g. **United States—Race relations;** names of places with the subdivision *Ethnic relations,* e.g. **United States—Ethnic relations;** and headings for minorities in various industries and fields of en-

---

BT = Broader Term   NT = Narrower Term   RT = Related Term   SA = See Also   UF = Used For

Minorities—*Continued*

  deavor, e.g., **Minorities in broadcasting;** to be added as needed

NT **Aliens**
  Immigrants
  Mexican Americans
  Mexicans—United States
  Minorities in broadcasting
  Minorities in television
  Minorities in television broadcasting
  Minority business enterprises

RT **Discrimination**
  Ethnic relations
  Race relations
  Segregation

Minorities in broadcasting 384.5; 791.4

Use for materials on minority involvement in the broadcasting industry.

UF Minority groups in broadcasting
SA names of particular minority groups in broadcasting or in particular broadcast media, e.g. **African Americans in television broadcasting;** to be added as needed
BT **Broadcasting**
  Minorities
NT **Minorities in television broadcasting**

Minorities in engineering 620

UF Minority groups in engineering
BT **Engineering**

Minorities in television 791.45

Use for materials on the portrayal of minorities in television programs. Materials on all aspects of minority involvement in television are entered under **Minorities in television broadcasting.**

UF Minorities on television
SA names of particular minority groups in television, e.g. **African Americans in television;** to be added as needed
BT **Minorities**
  Television

Minorities in television broadcasting
 791.45

Use for materials on all aspects of minority involvement in television. Materials on the portrayal of minorities in television programs are entered under **Minorities in television.**

UF Minorities in the television industry
SA names of particular minority groups in television broadcasting, e.g. **African Americans in television broadcasting;** to be added as needed
BT **Minorities**
  Minorities in broadcasting
  Television broadcasting

Minorities in the television industry
USE **Minorities in television broadcasting**

Minorities on television
USE **Minorities in television**

Minority business enterprises 338.6

UF Business enterprises, Minority
  Minority businesses
  Minority-owned business enterprises
BT **Business enterprises**
  Minorities
NT **Federal aid to minority business enterprises**

Minority business enterprises—Federal aid
USE **Federal aid to minority business enterprises**

Minority businesses
USE **Minority business enterprises**

Minority groups
USE **Minorities**

Minority groups in broadcasting
USE **Minorities in broadcasting**

Minority groups in engineering
USE **Minorities in engineering**

Minority-owned business enterprises
USE **Minority business enterprises**

Minstrels 791.092; 920

BT **Poets**
NT **Troubadours**

Mints 332.4

BT **Money**
RT **Coinage**

Miracle plays
USE **Mysteries and miracle plays**

Miracles 291.2

UF Bible—Miracles
RT **Spiritual healing**
  Supernatural

BT = Broader Term NT = Narrower Term RT = Related Term SA = See Also UF = Used For

Miracles—Christianity   231.7
UF   Bible. N.T.—Miracles
BT   **Christianity**
     Church history
Mirrors   748.8
UF   Looking glasses
BT   **Furniture**
MIS (Information systems)
USE   **Management information sys-
       tems**
Miscarriage   618.3
UF   Abortion, Spontaneous
     Fetal death
     Spontaneous abortion
BT   **Pregnancy**
Miscellanea
USE   subjects with the subdivision
       Miscellanea, e.g. **Medicine—
       Miscellanea;** to be added as
       needed
Miscellaneous facts
USE   **Curiosities and wonders**
Misconduct in office   353.4
UF   Malfeasance in office
     Official misconduct
SA   names of specific incidents and
       offenses, to be added as need-
       ed
BT   **Conflict of interests**
     Criminal law
NT   **Police corruption**
     Watergate Affair, 1972-1974
RT   **Political corruption**
Misdemeanors (Law)
USE   **Criminal law**
Misleading advertising
USE   **Deceptive advertising**
Misrepresentation in advertising
USE   **Deceptive advertising**
Missiles, Ballistic
USE   **Ballistic missiles**
Missiles, Guided
USE   **Guided missiles**
Missing children   362.82; 363.2
UF   Lost children
BT   **Children**
     Criminal investigation
     Missing persons
NT   **Runaway children**

Missing in action
UF   M.I.A.'s
     MIA's
     Military personnel missing in ac-
       tion
SA   names of wars with the subdivi-
       sion *Missing in action,* to be
       added as needed
BT   **Prisoners of war**
     Soldiers
NT   **World War, 1939-1945—Miss-
       ing in action**
Missing persons (May subdiv. geog.)
     363.2
BT   **Criminal investigation**
NT   **Missing children**
     Runaway adults
     Runaway teenagers
Missionaries, Christian
USE   **Christian missionaries**
Missions
USE   names of Christian churches, de-
       nominations, religious orders,
       etc., with the subdivision *Mis-
       sions,* e.g. **Catholic Church—
       Missions;** and names of peo-
       ples evangelized with the sub-
       division *Christian missions,*
       e.g. **Indians of North Ameri-
       ca—Christian missions;** to
       be added as needed
Missions, Christian
USE   **Christian missions**
Missions, Indian
USE   **Indians of North America—
       Christian missions**
Missions, Medical
USE   **Medical missions**
Mississippi River Valley   977
UF   Mississippi Valley
BT   **United States**
NT   **Middle West**
Mississippi River Valley—History   977
UF   New France—History
Mississippi Valley
USE   **Mississippi River Valley**
Mistakes
USE   **Errors**
Misuse of therapeutic drugs
USE   **Medication abuse**

BT = Broader Term   NT = Narrower Term   RT = Related Term   SA = See Also   UF = Used For

Mixed marriage
  USE   **Interfaith marriage**
            Intermarriage
            Interracial marriage
Mnemonics
  USE   **Memory**
Mobile home living   **643; 728.7**
  BT   **Home economics**
          Mobile homes
  NT   **Trailer parks**
          Van life
Mobile home parks
  USE   **Trailer parks**
Mobile homes   **643; 728.7**
     Use for materials on stationary transportable structures designed for year-round living. Materials on structures mounted upon a truck or towed by a truck or automobile for the purpose of temporary dwelling or cargo hauling are entered under **Travel trailers and campers.**
  UF   Homes, Mobile
          House trailers
          Trailers, Home
  BT   **Housing**
  NT   **Mobile home living**
  RT   **Travel trailers and campers**
Mobiles (Sculpture)   **731**
  BT   **Kinetic sculpture**
          Sculpture
Mobilization, Industrial
  USE   **Industrial mobilization**
Mobs
  USE   **Crowds**
           Riots
Mock epic literature
  USE   **Mock-heroic literature**
Mock-heroic literature   **800**
     May be used for individual works, collections, or materials about mock-heroic literature.
  UF   Comic epic literature
          Mock epic literature
  BT   **Literature**
          Wit and humor
  RT   **Epic literature**
          Humorous fiction
Model airplanes
  USE   **Airplanes—Models**
Model cars
  USE   **Automobiles—Models**
Model making
  USE   **Models and model making**

Model ships
  USE   **Ships—Models**
Model trains
  USE   **Locomotives—Models**
           Railroads—Models
Modeling   **731.4; 738.1**
  UF   Clay modeling
  BT   **Clay**
          Sculpture
  NT   **Soap sculpture**
  RT   **Sculpture—Technique**
Modelmaking
  USE   **Models and model making**
Models
  USE   **Artists' models**
          Fashion models
          Mathematical models
          Models and model making
          and types of objects with the subdivision *Models,* e.g. **Airplanes—Models;** to be added as needed
Models and model making   **688**
  UF   Model making
          Modelmaking
          Models
          Models and modelmaking
  SA   types of objects with the subdivision *Models,* e.g. **Airplanes—Models;** to be added as needed
  BT   **Handicraft**
          Miniature objects
  NT   **Airplanes—Models**
          Automobiles—Models
          Locomotives—Models
          Machinery—Models
          Motorboats—Models
          Pattern making
          Railroads—Models
          Ships—Models
Models and modelmaking
  USE   **Models and model making**
Models, Artists'
  USE   **Artists' models**
Models, Fashion
  USE   **Fashion models**
Models, Mathematical
  USE   **Mathematical models**

BT = Broader Term   NT = Narrower Term   RT = Related Term   SA = See Also   UF = Used For

Models, Mechanical
USE   Machinery—Models
Models (Persons)
USE   Artists' models
          Fashion models
Modern architecture   724
    UF   Architecture, Modern [Former
              heading]
    BT   Architecture
Modern architecture—1600-1799 (17th
      and 18th centuries)   724
Modern architecture—1800-1899 (19th
      century)   724
    UF   Architecture, Modern—19th
              century
Modern architecture—1900-1999 (20th
      century)   724
    UF   Architecture, Modern—20th
              century
Modern art   709.03; 709.04
    UF   Art, Modern [Former heading]
    BT   Art
    RT   Modernism (Arts)
Modern art—1800-1899 (19th century)
          709.03
    UF   Art, Modern—19th century
    BT   Art
    NT   Impressionism (Art)
              Postimpressionism (Art)
Modern art—1900-1999 (20th century)
          709.04
    UF   Art, Modern—20th century
              Contemporary art
    SA   types of modern art, to be added
              as needed
    BT   Art
    NT   Abstract art
              Computer art
              Earthworks (Art)
              Kinetic art
              Performance art
              Postimpressionism (Art)
              Video art
Modern church history
    USE   Church history—1500- , Mod-
                ern period
Modern civilization   306.09; 909
    Use for materials covering the period after
    1453.
    UF   Civilization, Modern [Former
              heading]

    BT   Civilization
    NT   Renaissance
    RT   Modern history
Modern civilization—1950-   306.09;
          909.82
Modern dance   792.8
    UF   Interpretive dance
    BT   Dance
Modern Greek language   489
    May be subdivided like English language.
    UF   Greek language, Modern [For-
              mer heading]
              Romaic language
    BT   Language and languages
    RT   Greek language
Modern Greek literature   889
    May use same subdivisions and names of
    literary forms as for English literature.
    UF   Greek literature, Modern [For-
              mer heading]
              Neo-Greek literature
              Romaic literature
    BT   Literature
Modern history   909.08
    Use for materials covering the period after
    1453.
    UF   History, Modern [Former head-
              ing]
    BT   History
              World history
    NT   Eighteenth century
              Reformation
              Renaissance
              Seventeenth century
    RT   Modern civilization
Modern history—1800-1899 (19th
          century)   909.81
    UF   History, Modern—19th century
    NT   Nineteenth century
Modern history—1900-1999 (20th
          century)   909.82
    UF   History, Modern—20th century
    NT   Italo-Ethiopian War, 1935-1936
              Korean War, 1950-1953
              Twentieth century
              World War, 1914-1918
              World War, 1939-1945
Modern history—1945-   909.82
Modern history—Study and teaching
          907
    NT   Current events

BT = Broader Term   NT = Narrower Term   RT = Related Term   SA = See Also   UF = Used For

Modern languages 410

Use for materials dealing collectively with living literary languages. May be subdivided like **English language.**

UF　Languages, Modern *[Former heading]*

BT　**Language and languages**

Modern languages—Conversation and phrase books 418

Use for instructional materials or for books of convenient conversations and phrases for travelers. Materials on foreign words and phrases incorporated into a language are entered under the name of the language with the subdivision *Foreign words and phrases,* e.g. **English language—Foreign words and phrases.**

UF　Conversation and phrase books

Conversation in foreign languages

Conversations and phrases

Foreign language phrases

Modern languages—Conversations and phrases *[Former heading]*

SA　names of languages with the subdivision *Conversation and phrase books,* e.g. **French language—Conversation and phrase books; English language—Conversation and phrase books;** etc., to be added as needed

Modern languages—Conversations and phrases

USE　**Modern languages—Conversation and phrase books**

Modern languages—Study and teaching 418

RT　**Language laboratories**

Modern painting 759.06

UF　Painting, Modern *[Former heading]*

BT　**Painting**

Modern painting—1800-1899 (19th century) 759.05

UF　Painting, Modern—19th century

Modern painting—1900-1999 (20th century) 759.06

UF　Painting, Modern—20th century

Modern philosophy 190

UF　Philosophy, Modern *[Former heading]*

BT　**Philosophy**

NT　**Enlightenment**

Existentialism

Phenomenology

Modern sculpture 735

UF　Sculpture, Modern *[Former heading]*

BT　**Sculpture**

Modern sculpture—1900-1999 (20th century) 735

UF　Sculpture, Modern—20th century

Modernism

USE　**Modernism (Arts)**

Modernism (Theology)

Modernism (Aesthetics)

USE　**Modernism (Arts)**

Modernism (Art)

USE　**Modernism (Arts)**

Modernism (Arts) 700.1

Use for materials on the philosophy and practice of the arts since the nineteenth century characterized by a self-conscious break with the past and a search for new forms of expression.

UF　Art, Modern

Modernism

Modernism (Aesthetics)

Modernism (Art)

Modernism (Literature)

BT　**Aesthetics**

RT　**Literature**

Modern art

Postmodernism

Modernism (Literature)

USE　**Modernism (Arts)**

Modernism (Theology) 230; 273

Use for materials on the movement in the Christian churches that applies modern critical methods to biblical study and the history of dogma, and emphasizes the spiritual and ethical side of religion over historic dogmas and creeds.

UF　Modernism *[Former heading]*

Modernist-fundamentalist controversy

BT　**Christianity—Doctrines**

RT　**Christian fundamentalism**

Modernist-fundamentalist controversy

USE　**Christian fundamentalism**

Modernism (Theology)

Modernization

USE　**Modernization (Sociology)**

BT = Broader Term　　NT = Narrower Term　　RT = Related Term　　SA = See Also　　UF = Used For

Modernization (Sociology) (May subdiv. geog.) **303.44**

Use for materials on the process by which traditional societies achieve the political, cultural, economic, and social characteristics of modernity.

UF Development

Modernization *[Former heading]*

BT **Social change**

RT **Industrialization**

Mohammedan art

USE **Islamic art**

Mohammedanism

USE **Islam**

Mohammedans

USE **Muslims**

Mold (Fungi)

USE **Molds (Fungi)**

Molding (Metal)

USE **Founding**

Molds (Botany)

USE **Molds (Fungi)**

Molds (Fungi) 579.5

UF Mold (Fungi)

Molds (Botany) *[Former heading]*

BT **Fungi**

Molecular biochemistry

USE **Molecular biology**

Molecular biology 591.6

UF Biology, Molecular

Molecular biochemistry

Molecular biophysics

BT **Biochemistry**

Biophysics

NT **Genetic code**

Molecular biophysics

USE **Molecular biology**

Molecular cloning 174; 572.8

UF Cloning, Molecular

DNA cloning

BT **Cloning**

Genetic engineering

Molecular physiology

USE **Biophysics**

Molecules 539; 541.2

BT **Physical chemistry**

Molesting of children

USE **Child sexual abuse**

Mollusks 594

Use for materials on mollusks and for systematic and comprehensive materials on shells. Popular materials on shells and shell collecting are entered under **Shells.**

BT **Invertebrates**

Shellfish

RT **Shells**

Monarchs

USE **Kings and rulers**

Monarchy (May subdiv. geog.) **321; 321.8**

UF Royal houses

Royalty

Sovereigns

BT **Constitutional history**

Constitutional law

Executive power

Political science

NT **Empresses**

Queens

RT **Kings and rulers**

Monasteries (May subdiv. geog.) **255; 271; 726**

UF Cloisters

BT **Church architecture**

Church history

NT **Abbeys**

Convents

RT **Monasticism and religious orders**

Monastic orders

USE **Monasticism and religious orders**

Monasticism

USE **Monasticism and religious orders**

Monasticism and religious orders (May subdiv. geog.) **255; 271**

Use for materials on the institution of monasticism and for general materials on religious orders not limited to orders for a single sex. This heading may be subdivided by religion or denomination as needed.

UF Monastic orders

Monasticism *[Former heading]*

Orders, Monastic

Religious orders *[Former heading]*

SA names of monastic and religious orders, e.g. **Franciscans;** to be added as needed

---

BT = Broader Term   NT = Narrower Term   RT = Related Term   SA = See Also   UF = Used For

Monasticism and religious orders—*Continued*

NT   Franciscans

       Monasticism and religious orders for men

       Monasticism and religious orders for women

RT   Hermits

       Religious life

Monasticism and religious orders for men   255; 271

This heading may be subdivided by religion or denomination as needed.

UF   Religious orders for men *[Former heading]*

BT   **Monasticism and religious orders**

RT   **Monks**

Monasticism and religious orders for women   255; 271

This heading may be subdivided by religion or denomination as needed.

UF   Religious orders for women *[Former heading]*

       Sisterhoods

BT   **Convents**

       Monasticism and religious orders

RT   **Nuns**

Monetary policy (May subdiv. geog.) **332.4**

UF   Bimetallism

       Currency devaluation

       Devaluation of currency

       Free coinage

BT   **Economic policy**

RT   **Finance**

       Fiscal policy

       Inflation (Finance)

       Money

Monetary policy—United States   332.4

UF   United States—Monetary policy

Money   332.4

Use for materials on currency as a medium of exchange or measure of value and for general materials on various types of money.

UF   Currency

       Standard of value

BT   **Economics**

       Exchange

       Finance

NT   **Barter**

       Children's allowances

       Coinage

       Coins

       Counterfeits and counterfeiting

       Credit

       Foreign exchange

       Mints

       Paper money

RT   **Banks and banking**

       Gold

       Monetary policy

       Silver

       Wealth

Money raising

USE   **Fund raising**

Moneymaking projects for children   332.024; 650.1

UF   Children's moneymaking projects

BT   **Children—Employment**

RT   **Children's allowances**

Monkeys   599.8

BT   **Primates**

Monkeys—Behavior   599.8

UF   Monkeys—Habits and behavior *[Former heading]*

BT   **Animal behavior**

Monkeys—Habits and behavior

USE   **Monkeys—Behavior**

Monks   255; 271

RT   **Monasticism and religious orders for men**

Monograms   745.6

UF   Ciphers (Lettering)

BT   **Alphabets**

       Decoration and ornament

       Lettering

RT   **Initials**

Monologues   808.85; 815, etc.

May be used for individual works, collections, or materials about monologues. Monologues with incidental musical background and musical works in which spoken language is an integral part are entered under **Monologues with music.**

UF   Declamations

       Narrations

BT   **Recitations**

RT   **Monologues with music**

Monologues with music   808.85; 815, etc.; 782.2

Use for musical scores and for materials about monologues with incidental musical

---

BT = Broader Term   NT = Narrower Term   RT = Related Term   SA = See Also   UF = Used For

Monologues with music—*Continued*
background and musical works in which spoken language is an integral part. Individual monologues without music, collections, and materials about monologues without music are entered under **Monologues.**
- UF Declamations, Musical
  - Narration with music
  - Recitations with music
- BT **Recitations**
- RT **Monologues**

Monopolies   338.8
- BT **Commerce**
  - **Economics**
- NT **Railroads—Consolidation**
- RT **Competition**
  - **Corporation law**
  - **Industrial trusts**
  - **Restraint of trade**

Monorail railroads   385; 625.1
- UF Railroads, Single rail
  - Single rail railroads
- BT **Railroads**

Monroe Doctrine   327.73
- BT **International relations**
  - **Intervention (International law)**
  - **Pan-Americanism**
  - **United States—Foreign relations**

Monster films
- USE **Horror films**

Monsters   001.9; 398.2
  Use for materials on legendary animals combining features of human and animal form or having the forms of various animals in combination. Materials on human abnormalities are entered under either **Birth defects** or **Growth disorders.**
- BT **Animals—Folklore**
  - **Curiosities and wonders**
  - **Folklore**
  - **Mythology**
- NT **Dragons**
  - **Giants**
  - **Sasquatch**
  - **Yeti**

Montessori method of education   371.39
- BT **Elementary education**
  - **Kindergarten**
  - **Teaching**

Months   529
- SA names of the months, to be added as needed

- BT **Calendars**
  - **Chronology**

Monumental brasses
- USE **Brasses**

Monuments (May subdiv. geog.)   **725**
- UF Statues
- SA ethnic groups, classes of persons, individual persons, families, and wars with the subdivision *Monuments,* e.g. **World War, 1939-1945—Monuments;** to be added as needed
- BT **Architecture**
  - **Sculpture**
- NT **Historic buildings**
  - **National monuments**
  - **Obelisks**
  - **Pyramids**
  - **Tombs**
  - **World War, 1939-1945—Monuments**

Monuments, National
- USE **National monuments**

Monuments, Natural
- USE **Natural monuments**

Moon   523.3
- BT **Astronomy**
  - **Solar system**
- NT **Tides**

Moon bases
- USE **Lunar bases**

Moon cars   629.2
- UF Lunar cars
  - Lunar rover vehicles
  - Lunar surface vehicles
- BT **Vehicles**

Moon—Eclipses
- USE **Lunar eclipses**

Moon—Exploration   629.45
- UF Lunar exploration
- BT **Space flight to the moon**

Moon—Geology
- USE **Lunar geology**

Moon (in religion, folklore, etc.)
- USE **Moon worship**

Moon—Maps   523.3022
- BT **Maps**

Moon—Photographs
- USE **Moon—Pictorial works**

BT = Broader Term   NT = Narrower Term   RT = Related Term   SA = See Also   UF = Used For

Moon—Pictorial works 523.3; 778.3
  UF   Moon—Photographs *[Former heading]*
  BT   **Space photography**
Moon probes
  USE **Lunar probes**
Moon rocks
  USE **Lunar petrology**
Moon soil
  USE **Lunar soil**
Moon—Surface 523.3
  UF   Lunar surface
  RT   **Lunar soil**
Moon, Voyages to
  USE **Space flight to the moon**
Moon worship 291.2
  UF   Moon (in religion, folklore, etc.)
  BT   **Religion**
Moonlighting
  USE **Supplementary employment**
Moons
  USE **Satellites**
Moorish architecture
  USE **Islamic architecture**
Moors 305.892; 909
  BT   **Arabs**
Moral and philosophic stories
  USE **Didactic fiction**
        Fables
        Parables
Moral conditions 301; 306; 900
  UF   Morals
  SA   names of countries, cities, etc., with the subdivision *Moral conditions,* to be added as needed
  BT   **Social conditions**
  NT   **Chicago (Ill.)—Moral conditions**
        Ohio—Moral conditions
        United States—Moral conditions
Moral education 370.11
  UF   Character education
        Education, Character
        Education, Ethical
        Education, Moral
        Ethical education
  BT   **Education**
        Ethics

  RT   **Religious education**
Moral philosophy
  USE **Ethics**
Moral theology, Christian
  USE **Christian ethics**
Morale 152.4
  SA   types of morale, e.g. **Employee morale;** to be added as needed
  BT   **Courage**
  NT   **Employee morale**
        Psychological warfare
Moralities
  USE **Morality plays**
Morality
  USE **Ethics**
Morality plays 792.1; 808.82; 812, etc.
    May be used for individual works, collections, or materials about plays in which the chief characters are personifications of abstract qualities.
  UF   Moralities
  BT   **Drama**
        English drama
        Religious drama
        Theater
  RT   **Mysteries and miracle plays**
Morality stories
  USE **Didactic fiction**
Morality tales
  USE **Parables**
Morals
  USE **Conduct of life**
        Ethics
        Human behavior
        Moral conditions
Moravians 284
  UF   United Brethren
  BT   **Christian sects**
Mormon Church
  USE **Church of Jesus Christ of Latter-day Saints**
Mormons 289.3092
  RT   **Church of Jesus Christ of Latter-day Saints**
Morphine 362.29; 615
  BT   **Narcotics**
  NT   **Heroin**
  RT   **Opium**
Morphology
  USE **Anatomy**

BT = Broader Term   NT = Narrower Term   RT = Related Term   SA = See Also   UF = Used For

Morphology—*Continued*
>> **Animals—Anatomy**
>> **Biology**
>> **Comparative anatomy**
>> **Plants—Anatomy**

Morse code
> USE **Cipher and telegraph codes**

Mortality (May subdiv. geog.)   **304.6**
> UF Burial statistics
>> Death rate
>> Mortuary statistics
> SA ethnic groups, classes of persons, diseases, and animals with the subdivision *Mortality*, for works on the number of deaths during a given time among a particular groups or due to a particular cause, e.g. **Infants—Mortality; Tuberculosis—Mortality;** etc. to be added as needed
> BT **Population**
>> **Vital statistics**
> NT **Infants—Mortality**
> RT **Death**

Mortar   **666; 691**
> BT **Adhesives**
>> **Plaster and plastering**

Mortgage loans
> USE **Mortgages**

Mortgages   **332.63; 332.7**
> UF Chattel mortgages
>> Home loans
>> Housing loans
>> Mortgage loans
> BT **Commercial law**
>> **Contracts**
>> **Credit**
>> **Investments**
>> **Loans**
>> **Personal loans**
>> **Real estate**
>> **Securities**
> NT **Agricultural credit**

Morticians
> USE **Undertakers and undertaking**

Mortuary customs
> USE **Cremation**
>> **Funeral rites and ceremonies**

Mortuary statistics
> USE **Mortality**
>> **Vital statistics**

Mosaics   **729; 738.5; 748.5**
> BT **Decoration and ornament**
>> **Decorative arts**
> RT **Mural painting and decoration**

Moslem countries
> USE **Islamic countries**

Moslemism
> USE **Islam**

Moslems
> USE **Muslims**

Mosques   **726**
> BT **Church architecture**
>> **Islamic architecture**
>> **Temples**
> RT **Asian architecture**

Mosquitoes   **595.77**
> BT **Insects**

Mosquitoes—Control   **363.7**
> BT **Pest control**

Mosses   **588**
> BT **Plants**

Motels
> USE **Hotels and motels**

Mother and child   **306.874**
> UF Child and mother
>> Mother-child relationship
> BT **Parent and child**
> NT **Mothers and daughters**
>> **Mothers and sons**

Mother-child relationship
> USE **Mother and child**

Mother Goddess religion
> USE **Goddess religion**

Mothers   **306.874**
> UF Maternity
> BT **Family**
>> **Homemakers**
>> **Women**
> NT **Surrogate mothers**
>> **Teenage mothers**
>> **Unmarried mothers**

Mothers and daughters   **305.4; 306.874**
> UF Daughters and mothers
> BT **Girls**
>> **Mother and child**

Mothers and sons   **306.874**
> UF Sons and mothers

BT = Broader Term   NT = Narrower Term   RT = Related Term   SA = See Also   UF = Used For

Mothers and sons—*Continued*
BT   Boys
       Mother and child
Mothers' pensions
USE   Child welfare
Mothers, Single parent
USE   Single parent family
Moths   595.78
UF   Cocoons
       Lepidoptera
BT   Insects
NT   Caterpillars
       Silkworms
RT   Butterflies
Motion   531
UF   Kinetics
BT   Dynamics
NT   Mechanical movements
       Speed
RT   Force and energy
       Kinematics
       Mechanics
Motion picture actors
USE   Actors
Motion picture adaptations
USE   Film adaptations
Motion picture cameras   778.5
UF   Movie cameras
BT   Cameras
       Cinematography
RT   Amateur films
Motion picture cartoons
USE   Animated films
Motion picture direction
USE   Motion pictures—Production
       and direction
Motion picture directors
USE   Motion picture producers and
       directors
Motion picture festivals
USE   Film festivals
Motion picture industry (May subdiv.
    geog.)   384; 791.43
UF   Film industry (Motion pictures)
BT   Industries
NT   African Americans in the mo-
       tion picture industry
       Blacks in the motion picture
       industry

       Motion picture producers and
       directors
       Motion pictures—Production
       and direction
       Women in the motion picture
       industry
RT   Motion pictures
Motion picture musicals
USE   Musical films
Motion picture photography
USE   Cinematography
Motion picture plays   808.82; 812, etc.
    May be used for individual works, collec-
tions, or materials about motion picture plays.
UF   Film scripts
       Filmscripts
       Photoplays
       Scenarios
       Screen plays
       Screenplays
BT   Drama
Motion picture plays—Technique   808.2
UF   Motion pictures—Play writing
       Play writing
       Playwriting
BT   Drama—Technique
Motion picture posters
USE   Film posters
Motion picture producers
USE   Motion picture producers and
       directors
Motion picture producers and directors
    791.43; 920
UF   Film directors
       Film producers
       Motion picture directors
       Motion picture producers
BT   Motion picture industry
RT   Motion pictures—Production
       and direction
Motion picture production
USE   Motion pictures—Production
       and direction
Motion picture projectors
USE   Projectors
Motion picture serials   791.43
    May be used for individual works, collec-
tions, or materials about motion picture seri-
als.
BT   Motion pictures

BT = Broader Term   NT = Narrower Term   RT = Related Term   SA = See Also   UF = Used For

Motion pictures (May subdiv. geog.)
384; 791.43

Use for general materials on motion pictures, including motion pictures as an art form. Materials on the technical aspects of making motion pictures and their projection onto a screen are entered under **Cinematography.** For materials on motion pictures produced by the motion picture industry of an individual country or on the motion pictures shown in a country, subdivide geographically, e.g. **Motion pictures—United States.**

UF   Cinema

      Films

      Movies

      Moving pictures

      Talking pictures

SA   types of motion pictures, e.g. **Documentary films; Horror films;** motion pictures and particular groups of persons, e.g., **Motion pictures and children;** motion pictures as used in various industries or fields of endeavor, e.g. **Motion pictures in education;** subjects and groups of persons portrayed in motion pictures, e.g. **Animals in motion pictures; Women in motion pictures;** groups of persons in the motion picture industry, e.g. **Women in the motion picture industry;** and names of individual motion pictures, to be added as needed

BT   **Amusements**

      Audiovisual materials

      Mass media

NT   **Adventure films**

      African Americans in motion pictures

      Amateur films

      Animals in motion pictures

      Animated films

      Bible films

      Biographical films

      Blacks in motion pictures

      Comedy films

      Documentary films

      Epic films

      Erotic films

      Experimental films

      Fantasy films

      Film adaptations

      Film noir

      Gangster films

      Horror films

      Legal drama (Films)

      Libraries and motion pictures

      Medical drama (Films)

      Motion picture serials

      Motion pictures and children

      Motion pictures in education

      Musical films

      Mystery films

      Science fiction films

      Sherlock Holmes films

      Short films

      Silent films

      Sports drama (Films)

      Spy films

      Star Wars films

      Television movies

      Three Stooges films

      Vampire films

      War films

      Western films

      Women in motion pictures

      World War, 1939-1945—Motion pictures and the war

RT   **Motion picture industry**

Motion pictures, Amateur

USE   **Amateur films**

Motion pictures, American

USE   **Motion pictures—United States**

Motion pictures and children   305.23; 649; 791.43

Use for materials on the effect of motion pictures on children and youth.

UF   Children and motion pictures

BT   **Children**

      Motion pictures

Motion pictures and libraries

USE   **Libraries and motion pictures**

Motion pictures—Biography   791.43092; 920

BT   **Biography**

Motion pictures—Catalogs   016.79143

UF   Catalogs, Film

      Film catalogs

      Filmography

BT = Broader Term   NT = Narrower Term   RT = Related Term   SA = See Also   UF = Used For

Motion pictures—Catalogs—*Continued*
SA   types of motion pictures with
        the subdivision *Catalogs*, e.g.
        **Science fiction films—Cata-
        logs;** and subjects, classes of
        persons, corporate entities,
        and names of individual per-
        sons with the subdivision
        Filmography, e.g. **Animals—
        Filmography; Shakespeare,
        William, 1564-1616—Filmog-
        raphy;** etc., to be added as
        needed
Motion pictures—Censorship   791.43
BT   **Censorship**
**Motion pictures—Ethical aspects
    791.43**
UF   Motion pictures—Moral and reli-
        gious aspects *[Former head-
        ing]*
BT   **Ethics**
Motion pictures, Experimental
USE   **Experimental films**
Motion pictures in education   371.33
UF   Educational films
BT   **Audiovisual education
        Motion pictures
        Teaching—Aids and devices**
NT   **Libraries and motion pictures**
Motion pictures—Moral and religious as-
    pects
USE   **Motion pictures—Ethical as-
        pects
        Motion pictures—Religious as-
        pects**
Motion pictures—Play writing
USE   **Motion picture plays—Tech-
        nique**
Motion pictures—Posters
USE   **Film posters**
**Motion pictures—Production and direc-
    tion   384; 791.43**
UF   Direction (Motion pictures)
        Film direction
        Film production
        Filmmaking
        Motion picture direction
        Motion picture production
BT   **Motion picture industry**

RT   **Motion picture producers and
        directors**
**Motion pictures—Religious aspects
    248.4; 291.4; 791.43**
UF   Motion pictures—Moral and reli-
        gious aspects *[Former head-
        ing]*
Motion pictures—Television adaptations
USE   **Television adaptations**
**Motion pictures—United States
    791.430973**
    Use for materials on motion pictures pro-
    duced by the motion picture industry of the
    United States or on motion pictures shown in
    the United States.
UF   American films
        American motion pictures
        Motion pictures, American
Motion study   658.5
BT   **Factory management
        Industrial efficiency
        Job analysis
        Personnel management
        Production standards**
RT   **Time study**
Motivation (Psychology)   153.8
UF   Incentive (Psychology)
BT   **Psychology**
NT   **Burn out (Psychology)
        Wishes**
Motor boats
USE   **Motorboats**
Motor buses
USE   **Buses**
Motor cars
USE   **Automobiles**
Motor coordination
USE   **Movement education**
Motor courts
USE   **Hotels and motels**
Motor cycles
USE   **Motorcycles**
Motor trucks
USE   **Trucks**
Motor vehicle industry
USE   **Automobile industry**
Motorboats   623.8
UF   Motor boats
        Outboard motorboats
        Power boats
BT   **Boats and boating**

Motorboats—Models 623.8
BT Models and model making
Motorcycles 629.227
UF Cycles, Motor
Motor cycles
SA specific makes and models of
motorcycles, to be added as
needed
BT Bicycles
NT Minibikes
RT Motorcycling
Motorcycling 796.7
BT Cycling
RT Motorcycles
Motoring
USE Automobile travel
Motorization, Military
USE Military transportation
Motors
USE Electric motors
Engines
Motorways
USE Express highways
Mottoes 808.88; 818.008, etc.; 929.8
May be used for collections of mottoes and
for materials about mottoes.
UF Emblems
BT Heraldry
RT National emblems
Moulding (Metal)
USE Founding
Mound-builders
USE Mounds and mound builders
Mounds and mound builders 930.1;
970.004
UF Barrows
Graves
Mound-builders
BT Archeology
Burial
Indians of North America
Indians of North America—
Antiquities
Tombs
RT Excavations (Archeology)
Mount Rainier (Wash.) 979.7
BT Mountains
Mountain animals 591.75
UF Alpine animals [Former head-
ing]
Alpine fauna

Mountain fauna
BT Animals
Wildlife
Mountain bicycles
USE Mountain bikes
Mountain bikes 629.227
UF All terrain bicycles
Bicycles, All terrain
Bikes, Mountain
Mountain bicycles
BT All terrain vehicles
Bicycles
Mountain climbing
USE Mountaineering
Mountain fauna
USE Mountain animals
Mountain flora
USE Mountain plants
Mountain life 307.72
BT Country life
Mountain plants 581.7; 635.9
UF Alpine flora
Alpine plants [Former heading]
Mountain flora
BT Plant ecology
Plants
Mountaineering 796.52
UF Mountain climbing
Rock climbing
BT Mountains
Outdoor life
Mountains (May subdiv. geog.) 551.43
SA names of mountain ranges and
of individual mountains, to be
added as needed
BT Landforms
Physical geography
NT Mount Rainier (Wash.)
Mountaineering
Rocky Mountains
Volcanoes
Mourning
USE Bereavement
Mourning customs
USE Funeral rites and ceremonies
Mouse
USE Mice
Movable books
USE Toy and movable books

BT = Broader Term   NT = Narrower Term   RT = Related Term   SA = See Also   UF = Used For

Movement education   152.3; 153.7;
        372.86
  UF   Creative movement
          Motor coordination
  BT   **Physical education**
Movement, Freedom of
  USE   **Freedom of movement**
Movements of animals
  USE   **Animal locomotion**
Movie cameras
  USE   **Motion picture cameras**
Movie festivals
  USE   **Film festivals**
Movie novelizations
  USE   **Movie novels**
Movie novels   813, etc.
    May be used for individual works, collections, or materials about novels based on movies.
  UF   Movie novelizations
          Movie tie-ins
  BT   **Fiction**
  RT   **Radio and television novels**
Movie posters
  USE   **Film posters**
Movie tie-ins
  USE   **Movie novels**
Movies
  USE   **Motion pictures**
Moving   648
    Use for materials on changing the location of possessions, household, office, etc.
  UF   Household moving
          Moving, household *[Former heading]*
  BT   **Home economics**
Moving, household
  USE   **Moving**
Moving pictures
  USE   **Motion pictures**
Muhammedanism
  USE   **Islam**
Muhammedans
  USE   **Muslims**
Multi-age grouping
  USE   **Nongraded schools**
Multicultural education   370.117
    Use for materials on the attempt to eradicate racial and religious prejudices through the study of various races, creeds, and immigrant cultures.

  UF   Intercultural education *[Former heading]*
  BT   **Acculturation**
          Education
          Multiculturalism
  NT   **Bilingual education**
  RT   **International education**
          Multicultural literature
Multicultural literature   808.8
    Use for collections that bring together literatures of various cultures for the purpose of illustrating racial, religious, or ethnic diversity.
  UF   Intercultural literature
          Literature, Intercultural
          Literature, Multicultural
  BT   **Literature**
          Multiculturalism
  RT   **Multicultural education**
Multiculturalism (May subdiv. geog.)
        306.44
    Use for materials on the preservation of various cultures or cultural identities within a unified society. Materials on the presence of two distinct cultures within a single country or region are entered under **Biculturalism.**
  UF   Cultural pluralism
          Diversity movement
          Pluralism (Social sciences)
  BT   **Ethnic relations**
          Race relations
  NT   **Multicultural education**
          Multicultural literature
  RT   **Biculturalism**
          Ethnicity
Multilingual dictionaries
  USE   **Polyglot dictionaries**
Multilingual glossaries, phrase books, etc.
  USE   **Polyglot dictionaries**
Multimedia centers
  USE   **Instructional materials centers**
Multimedia computing
  USE   **Multimedia systems**
Multimedia information systems
  USE   **Multimedia systems**
Multimedia knowledge systems
  USE   **Multimedia systems**
Multimedia materials
  USE   **Audiovisual materials**
Multimedia systems   006.7
    Use for materials on computer systems that integrate diverse media, such as text, graphics,

---

BT = Broader Term   NT = Narrower Term   RT = Related Term   SA = See Also   UF = Used For

Multimedia systems—*Continued*
sound, etc., which can be interactively manipulated by individual users.
- UF   Computer-based multimedia information systems
  - Interactive multimedia
  - Multimedia computing
  - Multimedia information systems
  - Multimedia knowledge systems
- BT   **Information systems**
- NT   **Hypertext**

Multinational corporations   338.8; 658
- UF   Business enterprises, International
  - Business—International aspects
  - Corporations, International
  - Corporations, Multinational
  - International business enterprises *[Former heading]*
- BT   **Business enterprises**
  - **Commerce**
  - **Corporations**
  - **International economic relations**
- NT   **Foreign investments**

Multiple birth   618.2
- UF   Birth, Multiple *[Former heading]*
- SA   types of multiple births, e.g. **Twins;** to be added as needed
- BT   **Childbirth**
- NT   **Twins**

Multiple personalities
- USE   **Multiple personality**

Multiple personality   616.85
- UF   Double consciousness
  - Multiple personalities
  - Personality, Multiple
  - Split personality
- BT   **Abnormal psychology**
  - **Mental illness**
  - **Personality disorders**
  - **Psychology**

Multiple plot stories
- USE   **Plot-your-own stories**

Multiplication   513.2
- BT   **Arithmetic**

Mummies   393
- BT   **Archeology**
  - **Burial**

Municipal administration
- USE   **Municipal government**

Municipal art   711
- UF   Art, Municipal *[Former heading]*
  - Civic art
  - Municipal improvements
- BT   **Art**
  - **Cities and towns**
- RT   **City planning**

Municipal civil service
- USE   **Municipal officials and employees**

Municipal employees
- USE   **Municipal officials and employees**

Municipal engineering   628
- BT   **Engineering**
  - **Public works**
- NT   **Drainage**
  - **Refuse and refuse disposal**
  - **Sewerage**
  - **Street cleaning**
  - **Water supply**
- RT   **Sanitary engineering**

Municipal-federal relations
- USE   **Federal-city relations**

Municipal finance   336
Use for general materials on city finance. Materials on the finance of a particular city are entered under **Public finance** subdivided geographically.
- UF   Finance, Municipal
- BT   **Municipal government**
  - **Public finance**
- NT   **Metropolitan finance**

Municipal government (May subdiv. geog.)   **320.8; 352.16**
Use for materials on the government of cities in general and, when subdivided by country, state, or region, for general consideration of municipal government in those places. Materials on the government of individual cities, towns, or metropolitan areas are entered under the name of the city, town, or area with the subdivision *Politics and government.*
- UF   City government
  - Government, Municipal
  - Municipal administration
  - Municipalities
- SA   names of cities with the subdivision *Politics and government,* to be added as needed
- BT   **Local government**

BT = Broader Term   NT = Narrower Term   RT = Related Term   SA = See Also   UF = Used For

Municipal government—*Continued*
 Political science
NT Chicago (Ill.)—Politics and
  government
 Cities and towns
 Federal-city relations
 Municipal finance
 Municipal government by city
  manager
 Municipal government by com-
  mission
 Public administration
 State-local relations
RT Metropolitan government
 Municipal officials and em-
  ployees
Municipal government by city manager
 320.8; 352.16
UF City manager
 Commission government with
  city manager
BT Municipal government
Municipal government by commission
 320.8; 352.16
UF Commission government
 Government by commission
BT Municipal government
Municipal government—United States
 320.8; 352.160973
UF United States—Municipal gov-
  ernment
Municipal improvements
USE Cities and towns—Civic im-
  provement
 Municipal art
Municipal officers
USE Municipal officials and em-
  ployees
Municipal officials and employees
 352.16
UF Municipal civil service
 Municipal employees
 Municipal officers
 Town officers
SA names of cities with the subdivi-
  sion *Officials and employees,*
  e.g. **Chicago (Ill.)—Officials
  and employees;** to be added
  as needed
BT Civil service

RT Municipal government
Municipal ownership 338.9; 352.5
UF Public ownership
BT Corporations
 Economic policy
 Government ownership
Municipal planning
USE City planning
Municipal transit
USE Local transit
Municipalities
USE Cities and towns
 Municipal government
Munitions
USE Defense industries
 Military weapons
Mural painting and decoration 729;
 751.7
UF Fresco painting
 Wall decoration
 Wall painting
BT Decoration and ornament
 Interior design
 Painting
 Walls
NT Cave drawings
 Rock drawings, paintings, and
  engravings
RT Mosaics
Murder
USE Homicide
Murder mysteries
USE Mystery and detective plays
 Mystery fiction
 Mystery films
 Mystery radio programs
 Mystery television programs
Murder trials
USE Trials (Homicide)
Muscles 611; 612.7
BT Musculoskeletal system
Muscular system
USE Musculoskeletal system
Musculoskeletal system 611; 612.7
UF Muscular system
BT Anatomy
 Physiology
NT Bones
 Muscles
 Skeleton

BT = Broader Term NT = Narrower Term RT = Related Term SA = See Also UF = Used For

Musculoskeletal system—*Continued*
RT   **Human locomotion**
Museums (May subdiv. geog.)   **069; 708**
SA   appropriate subjects and names
          of wars and of corporate bod-
          ies with the subdivision *Mu-*
          seums, e.g. **World War,**
          1939-1945—Museums; and
          names of individual galleries
          and museums, to be added as
          needed
NT   **Art museums**
          Museums and schools
          World War, 1939-1945—Muse-
          ums
Museums and schools   069
UF   Schools and museums
BT   **Museums**
          Schools
Museums—Ohio   708.171
UF   Ohio—Museums
Museums—United States   708.13
UF   United States—Museums
Mushrooms   579.6; 635
UF   Toadstools
BT   **Plants**
RT   **Fungi**
Music   780
UF   Classical music
SA   music of particular countries,
          e.g. **American music;** types
          of music, e.g. **Vocal music;**
          subjects, classes of persons,
          and names of persons, corpo-
          rate bodies, places, or wars,
          with the subdivision *Songs* for
          collections or individual songs
          about the topic or entity
          named, e.g. **Surfing—Songs;**
          and ethnic groups with the
          subdivision *Music* for music
          of the group, e.g. **Indians of**
          North America—Music; to
          be added as needed
BT   **Humanities**
NT   **African American music**
          American music
          Black music
          Chamber music
          Church music

Composition (Music)
Computer music
Concerts
Conducting
Cowhands—Songs
Dance music
Electronic music
Ensembles (Music)
Folk music
Harmony
Indians of North America—
    Music
Instrumental music
Instrumentation and orchestra-
    tion
Jazz music
Military music
Music and literature
Musical notation
Musicians
Orchestral music
Organ music
Piano music
Popular music
Radio and music
Rock music
Singing
Violin music
Vocal music
RT   **Romanticism**
Music—Acoustics and physics   781.2
UF   Acoustics
BT   **Music—Theory**
          Physics
RT   **Sound**
Music, African American
USE   **African American music**
Music, American
USE   **American music**
Music—Analysis, appreciation
USE   **Music appreciation**
          Music—History and criticism
Music and literature   780
UF   Literature and music
          Music and poetry
          Poetry and music
BT   **Literature**
          Music
Music and poetry
USE   **Music and literature**

Music and radio
    USE   **Radio and music**
Music—Anecdotes   780
    UF   Music—Anecdotes, facetiae, sat-
            ire, etc. *[Former heading]*
    BT   **Anecdotes**
Music—Anecdotes, facetiae, satire, etc.
    USE   **Music—Anecdotes**
            Music—Humor
Music appreciation   781.1
    UF   Appreciation of music
            Music—Analysis, appreciation
            [Former heading]
            Musical appreciation
    BT   **Music—Study and teaching**
    RT   **Music—History and criticism**
Music, Black
    USE   **Black music**
Music box
    USE   **Music boxes**
Music boxes   786.6
    UF   Music box *[Former heading]*
    BT   **Mechanical musical instru-
            ments**
Music—Cataloging
    USE   **Cataloging of music**
Music, Choral
    USE   **Choral music**
Music—Composition
    USE   **Composition (Music)**
Music, Computer
    USE   **Computer music**
Music conductors
    USE   **Conductors (Music)**
Music—Discography   016.78
Music education
    USE   **Music—Study and teaching**
Music, Electronic
    USE   **Electronic music**
Music—Examinations   780.76
    UF   Music—Examinations, questions,
            etc. *[Former heading]*
    BT   **Examinations**
Music—Examinations, questions, etc.
    USE   **Music—Examinations**
Music festivals   780.79
    UF   Musical festivals
    BT   **Festivals**
    RT   **Concerts**

Music, Gospel
    USE   **Gospel music**
Music—History and criticism   780.9
    UF   Music—Analysis, appreciation
            Musical criticism
    RT   **Music appreciation**
Music—Humor   780
    UF   Music—Anecdotes, facetiae, sat-
            ire, etc. *[Former heading]*
    BT   **Wit and humor**
Music, Indian
    USE   **Indians of North America—
            Music**
Music, Influence of
    USE   **Music—Psychological aspects**
Music—Instruction and study
    USE   **Music—Study and teaching**
Music, Instrumental
    USE   **Instrumental music**
Music libraries   026
    UF   Libraries, Music
    BT   **Special libraries**
Music, Military
    USE   **Military music**
Music—Notation
    USE   **Musical notation**
Music, Popular (Songs, etc.)
    USE   **Popular music**
Music—Psychological aspects   781
    UF   Music, Influence of
            Psychology of music
    BT   **Psychology**
Music—Study and teaching   780.7
    UF   Education, Musical
            Music education
            Music—Instruction and study
            Musical education
            Musical instruction
            School music
    NT   **Music appreciation**
Music—Theory   781
    NT   **Composition (Music)**
            Counterpoint
            Harmony
            Music—Acoustics and physics
            Musical form
            Musical meter and rhythm
Music videos   384.55; 778.59
    May be used for individual works, collec-
    tions, or materials about music videos.
    UF   Videos, Music

BT = Broader Term   **NT** = Narrower Term   **RT** = Related Term   **SA** = See Also   **UF** = Used For

Music videos—*Continued*
   BT   Television programs
          Videodiscs
          Videotapes
Music, Vocal
   USE   **Vocal music**
Musical ability   780.7
   UF   Musical talent
          Talent
   BT   **Ability**
Musical accompaniment   781.47
   UF   Accompaniment, Musical
   BT   **Composition (Music)**
Musical appreciation
   USE   **Music appreciation**
Musical comedies
   USE   **Musicals**
Musical composition
   USE   **Composition (Music)**
Musical criticism
   USE   **Music—History and criticism**
Musical education
   USE   **Music—Study and teaching**
Musical ensembles
   USE   **Ensembles (Music)**
Musical festivals
   USE   **Music festivals**
Musical films   791.43
     May be used for individual works, collections, or materials about musical films.
   UF   Motion picture musicals
          Musicals (Motion pictures)
   BT   **Motion pictures**
   RT   **Musicals**
Musical form   784.18
   UF   Form, Musical
   SA   names of musical forms expressed in the singular, to be used both for musical scores and for materials about the musical form, e.g. **Concerto;** to be added as needed
   BT   **Composition (Music)**
          Music—Theory
   NT   **Concerto**
          Ensembles (Music)
          Fugue
          Opera
          Operetta
          Oratorio
          Sonata

          Suite (Music)
          Symphony
Musical instruction
   USE   **Music—Study and teaching**
Musical instruments   784.19
   UF   Instruments, Musical
   SA   types of instruments, e.g. **Percussion instruments;** to be added as needed
   NT   **Bells**
          Drums
          Electronic musical instruments
          Mechanical musical instruments
          Organs (Musical instruments)
          Percussion instruments
          Stringed instruments
          Wind instruments
   RT   **Instrumental music**
          Instrumentation and orchestration
          Orchestra
          Tuning
Musical instruments, Electronic
   USE   **Electronic musical instruments**
Musical instruments, Mechanical
   USE   **Mechanical musical instruments**
Musical meter and rhythm   781.2
   UF   Meter
   BT   **Music—Theory**
          Rhythm
Musical notation   780.1
   UF   Music—Notation
          Notation, Music
   BT   **Music**
Musical revues, comedies, etc.
   USE   **Musicals**
Musical talent
   USE   **Musical ability**
Musicals   782.1; 792.6
     Use for scores and for materials about musical comedies and revues.
   UF   Dramatic music
          Musical comedies
          Musical revues, comedies, etc.
          [Former heading]
   BT   **Theater**
   RT   **Musical films**
          Operetta

BT = Broader Term   NT = Narrower Term   RT = Related Term   SA = See Also   UF = Used For

Musicals (Motion pictures)
  USE   **Musical films**
Musicians   780.92; 920
  SA   musicians of particular countries,
         e.g. **American musicians;**
         types of musicians; and
         names of individual musi-
         cians, to be added as needed
  BT   **Music**
  NT   **African American musicians**
         American musicians
         Black musicians
         Composers
         Conductors (Music)
         Ensembles (Music)
         Instrumentalists
         Singers
Musicians, African American
  USE   **African American musicians**
Musicians, American
  USE   **American musicians**
Musicians—Biography   780.92; 920
  BT   **Biography**
Musicians, Black
  USE   **Black musicians**
Musicians—Portraits   780.92
Muslim architecture
  USE   **Islamic architecture**
Muslim art
  USE   **Islamic art**
Muslim countries
  USE   **Islamic countries**
Muslim law
  USE   **Islamic law**
Muslimism
  USE   **Islam**
Muslims (May subdiv. geog.)   **297.092**
  UF   Mohammedans
         Moslems
         Muhammedans
  RT   **Islam**
Muslims—United States   297.092
  UF   United States—Muslims
  NT   **Black Muslims**
Mutation (Biology)
  USE   **Evolution**
         Variation (Biology)
Mutual defense assistance program
  USE   **Military assistance**

Mutual funds   332.63
  UF   Investment companies
         Investment trusts *[Former head-
         ing]*
         Open-end mutual funds
         Profit-sharing trusts
  BT   **Investments**
Mutualism (Biology)
  USE   **Symbiosis**
Mycology
  USE   **Fungi**
Myocardial infarction
  USE   **Heart attack**
Myotherapy
  USE   **Acupressure**
Mysteries
  USE   **Mysteries and miracle plays**
         Mystery and detective plays
         Mystery fiction
         Mystery films
         Mystery radio programs
         Mystery television programs
**Mysteries and miracle plays   792.1;
         808.82; 822, etc.**
     May be used for individual plays, collec-
     tions, or materials about medieval plays de-
     picting the life of Jesus or legends of the
     saints.
  UF   Miracle plays
         Mysteries
         Mystery plays
  BT   **Bible plays**
         English drama
         Pageants
         Religious drama
         Theater
  NT   **Passion plays**
  RT   **Morality plays**
Mystery and detective comics
  USE   **Mystery comic books, strips,
         etc.**
Mystery and detective films
  USE   **Mystery films**
**Mystery and detective plays   808.82;
         812, etc.**
     May be used for individual works, collec-
     tions, or materials about mystery and detective
     dramas.
  UF   Crime plays
         Detective and mystery plays
         Murder mysteries
         Mysteries

BT = Broader Term   NT = Narrower Term   RT = Related Term   SA = See Also   UF = Used For

Mystery and detective plays—*Continued*

    Mystery plays

    Private eye stories

    Whodunits

  BT   **Drama**

Mystery and detective radio programs

  USE   **Mystery radio programs**

Mystery and detective stories

  USE   **Mystery fiction**

Mystery and detective television programs

  USE   **Mystery television programs**

Mystery comic books, strips, etc.   741.5

    May be used for individual works, collections, or materials about mystery and detective comics.

  UF   Crime comics

    Detective and mystery comic books, strips, etc.

    Detective comics

    Mystery and detective comics

  BT   **Comic books, strips, etc.**

Mystery fiction   808.83; 813, etc.

    May be used for individual works, collections, or materials about mystery fiction.

  UF   Crime stories

    Detective and mystery stories

    Detective fiction

    Detective stories

    Murder mysteries

    Mysteries

    Mystery and detective stories

      [Former heading]

    Mystery stories

    Private eye stories

    Suspense novels

    Whodunits

  BT   **Fiction**

  RT   **Ghost stories**

    Horror fiction

    Romantic suspense novels

    Spy stories

Mystery films   791.43

    May be used for individual works, collections, or materials about mystery and detective films.

  UF   Crime films

    Detective and mystery films

    Murder mysteries

    Mysteries

    Mystery and detective films

    Private eye stories

    Suspense films

    Whodunits

  SA   particular kinds of detective and mystery films, e.g. **Sherlock Holmes films;** to be added as needed

  BT   **Motion pictures**

  NT   **Sherlock Holmes films**

  RT   **Film noir**

    Gangster films

    Spy films

Mystery plays

  USE   **Mysteries and miracle plays**

    Mystery and detective plays

Mystery radio programs

    May be used for individual works, collections, or materials about mystery and detective radio programs.

  UF   Crime programs

    Detective and mystery radio programs

    Murder mysteries

    Mysteries

    Mystery and detective radio programs

    Private eye stories

    Suspense programs

    Whodunits

  BT   **Radio programs**

Mystery stories

  USE   **Mystery fiction**

Mystery television programs   791.45

    May be used for individual works, collections, or materials about mystery and detective television programs.

  UF   Crime programs

    Detective and mystery television programs

    Murder mysteries

    Mysteries

    Mystery and detective television programs

    Private eye stories

    Suspense programs

    Whodunits

  BT   **Television programs**

  RT   **Spy television programs**

Mystical theology

  USE   **Mysticism**

Mysticism   248.2; 291.4

  UF   Dark night of the soul

    Mystical theology

BT = Broader Term   NT = Narrower Term   RT = Related Term   SA = See Also   UF = Used For

Mysticism—*Continued*
  BT   Spiritual life
  NT   Cabala
          Theosophy
Mythical animals   398.24
  UF   Animal lore
          Animals, Imaginary
          Animals, Mythical *[Former heading]*
          Creatures, Imaginary
          Imaginary animals
  SA   types of mythical animals, to be added as needed
  BT   **Mythology**
  NT   **Dragons**
          Mermaids and mermen
          Sasquatch
          Yeti
  RT   **Animals—Folklore**
Mythology   291.1; 398.2
  UF   Myths
  SA   mythology of particular national or ethnic groups or of particular geographic areas, e.g. **Celtic mythology;** to be added as needed
  BT   **Legends**
          Religion
          Religions
  NT   **Art and mythology**
          Celtic mythology
          Classical mythology
          Geographical myths
          Monsters
          Mythical animals
          Symbolism
          Totems and totemism
  RT   **Folklore**
          Gods and goddesses
          Heroes and heroines
Mythology, Celtic
  USE   **Celtic mythology**
Mythology, Classical
  USE   **Classical mythology**
Mythology in art
  USE   **Art and mythology**
Myths
  USE   **Mythology**

N.A.T.O.
  USE   **North Atlantic Treaty Organization**
Names   929.4
  UF   Epithets
          Nomenclature
          Proper names
          Terminology
  SA   types of names, e.g. **Geographic names;** and types of objects, domestic animals, events, organization, and institutions with the subdivision *Names,* for materials on the naming of those items, e.g. **Pets—Names;** to be added as needed
  NT   **Code names**
          Geographic names
          Indians of North America—Names
          Personal names
          Pseudonyms
          Terms and phrases
Names, Fictitious
  USE   **Pseudonyms**
Names, Geographical
  USE   **Geographic names**
Names, Personal
  USE   **Personal names**
Names—Pronunciation   421
  UF   Pronunciation
Napoleon I, Emperor of the French, 1769-1821—Drama   808.82; 812, etc.

May be used for individual works or collections of plays about Napoleon. Materials on Napoleon as a character in drama are entered under **Napoleon I, Emperor of the French, 1769-1821—In literature.**

Napoleon I, Emperor of the French, 1769-1821—Fiction   813, etc.

May be used for individual works or collections of fiction about Napoleon. Materials on Napoleon as a character in fiction are entered under **Napoleon I, Emperor of the French, 1769-1821—In literature.**

Napoleon I, Emperor of the French, 1769-1821—In literature   809

Use for materials about Napoleon as a character or as he is portrayed in works of fiction, drama, or poetry. Individual works or collections in which Napoleon is a character are en-

---

BT = Broader Term   NT = Narrower Term   RT = Related Term   SA = See Also   UF = Used For

Napoleon I, Emperor of the French, 1769-
1821—In literature—*Continued*
  tered under **Napoleon I, Emperor of the
  French, 1769-1821—Fiction; Napoleon I,
  Emperor of the French, 1769-1821—Dra-
  ma;** or **Napoleon I, Emperor of the French,
  1769-1821—Poetry;** as appropriate.
  UF   Napoleon in fiction, drama, po-
          etry, etc.
**Napoleon I, Emperor of the French,
    1769-1821—Poetry   808.81; 811,
    etc.**
  May be used for individual works or collec-
  tions of poetry about Napoleon. Materials on
  Napoleon as portrayed in poetry are entered
  under **Napoleon I, Emperor of the French,
  1769-1821—In literature.**
Napoleon in fiction, drama, poetry, etc.
  USE   **Napoleon I, Emperor of the
          French, 1769-1821—In liter-
          ature**
Napoleonic Wars
  USE   **Europe—History—1789-1815
          France—History—1789-1799,
          Revolution
          France—History—1799-1815**
Narcotic abuse
  USE   **Drug abuse**
Narcotic addiction
  USE   **Drug abuse**
Narcotic addiction counseling
  USE   **Drug abuse counseling**
Narcotic addicts
  USE   **Drug addicts**
Narcotic habit
  USE   **Drug abuse**
Narcotic traffic
  USE   **Drug traffic**
Narcotics   178; 394.1; 615
  Use for materials limited to those drugs that
  induce sleep or lethargy or deaden pain.
  UF   Opiates
          Soporifics
  SA   types of narcotics, to be added
          as needed
  BT   **Drugs
          Materia medica
          Psychotropic drugs**
  NT   **Cocaine
          Endorphins
          Heroin
          Marijuana
          Morphine**

  Opium
Narcotics and crime
  USE   **Drugs and crime**
Narcotics and criminals
  USE   **Criminals—Drug use**
Narcotics and teenagers
  USE   **Teenagers—Drug use**
Narcotics and youth
  USE   **Youth—Drug use**
Narration with music
  USE   **Monologues with music**
Narrations
  USE   **Monologues
          Recitations**
Narrative poetry   808.81; 811, etc.
  May be used for individual works, collec-
  tions, or materials about narrative poetry.
  Rhyming stories for very young children are
  entered under the form heading **Stories in
  rhyme.**
  BT   **Poetry**
  NT   **Epic poetry
          Historical poetry
          Stories in rhyme**
Nation of Islam
  USE   **Black Muslims**
National anthems
  USE   **National songs**
National book week
  USE   **National Book Week**
National Book Week   021.7
  UF   Book Week, National
          National book week *[Former
            heading]*
  BT   **Books and reading**
National characteristics
  UF   Characteristics, National
          Images, National
          National images
          National psychology
          Psychology, National
  SA   national characteristics of partic-
          ular countries, e.g. **American
          national characteristics;** to
          be added as needed
  BT   **Anthropology
          Nationalism
          Social psychology**
  NT   **American national characteris-
          tics**
  RT   **Ethnopsychology**

BT = Broader Term   NT = Narrower Term   RT = Related Term   SA = See Also   UF = Used For

National characteristics, American
    USE   **American national characteristics**

National community service
    USE   **National service**

National consciousness
    USE   **Nationalism**

National dances
    USE   **Folk dancing**

National debts
    USE   **Public debts**

National defenses
    USE   **Industrial mobilization**
            Military readiness

National emblems (May subdiv. geog.) **929.9**
    UF   Emblems, National
            National symbols
    SA   types of national emblems and national symbols, e.g. **Flags;** to be added as needed
    BT   **Signs and symbols**
    RT   **Flags**
            Heraldry
            Insignia
            Mottoes
            Seals (Numismatics)
            State emblems

National forests
    USE   **Forest reserves**

National Guard (U.S.)
    USE   **United States. National Guard**

National health insurance (May subdiv. geog.) **368.4**
    UF   Government health insurance
            Health insurance, Government
            Health insurance, National
            Medical insurance, National
            National health service
            Socialized medicine
    BT   **Health insurance**
    NT   **Medicaid**
            Medicare
    RT   **State medicine**

National health service
    USE   **National health insurance**
            State medicine

National holidays
    USE   **Holidays**

National hymns
    USE   **National songs**

National images
    USE   **National characteristics**

National interest
    USE   **Public interest**

National landmarks
    USE   **National monuments**

National liberation movements (May subdiv. geog. except U.S.) **320.5**
    UF   Liberation movements, National
    SA   names of individual liberation movements, to be added as needed
    BT   **Nationalism**
            Revolutions
    NT   **Guerrillas**

National libraries   **027.5**
    Use for materials on libraries maintained by government funds that serve a country as a whole, particularly in collecting and preserving that country's publications.
    UF   Libraries, National
    SA   names of individual national libraries, to be added as needed
    BT   **Government libraries**

National monuments   **917.3**
    Use for materials on monuments, such as historic sites or geographic areas, that are owned and maintained in the public interest by the federal government.
    UF   Landmarks, Preservation of
            Monuments, National
            National landmarks
    SA   names of individual national monuments, to be added as needed
    BT   **Monuments**
            National parks and reserves
    RT   **Historic sites**
            Natural monuments

National parks and reserves (May subdiv. geog.) **338.78; 363.6; 719**
    SA   names of individual national parks, to be added as needed
    BT   **Parks**
            Public lands
    NT   **National monuments**
    RT   **Conservation of natural resources**
            Forest reserves
            Natural monuments

BT = Broader Term   NT = Narrower Term   RT = Related Term   SA = See Also   UF = Used For

National parks and reserves—*Continued*
    Wilderness areas
National parks and reserves—United
    States 719; 917.3
    UF   United States—National parks
           and reserves
    NT   **Yosemite National Park (Calif.)**
National planning
    USE   **Economic policy**
           Social policy
National psychology
    USE   **Ethnopsychology**
           National characteristics
National resources
    USE   **Economic conditions**
           Natural resources
           United States—Economic con-
              ditions
National security (May subdiv. geog.)
    355
    RT   **Economic policy**
           International relations
           Military policy
National security—United States   355
    UF   United States—National security
           [Former heading]
National service
    UF   Alternative military service
           National community service
    BT   **Public welfare**
    RT   **Volunteer work**
National socialism   320.5; 335.6
    Use for materials limited to fascism in Germany during the Nazi regime.
    UF   Nazism
    BT   **Fascism**
           World War, 1939-1945—
              Causes
    RT   **Neo-Nazis**
           Socialism
National songs (May subdiv. geog.)
    782.42
    UF   Anthems, National
           National anthems
           National hymns
           Patriotic songs
           Songs, National
    BT   **Songs**
    NT   **War songs**
    RT   **Folk songs**
           Patriotic poetry

National songs, American
    USE   **National songs—United States**
National songs—United States   782.42
    UF   American national songs
           National songs, American *[Former heading]*
           United States—National songs
    BT   **American songs**
National symbols
    USE   **National emblems**
Nationalism (May subdiv. geog.)   320.5
    UF   Internationalism
           National consciousness
    BT   **International relations**
           Political science
    NT   **National characteristics**
           National liberation movements
    RT   **Patriotism**
           Regionalism
Nationalism, Black
    USE   **Black nationalism**
Nationalism—United States   320.5
Nationalist China
    USE   **Taiwan**
Nationality (Citizenship)
    USE   **Citizenship**
Nationalization
    USE   **Government ownership**
Nationalization of railroads
    USE   **Railroads—Government policy**
Native American women
    USE   **Indians of North America—**
           Women
Native Americans
    USE   **Indians of North America**
Native peoples (May subdiv. geog.)
    305.8
    Use for materials on indigenous groups within a colonial area or modern state where the group does not control the government. General materials on people bound together by common ancestry and culture are entered under **Ethnic groups.** Materials on the various ethnic groups or native peoples in a particular region or country are entered under **Ethnology** subdivided geographically. Materials on individual native peoples are entered under the name of the group, e.g. **Yoruba (African people).**
    UF   Aborigines
           Indigenous peoples
           Natives
           People

BT = Broader Term   **NT** = Narrower Term   **RT** = Related Term   **SA** = See Also   **UF** = Used For

Native peoples—*Continued*
    BT   Ethnology
    NT   **Australian aborigines**
          Indians of North America
          Inuit
          Yoruba (African people)
Natives
    USE   **Native peoples**
Nativity of Christ
    USE   **Jesus Christ—Nativity**
NATO
    USE   **North Atlantic Treaty Organi-
          zation**
Natural beauty conservation
    USE   **Landscape protection**
Natural childbirth   **618.4**
    UF   Childbirth, Natural
          Lamaze method of childbirth
    BT   **Childbirth**
    NT   **Midwives**
Natural cycles
    USE   **Cycles**
Natural disasters (May subdiv. geog.)
          904
    SA   types of natural disasters, to be
          added as needed
    BT   **Disasters**
    NT   **Earthquakes**
          Floods
          Storms
          Tsunamis
Natural disasters—United States   **973**
    UF   United States—Natural disasters
Natural food cooking
    USE   **Cooking—Natural foods**
Natural foods   **641.3**
    UF   Food, Natural *[Former heading]*
          Health foods
          Organically grown foods
    BT   **Food**
    RT   **Cooking—Natural foods**
Natural gardening
    USE   **Organic gardening**
Natural gas   **553.2; 665.7**
    UF   Gas, Natural
    BT   **Fuel**
          Gases
Natural history (May subdiv. geog.)
          508
    Use for materials on the unsystematic study
of zoology, botany, mineralogy, etc., the collecting of specimens, and, with a geographic
subdivision, the description of nature in a particular place. Materials on the study of animals and plants as an elementary school subject are entered under **Nature study.** General
and theoretical materials on the natural world
are entered under **Nature.**
    UF   Animal lore
          Mineralogy
    BT   **Science**
    NT   **Aquariums**
          Bible—Natural history
          Bird watching
          Fossils
          Nature photography
    RT   **Biogeography**
          Botany
          Minerals
          Nature
          Zoology
Natural history, Biblical
    USE   **Bible—Natural history**
Natural history—United States   **508.73**
    UF   Nature study—United States
          [Former heading]
          United States—Natural history
Natural law   **340**
    UF   Law of nature
          Natural rights
    BT   **Ethics**
          Law
    RT   **International law**
Natural monuments (May subdiv. geog.)
          719
    Use for general materials on natural objects
of historic or scientific interest such as caves,
cliffs, and natural bridges.
    UF   Landmarks, Preservation of
          Monuments, Natural
          Preservation of natural scenery
          Protection of natural scenery
          Scenery
    SA   names of individual natural
          monuments, to be added as
          needed
    BT   **Landscape protection**
          Nature conservation
    RT   **National monuments**
          National parks and reserves
Natural monuments—United States
          719; 917.3
    UF   United States—Natural monu-
          ments

BT = Broader Term   NT = Narrower Term   RT = Related Term   SA = See Also   UF = Used For

Natural parents
USE   Birthparents
Natural pesticides   668
BT   Pesticides
Natural religion
USE   **Natural theology**
Natural resources (May subdiv. geog.)
        333.7
UF   National resources
        Resources, Natural
SA   types of natural resources, to be
          added as needed
BT   **Economic conditions**
NT   **Conservation of natural re-
          sources**
        Energy resources
        Fisheries
        Forests and forestry
        Marine resources
        Mines and mineral resources
        Water resources development
RT   **Public lands**
Natural resources—Management   333.7
BT   **Management**
Natural resources—United States   333.7
UF   United States—Natural resources
RT   **United States—Economic con-
          ditions**
Natural rights
USE   **Natural law**
Natural satellites
USE   **Satellites**
Natural selection   576.8
UF   Selection, Natural
        Survival of the fittest
BT   **Genetics**
        Variation (Biology)
RT   **Evolution**
        Heredity
Natural steam energy
USE   **Geothermal resources**
Natural theology   210
  Use for materials on the knowledge of
God's existence obtained by observing the
visible processes of nature.
UF   Natural religion
BT   **Apologetics**
        Theology
NT   **Creation**
RT   **Religion and science**

Natural therapy
USE   **Naturopathy**
Naturalism in art
USE   **Realism in art**
Naturalism in literature
USE   **Realism in literature**
Naturalists   508.092; 920
SA   types of naturalists, e.g. **Bota-
          nists;** to be added as needed
BT   **Scientists**
NT   **Biologists**
        Botanists
Naturalization   323.6
BT   **Immigration and emigration**
        International law
        Suffrage
RT   **Aliens**
        Americanization
        Citizenship
Nature   508
  Use for general and theoretical materials on
the natural world. Materials on the study of
animals and plants as an elementary school
subject are entered under **Nature study.** Ma-
terials on the unsystematic study of zoology,
botany, mineralogy, etc., the collecting of
specimens, and the description of nature in a
particular place are entered under **Natural
history.**
RT   **Natural history**
        Nature study
Nature conservation   333.7
UF   Conservation of nature
        Nature protection
        Preservation of natural scenery
        Protection of natural scenery
BT   **Conservation of natural re-
          sources**
NT   **Endangered species**
        Landscape protection
        Natural monuments
        Plant conservation
        Wildlife conservation
Nature craft   745.5
  Use for materials on crafts using objects
found in nature, such as leaves, shells, etc.
UF   Naturecraft
BT   **Handicraft**
Nature, Effect of man on
USE   **Human influence on nature**
Nature in literature   809
BT   **Literature**
NT   **Animals in literature**

BT = Broader Term   NT = Narrower Term   RT = Related Term   SA = See Also   UF = Used For

Nature in literature—*Continued*
    Birds in literature
    Nature poetry
Nature in poetry
  USE   **Nature poetry**
Nature in the bible
  USE   **Bible—Natural history**
Nature photography   778.9
  UF   Photography of nature
  SA   photography of particular sub-
       jects in nature, e.g. **Photogra-
       phy of birds;** to be added as
       needed
  BT   **Natural history**
       Photography
  NT   **Photography of animals**
       Photography of birds
       Photography of fishes
       Photography of plants
  RT   **Outdoor photography**
Nature—Poetry
  USE   **Nature poetry**
Nature poetry   809.1; 811, etc.
    May be used for individual works or collec-
    tions of nature poetry and for materials about
    the theme of nature in poetry.
  UF   Nature in poetry *[Former head-
       ing]*
       Nature—Poetry
  BT   **Nature in literature**
       Poetry
Nature protection
  USE   **Nature conservation**
Nature study   372.3; 508.07
    Use for materials on the study of animals
    and plants as an elementary school subject.
    Materials on the unsystematic study of zoolo-
    gy, botany, mineralogy, etc., the collecting of
    specimens, and the description of nature in a
    particular place are entered under **Natural
    history.** General and theoretical materials on
    the natural world are entered under **Nature.**
  BT   **Education**
       Science—Study and teaching
  RT   **Nature**
       Outdoor education
       Outdoor life
Nature study—United States
  USE   **Natural history—United States**
Naturecraft
  USE   **Nature craft**
Naturopathy   615.5
  UF   Natural therapy

  BT   **Alternative medicine**
       Therapeutics
  RT   **Chiropractic**
Nautical almanacs   528
  BT   **Almanacs**
       Navigation
Nautical astronomy   527
  UF   Astronomy, Nautical
  BT   **Astronomy**
  NT   **Latitude**
       Longitude
  RT   **Navigation**
       Time
Navaho Indians
  USE   **Navajo Indians**
Navaho language
  USE   **Navajo language**
Navajo Indians   970.004
  UF   Navaho Indians
  BT   **Indians of North America**
Navajo language   497
  UF   Navaho language
  BT   **Indians of North America—
       Languages**
Naval administration
  USE   **Naval art and science**
       and names of countries with the
       subhead *Navy,* e.g. **United
       States. Navy;** to be added as
       needed
Naval aeronautics
  USE   **Military aeronautics**
Naval air bases
  USE   **Air bases**
Naval airplanes
  USE   **Military airplanes**
Naval architecture   623.8
  UF   Architecture, Naval
       Marine architecture
  BT   **Architecture**
  NT   **Boatbuilding**
       Marine engineering
       Ships
       Steamboats
       Warships
  RT   **Shipbuilding**
Naval art and science   359
  UF   Fighting
       Naval administration
       Naval science

BT = Broader Term   NT = Narrower Term   RT = Related Term   SA = See Also   UF = Used For

Naval art and science—*Continued*
    Naval warfare
    Navy
  SA names of wars with the subdivision *Naval operations,* e.g. **World War, 1939-1945—Naval operations;** to be added as needed
  NT **Camouflage (Military science)**
       Marine engineering
       Navy yards and naval stations
       Privateering
       Sailors
       Sea power
       Shipbuilding
       Signals and signaling
       Submarine warfare
       Torpedoes
       Warships
  RT **Military art and science**
       Navies
       Navigation
       Strategy
       War

Naval art and science—Study and teaching
  USE **Naval education**

Naval bases
  USE **Navy yards and naval stations**

Naval battles   359.4; 904
  UF Naval warfare
  SA names of countries with the subdivision *Naval history;* names of wars with the subdivision *Naval operations,* e.g. **World War, 1939-1945—Naval operations;** and names of specific naval battles, to be added as needed
  BT **Sea power**
  NT **United States—Naval history**
  RT **Battles**
       Naval history

Naval biography
  USE names of navies with the subdivision *Biography,* e.g. **United States. Navy—Biography;** to be added as needed

Naval education   359.007
  UF Education, Naval

Naval art and science—Study and teaching
    Naval schools
  BT **Education**

Naval engineering
  USE **Marine engineering**

Naval history   359.009
  UF History, Naval
       Wars
  SA names of countries with the subhead *Navy* or the subdivision *Naval history,* to be added as needed
  BT **History**
  NT **Pirates**
       Privateering
       United States—Naval history
       United States. Navy
  RT **Military history**
       Naval battles
       Sea power

Naval law
  USE **Maritime law**

Naval offenses
  USE **Military offenses**

Naval pensions
  USE **Military pensions**

Naval personnel
  USE **Sailors**

Naval power
  USE **Sea power**

Naval schools
  USE **Naval education**

Naval science
  USE **Naval art and science**

Naval shipyards
  USE **Navy yards and naval stations**

Naval signaling
  USE **Signals and signaling**

Naval strategy
  USE **Strategy**

Naval uniforms
  USE **Military uniforms**

Naval warfare
  USE **Naval art and science**
       Naval battles
       Submarine warfare

Navies   359.3
  UF Military power
       Navy

BT = Broader Term   NT = Narrower Term   RT = Related Term   SA = See Also   UF = Used For

Navies—*Continued*
         Sea life
    SA   names of countries with the sub-
         head *Navy*, e.g. **United
         States. Navy;** to be added as
         needed
    BT   **Armed forces**
         Military personnel
    NT   **Admirals**
         Sailors
         United States. Navy
    RT   **Naval art and science**
         Sea power
         Warships
Navigation   623.89; 629.04
    UF   Pilots and pilotage *[Former
         heading]*
         Seamanship
    BT   **Locomotion**
    NT   **Compass**
         Harbors
         Inland navigation
         Knots and splices
         Lighthouses
         Loran
         Nautical almanacs
         Ocean currents
         Orienteering
         Pilot guides
         Radar
         Shipwrecks
         Signals and signaling
         Steam navigation
         Tides
         Winds
    RT   **Direction sense**
         Nautical astronomy
         Naval art and science
         Sailing
         Ship pilots
Navigation, Aerial
    USE **Navigation (Aeronautics)**
Navigation (Aeronautics)   629.132
    UF   Aerial navigation
         Aeronautics—Navigation
         Air navigation
         Navigation, Aerial
    BT   **Aeronautics**
    NT   **Airplanes—Piloting**
         Radio in aeronautics

Navigation (Astronautics)   629.45
    UF   Astronavigation
         Space navigation
    BT   **Astrodynamics**
         Astronautics
    NT   **Astronautical instruments**
         Radio in astronautics
         Space vehicles—Piloting
    RT   **Space flight**
Navigation, Inland
    USE **Inland navigation**
Navigation—Law and legislation
    USE **Maritime law**
Navigators
    USE **Exploration**
         Explorers
         Sailors
Navy
    USE **Naval art and science**
         Navies
         Sea power
         and names of countries with the
         subhead *Navy,* e.g. **United
         States. Navy;** to be added as
         needed
Navy Sealab project
    USE **Sealab project**
Navy yards and naval stations   359.7
    UF   Naval bases
         Naval shipyards
    BT   **Naval art and science**
Nazism
    USE **National socialism**
Near-death experiences   133.9; 155.9
         Use for materials on the paranormal experi-
         ences of those who have survived near death
         or apparent death.
    UF   Death, Apparent
         Experiences, Near-death
    BT   **Death**
    RT   **Parapsychology**
Near East
    USE **Middle East**
Neatness
    USE **Cleanliness**
Nebulae, Extragalactic
    USE **Galaxies**
Necrologies
    USE **Obituaries**
Necromancy
    USE **Divination**

BT = Broader Term   NT = Narrower Term   RT = Related Term   SA = See Also   UF = Used For

Necromancy—*Continued*
>> **Magic**
>> **Witchcraft**
Needlepoint 746.44
>> UF Canvas embroidery
>> BT **Embroidery**
>> **Needlework**
Needlework 746.4
>> SA types of needlework, to be added as needed
>> BT **Decoration and ornament**
>> **Decorative arts**
>> NT **Crocheting**
>> **Embroidery**
>> **Knitting**
>> **Lace and lace making**
>> **Needlepoint**
>> **Samplers**
>> **Tapestry**
>> RT **Dressmaking**
>> **Sewing**
Negotiable instruments 332.7
>> UF Bills and notes
>> Bills of credit
>> Commercial paper
>> Instruments, Negotiable
>> Letters of credit
>> BT **Banks and banking**
>> **Commercial law**
>> **Contracts**
>> **Credit**
>> NT **Bonds**
Negotiation 158; 302.3
>> UF Bargaining
>> Discussion
>> BT **Applied psychology**
>> NT **Collective bargaining**
>> **Hostage negotiation**
>> **Industrial arbitration**
Negritude
>> USE **Blacks—Race identity**
Negroes
>> USE **African Americans**
>> **Blacks**
Neighborhood
>> USE **Community life**
Neighborhood centers
>> USE **Community centers**
>> **Social settlements**

Neighborhood development
>> USE **Community development**
Neighborhood schools
>> USE **Public schools**
Neo-fascism
>> USE **Fascism**
>> **Neo-Nazis**
Neo-Greek literature
>> USE **Modern Greek literature**
Neo-impressionism (Art)
>> USE **Impressionism (Art)**
Neo-Latin languages
>> USE **Romance languages**
Neo-Nazis 320.5
>> Use for materials on political groups whose social beliefs or political agendas are reminiscent of those of Hitler's Nazis.
>> UF Neo-fascism
>> Neo-nazism
>> BT **Fascism**
>> RT **National socialism**
Neo-nazism
>> USE **Neo-Nazis**
Neolithic period
>> USE **Stone Age**
Neon tubes 621.32
>> BT **Electric signs**
Nero, Emperor of Rome, 37-68 92; B
>> BT **Emperors—Rome**
Nerves 611; 612.8
>> BT **Nervous system**
Nerves—Diseases
>> USE **Nervous system—Diseases**
Nervous breakdown
>> USE **Mental illness**
>> **Neurasthenia**
Nervous exhaustion
>> USE **Neurasthenia**
Nervous prostration
>> USE **Neurasthenia**
Nervous system 611; 612.8
>> UF Neurology
>> BT **Anatomy**
>> **Physiology**
>> NT **Abnormal psychology**
>> **Brain**
>> **Nerves**
>> **Psychophysiology**
Nervous system—Diseases 616.8
>> UF Nerves—Diseases
>> Neuropathology

Nervous system—Diseases—*Continued*
   BT   Diseases
   NT   Epilepsy
          Neurasthenia
Netherlands   949.2
    May be subdivided like United States except for *History.*
   UF   Holland
Netherlands—History   949.2
Netherlands—History—1940-1945, German occupation   949.207
   UF   German occupation of Netherlands, 1940-1945
   BT   Military occupation
          World War, 1939-1945—Occupied territories
Network theory
   USE   System analysis
Networks (Associations, institutions, etc.)
   USE   Associations
Networks, Computer
   USE   Computer networks
Networks, Information
   USE   Information networks
Networks, Library
   USE   Library information networks
Neurasthenia   616.85
   UF   Nervous breakdown
          Nervous exhaustion
          Nervous prostration
   BT   Nervous system—Diseases
Neurology
   USE   Nervous system
Neuropathology
   USE   Nervous system—Diseases
Neuroses   616.85
   BT   Abnormal psychology
   NT   Anxiety
          Depression (Psychology)
          Phobias
          Post-traumatic stress disorder
          Psychosomatic medicine
Neurotic children
   USE   Emotionally disturbed children
Neutrality (May subdiv. geog.)   327.1; 341.6
   UF   Nonalignment
   BT   International law
          International relations
          International security
   RT   Intervention (International law)

Neutrality—United States   327.73
   UF   United States—Neutrality *[Former heading]*
   RT   United States—Foreign relations
Neutron bomb   623.4
   UF   Neutron bombs *[Former heading]*
   BT   Bombs
          Neutron weapons
Neutron bombs
   USE   Neutron bomb
Neutron weapons   623.4
   UF   Enhanced radiation weapons
          Weapons, Enhanced radiation
          Weapons, Neutron
   BT   Nuclear weapons
   NT   Neutron bomb
Neutrons   539.7
   BT   Atoms
          Particles (Nuclear physics)
New Age movement   131; 133; 299
    Use for materials on any of various post-1970 cults and organizations that incorporate Eastern or Native American religions, occult beliefs and practices, mysticism, or meditation techniques in an attempt to enhance consciousness and develop human potential.
   UF   Aquarian Age movement
   BT   Cults
          Occultism
          Social movements
   NT   Wicca
   RT   Goddess religion
New birth (Theology)
   USE   Regeneration (Christianity)
New business enterprises   338.7
   UF   Business enterprises, New
          How to start a business
          Starting a business
   BT   Business enterprises
New England   974
   BT   United States
New France—History
   USE   Canada—History—0-1763 (New France)
           Mississippi River Valley—History
New nations
   USE   New states
New Negro Movement
   USE   Harlem Renaissance

BT = Broader Term   NT = Narrower Term   RT = Related Term   SA = See Also   UF = Used For

New states 321
  UF New nations
      States, New [Former heading]
  BT Developing countries
New Testament
  USE Bible. N.T.
New words 417; 427, etc.
  UF Coinage of words
      Words, New [Former heading]
  BT Vocabulary
New York (N.Y.)—Streets
  USE Streets—New York (N.Y.)
Newbery Award
  USE Newbery Medal
Newbery Medal 028.5
  UF Newbery Award
      Newbery Medal books [Former
        heading]
      Newbery Prize books
  BT Children's literature
      Literary prizes
Newbery Medal books
  USE Newbery Medal
Newbery Prize books
  USE Newbery Medal
News agencies 070.4
  UF News services
      Wire agencies
  BT Press
News editing
  USE Journalism—Editing
News photography
  USE Photojournalism
News services
  USE News agencies
Newspaper advertising 659.13
    Use for materials on advertising in newspa-
    pers. Materials on the advertising of newspa-
    pers are entered under Advertising—Newspa-
    pers.
  UF Advertising, Newspaper
  BT Advertising
      Newspapers
Newspaper clippings
  USE Clippings (Books, newspapers,
        etc.)
Newspaper work
  USE Reporters and reporting
Newspapers 070
    Use for materials limited to the history, or-
    ganization, and management of newspapers.

Materials on writing for the periodical press,
on the editing of such writing, and on journal-
ism as an occupation, are entered under Jour-
nalism.
  SA newspapers of particular coun-
        tries, e.g. American newspa-
        pers; English newspapers;
        etc.; and names of individual
        newspapers, to be added as
        needed
  BT Mass media
      Serial publications
  NT American newspapers
      Clippings (Books, newspapers,
        etc.)
      English newspapers
      Newspaper advertising
      Reporters and reporting
  RT Journalism
      Periodicals
      Press
Newspapers—Advertising
  USE Advertising—Newspapers
Newspapers—Editing
  USE Journalism—Editing
Newspapers—Indexes 070.1
Nicene Creed 238
  BT Creeds
Nicknames 929.4
  UF Epithets
      Sobriquets
      Soubriquets
  BT Personal names
Nicotine habit
  USE Tobacco habit
Night 529
  BT Chronology
      Time
  NT Bedtime
  RT Day
Night schools
  USE Evening and continuation
        schools
Nike rocket 623.4
  BT Guided missiles
Nineteenth century 909.81
    Use for general materials covering progress
    and development during this period in one or
    in several countries.
  UF 1800-1899 (19th century)
  BT Modern history—1800-1899
      (19th century)

Nitrates   553.6
   BT   Fertilizers
Nitrogen   546; 665
   BT   Gases
NMR imaging
   USE   Magnetic resonance imaging
No fault automobile insurance
   USE   Automobile insurance
Nobel prizes
   USE   Nobel Prizes
Nobel Prizes   001.4; 807.9
   UF   Nobel prizes *[Former heading]*
   BT   Awards
Nobility   305.5; 929.7
   UF   Baronage
         Peerage
   BT   Upper class
   NT   Knights and knighthood
   RT   Aristocracy
         Heraldry
Noise   363.74
   SA   subjects with the subdivision
         Noise, to be added as needed
   BT   Public health
         Sound
   NT   Airplanes—Noise
Noise pollution   363.74
   SA   subjects with the subdivision
         Noise, to be added as needed
   BT   Pollution
   NT   Airplanes—Noise
Nomadic peoples
   USE   Nomads
Nomads (May subdiv. geog.)   304.2;
         306.08
   UF   Nomadic peoples
         Pastoral peoples
   BT   Primitive societies
Nomenclature
   USE   Names
         and scientific and technical sub-
         jects with the subdivision *Ter-*
         minology, e.g. **Botany—Ter-**
         minology; to be added as
         needed
Nomination of presidents
   USE   Presidents—United States—
         Nomination
Non-professional theater
   USE   Amateur theater

Non-proliferation of nuclear weapons
   USE   Arms control
Non-promotion (School)
   USE   Promotion (School)
Non-victim crimes
   USE   Crimes without victims
Non-wage payments
   USE   Nonwage payments
Nonalignment
   USE   Neutrality
Nonbook materials
   USE   Audiovisual materials
Noncitizens
   USE   Aliens
Nonconformity
   USE   Conformity
         Counter culture
         Dissent
Nondenominational churches
   USE   Community churches
Nonfamily households
   USE   Shared housing
Nonfiction films
   USE   Documentary films
Nonformal colleges and universities
   USE   Free universities
Nonformal schools
   USE   Experimental schools
Nonfossil fuels
   USE   Synthetic fuels
Nongraded schools   371.2
   UF   Multi-age grouping
         Schools, Nongraded
         Schools, Ungraded
         Ungraded schools
   BT   Ability grouping in education
         Education—Experimental
         methods
Noninstitutional churches   289.9
   UF   Avant-garde churches
         Churches, Avant-garde
         Churches, Noninstitutional
   BT   Christian sects
Nonlinguistic communication
   USE   Nonverbal communication
Nonliterate folk society
   USE   Primitive societies
Nonliterate man
   USE   Primitive societies

BT = Broader Term   NT = Narrower Term   RT = Related Term   SA = See Also   UF = Used For

Nonnationals
  USE   Aliens
Nonnutritive sweeteners
  USE   Sugar substitutes
Nonobjective art
  USE   Abstract art
Nonprescription drugs   615
  UF   Drugs, Nonprescription *[Former heading]*
        Over-the-counter drugs
        Patent medicines
  BT   **Drugs**
Nonprint materials
  USE   Audiovisual materials
Nonprofit corporations
  USE   Nonprofit organizations
Nonprofit organizations   346; 658
  UF   Corporations, Nonprofit
        Nonprofit corporations
        Nonprofit sector
        Nonprofits
        Not-for-profit organizations
        Organizations, Nonprofit
  BT   **Associations**
Nonprofit sector
  USE   Nonprofit organizations
Nonprofitable drugs
  USE   Orphan drugs
Nonprofits
  USE   Nonprofit organizations
Nonpublic schools
  USE   Church schools
        Private schools
Nonsense verses   808.81; 811, etc.; 811.008, etc.
    May be used for individual works, collections, or materials about nonsense verse.
  UF   Rhymes
  BT   **Children's poetry**
        Humorous poetry
        Wit and humor
  NT   **Tongue twisters**
  RT   **Limericks**
Nonsupport
  USE   Desertion and nonsupport
Nonverbal communication   153.6; 302.2
  UF   Body language *[Former heading]*
        Nonlinguistic communication
  BT   **Communication**
  NT   **Hugging**

        Personal space
  RT   Deaf—Means of communication
Nonvictim crimes
  USE   Crimes without victims
Nonviolence   179; 303.6
  NT   **Hunger strikes**
  RT   **Pacifism**
        Passive resistance
Nonviolent noncooperation
  USE   Passive resistance
Nonwage payments   331.25
  UF   Employee benefits
        Fringe benefits
        Non-wage payments
  BT   **Wages**
Nonword stories
  USE   Stories without words
Nordic peoples
  USE   Teutonic peoples
Normal schools
  USE   Teachers colleges
Normandy (France), Attack on, 1944 940.54
  UF   D Day
  BT   **World War, 1939-1945—Campaigns**
Normans   941.02
  BT   **Great Britain—History—1066-1154, Norman period**
  RT   **Vikings**
Norse languages
  USE   Old Norse language
        Scandinavian languages
Norse legends   398.2
  UF   Legends, Norse *[Former heading]*
  BT   **Legends**
Norse literature
  USE   Old Norse literature
        Scandinavian literature
Norsemen
  USE   Vikings
North Africa   961
    Use for materials dealing collectively with Morocco, Algeria, Tunisia, and Libya.
  UF   Africa, North *[Former heading]*
        Barbary States
        Maghreb
  BT   **Africa**

BT = Broader Term   NT = Narrower Term   RT = Related Term   SA = See Also   UF = Used For

505

North America   970
  BT   America
  NT   Central America
        Northwest Coast of North
          America
        Pacific Northwest
North American Indians
  USE   Indians of North America
North Atlantic Treaty Organization
    341.7
  UF   N.A.T.O.
        NATO
  BT   International organization
North Central States
  USE   Middle West
North Korea
  USE   Korea (North)
North Pole   910.9163; 998
  BT   Polar regions
  RT   Arctic regions
Northeast Africa   960
    Use for materials dealing collectively with
    Sudan, Ethiopia, Eritrea, Somalia, and Djibou-
    ti.
  UF   Africa, Northeast [Former head-
          ing]
  BT   Africa
Northeast Passage   998
  BT   Arctic regions
        Exploration
        Voyages and travels
Northern lights
  USE   Auroras
Northmen
  USE   Vikings
Northwest Africa   964
    Use for materials dealing collectively with
    the area extending eastward from Morocco,
    Western Sahara, and Mauritania to include
    Libya and Chad. Northwest Africa includes
    the political entities of Morocco, Western Sa-
    hara, Mauritania, Algeria, Mali, Tunisia, Lib-
    ya, Niger, and Chad.
  UF   Africa, Northwest [Former head-
          ing]
  BT   Africa
Northwest coast of North America
  USE   Northwest Coast of North
          America
Northwest Coast of North America
    979.5
  UF   Northwest coast of North Ameri-
          ca [Former heading]

Northwest, Pacific coast
Pacific Northwest coast
  BT   North America
Northwest, Old
  USE   Old Northwest
Northwest, Pacific
  USE   Pacific Northwest
Northwest, Pacific coast
  USE   Northwest Coast of North
          America
Northwest Passage   971.9
  BT   America—Exploration
        Arctic regions
Northwest Territory
  USE   Old Northwest
Norwegian language   439.8
    May be subdivided like English language.
  BT   Language and languages
        Scandinavian languages
  NT   Danish language
Norwegian language—0-1350
  USE   Old Norse language
Norwegian literature   839.82
    May use same subdivisions and names of
    literary forms as for English literature.
  BT   Literature
        Scandinavian literature
Nose   611; 612.2
  BT   Face
        Head
  RT   Smell
Not-for-profit organizations
  USE   Nonprofit organizations
Notation, Mathematical
  USE   Mathematical notation
Notation, Music
  USE   Musical notation
Novelists   809.3; 920
  SA   novelists of particular countries,
          e.g. American novelists; and
          names of individual novelists,
          to be added as needed
  BT   Authors
  NT   American novelists
Novelists, American
  USE   American novelists
Novels
  USE   Fiction
Novels in letters
  USE   Epistolary fiction

BT = Broader Term   NT = Narrower Term   RT = Related Term   SA = See Also   UF = Used For

Novels—Plots
 USE   Plots (Drama, fiction, etc.)
Nuclear bomb shelters
 USE   Air raid shelters
Nuclear energy   333.792; 539.7
 UF   Atomic energy
        Atomic power
        Nuclear power
 BT   Nuclear physics
 NT   Nuclear engineering
        Nuclear industry
        Nuclear propulsion
        Nuclear reactors
 RT   Nuclear power plants
Nuclear engineering   621.48
 BT   Engineering
        Nuclear energy
        Nuclear physics
 NT   Nuclear reactors
        Radioactive waste disposal
        Radioisotopes
Nuclear freeze movement
 USE   Antinuclear movement
Nuclear industry   333.792
 UF   Atomic industry
 BT   Nuclear energy
Nuclear magnetic resonance imaging
 USE   Magnetic resonance imaging
Nuclear medicine   616.07
 UF   Atomic medicine
        Medicine, Atomic
        Medicine, Nuclear
 BT   Medicine
 RT   Radiation—Physiological effect
Nuclear medicine—Practice   616.07
 BT   Medical practice
Nuclear non-proliferation
 USE   Arms control
Nuclear particles
 USE   Particles (Nuclear physics)
Nuclear physics   539.7
 UF   Atomic nuclei
        Physics, Nuclear
 BT   Physics
 NT   Cosmic rays
        Cyclotron
        Nuclear energy
        Nuclear engineering
        Nuclear reactors
        Particles (Nuclear physics)

 Radiobiology
 Transmutation (Chemistry)
 RT   Physical chemistry
        Radioactivity
Nuclear pollution
 USE   Radioactive pollution
Nuclear power
 USE   Nuclear energy
Nuclear power plants   621.48
 UF   Atomic power plants
        Power plants, Atomic
 BT   Power plants
 RT   Nuclear energy
Nuclear power plants—Accidents
        363.17
Nuclear power plants—Environmental
        aspects   333.792; 621.48
 BT   Environment
        Environmental health
 NT   Radioactive waste disposal
 RT   Antinuclear movement
Nuclear power plants—Fires and fire
        prevention   363.37; 628.9
 BT   Fire prevention
        Fires
Nuclear power plants—Security mea-
        sures   621.48
Nuclear propulsion   621.48
 UF   Atomic powered vehicles
 SA   specific applications of nuclear
        propulsion, e.g. Nuclear sub-
        marines; to be added as
        needed
 BT   Nuclear energy
 NT   Nuclear submarines
 RT   Nuclear reactors
Nuclear reactors   621.48
 UF   Atomic piles
        Breeder reactors
        Fast breeder reactors
        Reactors (Nuclear physics)
 BT   Nuclear energy
        Nuclear engineering
        Nuclear physics
 RT   Nuclear propulsion
Nuclear submarines   623.8
 UF   Atomic submarines
        Submarines, Nuclear
 BT   Nuclear propulsion
        Submarines

BT = Broader Term   NT = Narrower Term   RT = Related Term   SA = See Also   UF = Used For

Nuclear test ban
USE **Arms control**
Nuclear warfare   355.02
UF Atomic warfare
BT **War**
NT **Atomic bomb**
Hydrogen bomb
RT **Nuclear weapons**
Nuclear waste disposal
USE **Radioactive waste disposal**
Nuclear weapons   355.8; 623.4
UF Atomic weapons
Weapons, Atomic
Weapons, Nuclear
SA types of nuclear weapons, e.g.
Atomic bomb; to be added
as needed
BT **Military weapons**
Ordnance
NT **Antinuclear movement**
Atomic bomb
Ballistic missiles
Hydrogen bomb
Neutron weapons
RT **Nuclear warfare**
Nucleic acids   547; 572.8
UF Polynucleotides
BT **Biochemistry**
NT **DNA**
RNA
Nucleons
USE **Particles (Nuclear physics)**
Nude in art   704.9; 743.4
UF Human anatomy in art
Human figure in art
BT **Art**
NT **Artistic anatomy**
Number concept   119; 155.4; 372.7
Use for materials on the apperception and
conceptualization of numbers. Materials on
numbers, numbering, and systems of numera-
tion are entered under **Numbers**. Materials on
counting, including counting books, are en-
tered under **Counting**.
BT **Apperception**
Psychology
RT **Numbers**
Number games   793.7
BT **Arithmetic—Study and teach-**
ing
Counting
Mathematical recreations

Number patterns
USE **Patterns (Mathematics)**
Number readiness
USE **Mathematical readiness**
Number symbolism
USE **Numerology**
Symbolism of numbers
Number systems
USE **Numbers**
Number theory   512
Use for materials on that branch of mathe-
matics that involves the study of integers and
their relation to one another.
UF Numbers, Theory of
Theory of numbers
BT **Algebra**
Mathematics
Set theory
NT **Group theory**
RT **Numbers**
Numbers   119; 513
Use for materials on numbers, numbering,
and systems of numeration. Materials on the
conceptualization of numbers are entered un-
der **Number concept**. Materials on counting,
including counting books, are entered under
Counting. Materials on the graphic represen-
tation of numbers are entered under **Numer-**
als.
UF Number systems
Numeration *[Former heading]*
SA names of individual numbers,
e.g. **Three (The number)**;
and systems of numeration,
e.g. **Decimal system**; to be
added an needed
NT **Binary system (Mathematics)**
Decimal system
Three (The number)
RT **Arithmetic**
Counting
Number concept
Number theory
Numerals
Symbolism of numbers
Numbers, Theory of
USE **Number theory**
Numeral formation
USE **Writing of numerals**
Numeral writing
USE **Writing of numerals**

Numerals 513

Use for materials on the graphic representation of numbers.

SA   types of numerals, e.g. **Roman numerals;** to be added as needed

NT   **Roman numerals**

       Writing of numerals

RT   **Numbers**

Numerals, Writing of

USE   **Writing of numerals**

Numeration

USE   **Numbers**

Numerical analysis 515

BT   **Mathematical analysis**

NT   **Approximate computation**

Numerical sequences

USE   **Sequences (Mathematics)**

Numerology 133.3

Use for materials on the occult significance of numbers. General materials on the symbolism of numbers, as in philosophy, religion, or literature, are entered under **Symbolism of numbers.**

UF   Number symbolism

       Sacred numbers

       Symbolic numbers

BT   **Occultism**

       Symbolism of numbers

Numismatics 737

Use for materials on coins, paper money, medals, and tokens considered as works of art, as historical specimens, or as aids to the study of history, archeology, etc.

BT   **Ancient history**

       Archeology

       History

NT   **Seals (Numismatics)**

RT   **Coins—Collectors and collecting**

       Medals

Nunneries

USE   **Convents**

Nuns 255; 271

UF   Sisters (Religious)

BT   **Women**

NT   **Ex-nuns**

RT   **Monasticism and religious orders for women**

Nurse clinicians

USE   **Nurse practitioners**

Nurse practitioners 610.73092; 920

UF   Nurse clinicians

BT   **Allied health personnel**

       Nurses

Nurse widwives

USE   **Midwives**

Nurseries, Day

USE   **Day care centers**

Nurseries (Horticulture) 631.5; 635

BT   **Fruit culture**

       Gardening

NT   **Plant propagation**

Nursery rhymes 398.8

May be used for collections of nursery rhymes or for materials about nursery rhymes.

UF   Poetry for children

       Rhymes

BT   **Children's poetry**

       Children's songs

       Folklore

Nursery schools 372.21

BT   **Elementary education**

       Schools

RT   **Day care centers**

       Kindergarten

       Preschool education

Nurses 610.73092; 920

UF   District nurses

       Trained nurses

SA   types of nurses, to be added as needed

NT   **Midwives**

       Nurse practitioners

       Practical nurses

       School nurses

RT   **Nursing**

Nursing 610.73; 649.8

SA   types of nursing, e.g. **Home nursing;** and diseases and medical procedures with the subdivision *Nursing,* to be added as needed

BT   **Medicine**

       Therapeutics

NT   **Cancer—Nursing**

       Cooking for the sick

       First aid

       Heart—Surgery—Nursing

       Home nursing

       Practical nursing

RT   **Nurses**

       Sick

BT = Broader Term   NT = Narrower Term   RT = Related Term   SA = See Also   UF = Used For

Nursing homes   362.1
   BT   Elderly—Care
          Hospitals
          Institutional care
          Long-term care facilities
Nursing (Infant feeding)
   USE   Breast feeding
Nutrition   613.2
   UF   Meal planning
   SA   subjects and classes of persons
          with the subdivision *Nutrition,*
          e.g. **Children—Nutrition;** to
          be added as needed
   BT   Health self-care
          Physiology
          Therapeutics
   NT   Astronauts—Nutrition
          Children—Nutrition
          Eating customs
          Infants—Nutrition
          Malnutrition
          Plants—Nutrition
          Vitamins
   RT   Diet
          Digestion
          Food
          Metabolism
Nuts   581.4; 634
    Use the names of specific kinds of nuts, expressed in the singular form, for materials on the nut or the tree or both.
   SA   types of nuts, e.g. **Pecan;** to be
          added as needed, in the singular form
   BT   Food
          Seeds
          Trees
   NT   Pecan
Nylon   677
   BT   Synthetic fabrics
Oak   583
   UF   Oaks
   BT   Trees
          Wood
Oaks
   USE   Oak
Oats   633.1
   BT   Feeds
Obedience   179
   UF   Disobedience
   BT   Virtue

Obelisks   721
   BT   Archeology
          Architecture
          Monuments
          Pyramids
Obesity   613.2; 616.3
   UF   Corpulence
          Fatness
          Overweight
   BT   Body weight
Obituaries (May subdiv. geog.)   920
   UF   Death notices
          Necrologies
   SA   ethnic groups and classes of persons with the subdivision *Obituaries,* to be added as needed
   BT   Biography
Objective tests
   USE   Examinations
Objets d'art
   USE   Art objects
Obscene materials
   USE   Obscenity (Law)
          Pornography
Obscenity (Law)   345
   UF   Obscene materials
   BT   Criminal law
          Erotica
          Pornography
Observatories, Astronomical
   USE   Astronomical observatories
Observatories, Meteorological
   USE   Meteorological observatories
Obstetrics
   USE   Childbirth
Occidental civilization
   USE   Western civilization
Occult fiction   808.83; 813, etc.
    May be used for individual works, collections, or materials about fiction dealing with supernatural powers.
   BT   Fiction
   NT   Ghost stories
          Gothic novels
   RT   Fantasy fiction
Occult sciences
   USE   Occultism
Occult, The
   USE   Occultism

BT = Broader Term   NT = Narrower Term   RT = Related Term   SA = See Also   UF = Used For

Occultism   133
  UF   Hermetic art and philosophy
       Occult sciences [Former head-
         ing]
       Occult, The
       Sorcery
  BT   Religions
       Supernatural
  NT   Alchemy
       Astrology
       Cabala
       Clairvoyance
       Divination
       Fortune telling
       Magic
       New Age movement
       Numerology
       Oracles
       Palmistry
       Prophecies
       Spiritualism
       Witchcraft
  RT   Demonology
       Parapsychology
       Superstition
Occupation, Military
  USE Military occupation
Occupational accidents
  USE Industrial accidents
Occupational crimes
  USE White collar crimes
Occupational diseases   616.9
  UF   Diseases, Industrial
       Diseases, Occupational
       Diseases of occupation
       Industrial diseases
       Occupations—Diseases
  SA   occupational groups with the
       subdivision Diseases, e.g.
       Miners—Diseases; types of
       industries with the subdivi-
       sions Employees—Diseases;
       e.g. Chemical industry—Em-
       ployees—Diseases; and names
       of occupational diseases, to be
       added as needed
  BT   Diseases
  NT   Chemical industry—Employ-
         ees—Diseases
       Lead poisoning

       Miners—Diseases
  RT   Hazardous occupations
       Occupational health and safety
Occupational forecasting
  USE Employment forecasting
Occupational guidance
  USE Vocational guidance
Occupational health and safety   363.11;
       658.3
  UF   Health, Industrial
       Hygiene, Industrial
       Industrial health
       Industrial safety
       Safety, Industrial
  BT   Environmental health
       Management
       Public health
  NT   Burn out (Psychology)
  RT   Hazardous occupations
       Occupational diseases
       Occupational health services
Occupational health services   362.1;
       613.6; 658.3
       Use for materials on health services for em-
       ployees, usually provided at the place of
       work.
  UF   Employee health services
  BT   Medical care
  RT   Occupational health and safety
Occupational injuries
  USE Industrial accidents
Occupational literacy
  USE Functional literacy
Occupational retraining   331.25
  UF   Job retraining
       Retraining, Occupational
  BT   Employees—Training
       Labor supply
       Manpower policy
       Occupational training
       Technical education
       Unemployed
       Vocational education
Occupational stress
  USE Job stress
Occupational therapy   615.8
  BT   Mental health
       Physical therapy
       Physically handicapped—Reha-
         bilitation
       Therapeutics

BT = Broader Term   NT = Narrower Term   RT = Related Term   SA = See Also   UF = Used For

Occupational therapy—*Continued*
RT   **Handicraft**
Occupational training   331.25; 374
   Use for materials on teaching people a skill after formal education. Materials on teaching a skill during the educational process are entered under **Vocational education.** Materials discussing on-the-job training are entered under **Employees—Training.** Materials on retraining are entered under **Occupational retraining.**
UF   Job training
       Training, Occupational
       Training, Vocational
       Vocational training
BT   **Manpower policy**
       Technical education
       Vocational education
NT   **Employees—Training**
       Occupational retraining
Occupations (May subdiv. geog.)   **331.7**
   Use for descriptions and lists of occupations.
UF   Careers
       Jobs
       Trades
       Vocations
SA   fields of knowledge, professions, industries, and trades with the subdivision *Vocational guidance,* to be added as needed
BT   **Business**
       Labor
NT   **Hazardous occupations**
       Job analysis
       Paraprofessionals
       Professions
RT   **Employment**
       Vocational guidance
       Work
Occupations—Chicago (Ill.)   331.7
UF   Chicago (Ill.)—Occupations
       [Former heading]
Occupations, Dangerous
USE   **Hazardous occupations**
Occupations—Diseases
USE   **Occupational diseases**
Occupations—Ohio   331.7
UF   Ohio—Occupations *[Former heading]*
Occupations—United States   331.7
UF   United States—Occupations
       [Former heading]

Occupied territory
USE   **Military occupation**
Ocean   551.46
UF   Oceans
       Sea
SA   names of oceans and seas, to be added as needed
BT   **Earth**
       Physical geography
       Water
NT   **Atlantic Ocean**
       Icebergs
       Ocean bottom
       Ocean currents
       Ocean waves
       Oceanography
       Tides
RT   **Seashore**
Ocean bottom   551.46
UF   Ocean floor
       Sea bed
BT   **Ocean**
       Submarine geology
NT   **Marine mineral resources**
Ocean cables
USE   **Submarine cables**
Ocean currents   551.47
UF   Currents, Ocean
BT   **Navigation**
       Ocean
Ocean—Economic aspects
USE   **Marine resources**
       Shipping
Ocean energy resources   333.91
UF   Energy resources, Ocean
BT   **Energy resources**
       Marine resources
       Ocean engineering
NT   **Geothermal resources**
RT   **Marine mineral resources**
Ocean engineering   627
   Use for materials on engineering beneath the surface of the ocean.
UF   Deep sea engineering
       Submarine engineering
       Undersea engineering
BT   **Engineering**
       Marine resources
       Oceanography
NT   **Drilling platforms**
       Marine mineral resources

BT = Broader Term   NT = Narrower Term   RT = Related Term   SA = See Also   UF = Used For

Ocean engineering—*Continued*
>> Ocean energy resources
>> Ocean mining
>> Offshore oil well drilling

Ocean farming
>> USE **Aquaculture**

Ocean floor
>> USE **Ocean bottom**

Ocean life
>> USE **Marine biology**

Ocean mineral resources
>> USE **Marine mineral resources**

Ocean mining   622
>> UF   Deep sea mining
>> Mining, Ocean
>> BT   Marine mineral resources
>> Mining engineering
>> Ocean engineering

Ocean pollution
>> USE **Marine pollution**

Ocean resources
>> USE **Marine resources**

Ocean routes
>> USE **Trade routes**

Ocean transportation
>> USE **Shipping**

Ocean travel   910.4
>> UF   Cruises
>> Sea travel
>> BT   Transportation
>> Travel
>> Voyages and travels
>> NT   Ships
>> Steamboats
>> Yachts and yachting

Ocean waves   551.47
>> UF   Breakers
>> Sea waves
>> Surf
>> Swell
>> Tidal waves
>> BT   Ocean
>> Waves
>> NT   Tsunamis

Oceanariums
>> USE **Marine aquariums**

Oceania   995
>> Use for comprehensive materials on the lands and area of the central and southern Pacific Ocean, including Micronesia, Melanesia,

and Polynesia. Comprehensive works on all the islands of the Pacific Ocean are entered under **Islands of the Pacific.**
>> UF   South Pacific region
>> South Sea Islands
>> South Seas
>> Southwest Pacific region
>> BT   **Islands of the Pacific**

Oceanographic research
>> USE **Oceanography—Research**

Oceanographic submersibles
>> USE **Submersibles**

Oceanography (May subdiv. geog. by ocean or area)   **551.46**
>> UF   Deep sea technology
>> Oceanology
>> Undersea technology
>> BT   **Earth**
>> **Earth sciences**
>> **Geology**
>> **Geophysics**
>> **Ocean**
>> NT   **Marine biology**
>> **Marine pollution**
>> **Marine resources**
>> **Ocean engineering**
>> **Submarine geology**
>> **Underwater exploration**

Oceanography—Atlantic Ocean   551.46

Oceanography—Computer programs   551.46
>> BT   **Computer software**

Oceanography—Research   551.46
>> UF   Oceanographic research
>> BT   **Research**
>> NT   **Bathyscaphe**
>> **Undersea research stations**

Oceanology
>> USE **Oceanography**

Oceans
>> USE **Ocean**

Oddities
>> USE **Curiosities and wonders**

Offenses against public safety   364.1
>> UF   Crimes against public safety
>> Public safety, Crimes against
>> SA   types of offenses, e.g. **Hijacking of airplanes;** to be added as needed
>> BT   **Criminal law**
>> NT   **Bombings**

BT = Broader Term   NT = Narrower Term   RT = Related Term   SA = See Also   UF = Used For

Offenses against public safety—*Continued*
    Hijacking of airplanes
    Riots
    Sabotage
Offenses against the person   **364.15**
    UF   Abuse of persons
           Assault, Criminal
           Crimes against the person
           Criminal assault
           Persons, Crimes against
    SA   types of offenses, to be added
           as needed
    BT   **Crime**
           Criminal law
    NT   **Homicide**
           Kidnapping
           Rape
Offenses, Military
    USE   **Military offenses**
Office buildings (May subdiv. geog.)
    725
    UF   Buildings, Office
    BT   **Buildings**
Office employees
    USE   **Office workers**
Office equipment and supplies   **651**
    UF   Business machines
           Office machines
           Office supplies
    SA   types of office equipment and
           supplies, to be added as need-
           ed
    BT   **Bookkeeping**
           Office management
    NT   **Calculators**
           Copying machines
           Keyboards (Electronics)
           Typewriters
Office machines
    USE   **Office equipment and supplies**
Office management   **651.3**
    UF   Office procedures
    BT   **Business**
           Factory management
           Industrial efficiency
           Management
    NT   **Files and filing**
           Office equipment and supplies
           Office practice
           Secretaries

           Word processing
    RT   **Personnel management**
Office practice   **651.3**
    UF   Secretarial practice
    BT   **Office management**
    NT   **Keyboarding (Electronics)**
           Shorthand
           Typewriting
           Word processing
    RT   **Office workers**
Office procedures
    USE   **Office management**
Office romance
    USE   **Sex in the workplace**
Office supplies
    USE   **Office equipment and supplies**
Office work—Training
    USE   **Business education**
Office workers   **331.7; 651.3**
    UF   Clerical employees
           Clerks
           Commercial employees
           Employees, Clerical
           Office employees *[Former head-
           ing]*
    BT   **Employees**
    RT   **Office practice**
Official misconduct
    USE   **Misconduct in office**
Official publications
    USE   **Government publications**
Officials and employees
    USE   **Civil service**
           and names of countries, states,
           cities, etc., and corporate bod-
           ies with the subdivision *Offi-
           cials and employees,* e.g.
           **United States—Officials and
           employees; Ohio—Officials
           and employees; Chicago
           (Ill.)—Officials and employ-
           ees; United Nations—Offi-
           cials and employees;** etc., to
           be added as needed
Offset printing   **686.2**
    UF   Lithoprinting
           Printing, Offset
    BT   **Lithography**
           Printing

BT = Broader Term   NT = Narrower Term   RT = Related Term   SA = See Also   UF = Used For

Offshore oil industry   338.2
   UF   Oil industry, Offshore
         Petroleum industry, Offshore
   BT   **Petroleum industry**
   NT   **Offshore oil well drilling**
Offshore oil well drilling   622
   UF   Deep sea drilling (Petroleum)
         Oil well drilling, Offshore
         Oil well drilling, Submarine
         [Former heading]
         Submarine oil well drilling
         Underwater drilling (Petroleum)
   BT   **Ocean engineering**
        Offshore oil industry
        Oil well drilling
   NT   **Drilling platforms**
Offshore structures
   USE   **Drilling platforms**
Offshore water pollution
   USE   **Marine pollution**
Ohio   977.1

   The subdivisions under **Ohio** may be used under the name of any state of the United States or province of Canada. The subdivisions under **United States** may be further consulted as a guide for formulating other headings as needed.

Ohio—African Americans
   USE   **African Americans—Ohio**
Ohio—Antiquities   977.1
   BT   **Antiquities**
Ohio—Bibliography   015.771; 016.9771
Ohio—Bio-bibliography   012
Ohio—Biography   920.0771
   BT   **Biography**
Ohio—Biography—Dictionaries
    920.0771
Ohio—Biography—Portraits   920.0771
Ohio—Boundaries   977.1
   BT   **Boundaries**
Ohio—Census   317.71
   BT   **Census**
Ohio—Church history   277.71
   UF   Church history—Ohio
         Ohio—Religious history
   BT   **Church history**
   RT   **Ohio—Religion**
Ohio—Civilization   977.1
   BT   **Civilization**
Ohio—Climate   551.69771
   BT   **Climate**

Ohio—Commerce   381
   BT   **Commerce**
Ohio—Constitution
   USE   **Constitutions—Ohio**
Ohio—Constitutional history
   USE   **Constitutional history—Ohio**
Ohio—Constitutional law
   USE   **Constitutional law—Ohio**
Ohio—Description   917.71
   UF   Ohio—Description and travel
         [Former heading]
         Ohio—Travel
Ohio—Description and travel
   USE   **Ohio—Description**
Ohio—Description—Guidebooks
   USE   **Ohio—Guidebooks**
Ohio—Description—Views
   USE   **Ohio—Pictorial works**
Ohio—Directories   917.710025

   Use for lists of names and addresses. Lists of names without addresses are entered under **Ohio—Registers.**

   BT   **Directories**
   RT   **Ohio—Registers**
Ohio—Economic conditions   330.9771
   BT   **Economic conditions**
Ohio—Economic policy   338.9771
   BT   **Economic policy**
Ohio—Employees
   USE   **Ohio—Officials and employees**
Ohio—Executive departments
   USE   **Executive departments—Ohio**
Ohio—Executive departments—Reorganization
   USE   **Administrative agencies—Reorganization—Ohio**
Ohio—Fiction   808.83; 813, etc.
Ohio—Folk songs
   USE   **Folk songs—Ohio**
Ohio—Gazetteers   917.71
   BT   **Gazetteers**
Ohio—Government employees
   USE   **Ohio—Officials and employees**
Ohio—Government publications
   USE   **Government publications—Ohio**
Ohio—Guidebooks   917.7104
   UF   Ohio—Description—Guidebooks
         [Former heading]
Ohio—Historic buildings
   USE   **Historic buildings—Ohio**

BT = Broader Term   **NT** = Narrower Term   **RT** = Related Term   **SA** = See Also   **UF** = Used For

Ohio—History   977.1
  NT   Constitutional history—Ohio
Ohio—History, Local
  USE   Ohio—Local history
Ohio—History—Societies   977.106
  BT   History—Societies
Ohio—History—Sources   977.1
  BT   History—Sources
Ohio—Industries
  USE   Industries—Ohio
Ohio—Intellectual life   977.1
  BT   Intellectual life
Ohio—Local history   977.1
  UF   Ohio—History, Local *[Former
         heading]*
  BT   Local history
Ohio—Manufactures
  USE   Industries—Ohio
Ohio—Maps   912.771
  BT   Maps
Ohio—Militia   355.3
  BT   Armed forces
Ohio—Moral conditions   977.1
  BT   Moral conditions
Ohio—Museums
  USE   Museums—Ohio
Ohio—Occupations
  USE   Occupations—Ohio
Ohio—Officials and employees   351.771
  UF   Ohio—Employees
         Ohio—Government employees
Ohio—Pictorial works   917.710022
  UF   Ohio—Description—Views *[For-
         mer heading]*
Ohio—Politics and government   977.1
  BT   State governments
Ohio—Population   304.609771
  BT   Population
Ohio—Public buildings
  USE   Public buildings—Ohio
Ohio—Public lands
  USE   Public lands—Ohio
Ohio—Public works
  USE   Public works—Ohio
Ohio—Race relations   305.8009771
  BT   Race relations
Ohio—Registers   917.710025
     Use for lists of names without addresses.
     Lists of names that include addresses are en-
     tered under **Ohio—Directories.**
  RT   Ohio—Directories

Ohio—Religion   277.71
  BT   Religion
  RT   Ohio—Church history
Ohio—Religious history
  USE   Ohio—Church history
Ohio—Rural conditions   307.7209771
  BT   Rural sociology
Ohio—Social conditions   977.1
  BT   Social conditions
Ohio—Social life and customs   977.1
  BT   Manners and customs
Ohio—Social policy   361.6; 977.1
  BT   Social policy
Ohio—Statistics   317.71
  BT   Statistics
Ohio—Travel
  USE   Ohio—Description
Oil
  USE   Oils and fats
         Petroleum
Oil burners   697
  BT   Heating
         Petroleum as fuel
Oil engines
  USE   Internal combustion engines
Oil fuel
  USE   Petroleum as fuel
Oil industry
  USE   Petroleum industry
Oil industry, Offshore
  USE   Offshore oil industry
Oil painting
  USE   Painting
Oil pollution of rivers, harbors, etc.
  USE   Oil pollution of water
Oil pollution of water   363.739; 628.1
  UF   Oil pollution of rivers, harbors,
         etc. *[Former heading]*
         Petroleum pollution of water
         Water—Oil pollution
  BT   Water pollution
  NT   Oil spills
  RT   Marine pollution
Oil spills   363.738
  BT   Oil pollution of water
Oil well drilling   622
  UF   Drilling, Oil well
         Petroleum—Well boring
         Well drilling, Oil
  BT   Petroleum industry

BT = Broader Term   NT = Narrower Term   RT = Related Term   SA = See Also   UF = Used For

Oil well drilling—*Continued*
   NT   **Offshore oil well drilling**
           Oil wells—Blowouts
   RT   **Oil wells**
Oil well drilling, Offshore
   USE **Offshore oil well drilling**
Oil well drilling, Submarine
   USE **Offshore oil well drilling**
Oil wells   622
   BT   **Petroleum industry**
   RT   **Oil well drilling**
Oil wells—Blowouts   622
   UF   Blowouts, Oil well
   BT   **Oil well drilling**
Oils and fats   665
   UF   Animal oils
           Fat
           Fats
           Grease
           Oil
           Vegetable oils
   NT   **Essences and essential oils**
           Petroleum
   RT   **Coal tar products**
           Lubrication and lubricants
Oils, Essential
   USE **Essences and essential oils**
Old age   305.26
   BT   **Age**
   NT   **Aging**
           Retirement
   RT   **Elderly**
           Gerontology
           Longevity
Old age homes
   USE **Elderly—Institutional care**
Old age pensions   331.25; 368.3
   UF   Insurance, Old age
           Labor—Insurance
   BT   **Pensions**
           Retirement income
           Saving and thrift
           Social security
Old English language
   USE **Anglo-Saxon language**
Old English literature
   USE **Anglo-Saxon literature**
Old Icelandic language
   USE **Old Norse language**

Old Norse language   439
   UF   Icelandic language—0-1500
           Norse languages
           Norwegian language—0-1350
           Old Icelandic language
           Old Norwegian language
   BT   **Language and languages**
           Scandinavian languages
Old Norse literature   839
   UF   Norse literature
   BT   **Literature**
           Medieval literature
   NT   **Eddas**
           Sagas
   RT   **Icelandic literature**
           Scandinavian literature
Old Northwest   977
     Use for materials on the region between the Ohio and Mississippi rivers and the Great Lakes.
   UF   Northwest, Old
           Northwest Territory
   BT   **United States**
   RT   **Middle West**
Old Norwegian language
   USE **Old Norse language**
Old Southwest   976
     Use for materials on that section of the United States that comprised the southwestern part before the cessions of land from Mexico following the Mexican War. It included Louisiana, Texas, Arkansas, Tennessee, Kentucky and Missouri.
   UF   Southwest, Old
   BT   **United States**
Old Testament
   USE **Bible. O.T.**
Older persons
   USE **Elderly**
Oldest child
   USE **Birth order**
Oleomargarine
   USE **Margarine**
Olympic games   796.48; 796.98
   UF   Olympics
   SA   topical headings for Olympic events of a particular year, e.g. **Olympic games, 1996 (Atlanta, Ga.); to be added as needed**
   BT   **Athletics**
           Contests

BT = Broader Term   NT = Narrower Term   RT = Related Term   SA = See Also   UF = Used For

Olympic games—*Continued*
    Games
    Sports
  NT **Olympic games, 1996 (Atlanta, Ga.)**
    Special Olympics
Olympic games, 1996 (Atlanta, Ga.) **796.48**
  BT **Olympic games**
Olympics
  USE **Olympic games**
Ombudsman (May subdiv. geog.) **328.3; 342; 352.8**
  UF Citizen's defender
    Grievance procedures (Public administration)
  BT **Administrative law**
    Public interest
On the job stress
  USE **Job stress**
One act plays **808.82; 812, etc.**
  May be used for individual works, collections, or materials about one-act plays.
  UF Plays
    Short plays
  BT **Amateur theater**
    Drama
One parent family
  USE **Single parent family**
Online catalogs **025.3**
  UF Catalogs, Online *[Former heading]*
    Online public access catalogs
    OPACs (Online public access catalogs)
  BT **Library catalogs**
  RT **Libraries—Automation**
Online data processing **004**
  BT **Electronic data processing**
  NT **Computer bulletin boards**
Online public access catalogs
  USE **Online catalogs**
Online publishing
  USE **Electronic publishing**
Online reference services
  USE **Reference services (Libraries)**
Only child **155.44; 306.874**
  UF Single child
  BT **Children**
    Family size

OPACs (Online public access catalogs)
  USE **Online catalogs**
Opaque projectors
  USE **Projectors**
Open and closed shop **331.88**
  UF Closed shop
    Right to work
    Union shop
  BT **Labor**
    Labor contract
    Labor unions
Open classroom approach to teaching
  USE **Open plan schools**
Open education
  USE **Open plan schools**
Open-end mutual funds
  USE **Mutual funds**
Open heart surgery
  USE **Heart—Surgery**
Open housing
  USE **Discrimination in housing**
Open plan schools **371.2**
  Use for materials on schools without interior walls.
  UF Interest centers approach to teaching
    Learning center approach to teaching
    Open classroom approach to teaching
    Open education
  BT **Education—Experimental methods**
  NT **Individualized instruction**
  RT **Experimental schools**
Open universities
  USE **Free universities**
Opera (May subdiv. geog.) **782.1; 792.5**
  Use for musical scores and for materials about the opera.
  UF Comic opera
    Dramatic music
    Lyric drama
    Operas *[Former heading]*
  BT **Drama**
    Musical form
    Performing arts
    Vocal music
  NT **Operetta**

BT = Broader Term   NT = Narrower Term   RT = Related Term   SA = See Also   UF = Used For

Opera librettos   782.1026

Use for individual opera librettos and for collections of opera librettos.

UF   Operas—Librettos *[Former heading]*

BT   **Librettos**

RT   **Opera—Stories, plots, etc.**

Opera—Stories, plots, etc.   782.1026

Use for collections of opera plots.

RT   **Literature—Stories, plots, etc.**

Opera librettos

Operas

USE   **Opera**

Operas—Librettos

USE   **Opera librettos**

Operating systems (Computers)

USE   **Computer operating systems**

Operation Desert Storm

USE   **Persian Gulf War, 1991**

Operational analysis

USE   **Operations research**

Operational research

USE   **Operations research**

Operations research   658.5

UF   Operational analysis

Operational research

BT   **Research**

System theory

RT   **Management**

Systems engineering

Operations, Surgical

USE   **Surgery**

Operetta   782.1; 792.5

Use for musical scores and for materials on the operetta as a musical form.

UF   Comic opera

Dramatic music

Operettas

BT   **Musical form**

Opera

Vocal music

RT   **Musicals**

Operettas

USE   **Operetta**

Opiates

USE   **Narcotics**

Opinion polls

USE   **Public opinion polls**

Opinion, Public

USE   **Public opinion**

Opioids, Brain

USE   **Endorphins**

Opium   615

BT   **Narcotics**

RT   **Morphine**

Opium—Physiological effect   615

BT   **Drugs—Physiological effect**

Opposites   153.2

UF   Antonyms

Polarity

BT   **Concepts**

RT   **English language—Synonyms and antonyms**

Optical data processing   006.4; 621.36; 621.39

UF   Visual data processing

BT   **Bionics**

Electronic data processing

Optical discs

USE   **Optical storage devices**

Optical illusions   152.14

UF   Illusions

BT   **Hallucinations and illusions**

Psychophysiology

Vision

Optical instruments   681

UF   Instruments, Optical

BT   **Scientific apparatus and instruments**

NT   **Lenses**

Microscopes

Telescopes

RT   **Optics**

Space optics

Optical masers

USE   **Lasers**

Optical storage devices   004.5; 621.39

Use for materials on data storage devices in which audio, video, or other data are optically encoded.

UF   Discs, Optical

Optical discs

BT   **Computer storage devices**

Optics

NT   **CD-I technology**

CD-ROMs

Compact discs

Videodiscs

RT   **Laser recording**

Magnetic recorders and recording

BT = Broader Term   NT = Narrower Term   RT = Related Term   SA = See Also   UF = Used For

Optical storage devices—*Continued*
          Sound—Recording and repro-
            ducing
Optics   535; 621.36
  BT   **Physics**
  NT   **Color**
         Optical storage devices
         Perspective
         Radiation
         Refraction
         Space optics
         Spectrum analysis
         Vision
  RT   **Light**
         Optical instruments
         Photometry
Optometry   617.7
  RT   **Eye**
Oracles   133.3
  BT   **Occultism**
  RT   **Divination**
         Prophecies
Oral arithmetic
  USE   **Mental arithmetic**
Oral history   907

    Use for materials on recording oral recollec-
tions of places, events, etc., from persons
drawing on their own life experiences. Oral
histories that focus on a particular subject are
entered under that subject.

  UF   History, Oral
  BT   **History**
Oral interpretation
  USE   **Recitations**
Orange
  USE   **Orange (Fruit)**
Orange (Fruit)   634 ; 641.3
  UF   Orange *[Former heading]*
         Oranges
  BT   **Citrus fruits**
         Trees
Oranges
  USE   **Orange (Fruit)**
Orations
  USE   **Speeches**
Oratorio   782.23

    Use for musical scores and for materials on
the oratorio as a musical form.

  UF   Oratorios *[Former heading]*
  BT   **Church music**
         Musical form
         Vocal music

Oratorios
  USE   **Oratorio**
Oratory
  USE   **Public speaking**
Orbital debris
  USE   **Space debris**
Orbital laboratories
  USE   **Space stations**
Orbital rendezvous (Space flight)
         629.45
  UF   Rendezvous in space
         Space orbital rendezvous
  SA   names of projects, e.g. **Apollo
         project; Gemini project;** etc.;
         and names of specific space
         ships, to be added as needed
  BT   **Space flight**
         Space stations
         Space vehicles
  NT   **Apollo project**
         Gemini project
Orbiting vehicles
  USE   **Artificial satellites**
         Space stations
Orchards
  USE   **Fruit culture**
Orchestra   784.2
  SA   types of orchestras, to be added
         as needed
  NT   **Conductors (Music)**
         **Instrumentation and orchestra-
         tion**
         Orchestral music
  RT   **Bands (Music)**
         Conducting
         Ensembles (Music)
         Musical instruments
Orchestral music   784.2
  SA   types of orchestral music, e.g.
         Symphony; to be added as
         needed
  BT   **Instrumental music**
         Music
         Orchestra
  NT   **Concerto**
         String orchestra music
         Suite (Music)
         Symphonic poems
         Symphony

BT = Broader Term   NT = Narrower Term   RT = Related Term   SA = See Also   UF = Used For

Orchestration
    USE   Instrumentation and orchestra-
             tion
Orders, Monastic
    USE   Monasticism and religious or-
             ders
Ordination   262; 265
    BT   **Rites and ceremonies**
            Sacraments
    NT   **Ordination of women**
    RT   **Clergy**
Ordination of women   262
    UF   Women—Ordination
    BT   **Ordination**
    RT   **Women clergy**
Ordnance   355.8; 623.4
    Use for materials on military supplies
including weapons, ammunition, and vehicles,
and the task of procuring, testing, storing, and
issuing such supplies.
    UF   Cannon
            Guns
    SA   types of military ordnance, e.g.
            Bombs; names of armies with
            the subdivision *Ordnance,* e.g.
            **United States. Army—Ord-
            nance;** and names of wars
            with the subdivision *Equip-
            ment and supplies,* e.g. **World
            War, 1939-1945—Equipment
            and supplies;** to be added as
            needed
    BT   **Military art and science**
    NT   **Ammunition**
            Bombs
            Nuclear weapons
            **United States. Army—Ord-
            nance**
    RT   **Artillery**
            Defense industries
            Military weapons
            Projectiles
Ore deposits   553
    SA   types of ores, e.g. **Iron ores;** to
            be added as needed
    BT   **Geology**
    NT   **Iron ores**
    RT   **Ores**
Ore dressing   622
    UF   Dressing of ores
    BT   **Smelting**

Oregon country
    USE   Pacific Northwest
Oregon Trail   978
    BT   **Overland journeys to the Pa-
            cific**
            United States
Ores   553
    SA   types of ores, e.g. **Iron ores;** to
            be added as needed
    BT   **Minerals**
    NT   **Iron ores**
            Metals
    RT   **Metallurgy**
            Ore deposits
Organ
    USE   **Organs (Musical instruments)**
Organ donation
    USE   **Donation of organs, tissues,
            etc.**
Organ music   786.5
    BT   **Church music**
            Instrumental music
            Music
Organ preservation (Anatomy)
    USE   **Preservation of organs, tissues,
            etc.**
Organ transplantation
    USE   **Transplantation of organs, tis-
            sues, etc.**
Organ transplants
    USE   **Transplantation of organs, tis-
            sues, etc.**
Organic agriculture
    USE   **Organic farming**
Organic chemistry   547
    UF   Chemistry, Organic *[Former
            heading]*
    BT   **Chemistry**
Organic chemistry—Synthesis   547
    UF   Chemistry, Synthetic
            Synthetic chemistry
    NT   **Polymers**
            Synthetic products
    RT   **Plastics**
Organic farming   631.5
    UF   Ecological agriculture
            Farming, Organic
            Organic agriculture
            Organiculture *[Former heading]*
    BT   **Agriculture**

BT = Broader Term   NT = Narrower Term   RT = Related Term   SA = See Also   UF = Used For

Organic gardening   635
    UF   Gardening, Organic
            Natural gardening
            Organiculture *[Former heading]*
    BT   **Gardening**
            Horticulture
    RT   **Compost**
Organic waste as fuel
    USE   **Waste products as fuel**
Organically grown foods
    USE   **Natural foods**
Organiculture
    USE   **Organic farming**
            Organic gardening
Organists   786.5092; 920
    BT   **Instrumentalists**
Organization and management
    USE   **Management**
Organization development
    USE   **Organizational change**
Organization, International
    USE   **International organization**
Organization (Sociology)
    USE   **Organizational sociology**
Organization theory
    USE   **Organizational sociology**
Organizational change   338.7; 658.4
    UF   Change, Organizational
            Organization development
            Organizational development
            Organizational innovation
    BT   **Management**
    NT   **Downsizing of organizations**
Organizational development
    USE   **Organizational change**
Organizational downsizing
    USE   **Downsizing of organizations**
Organizational innovation
    USE   **Organizational change**
Organizational retrenchment
    USE   **Downsizing of organizations**
Organizational sociology   302.3
    UF   Organization (Sociology)
            Organization theory
            Sociology of organizations
    BT   **Sociology**
    RT   **Bureaucracy**
Organizational stress
    USE   **Job stress**

Organizations
    USE   **Associations**
Organizations, Business
    USE   **Business enterprises**
Organizations, Nonprofit
    USE   **Nonprofit organizations**
Organized crime   364.106
    UF   Crime syndicates
    SA   types of organized crime, e.g.
            Racketeering; to be added as
            needed
    BT   **Crime**
    NT   **Gangs**
            Racketeering
Organized labor
    USE   **Labor unions**
Organs (Anatomy)—Preservation
    USE   **Preservation of organs, tissues,**
            etc.
Organs, Artificial
    USE   **Artificial organs**
Organs (Musical instruments)   786.5
    UF   Organ *[Former heading]*
            Pipe organs
    BT   **Musical instruments**
    NT   **Keyboards (Musical instru-**
            ments)
Orient
    USE   **Asia**
            East Asia
            Middle East
Oriental architecture
    USE   **Asian architecture**
Oriental art
    USE   **Asian art**
Oriental civilization
    USE   **Asia—Civilization**
Oriental rugs   746.7
    UF   Rugs, Oriental *[Former heading]*
    SA   types of Oriental rugs, to be
            added as needed
    BT   **Rugs**
Orientation
    USE   **Direction sense**
Orienteering   796.58
    Use for materials on the cross-country sport in which competitors using maps and compasses proceed on foot to checkpoints through unknown terrain.
    BT   **Hiking**
            Navigation

BT = Broader Term   NT = Narrower Term   RT = Related Term   SA = See Also   UF = Used For

Orienteering—*Continued*
   Racing
   Running
   Sports
 RT **Direction sense**
Origami 736
 UF Japanese paper folding
   Paper folding, Japanese
 BT **Paper crafts**
Origin
 USE subjects, ethnic groups, classes
   of persons, animals, plants,
   crops, and religions with the
   subdivision *Origin,* e.g.
   Life—Origin; Indians of
   North America—Origin; etc.,
   to be added as needed
Origin of life
 USE **Life—Origin**
Origin of man
 USE **Human origins**
Origin of species
 USE **Evolution**
Ornament
 USE **Decoration and ornament**
Ornamental alphabets
 USE **Alphabets**
   Illumination of books and
   manuscripts
   Lettering
Ornamental plants 635.9; 715
 UF Plants, Ornamental *[Former*
   heading]
 BT **Cultivated plants**
   Flower gardening
   Landscape gardening
 RT **Shrubs**
Ornithology
 USE **Birds**
Orphan drugs 615
 Use for materials on drugs that appear to be
 useful for the treatment of rare disorders but
 owing to their limited commercial value have
 difficulty in finding funding for research and
 marketing.
 UF Drugs, Orphan
   Nonprofitable drugs
 BT **Drugs**
Orphanages (May subdiv. geog.) **362.73**
 UF Charitable institutions
   Homes (Institutions)
 BT **Charities**

   Children—Institutional care
 RT **Child welfare**
Orphans 362.73
 UF Foundlings
 BT **Children**
 RT **Abandoned children**
   Adopted children
Orthodox Eastern Church 281.9
 UF Greek Church
 BT **Christian sects**
   Eastern churches
Orthodox Eastern Church, Russian
 USE **Russian Orthodox Church**
Orthography
 USE **Spelling reform**
   and names of languages with
   the subdivision *Spelling,* e.g.
   English language—Spelling;
   to be added as needed
Orthopedic surgery
 USE **Orthopedics**
Orthopedics 616.7; 617.4
 UF Orthopedic surgery
   Surgery, Orthopedic
 BT **Medicine**
   Surgery
 NT **Artificial limbs**
 RT **Physically handicapped**
Osteology
 USE **Bones**
   Skeleton
Osteopathic medicine 610; 615.5
 Use for materials on the therapeutic system
 based on the theory that disease is caused by
 loss of a structural integrity that can be re-
 stored by manipulation of the bones and mus-
 cles.
 UF Osteopathy *[Former heading]*
 BT **Alternative medicine**
 NT **Chiropractic**
 RT **Massage**
Osteopathy
 USE **Osteopathic medicine**
Ostrogoths
 USE **Goths**
Out-of-doors education
 USE **Outdoor education**
Out-of-work people
 USE **Unemployed**
Outboard motorboats
 USE **Motorboats**

BT = Broader Term NT = Narrower Term RT = Related Term SA = See Also UF = Used For

Outdoor cookery
  USE   Outdoor cooking
Outdoor cooking   641.5
  UF   Camp cooking
       Cooking, Outdoor
       Outdoor cookery *[Former head-
           ing]*
  BT   Camping
       Cooking
  NT   Barbecue cooking
Outdoor education   371.3
  UF   Education, Outdoor
       Out-of-doors education
  BT   Education
  RT   Nature study
       Outdoor life
Outdoor life   796.5
  UF   Rural life
  SA   types of outdoor life, education,
           or activities, to be added as
           needed
  NT   Hiking
       Mountaineering
       Wilderness survival
  RT   Camping
       Country life
       Nature study
       Outdoor education
       Sports
Outdoor photography   778.7
  UF   Field photography
       Photography, Outdoor
  BT   Photography
  RT   Nature photography
Outdoor recreation   796
  SA   types of outdoor recreation, e.g.
           Camping; to be added as
           needed
  BT   Recreation
  NT   Camping
       Cycling
       Parks
       Recreational vehicles
       Roller skating
Outdoor survival
  USE   Wilderness survival
Outer space   523.1
  UF   Space, Outer
  BT   Astronautics
       Astronomy

Space sciences
  NT   Space environment
       Space warfare
Outer space and civilization
  USE   Astronautics and civilization
Outer space—Colonies
  USE   Space colonies
Outer space—Communication
  USE   Interstellar communication
Outer space—Exploration   629.4
  UF   Exploration, Space
       Space exploration (Astronautics)
       Space research
  BT   Exploration
       Interplanetary voyages
       Space flight
  NT   Planets—Exploration
       Space probes
Outer space—Pollution
  USE   Space debris
Outer space travel
  USE   Interplanetary voyages
Outlaws
  USE   Criminals
       Thieves
Outlines, syllabi, etc.
  USE   subjects with the subdivision
           Outlines, syllabi, etc., e.g.
           English literature—Outlines,
           syllabi, etc.; to be added as
           needed
Output equipment (Computers)
  USE   Computer peripherals
Output standards
  USE   Production standards
Over-the-counter drugs
  USE   Nonprescription drugs
Overactive children
  USE   Hyperactive children
Overactivity
  USE   Hyperactivity
Overland journeys to the Pacific   978
       Use for materials on the pioneers' crossing
       of the American continent toward the Pacific
       by foot, horseback, wagon, etc.
  UF   Transcontinental journeys
           (American continent)
  BT   Frontier and pioneer life
       Voyages and travels
  NT   Oregon Trail
  RT   West (U.S.)—Exploration

BT = Broader Term   NT = Narrower Term   RT = Related Term   SA = See Also   UF = Used For

Overseas study
USE **Foreign study**
Oversize books
USE **Big books**
Oversized books for shared reading
USE **Big books**
Overtime
USE **Hours of labor**
Wages
Overweight
USE **Obesity**
Ownership
USE **Property**
Oxyacetylene welding
USE **Welding**
Oxygen 546; 547; 665.8
BT **Chemical elements**
Gases
NT **Ozone**
Ozone 665.8
BT **Oxygen**
Ozone layer 363.738; 551.51
UF Ozonosphere
Stratospheric ozone
BT **Stratosphere**
Ozonosphere
USE **Ozone layer**
P.C. (Political correctness)
USE **Political correctness**
P.O.W.'s
USE **Prisoners of war**
P.T.A.'s
USE **Parent-teacher associations**
Pacific cable
USE **Submarine cables**
Pacific Islands
USE **Islands of the Pacific**
Pacific Northwest 979.5
Use for materials on the old Oregon coun-
try, comprising the present states of Oregon,
Washington, and Idaho, parts of Montana and
Wyoming, and the province of British Colum-
bia.
UF Northwest, Pacific
Oregon country
BT **North America**
United States
West (U.S.)
Pacific Northwest coast
USE **Northwest Coast of North**
America

Pacific Ocean Islands
USE **Islands of the Pacific**
Pacific rim 330.99; 990
Use for materials on the periphery of the
Pacific Ocean, especially as a region of inter-
dependent economies.
RT **East Asia**
Islands of the Pacific
Pacific States 979
BT **West (U.S.)**
Pacifism 174; 303.6
Use for materials on the renunciation of of-
fensive or defensive military actions on moral
grounds. Materials on social movements
adovcating peace are entered under **Peace**
movements.
BT **War—Religious aspects**
RT **Conscientious objectors**
Nonviolence
Peace
Peace movements
Pack transportation
USE **Backpacking**
Packaged houses
USE **Prefabricated houses**
Packaging 658.5; 658.7; 658.8
SA types of packaging and packag-
ing materials, to be added as
needed
BT **Advertising**
Retail trade
NT **Aluminum foil**
Boxes
Gift wrapping
Packing industry
USE **Meat industry**
PACs (Political action committees)
USE **Political action committees**
Paganism 291; 292
UF Heathenism
BT **Christianity and other religions**
Religions
NT **Goddess religion**
Wicca
Pageants 394; 791.6
BT **Acting**
NT **Masks (Plays)**
Mysteries and miracle plays
Parades
RT **Festivals**
Pain 152.1; 612.8
BT **Diagnosis**

BT = Broader Term   NT = Narrower Term   RT = Related Term   SA = See Also   UF = Used For

Pain—*Continued*
    Emotions
    Psychophysiology
    Senses and sensation
  NT   Anesthetics
  RT   Pleasure
    Suffering
Paint   645; 667
  UF   Finishes and finishing
  BT   **House painting**
    Industrial painting
  RT   **Corrosion and anticorrosives**
    Pigments
Paint sniffing
  USE   **Solvent abuse**
Painted glass
  USE   **Glass painting and staining**
Painters   759; 920
  SA   painters of particular countries,
      e.g. **American painters;** and
      names of individual painters,
      to be added as needed
  BT   **Artists**
  NT   **American painters**
Painters, American
  USE   **American painters**
Painters' materials
  USE   **Artists' materials**
Painting   750
  UF   Oil painting
    Paintings
  SA   painting of particular countries,
      e.g. **American painting;** and
      types of painting, e.g. **Land-
      scape painting;** to be added
      as needed
  BT   **Art**
    Graphic arts
  NT   **American painting**
    **Animal painting and illustra-
    tion**
    China painting
    Color
    Cubism
    Expressionism (Art)
    Figure painting
    Finger painting
    Futurism (Art)
    Glass painting and staining
    House painting

    Impressionism (Art)
    Industrial painting
    Landscape painting
    Marine painting
    Miniature painting
    Modern painting
    Mural painting and decoration
    Perspective
    Portrait painting
    Postimpressionism (Art)
    Scene painting
    Stencil work
    Textile painting
    Watercolor painting
  RT   **Composition (Art)**
    Decoration and ornament
    Drawing
    Pictures
Painting, Abstract
  USE   **Abstract art**
Painting, American
  USE   **American painting**
Painting books
  USE   **Coloring books**
Painting—Color reproductions
  USE   **Color prints**
Painting—Conservation and restoration
    751.6
Painting, Decorative
  USE   **Decoration and ornament**
Painting, Finger
  USE   **Finger painting**
Painting, Industrial
  USE   **Industrial painting**
Painting, Mechanical
  USE   **Industrial painting**
Painting, Modern
  USE   **Modern painting**
Painting, Modern—19th century
  USE   **Modern painting—1800-1899
    (19th century)**
Painting, Modern—20th century
  USE   **Modern painting—1900-1999
    (20th century)**
Painting, Romanesque
  USE   **Romanesque painting**
Painting—Technique   751.4
Paintings
  USE   **Painting**

BT = Broader Term   NT = Narrower Term   RT = Related Term   SA = See Also   UF = Used For

Pair system
    USE   **Binary system (Mathematics)**

Palaces (May subdiv. geog.)   **728.8**
    BT   **Buildings**

Paleobiogeography
    USE   **Biogeography**

Paleobotany
    USE   **Fossil plants**

Paleolithic period
    USE   **Stone Age**

Paleontology
    USE   **Fossils**

Palestine problem, 1917-
    USE   **Israel-Arab conflicts**

Palestinian Arabs   **305.892; 956.94**
    UF   Arabs—Palestine
            Palestinians
    BT   **Arabs**
    RT   **Jewish-Arab relations**

Palestinian-Israeli conflict, 1987-
    USE   **Intifada, 1987-**

Palestinian uprising, 1987-
    USE   **Intifada, 1987-**

Palestinians
    USE   **Palestinian Arabs**

Palmistry   **133.6**
    BT   **Divination**
            Fortune telling
            Occultism

Palsy, Cerebral
    USE   **Cerebral palsy**

Pamphlets   **025.17**
    UF   Street literature
    BT   **Press**
    NT   **Chapbooks**

Pamphlets—Design   **686.2**

Pan-Africanism   **320.5; 327**
    Use for materials on the advocacy of either political alliance or close economic, cultural, and military cooperation among the countries of Africa.
    UF   African relations
    BT   **Africa**

Pan-Americanism   **320.5; 327**
    Use for materials on the advocacy of either political alliance or close economic, cultural, and military cooperation among the countries of North and South America.
    UF   Inter-American relations
    BT   **Latin America**
    NT   **Monroe Doctrine**

    RT   **America—Politics and government**

Pan-Arabism   **320.5**
    Use for materials on the advocacy of either political alliance or close economic, cultural, and military cooperation among the Arab countries.
    UF   Panarabism *[Former heading]*
    BT   **Arab countries—Politics and government**

Panama Canal   **972.87**
    BT   **Canals**

Panarabism
    USE   **Pan-Arabism**

Panel discussions
    USE   **Discussion groups**

Panel heating
    USE   **Radiant heating**

Paneuropean federation
    USE   **European federation**

Panhandling
    USE   **Begging**

Panics (Finance)
    USE   **Financial crises**

Pantomimes   **792.3**
    BT   **Acting**
            Amateur theater
            Drama
            Theater
    NT   **Shadow pantomimes and plays**
    RT   **Ballet**
            Mime

Papacy   **262**
    UF   Holy See
    BT   **Catholic Church**
            Church history
    RT   **Popes**

Papal encyclicals   **262.9**
    UF   Encyclicals, Papal *[Former heading]*
    BT   **Christian literature**

Papal visits   **262**
    UF   Popes—Travel
            Popes—Voyages and travels *[Former heading]*
    BT   **Voyages and travels**

Paper   **676**
    BT   **Fibers**
    NT   **Papermaking**

Paper airplanes
    USE   **Airplanes—Models**

BT = Broader Term   NT = Narrower Term   RT = Related Term   SA = See Also   UF = Used For

Paper bound books
USE **Paperback books**
Paper crafts   745.54
UF   Paper folding
Paper sculpture
Paper work
Papier-mâché
SA   types of paper crafts, to be added as needed
BT   **Handicraft**
NT   **Decoupage**
Gift wrapping
Origami
RT   **Papermaking**
Paper folding
USE   **Paper crafts**
Paper folding, Japanese
USE   **Origami**
Paper hanging
USE   **Paperhanging**
Paper industry   338.4
Use for materials on the business of making and selling paper. Materials on the technology and craft of making paper are entered under **Papermaking.**
UF   Paper making and trade *[Former heading]*
Paper trade
Papermaking industry
BT   **Industries**
RT   **Book industries**
Paper making
USE   **Papermaking**
Paper making and trade
USE   **Paper industry**
Paper manufacture
USE   **Papermaking**
Paper money   332.4
UF   Bills of credit
Fiat money
Legal tender
BT   **Money**
RT   **Inflation (Finance)**
Paper sculpture
USE   **Paper crafts**
Paper trade
USE   **Paper industry**
Paper work
USE   **Paper crafts**
Paperback books   070.5
UF   Paper bound books

BT   **Books**
Editions
Paperhanging   698
UF   Paper hanging *[Former heading]*
BT   **Interior design**
RT   **Wallpaper**
Papermaking   676
Use for materials on the technology and craft of making paper. Materials on the business of making and selling paper are entered under **Paper industry.**
UF   Paper making
Paper manufacture
BT   **Manufactures**
Paper
RT   **Paper crafts**
Papermaking industry
USE   **Paper industry**
Papers, Collected (Anthologies)
USE   **Anthologies**
Papier-mâché
USE   **Paper crafts**
Parables   808
May be used for individual works, collections, or materials about parables.
UF   Cautionary tales and verse
Moral and philosophic stories
Morality tales
NT   **Bible—Parables**
Jesus Christ—Parables
RT   **Allegories**
Didactic fiction
Didactic poetry
Fables
Parachute troops   356
UF   Paratroops
SA   names of armies with the subdivision *Parachute troops,* e.g. **United States. Army—Parachute troops;** to be added as needed
BT   **Military aeronautics**
Parachutes
NT   **United States. Army—Parachute troops**
Parachutes   629.134
BT   **Aeronautics**
NT   **Parachute troops**
Parade floats
USE   **Parades**

BT = Broader Term   NT = Narrower Term   RT = Related Term   SA = See Also   UF = Used For

Parades 791.6
   UF   Floats (Parades)
           Parade floats
           Pomp
           Processions
   BT   **Festivals**
           Pageants
Paradise 236; 291.2
     Use for materials on the earthly paradise or on a blessed intermediate state in the afterlife.
   UF   Earthly paradise
           Eden
           Garden of Eden
   BT   **Future life**
   RT   **Heaven**
           Utopias
Parallel economy
   USE   **Underground economy**
Paralysis, Anterior spinal
   USE   **Poliomyelitis**
Paralysis, Cerebral
   USE   **Cerebral palsy**
Paralysis, Infantile
   USE   **Poliomyelitis**
Paralysis, Spastic
   USE   **Cerebral palsy**
Paramedical personnel
   USE   **Allied health personnel**
           Emergency medical technicians
Paramedics, Emergency
   USE   **Emergency medical technicians**
Paramilitary militia movements
   USE   **Militia movements**
Paranormal phenomena
   USE   **Parapsychology**
Paraphilia
   USE   **Sexual deviation**
Paraprofessional librarians
   USE   **Library technicians**
Paraprofessionals 331.7
   UF   Paraprofessions and paraprofessionals *[Former heading]*
   SA   types of paraprofessional personnel, e.g. **Library technicians;** and fields of knowledge, professions, industries, and trades with the subdivision *Vocational guidance,* to be added as needed
   BT   **Occupations**

           Professions
   NT   **Library technicians**
Paraprofessions and paraprofessionals
   USE   **Paraprofessionals**
Parapsychology 133
     Use for materials on investigations of phenomena that appear to be contrary to physical laws and beyond the normal sense perceptions.
   UF   Paranormal phenomena
           Psi (Parapsychology)
           Psychic phenomena
           Psychical research *[Former heading]*
   BT   **Psychology**
           Research
           Supernatural
   NT   **Apparitions**
           Clairvoyance
           Extrasensory perception
           Hallucinations and illusions
           Mental suggestion
           Mind and body
           Psychokinesis
           Subconsciousness
           Telepathy
           Visions
   RT   **Ghosts**
           Occultism
           Spiritualism
Parasites 577.8; 578.6; 581.6; 591.6
   UF   Animal parasites
           Diseases and pests
           Entozoa
           Epizoa
   BT   **Pests**
   NT   **Bacteria**
           Ticks
   RT   **Insect pests**
           Symbiosis
Parasols
   USE   **Umbrellas and parasols**
Paratroops
   USE   **Parachute troops**
Parcel post
   USE   **Postal service**
Pardon 364.6
   BT   **Administration of criminal justice**
           Executive power
   RT   **Amnesty**

BT = Broader Term   NT = Narrower Term   RT = Related Term   SA = See Also   UF = Used For

Pardon—*Continued*
>Forgiveness

Parent abuse
>USE **Elderly abuse**

Parent and child   306.874
>Use for materials on the psychological and social interaction between parents and their minor children. Materials on the skills, attributes, and attitudes needed for parenthood are entered under **Parenting.** Materials on the principles and techniques of rearing children are entered under **Child rearing.** Materials restricted to the legal right of parents to visit their children in situations of separation, divorce, etc., are entered under **Visitation rights (Domestic relations).**
>
>UF Child and parent
>
>BT **Children and adults**
>**Domestic relations**
>**Family**
>**Human relations**
>
>NT **Adoption**
>**Adult children of alcoholics**
>**Birthparents**
>**Child abuse**
>**Child custody**
>**Child rearing**
>**Children of alcoholics**
>**Children of divorced parents**
>**Children of drug addicts**
>**Children of immigrants**
>**Children of working parents**
>**Father and child**
>**Inheritance and succession**
>**Mother and child**
>**Parenting**
>
>RT **Conflict of generations**

Parent-teacher associations   371.19
>UF P.T.A.'s
>Parents' and teachers' associations *[Former heading]*
>PTAs
>
>BT **Community and school**
>**Educational associations**
>**Parent-teacher relationships**
>**Societies**
>
>RT **Home and school**

Parent-teacher conferences   371.103
>UF Conferences, Parent-teacher
>Interviews, Parent-teacher
>Teacher-parent conferences
>
>BT **Parent-teacher relationships**

Parent-teacher relationships   371.19
>UF Parents and teachers
>Teacher-parent relationships
>Teachers and parents
>
>NT **Parent-teacher associations**
>**Parent-teacher conferences**
>
>RT **Home and school**

Parental behavior
>USE **Parenting**

Parental custody
>USE **Child custody**

Parental kidnapping   362.82
>UF Child snatching by parents
>Custody kidnapping
>Kidnapping, Parental *[Former heading]*
>
>BT **Child custody**

Parenting   306.874; 649
>Use for materials on the skills, attributes, and attitudes needed for parenthood. Materials on the psychological and social interaction between parents and their minor children are entered under **Parent and child.** Materials on the principles and techniques of rearing children are entered under **Child rearing.**
>
>UF Parental behavior
>
>BT **Parent and child**
>
>NT **Part-time parenting**
>
>RT **Child rearing**

Parenting, Part-time
>USE **Part-time parenting**

Parents, Aging
>USE **Aging parents**

Parents and teachers
>USE **Parent-teacher relationships**

Parents' and teachers' associations
>USE **Parent-teacher associations**

Parents, Biological
>USE **Birthparents**

Parents' choice of school
>USE **School choice**

Parents, Single
>USE **Single parent family**

Parents, Unmarried
>USE **Unmarried fathers**
>**Unmarried mothers**

Parents without partners
>USE **Single parent family**

Parish libraries
>USE **Church libraries**

Parish registers
>USE **Registers of births, etc.**

BT = Broader Term   NT = Narrower Term   RT = Related Term   SA = See Also   UF = Used For

Parks (May subdiv. geog.)   363.6; 712
   BT   Cities and towns
        Landscape architecture
        Outdoor recreation
   NT   Amusement parks
        Botanical gardens
        National parks and reserves
        Zoos
   RT   Playgrounds
Parks—United States   363.6; 712; 917.3
   UF   United States—Parks
Parkways
   USE   Express highways
Parliamentary government
   USE   Representative government and
          representation
Parliamentary practice   060.4
   UF   Rules of order
   BT   Debates and debating
        Legislation
        Legislative bodies
        Public meetings
Parliaments
   USE   Legislative bodies
Parochial schools
   USE   Church schools
Parodies   **808.87; 817, etc.**
   Use for collections of parodies. Materials on the literary form of parody, that is, satirical or humorous imitation of a serious piece of literature, are entered under **Parody.**
   UF   Travesties
   SA   types of literature, individual literary works entered under title, and names of prominent authors with the subdivision *Parodies, imitations, etc.,* e.g. **Shakespeare, William, 1564-1616—Parodies, imitations, etc.;** to be added as needed
   BT   Literature—Collections
Parodies, imitations, etc.
   USE   types of literature, individual literary works entered under title, and names of prominent authors with the subdivision *Parodies, imitations, etc.,* e.g. **Shakespeare, William, 1564-1616—Parodies, imitations, etc.;** to be added as needed

Parody   808.7
   Use for materials about the literary form of parody, that is, satirical or humorous imitation of a serious piece of literature. Collections of parodies are entered under **Parodies.**
   UF   Comic literature
   BT   Literature
        Satire
        Wit and humor
Parole   364.6
   BT   Administration of criminal justice
        Corrections
        Punishment
        Social case work
   RT   Probation
Part-time employment   331.25
   UF   Alternative work schedules
        Employment, Part-time
   BT   Employment
        Hours of labor
        Labor
   NT   Job sharing
        Supplementary employment
Part-time parenting   306.874; 649
   Use for materials on parenting skills for separated, divorced, or surrogate parents who live apart from their children and spend less than full time with them.
   UF   Co-parenting
        Joint custody of children
        Parenting, Part-time *[Former heading]*
        Shared parenting
        Single parents
   BT   Parenting
   RT   Children of divorced parents
Partial hearing
   USE   Hearing impaired
Partially hearing
   USE   Hearing impaired
Participative management   331.89; 658.3
   UF   Consultative management
        Employees' representation in management
        Industrial councils
        Labor participation in management
        Management—Employee participation *[Former heading]*

BT = Broader Term   NT = Narrower Term   RT = Related Term   SA = See Also   UF = Used For

Participative management—*Continued*
        Workers' participation in management
        Workshop councils
  BT   **Factory management**
        Industrial relations
        Personnel management
  RT   **Collective bargaining**
Particles (Nuclear physics) 539.7
  UF   Elementary particles (Physics)
        Nuclear particles
        Nucleons
  SA   names of particles, to be added
        as needed
  BT   **Nuclear physics**
  NT   **Electrons**
        Neutrons
        Protons
        Quarks
Parties 793.2
  SA   types of parties, to be added as
        needed
  BT   **Entertaining**
  NT   **Children's parties**
        Showers (Parties)
Parties, Political
  USE   **Political parties**
Partisans
  USE   **Guerrillas**
Partita
  USE   **Suite (Music)**
Passion plays 792.1; 808.82; 822, etc.
    May be used for individual plays, collections, or materials about medieval plays depicting the Passion of Christ.
  BT   **Bible plays**
        Jesus Christ—Drama
        Mysteries and miracle plays
        Religious drama
        Theater
Passions
  USE   **Emotions**
Passive resistance 303.6; 322.4
  UF   Civil disobedience
        Nonviolent noncooperation
  BT   **Resistance to government**
  NT   **Boycotts**
        Hunger strikes
  RT   **Nonviolence**
Passover 296.4; 394.267
  UF   Pesach

  BT   **Jewish holidays**
Pastel drawing 741.2
  BT   **Drawing**
  RT   **Crayon drawing**
Pastimes
  USE   **Amusements**
        Games
        Recreation
Pastoral drama 808.82; 812, etc.
    May be used for individual works, collections, or materials about pastoral drama.
  UF   Rural comedies
  BT   **Drama**
Pastoral fiction 808.83; 813, etc.
    May be used for individual works, collections, or materials about novels or short stories with a rural setting and a tone of romantic nostalgia.
  UF   Pastoral romances
        Rural comedies
  BT   **Fiction**
Pastoral peoples
  USE   **Nomads**
Pastoral poetry 808.81; 811, etc.
    May be used for individual works, collections, or materials about pastoral poetry.
  UF   Bucolic poetry
        Eclogues
        Idyllic poetry
        Rural poetry
  BT   **Poetry**
Pastoral psychiatry
  USE   **Pastoral psychology**
Pastoral psychology 253.5; 291.6
    Use for materials on the application of psychology and psychiatry by the clergy to the spiritual problems of individuals.
  UF   Clerical psychology
        Pastoral psychiatry
        Psychology, Pastoral *[Former heading]*
        Psychology, Religious
  BT   **Applied psychology**
        Church work
        Psychology of religion
  RT   **Pastoral theology**
Pastoral romances
  USE   **Pastoral fiction**
Pastoral theology 253; 291.6
  UF   Pastoral work *[Former heading]*
        Theology, Pastoral
  BT   **Theology**

BT = Broader Term   NT = Narrower Term   RT = Related Term   SA = See Also   UF = Used For

Pastoral theology—*Continued*
NT   Ministry
       Preaching
RT   Church work
       Clergy
       Pastoral psychology
Pastoral work
USE   Pastoral theology
Pastors
USE   Clergy
       Priests
Pastry   641.8
BT   Baking
       Cooking
RT   Cake
Pastures   333.74
BT   Agriculture
       Land use
Patchwork quilts
USE   Quilts
Patent medicines
USE   Nonprescription drugs
Patents   608
UF   Discoveries in science
       Intellectual property
BT   Manufactures
RT   Inventions
       Trademarks
Pathological botany
USE   Plant diseases
Pathological psychology
USE   Abnormal psychology
Pathology   616.07
UF   Disease (Pathology)
BT   Medicine
NT   Birth defects
       Fever
       Immunity
       Medical genetics
       Therapeutics
RT   Diseases
       Preventive medicine
Patience   179
BT   Human behavior
       Virtue
Patience (Game)
USE   Solitaire (Game)
Patients   362.1
SA   diseases with the subdivision
         Patients, e.g. **Cancer—Pa-**

tients; and organs or regions
of the body with the subdivi-
sions *Surgery—Patients,* or
Transplantation—Patients, to
be added as needed
NT   Cancer—Patients
RT   Sick
Patios   643
UF   Decks (Domestic architecture)
BT   Landscape architecture
Patriotic poetry   808.81; 811, etc.;
        811.008, etc.
   May be used for individual works, collec-
tions, or materials about patriotic poetry.
BT   Poetry
RT   National songs
Patriotic songs
USE   National songs
Patriotism   172
BT   Citizenship
       Human behavior
       Loyalty
RT   Nationalism
Patristic philosophy
USE   Fathers of the church
Patristics
USE   Fathers of the church
Patronage of the arts
USE   Art patronage
Pattern making   671.2
BT   Models and model making
NT   Mechanical drawing
RT   Design
       Founding
Patterns for crafts
USE   subjects with the subdivision
         Patterns, e.g. **Dressmaking—**
         Patterns; to be added as
         needed
Patterns (Language arts)
USE   Language arts—Patterning
Patterns (Mathematics)   372.7
UF   Geometric patterns
       Number patterns
BT   Mathematics
Paul Bunyan
USE   Bunyan, Paul (Legendary char-
         acter)
Pauperism
USE   Poverty

BT = Broader Term   NT = Narrower Term   RT = Related Term   SA = See Also   UF = Used For

Pavements   625.8
  RT   Roads
        Streets
Pay equity
  USE   Equal pay for equal work
Pay television, Cable
  USE   Cable television
Pay television, Subscription
  USE   Subscription television
Payroll taxes
  USE   Income tax
        Unemployment insurance
PC computers
  USE   Microcomputers
PC (Political correctness)
  USE   Political correctness
PC's
  USE   Microcomputers
Peace   172; 327.1; 341.7
  SA   names of wars with the subdivi-
        sion *Peace*, to be added as
        needed
  BT   International relations
  NT   World War, 1914-1918—Peace
        World War, 1939-1945—Peace
  RT   Arms control
        International arbitration
        International security
        Pacifism
        Peace movements
        War
Peace keeping forces
  USE   United Nations—Armed forces
Peace movements (May subdiv. geog.)
        327.1
    Use for materials on social movements ad-
  vocating peace. Materials on the renunciation
  of offensive or defensive military actions on
  moral grounds are entered under **Pacifism.**
  UF   Antiwar movements
        Protest movements
        War protest movements
  SA   names of wars with the subdivi-
        sion *Protests movements*, e.g.
        World War, 1939-1945—
        Protests movements; to be
        added as needed
  BT   Social movements
  RT   Demonstrations
        Pacifism
        Peace

Peaceful coexistence
  USE   International relations
Peacocks   598.6
  UF   Peafowl
        Peahens
  BT   Birds
Peafowl
  USE   Peacocks
Peahens
  USE   Peacocks
Pearl fisheries   338.3; 639
  UF   Pearlfisheries *[Former heading]*
  BT   Fisheries
Pearl Harbor (Oahu, Hawaii), Attack on,
      1941   940.54
  BT   World War, 1939-1945—Cam-
        paigns
Pearlfisheries
  USE   Pearl fisheries
Peasant art
  USE   Folk art
Peasantry (May subdiv. geog.)   305.5;
        307.72
  BT   Feudalism
        Labor
  RT   Agricultural laborers
        Land tenure
        Rural sociology
Pecan   583; 634
  UF   Pecans
  BT   Nuts
        Trees
Pecans
  USE   Pecan
Pedagogy
  USE   Education
        Education—Study and teaching
        Teaching
Peddlers and peddling   658.8
  UF   Door to door selling
  BT   Direct selling
        Sales personnel
Pediatric psychiatry
  USE   Child psychiatry
Pediatric surgery
  USE   Children—Surgery
Pediatrics
  USE   Children—Diseases
        Children—Health and hygiene
        Infants—Diseases

BT = Broader Term   NT = Narrower Term   RT = Related Term   SA = See Also   UF = Used For

Pediatrics—*Continued*
    Infants—Health and hygiene
Pedigrees
  USE   **Genealogy**
        Heraldry
Peer counseling   158; 361.3
  UF   Peer counseling in rehabilitation
        Peer counseling of students
        Peer group counseling
        Rehabilitation peer counseling
        Student to student counseling
  BT   **Counseling**
Peer counseling in rehabilitation
  USE   **Peer counseling**
Peer counseling of students
  USE   **Peer counseling**
Peer group counseling
  USE   **Peer counseling**
Peer group influence
  USE   **Peer pressure**
Peer pressure   303.3; 364.2
  UF   Peer group influence
  BT   **Socialization**
Peerage
  USE   **Nobility**
Pelts
  USE   **Hides and skins**
Pen drawing   741.2
  UF   Ink drawing
  BT   **Drawing**
Pen names
  USE   **Pseudonyms**
Penal codes
  USE   **Criminal law**
Penal colonies   365
  UF   Expulsion
        Transportation of criminals
  BT   **Colonies**
        Correctional institutions
Penal institutions
  USE   **Correctional institutions**
        Prisons
        Reformatories
Penal law
  USE   **Criminal law**
Penal reform
  USE   **Prison reform**
Penance   265
  UF   Contrition
        Forgiveness of sin

        Reconciliation, Sacrament of
        Sacrament of Reconciliation
  BT   **Sacraments**
  RT   **Confession**
Pencil drawing   741.2
  BT   **Drawing**
Penicillin   615
  BT   **Antibiotics**
Peninsulas (May subdiv. geog.)   **551.41**
  SA   names of peninsulas, to be add-
        ed as needed
  NT   **Arabian Peninsula**
Penitentiaries
  USE   **Prisons**
Penmanship
  USE   **Handwriting**
Pennsylvania Dutch   974.8
  UF   Pennsylvania Germans
Pennsylvania Germans
  USE   **Pennsylvania Dutch**
Penology
  USE   **Corrections**
        Punishment
Pensions (May subdiv. geog.)   **331.25;**
        353.5; 658.3
  UF   Compensation
  SA   ethnic groups, classes of per-
        sons, and employees in partic-
        ular industries with the subdi-
        vision *Pensions,* e.g. **Teach-**
        ers—Pensions; Chemical in-
        dustry—Employees—Pen-
        sions; etc., to be added as
        needed
  BT   **Annuities**
        Retirement income
  NT   **Individual retirement accounts**
        Military pensions
        Old age pensions
        Social security
Pensions, Military
  USE   **Military pensions**
Pensions, Naval
  USE   **Military pensions**
Pentecostal churches   289.9
      Use for general materials on Christian de-
nominations of the Pentecostal type. Materials
on Christian movements that stress the person-
al experience of the Holy Spirit in daily life,
with emphasis on personal holiness and spiritual gifts, especially the gift of tongues, are
entered under **Pentecostalism.**

BT = Broader Term   NT = Narrower Term   RT = Related Term   SA = See Also   UF = Used For

Pentecostal churches—*Continued*
    BT   **Christian sects**
               Protestantism
    RT   **Pentecostalism**
Pentecostal movement
    USE   **Pentecostalism**
Pentecostalism (May subdiv. geog.)
    270.8

    Use for materials on Christian movements that stress the personal experience of the Holy Spirit in daily life, with emphasis on personal holiness and spiritual gifts, especially the gift of tongues. General materials on Christian denominations of the Pentecostal type are entered under **Pentecostal churches.**

    UF   Charismatic movement
               Charismatic renewal movement
               Pentecostal movement
    BT   **Christianity**
    RT   **Catholic charismatic movement**
               Glossolalia
               Pentecostal churches
               Spiritual gifts
Peonage   **306.3; 331.5**
    UF   Compulsory labor
               Forced labor
               Servitude
    BT   **Labor**
    RT   **Contract labor**
               Convict labor
               Slavery
People
    USE   **Ethnic groups**
              Native peoples
              Persons
          and racial and ethnic groups
            and native peoples, e.g.
            African Americans; Mexican Americans; Yoruba (African people); etc., and classes of persons, e.g. **Elderly; Handicapped; Explorers; Drug addicts;** etc., to be added as needed
People in space
    USE   **Interplanetary voyages**
              Space flight
People's banks
    USE   **Cooperative banks**
People's democracies
    USE   **Communist countries**

People's Republic of China
    USE   **China**
Pep pills
    USE   **Amphetamines**
Percentage   **513.2**
    BT   **Arithmetic**
Perception   **152.1; 153.7**
    UF   Feeling
    SA   types of concepts and images, e.g. **Size; Shape;** etc., to be added as needed
    BT   **Intellect**
               Psychology
               Senses and sensation
               Theory of knowledge
               Thought and thinking
    NT   **Concepts**
               Consciousness
               Gestalt psychology
               Shape
               Size
    RT   **Apperception**
               Intuition
Percussion instruments   **786.8**
    SA   types of percussion instruments, e.g. **Drums;** to be added as needed
    BT   **Musical instruments**
    NT   **Drums**
               Pianos
Perennials   **635.9**
    BT   **Cultivated plants**
               Flower gardening
               Flowers
Perfectionism (Personality trait)   **155.2**
    UF   Self-expectations, Perfectionist
    BT   **Personality**
Performance art   **700**

    Use for materials on live performances by artists, drawing on literature, theater, music, film, etc., and combining elements of the various arts in untraditional ways.

    UF   Happening (Art)
    BT   **Modern art—1900-1999 (20th century)**
               Performing arts
Performance standards   **658.5**
    UF   Job performance standards
               Rating
               Work performance standards

BT = Broader Term   NT = Narrower Term   RT = Related Term   SA = See Also   UF = Used For

Performance standards—*Continued*
- SA   subjects and classes of persons with the subdivision *Rating,* e.g. **Bonds—Rating; Employees—Rating;** etc., to be added as needed
- NT   **Bonds—Rating**
  Employees—Rating
  Librarians—Rating

Performing arts   790.2
- UF   Show business
- SA   specific art forms performed on stage or screen, to be added as needed
- BT   **Arts**
- NT   **Ballet**
  Centers for the performing arts
  Dance
  Opera
  Performance art
  Theater

Perfumes   391.6; 668
- BT   **Cosmetics**
  Essences and essential oils

Periodic health examinations   616.07
- UF   Health examinations
  Medical examinations
  Physical examinations (Medicine)
- SA   subjects, classes of persons, ethnic groups, and military services with the subdivision *Medical examinations,* e.g. **Children—Medical examinations;** to be added as needed
- BT   **Medicine**

Periodic law   541.2
- BT   **Physical chemistry**
- RT   **Chemical elements**

Periodicals   050
- UF   Annuals
  Journals
  Magazines
  Yearbooks
- SA   periodicals of particular countries, e.g. **American periodicals;** subjects with the subdivision *Periodicals,* e.g. **Engineering—Periodicals;** and

names of individual periodicals, to be added as needed
- BT   **Mass media**
  Serial publications
- NT   **American periodicals**
  Chapbooks
  English periodicals
- RT   **Journalism**
  Newspapers
  Press

Periodicals—Editing
- USE   **Journalism—Editing**

Periodicals—Indexes   050

Periodicity
- USE   **Cycles**

Permanent education
- USE   **Continuing education**

Persecution   291; 909
- UF   Religious persecution
- SA   religious groups with the subdivision *Persecutions,* e.g. **Christians—Persecutions; Jews—Persecutions;** etc., to be added as needed
- BT   **Atrocities**
- NT   **Christians—Persecutions**
  Jews—Persecutions
  Massacres
- RT   **Freedom of religion**
  Martyrs

Persia
- USE   **Iran**

Persian Gulf War, 1991   956.7044
- UF   Gulf War, 1991
  Middle East War, 1991
  Operation Desert Storm
- BT   **United States—History—1989-**

Personal actions (Law)
- USE   **Litigation**

Personal appearance   391.6
- UF   Appearance, Personal
  Beauty, Personal
  Physical appearance
  Self image
- NT   **Personal grooming**
  Tattooing
- RT   **Clothing and dress**

Personal cleanliness
- USE   **Hygiene**

BT = Broader Term   NT = Narrower Term   RT = Related Term   SA = See Also   UF = Used For

Personal computers
　　USE　**Microcomputers**
Personal conduct
　　USE　**Conduct of life**
Personal development
　　USE　**Personality**
　　　　　Self-improvement
　　　　　Success
Personal films
　　USE　**Amateur films**
　　　　　Experimental films
Personal finance　332.024
　　UF　Budgets, Personal
　　　　　Domestic finance
　　　　　Family finance
　　　　　Finance, Personal *[Former head-ing]*
　　　　　Financial planning, Personal
　　SA　ethnic groups, classes of per-sons, and names of individual persons with the subdivision *Personal finance,* e.g. **Retir-ees—Personal finance;** to be added as needed
　　BT　**Finance**
　　NT　**Children's allowances**
　　　　　Consumer credit
　　　　　Estate planning
　　　　　Household budgets
　　　　　Insurance
　　　　　Saving and thrift
　　　　　Tax planning
Personal freedom
　　USE　**Freedom**
Personal grooming　391.6; 646.7
　　UF　Beauty, Personal
　　　　　Good grooming
　　　　　Grooming
　　　　　Grooming for men
　　　　　Grooming for women
　　　　　Grooming, Personal *[Former heading]*
　　BT　**Hygiene**
　　　　　Personal appearance
　　NT　**Cosmetics**
　　　　　Hair
　　　　　Toiletries
　　RT　**Clothing and dress**
Personal growth
　　USE　**Self-improvement**

Personal health
　　USE　**Health**
Personal health services
　　USE　**Medical care**
Personal hygiene
　　USE　**Hygiene**
Personal life skills
　　USE　**Life skills**
Personal loans　332.7
　　　　Use for materials on loans to individuals for personal rather than business uses.
　　UF　Consumer loans
　　　　　Loans, Personal
　　　　　Small loans
　　BT　**Consumer credit**
　　　　　Loans
　　NT　**Cooperative banks**
　　　　　Mortgages
　　　　　Savings and loan associations
Personal names (May subdiv. geog.)
　　　929.4
　　UF　Christian names
　　　　　Family names
　　　　　Forenames
　　　　　Names, Personal *[Former head-ing]*
　　　　　Surnames
　　SA　personal names of particular na-tional or ethnic origins re-gardless of the place where they are found, e.g. **Scottish personal names;** to be added as needed
　　BT　**Names**
　　NT　**Nicknames**
　　　　　Pseudonyms
　　　　　Scottish personal names
Personal names, Scottish
　　USE　**Scottish personal names**
Personal names—United States
　　　929.40973
　　UF　American personal names
　　　　　United States—Personal names
Personal narratives
　　USE　**Autobiographies**
　　　　　Biography
　　　　　and subjects with the subdivi-sion *Biography* or *Correspon-dence;* and names of diseases, events, and wars with the

---

Personal narratives—*Continued*
    subdivision *Personal narra-
    tives,* e.g. **World War, 1939-
    1945—Personal narratives;**
    to be added as needed

Personal space   153.6; 302.2
Use for materials on the sense of physical space required for psychological comfort.
    UF   Space, Personal
    BT   **Human relations**
          Nonverbal communication
          Space and time

Personal time management
    USE   **Time management**

Personality   155.2
    UF   Identity
          Personal development
    BT   **Consciousness**
          Psychology
    NT   **Body image**
          Character
          Eccentrics and eccentricities
          Identity (Psychology)
          **Perfectionism (Personality
            trait)**
          Self
    RT   **Individuality**
          Persons

Personality disorders   616.85
    BT   **Abnormal psychology**
    NT   **Multiple personality**
    RT   **Hallucinations and illusions**
          Mental illness

Personality, Multiple
    USE   **Multiple personality**

Personnel administration
    USE   **Personnel management**

Personnel classification
    USE   **Job analysis**

Personnel management   658.3
Use for materials on problems of personnel in factories, business, etc., hiring and dismissing employees, and general questions of the relationship between officials and employees.
    UF   Career development
          Employment management
          Human resource management
          Personnel administration
          Supervision of employees
    BT   **Human relations**
          Industrial relations
          Management

    NT   **Absenteeism (Labor)**
          Affirmative action programs
          Applications for positions
          Counseling
          Employee morale
          Employees—Dismissal
          Employees—Training
          Employment agencies
          Job analysis
          Job satisfaction
          Job security
          Labor turnover
          Motion study
          Participative management
          Recruiting of employees
          Supervisors
          Time study
    RT   **Employees**
          Factory management
          Industrial efficiency
          Office management

Personnel service in education
    USE   **Educational counseling**

Persons   128
Use for materials on human beings as individuals. Materials on the human species from the point of view of biology or anthropology are entered under **Human beings.**
    UF   Categories of persons
          Classes of persons
          Groups of persons
          People
    SA   classes of persons, e.g. **Elderly;
            Handicapped; Explorers;
            Drug addicts;** etc., to be
            added as needed
    BT   **Human beings**
    NT   **Celebrities**
          Intellectuals
    RT   **Individualism**
          Personality

Persons, Crimes against
    USE   **Offenses against the person**

Perspective   701
    UF   Architectural perspective
    BT   **Descriptive geometry**
          Geometrical drawing
          Optics
          Painting
    RT   **Drawing**

BT = Broader Term   NT = Narrower Term   RT = Related Term   SA = See Also   UF = Used For

Persuasion (Rhetoric)
    USE   **Public speaking**
              Rhetoric
Perversion, Sexual
    USE   **Sexual deviation**
Pesach
    USE   **Passover**
Pest control   363.7; 628.9; 632
    UF   Extermination of pests
           Pest extermination
           Pests—Biological control *[Former heading]*
           Pests—Control *[Former heading]*
           Pests—Extermination
    SA   types of pests with the subdivision *Control,* e.g. **Mosquitoes—Control;** to be added as needed
    BT   **Agricultural pests**
           Economic zoology
           Pests
    NT   **Mosquitoes—Control**
           Pesticides
Pest extermination
    USE   **Pest control**
Pesticide pollution
    USE   **Pesticides—Environmental aspects**
Pesticides   632; 668
    BT   **Agricultural chemicals**
           Pest control
           Poisons and poisoning
    NT   **Fungicides**
           Herbicides
           Insecticides
           Natural pesticides
Pesticides and wildlife   590
    UF   Wildlife and pesticides
    BT   **Pesticides—Environmental aspects**
           Wildlife conservation
Pesticides—Environmental aspects   363.7; 632
    UF   Environment and pesticides
           Pesticide pollution
    BT   **Environment**
           Pollution
    NT   **Pesticides and wildlife**
Pestilences
    USE   **Epidemics**

Pests   591.6; 632
    Use for materials on detrimental or annoying animals or organisms.
    UF   Vermin
    SA   types of pests, e.g. **Agricultural pests; Flies;** etc., and names of crops, trees, etc., with the subdivision *Diseases and pests,* e.g. **Fruit—Diseases and pests;** to be added as needed
    BT   **Economic zoology**
    NT   **Agricultural pests**
           Flies
           Fruit—Diseases and pests
           Fungi
           Household pests
           Insect pests
           Parasites
           Pest control
Pests—Biological control
    USE   **Pest control**
Pests—Control
    USE   **Pest control**
Pests—Extermination
    USE   **Pest control**
Pet-facilitated psychotherapy
    USE   **Pet therapy**
Pet therapy   615.8
    UF   Animal-facilitated therapy
           Companion-animal partnership
           Pet-facilitated psychotherapy
    BT   **Animals and the handicapped**
           Therapeutics
Petrochemicals   661
    UF   Petroleum chemicals
    BT   **Chemicals**
Petroglyphs
    USE   **Rock drawings, paintings, and engravings**
Petroleum (May subdiv. geog.)   553.2; 665.5
    UF   Coal oil
           Crude oil
           Oil
    BT   **Oils and fats**
    NT   **Coal tar products**
           Gasoline
    RT   **Petroleum geology**
Petroleum as fuel   338.4; 665.5
    UF   Fuel, Liquid

BT = Broader Term   NT = Narrower Term   RT = Related Term   SA = See Also   UF = Used For

Petroleum as fuel—*Continued*
　　Fuel oil
　　Liquid fuel
　　Oil fuel
　BT　**Fuel**
　NT　**Oil burners**
Petroleum chemicals
　USE　**Petrochemicals**
Petroleum engines
　USE　**Internal combustion engines**
Petroleum geology　**553.2**
　UF　Geology, Petroleum
　BT　**Economic geology**
　　Prospecting
　RT　**Petroleum**
Petroleum industry　**338.2**
　UF　Oil industry
　　Petroleum industry and trade
　　　[Former heading]
　　Petroleum trade
　BT　**Industries**
　NT　**Offshore oil industry**
　　Oil well drilling
　　Oil wells
　　Service stations
Petroleum industry and trade
　USE　**Petroleum industry**
Petroleum industry, Offshore
　USE　**Offshore oil industry**
Petroleum—Pipelines
　USE　**Petroleum pipelines**
Petroleum pipelines　**338.2; 665.5**
　UF　Petroleum—Pipelines *[Former heading]*
　　Pipelines, Petroleum
　BT　**Pipelines**
Petroleum pollution of water
　USE　**Oil pollution of water**
Petroleum trade
　USE　**Petroleum industry**
Petroleum—United States　**553.2; 665.5**
　UF　United States—Petroleum
Petroleum—Well boring
　USE　**Oil well drilling**
Petrology　**552**
　SA　types of rocks, e.g. **Granite;** to be added as needed
　BT　**Science**
　NT　**Geochemistry**
　　Lunar petrology

　RT　**Geology**
　　Minerals
　　Rocks
　　Stone
Pets　**636.088**
　SA　types of animals not ordinarily kept as pet, e.g. **Snakes as pets;** to be added as needed
　BT　**Animals**
　NT　**Snakes as pets**
　RT　**Domestic animals**
Pets and the handicapped
　USE　**Animals and the handicapped**
Pets—Housing　**690**
　BT　**Animal housing**
Pets—Names　**636.088**
Petting zoos　**590.73**
　UF　Animals—Petting zoos
　BT　**Zoos**
Pewter　**673; 739.5**
　BT　**Alloys**
　　Art metalwork
　　Metals
Phantoms
　USE　**Apparitions**
　　Ghosts
Pharmaceutical abuse
　USE　**Medication abuse**
Pharmaceutical chemistry　**615**
　UF　Chemistry, Medical and pharmaceutical *[Former heading]*
　　Chemistry, Pharmaceutical
　　Drugs—Chemistry
　　Medicinal chemistry
　BT　**Chemistry**
　NT　**Disinfection and disinfectants**
　RT　**Pharmacy**
　　Therapeutics
Pharmaceuticals
　USE　**Drugs**
Pharmacies
　USE　**Drugstores**
Pharmacodynamics
　USE　**Pharmacology**
Pharmacology　**615**
　　Use for materials on the action and properties of drugs in general. Materials limited to the effect of drugs on the functions of living organisms are entered under **Drugs—Physiological effect.** Materials on the art or practice of preparing, preserving, and dispensing drugs are entered under **Pharmacy.**

BT = Broader Term　　NT = Narrower Term　　RT = Related Term　　SA = See Also　　UF = Used For

Pharmacology—*Continued*
   UF   Drugs—Adulteration and analysis
         [Former heading]
         Medicine—Physiological effect
         Pharmacodynamics
   BT   **Materia medica**
         Medicine
   NT   **Drugs—Physiological effect**
         Drugs—Testing
   RT   **Drug therapy**
         Drugs
         Pharmacy
Pharmacopoeias
   USE   **Materia medica**
Pharmacotherapy
   USE   **Drug therapy**
Pharmacy   615
      Use for materials on the art or practice of
   preparing, preserving, and dispensing drugs.
   Materials on the action and properties of
   drugs are entered under **Pharmacology**. Mate-
   rials on business establishments that sell drugs
   are entered under **Drugstores**.
   BT   **Chemistry**
         Medicine
   NT   **Drugs**
         Homeopathy
         Medical botany
   RT   **Materia medica**
         Pharmaceutical chemistry
         Pharmacology
Pheasants   598.6; 636.5
   BT   **Birds**
         Game and game birds
Phenomenology   142
   BT   **Modern philosophy**
   NT   **Existentialism**
Philanthropists   361.7092; 920
   UF   Altruists
         Humanitarians
Philanthropy
   USE   **Charities**
         Charity organization
         Endowments
         Gifts
         Social work
Philately
   USE   **Stamp collecting**
Philology
   USE   **Language and languages**
         Linguistics

Philology, Comparative
   USE   **Linguistics**
Philosophers   180; 190; 920
   SA   philosophers of particular coun-
         tries, e.g. **American philoso-
         phers;** to be added as needed
   NT   **American philosophers**
   RT   **Philosophy**
Philosophers, American
   USE   **American philosophers**
Philosophers' stone
   USE   **Alchemy**
Philosophy   100
   SA   movements in philosophy, e.g.
         Positivism; philosophy of par-
         ticular countries, e.g.
         American philosophy; philos-
         ophy associated with particu-
         lar religions, e.g. **Christian
         philosophy;** and subjects with
         the subdivision *Philosophy,*
         e.g. **History—Philosophy;** to
         be added as needed
   BT   **Humanities**
   NT   **American philosophy**
         Ancient philosophy
         Belief and doubt
         Christian philosophy
         Empiricism
         Ethics
         Evolution
         Fate and fatalism
         Free will and determinism
         Gnosticism
         Good and evil
         Hindu philosophy
         History—Philosophy
         Humanism
         Idealism
         Ideology
         Intuition
         Logic
         Marxism
         Materialism
         Medieval philosophy
         Metaphysics
         Mind and body
         Modern philosophy
         Philosophy and religion
         Positivism

BT = Broader Term   NT = Narrower Term   RT = Related Term   SA = See Also   UF = Used For

Philosophy—*Continued*

       Pragmatism
       Psychology
       Rationalism
       Realism
       Reality
       Skepticism
       Soul
       Theism
       Theory of knowledge
       Transcendentalism
       Truth
  RT   **Philosophers**

Philosophy, American
  USE   **American philosophy**

Philosophy, Ancient
  USE   **Ancient philosophy**

Philosophy and religion   210
    Use for materials on the reciprocal relationship and influence between philosophy and religion. Materials on the nature, origin, or validity of religion from a philosophical point of view are entered under **Religion—Philosophy.**
  UF   Religion and philosophy
  BT   **Philosophy**
        Religion
  RT   **Religion—Philosophy**

Philosophy—Encyclopedias   103
  BT   **Encyclopedias and dictionaries**

Philosophy, Greek
  USE   **Ancient philosophy**

Philosophy, Hindu
  USE   **Hindu philosophy**

Philosophy—Historiography   109
  BT   **Historiography**

Philosophy, Medieval
  USE   **Medieval philosophy**

Philosophy, Modern
  USE   **Modern philosophy**

Philosophy, Moral
  USE   **Ethics**

Philosophy of history
  USE   **History—Philosophy**

Philosophy of religion
  USE   **Religion—Philosophy**

Philosophy, Roman
  USE   **Ancient philosophy**

Phobias   616.85
  BT   **Fear**
        Neuroses

Phonetic spelling
  USE   **Spelling reform**

Phonetics   414
  UF   Phonics
        Phonology
  SA   names of languages with the subdivision *Pronunciation,* to be added as needed
  BT   **Language and languages**
        Sound
  NT   **English language—Pronunciation**
  RT   **Reading—Phonetic method**
        Speech
        Voice

Phonics
  USE   **Phonetics**
        Reading—Phonetic method

Phonograph   621.389
  UF   Gramophone
  BT   **Sound—Recording and reproducing**
  NT   **Compact disc players**
        Sound—Recording and reproducing
  RT   **High-fidelity sound systems**

Phonograph records
  USE   **Sound recordings**

Phonology
  USE   **Phonetics**
        and names of languages with the subdivision *Pronunciation,* e.g. **English language—Pronunciation;** to be added as needed

Phosphates   546; 553.6; 631.8
  BT   **Fertilizers**

Phosphorescence   535
  BT   **Luminescence**
        Radioactivity

Photo journalism
  USE   **Photojournalism**

Photocopying   686.4
  UF   Photocopying processes
        Photoduplication
        Photographic reproduction
        Xerography *[Former heading]*
  BT   **Copying processes**
  RT   **Copy art**

Photocopying machines
  USE   **Copying machines**

BT = Broader Term   NT = Narrower Term   RT = Related Term   SA = See Also   UF = Used For

Photocopying processes
USE **Photocopying**
Photoduplication
USE **Photocopying**
Photoelectric cells   537.5; 621.3815
UF   Electric eye
Photoengraving   686.2
UF   Halftone process
BT   **Engraving**
RT   **Photomechanical processes**
Photographic chemistry   771
> Use for materials on the chemical processes employed in photography.

UF   Chemistry, Photographic
BT   **Chemistry**
NT   **Photography—Processing**
RT   **Photography**
Photographic film
USE   **Photography—Film**
Photographic reproduction
USE   **Photocopying**
Photographic slides
USE   **Slides (Photography)**
Photographic supplies
USE   **Photography—Equipment and supplies**
Photographs from space
USE   **Space photography**
Photography   770
SA   kinds of photography, e.g. **Portrait photography;** photography of particular subjects, e.g. **Photography of birds;** and subjects and names of cities, states, countries, and named entities, such as individual parks, structures, etc., with the subdivision *Pictorial works,* to be added as needed
BT   **Graphic arts**
NT   **Aerial photography**
Artistic photography
Astronomical photography
Cameras
Cinematography
Color photography
Commercial photography
Filmstrips
Holography
Medical photography
Microphotography

Nature photography
Outdoor photography
Photojournalism
Photomechanical processes
Photomicrography
Portrait photography
Slides (Photography)
Space photography
Telephotography
Three dimensional photography
Underwater photography
RT   **Photographic chemistry**
Pictures
Photography, Aerial
USE   **Aerial photography**
Photography—Aesthetics
USE   **Artistic photography**
Photography, Artistic
USE   **Artistic photography**
Photography, Astronomical
USE   **Astronomical photography**
Photography, Color
USE   **Color photography**
Photography, Commercial
USE   **Commercial photography**
Photography—Darkroom technique
USE   **Photography—Processing**
Photography—Developing and developers   771
BT   **Photography—Processing**
Photography—Enlarging   771
UF   Enlarging (Photography)
Photography—Equipment and supplies   771
UF   Photographic supplies
NT   **Cameras**
Photography—Film   771
UF   Photographic film
Photography from space
USE   **Space photography**
Photography—Handbooks, manuals, etc.   770.2
Photography in astronautics
USE   **Space photography**
Photography, Journalistic
USE   **Photojournalism**
Photography, Laser
USE   **Holography**

BT = Broader Term   NT = Narrower Term   RT = Related Term   SA = See Also   UF = Used For

Photography, Lensless
USE **Holography**
Photography—Lighting   771; 778.7
BT **Lighting**
Photography, Medical
USE **Medical photography**
Photography—Motion pictures
USE **Cinematography**
Photography of animals   778.9
Use for materials on the technique of photographing animals. Materials consisting of photographs and pictures of animals are entered under **Animals—Pictorial works.**
UF Animal photography
Animals—Photography
BT **Nature photography**
RT **Animal painting and illustration**
Animals—Pictorial works
Photography of birds   778.9
UF Bird photography
Birds—Photography
BT **Nature photography**
Photography of fishes   778.9
UF Fishes—Photography
BT **Nature photography**
Photography of nature
USE **Nature photography**
Photography of plants   778.9
UF Plants—Photography
BT **Nature photography**
Photography, Outdoor
USE **Outdoor photography**
Photography—Portraits
USE **Portrait photography**
Photography—Printing processes   771
BT **Photography—Processing**
Photography—Processing   771
UF Darkroom technique in photography
Photography—Darkroom technique
SA types of photographic processing techniques, e.g. **Photography—Developing and developers; Photography—Printing processes;** etc., to be added as needed
BT **Photographic chemistry**
NT **Photography—Developing and developers**

Photography—Printing processes
Photography—Retouching   771
UF Retouching (Photography)
Photography—Scientific applications   778.3
SA specific applications, e.g. **Medical photography;** to be added as needed
NT **Medical photography**
Space photography
Photography, Space
USE **Space photography**
Photography, Stereoscopic
USE **Three dimensional photography**
Photography, Underwater
USE **Underwater photography**
Photojournalism   070.4; 779
UF Journalistic photography
News photography
Photo journalism
Photography, Journalistic *[Former heading]*
BT **Commercial photography**
Journalism
Photography
Photomechanical processes   686.2
SA types of photomechanical processes, e.g. **Photoengraving;** to be added as needed
BT **Illustration of books**
Photography
RT **Photoengraving**
Photometry   535
UF Electric light
BT **Measurement**
NT **Color**
RT **Light**
Optics
Photomicrography   778.3
Use for materials on the photographing of minute objects through a miscroscope. Materials on the photographing of objects of any size to produce minute images are entered under **Microphotography.**
BT **Photography**
RT **Microscopes**
Photoplays
USE **Motion picture plays**

BT = Broader Term   NT = Narrower Term   RT = Related Term   SA = See Also   UF = Used For

545

Photosynthesis 572
  BT   Botany
Phototherapy 615.8
  UF   Electric light
       Light—Therapeutic use
  BT   **Physical therapy**
       Therapeutics
  RT   **Radiotherapy**
       Ultraviolet rays
Photovoltaic power generation 621.31
  UF   Solar cells
  BT   **Solar energy**
  NT   **Solar batteries**
Phrenology 139
  BT   **Brain**
       Head
       Psychology
  RT   **Mind and body**
       Physiognomy
Physical anthropology 599.9
  UF   Anthropology, Physical
       Biological anthropology
       Somatology
  BT   **Anthropology**
       Ethnology
  NT   **Human origins**
Physical appearance
  USE **Personal appearance**
Physical chemistry 541
  UF   Chemistry, Physical and theoreti-
       cal *[Former heading]*
       Theoretical chemistry
  BT   **Chemistry**
       Physics
  NT   **Atomic theory**
       Atoms
       Catalysis
       Colloids
       Crystals
       Electrochemistry
       Molecules
       Periodic law
       Polymers
       Radiochemistry
       Solids
       Thermodynamics
  RT   **Nuclear physics**
       Quantum theory
Physical culture
  USE **Physical education**

Physical education 613.7; 796.07
  UF   Calisthenics
       Physical culture
       Physical education and training
       Physical training
  SA   types of sports activities with
       the subdivision *Training,* e.g.
       Soccer—Training; and names
       of sports and types of physi-
       cal exercise, to be added as
       needed
  BT   **Education**
  NT   **Coaching (Athletics)**
       Fencing
       Games
       Judo
       Marching drills
       Movement education
       Physical fitness
       Posture
       Soccer—Training
  RT   **Athletics**
       Exercise
       Gymnastics
       Sports
Physical education and training
  USE **Physical education**
Physical education—Medical aspects
  USE **Sports medicine**
Physical examinations (Medicine)
  USE **Periodic health examinations**
Physical fitness 613.7
  UF   Endurance, Physical
       Fitness
       Physical stamina
       Stamina, Physical
  BT   **Exercise**
       Health
       Health self-care
       Physical education
  NT   **Bodybuilding**
       Kinesiology
       Physical fitness centers
Physical fitness centers (May subdiv.
     geog.) **613.7**
  UF   Health clubs
       Health resorts, spas, etc.
       Health spas
       Recreation centers
       Spas

BT = Broader Term   NT = Narrower Term   RT = Related Term   SA = See Also   UF = Used For

Physical fitness centers—*Continued*
  BT   Physical fitness
Physical geography (May subdiv. geog.)
    910
  Use for materials on the physical features
  of the earth's surface and its atmosphere.
  General materials, frequently school materials,
  describing the surface of the earth and its in-
  terrelationship with various peoples, animals,
  natural products, and industries are entered
  under **Geography.**
  UF   Geography, Physical
       Physiography
  BT   Geography
       Geology
  NT   Deserts
       Earthquakes
       Geysers
       Glaciers
       Ice
       Icebergs
       Lakes
       Mountains
       Ocean
       Rivers
       Tides
       Volcanoes
       Winds
  RT   Earth
Physical geography—United States
    917.3
  UF   United States—Physical geogra-
       phy
Physical sciences   500.2
  BT   Science
  NT   Astronomy
       Chemistry
       Earth sciences
       Physics
Physical stamina
  USE   Physical fitness
Physical therapy   615.8
  UF   Physiotherapy
  SA   types of physical therapy, e.g.
       Hydrotherapy; and types of
       disabilities, injuries, or dis-
       eases with the subdivision
       Physical therapy, e.g. **Arthri-
       tis—Physical therapy;** to be
       added as needed
  BT   Therapeutics
  NT   Baths

       Electrotherapeutics
       Hydrotherapy
       Massage
       Occupational therapy
       Phototherapy
       Radiotherapy
Physical training
  USE   Physical education
Physically handicapped   362.4
  UF   Crippled people
       Invalids
  SA   types of physically handicapped
       persons, e.g. **Blind; Deaf;**
       etc., to be added as needed
  BT   Handicapped
  NT   Blind
       Deaf
       Hearing impaired
       Physically handicapped chil-
       dren
  RT   Orthopedics
Physically handicapped children
    155.45; 362.4
  UF   Children, Crippled
       Crippled children
  BT   Handicapped children
       Physically handicapped
Physically handicapped—Housing   362.4
  UF   Housing for the physically hand-
       icapped
  BT   Housing
Physically handicapped—Rehabilitation
    362.4
  NT   Occupational therapy
Physicians   610.69; 920
  UF   Doctors
       Medical profession
  SA   types of medical specialists, to
       be added as needed
  NT   Radiologists
       Surgeons
       Women physicians
  RT   Medicine
Physicians—Directories   610.69
  BT   Directories
Physicians—Drug use   362.29; 610.69
  UF   Drug abusing physicians
       Drug addicted physicians
Physicians—Malpractice   346.03
  UF   Medical errors

BT = Broader Term   NT = Narrower Term   RT = Related Term   SA = See Also   UF = Used For

Physicians—Malpractice—*Continued*
  BT   **Malpractice**
          Medical ethics
          Medicine—Law and legislation
Physicists   530.092; 920
  BT   **Scientists**
Physics   530
  BT   **Physical sciences**
          Science
  NT   **Astrophysics**
          Biophysics
          Electricity
          Electronics
          Gases
          Geophysics
          Gravitation
          Hydraulics
          Hydrostatics
          Light
          Liquids
          Magnetism
          Matter
          Mechanics
          Music—Acoustics and physics
          Nuclear physics
          Optics
          Physical chemistry
          Pneumatics
          Quantum theory
          Radiation
          Radioactivity
          Relativity (Physics)
          Solids
          Sound
          Statics
          Thermodynamics
          Weights and measures
  RT   **Dynamics**
Physics, Astronomical
  USE   **Astrophysics**
Physics, Biological
  USE   **Biophysics**
Physics—Congresses   530
Physics, Nuclear
  USE   **Nuclear physics**
Physics, Terrestrial
  USE   **Geophysics**
Physiognomy   138
  BT   **Psychology**
  RT   **Face**

Phrenology
Physiography
  USE   **Physical geography**
Physiological aspects
  USE   types of activities and mental
          conditions with the subdivi-
          sion **Physiological aspects,**
          e.g. **Mental illness—Physio-**
          logical aspects; to be added
          as needed
Physiological chemistry
  USE   **Biochemistry**
Physiological effect
  USE   drugs, chemicals, or environmen-
          tal phenomena or conditions
          with the subdivision *Physio-*
          logical effect, e.g. **Alcohol—**
          Physiological effect; Radia-
          tion—Physiological effect;
          etc., to be added as needed
Physiological psychology
  USE   **Psychophysiology**
Physiological stress
  USE   **Stress (Physiology)**
Physiology   571; 612
    Use for general materials on physiology and
for materials on human physiology. Materials
on the physiology of other animals or of
plants are entered under the appropriate head-
ing with the subdivision *Physiology.*
  UF   Human physiology
  SA   names of organs and regions of
          the body, types of plants and
          animals, and classes of per-
          sons with the subdivision
          Physiology, e.g. **Heart—Phys-**
          iology; Reptiles—Physiology;
          etc.; activities and mental
          conditions with the subdivi-
          sion *Physiological aspects,*
          e.g. **Mental illness—Physio-**
          logical aspects; and drugs,
          chemicals, and environmental
          phenomena or conditions with
          the subdivision *Physiological*
          effect, e.g. **Alcohol—Physio-**
          logical effect; Radiation—
          Physiological effect; etc., to
          be added as needed
  BT   **Biology**
          Medicine

BT = Broader Term   NT = Narrower Term   RT = Related Term   SA = See Also   UF = Used For

Physiology—*Continued*
       Science
NT   Blood
       Body temperature
       Cardiovascular system
       Cells
       Comparative physiology
       Digestion
       Fatigue
       Glands
       Growth
       Health
       Heart—Physiology
       Human locomotion
       Immune system
       Lymphatic system
       Mental illness—Physiological
         aspects
       Musculoskeletal system
       Nervous system
       Nutrition
       Psychophysiology
       Reproduction
       Reproductive system
       Reptiles—Physiology
       Respiration
       Respiratory system
       Senses and sensation
       Skin
       Stress (Physiology)
RT   Anatomy
       Human body
Physiology, Comparative
  USE   Comparative physiology
Physiology, Molecular
  USE   Biophysics
Physiology of plants
  USE   Plant physiology
Physiotherapy
  USE   Physical therapy
Physique
  USE   Bodybuilding
Phytogeography
  USE   Plants—Geographical distribu-
       tion
Pianists   786.2092; 920
  BT   Instrumentalists
Piano
  USE   Pianos

Piano music   786.2
  BT   Instrumental music
       Music
Pianos   786.2
  UF   Piano *[Former heading]*
  BT   Percussion instruments
  NT   Keyboards (Musical instru-
       ments)
Pianos—Tuning   786.2
  BT   Tuning
Picaresque literature   800
     May be used for individual works, collec-
    tions, or materials about episodic accounts of
    the adventures of an engagingly roguish hero.
  UF   Picaresque novels
  BT   Fiction
       Literature
Picaresque novels
  USE   Picaresque literature
Picketing
  USE   Strikes
Pickling
  USE   Canning and preserving
Pickup campers
  USE   Travel trailers and campers
Pictographs
  USE   Picture writing
Pictorial works
  USE   Pictures
       and subjects, names of cities,
       states, and countries, and
       named entities, such as indi-
       vidual parks, structures, etc.,
       with the subdivision *Pictorial
       works,* e.g. **Animals—Pictori-
       al works; United States—
       History—1861-1865, Civil
       War—Pictorial works; Chi-
       cago (Ill.)—Pictorial works;
       United States—Pictorial
       works; Yosemite National
       Park (Calif.)—Pictorial
       works;** etc.; and names of
       persons or groups of persons
       with the subdivisions *Car-
       toons and caricatures; Picto-
       rial works;* or *Portraits;* to be
       added as needed
Picture books
  USE   Pictures

BT = Broader Term   NT = Narrower Term   RT = Related Term   SA = See Also   UF = Used For

Picture books for children
  BT Children's literature
  NT Coloring books
      Glow-in-the-dark books
      Stories without words
      Toy and movable books
  RT Illustration of books
Picture books for children, Wordless
  USE Stories without words
Picture dictionaries   413; 423, etc.
  UF Dictionaries, Picture
      Word books
  BT Encyclopedias and dictionaries
Picture frames and framing   684; 749
  UF Framing of pictures
  BT Decoration and ornament
      Handicraft
Picture galleries
  USE Art museums
Picture postcards
  USE Postcards
Picture posters
  USE Posters
Picture telephone
  USE Video telephone
Picture writing   411
      Use for materials on the recording of events
      or the expression of messages by pictures rep-
      resenting actions or facts.
  UF Pictographs
  BT Writing
  NT Cave drawings
      Rock drawings, paintings, and
        engravings
  RT Hieroglyphics
Pictures   025.17; 760
      Use for general materials on the study and
      use of pictures and for miscellaneous collec-
      tions of pictures.
  UF Pictorial works
      Picture books
  SA subjects and names of cities,
      states, countries, and named
      entities, such as individual
      parks, structures, etc., with
      the subdivision *Pictorial
      works;* and names of persons
      or groups of persons with the
      subdivisions *Cartoons and
      caricatures; Pictorial works;*

or *Portraits;* to be added as
      needed
  BT Art
  NT Cartoons and caricatures
      Engraving
      Etching
      Libraries and pictures
      Portraits
      Views
  RT Painting
      Photography
Pictures, Humorous
  USE Cartoons and caricatures
Pigments   547; 667; 751.2
  NT Dyes and dyeing
  RT Color
      Paint
Pigs   599.63; 636.4
  UF Hogs
      Swine
  BT Domestic animals
      Mammals
Pilgrims and pilgrimages   263; 291.3
  BT Voyages and travels
  RT Saints
      Shrines
Pilgrims (New England colonists)   974.4
  BT Puritans
      United States—History—1600-
        1775, Colonial period
Pilot guides   623.89
  UF Coast pilot guides
  BT Navigation
Piloting (Aeronautics)
  USE types of aircraft with the subdi-
      vision *Piloting,* e.g. **Air-
      planes—Piloting;** to be added
      as needed
Piloting (Astronautics)
  USE Space vehicles—Piloting
Pilots
  USE Air pilots
      Ship pilots
Pilots and pilotage
  USE Navigation
      Ship pilots
Pimples (Acne)
  USE Acne
Ping-pong
  USE Table tennis

BT = Broader Term   NT = Narrower Term   RT = Related Term   SA = See Also   UF = Used For

Pioneer life
  USE   Frontier and pioneer life
Pipe fitting   696
  UF   Steam fitting
  RT   **Plumbing**
Pipe lines
  USE   **Pipelines**
Pipe organs
  USE   **Organs (Musical instruments)**
Pipelines   388.5; 621.8
  UF   Pipe lines
  SA   types of pipelines, to be added
            as needed
  BT   **Hydraulic structures**
            Transportation
  NT   **Petroleum pipelines**
Pipelines, Petroleum
  USE   **Petroleum pipelines**
Pipes, Tobacco
  USE   **Tobacco pipes**
Pirates   364.16; 910.4
  UF   Barbary corsairs
            Buccaneers
            Corsairs
            Freebooters
  BT   **Criminals**
            International law
            Maritime law
            Naval history
  NT   **Privateering**
            United States—History—1801-
            1805, Tripolitan War
Pistols
  USE   **Handguns**
Place names
  USE   **Geographic names**
Places, Imaginary
  USE   **Geographical myths**
Places of retirement
  USE   **Retirement communities**
Places of work
  USE   **Work environment**
Plague   616.9
  UF   Black death
            Bubonic plague
  BT   **Communicable diseases**
            Epidemics
Plain chant
  USE   **Chants (Plain, Gregorian, etc.)**

Plainsong
  USE   **Chants (Plain, Gregorian, etc.)**
Plane crashes
  USE   **Aircraft accidents**
Plane geometry
  USE   **Geometry**
Plane trigonometry
  USE   **Trigonometry**
Planetariums   520.74
  BT   **Astronomy**
Planetary satellites
  USE   **Satellites**
Planetoids
  USE   **Asteroids**
Planets   523.4
  SA   names of planets, e.g. **Saturn**
            (Planet); to be added as
            needed
  BT   **Astronomy**
            Solar system
  NT   **Earth**
            Life on other planets
            Mars (Planet)
            Saturn (Planet)
  RT   **Asteroids**
Planets—Exploration   523.4
  SA   names of planets with the subdi-
            vision *Exploration,* to be add-
            ed as needed
  BT   **Outer space—Exploration**
  NT   **Mars (Planet)—Exploration**
Planets, Life on other
  USE   **Life on other planets**
Planets, Minor
  USE   **Asteroids**
Planets—Satellites
  USE   **Satellites**
Planing machines   621.9
  BT   **Machine tools**
Planned parenthood
  USE   **Birth control**
Planning (May subdiv. geog.)   **338.9;**
            658.4
  SA   types of planning, e.g. **Curricu-**
            lum planning; and types of
            activities, facilities, industries,
            services, and undertakings
            with the subdivision *Planning,*
            e.g. **Transportation—Plan-**
            ning; to be added as needed

BT = Broader Term   NT = Narrower Term   RT = Related Term   SA = See Also   UF = Used For

Planning—*Continued*
- BT Creation (Literary, artistic, etc.)
- Executive ability
- Management
- NT City planning
- Curriculum planning
- Economic policy
- Estate planning
- Regional planning
- Social policy
- Tax planning
- Transportation—Planning

Plans
- USE Architectural drawing
- Geometrical drawing
- Map drawing
- Maps
- Mechanical drawing

Plant anatomy
- USE Plants—Anatomy

Plant breeding 631.5

Use for materials on attempts to produce new or improved varieties of plants through controlled reproduction. Materials on the continuance or multiplication of plants by successive production are entered under **Plant propagation.**
- UF Hybridization
- BT Agriculture
- Breeding
- Horticulture
- NT Fertilization of plants
- RT Plant propagation

Plant chemistry
- USE Botanical chemistry
- Plants—Analysis

Plant classification
- USE Botany—Classification

Plant conservation 333.95; 639.9
- UF Conservation of plants
- Plants—Conservation
- Protection of plants
- Wild flowers—Conservation
- BT Conservation of natural resources
- Economic botany
- Endangered species
- Nature conservation
- NT Scarecrows
- RT Rare plants

Plant diseases 571.9; 632
- UF Botany—Pathology
- Diseases and pests
- Diseases of plants
- Garden pests
- Pathological botany
- Plant pathology
- Plants—Diseases *[Former heading]*
- Vegetable pathology
- SA types of crops, plants, trees, etc., with the subdivision *Diseases and pests,* to be added as needed
- BT Agricultural pests
- Diseases
- Fungi
- NT Fruit—Diseases and pests

Plant distribution
- USE Plants—Geographical distribution

Plant ecology 571.7
- UF Botany—Ecology *[Former heading]*
- Plants—Ecology *[Former heading]*
- SA types of plants and crops with the subdivision *Ecology,* to be added as needed
- BT Ecology
- NT Desert plants
- Forest plants
- Mountain plants
- RT Forest influences
- Symbiosis

Plant introduction 581.6; 631.5
- BT Economic botany

Plant lore
- USE Plants—Folklore

Plant names, Popular
- USE Popular plant names

Plant names, Scientific
- USE Botany—Terminology

Plant nutrition
- USE Plants—Nutrition

Plant pathology
- USE Plant diseases

Plant physiology 571.2
- UF Botany—Physiology
- Physiology of plants

BT = Broader Term   NT = Narrower Term   RT = Related Term   SA = See Also   UF = Used For

Plant physiology—*Continued*
  BT   Botany
  NT   Fertilization of plants
       Germination
       Plants—Growth
       Plants—Nutrition
Plant propagation   631.5
  Use for materials on the continuance or
  multiplication of plants by successive produc-
  tion. Materials on attempts to produce new or
  improved varieties of plants through con-
  trolled reproduction are entered under **Plant
  breeding.**
  UF   Plants—Propagation
       Propagation of plants
  BT   Fruit culture
       Gardening
       Nurseries (Horticulture)
  NT   Grafting
       Seeds
  RT   Plant breeding
Plant taxonomy
  USE   Botany—Classification
Plantation life   307.72
  BT   Country life
Planting
  USE   Agriculture
        Gardening
        Landscape gardening
        Tree planting
Plants (May subdiv. geog.)   **580**
  Use for nonscientific materials. Materials on
  the science of plants are entered under **Bota-
  ny.** Subdivisions used under this heading may
  be used under the names of orders, classes, or
  individual species of plants.
  UF   Flora
       Vegetable kingdom
  SA   types of plants characterized by
       their physical characteristics,
       environment, or use, e.g.
       **Climbing plants; Desert
       plants; Forage plants; etc.;**
       and names of botanical cate-
       gories of plants, e.g. **Ferns;**
       to be added as needed
  NT   **Bulbs**
       Carnivorous plants
       Climbing plants
       Desert plants
       Edible plants
       Ferns
       Fertilization of plants

       Flowers
       Forage plants
       Forest plants
       Fossil plants
       Freshwater plants
       Fruit
       Fungi
       Grasses
       Herbs
       Horticulture
       House plants
       Leaves
       Marine plants
       Mosses
       Mountain plants
       Mushrooms
       Poisonous plants
       Popular plant names
       Rare plants
       Seeds
       Shrubs
       Tobacco
       Trees
       Vegetables
       Weeds
  RT   Botany
       Gardening
       Herbicides
Plants—Analysis   572
  UF   Plant chemistry
       Plants—Chemical analysis
  BT   **Botanical chemistry**
Plants—Anatomy   571.3
  UF   Anatomy of plants
       Botany—Anatomy *[Former
          heading]*
       Botany—Structure
       Morphology
       Plant anatomy
       Structural botany
       Vegetable anatomy
  BT   **Anatomy**
       Botany
Plants—Chemical analysis
  USE   **Plants—Analysis**
Plants—Classification
  USE   **Botany—Classification**

BT = Broader Term   NT = Narrower Term   RT = Related Term   SA = See Also   UF = Used For

Plants—Collection and preservation
    580.75
  UF   Botanical specimens—Collection
       and preservation
       Collections of natural specimens
       Herbaria
       Preservation of botanical speci-
        mens
       Specimens, Preservation of
  BT   **Collectors and collecting**
  NT   **Flowers—Drying**
Plants—Conservation
  USE **Plant conservation**
Plants, Cultivated
  USE **Cultivated plants**
Plants—Diseases
  USE **Plant diseases**
Plants—Ecology
  USE **Plant ecology**
Plants, Edible
  USE **Edible plants**
Plants—Effect of poisons on
  USE **Herbicides**
Plants, Extinct
  USE **Fossil plants**
Plants—Fertilization
  USE **Fertilization of plants**
Plants—Folklore   398.24
  UF   Plant lore
  BT   **Folklore**
       Popular plant names
  NT   **Ethnobotany**
Plants, Fossil
  USE **Fossil plants**
Plants—Geographical distribution
    581.9
  UF   Geographical distribution of
       plants
       Phytogeography
       Plant distribution
  SA   types of plants with the subdivi-
       sion *Geographical distribu-*
       tion, to be added as needed
  BT   **Biogeography**
Plants—Growth   571.8
  BT   **Plant physiology**
Plants in art   704.9
  SA   types of plants in art, e.g. **Flow-**
       ers in art; to be added as
       needed

  BT   **Art**
       Decoration and ornament
  NT   **Flowers in art**
  RT   **Botanical illustration**
Plants, Industrial
  USE **Factories**
Plants, Medicinal
  USE **Medical botany**
Plants—Nutrition   575.7; 631.5
  UF   Plant nutrition
  BT   **Nutrition**
       Plant physiology
Plants, Ornamental
  USE **Ornamental plants**
Plants—Photography
  USE **Photography of plants**
Plants, Poisonous
  USE **Poisonous plants**
Plants—Propagation
  USE **Plant propagation**
Plants—Soilless culture
  USE **Hydroponics**
Plants—United States   581.973
  UF   Botany—United States *[Former*
       heading]
       United States—Plants
Plants, Useful
  USE **Economic botany**
      Edible plants
Plaster and plastering   693
  UF   Plastering
  BT   **Masonry**
  NT   **Cement**
       Concrete
       Mortar
       Stucco
Plaster casts   731.4
  UF   Casting
       Casts, Plaster
  BT   **Sculpture**
Plastering
  USE **Plaster and plastering**
Plastic industries
  USE **Plastics industry**
Plastic materials
  USE **Plastics**
Plastic surgery   617.9
  UF   Cosmetic surgery
       Surgery, Cosmetic

BT = Broader Term   NT = Narrower Term   RT = Related Term   SA = See Also   UF = Used For

Plastic surgery—*Continued*

       Surgery, Plastic *[Former heading]*

  BT   **Surgery**

       Transplantation of organs, tissues, etc.

Plastics   668.4

  UF   Plastic materials

  SA   names of specific plastics, to be added as needed

  BT   **Polymers**

  NT   **Gums and resins**

       Synthetic rubber

  RT   **Organic chemistry—Synthesis**

       Plastics industry

       Synthetic products

Plastics industry   338.4; 668.4

  UF   Plastic industries

       Plastics trade

  BT   **Chemical industry**

  RT   **Plastics**

Plastics trade

  USE **Plastics industry**

Plate   739.2

  UF   Gold plate

       Silver plate

  BT   **Goldwork**

       Silverwork

  NT   **Hallmarks**

       Sheffield plate

Plate metalwork   671.8

  BT   **Metalwork**

       Sheet metalwork

Plate tectonics   551.1

  BT   **Earth—Crust**

       Geophysics

  RT   **Continental drift**

       Submarine geology

Platforms, Drilling

  USE **Drilling platforms**

Play   790

  BT   **Recreation**

  NT   **Finger play**

       Imaginary playmates

       Sports

  RT   **Amusements**

       Games

Play centers

  USE **Community centers**

       Playgrounds

Play direction (Theater)

  USE **Theater—Production and direction**

Play production

  USE **Amateur theater**

       Theater—Production and direction

Play writing

  USE **Drama—Technique**

       Motion picture plays—Technique

       Radio plays—Technique

       Television plays—Technique

Playbills

  USE **Film posters**

Playgrounds   796.06

  UF   Play centers

       Public playgrounds

       School playgrounds

  BT   **Recreation**

       Sports facilities

  RT   **Community centers**

       Parks

Playhouses

  USE **Theaters**

Playing cards

  USE **Card games**

Playmates, Imaginary

  USE **Imaginary playmates**

Plays

  USE **Drama—Collections**

       One act plays

Plays, Bible

  USE **Bible plays**

Plays, Christmas

  USE **Christmas plays**

Plays, College

  USE **College and school drama—Collections**

Plays for children

  USE **Children's plays**

Playwrights

  USE **Dramatists**

Playwriting

  USE **Drama—Technique**

       Motion picture plays—Technique

       Radio plays—Technique

       Television plays—Technique

BT = Broader Term   NT = Narrower Term   RT = Related Term   SA = See Also   UF = Used For

Pleasure   152.4
  BT   **Emotions**
       Joy and sorrow
       Senses and sensation
  RT   **Happiness**
       Pain
Plot-your-own stories   808.3; 813, etc.
  UF   Choose-your-own story plots
       Making-choices stories
       Multiple plot stories
       Which-way stories
  BT   **Children's literature**
       Fiction
       Literary recreations
Plots (Drama, fiction, etc.)   808
    Use for materials that analyze plots or dis-
    cuss the technique of constructing plots. Col-
    lections of plots of a specific literary or musi-
    cal form are entered under that form with the
    subdivision *Stories, plots, etc.* Collections of
    literary plots are entered under **Literature—
    Stories, plots, etc.**
  UF   Drama—Plots
       Dramatic plots
       Fiction—Plots
       Novels—Plots
       Scenarios
  SA   national literatures and literary
         or musical forms with the
         subdivision *Stories, plots, etc.,*
         e.g. **Ballet—Stories, plots,
         etc.; Opera—Stories, plots,
         etc.;** to be added as needed
  BT   **Authorship**
       **Characters and characteristics
         in literature**
       Drama
       Fiction
       Literature
Plows   631.3
  BT   **Agricultural machinery**
Plumbing   696
  BT   **Building**
  NT   **Sewerage**
  RT   **House drainage**
       Household sanitation
       Pipe fitting
Pluralism (Social sciences)
  USE   **Biculturalism**
        Multiculturalism
Plywood   674
  BT   **Wood**

PMS (Gynecology)
  USE   **Premenstrual syndrome**
Pneumatic transmission
  USE   **Compressed air**
Pneumatics   533; 621.5
  BT   **Physics**
  NT   **Aerodynamics**
       Compressed air
       Ground cushion phenomena
       Sound
  RT   **Gases**
Pneumonia   616.2
  BT   **Lungs—Diseases**
Pocket calculators
  USE   **Calculators**
Podiatry   617.5
  UF   Chiropody
  BT   **Medicine**
  NT   **Foot—Care**
  RT   **Foot—Wounds and injuries**
Poetics   808.1
    Use for materials on the art and technique
    of poetry. General materials on the apprecia-
    tion, philosophy, etc. of poetry are entered un-
    der **Poetry.**
  UF   Poetry—Technique
  BT   **Poetry**
  NT   **Rhyme**
       Rhythm
       Versification
Poetry   809.1
    Use for general materials on poetry, not for
    individual works. Materials on the history and
    criticism of poetry from more than one litera-
    ture are entered under **Poetry—History and
    criticism.** Materials on the art and technique
    of poetry are entered under **Poetics.** Collec-
    tions of poetry are entered under **Poetry—
    Collections; English poetry—Collections;**
    etc.
  UF   Poetry—Philosophy
  SA   types of poetry, e.g. **Haiku;** and
         subjects, historical events,
         names of places, ethnic
         groups, classes of persons,
         and names of individual per-
         sons with the subdivision *Po-
         etry,* to express the theme or
         subject content of individual
         works or collections of poet-
         ry, e.g. **Animals—Poetry;
         Bunker Hill (Boston, Mass.),
         Battle of, 1775—Poetry;** Na-

BT = Broader Term   NT = Narrower Term   RT = Related Term   SA = See Also   UF = Used For

Poetry—*Continued*

        poleon I, Emperor of the
French, 1769-1821—Poetry;
etc., to be added as needed

BT   Literature

NT   American poetry

      Animals—Poetry

      Ballads

      Chicago (Ill.)—Poetry

      Children's poetry

      Christmas poetry

      Didactic poetry

      Eddas

      Elegiac poetry

      English poetry

      Epistolary poetry

      Erotic poetry

      Fantasy poetry

      Free verse

      French poetry

      Haiku

      Humorous poetry

      Indians of North America—Poetry

      Love poetry

      Narrative poetry

      Nature poetry

      Pastoral poetry

      Patriotic poetry

      Poetics

      Religious poetry

      Science fiction poetry

      Sea poetry

      Songs

      War poetry

Poetry and music

USE   Music and literature

Poetry—Collections   808.81; 811.08, etc.

UF   Poetry—Selections

      Rhymes

Poetry—Editing   070.5

BT   Editing

Poetry for children

USE   Children's poetry

      Nursery rhymes

Poetry, Historical

USE   Historical poetry

Poetry—History and criticism   809.1

Poetry—Philosophy

USE   Poetry

Poetry—Selections

USE   Poetry—Collections

Poetry—Technique

USE   Poetics

Poets   809.1; 920

    Use for materials on the personal lives of several poets, not limited to a single national literature. Materials about their literary productions are entered under **Poetry—History and criticism; English poetry—History and criticism;** etc.

SA   poets of particular countries, e.g. **American poets;** to be added as needed

BT   Authors

NT   American poets

      Lyricists

      Minstrels

      Troubadours

Poets, American

USE   American poets

Point Four program

USE   Reconstruction (1939-1951)

Poison ivy   583

BT   Poisonous plants

Poisonous animals   591.6

SA   names of poisonous animals, e.g. **Rattlesnakes;** to be added as needed

BT   Animals

      Dangerous animals

      Economic zoology

      Poisons and poisoning

NT   Rattlesnakes

Poisonous gases   363.17

UF   Asphyxiating gases

      Gases, Asphyxiating and poisonous

      Gases, Poisonous

BT   Gases

      Poisons and poisoning

NT   Radon

Poisonous gases—War use

USE   Chemical warfare

Poisonous plants   581.6

UF   Plants, Poisonous

      Toxic plants

SA   names of poisonous plants, e.g. **Poison ivy;** to be added as needed

BT   Economic botany

      Plants

BT = Broader Term   NT = Narrower Term   RT = Related Term   SA = See Also   UF = Used For

Poisonous plants—*Continued*
      Poisons and poisoning
NT   **Poison ivy**
Poisonous substances
  USE   **Poisons and poisoning**
Poisons and poisoning   363.17; 615.9
  UF   Poisonous substances
        Toxic substances
        Toxicology
  SA   types of poisons, to be added as
        needed; and, for the influence
        of particular substances on
        humans and animals, types of
        poisonous substances with the
        subdivision *Toxicology,* e.g.
        Insecticides—Toxicology; to
        be added as needed
  BT   **Accidents**
        Chemistry
        Hazardous substances
        Homicide
        Medical jurisprudence
  NT   **Food poisoning**
        Insecticides—Toxicology
        Lead poisoning
        Pesticides
        Poisonous animals
        Poisonous gases
        Poisonous plants
Polar expeditions
  USE   **Antarctica—Exploration**
        Arctic regions—Exploration
        Scientific expeditions
Polar lights
  USE **Auroras**
Polar regions   998
    Use for materials on both the Antarctic and
Arctic regions.
  NT   **Antarctica**
        Arctic regions
        North Pole
        South Pole
Polarity
  USE   **Opposites**
Police (May subdiv. geog.)   **363.2**
  UF   Police officers
        Policemen
  BT   **Administration of criminal jus-
tice**
        Law enforcement
  NT   **Animals in police work**

        Detectives
        Police brutality
        Police corruption
        Policewomen
        Secret service
        State police
  RT   **Crime**
        Criminal investigation
Police brutality (May subdiv. geog.)
    363.2
  UF   Police—Complaints against *[For-
mer heading]*
        Police cruelty
        Police repression
        Police violence
  BT   **Police**
Police—Complaints against
  USE   **Police brutality**
        Police corruption
Police—Corrupt practices
  USE   **Police corruption**
Police corruption (May subdiv. geog.)
    363.2
  UF   Corruption, Police
        Police—Complaints against *[For-
mer heading]*
        Police—Corrupt practices *[For-
mer heading]*
  BT   **Misconduct in office**
        Police
Police cruelty
  USE   **Police brutality**
Police, International
  USE   **International police**
Police officers
  USE   **Police**
Police repression
  USE   **Police brutality**
Police, State
  USE   **State police**
Police—United States   363.20973
  UF   United States—Police
Police violence
  USE   **Police brutality**
Policemen
  USE   **Police**
Policewomen   363.2
  UF   Women police officers
  BT   **Police**
        Women

BT = Broader Term   NT = Narrower Term   RT = Related Term   SA = See Also   UF = Used For

Polio
    USE   **Poliomyelitis**
Poliomyelitis   616.8
    UF   Infantile paralysis
          Paralysis, Anterior spinal
          Paralysis, Infantile
          Polio
          Spinal paralysis, Anterior
    BT   **Diseases**
Poliomyelitis vaccine   614.4; 615
    UF   Live poliovirus vaccine
          Sabin vaccine
          Salk vaccine
    BT   **Vaccination**
Polishing
    USE   **Grinding and polishing**
Politeness
    USE   **Courtesy**
          Etiquette
Political action committees (May subdiv.
    geog.)   **322.4; 324**

    Use for materials on special interest groups that support sympathetic candidates for public office through campaign contributions. Materials on groups that promote their own interests with public officials are entered under **Lobbying.**

    UF   Interest groups
          PACs (Political action committees)
          Pressure groups
    BT   **Political participation**
    RT   **Lobbying**
Political activity
    USE   **Political participation**
          and corporate bodies, families, classes of persons, industries, military services, and religious denominations with the subdivision *Political activity,* e.g. **Women—Political activity;** to be added as needed
Political aspects
    USE   subjects with the subdivision *Political aspects,* e.g. **Ethnic relations—Political aspects;** to be added as needed
Political assessments
    USE   **Campaign funds**
Political asylum
    USE   **Asylum**

Political behavior
    USE   **Political participation**
          Political psychology
Political boundaries
    USE   **Boundaries**
Political campaign literature
    USE   **Campaign literature**
Political campaigns
    USE   **Politics**
Political conventions   324.5
    UF   Conventions, Political
    BT   **Political science**
          Politics
    NT   **Primaries**
    RT   **Political parties**
Political correctness   306
    UF   Correctness, Political
          P.C. (Political correctness)
          PC (Political correctness)
    BT   **Ideology**
Political corruption   324; 353.4
    UF   Boss rule
          Corruption in politics *[Former heading]*
          Graft in politics
          Political scandals
          Politics—Corrupt practices
          Spoils system
    SA   names of specific incidents, e.g. **Watergate Affair, 1972-1974;** to be added as needed
    BT   **Conflict of interests**
          Political crimes and offenses
          Political ethics
          Politics
    NT   **Iran-Contra Affair, 1985-1990**
          Watergate Affair, 1972-1974
          Whistle blowing
    RT   **Campaign funds**
          Misconduct in office
Political crimes and offenses   364.1
    UF   Crimes, Political
          Sedition
    BT   **Political ethics**
          Subversive activities
    NT   **Anarchism and anarchists**
          Assassination
          Bombings
          Concentration camps
          Political corruption

BT = Broader Term   NT = Narrower Term   RT = Related Term   SA = See Also   UF = Used For

Political crimes and offenses—*Continued*
    Political prisoners
    Resistance to government
    Terrorism
    Treason
Political defectors
  USE   Defectors
Political economy
  USE   Economics
Political ethics   172
  UF   Ethics, Political
  BT   Political science
       Politics
       Social ethics
  NT   Citizenship
       Conflict of interests
       Political corruption
       Political crimes and offenses
       Resistance to government
Political extremism
  USE   Radicalism
Political geography
  USE   Boundaries
       Geopolitics
Political participation (May subdiv. geog.)
    323
  UF   Citizen participation
       Civic involvement
       Community action
       Mass political behavior
       Political activity
       Political behavior
  SA   subjects designating government
       activity with the subdivision
       Citizen participation, e.g.
       Crime prevention—Citizen
       participation; and corporate
       bodies, families, classes of
       persons, industries, military
       services, and religious denom-
       inations with the subdivision
       Political activity, e.g. **Wom-**
       en—Political activity; to be
       added as needed
  BT   **Politics**
  NT   **African Americans—Political**
       activity
       Blacks—Political activity
       City planning—Citizen partici-
       pation

       Clergy—Political activity
       College students—Political ac-
        tivity
       Crime prevention—Citizen par-
        ticipation
       Jews—Political activity
       Political action committees
       Students—Political activity
       Women—Political activity
  RT   Social action
Political parties (May subdiv. geog.)
    324.2
  UF   Parties, Political
  SA   names of parties, to be added as
       needed
  BT   **Political science**
       Politics
  NT   **Democratic Party (U.S.)**
       Politics
       Republican Party (U.S.)
       Right and left (Political sci-
       ence)
       Third parties (United States
       politics)
  RT   **Political conventions**
Political parties—Finance
  USE   **Campaign funds**
Political prisoners   365
  UF   Prisoners, Political
  BT   **Political crimes and offenses**
       Prisoners
Political psychology   302
  UF   Political behavior
       Politics—Psychological aspects
       Psychology, Political
  BT   **Political science**
       Psychology
       Social psychology
  NT   **Propaganda**
       Public opinion
Political refugees (May subdiv. geog.)
    325
  UF   Displaced persons
       Refugees, Political *[Former*
        heading]
  SA   refugees of particular countries,
       geographic regions, or ethnic
       groups, e.g. **Vietnamese refu-**
       gees; Arab refugees; etc.,

BT = Broader Term   NT = Narrower Term   RT = Related Term   SA = See Also   UF = Used For

Political refugees—*Continued*
>and names of wars with the
>subdivision *Refugees,* e.g.
>**World War, 1939-1945—**
>**Refugees;** to be added as
>needed
- BT Asylum
>International law
>International relations
>Refugees
- NT Defectors
>World War, 1939-1945—Refu-
>gees

Political scandals
- USE Political corruption

Political science   320

Use for materials on the science of politics. Materials on the various aspects of practical politics, such as electioneering, political machines, etc., are entered under **Politics.** Materials on the political processes of particular regions, countries, cities, etc., are entered under the place with the subdivision *Politics and government.*

- UF Administration
>Civics
>Civil government
>Commonwealth, The
>Government
- SA movements in political philoso-
>phy, e.g. **Marxism;** topics
>with the subdivision *Political*
>*aspects,* e.g. **Ethnic rela-**
>**tions—Political aspects;** and
>names of continents, areas,
>countries, cities, etc., and na-
>tive peoples with the subdivi-
>sion *Politics and government,*
>e.g. **United States—Politics**
>**and government; Indians of**
>**North America—Politics and**
>**government;** to be added as
>needed
- BT Social sciences
- NT Anarchism and anarchists
>Aristocracy
>Bureaucracy
>Citizenship
>Civil rights
>Civil service
>Communism
>Comparative government

>Conservatism
>Democracy
>Equality
>Executive power
>Federal government
>Freedom
>Geopolitics
>Government ownership
>Ideology
>Imperialism
>Individualism
>Law
>Legislation
>Liberalism
>Local government
>Marxism
>Monarchy
>Municipal government
>Nationalism
>Political conventions
>Political ethics
>Political parties
>Political psychology
>Power (Social sciences)
>Public administration
>Public opinion
>Radicalism
>Representative government and
>representation
>Republics
>Resistance to government
>Revolutions
>Right and left (Political sci-
>ence)
>Separation of powers
>Social contract
>Socialism
>State governments
>State rights
>Suffrage
>Taxation
>Totalitarianism
>United States—Politics and
>government
>Utopias
>World politics
- RT Constitutional history
>Constitutional law
>Politics
>State, The

BT = Broader Term   NT = Narrower Term   RT = Related Term   SA = See Also   UF = Used For

Political science—Religious aspects
USE **Religion and politics**
Political violence
USE **Sabotage**
Terrorism
Politicians (May subdiv. geog.)
324.2092; 920
BT **Statesmen**
NT **Women politicians**
Politicians, American
USE **Politicians—United States**
Politicians—United States 324.2092;
920
UF American politicians
Politicians, American
United States—Politicians
Politics 324.7

Use for materials on the various aspects of practical politics, such as electioneering, political machines, etc. Materials on the science of politics are entered under **Political science.**

UF Campaigns, Political
Electioneering
Political campaigns
Politics, Practical *[Former heading]*
Practical politics
SA subjects with the subdivision *Political aspects,* e.g. **Ethnic relations—Political aspects;** names of continents, areas, countries, cities, etc., and native peoples, with the subdivision *Politics and government;* and ethnic groups and classes of persons with the subdivision *Political activity,* e.g. **College students—Political activity;** to be added as needed
BT **Political parties**
NT **Arab countries—Politics and government**
Asia—Politics and government
Business and politics
Campaign funds
Campaign literature
Chicago (Ill.)—Politics and government
Elections

Indians of North America—Politics and government
Latin America—Politics and government
Lobbying
Political conventions
Political corruption
Political ethics
Political participation
Political parties
Primaries
Regionalism
Religion and politics
Television and politics
United States—Politics and government
RT **Political science**
Politics and business
USE **Business and politics**
Politics and Christianity
USE **Christianity and politics**
Politics and government
USE names of continents, areas, countries, cities, etc., and native peoples with the subdivision *Politics and government,* e.g. **United States—Politics and government; Arab countries—Politics and government; Indians of North America—Politics and government;** etc., to be added as needed
Politics and religion
USE **Religion and politics**
Politics and students
USE **Students—Political activity**
Politics and television
USE **Television and politics**
Politics—Corrupt practices
USE **Political corruption**
Politics, Practical
USE **Politics**
Politics—Psychological aspects
USE **Political psychology**
Politics—Religious aspects
USE **Religion and politics**
Pollination
USE **Fertilization of plants**

BT = Broader Term   NT = Narrower Term   RT = Related Term   SA = See Also   UF = Used For

Polls, Election
   USE   **Elections**
Polls, Public opinion
   USE   **Public opinion polls**
Pollution   304.2; 363.73
   UF   Chemical pollution
        Contamination of environment
        Environmental pollution
   SA   types of pollution, e.g. **Air pol-**
        lution; to be added as needed
   BT   **Environmental health**
        Human influence on nature
        Public health
        Sanitary engineering
        Sanitation
   NT   **Air pollution**
        Noise pollution
        Pesticides—Environmental as-
        pects
        Pollution control industry
        Radioactive pollution
        Space debris
        Water pollution
   RT   **Environmental protection**
        Hazardous wastes
        Industrial wastes
        Refuse and refuse disposal
Pollution control
   USE   **Pollution control industry**
Pollution control devices (Motor vehicles)
   USE   **Automobiles—Pollution control**
        devices
Pollution control industry   338.4;
        363.73
   UF   Pollution control
        Pollution—Prevention
   BT   **Pollution**
   NT   **Automobiles—Pollution control**
        devices
        Recycling
   RT   **Refuse and refuse disposal**
Pollution—Mathematical models   304.2;
        363.73
   BT   **Mathematical models**
Pollution of air
   USE   **Air pollution**
Pollution of water
   USE   **Water pollution**
Pollution—Prevention
   USE   **Pollution control industry**

Pollution, Radioactive
   USE   **Radioactive pollution**
Pollution, Space
   USE   **Space debris**
Poltergeists
   USE   **Ghosts**
Polyglot dictionaries   413
   UF   Dictionaries, Multilingual
        Dictionaries, Polyglot
        Multilingual dictionaries
        Multilingual glossaries, phrase
          books, etc.
        Polyglot glossaries, phrase
          books, etc.
   BT   **Encyclopedias and dictionaries**
Polyglot glossaries, phrase books, etc.
   USE   **Polyglot dictionaries**
Polygraph
   USE   **Lie detectors and detection**
Polymers   541.3; 547; 668.9
   UF   Polymers and polymerization
        [Former heading]
   SA   types of polymers, e.g. **Plastics;**
        to be added as needed
   BT   **Organic chemistry—Synthesis**
        Physical chemistry
   NT   **Plastics**
Polymers and polymerization
   USE   **Polymers**
Polynucleotides
   USE   **Nucleic acids**
Pomp
   USE   **Parades**
Ponds   551.48
   BT   **Water**
Ponies   636.1
   UF   Foals
   BT   **Horses**
Pontiac's Conspiracy, 1763-1765   973.2
   BT   **Indians of North America—**
        Wars
        United States—History—1600-
        1775, Colonial period
        United States—History—1755-
        1763, French and Indian
        War
Pony express   383
   BT   **Express service**
        Postal service

BT = Broader Term   NT = Narrower Term   RT = Related Term   SA = See Also   UF = Used For

Pools
USE   Swimming pools
Poor (May subdiv. geog.)   305.5; 362.5
   BT   **Poverty**
          Public welfare
   NT   **Begging**
          Homeless persons
          Tramps
          Unemployed
Poor—Medical care   362.1
   UF   Medical care for the poor
   BT   **Medical care**
   NT   **Medicaid**
Poor relief
   USE   **Charities**
           Domestic economic assistance
           Public welfare
Pop culture
   USE   **Popular culture**
Pop-up books
   USE   **Toy and movable books**
Popes   262; 920
   UF   Holy See
   BT   **Church history**
   RT   **Papacy**
Popes—Infallibility   262
   UF   Infallibility of the Pope
Popes—Temporal power   262
   UF   Temporal power of the Pope
   BT   **Church history—600-1500,**
           Middle Ages
   RT   **Church and state**
Popes—Travel
   USE   **Papal visits**
Popes—Voyages and travels
   USE   **Papal visits**
Popular arts
   USE   **Popular culture**
Popular culture (May subdiv. geog.)
   306.4

   Use for materials on literature, art, music, motion pictures, etc. produced for a mass audience. General materials on learning and scholarship, literature, the arts, etc. are entered under **Intellectual life.**

   UF   Culture, Popular
          Mass culture
          Pop culture
          Popular arts
   BT   **Civilization**
          Communication

          Culture
          Intellectual life
          Manners and customs
          Recreation
   RT   **Mass media**
Popular culture—Chicago (Ill.)   977.3
   UF   Chicago (Ill.)—Popular culture
           [Former heading]
Popular culture—United States   973
   UF   United States—Popular culture
           [Former heading]
   NT   **Americana**
Popular government
   USE   **Democracy**
Popular medicine   616.02

   Use for medical books written for the layman.

   UF   Medicine, Popular *[Former heading]*
   BT   **Medicine**
   NT   **Traditional medicine**
   RT   **Health self-care**
Popular music   781.64; 782.42164
   UF   Music, Popular (Songs, etc.)
           [Former heading]
          Popular songs
   SA   types of popular music, to be added as needed
   BT   **Music**
          Songs
   NT   **Blues music**
          Country music
          Gospel music
          Rap music
          Rock music
Popular music—Texts   782.42164
   UF   Lyrics
          Popular song lyrics
          Song lyrics
Popular music—Writing and publishing
   070.5; 781.3
   UF   Song writing
          Songwriting
   BT   **Composition (Music)**
Popular plant names   580.1

   Use for materials on the common or vernacular names of plants. Materials on the scientific names are entered under **Botany—Terminology.**

   UF   Botany—Nomenclature

Popular plant names—*Continued*
　　　　Plant names, Popular *[Former heading]*
　BT　**Plants**
　NT　**Plants—Folklore**
　RT　**Botany—Terminology**
Popular song lyrics
　USE　**Popular music—Texts**
Popular songs
　USE　**Popular music**
Popularity　158
　BT　**Social psychology**
Population　304.6; 363.9
　UF　Demography
　　　Foreign population
　SA　names of countries, cities, etc., with the subdivision *Population,* to be added as needed
　BT　**Economics**
　　　Human ecology
　　　Sociology
　　　Vital statistics
　NT　**Birth control**
　　　Census
　　　Chicago (Ill.)—Population
　　　Cities and towns—Growth
　　　Eugenics
　　　Human fertility
　　　Immigration and emigration
　　　Internal migration
　　　Mortality
　　　Ohio—Population
　　　United States—Population
　RT　**Birth rate**
Porcelain　738.2
　Use for materials on chinaware and porcelain for the table or decorative use. Materials on the technology of fired earthen products or on clay products intended for industrial use are entered under **Ceramics.**
　UF　China (Porcelain)
　　　Chinaware
　　　Dishes
　SA　types of porcelain, to be added as needed
　BT　**Decorative arts**
　　　Pottery
　　　Tableware
　NT　**China painting**
Porcelain enamels
　USE　**Enamel and enameling**

Porcelain painting
　USE　**China painting**
Pornography　176; 363.4; 364.1
　UF　Immoral literature
　　　Obscene materials
　NT　**Obscenity (Law)**
　RT　**Erotica**
Portable computers　004.16
　UF　Computers, Portable
　　　Handheld computers
　　　Laptop computers
　BT　**Computers**
　　　Microcomputers
Portrait miniatures
　USE　**Miniature painting**
Portrait painting　757
　UF　Portraiture
　BT　**Painting**
　　　Portraits
　RT　**Figure painting**
　　　Miniature painting
Portrait photography　778.9; 779
　UF　Photography—Portraits *[Former heading]*
　　　Portraiture
　BT　**Photography**
　　　Portraits
Portraits　704.9; 757
　UF　Iconography
　SA　headings for collective and individual biography, classes of persons, and names of individuals with the subdivision *Portraits,* e.g. **United States—Biography—Portraits; Musicians—Portraits; Shakespeare, William, 1564-1616—Portraits;** etc., to be added as needed
　BT　**Art**
　　　Biography
　　　Pictures
　NT　**Cartoons and caricatures**
　　　Portrait painting
　　　Portrait photography
Portraiture
　USE　**Portrait painting**
　　　Portrait photography
Ports
　USE　**Harbors**

BT = Broader Term　　NT = Narrower Term　　RT = Related Term　　SA = See Also　　UF = Used For

565

Portuguese literature   869
    BT   Literature
          Romance literature
    RT   Brazilian literature
Position analysis
    USE   Topology
Positivism   146
    BT   Philosophy
          Rationalism
    NT   Materialism
          Pragmatism
    RT   Agnosticism
          Deism
          Realism
Possessions, Lost and found
    USE   Lost and found possessions
Post cards
    USE   Postcards
Post-impressionism
    USE   Postimpressionism (Art)
Post-modernism
    USE   Postmodernism
Post office
    USE   Postal service
Post-traumatic stress disorder   616.85
    UF   Posttraumatic stress disorder
          Traumatic stress syndrome
    BT   Anxiety
          Neuroses
          Stress (Psychology)
Postage stamp collecting
    USE   Stamp collecting
Postage stamps   383; 769.56
    UF   Stamps, Postage
    RT   Stamp collecting
Postage stamps—Collectors and collecting
    USE   Stamp collecting
Postal cards
    USE   Postcards
Postal delivery code
    USE   Zip code
Postal service (May subdiv. geog.)
    354.75; 383
    UF   Mail service
          Parcel post
          Post office
    BT   Communication
          Transportation
    NT   Air mail service
          Pony express

          Zip code
Postal service—United States   354.75;
    383
    UF   United States—Mail
          United States—Postal service
Postcards   383; 741.6
    UF   Picture postcards
          Post cards
          Postal cards
Postcards—Collectors and collecting
    790.1
Posters   741.6
    UF   Advertising, Pictorial
          Picture posters
    SA   types of posters, e.g. **Film post-**
          ers; and subjects, ethnic
          groups, classes of persons, in-
          dividual persons, corporate
          bodies, and names of wars
          with the subdivision *Posters,*
          to be added as needed
    BT   **Advertising**
          Commercial art
    NT   **Film posters**
    RT   **Signs and signboards**
Posters, Film
    USE   **Film posters**
Postimpressionism (Art)   709.03
    UF   Post-impressionism
    BT   **Modern art—1800-1899 (19th**
          century)
          Modern art—1900-1999 (20th
          century)
          Painting
    RT   **Cubism**
          Expressionism (Art)
          Futurism (Art)
          Impressionism (Art)
          Surrealism
Postmodernism   190; 700.1
    UF   Post-modernism
    BT   **Aesthetics**
    RT   **Modernism (Arts)**
Posttraumatic stress disorder
    USE   **Post-traumatic stress disorder**
Posture   613.7
    BT   **Physical education**
Pot (Drug)
    USE   **Marijuana**

BT = Broader Term   NT = Narrower Term   RT = Related Term   SA = See Also   UF = Used For

Potable water
    USE   **Drinking water**
Potash   631.8; 668
    BT   **Fertilizers**
Potatoes   635; 641.3
    BT   **Vegetables**
Potters   738.092; 920
    BT   **Artists**
Potters' marks
    USE   **Pottery—Marks**
Pottery   666; 738
    Use for materials on pottery for the table or for decorative use. Materials on the technology of fired earthen products or on clay products intended for industrial use are entered under **Ceramics.**
    UF   Crockery
           Dishes
           Earthenware
           Faience
           Stoneware
    SA   types of pottery and pottery of particular countries, e.g. **American pottery;** to be added as needed
    BT   **Ceramics**
           Clay industries
           Decoration and ornament
           Decorative arts
           Tableware
    NT   **American pottery**
           Glazes
           Porcelain
           Terra cotta
           Tiles
    RT   **Vases**
Pottery, American
    USE   **American pottery**
Pottery—Marks   738
    UF   Potters' marks
Poultry   598.6; 636.5
    SA   types of domesticated birds, e.g. **Ducks;** to be added as needed
    BT   **Birds**
           Domestic animals
    NT   **Ducks**
           Geese
           Turkeys
Poverty   305.5; 362.5
    UF   Destitution

Pauperism
    SA   names of countries with the subdivisions *Economic conditions* and *Social conditions,* to be added as needed
    BT   **Economic conditions**
           Social problems
    NT   **Homelessness**
           Poor
    RT   **Domestic economic assistance**
           Public welfare
           Subsistence economy
Powder, Smokeless
    USE   **Gunpowder**
Powdered milk
    USE   **Dried milk**
Power blackouts
    USE   **Electric power failures**
Power boats
    USE   **Motorboats**
Power failures
    USE   **Electric power failures**
Power (Mechanics)   531; 621
    Use for materials on the physics and engineering aspects of power. Materials on the available sources of mechanical power in general are entered under **Energy resources.**
    UF   Energy technology
    BT   **Mechanical engineering**
           Mechanics
    NT   **Compressed air**
           Electric power
           Energy resources
           Force and energy
           Machinery
           Power transmission
           Steam
           Water power
           Wind power
Power plants   621.4
    UF   Power stations
    SA   types of power plants, to be added as needed
    NT   **Electric power plants**
           Nuclear power plants
           Steam power plants
Power plants, Atomic
    USE   **Nuclear power plants**
Power plants, Electric
    USE   **Electric power plants**

Power plants, Hydroelectric
    USE   **Hydroelectric power plants**
Power plants, Steam
    USE   **Steam power plants**
Power politics
    USE   **Balance of power**
                Cold war
Power resources
    USE   **Energy resources**
Power resources conservation
    USE   **Energy conservation**
Power resources development
    USE   **Energy development**
Power (Social sciences)   303.3
    BT   **Political science**
    NT   **Elite (Social sciences)**
Power stations
    USE   **Power plants**
Power supply
    USE   **Energy resources**
Power tools   621.9
    BT   **Tools**
Power transmission   621.8
    UF   Transmission of power
    BT   **Mechanical engineering**
                Power (Mechanics)
    NT   **Cables**
                Electric power distribution
                Gearing
    RT   **Belts and belting**
                Machinery
Power transmission, Electric
    USE   **Electric lines**
                Electric power distribution
Powerlifting
    USE   **Weight lifting**
Powers, Separation of
    USE   **Separation of powers**
POWs
    USE   **Prisoners of war**
Powwows   394.2; 970.004
    BT   **Festivals**
                Indians of North America—Rites and ceremonies
                Indians of North America—Social life and customs
Practical jokes   818, etc.
    UF   Pranks
    BT   **Jokes**
                Wit and humor

Practical nurses   610.73; 920
    BT   **Nurses**
Practical nursing   610.73; 649.8
    BT   **Nursing**
Practical politics
    USE   **Politics**
Practical Psychology
    USE   **Applied psychology**
Practice
    USE   types of professions with the subdivision *Practice*, e.g. **Nuclear medicine—Practice;** to be added as needed
Practice teaching
    USE   **Student teaching**
Pragmatism   144
    BT   **Philosophy**
                Positivism
                Realism
                Theory of knowledge
    RT   **Empiricism**
                Reality
                Truth
                Utilitarianism
Prairies   577.4; 578.74
    BT   **Grasslands**
Pranks
    USE   **Practical jokes**
Prayer   248.3; 291.4
    UF   Devotion
                Devotional theology
    BT   **Worship**
    RT   **Devotional exercises**
                Prayers
Prayer-books
    USE   **Prayers**
Prayer-books and devotions
    USE   **Prayers**
Prayer in the public schools
    USE   **Religion in the public schools**
Prayers   242; 264; 291.4
    UF   Collects
                Prayer-books
                Prayer-books and devotions
    SA   names of religions, denominations, religious orders, classes of persons for whose use the prayers are intended, and names of saints and deities to

---

BT = Broader Term   NT = Narrower Term   RT = Related Term   SA = See Also   UF = Used For

Prayers—*Continued*
     whom the prayers are directed
     with the subdivision *Prayers,*
     e.g. **Buddhism—Prayers;**
     Sick—Prayers; Mary,
     Blessed Virgin, Saint—
     Prayers; etc., to be added as
     needed
  BT   **Devotional literature**
  NT   **Buddhism—Prayers**
       Mary, Blessed Virgin, Saint—
         Prayers
       Meditations
       Sick—Prayers
  RT   **Prayer**
Prayers in the public schools
  USE **Religion in the public schools**
Pre-Columbian Americans
  USE **Indians of North America**
Pre-Lenten festivities
  USE **Carnival**
Preachers
  USE **Clergy**
Preaching   251; 291.6
  UF   Speaking
  BT   **Pastoral theology**
       Public speaking
       Rhetoric
  RT   **Sermons**
Precious metals   553.4; 669
  UF   Bullion
  BT   **Metals**
       Mines and mineral resources
  NT   **Gold**
       Silver
Precious stones   553.8
    Use for mineralogical or technological materials on gem stones. Materials on cut and polished precious stones treated from the point of view of art or antiquity are entered under **Gems.** Materials on gems in which the emphasis is on the setting are entered under **Jewelry.**
  UF   Gemstones
       Jewels
  SA   names of precious stones, to be
       added as needed
  BT   **Minerals**
  NT   **Diamonds**
  RT   **Gems**
Precipitation forecasting
  USE **Weather forecasting**

Precipitation (Meteorology)
  USE **Rain**
        Snow
Precocious children
  USE **Gifted children**
Precolumbian Americans
  USE **Indians of North America**
Predaceous animals
  USE **Predatory animals**
Predacious animals
  USE **Predatory animals**
Predators
  USE **Predatory animals**
Predatory animals   591.5
  UF   Predaceous animals
       Predacious animals
       Predators
  SA   types of predatory animals, to be
       added as needed
  BT   **Animals**
  NT   **Birds of prey**
Predestination   234; 291.2
  UF   Election (Theology)
       Foreordination
  BT   **Theology**
  RT   **Fate and fatalism**
       Free will and determinism
Predictions
  USE **Forecasting**
        Prophecies
Prefabricated buildings   693
  UF   Buildings, Prefabricated *[Former heading]*
  BT   **Buildings**
  NT   **Prefabricated houses**
Prefabricated houses   693; 728
  UF   Houses, Prefabricated
       Packaged houses
  BT   **Domestic architecture**
       House construction
       Houses
       Prefabricated buildings
Pregnancy   599; 612.6; 618.2
  BT   **Reproduction**
  NT   **Miscarriage**
       Prenatal care
       Teenage pregnancy
  RT   **Childbirth**
Pregnancy, Adolescent
  USE **Teenage pregnancy**

BT = Broader Term   NT = Narrower Term   RT = Related Term   SA = See Also   UF = Used For

Pregnancy, Teenage
USE **Teenage pregnancy**
Pregnancy, Termination of
USE **Abortion**
Prehistoric animals   560
UF   Animals, Prehistoric
BT   **Animals**
      Fossils
NT   **Dinosaurs**
RT   **Extinct animals**
Prehistoric art   709.01
UF   Art, Prehistoric *[Former heading]*
BT   **Art**
NT   **Rock drawings, paintings, and engravings**
Prehistoric man
USE   **Fossil hominids**
       Prehistoric peoples
Prehistoric peoples (May subdiv. geog.)
       930.1
UF   Man, Prehistoric *[Former heading]*
      Prehistoric man *[Former heading]*
      Prehistory
SA   names of prehistoric peoples,
       e.g. **Cro-Magnons;** etc.; and
       names of countries, cities,
       etc., with the subdivision *Antiquities,* e.g. **United States—Antiquities;** to be added as
       needed
BT   **Antiquities**
      Archeology
      Human beings
NT   **Cave dwellers**
      Cro-Magnons
RT   **Human origins**
Prehistory
USE   **Archeology**
       Fossil hominids
       Prehistoric peoples
Preimplantational ectogenesis
USE   **Fertilization in vitro**
Prejudgments
USE   **Prejudices**
Prejudice
USE   **Prejudices**

Prejudice-motivated crimes
USE   **Hate crimes**
Prejudices   152.4; 177; 303.3
UF   Antipathies
      Bias (Psychology)
      Bigotry
      Prejudgments
      Prejudice
SA   types of prejudice, to be added
       as needed
BT   **Attitude (Psychology)**
      Emotions
      Human relations
NT   **Antisemitism**
      Discrimination
      Racism
      Sexism
Prejudicial publicity
USE   **Freedom of the press and fair trial**
Prelude and fugue
USE   **Fugue**
Preludes and fugues
USE   **Fugue**
Premarital contracts
USE   **Marriage contracts**
Premarital counseling
USE   **Marriage counseling**
Premenstrual syndrome   618.1
UF   PMS (Gynecology)
      Premenstrual tension
      Tension, Premenstrual
BT   **Menstruation**
Premenstrual tension
USE   **Premenstrual syndrome**
Premiers
USE   **Prime ministers**
Prenatal care   618.2
BT   **Pregnancy**
Prenatal diagnosis   618.3
BT   **Diagnosis**
NT   **Amniocentesis**
      Genetic counseling
Prenuptial contracts
USE   **Marriage contracts**
Prepaid group medical practice
USE   **Health maintenance organizations**
Prepaid health plans
USE   **Health insurance**

BT = Broader Term   NT = Narrower Term   RT = Related Term   SA = See Also   UF = Used For

Prepaid medical care
USE **Health insurance**
Prepared cereals   641.3; 664
UF   Breakfast cereals
Cereals, Prepared *[Former heading]*
BT   **Breakfasts**
Food
Preprimers
USE   **Easy reading materials**
Presbyterian Church   285
BT   **Christian sects**
Preschool children
USE   **Children**
Preschool education   372.21
UF   Children—Education
Education, Preschool *[Former heading]*
Infants—Education
BT   **Education**
NT   **Readiness for school**
RT   **Kindergarten**
Nursery schools
Preschool reading materials
USE   **Easy reading materials**
Prescription drug abuse
USE   **Medication abuse**
Presents
USE   **Gifts**
Preservation
USE   types of foods and other things preserved with the subdivision *Preservation,* e.g. **Fruit—Preservation; Wood—Preservation;** etc.; antiquities and types of natural objects, including animal specimens and plant specimens, with the subdivision *Collection and preservation,* e.g. **Birds—Collection and preservation;** and types of art objects, library materials, architecture, and land vehicles with the subdivision *Conservation and restoration,* e.g. **Automobiles—Conservation and restoration;** to be added as needed

Preservation of antiquities
USE   **Antiquities—Collection and preservation**
Preservation of botanical specimens
USE   **Plants—Collection and preservation**
Preservation of buildings
USE   **Architecture—Conservation and restoration**
Preservation of food
USE   **Food—Preservation**
Preservation of forests
USE   **Forest conservation**
Preservation of historical records
USE   **Archives**
Preservation of library resources
USE   **Library resources—Conservation and restoration**
Preservation of natural resources
USE   **Conservation of natural resources**
Preservation of natural scenery
USE   **Landscape protection**
Natural monuments
Nature conservation
Preservation of organs, tissues, etc.
617.9
UF   Organ preservation (Anatomy)
Organs (Anatomy)—Preservation
RT   **Transplantation of organs, tissues, etc.**
Preservation of specimens
USE   **Taxidermy**
Preservation of wildlife
USE   **Wildlife conservation**
Preservation of wood
USE   **Wood—Preservation**
Preservation of works of art
USE   subjects with the subdivision *Conservation and restoration,* e.g. **Painting—Conservation and restoration;** to be added as needed
Preservation of zoological specimens
USE   **Zoological specimens—Collection and preservation**
Preserving
USE   **Canning and preserving**

BT = Broader Term   NT = Narrower Term   RT = Related Term   SA = See Also   UF = Used For

Presidential aides
USE **Presidents—United States—Staff**

Presidential campaigns—United States
USE **Presidents—United States—Election**

Presidential libraries
USE **Presidents—United States—Archives**

Presidents (May subdiv. geog.)   **352.23; 920**
SA   names of presidents, to be added as needed
BT   **Heads of state**
NT   **Vice-presidents**
RT   **Executive power**

Presidents—Mexico   920; 972
UF   Mexico—Presidents

Presidents—Powers
USE   **Executive power**

Presidents' spouses—United States   920
UF   First ladies—United States
Presidents—United States—Spouses *[Former heading]*
Presidents' wives—United States
Wives of presidents—United States

Presidents—United States   352.230973; 920
When applicable, the subdivisions under this heading may be used under names of presidents, prime ministers, and other rulers.
UF   United States—Presidents
SA   names of presidents, to be added as needed
NT   **Lincoln, Abraham, 1809-1865**

Presidents—United States—Appointment   352.23

Presidents—United States—Archives   026
UF   Libraries, Presidential
Presidential libraries
Presidents—United States—Libraries
SA   names of individual libraries, to be added as needed
BT   **Archives**
NT   **Harry S. Truman Library**

Presidents—United States—Assassination   364.15; 973
BT   **Assassination**

Presidents—United States—Death and burial

Presidents—United States—Burial
USE   **Presidents—United States—Death and burial**

Presidents—United States—Children   920

Presidents—United States—Death and burial   393; 973
UF   Presidents—United States—Burial
Presidents—United States—Funeral and memorial services *[Former heading]*
Presidents—United States—Memorial services
NT   **Presidents—United States—Assassination**

Presidents—United States—Election   324.973
May further subdivide by date.
UF   Campaigns, Presidential—United States
Electoral college
Presidential campaigns—United States
BT   **Elections**

Presidents—United States—Family   920

Presidents—United States—Fathers   920

Presidents—United States—Friends and associates   920

Presidents—United States—Funeral and memorial services
USE   **Presidents—United States—Death and burial**

Presidents—United States—Health   352.23; 920
UF   Presidents—United States—Illness

Presidents—United States—Homes   728

Presidents—United States—Illness
USE   **Presidents—United States—Health**

Presidents—United States—Impeachment   342

Presidents—United States—Inability
USE   **Presidents—United States—Succession**

Presents—United States—Inaugural addresses 352.23
   BT   Presidents—United States—Inauguration
         Speeches
Presidents—United States—Inauguration 352.23
   NT   Presidents—United States—Inaugural addresses
Presidents—United States—Libraries
   USE   Presidents—United States—Archives
Presidents—United States—Medals 352.23
Presidents—United States—Memorial services
   USE   Presidents—United States—Death and burial
Presidents—United States—Messages 352.23
   UF   Messages to Congress
         Presidents—United States—State of the Union message
         State of the Union messages
Presidents—United States—Mothers 920
Presidents—United States—Nomination 324.50973
   UF   Nomination of presidents
Presidents—United States—Portraits 973
Presidents—United States—Power
   USE   Executive power—United States
Presidents—United States—Press relations 070.4; 352.230973
Presidents—United States—Protection 352.23
Presidents—United States—Quotations 818
   BT   Quotations
Presidents—United States—Relations with Congress 328.73; 352.23
Presidents—United States—Religion 920
Presidents—United States—Resignation 352.23
Presidents—United States—Sports 920

Presidents—United States—Spouses
   USE   Presidents' spouses—United States
Presidents—United States—Staff 352.23
   UF   Presidential aides
   BT   Executive departments—United States
Presidents—United States—State of the Union message
   USE   Presidents—United States—Messages
Presidents—United States—Succession 342; 352.23
   UF   Presidents—United States—Inability
Presidents—United States—Tombs 917.3
Presidents—United States—Travel 352.23
   UF   Presidents—United States—Voyages and travels *[Former heading]*
Presidents—United States—Voyages and travels
   USE   Presidents—United States—Travel
Presidents' wives—United States
   USE   Presidents' spouses—United States
Press 070
   BT   Journalism
         Propaganda
         Publicity
   NT   Alternative press
         Broadcast journalism
         Freedom of the press
         Freedom of the press and fair trial
         News agencies
         Pamphlets
   RT   Newspapers
         Periodicals
         Public opinion
Press, Alternative
   USE   Alternative press
Press and government
   USE   Press—Government policy
Press censorship
   USE   Freedom of the press

BT = Broader Term   NT = Narrower Term   RT = Related Term   SA = See Also   UF = Used For

Press clippings
  USE   Clippings (Books, newspapers, etc.)
Press—Government policy   323.44
  UF   Government and the press
       Press and government
  BT   Freedom of information
Press, Underground
  USE   Alternative press
Press working of metal
  USE   Sheet metalwork
Pressure groups
  USE   Lobbying
       Political action committees
Prestidigitation
  USE   Magic tricks
Pretenders
  USE   Impostors and imposture
Prevention
  USE   diseases, medical conditions, and situations to be avoided with the subdivision *Prevention*, e.g. **AIDS (Disease)—Prevention; Accidents—Prevention;** etc., to be added as needed
Prevention of accidents
  USE   Accidents—Prevention
Prevention of crime
  USE   Crime prevention
Prevention of cruelty to animals
  USE   Animal welfare
Prevention of disease
  USE   Preventive medicine
Prevention of fire
  USE   Fire prevention
Prevention of smoke
  USE   Smoke prevention
Preventive medicine   613
  UF   Diseases—Prevention
       Medicine, Preventive *[Former heading]*
       Prevention of disease
  SA   names of diseases with the subdivision *Prevention*, e.g. **AIDS (Disease)—Prevention;** to be added as needed
  BT   Medicine
  NT   Communicable diseases—Prevention
       Health

Heart diseases—Prevention
       Hygiene
       Immunity
       Vaccination
  RT   Pathology
       Public health
Price controls
  USE   Wage-price policy
Price indexes, Consumer
  USE   Consumer price indexes
Price-wage policy
  USE   Wage-price policy
Prices   338.5
  SA   subjects with the subdivision *Prices*, e.g. **Art—Prices;** to be added as needed
  BT   Commerce
       Consumption (Economics)
       Economics
       Finance
       Manufactures
  NT   Art—Prices
       Books—Prices
       Consumer price indexes
       Farm produce—Marketing
       Wage-price policy
  RT   Cost and standard of living
       Wages
Priests   200.92; 270.092
  UF   Pastors
  SA   names of church denominations with the subdivision *Clergy*, e.g. **Catholic Church—Clergy;** to be added as needed
  BT   Clergy
  NT   Catholic Church—Clergy
       Ex-priests
Primaries   324.5
  UF   Direct primaries
       Elections, Primary
  BT   Elections
       Political conventions
       Politics
Primary education
  USE   Elementary education
Primates   599.8
  SA   types of primates, e.g. **Monkeys;** to be added as needed
  BT   Mammals
  NT   Human beings

BT = Broader Term   NT = Narrower Term   RT = Related Term   SA = See Also   UF = Used For

Primates—*Continued*
  Monkeys
Primates—Behavior   599.8
  UF   Primates—Habits and behavior
        [Former heading]
  BT   Animal behavior
Primates—Habits and behavior
  USE   Primates—Behavior
Prime ministers (May subdiv. geog.)
        352.23; 920
    May use same subdivisions, following geographic subdivision, as for **Presidents—United States.**
  UF   Premiers
  BT   Cabinet officers
        Executive power
Prime ministers—Great Britain
        352.230941; 920
  UF   Great Britain—Prime ministers
Primers
  USE   Easy reading materials
Primitive Christianity
  USE   Church history—30-600, Early
        church
Primitive man
  USE   Primitive societies
Primitive societies (May subdiv. geog.)
        306; 305.8
    Use for materials on nonliterate, nonindustrialized peoples who, according to nineteenth-century theories, represented an early or primitive stage of social evolution.
  UF   Man, Primitive *[Former heading]*
        Nonliterate folk society *[Former heading]*
        Nonliterate man *[Former heading]*
        Primitive man
        Primitive society
        Society, Primitive
  BT   Civilization
        Ethnology
  NT   Nomads
Primitive society
  USE   Primitive societies
Princes (May subdiv. geog.)   920
  UF   Princes and princesses *[Former heading]*
        Royalty
  BT   Courts and courtiers

Princes and princesses
  USE   Princes
        Princesses
Princesses (May subdiv. geog.)   920
  UF   Princes and princesses *[Former heading]*
        Royalty
  BT   Courts and courtiers
Printing (May subdiv. geog.)   686.2
  SA   types of printing processes, to
        be added as needed
  BT   Bibliography
        Book industries
        Graphic arts
        Industrial arts
        Publishers and publishing
  NT   Advertising layout and typography
        Color printing
        Electrotyping
        Linoleum block printing
        Linotype
        Lithography
        Offset printing
        Proofreading
        Textile printing
        Type and type founding
        Typesetting
        Typography
  RT   Books
        Prints
Printing—Exhibitions   686.2074
  UF   Books—Exhibitions
  BT   Exhibitions
  RT   Book industries—Exhibitions
Printing, Offset
  USE   Offset printing
Printing—Specimens   686.2
  UF   Type specimens
  BT   Advertising
        Initials
  RT   Type and type founding
Printing—Style manuals   686.02
  UF   Style manuals
  RT   Authorship—Handbooks, manuals, etc.
Printing, Textile
  USE   Textile printing

BT = Broader Term   NT = Narrower Term   RT = Related Term   SA = See Also   UF = Used For

Prints   769
   SA   prints of particular countries, e.g.
         American prints; to be add-
         ed as needed
   BT   **Graphic arts**
   NT   **American prints**
         Bookplates
         Color prints
         Linoleum block printing
         Lithography
         Woodcuts
   RT   **Printing**
Prints, American
   USE   **American prints**
Prison escapes
   USE   **Escapes**
Prison labor
   USE   **Convict labor**
Prison reform   365
   UF   Penal reform
   BT   **Social problems**
Prison schools
   USE   **Prisoners—Education**
Prisoners   365
   UF   Convicts
   BT   **Criminals**
   NT   **Political prisoners**
         United States—History—1861-
         1865, Civil War—Prisoners
         and prisons
   RT   **Prisons**
Prisoners—Education   365
   UF   Education of criminals
         Education of prisoners
         Prison schools
   BT   **Adult education**
         Prisons
Prisoners of war   341.6; 355.7
   UF   Exchange of prisoners of war
         P.O.W.'s
         POWs
   SA   prisoners of war from particular
         countries, e.g. **American pris-**
         oners of war; and names of
         wars with the subdivision
         Prisoners and prisons, to be
         added as needed
   NT   **American prisoners of war**
         Missing in action

         World War, 1939-1945—Pris-
         oners and prisons
   RT   **Concentration camps**
Prisoners of war, American
   USE   **American prisoners of war**
Prisoners, Political
   USE   **Political prisoners**
Prisons (May subdiv. geog.)   365
   UF   Dungeons
         Imprisonment
         Jails
         Penal institutions
         Penitentiaries
   SA   types of prisons and names of
         individual prisons, to be add-
         ed as needed
   BT   **Administration of criminal jus-**
         tice
         Correctional institutions
         Punishment
   NT   **Escapes**
         Prisoners—Education
         Probation
         Reformatories
         United States—History—1861-
         1865, Civil War—Prisoners
         and prisons
   RT   **Convict labor**
         Crime
         Prisoners
Prisons—United States   365
   UF   United States—Prisons
Privacy, Right of
   USE   **Right of privacy**
Private art collections
   USE   **Art collections**
Private enterprise
   USE   **Free enterprise**
Private eye stories
   USE   **Mystery and detective plays**
         Mystery fiction
         Mystery films
         Mystery radio programs
         Mystery television programs
Private funding of the arts
   USE   **Art patronage**
Private schools   371.02; 373.2
   UF   Boarding schools
         Independent schools
         Nonpublic schools

BT = Broader Term   NT = Narrower Term   RT = Related Term   SA = See Also   UF = Used For

Private schools—*Continued*
  BT   Schools
  NT   Church schools
        English public schools
Private theater
  USE   Amateur theater
Privateering   341
  UF   Letters of marque
  BT   International law
        Naval art and science
        Naval history
        Pirates
Privatisation
  USE   Privatization
Privatization (May subdiv. geog.)   338.9
     Use for materials on the transfer of public
  assets and service functions to the private sec-
  tor.
  UF   Denationalization
        Privatisation
  BT   Economic policy
        Industrial policy
  RT   Government ownership
Prize fighting
  USE   Boxing
Prizes (Rewards)
  USE   Awards
Pro-abortion movement
  USE   Pro-choice movement
Pro-choice movement   179.7; 363.46
  UF   Abortion rights movement
        Freedom of choice movement
        Pro-abortion movement
        Right to choose movement
  BT   Social movements
  RT   Abortion—Ethical aspects
        Abortion—Religious aspects
        Women's rights
Pro-life movement   179.7; 363.46
  UF   Anti-abortion movement
        Antiabortion movement
        Right-to-life movement (Anti-
          abortion movement)
  BT   Social movements
  RT   Abortion—Ethical aspects
        Abortion—Religious aspects
        Women's rights
Probabilities   519.2
  UF   Certainty
        Fortune
        Statistical inference

  BT   Algebra
        Logic
        Mathematics
        Statistics
  NT   Average
        Game theory
        Reliability (Engineering)
        Sampling (Statistics)
Probation   364.6
  UF   Reform of criminals
        Suspended sentence
  BT   Corrections
        Criminal law
        Prisons
        Punishment
        Reformatories
        Social case work
  RT   Juvenile courts
        Parole
Probes, Space
  USE   Space probes
Problem children
  USE   Emotionally disturbed children
Problem drinking
  USE   Alcoholism
Problem families—Counseling of
  USE   Family therapy
Problem solving   153.4; 510.76
  UF   Solution achievement
  BT   Psychology
  NT   Crisis management
        Critical thinking
        Group problem solving
  RT   Decision making
Problem solving, Group
  USE   Group problem solving
Problems, exercises, etc.
  USE   subjects with the subdivision
          Problems, exercises, etc., for
          compilations of practice prob-
          lems or exercises for use in
          the study of a topic, e.g.
          **Chemistry—Problems, exer-
          cises, etc.;** to be added as
          needed
Procedural due process
  USE   Due process of law
Processing (Libraries)
  USE   Library technical processes

BT = Broader Term   NT = Narrower Term   RT = Related Term   SA = See Also   UF = Used For

Processions
USE **Parades**
Procurement, Government
USE **Government purchasing**
Producers
USE producers and directors in specific media, e.g. **Motion picture producers and directors; Theatrical producers and directors;** etc., to be added as needed
Product recall 658.5
UF Commercial products recall
Manufactures—Defects
Manufactures recall
Recall of products
BT **Consumer protection**
Product safety 363.19; 658.5
UF Commercial products—Safety measures
BT **Consumer protection**
Production
USE **Economics**
Industries
Production engineering
USE **Factory management**
Production standards 658.5
Use for materials on the unit time value for the accomplishment of a work task as determined by work measurement techniques.
UF Output standards
Standards of output
Time production standards
Work standards
SA types of industries and processes with the subdivision *Production standards,* e.g. **Automobile industry—Production standards;** to be added as needed
BT **Labor productivity**
Management
NT **Automobile industry—Production standards**
Motion study
Time study
Productivity of labor
USE **Labor productivity**
Products, Animal
USE **Animal products**

Products, Brand name
USE **Brand name products**
Products, Commercial
USE **Commercial products**
Products, Dairy
USE **Dairy products**
Products, Generic
USE **Generic products**
Professional associations
USE **Trade and professional associations**
Professional education 378
SA types of professions with the subdivision *Study and teaching,* e.g. **Medicine—Study and teaching;** to be added as needed
BT **Education**
Higher education
Learning and scholarship
NT **Colleges and universities**
Library education
RT **Technical education**
Vocational education
Professional ethics 174
UF Ethics, Professional
SA types of professional ethics, e.g. **Medical ethics;** professions and types of professional personnel with the subdivision *Ethics,* e.g. **Librarians—Ethics;** and subjects with the subdivision *Ethical aspects;* to be added as needed
BT **Ethics**
NT **Business ethics**
Journalism—Objectivity
Legal ethics
Librarians—Ethics
Medical ethics
Professional liability
USE **Malpractice**
Professional liability insurance
USE **Malpractice insurance**
Professional sports 796
SA types of sports, to be added as needed
BT **Sports**
Professions 331.7
UF Careers

Professions—*Continued*

        Jobs

        Vocations

  SA   types of professions with the subdivision *Vocational guidance,* e.g. **Law—Vocational guidance;** to be added as needed

  BT   **Occupations**

        Self-employed

  NT   **College graduates**

        Law—Vocational guidance

        Paraprofessionals

  RT   **Vocational guidance**

Professions—Tort liability

  USE **Malpractice**

Professors

  USE **Educators**

       Teachers

Profit   338.5; 658.15

  BT   **Business**

        Capital

        Economics

        Wealth

  NT   **Capitalism**

  RT   **Income**

Profit sharing   658.3; 331.2

  BT   **Commerce**

        Wages

  RT   **Cooperation**

Profit-sharing trusts

  USE **Mutual funds**

Program evaluation in education

  USE **Educational evaluation**

Programmed instruction   371.39

  UF   Programmed textbooks

  SA   subjects with the subdivision *Programmed instruction,* to be added as needed

  BT   **Teaching—Aids and devices**

  NT   **Computer assisted instruction**

        English language—Programmed instruction

        Teaching machines

Programmed textbooks

  USE **Programmed instruction**

Programming (Computers)   005.1

  UF   Computer programming

        Computers—Programming

        Flow charts (Computer science)

        Flowcharting (Computer science)

  SA   subjects with the subdivision *Computer programs,* e.g. **Database management—Computer programs;** to be added as needed

  BT   **Electronic data processing**

        Mathematical analysis

        Mathematical models

  NT   **Programming languages (Computers)**

  RT   **Computer software**

Programming languages (Computers)   005.13

  UF   Autocodes

        Automatic programming languages

        Computer program languages

        Machine language

  SA   names of specific languages, e.g. **FORTRAN (Computer language);** to be added as needed

  BT   **Computer software**

        Electronic data processing

        Language and languages

        Programming (Computers)

  NT   **FORTRAN (Computer language)**

Programs, Computer

  USE **Computer software**

Programs, Radio

  USE **Radio programs**

Programs, Television

  USE **Television programs**

Programs, Twelve-step

  USE **Twelve-step programs**

Progress   303.44

  BT   **Civilization**

  NT   **Science and civilization**

Progressive education

  USE **Education—Experimental methods**

Prohibited books

  USE **Books—Censorship**

Prohibition   344

    Use for materials on the legal prohibition of liquor traffic and liquor manufacture.

  BT   **Criminal law**

  RT   **Temperance**

BT = Broader Term   NT = Narrower Term   RT = Related Term   SA = See Also   UF = Used For

Project Apollo
USE **Apollo project**
Project Gemini
USE **Gemini project**
Project method in teaching   371.3
BT **Teaching**
Project Ranger   629.43
UF Ranger project
BT **Lunar probes**
Project schools
USE **Experimental schools**
Project Sealab
USE **Sealab project**
Project Telstar
USE **Telstar project**
Project Voyager   629.43
UF Voyager project
BT **Astronautics—United States**
Projectiles   623.4
UF Bullets
Shells (Projectiles)
NT **Ammunition**
Bombs
Guided missiles
Rockets (Aeronautics)
RT **Ordnance**
Projective geometry   516
UF Geometry, Projective *[Former heading]*
BT **Geometry**
Projectors   778.2
UF Film projectors
Lantern projection
Motion picture projectors
Opaque projectors
Slide projectors
Projects, Science
USE **Science projects**
Proletariat   305.5
BT **Labor**
Socialism
Working class
Proliferation of arms
USE **Arms race**
Promotion in school
USE **Promotion (School)**
Promotion (School)   371.2
UF Grade repetition
Grade retention
Non-promotion (School)

Promotion in school
Retention, Grade
School grade retention
School promotion
Student promotion
BT **Grading and marking (Education)**
Promptness
USE **Punctuality**
Pronunciation
USE **Names—Pronunciation**
and names of languages with the subdivision *Pronunciation*, e.g. **English language—Pronunciation;** to be added as needed
Proofreading   070.5; 686.2
BT **Printing**
Propaganda   303.3; 327.1
SA propaganda of particular countries, e.g. **American propaganda;** to be added as needed
BT **Political psychology**
Public opinion
NT **American propaganda**
Lobbying
Press
Psychological warfare
World War, 1939-1945—Propaganda
RT **Advertising**
Publicity
Propaganda, American
USE **American propaganda**
Propagation of plants
USE **Plant propagation**
Propellers, Aerial
USE **Aerial propellers**
Proper names
USE **Names**
Property   330.1
UF Ownership
BT **Economics**
NT **Airspace law**
Eminent domain
Income
Lost and found possessions
Real estate
Surplus government property
RT **Wealth**

BT = Broader Term   NT = Narrower Term   RT = Related Term   SA = See Also   UF = Used For

Property, Literary
USE   **Copyright**
Property, Real
USE   **Real estate**
Property tax—Assessment
USE   **Tax assessment**
Prophecies   133.3; 291.2
UF   Predictions
       Prophecies (Occult sciences)
       [Former heading]
       Prophecies (Occultism) *[Former heading]*
       Prophecy
SA   subjects, titles of sacred works, and names of persons with the subdivision *Prophecies,* e.g. **Bible—Prophecies;** to be added as needed
BT   **Occultism**
       Supernatural
NT   **Fortune telling**
RT   **Divination**
       Oracles
Prophecies (Bible)
USE   **Bible—Prophecies**
Prophecies (Occult sciences)
USE   **Prophecies**
Prophecies (Occultism)
USE   **Prophecies**
Prophecy
USE   **Prophecies**
Prophets   200.92
RT   **Saints**
Proportion (Architecture)
USE   **Architecture—Composition, proportion, etc.**
Proportional representation   328.3
UF   Representation, Proportional
BT   **Constitutional law**
       Representative government and representation
RT   **Elections**
Prose literature, American
USE   **American prose literature**
Prose literature, English
USE   **English prose literature**
Prosody
USE   **Versification**
Prospecting   622
BT   **Gold mines and mining**

       Mines and mineral resources
       Silver mines and mining
NT   **Mine surveying**
       Petroleum geology
Prosthesis
USE   **Artificial limbs**
       Artificial organs
Prostitution   176; 306.74; 363.4; 364.1
BT   **Sexual ethics**
       Social problems
       Women—Social conditions
NT   **Juvenile prostitution**
Prostitution, Juvenile
USE   **Juvenile prostitution**
Protection
USE   subjects with the subdivision *Protection,* e.g. **Birds—Protection;** to be added as needed
Protection against burglary
USE   **Burglary protection**
Protection of animals
USE   **Animal welfare**
Protection of birds
USE   **Birds—Protection**
Protection of children
USE   **Child welfare**
Protection of environment
USE   **Environmental protection**
Protection of game
USE   **Game protection**
Protection of natural scenery
USE   **Landscape protection**
       Natural monuments
       Nature conservation
Protection of plants
USE   **Plant conservation**
Protection of wildlife
USE   **Wildlife conservation**
Protectionism (May subdiv. geog.)   382
UF   Free trade and protection *[Former heading]*
       Tariff question—Free trade and protection
BT   **Commercial policy**
RT   **Free trade**
       Tariff
Proteins   547; 572
BT   **Biochemistry**
NT   **Enzymes**

BT = Broader Term   NT = Narrower Term   RT = Related Term   SA = See Also   UF = Used For

Protest
USE   **Dissent**
Protest marches and rallies
USE   **Demonstrations**
Protest movements
USE   **Demonstrations**
      Peace movements
      and names of wars and other
      objects of protest with the
      subdivision *Protest move-*
      ments, e.g. **World War,**
      1939-1945—Protest move-
      ments; to be added as needed

Protestant churches (May subdiv. geog.)
   280

Use for materials on Protestant denominations treated collectively. Works on Protestant church buildings are entered under **Church buildings.**

UF   Denominations, Protestant
      Protestant denominations
SA   names of Protestant churches,
      e.g. **Presbyterian Church;** to
      be added as needed
BT   **Christian sects**
      Church history
      Protestantism
Protestant denominations
USE   **Protestant churches**
Protestant Episcopal Church in the U.S.A.
USE   **Episcopal Church**
Protestant Reformation
USE   **Reformation**
Protestant work ethic
USE   **Work ethic**
Protestantism   **280**
BT   **Christianity**
      Church history
NT   **Pentecostal churches**
      Protestant churches
RT   **Reformation**
Protests, demonstrations, etc.
USE   **Demonstrations**
Protests, demonstrations, etc.—Chicago
   (Ill.)
USE   **Demonstrations—Chicago (Ill.)**
Protests, demonstrations, etc.—United
   States
USE   **Demonstrations—United States**
Protons   **539.7**
UF   Hydrogen nucleus

BT   **Atoms**
      Particles (Nuclear physics)
Protoplasm   **571.6**
BT   **Biology**
      Life (Biology)
RT   **Cells**
      Embryology
Protozoa   **579.4**
BT   **Cells**
      Invertebrates
      Microorganisms
Proverbs   **398.9**
UF   Adages
      Maxims
      Sayings
BT   **Folklore**
      Quotations
RT   **Epigrams**
Providence and government of God
   214; 231; 291.2
UF   God—Providence and govern-
      ment
      God—Sovereignty
BT   **God**
Provincialism
USE   **Regionalism**
Provincialisms
USE   names of languages with the
      subdivision *Provincialisms,*
      e.g. **English language—Pro-**
      vincialisms; to be added as
      needed
Pruning   **631.5**
BT   **Forests and forestry**
      Fruit culture
      Gardening
      Trees
Pseudonyms   **929.4**
UF   Anonyms
      Fictitious names
      Names, Fictitious
      Pen names
BT   **Names**
      Personal names
Psi (Parapsychology)
USE   **Parapsychology**
Psychiatric hospitals   **362.2**
UF   Mental hospitals
BT   **Hospitals**
RT   **Mentally ill—Institutional care**

BT = Broader Term   NT = Narrower Term   RT = Related Term   SA = See Also   UF = Used For

Psychiatrists 920; 926
  UF   Psychopathologists
  BT   **Psychologists**
Psychiatry 616.89
  Use for materials on clinical aspects of mental disorders, including therapy. Popular materials and materials on regional or social aspects of mental disorders are entered under **Mental illness.** Systematic descriptions of mental disorders are entered under **Abnormal psychology.**
  BT   **Medicine**
  NT   **Adolescent psychiatry**
        Child psychiatry
        Psychotherapy
  RT   **Abnormal psychology**
        Mental health
        Mental illness
Psychiatry, Adolescent
  USE   **Adolescent psychiatry**
Psychic healing
  USE   **Mental healing**
Psychic phenomena
  USE   **Parapsychology**
Psychical research
  USE   **Parapsychology**
Psychoactive drugs
  USE   **Psychotropic drugs**
Psychoanalysis 150.19; 616.89
  BT   **Psychology**
  NT   **Psychosomatic medicine**
  RT   **Abnormal psychology**
        Hypnotism
        Mind and body
        Subconsciousness
Psychogenetics
  USE   **Behavior genetics**
Psychokinesis 133.8
  UF   Telekinesis
  BT   **Parapsychology**
        Spiritualism
Psychological aspects
  USE   subjects with the subdivision *Psychological aspects,* e.g. **Drugs—Psychological aspects; World War, 1939-1945—Psychological aspects;** etc., to be added as needed
Psychological stress
  USE   **Stress (Psychology)**
Psychological tests
  UF   Mental tests *[Former heading]*

  BT   **Psychology**
  NT   **Ability—Testing**
  RT   **Educational tests and measurements**
Psychological warfare 355.3
  Use for materials on methods used to undermine the morale of the civilian population and the military forces of an enemy country.
  UF   War of nerves
  SA   names of wars with the subdivision *Psychological aspects,* to be added as needed
  BT   **Applied psychology**
        Military art and science
        Morale
        Propaganda
        War
  NT   **Brainwashing**
        World War, 1939-1945—Psychological aspects
Psychologists 150.92; 920
  NT   **Psychiatrists**
        School psychologists
  RT   **Psychology**
Psychology 150
  UF   Mind
  SA   religions, theological topics, titles of individual sacred works, types of animals, classes of persons, ethnic groups, and names of individual persons, including individual literary authors, with the subdivision *Psychology,* e.g. **Christianity—Psychology; Women—Psychology;** etc.; and subjects with the subdivision *Psychological aspects* for materials on the influence of particular situations, conditions, activities, environments, or objects on the mental condition or personality of the individual, e.g. **Color—Psychological aspects;** to be added as needed
  BT   **Brain**
        Philosophy
        Soul
  NT   **Adjustment (Psychology)**
        Adolescent psychology

BT = Broader Term   NT = Narrower Term   RT = Related Term   SA = See Also   UF = Used For

Psychology—*Continued*

Aggressiveness (Psychology)
Apperception
Applied psychology
Assertiveness (Psychology)
Attention
Attitude (Psychology)
Behavior genetics
Behaviorism
Bible—Psychology
Child psychology
Choice (Psychology)
Color—Psychological aspects
Consciousness
Dogs—Psychology
Educational psychology
Emotions
Ethnopsychology
Genius
Gestalt psychology
Habit
Human behavior
Identity (Psychology)
Ideology
Imagination
Indians of North America—
Psychology
Individuality
Instinct
Intellect
Intuition
Memory
Men—Psychology
Motivation (Psychology)
Multiple personality
Music—Psychological aspects
Number concept
Parapsychology
Perception
Personality
Phrenology
Physiognomy
Political psychology
Problem solving
Psychoanalysis
Psychological tests
Psychology of religion
Psychophysiology
Reasoning
Self-acceptance

Self-consciousness
Self-control
Self-esteem
Self-perception
Self-realization
Senses and sensation
Sex differences (Psychology)
Shakespeare, William, 1564-
1616—Psychology
Social psychology
Stress (Psychology)
Subconsciousness
Temperament
Thought and thinking
Values
Women—Psychology
RT   Mental health
Psychologists
Psychology, Abnormal
USE   Abnormal psychology
Psychology, Adolescent
USE   Adolescent psychology
Psychology and religion
USE   Psychology of religion
Psychology, Applied
USE   Applied psychology
Psychology, Biblical
USE   Bible—Psychology
Psychology, Comparative
USE   Comparative psychology
Psychology—Computer simulation   150
BT   Computer simulation
Psychology, Criminal
USE   Criminal psychology
Psychology, Educational
USE   Educational psychology
Psychology, Ethnic
USE   Ethnopsychology
Psychology, Experimental
USE   Psychophysiology
Psychology, Industrial
USE   Applied psychology
Psychology, Medical
USE   Abnormal psychology
Psychology, National
USE   Ethnopsychology
National characteristics
Psychology of color
USE   Color—Psychological aspects

BT = Broader Term   NT = Narrower Term   RT = Related Term   SA = See Also   UF = Used For

Psychology of learning   153.1
    UF   Learning, Psychology of *[Former heading]*
    BT   **Animal intelligence**
           Child psychology
           Education
           Educational psychology
           Memory
    NT   **Behavior modification**
           Biofeedback training
           Brainwashing
           Concept learning
           Feedback (Psychology)
           Learning disabilities
           Reading comprehension
           Verbal learning
Psychology of music
    USE   **Music—Psychological aspects**
Psychology of religion   200.1
    UF   Psychology and religion
           Psychology, Religious *[Former heading]*
           Religion and psychology
           Religion—Psychological aspects
           Religious psychology
    SA   religious topics, titles of individual sacred works, and names of religions with the subdivision *Psychology,* to be added as needed
    BT   **Psychology**
           Religion
    NT   **Christianity—Psychology**
           Faith—Psychology
           Pastoral psychology
Psychology, Pastoral
    USE   **Pastoral psychology**
Psychology, Pathological
    USE   **Abnormal psychology**
Psychology, Physiological
    USE   **Psychophysiology**
Psychology, Political
    USE   **Political psychology**
Psychology, Practical
    USE   **Applied psychology**
Psychology, Racial
    USE   **Ethnopsychology**
Psychology, Religious
    USE   **Pastoral psychology**
              Psychology of religion

Psychology, Social
    USE   **Social psychology**
Psychology, Structural
    USE   **Gestalt psychology**
Psychopathologists
    USE   **Psychiatrists**
Psychopathology
    USE   **Abnormal psychology**
Psychopathy
    USE   **Abnormal psychology**
Psychopharmaceuticals
    USE   **Psychotropic drugs**
Psychophysics
    USE   **Psychophysiology**
Psychophysiology   152
        Use for materials on the relationship between psychological and physiological processes.
    UF   Experimental psychology
           Physiological psychology
           Psychology, Experimental
           Psychology, Physiological *[Former heading]*
           Psychophysics
    BT   **Nervous system**
           Physiology
           Psychology
    NT   **Behaviorism**
           Color sense
           Emotions
           Human engineering
           Hypnotism
           Left- and right-handedness
           Memory
           Optical illusions
           Pain
           Senses and sensation
           Sleep
           Temperament
    RT   **Mind and body**
Psychoses
    USE   **Mental illness**
Psychosomatic medicine   616.08
    UF   Medicine, Psychosomatic *[Former heading]*
    BT   **Abnormal psychology**
           Medicine
           Mind and body
           Neuroses
           Psychoanalysis

BT = Broader Term   NT = Narrower Term   RT = Related Term   SA = See Also   UF = Used For

Psychotherapy   616.89
    UF   Therapy, Psychological
    BT   Psychiatry
           Therapeutics
    NT   Biofeedback training
           Family therapy
           Sex therapy
           Transactional analysis
    RT   Mental healing
           Suggestive therapeutics
Psychotic children
    USE   Emotionally disturbed children
Psychotics
    USE   Mentally ill
Psychotropic drugs   615
    Use for general materials on the group of drugs that act on the central nervous system to affect behavior, mental activity, or perception, including the antipsychotic drugs, antidepressants, hallucinogenic agents, and tranquilizers.
    UF   Drugs, Psychotropic
           Psychoactive drugs
           Psychopharmaceuticals
    SA   types of drugs and names of individual drugs, to be added as needed
    BT   Drugs
    NT   Hallucinogens
           Narcotics
           Stimulants
PTAs
    USE   Parent-teacher associations
Public accommodations, Discrimination in
    USE   Discrimination in public accommodations
Public administration   351
    Use for general materials on the principles and techniques involved in the conduct of public business. Materials limited to the governmental process of individual countries, states, cities, etc., are entered under the name of the place with the subdivision *Politics and government.*
    UF   Administration
    SA   names of countries, states, cities, etc., with the subdivision *Politics and government,* to be added as needed
    BT   Local government
           Municipal government
           Political science
    NT   Administrative agencies

           Bureaucracy
           Civil service
           Intelligence service
           Military government
           United States—Politics and government
    RT   Administrative law
Public assistance
    USE   Public welfare
Public buildings (May subdiv. geog.)
    352.5; 725
    Use for materials on buildings owned by the public and maintained at public expense, such as government office buildings, public libraries, public schools, etc. Materials on buildings that are privately owned and maintained and are open to the public for business or entertainment are entered under **Buildings** or under the specific type of building.
    UF   Buildings, Public
           Government buildings
    SA   names of individual public buildings, to be added as needed
    BT   Buildings
           Public works
    NT   Capitols
Public buildings, American
    USE   Public buildings—United States
Public buildings—Chicago (Ill.)
    725.09773
    UF   Chicago (Ill.)—Public buildings *[Former heading]*
Public buildings—Ohio   725.09771
    UF   Ohio—Public buildings *[Former heading]*
Public buildings—United States   352.5;
    725.0973
    Use for materials on U.S. federal government buildings located in or outside of the United States, including materials on U.S embassy or consulate buildings abroad.
    UF   Public buildings, American
           United States—Government buildings
           United States—Public buildings *[Former heading]*
Public charities
    USE   Public welfare
Public debts (May subdiv. geog.)   336.3
    Use for materials on government debts.
    UF   Debts, Government
           Debts, Public *[Former heading]*

BT = Broader Term   **NT** = Narrower Term   **RT** = Related Term   **SA** = See Also   **UF** = Used For

Public debts—*Continued*
    Federal debt
    Government debts
    National debts
    State debts
    War debts
  SA   names of wars with the subdivision *Finance,* e.g. **World War, 1939-1945—Finance;** to be added as needed
  BT   **Debt**
        Loans
        Public finance
  RT   **Bonds**
        Deficit financing
Public debts—United States   336.3
  UF   United States—Public debts
Public demonstrations
  USE   **Demonstrations**
Public documents
  USE   **Government publications**
Public domain
  USE   **Public lands**
Public figures
  USE   **Celebrities**
Public finance (May subdiv. geog.)   336
    Use for materials on the raising and expenditure of funds in the public sector.
  UF   Finance, Public
  BT   **Finance**
  NT   **Budget**
        Deficit financing
        Fiscal policy
        Government lending
        Grants-in-aid
        Metropolitan finance
        Municipal finance
        Public debts
        Tariff
        Taxation
Public health (May subdiv. geog.)   362.1; 614
  UF   Health, Public
        Hygiene, Social
        Public hygiene
        Social hygiene
  BT   **Health**
        Social problems
        State medicine
  NT   **Burial**
        Cemeteries

        Communicable diseases
        Community health services
        Cremation
        Disinfection and disinfectants
        Environmental health
        Epidemics
        Food adulteration and inspection
        Health boards
        Hospitals
        Meat inspection
        Medical care
        Medical charities
        Milk supply
        Noise
        Occupational health and safety
        Pollution
        Refuse and refuse disposal
        School hygiene
        Sewage disposal
        Social medicine
        Street cleaning
        Vaccination
        Water pollution
        Water supply
  RT   **Preventive medicine**
        Sanitation
Public health boards
  USE   **Health boards**
Public health—Evaluation   362.1
  UF   Health program evaluation
Public health—United States   362.10973; 614
  UF   United States—Public health
Public housing (May subdiv. geog.)   363.5
  UF   Government housing
        Housing projects, Government
        Low income housing
  BT   **Housing**
Public hygiene
  USE   **Public health**
Public interest   172; 320.01; 344
  UF   National interest
  BT   **State, The**
  NT   **Ombudsman**
        Whistle blowing
Public lands (May subdiv. geog.)   333.1
  UF   Crown lands
        Public domain

BT = Broader Term   **NT** = Narrower Term   **RT** = Related Term   **SA** = See Also   **UF** = Used For

Public lands—*Continued*
    BT   Colonization
           Land use
    NT   Forest reserves
           National parks and reserves
    RT   Natural resources
Public lands—Ohio   333.109771
    UF   Ohio—Public lands *[Former*
           heading]
Public lands—United States   333.10973
    UF   United States—Public lands
           [Former heading]
Public libraries (May subdiv. geog.)
           027.4
    UF   Libraries, Public
    BT   **Libraries**
    NT   **County libraries**
           Regional libraries
Public meetings   302.3
    UF   Meetings, Public
    BT   **Freedom of assembly**
    NT   **Demonstrations**
           Parliamentary practice
Public opinion   303.3
    UF   Opinion, Public
    SA   subjects with the subdivision
           Public opinion, e.g. **World**
           War, 1939-1945—Public
           opinion; and names of coun-
           tries with the subdivision *For-*
           eign opinion for materials
           dealing with foreign public
           opinion about the country,
           e.g. **United States—Foreign**
           opinion; to be added as need-
           ed
    BT   **Freedom of conscience**
           Political psychology
           Political science
           Social psychology
    NT   **Propaganda**
           Public opinion polls
           Publicity
           United States—Foreign opinion
           World War, 1939-1945—Public
           opinion
    RT   **Attitude (Psychology)**
           Press
           Public relations

Public opinion polls   303.3
    UF   Opinion polls
           Polls, Public opinion
           Straw votes
    BT   **Public opinion**
    RT   **Market surveys**
Public ownership
    USE   **Government ownership**
            Municipal ownership
Public playgrounds
    USE   **Playgrounds**
Public procurement
    USE   **Government purchasing**
Public records—Preservation
    USE   **Archives**
Public relations   659.2
      May be subdivided by topic, e.g. **Public re-**
    lations—Libraries; etc.
    NT   **Business entertaining**
           Customer relations
    RT   **Advertising**
           Public opinion
           Publicity
Public relations—Libraries   021.7
    UF   Libraries—Public relations
    BT   **Libraries and community**
    NT   **Book talks**
Public safety, Crimes against
    USE   **Offenses against public safety**
Public schools (May subdiv. geog.)
           371.01
      Use for materials on preschool, elementary,
    and secondary schools supported by state and
    local government. Materials on British en-
    dowed secondary schools that are open to
    public admission but are not financed or ad-
    ministered by any government body are en-
    tered under **English public schools.**
    UF   Common schools
           Community schools
           Grammar schools
           Neighborhood schools
    BT   **Schools**
    NT   **Evening and continuation**
           schools
           High schools
           Junior high schools
           Magnet schools
           Religion in the public schools
           Rural schools
           Summer schools

BT = Broader Term   NT = Narrower Term   RT = Related Term   SA = See Also   UF = Used For

Public schools and religion
 USE **Religion in the public schools**
Public schools, Endowed (Great Britain)
 USE **English public schools**
Public schools, English
 USE **English public schools**
Public schools—United States
 371.010973
 UF United States—Public schools
Public service commissions (May subdiv.
 geog.) **354.72**
 Use for materials on bodies appointed to
 regulate or control public utilities.
 UF Public utility commissions
 BT **Corporation law**
 Corporations
 Industrial policy
Public service corporations
 USE **Public utilities**
Public shelters
 USE **Air raid shelters**
Public speaking 808.5
 Use for materials on the art of delivering
 speeches. Collections of speeches on several
 subjects and materials about speeches that
 have already been delivered are entered under
 Speeches. Materials limited to scholarly lec-
 tures are entered under **Lectures and lectur-
 ing.**
 UF Elocution
 Oratory
 Persuasion (Rhetoric)
 Speaking
 BT **Communication**
 NT **Acting**
 Book talks
 Chalk talks
 Debates and debating
 Lectures and lecturing
 Preaching
 RT **Speeches**
 Voice
Public television 384.55
 UF Educational television
 BT **Television broadcasting**
Public transit
 USE **Local transit**
Public utilities 343.09; 354.72; 363.6
 UF Electric utilities
 Gas companies
 Public service corporations
 Utilities, Public

 NT **Electric railroads**
 Gas
 Railroads
 Railroads—Government policy
 Street railroads
 Telegraph
 Telephone
 Water supply
 RT **Corporations**
Public utility commissions
 USE **Public service commissions**
Public welfare 361.6
 Use for materials on tax-supported welfare
 activities. Materials on privately supported
 welfare activities are entered under **Charities.**
 Materials on the methods employed in welfare
 work, public or private, are entered under **So-
 cial work.**
 UF Charities, Public
 Poor relief
 Public assistance
 Public charities
 Relief, Public
 Social welfare
 Welfare work
 BT **Social work**
 NT **Child welfare**
 Disaster relief
 Food relief
 Institutional care
 Legal aid
 National service
 Poor
 Social medicine
 Volunteer work
 Welfare state
 RT **Charities**
 Poverty
Public works (May subdiv. geog.)
 352.7; 363
 BT **Civil engineering**
 Domestic economic assistance
 NT **Municipal engineering**
 Public buildings
 RT **City planning**
Public works—Chicago (Ill.) 363.09773
 UF Chicago (Ill.)—Public works
 [Former heading]
Public works—Ohio 352.7; 363.09771
 UF Ohio—Public works *[Former
 heading]*

BT = Broader Term   NT = Narrower Term   RT = Related Term   SA = See Also   UF = Used For

Public works—United States   352.7;
    363.0973
    UF   United States—Public works
           [Former heading]
Public worship   264; 291.3
    UF   Church attendance
    BT   **Worship**
Publicity   659
    BT   **Public opinion**
    NT   **Press**
    RT   **Advertising**
           Propaganda
           Public relations
Publishers and authors
    USE   **Authors and publishers**
Publishers and publishing (May subdiv.
    geog.)   070.5
    UF   Book trade
           Publishing
    NT   **Authors and publishers**
           Editing
           Electronic publishing
           Printing
           Publishers' catalogs
           **Publishers' standard book
              numbers**
           Serial publications
    RT   **Book industries**
           Books
           Booksellers and bookselling
           Copyright
Publishers' catalogs   015
    Use for catalogs produced by publishers and
for materials about such catalogs. Retail book
catalogs and book auction catalogs and materials about such catalogs are entered under
Booksellers' catalogs.
    UF   Books—Catalogs
           Catalogs
           Catalogs, Publishers' *[Former
              heading]*
    BT   **Publishers and publishing**
Publishers' standard book numbers
    070.5
    UF   Book numbers, Publishers' stan-
              dard
           Standard book numbers
    BT   **Publishers and publishing**
    NT   **International Standard Book
              Numbers**

Publishing
    USE   **Publishers and publishing**
Pubs
    USE   **Bars**
Pugilism
    USE   **Boxing**
Pulmonary resuscitation
    USE   **Artificial respiration**
Pulsars   523.8
    UF   Pulsating radio sources
    BT   **Astronomy**
Pulsating radio sources
    USE   **Pulsars**
Pumping iron
    USE   **Weight lifting**
Pumping machinery   621.6
    UF   Force pumps
           Pumps
           Steam pumps
    SA   types of pumping machinery,
              e.g. **Heat pumps;** to be add-
              ed as needed
    BT   **Engines**
           Hydraulic engineering
    NT   **Heat pumps**
Pumps
    USE   **Pumping machinery**
Punched card systems
    USE   **Information systems**
Punctuality
    UF   Lateness
           Promptness
           Tardiness
    BT   **Time**
           Virtue
Punctuation   411; 421, etc.
    UF   English language—Punctuation
    BT   **Rhetoric**
Punishment   364.6
    UF   Discipline
           Penology
    BT   **Administration of criminal jus-
              tice**
           Corrections
    NT   **Capital punishment**
           Correctional institutions
           Parole
           Prisons
           Probation
           Reformatories

BT = Broader Term   NT = Narrower Term   RT = Related Term   SA = See Also   UF = Used For

Punishment—*Continued*
　　　　Torture
　RT　Crime
　　　　Criminal law
Punishment in schools
　USE　School discipline
Puns　808.88; 818, etc.
　　　May be used for collections of puns or for materials about puns.
　UF　Puns and punning *[Former heading]*
　BT　Wit and humor
Puns and punning
　USE　Puns
Pupil-teacher relationships
　USE　Teacher-student relationships
Puppets and puppet plays　791.5
　UF　Marionettes
　SA　types of puppets or puppet plays, to be added as needed
　BT　Drama
　　　　Folk drama
　　　　Theater
　NT　Shadow pantomimes and plays
Puppies
　USE　Dogs
Purchase tax
　USE　Sales tax
Purchasing
　USE　Buying
　　　　Shopping
Purchasing, Government
　USE　Government purchasing
Pure food
　USE　Food adulteration and inspection
Purgatory　236; 291.2
　BT　Eschatology
Purification of water
　USE　Water purification
Puritans　285
　BT　Christian sects
　　　　United States—History—1600-1775, Colonial period
　NT　Pilgrims (New England colonists)
　RT　Calvinism
　　　　Church of England—United States
　　　　Congregationalism

Puzzles　793.73
　BT　Amusements
　NT　Crossword puzzles
　　　　Mathematical recreations
　RT　Riddles
Pyramids　722; 909
　BT　Ancient architecture
　　　　Archeology
　　　　Monuments
　NT　Obelisks
Quacks and quackery　615.8
　BT　Impostors and imposture
　　　　Medicine
　　　　Swindlers and swindling
Quakers
　USE　Society of Friends
Qualitative analysis
　USE　Analytical chemistry
Quality control　519.8; 658.5
　SA　industries, processes, and materials with the subdivision *Quality control*, to be added as needed
　BT　Reliability (Engineering)
　　　　Sampling (Statistics)
　NT　Steel industry—Quality control
Quality of life　303.3
　　　Use for materials on the objective standards and subjective attitudes by which individuals and groups assess their life situations.
　UF　Life quality
　BT　Economic conditions
　　　　Social conditions
　NT　Cost and standard of living
　　　　Lifestyles
　RT　Social values
Quantitative analysis
　USE　Analytical chemistry
Quantity cookery
　USE　Quantity cooking
Quantity cooking　641.5
　　　Use for materials limited to the preparation and cooking of food in large quantities. Materials on the preparation, delivery, and serving of ready-to-eat foods in large quantities outside of the home are entered under **Food service**.
　UF　Cooking for large numbers
　　　　Quantity cookery *[Former heading]*
　BT　Cooking
　RT　Food service

BT = Broader Term　　NT = Narrower Term　　RT = Related Term　　SA = See Also　　UF = Used For

Quantum mechanics
USE **Quantum theory**
Quantum theory   530.12
   UF   Quantum mechanics
   BT   **Dynamics**
         Physics
   NT   **Wave mechanics**
   RT   **Atomic theory**
         Force and energy
         Physical chemistry
         Radiation
         Relativity (Physics)
         Thermodynamics
Quarantine
USE **Communicable diseases**
Quarks   539.7
   BT   **Particles (Nuclear physics)**
Quarries and quarrying   622
   UF   **Stone quarries**
   BT   **Economic geology**
   RT   **Stone**
Quartz   549
   UF   Rock crystal
   BT   **Crystals**
         Minerals
Quasars   523.1
   UF   Quasi-stellar radio sources
   BT   **Astronomy**
         Radio astronomy
Quasi-stellar radio sources
USE **Quasars**
Québec (Province)   971.4
Québec (Province)—History   971.4
Québec (Province)—History—Autonomy and independence movements 971.4
   UF   Québec (Province)—Separatist movement
         Separatist movement in Québec (Province)
   BT   **Canada—English-French relations**
Québec (Province)—Separatist movement
USE **Québec (Province)—History—Autonomy and independence movements**
Queens (May subdiv. geog.)
   Use for materials on women monarchs as well as on wives or consorts of monarchs.
   UF   Royalty
         Rulers

         Sovereigns
   SA   names of queens, e.g. **Elizabeth II, Queen of Great Britain, 1926- ;** ethnic groups with the subdivision *Queens,* and countries, cities, etc., with the subdivision *Kings and rulers,* to be added as needed
   BT   **Monarchy**
   RT   **Courts and courtiers**
         Empresses
         Kings and rulers
Queens—Great Britain   920; 941
   UF   Great Britain—Queens
   SA   names of British queens, e.g. **Elizabeth II, Queen of Great Britain, 1926- ;** to be added as needed
   NT   **Elizabeth II, Queen of Great Britain, 1926-**
Queries
USE **Questions and answers**
Questions and answers   793.73
   Use for collections of informal quizzes on various subjects. Informal quizzes on a particular subject are entered under the subject with the subdivision *Miscellanea.* Materials on formal examinations are entered under **Examinations.** Examination questions on a particular subject are entered under the subject with the subdivision *Examinations,* e.g. **Music—Examinations.** Compilations of practice problems or exercises for use in the study of a topic are entered under the topic with the subdivision *Problems, exercises, etc.,* e.g. **Chemistry—Problems, exercises, etc.**
   UF   Answers to questions
         Queries
         Quizzes
         Trivia
   SA   subjects with the subdivision *Miscellanea,* e.g. **Medicine—Miscellanea;** to be added as needed
   NT   **Examinations**
Quick and easy cookery
USE **Quick and easy cooking**
Quick and easy cooking   641.5
   Use for materials containing recipes or cooking techniques emphasizing economy of preparation time and the use of readily available ingredients.
   UF   Convenience cooking
         Easy and quick cooking

BT = Broader Term   NT = Narrower Term   RT = Related Term   SA = See Also   UF = Used For

Quick and easy cooking—*Continued*

    Quick and easy cookery *[Former heading]*

    Quick-meal cooking

    Time saving cooking

  BT **Cooking**

Quick-meal cooking

  USE **Quick and easy cooking**

Quicksilver

  USE **Mercury**

Quilt designing

  USE **Quilts—Design**

Quilting 746.46

  BT **Handicraft**

  RT **Quilts**

Quilts 746.46

  UF Coverlets

    Patchwork quilts

  BT **Interior design**

  RT **Quilting**

Quilts—Design 746.46

  UF Quilt designing

  BT **Design**

Quintets 785

  BT **Chamber music**

Quislings

  USE **World War, 1939-1945—Collaborationists**

Quit-smoking programs

  USE **Smoking cessation programs**

Quizzes

  USE **Questions and answers**

Qumran texts

  USE **Dead Sea scrolls**

Quotations 080; 808.88

  UF Sayings

  SA subjects, classes of persons, ethnic groups, and names of individuals with the subdivision *Quotations,* to be added as needed

  BT **Epigrams**

    Literature—Collections

  NT **Presidents—United States—Quotations**

    Proverbs

Qur'an

  USE **Koran**

R.V.'s

  USE **Recreational vehicles**

Rabbis 296.6; 920

  BT **Clergy**

    Judaism

Rabbits 599.32; 636

  UF Bunnies

    Bunny rabbits

    Hares

  BT **Mammals**

Rabies 616.9; 636.089

  UF Hydrophobia

  BT **Communicable diseases**

Race 599.97

  BT **Ethnology**

Race awareness 305.8

  UF Race identity

    Racial identity

  SA names of racial groups with the subdivision *Race identity,* to be added as needed

  BT **Race relations**

  NT **African Americans—Race identity**

    Blacks—Race identity

    Racism

Race discrimination 305.8

  Use for materials on the restriction or denial of rights, privileges, or choice because of race. Materials on prejudicial attitudes about particular groups because of their race are entered under **Racism**.

  UF Discrimination, Racial

    Racial discrimination

  SA types of discrimination, e.g. **Discrimination in education;** to be added as needed

  BT **Discrimination**

    Race relations

    Racism

    Social problems

Race identity

  USE **Race awareness**

    and names of racial groups with the subdivision *Race identity,* e.g. **Blacks—Race identity; African Americans—Race identity;** etc., to be added as needed

Race prejudice

  USE **Racism**

Race problems

  USE **Race relations**

BT = Broader Term   NT = Narrower Term   RT = Related Term   SA = See Also   UF = Used For

Race psychology
　　USE　Ethnopsychology
Race relations　　305.8
　　UF　Integration, Racial
　　　　Interracial relations
　　　　Race problems
　　　　Racial integration
　　SA　names of countries, cities, etc.,
　　　　with the subdivision *Race re-*
　　　　lations, e.g. **United States—**
　　　　Race relations; to be added
　　　　as needed
　　BT　Acculturation
　　　　Ethnology
　　　　Sociology
　　NT　Chicago (Ill.)—Race relations
　　　　Culture conflict
　　　　Discrimination
　　　　Interracial adoption
　　　　Multiculturalism
　　　　Ohio—Race relations
　　　　Race awareness
　　　　Race discrimination
　　　　Racism
　　　　School integration
　　　　Segregation
　　　　South Africa—Race relations
　　　　United States—Race relations
　　　　White supremacy movements
　　RT　Ethnic relations
　　　　Minorities
Race relations and the church
　　USE　Church and race relations
Races of people
　　USE　Ethnology
Racial balance in schools
　　USE　School integration
　　　　Segregation in education
Racial bias
　　USE　Racism
Racial discrimination
　　USE　Race discrimination
Racial identity
　　USE　Race awareness
Racial integration
　　USE　Race relations
Racial intermarriage
　　USE　Interracial marriage

Racing　　796
　　SA　types of racing, to be added as
　　　　needed
　　BT　Sports
　　NT　Airplane racing
　　　　Automobile racing
　　　　Bicycle racing
　　　　Boat racing
　　　　Horse racing
　　　　Orienteering
　　　　Soap box derbies
　　RT　Running
Racism　　305.8; 320.5
　　Use for materials on prejudicial attitudes
　about particular groups because of their race.
　Materials on the restriction or denial of rights,
　privileges, or choice because of race are en-
　tered under **Race discrimination.**
　　UF　Race prejudice
　　　　Racial bias
　　BT　Attitude (Psychology)
　　　　Prejudices
　　　　Race awareness
　　　　Race relations
　　NT　Race discrimination
　　　　White supremacy movements
Racketeering　　364.106
　　UF　Crime syndicates
　　BT　Crime
　　　　Organized crime
Radar　　621.3848
　　BT　Navigation
　　　　Radio
　　　　Remote sensing
Radar defense networks　　623
　　UF　Defenses, Radar
　　BT　Air defenses
　　NT　Ballistic missile early warning
　　　　system
Radiant heating　　697
　　UF　Panel heating
　　BT　Heating
Radiation　　539.2
　　BT　Optics
　　　　Physics
　　　　Waves
　　NT　Cosmic rays
　　　　Electromagnetic waves
　　　　Gamma rays
　　　　Infrared radiation
　　　　Luminescence

BT = Broader Term　　NT = Narrower Term　　RT = Related Term　　SA = See Also　　UF = Used For

Radiation—*Continued*
>> Radioactivity
>> Radium
>> Sound
>> Spectrum analysis
>> Ultraviolet rays
>> X-rays
> RT Light
>> Quantum theory

Radiation biology
> USE **Radiobiology**

Radiation—Physiological effect 612
> RT **Atomic bomb—Physiological effect**
>> **Nuclear medicine**

Radiation—Safety measures 363.1; 612
> BT **Accidents—Prevention**

Radiation, Solar
> USE **Solar radiation**

Radiation therapy
> USE **Radiotherapy**

Radicalism (May subdiv. geog.) 320.5
> Use for materials on extremist social and political movements of either the right or the left.
> UF Extremism (Political science)
>> Political extremism
>> Radicals and radicalism *[Former heading]*
> BT **Political science**
>> **Revolutions**
>> **Right and left (Political science)**
> NT **Militia movements**
> RT **Counter culture**

Radicals and radicalism
> USE **Radicalism**

Radio 621.384
> UF Wireless
> SA radio and other subjects, e.g. **Radio and music;** and radio in various industries or fields of endeavor, e.g. **Radio in aeronautics;** to be added as needed
> BT **Electric engineering**
>> **Telecommunication**
> NT **Radar**
>> **Radio and music**
>> **Radio frequency modulation**
>> **Radio in aeronautics**

>> **Radio in astronautics**
>> **Radio in education**
>> **Shortwave radio**

Radio addresses, debates, etc. 384.54; 808.5; 808.85
> UF Radio lectures
> BT **Debates and debating**
>> **Lectures and lecturing**
>> **Radio broadcasting**
>> **Radio scripts**

Radio advertising 659.14
> UF Advertising, Radio
>> Commercials, Radio
>> Radio commercials
> BT **Advertising**
>> **Radio broadcasting**

Radio and music 780; 781.5
> UF Music and radio
> BT **Music**
>> **Radio**

Radio and television novels 813, etc.
> May be used for individual works, collections, or materials about novels based on radio or television programs.
> UF Radio novels
>> Television novels
> BT **Fiction**
> RT **Movie novels**

Radio apparatus industry
> USE **Radio supplies industry**

Radio astronomy 522
> SA names of celestial radio sources, e.g. **Quasars;** to be added as needed
> BT **Astronomy**
>> **Interstellar communication**
> NT **Quasars**

Radio authorship 808
> UF Radio script writing
>> Radio writing
> BT **Authorship**
>> **Radio broadcasting**
> NT **Radio plays—Technique**
> RT **Radio scripts**

Radio broadcasting 384.54
> UF Radio industry
> SA radio broadcasting of particular kinds of programs, e.g. **Radio broadcasting of sports;** to be added as needed
> BT **Broadcasting**

BT = Broader Term   NT = Narrower Term   RT = Related Term   SA = See Also   UF = Used For

Radio broadcasting—*Continued*
  Mass media
  NT   Radio addresses, debates, etc.
       Radio advertising
       Radio authorship
       Radio broadcasting of sports
       Radio programs
       Radio stations
Radio broadcasting of sports   070.4
  UF   Sports broadcasting
       Sports in radio
  BT   **Broadcast journalism**
       Radio broadcasting
Radio chemistry
  USE   **Radiochemistry**
Radio comedies
  USE   **Comedy radio programs**
Radio comedy programs
  USE   **Comedy radio programs**
Radio commercials
  USE   **Radio advertising**
Radio drama
  USE   **Radio plays**
Radio—Equipment and supplies
       621.384028
  BT   **Radio supplies industry**
  NT   **Radio—Receivers and reception**
       Radio supplies industry
Radio equipment industry
  USE   **Radio supplies industry**
Radio frequency modulation   621.384
  UF   F.M. radio
       FM radio
       Frequency modulation, Radio
  BT   **Radio**
  NT   **Shortwave radio**
Radio in aeronautics   629.135
  BT   **Aeronautics**
       Navigation (Aeronautics)
       Radio
Radio in astronautics   629.4
  UF   Lunar surface radio communication
  BT   **Astronautics—Communication systems**
       Navigation (Astronautics)
       Radio
Radio in education   371.33
  UF   Education and radio

  BT   **Audiovisual education**
       Radio
       Teaching—Aids and devices
Radio industry
  USE   **Radio broadcasting**
Radio industry and trade
  USE   **Radio supplies industry**
Radio journalism
  USE   **Broadcast journalism**
Radio lectures
  USE   **Radio addresses, debates, etc.**
Radio novels
  USE   **Radio and television novels**
Radio operators   621.3841
Radio plays   808.82; 812, etc.
  May be used for individual works, collections, or materials about radio plays. Works on how to write radio plays are entered under **Radio plays—Technique.**
  UF   Radio drama
       Scenarios
  BT   **Drama**
       Radio programs
  NT   **Soap operas**
  RT   **Radio scripts**
Radio plays—Technique   808.2
  UF   Play writing
       Playwriting
  BT   **Drama—Technique**
       Radio authorship
  RT   **Television plays—Technique**
Radio programs   384.54
  May be used for individual works, collections, or materials about radio programs.
  UF   Programs, Radio
  SA   types of programs and names of specific programs, to be added as needed
  BT   **Radio broadcasting**
  NT   **Adventure radio programs**
       Biographical radio programs
       Comedy radio programs
       Fantasy radio programs
       Horror radio programs
       Legal drama (Radio programs)
       Medical drama (Radio programs)
       Mystery radio programs
       Radio plays
       Radio serials
       Science fiction radio programs

BT = Broader Term   NT = Narrower Term   RT = Related Term   SA = See Also   UF = Used For

Radio programs—*Continued*
>> Sports drama (Radio programs)
>> Spy radio programs
>> Talk shows
>> Variety shows (Radio programs)
>> War radio programs
>> Westerns (Radio programs)
> RT **Radio scripts**
Radio—Receivers and reception
>> 621.384
> UF Radio reception
>> Radios
> BT **Radio—Equipment and supplies**
Radio reception
> USE **Radio—Receivers and reception**
Radio—Repairing 621.384
> UF Radio repairs
>> Radio servicing
Radio repairs
> USE **Radio—Repairing**
Radio script writing
> USE **Radio authorship**
Radio scripts 791.44; 808.8; 818, etc.
> May be used for individual works, collections, or materials about radio scripts.
> NT **Radio addresses, debates, etc.**
> RT **Radio authorship**
>> **Radio plays**
>> **Radio programs**
Radio serials 791.44
> May be used for individual works, collections, or materials about radio serials.
> BT **Radio programs**
> RT **Soap operas**
Radio servicing
> USE **Radio—Repairing**
Radio, Shortwave
> USE **Shortwave radio**
Radio stations 384.54
> SA names of specific radio stations, to be added as needed
> BT **Radio broadcasting**
Radio stations, Amateur
> USE **Amateur radio stations**
Radio supplies industry 338.4
> UF Radio apparatus industry
>> Radio equipment industry

Radio industry and trade *[Former heading]*
> BT **Radio—Equipment and supplies**
> NT **Radio—Equipment and supplies**
Radio waves
> USE **Electric waves**
Radio writing
> USE **Radio authorship**
Radioactive fallout 539.7
> UF Dust, Radioactive
>> Fallout, Radioactive
> BT **Atomic bomb**
>> **Hydrogen bomb**
>> **Radioactive pollution**
Radioactive isotopes
> USE **Radioisotopes**
Radioactive pollution 363.17; 363.73; 621.48
> UF Environmental radioactivity
>> Nuclear pollution
>> Pollution, Radioactive
> BT **Pollution**
>> **Radioactivity**
> NT **Radioactive fallout**
> RT **Radioactive waste disposal**
Radioactive substances
> USE **Radioactivity**
Radioactive waste disposal 363.72; 621.48
> UF Nuclear waste disposal
> BT **Nuclear engineering**
>> **Nuclear power plants—Environmental aspects**
>> **Radioactivity**
>> **Refuse and refuse disposal**
> RT **Radioactive pollution**
Radioactivity 539.7
> UF Radioactive substances
> BT **Physics**
>> **Radiation**
> NT **Cosmic rays**
>> **Phosphorescence**
>> **Radioactive pollution**
>> **Radioactive waste disposal**
>> **Radiobiology**
>> **Radiochemistry**
>> **Radiotherapy**
>> **Transmutation (Chemistry)**

BT = Broader Term   NT = Narrower Term   RT = Related Term   SA = See Also   UF = Used For

Radioactivity—*Continued*
RT Nuclear physics
    Radium
    Radon
    Uranium
Radiobiology 571.4
UF Radiation biology
BT Biology
    Biophysics
    Nuclear physics
    Radioactivity
Radiocarbon dating 539.7
UF Carbon 14 dating
    Dating, Radiocarbon
BT Archeology
Radiochemistry 541.3
UF Radio chemistry
BT Physical chemistry
    Radioactivity
Radiography
USE X-rays
Radioisotopes 621.48
UF Radioactive isotopes
BT Isotopes
    Nuclear engineering
Radiologists 920
UF Roentgenologists
BT Physicians
RT Radiotherapy
Radios
USE Radio—Receivers and recep-
      tion
Radiotherapy 615.8
UF Radiation therapy
BT Electrotherapeutics
    Physical therapy
    Radioactivity
    Therapeutics
RT Phototherapy
    Radiologists
    Radium
    Ultraviolet rays
    X-rays
Radium 546; 661; 669
BT Chemical elements
    Radiation
RT Radioactivity
    Radiotherapy
Radium emanation
USE Radon

Radon 363.738; 546
UF Radium emanation
BT Poisonous gases
RT Radioactivity
Railroad accidents 363.12
UF Collisions, Railroad
    Derailments
    Railroads—Accidents *[Former
      heading]*
    Train wrecks
BT Accidents
    Disasters
Railroad construction
USE Railroad engineering
Railroad engineering 625.1
UF Railroad construction
BT Civil engineering
    Engineering
    Railroads
Railroad fares
USE Railroads—Rates
Railroad mergers
USE Railroads—Consolidation
Railroad rates
USE Railroads—Rates
Railroad workers
USE Railroads—Employees
**Railroads (May subdiv. geog.) 385;
    625.1**
UF Railways
    Trains
SA names of individual railroads, to
      be added as needed
BT Public utilities
    Transportation
NT Cable railroads
    Electric railroads
    Express service
    Freight
    Monorail railroads
    Railroad engineering
    Street railroads
Railroads—Accidents
USE Railroad accidents
Railroads and state
USE Railroads—Government policy
Railroads, Cable
USE Cable railroads
Railroads—Consolidation 338.8
UF Industrial mergers

BT = Broader Term   NT = Narrower Term   RT = Related Term   SA = See Also   UF = Used For

Railroads—Consolidation—*Continued*
      Mergers, Industrial
      Railroad mergers
  BT **Industrial trusts**
      Monopolies
Railroads, Electric
  USE **Electric railroads**
Railroads—Electrification   621.33
  UF Electrification of railroads
  RT **Electric railroads**
Railroads—Employees   331.7
  UF Railroad workers
  BT **Employees**
Railroads—Fares
  USE **Railroads—Rates**
Railroads—Finance   385
  BT **Finance**
  NT **Railroads—Rates**
Railroads—Government ownership
  USE **Railroads—Government policy**
Railroads—Government policy   354.6;
     385
  UF Government ownership of rail-
      roads
      Government regulation of rail-
      roads
      Nationalization of railroads
      Railroads and state
      Railroads—Government owner-
      ship
      Railroads, Nationalization of
      State and railroads
      State ownership of railroads
  BT **Government ownership**
     Industrial policy
     Public utilities
  NT **Railroads—Rates**
Railroads—Models   625.1
  UF Model trains
  BT **Models and model making**
Railroads, Nationalization of
  USE **Railroads—Government policy**
Railroads—Rates   385
  UF Railroad fares
      Railroad rates
      Railroads—Fares
      Rebates (Railroads)
  BT **Railroads—Finance**
     Railroads—Government policy
  RT **Freight**

Railroads—Safety appliances
  USE **Railroads—Safety devices**
Railroads—Safety devices   625.10028
  UF Railroads—Safety appliances
      [Former heading]
  BT **Accidents—Prevention**
     Safety devices
  NT **Railroads—Signaling**
Railroads—Signaling   625.1
  UF Block signal systems
      Interlocking signals
  BT **Railroads—Safety devices**
     Signals and signaling
Railroads, Single rail
  USE **Monorail railroads**
Railroads—Statistics   385
  BT **Statistics**
Railroads, Street
  USE **Street railroads**
Railroads, Underground
  USE **Subways**
Railways
  USE **Railroads**
Rain   551.57
  UF Precipitation (Meteorology)
      Rain and rainfall *[Former head-*
      ing]
      Rainfall
  BT **Meteorology**
     Water
     Weather
  NT **Acid rain**
     Floods
  RT **Droughts**
     Forest influences
     Storms
Rain and rainfall
  USE **Rain**
Rain forests (May subdiv. geog.)
     577.34; 634.9
    Use for materials on forests of broad-
leaved, mainly evergreen trees found in moist
climates in the tropics, subtropics, and some
parts of the temperate zones. Materials on im-
penetrable thickets of second-growth vegeta-
tion replacing tropical rain forests that have
been disturbed or degraded are entered under
Jungles.
  UF Rainforests
      Tropical rain forests
  BT **Forests and forestry**
  RT **Jungles**

BT = Broader Term   NT = Narrower Term   RT = Related Term   SA = See Also   UF = Used For

Rain making
   USE   **Weather control**
Rainbow   551.56
   BT   Meteorology
   RT   Refraction
Rainfall
   USE   **Rain**
Rainfall and forests
   USE   **Forest influences**
Rainforests
   USE   **Rain forests**
Rallies (Protest)
   USE   **Demonstrations**
Ranch life   307.72; 636
   BT   Farm life
          Frontier and pioneer life
   NT   Cowhands
Random access memories (Data processing)
   USE   **Computer storage devices**
Random access storage devices (Data processing)
   USE   **Computer storage devices**
Random sampling
   USE   **Sampling (Statistics)**
Ranger project
   USE   **Project Ranger**
Rank
   USE   **Social classes**
Rap music   782.421649
   UF   Rap songs
          Rapping (Music)
   BT   African American music
          Popular music
Rap songs
   USE   **Rap music**
Rape   362.883; 364.15
   UF   Assault, Sexual
          Sexual assault
   BT   Offenses against the person
          Sex crimes
   NT   Date rape
Rapid reading
   USE   **Speed reading**
Rapid transit
   USE   **Local transit**
Rapping (Music)
   USE   **Rap music**
Rare animals   591.68
   UF   Animals, Rare

   SA   names of specific animals, e.g.
          Bison; to be added as needed
   BT   Animals
          Wildlife
   RT   Endangered species
          Extinct animals
          Wildlife conservation
Rare books   090
   UF   Antiquarian books
          Book rarities
          Early printed books
   BT   Books
   RT   Editions
          First editions
Rare plants   581.68
   BT   Plants
   RT   Endangered species
          Plant conservation
Rating
   USE   **Performance standards**
          and subjects and classes of persons with the subdivision *Rating,* e.g. **Bonds—Rating; Employees—Rating;** etc., to be added as needed
Ratio and proportion   513.2
   BT   Arithmetic
          Geometry
Rationalism   149; 211
   BT   Philosophy
          Religion
          Secularism
          Theory of knowledge
   NT   Empiricism
          Enlightenment
          Intuition
          Positivism
          Reason
          Skepticism
   RT   Agnosticism
          Atheism
          Belief and doubt
          Deism
          Free thought
          Realism
Rattlesnakes   597.96
   BT   Poisonous animals
          Snakes
Raw materials   333.7
   Use for works on unprocessed minerals and unprocessed animal and vegetable products.

BT = Broader Term   NT = Narrower Term   RT = Related Term   SA = See Also   UF = Used For

Raw materials—*Continued*
Comprehensive works on the basic processed materials used in engineering and industry are entered under **Materials.**

BT   **Commercial products**

NT   **Farm produce**

       Forest products

       Mines and mineral resources

Rayon   677

BT   **Synthetic fabrics**

Rays, Ultra-violet

USE   **Ultraviolet rays**

Re-enlistment

USE   **Recruiting and enlistment**

Reaction (Political science)

USE   **Conservatism**

Reactions, Chemical

USE   **Chemical reactions**

Reactors (Nuclear physics)

USE   **Nuclear reactors**

Reader services (Libraries)

USE   **Library services**

Readers

USE   **Reading materials**

Readers and libraries

USE   **Library services**

Readers' theater   792

     Use for materials on the dramatic reading of plays before an audience.

UF   Chamber theater

       Story theater

BT   **Amateur theater**

       Theater

Readiness for mathematics

USE   **Mathematical readiness**

Readiness for reading

USE   **Reading readiness**

Readiness for school   372.21

UF   School readiness

BT   **Elementary education**

       Preschool education

Reading   372.4; 418

     Use for materials on methods of teaching reading and for general materials on the art of reading. Materials on teaching slow readers are entered under **Reading—Remedial teaching.** Materials on the cultural or informational aspects of reading and general discussions of books are entered under **Books and reading.**

UF   Children's reading

       Reading—Study and teaching

BT   **Language arts**

NT   **Books and reading**

       Reading comprehension

       Reading disability

       Reading—Phonetic method

       Reading readiness

       Speed reading

       Whole language

       Word skills

Reading clinics

USE   **Reading—Remedial teaching**

Reading comprehension   372.48

BT   **Psychology of learning**

       Reading

       Verbal learning

Reading disability   371.91

UF   Disability, Reading

       Reading retardation

       Retarded readers

SA   types of reading disabilities, e.g. **Dyslexia;** to be added as needed

BT   **Learning disabilities**

       Reading

NT   **Dyslexia**

Reading interests

USE   **Books and reading**

Reading interests of children

USE   **Children—Books and reading**

Reading interests of teenagers

USE   **Teenagers—Books and reading**

Reading interests of young adults

USE   **Teenagers—Books and reading**

Reading materials   372.41; 418

     Use for materials in English intended to be used in teaching reading or language skills. Such materials in other languages are entered under the language with the subdivision *Reading materials,* e.g. **French language—Reading materials.**

UF   English language—Reading materials

       Readers

BT   **Children's literature**

NT   **Basal readers**

       Big books

       Easy reading materials

       Hornbooks

       Recitations

RT   **Books and reading**

Reading—Patterning

USE   **Language arts—Patterning**

Reading—Phonetic method   372.46

UF   Letter-sound association

BT = Broader Term   NT = Narrower Term   RT = Related Term   SA = See Also   UF = Used For

Reading—Phonetic method—*Continued*
  Phonics
 BT **English language—Pronuncia-**
   tion
   Reading
 RT **Phonetics**
Reading readiness 372.41
 UF Readiness for reading
 BT **Reading**
Reading—Remedial teaching 372.43
 UF Reading clinics
   Remedial reading
Reading retardation
 USE **Reading disability**
Reading—Study and teaching
 USE **Reading**
Readings and recitations
 USE **Recitations**
Readings (Anthologies)
 USE **Anthologies**
Ready reckoners
 USE **Mathematics—Tables**
Real estate 333.3
  Use for materials on land and buildings considered as property. Materials on the buying and selling of real property are entered under **Real estate business.** General materials on land apart from the aspect of ownership are entered under **Land use.**
 UF Property, Real
   Real property
   Realty
 BT **Land use**
   Property
 NT **Farms**
   Landlord and tenant
   Mortgages
   Real estate business
   Real estate investment
 RT **Land tenure**
Real estate business 333.33; 346.04
  Use for materials limited to the buying and selling of real property. General materials on land and buildings considered as property are entered under **Real estate.**
 BT **Business**
   Real estate
 NT **Houses—Buying and selling**
Real estate investment 332.63
 UF Investment in real estate
   Real property investment
 BT **Investments**
   Real estate

  Speculation
Real estate investment—Taxation
  343.05
 BT **Taxation**
Real estate timesharing
 USE **Timesharing (Real estate)**
Real property
 USE **Real estate**
Real property investment
 USE **Real estate investment**
Real property tax—Assessment
 USE **Tax assessment**
Realism 149
 BT **Philosophy**
 NT **Pragmatism**
 RT **Idealism**
   Materialism
   Positivism
   Rationalism
Realism in art 709
 UF Naturalism in art
 BT **Art**
Realism in literature 809
 UF Naturalism in literature
 BT **Literature**
 RT **Romanticism**
Reality 111
 BT **Philosophy**
   Truth
 RT **Pragmatism**
   Theory of knowledge
Realty
 USE **Real estate**
Reapers
 USE **Harvesting machinery**
Reapportionment (Election law)
 USE **Apportionment (Election law)**
Reason 128; 160
 BT **Intellect**
   Rationalism
 NT **Reasoning**
Reasoning 153.4; 160
 BT **Psychology**
   Reason
   Thought and thinking
 NT **Critical thinking**
 RT **Intellect**
   Logic
Rebates (Railroads)
 USE **Railroads—Rates**

BT = Broader Term NT = Narrower Term RT = Related Term SA = See Also UF = Used For

Rebellions
USE Insurgency
Revolutions
Rebels (Social psychology)
USE Alienation (Social psychology)
Rebirth
USE Reincarnation
Rebirth (Theology)
USE Regeneration (Christianity)
Rebuses
USE Riddles
Recall of products
USE Product recall
Recall (Political science) 324.6
BT Impeachments
Representative government and representation
Recessions (May subdiv. geog.) 338.5
UF Business recessions
Economic recessions
Recessions, Economic
SA names of countries, states, cities, etc., with the subdivision *Economic conditions,* to be added as needed
BT Business cycles
Recessions, Economic
USE Recessions
Recipes
USE Cooking
Reciprocity
USE Commercial policy
Recitations 808.85
Use for collections of material written or selected for oral presentation and for materials about recitation.
UF Declamations
Narrations
Oral interpretation
Readings and recitations *[Former heading]*
Speakers (Recitation books)
BT Reading materials
School assembly programs
NT Choral speaking
Monologues
Monologues with music
Recitations with music
USE Monologues with music

Reclamation of land 627; 631.6
Use for general materials on reclamation, including drainage and irrigation.
UF Clearing of land
Land, Reclamation of
BT Agriculture
Civil engineering
Hydraulic engineering
Land use
NT Drainage
RT Irrigation
Wetlands
Recluses
USE Hermits
Recombinant DNA 572.8
UF Gene splicing
BT DNA
Genetic engineering
Genetic recombination
Recombination, Genetic
USE Genetic recombination
Recommendations for positions
USE Applications for positions
Reconciliation, Sacrament of
USE Penance
Reconnaissance, Aerial
USE Aerial reconnaissance
Reconstruction (1865-1876) 973.8
UF Carpetbag rule
United States—History—1861-1865, Civil War—Reconstruction
BT United States—History—1865-1898
RT Ku Klux Klan
Reconstruction (1914-1939) 940.3
UF World War, 1914-1918—Reconstruction
NT Veterans—Education
Veterans—Employment
RT Foreign aid
International cooperation
World War, 1914-1918—Economic aspects
Reconstruction (1939-1951) (May subdiv. geog. except U.S.) 940.53
UF Marshall Plan
Point Four program
World War, 1939-1945—Reconstruction
NT Veterans—Education

BT = Broader Term NT = Narrower Term RT = Related Term SA = See Also UF = Used For

Reconstruction (1939-1951)—*Continued*
    Veterans—Employment
    World War, 1939-1945—Civilian relief
    World War, 1939-1945—Reparations
  RT Foreign aid
    International cooperation
    World War, 1939-1945—Economic aspects
Recorders, Tape
  USE **Magnetic recorders and recording**
Recording, Laser
  USE **Laser recording**
Recordings, Sound
  USE **Sound recordings**
Records of achievement
  USE **World records**
Records of births, etc.
  USE **Registers of births, etc.**
    Vital statistics
Records, Phonograph
  USE **Sound recordings**
Records—Preservation
  USE **Archives**
Records, Sports
  USE **Sports records**
Records, World
  USE **World records**
Recovered memories
  USE **Recovered memory**
Recovered memory 616.85
  UF Delayed memory
    Recovered memories
    Repressed memory
  BT **Memory**
  RT **False memory syndrome**
Recovering addicts 362.29; 616.86
  BT **Drug addicts**
  RT **Recovering alcoholics**
Recovering alcoholics 362.292; 616.86
  BT **Alcoholics**
  RT **Recovering addicts**
Recovery of space vehicles
  USE **Space vehicles—Recovery**
Recovery of waste products
  USE **Recycling**
Recreation (May subdiv. geog.) **790**
  UF Pastimes

    Relaxation
  SA classes of persons with the subdivision *Recreation*, e.g. **Elderly—Recreation;** to be added as needed
  BT **Leisure**
  NT **Camps**
    Community centers
    Elderly—Recreation
    Games
    Hobbies
    Leisure
    Outdoor recreation
    Play
    Playgrounds
    Popular culture
    Resorts
    Sports
    Vacations
  RT **Amusements**
    Sports facilities
Recreation centers
  USE **Community centers**
    Physical fitness centers
Recreational vehicles 629.226
  UF R.V.'s
    RVs
    Vehicles, Recreational
  SA types of recreational vehicles, e.g. **Travel trailers and campers;** to be added as needed
  BT **Outdoor recreation**
    Vehicles
  NT **Travel trailers and campers**
Recreations
  USE **Hobbies**
Recreations, Literary
  USE **Literary recreations**
Recreations, Mathematical
  USE **Mathematical recreations**
Recreations, Scientific
  USE **Scientific recreations**
Recruiting and enlistment 355.2
  UF Armed forces—Recruiting, enlistment, etc.
    Enlistment
    Re-enlistment

BT = Broader Term   NT = Narrower Term   RT = Related Term   SA = See Also   UF = Used For

Recruiting and enlistment—*Continued*

SA   names of armed forces and of armies and navies with the subdivision *Recruiting, enlistment, etc.,* e.g. **United States—Armed Forces—Recruiting, enlistment, etc.; United States. Army—Recruiting, enlistment, etc.;** etc., to be added as needed

BT   **Armed forces**

Military personnel

NT   **Draft**

United States—Armed Forces—Recruiting, enlistment, etc.

United States. Army—Recruiting, enlistment, etc.

United States. Navy—Recruiting, enlistment, etc.

Voluntary military service

Recruiting of employees   658.3

SA   types of employees and professions with the subdivision *Recruiting,* e.g. **Librarians—Recruiting;** to be added as needed

BT   **Personnel management**

NT   **Employment agencies**

Librarians—Recruiting

Rectors

USE   **Clergy**

Recurrent education

USE   **Continuing education**

Recycling   628.4

Use for materials on the recovery and processing of waste paper, cans, bottles, etc. Materials on the recycling or reuse of a specific waste products are entered under that product with the subdivision *Recycling.*

UF   Conversion of waste products

Recovery of waste products

Recycling (Waste, etc.) *[Former heading]*

Reuse of waste

Utilization of waste

Waste products—Recycling

Waste reclamation

SA   subjects with the subdivision *Recycling,* e.g. **Aluminum—Recycling;** to be added as needed

BT   **Energy conservation**

Pollution control industry

Salvage

NT   **Aluminum—Recycling**

RT   **Refuse and refuse disposal**

Waste products

Recycling (Waste, etc.)

USE   **Recycling**

Red   535.6; 752

BT   **Color**

Redemption

USE   **Salvation**

Reducing

USE   **Weight loss**

Reference books   028.7

Use for materials about reference books. Reference books themselves are entered under **Encyclopedias and dictionaries;** or under the appropriate subjects with the subdivisions *Dictionaries; Bibliography;* etc., as needed.

BT   **Bibliography**

Books

Books and reading

NT   **Encyclopedias and dictionaries**

Reference services (Libraries)   025.5

Use for materials on activities designed to make information available to library users, including direct personal assistance.

UF   Library reference services

Online reference services

Reference work (Libraries)

BT   **Information services**

Library services

Reference work (Libraries)

USE   **Reference services (Libraries)**

Referendum   328.2

UF   Direct legislation

Initiative and referendum

Legislation, Direct

BT   **Constitutional law**

Democracy

Elections

Refinishing furniture

USE   **Furniture finishing**

Reforestation   333.75; 634.9

BT   **Forests and forestry**

RT   **Tree planting**

Reform, Agrarian

USE   **Land reform**

Reform of criminals

USE   **Criminals**

Probation

Reform of criminals—*Continued*
    Reformatories
Reform of health care delivery
  USE   **Health care reform**
Reform of medical care delivery
  USE   **Health care reform**
Reform schools
  USE   **Reformatories**
Reform, Social
  USE   **Social problems**
Reformation   270.6
  UF   Church history—1517-1648, Reformation
        Protestant Reformation
  SA   names of religious sects, e.g.
        Huguenots; to be added as
        needed
  BT   **Christianity**
        Modern history
  NT   **Calvinism**
        Huguenots
  RT   **Church history—1500- , Modern period**
        Counter-Reformation
        Protestantism
        Sixteenth century
Reformatories   365
  UF   Penal institutions
        Reform of criminals
        Reform schools
  BT   **Children—Institutional care**
        Correctional institutions
        Prisons
        Punishment
  NT   **Probation**
  RT   **Juvenile delinquency**
Reformers   920
    Use for materials about political, social, or
  religious reformers.
  NT   **Abolitionists**
        Suffragists
Refraction   535
  UF   Dioptrics
  BT   **Light**
        Optics
  RT   **Rainbow**
Refrigeration   621.5
  UF   Cooling appliances
        Freezing
        Ice manufacture

        Refrigeration and refrigerating
          machinery *[Former heading]*
        Refrigerators
  BT   **Frost**
  RT   **Air conditioning**
        Cold storage
        Low temperatures
Refrigeration and refrigerating machinery
  USE   **Refrigeration**
Refrigerators
  USE   **Refrigeration**
Refugees (May subdiv. geog.)   **325;**
        341.4; 362.87
  UF   Displaced persons
        Exiles
  SA   refugees of particular countries,
        geographic regions, or ethnic
        groups, e.g. **Vietnamese refugees; Arab refugees;** etc.,
        and names of wars with the
        subdivision *Refugees,* e.g.
        World War, 1939-1945—Refugees; to be added as
        needed
  BT   **Aliens**
        Homeless persons
        Immigration and emigration
  NT   **Arab refugees**
        Political refugees
        Vietnamese refugees
  RT   **Sanctuary movement**
Refugees, Arab
  USE   **Arab refugees**
Refugees, Political
  USE   **Political refugees**
Refugees, Vietnamese
  USE   **Vietnamese refugees**
Refuges, Wildlife
  USE   **Wildlife refuges**
Refuse and refuse disposal   363.72;
        628.4
  UF   Disposal of refuse
        Garbage
        Garbage disposal
        Incineration
        Littering
        Solid waste disposal
        Waste disposal

BT = Broader Term   NT = Narrower Term   RT = Related Term   SA = See Also   UF = Used For

Refuse and refuse disposal—*Continued*

- SA   types of refuse, e.g. **Industrial wastes;** types of waste disposal, e.g. **Radioactive waste disposal; Sewage disposal;** etc., and types of industries, plants, and facilities with the subdivision *Waste disposal,* e.g. **Chemical industry—Waste disposal;** to be added as needed
- BT   **Municipal engineering**
         Public health
         Sanitary engineering
         Sanitation
- NT   **Chemical industry—Waste disposal**
         Hazardous wastes
         Industrial wastes
         Medical wastes
         Radioactive waste disposal
         Sewage disposal
- RT   **Pollution**
         Pollution control industry
         Recycling
         Salvage
         Street cleaning
         Waste products

Regattas
- USE   **Rowing**
         Yachts and yachting

Regency novels   813, etc.

     May be used for individual works, collections, or materials about historical novels set during or around the period when the future George IV of England acted as Regent for George III (1811-1820).
- BT   **Historical fiction**

Regeneration (Christianity)   234; 248.2
- UF   Born again Christianity
         Christian new birth
         Christian regeneration
         New birth (Theology)
         Rebirth (Theology)
         Regeneration (Theology) *[Former heading]*
- BT   **Christianity—Doctrines**
         Salvation
- RT   **Conversion**

Regeneration (Theology)
- USE   **Regeneration (Christianity)**

Regional history
- USE   **Local history**

Regional libraries   027.4

     Use for materials on public libraries serving a group of communities, several counties, or other regions.
- UF   District libraries
         Libraries, Regional
- BT   **Public libraries**
- NT   **County libraries**

Regional planning (May subdiv. geog.)   307.1; 711
- UF   County planning
         Metropolitan planning
         State planning
- BT   **Land use**
         Planning
- RT   **City planning**
         Landscape protection

Regionalism (May subdiv. geog.)   320.4; 330.9

     Use for materials on the political or economic power or interests of geographic areas within nations or beyond national boundaries.
- UF   Localism
         Provincialism
         Sectionalism
- BT   **Geography**
         Politics
- RT   **Nationalism**

Regionalism—United States   917.3; 973
- UF   Sectionalism (U.S.) *[Former heading]*
         Sectionalism (United States) *[Former heading]*

Registers
- USE   subjects, ethnic groups, classes of persons, names of countries, cities, etc., and names of families and of corporate bodies, such as colleges and universities, with the subdivision *Registers,* for lists of persons or organizations without addresses or other identifying data, e.g. **United States—Registers; United States Military Academy—Registers;** etc., to be added as needed

---

BT = Broader Term   NT = Narrower Term   RT = Related Term   SA = See Also   UF = Used For

Registers of births, etc.   929
    UF   Birth records
           Births, Registers of
           Burial statistics
           Deaths, Registers of
           Marriage registers
           Parish registers
           Records of births, etc.
           Vital records
    BT   **Genealogy**
    NT   **Wills**
    RT   **Vital statistics**
Registration of voters
    USE   **Voter registration**
Regulatory agencies
    USE   **Administrative agencies**
Rehabilitation
    USE   classes of persons with the sub-
           division *Rehabilitation,* e.g.
           Drug addicts—Rehabilita-
           tion; Physically handi-
           capped—Rehabilitation; etc.,
           to be added as needed
Rehabilitation peer counseling
    USE   **Peer counseling**
Reign of Terror
    USE   **France—History—1789-1799,**
           Revolution
Reincarnation   129
    UF   Rebirth
    BT   **Theosophy**
    RT   **Soul**
Reindeer   599.65; 636.2
    BT   **Deer**
           Domestic animals
           Mammals
Reinforced concrete   691
    BT   **Building materials**
           Concrete
Relations among ethnic groups
    USE   **Ethnic relations**
Relative humidity
    USE   **Humidity**
Relativity (Physics)   530.11
    BT   **Physics**
    RT   **Gravitation**
           Quantum theory
           Space and time
Relaxation
    USE   **Recreation**

           Rest
Reliability (Engineering)   620
    UF   Reliability of equipment
           Systems reliability
           Testing
    BT   **Engineering**
           Probabilities
           Systems engineering
    NT   **Quality control**
           Structural failures
Reliability of equipment
    USE   **Reliability (Engineering)**
Relief, Public
    USE   **Public welfare**
Religion   200
    SA   names of peoples, ethnic groups,
           countries, states, etc., and in-
           dividual persons with the sub-
           division *Religion,* e.g. **Indians**
           of North America—Religion;
           African Americans—Reli-
           gion; United States—Reli-
           gion; Shakespeare, William,
           1564-1616—Religion; etc.; re-
           ligious subjects subdivided by
           religion or sect, e.g. **Laity—**
           Catholic Church; and other
           subjects with the subdivision
           Religious aspects, e.g. **Ethnic**
           relations—Religious aspects;
           Love—Religious aspects; etc.,
           which may be further subdi-
           vided by religion or sect, to
           be added as needed
    NT   **African Americans—Religion**
           Agnosticism
           Ancestor worship
           Art and religion
           Atheism
           Blacks—Religion
           Communism and religion
           Deism
           Faith
           Indians of North America—
           Religion
           Liturgies
           Moon worship
           Mythology
           Ohio—Religion
           Philosophy and religion

BT = Broader Term   NT = Narrower Term   RT = Related Term   SA = See Also   UF = Used For

Religion—*Continued*
      Psychology of religion
      Rationalism
      Religion and politics
      Religion and science
      Religion and sociology
      Religion in literature
      Religious awakening
      Religious education
      Religious fundamentalism
      Religious life
      Shakespeare, William, 1564-
        1616—Religion
      Sun worship
      Supernatural
      Theism
      United States—Religion
      Visions
      War—Religious aspects
      Worship
  RT God
      Religions
      Theology
Religion and art
  USE **Art and religion**
Religion and communism
  USE **Communism and religion**
Religion and education
  USE **Church and education**
Religion and literature
  USE **Religion in literature**
      Religious literature
Religion and medicine
  USE **Medicine—Religious aspects**
Religion and philosophy
  USE **Philosophy and religion**
Religion and politics   261.7; 291.1; 322
  UF Evangelism and politics
      Political science—Religious as-
        pects
      Politics and religion
      Politics—Religious aspects
      Religion—Political aspects
      Religions—Political aspects
  BT **Politics**
      Religion
  NT **Christianity and politics**
Religion and psychology
  USE **Psychology of religion**

Religion and science (May subdiv. geog.)
    215
  UF Science and religion
      Science—Religious aspects
  BT **Religion**
      Science
  NT **Bible and science**
  RT **Creationism**
      Evolution
      Natural theology
Religion and social problems
  USE **Church and social problems**
Religion and society
  USE **Religion and sociology**
Religion and sociology   306.6
    Use for materials on religious sociology in
    general. Materials on the sociology of Chris-
    tian denominations and on social theory from
    a Christian point of view are entered under
    Christian sociology. Materials on the practi-
    cal treatment of social problems from the
    point of view of the church are entered under
    Church and social problems.
  UF Religion and society
      Religion—Social aspects
      Religious sociology
      Society and religion
      Society—Religious aspects
      Sociology and religion
      Sociology of religion
      Sociology—Religious aspects
  SA sociology associated with partic-
      ular religions, e.g. **Christian**
      sociology; to be added as
      needed
  BT **Religion**
      Sociology
  NT **Christian sociology**
Religion and state
  USE **Church and state**
Religion and war
  USE **War—Religious aspects**
Religion in literature   809
  UF Religion and literature
  BT **Literature**
      Religion
  RT **Bible in literature**
Religion in the public schools   379.2
  UF Bible in the schools
      Fundamentalism and education
      [Former heading]
      Prayer in the public schools

BT = Broader Term   NT = Narrower Term   RT = Related Term   SA = See Also   UF = Used For

Religion in the public schools—*Continued*

> Prayers in the public schools
> Public schools and religion
> School prayer

BT   **Church and education**

Church and state

Public schools

Religious education

Religion—Philosophy   210

> Use for materials on the nature, origin, or validity of religion from a philosophical point of view. Materials on the reciprocal relationship and influence between philosophy and religion are entered under **Philosophy and religion.**

UF   Philosophy of religion

RT   **Philosophy and religion**

Religion—Political aspects

USE   **Religion and politics**

Religion—Psychological aspects

USE   **Psychology of religion**

Religion—Social aspects

USE   **Religion and sociology**

Religion—Study and teaching

USE   **Theology—Study and teaching**

Religions   291

> Use for materials on the major world religions. Materials on independent religious groups whose teachings or practices fall within the normative bounds of the major world religions are entered under **Sects.** Materials on groups or movements whose beliefs or practices differ significantly from the traditional religions, often focused upon a charismatic leader, are entered under **Cults.**

UF   Comparative religion

SA   names of religions and of sects within the major world religions, to be added as needed

BT   **Civilization**

NT   **Bahai Faith**

Brahmanism

Buddhism

Christianity

Christianity and other religions

Confucianism

Cults

Druids and Druidism

Gnosticism

Hinduism

Islam

Judaism

Mythology

Occultism

Paganism

Sects

Shinto

Taoism

Theosophy

Voodooism

RT   **Gods and goddesses**

Religion

Religions—Biography

USE   **Religious biography**

Religions—Political aspects

USE   **Religion and politics**

Religious art

USE   **Church architecture**

Religious art and symbolism

Religious art and symbolism   291.3; 704.9

UF   Iconography

Religious art

Religious painting

Religious sculpture

Religious symbolism

Sacred art

BT   **Art**

Symbolism

NT   **Christian art and symbolism**

RT   **Art and religion**

Religious aspects

USE   subjects with the subdivision *Religious aspects,* e.g. **Ethnic relations—Religious aspects; Love—Religious aspects;** etc., which may be further subdivided by the names of religions or sects, to be added as needed

Religious awakening (May subdiv. geog.) **269; 291.4**

> Use for materials on a renewal of interest in religion.

UF   Awakening, Religious

Revival (Religion)

BT   **Religion**

Religious belief

USE   **Faith**

Religious biography   200.92; 920

UF   Religions—Biography *[Former heading]*

SA   biography of particular religions, e.g. **Christian biography;** to be added as needed

---

BT = Broader Term   NT = Narrower Term   RT = Related Term   SA = See Also   UF = Used For

Religious biography—*Continued*
    BT   **Biography**
    NT   **Christian biography**
Religious ceremonies
    USE   **Rites and ceremonies**
Religious cults
    USE   **Cults**
Religious denominations
    USE   **Sects**
Religious drama   792.1; 808.82; 812, etc.

    May be used for collections or materials about religious drama, not for individual works.

    UF   Drama, Religious
    BT   **Drama**
           Religious literature
    NT   **Bible plays**
           Christmas plays
           Easter—Drama
           Jesus Christ—Drama
           Morality plays
           Mysteries and miracle plays
           Passion plays
Religious education   291.7

    Use for materials on the instruction of religion in schools and private life. Materials limited to the instruction of Christian religion in schools and private life are entered under **Christian education.** Materials on the relation of the church to education and on the history of the part that the church has taken in secular education are entered under **Church and education.** Materials on church supported and controlled elementary and secondary schools are entered under **Church schools.**

    UF   Theological education
    BT   **Education**
           Religion
    NT   **Christian education**
           Religion in the public schools
           Sunday schools
    RT   **Moral education**
           Theology—Study and teaching
Religious festivals
    USE   **Religious holidays**
Religious fiction   808.83; 813, etc.

    Use for individual works, collections, or materials about fiction that promotes religious teachings or exemplifies a religious way of life.

    SA   fiction associated with particular religions, e.g. **Christian fiction;** to be added as needed
    BT   **Fiction**

    NT   **Christian fiction**
           Jewish religious fiction
Religious freedom
    USE   **Freedom of religion**
Religious fundamentalism (May subdiv. geog.)   291

    Use for religious groups opposed to modernity and secularism and seeking a revival of orthodox or conservative beliefs and practices.

    UF   Fundamentalism *[Former heading]*
           Fundamentalisms
           Fundamentalist movements
    SA   fundamentalism of various religions, e.g. **Islamic fundamentalism;** to be added as needed
    BT   **Religion**
    NT   **Christian fundamentalism**
           Islamic fundamentalism
Religious history
    USE   **Church history**
Religious holidays   263; 394.265

    Use for materials on religious holidays in general. Materials on secular holidays are entered under **Holidays.** Materials on secular festivals other than holidays are entered under **Festivals.**

    UF   Church festivals
           Ecclesiastical fasts and feasts
           Fasts and feasts *[Former heading]*
           Feasts
           Fiestas
           Holy days
           Religious festivals
    SA   holidays of particular religions, e.g. **Jewish holidays;** and names of specific religious holidays and observances, e.g. **Christmas; Lent;** etc., to be added as needed
    BT   **Holidays**
           Rites and ceremonies
    NT   **Christian holidays**
           Church year
           Jewish holidays
           Thanksgiving Day
    RT   **Fasting**
           Festivals
Religious liberty
    USE   **Freedom of religion**

BT = Broader Term   NT = Narrower Term   RT = Related Term   SA = See Also   UF = Used For

Religious life   248.4; 291.4

Use for materials that describe or promote personal or community religious and devotional life.

SA   groups and classes of persons with the subdivision *Religious life,* to be added as needed

BT   **Religion**

NT   **Asceticism**
        Celibacy
        Christian life
        Family—Religious life
        Spiritual life
        Teenagers—Religious life
        Women—Religious life
        Youth—Religious life

RT   **Monasticism and religious orders**

Religious life (Christian)
  USE   **Christian life**

Religious literature   800

UF   Religion and literature

SA   literatures of particular religions or denominations, e.g. **Catholic literature;** to be added as needed

BT   **Literature**

NT   **Christian literature**
        Devotional literature
        Jewish literature
        Religious drama
        Religious poetry
        Sacred books

RT   **Bible as literature**

Religious music
  USE   **Church music**

Religious orders
  USE   **Monasticism and religious orders**

Religious orders for men
  USE   **Monasticism and religious orders for men**

Religious orders for women
  USE   **Monasticism and religious orders for women**

Religious painting
  USE   **Religious art and symbolism**

Religious persecution
  USE   **Persecution**

Religious poetry   808.81; 811, etc.; 811.008, etc.

May be used for collections or materials about religious poetry, not for individual works.

BT   **Poetry**
        Religious literature

RT   **Hymns**

Religious psychology
  USE   **Psychology of religion**

Religious sculpture
  USE   **Religious art and symbolism**

Religious sociology
  USE   **Religion and sociology**

Religious summer schools   268; 291.7

UF   Bible classes
        Summer schools, Religious *[Former heading]*
        Vacation church schools
        Vacation schools, Religious

BT   **Schools**
        Summer schools

Religious symbolism
  USE   **Religious art and symbolism**

Remarriage   306.84

BT   **Marriage**

Remedial reading
  USE   **Reading—Remedial teaching**

Remodeling
  USE   types of buildings and parts of buildings with the subdivision *Remodeling,* e.g. **Houses—Remodeling; Kitchens—Remodeling;** etc., to be added as needed

Remodeling (Architecture)
  USE   **Houses—Remodeling**

Remodeling of dwellings
  USE   **Houses—Remodeling**

Remodeling of houses
  USE   **Houses—Remodeling**

Remodeling of kitchens
  USE   **Kitchens—Remodeling**

Remote sensing   621.36

UF   Sensing, Remote
        Terrain sensing, Remote

BT   **Aerial photography**

NT   **Aerial reconnaissance**
        Radar

RT   **Space optics**

BT = Broader Term   NT = Narrower Term   RT = Related Term   SA = See Also   UF = Used For

Renaissance   940.2
  UF   Revival of letters
  BT   **Modern civilization**
        Modern history
  NT   **Fifteenth century**
        Renaissance architecture
        Renaissance art
        Sixteenth century
  RT   **Humanism**
        Middle Ages

Renaissance architecture   724
  UF   Architecture, Renaissance *[For-*
        mer heading]
  BT   **Architecture**
        Renaissance

Renaissance art   709.02
  UF   Art, Renaissance *[Former head-*
        ing]
  BT   **Art**
        Renaissance

Renaissance decoration and ornament
    745.4
  UF   Decoration and ornament, Re-
        naissance
  BT   **Decoration and ornament**

Renaissance, Harlem
  USE **Harlem Renaissance**

Rendezvous in space
  USE **Orbital rendezvous (Space**
        flight)

Renewable energy resources   333.79
  UF   Alternate energy resources
        Alternative energy resources
        Energy resources, Renewable
  SA   types of renewable resources, to
        be added as needed
  BT   **Energy resources**
  NT   **Geothermal resources**
        Solar energy
        Water power
        Wind power

Rental services
  USE **Lease and rental services**

Reorganization of administrative agencies
  USE **Administrative agencies—Reor-**
        ganization

Repairing   620
  UF   Fixing
        Maintenance and repair
        Mending

Repairs
  SA   types of things that require
        maintenance with the subdivi-
        sion *Maintenance and repair,*
        e.g. **Automobiles—Mainte-**
        nance and repair; Build-
        ings—Maintenance and re-
        pair; etc., and types of things
        that require no maintenance
        with the subdivision *Repair-*
        ing, e.g. **Radio—Repairing;**
        to be added as needed

Repairs
  USE **Repairing**

Reparations (World War, 1939-1945)
  USE **World War, 1939-1945—Repa-**
        rations

Report writing   808
  UF   Reports—Preparation
        Research paper writing
        Term paper writing
  BT   **Authorship**
  NT   **School reports**

Reporters and reporting   070.4
  UF   Interviewing (Journalism)
        Newspaper work
  BT   **Journalism**
        Newspapers

Reports—Preparation
  USE **Report writing**

Reports, Teachers'
  USE **School reports**

Representation
  USE **Representative government and**
        representation

Representation, Proportional
  USE **Proportional representation**

Representative government and represen-
    tation   321.8
  UF   Parliamentary government
        Representation
        Self-government
  BT   **Constitutional history**
        Constitutional law
        Political science
  NT   **Apportionment (Election law)**
        Legislative bodies
        Proportional representation
        Recall (Political science)
  RT   **Democracy**

BT = Broader Term   NT = Narrower Term   RT = Related Term   SA = See Also   UF = Used For

Representative government and represen-
tation—*Continued*
      Elections
      Republics
      Suffrage
Representatives, House of (U.S.)
  USE   United States. Congress. House
Repressed memory
  USE   Recovered memory
Reprints
  USE   Editions
Reproduction   573.6; 612.6
  UF   Generation
  BT   Biology
        Life (Biology)
        Physiology
  NT   Animal reproduction
        Artificial insemination
        Breeding
        Cells
        Fertility
        Fertilization in vitro
        Fetus
        Genetics
        Human artificial insemination
        Infertility
        Menstruation
        Pregnancy
  RT   Embryology
        Reproductive system
        Sex (Biology)
Reproduction processes
  USE   Copying processes
Reproductive behavior
  USE   Sexual behavior in animals
Reproductive organs
  USE   Reproductive system
Reproductive system   573.6; 611; 612.6
  UF   Generative organs
        Genitalia
        Reproductive organs
        Sex organs
  BT   Anatomy
        Physiology
        Sex (Biology)
  RT   Reproduction
Reprographic art
  USE   Copy art
Reprography
  USE   Copying processes

Reptiles   597.9
  BT   Vertebrates
  NT   Alligators
        Crocodiles
        Fossil reptiles
        Lizards
        Snakes
        Turtles
Reptiles, Fossil
  USE   Fossil reptiles
Reptiles—Physiology   597.9
  BT   Physiology
Republic of China, 1949-
  USE   Taiwan
Republic of South Africa
  USE   South Africa
Republican Party (U.S.)   324.2734
  BT   Political parties
Republics   321.8
  UF   Commonwealth, The
  BT   Constitutional history
        Constitutional law
        Political science
  NT   Federal government
  RT   Democracy
        Representative government and
          representation
Rescue of Jews, 1939-1945
  USE   World War, 1939-1945—
        Jews—Rescue
Rescue operations, Space
  USE   Space rescue operations
Rescue work   363.3
  UF   Search and rescue operations
  BT   Civil defense
  NT   First aid
        Lifesaving
        Space rescue operations
Research   001.4
  UF   Research and development
  SA   subjects with the subdivision *Re-
        search*, to be added as needed
  NT   Agriculture—Research
        Animal experimentation
        Evaluation
        Intelligence service
        Medicine—Research
        Oceanography—Research
        Operations research
        Parapsychology

BT = Broader Term   NT = Narrower Term   RT = Related Term   SA = See Also   UF = Used For

Research—*Continued*
         Surveys
  RT   Information services
         Learning and scholarship
Research and development
  USE   Research
Research paper writing
  USE   Report writing
Reservations, Indian
  USE   Indians of North America—
         Reservations
Reservoirs 627; 628.1
  BT   Hydraulic structures
  NT   Irrigation
  RT   Water supply
Resettlement
  USE   Land settlement
Residences
  USE   Domestic architecture
         Houses
Residential construction
  USE   House construction
Residential security
  USE   Burglary protection
Residential treatment centers
  USE   Group homes
Resins
  USE   Gums and resins
Resistance of materials
  USE   Strength of materials
Resistance to government 322.4
  UF   Civil disobedience
         Government, Resistance to *[For-
          mer heading]*
  BT   Political crimes and offenses
         Political ethics
         Political science
  NT   Hunger strikes
         Passive resistance
  RT   Insurgency
         Revolutions
Resistance welding
  USE   Electric welding
Resorts (May subdiv. geog.) 790
  BT   Recreation
  NT   Health resorts
         Summer resorts
         Winter resorts

Resource management
  USE   Conservation of natural re-
         sources
Resources, Marine
  USE   Marine resources
Resources, Natural
  USE   Natural resources
Respiration 573.2; 612.2
  UF   Breathing
  BT   Physiology
  RT   Respiratory system
Respiration, Artificial
  USE   Artificial respiration
Respiratory organs
  USE   Respiratory system
Respiratory system 573.2; 611; 612.2
  UF   Respiratory organs
  BT   Anatomy
         Physiology
  NT   Lungs
  RT   Respiration
Respite care
  USE   Home care services
Responsibility, Legal
  USE   Liability (Law)
Rest 613.7
  UF   Relaxation
  BT   Health
         Hygiene
  NT   Sleep
  RT   Fatigue
Restaurants (May subdiv. geog.) 647.95
  UF   Coffee shops
         Lunchrooms
         Restaurants, bars, etc. *[Former
          heading]*
         Tea rooms
         Tearooms
  SA   types of restaurants, to be added
         as needed
  BT   Food service
  NT   Coffeehouses
  RT   Bars
Restaurants, bars, etc.
  USE   Bars
         Restaurants
Restoration of automobiles
  USE   Automobiles—Conservation
         and restoration

BT = Broader Term   NT = Narrower Term   RT = Related Term   SA = See Also   UF = Used For

Restoration of buildings
USE   **Architecture—Conservation**
       and restoration
Restoration of furniture
USE   **Furniture finishing**
       Furniture—Repairing
Restoration of works of art
USE   subjects with the subdivision
       Conservation and restoration,
       e.g. **Painting—Conservation**
       and restoration; to be added
       as needed
Restraint of trade   338.6
UF   Combinations in restraint of
       trade
       Restrictive trade practices
       Trade, Restraint of
BT   **Commerce**
       Commercial law
RT   **Boycotts**
       Corporation law
       Industrial trusts
       Monopolies
       Unfair competition
Restrictive trade practices
USE   **Restraint of trade**
Résumés (Employment)   650.14; 808
UF   Job résumés
BT   **Applications for positions**
       Job hunting
Resurrection
USE   **Future life**
       Jesus Christ—Resurrection
Resurrection of Jesus Christ
USE   **Jesus Christ—Resurrection**
Resuscitation, Heart
USE   **Cardiac resuscitation**
Resuscitation, Pulmonary
USE   **Artificial respiration**
Retail sales tax
USE   **Sales tax**
Retail stores
USE   **Stores**
Retail trade   381; 658.8
UF   Merchandising
BT   **Commerce**
NT   **Advertising**
       Chain stores
       Department stores
       Direct selling

       Discount stores
       Drugstores
       Inventory control
       Packaging
       Sales personnel
       Selling
       Shopping centers and malls
       Stores
       Supermarkets
Retarded children
USE   **Mentally handicapped children**
Retarded readers
USE   **Reading disability**
Retention, Grade
USE   **Promotion (School)**
Retired people
USE   **Retirees**
Retired persons
USE   **Retirees**
Retirees (May subdiv. geog.)   155.67;
       305.9
UF   Retired people
       Retired persons
RT   **Elderly**
       Retirement
Retirees—Personal finance   332.024
Retirement   305.26; 306.3
BT   **Leisure**
       Old age
NT   **Retirement income**
RT   **Elderly—Life skills guides**
       Retirees
Retirement communities   307.7
UF   Life care communities
       Places of retirement
       Retirement places
BT   **Elderly—Housing**
Retirement income   331.25; 353.5
BT   **Income**
       Retirement
NT   **Annuities**
       Individual retirement accounts
       Old age pensions
       Pensions
Retirement places
USE   **Retirement communities**
Retouching (Photography)
USE   **Photography—Retouching**
Retraining, Occupational
USE   **Occupational retraining**

BT = Broader Term   NT = Narrower Term   RT = Related Term   SA = See Also   UF = Used For

Retrenchment of organizations
USE **Downsizing of organizations**
Retribution
USE **Future life**
Hell
Reunions, Family
USE **Family reunions**
Reusable space vehicles
USE **Space shuttles**
Reuse of waste
USE **Recycling**
Revelation 231.7; 291.2
BT **God**
Supernatural
Theology
Revenue
USE **Tariff**
Taxation
Revenue, Internal
USE **Internal revenue**
Revenue sharing 336.1

Use for materials on the practice of return-
ing a percentage of federal tax money to state
and local governments for locally directed and
controlled public service programs.

UF Federal revenue sharing
Tax sharing
BT **Intergovernmental tax relations**
Reviews
USE subjects with the subdivision *Re-
views*, e.g. **Books—Reviews;**
to be added as needed
Revival of letters
USE **Renaissance**
Revival (Religion)
USE **Evangelistic work**
Religious awakening
Revivals
Revivals 269; 291.4
UF Revival (Religion)
BT **Evangelistic work**
Revivals—Music
USE **Gospel music**
Revolution, American
USE **United States—History—1775-
1783, Revolution**
Revolution, French
USE **France—History—1789-1799,
Revolution**

Revolution, Russian
USE **Soviet Union—History—1917-
1921, Revolution**
Revolutions 303.6
UF Coups d'état
Rebellions
Sedition
SA names of countries with the sub-
division *History—[dates], Rev-
olution*, e.g. **France—His-
tory—1789-1799, Revolution;**
to be added as needed
BT **Political science**
NT **France—History—1789-1799,
Revolution**
**Hungary—History—1956, Rev-
olution**
Insurgency
National liberation movements
Radicalism
**Soviet Union—History—1917-
1921, Revolution**
**United States—History—1775-
1783, Revolution**
RT **Resistance to government**
Revolvers
USE **Handguns**
Rewards (Prizes, etc.)
USE **Awards**
Rh factor
USE **Blood groups**
Rhetoric 808
UF Composition (Rhetoric)
English language—Rhetoric
Persuasion (Rhetoric)
Speaking
SA names of languages with the
subdivision *Composition and
exercises,* e.g. **English lan-
guage—Composition and ex-
ercises;** to be added as need-
ed
BT **Language and languages**
NT **Criticism**
Debates and debating
Lectures and lecturing
Letter writing
Preaching
Punctuation
Satire

BT = Broader Term   NT = Narrower Term   RT = Related Term   SA = See Also   UF = Used For

Rhetoric—*Continued*
- RT English language—Composition and exercises
  - Literary style

Rheumatism 616.7
- BT Diseases
- NT Gout

Rhyme 808.1
- SA names of languages with the subdivision *Rhyme,* to be added as needed
- BT Poetics
  - Versification
- NT English language—Rhyme
  - Stories in rhyme

Rhymes
- USE Limericks
  - Nonsense verses
  - Nursery rhymes
  - Poetry—Collections

Rhythm 808.1
- BT Aesthetics
  - Poetics
- NT Musical meter and rhythm
  - Versification
- RT Cycles

Ribonucleic acid
- USE **RNA**

Ribose nucleic acid
- USE **RNA**

Ribozymes
- USE **Catalytic RNA**

Riches
- USE **Wealth**

Riddles 398.6; 793.735; 808.88; 818, etc.

Use for collections of riddles considered as folklore, as games, or as literary exercises, by one or several authors, and for materials about riddles.
- UF Conundrums
  - Enigmas
  - Rebuses
- BT Amusements
  - Literary recreations
- NT Charades
- RT Puzzles

Ride sharing
- USE **Car pools**

Riding
- USE **Horsemanship**

Rifles 683.4
- UF Carbines
  - Guns
- BT Firearms

Right and left
- USE **Left and right (Direction)**
  - **Right and left (Political science)**

Right- and left-handedness
- USE **Left- and right-handedness**

Right and left (Political science) 320.5

Use for general materials on political views or attitudes, i.e. conservative, traditional, liberal, radical, etc. Materials on the physical characteristics of favoring one hand or the other are entered under **Left- and right-handedness.** Materials on left and right as indications of location or direction are entered under **Left and right (Direction).**
- UF Left and right
  - Left (Political science)
  - Right and left
  - Right (Political science)
- BT Political parties
  - Political science
- NT Radicalism
- RT Conservatism
  - Liberalism

Right of assembly
- USE **Freedom of assembly**

Right of association
- USE **Freedom of association**

Right of asylum
- USE **Asylum**

Right of privacy 323.44
- UF Invasion of privacy
  - Privacy, Right of *[Former heading]*
- BT Civil rights
- NT Eavesdropping
  - Trade secrets
  - Wiretapping
- RT Computer crimes
  - Libel and slander

Right (Political science)
- USE **Conservatism**
  - **Right and left (Political science)**

Right to a fair trial
- USE **Fair trial**

Right to bear arms
- USE **Gun control**

BT = Broader Term   NT = Narrower Term   RT = Related Term   SA = See Also   UF = Used For

Right to choose movement
    USE   **Pro-choice movement**
Right to die   179.7
    BT   **Death**
          Medical ethics
          Medicine—Law and legislation
    RT   **Euthanasia**
          Living wills
          Suicide
Right to know
    USE   **Freedom of information**
Right-to-life movement (Anti-abortion
    movement)
    USE   **Pro-life movement**
Right to work
    USE   **Discrimination in employment**
          Open and closed shop
Rights, Civil
    USE   **Civil rights**
Rights, Human
    USE   **Human rights**
Rights of animals
    USE   **Animal rights**
Rights of man
    USE   **Human rights**
Rights of women
    USE   **Women's rights**
Riot control   303.6
    UF   Riots—Control *[Former head-
          ing]*
    BT   **Crowds**
          Riots
Riots (May subdiv. geog.)   **303.6**
    UF   Civil disorders
          Mobs
    SA   names of institutions with the
          subdivision *Riots;* and names
          of specific riots, to be added
          as needed
    BT   **Crime**
          Freedom of assembly
          Offenses against public safety
    NT   **Riot control**
    RT   **Crowds**
          Demonstrations
Riots—Control
    USE   **Riot control**
Ripoffs
    USE   **Fraud**

Rites and ceremonies (May subdiv. geog.)
    390
    UF   Ceremonies
          Ecclesiastical rites and ceremo-
          nies
          Religious ceremonies
          Ritual
          Traditions
    SA   classes of persons and ethnic
          groups with the subdivision
          Rites and ceremonies, e.g. **In-
          dians of North America—
          Rites and ceremonies;** etc.;
          and names of individual reli-
          gions and denominations with
          the subdivisions *Liturgy* and
          Customs and practices, e.g.
          **Catholic Church—Liturgy;
          Judaism—Customs and
          practices;** etc., to be added
          as needed
    NT   **Catholic Church—Liturgy**
          Funeral rites and ceremonies
          **Indians of North America—
          Rites and ceremonies**
          **Judaism—Customs and prac-
          tices**
          Liturgies
          Lord's Supper
          Marriage customs and rites
          Ordination
          Religious holidays
          Sacraments
          Secret societies
    RT   **Manners and customs**
Ritual
    USE   **Liturgies**
          Rites and ceremonies
River animals
    USE   **Stream animals**
River pollution
    USE   **Water pollution**
Rivers   551.48
    SA   names of rivers, to be added as
          needed
    BT   **Physical geography**
          Water
          Waterways
    NT   **Dams**
          Stream animals

BT = Broader Term   NT = Narrower Term   RT = Related Term   SA = See Also   UF = Used For

Rivers—*Continued*
      Water power
  RT   Floods
      Hydraulic engineering
      Inland navigation
RNA   572.8
  UF   Ribonucleic acid *[Former heading]*
      Ribose nucleic acid
  BT   **Nucleic acids**
  NT   **Catalytic RNA**
RNA, Catalytic
  USE   **Catalytic RNA**
Road construction
  USE   **Roads**
Road engineering
  USE   **Highway engineering**
Road maps   912
  UF   Maps, Road
      Roads—Maps
  SA   names of countries, areas, states, cities, etc., with the subdivision *Maps,* to be added as needed
  BT   **Maps**
  RT   **Automobile travel—Guidebooks**
Road signs
  USE   **Signs and signboards**
Roads   388.1; 625.7
  UF   Construction of roads
      Highway construction
      Highways
      Road construction
      Thoroughfares
  BT   **Civil engineering**
      Transportation
  NT   **Alaska Highway (Alaska and Canada)**
      Express highways
      Roadside improvement
      Street cleaning
  RT   **Highway engineering**
      Pavements
      Soil mechanics
      Streets
Roads—Maps
  USE   **Road maps**
Roadside improvement   713
  UF   Highway beautification
  BT   **Grounds maintenance**

      Landscape architecture
      Roads
Robbers and outlaws
  USE   **Thieves**
Robins   598.8
  BT   **Birds**
Robinsonades   808.83; 813, etc.
    May be used for individual works, collections, or materials about fictional works describing a character's survival without the aid of civilization, as on a desert island.
  UF   Apocalyptic fantasies
      End-of-the-world fantasies
  BT   **Adventure fiction**
      Imaginary voyages
Robotics
  USE   **Robots**
Robots   629.8
    Use for general materials on robots and robotics. Materials limited to robots in industry are entered under **Industrial robots.**
  UF   Automata
      Automatons
      Robotics *[Former heading]*
  BT   **Machinery**
      Mechanical movements
  NT   **Industrial robots**
Robots, Industrial
  USE   **Industrial robots**
Rochdale system
  USE   **Cooperation**
Rock and roll music
  USE   **Rock music**
Rock climbing
  USE   **Mountaineering**
Rock crystal
  USE   **Quartz**
Rock drawings, paintings, and engravings   759.01
  UF   Petroglyphs
      Rock engravings
      Rock paintings
  BT   **Archeology**
      Art
      Mural painting and decoration
      Picture writing
      Prehistoric art
  RT   **Cave drawings**
Rock engravings
  USE   **Rock drawings, paintings, and engravings**

BT = Broader Term   NT = Narrower Term   RT = Related Term   SA = See Also   UF = Used For

Rock gardens 635.9
BT Gardens
Rock music 781.66; 782.42166
UF Rock and roll music
BT Music
Popular music
Rock paintings
USE **Rock drawings, paintings, and engravings**
Rock tombs
USE **Tombs**
Rocket airplanes
USE **Rocket planes**
Rocket flight
USE **Space flight**
Rocket planes 629.133
UF Airplanes, Rocket propelled
Rocket airplanes
SA names of rocket planes, e.g.
X-15 (Rocket aircraft); to be added as needed
BT **High speed aeronautics**
Space vehicles
NT **X-15 (Rocket aircraft)**
Rocketry 621.43
BT **Aeronautics**
Astronautics
NT **Guided missiles**
Rockets (Aeronautics)
Space vehicles
Rockets (Aeronautics) 629.133
UF Aerial rockets
SA types of rockets and missiles and names of specific rockets and missiles, to be added as needed
BT **Aeronautics**
High speed aeronautics
Projectiles
Rocketry
NT **Artificial satellites—Launching**
Ballistic missiles
Guided missiles
RT **Interplanetary voyages**
Jet propulsion
Rocks 552
Use for general materials on naturally occurring solid minerals. Materials on stone as a building material are entered under **Stone**.
UF Crystalline rocks
Metamorphic rocks

SA varieties of rock, e.g. **Granite;** to be added as needed
NT **Granite**
Marble
RT **Geology**
Petrology
Stone
Rocks, Moon
USE **Lunar petrology**
Rocky Mountains 978
BT **Mountains**
Rodeos 791.8
BT **Sports**
RT **Cowhands**
Horsemanship
Roentgen rays
USE **X-rays**
Roentgenologists
USE **Radiologists**
Role conflict 302.5
Use for materials on the conflict within one person who is being called upon to fulfill two or more competing roles.
BT **Social conflict**
Social role
Role playing 302
BT **Social role**
Role, Social
USE **Social role**
Roller skating 796.2
UF Figure skating
Skating
BT **Outdoor recreation**
NT **In-line skating**
Rollerblading
USE **In-line skating**
Romaic language
USE **Modern Greek language**
Romaic literature
USE **Modern Greek literature**
Roman antiquities
USE **Classical antiquities**
Rome—Antiquities
Rome (Italy)—Antiquities
Roman architecture 722
UF Architecture, Roman [*Former heading*]
BT **Ancient architecture**
Architecture
Roman art 709.37
UF Art, Roman [*Former heading*]

BT = Broader Term   NT = Narrower Term   RT = Related Term   SA = See Also   UF = Used For

Roman art—*Continued*
　　Classical art
　BT　**Ancient art**
　　　Art
　　　Classical antiquities
Roman Catholic Church
　USE　**Catholic Church**
Roman civilization
　USE　**Rome—Civilization**
Roman emperors
　USE　**Emperors—Rome**
Roman Empire
　USE　**Rome**
Roman literature
　USE　**Latin literature**
Roman mythology
　USE　**Classical mythology**
Roman numerals　513
　BT　**Numerals**
Roman philosophy
　USE　**Ancient philosophy**
Romance languages　440
　UF　Neo-Latin languages
　SA　names of languages belonging to
　　　the Romance group, e.g.
　　　French language; to be add-
　　　ed as needed
　BT　**Language and languages**
　NT　**French language**
　　　Spanish language
　RT　**Latin language**
Romance literature　840
　SA　names of literatures belonging to
　　　the Romance group, e.g.
　　　French literature; to be add-
　　　ed as needed
　BT　**Literature**
　NT　**French literature**
　　　Portuguese literature
　　　Spanish literature
Romance novels
　USE　**Love stories**
Romances　808.8; 821, etc.; 823, etc.
　　May be used for individual works, collec-
　tions, or materials about medieval tales deal-
　ing with the age of chivalry or the supernatu-
　ral. They may be either in verse or in prose
　and may or may not have a basis in fact.
　Contemporary romance novels are entered un-
　der **Love stories** or **Romantic suspense nov-
　els.**
　UF　Chivalry—Romances

　　Metrical romances
　　Stories
　SA　names of historic persons with
　　　the subdivision *Romances,* to
　　　be added as needed
　BT　**Fiction**
　　　Literature
　NT　**Arthurian romances**
　RT　**Chivalry**
　　　Epic poetry
　　　Fables
　　　Legends
Romances (Love stories)
　USE　**Love stories**
Romanesque architecture　723
　UF　Architecture, Romanesque *[For-
　　　mer heading]*
　BT　**Architecture**
　　　Medieval architecture
Romanesque art　709.02
　UF　Art, Romanesque *[Former head-
　　　ing]*
　BT　**Medieval art**
　NT　**Romanesque painting**
Romanesque painting　759.02
　UF　Painting, Romanesque *[Former
　　　heading]*
　BT　**Romanesque art**
Romanies
　USE　**Gypsies**
Romans à clef　808.83; 813, etc.
　　May be used for individual works, collec-
　tions, or materials about novels in which fic-
　tional characters and events can be readily
　identified with real persons and events.
　UF　Livres à clef
　BT　**Fiction**
Romantic fiction
　USE　**Love stories**
Romantic stories
　USE　**Love stories**
Romantic suspense novels　813, etc.
　　May be used for individual works, collec-
　tions, or materials about modern romantic sus-
　pense novels. Medieval tales are entered under
　Romances.
　UF　Suspense novels
　BT　**Adventure fiction**
　RT　**Gothic novels**
　　　Love stories
　　　Mystery fiction
　　　Spy stories

BT = Broader Term　　NT = Narrower Term　　RT = Related Term　　SA = See Also　　UF = Used For

Romanticism 141; 709.03; 809
  BT   Aesthetics
  RT   Literature
       Music
       Realism in literature

Rome 937

Use for materials about the city of Rome in antiquity or about the Roman Empire. Materials on the modern city of Rome are entered under **Rome (Italy)**. Materials on the ruins and remains of ancient Rome, the city and its environs, are entered under **Rome (Italy)— Antiquities.** Materials on Roman antiquities in several countries are entered under **Rome— Antiquities.** Materials on Roman antiquities limited to one modern country are entered under the country with the subdivision *Antiquities.*

  UF   Roman Empire

Rome—Antiquities 937

Use for materials on Roman antiquities in several countries. Materials on Roman antiquities limited to one place are entered under the place with the subdivision *Antiquities.* Materials on the ruins and remains of ancient Rome, the city and its environs, are entered under **Rome (Italy)—Antiquities.**

  UF   Roman antiquities
  BT   **Classical antiquities**

Rome—Biography 920.037
  UF   Classical biography
  BT   **Biography**

Rome—Civilization 937

Use for materials on the civilization of ancient Rome. Materials on both ancient Greek and Roman civilizations are entered under **Classical civilization.**

  UF   Latin civilization
       Roman civilization
  BT   **Classical civilization**

Rome—Description 913.7; 937

Use for descriptive materials on the Roman Empire including accounts by travelers of ancient times.

  UF   Rome—Description and geography *[Former heading]*

Rome—Description and geography
  USE **Rome—Description**
          Rome—Geography

Rome—Geography 913.7

Use for geographic materials on ancient Rome.

  UF   Classical geography
       Rome—Description and geography *[Former heading]*
  BT   **Ancient geography**
       Historical geography

Rome—History 937
Rome (Italy) 945

Use for materials on the modern city of Rome. Materials about the city of Rome in antiquity or about the Roman Empire are entered under **Rome.**

Rome (Italy)—Antiquities 937

Use for materials on the ruins and remains of ancient Rome, the city and its environs. Materials on Roman antiquities in several countries are entered under **Rome—Antiquities.** Materials on Roman antiquities limited to one place are entered under the place with the subdivision *Antiquities.*

  UF   Roman antiquities
  BT   **Classical antiquities**

Rome (Italy)—Description 914.5
Rome (Italy)—History 945
Roofs 690; 695; 721
  BT   **Architecture—Details**
       Building
       Buildings

Rooming houses
  USE **Hotels and motels**

Rooms 643; 645
  SA   types of rooms, to be added as needed
  BT   **Buildings**
       Houses
  NT   **Garden rooms**
       Kitchens
  RT   **Interior design**

Root crops 633; 635
  BT   **Vegetables**
  RT   **Feeds**

Rope 623.88; 677
  NT   **Cables**
       Knots and splices
  RT   **Hemp**

Roses 583; 635.9
  BT   **Flowers**

Rosetta stone inscription 493
  BT   **Hieroglyphics**

Rosin
  USE **Gums and resins**

Rotating memory devices (Data processing)
  USE **Computer storage devices**

Rotation of crops
  USE **Crop rotation**

Roughage
  USE **Food—Fiber content**

Round stage
  USE **Arena theater**

BT = Broader Term   NT = Narrower Term   RT = Related Term   SA = See Also   UF = Used For

Routes of trade
USE   **Trade routes**
Rowing   797.1
   UF   Regattas
         Sculling
   BT   **Athletics**
         Boats and boating
         Exercise
         Sports
         Water sports
Royal houses
USE   **Kings and rulers**
         Monarchy
Royalty
USE   **Kings and rulers**
         Monarchy
         Princes
         Princesses
         Queens
Rubber   678
   UF   India rubber
   BT   **Forest products**
Rubber, Artificial
USE   **Synthetic rubber**
Rubber sheet geometry
USE   **Topology**
Rubber, Synthetic
USE   **Synthetic rubber**
Rubber tires
USE   **Tires**
Rugs   645; 677; 746.7

     Use for materials on one-piece floor coverings, such as woven fabrics, animal skins, etc. Materials on heavy woven or felted fabrics used as floor coverings, usually covering large areas, are entered under **Carpets.**

   BT   **Decorative arts**
         Interior design
   NT   **Hooked rugs**
         Oriental rugs
   RT   **Carpets**
Rugs, Hooked
USE   **Hooked rugs**
Rugs, Oriental
USE   **Oriental rugs**
Ruins
USE   **Antiquities**
         Excavations (Archeology)
         Extinct cities
Rule of equal time (Broadcasting)
USE   **Equal time rule (Broadcasting)**

Rulers
USE   **Emperors**
         Heads of state
         Kings and rulers
         Queens
Rules of order
USE   **Parliamentary practice**
Runaway adults   173; 306.88
   UF   Adults, Runaway
         Desertion
         Husbands, Runaway
         Wives, Runaway
   BT   **Desertion and nonsupport**
         Homeless persons
         Missing persons
Runaway children   362.74
   BT   **Children**
         Homeless persons
         Missing children
Runaway teenagers   362.74
   BT   **Homeless persons**
         Missing persons
         Teenagers
Running   796.42
   BT   **Track athletics**
   NT   **Jogging**
         Marathon running
         Orienteering
   RT   **Racing**
Rural architecture
USE   **Domestic architecture**
         Farm buildings
Rural churches   254
   UF   Church work, Rural
         Churches, Country
         Churches, Rural
         Country churches
   BT   **Church work**
Rural comedies
USE   **Pastoral drama**
         Pastoral fiction
Rural conditions
USE   names of countries, states, etc., with the subdivision *Rural conditions,* e.g. **United States—Rural conditions; Ohio—Rural conditions;** etc., to be added as needed
Rural credit
USE   **Agricultural credit**

BT = Broader Term   NT = Narrower Term   RT = Related Term   SA = See Also   UF = Used For

Rural electrification
    USE   **Electric power distribution**
           Electricity in agriculture
Rural high schools
    USE   **Rural schools**
Rural life
    USE   **Country life**
           Farm life
           Outdoor life
Rural poetry
    USE   **Pastoral poetry**
Rural schools   371
    UF   Country schools
          District schools
          High schools, Rural
          Rural high schools
    BT   **Public schools**
          Schools
Rural sociology   307.72
    Use for materials on the discipline of rural sociology and the theory of social organization in rural areas. Materials on the rural conditions of particular regions, countries, cities, etc., are entered under the place with the subdivision *Rural conditions.* Descriptive, popular, and literary materials on living in the country are entered under **Country life.**
    UF   Sociology, Rural *[Former heading]*
    SA   names of countries, states, etc., with the subdivision *Rural conditions,* to be added as needed
    BT   **Sociology**
    NT   **Ohio—Rural conditions**
          United States—Rural conditions
          Urbanization
    RT   **Country life**
          Farm family
          Farm life
          Peasantry
Rural-urban migration
    USE   **Internal migration**
Russia   947
    Use for materials on Russia (including the Russian Empire) prior to 1917. Materials on the Union of Soviet Socialist Republics from its inception in 1917 until its dissolution in December 1991 are entered under **Soviet Union.** Materials on the independent republic of Russia since its establishment in December 1991 are entered under **Russia (Federation).**
    UF   Russian Empire

    NT   **Russians**
    RT   **Russia (Federation)**
          Soviet Union
Russia (Federation)   947.086
    Use for materials on the independent republic, established in December 1991. Materials on Russia and the Russian Empire before 1917 are entered under **Russia.** Materials on the Union of Soviet Socialist Republics between 1917 and 1991 are entered under **Soviet Union.**
    UF   Russia (Republic) *[Former heading]*
    NT   **Russians**
    RT   **Commonwealth of Independent States**
          Russia
          Soviet Union
Russia—History   947
    Use for materials on the history of Russia and the Russian empire before 1917.
Russia—History—1905, Revolution   947.08
    UF   Soviet Union—History—1905, Revolution *[Former heading]*
Russia (Republic)
    USE   **Russia (Federation)**
Russian Church
    USE   **Russian Orthodox Church**
Russian communism
    USE   **Communism—Soviet Union**
Russian Empire
    USE   **Russia**
Russian intervention in Czechoslovakia
    USE   **Czechoslovakia—History—1968-1989**
Russian language   491.7
    May be subdivided like **English language.**
    BT   **Language and languages**
Russian literature   891.7
    Use for materials on literature in the Russian language. Materials on several of the literatures of the Soviet Union are entered under **Soviet literature.** May use same subdivisions and names of literary forms as for **English literature.**
    BT   **Literature**
    RT   **Soviet literature**
Russian Orthodox Church   281.9
    UF   Orthodox Eastern Church, Russian *[Former heading]*
          Russian Church
    BT   **Christian sects**
          Eastern churches

BT = Broader Term   NT = Narrower Term   RT = Related Term   SA = See Also   UF = Used For

Russian revolution
    USE   **Soviet Union—History—1917-**
           1921, Revolution
Russian satellite countries
    USE   **Communist countries**
Russians (May subdiv. geog.)   **920; 947**

    Use for materials on the dominant Slavic-speaking ethnic group of Russia. Materials on the citizens of the Soviet Union between 1917 and 1991, not limited to a single national or linguistic group, are entered under **Soviets (People)**.

    BT   **Russia**
           Russia (Federation)
           Soviet Union
Russo-Finnish War, 1939-1940
           948.9703
    UF   Finno-Russian War, 1939-1940
           Soviet Union—History—1939-
           1940, War with Finland
    BT   **Europe—History—1918-1945**
Russo-Turkish War, 1853-1856
    USE   **Crimean War, 1853-1856**
Rust
    USE   **Corrosion and anticorrosives**
Rustless coatings
    USE   **Corrosion and anticorrosives**
RVs
    USE   **Recreational vehicles**
S.A.T.
    USE   **Scholastic Aptitude Test**
S.S.T.'s
    USE   **Supersonic transport planes**
Sabbath   **263; 296.4**
    UF   Lord's Day
    BT   **Judaism**
Sabin vaccine
    USE   **Poliomyelitis vaccine**
Sabotage   **331.89; 364.16**
    UF   Political violence
    BT   **Offenses against public safety**
           Strikes
           Subversive activities
           Terrorism
Sacrament of Reconciliation
    USE   **Penance**
Sacraments   **234; 265**
    BT   **Church**
           Grace (Theology)
           Rites and ceremonies
    NT   **Anointing of the sick**
           Baptism

           Confirmation
           Lord's Supper
           Marriage
           Ordination
           Penance
Sacred art
    USE   **Christian art and symbolism**
           Religious art and symbolism
Sacred books   **291.8**
    UF   Books, Sacred
    SA   names of sacred books, to be
           added as needed
    BT   **Religious literature**
    NT   **Bible**
           Koran
           Vedas
Sacred music
    USE   **Church music**
Sacred numbers
    USE   **Numerology**
           Symbolism of numbers
Sacrifice   **291.3**
    UF   Burnt offering
    BT   **Worship**
    NT   **Atonement—Christianity**
Safe sex
    USE   **Safe sex in AIDS prevention**
Safe sex in AIDS prevention   **613.9;**
           616.97
    UF   Safe sex
    BT   **AIDS (Disease)—Prevention**
           Sexual hygiene
Safety appliances
    USE   **Safety devices**
Safety devices   **363.19; 620.8**
    UF   Safety appliances *[Former heading]*
           Safety equipment
    SA   subjects with the subdivision
           Safety devices, e.g. **Rail-**
           roads—Safety devices; to be
           added as needed
    NT   **Railroads—Safety devices**
    RT   **Accidents—Prevention**
Safety education   **363.1; 371.7**
    BT   **Accidents—Prevention**
Safety equipment
    USE   **Safety devices**
Safety, Industrial
    USE   **Occupational health and safety**

BT = Broader Term   NT = Narrower Term   RT = Related Term   SA = See Also   UF = Used For

Safety measures
USE   **Accidents—Prevention**
    and subjects with the subdivision *Safety measures*, e.g. **Aeronautics—Safety measures;** to be added as needed
Sagas   398.22; 839
  BT   **Folklore**
        Literature
        Old Norse literature
        Scandinavian literature
Sailboarding
  USE   **Windsùrfing**
Sailing   623.88; 797.1
  BT   **Ships**
        Water sports
  NT   **Windsurfing**
  RT   **Boats and boating**
        Navigation
        Yachts and yachting
Sailors   387.5092; 623.88092; 920
  UF   Mariners
        Naval personnel
        Navigators
        Sailors' life
        Sea life
        Seamen
  SA   names of navies, e.g. **United States. Navy;** to be added as needed
  BT   **Military personnel**
        Naval art and science
        Navies
  NT   **Merchant marine**
        Ship pilots
        United States. Navy
        United States. Navy—Officers
  RT   **Seafaring life**
Sailors' handbooks
  USE   **United States. Navy—Handbooks, manuals, etc.**
Sailors' life
  USE   **Sailors**
        Seafaring life
Sailors' song
  USE   **Sea songs**
Sailplanes (Aeronautics)
  USE   **Gliders (Aeronautics)**

Saint Bartholomew's Day, Massacre of, 1572   944
  UF   St. Bartholomew's Day, Massacre of, 1572
  BT   **France—History—1328-1589, House of Valois**
        Huguenots
        Massacres
Saint Francis, Order of
  USE   **Franciscans**
Saint Valentine's Day
  USE   **Valentine's Day**
Saints   200.092; 920
  SA   saints of particular religions, e.g. **Christian saints;** and names of individual saints, to be added as needed
  BT   **Heroes and heroines**
  NT   **Christian saints**
        Mary, Blessed Virgin, Saint
  RT   **Hermits**
        Legends
        Martyrs
        Pilgrims and pilgrimages
        Prophets
        Shrines
Salads   641.8
  BT   **Cooking**
  RT   **Cooking—Vegetables**
Salamanders   597.6
  BT   **Amphibians**
Salaries
  USE   **Wages**
Sale of infants
  USE   **Adoption—Corrupt practices**
Sales, Auction
  USE   **Auctions**
Sales management   658.8
  UF   Management, Sales
  BT   **Management**
        Marketing
        Selling
Sales personnel   381.092; 658.85
  UF   Agents, Sales
        Clerks (Retail trade)
        Salesmen
        Saleswomen
        Traveling sales personnel
  BT   **Retail trade**
  NT   **Booksellers and bookselling**

BT = Broader Term   NT = Narrower Term   RT = Related Term   SA = See Also   UF = Used For

Sales personnel—*Continued*
        Peddlers and peddling
Sales tax   336.2
    UF   Purchase tax
          Retail sales tax
          Taxation of sales
    BT   **Taxation**
Salesmanship
    USE **Selling**
Salesmen
    USE **Sales personnel**
Saleswomen
    USE **Sales personnel**
Saline water
    USE **Sea water**
Salk vaccine
    USE **Poliomyelitis vaccine**
Salmon   597.5
    BT   **Fishes**
Saloons
    USE **Bars**
Salt free diet
    USE **Salt-free diet**
Salt-free diet   613.2
    UF   Low sodium diet
          Salt free diet *[Former heading]*
    BT   **Cooking for the sick**
          Diet
          Diet in disease
Salt water
    USE **Sea water**
Salt water aquariums
    USE **Marine aquariums**
Salutations
    USE **Etiquette**
          Letter writing
Salvage   627; 628.4
    Use for materials on the recovery of equipment, parts, cargo, merchandise, structures, or waste.
    UF   Salvage (Waste, etc.) *[Former heading]*
          Utilization of waste
          Waste reclamation
    NT   **Marine salvage**
          Recycling
          Waste products as fuel
    RT   **Refuse and refuse disposal**
Salvage, Marine
    USE **Marine salvage**

Salvage (Waste, etc.)
    USE **Salvage**
Salvation   234; 291.2
    UF   Redemption
    BT   **Doctrinal theology**
    NT   **Atonement—Christianity**
          Conversion
          Faith
          Grace (Theology)
          Regeneration (Christianity)
          Sanctification
Salvation Army   287.9
    BT   **Christian missions**
          Christian sects
Samplers   746.3
    BT   **Embroidery**
          Needlework
Sampling (Statistics)   519.5
    UF   Random sampling
    BT   **Probabilities**
          Statistics
    NT   **Quality control**
Sanatoriums
    USE **Health resorts**
          Hospitals
Sanctification   234; 291.2
    BT   **Salvation**
Sanctions (International law)   341.5
    UF   Economic sanctions
    BT   **Economic policy**
          International economic relations
          International law
Sanctuaries, Wildlife
    USE **Wildlife refuges**
Sanctuary (Law)
    USE **Asylum**
Sanctuary movement   261.8
    Use for materials on any network of religious congregations or churches that shelter refugees or illegal aliens.
    UF   Sanctuary movement (Refugee aid) *[Former heading]*
    BT   **Asylum**
          Church and social problems
          Social movements
    RT   **Illegal aliens**
          Refugees
Sanctuary movement (Refugee aid)
    USE **Sanctuary movement**

Sand dunes   551.3
UF   Dunes
BT   Seashore
Sandwiches   641.8
BT   Cooking
Sanitary affairs
USE   **Sanitary engineering**
      Sanitation
Sanitary engineering   628
UF   Environmental health engineering
      Sanitary affairs
BT   **Engineering**
NT   **Drainage**
      Pollution
      Refuse and refuse disposal
      Sewerage
      Soil microbiology
      Street cleaning
      Water supply
RT   **Municipal engineering**
      Sanitation
Sanitary landfills
USE   **Landfills**
Sanitation   363.72; 648
UF   Sanitary affairs
NT   **Cemeteries**
      Cleaning
      Cleanliness
      Cremation
      Disinfection and disinfectants
      Household sanitation
      Military health
      Pollution
      Refuse and refuse disposal
      School hygiene
      Smoke prevention
      Ventilation
      Water purification
      Water supply
      World War, 1939-1945—Health
        aspects
RT   **Hygiene**
      Public health
      Sanitary engineering
Sanitation, Household
USE   **Household sanitation**
Santa Claus   394.2663
BT   **Christmas**
Saracenic architecture
USE   **Islamic architecture**

Saracenic art
USE   **Islamic art**
Sasquatch   001.9
UF   Big foot
      Bigfoot
BT   **Monsters**
      Mythical animals
SAT
USE   **Scholastic Aptitude Test**
Satan
USE   **Devil**
Satellite communication systems
USE   **Artificial satellites in telecom-**
        munication
Satellites   523.9
UF   Moons
      Natural satellites
      Planetary satellites
      Planets—Satellites
SA   names of planets with the subdi-
      vision *Satellites,* e.g. **Mars**
      (Planet)—Satellites; to be
      added as needed
BT   **Solar system**
NT   **Mars (Planet)—Satellites**
Satellites, Artificial
USE   **Artificial satellites**
Satellites—Mars
USE   **Mars (Planet)—Satellites**
Satire   808.7; 808.87
UF   Comic literature
SA   satire of particular countries, e.g.
      American satire; to be added
      as needed
BT   **Literature**
      Rhetoric
      Wit and humor
NT   **American satire**
      English satire
      Invective
      Parody
Satire, American
USE   **American satire**
Satire, English
USE   **English satire**
Satisfaction in work
USE   **Job satisfaction**
Saturn (Planet)   523.46
BT   **Planets**

BT = Broader Term   NT = Narrower Term   RT = Related Term   SA = See Also   UF = Used For

Saucers, Flying
USE   Unidentified flying objects
Sauces   641.8
  BT   **Cooking**
Saving and thrift   332.024
  UF   Economy
         Thrift
  BT   **Economics**
         Insurance
         Personal finance
         Success
  NT   **Old age pensions**
         Savings and loan associations
  RT   **Cost and standard of living**
         Investments
Savings and loan associations   332.3
  UF   Building and loan associations
         Cooperative building associations
         Loan associations
  BT   **Banks and banking**
         Cooperation
         Cooperative societies
         Investments
         Loans
         Personal loans
         Saving and thrift
  RT   **Cooperative banks**
Savings banks
  USE   **Banks and banking**
Saws   621.9
  BT   **Carpentry tools**
         Tools
Saxons
  USE   **Anglo-Saxons**
Sayings
  USE   **Epigrams**
         Proverbs
         Quotations
Scandinavian languages   439
  UF   Norse languages
  BT   **Language and languages**
  NT   **Danish language**
         Icelandic language
         Norwegian language
         Old Norse language
         Swedish language
Scandinavian literature   839
  UF   Norse literature
  BT   **Literature**
  NT   **Danish literature**

         Eddas
         Icelandic literature
         Norwegian literature
         Sagas
         Swedish literature
  RT   **Old Norse literature**
Scandinavians   920; 948
    Use for materials on the people of Scandinavia since the tenth century. Materials on earlier Scandinavians are entered under **Vikings.**
  NT   **Vikings**
Scarecrows   632
  BT   **Plant conservation**
Scenarios
  USE   **Motion picture plays**
         Plots (Drama, fiction, etc.)
         Radio plays
         Television plays
Scene painting   751.7
  BT   **Painting**
         Theaters—Stage setting and scenery
Scenery
  USE   **Landscape protection**
         Natural monuments
         Views
         Wilderness areas
Scenery (Stage)
  USE   **Theaters—Stage setting and scenery**
Scepticism
  USE   **Skepticism**
Scholarship
  USE   **Learning and scholarship**
Scholarship funds
  USE   **Scholarships**
Scholarships   371.2; 378.3
  UF   Bursaries
         Fellowships
         Funds, Scholarship
         Scholarship funds
         Scholarships, fellowships, etc.
         [Former heading]
  SA   fields of study, ethnic groups, and classes of persons with the subdivision *Scholarships,,* to be added as needed
  BT   **Education**
         Endowments
         Student aid

BT = Broader Term   NT = Narrower Term   RT = Related Term   SA = See Also   UF = Used For

Scholarships, fellowships, etc.
    USE   **Scholarships**
Scholastic achievement
    USE   **Academic achievement**
Scholastic Aptitude Test   378.1
    UF   S.A.T.
           SAT
           Scholastic aptitude test *[Former*
               heading]
    BT   **Colleges and universities—En-**
            trance examinations
            Examinations
Scholastic aptitude test
    USE   **Scholastic Aptitude Test**
School administration and organization
    USE   **Schools—Administration**
School age fathers
    USE   **Teenage fathers**
School age mothers
    USE   **Teenage mothers**
School and community
    USE   **Community and school**
School and home
    USE   **Home and school**
School architecture
    USE   **School buildings**
School assembly programs   371.8
    UF   Assembly programs, School
           School entertainments
           Schools—Exercises and recre-
              ations
           Schools—Opening exercises
    BT   **Student activities**
    NT   **Commencements**
           Recitations
    RT   **Drama in education**
School athletics
    USE   **School sports**
School attendance   371.2
    UF   Absence from school
           Absenteeism (School)
           Attendance, School
           Compulsory school attendance
           School enrollment
           Truancy (Schools)
    BT   **Schools—Administration**
    RT   **Compulsory education**
           Dropouts
School boards   353.8
    UF   Boards of education

    BT   **Schools—Administration**
School books
    USE   **Textbooks**
School buildings   371.6; 727
    UF   Buildings, School
           School architecture
           School houses
           Schoolhouses
    BT   **Buildings**
           Schools
School buildings as recreation centers
    USE   **Community centers**
School busing
    USE   **Busing (School integration)**
           School children—Transporta-
            tion
School children   155.42; 305.234
    BT   **Children**
           Students
School children—Food   371.7
    UF   Food for school children
           Meals for school children
           School lunches
    BT   **Children—Nutrition**
           Diet
           Food
School children—Medical examinations
    USE   **Children—Medical examina-**
            tions
School children—Transportation   371.8
    UF   School busing
    BT   **Transportation**
    NT   **Busing (School integration)**
School choice   379.1
       Use for materials on choosing a school and
on the right of parents to choose their children's school.
    UF   Choice of school
           Parents' choice of school
           Schools—Selection
    BT   **Education**
    NT   **College choice**
School clubs
    USE   **Students—Societies**
School counseling   371.4
       Use for materials on the assistance given to
students by schools, colleges, or universities
in understanding and coping with adjustment
problems. Materials on the assistance given to
students in the selection of a program of
studies are entered under **Educational coun-**
seling.
    UF   Guidance counseling, School

BT = Broader Term   NT = Narrower Term   RT = Related Term   SA = See Also   UF = Used For

School counseling—*Continued*
- BT Counseling
- RT Educational counseling
  School psychologists

School desegregation
- USE School integration

School discipline 371.5
- UF Discipline of children
  Punishment in schools
- BT Schools—Administration
  Teaching
- NT Classroom management
  Student government

School drama
- USE College and school drama

School dropouts
- USE Dropouts

School enrollment
- USE School attendance

School entertainments
- USE School assembly programs

School excursions
- USE Field trips

School fiction
- USE School stories

School finance
- USE Education—Finance

School furniture
- USE Schools—Equipment and supplies

School grade retention
- USE Promotion (School)

School houses
- USE School buildings

School hygiene 371.7
- UF Hygiene, School
- BT Children—Health and hygiene
  Health education
  Hygiene
  Public health
  Sanitation
- RT School nurses

School inspection
- USE School supervision
  Schools—Administration

School integration (May subdiv. geog.)
371.2
- UF Desegregated schools
  Desegregation in education
  Education—Integration
  Integrated schools
  Integration in education
  Racial balance in schools
  School desegregation
- BT Race relations
- NT Busing (School integration)
  Magnet schools
- RT Segregation in education

School journalism
- USE College and school journalism

School libraries 027.8
- UF Libraries, School
- BT Instructional materials centers
  Libraries
- NT Children's libraries
  Elementary school libraries
  High school libraries
  Libraries and students
- RT Libraries and schools

School libraries (Elementary school)
- USE Elementary school libraries

School libraries (High school)
- USE High school libraries

School life
- USE Students

School lunches
- USE School children—Food

School management and organization
- USE Schools—Administration

School media centers
- USE Instructional materials centers

School music
- USE Music—Study and teaching
  School songbooks
  Singing

School newspapers
- USE College and school journalism

School nurses 371.7
- BT Nurses
- RT Health education
  School hygiene

School organization
- USE Schools—Administration

School playgrounds
- USE Playgrounds

School plays
- USE Children's plays
  College and school drama—
  Collections

BT = Broader Term   NT = Narrower Term   RT = Related Term   SA = See Also   UF = Used For

School prayer
USE **Religion in the public schools**
School principals
USE **School superintendents and principals**
School promotion
USE **Promotion (School)**
School prose
USE **Children's writings**
School psychologists   371.7
BT **Psychologists**
RT **School counseling**
School readiness
USE **Readiness for school**
School reports   371.2
UF Educational reports
Reports, Teachers'
Teachers' reports
BT **Report writing**
RT **Grading and marking (Education)**
School science projects
USE **Science projects**
School shops   373.2
UF Industrial arts shops
BT **Technical education**
School songbooks   782.42
UF School music
Songbooks, School
BT **Songbooks**
Songs
NT **Children's songs**
School sports   371.8
UF Interscholastic sports
School athletics
BT **Sports**
Student activities
RT **College sports**
School stories   808.83; 813, etc.
May be used for individual works, collections, or materials about school stories.
UF School fiction
Schools—Fiction
BT **Fiction**
School superintendents and principals
371.2
UF School principals
Superintendents of schools
BT **Schools—Administration**
RT **School supervision**

School supervision   371.2
Use for materials on the supervision of instruction. Materials on the management and organization of schools and on the administrative duties of educators are entered under Schools—Administration.
UF Inspection of schools
Instructional supervision
School inspection
Supervision of schools
BT **Schools—Administration**
Teaching
RT **School superintendents and principals**
School surveys
USE **Educational surveys**
School taxes
USE **Education—Finance**
School teaching
USE **Teaching**
School trips
USE **Field trips**
School vandalism
USE **School violence**
School verse
USE **Children's writings**
School violence   371.7
UF School vandalism
Student violence
Violence in schools
BT **Juvenile delinquency**
Violence
School yearbooks   371.8
UF Annuals
College yearbooks
High school yearbooks
Senior yearbooks
Student yearbooks
Students—Yearbooks
Yearbooks, Student
BT **Serial publications**
Schoolboy fathers
USE **Teenage fathers**
Schoolgirl mothers
USE **Teenage mothers**
Schoolhouses
USE **School buildings**
Schools (May subdiv. geog.)   371
SA types of schools, e.g. **Church schools; Rural schools;** etc.; subjects with the subdivision

---

BT = Broader Term   NT = Narrower Term   RT = Related Term   SA = See Also   UF = Used For

Schools—*Continued*

Study and teaching, e.g. **Science—Study and teaching;** and names of individual schools, to be added as needed

NT **Business schools**
  Church schools
  Colleges and universities
  Correspondence schools and courses
  Evening and continuation schools
  Experimental schools
  High schools
  Junior high schools
  Kindergarten
  Libraries and schools
  Magnet schools
  Museums and schools
  Nursery schools
  Private schools
  Public schools
  Religious summer schools
  Rural schools
  School buildings
  Summer schools
RT **Education**

Schools—Accreditation
USE **Accreditation (Education)**

Schools—Administration 371.2

Use for materials on the management and organization of schools and on the administrative duties of educators. Materials on the supervision of instruction are entered under **School supervision.**

UF Educational administration
  Inspection of schools
  School administration and organization
  School inspection
  School management and organization
  School organization
  Schools—Management and organization
NT **Articulation (Education)**
  School attendance
  School boards
  School discipline
  School superintendents and principals

  School supervision
  Schools—Centralization
  Schools—Decentralization
  Student government

Schools and libraries
USE **Libraries and schools**

Schools and museums
USE **Museums and schools**

Schools as social centers
USE **Community centers**

Schools, Business
USE **Business schools**

Schools—Centralization 379.1
UF Centralization of schools
  Consolidation of schools
BT **Schools—Administration**

Schools—Curricula
USE **Education—Curricula**

Schools—Decentralization 379.1
UF Decentralization of schools
BT **Schools—Administration**

Schools—Equipment and supplies 371.6
UF School furniture
BT **Furniture**

Schools—Exercises and recreations
USE **School assembly programs**

Schools—Fiction
USE **School stories**

Schools, Magnet
USE **Magnet schools**

Schools—Management and organization
USE **Schools—Administration**

Schools, Military
USE **Military education**

Schools, Nonformal
USE **Experimental schools**

Schools, Nongraded
USE **Nongraded schools**

Schools—Opening exercises
USE **School assembly programs**

Schools, Parochial
USE **Church schools**

Schools—Selection
USE **School choice**

Schools, Ungraded
USE **Nongraded schools**

Schools—United States 371.0973
UF United States—Schools

BT = Broader Term NT = Narrower Term RT = Related Term SA = See Also UF = Used For

Science (May subdiv. geog.)　500
　　UF　Discoveries in science
　　NT　**Astronomy**
　　　　Bible and science
　　　　Biology
　　　　Botany
　　　　Chaos (Science)
　　　　Chemistry
　　　　Computer science
　　　　Earth sciences
　　　　Forensic sciences
　　　　Fossils
　　　　Geology
　　　　Life sciences
　　　　Mathematics
　　　　Natural history
　　　　Petrology
　　　　Physical sciences
　　　　Physics
　　　　Physiology
　　　　Religion and science
　　　　Science and civilization
　　　　Science and state
　　　　Science and the humanities
　　　　Space sciences
　　　　System theory
　　　　Zoology
　　RT　**Scientific apparatus and in-**
　　　　　struments
　　　　Scientists
Science and civilization　306.4
　　UF　Civilization and science
　　　　Science and society
　　BT　**Civilization**
　　　　Progress
　　　　Science
Science and religion
　　USE　**Religion and science**
Science and society
　　USE　**Science and civilization**
Science and space
　　USE　**Space sciences**
Science and state　353.7; 500
　　UF　Science—Government policy
　　　　　[Former heading]
　　　　Science policy
　　　　State and science
　　BT　**Science**
　　　　State, The

Science and the Bible
　　USE　**Bible and science**
Science and the humanities　001.3
　　UF　Humanities and science
　　BT　**Humanities**
　　　　Science
Science exhibition projects
　　USE　**Science projects**
Science—Exhibitions　507.4
　　UF　Science fairs
　　BT　**Exhibitions**
　　NT　**Science projects**
Science experiments
　　USE　**Science—Experiments**
Science—Experiments　507
　　UF　Experiments, Scientific
　　　　Science experiments
　　　　Scientific experiments
　　SA　branches of science with the
　　　　　subdivision *Experiments*, e.g.
　　　　　Chemistry—Experiments; to
　　　　　be added as needed
　　RT　**Science projects**
Science fair projects
　　USE　**Science projects**
Science fairs
　　USE　**Science—Exhibitions**
Science fiction　808.83; 813, etc.
　　　May be used for individual works, collec-
　　　tions, or materials about fiction based on
　　　imagined developments in science and tech-
　　　nology.
　　UF　Apocalyptic fantasies
　　　　End-of-the-world fantasies
　　　　Space flight (Fiction)
　　　　Time travel (Fiction)
　　BT　**Adventure fiction**
　　　　Fiction
　　NT　**Dystopias**
　　　　Imaginary voyages
　　　　Utopian fiction
　　RT　**Fantasy fiction**
　　　　Interplanetary voyages
Science fiction comic books, strips, etc.
　　　741.5
　　　May be used for individual works, collec-
　　　tions, or materials about science fiction com-
　　　ics.
　　BT　**Comic books, strips, etc.**
Science fiction films　791.43
　　　May be used for individual works, collec-
　　　tions, or materials about science fiction films.

BT = Broader Term　　NT = Narrower Term　　RT = Related Term　　SA = See Also　　UF = Used For

Science fiction films—*Continued*

SA   types of science fiction films,
       e.g. **Star Wars films;** to be
       added as needed
BT   **Motion pictures**
NT   **Star Wars films**
RT   **Fantasy films**
Science fiction films—Catalogs
       016.79143
Science fiction plays   808.82; 812, etc.
    May be used for individual works, collec-
    tions, or materials about science fiction plays.
UF   Time travel (Fiction)
BT   **Drama**
Science fiction poetry   808.81; 811, etc.
    May be used for individual works, collec-
    tions, or materials about science fiction poet-
    ry.
BT   **Poetry**
Science fiction radio programs   791.44
    May be used for individual works, collec-
    tions, or materials about science fiction radio
    programs.
UF   Time travel (Fiction)
BT   **Radio programs**
Science fiction television programs
       791.45
    May be used for individual works, collec-
    tions, or materials about science fiction televi-
    sion programs.
UF   Time travel (Fiction)
BT   **Television programs**
RT   **Fantasy television programs**
Science—Government policy
USE   **Science and state**
Science journalism
USE   **Scientific journalism**
Science—Methodology   501
UF   Scientific method
NT   **Logic**
Science policy
USE   **Science and state**
Science projects   507.8
UF   Projects, Science
       School science projects
       Science exhibition projects
       Science fair projects
BT   **Science—Exhibitions**
RT   **Science—Experiments**
Science—Religious aspects
USE   **Religion and science**
Science—Societies   506
UF   Scientific societies

BT   **Societies**
Science—Study and teaching   507
UF   Scientific education
NT   **Nature study**
Science—Study and teaching—Audiovisu-
    al aids   507.8
Science—Study and teaching—Evaluation
    507.6
Science—United States   509.73
UF   American science
       United States—Science
Scientific apparatus and instruments
       502.8
UF   Apparatus, Scientific
       Instruments, Scientific
       Scientific instruments
SA   types of instruments, e.g. **Aero-
       nautical instruments;** and
       names of specific instruments,
       to be added as needed
NT   **Aeronautical instruments**
       Astronomical instruments
       Chemical apparatus
       **Electric apparatus and appli-
       ances**
       **Electronic apparatus and ap-
       pliances**
       Engineering instruments
       Meteorological instruments
       Optical instruments
RT   **Science**
Scientific creationism
USE   **Creationism**
Scientific education
USE   **Science—Study and teaching**
Scientific errors
USE   **Errors**
Scientific expeditions   508
UF   Expeditions, Scientific
       Polar expeditions
SA   names of regions explored with
       the subdivision *Exploration*
       for materials on scientific ex-
       peditions to regions that are
       unsettled or sparsely settled
       and largely unknown to the
       world at large, e.g. **Antarcti-
       ca—Exploration;** names of
       countries, states, etc., with the

BT = Broader Term   NT = Narrower Term   RT = Related Term   SA = See Also   UF = Used For

Scientific expeditions—*Continued*
　　　　　subdivision *Exploring expedi-*
　　　　　tions for materials on explora-
　　　　　tions sponsored by those gov-
　　　　　ernments; and names of expe-
　　　　　ditions, to be added as needed
　BT　Voyages and travels
　NT　Antarctica—Exploration
　　　　Arctic regions—Exploration
　RT　Exploration
Scientific experiments
　USE　Science—Experiments
Scientific instruments
　USE　Scientific apparatus and in-
　　　　struments
Scientific journalism　　070.4
　UF　Journalism, Scientific *[Former*
　　　　heading]
　　　　Science journalism
　BT　Journalism
Scientific management
　USE　Management
Scientific method
　USE　Science—Methodology
Scientific recreations　　793.8
　UF　Recreations, Scientific
　BT　Amusements
　NT　Mathematical recreations
Scientific societies
　USE　Science—Societies
Scientific writing
　USE　Technical writing
Scientists　　509.2; 920
　SA　types of scientists and names of
　　　　individual scientists, to be
　　　　added as needed
　NT　Astronomers
　　　　Biologists
　　　　Chemists
　　　　Geologists
　　　　Mathematicians
　　　　Naturalists
　　　　Physicists
　RT　Science
Scottish clans
　USE　Clans—Scotland
Scottish personal names　　929.4
　UF　Personal names, Scottish *[For-*
　　　　mer heading]
　BT　Personal names

Scottish tartans
　USE　Tartans
Scouts and scouting　　369.4
　BT　Clubs
　　　　Community life
　NT　Boy Scouts
　　　　Girl Scouts
Screen plays
　USE　Motion picture plays
Screen printing
　USE　Silk screen printing
Screening for drug abuse
　USE　Drug testing
Screenplays
　USE　Motion picture plays
　　　　Television scripts
Scriptures, Holy
　USE　Bible
Scuba diving　　797.2
　　　Use for materials on free diving with the
　　aid of a self-contained underwater breathing
　　apparatus. Materials on free diving with mask,
　　fins, and snorkel are entered under **Skin div-**
　　ing.
　UF　Free diving
　BT　Deep diving
Sculling
　USE　Rowing
Sculptors　　730.92; 920
　SA　sculptors of particular countries,
　　　　e.g. **American sculptors;** to
　　　　be added as needed
　BT　Artists
　NT　American sculptors
Sculptors, American
　USE　American sculptors
Sculpture　　730
　UF　Statues
　SA　sculpture of particular countries,
　　　　e.g. **Greek sculpture;** and
　　　　specific types of sculpture, to
　　　　be added as needed
　BT　Art
　　　　Decoration and ornament
　NT　American sculpture
　　　　Brasses
　　　　Bronzes
　　　　Greek sculpture
　　　　Kinetic sculpture
　　　　Masks (Sculpture)
　　　　Mobiles (Sculpture)

BT = Broader Term　　NT = Narrower Term　　RT = Related Term　　SA = See Also　　UF = Used For

Sculpture—*Continued*

        Modeling

        Modern sculpture

        Monuments

        Plaster casts

        Soap sculpture

    RT   Carving (Decorative arts)

Sculpture, American

    USE   American sculpture

Sculpture, Greek

    USE   Greek sculpture

Sculpture in motion

    USE   Kinetic sculpture

Sculpture, Kinetic

    USE   Kinetic sculpture

Sculpture, Modern

    USE   Modern sculpture

Sculpture, Modern—20th century

    USE   Modern sculpture—1900-1999

            (20th century)

Sculpture—Technique   731.4

    RT   Modeling

SDI (Ballistic missile defense system)

    USE   Strategic Defense Initiative

Sea

    USE   Ocean

Sea animals

    USE   Marine animals

Sea bed

    USE   Ocean bottom

Sea farming

    USE   Aquaculture

Sea fisheries

    USE   Fisheries

Sea food

    USE   Seafood

Sea in art

    USE   Marine painting

Sea laboratories

    USE   Undersea research stations

Sea laws

    USE   Maritime law

Sea life

    USE   Marine biology

        Navies

        Sailors

        Seafaring life

Sea lions

    USE   Seals (Animals)

Sea mosses

    USE   Algae

Sea poetry   808.81; 811, etc.; 811.008, etc.

    May be used for individual works, collections, or materials about poetry about the sea.

    BT   Poetry

    NT   Sea songs

Sea pollution

    USE   Marine pollution

Sea power   359

    UF   Dominion of the sea

        Military power

        Naval power

        Navy

    SA   names of countries with the subhead *Navy* or the subdivision *Naval history,* e.g. **United States. Navy; United States—Naval history;** etc., to be added as needed

    BT   Naval art and science

    NT   Naval battles

        United States. Navy

        Warships

    RT   Naval history

        Navies

Sea resources

    USE   Marine resources

Sea routes

    USE   Trade routes

Sea shells

    USE   Shells

Sea-shore

    USE   Seashore

Sea songs   782.42

    UF   Chanties

        Sailors' song

    BT   Sea poetry

        Songs

Sea stories   808.83; 813, etc.

    May be used for individual works, collections, or materials about sea stories.

    BT   Adventure and adventurers

        Adventure fiction

        Fiction

Sea transportation

    USE   Shipping

Sea travel

    USE   Ocean travel

BT = Broader Term   NT = Narrower Term   RT = Related Term   SA = See Also   UF = Used For

Sea water   551.46
UF   Saline water
     Salt water
BT   **Water**
Sea water aquariums
USE   **Marine aquariums**
Sea water conversion   628.1
UF   Conversion of saline water
     Demineralization of salt water
     Desalination of water
     Desalting of water
BT   **Water purification**
Sea waves
USE   **Ocean waves**
Seafaring life   910.4
UF   Sailors' life
     Sea life
SA   names of countries with the sub-
     head *Navy*, e.g. **United
     States. Navy;** to be added as
     needed
BT   **Adventure and adventurers
     Manners and customs
     Voyages and travels**
RT   **Sailors**
Seafood   641.3
UF   Sea food
SA   names of marine fish, shellfish,
     etc., used as food, to be add-
     ed as needed
BT   **Food
     Marine resources**
RT   **Fish as food**
Sealab project   551.46
UF   Navy Sealab project
     Project Sealab
     United States. Navy—Sealab
     project
BT   **Undersea research stations**
Seals (Animals)   599.79
UF   Fur seals
     Sea lions
BT   **Mammals
     Marine mammals**
Seals (Numismatics)   737; 929.8
UF   Emblems
     Signets
BT   **Heraldry
     History
     Inscriptions**

Numismatics
RT   **National emblems**
Seamanship
USE   **Navigation**
Seamen
USE   **Sailors**
Search and rescue operations
USE   **Rescue work**
Seascapes
USE   **Marine painting**
Seashore (May subdiv. geog.)   551.45
UF   Sea-shore
BT   **Landforms**
NT   **Beaches
     Sand dunes**
RT   **Coasts
     Ocean**
Seasons   508.2; 525
SA   names of the seasons, to be add-
     ed as needed
BT   **Astronomy
     Climate
     Meteorology**
NT   **Autumn**
Seaweeds
USE   **Algae**
Secession
USE   **State rights
     United States—History—1861-
     1865, Civil War—Causes**
Second Advent   236
UF   Jesus Christ—Second Advent
     Second coming of Christ
BT   **Eschatology
     Jesus Christ**
RT   **Millennium**
Second coming of Christ
USE   **Second Advent**
Second economy
USE   **Underground economy**
Second hand trade
USE   **Secondhand trade**
Second job
USE   **Supplementary employment**
Secondary education   373
   Use for materials on those levels of educa-
   tion higher than elementary and lower than
   college or university.
UF   Education, Secondary *[Former
        heading]*
     High school education

BT = Broader Term   NT = Narrower Term   RT = Related Term   SA = See Also   UF = Used For

Secondary education—*Continued*
    Secondary schools
  BT   **Education**
  NT   **Adult education**
      Evening and continuation schools
  RT   **High schools**
      Junior high schools
Secondary employment
  USE **Supplementary employment**
Secondary school libraries
  USE **High school libraries**
Secondary schools
  USE **High schools**
      Junior high schools
      Secondary education
Secondhand trade   381
  UF   Second hand trade
      Used merchandise
  SA   types of secondhand trade, e.g.
      Garage sales; to be added as needed
  BT   **Selling**
  NT   **Garage sales**
Secret service (May subdiv. geog.)
    363.28
  Use for materials on governmental service of a secret nature.
  SA   names of wars with the subdivision *Secret service,* to be added as needed
  BT   **Police**
  NT   **Espionage**
      World War, 1939-1945—Secret service
  RT   **Detectives**
      Intelligence service
      Spies
Secret service—United States   363.28
  UF   United States—Secret service
Secret societies   366; 371.8
  SA   names of secret societies, e.g.
      Freemasons; to be added as needed
  BT   **Rites and ceremonies**
      Societies
  NT   **Freemasons**
      Ku Klux Klan
  RT   **Fraternities and sororities**
Secret writing
  USE **Cryptography**

Secretarial practice
  USE **Office practice**
Secretaries   651.3
  BT   **Business education**
      Office management
Secrets, Trade
  USE **Trade secrets**
Sectionalism
  USE **Regionalism**
Sectionalism (U.S.)
  USE **Regionalism—United States**
Sectionalism (United States)
  USE **Regionalism—United States**
Sects   280; 291.9
  Use for materials on independent religious groups whose teachings or practices fall within the normative bounds of the major world religions. Materials on the major world religions are entered under **Religions.** Materials on groups or movements whose beliefs or practices differ significantly from the traditional religions, often focused upon a charismatic leader, are entered under **Cults.**
  UF   Church denominations
      Denominations, Religious
      Religious denominations
  SA   names of churches and sects within the major world religions, e.g. **Presbyterian Church; Hasidim;** etc., to be added as needed
  BT   **Church history**
      Religions
  NT   **Christian sects**
  RT   **Cults**
Sects, Christian
  USE **Christian sects**
Secular humanism
  USE **Secularism**
Secularism   171; 211
  Use for materials on any intellectual or philosophical movement or set of beliefs that promotes human values as separate and distinct from religious doctrines.
  UF   Humanism—1900-1999 (20th century) *[Former heading]*
      Humanism, Secular
      Secular humanism
  BT   **Ethics**
      Theology
      Utilitarianism
  NT   **Atheism**
      Rationalism

BT = Broader Term   **NT** = Narrower Term   **RT** = Related Term   **SA** = See Also   **UF** = Used For

Secularism—*Continued*
RT   Humanism
Securities   332.63
   UF   Capitalization (Finance)
        Dividends
   SA   types of securities, to be added
        as needed
   BT   **Finance**
        Investments
        Stock exchange
   NT   **Bonds**
        Insider trading
        Mortgages
        Stocks
Securities exchange
   USE   **Stock exchange**
Securities trading, Insider
   USE   **Insider trading**
Security, Internal
   USE   **Internal security**
Security, International
   USE   **International security**
Security, Job
   USE   **Job security**
Security measures
   USE   subjects with the subdivision *Se-*
        curity measures, e.g. **Nuclear**
        power plants—Security mea-
        sures; to be added as needed
Security, Social
   USE   **Social security**
Sedition
   USE   **Political crimes and offenses**
        Revolutions
Seeds   581.4
   BT   **Plant propagation**
        Plants
   NT   **Nuts**
Seeds—Germination
   USE   **Germination**
Seeing eye dogs
   USE   **Guide dogs**
Segregation   305.8
   UF   Desegregation
   SA   segregation in particular areas,
        e.g. **Segregation in educa-**
        tion; and racial and ethnic
        groups and classes of persons
        with the subdivision *Segrega-*

tion, e.g. **African Ameri-**
cans—Segregation; to be
added as needed
   BT   **Race relations**
   NT   **African Americans—Segrega-**
        tion
        Apartheid
        Blacks—Segregation
        Segregation in education
   RT   **Discrimination**
        Minorities
Segregation in education   379.2
   UF   Education, Segregation in
        Integration in education
        Racial balance in schools
   BT   **Segregation**
   RT   **Discrimination in education**
        School integration
Segregation in housing
   USE   **Discrimination in housing**
Segregation in public accommodations
   USE   **Discrimination in public ac-**
        commodations
Seismic sea waves
   USE   **Tsunamis**
Seismography
   USE   **Earthquakes**
Seismology
   USE   **Earthquakes**
Selection, Artificial
   USE   **Breeding**
Selection, Natural
   USE   **Natural selection**
Selective service
   USE   **Draft**
Self   126; 155.2
   BT   **Consciousness**
        Individuality
        Personality
   NT   **Human body**
        Identity (Psychology)
Self-acceptance   155.2
   UF   Self-love (Psychology)
   BT   **Psychology**
   RT   **Self-confidence**
        Self-esteem
        Self-perception
Self-actualization
   USE   **Self-realization**

BT = Broader Term   NT = Narrower Term   RT = Related Term   SA = See Also   UF = Used For

Self-assurance
    USE   **Self-confidence**
               Self-reliance
Self-awareness
    USE   **Self-perception**
Self-care, Health
    USE   **Health self-care**
Self-care, Medical
    USE   **Health self-care**
Self-concept
    USE   **Self-perception**
Self-confidence   155.2
    UF   Self-assurance
    BT   **Emotions**
    RT   **Assertiveness (Psychology)**
               Self-acceptance
               Self-consciousness
               Self-esteem
               Self-reliance
Self-consciousness   155.2
    UF   Embarrassment
    BT   **Psychology**
    RT   **Self-confidence**
               Self-esteem
               Self-perception
Self-control   153.8
    UF   Control of self
               Discipline, Self
               Self-discipline
               Self-mastery
               Will power
               Willpower
    BT   **Psychology**
Self-culture
    USE   **Self-improvement**
               Self-instruction
Self-defense   613.6; 796.8
    UF   Fighting
    NT   **Boxing**
               Judo
               Karate
               Self-defense for women
    RT   **Martial arts**
Self-defense for women   613.6; 796.8
    UF   Fighting
               Women—Self-defense
               Women's self-defense
    BT   **Self-defense**
    RT   **Martial arts**

Self-defense in animals
    USE   **Animal defenses**
Self-development
    USE   **Self-improvement**
               Self-instruction
Self-discipline
    USE   **Self-control**
Self-education
    USE   **Self-instruction**
Self-employed   331.12
    UF   Freelancers
    BT   **Business people**
    NT   **Entrepreneurs**
               Home business
               Professions
Self-employed women   331.4
    UF   Women, Self-employed
    BT   **Women—Employment**
Self-esteem   155.2
    UF   Self-love (Psychology)
               Self-respect *[Former heading]*
    BT   **Psychology**
    RT   **Self-acceptance**
               Self-confidence
               Self-consciousness
               Self-perception
Self-evaluation in education
    USE   **Educational evaluation**
Self-examination, Medical
    USE   **Health self-care**
Self-expectations, Perfectionist
    USE   **Perfectionism (Personality trait)**
Self-fulfillment
    USE   **Self-realization**
Self-government
    USE   **Democracy**
               Representative government and representation
Self-government (in education)
    USE   **Student government**
Self health care
    USE   **Health self-care**
Self-help medical care
    USE   **Health self-care**
Self image
    USE   **Personal appearance**
Self-improvement   158
    UF   Personal development
               Personal growth

BT = Broader Term   NT = Narrower Term   RT = Related Term   SA = See Also   UF = Used For

Self-improvement—*Continued*
    Self-culture *[Former heading]*
    Self-development
  BT **Life skills**
  RT **Self-instruction**
Self-instruction **371.39**
  UF Home education
    Home study courses
    Self-culture *[Former heading]*
    Self-development
    Self-education
    Teach yourself courses
  SA subjects with the subdivision
    Programmed instruction, e.g.
    **English language—Pro-
    grammed instruction;** to be
    added as needed
  BT **Education**
    Study skills
  RT **Correspondence schools and
    courses**
    Self-improvement
Self-love (Psychology)
  USE **Self-acceptance**
    Self-esteem
Self-mastery
  USE **Self-control**
Self-medication
  USE **Health self-care**
Self-perception **155.2**
  UF Self-awareness
    Self-concept
  BT **Psychology**
  NT **Body image**
  RT **Self-acceptance**
    Self-consciousness
    Self-esteem
Self-protection in animals
  USE **Animal defenses**
Self-realization **155.2; 158**
  UF Fulfillment, Self
    Self-actualization
    Self-fulfillment
  BT **Psychology**
  RT **Success**
Self-reliance **179**
  UF Self-assurance
  RT **Self-confidence**
    Survival skills

Self-respect
  USE **Self-esteem**
Self-starvation
  USE **Anorexia nervosa**
Selling **380.1; 658.8**
  UF Salesmanship
  BT **Business**
    Retail trade
  NT **Auctions**
    Booksellers and bookselling
    Direct selling
    Mail-order business
    Sales management
    Secondhand trade
  RT **Advertising**
    Marketing
Selling of infants
  USE **Adoption—Corrupt practices**
Semantics **121; 302.2; 401**
  BT **Language and languages**
    Linguistics
  NT **Semiotics**
Semiconductors **621.3815**
  BT **Electric conductors**
    Electronics
  NT **Microelectronics**
    Transistors
Semiotics **302.2; 401**
    Use for materials on the relationship be-
    tween signs and symbols and whatever it is
    they stand for.
  BT **Semantics**
  NT **Visual literacy**
  RT **Signs and symbols**
Semitic peoples **305.892**
  BT **Ethnology**
Senate (U.S.)
  USE **United States. Congress. Senate**
Senescence
  USE **Aging**
Senior citizens
  USE **Elderly**
Senior yearbooks
  USE **School yearbooks**
Sense of direction
  USE **Direction sense**
Senses and sensation **152.1; 612.8**
  BT **Intellect**
    Physiology
    Psychology
    Psychophysiology

BT = Broader Term   NT = Narrower Term   RT = Related Term   SA = See Also   UF = Used For

Senses and sensation—*Continued*
    Theory of knowledge
NT   Color sense
    Gestalt psychology
    Hearing
    Pain
    Perception
    Pleasure
    Smell
    Taste
    Touch
    Vision
Sensing, Remote
  USE   Remote sensing
Sensitivity training
  USE   Group relations training
Separate development (Race relations)
  USE   Apartheid
Separation anxiety in children   155.4
  BT   Anxiety
    Child psychology
Separation (Law)
  USE   Divorce
Separation of church and state
  USE   Church and state
Separation of powers (May subdiv. geog.)
    320.4; 342
  UF   Division of powers
    Powers, Separation of
  BT   Constitutional law
    Executive power
    Political science
Separation of powers—United States
    320.473
  UF   United States—Separation of
    powers
Separatism, Black
  USE   Black nationalism
Separatist movement in Québec (Province)
  USE   Québec (Province)—History—
    Autonomy and independence
    movements
Sepulchers
  USE   Tombs
Sepulchral brasses
  USE   Brasses
Sequences (Mathematics)   510
  UF   Mathematical sequences
    Numerical sequences
  BT   Algebra

    Mathematics
Serial publications   050
    Use for general materials on publications in any medium issued in successive parts bearing numerical or chronological designations and intended to be continued indefinitely.
  BT   Bibliography
    Publishers and publishing
  NT   Almanacs
    Newspapers
    Periodicals
    School yearbooks
  RT   International Standard Serial
    Numbers
Serigraphy
  USE   Silk screen printing
Sermon on the mount   226.9
  UF   Jesus Christ—Sermon on the
    mount
Sermons   252; 291.4
  BT   Christian literature
  RT   Preaching
Serpents
  USE   Snakes
Servants
  USE   Household employees
Service books (Liturgy)
  USE   Liturgies
Service, Customer
  USE   Customer service
Service dogs
  USE   Animals and the handicapped
Service (in industry)
  USE   Customer service
Service industries   338.4
  UF   Industries, Service
  SA   types of service industries, to be
    added as needed
  BT   Industries
  NT   Food service
    Hotels and motels
    Lease and rental services
    Undertakers and undertaking
Service stations   629.28
  UF   Automobile service stations
    Automobiles—Service stations
    [Former heading]
    Filling stations
    Gas stations
  BT   Automobile industry
    Petroleum industry

BT = Broader Term   NT = Narrower Term   RT = Related Term   SA = See Also   UF = Used For

Servicemen
USE   Military personnel
Services, Customer
USE   Customer service
Servicewomen
USE   Military personnel
Servitude
USE   Peonage
        Slavery
Servomechanisms   629.8
UF   Automatic control
BT   Automation
        Feedback control systems
Set theory   511.3
UF   Aggregates
        Classes (Mathematics)
        Ensembles (Mathematics)
        Mathematical sets
        Sets (Mathematics)
BT   Mathematics
NT   Arithmetic
        Boolean algebra
        Fractals
        Number theory
        Topology
RT   Symbolic logic
Sets, Fractal
USE   Fractals
Sets (Mathematics)
USE   Set theory
Sets of fractional dimension
USE   Fractals
Settlement of land
USE   Land settlement
Settlements, Social
USE   Social settlements
Seven Years' War, 1756-1763   940.2
BT   Europe—History—1492-1789
NT   United States—History—1755-
        1763, French and Indian
        War
Seventeen-year locusts
USE   Cicadas
Seventeenth century   909
    Use for general materials covering progress
    and development during this period in one or
    in several countries.
UF   1600-1699 (17th century)
BT   Modern history
Seville (Spain). World's Fair, 1992
USE   Expo 92 (Seville, Spain)

Sewage disposal   628.3
BT   Public health
        Refuse and refuse disposal
RT   Water pollution
Sewerage   628
UF   Sewers
BT   House drainage
        Municipal engineering
        Plumbing
        Sanitary engineering
RT   Drainage
Sewers
USE   Sewerage
Sewing   646.2
BT   Home economics
NT   Embroidery
RT   Dressmaking
        Needlework
Sex
USE   Sexual behavior
Sex bias
USE   Sexism
Sex (Biology)   571.8; 612.6
    Use for materials on the physiological traits
    that distinguish the males and females of a
    species. Materials on sexuality and sexual be-
    havior are entered under Sexual behavior.
BT   Biology
NT   Reproductive system
        Sexual disorders
RT   Reproduction
        Sexual behavior
Sex change
USE   Transsexuality
Sex crimes   364.15
UF   Crimes, Sex
        Sexual abuse
        Sexual crimes
SA   types of sex crimes, to be added
        as needed
BT   Crime
        Sexual behavior
NT   Child sexual abuse
        Incest
        Rape
Sex customs
USE   Sexual behavior
Sex differences (Psychology)   155.3
BT   Psychology
NT   Androgyny
        Sex role

BT = Broader Term   NT = Narrower Term   RT = Related Term   SA = See Also   UF = Used For

Sex differences (Psychology)—*Continued*
RT Sex discrimination
Sexual behavior
Sex discrimination 305.3

Use for materials on the restriction or denial of rights, privileges, or choice because of one's sex. Materials on prejudicial attitudes toward people because of their sex are entered under **Sexism.**

UF Discrimination, Sex
BT **Discrimination**
Sexism
NT **Equal rights amendments**
Women's rights
RT **Sex differences (Psychology)**
Sex disorders
USE **Sexual disorders**
Sex education 372.3; 613.9071; 649
UF Human life education
Sex instruction
BT **Family life education**
RT **Sexual hygiene**
Sex in art
USE **Erotic art**
Sex in business
USE **Sex in the workplace**
Sex in the office
USE **Sex in the workplace**
Sex in the workplace 306.7; 658
UF Employee sex in the workplace
Office romance
Sex in business
Sex in the office
BT **Sexual behavior**
Work
RT **Sexual harassment**
Sex instruction
USE **Sex education**
Sex organs
USE **Reproductive system**
Sex (Psychology)
USE **Sexual behavior**
Sex role 305.3

Use for materials on the patterns of attitudes and behavior that are regarded as appropriate to one sex rather than the other.

UF Female role
Gender identity
Male role
Sexual identity
BT **Sex differences (Psychology)**
Sexual behavior

Social role
NT Androgyny
Transsexuality
RT Sexism
Sex therapy 616.6; 616.85
BT **Psychotherapy**
RT **Sexual disorders**
Sexism 305.3

Use for materials on prejudicial attitudes toward people because of their sex. Materials on the restriction or denial of rights, privileges, or choice because of one's sex are entered under **Sex discrimination.**

UF Sex bias
BT **Attitude (Psychology)**
Prejudices
NT **Sex discrimination**
RT **Sex role**
Sexual abstinence 176; 306.73

Use for materials on abstinence from sexual activity. Materials on the virtue that moderates and regulates the sexual appetite in human beings are entered under **Chastity.** Materials on the renunciation of marriage for religious reasons are entered under **Celibacy.**

UF Abstinence, Sexual
BT **Asceticism**
Sexual behavior
RT **Birth control**
Celibacy
Chastity
Sexual abuse
USE **Child sexual abuse**
Sex crimes
Sexual harassment
Sexual assault
USE **Rape**
Sexual behavior 155.3

Use for materials on sexuality or sexual behavior. Materials on the physiological traits that distinguish the males and females of a species are entered under **Sex (Biology).**

UF Behavior, Sexual
Sex
Sex customs
Sex (Psychology)
Sexuality
SA social groups and classes of persons with the subdivision *Sexual behavior,* e.g. **College students—Sexual behavior;** to be added as needed
BT **Human behavior**

BT = Broader Term   NT = Narrower Term   RT = Related Term   SA = See Also   UF = Used For

Sexual behavior—*Continued*
  NT   College students—Sexual be-
          havior
        Homosexuality
        Sex crimes
        Sex in the workplace
        Sex role
        Sexual abstinence
        Sexual behavior in animals
        Sexual deviation
        Sexual harassment
  RT   Sex (Biology)
        Sex differences (Psychology)
        Sexual disorders
        Sexual ethics
Sexual behavior in animals   591.56
  UF   Animal sexual behavior
        Animals—Sexual behavior
        Breeding behavior
        Mating behavior
        Reproductive behavior
  BT   Animal behavior
        Sexual behavior
  NT   Animal courtship
Sexual crimes
  USE   Sex crimes
Sexual deviation   306.7; 616.85
  UF   Deviation, Sexual
        Paraphilia
        Perversion, Sexual
        Sexual perversion
  BT   Sexual behavior
        Sexual disorders
Sexual disorders   616.6; 616.85
  UF   Sex disorders
  BT   Sex (Biology)
  NT   Sexual deviation
  RT   Sex therapy
        Sexual behavior
Sexual ethics   176
  UF   Ethics, Sexual
  BT   Social ethics
  NT   Adultery
        Chastity
        Free love
        Prostitution
        Sexual harassment
        Sexual hygiene
  RT   Birth control
        Human artificial insemination

        Sexual behavior
Sexual harassment   331.13; 344
  UF   Harassment, Sexual
        Sexual abuse
  BT   Sexual behavior
        Sexual ethics
  RT   Sex in the workplace
Sexual hygiene   613.9
  UF   Hygiene, Sexual
        Social hygiene
  BT   Hygiene
        Sexual ethics
  NT   Birth control
        Safe sex in AIDS prevention
  RT   AIDS (Disease)—Prevention
        Sex education
        Sexually transmitted diseases
Sexual identity
  USE   Sex role
Sexual perversion
  USE   Sexual deviation
Sexuality
  USE   Sexual behavior
Sexually abused children
  USE   Child sexual abuse
Sexually transmitted diseases   616.95
  UF   V.D.
        VD
        Venereal diseases [*Former head-
          ing*]
  SA   types of sexually transmitted dis-
          eases, to be added as needed
  BT   Communicable diseases
  NT   Syphilis
  RT   Sexual hygiene
Shade gardens
  USE   Gardening in the shade
Shades and shadows   741.2
  UF   Light and shade
        Shadows
  BT   Drawing
Shadow economy
  USE   Underground economy
Shadow pantomimes and plays   791.5
  BT   Amateur theater
        Pantomimes
        Puppets and puppet plays
        Shadow pictures
        Theater

BT = Broader Term   NT = Narrower Term   RT = Related Term   SA = See Also   UF = Used For

Shadow pictures   793
UF   Hand shadows
      Shadowplay
BT   Amusements
NT   Shadow pantomimes and plays

Shadowplay
USE   Shadow pictures

Shadows
USE   Shades and shadows

Shady gardens
USE   Gardening in the shade

Shaft sinking
USE   Boring

Shakers   289
BT   Christian sects

Shakespeare, William, 1564-1616   822.3
When applicable, the subdivisions provided with this heading may be used for other voluminous authors, e.g. **Dante; Goethe;** etc. These headings are to be used for materials about Shakespeare and about his writings. The texts of his plays, etc., are not given subject headings.

Shakespeare, William, 1564-1616—Adaptations   822.3
May be used for individual works, collections, or materials about literary, cinematic, video, or television adaptations of Shakespeare's works.
UF   Shakespeare, William, 1564-1616—Paraphrases

Shakespeare, William, 1564-1616—Allusions   822.3

Shakespeare, William, 1564-1616—Anniversaries   822.3

Shakespeare, William, 1564-1616—Authorship   822.3
UF   Bacon-Shakespeare controversy

Shakespeare, William, 1564-1616—Bibliography   016.8223

Shakespeare, William, 1564-1616—Biography   92; B
BT   Biography
NT   Shakespeare, William, 1564-1616—Psychology

Shakespeare, William, 1564-1616—Biography—Psychology
USE   Shakespeare, William, 1564-1616—Psychology

Shakespeare, William, 1564-1616—Characters   822.3

Shakespeare, William, 1564-1616—Comedies   822.3
Use for materials about the comedies, not for the texts of the plays.

Shakespeare, William, 1564-1616—Concordances   822.303
UF   Shakespeare, William, 1564-1616—Indexes

Shakespeare, William, 1564-1616—Contemporary England   822.3; 942.05
UF   Shakespeare's England

Shakespeare, William, 1564-1616—Criticism   822.3
Use for criticism of the works in general; criticism of the comedies is entered under **Shakespeare, William, 1564-1616—Comedies;** criticism of the tragedies under **Shakespeare, William, 1564-1616—Tragedies;** criticism of an individual play is entered under **Shakespeare, William, 1564-1616,** followed by the title of the play. Materials limited to criticism of the sonnets are entered under **Shakespeare, William, 1564-1616—Sonnets.**
UF   Shakespeare, William, 1564-1616—Criticism, interpretation, etc. *[Former heading]*
      Shakespeare, William, 1564-1616—Psychological studies

Shakespeare, William, 1564-1616—Criticism, interpretation, etc.
USE   **Shakespeare, William, 1564-1616—Criticism**

Shakespeare, William, 1564-1616—Dictionaries   822.303
BT   Encyclopedias and dictionaries

Shakespeare, William, 1564-1616—Discography   016.8223

Shakespeare, William, 1564-1616—Dramatic production   822.3
UF   Shakespeare, William, 1564-1616—Stage setting and scenery

Shakespeare, William, 1564-1616—Ethics   822.3
UF   Shakespeare, William, 1564-1616—Moral ideas
      Shakespeare, William, 1564-1616—Religion and ethics *[Former heading]*
BT   Ethics

BT = Broader Term   NT = Narrower Term   RT = Related Term   SA = See Also   UF = Used For

Shakespeare, William, 1564-1616—Filmography   016.8223

Shakespeare, William, 1564-1616—Histories   822.3

Use for materials about the histories, not for
the texts of the plays.

Shakespeare, William, 1564-1616—Indexes
USE   Shakespeare, William, 1564-
1616—Concordances

Shakespeare, William, 1564-1616—Influence   822.3

Use for materials on Shakespeare's influence on national literatures, literary movements, or specific persons.

Shakespeare, William, 1564-1616—
Knowledge   822.3

Use for materials on Shakespeare's knowledge or treatment of specific subjects. May be
subdivided by subject, e.g. Shakespeare, William, 1564-1616—Knowledge—Animals; etc.

Shakespeare, William, 1564-1616—Moral
ideas
USE   Shakespeare, William, 1564-
1616—Ethics

Shakespeare, William, 1564-1616—Paraphrases
USE   Shakespeare, William, 1564-
1616—Adaptations

Shakespeare, William, 1564-1616—Parodies, imitations, etc.   822.3
UF   Shakespeare, William, 1564-
1616—Parodies, travesties,
etc. [Former heading]

Shakespeare, William, 1564-1616—Parodies, travesties, etc.
USE   Shakespeare, William, 1564-
1616—Parodies, imitations,
etc.

Shakespeare, William, 1564-1616—Poetic
works   822.3

Use for materials about the poetic works,
not for the poetic texts themselves.

Shakespeare, William, 1564-1616—Portraits   822.3022

Shakespeare, William, 1564-1616—Psychological studies
USE   Shakespeare, William, 1564-
1616—Criticism
Shakespeare, William, 1564-
1616—Psychology

Shakespeare, William, 1564-1616—Psy-
chology   92; B
UF   Shakespeare, William, 1564-
1616—Biography—Psychology
[Former heading]
Shakespeare, William, 1564-
1616—Psychological studies
BT   Biography
Psychology
Shakespeare, William, 1564-
1616—Biography

Shakespeare, William, 1564-1616—Quotations   822.3

Shakespeare, William, 1564-1616—Reli-
gion   822.3
UF   Shakespeare, William, 1564-
1616—Religion and ethics
[Former heading]
BT   Religion

Shakespeare, William, 1564-1616—Religion
and ethics
USE   Shakespeare, William, 1564-
1616—Ethics
Shakespeare, William, 1564-
1616—Religion

Shakespeare, William, 1564-1616—Sonnets   822.3

Use for materials about the sonnets, not for
the texts of the sonnets.

Shakespeare, William, 1564-1616—Stage
history   792; 822.3
BT   Theater

Shakespeare, William, 1564-1616—Stage
setting and scenery
USE   Shakespeare, William, 1564-
1616—Dramatic production

Shakespeare, William, 1564-1616—Style
USE   Shakespeare, William, 1564-
1616—Technique

Shakespeare, William, 1564-1616—Technique   822.3
UF   Shakespeare, William, 1564-
1616—Style

Shakespeare, William, 1564-1616—Tragedies   822.3

Use for materials about the tragedies, not
for the texts of the plays.

Shakespeare's England
USE   Shakespeare, William, 1564-
1616—Contemporary Eng-
land

BT = Broader Term   NT = Narrower Term   RT = Related Term   SA = See Also   UF = Used For

Shape   516
 UF   Shapes
       Size and shape *[Former head-ing]*
 SA   types of geometric shapes, e.g.
       Square; to be added as need-ed
 BT   **Concepts**
       Geometry
       Perception
 NT   **Square**
Shapes
 USE   **Shape**
Sharecropping
 USE   **Farm tenancy**
Shared custody
 USE   **Child custody**
Shared housing   363.5
    Use for materials on two or more single, unrelated adults who live together.
 UF   Home sharing
       House sharing
       Nonfamily households
 BT   **Housing**
 NT   **Unmarried couples**
Shared parenting
 USE   **Part-time parenting**
Shared reading books
 USE   **Big books**
Shares of stock
 USE   **Stocks**
Sharing of jobs
 USE   **Job sharing**
Sheep   599.649; 636.3
 UF   Lambs
 BT   **Domestic animals**
       Mammals
Sheet metalwork   671.8
 UF   Press working of metal
 BT   **Metalwork**
 NT   **Plate metalwork**
Sheffield plate   739.2
 BT   **Plate**
Shellfish   594; 641.3
 BT   **Cooking**
       Food
       Invertebrates
 NT   **Crabs**
       Crustacea
       Lobsters
       Mollusks

Shells   591.47; 594.147
    Use for popular materials on seashells and shell collecting. Systematic and comprehensive materials on shells are entered under **Mollusks.**
 UF   Sea shells
 RT   **Mollusks**
Shells (Projectiles)
 USE   **Projectiles**
Shelterbelts
 USE   **Windbreaks**
Shelters, Air raid
 USE   **Air raid shelters**
Shelters, Animal
 USE   **Animal shelters**
Sherlock Holmes (Fictitious character)
 USE   **Holmes, Sherlock (Fictitious character)**
Sherlock Holmes films   791.43
    May be used for individual works, collec-tions, or materials about Sherlock Holmes films.
 BT   **Motion pictures**
       Mystery films
Shinto   299
 BT   **Religions**
 RT   **Ancestor worship**
Ship building
 USE   **Shipbuilding**
Ship models
 USE   **Ships—Models**
Ship pilots   623.89
 UF   Pilots
       Pilots and pilotage *[Former heading]*
 BT   **Sailors**
 RT   **Navigation**
Ship salvage
 USE   **Marine salvage**
Shipbuilding   623.8
 UF   Architecture, Naval
       Marine architecture
       Ship building
       Ships—Construction
 BT   **Industrial arts**
       Naval art and science
 NT   **Marine engines**
       Steamboats
 RT   **Boatbuilding**
       Naval architecture
       Ships

BT = Broader Term   NT = Narrower Term   RT = Related Term   SA = See Also   UF = Used For

Shipping (May subdiv. geog.)   387.5
UF   Marine transportation
    Ocean—Economic aspects
    Ocean transportation
    Sea transportation
    Water transportation
BT   **Transportation**
NT   **Harbors**
    Inland navigation
    Marine insurance
    Maritime law
    Territorial waters
RT   **Merchant marine**
Shipping—United States   387.00973
UF   United States—Shipping
Ships   387.2; 623.8
UF   Vessels (Ships)
SA   types of ships and vessels and
    names of individual ships, to
    be added as needed
BT   **Naval architecture**
    Ocean travel
NT   **Clipper ships**
    Hospital ships
    Lightships
    Merchant marine
    Sailing
    Steamboats
    Submarines
    Warships
    Yachts and yachting
RT   **Boats and boating**
    Shipbuilding
Ships—Construction
USE   **Shipbuilding**
Ships in art
USE   **Marine painting**
Ships—Models   623.8
UF   Model ships
    Ship models
BT   **Models and model making**
Shipwrecks   363.12; 910.4
UF   Marine disasters
    Wrecks
SA   names of wrecked ships, to be
    added as needed
BT   **Accidents**
    Adventure and adventurers
    Disasters
    Navigation

    Voyages and travels
NT   Survival after airplane acci-
    dents, shipwrecks, etc.
RT   Marine salvage
Shoe industry   338.4; 685
BT   **Clothing industry**
    Leather industry
    Shoes
Shoes   391.4; 646; 685
UF   Boots
    Footwear
BT   **Clothing and dress**
NT   **Shoe industry**
Shooting   799.3
    Use for materials on the use of firearms.
    Materials on shooting game are entered under
    Hunting.
UF   Gunning
NT   **Archery**
    Decoys (Hunting)
RT   **Firearms**
    Hunting
Shooting stars
USE   **Meteors**
Shop management
USE   **Factory management**
Shop practice
USE   **Machine shop practice**
Shop windows
USE   **Show windows**
Shoplifting   364.16
BT   **Stealing**
Shoppers' guides
USE   **Consumer education**
    Shopping
Shopping   381; 640.73
    Use for materials on buying by the consum-
    er. Materials on buying by government agen-
    cies and by commercial and industrial enter-
    prises are entered under **Buying.**
UF   Buyers' guides
    Marketing (Home economics)
    Purchasing
    Shoppers' guides
BT   **Home economics**
NT   **Grocery shopping**
RT   **Buying**
    Consumer education
    Consumers
Shopping centers and malls (May subdiv.
    geog.)   658.8
UF   Malls, Shopping

BT = Broader Term   NT = Narrower Term   RT = Related Term   SA = See Also   UF = Used For

Shopping centers and malls—*Continued*
    Shopping malls
  BT   Commercial buildings
       Retail trade
  RT   Stores
Shopping malls
  USE   Shopping centers and malls
Shops
  USE   Stores
Short films   791.43
    May be used for individual works, collections, or materials about short films.
  BT   Motion pictures
Short plays
  USE   One act plays
Short stories   808.83; 813, etc.
    Use for collections of short stories by one author or by several authors. Materials on the short story as a literary form and on the technique of writing short stories are entered under **Short story.**
  UF   Stories
  BT   Fiction
       Literature—Collections
Short stories—Indexes   016.80883
Short story   808.3
    Use for materials on the short story as a literary form and on the technique of writing short stories. Collections of stories are entered under **Short stories.**
  BT   Authorship
       Fiction
       Literature
  RT   Storytelling
**Short take off and landing aircraft
    629.133**
  UF   STOL aircraft
  BT   Jet planes
Shorthand   653
  UF   Stenography
  BT   Business education
       Office practice
       Writing
  RT   Abbreviations
Shortwave radio   621.3841
  UF   High-frequency radio
       Radio, Shortwave *[Former heading]*
       UHF radio
       Ultrahigh frequency radio
       Very high frequency radio
       VHF radio
  BT   Radio

       Radio frequency modulation
  NT   Amateur radio stations
       Citizens band radio
       Microwave communication systems
       Microwaves
Shotguns   683.4
  UF   Guns
  BT   Firearms
Show business
  USE   Performing arts
Show windows   659.1
  UF   Shop windows
       Window dressing
  BT   Advertising
       Decoration and ornament
       Windows
Showers (Parties)   793.2
  BT   Parties
Shows, Craft
  USE   Craft shows
Shrines (May subdiv. geog.)   263; 291.3;
    726
  NT   Tombs
  RT   Pilgrims and pilgrimages
       Saints
Shrubs   582.1; 635.9
  BT   Plants
       Trees
  NT   Evergreens
  RT   Landscape gardening
       Ornamental plants
Shuttles, Space
  USE   Space shuttles
Shyness   155.2
  UF   Bashfulness *[Former heading]*
  BT   Emotions
Sibling rivalry   306.875
  BT   Brothers and sisters
       Child psychology
Sibling sequence
  USE   Birth order
Siblings
  USE   Brothers and sisters
Sick   362.1
  UF   Invalids
  BT   Handicapped
  NT   Church work with the sick
       Cooking for the sick
       First aid

BT = Broader Term   NT = Narrower Term   RT = Related Term   SA = See Also   UF = Used For

Sick—*Continued*
Mentally ill
Terminally ill
RT Diseases
Home nursing
Nursing
Patients
Sick—Prayers 242; 291.4
BT Prayers
Sickness
USE Diseases
Sickness insurance
USE Health insurance
SIDS (Disease)
USE Sudden infant death syndrome
Sieges
USE Battles
Sight
USE Vision
Sight saving books
USE Large print books
Sign boards
USE Signs and signboards
Sign language 419
UF Deaf—Sign language
BT Language and languages
NT Indians of North America—
Sign language
RT Deaf—Means of communica-
tion
Signs and symbols
Sign painting 667
BT Advertising
Industrial painting
NT Alphabets
RT Lettering
Signs and signboards
Signals and signaling 388; 621.382
UF Coastal signals
Fog signals
Military signaling
Naval signaling
BT Communication
Military art and science
Naval art and science
Navigation
Signs and symbols
NT Railroads—Signaling
Sonar
RT Flags

Signboards
USE Signs and signboards
Signets
USE Seals (Numismatics)
Signs (Advertising)
USE Electric signs
Signs and signboards
Signs and signboards 659.13
UF Billboards
Guide posts
Road signs
Sign boards
Signboards
Signs (Advertising)
BT Advertising
NT Electric signs
RT Posters
Sign painting
Signs and symbols 302.2; 419
UF Emblems
Symbols
BT Communication
NT Ciphers
Cryptography
Heraldry
National emblems
Signals and signaling
State emblems
RT Abbreviations
Semiotics
Sign language
Symbolism
Signs and symbols in literature
USE Symbolism in literature
Signs, Electric
USE Electric signs
Silage and silos 633.2
UF Ensilage
Silos
BT Feeds
Forage plants
Silent films 791.43
May be used for individual works, collec-
tions, or materials about films made before
the development of films with sound.
UF Silent motion pictures
BT Motion pictures
Silent motion pictures
USE Silent films
Silk 677
BT Fabrics

BT = Broader Term   NT = Narrower Term   RT = Related Term   SA = See Also   UF = Used For

653

Silk—*Continued*
Fibers
RT   Silkworms
Silk screen printing   764
UF   Screen printing
Serigraphy
BT   Color printing
Stencil work
RT   Textile printing
Silkworms   595.78; 638
UF   Cocoons
BT   Beneficial insects
Insects
Moths
RT   Silk
Silos
USE   Silage and silos
Silver   332.4; 669
UF   Bimetallism
Bullion
BT   Chemical elements
Precious metals
NT   Silverware
Silverwork
RT   Coinage
Money
Silver articles
USE   Silverwork
Silver mines and mining   622
BT   Mines and mineral resources
NT   Prospecting
Silver plate
USE   Plate
Silverware
Silver work
USE   Silverwork
Silversmithing
USE   Silverwork
Silverware   642; 739.2
UF   Flatware, Silver
Silver plate
BT   Decorative arts
Silver
Silverwork
Tableware
Silverwork   739.2
UF   Silver articles
Silver work
Silversmithing
BT   Art metalwork

Metalwork
Silver
NT   Indians of North America—Sil-
verwork
Plate
Silverware
RT   Jewelry
Simple machines   621.8
UF   Machines, Simple
SA   types of simple machines, e.g.
Wheels; to be added as need-
ed
BT   Machinery
Mechanical movements
Mechanics
NT   Wheels
Simulation, computer
USE   Computer simulation
Simulation games in education   371.39
UF   Educational gaming
Educational simulation games
Gaming, Educational
BT   Education
Educational games
Game theory
Sin   241; 291.5
BT   Ethics
Good and evil
Theology
Sinai Campaign, 1956   956.04
UF   Anglo-French intervention in
Egypt, 1956
Arab-Israel War, 1956
Israel-Arab War, 1956
BT   Egypt—History
Israel-Arab conflicts
Singers   782.0092; 920
BT   Musicians
Singing   782; 783
UF   School music
Vocal culture
Voice culture
BT   Music
NT   Songbooks
RT   Choirs (Music)
Vocal music
Voice
Singing games   796.1
BT   Games

BT = Broader Term   NT = Narrower Term   RT = Related Term   SA = See Also   UF = Used For

Singing societies
USE   **Choral societies**

Single child
USE   **Only child**

Single men   155.6; 305.38
UF   Men, Single
       Unmarried men
BT   **Men**
       Single people
NT   **Widowers**

Single parent family   306.85

Use for materials on households in which a parent living without a partner is rearing children. Materials on parents who were not married at the time of the birth of their children are entered under **Unmarried fathers; Unmarried mothers.**

UF   Children of single parents
       Fathers, Single parent
       Mothers, Single parent
       One parent family
       Parents, Single
       Parents without partners
       Single parents
BT   **Family**
NT   **Children of divorced parents**
RT   **Unmarried fathers**
       Unmarried mothers
       Widowers
       Widows

Single parents
USE   **Part-time parenting**
       Single parent family

Single people   155.6; 305.9
UF   Unmarried people
NT   **Single men**
       Single women
RT   **Celibacy**

Single rail railroads
USE   **Monorail railroads**

Single women   155.6; 305.48
UF   Unmarried women
       Women, Single
BT   **Single people**
       Women
NT   **Widows**

Sirius   523.8
BT   **Stars**

Sisterhoods
USE   **Monasticism and religious orders for women**

Sisters and brothers
USE   **Brothers and sisters**

Sisters (Religious)
USE   **Nuns**

Sit-down strikes
USE   **Strikes**

Sit-ins for civil rights
USE   **Civil rights demonstrations**

Sitcoms
USE   **Comedy television programs**

Site oriented art
USE   **Earthworks (Art)**

Sitters (Babysitters)
USE   **Babysitters**

Situation comedies
USE   **Comedy television programs**

Six Day War, 1967
USE   **Israel-Arab War, 1967**

Sixteenth century   909

Use for general materials covering progress and development during this period in one or in several countries.

UF   1500-1599 (16th century)
BT   **Renaissance**
RT   **Reformation**

Size   530.8
UF   Large and small
       Size and shape *[Former heading]*
       Small and large
BT   **Concepts**
       Perception

Size and shape
USE   **Shape**
       Size

Skating
USE   **Ice skating**
       Roller skating

Skeletal remains
USE   **Anthropometry**

Skeleton   573.7; 611

Use for materials limited to the morphology or mechanics of the skeleton, human or animal. Comprehensive and systematic materials on the anatomy of bones are entered under **Bones.**

UF   Osteology
BT   **Musculoskeletal system**
RT   **Bones**

Skepticism   149; 186; 211
UF   Scepticism
       Unbelief

BT = Broader Term   NT = Narrower Term   RT = Related Term   SA = See Also   UF = Used For

Skepticism—*Continued*
  BT   Free thought
        Philosophy
        Rationalism
  RT   Agnosticism
        Belief and doubt
        Truth
Sketching
  USE   Drawing
Skidoos
  USE   Snowmobiles
Skiing   796.93
  UF   Skis and skiing *[Former head-ing]*
        Snow skiing
  BT   **Winter sports**
Skiing, Water
  USE   **Water skiing**
Skilled workers
  USE   **Labor**
        Working class
Skin   611; 612.7
  BT   **Anatomy**
        Physiology
Skin—Care   616.5; 646.7
  UF   Skin care
        Skin—Care and hygiene *[For-mer heading]*
Skin care
  USE   **Skin—Care**
Skin—Care and hygiene
  USE   **Skin—Care**
Skin—Diseases   616.5
  UF   Dermatitis
  SA   types of skin diseases, to be added as needed
  BT   **Diseases**
  NT   **Acne**
Skin diving   797.2
    Use for materials on free diving with mask, fins, and snorkel. Materials on free diving with the aid of a self-contained underwater breathing apparatus are entered under **Scuba diving.**
  UF   Free diving
        Snorkeling
        Underwater swimming
  BT   **Deep diving**
Skin garments
  USE   **Leather garments**
Skinheads
  USE   **White supremacy movements**

Skins
  USE   **Hides and skins**
Skis and skiing
  USE   **Skiing**
Skits   791
  BT   **Amusements**
        Theater
Sky   520; 551.5
  BT   **Astronomy**
        Atmosphere
  NT   **Constellations**
Sky diving
  USE   **Skydiving**
Sky hijacking
  USE   **Hijacking of airplanes**
Sky laboratories
  USE   **Space stations**
Skydiving   797.5
  UF   Sky diving
  BT   **Aeronautical sports**
Skyjacking
  USE   **Hijacking of airplanes**
Skyscrapers   690; 720
  UF   High rise buildings
  BT   **Buildings**
Skyscrapers—Earthquake effects   690; 725
  BT   **Buildings—Earthquake effects**
        Earthquakes
Slander (Law)
  USE   **Libel and slander**
Slang
  USE   names of languages with the subdivision *Slang*, e.g. **English language—Slang;** to be added as needed
Slanted journalism
  USE   **Journalism—Objectivity**
Slapstick comedies
  USE   **Comedies**
        Comedy films
        Comedy television programs
Slave trade   341; 345; 380.1
  BT   **International law**
        Slavery
Slavery (May subdiv. geog.)   177; 306.3; 326; 342
  UF   Abolition of slavery
        Antislavery
        Compulsory labor

BT = Broader Term   NT = Narrower Term   RT = Related Term   SA = See Also   UF = Used For

Slavery—*Continued*
      Emancipation of slaves
      Forced labor
      Servitude
  BT   **Labor**
  NT   **Slave trade**
        Slaves
  RT   **Abolitionists**
        Peonage

Slavery—United States 306.3; 326.0973
  UF   Emancipation of slaves
  RT   **African Americans**
        Southern States—History
        Underground railroad

Slavery—United States—Fiction
    808.83; 813, etc.
  May be used for individual works, collections, or materials about fiction dealing with slavery in the United States.

Slaves (May subdiv. geog.) 305.5
  BT   **Slavery**

Sledding 796.9
  UF   Sledges
      Sleds and sledding *[Former heading]*
      Sleighs and sledges
  BT   **Winter sports**

Sledges
  USE **Sledding**

Sleds and sledding
  USE **Sledding**

Sleep 154.6; 612.8; 613.7
  BT   **Brain**
        Health
        Hygiene
        Mind and body
        Psychophysiology
        Rest
        Subconsciousness
  NT   **Bedtime**
  RT   **Dreams**
        Insomnia

Sleeplessness
  USE **Insomnia**

Sleighs and sledges
  USE **Sledding**

Sleight of hand
  USE **Juggling**
       Magic tricks

Slide projectors
  USE **Projectors**

Slide rule 510.28
  BT   **Calculators**
        Logarithms

Slides (Photography) 778.2
  UF   Color slides
      Lantern slides
      Photographic slides
  BT   **Photography**
  RT   **Filmstrips**

Slovakia 943.73
  May be subdivided like United States except for *History.*
  RT   **Czechoslovakia**

Slow learning children 155.4; 371.92
  Use for materials on children with less than average intelligence and slow social development who can nonetheless be educated and lead a normal life.
  BT   **Exceptional children**
  NT   **Learning disabilities**
  RT   **Mentally handicapped children**

Slum clearance
  USE **City planning**
       Housing
       Urban renewal

Slumber songs
  USE **Lullabies**

Small and large
  USE **Size**

Small arms
  USE **Firearms**

Small business 338.6; 658.02
  Use for materials on small independent business enterprises.
  UF   Business, Small
  BT   **Business**
  NT   **Entrepreneurship**
        Home business
        Underground economy

Small cars
  USE **Compact cars**

Small loans
  USE **Personal loans**

Smell 152.1
  BT   **Senses and sensation**
  RT   **Nose**

Smelting 669
  BT   **Furnaces**
  NT   **Blast furnaces**
        Electrometallurgy
        Ore dressing
  RT   **Metallurgy**

BT = Broader Term   NT = Narrower Term   RT = Related Term   SA = See Also   UF = Used For

Smoke-ending programs
USE   Smoking cessation programs
Smoke prevention   363.738; 628.5
UF   Prevention of smoke
BT   Sanitation
Smoke stacks
USE   Chimneys
Smokeless powder
USE   Gunpowder
Smoking   178; 613.85
NT   Cigarettes
    Cigars
    Tobacco habit
    Tobacco pipes
RT   Tobacco
Smoking cessation programs   613.85
UF   How-to-stop-smoking programs
    Quit-smoking programs
    Smoke-ending programs
BT   Tobacco habit
Smuggling   364.1
UF   Contraband trade
BT   Crime
    Tariff
Smuggling of drugs
USE   Drug traffic
Snakes   597.96
UF   Serpents
    Vipers
SA   types of snakes, e.g. **Rattle-snakes;** to be added as need-ed
BT   Reptiles
NT   Rattlesnakes
    Snakes as pets
Snakes as pets   636.088
BT   Pets
    Snakes
Snorkeling
USE   Skin diving
Snow   551.57
UF   Precipitation (Meteorology)
BT   Meteorology
    Water
    Weather
RT   Blizzards
    Storms
Snow skiing
USE   Skiing

Snowmobiles   629.22; 796.94
UF   Skidoos
BT   All terrain vehicles
Soap   668
BT   Cleaning compounds
RT   Detergents
Soap box derbies   796.6
BT   Racing
Soap carving
USE   Soap sculpture
Soap operas   791.44; 791.45
May be used for individual works, collec-tions, or materials about soap operas.
BT   Radio plays
    Television plays
RT   Radio serials
    Television serials
Soap sculpture   736
UF   Soap carving
BT   Modeling
    Sculpture
Soaring flight
USE   Gliding and soaring
Sobriquets
USE   Nicknames
Soccer   796.334
BT   Ball games
    Football
    Sports
Soccer—Training   796.334
BT   Physical education
Social action   361.2
UF   Social activism
SA   subjects with the subdivision *Citizen participation,* e.g. **City planning—Citizen participa-tion;** to be added as needed
BT   Social policy
NT   City planning—Citizen partici-pation
RT   Political participation
    Social problems
    Social work
Social activism
USE   Social action
Social adjustment   158; 303.3
UF   Adjustment, Social
BT   Human behavior
    Human relations
    Social psychology
NT   Socially handicapped

BT = Broader Term   **NT** = Narrower Term   **RT** = Related Term   **SA** = See Also   **UF** = Used For

Social alienation
　USE　**Alienation (Social psychology)**
Social anthropology
　USE　**Ethnology**
Social aspects
　USE　subjects with the subdivision *Social aspects,* e.g. **Genetic engineering—Social aspects; to** be added as needed
Social behavior
　USE　**Human behavior**
Social case work　361.3
　UF　Case work, Social
　　　Family social work
　BT　**Social work**
　NT　**Parole**
　　　Probation
　RT　**Counseling**
Social change (May subdiv. geog.)
　　　303.4; 909
　UF　Change, Social
　　　Cultural change
　　　Social evolution
　BT　**Anthropology**
　　　Social sciences
　　　Sociology
　NT　**Community development**
　　　Modernization (Sociology)
　　　Urbanization
Social classes　305.5; 323.3
　UF　Class distinction
　　　Rank
　　　Social distinctions
　BT　**Caste**
　　　Sociology
　NT　**Class consciousness**
　　　Elite (Social sciences)
　　　Intellectuals
　　　Middle class
　　　Upper class
　　　Working class
Social compact
　USE　**Social contract**
Social conditions　306.09; 909
　　Use for materials on the social aspects of several of the following topics: labor, poverty, education, health, housing, recreation, moral conditions.
　UF　Social history

　SA　racial and ethnic groups, classes of persons, and names of countries, cities, etc., with the subdivision *Social conditions,* to be added as needed
　BT　**Social ethics**
　　　Sociology
　NT　**African Americans—Social conditions**
　　　Blacks—Social conditions
　　　Chicago (Ill.)—Social conditions
　　　Cost and standard of living
　　　Counter culture
　　　Economic conditions
　　　Indians of North America—Social conditions
　　　Jews—Social conditions
　　　Labor
　　　Men—Social conditions
　　　Moral conditions
　　　Ohio—Social conditions
　　　Quality of life
　　　Social movements
　　　Social policy
　　　Social problems
　　　United States—Social conditions
　　　Urbanization
　　　Women—Social conditions
Social conflict　303.6
　UF　Class conflict
　　　Class struggle
　　　Conflict, Social
　BT　**Social psychology**
　　　Sociology
　NT　**Conflict of generations**
　　　Role conflict
Social conformity
　USE　**Conformity**
Social contract　320.01; 320.1
　UF　Social compact
　BT　**Political science**
　　　Sociology
Social customs
　USE　**Manners and customs**
Social democracy
　USE　**Socialism**
Social distinctions
　USE　**Social classes**

Social drinking
    USE   **Drinking of alcoholic beverages**
Social ecology
    USE   **Human ecology**
Social equality
    USE   **Equality**
Social ethics   170
    UF   Ethics, Social
    BT   **Ethics**
    NT   **Bioethics**
           Citizenship
           Crime
           Friendship
           Political ethics
           Sexual ethics
           Social conditions
    RT   **Social problems**
Social evolution
    USE   **Social change**
Social group work   361.4; 362
    UF   Group social work
           Group work, Social
           Social work with groups
    BT   **Counseling**
           Social work
Social groups   302.3; 305
    UF   Group dynamics
           Groups, Social
    BT   **Sociology**
    NT   **Elite (Social sciences)**
           Leadership
           Social psychology
Social history
    USE   **Social conditions**
Social hygiene
    USE   **Public health**
           Sexual hygiene
Social insurance
    USE   **Social security**
Social isolation
    USE   **Loneliness**
Social learning
    USE   **Socialization**
Social life and customs
    USE   **Manners and customs**
           and names of ethnic groups,
           countries, cities, etc., with the
           subdivision *Social life and*
           customs, e.g. **Indians of**

           **North America—Social life
           and customs; Jews—Social
           life and customs; United
           States—Social life and cus-
           toms;** etc., to be added as
           needed
Social medicine (May subdiv. geog.)
        306.4; 362.1
    Use for materials on the study of social, ge-
netic, and environmental influences on human
disease and disability, as well as the promotion of health measures to protect both the individual and the community.
    UF   Medical care—Social aspects
           Medical sociology
           Medicine, Social
           Medicine—Social aspects
    BT   **Medicine**
           Public health
           Public welfare
           Sociology
    NT   **Hospices**
    RT   **Medical ethics**
Social movements   303.48
    SA   types of social movements, e.g.
           Environmental movement; to
           be added as needed
    BT   **Social conditions**
           Social psychology
    NT   **Animal rights movements**
           Anti-apartheid movement
           Antinuclear movement
           Environmental movement
           Labor movement
           Militia movements
           New Age movement
           Peace movements
           Pro-choice movement
           Pro-life movement
           Sanctuary movement
           Survivalism
           White supremacy movements
           Youth movement
Social planning
    USE   **Social policy**
Social policy   361.6
    Use for materials on the ways a society reg-
ulates the relationships among individuals,
groups, communities, and institutions, and on
systematic procedures for achieving social
goals and managing available resources to at-
tain social change.
    UF   National planning

BT = Broader Term   NT = Narrower Term   RT = Related Term   SA = See Also   UF = Used For

Social policy—*Continued*
>Social planning
>State planning
- SA names of countries, states, cities, etc., with the subdivision *Social policy,* e.g. **United States—Social policy;** subjects with the subdivision *Government policy,* e.g. **Homeless persons—Government policy;** and types of activities, facilities, industries, services, and undertakings with the subdivision *Planning,* e.g. **Transportation—Planning;** to be added as needed
- BT **Planning**
>**Social conditions**
- NT **Arts—Government policy**
>**Chicago (Ill.)—Social policy**
>**Education and state**
>**Homeless persons—Government policy**
>**Land reform**
>**Libraries—Government policy**
>**Ohio—Social policy**
>**Social action**
>**United States—Social policy**
>**Welfare state**
- RT **Economic policy**

Social problems   361.1
- UF Reform, Social
>Social reform
>Social welfare
- BT **Social conditions**
>**Sociology**
- NT **Alcoholism**
>**Children—Employment**
>**Church and social problems**
>**Crime**
>**Discrimination**
>**Drug abuse**
>**Homelessness**
>**Illegitimacy**
>**Juvenile delinquency**
>**Poverty**
>**Prison reform**
>**Prostitution**
>**Public health**
>**Race discrimination**

>**Solvent abuse**
>**Suicide**
>**Unemployment**
- RT **Social action**
>**Social ethics**

Social problems and the church
- USE **Church and social problems**

Social problems in education
- USE **Educational sociology**

Social psychology   302
- UF Mass psychology
>Psychology, Social
- BT **Human ecology**
>**Psychology**
>**Social groups**
>**Sociology**
- NT **Alienation (Social psychology)**
>**Class consciousness**
>**Discrimination**
>**Human relations**
>**Interviewing**
>**National characteristics**
>**Political psychology**
>**Popularity**
>**Public opinion**
>**Social adjustment**
>**Social conflict**
>**Social movements**
>**Social role**
>**Stereotype (Psychology)**
>**Violence**
- RT **Applied psychology**
>**Crowds**
>**Ethnopsychology**

Social reform
- USE **Social problems**

Social role   302
- UF Role, Social
- BT **Social psychology**
- NT **Role conflict**
>**Role playing**
>**Sex role**

Social sciences   300
>Use for general and comprehensive materials on the various branches of knowledge dealing with human society, such as sociology, political science, economics, etc.
- UF Social studies
- BT **Civilization**
- NT **Anthropology**
>**Conservatism**

BT = Broader Term   NT = Narrower Term   RT = Related Term   SA = See Also   UF = Used For

Social sciences—*Continued*
>   Cross cultural studies
>   Economics
>   Gerontology
>   History
>   Human behavior
>   Liberalism
>   Political science
>   Social change
>   Social surveys
>   Sociology

Social security   362; 368.4
>   UF   Insurance, Social
>   Insurance, State and compulsory
>   Insurance, Workers'
>   Labor—Insurance
>   Security, Social
>   Social insurance
>   State and insurance
>   BT   **Pensions**
>   NT   **Old age pensions**
>   **Workers' compensation**

Social service
>   USE   **Social work**

Social settlements   361.7; 362.5
>   UF   Church settlements
>   Neighborhood centers
>   Settlements, Social
>   SA   names of settlements, e.g. **Hull House (Chicago, Ill.)**; to be added as needed
>   BT   **Charities**
>   **Industrial welfare**
>   **Social work**
>   NT   **Boys' clubs**
>   **Community centers**
>   **Girls' clubs**
>   **Hull House (Chicago, Ill.)**

Social studies
>   USE   **Geography**
>   **History**
>   **Social sciences**

Social surveys (May subdiv. geog.)
>   300.7
>   Use for materials on the methods employed in conducting surveys of social and economic conditions.
>   UF   Community surveys
>   SA   names of regions, countries, cities, etc., with the subdivision

Social conditions, to be added as needed
>   BT   **Social sciences**
>   **Surveys**

Social surveys—United States   301
>   UF   United States—Social surveys

Social values   303.3
>   Use for materials on the principles and standards of human interaction within a particular group.
>   UF   Group values
>   BT   **Human relations**
>   **Values**
>   RT   **Quality of life**

Social welfare
>   USE   **Charities**
>   **Public welfare**
>   **Social problems**
>   **Social work**

Social work   361.3
>   Use for materials on the methods employed in welfare work, public or private. Materials on privately supported welfare activities are entered under **Charities.** Materials on tax-supported welfare activities are entered under **Public welfare.**
>   UF   Philanthropy
>   Social service
>   Social welfare
>   Welfare work
>   SA   social work with particular groups of people, e.g. **Social work and the elderly;** to be added as needed
>   NT   **Charities**
>   **Child welfare**
>   **Community organization**
>   **Community services**
>   **Crisis centers**
>   **Group homes**
>   **Hotlines (Telephone counseling)**
>   **Industrial welfare**
>   **Public welfare**
>   **Social case work**
>   **Social group work**
>   **Social settlements**
>   **Social work with the elderly**
>   RT   **Social action**

Social work with groups
>   USE   **Social group work**

Social work with the elderly   362.6
>   BT   **Elderly**

BT = Broader Term   NT = Narrower Term   RT = Related Term   SA = See Also   UF = Used For

Social work with the elderly—*Continued*
    Social work
Socialism (May subdiv. geog.)   320.5;
    335
  UF   Collectivism
       Social democracy
  BT   **Economics**
       Political science
  NT   **Collective settlements**
       Dialectical materialism
       Government ownership
       Labor unions
       Proletariat
       Utopias
  RT   **Communism**
       Marxism
       National socialism
Socialism—United States   320.5;
    335.00973
  UF   United States—Socialism
Socialization   303.3
   Use for materials on the process by which individuals acquire group values and learn to function effectively in society.
  UF   Children—Socialization
       Social learning
  BT   **Acculturation**
       Child rearing
       Education
       Sociology
  NT   **Americanization**
       Peer pressure
Socialization of industry
  USE **Government ownership**
       Industrial policy
Socialized medicine
  USE **Medical charities**
       National health insurance
       State medicine
Socially handicapped   362
  UF   Culturally deprived
       Culturally handicapped
       Disadvantaged
       Underprivileged
  BT   **Handicapped**
       Social adjustment
  NT   **Socially handicapped children**
Socially handicapped children   362.74
  UF   Culturally deprived children
       Culturally handicapped children
       Disadvantaged children

       Underprivileged children
  BT   **Handicapped children**
       Socially handicapped
  RT   **At risk students**
Socials
  USE **Church entertainments**
Societies   060
  UF   Learned societies
  SA   types of societies, e.g. **Choral societies;** subjects, ethnic groups, classes of persons, corporate bodies, individual persons, and sacred works with the subdivision *Societies,* e.g. **Agriculture—Societies; Women—Societies;** etc.; and names of individual societies, to be added as needed
  BT   **Associations**
  NT   **Agriculture—Societies**
       Boys' clubs
       Chemistry—Societies
       Choral societies
       Cooperative societies
       Educational associations
       Elderly—Societies
       Girls' clubs
       History—Societies
       Labor unions
       Men—Societies
       Parent-teacher associations
       Science—Societies
       Secret societies
       Students—Societies
       Women—Societies
  RT   **Clubs**
Society and art
  USE **Art and society**
Society and language
  USE **Sociolinguistics**
Society and religion
  USE **Religion and sociology**
Society of Friends   289.6
  UF   Friends, Society of
       Quakers
  BT   **Christian sects**
Society, Primitive
  USE **Primitive societies**
Society—Religious aspects
  USE **Religion and sociology**

Sociobiology   304.5; 577.8; 591.56

Use for materials on the biological basis of social behavior, especially as transmitted genetically.

UF   Biology—Social aspects

Biosociology

BT   **Comparative psychology**

Sociology

Sociolinguistics   306.44

Use for materials on the study of the social aspects of language, particularly linguistic behavior as determined by sociocultural factors.

UF   Language and society

Society and language

Sociology and language

BT   **Language and languages**

Sociology

Sociology   301

Use for systematic studies on the structure of society. General materials on sociology, political science, economics, etc., are entered under **Social sciences.**

SA   sociology of particular religions, e.g. **Christian sociology; to** be added as needed

BT   **Social sciences**

NT   **Christian sociology**

Cities and towns

Communication

Educational sociology

Equality

Ethnic relations

Ethnopsychology

Family

Human ecology

Individualism

Labor

Marxism

Organizational sociology

Population

Race relations

Religion and sociology

Rural sociology

Social change

Social classes

Social conditions

Social conflict

Social contract

Social groups

Social medicine

Social problems

Social psychology

Socialization

Sociobiology

Sociolinguistics

Urban sociology

RT   **Civilization**

Culture

Sociology and art

USE   **Art and society**

Sociology and language

USE   **Sociolinguistics**

Sociology and religion

USE   **Religion and sociology**

Sociology, Christian

USE   **Christian sociology**

Sociology, Educational

USE   **Educational sociology**

Sociology of organizations

USE   **Organizational sociology**

Sociology of religion

USE   **Religion and sociology**

Sociology—Religious aspects

USE   **Religion and sociology**

Sociology, Rural

USE   **Rural sociology**

Sociology, Urban

USE   **Urban sociology**

Sodium content of food

USE   **Food—Sodium content**

Softball   796.357

BT   **Ball games**

Baseball

Software, Computer

USE   **Computer software**

Software viruses

USE   **Computer viruses**

Soil conservation   631.4

UF   Conservation of the soil

BT   **Conservation of natural resources**

Environmental protection

RT   **Erosion**

Soil erosion

Soil engineering

USE   **Soil mechanics**

Soil erosion   631.4

UF   Top soil loss

BT   **Erosion**

RT   **Soil conservation**

Soil fertility

USE   **Soils**

BT = Broader Term   NT = Narrower Term   RT = Related Term   SA = See Also   UF = Used For

Soil mechanics   620.1
    UF   Earthwork
            Geotechnique
            Soil engineering
            Soils (Engineering) *[Former heading]*
    BT   **Mechanics**
            Structural engineering
    RT   **Foundations**
            Roads
            Soils
Soil microbiology   631.4
    UF   Soils—Bacteriology *[Former heading]*
    BT   **Microbiology**
            Sanitary engineering
    RT   **Agricultural bacteriology**
Soilless agriculture
    USE   **Hydroponics**
Soils   631.4
    UF   Soil fertility
    BT   **Agriculture**
            Economic geology
    NT   **Clay**
            Compost
            Fertilizers
    RT   **Agricultural chemistry**
            Soil mechanics
Soils—Bacteriology
    USE   **Soil microbiology**
Soils (Engineering)
    USE   **Soil mechanics**
Soils, Lunar
    USE   **Lunar soil**
Solace
    USE   **Consolation**
Solar batteries   621.31
    UF   Batteries, Solar
            Solar cells
            Sun powered batteries
    BT   **Electric batteries**
            Photovoltaic power generation
            Solar radiation
Solar cells
    USE   **Photovoltaic power generation**
            Solar batteries
Solar eclipses   523.7
    UF   Eclipses, Solar *[Former heading]*
            Sun—Eclipses
    BT   **Astronomy**

Solar energy   333.792; 621.47
    UF   Solar power
    BT   **Energy resources**
            Renewable energy resources
            Solar radiation
            Sun
    NT   **Photovoltaic power generation**
            Solar engines
            Solar heating
Solar engines   621.47
    BT   **Engines**
            Solar energy
Solar heat
    USE   **Solar heating**
Solar heating   621.47; 697
    UF   Solar heat
    SA   types of solar heating applications, e.g. **Solar homes;** to be added as needed
    BT   **Heating**
            Solar energy
    NT   **Solar homes**
Solar homes   697; 728
    BT   **Domestic architecture**
            Houses
            Solar heating
Solar physics
    USE   **Sun**
Solar power
    USE   **Solar energy**
Solar radiation   523.7; 621.47
    UF   Radiation, Solar
            Sun—Radiation
    BT   **Meteorology**
            Space environment
    NT   **Greenhouse effect**
            Solar batteries
            Solar energy
            Sunspots
Solar system   523.2
    SA   names of planets, e.g. **Saturn (Planet);** to be added as needed
    BT   **Astronomy**
            Stars
    NT   **Asteroids**
            Comets
            Earth
            Meteors
            Moon

BT = Broader Term   NT = Narrower Term   RT = Related Term   SA = See Also   UF = Used For

Solar system—*Continued*
    Planets
    Satellites
    Sun
Solder and soldering
  USE   **Soldering**
Soldering   671.5
  UF   Brazing
       Solder and soldering *[Former
         heading]*
  BT   **Metals**
       Metalwork
  RT   **Welding**
Soldiers (May subdiv. geog.)   355.0092;
    920
  UF   Army life
       Soldiers' life
  SA   names of countries with the sub-
       division *Army—Military life,*
       to be added as needed
  BT   **Armies**
       Military personnel
  NT   **Mercenary soldiers**
       Missing in action
       **United States. Army—Military
        life**
       United States. Army—Officers
  RT   **Veterans**
Soldiers' handbooks
  USE   **United States. Army—Hand-
       books, manuals, etc.**
Soldiers—Hygiene
  USE   **Military health**
Soldiers' life
  USE   **Soldiers**
       and names of countries with the
       subdivision *Army—Military
       life,* e.g. **United States.
       Army—Military life;** to be
       added as needed
Soldiers of fortune
  USE   **Mercenary soldiers**
Soldiers' songs
  USE   **War songs**
Soldiers—United States   355.0092; 920
  UF   G.I.'s
       GIs
       United States—Soldiers
Solicitors
  USE   **Lawyers**

Solid geometry
  USE   **Geometry**
Solid waste disposal
  USE   **Refuse and refuse disposal**
Solids   530.4; 531; 541
  BT   **Physical chemistry**
       Physics
  NT   **Crystals**
Solitaire (Game)   795.4
  UF   Patience (Game)
  BT   **Card games**
Solitude
  USE   **Loneliness**
Solution achievement
  USE   **Problem solving**
Solvent abuse   362.29
  UF   Aerosol sniffing
       Glue sniffing
       Inhalant abuse
       Inhalation abuse of solvents
       Paint sniffing
       Substance abuse *[Former head-
        ing]*
  BT   **Social problems**
  RT   **Drug abuse**
Somatology
  USE   **Physical anthropology**
Sonar   621.389
  UF   Echo ranging
       Sound navigation
  BT   **Signals and signaling**
Sonata   784.18
    Use for musical scores and for materials on
  the sonata as a musical form.
  UF   Sonatas *[Former heading]*
  BT   **Musical form**
Sonatas
  USE   **Sonata**
Song books
  USE   **Songbooks**
Song lyrics
  USE   **Popular music—Texts**
Song writing
  USE   **Composition (Music)**
       **Popular music—Writing and
       publishing**
Songbooks   782.42
    Use for general collections of songs that
  contain both words and music. Similar collec-
  tions limited to sacred songs are entered under
  Hymnals. Materials about songs are entered

BT = Broader Term   NT = Narrower Term   RT = Related Term   SA = See Also   UF = Used For

Songbooks—*Continued*
under **Songs.** Collections of songs on a single subject are entered under the subject with the subdivision *Songs.*

- UF   Community songbooks
  Song books
- BT   **Singing**
  Songs
- NT   **Hymnals**
  School songbooks

Songbooks, School
- USE   **School songbooks**

Songs   782.42
Use for materials about songs. General collections of songs that contain both words and music are entered under **Songbooks.** Collections of songs that contain the words but not the music are entered under **Poetry—Collections** for classical songs and under **Popular music—Texts** for popular songs.

- SA   types of songs, e.g. **Children's Songs;** songs of particular countries, e.g. **American songs;** subjects, classes of persons, and names of persons, corporate bodies, places, or wars, with the subdivision *Songs,* for collections or individual songs about the topic or associated with the entity named, e.g. **Cowhands—Songs; Surfing—Songs; United States Military Academy—Songs; World War, 1939-1945—Songs;** etc.; and names of individual songs, to be added as needed
- BT   **Poetry**
  Vocal music
- NT   **African songs**
  American songs
  Ballads
  Carols
  Children's songs
  Cowhands—Songs
  Folk songs
  Hymns
  Lullabies
  National songs
  Popular music
  School songbooks
  Sea songs
  Songbooks

Spirituals (Songs)
State songs
Students' songs
Surfing—Songs
United States. Army—Songs
War songs

Songs, African
- USE   **African songs**

Songs, African American
- USE   **African American music**

Songs, American
- USE   **American songs**

Songs and music
- USE   subjects, classes of persons, and names of persons, corporate bodies, places, or wars, with the subdivision *Songs,* for collections or individual songs about the topic or entity named, e.g. **Cowhands—Songs; Surfing—Songs; United States Military Academy—Songs; World War, 1939-1945—Songs;** and ethnic groups with the subdivision *Music* for music of the group, e.g. **Indians of North America—Music;** to be added as needed

Songs for children
- USE   **Children's songs**

Songs, National
- USE   **National songs**

Songwriters
- USE   **Composers**
  Lyricists

Songwriting
- USE   **Composition (Music)**
  Popular music—Writing and publishing

Sons and fathers
- USE   **Fathers and sons**

Sons and mothers
- USE   **Mothers and sons**

Soothsaying
- USE   **Divination**

Soporifics
- USE   **Narcotics**

Sorcery
- USE   **Magic**

BT = Broader Term   NT = Narrower Term   RT = Related Term   SA = See Also   UF = Used For

Sorcery—*Continued*
> Occultism
> Witchcraft

Sororities
> USE   **Fraternities and sororities**

Sorrow
> USE   **Bereavement**
> **Grief**
> **Joy and sorrow**

Soubriquets
> USE   **Nicknames**

Soul   128; 233
> UF   Spirit
> BT   **Future life**
> **Man (Theology)**
> **Philosophy**
> NT   **Immortality**
> **Psychology**
> RT   **Reincarnation**

Sound   534; 620.2
> UF   Acoustics
> BT   **Physics**
> **Pneumatics**
> **Radiation**
> NT   **Architectural acoustics**
> **Computer sound processing**
> **Hearing**
> **Noise**
> **Phonetics**
> **Sound effects**
> **Soundproofing**
> **Sounds**
> **Ultrasonics**
> **Vibration**
> RT   **Music—Acoustics and physics**

Sound effects   534; 620.2
> BT   **Sound**

Sound insulation
> USE   **Soundproofing**

Sound navigation
> USE   **Sonar**

Sound processing, Computer
> USE   **Computer sound processing**

Sound recording
> USE   **Sound—Recording and reproducing**

Sound—Recording and reproducing
>   621.389

Use for materials on the equipment or the process by which sound is recorded. Materials on sound recordings that emphasize the content of the recording rather than the equipment, process, or format are entered under **Sound recordings**. Materials about the format are entered under the format, e.g. **Compact discs**.
> UF   Sound recording
> SA   methods of recording, e.g. **Magnetic recorders and recording**; to be added as needed
> BT   **Phonograph**
> NT   **Compact disc players**
> **High-fidelity sound systems**
> **Phonograph**
> **Stereophonic sound systems**
> RT   **Magnetic recorders and recording**
> **Optical storage devices**
> **Sound recordings**

Sound recordings   621.389; 780.26

Use for general materials and for materials on sound recordings that emphasize the content of the recording rather than the format. Materials about the format are entered under the format, e.g. **Compact discs**. Materials about the equipment or the process by which sound is recorded are entered under **Sound—Recording and reproducing**.
> UF   Audio cassettes
> Audiotapes
> Cassette tapes, Audio
> Discography
> Discs, Sound
> Phonograph records
> Recordings, Sound
> Records, Phonograph
> Tape recordings, Audio
> SA   types of sound recordings, e.g. **Compact discs**; to be added as needed
> BT   **Audiovisual materials**
> NT   **Compact discs**
> **Talking books**
> RT   **Sound—Recording and reproducing**

Sound waves   534; 620.2
> BT   **Vibration**
> **Waves**
> NT   **Ultrasonic waves**

Soundproofing   620.2; 693.8
> UF   Insulation (Sound)
> Sound insulation
> BT   **Architectural acoustics**
> **Sound**

BT = Broader Term   NT = Narrower Term   RT = Related Term   SA = See Also   UF = Used For

Sounds 534; 620.2
  BT Sound
Soups 641.8
  BT Cooking
Sources
  USE historical subjects, periods of
      history, individual literary and
      sacred works, and names of
      wars with the subdivision
      Sources, e.g. **World War,
      1939-1945—Sources;** and
      subjects, ethnic groups, class-
      es of persons, coporate bod-
      ies, and names of countries,
      states, etc., with the subdivi-
      sion *History—Sources;* e.g.
      **United States—History—
      Sources;** to be added as
      needed
South Africa 968
  Use for materials on the Republic of South
  Africa.
  UF Africa, South
      Republic of South Africa
      Union of South Africa
  BT **Africa**
      Southern Africa
South Africa—History 968
South Africa—Race relations
      305.800968; 968
  BT **Race relations**
  NT **Anti-apartheid movement**
      Apartheid
South African Dutch
  USE **Afrikaners**
South Africans, Afrikaans-speaking
  USE **Afrikaners**
South America 980
  BT **America**
South American Indians
  USE **Indians of South America**
South American literature
  USE **Latin American literature**
South Atlantic States
  USE **Atlantic States**
South Korea
  USE **Korea (South)**
South Pacific region
  USE **Oceania**
South Pole 998
  BT **Polar regions**

  RT **Antarctica**
South Sea Islands
  USE **Oceania**
South Seas
  USE **Oceania**
South (U.S.)
  USE **Southern States**
Southeast Asia 959
  Use for materials on Southeast Asia includ-
  ing Burma, Thailand, Malaysia, Singapore, In-
  donesia, Vietnam, Cambodia, Laos, and the
  Philippines.
  UF Asia, Southeast
  BT **Asia**
  NT **Indochina**
Southern Africa 968
  Use for materials dealing collectively with
  the area south of the countries of Zaire and
  Tanzania. Southern Africa includes the politi-
  cal entities of Angola, Botswana, Comoros,
  Lesotho, Madagascar, Malawi, Mozambique,
  Namibia, South Africa, Swaziland, Zambia,
  and Zimbabwe. Materials on the Republic of
  South Africa are entered under **South Africa.**
  UF Africa, Southern *[Former head-
      ing]*
  BT **Africa**
  NT **South Africa**
Southern cooking 641.5975
  UF Cooking—Southern States *[For-
      mer heading]*
      Southern States—Cooking
  BT **Cooking**
Southern lights
  USE **Auroras**
Southern literature
  USE **American literature—Southern
      States**
Southern States 975
  UF South (U.S.)
  BT **United States**
Southern States—African Americans
  USE **African Americans—Southern
      States**
Southern States—Cooking
  USE **Southern cooking**
Southern States—History 975
  BT **United States—History**
  RT **Slavery—United States**
Southwest, New
  USE **Southwestern States**
Southwest, Old
  USE **Old Southwest**

BT = Broader Term   NT = Narrower Term   RT = Related Term   SA = See Also   UF = Used For

Southwest Pacific region

USE   **Oceania**

Southwestern States   **979**

Use for materials on that part of the United States that corresponds roughly with the old Spanish province of New Mexico, including the present Arizona, New Mexico, southern Colorado, Utah, Nevada, and California.

UF   Southwest, New

BT   **United States**

Sovereigns

USE   **Emperors**

        Kings and rulers

        Monarchy

        Queens

Soviet artificial satellites   **629.43; 629.46**

UF   Artificial satellites, Soviet *[Former heading]*

        Sputniks

BT   **Artificial satellites**

Soviet bloc

USE   **Communist countries**

Soviet communism

USE   **Communism—Soviet Union**

Soviet intervention in Czechoslovakia

USE   **Czechoslovakia—History—1968-1989**

Soviet literature   **890**

Use for materials on several of the literatures of the Soviet Union. Materials on the individual literatures of the republics that made up the Soviet Union are entered with the appropriate adjective, e.g. **Russian literature;** etc.

UF   Literatures of the Soviet Union

        Soviet Union—Literatures *[Former heading]*

BT   **Literature**

RT   **Russian literature**

Soviet people

USE   **Soviets (People)**

Soviet Union   **947.084**

Use for materials on the Union of Soviet Socialist Republics between 1917 and 1991. Materials on Russia or the Russian empire before 1917 are entered under **Russia**. Materials on the independent republic of Russia since its establishment in December 1991 are entered under **Russia (Federation)**. Materials on several or all of the countries that emerged from the dissolution of the Soviet Union in 1991 are entered under **Former Soviet republics**. Material specifically on the federation of former Soviet republics that was established in December 1991 and does not include Georgia or the Baltic states are entered under **Commonwealth of Independent States**. The Bal-

tic states and the other republics of the former Soviet Union are: Armenia (Republic); Azerbaijan; Belarus; Estonia; Georgia (Republic); Kazakstan; Kyrgyzstan; Latvia; Lithuania; Moldova; Tajikistan; Turkmenistan; Ukraine; and Uzbekistan; to be added as needed. The adjective **Soviet** is used to refer to the Soviet Union as a whole between 1917 and 1991, e.g. **Soviet artificial satellites.** Materials on the citizens of the Soviet Union between 1917 and 1991 are entered under **Soviets (People).** Materials on topics pertaining to individual republics, nationalities, or ethnic groups of the former Soviet Union are to be added as needed with the appropriate qualifier, e.g., **Russians; Russian language;** etc.

UF   U.S.S.R.

        Union of Soviet Socialist Republics

        USSR

NT   **Russians**

        Soviets (People)

RT   **Commonwealth of Independent States**

        Former Soviet republics

        Russia

        Russia (Federation)

Soviet Union—Communism

USE   **Communism—Soviet Union**

Soviet Union—History   **947.084**

UF   Soviet Union—History—1917- *[Former heading]*

Soviet Union—History—1905, Revolution

USE   **Russia—History—1905, Revolution**

Soviet Union—History—1917-

USE   **Soviet Union—History**

Soviet Union—History—1917-1921, Revolution   **947.084**

UF   Revolution, Russian

        Russian revolution

BT   **Revolutions**

Soviet Union—History—1917-1925   **947.084**

Soviet Union—History—1925-1953   **947.084**

Soviet Union—History—1939-1940, War with Finland

USE   **Russo-Finnish War, 1939-1940**

Soviet Union—History—1953-

USE   **Soviet Union—History—1953-1991**

Soviet Union—History—1953-1985   **947.085**

BT = Broader Term   NT = Narrower Term   RT = Related Term   SA = See Also   UF = Used For

Soviet Union—History—1953-1991
    947.085
    UF   Soviet Union—History—1953-
        [Former heading]
Soviet Union—History—1985-
    USE   **Soviet Union—History—1985-
        1991**
Soviet Union—History—1985-1991
    947.085
    UF   Soviet Union—History—1985-
        [Former heading]
Soviet Union—Literatures
    USE   **Soviet literature**
Soviets (People)   920; 947.084
    Use for materials on the citizens of the So-
    viet Union between 1917 and 1991, not limit-
    ed to a single national or ethnic group. Mate-
    rials on the individual ethnic groups of the
    former Soviet Union are entered under the
    name for the ethnic group, e.g. **Russians;** etc.
    UF   Soviet people
    BT   **Soviet Union**
Soybean   633.3
    BT   **Forage plants**
Space age
    USE   **Astronautics and civilization**
Space and time   115
    UF   Time and space
    BT   **Fourth dimension**
        Metaphysics
        Space sciences
        Time
    NT   **Personal space**
    RT   **Relativity (Physics)**
Space-based weapons
    USE   **Space weapons**
Space biology   571.0919; 612
    Use for materials on the biology of humans
    or other earth creatures while in outer space.
    Materials on the possibility of indigenous life
    in outer space are entered under **Life on oth-
    er planets.**
    UF   Astrobiology
        Bioastronautics
        Cosmobiology
        Exobiology
    BT   **Biology**
        Space sciences
    NT   **Life on other planets**
        Space medicine
Space chemistry   523
    UF   Cosmic chemistry
        Cosmochemistry

    BT   **Chemistry**
Space colonies   629.44; 999
    Use for materials on communities estab-
    lished in space or on natural extraterrestrial
    bodies. Materials on bases established on nat-
    ural extraterrestrial bodies for specific func-
    tions other than colonization are entered under
    Extraterrestrial bases. Materials on manned
    installations orbiting in space for specific
    functions, such as servicing space ships, are
    entered under **Space stations.**
    UF   Colonies, Space
        Communities, Space
        Outer space—Colonies
    BT   **Astronautics and civilization**
    RT   **Extraterrestrial bases**
Space commercialization
    USE   **Space industrialization**
Space communication
    USE   **Astronautics—Communication
        systems**
        Interstellar communication
Space craft
    USE   **Space vehicles**
Space debris   629.4
    UF   Debris, Space
        Junk in space
        Orbital debris
        Outer space—Pollution
        Pollution, Space
        Space pollution
    BT   **Pollution**
        Space environment
Space environment   629.4
    UF   Environment, Space
        Extraterrestrial environment
        Space weather
    BT   **Astronomy**
        Outer space
    NT   **Cosmic rays**
        Solar radiation
        Space debris
Space exploration (Astronautics)
    USE   **Outer space—Exploration**
Space flight   629.4
    Use for materials on the physics and techni-
    cal details of flight beyond the earth's atmo-
    sphere. General materials and imaginary ac-
    counts of travel to other planets are entered
    under **Interplanetary voyages.**
    UF   Humans in space
        Man in space
        Manned space flight
        People in space

Space flight—*Continued*
> Rocket flight
> Space flight, Manned
> Space travel
> SA   names of projects, e.g. **Gemini project;** and space flight to particular places, e.g. **Space flight to the moon;** to be added as needed
> BT   **Aeronautics—Flights**
>   **Astronautics**
> NT   **Astronauts**
>   **Extravehicular activity (Space flight)**
>   **Gemini project**
>   **Orbital rendezvous (Space flight)**
>   **Outer space—Exploration**
>   **Space flight to the moon**
> RT   **Astrodynamics**
>   **Interplanetary voyages**
>   **Navigation (Astronautics)**
>   **Space medicine**
>   **Space vehicles**

Space flight (Fiction)
> USE   **Imaginary voyages**
>   **Science fiction**

Space flight—Law and legislation
> USE   **Space law**

Space flight, Manned
> USE   **Space flight**

Space flight—Rescue work
> USE   **Space rescue operations**

Space flight to the moon   629.45
> UF   Flight to the moon
>   Lunar expeditions
>   Moon, Voyages to
>   Voyages to the moon
> BT   **Astronautics**
>   **Space flight**
> NT   **Apollo project**
>   **Moon—Exploration**

Space heaters   644; 697
> BT   **Heating**
> NT   **Fireplaces**
>   **Stoves**

Space industrial processing
> USE   **Space industrialization**

Space industrialization   629.44
> UF   Commercial endeavors in space

Industrial uses of space
Manufacturing in space
Space commercialization
Space industrial processing
Space manufacturing
Space stations—Industrial applications
> BT   **Industrialization**

Space laboratories
> USE   **Space stations**

Space law   341.4
> UF   Aerospace law
>   Artificial satellites—Law and legislation
>   Astronautics—Law and legislation
>   Law, Space
>   Space flight—Law and legislation
>   Space stations—Law and legislation
> BT   **Astronautics and civilization**
>   **International law**
>   **Law**

Space manufacturing
> USE   **Space industrialization**

Space medicine   616.9
> UF   Aerospace medicine
>   Bioastronautics
> BT   **Medicine**
>   **Space biology**
>   **Space sciences**
> NT   **Life support systems (Space environment)**
>   **Weightlessness**
> RT   **Aviation medicine**
>   **Space flight**

Space navigation
> USE   **Navigation (Astronautics)**

Space nutrition
> USE   **Astronauts—Nutrition**

Space optics   535
> BT   **Optics**
>   **Space sciences**
> NT   **Astronautical instruments**
>   **Astronomical instruments**
> RT   **Optical instruments**
>   **Remote sensing**

BT = Broader Term   NT = Narrower Term   RT = Related Term   SA = See Also   UF = Used For

Space orbital rendezvous
   USE   **Orbital rendezvous (Space flight)**
Space, Outer
   USE   **Outer space**
Space, Personal
   USE   **Personal space**
Space photography   778.3
   UF   Astronautics, Photography in
        Photographs from space
        Photography from space
        Photography in astronautics
        Photography, Space
   SA   celestial bodies or objects in
        space with the subdivision
        Pictorial works, to be added
        as needed
   BT   **Photography**
        Photography—Scientific applications
   NT   **Mars (Planet)—Pictorial works**
        Moon—Pictorial works
Space platforms
   USE   **Space stations**
Space pollution
   USE   **Space debris**
Space power
   USE   **Astronautics and civilization**
Space probes   629.43
   Use for materials on space exploration by
   remote control from earth.
   UF   Probes, Space
   SA   types of probes, e.g. **Lunar probes; Mars probes;** etc.;
        and names of space vehicles
        and space projects, e.g.
        Project Voyager; to be added
        as needed
   BT   **Outer space—Exploration**
        Space vehicles
   NT   **Lunar probes**
        Mars probes
Space rescue operations   629.45
   UF   Rescue operations, Space
        Space flight—Rescue work
        Space vehicles—Rescue work
   BT   **Rescue work**
Space research
   USE   **Outer space—Exploration**
        Space sciences

Space rockets
   USE   **Space vehicles**
Space sciences   500.5
   Use for general materials and for scientific
   results of space exploration and scientific ap-
   plications of space flight.
   UF   Science and space
        Space research
   BT   **Science**
   NT   **Outer space**
        Space and time
        Space biology
        Space medicine
        Space optics
   RT   **Astronautics**
        Astronomy
Space sciences—International cooperation   500.5
   BT   **International cooperation**
Space ships
   USE   **Space vehicles**
Space shuttles   629.44
   Use for materials on reusable vehicles that
   transport equipment and personnel in space.
   UF   Reusable space vehicles
        Shuttles, Space
        Space vehicles, Reusable
   SA   names of individual space shut-
        tles, to be added as needed
   BT   **Space vehicles**
   NT   **Challenger (Spacecraft)**
Space stations   629.44
   Use for materials on manned installations
   orbiting in space for specific functions, such
   as servicing space ships. Materials on bases
   established on natural extraterrestrial bodies
   for specific functions other than colonization
   are entered under **Extraterrestrial bases.** Ma-
   terials on communities established in space or
   on natural extraterrestrial bodies are entered
   under **Space colonies.**
   UF   Laboratories, Space
        Orbital laboratories
        Orbiting vehicles
        Sky laboratories
        Space laboratories
        Space platforms
   BT   **Artificial satellites**
        Astronautics
        Space vehicles
   NT   **Orbital rendezvous (Space flight)**
Space stations—Industrial applications
   USE   **Space industrialization**

BT = Broader Term   NT = Narrower Term   RT = Related Term   SA = See Also   UF = Used For

Space stations—Law and legislation
   USE   **Space law**
Space suits   629.47
   UF   Astronauts—Clothing *[Former heading]*
   BT   **Life support systems (Space environment)**
Space telecommunication
   USE   **Interstellar communication**
Space television
   USE   **Television in astronautics**
Space travel
   USE   **Interplanetary voyages**
           Space flight
Space vehicle accidents   363.12; 629.4
   UF   Astronautical accidents
           Astronautics—Accidents *[Former heading]*
           Space vehicles—Accidents
   BT   **Accidents**
Space vehicles   629.47
   UF   Space craft
           Space rockets
           Space ships *[Former heading]*
           Spacecraft
   BT   **Rocketry**
   NT   **Lunar excursion module**
           Orbital rendezvous (Space flight)
           Rocket planes
           Space probes
           Space shuttles
           Space stations
   RT   **Artificial satellites**
           Astronautics
           Space flight
Space vehicles—Accidents
   USE   **Space vehicle accidents**
Space vehicles—Extravehicular activity
   USE   **Extravehicular activity (Space flight)**
Space vehicles—Guidance systems
           629.47
Space vehicles—Instruments
   USE   **Astronautical instruments**
Space vehicles—Piloting   629.45
   UF   Piloting (Astronautics)
   BT   **Astronauts**
           Navigation (Astronautics)

Space vehicles—Propulsion systems
           629.47
Space vehicles—Recovery   629.4
   UF   Recovery of space vehicles
Space vehicles—Rescue work
   USE   **Space rescue operations**
Space vehicles, Reusable
   USE   **Space shuttles**
Space vehicles—Thermodynamics
           629.47
   BT   **Thermodynamics**
Space vehicles—Tracking   629.4
   UF   Tracking of satellites
Space walk
   USE   **Extravehicular activity (Space flight)**
Space warfare   358
      Use for materials on interplanetary warfare, attacks on earth from outer space, and warfare among the nations of earth in outer space.
   UF   Earth—Space attack and defense
           Interplanetary warfare
           Interstellar warfare
           Space wars
           War, Space
           Warfare, Space
   BT   **Outer space**
   NT   **Space weapons**
           Strategic Defense Initiative
Space wars
   USE   **Space warfare**
Space weapons   358
   UF   Space-based weapons
           Star Wars weapons
           Weapons, Space
   BT   **Military weapons**
           Space warfare
   RT   **Strategic Defense Initiative**
Space weather
   USE   **Space environment**
Spacecraft
   USE   **Space vehicles**
Spain   946
      May be subdivided like United States except for *History.*
Spain—History   946
   NT   **Spanish-American War, 1898**
           Spanish Armada, 1588
Spain—History—1898, War of 1898
   USE   **Spanish-American War, 1898**

BT = Broader Term   NT = Narrower Term   RT = Related Term   SA = See Also   UF = Used For

Spain—History—1936-1939, Civil War
    946.081
Spain—History—1939-1975   946.082
Spain—History—1975-   946.083
Spanish America
   USE   **Latin America**
Spanish American literature
   USE   **American literature (Spanish)**
           Latin American literature
Spanish-American War, 1898   973.8
   UF   American-Spanish War, 1898
        Hispano-American War, 1898
        Spain—History—1898, War of
          1898
        United States—History—1898,
          War of 1898 *[Former head-*
          ing]
   BT   **Spain—History**
         United States—History—1865-
         1898
         United States—History—1898-
         1919
Spanish Armada, 1588   942.05; 946
   UF   Armada, 1588 *[Former heading]*
        Invincible Armada
   BT   **Great Britain—History—1485-**
         1603, Tudors
         Spain—History
Spanish language   460
   May be subdivided like **English language.**
   BT   **Language and languages**
         Romance languages
Spanish literature   860
   May use same subdivisions and names of
literary forms as for **English literature.**
   BT   **Literature**
         Romance literature
   RT   **Latin American literature**
Sparring
   USE   **Boxing**
Spas
   USE   **Health resorts**
         Physical fitness centers
Spastic paralysis
   USE   **Cerebral palsy**
Speakers (Recitation books)
   USE   **Recitations**
Speaking
   USE   **Debates and debating**
         Lectures and lecturing
         Preaching

         Public speaking
         Rhetoric
         Voice
Speaking choirs
   USE   **Choral speaking**
Speaking in tongues
   USE   **Glossolalia**
Speaking with tongues
   USE   **Glossolalia**
Spear fishing   799.1
   BT   **Fishing**
Special collections in libraries
   USE   **Libraries—Special collections**
Special education   371.9
   UF   Education, Special
   SA   classes of exceptional children
         with the subdivision *Educa-*
         tion, to be added as needed
   BT   **Education**
   NT   **Mentally handicapped chil-**
         dren—Education
   RT   **Mainstreaming in education**
Special libraries   026; 027.6
   Use for materials on libraries covering spe-
cialized subjects, containing special format
materials, or serving a specialized clientele.
   UF   Libraries, Special
   SA   types of special libraries, e.g.
         Business libraries; to be add-
         ed as needed
   BT   **Libraries**
   NT   **Business libraries**
         Corporate libraries
         Government libraries
         Music libraries
Special Olympics   796.087
   BT   **Olympic games**
         Sports for the handicapped
Specialists exchange programs
   USE   **Exchange of persons programs**
Specie
   USE   **Coins**
Specifications
   USE   types of engineering, construc-
         tion, industries, products, and
         merchandise with the subdivi-
         sion *Specifications,* for works
         on the particular qualities pre-
         scribed for a product to meet
         specific requirements, to be
         added as needed

BT = Broader Term   NT = Narrower Term   RT = Related Term   SA = See Also   UF = Used For

Specimens, Preservation of
    USE   **Plants—Collection and preser-**
           vation
           Taxidermy
           Zoological specimens—Collec-
           tion and preservation
           and types of natural specimens
           with the subdivision *Collec-*
           tion and preservation, e.g.
           Birds—Collection and pres-
           ervation; to be added as
           needed
Spectacles
    USE   **Eyeglasses**
Specters
    USE   **Apparitions**
           Ghosts
Spectra
    USE   **Spectrum analysis**
Spectrochemical analysis
    USE   **Spectrum analysis**
Spectrochemistry
    USE   **Spectrum analysis**
Spectroscopy
    USE   **Spectrum analysis**
Spectrum analysis   535.8
    UF   Analysis, Spectrum
          Spectra
          Spectrochemical analysis
          Spectrochemistry
          Spectroscopy
    BT   **Astronomy**
          Astrophysics
          Chemistry
          Optics
          Radiation
    NT   **Mass spectrometry**
    RT   **Light**
Speculation   332.64
    BT   **Finance**
    NT   **Real estate investment**
    RT   **Investments**
          Stock exchange
Speech   302.2; 372.62; 410; 612.7
    BT   **Language arts**
    NT   **Speech disorders**
          Speech processing systems
          Speech therapy
    RT   **Language and languages**
          Phonetics

          Voice
Speech correction
    USE   **Speech therapy**
Speech disorders   616.85
    UF   Defective speech
          Speech pathology
          Stammering
          Stuttering
    BT   **Speech**
Speech, Freedom of
    USE   **Freedom of speech**
Speech pathology
    USE   **Speech disorders**
Speech processing systems   006.5
    UF   Computer speech processing sys-
          tems
          Electronic speech processing sys-
          tems
          Speech scramblers
          Speech synthesis
    BT   **Speech**
          Telecommunication
    NT   **Automatic speech recognition**
    RT   **Computer sound processing**
Speech recognition, Automatic
    USE   **Automatic speech recognition**
Speech scramblers
    USE   **Speech processing systems**
Speech synthesis
    USE   **Speech processing systems**
Speech therapy   616.85
    UF   Speech correction
    BT   **Speech**
Speeches   808.85; 815.008, etc.
    Use for collections of speeches on several
    subjects and materials about speeches that
    have already been delivered. Materials on the
    art of delivering speeches are entered under
    Public speaking or under **Lectures and lec-**
    turing. Collections of speeches on a single
    subject are entered under that subject.
    UF   Addresses
          Orations
          Speeches, addresses, etc. *[For-*
          mer heading]
    SA   speeches of particular countries,
          e.g. **American speeches;** to
          be added as needed
    BT   **Literature**
    NT   **After dinner speeches**
          American speeches
          English speeches

BT = Broader Term   **NT** = Narrower Term   **RT** = Related Term   **SA** = See Also   **UF** = Used For

Speeches—*Continued*

    Presidents—United States—In-
        augural addresses
    Toasts
  RT Lectures and lecturing
      Public speaking

Speeches, addresses, etc.
  USE **Speeches**

Speeches, addresses, etc., American
  USE **American speeches**

Speeches, addresses, etc., English
  USE **English speeches**

Speed 531
  UF Velocity
  BT **Motion**

Speed (Drug)
  USE **Methamphetamine**

Speed reading 372.45
  UF Accelerated reading
      Faster reading
      Rapid reading *[Former heading]*
  BT **Reading**

Speed, Supersonic
  USE **Supersonic aerodynamics**

Speleology
  USE **Caves**

Spellers 418; 428.1, etc.
  BT **English language—Spelling**

Spelling
  USE names of languages with the
      subdivision *Spelling*, e.g. **Eng-
      lish language—Spelling;** to
      be added as needed

Spelling reform 418; 428.1, etc.
  UF English language—Spelling re-
      form
      Orthography
      Phonetic spelling
  BT **English language—Spelling**

Spells
  USE **Charms**
      Magic

Spherical trigonometry
  USE **Trigonometry**

Spices 641.3
  SA types of spices, to be added as
      needed
  BT **Food**

Spiders 595.4
  UF Arachnida

  BT **Invertebrates**

Spies 327.12; 353.1; 355.3
  UF Intelligence agents
      Spying
  BT **Espionage**
      Subversive activities
  RT **Secret service**

Spinal paralysis, Anterior
  USE **Poliomyelitis**

Spinning 677; 746.1
  BT **Textile industry**

Spiral gearing
  USE **Gearing**

Spires 721
  UF Steeples
  BT **Architecture**
      Church architecture

Spirit
  USE **Soul**

Spiritism
  USE **Spiritualism**

Spirits
  USE **Angels**
      Apparitions
      Demonology
      Ghosts
      Spiritualism
      Witchcraft

Spirits, Alcoholic
  USE **Liquors**

Spiritual gifts 234

    Use for materials on extraordinary phenom-
  ena, such as glossolalia, visions, prophecies
  and interpretations, healings, discernment of
  spirits, etc. Materials dealing collectively with
  ordinary spiritual phenomena, such as faith,
  hope, love, patience, temperance, etc., are entered under **Virtue.**
  UF Charismata
      Gifts of grace
      Gifts of the Holy Spirit
      Gifts, Spiritual
  BT **Grace (Theology)**
  NT **Glossolalia**
      Spiritual healing
      Visions
  RT **Catholic charismatic movement**
      Holy Spirit
      Pentecostalism

Spiritual healing 234; 291.2; 615.8
    Use for materials on the use of faith,
  prayer, or other religious means to treat ill-

BT = Broader Term   NT = Narrower Term   RT = Related Term   SA = See Also   UF = Used For

Spiritual healing—*Continued*

ness. Materials on psychic or psychological means to treat illness are entered under **Mental healing.**

    UF   Divine healing

            Evangelistic healing

            Faith cure

            Faith healing

            Healing, Spiritual

    BT   **Medicine—Religious aspects**

            Spiritual gifts

    RT   **Christian Science**

            Mental healing

            Mind and body

            Miracles

            Subconsciousness

            Suggestive therapeutics

Spiritual life   248; 291.4

    Use for materials on spiritual practices and on the relationship that individuals may attain with the sacred.

    BT   **Religious life**

    NT   **Conversion**

            Faith

            Hope

            Meditation

            Mysticism

Spiritualism   133.9

    Use for materials on extraordinary spiritual phenomena, especially contact with the spirits of the dead.

    UF   Spiritism

            Spirits

    BT   **Future life**

            Occultism

            Supernatural

    NT   **Clairvoyance**

            Psychokinesis

    RT   **Apparitions**

            Ghosts

            Parapsychology

Spirituals (Songs)   782.25

    BT   **American songs**

            Folk songs—United States

            Hymns

            Songs

    RT   **African American music**

            Gospel music

Splicing

    USE   **Knots and splices**

Splicing of genes

    USE   **Genetic engineering**

Split personality

    USE   **Multiple personality**

Spoils system

    USE   **Political corruption**

Sponges   593.4

    BT   **Invertebrates**

Spontaneous abortion

    USE   **Miscarriage**

Sport cars

    USE   **Sports cars**

Sporting equipment

    USE   **Sporting goods**

Sporting goods   796.028

    UF   Sporting equipment

            Sports—Equipment and supplies

            [Former heading]

    RT   **Sports**

Sports (May subdiv. geog.)   796

    SA   types of sports and names of sports competitions, to be added as needed

    BT   **Play**

            Recreation

    NT   **Aeronautical sports**

            Baseball

            Basketball

            Bullfights

            Coaching (Athletics)

            College sports

            Cycling

            Field hockey

            Football

            Gymnastics

            Olympic games

            Orienteering

            Professional sports

            Racing

            Rodeos

            Rowing

            School sports

            Soccer

            Sports cards

            Sports records

            Sportsmanship

            Tennis

            Track athletics

            Water sports

            Winter sports

    RT   **Amusements**

            Athletes

BT = Broader Term   NT = Narrower Term   RT = Related Term   SA = See Also   UF = Used For

Sports—*Continued*
>
> Athletics
> Games
> Outdoor life
> Physical education
> Sporting goods
> Sports facilities

Sports and drugs
>
> USE   **Athletes—Drug use**

Sports broadcasting
>
> USE   **Radio broadcasting of sports**
> **Television broadcasting of sports**

Sports cards   769
>
> UF   Cards, Sports
> SA   types of cards for specific sports, e.g. **Baseball cards;** to be added as needed
> BT   **Sports**
> NT   **Baseball cards**

Sports cars   629.222
>
> UF   Sport cars
> SA   names of specific sports cars, to be added as needed
> BT   **Automobiles**

Sports coaching
>
> USE   **Coaching (Athletics)**

Sports—Corrupt practices   796
>
> UF   Cheating in sports
> Corruption in sports
> Sports scandals

Sports drama (Films)   791.43
>
> May be used for individual works, collections, or materials about sports drama on film.
> BT   **Motion pictures**

Sports drama (Radio programs)   791.44
>
> May be used for individual works, collections, or materials about sports drama on the radio.
> BT   **Radio programs**

Sports drama (Television programs)
>   791.45
> May be used for individual works, collections, or materials about sports drama on television.
> BT   **Television programs**

Sports—Equipment and supplies
>
> USE   **Sporting goods**

Sports facilities   796.06
>
> SA   types of sports facilities, to be added as needed
> NT   **Playgrounds**

> Stadiums
> Swimming pools
> RT   **Recreation**
> **Sports**

Sports—Fiction   808.83; 813, etc.
>
> May be used for individual works, collections, or materials about sports stories.
> UF   Sports stories *[Former heading]*
> SA   types of sports with the subdivision *Fiction,* e.g. **Baseball—Fiction;** to be added as needed

Sports for the handicapped   796.01
>
> BT   **Handicapped**
> NT   **Special Olympics**

Sports in radio
>
> USE   **Radio broadcasting of sports**

Sports in television
>
> USE   **Television broadcasting of sports**

Sports—Medical aspects
>
> USE   **Sports medicine**

Sports medicine   613.7; 617.1
>
> UF   Athletic medicine
> Physical education—Medical aspects
> Sports—Medical aspects
> BT   **Medical care**
> **Medicine**

Sports records   796
>
> Use for materials on top performances or achievements.
> UF   Records, Sports
> BT   **Sports**
> RT   **Sports—Statistics**
> **World records**

Sports scandals
>
> USE   **Sports—Corrupt practices**

Sports—Statistics   796
>
> SA   types of sports with the subdivision *Statistics,* to be added as needed
> BT   **Statistics**
> RT   **Sports records**

Sports stories
>
> USE   **Sports—Fiction**

Sportsmanship   175
>
> BT   **Human behavior**
> **Sports**

Spot welding
>
> USE   **Electric welding**

BT = Broader Term   NT = Narrower Term   RT = Related Term   SA = See Also   UF = Used For

Spouses
USE   Husbands
       Wives
Spraying and dusting   632
    UF   Dusting and spraying
    BT   **Agricultural pests**
          Fruit—Diseases and pests
    NT   **Aeronautics in agriculture**
    RT   **Fungicides**
          Herbicides
          Insecticides
Spread sheets, Electronic
    USE   **Electronic spreadsheets**
Spreadsheeting, Electronic
    USE   **Electronic spreadsheets**
Spreadsheets, Electronic
    USE   **Electronic spreadsheets**
Spun glass
    USE   **Glass fibers**
Sputniks
    USE   **Soviet artificial satellites**
Spy films   791.43
    May be used for individual works, collections, or materials about spy films.
    UF   Espionage films
          Suspense films
    BT   **Motion pictures**
    RT   **Mystery films**
Spy novels
    USE   **Spy stories**
Spy radio programs   791.44
    May be used for individual works, collections, or materials about spy radio programs.
    UF   Suspense programs
    BT   **Radio programs**
Spy stories   808.83; 813, etc.
    May be used for individual works, collections, or materials about spy stories.
    UF   Espionage stories
          Spy novels
    BT   **Adventure fiction**
    RT   **Mystery fiction**
          Romantic suspense novels
Spy television programs   791.45
    May be used for individual works, collection, or materials about spy television programs.
    UF   Espionage television programs
          Suspense programs
    BT   **Television programs**
    RT   **Mystery television programs**

Spying
    USE   **Espionage**
           Spies
Square   516
    BT   **Geometry**
          Shape
Square dancing   793.3
    BT   **Folk dancing**
Square root   513.2
    BT   **Arithmetic**
Squirrels   599.36
    BT   **Mammals**
    NT   **Chipmunks**
SSTs
    USE   **Supersonic transport planes**
St. Bartholomew's Day, Massacre of, 1572
    USE   **Saint Bartholomew's Day,**
           Massacre of, 1572
St. Francis, Order of
    USE   **Franciscans**
St. Valentine's Day
    USE   **Valentine's Day**
Stabilization in industry
    USE   **Business cycles**
           Economic conditions
Stadia
    USE   **Stadiums**
Stadiums   796.06
    UF   Ballparks
          Stadia
    BT   **Sports facilities**
Stage
    USE   **Acting**
           Actors
           Drama
           Theater
Stage lighting   792
    UF   Television—Stage lighting
          Theaters—Stage lighting
    BT   **Lighting**
Stage scenery
    USE   **Theaters—Stage setting and**
           scenery
Stage setting
    USE   **Theaters—Stage setting and**
           scenery
Stagecoaches
    USE   **Carriages and carts**
Stained glass
    USE   **Glass painting and staining**

BT = Broader Term   NT = Narrower Term   RT = Related Term   SA = See Also   UF = Used For

Stamina, Physical
    USE   **Physical fitness**
Stammering
    USE   **Speech disorders**
Stamp collecting   769.56
    Use for materials on the collecting, buying,
and selling of postage stamps.
    UF   Philately
           Postage stamp collecting
           Postage stamps—Collectors and
              collecting *[Former heading]*
           Stamps—Collectors and collect-
              ing
    BT   **Collectors and collecting**
    RT   **Postage stamps**
Stamps—Collectors and collecting
    USE   **Stamp collecting**
Stamps, Postage
    USE   **Postage stamps**
Standard book numbers
    USE   **Publishers' standard book**
              numbers
Standard of living
    USE   **Cost and standard of living**
Standard of value
    USE   **Money**
Standard time
    USE   **Time**
Standards of output
    USE   **Production standards**
Star Wars (Ballistic missile defense sys-
    tem)
    USE   **Strategic Defense Initiative**
Star Wars films   791.43
    May be used for individual works, collec-
tions, or materials about Star Wars films.
    BT   **Motion pictures**
           Science fiction films
Star Wars weapons
    USE   **Space weapons**
Stars   523.8
    SA   names of constellations and of
           individual stars, e.g. **Sirius;** to
           be added as needed
    NT   **Black holes (Astronomy)**
           Galaxies
           Meteors
           Sirius
           Solar system
           Supernovas
    RT   **Astronomy**

           Constellations
Stars—Atlases   523.8022
    UF   Astronomy—Atlases
           Atlases, Astronomical
    BT   **Atlases**
Stars, Falling
    USE   **Meteors**
Starting a business
    USE   **New business enterprises**
Starvation   363.8
    NT   **Famines**
    RT   **Fasting**
           Hunger
           Malnutrition
Starvation, Self-imposed
    USE   **Anorexia nervosa**
State aid to education   379.1
    UF   Education—State aid
    BT   **Education and state**
           Education—Finance
State aid to libraries   021.8
    UF   Libraries—State aid
    BT   **Libraries—Government policy**
           Library finance
State and agriculture
    USE   **Agricultural subsidies**
           Agriculture—Government poli-
              cy
State and church
    USE   **Church and state**
State and education
    USE   **Education and state**
State and energy
    USE   **Energy policy**
State and environment
    USE   **Environmental policy**
State and industry
    USE   **Industrial policy**
State and insurance
    USE   **Social security**
State and railroads
    USE   **Railroads—Government policy**
State and science
    USE   **Science and state**
State and the arts
    USE   **Arts—Government policy**
           Federal aid to the arts
State birds   598
    BT   **Birds**
           State emblems

BT = Broader Term   NT = Narrower Term   RT = Related Term   SA = See Also   UF = Used For

State church
  USE   **Church and state**
State constitutions
  USE   **Constitutions**
           Constitutions—United States
State debts
  USE   **Public debts**
State emblems (May subdiv. geog.)
    929.9
  UF   Emblems, State
         State symbols
  SA   types of state emblems and state
         symbols, e.g. **State birds;**
         State flowers; to be added as
         needed
  BT   **Signs and symbols**
  NT   **State birds**
         State flowers
  RT   **National emblems**
State encouragement of the arts
  USE   **Arts—Government policy**
           Federal aid to the arts
State-federal relations
  USE   **Federal-state relations**
State flowers   **582.13**
  UF   Flowers, State
  BT   **Flowers**
         State emblems
State governments   **352.13**
    Use for general materials on state govern-
    ment. Materials on the government of a par-
    ticular state are entered under the name of the
    state with the subdivision *Politics and govern-*
    ment.
  UF   United States—State govern-
         ments
  SA   names of states with the subdi-
         vision *Politics and govern-*
         ment, to be added as needed
  BT   **Political science**
  NT   **Federal-state relations**
         Governors
         Ohio—Politics and government
         State-local relations
  RT   **Federal government**
State, Heads of
  USE   **Heads of state**
State libraries   **027.5**
    Use for materials on government libraries,
    maintained by state funds, that preserve state
    records and publications.
  BT   **Government libraries**

State-local relations   **342; 352.13**
  UF   City-state relations
         Local-state relations
  BT   **Local government**
         Municipal government
         State governments
State-local tax relations
  USE   **Intergovernmental tax relations**
State medicine   **362.1; 368.4; 614**
    Use for general materials on the relations of
    the state to medicine, public health, medical
    legislation, examinations of physicians by
    state boards, etc.
  UF   Medicine, State *[Former head-*
         ing]
         National health service
         Socialized medicine
  BT   **Medicine**
  NT   **Medicaid**
         Medicare
         Public health
  RT   **National health insurance**
State ministries
  USE   **Executive departments**
State of the Union messages
  USE   **Presidents—United States—**
           Messages
State ownership
  USE   **Government ownership**
State ownership of railroads
  USE   **Railroads—Government policy**
State planning
  USE   **Economic policy**
           Regional planning
           Social policy
State police   **363.2**
  UF   Police, State *[Former heading]*
  BT   **Police**
State regulation of industry
  USE   **Industrial policy**
State rights   **321.02; 342**
  UF   Secession
         States' rights
  BT   **Political science**
State songs   **782.42**
  BT   **Songs**
State symbols
  USE   **State emblems**
State, The   **320.1**
  UF   Administration
         Commonwealth, The

State, The—*Continued*
  NT   Church and state
          Education and state
          Public interest
          Science and state
          Welfare state
  RT   Political science
States, New
  USE   New states
States' rights
  USE   State rights
Statesmen (May subdiv. geog.)   **920**
  NT   **Diplomats**
          Heads of state
          Politicians
Statics   **531**
  BT   **Mechanics**
          Physics
  NT   **Hydrostatics**
          Strains and stresses
  RT   **Dynamics**
Statistical inference
  USE   **Probabilities**
Statistics   **001.4; 310**
    Use for materials on the theory and methods of statistics.
  SA   subjects and names of countries, cities, etc., with the subdivision *Statistics,* to be added as needed
  BT   **Economics**
  NT   **Agriculture—Statistics**
          Average
          Census
          Chicago (Ill.)—Statistics
          Education—Statistics
          Libraries—Statistics
          Ohio—Statistics
          Probabilities
          Railroads—Statistics
          Sampling (Statistics)
          Sports—Statistics
          United States—Statistics
          Vital statistics
Statistics—Graphic methods   **001.4**
  UF   Diagrams, Statistical
  BT   **Graphic methods**
Statues
  USE   **Monuments**
          Sculpture

Statutes
  USE   **Law**
Stealing   **364.16**
  UF   Larceny
          Theft
  BT   **Crime**
  NT   **Shoplifting**
  RT   **Thieves**
Steam   **536; 621.1**
  BT   **Heat**
          Power (Mechanics)
          Water
  RT   **Steam engineering**
Steam engineering   **621.1**
  BT   **Engineering**
  NT   **Steam engines**
          Steam navigation
          Steam power plants
  RT   **Mechanical engineering**
          Steam
Steam engines   **621.1**
  BT   **Engines**
          Heat engines
          Machinery
          Mechanics
          Steam engineering
  NT   **Condensers (Steam)**
          Locomotives
          Marine engines
          Steam turbines
Steam fitting
  USE   **Pipe fitting**
Steam heating   **697**
  BT   **Heating**
Steam navigation   **387; 623.8**
  BT   **Navigation**
          Steam engineering
          Transportation
  NT   **Marine engineering**
          Steam turbines
  RT   **Steamboats**
Steam power plants   **621.1**
  UF   Power plants, Steam
  BT   **Power plants**
          Steam engineering
Steam pumps
  USE   **Pumping machinery**
Steam turbines   **621.1**
  BT   **Steam engines**
          Steam navigation

BT = Broader Term   NT = Narrower Term   RT = Related Term   SA = See Also   UF = Used For

Steam turbines—*Continued*
  Turbines
Steamboats   387.2; 623.8
  UF   Steamships
  BT   **Boats and boating**
        Naval architecture
        Ocean travel
        Shipbuilding
        Ships
  RT   **Steam navigation**
Steamships
  USE   **Steamboats**
Steel   669; 672
  BT   **Iron**
        Metalwork
  NT   **Structural steel**
Steel construction   693
  UF   Building, Iron and steel *[Former*
        heading]
        Iron and steel building
  BT   **Building**
        Structural engineering
  RT   **Structural steel**
Steel engraving
  USE   **Engraving**
Steel industry   338.4; 672
  UF   Steel industry and trade *[Former*
        heading]
        Steel trade
  BT   **Industries**
  RT   **Iron industry**
Steel industry and trade
  USE   **Steel industry**
Steel industry—Labor productivity
        338.4
  BT   **Labor productivity**
Steel industry—Quality control   338.4;
        672
  BT   **Quality control**
Steel, Structural
  USE   **Structural steel**
Steel trade
  USE   **Steel industry**
Steeples
  USE   **Spires**
Steers
  USE   **Beef cattle**
Stencil work   686.2; 745.7
  BT   **Decoration and ornament**
        Painting

  NT   **Silk screen printing**
Stenography
  USE   **Shorthand**
Step-family
  USE   **Stepfamily**
Stepfamilies
  USE   **Stepfamily**
Stepfamily   306.85
  UF   Blended family
        Step-family
        Stepfamilies
  BT   **Family**
Stereo photography
  USE   **Three dimensional photogra-**
        phy
Stereo sound systems
  USE   **Stereophonic sound systems**
Stereophonic sound systems   621.389
  UF   Stereo sound systems
  BT   **High-fidelity sound systems**
        Sound—Recording and repro-
        ducing
Stereophotography
  USE   **Three dimensional photogra-**
        phy
Stereoscopic photography
  USE   **Three dimensional photogra-**
        phy
Stereotype (Psychology)   303.3
  UF   Mental stereotype
        Stereotyped behavior
  BT   **Attitude (Psychology)**
        Social psychology
        Thought and thinking
Stereotyped behavior
  USE   **Stereotype (Psychology)**
Sterility in animals
  USE   **Infertility**
Sterility in humans
  USE   **Infertility**
Sterilization (Birth control)   363.9;
        613.9
  BT   **Birth control**
  NT   **Vasectomy**
Steroids   572; 612
  UF   Anabolic steroids
  BT   **Biochemistry**
        Drugs
  RT   **Athletes—Drug use**
        Hormones

BT = Broader Term   NT = Narrower Term   RT = Related Term   SA = See Also   UF = Used For

Stewardesses, Airline
USE **Flight attendants**
Stewards, Airline
USE **Flight attendants**
Stills
USE **Distillation**
Stimulants   613.8; 615
SA types of stimulants, e.g. **Amphetamines;** and names of individual stimulants, to be added as needed
BT **Drugs**
Psychotropic drugs
NT **Amphetamines**
Hallucinogens
Stock and stock breeding
USE **Livestock industry**
Stock control
USE **Inventory control**
Stock exchange   332.64
UF Securities exchange
Stock market
BT **Commerce**
Exchange
Finance
NT **Bonds**
Foreign exchange
Insider trading
Securities
Wall Street (New York, N.Y.)
RT **Investments**
Speculation
Stocks
Stock exchange crashes
USE **Financial crises**
Stock judging
USE **Livestock judging**
Stock market
USE **Stock exchange**
Stock market panics
USE **Financial crises**
Stock raising
USE **Livestock industry**
Stockings
USE **Hosiery**
Stocks   332.63
UF Dividends
Shares of stock
BT **Commerce**
Securities

NT **Corporations**
RT **Bonds**
Investments
Stock exchange
Stocks—Insider trading
USE **Insider trading**
Stockyards
USE **Meat industry**
Stoics   188
BT **Ancient philosophy**
Ethics
STOL aircraft
USE **Short take off and landing aircraft**
Stomach   612.3
BT **Anatomy**
RT **Digestion**
Stone   553.5; 693
Use for materials on stone as a building material. General materials on naturally occurring solid minerals are entered under **Rocks.**
SA types of stone, e.g. **Marble;** to be added as needed
BT **Building materials**
Economic geology
NT **Granite**
Marble
Masonry
Stonecutting
RT **Petrology**
Quarries and quarrying
Rocks
Stone Age   930.1
UF Eolithic period
Neolithic period
Paleolithic period
NT **Stone implements**
RT **Archeology**
Stone-cutting
USE **Stonecutting**
Stone implements   930.1
UF Flint implements
Implements, utensils, etc.
BT **Archeology**
Stone Age
Stone quarries
USE **Quarries and quarrying**
Stonecutting   693
UF Stone-cutting
BT **Masonry**
Stone

BT = Broader Term   NT = Narrower Term   RT = Related Term   SA = See Also   UF = Used For

Stoneware
USE   Pottery
Storage batteries   621.31
UF   Batteries, Electric
BT   Electric apparatus and appli-
ances
RT   Electric batteries
Storage devices, Computer
USE   Computer storage devices
Storage in the home   648
UF   Home storage
BT   Home economics
Store buildings
USE   Commercial buildings
Stores (May subdiv. geog.)   381
UF   Retail stores
Shops
SA   types of stores, e.g. Drugstores;
to be added as needed
BT   Commercial buildings
Retail trade
NT   Chain stores
Department stores
Discount stores
Drugstores
Supermarkets
RT   Shopping centers and malls
Stories
USE   Anecdotes
Bible stories
Fairy tales
Fiction
Legends
Romances
Short stories
Stories in rhyme
Stories without words
Storytelling
and for collections of plots,
Literature—Stories, plots,
etc.; and literary and musical
forms with the subdivision
Stories, plots, etc., e.g. Bal-
let—Stories, plots, etc.; Op-
era—Stories, plots, etc.; etc.,
to be added as needed
Stories in rhyme   811, etc.
Use as a form heading for narrative poems
for very young children. Narrative poetry and
materials about narrative poetry for older chil-

dren and for adults are entered under Narra-
tive poetry.
UF   Stories
BT   Narrative poetry
Rhyme
Stories, plots, etc.
USE   Literature—Stories, plots, etc.
and literary and musical forms
with the subdivision Stories,
plots, etc., e.g. Ballet—Sto-
ries, plots, etc.; Opera—Sto-
ries, plots, etc.; etc., to be
added as needed
Stories without words
Use as a form heading for stories for chil-
dren told only through a sequence of pictures.
UF   Nonword stories
Picture books for children,
Wordless
Stories
Wordless stories
BT   Picture books for children
Storms (May subdiv. geog.)   551.55
SA   types of storms, to be added as
needed
BT   Meteorology
Natural disasters
Weather
NT   Blizzards
Cyclones
Dust storms
Hurricanes
Thunderstorms
Tornadoes
Typhoons
RT   Rain
Snow
Winds
Story theater
USE   Readers' theater
Storytelling   027.62; 372.67
UF   Stories
BT   Children's literature
RT   Folklore
Short story
Storytelling—Collections   808.85
Use for collections of stories compiled pri-
marily for oral presentation.
UF   Collected works
Collections of literature

BT = Broader Term   NT = Narrower Term   RT = Related Term   SA = See Also   UF = Used For

Stoves   697
  BT   Heating
        Space heaters
Strain (Psychology)
  USE   Stress (Psychology)
Strains and stresses   531; 620.1; 624.1
  UF   Architectural engineering
        Stresses
  BT   Mechanics
        Statics
        Structural analysis (Engineer-
          ing)
  RT   Strength of materials
Strangers and children
  USE   Children and strangers
Strategic Defense Initiative   358.1
  UF   SDI (Ballistic missile defense
          system)
        Star Wars (Ballistic missile de-
          fense system)
  BT   Space warfare
        United States—Defenses
        United States—Military policy
  RT   Space weapons
Strategic materials
  USE   Materials
Strategy   355.4
  UF   Military strategy
        Naval strategy
  SA   countries and areas of the world
          with the subdivision *Strategic
          aspects*, e.g. **Middle East—
          Strategic aspects**; to be add-
          ed as needed
  BT   War
  NT   Middle East—Strategic aspects
        Tactics
  RT   Military art and science
        Naval art and science
Stratigraphic geology   551.7
  UF   Geology, Historical
        Geology, Stratigraphic *[Former
          heading]*
        Historical geology
  BT   Geology
  NT   Fossils
Stratosphere   551.5
  BT   Upper atmosphere
  NT   Ozone layer

Stratospheric ozone
  USE   Ozone layer
Straw votes
  USE   Public opinion polls
Strawberries   634
  BT   Berries
Stream animals   578.76
  UF   River animals
        Stream fauna
  BT   Animals
        Rivers
        Wildlife
Stream fauna
  USE   Stream animals
Streamlining
  USE   Aerodynamics
Street cars
  USE   Street railroads
Street cleaning   363.72; 628.4
  BT   Cleaning
        Municipal engineering
        Public health
        Roads
        Sanitary engineering
        Streets
  RT   Refuse and refuse disposal
Street gangs
  USE   Gangs
Street lighting
  USE   Streets—Lighting
Street literature
  USE   Pamphlets
Street people
  USE   Homeless persons
Street railroads   388.4; 625.6
  UF   Interurban railroads
        Railroads, Street
        Street cars
        Trams
        Trolley cars
  BT   Local transit
        Public utilities
        Railroads
        Transportation
  NT   Subways
  RT   Cable railroads
        Electric railroads
Street traffic
  USE   City traffic
        Traffic engineering

BT = Broader Term   NT = Narrower Term   RT = Related Term   SA = See Also   UF = Used For

687

Street traffic—*Continued*
> **Traffic regulations**

Streets (May subdiv. geog.) 388.4;
625.7
- UF   Alleys
  - Avenues
  - Boulevards
  - Thoroughfares
- BT   **Cities and towns**
  - **Civil engineering**
  - **Transportation**
- NT   **City traffic**
  - **Street cleaning**
- RT   **Pavements**
  - **Roads**

Streets—Chicago (Ill.) 977.3
- UF   Chicago (Ill.)—Streets

Streets—Lighting 628.9
- UF   Cities and towns—Lighting
  - Street lighting
- BT   **Lighting**

Streets—New York (N.Y.) 974.7
- UF   New York (N.Y.)—Streets
- RT   **Wall Street (New York, N.Y.)**

Strength of materials 620.1
- UF   Materials, Strength of
  - Resistance of materials
  - Testing
- SA   types of materials with the subdivision *Testing,* e.g. **Concrete—Testing;** to be added as needed
- BT   **Building**
  - **Civil engineering**
  - **Materials**
  - **Mechanics**
  - **Structural analysis (Engineering)**
- NT   **Concrete—Testing**
- RT   **Building materials**
  - **Strains and stresses**

Strength training
- USE   **Weight lifting**

Stress (Physiology) 612; 616.8
- UF   Physiological stress
  - Tension (Physiology)
- BT   **Adaptation (Biology)**
  - **Physiology**
- NT   **Job stress**

Stress (Psychology) 155.9; 616.89
- UF   Emotional stress
  - Mental stress
  - Psychological stress
  - Strain (Psychology)
  - Tension (Psychology)
- BT   **Mental health**
  - **Psychology**
- NT   **Anxiety**
  - **Burn out (Psychology)**
  - **Job stress**
  - **Post-traumatic stress disorder**

Stresses
- USE   **Strains and stresses**

Strikes (May subdiv. geog.) 331.892
> This heading may also be subdivided by industry or occupation and then geographically, e.g. **Strikes—Automobile industry—United States.**

- UF   Lockouts
  - Picketing
  - Sit-down strikes
  - Strikes and lockouts *[Former heading]*
  - Work stoppages
- BT   **Industrial relations**
  - **Labor disputes**
- NT   **Sabotage**
- RT   **Collective bargaining**
  - **Industrial arbitration**
  - **Injunctions**
  - **Labor unions**

Strikes and lockouts
- USE   **Strikes**

Strikes—Automobile industry—United States 331.892

Strikes—United States 331.892
- UF   United States—Strikes
  - United States—Strikes and lockouts

String orchestra music 784.7
- BT   **Orchestral music**

Stringed instruments 787
- UF   Bowed instruments
- SA   types of stringed instruments, to be added as needed
- BT   **Musical instruments**
- NT   **Guitars**
  - **Violins**
  - **Violoncellos**

BT = Broader Term   NT = Narrower Term   RT = Related Term   SA = See Also   UF = Used For

Strip films
  USE   **Filmstrips**
Stroke   616.8
  UF   Apoplexy
         Cerebrovascular disease
  BT   **Brain—Diseases**
Structural analysis (Engineering)   624
  UF   Architectural engineering
         Theory of structures *[Former
            heading]*
  BT   **Structural engineering**
  NT   **Strains and stresses**
         Strength of materials
Structural botany
  USE   **Plants—Anatomy**
Structural drafting
  USE   **Mechanical drawing**
Structural engineering   624.1
  UF   Engineering, Structural
  BT   **Civil engineering**
         Engineering
  NT   **Building**
         Foundations
         Hydraulic structures
         Soil mechanics
         Steel construction
         **Structural analysis (Engineer-
            ing)**
Structural failures   624.1
  UF   Collapse of structures
         Failures, Structural
  SA   types of structural failures, e.g.
         Building failures; to be add-
            ed as needed
  BT   **Reliability (Engineering)**
  NT   **Building failures**
Structural materials
  USE   **Building materials**
Structural psychology
  USE   **Gestalt psychology**
Structural steel   691
  UF   Steel, Structural *[Former head-
            ing]*
  BT   **Building materials**
         Civil engineering
         Steel
  RT   **Steel construction**
Structural zoology
  USE   **Animals—Anatomy**

Structures
  USE   **Buildings**
Structures, Offshore
  USE   **Drilling platforms**
Stucco   693
  BT   **Building materials**
         Decoration and ornament
         Plaster and plastering
Student activities   371.8
  UF   Extracurricular activities
  BT   **Student life**
  NT   **After school programs**
         Cheerleading
         College and school drama
         College and school journalism
         College sports
         Field trips
         School assembly programs
         School sports
Student aid   371.2; 378.3
  UF   Financial aid, Student
         Financial aid to students
         Student financial aid
         Student financial assistance
  BT   **College costs**
         Loans
  NT   **Scholarships**
         Student loan funds
Student busing
  USE   **Busing (School integration)**
Student clubs
  USE   **Students—Societies**
Student councils
  USE   **Student government**
Student customs
  USE   **Student life**
Student dropouts
  USE   **Dropouts**
Student evaluation of teachers   371.14
  UF   Student rating of teachers
         Teachers, Student rating of
  BT   **Teacher-student relationships**
Student financial aid
  USE   **Student aid**
Student financial assistance
  USE   **Student aid**
Student government   371.5
  UF   Honor system
         Self-government (in education)
            [Former heading]

BT = Broader Term   NT = Narrower Term   RT = Related Term   SA = See Also   UF = Used For

Student government—*Continued*
Student councils
Student self-government
BT **School discipline**
Schools—Administration
Student guidance
USE **Educational counseling**
Student life   371.8
UF Student customs
BT **Students**
NT **Student activities**
Student loan funds   371.2; 378.3
UF Loan funds, Student
BT **College costs**
Student aid
Student movement
USE **Youth movement**
Student promotion
USE **Promotion (School)**
Student protests, demonstrations, etc.
USE **Students—Political activity**
Youth movement
Student rating of teachers
USE **Student evaluation of teachers**
Student revolt
USE **Students—Political activity**
Youth movement
Student self-government
USE **Student government**
Student societies
USE **Students—Societies**
Student songs
USE **Students' songs**
Student-teacher interaction
USE **Teacher-student relationships**
Student teaching   370.71
UF Practice teaching
Teachers—Practice teaching
BT **Teachers—Training**
Teaching
Student to student counseling
USE **Peer counseling**
Student violence
USE **School violence**
Student yearbooks
USE **School yearbooks**
Students (May subdiv. geog.)   **371.8**
UF School life

SA types of students, e.g. **College students;** to be added as needed
NT **At risk students**
College students
Dropouts
Foreign students
High school students
School children
Student life
Students and libraries
USE **Libraries and students**
Students— Counseling
USE **Educational counseling**
Students, Foreign
USE **Foreign students**
Students—Grading and marking
USE **Grading and marking (Education)**
Students' military training camps
USE **Military training camps**
Students—Political activity   324; 371.8
UF Politics and students
Student protests, demonstrations, etc.
Student revolt
BT **Political participation**
Youth movement
Students—Societies   371.8
UF School clubs
Student clubs
Student societies
BT **Societies**
NT **Fraternities and sororities**
Students' songs   782.42
UF College songs
Student songs
BT **Songs**
NT **United States Military Academy—Songs**
Students—United States   371.80973
UF United States—Students
Students with problems
USE **At risk students**
Students—Yearbooks
USE **School yearbooks**
Study abroad
USE **Foreign study**
Study and teaching
USE **Education**

BT = Broader Term   NT = Narrower Term   RT = Related Term   SA = See Also   UF = Used For

Study and teaching—*Continued*
    and subjects with the subdivision *Study and teaching,* e.g. **Science—Study and teaching;** to be added as needed
Study, Foreign
  USE **Foreign study**
Study, Method of
  USE **Study skills**
Study overseas
  USE **Foreign study**
Study skills 371.3028
  UF Learning, Art of
      Method of study
      Study, Method of *[Former heading]*
      Study strategies
  SA subjects with the subdivision *Study and teaching,* e.g. **Art—Study and teaching;** to be added as needed
  BT **Education**
      Teaching
  NT **Homework**
      Independent study
      Self-instruction
Study strategies
  USE **Study skills**
Stunt flying 797.5
  UF Aerobatic flying
      Aerobatics
  BT **Airplanes—Piloting**
Stunt men
  USE **Stunt performers**
Stunt men and women
  USE **Stunt performers**
Stunt performers 791.4
  UF Stunt men
      Stunt men and women *[Former heading]*
  BT **Actors**
Stuttering
  USE **Speech disorders**
Style in dress
  USE **Costume**
      Fashion
Style, Literary
  USE **Literary style**
Style manikins
  USE **Fashion models**

Style manuals
  USE **Printing—Style manuals**
Sub-Saharan Africa 960
  UF Africa, Sub-Saharan *[Former heading]*
      Black Africa
  BT **Africa**
Subconsciousness 127; 154.2
  BT **Parapsychology**
      Psychology
  NT **Hallucinations and illusions**
      Mental suggestion
      Sleep
  RT **Consciousness**
      Dreams
      Hypnotism
      Mental healing
      Mind and body
      Psychoanalysis
      Spiritual healing
      Telepathy
Subculture
  USE **Counter culture**
Subgravity state
  USE **Weightlessness**
Subject catalogs 016; 017
  UF Catalogs, Subject *[Former heading]*
  BT **Library catalogs**
  NT **Subject headings**
Subject dictionaries
  USE **Encyclopedias and dictionaries**
Subject headings 025.4
  UF Thesauri
  BT **Cataloging**
      Indexes
      Subject catalogs
Submarine boats
  USE **Submarines**
      Submersibles
Submarine cables 384.1; 384.6
  UF Atlantic cable
      Cables, Submarine *[Former heading]*
      Ocean cables
      Pacific cable
      Submarine telegraph
      Telegraph, Submarine
  BT **Telecommunication**
      Telegraph

BT = Broader Term   NT = Narrower Term   RT = Related Term   SA = See Also   UF = Used For

Submarine diving
   USE   **Deep diving**
Submarine engineering
   USE   **Ocean engineering**
Submarine exploration
   USE   **Underwater exploration**
Submarine geology   551.46
   UF   Geology, Submarine
         Marine geology
         Underwater geology
   BT   **Geology**
         Oceanography
   NT   **Ocean bottom**
   RT   **Plate tectonics**
Submarine medicine   616.9
   UF   Medicine, Submarine
         Underwater medicine
         Underwater physiology
   BT   **Medicine**
Submarine oil well drilling
   USE   **Offshore oil well drilling**
Submarine photography
   USE   **Underwater photography**
Submarine research stations
   USE   **Undersea research stations**
Submarine telegraph
   USE   **Submarine cables**
Submarine vehicles
   USE   **Submersibles**
Submarine warfare   359.9
   UF   Naval warfare
         Warfare, Submarine
   BT   **Naval art and science**
         War
   NT   **Submarines**
         Torpedoes
         World War, 1939-1945—Naval
         operations—Submarine
Submarines   359.9; 623.8
   Use for materials on submarines only. Materials on other underwater craft are entered under **Submersibles.**
   UF   Boats, Submarine
         Submarine boats
         U boats
   BT   **Ships**
         Submarine warfare
         Submersibles
         Warships
   NT   **Nuclear submarines**

Submarines, Nuclear
   USE   **Nuclear submarines**
Submersibles   623.8
   UF   Boats, Submarine
         Deep diving vehicles
         Deep sea vehicles
         Deep submergence vehicles
         Oceanographic submersibles
         Submarine boats
         Submarine vehicles
         Undersea vehicles
         Underwater exploration devices
   SA   types of submersibles, to be
         added as needed
   BT   **Vehicles**
   NT   **Bathyscaphe**
         Submarines
Subscription television   384.55
   UF   Pay television, Subscription
         Television, Subscription
   BT   **Television broadcasting**
   NT   **Home Box Office**
Subsidies   338.9
   UF   Bounties
         Federal aid
         Grants
         Subventions
   SA   types of subsidies, e.g. **Agricul-**
         tural subsidies; and federal
         aid to specific endeavors, e.g.
         Federal aid to the arts; to
         be added as needed
   BT   **Domestic economic assistance**
         Economic policy
         Industrial policy
   NT   **Agricultural subsidies**
         Federal aid to education
         Federal aid to libraries
         Federal aid to minority busi-
         ness enterprises
         Federal aid to the arts
         Transfer payments
Subsidies, Agricultural
   USE   **Agricultural subsidies**
Subsidies, Farm
   USE   **Agricultural subsidies**
Subsistence economy   330.9
   BT   **Cost and standard of living**
   NT   **Barter**
   RT   **Poverty**

BT = Broader Term   NT = Narrower Term   RT = Related Term   SA = See Also   UF = Used For

Substance abuse
   USE   **Drug abuse**
           Solvent abuse
Substantive due process
   USE   **Due process of law**
Substitute products
   UF   Ersatz products
   SA   types of substitute products, e.g.
           Sugar substitutes; to be add-
           ed as needed
   BT   **Commercial products**
   NT   **Sugar substitutes**
   RT   **Synthetic products**
Subterranean voyages
   USE   **Imaginary voyages**
Subtraction   513.2
   BT   **Arithmetic**
Suburban areas
   USE   **Suburbs**
Suburban life   307.74
   BT   **Suburbs**
Suburbs (May subdiv. geog.)   307.76
   UF   Suburban areas
           Suburbs and environs
   SA   names of suburban areas, e.g.
           Chicago Suburban Area
           (Ill.); to be added as needed
   BT   **Cities and towns—Growth**
           City planning
           Metropolitan areas
   NT   **Suburban life**
Suburbs and environs
   USE   **Suburbs**
Subventions
   USE   **Subsidies**
Subversive activities (May subdiv. geog.)
       322.4; 327.12

   Use for materials on any attempt to subvert, overthrow, or cause the destruction of any established or legally constituted government. Materials on the offense of acting to overthrow one's own government or to harm or kill its sovereign are entered under **Treason.**

   UF   Fifth column
   BT   **Insurgency**
   NT   **Espionage**
           Political crimes and offenses
           Sabotage
           Spies
           Terrorism
           Treason
   RT   **Internal security**

Subways   388.4; 625.4
   UF   Railroads, Underground
           Underground railroads
   BT   **Local transit**
           Street railroads
Success   158; 646.7
   UF   Fortune
           Personal development
   BT   **Business ethics**
           Wealth
   NT   **Academic achievement**
           Leadership
           Life skills
           Saving and thrift
   RT   **Ability**
           Self-realization
Succession, Intestate
   USE   **Inheritance and succession**
Sudden death in infants
   USE   **Sudden infant death syndrome**
Sudden infant death
   USE   **Sudden infant death syndrome**
Sudden infant death syndrome   618.92
   UF   Cot death
           Crib death
           Infant sudden death
           SIDS (Disease)
           Sudden death in infants
           Sudden infant death
   BT   **Infants—Death**
Suffering   128; 152.1; 214
   UF   Affliction
   RT   **Joy and sorrow**
           Pain
Suffrage   324.6
   UF   Franchise
           Voting
   SA   ethnic groups and classes of persons with the subdivision *Suffrage,* to be added as needed
   BT   **Citizenship**
           Constitutional law
           Democracy
           Elections
           Political science
   NT   **African Americans—Suffrage**
           Blacks—Suffrage
           Naturalization
           Voter registration
           Women—Suffrage

BT = Broader Term   **NT** = Narrower Term   **RT** = Related Term   **SA** = See Also   **UF** = Used For

Suffrage—*Continued*
   RT   **Representative government and representation**
Suffragettes
   USE   **Suffragists**
Suffragists (May subdiv. geog.) **324.6; 920**
   UF   Suffragettes
   BT   **Reformers**
   RT   **Feminism**
        Women—Suffrage
Sugar **641.3; 664**
   SA   types of sugar, to be added as needed
   BT   **Food**
   NT   **Maple sugar**
        Syrups
Sugar substitutes **641.3; 664**
   UF   Artificial sweeteners
        Nonnutritive sweeteners
   BT   **Substitute products**
Suggestion, Mental
   USE   **Mental suggestion**
Suggestive therapeutics **615.8**
   UF   Therapeutics, Suggestive *[Former heading]*
   BT   **Therapeutics**
   RT   **Hypnotism**
        Mental healing
        Mental suggestion
        Psychotherapy
        Spiritual healing
Suicide **179.7; 362.28**
   BT   **Medical jurisprudence**
        Social problems
   RT   **Homicide**
        Right to die
Suing (Law)
   USE   **Litigation**
Suite (Music) **784.18**
   Use for musical scores and for materials on the suite as a musical form.
   UF   Partita
        Suites *[Former heading]*
   BT   **Musical form**
        Orchestral music
Suites
   USE   **Suite (Music)**
Suits (Law)
   USE   **Litigation**

Suits of armor
   USE   **Armor**
Sulfa drugs
   USE   **Sulfonamides**
Sulfonamides **615**
   UF   Sulfa drugs
   BT   **Drugs**
Sulfur
   USE   **Sulphur**
Sulphur **546; 553.6; 661**
   UF   Sulfur
   BT   **Chemical elements**
Summer camps
   USE   **Camps**
Summer employment **331.1**
   BT   **Employment**
   RT   **Teenagers—Employment**
        Youth—Employment
Summer resorts **790**
   BT   **Resorts**
Summer schools **371.2**
   UF   Vacation schools
   BT   **Public schools**
        Schools
   NT   **Religious summer schools**
Summer schools, Religious
   USE   **Religious summer schools**
Sun **523.7**
   UF   Solar physics
   BT   **Astronomy**
        Solar system
   NT   **Solar energy**
        Sunspots
Sun-dials
   USE   **Sundials**
Sun—Eclipses
   USE   **Solar eclipses**
Sun (in religion, folklore, etc.)
   USE   **Sun worship**
Sun powered batteries
   USE   **Solar batteries**
Sun—Radiation
   USE   **Solar radiation**
Sun-spots
   USE   **Sunspots**
Sun worship **291.2**
   UF   Sun (in religion, folklore, etc.)
   BT   **Religion**
Sunday schools **268**
   UF   Bible classes

BT = Broader Term   NT = Narrower Term   RT = Related Term   SA = See Also   UF = Used For

Sunday schools—*Continued*
  BT   Church work
          Religious education
  NT   Bible—Study and teaching
Sundials   681.1
  UF   Horology
          Sun-dials
  BT   Clocks and watches
          Garden ornaments and furni-
            ture
          Time
Sunken cities
  USE   Extinct cities
Sunken treasure
  USE   Buried treasure
Sunspots   523.7
  UF   Sun-spots
  BT   Meteorology
          Solar radiation
          Sun
Super markets
  USE   Supermarkets
Supercomputers   004.1
    Use for materials on extraordinarily power-
    ful computers.
  BT   Computers
Superconducting materials
  USE   Superconductors
Superconductive devices
  USE   Superconductors
Superconductivity
  USE   Superconductors
Superconductors   537.6; 621.3
  UF   Superconducting materials
          Superconductive devices
          Superconductivity
  BT   Electric conductors
          Electronics
Superhero comic books, strips, etc.
      741.5
    May be used for individual works, collec-
    tions, or materials about superhero comics.
  BT   Comic books, strips, etc.
Superhero films   791.43
    May be used for individual works, collec-
    tions, or materials about superhero films.
  SA   films with particular superheroes,
          e.g. **Superman films**; to be
          added as needed
  BT   Adventure films
  NT   Superman films

Superhero radio programs   791.44
    May be used for individual works, collec-
    tions, or materials about superhero radio pro-
    grams.
  BT   Adventure radio programs
Superhero television programs   791.45
    May be used for individual works, collec-
    tions, or materials about superhero television
    programs.
  BT   Adventure television programs
Superhighways
  USE   Express highways
Superintendents of schools
  USE   School superintendents and
            principals
Superior children
  USE   Gifted children
Superman films   791.43
    May be used for individual works, collec-
    tions, or materials about Superman films.
  BT   Superhero films
Supermarket shopping
  USE   Grocery shopping
Supermarkets   658.8
  UF   Super markets
  BT   Grocery trade
          Retail trade
          Stores
Supernatural   133; 291.2; 398.2
  BT   Religion
  NT   Divination
          Occultism
          Parapsychology
          Prophecies
          Revelation
          Spiritualism
  RT   Miracles
Supernovae
  USE   Supernovas
Supernovas   523.8
  UF   Supernovae
  BT   Stars
Supersonic aerodynamics   629.132
  UF   Aerodynamics, Supersonic *[For-
            mer heading]*
          High speed aerodynamics
          Speed, Supersonic
  BT   Aerodynamics
          High speed aeronautics
  NT   Aerothermodynamics
Supersonic airliners
  USE   Supersonic transport planes

BT = Broader Term   NT = Narrower Term   RT = Related Term   SA = See Also   UF = Used For

Supersonic transport planes 629.133
    UF   S.S.T.'s
           SSTs
           Supersonic airliners
    BT   **Jet planes**
Supersonic waves
    USE   **Ultrasonic waves**
Supersonics
    USE   **Ultrasonics**
Superstition 001.9; 398
    UF   Traditions
    BT   **Folklore**
    NT   **Alchemy**
           Apparitions
           Astrology
           Charms
           Exorcism
           Fairies
           Fortune telling
           Vampires
           Witchcraft
    RT   **Demonology**
           Divination
           Errors
           Ghosts
           Occultism
Supervision of employees
    USE   **Personnel management**
Supervision of schools
    USE   **School supervision**
Supervisors 331.7; 658.3
    UF   Foremen
           Managers
    BT   **Factory management**
           Personnel management
Supplementary employment 331.1
    UF   Double employment
           Dual employment
           Employment, Supplementary
           Moonlighting
           Second job
           Secondary employment
    BT   **Labor**
           Part-time employment
Support of children
    USE   **Child support**
Supreme Court—United States
    USE   **United States. Supreme Court**
Surf
    USE   **Ocean waves**

Surf riding
    USE   **Surfing**
Surface effect machines
    USE   **Ground effect machines**
Surface of the earth
    USE   **Earth—Surface**
Surfing 797.3
    UF   Surf riding
    BT   **Water sports**
Surfing—Songs 782.42
    UF   Surfing—Songs and music *[For-*
                mer heading]
    BT   **Songs**
Surfing—Songs and music
    USE   **Surfing—Songs**
Surgeons 610.69; 617.092; 920
    UF   Medical profession
    BT   **Physicians**
Surgery 617
    UF   Operations, Surgical
    SA   classes of persons, names of dis-
           eases, and names of organs
           and regions of the body with
           the subdivision *Surgery,* to be
           added as needed
    BT   **Medicine**
    NT   **Anesthetics**
           Antiseptics
           Artificial organs
           Cancer—Surgery
           Children—Surgery
            Cryosurgery
            Heart—Surgery
           Orthopedics
           Plastic surgery
           Transplantation of organs, tis-
              sues, etc.
           Vivisection
Surgery, Cosmetic
    USE   **Plastic surgery**
Surgery, Orthopedic
    USE   **Orthopedics**
Surgery, Pediatric
    USE   **Children—Surgery**
Surgery, Plastic
    USE   **Plastic surgery**
Surgical transplantation
    USE   **Transplantation of organs, tis-**
              sues, etc.

BT = Broader Term   NT = Narrower Term   RT = Related Term   SA = See Also   UF = Used For

Surnames
USE   Personal names
Surplus government property   352.5
   UF   Excess government property
           Government property, Surplus
   BT   **Property**
Surrealism   709.04; 759.06
   BT   **Art**
   RT   **Postimpressionism (Art)**
Surrogate mothers   176; 306.874;
        346.01
   BT   **Mothers**
Surveillance, Electronic
   USE   **Eavesdropping**
Surveying   526.9
   UF   Land surveying
           Land surveys
   SA   names of countries, cities, etc.,
           with the subdivision *Surveys,*
           for works containing the re-
           sults of land surveys in those
           places, e.g. **United States—**
           Surveys; to be added as
           needed
   BT   **Civil engineering**
           Geography
           Measurement
   NT   **Mine surveying**
           Topographical drawing
   RT   **Geodesy**
Surveys   001.4
   UF   Government surveys
   SA   types of surveys, e.g. **Market**
           surveys; and names of coun-
           tries, cities, etc., with the sub-
           division *Surveys,* for works
           containing the results of land
           surveys in those places, to be
           added as needed
   BT   **Research**
   NT   **Educational surveys**
           Library surveys
           Market surveys
           Social surveys
Survival (after airplane accidents, ship-
       wrecks, etc.)
   USE   **Survival after airplane acci-**
           dents, shipwrecks, etc.

Survival after airplane accidents, ship-
       wrecks, etc.   613.6
   UF   Castaways
           Survival (after airplane accidents,
           shipwrecks, etc.) *[Former*
           heading]
   BT   **Aircraft accidents**
           Shipwrecks
   RT   **Wilderness survival**
Survival of the fittest
   USE   **Natural selection**
Survival skills   613.6
       Use for materials on skills needed to sur-
    vive in a hazardous environment, usually
    stressing self-reliance and economic self-
    sufficiency.
   UF   Emergency survival
           Human survival skills
   SA   types of survival, e.g. **Wilder-**
           ness survival; to be added as
           needed
   BT   **Civil defense**
           Environmental influence on
           humans
           Human ecology
           Life skills
   NT   **Wilderness survival**
   RT   **Self-reliance**
Survivalism   320.5; 613.6
   UF   Survivalist movements
   BT   **Social movements**
Survivalist movements
   USE   **Survivalism**
Suspended sentence
   USE   **Probation**
Suspense films
   USE   **Adventure films**
           Mystery films
           Spy films
Suspense novels
   USE   **Adventure fiction**
           Mystery fiction
           Romantic suspense novels
Suspense programs
   USE   **Mystery radio programs**
           Mystery television programs
           Spy radio programs
           Spy television programs
Suspension bridges
   USE   **Bridges**

BT = Broader Term   NT = Narrower Term   RT = Related Term   SA = See Also   UF = Used For

Sustainable development (May subdiv. geog.) **333.7; 338.9**

Use for materials on economic development that satisfies the needs of the present generation without depleting natural resources for the future or having adverse environmental effects. General materials on the environmental impact of economic development are entered under **Economic development—Environmental aspects.**

UF   Economic sustainability

Sustainable economic development

BT   **Economic development**

Sustainable economic development

USE   **Sustainable development**

Swamp animals   578.768

UF   Swamp fauna

BT   **Animals**

Marshes

Wildlife

Swamp fauna

USE   **Swamp animals**

Swamps

USE   **Marshes**

Wetlands

Swashbucklers

USE   **Adventure fiction**

Adventure films

Swedish language   439.7

May be subdivided like **English language.**

BT   **Language and languages**

Scandinavian languages

Swedish literature   839.7

May use same subdivisions and names of literary forms as for **English literature.**

BT   **Literature**

Scandinavian literature

Sweets

USE   **Confectionery**

Swell

USE   **Ocean waves**

Swimming   797.2

BT   **Water sports**

NT   **Diving**

Marathon swimming

Synchronized swimming

Swimming pools   690; 725; 797.2

UF   Pools

BT   **Sports facilities**

Swindlers and swindling   364.16

UF   Con artists

Con game

Confidence game

BT   **Crime**

Criminals

NT   **Counterfeits and counterfeiting**

Credit card crimes

Quacks and quackery

RT   **Fraud**

Impostors and imposture

Swine

USE   **Pigs**

Switchboard hotlines

USE   **Hotlines (Telephone counseling)**

Switches, Electric

USE   **Electric switchgear**

Symbiosis   577.8

UF   Mutualism (Biology)

BT   **Biology**

Ecology

RT   **Parasites**

Plant ecology

Symbolic logic   511.3

UF   Logic, Symbolic and mathematical *[Former heading]*

Mathematical logic

BT   **Logic**

Mathematics

NT   **Boolean algebra**

RT   **Set theory**

Symbolic numbers

USE   **Numerology**

Symbolism of numbers

Symbolism   291.3; 700

SA   types of symbolism in religions, e.g. **Christian art and symbolism; Religious art and symbolism;** and symbolism in particular subjects, e.g. **Symbolism in literature;** to be added as needed

BT   **Art**

Mythology

NT   **Christian art and symbolism**

Heraldry

Religious art and symbolism

Symbolism in literature

Symbolism of numbers

RT   **Signs and symbols**

Symbolism in literature   809

UF   Signs and symbols in literature

BT   **Literature**

BT = Broader Term   NT = Narrower Term   RT = Related Term   SA = See Also   UF = Used For

Symbolism in literature—*Continued*
     Symbolism
  RT   Allegory
Symbolism of numbers   246; 291.3; 809
    Use for general materials on the symbolism of numbers, as in philosophy, religion, or literature. Materials on the occult significance of numbers are entered under **Numerology.**
  UF   Number symbolism
        Sacred numbers
        Symbolic numbers
  BT   **Christian art and symbolism**
        Symbolism
  NT   **Numerology**
  RT   **Cabala**
        Numbers
Symbols
  USE **Abbreviations**
        Signs and symbols
Symbols, Mathematical
  USE **Mathematical notation**
Sympathy
  USE **Bereavement**
        Consolation
Symphonic poems   784.2
  BT   **Orchestral music**
Symphonies
  USE **Symphony**
Symphony   784.18; 784.2
    Use for musical scores and for materials on the symphony as a musical form.
  UF   Symphonies *[Former heading]*
  BT   **Musical form**
        Orchestral music
Symptoms
  USE **Diagnosis**
Synagogues (May subdiv. geog.)   **296.6; 726**
  BT   **Buildings**
  RT   **Judaism**
Synchronized swimming   797.2
  UF   Ballet, Water
        Water ballet
  BT   **Swimming**
Synfuels
  USE **Synthetic fuels**
Synods
  USE **Councils and synods**
Synonyms
  USE names of languages with the subdivision *Synonyms and*

antonyms, e.g. **English language—Synonyms and antonyms;** to be added as needed
Synthesizer music
  USE **Electronic music**
Synthesizer (Musical instrument)
  USE **Synthesizers (Musical instruments)**
Synthesizers (Musical instruments)   786.7
  UF   Synthesizer (Musical instrument)
        [Former heading]
  BT   **Electronic musical instruments**
Synthetic chemistry
  USE **Organic chemistry—Synthesis**
Synthetic detergents
  USE **Detergents**
Synthetic drugs of abuse
  USE **Designer drugs**
Synthetic fabrics   677
  UF   Fabrics, Synthetic
  SA   types of synthetic fabrics, to be added as needed
  BT   **Fabrics**
        Synthetic products
  NT   **Nylon**
        Rayon
Synthetic foods
  USE **Artificial foods**
Synthetic fuels   662
  UF   Artificial fuels
        Nonfossil fuels
        Synfuels
  BT   **Fuel**
        Synthetic products
Synthetic products   670
  SA   types of synthetic products and names of specific products, to be added as needed
  BT   **Industrial chemistry**
        Organic chemistry—Synthesis
  NT   **Artificial foods**
        Synthetic fabrics
        Synthetic fuels
        Synthetic rubber
  RT   **Plastics**
        Substitute products

BT = Broader Term   NT = Narrower Term   RT = Related Term   SA = See Also   UF = Used For

Synthetic rubber   678
   UF   Rubber, Artificial *[Former heading]*
          Rubber, Synthetic
   BT   Plastics
          Synthetic products
Syphilis   616.95
   BT   Sexually transmitted diseases
Syrups   641.3
   BT   Sugar
System analysis   003; 004.2; 658.4
   UF   Flow charts
          Flowcharting
          Linear system theory
          Network theory
          Systems analysis
   BT   Cybernetics
          Mathematical models
          System theory
   NT   Fuzzy systems
          System design
          Systems engineering
System design   003; 004.2; 621.39
   UF   Design, System
          Systems design
   BT   Electronic data processing
          System analysis
System engineering
   USE   Systems engineering
System theory   003
   UF   Systems, Theory of
          Theory of systems
   BT   Science
   NT   Chaos (Science)
          Cybernetics
          Operations research
          System analysis
          Systems engineering
Systematic botany
   USE   Botany—Classification
Systematic theology
   USE   Doctrinal theology
Systems analysis
   USE   System analysis
Systems, Database management
   USE   Database management
Systems design
   USE   System design
Systems engineering   620
   UF   System engineering

   BT   Automation
          Cybernetics
          Engineering
          Industrial design
          System analysis
          System theory
   NT   Bionics
          Reliability (Engineering)
   RT   Operations research
Systems, Expert (Computer science)
   USE   Expert systems (Computer science)
Systems, Fuzzy
   USE   Fuzzy systems
Systems reliability
   USE   Reliability (Engineering)
Systems, Theory of
   USE   System theory
T groups
   USE   Group relations training
T.I.R.O.S. (Meteorological satellite)
   USE   Tiros (Meteorological satellite)
T.V.
   USE   Television
Table decoration
   USE   Table setting and decoration
Table etiquette   395.5
   BT   Eating customs
          Etiquette
   RT   Dining
Table setting and decoration   642
   UF   Table decoration
   BT   Decoration and ornament
   NT   Flower arrangement
          Tableware
Table talk
   USE   Conversation
Table tennis   796.34
   UF   Ping-pong *[Former heading]*
   BT   Ball games
Tables (Systematic lists)
   USE   scientific and economic subjects with the subdivision *Tables,* e.g. **Trigonometry—Tables;** to be added as needed
Tableware   642
   UF   Dishes
   BT   Table setting and decoration
   NT   Glassware
          Porcelain

BT = Broader Term   NT = Narrower Term   RT = Related Term   SA = See Also   UF = Used For

Tableware—*Continued*
    Pottery
    Silverware
Tactics 355.4
  UF   Military tactics
  BT   **Military art and science**
        Strategy
  NT   **Biological warfare**
        Drill and minor tactics
        Guerrilla warfare
Tadpoles
  USE **Frogs**
Tailoring 646.4; 687
  UF   Garment making
  BT   **Clothing and dress**
        Clothing industry
        Fashion
  NT   **Military uniforms**
  RT   **Dressmaking**
Taiwan 951.24
    Use for materials dealing with the island of Taiwan, regardless of time period, or with the post-1948 Republic of China. Materials dealing with mainland China, regardless of time period, or with the People's Republic of China and comprehensive materials on China including Taiwan are entered under **China.** May be subdivided like United States except for *History.*
  UF   China (Republic of China, 1949-   )
        Formosa
        Nationalist China
        Republic of China, 1949-
Takeovers, Corporate
  USE **Corporate mergers and acquisitions**
Talent
  USE **Genius**
        Gifted children
        Musical ability
Tales
  USE **Fables**
        Fairy tales
        Folklore
        Legends
Talismans
  USE **Charms**
Talk shows 791.44; 791.45
    May be used for individual works, collections, or materials about talk shows.
  BT   **Interviewing**
        Radio programs

        Television programs
Talking
  USE **Conversation**
Talking books 011; 027.6
  UF   Books, Talking
        Cassette books
  BT   **Blind—Books and reading**
        Sound recordings
Talking pictures
  USE **Motion pictures**
Tall tales 398.2; 808.83; 813, etc.
    May be used for individual works, collections, or materials about tall tales.
  BT   **Folklore**
        Legends
        Wit and humor
Talmud 296.1
  BT   **Hebrew literature**
        Jewish literature
        Judaism
Tanks (Military science)
  USE **Military tanks**
Tanning 675
  BT   **Industrial chemistry**
  RT   **Hides and skins**
        Leather
Taoism 299
  BT   **Religions**
Tap dancing 792.7
  BT   **Dance**
Tap water
  USE **Drinking water**
Tape recorder music
  USE **Electronic music**
Tape recorders
  USE **Magnetic recorders and recording**
Tape recordings, Audio
  USE **Sound recordings**
Tape recordings, Video
  USE **Videotapes**
Tapestry 677; 746.3
  BT   **Decoration and ornament**
        Decorative arts
        Interior design
        Needlework
Tardiness
  USE **Punctuality**
Tariff (May subdiv. geog.) 336.2; 382
  UF   Custom duties
        Customs (Tariff)

BT = Broader Term   NT = Narrower Term   RT = Related Term   SA = See Also   UF = Used For

Tariff—*Continued*

  Duties
  Government regulation of commerce
  Revenue
  Tariff question—Free trade and protection
 BT **Commercial policy**
   Economic policy
   Public finance
 NT **Balance of trade**
   Smuggling
 RT **Free trade**
   Protectionism
Tariff question—Free trade and protection
 USE **Free trade**
   Protectionism
   Tariff
Tariff—United States   336.2; 382
 UF United States—Tariff
Tarot   133.3; 795.4
  Use for materials on the cards and the game.
 UF Tarot (Game)
 BT **Card games**
   Fortune telling
Tarot (Game)
 USE **Tarot**
Tartans   391; 929.6
 UF Highland costume
   Scottish tartans
 BT **Clans**
Taste   152.1
 BT **Senses and sensation**
Taste (Aesthetics)
 USE **Aesthetics**
Tattooing   391.6
 UF Tattoos (Body markings)
 BT **Manners and customs**
   Personal appearance
Tattoos (Body markings)
 USE **Tattooing**
Taverns
 USE **Bars**
Tax assessment   336.2
  Use for general materials on the valuation of property for determining tax liability. Materials on the assessment of property for tax purposes in a particular place are entered under **Taxation** followed by the appropriate geographical subdivision.
 UF Appraisal

  Assessment *[Former heading]*
  Assessment, Tax
  Property tax—Assessment
  Real property tax—Assessment
 BT **Taxation**
   Valuation
Tax avoidance
 USE **Tax planning**
Tax credits   336.2
 BT **Income tax**
Tax planning   343.04
 UF Tax avoidance
   Tax saving
 BT **Personal finance**
   Planning
   Taxation
 RT **Estate planning**
Tax relations, Intergovernmental
 USE **Intergovernmental tax relations**
Tax saving
 USE **Tax planning**
Tax sharing
 USE **Intergovernmental tax relations**
   Revenue sharing
Taxation (May subdiv. geog.)   **336.2**
 UF Direct taxation
   Duties
   Revenue
   Taxes
 SA subjects with the subdivision
   Taxation, e.g. **Real estate investment—Taxation;** to be added as needed
 BT **Political science**
   Public finance
 NT **Income tax**
   Inheritance and transfer tax
   Intergovernmental tax relations
   Internal revenue
   Real estate investment—Taxation
   Sales tax
   Tax assessment
   Tax planning
   Tithes
Taxation of income
 USE **Income tax**
Taxation of legacies
 USE **Inheritance and transfer tax**

Taxation of sales
USE   Sales tax
Taxation—United States   336.200973
UF   United States—Taxation
Taxes
USE   Taxation
Taxidermy   590.75
UF   Preservation of specimens
Specimens, Preservation of
SA   types of specimens with the sub-
division *Collection and pres-
ervation,* e.g. **Birds—Collec-
tion and preservation;** to be
added as needed
RT   **Zoological specimens—Collec-
tion and preservation**
Taxonomy (Botany)
USE   **Botany—Classification**
Tea   633.7; 641.8
Use for materials on the plant or on the
beverage. Materials on the meal are entered
under **Afternoon teas.**
BT   **Beverages**
RT   **Afternoon teas**
Tea rooms
USE   **Restaurants**
Teach yourself courses
USE   **Self-instruction**
Teacher exchange   370.116
UF   Exchange of teachers
Interchange of teachers
Teachers, Exchange of
Teachers, Interchange of *[For-
mer heading]*
BT   **Exchange of persons programs
International education**
Teacher-parent conferences
USE   **Parent-teacher conferences**
Teacher-parent relationships
USE   **Parent-teacher relationships**
Teacher-student relationships   371.1;
378.1
UF   Pupil-teacher relationships
Student-teacher interaction
BT   **Children and adults
Human relations
Teaching**
NT   **Student evaluation of teachers**
Teacher training
USE   **Teachers colleges
Teachers—Training**

Teachers   371.1; 920
Use for materials on educators engaged in
classroom or other instruction. Materials on
people engaged professionally in the field of
education in general are entered under **Educa-
tors.**
UF   College teachers
Faculty (Education)
Professors
BT   **Educators**
NT   **Colleges and universities—Fac-
ulty
Educational associations**
RT   **Teaching**
Teachers and parents
USE   **Parent-teacher relationships**
Teachers colleges   378.1
Use for general and historical materials
about teachers colleges. Materials on their ed-
ucational functions are entered under **Teach-
ers—Training.**
UF   Normal schools
Teacher training
Training colleges for teachers
SA   names of teachers colleges, to
be added as needed
BT   **Colleges and universities
Education—Study and teaching**
RT   **Teachers—Training**
Teachers, Exchange of
USE   **Teacher exchange**
Teachers' institutes
USE   **Teachers' workshops**
Teachers, Interchange of
USE   **Teacher exchange**
Teachers—Pensions (May subdiv. geog.)
331.25
SA   types of educational institutions
and names of individual edu-
cational insititutions with the
subdivisions *Faculty—Pen-
sions,* e.g. **Colleges and uni-
versities—Faculty—Pensions;**
to be added as needed
Teachers—Practice teaching
USE   **Student teaching**
Teachers' reports
USE   **School reports**
Teachers, Student rating of
USE   **Student evaluation of teachers**
Teachers—Training   370.71
Use for materials on the history and meth-
ods of training teachers, including the educa-

BT = Broader Term   NT = Narrower Term   RT = Related Term   SA = See Also   UF = Used For

Teachers—Training—*Continued*

tional functions of teachers colleges. Materials on the study of education as a discipline are entered under **Education—Study and teaching.** Materials on the art of teaching and methods of teaching are entered under **Teaching.**

UF   Teacher training

        Teachers—Training of

BT   **Education—Study and teaching**

        Teaching

NT   **Student teaching**

        Teachers' workshops

RT   **Teachers colleges**

Teachers—Training of

USE   **Teachers—Training**

Teachers' workshops   371.1

UF   Teachers' institutes

        Workshops, Teachers'

BT   **Teachers—Training**

Teaching   371.102

Use for materials on the art of teaching and methods of teaching. Materials on the study of education as a discipline are entered under **Education—Study and teaching.** Materials on the history and methods of training teachers, including the educational functions of teachers colleges, are entered under **Teachers—Training.**

UF   Instruction

        Pedagogy

        School teaching

SA   subjects with the subdivision

        Study and teaching, e.g. **Science—Study and teaching;**

        to be added as needed

BT   **Education**

NT   **Classroom management**

        Cooperative learning

        Educational psychology

        Examinations

        Lectures and lecturing

        Montessori method of education

        Project method in teaching

        School discipline

        School supervision

        Student teaching

        Study skills

        Teacher-student relationships

        Teachers—Training

        Teaching teams

        Tutors and tutoring

RT   **Teachers**

Teaching—Aids and devices   371.33

UF   Educational media

        Instructional materials

        Teaching materials

NT   **Audiovisual materials**

        Bulletin boards

        Manipulatives

        Motion pictures in education

        Programmed instruction

        Radio in education

        Teaching machines

        Television in education

RT   **Educational technology**

Teaching, Computer

USE   **Computer assisted instruction**

Teaching—Data processing

USE   **Computer assisted instruction**

Teaching—Experimental methods

USE   **Education—Experimental methods**

Teaching, Freedom of

USE   **Academic freedom**

Teaching machines   371.33

UF   Automatic teaching

        Tutorial machines

BT   **Programmed instruction**

        Teaching—Aids and devices

Teaching materials

USE   **Teaching—Aids and devices**

Teaching teams   371.14

UF   Team teaching

BT   **Teaching**

Teachings of Jesus

USE   **Jesus Christ—Teachings**

Team problem solving

USE   **Group problem solving**

Team teaching

USE   **Teaching teams**

Tearooms

USE   **Restaurants**

Teas

USE   **Afternoon teas**

Technical assistance (May subdiv. geog.)   **338.91; 361.6**

Use for materials on foreign aid in the form of technical expertise. Materials on the transfer of innovations in technology from one country to another are entered under **Technology transfer.**

UF   Aid to developing areas

        Assistance to developing areas

Technical assistance—*Continued*
Foreign aid program
SA technical assistance from particular countries, e.g. **American technical assistance;** to be added as needed
BT **Foreign aid**
International economic relations
NT **American technical assistance**
RT **Community development**
Technology transfer
Technical assistance, American
USE **American technical assistance**
Technical chemistry
USE **Industrial chemistry**
Technical education   370.11; 373.246; 374
UF Education, Industrial
Education, Technical
Industrial education
Industrial schools
Technical schools
Trade schools
SA technical subjects with the subdivision *Study and teaching,* e.g. **Engineering—Study and teaching;** to be added as needed
BT **Education**
Higher education
Technology
NT **Apprentices**
Correspondence schools and courses
Engineering—Study and teaching
Evening and continuation schools
Occupational retraining
Occupational training
School shops
RT **Employees—Training**
Industrial arts education
Professional education
Vocational education
Technical schools
USE **Technical education**
Technical service
USE **Customer service**

Technical services (Libraries)
USE **Library technical processes**
Technical terms
USE **Technology—Dictionaries**
Technical writing   808
UF Scientific writing
BT **Authorship**
Technology—Language
Technique
USE subjects with the subdivision *Technique,* e.g. **Fiction—Technique; Love stories—Technique; Painting—Technique;** etc., to be added as needed
Technological transfer
USE **Technology transfer**
Technology   600
UF Applied science
Arts, Useful
High tech
High technology
Useful arts
SA technology and other subjects, e.g. **Technology and civilization;** to be added as needed
NT **Distillation**
Electronics
Engineering
Industrial chemistry
Inventions
Machinery
Manufactures
Mills
Technical education
Technology and civilization
Technology transfer
RT **Industrial arts**
Technology and civilization   303.4
UF Civilization and technology
BT **Civilization**
Technology
NT **Computers and civilization**
RT **Industrial revolution**
Technology—Dictionaries   603
UF Technical terms
BT **Encyclopedias and dictionaries**
Technology in the workplace
USE **Machinery in the workplace**

BT = Broader Term   NT = Narrower Term   RT = Related Term   SA = See Also   UF = Used For

Technology—Language   601; 603
NT   Technical writing
Technology transfer (May subdiv. geog.)
     338.9

Use for materials on the transfer of innovations in technology from one country to another. Materials on foreign aid in the form of technical expertise are entered under **Technical assistance.** May be subdivided by the region or country receiving the technology. Where applicable, make an additional entry under this heading subdivided by the region or country transferring the technology.

UF   Technological transfer
     Transfer of technology
BT   **Inventions**
     Technology
RT   **International cooperation**
     International relations
     Technical assistance

Teen age
USE   **Adolescence**
Teen-agers
USE   **Teenagers**
Teenage consumers
USE   **Young consumers**
Teenage drinking
USE   **Teenagers—Alcohol use**
Teenage dropouts
USE   **Dropouts**
Teenage fathers   306.874; 362.7

Use for materials focusing on fathers who are teenagers. Materials on fathers who at the time of a child's birth were not married to the child's mother are entered under **Unmarried fathers.** Materials focusing on fathers rearing children without a partner in the household are entered under **Single parent family.**

UF   Adolescent fathers
     School age fathers
     Schoolboy fathers
BT   **Fathers**
     Teenage parents
Teenage gangs
USE   **Gangs**
Teenage literature
USE   **Young adult literature**
Teenage mothers   306.874; 362.7;
     362.83

Use for materials focusing on mothers who are teenagers. Materials on mothers who at the time of giving birth were not married to the child's father are entered under **Unmarried mothers.** Materials focusing on mothers rearing children without a partner in the household are entered under **Single parent family.**

UF   Adolescent mothers *[Former heading]*
     School age mothers
     Schoolgirl mothers
BT   **Mothers**
     Teenage parents
RT   **Teenage pregnancy**
Teenage parents   306.874; 362.7
BT   **Family**
     Teenagers
NT   **Teenage fathers**
     Teenage mothers
Teenage pregnancy   362.7; 618.2
UF   Adolescent pregnancy
     Pregnancy, Adolescent *[Former heading]*
     Pregnancy, Teenage
BT   **Pregnancy**
RT   **Teenage mothers**
Teenage prostitution
USE   **Juvenile prostitution**
Teenagers (May subdiv. geog.)   305.235

Use for materials about teen youth. Materials on the time of life extending from thirteen to twenty-five years, as well as on people in that general age range, are entered under **Youth.** Materials limited to people in the general age range of eighteen through twenty-five years of age are entered under **Young men** or **Young women.** Materials on the process or state of growing up are entered under **Adolescence.**

UF   Adolescents
     Boys, Teenage
     Girls, Teenage
     Teen-agers
     Teens
     Young adults
     Young people
     Young persons
BT   **Age**
     Youth
NT   **Runaway teenagers**
     Teenage parents
RT   **Boys**
     Girls
Teenagers—Alcohol use   362.292;
     613.81; 616.86
UF   Alcohol and teenagers
     Drinking and teenagers
     Teenage drinking

BT = Broader Term   NT = Narrower Term   RT = Related Term   SA = See Also   UF = Used For

706

Teenagers—Alcohol use—*Continued*
        Teenagers and alcohol
  NT   **Drinking age**
Teenagers and alcohol
  USE   **Teenagers—Alcohol use**
Teenagers and drugs
  USE   **Teenagers—Drug use**
Teenagers and narcotics
  USE   **Teenagers—Drug use**
Teenagers—Attitudes   155.5; 305.235
  BT   **Attitude (Psychology)**
Teenagers—Books and reading   011.62;
     028.5

Use for materials on the reading interests of teenagers and for lists of books for teenagers. Collections or materials about literature published for teenagers are entered under **Young adult literature.**

  UF   Books and reading for teenagers
       Books and reading for young
         adults
       Reading interests of teenagers
       Reading interests of young
         adults
       Young adults—Books and read-
         ing
  BT   **Books and reading**
Teenagers—Development
  USE   **Adolescence**
Teenagers—Drug use   362.29; 613.8;
     616.86
  UF   Drugs and teenagers
       Narcotics and teenagers
       Teenagers and drugs
       Teenagers and narcotics
  BT   **Youth—Drug use**
  RT   **Juvenile delinquency**
Teenagers—Employment   331.3
  UF   Child labor
       Employment of teenagers
  BT   **Age and employment**
       Labor
       Labor supply
       Youth—Employment
  RT   **Summer employment**
Teenagers' library services
  USE   **Young adults' library services**
Teenagers—Literature
  USE   **Young adult literature**
Teenagers, Psychiatry of
  USE   **Adolescent psychiatry**

Teenagers—Psychology
  USE   **Adolescent psychology**
Teenagers—Religious life   248.4; 291.4
  BT   **Religious life**
       Youth—Religious life
Teenagers—United States   305.2350973
  UF   American teenagers
       United States—Teenagers
  BT   **Youth—United States**
Teens
  USE   **Teenagers**
Teepees
  USE   **Indians of North America—**
       Dwellings
Teeth   611; 612.3; 617.6
  UF   Anatomy, Dental
  BT   **Head**
  RT   **Dentistry**
Teeth—Diseases   617.6
  UF   Medicine, Dental
  BT   **Diseases**
  RT   **Water fluoridation**
Telecommunication   384; 621.382
  UF   Electric communication
       Mass communication
  SA   subjects with the subdivision
       Communication systems, e.g.
       Astronautics—Communica-
       tion systems; to be added as
       needed
  BT   **Communication**
  NT   **Artificial satellites in telecom-**
       munication
       Astronautics—Communication
       systems
       Broadcasting
       Computer networks
       Data transmission systems
       Electronic mail systems
       Facsimile transmission
       Intercommunication systems
       Interstellar communication
       Microwave communication sys-
       tems
       Radio
       Speech processing systems
       Submarine cables
       Telecommuting
       Telegraph
       Telephone

BT = Broader Term   NT = Narrower Term   RT = Related Term   SA = See Also   UF = Used For

Telecommunication—*Continued*
 Television
Telecommuting 331.25
 Use for materials on employment at home
 with computers, word processors, etc., con-
 nected to a central work site, permitting em-
 ployees to substitute telecommunications for
 transportation.
 UF Alternate work sites
  At-home employment
  Home labor
  Work at home
  Working at home
 BT **Automation**
  Home business
  Telecommunication
Teleconferencing 384; 658.4
 UF Conference calls
   (Teleconferencing)
  Telephone—Conference calls
 BT **Telephone**
Telefax
 USE **Facsimile transmission**
Telegraph 384.1; 621.383
 BT **Electric engineering**
  Public utilities
  Telecommunication
 NT **Cipher and telegraph codes**
  Submarine cables
Telegraph codes
 USE **Cipher and telegraph codes**
Telegraph, Submarine
 USE **Submarine cables**
Telekinesis
 USE **Psychokinesis**
Telemarketing 381; 658.8
 Use for materials on the use of electronic
 media as a form of marketing that bypasses
 retail outlets in the advertising and selling of
 goods.
 UF Electronic marketing
 BT **Direct selling**
  Marketing
Telepathy 133.8
 UF Mental telepathy
  Mind reading *[Former heading]*
  Thought transference
 BT **Extrasensory perception**
  Parapsychology
 RT **Clairvoyance**
  Subconsciousness

Telephone 384.6; 621.385
 BT **Electric engineering**
  Public utilities
  Telecommunication
 NT **Teleconferencing**
  Video telephone
Telephone—Conference calls
 USE **Teleconferencing**
Telephone counseling
 USE **Hotlines (Telephone counseling)**
Telephone directories
 USE countries, cities, etc., corporate
   bodies, classes of persons,
   ethnic groups, and types of
   organizations and industries
   with the subdivision *Tele-
   phone directories,* e.g. **Chica-
   go (Ill.)—Telephone directo-
   ries;** to be added as needed
Telephotography 778.3
 BT **Photography**
Teleprocessing networks
 USE **Computer networks**
Telereference
 USE **Information networks**
  Teletext systems
  Videotex systems
Telescope
 USE **Telescopes**
Telescopes 522; 681
 UF Telescope *[Former heading]*
 BT **Astronomical instruments**
  Optical instruments
Teletext systems 004.692; 384.3
 Use for materials on the one-way transmis-
 sion of computer-based data, such as weather
 forecasts or stock quotations, from a central
 source to a television set.
 UF Telereference
 BT **Data transmission systems**
  Electronic publishing
  Information systems
  Television broadcasting
 RT **Videotex systems**
Television 302.23; 384.55; 621.388
 UF T.V.
  TV
 SA television and particular groups
   of people, e.g. **Television and
   children;** and television in

BT = Broader Term NT = Narrower Term RT = Related Term SA = See Also UF = Used For

Television—*Continued*
various industries or fields of
endeavor, e.g. **Television in
education;** to be added as
needed
BT **Telecommunication**
NT **African Americans in television**
Closed caption television
Closed-circuit television
Color television
High definition television
Home video systems
Minorities in television
Television and children
Television and politics
Television and youth
Television broadcasting
Television in astronautics
Television in education
Video art
Video telephone
Violence in television
RT **Videodiscs**
Videotapes
Television actors
USE **Actors**
Television adaptations   791.45
May be used for individual works, collec-
tions, or materials about television adaptations
of material from other media.
UF Adaptations
Adaptations, Television
Literature—Film and video adap-
tations
Motion pictures—Television ad-
aptations
SA names of literatures and literary
authors with the subdivision
Film and video adaptations,
to be added as needed
BT **Television plays**
Television programs
Television scripts
Television advertising   659.14
UF Advertising, Television
Commercials, Television
Television commercials
BT **Advertising**
Television broadcasting

Television and children   305.23; 384.55;
791.45
Use for materials on the effect of television
on children.
UF Children and television
BT **Children**
Television
Television and infrared observation satellite
USE **Tiros (Meteorological satellite)**
Television and politics   324
UF Politics and television
Television in politics [*Former
heading*]
BT **Politics**
Television
NT **Equal time rule (Broadcasting)**
**Fairness doctrine (Broadcast-
ing)**
Television and youth   305.235; 384.55;
791.45
UF Youth and television
BT **Television**
Youth
Television apparatus industry
USE **Television supplies industry**
Television authorship   808
UF Television writing
BT **Authorship**
NT **Television plays—Technique**
Television broadcasting   384.55
UF Television industry
SA television broadcasting of partic-
ular kinds of programs, e.g.
**Television broadcasting of
sports;** to be added as needed
BT **Broadcasting**
Mass media
Television
NT **African Americans in television
broadcasting**
Cable television
**Minorities in television broad-
casting**
Public television
Subscription television
Teletext systems
Television advertising
**Television broadcasting of
news**
**Television broadcasting of
sports**

Television broadcasting—*Continued*
      Television—Production and direction
      Television programs
      Television scripts
      Television stations
      Videotex systems
  RT Video recording
Television broadcasting of news 070.1
  UF Television coverage of news
      Television journalism
      Television news
  BT **Broadcast journalism**
      Television broadcasting
Television broadcasting of sports 070.4
  UF Sports broadcasting
      Sports in television
      Television sports
  BT **Broadcast journalism**
      Television broadcasting
Television broadcasting—Vocational guidance 384.55
  BT **Vocational guidance**
Television, Cable
  USE **Cable television**
Television cartoons
  USE **Animated television programs**
Television—Censorship 384.55
  BT **Censorship**
Television, Closed-circuit
  USE **Closed-circuit television**
Television, Color
  USE **Color television**
Television comedies
  USE **Comedy television programs**
Television comedy programs
  USE **Comedy television programs**
Television commercials
  USE **Television advertising**
Television coverage of news
  USE **Television broadcasting of news**
Television drama
  USE **Television plays**
Television—Equipment and supplies 621.388
  NT **Television—Receivers and reception**
      Videodisc players
  RT **Television supplies industry**

      Video recording
Television equipment industry
  USE **Television supplies industry**
Television films
  USE **Television movies**
Television games
  USE **Video games**
Television in astronautics 621.388; 629.47
  UF Space television
      Television, Space
  BT **Astronautics—Communication systems**
      Television
Television in education 371.33
  UF Education and television
      Educational television
  BT **Audiovisual education**
      Teaching—Aids and devices
      Television
Television in politics
  USE **Television and politics**
Television industry
  USE **Television broadcasting**
      Television supplies industry
Television journalism
  USE **Broadcast journalism**
      Television broadcasting of news
Television movies 791.45
    May be used for individual works, collections, or materials about television movies.
  UF Made-for-TV movies
      Television films
  BT **Motion pictures**
      Television programs
Television news
  USE **Television broadcasting of news**
Television novels
  USE **Radio and television novels**
Television plays 808.82; 812, etc.
    May be used for individual works, collections, or materials about television plays. Materials on how to write television plays are entered under **Television plays—Technique.**
  UF Scenarios
      Television drama
  BT **Drama**
      Television programs
  NT **Soap operas**

BT = Broader Term   NT = Narrower Term   RT = Related Term   SA = See Also   UF = Used For

Television plays—*Continued*
Television adaptations
RT   Television scripts
Television plays—Technique   808.2
UF   Play writing
Playwriting
BT   Drama—Technique
Television authorship
RT   Radio plays—Technique
Television—Production and direction
384.55; 791.45
BT   Television broadcasting
Television programs   791.45
May be used for individual works, collections, or materials about television programs.
UF   Programs, Television
SA   types of television programs and
names of specific programs,
to be added as needed
BT   Television broadcasting
NT   Adventure television programs
Animated television programs
Biographical television programs
Comedy television programs
Fantasy television programs
Horror television programs
Legal drama (Television programs)
Medical drama (Television programs)
Music videos
Mystery television programs
Science fiction television programs
Sports drama (Television programs)
Spy television programs
Talk shows
Television adaptations
Television movies
Television plays
Television serials
Variety shows (Television programs)
Violence in television
War television programs
Westerns (Television programs)
RT   Television scripts

Television—Receivers and reception
621.388
UF   Television reception
Television sets
BT   Television—Equipment and
supplies
NT   Video games
Television reception
USE   Television—Receivers and reception
Television—Repairing   621.388
Television scripts   791.45; 808.8; 818,
etc.
May be used for individual works, collections, or materials about television scripts.
UF   Screenplays
BT   Television broadcasting
NT   Television adaptations
RT   Television plays
Television programs
Television serials   791.45
May be used for individual works, collections, or materials about television serials.
BT   Television programs
RT   Soap operas
Television sets
USE   Television—Receivers and reception
Television, Space
USE   Television in astronautics
Television sports
USE   Television broadcasting of
sports
Television—Stage lighting
USE   Stage lighting
Television stations   384.55
BT   Television broadcasting
Television, Subscription
USE   Subscription television
Television supplies industry   338.4;
384.55
UF   Television apparatus industry
Television equipment industry
Television industry
RT   Television—Equipment and
supplies
Television writing
USE   Television authorship
Telstar project   621.382
UF   Bell System Telstar satellite
Project Telstar

BT = Broader Term   NT = Narrower Term   RT = Related Term   SA = See Also   UF = Used For

Telstar project—*Continued*
    BT   Artificial satellites in telecom-
            munication
Temperament   155.2
    BT   Mind and body
           Psychology
           Psychophysiology
    RT   Character
Temperance   178; 241; 613.81
    Use for materials on the virtue of temper-
ance or on the temperance movement.
    UF   Abstinence
           Drunkenness
           Intemperance
           Intoxication
           Total abstinence
    BT   Virtue
    RT   Alcoholism
           Drinking of alcoholic beverages
           Prohibition
Temperature   536
    NT   Low temperatures
    RT   Cold
           Heat
           Thermometers
Temperature, Animal and human
    USE   Body temperature
Temperature, Body
    USE   Body temperature
Temperatures, Low
    USE   Low temperatures
Temples (May subdiv. geog.)   291.3; 726
    BT   Ancient architecture
           Archeology
           Asian architecture
           Buildings
           Church architecture
    NT   Mosques
Temporal power of the Pope
    USE   Popes—Temporal power
Temporary employment   331.25
    UF   Employment, Temporary
    BT   Employment
Ten commandments   222
    UF   Commandments, Ten
           Decalogue
    BT   Bible. O.T.
Tenant and landlord
    USE   Landlord and tenant
Tenant farming
    USE   Farm tenancy

Tenement houses (May subdiv. geog.)
    647
    UF   Tenements (Apartment houses)
    BT   Apartment houses
Tenements (Apartment houses)
    USE   Tenement houses
Tennis   796.342
    UF   Lawn tennis
    BT   Sports
Tennis—Tournaments   796.342
    BT   Contests
Tenpins
    USE   Bowling
Tension (Physiology)
    USE   Stress (Physiology)
Tension, Premenstrual
    USE   Premenstrual syndrome
Tension (Psychology)
    USE   Stress (Psychology)
Tents   796.54
    BT   Camping
Tenure of land
    USE   Land tenure
Tenure of office
    USE   Civil service
Tepees
    USE   Indians of North America—
           Dwellings
Term paper writing
    USE   Report writing
Terminal care   362.1; 649.8
    UF   Care of the dying
    BT   Medical care
    NT   Hospices
           Life support systems (Medical
           environment)
           Terminally ill
    RT   Death
           Living wills
Terminally ill   362.1; 649.8
    UF   Dying patients
           Fatally ill patients
    BT   Sick
           Terminal care
    NT   Terminally ill children
    RT   Death
Terminally ill children   362.1; 649.8
    UF   Dying children
           Fatally ill children
    BT   Terminally ill

BT = Broader Term   NT = Narrower Term   RT = Related Term   SA = See Also   UF = Used For

Terminals, Computer
　USE　**Computer terminals**
Termination of pregnancy
　USE　**Abortion**
Terminology
　USE　**Names**
　　　　Terms and phrases
　　　　and names of languages with
　　　　the subdivision *Terms and*
　　　　phrases, e.g. **English lan-**
　　　　guage—Terms and phrases;
　　　　and subjects, classes of per-
　　　　sons, sacred works, or reli-
　　　　gious sects with the subdivi-
　　　　sion *Terminology,* e.g. **Bota-**
　　　　ny—Terminology; to be add-
　　　　ed as needed
Terms and phrases　030
　UF　Commonplaces
　　　　Terminology
　SA　names of languages with the
　　　　subdivision *Terms and*
　　　　phrases, e.g. **English lan-**
　　　　guage—Terms and phrases;
　　　　and subjects, classes of per-
　　　　sons, sacred works, or reli-
　　　　gious sects with the subdivi-
　　　　sion *Terminology,* e.g. **Bota-**
　　　　ny—Terminology; to be add-
　　　　ed as needed
　BT　**Names**
　RT　**Allusions**
Terns　598.3
　BT　**Birds**
　　　　Water birds
Terra cotta　620.1; 691
　BT　**Building materials**
　　　　Decoration and ornament
　　　　Pottery
Terrain sensing, Remote
　USE　**Remote sensing**
Terrapins
　USE　**Turtles**
Terrariums　635.9
　UF　Vivariums
　BT　**Indoor gardening**
　RT　**Miniature gardens**
Terrestrial physics
　USE　**Geophysics**

Territorial waters (May subdiv. geog.)
　　　　341.4
　UF　3 mile limit
　　　　200 mile limit
　　　　Economic zones (Maritime law)
　　　　Three mile limit
　　　　Two hundred mile limit
　BT　**Shipping**
　RT　**Continental shelf**
　　　　Maritime law
Territorial waters—United States　341.4
　UF　United States—Territorial waters
Terror, Reign of
　USE　**France—History—1789-1799,**
　　　　Revolution
Terror tales
　USE　**Ghost stories**
　　　　Horror fiction
Terrorism (May subdiv. geog.)　**303.6**
　UF　Political violence
　BT　**Insurgency**
　　　　Political crimes and offenses
　　　　Subversive activities
　NT　**Bombings**
　　　　Hostages
　　　　Sabotage
　RT　**Anarchism and anarchists**
Terrorism—United States　303.6; 322.4
　UF　United States—Terrorism
Terrorist bombings
　USE　**Bombings**
Test pilots
　USE　**Air pilots**
　　　　Airplanes—Testing
Test tube babies
　USE　**Fertilization in vitro**
Test tube fertilization
　USE　**Fertilization in vitro**
Testing
　USE　**Electric testing**
　　　　Reliability (Engineering)
　　　　Strength of materials
　　　　and things tested with the sub-
　　　　division *Testing,* e.g. **Abili-**
　　　　ty—Testing; Airplanes—
　　　　Testing; Concrete—Testing;
　　　　etc; and classes of persons
　　　　with the subdivision *Drug*
　　　　testing, e.g. **Employees—**

Testing—*Continued*

> Drug testing; to be added as needed

Testing for drug abuse

USE **Drug testing**

Tests

USE **Educational tests and measurements**

Examinations

Teutonic peoples   305.83

UF   Nordic peoples

Teutonic race

SA   names of particular Teutonic peoples, e.g. **Goths;** to be added as needed

NT   **Anglo-Saxons**

Goths

Teutonic race

USE   **Teutonic peoples**

Textbooks   371.3

Use for materials about textbooks. Textbooks themselves are entered under the subject only, e.g. **Arithmetic; Geography;** etc.

UF   School books

BT   **Books**

Textile chemistry   677

UF   Chemistry, Textile

BT   **Industrial chemistry**

Textile industry

NT   **Dyes and dyeing**

Textile design   746

UF   Fabric design

BT   **Commercial art**

Decoration and ornament

Design

NT   **Textile painting**

RT   **Textile printing**

Textile fibers

USE   **Fibers**

Textile industry   338.4; 677

SA   types of articles manufactured, e.g **Carpets; Hosiery;** etc., to be added as needed

BT   **Industries**

NT   **Bleaching**

Carpets

Cotton manufacture

Dyes and dyeing

Hosiery

Spinning

Textile chemistry

Textile printing

Yarn

RT   **Weaving**

Textile painting   746.6

BT   **Painting**

Textile design

Textile printing   746.6

UF   Block printing

Printing, Textile

BT   **Printing**

Textile industry

RT   **Silk screen printing**

Textile design

Textiles

USE   **Fabrics**

Texts

USE   lesser-known languages, dialects, early periods of languages, liturgies, and types of vocal music with the subdivision *Texts,* e.g. **Catholic Church—Liturgy—Texts; Popular music—Texts;** etc., for individual texts or collections of texts, to be added as needed

Thanksgiving Day   394.2649

BT   **Holidays**

Religious holidays

Theater (May subdiv. geog.)   792

Use for materials on drama as acted on the stage. Materials on drama as a literary form are entered under **Drama; American drama; English drama;** etc. Collections of plays are entered under **Drama—Collections; American drama—Collections;** etc. Materials on theater buildings are entered under **Theaters.**

UF   Histrionics

Stage

SA   names of wars with the subdivision *Theater and the war,* to be added as needed

BT   **Amusements**

Performing arts

NT   **Amateur theater**

Arena theater

Ballet

Children's plays

Experimental theater

Little theater movement

Masks (Plays)

BT = Broader Term   NT = Narrower Term   RT = Related Term   SA = See Also   UF = Used For

Theater—*Continued*
Morality plays
Musicals
Mysteries and miracle plays
Pantomimes
Passion plays
Puppets and puppet plays
Readers' theater
Shadow pantomimes and plays
Shakespeare, William, 1564-
1616—Stage history
Skits
Vaudeville
World War, 1939-1945—The-
ater and the war
RT Acting
Actors
Drama
Dramatic criticism
Theaters
Theater criticism
USE Dramatic criticism
Theater-in-the-round
USE Arena theater
Theater—Little theater movement
USE Little theater movement
Theater—Production and direction   792
UF Direction (Theater)
Play direction (Theater)
Play production
Theatrical direction
Theatrical production
RT Theatrical producers and di-
rectors
Theater—United States   792.0973
UF United States—Theater
Theaters (May subdiv. geog.)   725
Use for materials on theater buildings, their
architecture, technical fixtures, decoration, etc.
Materials on drama as a literary form are en-
tered under **Drama**. Materials on drama as
acted on the stage are entered under **Theater.**
UF Playhouses
SA types of theaters, to be added as
needed
BT **Buildings**
**Centers for the performing
arts**
RT **Theater**
Theaters—Stage lighting
USE **Stage lighting**

Theaters—Stage setting and scenery
792
UF Scenery (Stage)
Stage scenery
Stage setting
Theatrical scenery
NT **Scene painting**
Theatrical costume
USE **Costume**
Theatrical direction
USE **Theater—Production and di-
rection**
Theatrical directors
USE **Theatrical producers and di-
rectors**
Theatrical directors and producers
USE **Theatrical producers and di-
rectors**
Theatrical makeup   791.43; 791.45; 792
UF Makeup, Theatrical *[Former
heading]*
BT **Cosmetics**
Costume
Theatrical producers
USE **Theatrical producers and di-
rectors**
Theatrical producers and directors
792; 920
UF Theatrical directors
Theatrical directors and produc-
ers
Theatrical producers
RT **Theater—Production and di-
rection**
Theatrical production
USE **Theater—Production and di-
rection**
Theatrical scenery
USE **Theaters—Stage setting and
scenery**
Theatricals, College
USE **College and school drama**
Theft
USE **Stealing**
Thefts, Art
USE **Art thefts**
Theism   211
BT **Philosophy**
Religion
Theology

BT = Broader Term   NT = Narrower Term   RT = Related Term   SA = See Also   UF = Used For

715

Theism—*Continued*
    RT   **Atheism**
           Deism
           God
Theme parks
    USE   **Amusement parks**
Theological education
    USE   **Religious education**
           Theology—Study and teaching
Theology   230; 291.2
    NT   **Apologetics**
           Atheism
           Church
           Covenants
           Deism
           Doctrinal theology
           Eschatology
           Faith
           Feminist theology
           Good and evil
           Immortality
           Natural theology
           Pastoral theology
           Predestination
           Revelation
           Secularism
           Sin
           Theism
           Worship
    RT   **God**
           Religion
Theology, Doctrinal
    USE   **Doctrinal theology**
Theology, Feminist
    USE   **Feminist theology**
Theology of liberation
    USE   **Liberation theology**
Theology, Pastoral
    USE   **Pastoral theology**
Theology—Study and teaching   230.07;
      291.2
    UF   Education, Theological
           Religion—Study and teaching
           Theological education
    NT   **Catechisms**
    RT   **Religious education**
Theoretical chemistry
    USE   **Physical chemistry**
Theory of games
    USE   **Game theory**

Theory of graphs
    USE   **Graph theory**
Theory of knowledge   001.01; 121
      Use for materials on the origin, nature,
    methods, and limits of human knowledge.
    UF   Cognition
           Epistemology
           Knowledge, Theory of *[Former
             heading]*
           Understanding
    BT   **Consciousness**
           Logic
           Metaphysics
           Philosophy
    NT   **Belief and doubt**
           Empiricism
           Gestalt psychology
           Ideology
           Intuition
           Perception
           Pragmatism
           Rationalism
           Senses and sensation
    RT   **Apperception**
           Intellect
           Reality
           Truth
Theory of numbers
    USE   **Number theory**
Theory of structures
    USE   **Structural analysis (Engineer-
           ing)**
Theory of systems
    USE   **System theory**
Theosophy   299
    BT   **Mysticism**
           Religions
    NT   **Reincarnation**
           Yoga
Therapeutic systems
    USE   **Alternative medicine**
Therapeutic use
    USE   subjects with the subdivision
           Therapeutic use, e.g. **Cold—
           Therapeutic use;** to be added
           as needed
Therapeutics   615.5
    UF   Diseases—Treatment
           Therapy
           Treatment
           Treatment of diseases

BT = Broader Term   NT = Narrower Term   RT = Related Term   SA = See Also   UF = Used For

Therapeutics—*Continued*
    SA   types of therapies, e.g. **Hydro-**
           therapy; diseases with the
           subdivision *Treatment*, e.g.
           AIDS (Disease)—Treatment;
           subjects with the subdivision
           Therapeutic use, e.g. **Cold—**
           Therapeutic use; and types
           of drugs and names of specif-
           ic drugs, to be added as
           needed
    BT   **Medicine**
           Pathology
    NT   **AIDS (Disease)—Treatment**
           Antiseptics
           Cold—Therapeutic use
           Diet in disease
           Diet therapy
           Drug therapy
           Drugs
           Electrotherapeutics
           Gene therapy
           Hydrotherapy
           Materia medica
           Medicine
           Naturopathy
           Nursing
           Nutrition
           Occupational therapy
           Pet therapy
           Phototherapy
           Physical therapy
           Psychotherapy
           Radiotherapy
           Suggestive therapeutics
    RT   **Pharmaceutical chemistry**
Therapeutics, Suggestive
    USE   **Suggestive therapeutics**
Therapy
    USE   **Therapeutics**
Therapy, Gene
    USE   **Gene therapy**
Therapy, Psychological
    USE   **Psychotherapy**
Thermal insulation
    USE   **Insulation (Heat)**
Thermal waters
    USE   **Geothermal resources**
           Geysers

Thermoaerodynamics
    USE   **Aerothermodynamics**
Thermodynamics   **536**
    SA   subjects with the subdivision
           Thermodynamics, e.g. **Space**
           vehicles—Thermodynamics;
           to be added as needed
    BT   **Dynamics**
           Physical chemistry
           Physics
    NT   **Aerothermodynamics**
           Heat engines
           Heat pumps
           Space vehicles—Thermodynam-
           ics
    RT   **Heat**
           Heat engines
           Quantum theory
Thermometers   **536**
    UF   Thermometry
    BT   **Heat**
           Meteorological instruments
    RT   **Temperature**
Thermometry
    USE   **Thermometers**
Thermonuclear bomb
    USE   **Hydrogen bomb**
Thesauri
    USE   **Subject headings**
           and names of languages with
           the subdivision *Synonyms and*
           antonyms, e.g. **English lan-**
           guage—Synonyms and ant-
           onyms; to be added as need-
           ed
Theses
    USE   **Dissertations**
Thieves   **364.3**
    UF   Bandits
           Brigands
           Brigands and robbers
           Burglars
           Highwaymen
           Outlaws
           Robbers and outlaws *[Former*
           heading]
    BT   **Criminals**
    RT   **Stealing**
Think tanks
    USE   **Group problem solving**

BT = Broader Term   NT = Narrower Term   RT = Related Term   SA = See Also   UF = Used For

Thinking
  USE   **Thought and thinking**
Third parties (U.S. politics)
  USE   **Third parties (United States politics)**
Third parties (United States politics)
    324.273
  UF   Third parties (U.S. politics)
      [Former heading]
  BT   **Political parties**
      United States—Politics and government
Third World
  USE   **Developing countries**
Third World War
  USE   **World War III**
Thirteenth century   909
    Use for general materials covering progress and development during this period in one or in several countries.
  UF   1200-1299 (13th century)
  BT   **Middle Ages**
Thirty Years' War, 1618-1648   909.08; 940.2
  BT   **Europe—History—1492-1789**
      Germany—History—1517-1740
Thoroughfares
  USE   **Roads**
      Streets
Thought and thinking   153.4
  UF   Thinking
  BT   **Educational psychology**
      Psychology
  NT   **Attention**
      Critical thinking
      Ideology
      Memory
      Perception
      Reasoning
      Stereotype (Psychology)
  RT   **Intellect**
      Logic
Thought control
  USE   **Brainwashing**
Thought transference
  USE   **Telepathy**
Threatened species
  USE   **Endangered species**
Three dimensional computer graphics
  USE   **Virtual reality**

Three dimensional photography   778.4
  UF   3-D photography
      3D photography
      Photography, Stereoscopic *[Former heading]*
      Stereo photography
      Stereophotography
      Stereoscopic photography
  BT   **Photography**
  RT   **Holography**
Three mile limit
  USE   **Territorial waters**
Three Stooges films   791.43
    May be used for individual works, collections, or materials about Three Stooges films.
  BT   **Comedy films**
      Motion pictures
Three (The number)   513
  BT   **Numbers**
Thrift
  USE   **Saving and thrift**
Thrillers
  USE   **Adventure fiction**
      Adventure films
Throat   611; 612; 617.5
  BT   **Anatomy**
  NT   **Voice**
Thunderstorms   551.55
  BT   **Meteorology**
      Storms
  NT   **Lightning**
Tiananmen Square Incident, China, 1989
  USE   **China—History—1989, Tiananmen Square Incident**
Tiananmen Square Massacre, China
  USE   **China—History—1989, Tiananmen Square Incident**
Ticks   595.4
  UF   Arachnida
  BT   **Parasites**
  RT   **Lyme disease**
Tidal waves
  USE   **Ocean waves**
Tidal waves, Seismic
  USE   **Tsunamis**
Tides   551.47
  BT   **Astronomy**
      Moon
      Navigation
      Ocean
      Physical geography

Tie dyeing   746.6
   BT   **Dyes and dyeing**
Tiles   666; 693; 738.6
   BT   **Bricks**
        Building materials
        Ceramics
        Clay industries
        Pottery
Timber
   USE   **Forests and forestry**
        Lumber and lumbering
        Trees
        Wood
Time   529
   UF   Horology
        Standard time
   NT   **Calendars**
        Chronology
        Clocks and watches
        Day
        Night
        Punctuality
        Space and time
        Sundials
   RT   **Cycles**
        Nautical astronomy
Time and space
   USE   **Space and time**
Time management   640; 650.1
   UF   Allocation of time
        Personal time management
        Time—Organization
        Time, Use of
        Use of time
   BT   **Management**
Time—Organization
   USE   **Time management**
Time production standards
   USE   **Production standards**
Time saving cooking
   USE   **Quick and easy cooking**
Time sharing (Real estate)
   USE   **Timesharing (Real estate)**
Time study   658.5
   BT   **Factory management**
        Industrial efficiency
        Job analysis
        Personnel management
        Production standards
   RT   **Motion study**

Time travel
   USE   **Fourth dimension**
Time travel (Fiction)
   USE   **Fantasy fiction**
        Fantasy films
        Fantasy television programs
        Imaginary voyages
        Science fiction
        Science fiction plays
        Science fiction radio programs
        Science fiction television pro-
          grams
Time, Use of
   USE   **Time management**
Timesharing (Real estate)   333.3; 333.5;
        643
   UF   Condominium timesharing
        Real estate timesharing
        Time sharing (Real estate)
        Vacation home timesharing
   BT   **Condominiums**
        Housing
Tin   669
   BT   **Chemical elements**
        Metals
Tinsmithing
   USE   **Tinwork**
Tinwork   673
   UF   Tinsmithing
   BT   **Metalwork**
Tiny objects
   USE   **Miniature objects**
Tipis
   USE   **Indians of North America—**
        Dwellings
Tires   678
   UF   Rubber tires
   BT   **Wheels**
Tiros (Meteorological satellite)   551.5
   UF   T.I.R.O.S. (Meteorological satel-
        lite)
        Television and infrared observa-
        tion satellite
   BT   **Meteorological satellites**
Tissue donation
   USE   **Donation of organs, tissues,**
        etc.
Tissues—Transplantation
   USE   **Transplantation of organs, tis-**
        sues, etc.

Tithes   248; 254
  BT   Church finance
       Ecclesiastical law
       Taxation
Toadstools
  USE   Mushrooms
Toasts   808.5; 808.85
  UF   Healths, Drinking of
  BT   Epigrams
       Speeches
  RT   After dinner speeches
Tobacco   633.7
  BT   Plants
  NT   Cigarettes
       Cigars
  RT   Smoking
Tobacco habit   178; 613.85; 616.86
  UF   Addiction to nicotine
       Addiction to tobacco
       Nicotine habit
  BT   Habit
       Smoking
  NT   Smoking cessation programs
Tobacco pipes   688
  UF   Pipes, Tobacco
  BT   Smoking
Toilet preparations
  USE   Toiletries
Toilet training   649
  UF   Training, Toilet
  BT   Child rearing
Toiletries   646.7
  UF   Toilet preparations
  BT   Personal grooming
  RT   Cosmetics
Toleration   179; 323
  UF   Bigotry
       Intolerance
  BT   Human relations
  NT   Academic freedom
       Freedom of conscience
       Freedom of religion
  RT   Discrimination
Toll roads
  USE   Express highways
Tombs (May subdiv. geog.)   726
  UF   Graves
       Mausoleums
       Rock tombs
       Sepulchers

Vaults (Sepulchral)
  BT   Archeology
       Architecture
       Burial
       Monuments
       Shrines
  NT   Brasses
       Catacombs
       Epitaphs
       Mounds and mound builders
  RT   Cemeteries
Tomography   616.07; 621.36
  UF   CAT scan
       Computerized tomography
  BT   X-rays
Tongue twisters   398.8
  BT   Children's poetry
       Folklore
       Nonsense verses
Tools   621.9
  UF   Implements, utensils, etc.
  SA   types of tools, to be added as
       needed
  NT   Agricultural machinery
       Carpentry tools
       Machine tools
       Machinery
       Power tools
       Saws
       Weapons
Top soil loss
  USE   Soil erosion
Topographical drawing   526.022
  BT   Drawing
       Surveying
  RT   Map drawing
Topology   514
  UF   Analysis situs
       Position analysis
       Rubber sheet geometry
  BT   Geometry
       Set theory
  NT   Fractals
       Graph theory
  RT   Linear algebra
Tories, American
  USE   American Loyalists
Tornadoes (May subdiv. geog.)   551.55
  UF   Twisters (Tornadoes)
  BT   Meteorology

BT = Broader Term   NT = Narrower Term   RT = Related Term   SA = See Also   UF = Used For

Tornadoes—*Continued*
      Storms
      Winds
Torpedoes   623.4
  BT **Explosives**
        Naval art and science
        Submarine warfare
Tort liability of professions
  USE **Malpractice**
Tortoises
  USE **Turtles**
Torture (May subdiv. geog.)   **365**
  BT **Criminal procedure**
        Cruelty
        Punishment
Total abstinence
  USE **Temperance**
Totalitarianism   321.9
  UF Authoritarianism
  BT **Political science**
  NT **Communism**
        Dictators
        Fascism
Totem poles   299; 730.89
  BT **Totems and totemism**
Totems and totemism   299
  BT **Ethnology**
        Mythology
  NT **Totem poles**
Touch   152.1; 612
  UF Feeling
  BT **Senses and sensation**
  NT **Hugging**
Touring, Bicycle
  USE **Bicycle touring**
Tourism
  USE **Tourist trade**
Tourist accommodations
  USE **Hotels and motels**
        Youth hostels
Tourist trade   338.4
  UF Tourism
        Tourists
  BT **Commerce**
  RT **Travel**
Tourists
  USE **Tourist trade**
        Travelers

Tournaments
  USE subjects with the subdivision
        Tournaments, e.g. **Tennis—**
        Tournaments; to be added as
        needed
Town life
  USE **City life**
Town meeting
  USE **Local government**
Town officers
  USE **Municipal officials and em-**
        ployees
Town planning
  USE **City planning**
Towns
  USE **Cities and towns**
Towns, abandoned
  USE **Ghost towns**
Township government
  USE **Local government**
Toxic dumps
  USE **Hazardous waste sites**
Toxic plants
  USE **Poisonous plants**
Toxic substances
  USE **Hazardous substances**
        Poisons and poisoning
Toxic wastes
  USE **Hazardous wastes**
Toxicology
  USE **Poisons and poisoning**
Toy and movable books
  UF Movable books
        Pop-up books
  BT **Picture books for children**
  NT **Glow-in-the-dark books**
Toys   688.7; 790.1
  SA types of toys, to be added as
        needed
  BT **Amusements**
  NT **Dollhouses**
        Dolls
        Electric toys
        Electronic toys
  RT **Miniature objects**
Track and field
  USE **Track athletics**
Track athletics   796.42
  UF Field athletics
        Track and field

BT = Broader Term   NT = Narrower Term   RT = Related Term   SA = See Also   UF = Used For

Track athletics—*Continued*
  SA   types of track sports, to be add-
        ed as needed
  BT   **Athletics**
        Sports
  NT   **Running**
Tracking and trailing   799.2
  UF   Trailing
  BT   **Hunting**
  NT   **Animal tracks**
  RT   **Animal behavior**
Tracking of satellites
  USE   **Artificial satellites—Tracking**
        Space vehicles—Tracking
Tracks of animals
  USE   **Animal tracks**
Traction engines
  USE   **Tractors**
Tractors   629.225; 631.3
  UF   Traction engines
  BT   **Agricultural machinery**
Trade
  USE   **Business**
        Commerce
Trade agreements (Labor)
  USE   **Industrial arbitration**
        Labor contract
Trade and professional associations
        380.1; 650
    Use for materials on business or profession-
  al organizations whose aim is the protection
  or advancement of their common interests
  without regard to the relations of employer
  and employee.
  UF   Professional associations
  BT   **Associations**
Trade, Balance of
  USE   **Balance of trade**
Trade barriers
  USE   **Commercial policy**
Trade, Boards of
  USE   **Chambers of commerce**
Trade fairs
  USE   **Fairs**
Trade, International
  USE   **International trade**
Trade marks
  USE   **Trademarks**
Trade, Restraint of
  USE   **Restraint of trade**
Trade routes   387
  UF   Ocean routes

        Routes of trade
        Sea routes
  BT   **Commerce**
        Commercial geography
        Transportation
Trade schools
  USE   **Technical education**
Trade secrets   346.04; 658.4
  UF   Business secrets
        Commercial secrets
        Industrial secrets
        Secrets, Trade
  BT   **Right of privacy**
        Unfair competition
Trade shows
  USE   **Exhibitions**
Trade unions
  USE   **Labor unions**
Trade waste
  USE   **Industrial wastes**
        Waste products
Trademarks   346.04; 929.9
  UF   Company symbols
        Corporate symbols
        Trade marks
  BT   **Commerce**
        Manufactures
  RT   **Brand name products**
        Patents
Trades
  USE   **Industrial arts**
        Occupations
Traditional birth attendants
  USE   **Midwives**
Traditional medicine (May subdiv. geog.)
        615.8
  UF   Folk medicine *[Former heading]*
        Folklore, Medical
        Medical folklore
  SA   ethnic groups and groups of
        American Indians with the
        subdivision *Medicine,* e.g. **In-**
        dians of North America—
        Medicine; to be added as
        needed
  BT   **Medicine**
        Popular medicine
Traditions
  USE   **Folklore**
        Legends

BT = Broader Term   NT = Narrower Term   RT = Related Term   SA = See Also   UF = Used For

Traditions—*Continued*

    Manners and customs

    Rites and ceremonies

    Superstition

Traffic accidents   363.12

  UF   Automobile accidents

          Automobiles—Accidents

          Car accidents

          Car wrecks

          Highway accidents

  BT   **Accidents**

  RT   **Traffic regulations**

Traffic, City

  USE   **City traffic**

Traffic control

  USE   **Traffic engineering**

Traffic engineering   388.4

    Use for materials on the planning of the flow of traffic and related topics, largely as they concern street transportation in cities and metropolitan areas.

  UF   Street traffic

          Traffic control

          Traffic regulation

  BT   **Engineering**

          Highway engineering

          Transportation

  NT   **Car pools**

          City traffic

          Express highways

          Local transit

          Traffic regulations

Traffic regulation

  USE   **Traffic engineering**

Traffic regulations   388.4

  UF   Street traffic

  BT   **Traffic engineering**

          Transportation

  RT   **Automobiles—Law and legislation**

          Traffic accidents

Trafficking in drugs

  USE   **Drug traffic**

Trafficking in narcotics

  USE   **Drug traffic**

Tragedies   808.82; 812, etc.

    May be used for individual works or for collections. Materials about tragedy as a literary form are entered under **Tragedy.**

  BT   **Drama**

Tragedy   792.1; 809.2

    Use for materials on tragedy as a literary form. Individual works and collections of tragedies are entered under **Tragedies.**

  BT   **Drama**

Trailer camps

  USE   **Trailer parks**

Trailer parks   647; 796.54

  UF   Mobile home parks *[Former heading]*

          Trailer camps

  BT   **Campgrounds**

          Mobile home living

Trailers

  USE   **Travel trailers and campers**

Trailers, Home

  USE   **Mobile homes**

Trailing

  USE   **Tracking and trailing**

Train wrecks

  USE   **Railroad accidents**

Trained nurses

  USE   **Nurses**

Training

  USE   sports activites, plants and crops, animals, and classes of persons with the subdivision *Training,* e.g. **Soccer—Training; Horses—Training; Teachers—Training;** etc., to be added as needed

Training camps, Military

  USE   **Military training camps**

Training colleges for teachers

  USE   **Teachers colleges**

Training, Occupational

  USE   **Occupational training**

Training of animals

  USE   **Animals—Training**

Training of children

  USE   **Child rearing**

Training of employees

  USE   **Employees—Training**

Training, Toilet

  USE   **Toilet training**

Training, Vocational

  USE   **Occupational training**

Trains

  USE   **Railroads**

BT = Broader Term   NT = Narrower Term   RT = Related Term   SA = See Also   UF = Used For

Tramps   305.5

Use for materials on persons who travel about from place to place living on occasional jobs or gifts of money and food.

UF   Hoboes

Vagabonds

Vagrants

BT   **Homeless persons**

Poor

RT   **Begging**

Unemployed

Trams

USE   **Street railroads**

Transactional analysis   158

BT   **Human relations**

Psychotherapy

Transatlantic flights

USE   **Aeronautics—Flights**

Transcendental meditation   158

BT   **Meditation**

Transcendentalism   141

BT   **Philosophy**

RT   **Idealism**

Transcontinental journeys (American continent)

USE   **Overland journeys to the Pacific**

Transcultural studies

USE   **Cross cultural studies**

Transexuality

USE   **Transsexuality**

Transfer of technology

USE   **Technology transfer**

Transfer payments (May subdiv. geog.) **339.5**

UF   Government transfer payments

BT   **Domestic economic assistance**

Economic policy

Subsidies

Transfer tax

USE   **Inheritance and transfer tax**

Transformation (Genetics)

USE   **Genetic transformation**

Transformers, Electric

USE   **Electric transformers**

Transgenics

USE   **Genetic engineering**

Transistor amplifiers   621.3815

UF   Amplifiers, Transistor

Audio amplifiers, Transistor

Transistor audio amplifiers

BT   **Amplifiers (Electronics)**

Transistors

Transistor audio amplifiers

USE   **Transistor amplifiers**

Transistors   621.3815

BT   **Electronics**

Semiconductors

NT   **Transistor amplifiers**

Transit systems

USE   **Local transit**

Translating and interpreting   418

UF   Interpreting and translating

BT   **Language and languages**

Transmission of data

USE   **Data transmission systems**

Transmission of power

USE   **Electric lines**

Electric power distribution

Power transmission

Transmissions, Automobile

USE   **Automobiles—Transmission devices**

Transmutation (Chemistry)   539.7

Use for materials on the transmutation of metals in nuclear physics. Materials on medieval attempts to change base metals into gold are entered under **Alchemy.**

UF   Metals, Transmutation of

Transmutation of metals

BT   **Atoms**

Nuclear physics

Radioactivity

NT   **Cyclotron**

RT   **Alchemy**

Transmutation of metals

USE   **Alchemy**

Transmutation (Chemistry)

Transplantation of organs, tissues, etc. 617.9

UF   Medical transplantation

Organ transplantation

Organ transplants

Surgical transplantation

Tissues—Transplantation

SA   organs of the body with the subdivision *Transplantation,* to be added as needed

BT   **Surgery**

NT   **Heart—Transplantation**

Plastic surgery

BT = Broader Term   NT = Narrower Term   RT = Related Term   SA = See Also   UF = Used For

Transplantation of organs, tissues, etc.—
Continued
RT   Donation of organs, tissues,
      etc.
      Preservation of organs, tissues,
      etc.
Transplantation of organs, tissues, etc.—
      Ethical aspects   174
UF   Transplantation of organs, tis-
      sues, etc.—Moral and reli-
      gious aspects *[Former head-
      ing]*
BT   Bioethics
Transplantation of organs, tissues, etc.—
      Moral and religious aspects
USE   **Transplantation of organs, tis-
      sues, etc.—Ethical aspects**
      **Transplantation of organs, tis-
      sues, etc.—Religious aspects**
Transplantation of organs, tissues, etc.—
      Religious aspects   241; 291.1
UF   Transplantation of organs, tis-
      sues, etc.—Moral and reli-
      gious aspects *[Former head-
      ing]*
Transportation (May subdiv. geog.)   388
SA   subjects, classes of person, and
      names of wars with the sub-
      division *Transportation*, e.g.
      **Hazardous substances—
      Transportation; School chil-
      dren—Transportation;
      World War, 1939-1945—
      Transportation**; etc., to be
      added as needed
BT   Locomotion
NT   Boats and boating
      Bridges
      Canals
      Car pools
      Commercial aeronautics
      Electric railroads
      Express service
      Freight
      Harbors
      Hazardous substances—Trans-
      portation
      Highway transportation
      Inland navigation
      Local transit

      Merchant marine
      Military transportation
      Ocean travel
      Pipelines
      Postal service
      Railroads
      Roads
      School children—Transporta-
      tion
      Shipping
      Steam navigation
      Street railroads
      Streets
      Trade routes
      Traffic engineering
      Traffic regulations
      Trucking
      Vehicles
      Waterways
      World War, 1939-1945—Trans-
      portation
RT   Commerce
Transportation, Highway
USE   **Highway transportation**
Transportation, Military
USE   **Military transportation**
Transportation of criminals
USE   **Penal colonies**
Transportation—Planning (May subdiv.
      geog.)   338
BT   Planning
Transsexuality   305.3; 616.85
UF   Change of sex
      Sex change
      Transexuality
BT   Sex role
Trapping   639
NT   Fur trade
RT   Game and game birds
      Hunting
Traumatic stress syndrome
USE   **Post-traumatic stress disorder**
Travel   910
      Use for materials on the art and enjoyment
      of travel and advice for travelers. Descriptions
      of actual voyages are entered under **Voyages
      and travels** or under the name of a place with
      the subdivision *Description.* An account of an
      extinct city or town by a traveler in ancient
      times is entered under the name of the extinct
      city or town, without further subdivision, e.g.
      Delphi (Extinct city).
UF   Group travel

BT = Broader Term   NT = Narrower Term   RT = Related Term   SA = See Also   UF = Used For

Travel—*Continued*

    Journeys

  SA   names of cities (except extinct cities), countries, states, etc., with the subdivision *Description,* e.g. **United States—Description;** and ethnic groups, classes of persons, and names of individuals with the subdivision *Travel,* e.g. **Handicapped—Travel;** to be added as needed

  BT   **Manners and customs**

  NT   **Automobile travel**

        Bicycle touring

        Handicapped—Travel

        Ocean travel

        Travel in literature

        Voyages around the world

  RT   **Tourist trade**

        Voyages and travels

Travel books

  USE   **Voyages and travels**

        Voyages around the world

Travel guides

  USE   **Automobile travel—Guidebooks** and names of cities (except ancient cities), countries, states, etc., with the subdivision *Guidebooks,* e.g. **Chicago (Ill.)—Guidebooks; United States—Guidebooks;** etc., to be added as needed

Travel in literature   809

  Use for materials about the theme of travel in literature. Materials about non-fiction travel writing, collections of travel writings, and accounts of voyages and travels not limited to a single place are entered under **Voyages and travels.** Accounts of voyages and travels limited to a single place are entered under the name of the place with the subdivision *Description.*

  UF   Voyages and travels in literature

  BT   **Literature**

       Travel

  RT   **Voyages and travels**

Travel trailers and campers   629.226; 796.7

  Use for materials on structures mounted upon a truck or towed by a truck or automobile for the purpose of temporary dwelling or cargo hauling. Materials on stationary trans-portable structures designed for year-round living are entered under **Mobile homes.**

  UF   Automobiles—Trailers *[Former heading]*

       Campers and trailers

       House trailers

       Pickup campers

       Trailers

  BT   **Camping**

       Recreational vehicles

  NT   **Vans**

  RT   **Mobile homes**

Travelers   910.92; 920

  UF   Tourists

       Voyagers

  SA   travelers from particular countries, e.g. **American travelers;** and ethnic groups, classes of person, and names of individuals with the subdivision *Travel,* e.g. **Presidents—United States—Travel;** to be added as needed

  BT   **Voyages and travels**

  NT   **American travelers**

  RT   **Explorers**

Travelers, American

  USE   **American travelers**

Traveling carnivals

  USE   **Carnivals**

Traveling sales personnel

  USE   **Sales personnel**

Travels

  USE   **Voyages and travels**

Travesties

  USE   **Parodies**

Tray gardens

  USE   **Miniature gardens**

Treason (May subdiv. geog.)   **364.1**

  Use for materials on the offense of acting to overthrow one's own government or to harm or kill its sovereign. Materials on any attempt to subvert, overthrow, or cause the destruction of any established or legally constituted government are entered under **Subversive activities.**

  UF   Collaborationists

       High treason

  BT   **Crime**

       Political crimes and offenses

       Subversive activities

Treasure trove

  USE   **Buried treasure**

BT = Broader Term   NT = Narrower Term   RT = Related Term   SA = See Also   UF = Used For

Treaties   341; 341.3
   SA   names of countries with the sub-
          division *Foreign relations—*
          Treaties, and names of wars
          with the subdivision *Treaties,*
          to be added as needed
   BT   **Congresses and conventions**
          Diplomacy
          International law
          International relations
   NT   **International arbitration**
          United States—Foreign rela-
          tions—Treaties
          World War, 1939-1945—Trea-
          ties

Treatment
   USE   **Therapeutics**
          and types of diseases with the
          subdivision *Treatment,* e.g.
          AIDS (Disease)—Treatment;
          to be added as needed

Treatment of diseases
   USE   **Therapeutics**

Tree planting   635.9
   UF   Planting
   BT   **Forests and forestry**
   NT   **Windbreaks**
   RT   **Christmas tree growing**
          Reforestation
          Trees

Trees (May subdiv. geog.)   582.16; 635.9
   UF   Arboriculture
          Timber
   SA   types of trees, e.g. **Oak;** to be
          added as needed, in the sin-
          gular form
   BT   **Plants**
   NT   **Apple**
          Christmas trees
          Dwarf trees
          Evergreens
          Fruit culture
          Lemon
          Lime (Fruit)
          Lumber and lumbering
          Nuts
          Oak
          Orange (Fruit)
          Pecan
          Pruning

          Shrubs
          Wood
   RT   **Forests and forestry**
          Landscape gardening
          Tree planting

Trees—United States   582.160973
   UF   United States—Trees

Trent Affair, 1861   973.7
   BT   **United States—History—1861-**
          1865, Civil War

Trial by jury
   USE   **Jury**

Trial by publicity
   USE   **Freedom of the press and fair**
          trial

Trial marriage
   USE   **Unmarried couples**

Trials   345; 347
      May be qualified by topic, e.g. **Trials**
      (Homicide).
   BT   **Criminal law**
   NT   **Courts martial and courts of**
          inquiry
          Trials (Homicide)
          War crime trials
          Witnesses
   RT   **Crime**

Trials (Homicide)   345
   UF   Homicide trials
          Murder trials
          Trials (Murder) *[Former head-*
          ing]
   BT   **Homicide**
          Trials

Trials (Murder)
   USE   **Trials (Homicide)**

Tricks   793.5
   SA   types of tricks, to be added as
          needed
   BT   **Amusements**
   NT   **Card tricks**
          Juggling
          Magic tricks

Tricycles   629.227; 796.6
   UF   Trikes
   BT   **Vehicles**
   RT   **Cycling**

Trigonometry   516.24
   UF   Plane trigonometry
          Spherical trigonometry
   BT   **Geometry**

BT = Broader Term   **NT** = Narrower Term   **RT** = Related Term   **SA** = See Also   **UF** = Used For

Trigonometry—*Continued*
        Mathematics
Trigonometry—Tables   **516.24**
    BT   **Mathematics—Tables**
    NT   **Logarithms**
Trikes
    USE   **Tricycles**
Trinity   **231**
    BT   **Christianity—Doctrines**
           God—Christianity
    NT   **Holy Spirit**
    RT   **Jesus Christ—Divinity**
Tripoline War
    USE   **United States—History—1801-**
           1805, Tripolitan War
Trivia
    USE   **Curiosities and wonders**
           Questions and answers
Trolley cars
    USE   **Street railroads**
Tropical diseases
    USE   **Tropical medicine**
Tropical fish   **597.17**
    BT   **Fishes**
Tropical jungles
    USE   **Jungles**
Tropical medicine   **614**
    UF   Diseases, Tropical
           Hygiene, Tropical
           Medicine, Tropical
           Tropical diseases
    SA   types of tropical diseases, e.g.
           Yellow fever; to be added as
           needed
    BT   **Medicine**
    NT   **Yellow fever**
Tropical rain forests
    USE   **Rain forests**
Tropics   **910.913**
    SA   subjects with the subdivision
           Tropics, or *Tropical condi-*
           tions, to be added as needed
    BT   **Earth**
    NT   **Agriculture—Tropics**
Troubadours   **849.1; 920**
    BT   **French poetry**
           Minstrels
           Poets
Trout fishing   **799.1**
    BT   **Fishing**

Truancy (Schools)
    USE   **School attendance**
Truck crops
    USE   **Truck farming**
Truck farming   **635**
    UF   Garden farming
           Market gardening
           Truck crops
           Truck gardening
    BT   **Agriculture**
           Gardening
           Horticulture
    RT   **Vegetable gardening**
Truck freight
    USE   **Trucking**
Truck gardening
    USE   **Truck farming**
Trucking   **388.3**
    UF   Truck freight
    BT   **Freight**
           Transportation
Trucks   **629.224**
    UF   Automobile trucks
           Motor trucks
    SA   types of trucks and names of
           specific makes and models, to
           be added as needed
    BT   **Automobiles**
           Highway transportation
    RT   **Materials handling**
Trust companies   **332.2**
    UF   Companies, Trust
    BT   **Business**
           Corporations
    RT   **Banks and banking**
Trusts, Industrial
    USE   **Industrial trusts**
Truth   **121**
    UF   Certainty
    BT   **Belief and doubt**
           Philosophy
    NT   **Reality**
           Truthfulness and falsehood
    RT   **Pragmatism**
           Skepticism
           Theory of knowledge
Truth in advertising
    USE   **Deceptive advertising**
Truthfulness and falsehood   **177**
    UF   Credibility

BT = Broader Term   NT = Narrower Term   RT = Related Term   SA = See Also   UF = Used For

Truthfulness and falsehood—*Continued*
      Falsehood
      Lying
      Untruth
  BT   **Human behavior**
      Truth
  NT   **Lie detectors and detection**
  RT   **Honesty**

Tsunamis   551.47
    Use for materials on unusually large sea waves generated by earthquakes or undersea volcanic eruptions.
  UF   Earthquake sea waves
      Seismic sea waves
      Tidal waves, Seismic
  BT   **Natural disasters**
      Ocean waves

Tuberculosis   362.1; 616.9
  BT   **Lungs—Diseases**

Tuberculosis—Mortality (May subdiv. geog.)   **362.1**

Tuberculosis—Vaccination   614.4

Tugboats   623.8
  BT   **Boats and boating**

Tuition
  USE   **College costs**
      Colleges and universities—Finance
      Education—Finance

Tumbling   796.47
  BT   **Acrobats and acrobatics**

Tumors   616.99
  NT   **Cancer**

Tuning   784.192
  SA   types of instruments with the subdivision *Tuning,* to be added as needed
  NT   **Pianos—Tuning**
  RT   **Musical instruments**

Tunnels   388; 624.1
  BT   **Civil engineering**
  NT   **Boring**
      Excavation

Turbines   621.406
  BT   **Engines**
      Hydraulic machinery
  NT   **Gas turbines**
      Steam turbines

Turkeys   598.6; 636.5
  BT   **Birds**
      Poultry

Turncoats
  USE   **Defectors**

Turning   621.9
  UF   Lathe work
      Wood turning
  BT   **Carpentry**
  RT   **Lathes**
      Woodwork

Turnpikes (Modern)
  USE   **Express highways**

Turtles   597.92
  UF   Terrapins
      Tortoises
  BT   **Reptiles**

Tutorial machines
  USE   **Teaching machines**

Tutoring
  USE   **Tutors and tutoring**

Tutors
  USE   **Tutors and tutoring**

Tutors and tutoring   371.39
    Use for materials on individual one-on-one instruction. Materials on the adaptation of instruction to meet individual needs within a group are entered under **Individualized instruction.**
  UF   Tutoring
      Tutors
  BT   **Teaching**
  NT   **Independent study**
  RT   **Individualized instruction**

TV
  USE   **Television**

Twelve-step programs   362.29
    Use for materials on self-help programs to resolve addiction problems which are based on the twelve-step, group approach of Alcoholics Anonymous. Materials on specific twelve-step programs are entered under the name of the individual organization.
  UF   Programs, Twelve-step
      Twelve steps (Self-help)
  SA   names of specific twelve-step programs, to be added as needed
  BT   **Behavior modification**
  RT   **Alcoholism**
      Compulsive behavior
      Drug abuse

Twelve steps (Self-help)
  USE   **Twelve-step programs**

BT = Broader Term   NT = Narrower Term   RT = Related Term   SA = See Also   UF = Used For

Twentieth century   909.82
> Use for general materials covering progress and development during this period in one or in several countries.

UF   1900-1999 (20th century)

BT   **Modern history—1900-1999 (20th century)**

Twenty-first century   909.83

UF   2000-2099 (21st century)

Twins   155.44; 306.875

BT   **Multiple birth**

RT   **Brothers and sisters**

Twisters (Tornadoes)

USE   **Tornadoes**

Two-career couples

USE   **Dual career family**

Two-career families

USE   **Dual career family**

Two-career family

USE   **Dual career family**

Two hundred mile limit

USE   **Territorial waters**

Type and type founding   686.2

BT   **Founding**
       Printing

NT   **Linotype**

RT   **Initials**
       Printing—Specimens
       Typesetting
       Typography

Type design

USE   **Typography**

Type-setting

USE   **Typesetting**

Type specimens

USE   **Printing—Specimens**

Typefaces

USE   **Typography**

Typesetting   686.2

UF   Composition (Printing)
       Type-setting

BT   **Printing**

NT   **Linotype**

RT   **Type and type founding**

Typewriters   652.3; 681

BT   **Office equipment and supplies**

Typewriting   652.3

BT   **Business education**
       Office practice
       Writing

RT   **Keyboarding (Electronics)**

Typhoid fever   616.9

UF   Enteric fever

BT   **Diseases**
       Fever

Typhoons   551.55
> Use for cyclonic storms originating in the region of the China Seas and the Philippines.

BT   **Cyclones**
       Storms
       Winds

RT   **Hurricanes**

Typography   686.2

UF   Type design
       Typefaces

BT   **Graphic arts**
       Printing

NT   **Advertising layout and typography**

RT   **Type and type founding**

U boats

USE   **Submarines**

U.F.O.'s

USE   **Unidentified flying objects**

U.N.

USE   **United Nations**

U.S.

USE   **United States**

U.S.A.

USE   **United States**

U.S.M.A.

USE   **United States Military Academy**

U.S.S.R.

USE   **Soviet Union**

UFOs

USE   **Unidentified flying objects**

UHF radio

USE   **Shortwave radio**

Ultrahigh frequency radio

USE   **Shortwave radio**

Ultrasonic waves   534.5

UF   Supersonic waves
       Waves, Ultrasonic

BT   **Sound waves**
       Ultrasonics

Ultrasonic waves—Industrial applications   620.2

Ultrasonics   534.5

UF   Inaudible sound
       Supersonics

BT   **Sound**

BT = Broader Term   NT = Narrower Term   RT = Related Term   SA = See Also   UF = Used For

Ultrasonics—*Continued*
  NT   Ultrasonic waves
Ultraviolet rays   535.01; 621.36
  UF   Rays, Ultra-violet
  BT   Electromagnetic waves
        Radiation
  RT   Phototherapy
        Radiotherapy
Umbrellas and parasols   391.4; 685
  UF   Parasols
  BT   Costume
UN
  USE   United Nations
Unbelief
  USE   Skepticism
Unborn child
  USE   Fetus
Unconventional warfare
  USE   Guerrilla warfare
Unction, Extreme
  USE   Anointing of the sick
Undenominational churches
  USE   Community churches
Under water exploration
  USE   Underwater exploration
Underdeveloped areas
  USE   Developing countries
Undergraduates
  USE   College students
Underground aliens
  USE   Illegal aliens
Underground, Anticommunist
  USE   Anticommunist movements
Underground architecture   624.1; 690;
        720
  UF   Underground design
  BT   Architecture
  NT   Basements
        Earth sheltered houses
Underground design
  USE   Underground architecture
Underground economy   381
    Use for materials on goods and services
  that are produced and sold legally but not re-
  ported or taxed. Materials on illegal trade
  aimed at avoiding government regulations,
  such as fixed prices or rationing, are entered
  under **Black market.**
  UF   Economy, Underground
        Hidden economy
        Income, Untaxed
        Informal sector (Economics)

        Parallel economy
        Second economy
        Shadow economy
  BT   Economics
        Small business
  NT   Barter
        Illegal aliens
  RT   Black market
Underground films
  USE   Experimental films
Underground houses
  USE   Earth sheltered houses
Underground literature
  USE   Alternative press
Underground movements (World War,
        1939-1945)
  USE   World War, 1939-1945—Un-
        derground movements
Underground press
  USE   Alternative press
Underground railroad   326
  RT   Slavery—United States
Underground railroads
  USE   Subways
Underprivileged
  USE   Socially handicapped
Underprivileged children
  USE   Socially handicapped children
Underprivileged students
  USE   At risk students
Undersea engineering
  USE   Ocean engineering
Undersea exploration
  USE   Underwater exploration
Undersea research habitats
  USE   Undersea research stations
Undersea research stations   551.46
  UF   Aquanauts *[Former heading]*
        Manned undersea research sta-
        tions
        Sea laboratories
        Submarine research stations
        Undersea research habitats
        Underwater research stations
  SA   names of special research
        projects and stations, e.g.
        Sealab project; to be added
        as needed
  BT   Oceanography—Research
        Underwater exploration

BT = Broader Term   NT = Narrower Term   RT = Related Term   SA = See Also   UF = Used For

Undersea research stations—*Continued*
    NT   **Sealab project**
Undersea technology
    USE   **Oceanography**
Undersea vehicles
    USE   **Submersibles**
Understanding
    USE   **Intellect**
            Theory of knowledge
Undertakers and undertaking   **363.7;**
    393
    UF   Funeral directors
           Morticians
    BT   **Service industries**
Underwater diving
    USE   **Deep diving**
Underwater drilling (Petroleum)
    USE   **Offshore oil well drilling**
Underwater exploration   **551.46; 627**
    UF   Aquanauts *[Former heading]*
           Exploration, Submarine
           Exploration, Underwater
           Submarine exploration
           Under water exploration
           Undersea exploration
    BT   **Exploration**
           Oceanography
    NT   **Buried treasure**
           Deep diving
           Marine biology
           Undersea research stations
Underwater exploration devices
    USE   **Submersibles**
Underwater geology
    USE   **Submarine geology**
Underwater medicine
    USE   **Submarine medicine**
Underwater photography   **778.7**
    UF   Deep-sea Photography
           Photography, Underwater
           Submarine photography
    BT   **Photography**
Underwater physiology
    USE   **Submarine medicine**
Underwater research stations
    USE   **Undersea research stations**
Underwater swimming
    USE   **Skin diving**
Underwriting
    USE   **Insurance**

Undocumented aliens
    USE   **Illegal aliens**
Unemployed   **331.13**
    UF   Jobless people
           Out-of-work people
    BT   **Labor supply**
           Poor
           Unemployment
    NT   **Food relief**
           Occupational retraining
    RT   **Domestic economic assistance**
           Tramps
Unemployment   **331.13**
    UF   Joblessness
    BT   **Employment**
           Labor supply
           Manpower policy
           Social problems
    NT   **Employment agencies**
           Unemployed
Unemployment insurance   **368.4**
    UF   Insurance, Unemployment *[For-*
           mer heading]
           Labor—Insurance
           Payroll taxes
    BT   **Insurance**
Unfair competition   **338.6**
    UF   Competition, Unfair *[Former*
           heading]
           Fair trade
           Unfair trade practices
    BT   **Commercial law**
    NT   **Trade secrets**
    RT   **Restraint of trade**
Unfair trade practices
    USE   **Unfair competition**
Ungraded schools
    USE   **Nongraded schools**
Unicameral legislatures
    USE   **Legislative bodies**
Unidentified flying objects   **001.9**
    UF   Flying saucers
           Saucers, Flying
           U.F.O.'s
           UFOs
    BT   **Aeronautics**
           Astronautics
Uniforms, Military
    USE   **Military uniforms**

BT = Broader Term   NT = Narrower Term   RT = Related Term   SA = See Also   UF = Used For

Uniforms, Naval
USE   **Military uniforms**
Union churches
USE   **Community churches**
Union of South Africa
USE   **South Africa**
Union of Soviet Socialist Republics
USE   **Soviet Union**
Union shop
USE   **Open and closed shop**
Unions, Labor
USE   **Labor unions**
Unison speaking
USE   **Choral speaking**
Unitarianism   289.1
BT   **Christian sects**
          Congregationalism
United Brethren
USE   **Moravians**
United Nations   341.23
UF   U.N.
          UN
BT   **International arbitration**
          International cooperation
          International organization
United Nations—Armed forces   341.23
UF   Peace keeping forces
BT   **Armed forces**
United Nations—Employees
USE   **United Nations—Officials and**
          employees
United Nations—Finance   341.23
BT   **Finance**
United Nations—Information services
          341.23
BT   **Information services**
United Nations—Officials and employees
          341.23
UF   United Nations—Employees
United States   973
   The subdivisions under **United States**, with
the exception of the period divisions of his-
tory, may be used under the name of any
country or region. The subdivisions under
Ohio may be used under names of states, and
those under **Chicago (Ill.)** under cities. Corporate name headings for corporate entities within the United States government, such as government agencies and departments, which are
used either as authors or as subjects, have a
period rather than a dash between the parts,
e.g. **United States. Army;** and may be added
as needed.
UF   U.S.

U.S.A.
US
USA
SA   regions of the United States and
          groups of states, e.g. **New**
          England; Southern States;
          etc., to be added as needed
NT   **Atlantic States**
          Gulf States (U.S.)
          Middle West
          Mississippi River Valley
          New England
          Old Northwest
          Old Southwest
          Oregon Trail
          Pacific Northwest
          Southern States
          Southwestern States
          West (U.S.)
RT   **Americans**
United States—Agriculture
USE   **Agriculture—United States**
United States—Air pollution
USE   **Air pollution—United States**
United States—Animals
USE   **Animals—United States**
United States—Annexations
USE   **United States—Territorial ex-**
          pansion
United States—Antiques
USE   **Antiques—United States**
United States—Antiquities   973
BT   **Antiquities**
NT   **Indians of North America—**
          Antiquities
United States—Appropriations and ex-
          penditures   352.4
UF   Federal spending policy
          Government spending policy
BT   **Budget—United States**
United States—Archives
USE   **Archives—United States**
United States—Armed forces   355.00973
SA   official names and branches of
          the armed forces, e.g. **United**
          States. Army; United States.
          Navy; etc., to be added as
          needed
BT   **Armed forces**
NT   **United States. Army**

BT = Broader Term   NT = Narrower Term   RT = Related Term   SA = See Also   UF = Used For

733

United States—Armed forces—*Continued*
>United States. Navy
United States—Armed forces—Gays
>USE Gays and lesbians in the military
United States—Armed forces—Military life 355.10973
>BT Military personnel
United States—Armed Forces—Recruiting, enlistment, etc. 355.2
>BT Recruiting and enlistment
United States. Army 355
>Subdivisions used under this heading may be used under armies of other countries as appropriate.
>BT Armies
>Military history
>United States—Armed forces
>NT United States Military Academy
United States. Army—Appointments and retirements 355.1
>UF United States. Army—Retirements
United States. Army—Biography 920
>BT Biography
United States. Army—Chaplains 355.3; 920
>BT Chaplains
United States. Army—Crimes and misdemeanors
>USE Military offenses—United States
United States. Army—Demobilization 355.2
United States. Army—Desertions
>USE Military desertion—United States
United States. Army—Enlistment
>USE United States. Army—Recruiting, enlistment, etc.
United States. Army—Examinations 355.1
>UF Army tests
>BT Examinations
United States. Army—Handbooks, manuals, etc. 355
>UF Soldiers' handbooks
>United States. Army—Officers' handbooks

United States. Army—Soldiers' handbooks
United States. Army—Insignia 355.1
>BT Insignia
United States. Army—Medals, badges, decorations, etc. 355.1
>BT Insignia
>Medals
United States. Army—Military life 355.1
>BT Military personnel
>Soldiers
United States. Army—Music
>USE United States. Army—Songs
United States. Army—Officers 355.3
>BT Military personnel
>Soldiers
United States. Army—Officers' handbooks
>USE United States. Army—Handbooks, manuals, etc.
United States. Army—Ordnance 355.8
>UF United States. Army—Ordnance and ordnance stores *[Former heading]*
>BT Ordnance
United States. Army—Ordnance and ordnance stores
>USE United States. Army—Ordnance
United States. Army—Parachute troops 356
>UF United States—Parachute troops
>BT Parachute troops
United States. Army—Recruiting, enlistment, etc. 355.2
>UF United States. Army—Enlistment
>BT Recruiting and enlistment
United States. Army—Retirements
>USE United States. Army—Appointments and retirements
United States. Army—Soldiers' handbooks
>USE United States. Army—Handbooks, manuals, etc.
United States. Army—Songs 782.42
>UF United States. Army—Music
>United States. Army—Songs and music *[Former heading]*
>BT Songs
United States. Army—Songs and music
>USE United States. Army—Songs

BT = Broader Term   NT = Narrower Term   RT = Related Term   SA = See Also   UF = Used For

United States—Astronautics
  USE   Astronautics—United States
United States—Atlases
  USE   United States—Maps
United States—Banks and banking
  USE   Banks and banking—United
         States
United States—Bibliography   015.73;
       016.973
United States—Bicentennial celebrations
  USE   American Revolution Bicenten-
         nial, 1776-1976
United States—Biculturalism
  USE   Biculturalism—United States
United States—Bilingualism
  USE   Bilingualism—United States
United States—Bio-bibliography   012
United States—Biography   920.073
  BT   Biography
United States—Biography—Dictionaries
       920.073
United States—Biography—Portraits
       920.073
  UF   United States—History—Portraits
United States—Birds
  USE   Birds—United States
United States—Boundaries   973
  BT   Boundaries
United States—Budget
  USE   Budget—United States
United States—Campaign funds
  USE   Campaign funds—United
         States
United States—Capital punishment
  USE   Capital punishment—United
         States
United States—Cathedrals
  USE   Cathedrals—United States
United States—Catholic Church
  USE   Catholic Church—United
         States
United States—Catholics
  USE   Catholics—United States
United States—Census   317.3; 352.7
  BT   Census
United States—Centennial celebrations,
       etc.   973
  NT   American Revolution Bicenten-
         nial, 1776-1976

United States—Children
  USE   Children—United States
United States—Children—Employment
  USE   Children—Employment—Unit-
         ed States
United States—Christmas
  USE   Christmas—United States
United States—Church buildings
  USE   Church buildings—United
         States
United States—Church—Government policy
  USE   Church and state—United
         States
United States—Church history   277.3
  UF   Church history—United States
         United States—Religious history
  BT   Church history
  RT   United States—Religion
United States—Church of England
  USE   Church of England—United
         States
United States—Cities and towns
  USE   Cities and towns—United
         States
United States—City planning
  USE   City planning—United States
United States—Civil defense
  USE   Civil defense—United States
United States—Civil service
  USE   Civil service—United States
United States—Civilization   973
  BT   Civilization
  NT   Americana
United States—Civilization—1960-1970
       973.92
United States—Civilization—1970-
       973.92
United States—Civilization—Foreign in-
       fluences   973
United States—Climate   551.6973
  BT   Climate
United States—Collective settlements
  USE   Collective settlements—United
         States
United States—Colleges and universities
  USE   Colleges and universities—
         United States
United States—Colonies
  USE   United States—Territories and
         possessions

BT = Broader Term   NT = Narrower Term   RT = Related Term   SA = See Also   UF = Used For

United States—Commerce 380.1;
382.0973
BT Commerce
United States—Commerce—Japan 382
United States—Commercial policy
380.1; 381.3; 382
BT Commercial policy
Economic policy
United States—Communism
USE Communism—United States
United States. Congress 328.73
UF Congress (U.S.)
BT Legislative bodies
NT United States. Congress. House
United States. Congress. Senate
United States. Congress. House 328.73
UF House of Representatives (U.S.)
Representatives, House of (U.S.)
BT United States. Congress
United States. Congress. Senate 328.73
UF Senate (U.S.)
BT United States. Congress
United States—Constitution
USE Constitutional history—United
States
Constitutional law—United
States
Constitutions—United States
United States—Constitutional history
USE Constitutional history—United
States
United States—Constitutional law
USE Constitutional law—United
States
United States—Country life
USE Country life—United States
United States—Courts
USE Courts—United States
United States—Crime
USE Crime—United States
United States—Dance
USE Dance—United States
United States—Declaration of indepen-
dence 973.3
UF Declaration of independence
(U.S.)
United States—Decorative arts
USE Decorative arts—United States
United States—Defenses 355.4
BT Military readiness

NT Strategic Defense Initiative
United States—Demonstrations
USE Demonstrations—United States
United States—Description 917.3
UF United States—Description and
travel [Former heading]
United States—Travel
BT Geography
United States—Description and travel
USE United States—Description
United States—Description—Guidebooks
USE United States—Guidebooks
United States—Description—Views
USE United States—Pictorial works
United States—Diplomatic and consular
service
USE American diplomatic and con-
sular service
United States—Directories 917.30025
Use for lists of names and addresses. Lists
of names without addresses are entered under
United States—Registers.
BT Directories
RT United States—Registers
United States—Earthquakes
USE Earthquakes—United States
United States—Economic conditions
330.973
May be subdivided by period using the sub-
divisions under United States—History, e.g.
United States—Economic conditions—1600-
1775, Colonial period.
UF National resources
BT Economic conditions
RT Natural resources—United
States
United States—Economic policy
338.973
BT Economic policy
United States—Education
USE Education—United States
United States—Elderly
USE Elderly—United States
United States—Elections
USE Elections—United States
United States—Emigration and immigration
USE United States—Immigration
and emigration
United States—Employees
USE United States—Officials and
employees

BT = Broader Term   NT = Narrower Term   RT = Related Term   SA = See Also   UF = Used For

United States—Environmental policy
USE   **Environmental policy—United States**

United States—Ethnic relations   305.8

United States—Ethnology
USE   **Ethnology—United States**

United States—European War, 1914-1918
USE   **World War, 1914-1918—United States**

United States—Excavations (Archeology)
USE   **Excavations (Archeology)—United States**

United States—Executive departments
USE   **Executive departments—United States**

United States—Executive departments—Reorganization
USE   **Administrative agencies—Reorganization—United States**

United States—Executive power
USE   **Executive power—United States**

United States—Exploration   973
UF   Exploration—United States
BT   **America—Exploration**
        Exploration
NT   **West (U.S.)—Exploration**

United States—Exploring expeditions   910.973; 973

Use for materials on exploring expeditions sponsored by the United States. Materials on early exploration of a particular place are entered under the name of the place with the subdivision *Exploration*.

UF   American exploring expeditions
SA   names of expeditions, e.g. **Lewis and Clark Expedition (1804-1806)**; to be added as needed
BT   **Explorers**
NT   **Lewis and Clark Expedition (1804-1806)**

United States—Famines
USE   **Famines—United States**

United States—Farm life
USE   **Farm life—United States**

United States—Fascism
USE   **Fascism—United States**

United States—Festivals
USE   **Festivals—United States**

United States—Finance
USE   **Finance—United States**

United States—Fiscal policy
USE   **Fiscal policy—United States**

United States—Fisheries
USE   **Fisheries—United States**

United States—Fishes
USE   **Fishes—United States**

United States—Fishing
USE   **Fishing—United States**

United States—Flags
USE   **Flags—United States**

United States—Flowers
USE   **Flowers—United States**

United States—Folk music
USE   **Folk music—United States**

United States—Folk songs
USE   **Folk songs—United States**

United States—Folklore
USE   **Folklore—United States**

United States—Foreign economic relations   337.73
UF   Foreign economic relations—United States
BT   **International economic relations**

United States—Foreign opinion (May subdiv. geog.)   303.3; 973

Use for materials on foreign public opinion about the United States. May be further subdivided by the country holding the opinion, e.g. **United States—Foreign opinion—France.**

UF   Anti-Americanism
        Antiamericanism
        United States—Foreign public opinion
BT   **Public opinion**

United States—Foreign opinion—France   303.3; 973

Use for materials on French public opinion about the United States.

UF   French foreign opinion—United States
        United States—Foreign opinion, French *[Former heading]*
        United States—Foreign public opinion, French

United States—Foreign opinion, French
USE   **United States—Foreign opinion—France**

United States—Foreign policy
USE   **United States—Foreign relations**

United States—Foreign population
  USE   **Aliens—United States**
           Immigrants—United States
United States—Foreign public opinion
  USE   **United States—Foreign opinion**
United States—Foreign public opinion,
    French
  USE   **United States—Foreign opin-
           ion—France**
United States—Foreign relations (May
    subdiv. geog.)   **327.73**
    When further subdividing geographically,
    provide an additional subject entry with the
    two places in reversed positions, i.e. **United
    States—Foreign relations—Iran** and also
    Iran—Foreign relations—United States.
  UF   United States—Foreign policy
  BT   **Diplomacy**
          International relations
          World politics
  NT   **Monroe Doctrine**
  RT   **Neutrality—United States**
**United States—Foreign relations—Iran
    327.73055**
  NT   **Iran hostage crisis, 1979-1981**
**United States—Foreign relations—Trea-
    ties   327.73; 341.3**
  UF   United States—Treaties
  BT   **Treaties**
United States—Forests and forestry
  USE   **Forests and forestry—United
           States**
United States—Gazetteers   917.3003
  BT   **Gazetteers**
United States—Geographic names
  USE   **Geographic names—United
           States**
United States—Geography   917.3
  BT   **Geography**
United States—Geology
  USE   **Geology—United States**
United States—Government
  USE   **United States—Politics and
           government**
United States—Government buildings
  USE   **Public buildings—United States**
United States—Government employees
  USE   **United States—Officials and
           employees**

United States—Government publications
  USE   **Government publications—
           United States**
United States—Governmental investigations
  USE   **Governmental investigations—
           United States**
United States—Graphic arts
  USE   **Graphic arts—United States**
United States—Guidebooks   917.304
  UF   United States—Description—
          Guidebooks *[Former heading]*
United States—Hippies
  USE   **Hippies—United States**
United States—Historic buildings
  USE   **Historic buildings—United
           States**
**United States—Historical geography
    911**
  BT   **Historical geography**
**United States—Historical geography—
    Maps   911**
  BT   **United States—Maps**
United States—Historiography   973.07
  UF   United States—History—Histori-
          ography *[Former heading]*
  BT   **Historiography**
United States—History   973
  UF   American history
  NT   **Americana**
          **Constitutional history—United
            States**
          Southern States—History
          West (U.S.)—History
**United States—History—1600-1775, Colo-
    nial period   973.2**
    Use for materials on American history from
    the earliest permanent English settlements on
    the Atlantic coast up to the American Revolu-
    tion. Materials on the period of discovery are
    entered under **United States—Exploration.**
  UF   American colonies
          Colonial history (U.S.)
  NT   **Bacon's Rebellion, 1676**
          King Philip's War, 1675-1676
          **Pilgrims (New England colo-
           nists)**
          **Pontiac's Conspiracy, 1763-
           1765**
          Puritans
          **United States—History—1689-
           1697, King William's War**

BT = Broader Term   NT = Narrower Term   RT = Related Term   SA = See Also   UF = Used For

United States—History—1600-1775, Colonial period—*Continued*

> United States—History—1755-1763, French and Indian War

United States—History—1675-1676, King Philip's War
USE   **King Philip's War, 1675-1676**
United States—History—1689-1697, King William's War   **973.2**
   UF   King William's War, 1689-1697
   BT   **Indians of North America— Wars**
       United States—History—1600-1775, Colonial period
United States—History—1755-1763, French and Indian War   **973.2**
   UF   French and Indian War
   BT   **Indians of North America— Wars**
       Seven Years' War, 1756-1763
       United States—History—1600-1775, Colonial period
   NT   **Pontiac's Conspiracy, 1763-1765**
United States—History—1775-1783, Revolution   **973.3**
   May be subdivided like **United States—History—1861-1865, Civil War.**
   UF   American Revolution
       Revolution, American
       War of the American Revolution
   BT   **Revolutions**
   NT   **American Loyalists**
       Canadian Invasion, 1775-1776
       Fourth of July
United States—History—1775-1783, Revolution—Centennial celebrations, etc.
USE   **American Revolution Bicentennial, 1776-1976**
United States—History—1783-1809   **973.3; 973.4**
   UF   Confederation of American colonies
   NT   **Lewis and Clark Expedition (1804-1806)**
       Louisiana Purchase
   RT   **Constitutional history—United States**
United States—History—1783-1865   **973.3-973.7**

United States—History—1801-1805, Tripolitan War   **973.4**
   UF   Tripoline War
   BT   **Pirates**
United States—History—1812-1815, War of 1812   **973.5**
   UF   War of 1812
United States—History—1815-1861   **973.5; 973.6**
   NT   **Black Hawk War, 1832**
       Mexican War, 1846-1848
United States—History—1845-1848, War with Mexico
USE   **Mexican War, 1846-1848**
United States—History—1861-1865, Civil War   **973.7**
   UF   American Civil War
       Civil War—United States
       War of Secession (U.S.)
   NT   **Confederate States of America**
       Trent Affair, 1861
United States—History—1861-1865, Civil War—Biography   **920; 973.7092**
   BT   **Biography**
United States—History—1861-1865, Civil War—Campaigns   **973.7**
   SA   names of battles, e.g. **Gettysburg (Pa.), Battle of, 1863;** to be added as needed
   NT   **Gettysburg (Pa.), Battle of, 1863**
United States—History—1861-1865, Civil War—Causes   **973.7**
   UF   Secession
United States—History—1861-1865, Civil War—Centennial celebrations, etc.   **973.7**
United States—History—1861-1865, Civil War—Drama   **808.82; 812, etc.**
   May be used for individual works, collections, or materials about plays dealing with the Civil War.
   BT   **Historical drama**
United States—History—1861-1865, Civil War—Fiction   **808.83; 813, etc.**
   May be used for individual works, collections, or materials about fiction dealing with the Civil War.
United States—History—1861-1865, Civil War—Health aspects   **973.7**

BT = Broader Term   NT = Narrower Term   RT = Related Term   SA = See Also   UF = Used For

United States—History—1861-1865, Civil
    War—Historiography   973.7
  BT   Historiography
United States—History—1861-1865, Civil
    War—Medical care   973.7
  BT   Armies—Medical care
United States—History—1861-1865, Civil
    War—Naval operations   973.7
United States—History—1861-1865, Civil
    War—Personal narratives   973.7

Use for collective or individual eyewitness reports or autobiographical accounts of the war in general. Accounts limited to a specific topic are entered under that topic.

  BT   Autobiographies
        Biography
United States—History—1861-1865, Civil
    War—Pictorial works   973.7022
United States—History—1861-1865, Civil
    War—Prisoners and prisons
    973.7
  BT   Prisoners
        Prisons
United States—History—1861-1865, Civil
    War—Reconstruction
  USE   Reconstruction (1865-1876)
United States—History—1861-1865, Civil
    War—Sources   973.7
  BT   History—Sources
United States—History—1865-1898
    973.8
  NT   Reconstruction (1865-1876)
        Spanish-American War, 1898
United States—History—1898-1919
    973.9; 973.91
  NT   Spanish-American War, 1898
United States—History—1898, War of
  1898
  USE   Spanish-American War, 1898
United States—History—1900-1999 (20th
  century)   973.9
  UF   United States—History—20th
        century
United States—History—20th century
  USE   United States—History—1900-
       1999 (20th century)
United States—History—1914-1918, Euro-
  pean War
  USE   World War, 1914-1918—United
       States

United States—History—1914-1918, World
  War
  USE   World War, 1914-1918—United
       States
United States—History—1919-1933
    973.91
United States—History—1933-1945
    973.917
United States—History—1939-1945, World
  War
  USE   World War, 1939-1945—United
       States
United States—History—1945-   973.92
United States—History—1945-1953
    973.918
United States—History—1953-1961
    973.921
United States—History—1961-1974
    973.922-973.924
  NT   Vietnam War, 1961-1975
        Watergate Affair, 1972-1974
United States—History—1974-1989
    973.925-973.927
  NT   Iran-Contra Affair, 1985-1990
United States—History—1989-   973.928
  NT   Iran-Contra Affair, 1985-1990
        Persian Gulf War, 1991
United States—History—Bibliography
    016.973
United States—History—Chronology
    973
  BT   Historical chronology
United States—History—Dictionaries
    973.03
  BT   History—Dictionaries
United States—History—Drama
    808.82; 812, etc.

May be used for individual works, collections, or materials about plays dealing with American history.

  BT   Historical drama
United States—History—Examinations
    973.076
  UF   United States—History—Exami-
        nations, questions, etc. *[For-
        mer heading]*
  BT   United States—History—Study
        and teaching

United States—History—Examinations,
    questions, etc.
  USE   **United States—History—Exam-**
        inations
United States—History—Fiction
    808.83; 813, etc.
    May be used for individual works, collec-
    tions, or materials about fiction dealing with
    American history.
United States—History—Historiography
  USE   **United States—Historiography**
United States—History—Library re-
    sources 973.07
United States—History, Local
  USE   **United States—Local history**
United States—History, Military
  USE   **United States—Military history**
United States—History, Naval
  USE   **United States—Naval history**
United States—History—Outlines, syllabi,
    etc. 973.02
  BT   **United States—History—Study**
        and teaching
United States—History—Periodicals
    973.05
United States—History—Poetry 808.81;
    811, etc.; 811.008, etc.
    May be used for individual works, collec-
    tions, or materials about poetry dealing with
    American history.
  BT   **Historical poetry**
United States—History, Political
  USE   **United States—Politics and**
        government
United States—History—Portraits
  USE   **United States—Biography—**
        Portraits
United States—History—Societies
    973.06
  BT   **History—Societies**
United States—History—Sources 973
  BT   **History—Sources**
United States—History—Study and
    teaching 973.07
  NT   **United States—History—Exam-**
        inations
        United States—History—Out-
        lines, syllabi, etc.
United States—Hospitals
  USE   **Hospitals—United States**

United States—Hotels and motels
  USE   **Hotels and motels—United**
        States
United States—Hunting
  USE   **Hunting—United States**
United States—Immigration and emigra-
    tion 325; 325.73
  UF   United States—Emigration and
        immigration
  SA   names of nationality groups, e.g.
        Mexican Americans; Mexi-
        cans—United States; to be
        added as needed
  BT   **Americanization**
        Colonization
        Immigration and emigration
  RT   **Aliens—United States**
        Immigrants—United States
United States—Industries
  USE   **Industries—United States**
United States—Industries—Government pol-
    icy
  USE   **Industrial policy—United**
        States
United States—Insular possessions
  USE   **United States—Territories and**
        possessions
United States—Intellectual life 973
  BT   **Intellectual life**
United States—Intelligence service
  USE   **Intelligence service—United**
        States
United States—Internal security
  USE   **Internal security—United**
        States
United States—Irrigation
  USE   **Irrigation—United States**
United States—Labor
  USE   **Labor—United States**
United States—Labor unions
  USE   **Labor unions—United States**
United States—Lakes
  USE   **Lakes—United States**
United States—Land settlement
  USE   **Land settlement—United States**
United States—Land surveys
  USE   **United States—Surveys**
United States—Languages 306.44
    Use for materials on the several languages
    spoken in the United States.

BT = Broader Term   NT = Narrower Term   RT = Related Term   SA = See Also   UF = Used For

United States—Law
   USE   **Law—United States**
United States—Legends
   USE   **Legends—United States**
United States—Libraries
   USE   **Libraries—United States**
United States. Library of Congress
   USE   **Library of Congress**
United States—Literary landmarks
   USE   **Literary landmarks—United States**
United States—Local history   973
   UF   United States—History, Local
         [Former heading]
   BT   **Local history**
United States—Mail
   USE   **Postal service—United States**
United States—Manufactures
   USE   **Industries—United States**
United States—Maps   912.73
   UF   United States—Atlases
   BT   **Atlases**
         Maps
   NT   **United States—Historical geography—Maps**
United States—Medicine
   USE   **Medicine—United States**
United States—Merchant marine
   USE   **Merchant marine—United States**
United States Military Academy   355.0071
   UF   U.S.M.A.
         USMA
         West Point (Military academy)
   BT   **Colleges and universities**
         United States. Army
United States Military Academy—Registers   355.0071
United States Military Academy—Songs   782.42
   UF   United States Military Academy—Songs and music *[Former heading]*
   BT   **Students' songs**
United States Military Academy—Songs and music
   USE   **United States Military Academy—Songs**

United States—Military history   355.00973; 973
   UF   United States—History, Military
         [Former heading]
   BT   **Military history**
United States—Military offenses
   USE   **Military offenses—United States**
United States—Military personnel
   USE   **Military personnel—United States**
United States—Military policy   355
   BT   **Military policy**
   NT   **Strategic Defense Initiative**
United States—Militia   355.3
   BT   **Armed forces**
   NT   **United States. National Guard**
United States—Mines and mineral resources
   USE   **Mines and mineral resources—United States**
United States—Monetary policy
   USE   **Monetary policy—United States**
United States—Moral conditions   973
   BT   **Moral conditions**
United States—Municipal government
   USE   **Municipal government—United States**
United States—Museums
   USE   **Museums—United States**
United States—Muslims
   USE   **Muslims—United States**
United States—National characteristics
   USE   **American national characteristics**
United States. National Guard   355.3
   UF   National Guard (U.S.)
   BT   **United States—Militia**
United States—National parks and reserves
   USE   **National parks and reserves—United States**
United States—National security
   USE   **National security—United States**
United States—National songs
   USE   **National songs—United States**
United States—Natural disasters
   USE   **Natural disasters—United States**

BT = Broader Term   NT = Narrower Term   RT = Related Term   SA = See Also   UF = Used For

United States—Natural history
USE **Natural history—United States**
United States—Natural monuments
USE **Natural monuments—United States**
United States—Natural resources
USE **Natural resources—United States**
United States—Naval history 359.00973
UF United States—History, Naval *[Former heading]*
BT **Naval battles**
Naval history
United States. Navy 359
Subdivisions used under **United States. Army** may be used under this heading and under navies of other countries as appropriate.
BT **Naval history**
Navies
Sailors
Sea power
United States—Armed forces
Warships
United States. Navy—Biography 920
BT **Biography**
United States. Navy—Enlistment
USE **United States. Navy—Recruiting, enlistment, etc.**
United States. Navy—Handbooks, manuals, etc. 359
UF Sailors' handbooks
United States. Navy—Officers' handbooks
United States. Navy—Sailors' handbooks
United States. Navy—Insignia 359.1
BT **Insignia**
United States. Navy—Medals, badges, decorations, etc. 359.1
BT **Insignia**
Medals
United States. Navy—Officers 359.3
BT **Military personnel**
Sailors
United States. Navy—Officers' handbooks
USE **United States. Navy—Handbooks, manuals, etc.**
United States. Navy—Recruiting, enlistment, etc. 359.2
UF United States. Navy—Enlistment
BT **Recruiting and enlistment**

United States. Navy—Sailors' handbooks
USE **United States. Navy—Handbooks, manuals, etc.**
United States. Navy—Sealab project
USE **Sealab project**
United States—Neutrality
USE **Neutrality—United States**
United States—Occupations
USE **Occupations—United States**
United States of Europe (proposed)
USE **European federation**
United States—Officials and employees 351.73
UF United States—Employees
United States—Government employees
RT **Civil service—United States**
United States—Parachute troops
USE **United States. Army—Parachute troops**
United States—Parks
USE **Parks—United States**
United States—Peoples
USE **Ethnology—United States**
United States—Personal names
USE **Personal names—United States**
United States—Petroleum
USE **Petroleum—United States**
United States—Physical geography
USE **Physical geography—United States**
United States—Pictorial works 917.30022
UF United States—Description—Views *[Former heading]*
United States—Plants
USE **Plants—United States**
United States—Police
USE **Police—United States**
United States—Politicians
USE **Politicians—United States**
United States—Politics and government 973
May be subdivided by period using the subdivisions under **United States—History,** e.g. **United States—Politics and government—1600-1775, Colonial period.**
UF American government
American politics
Civics
Civil government

BT = Broader Term   NT = Narrower Term   RT = Related Term   SA = See Also   UF = Used For

United States—Politics and government—
Continued
       United States—Government
       United States—History, Political
  BT   **Political science**
       Politics
       Public administration
  NT   **Third parties (United States**
       politics)
United States—Popular culture
  USE **Popular culture—United States**
United States—Population   304.60973
  BT   **Population**
United States—Postal service
  USE **Postal service—United States**
United States—Pottery
  USE **American pottery**
United States—Presidents
  USE **Presidents—United States**
United States—Prisons
  USE **Prisons—United States**
United States—Public buildings
  USE **Public buildings—United States**
United States—Public debts
  USE **Public debts—United States**
United States—Public health
  USE **Public health—United States**
United States—Public lands
  USE **Public lands—United States**
United States—Public schools
  USE **Public schools—United States**
United States—Public works
  USE **Public works—United States**
United States—Race relations
       305.800973
  BT   **Race relations**
United States—Registers   917.30025
    Use for lists of names without addresses.
Lists of names that include addresses are en-
tered under **United States—Directories.**
  RT   **United States—Directories**
United States—Religion   200.973; 277.3
  BT   **Religion**
  RT   **United States—Church history**
United States—Religious history
  USE **United States—Church history**
United States—Rural conditions
       307.720973
  BT   **Rural sociology**
United States—Schools
  USE **Schools—United States**

United States—Science
  USE **Science—United States**
United States—Secret service
  USE **Secret service—United States**
United States—Separation of powers
  USE **Separation of powers—United**
       States
United States—Shipping
  USE **Shipping—United States**
United States—Social conditions   973
  BT   **Social conditions**
United States—Social life and customs
       973
  BT   **Manners and customs**
United States—Social policy   361.6; 973
  BT   **Social policy**
United States—Social surveys
  USE **Social surveys—United States**
United States—Socialism
  USE **Socialism—United States**
United States—Soldiers
  USE **Soldiers—United States**
United States—State governments
  USE **State governments**
United States—Statistics   317.3
  BT   **Statistics**
United States—Strikes
  USE **Strikes—United States**
United States—Strikes and lockouts
  USE **Strikes—United States**
United States—Students
  USE **Students—United States**
United States. Supreme Court   347.73
  UF   Supreme Court—United States
  BT   **Courts**
United States. Supreme Court—Biogra-
  phy   920
  BT   **Biography**
United States—Surveys   972
    Use for materials containing the results of
land surveys of the United States.
  UF   United States—Land surveys
United States—Tariff
  USE **Tariff—United States**
United States—Taxation
  USE **Taxation—United States**
United States—Teenagers
  USE **Teenagers—United States**

BT = Broader Term   NT = Narrower Term   RT = Related Term   SA = See Also   UF = Used For

United States—Territorial expansion
973
    UF   Expansion (United States poli-
tics)
           Manifest destiny (United States)
           United States—Annexations
           Westward movement
United States—Territorial waters
    USE   **Territorial waters—United
States**
**United States—Territories and posses-
sions   325; 973**
    UF   United States—Colonies *[Former
heading]*
           United States—Insular posses-
sions
United States—Terrorism
    USE   **Terrorism—United States**
United States—Theater
    USE   **Theater—United States**
United States—Travel
    USE   **United States—Description**
United States—Treaties
    USE   **United States—Foreign rela-
tions—Treaties**
United States—Trees
    USE   **Trees—United States**
United States—Universities
    USE   **Colleges and universities—
United States**
United States—Urban renewal
    USE   **Urban renewal—United States**
United States—Veterans
    USE   **Veterans—United States**
United States—Vice-presidents
    USE   **Vice-presidents—United States**
United States—Women
    USE   **Women—United States**
United States—World War, 1914-1918
    USE   **World War, 1914-1918—United
States**
United States—World War, 1939-1945
    USE   **World War, 1939-1945—United
States**
United States—Youth
    USE   **Youth—United States**
United Steelworkers of America   331.88
    BT   **Labor unions**
Universal bibliographic control
    USE   **Bibliographic control**

Universal history
    USE   **World history**
Universal language   401
    UF   International language
           Language, International
           Language, Universal *[Former
heading]*
           World language
    BT   **Language and languages
Linguistics**
    NT   **Esperanto**
Universal military training
    USE   **Draft**
Universe   113; 523.1
        Use for materials limited to the physical de-
scription of the universe. General and theoreti-
cal materials on the science or philosophy of
the universe are entered under **Cosmology.**
    UF   Cosmogony
           Cosmography
    NT   **Astronomy
Cosmology
Life on other planets**
    RT   **Creation**
Universities
    USE   **Colleges and universities**
Universities and colleges
    USE   **Colleges and universities**
University degrees
    USE   **Academic degrees**
University extension   378.1
    BT   **Colleges and universities
Distance education
Higher education**
    NT   **Adult education
Correspondence schools and
courses**
University graduates
    USE   **College graduates**
University libraries
    USE   **Academic libraries**
University students
    USE   **College students**
Unmarried couples   306.7
    UF   Cohabitation
           Common law marriage
           Living together
           Trial marriage
           Unmarried people
    BT   **Lifestyles
Shared housing**

BT = Broader Term   NT = Narrower Term   RT = Related Term   SA = See Also   UF = Used For

Unmarried fathers   306.85; 362.82

Use for materials on fathers who at the time of childbirth were not married to the child's mother. Materials on fathers rearing children without a partner in the household are entered under **Single parent family.** Materials on fathers who are teenagers are entered under **Teenage fathers.**

UF   Parents, Unmarried

       Unmarried parents

       Unwed fathers

BT   **Child welfare**

       Fathers

       Illegitimacy

RT   **Single parent family**

Unmarried men

USE   **Single men**

Unmarried mothers   306.85; 362.83

Use for materials on mothers who at the time of giving birth were not married to the child's father. Materials on mothers rearing children without a partner in the household are entered under **Single parent family.** Materials on mothers who are teenagers are entered under **Teenage mothers.**

UF   Parents, Unmarried

       Unmarried parents

       Unwed mothers

BT   **Child welfare**

       Illegitimacy

       Mothers

RT   **Single parent family**

Unmarried parents

USE   **Unmarried fathers**

        Unmarried mothers

Unmarried people

USE   **Single people**

        Unmarried couples

Unmarried women

USE   **Single women**

Unskilled workers

USE   **Labor**

        Working class

Untruth

USE   **Truthfulness and falsehood**

Unwed fathers

USE   **Unmarried fathers**

Unwed mothers

USE   **Unmarried mothers**

Upholstery   684.1; 747

BT   **Interior design**

NT   **Drapery**

RT   **Furniture**

Upper atmosphere   551.5

UF   Atmosphere, Upper *[Former heading]*

BT   **Atmosphere**

NT   **Stratosphere**

Upper class   305.5

UF   Fashionable society

       High society

       Upper classes *[Former heading]*

BT   **Social classes**

NT   **Aristocracy**

       Nobility

Upper classes

USE   **Upper class**

Uranium   669

BT   **Chemical elements**

RT   **Radioactivity**

Urban areas

USE   **Cities and towns**

        Metropolitan areas

Urban development

USE   **Cities and towns—Growth**

        City planning

        Urbanization

Urban-federal relations

USE   **Federal-city relations**

Urban homesteading (May subdiv. geog.)
    363.5

BT   **Houses—Buying and selling**

       Housing

       Urban renewal

Urban housing

USE   **Housing**

Urban life

USE   **City life**

Urban planning

USE   **City planning**

Urban renewal (May subdiv. geog.)
    307.3

Use for materials on the economic, sociological, and political aspects of urban redevelopment. Materials on the architectural and engineering aspects are entered under **City planning.**

UF   Slum clearance

BT   **Metropolitan areas**

       Urban sociology

NT   **Community development**

       Urban homesteading

RT   **City planning**

       Community organization

BT = Broader Term   NT = Narrower Term   RT = Related Term   SA = See Also   UF = Used For

Urban renewal—Chicago (Ill.)   307.3
    UF   Chicago (Ill.)—Urban renewal
Urban renewal—United States   307.3
    UF   United States—Urban renewal
Urban-rural migration
    USE   **Internal migration**
Urban sociology   307.76
    UF   Sociology, Urban *[Former heading]*
    BT   **Sociology**
    NT   **City life**
          Urban renewal
          Urbanization
    RT   **Cities and towns**
Urban traffic
    USE   **City traffic**
Urban transportation
    USE   **Local transit**
Urbanization (May subdiv. geog.)
    307.76
    Use for materials on the process by which town and communities acquire urban characteristics.
    UF   Cities and towns, Movement to
          Urban development
    BT   **Cities and towns**
          Rural sociology
          Social change
          Social conditions
          Urban sociology
    RT   **Cities and towns—Growth**
US
    USE   **United States**
USA
    USE   **United States**
Use of time
    USE   **Time management**
Used merchandise
    USE   **Secondhand trade**
Useful arts
    USE   **Industrial arts**
          Technology
Useful insects
    USE   **Beneficial insects**
USMA
    USE   **United States Military Academy**
USSR
    USE   **Soviet Union**
Utensils, Kitchen
    USE   **Kitchen utensils**

Utilitarianism   144
    BT   **Ethics**
    NT   **Secularism**
    RT   **Pragmatism**
Utilities (Computer programs)   005.4
    Use for materials on software used to perform standard computer system operations such as sorting data, searching for viruses, copying data from one file to another, etc.
    UF   Computer utility programs
          Computers—Utility programs
          Utility programs (Computer programs)
          Utility routines (Computer programs)
    BT   **Computer software**
Utilities, Public
    USE   **Public utilities**
Utility programs (Computer programs)
    USE   **Utilities (Computer programs)**
Utility routines (Computer programs)
    USE   **Utilities (Computer programs)**
Utilization of waste
    USE   **Recycling**
          Salvage
Utopian fiction   813, etc.
    May be used for individual works, collections, or materials about imaginative accounts of ideal societies. Theoretical materials about ideal societies and accounts of practical attempts to create such societies are entered under **Utopias.**
    UF   Ideal states
          Utopian literature
    BT   **Fantasy fiction**
          Science fiction
    RT   **Dystopias**
          Utopias
Utopian literature
    USE   **Utopian fiction**
          Utopias
Utopias   321; 335
    Use for theoretical materials on ideal societies and for accounts of practical attempts to create such societies. Imaginative accounts of ideal societies are entered under **Utopian fiction.**
    UF   Ideal states
          Utopian literature
    BT   **Political science**
          Socialism
    RT   **Collective settlements**
          Paradise
          Utopian fiction

BT = Broader Term   NT = Narrower Term   RT = Related Term   SA = See Also   UF = Used For

V.C.R.'s
USE **Video recording**
V.D.
USE **Sexually transmitted diseases**
V.T.O.L.'s
USE **Vertically rising airplanes**
Vacation church schools
USE **Religious summer schools**
Vacation home timesharing
USE **Timesharing (Real estate)**
Vacation schools
USE **Summer schools**
Vacation schools, Religious
USE **Religious summer schools**
Vacations   331.25; 658.3
BT **Recreation**
RT **Holidays**
Vaccination   614.4
UF Immunization
Inoculation
SA types of animals and diseases
with the subdivision *Vaccina-
tion*, e.g. **Tuberculosis—Vac-
cination;** to be added as
needed
BT **Communicable diseases**
Preventive medicine
Public health
NT **Poliomyelitis vaccine**
RT **Immunity**
Vacuum tubes   537.5; 621.3815
UF Electron tubes
BT **X-rays**
NT **Cathode ray tubes**
Vagabonds
USE **Tramps**
Vagrants
USE **Tramps**
Valentine's Day   394.2618
UF Saint Valentine's Day
St. Valentine's Day
BT **Holidays**
Valuation   338.5
Use for general materials on the appraisal
of property. Materials on valuation of particu-
lar types of property are entered under the
type of property, e.g. **Real estate.** Materials
on valuation for taxing purposes are entered
under **Tax assessment.**
UF Appraisal
Capitalization (Finance)
NT **Tax assessment**

Values   121; 170; 303.3
Use for materials on moral and aesthetic
values.
UF Axiology
Human values
Worth
BT **Aesthetics**
Ethics
Psychology
NT **Social values**
Vampire films   791.43
May be used for individual works, collec-
tions, or materials about vampire films.
UF Vampires in motion pictures
BT **Horror films**
Motion pictures
Vampires   398.21
BT **Superstition**
Vampires in motion pictures
USE **Vampire films**
Van life   796.7
UF Vanning
Vans—Social aspects
BT **Mobile home living**
Vans
Van pools
USE **Car pools**
Vanishing species
USE **Endangered species**
Vanning
USE **Van life**
Vans   728.7
BT **Travel trailers and campers**
NT **Van life**
Vans—Social aspects
USE **Van life**
Variation (Biology)   576.5
UF Mutation (Biology)
BT **Biology**
Genetics
Heredity
NT **Adaptation (Biology)**
Mendel's law
Natural selection
RT **Evolution**
**Variety shows (Radio programs)
791.44**
May be used for individual works, collec-
tions, or materials about variety shows on the
radio.
BT **Radio programs**

BT = Broader Term   NT = Narrower Term   RT = Related Term   SA = See Also   UF = Used For

748

Variety shows (Television programs)
791.45

May be used for individual works, collections, or materials about variety shows on television.

BT   Television programs

Varnish and varnishing   667; 698

UF   Finishes and finishing

BT   Industrial painting
       Wood finishing

RT   Lacquer and lacquering

Varsity sports

USE   College sports

Vascular system

USE   Cardiovascular system

Vasectomy   613.9

BT   Sterilization (Birth control)

Vases   731; 738

RT   Glassware
       Pottery

Vassals

USE   Feudalism

Vatican City   945.6

Use for geographical and descriptive materials on the independent papal state in Rome. Materials on the central administration of the Roman Catholic Church are entered under **Catholic Church.**

Vatican City—Foreign relations

USE   Catholic Church—Foreign relations

Vatican Council (2nd : 1962-1965)   262

BT   Councils and synods

Vaudeville   792.7

BT   Amusements
       Theater

Vaults (Sepulchral)

USE   Tombs

VCRs

USE   Video recording

VD

USE   Sexually transmitted diseases

VDTs

USE   Video display terminals

Vedas   294.5

BT   Hinduism
       Sacred books

Vegetable anatomy

USE   Plants—Anatomy

Vegetable gardening   635

UF   Kitchen gardens

BT   Gardening

       Horticulture

RT   Truck farming
       Vegetables

Vegetable kingdom

USE   Botany
       Plants

Vegetable oils

USE   Essences and essential oils
       Oils and fats

Vegetable pathology

USE   Plant diseases

Vegetables   635; 641.3

SA   types of vegetables, to be added as needed

BT   Food
       Plants

NT   Celery
       Cooking—Vegetables
       Potatoes
       Root crops

RT   Vegetable gardening

Vegetables—Canning

USE   Vegetables—Preservation

Vegetables—Preservation   641.4

UF   Vegetables—Canning

BT   Canning and preserving

Vegetarian cookery

USE   Vegetarian cooking

Vegetarian cooking   641.5

UF   Cooking, Vegetarian
       Vegetarian cookery *[Former heading]*

BT   Cooking

RT   Cooking—Vegetables

Vegetarianism   613.2

BT   Diet

Vehicles   388; 629.2

SA   types of vehicles and names of specific makes and models of vehicles, to be added as needed

BT   Transportation

NT   All terrain vehicles
       Automobiles
       Bicycles
       Carriages and carts
       Military vehicles
       Moon cars
       Recreational vehicles
       Submersibles

BT = Broader Term   NT = Narrower Term   RT = Related Term   SA = See Also   UF = Used For

Vehicles—*Continued*
>> Tricycles

Vehicles, Military
>> USE **Military vehicles**

Vehicles, Recreational
>> USE **Recreational vehicles**

Velocity
>> USE **Speed**

Veneers and veneering   674; 698
>> BT **Cabinetwork**
>> **Furniture**

Venereal diseases
>> USE **Sexually transmitted diseases**

Ventilation   697.9
>> BT **Air**
>> **Home economics**
>> **Household sanitation**
>> **Hygiene**
>> **Sanitation**
>> NT **Chimneys**
>> RT **Air conditioning**
>> **Heating**

Ventriloquism   793.8
>> BT **Amusements**
>> **Voice**

Verbal abuse
>> USE **Invective**

Verbal learning   153.1; 370.15
>> Use for materials on the process of learning and understanding written or spoken language, ranging from learning to associate two nonsense syllables to solving problems presented in verbal terms.
>> UF Learning, Verbal
>> BT **Language and languages**
>> **Psychology of learning**
>> NT **Reading comprehension**

Vermin
>> USE **Household pests**
>> **Pests**

Vers libre
>> USE **Free verse**

Verse epistles
>> USE **Epistolary poetry**

Versification   808.1
>> UF English language—Versification
>> Meter
>> Prosody
>> BT **Authorship**
>> **Poetics**
>> **Rhythm**
>> NT **Rhyme**

Vertebrates   596
>> BT **Animals**
>> NT **Amphibians**
>> **Birds**
>> **Fishes**
>> **Mammals**
>> **Reptiles**

Vertical take off airplanes
>> USE **Vertically rising airplanes**

Vertically rising airplanes   629.133
>> UF Airplanes, Vertically rising
>> V.T.O.L.'s
>> Vertical take off airplanes
>> VTOLs
>> BT **Airplanes**
>> **Ground effect machines**

Very high frequency radio
>> USE **Shortwave radio**

Vessels (Ships)
>> USE **Ships**

Vesta (Roman deity)   292.2
>> BT **Gods and goddesses**

Veterans (May subdiv. geog.)   **305.9; 920**
>> UF Ex-service men
>> War veterans
>> BT **Military art and science**
>> RT **Military hospitals**
>> **Military pensions**
>> **Military personnel**
>> **Soldiers**

Veterans Day   394.264
>> UF Armistice Day
>> BT **Holidays**

Veterans—Education   362.86
>> UF Education of veterans
>> BT **Education**
>> **Reconstruction (1914-1939)**
>> **Reconstruction (1939-1951)**

Veterans—Employment   331.5
>> UF Employment of veterans
>> BT **Employment**
>> **Reconstruction (1914-1939)**
>> **Reconstruction (1939-1951)**

Veterans—Hospitals
>> USE **Military hospitals**

Veterans—Legal status, laws, etc.   343
>> BT **Military law**

BT = Broader Term   NT = Narrower Term   RT = Related Term   SA = See Also   UF = Used For

Veterans—United States 305.9;
    353.5390973; 920
  UF   G.I.'s
         GIs
         United States—Veterans
Veterinary medicine 636.089
  SA   types of animals with the subdi-
         vision *Diseases,* e.g. **Horses—**
         Diseases; or with the subdivi-
         sion *Wounds and injuries,* e.g.
         Horses—Wounds and inju-
         ries; to be added as needed
  BT   **Medicine**
  RT   **Animals—Diseases**
VHF radio
  USE **Shortwave radio**
Viaducts
  USE **Bridges**
Vibration 531; 620.3
  BT   **Mechanics**
         Sound
  NT   **Sound waves**
         Waves
Vicarious atonement
  USE **Atonement—Christianity**
Vice 170
  UF   Vices
  SA   types of vices, to be added as
         needed
  BT   **Conduct of life**
         Ethics
         Human behavior
  RT   **Crime**
Vice-presidents (May subdiv. geog.)
    352.23; 920
  BT   **Presidents**
Vice-presidents—United States 352.23;
    920
  UF   United States—Vice-presidents
Vices
  USE **Vice**
Victimless crimes
  USE **Crimes without victims**
Victims of atomic bombings
  USE **Atomic bomb victims**
Victims of crime
  USE **Victims of crimes**
Victims of crimes 362.88
  UF   Crime victims

Victims of crime *[Former head-*
    ing]
  BT   **Crime**
  NT   **Abused women**
         Adult child abuse victims
Victoriana 745.1; 747.2
  BT   **Antiques**
         Decorative arts
Video art 700; 791.45
    Use for materials on works of art created
  with the use of television and video recording
  technology.
  UF   Art, Electronic
         Art, Video
         Electronic art
  BT   **Modern art—1900-1999 (20th**
         century)
         Television
         Video recording
Video cameras, Home
  USE **Camcorders**
Video cassette recorders and recording
  USE **Video recording**
Video cassettes
  USE **Videotapes**
Video disc players
  USE **Videodisc players**
Video discs
  USE **Videodiscs**
Video display terminals 004.7
  UF   CRT display terminals
         Display terminals, Video
         VDTs
  BT   **Computer peripherals**
         Computer terminals
Video games 688.7; 794.8
  UF   Electronic games
         Games, Electronic
         Television games
  SA   types of video games and names
         of individual games, to be
         added as needed
  BT   **Electronic toys**
         Games
         Television—Receivers and re-
         ception
Video recording 384.55; 621.388;
    778.59
    Use for materials on either the equipment
  or the process by which video or video and
  audio materials are recorded.

Video recording—*Continued*
  UF   V.C.R.'s
        VCRs
        Video cassette recorders and re-
          cording
        Videorecorders
        Videotape recorders and record-
          ing *[Former heading]*
  NT   **Camcorders**
        Video art
        Videodiscs
        Videotapes
  RT   **Home video systems**
        **Magnetic recorders and re-
          cording**
        Television broadcasting
        **Television—Equipment and
          supplies**
Video recordings
  USE   **Videodiscs**
        Videotapes
Video recordings, Closed caption
  USE   **Closed caption video record-
          ings**
Video recordings for the hearing impaired
  USE   **Closed caption video record-
          ings**
Video tapes
  USE   **Videotapes**
Video telephone   384.6; 621.386
  UF   Picture telephone
        Videophone
  BT   **Data transmission systems**
        Telephone
        Television
Videocassettes
  USE   **Videotapes**
Videodisc players   384.55; 621.388
  UF   Video disc players
  BT   **Television—Equipment and
          supplies**
Videodiscs   384.55; 621.388
  UF   Video discs
        Video recordings
  BT   **Audiovisual materials**
        Optical storage devices
        Video recording
  NT   **Closed caption video record-
          ings**
        Music videos

  RT   **Television**
Videophone
  USE   **Video telephone**
Videorecorders
  USE   **Video recording**
Videos, Music
  USE   **Music videos**
Videotape recorders and recording
  USE   **Video recording**
Videotapes   384.55; 778.59
  UF   Tape recordings, Video
        Video cassettes
        Video recordings
        Video tapes
        Videocassettes
  BT   **Audiovisual materials**
        Home video systems
        Video recording
  NT   **Closed caption video record-
          ings**
        Music videos
  RT   **Television**
Videotex systems   004.69; 384.3
      Use for materials on the transmission of
    computer-based data from a central source to
    a television set or personal computer allowing
    for two-way interactions, such as with home
    shopping or home banking.
  UF   Interactive videotex
        Telereference
        Viewdata systems
  BT   **Data transmission systems**
        Information systems
        Television broadcasting
  RT   **Teletext systems**
Vietnam War, 1961-1975   959.704
      May use appropriate subdivisions under
    World War, 1939-1945.
  UF   Vietnamese Conflict, 1961-1975
        Vietnamese War, 1961-1975
  BT   **United States—History—1961-
          1974**
Vietnamese Conflict, 1961-1975
  USE   **Vietnam War, 1961-1975**
Vietnamese refugees (May subdiv. geog.)
        325
  UF   Refugees, Vietnamese *[Former
          heading]*
  BT   **Refugees**
Vietnamese War, 1961-1975
  USE   **Vietnam War, 1961-1975**

BT = Broader Term   NT = Narrower Term   RT = Related Term   SA = See Also   UF = Used For

Viewdata systems
  USE   **Videotex systems**
Views 910.22
  Use for collections of pictures of many places.
  UF   Scenery
  SA   countries, states, cities, etc., and named entities, such as individual parks, structures, etc., with the subdivision *Pictorial works,* e.g. **Chicago (Ill.)—Pictorial works; United States—Pictorial works; Yosemite National Park (Calif.)—Pictorial works;** etc., to be added as needed
  BT   **Pictures**
Vigilance committees 364.1; 364.4
  UF   Vigilantes
  BT   **Crime**
       Criminal law
  RT   **Lynching**
Vigilantes
  USE   **Vigilance committees**
Vikings 948
  Use for materials on early Scandinavian people. Materials on the people since the tenth century are entered under **Scandinavians.**
  UF   Norsemen
       Northmen
  BT   **Scandinavians**
  RT   **Normans**
Villages 307.76
  BT   **Cities and towns**
Vines
  USE   **Climbing plants**
Vineyards (May subdiv. geog.) **634.8**
  UF   Viticulture
  BT   **Farms**
  RT   **Grapes**
       Wine and wine making
Violence 303.6
  SA   types of violence, to be added as needed
  BT   **Aggressiveness (Psychology)**
       Social psychology
  NT   **Family violence**
       Hate crimes
       School violence
Violence in schools
  USE   **School violence**

Violence in television 302.23; 791.45
  UF   Violence on television
  BT   **Television**
       Television programs
Violence on television
  USE   **Violence in television**
Violin
  USE   **Violins**
Violin music 787.2
  BT   **Music**
Violin players
  USE   **Violinists**
Violinists 787.2092; 920
  UF   Violin players
       Violinists, violoncellists, etc. *[Former heading]*
  BT   **Instrumentalists**
Violinists, violoncellists, etc.
  USE   **Violinists**
       Violoncellists
Violins 787.2
  UF   Fiddle
       Violin *[Former heading]*
  BT   **Stringed instruments**
Violoncellists 787.4092
  UF   Cellists
       Cello players
       Violinists, violoncellists, etc. *[Former heading]*
       Violoncello players
  BT   **Instrumentalists**
Violoncello
  USE   **Violoncellos**
Violoncello players
  USE   **Violoncellists**
Violoncellos 787.4
  UF   Cello
       Violoncello *[Former heading]*
  BT   **Stringed instruments**
Vipers
  USE   **Snakes**
Virgin Mary
  USE   **Mary, Blessed Virgin, Saint**
Virtual reality 006
  UF   Artificial reality
       Three dimensional computer graphics
  BT   **Computer simulation**
  RT   **Computer graphics**

Virtue 170
    UF   Virtues
    SA   types of virtues, to be added as
            needed
    BT   Conduct of life
            Ethics
            Human behavior
    NT   Charity
            Chastity
            Courage
            Courtesy
            Faith
            Forgiveness
            Hope
            Justice
            Loyalty
            Obedience
            Patience
            Punctuality
            Temperance

Virtues
    USE   Virtue

Viruses 579.2
    UF   Microbes
    BT   Microorganisms
    NT   Chickenpox

Viruses, Computer
    USE   Computer viruses

Visceral learning
    USE   Biofeedback training

Viscosity 532; 620.1
    BT   Hydrodynamics
            Mechanics

Vision 152.14; 573.8; 612.8; 617.7
    UF   Sight
    BT   Optics
            Senses and sensation
    NT   Color sense
            Optical illusions
            Vision disorders
    RT   Eye

Vision disorders 362.4; 617.7
    UF   Defective vision
            Impaired vision
            Visual handicaps
            Visual impairments
    BT   Vision
    NT   Blind
            Color blindness

Visions 133.8; 248.2; 291.4
    BT   Parapsychology
            Religion
            Spiritual gifts
    NT   Dreams
            Hallucinations and illusions
    RT   Apparitions

Visitation rights (Domestic relations) 306.8
    Use for materials on the legal right of parents or grandparents to visit their children or grandchildren in situations of separation, divorce, etc.
    BT   Domestic relations

Visitors' exchange programs
    USE   Exchange of persons programs

Visual data processing
    USE   Optical data processing

Visual handicaps
    USE   Vision disorders

Visual impairments
    USE   Vision disorders

Visual instruction
    USE   Audiovisual education

Visual literacy 153; 707
    Use for materials on the ability to interpret and evaluate visual objects and symbols, such as television, motion pictures, art works, etc.
    UF   Literacy, Visual
    BT   Arts
            Literacy
            Semiotics

Vital records
    USE   Registers of births, etc.

Vital statistics 304.6; 310
    UF   Burial statistics
            Death rate
            Marriage statistics
            Mortuary statistics
            Records of births, etc.
    BT   Statistics
    NT   Birth rate
            Census
            Mortality
            Population
    RT   Registers of births, etc.

Vitamins 572; 613.2; 615
    BT   Food
            Nutrition

Viticulture
    USE   Grapes
            Vineyards

BT = Broader Term   NT = Narrower Term   RT = Related Term   SA = See Also   UF = Used For

Viticulture—*Continued*
Wine and wine making
Vivariums
USE **Terrariums**
Vivisection   179
BT **Animal experimentation**
Surgery
Vocabulary   418; 428, etc.
UF English language—Vocabulary
Languages—Vocabulary
Words
BT **Language and languages**
NT **New words**
Vocal culture
USE **Singing**
Voice
Vocal ensembles
USE **Ensembles (Music)**
Vocal music   782
UF Music, Vocal
BT **Music**
NT **Cantatas**
Carols
Choral music
Folk songs
Hymns
Opera
Operetta
Oratorio
Songs
RT **Singing**
Vocation, Choice of
USE **Vocational guidance**
Vocational education   370.11; 373.246;
374

Use for materials on teaching a skill during the educational process. Materials on teaching people a skill after formal education are entered under **Occupational training**. Materials discussing on-the-job training are entered under **Employees—Training**. Materials on retraining are entered under **Occupational retraining.**

UF Career education
Education, Vocational
SA types of industries, professions, etc., with the subdivision *Study and teaching,* e.g. **Agriculture—Study and teaching;** to be added as needed
BT **Education**
Manpower policy

NT **Agriculture—Study and teaching**
Employees—Training
Industrial arts education
Occupational retraining
Occupational training
Vocational guidance
RT **Professional education**
Technical education
Vocational guidance   331.7; 371.4

Use for materials on the activities and programs designed to help people plan, choose, and succeed in their careers. Materials on the assistance given to students by schools, colleges, or universities in the selection of a program of studies suited to their abilities, interests, future plans, and general circumstances are entered under **Educational counseling.**

UF Career counseling
Career development
Career guidance
Careers
Choice of profession, occupation, vocation, etc.
Employment guidance
Guidance, Vocational
Job placement guidance
Occupational guidance
Vocation, Choice of
SA vocational guidance for particular classes of persons, e.g. **Vocational guidance for the handicapped;** and fields of knowledge, corporate bodies, military services, professions, and industries and trades with the subdivision *Vocational guidance,* to be added as needed
BT **Counseling**
Vocational education
NT **Career changes**
Job hunting
Law—Vocational guidance
Television broadcasting—Vocational guidance
Vocational guidance for the handicapped
RT **Educational counseling**
Employment
Occupations
Professions

BT = Broader Term   NT = Narrower Term   RT = Related Term   SA = See Also   UF = Used For

**Vocational guidance for the handicapped
371.4**
  BT   **Handicapped**
        Vocational guidance
Vocational training
  USE   **Occupational training**
Vocations
  USE   **Occupations**
        Professions
Vodun
  USE   **Voodooism**
Voice   783
  UF   Speaking
        Vocal culture
        Voice culture
  BT   **Language and languages**
        Throat
  NT   **Automatic speech recognition**
        Ventriloquism
  RT   **Phonetics**
        Public speaking
        Singing
        Speech
Voice culture
  USE   **Singing**
        Voice
Volatile oils
  USE   **Essences and essential oils**
Volcanoes (May subdiv. geog.)   **551.21**
  UF   Eruptions
  SA   names of volcanoes, to be added
         as needed
  BT   **Geology**
        Mountains
        Physical geography
Volleyball   796.325
  BT   **Ball games**
Volume (Cubic content)   389; 530.8
  UF   Cubic measurement
  BT   **Geometry**
        Measurement
        Weights and measures
Volume feeding
  USE   **Food service**
Voluntarism
  USE   **Volunteer work**
Voluntary associations
  USE   **Associations**

Voluntary military service   355.2
  UF   Military service, Voluntary *[For-*
         mer heading]
        Volunteer military service
  BT   **Armed forces**
        Recruiting and enlistment
Voluntary organizations
  USE   **Associations**
Volunteer military service
  USE   **Voluntary military service**
Volunteer work   361.3
  UF   Voluntarism *[Former heading]*
        Volunteering
        Volunteerism
        Volunteers
  SA   types of volunteer work and
         names of volunteer programs,
         e.g. **Meals on wheels pro-**
         grams; to be added as need-
         ed
  BT   **Public welfare**
  NT   **Caregivers**
        Foster grandparents
  RT   **Charities**
        National service
Volunteering
  USE   **Volunteer work**
Volunteerism
  USE   **Volunteer work**
Volunteers
  USE   **Volunteer work**
Volunteers in church work
  USE   **Lay ministry**
Voodoo
  USE   **Voodooism**
Voodooism (May subdiv. geog.)   **299**
  UF   Vodun
        Voodoo
        Voudou
        Voudouism
  BT   **Religions**
Voter registration   324.6
  UF   Registration of voters
  BT   **Elections**
        Suffrage
Voting
  USE   **Elections**
        Suffrage
Voudou
  USE   **Voodooism**

BT = Broader Term   NT = Narrower Term   RT = Related Term   SA = See Also   UF = Used For

Voudouism
USE   **Voodooism**
Voyager project
USE   **Project Voyager**
Voyagers
USE   **Explorers**
       Travelers
Voyages and travels   910.4
> Use for materials about non-fiction travel writing, for collections of travel writings, and for accounts of voyages and travels not limited to a single place. Materials about the theme of travel in literature are entered under **Travel in literature.** Materials on the art and enjoyment of travel and advice for travelers are entered under **Travel.**

UF   Journeys
       Travel books
       Travels
SA   names of cities (except extinct cities), states, countries, continents, etc., with the subdivision *Description;* e.g. **United States—Description;** names of extinct cities or towns, without further subdivision, for accounts of those places by travelers in ancient times, e.g. **Delphi (Extinct city);** names of individual ships; names of regions, e.g. **Arctic regions;** ethnic groups, classes of persons, and names of individuals with the subidivision *Travel,* e.g. **Handicapped—Travel;** names of countries sponsoring exploring expeditions with the subdivision *Exploring expeditions;* e.g. **United States—Exploring expeditions;** and names of places that were unsettled or sparsely settled and largely unknown to the world at large at the time of exploration, with the subdivision *Exploration,* e.g. **America—Exploration;** to be added as needed
BT   **Geography**
NT   **Aeronautics—Flights**
       Northeast Passage
       Ocean travel

       Overland journeys to the Pacific
       Papal visits
       Pilgrims and pilgrimages
       Scientific expeditions
       Seafaring life
       Shipwrecks
       Travelers
       Voyages around the world
       Whaling
       Yachts and yachting
RT   **Adventure and adventurers**
       Exploration
       Explorers
       Travel
       Travel in literature
Voyages and travels in literature
USE   **Travel in literature**
Voyages around the world   910.4
UF   Circumnavigation
       Travel books
BT   **Travel**
       Voyages and travels
Voyages, Imaginary
USE   **Imaginary voyages**
Voyages to the moon
USE   **Imaginary voyages**
       Space flight to the moon
VTOLs
USE   **Vertically rising airplanes**
Wage-price controls
USE   **Wage-price policy**
Wage-price policy   331.2
UF   Price controls
       Price-wage policy
       Wage-price controls
BT   **Inflation (Finance)**
       Prices
       Wages
Wages   331.2; 658.3
UF   Compensation
       Overtime
       Salaries
BT   **Income**
       Labor
       Labor contract
NT   **Equal pay for equal work**
       Job analysis
       Minimum wage
       Nonwage payments

BT = Broader Term   NT = Narrower Term   RT = Related Term   SA = See Also   UF = Used For

Wages—*Continued*
>> Profit sharing
>> Wage-price policy
> RT   Cost and standard of living
>> Prices

Wages—Minimum wage
> USE   **Minimum wage**

Wagons
> USE   **Carriages and carts**

Waiters and waitresses   642
> UF   Waitresses
> BT   **Food service**

Waitresses
> USE   **Waiters and waitresses**

Wakefulness
> USE   **Insomnia**

Walking   796.51
> BT   **Locomotion**
> RT   **Hiking**

Walking in space
> USE   **Extravehicular activity (Space flight)**

Wall decoration
> USE   **Mural painting and decoration**

Wall painting
> USE   **Mural painting and decoration**

Wall Street (New York, N.Y.)   332.6
> Use for materials on the activities of Wall Street as a financial district. Historical and descriptive materials on Wall Street as a street are entered under **Streets—New York (N.Y.)**.

> BT   **Stock exchange**
> RT   **Streets—New York (N.Y.)**

Wallpaper   676; 747
> BT   **Interior design**
> RT   **Paperhanging**

Walls   690; 721
> BT   **Building**
>> **Carpentry**
>> **Civil engineering**
> NT   **Mural painting and decoration**
> RT   **Foundations**
>> **Masonry**

Walt Disney World (Fla.)   791.06
> UF   Disney World (Fla.)
> BT   **Amusement parks**

War   172; 303.6; 355.02
> UF   Fighting
>> Wars

> SA   names of wars, battles, etc., e.g. **United States—History—1861-1865, Civil War; Gettysburg (Pa.), Battle of, 1863;** and war and other subjects, e.g. **War and civilization;** to be added as needed

> NT   **Arms control**
>> **Battles**
>> **Chemical warfare**
>> **Children and war**
>> **Guerrilla warfare**
>> **Intervention (International law)**
>> **Military aeronautics**
>> **Military occupation**
>> **Military personnel**
>> **Military weapons**
>> **Nuclear warfare**
>> **Psychological warfare**
>> **Strategy**
>> **Submarine warfare**
>> **War and civilization**
>> **War and emergency powers**
>> **War crimes**
>> **War—Religious aspects**
>> **World War III**

> RT   **Armed forces**
>> **International law**
>> **Military art and science**
>> **Military law**
>> **Naval art and science**
>> **Peace**

War and children
> USE   **Children and war**

War and civilization   172; 303.4
> UF   Civilization and war
> BT   **Civilization**
>> **War**

War and emergency powers   342
> UF   Emergency powers
>> War powers
> BT   **Constitutional law**
>> **Executive power**
>> **Legislative bodies**
>> **War**

War and industry
> USE   **War—Economic aspects**

War and religion
> USE   **War—Religious aspects**

BT = Broader Term   NT = Narrower Term   RT = Related Term   SA = See Also   UF = Used For

War, Articles of
USE   **Military law**
War crime trials   341.6
  BT   **Trials**
War crimes (May subdiv. geog.)   **341.6; 364.1**
  UF   Military atrocities
  SA   names of wars with the subdivision *Atrocities*, e.g. **World War, 1939-1945—Atrocities;** and names of specific atrocities, to be added as needed
  BT   **Crime**
       · **International law**
       War
War debts
USE   **Public debts**
War—Economic aspects   303.6
   Use for materials discussing the economic causes of war and the effect of war on industry and trade.
  UF   Economics of war
       Industry and war
       War and industry
  SA   names of wars with the subdivision *Economic aspects*, to be added as needed
  NT   **Industrial mobilization**
       World War, 1939-1945—Economic aspects
  RT   **International competition**
War films   791.43
   May be used for individual works, collections, or materials about war films in general, not limited to a particular war.
  UF   Anti-war films
       Apocalyptic fantasies
       End-of-the-world fantasies
  SA   names of wars with the subdivision *Motion pictures and the war;* e.g. **World War, 1939-1945—Motion pictures and the war;** to be added as needed
  BT   **Historical drama**
       Motion pictures
  NT   **World War, 1939-1945—Motion pictures and the war**
War of 1812
USE   **United States—History—1812-1815, War of 1812**

War of 1914
USE   **World War, 1914-1918**
War of 1939-1945
USE   **World War, 1939-1945**
War of nerves
USE   **Psychological warfare**
War of Secession (U.S.)
USE   **United States—History—1861-1865, Civil War**
War of the American Revolution
USE   **United States—History—1775-1783, Revolution**
War pensions
USE   **Military pensions**
War poetry   808.81; 811, etc.; 811.008, etc.
   May be used for individual works or collections of war poetry, or for materials about war poetry in general, not confined to a particular war.
  UF   Anti-war poetry
  SA   names of wars with the subdivision *Poetry*, to be added as needed
  BT   **Poetry**
  NT   **Bunker Hill (Boston, Mass.), Battle of, 1775—Poetry**
       World War, 1939-1945—Poetry
  RT   **War songs**
War powers
USE   **War and emergency powers**
War protest movements
USE   **Peace movements**
War radio programs   791.44
   May be used for individual works, collections, or materials about war radio programs.
  BT   **Radio programs**
War—Religious aspects   261.8; 291.1
  UF   Religion and war
       War and religion *[Former heading]*
  SA   names of wars with the subdivision *Religious aspects*, e.g. **World War, 1939-1945—Religious aspects;** to be added as needed
  BT   **Religion**
       War
  NT   **Conscientious objectors**
       Pacifism

BT = Broader Term   NT = Narrower Term   RT = Related Term   SA = See Also   UF = Used For

War ships
USE **Warships**
War songs 782.42
UF **Battle songs**
   Soldiers' songs
BT **National songs**
   Songs
NT **World War, 1939-1945—Songs**
RT **War poetry**
War, Space
USE **Space warfare**
War stories 808.83; 813, etc.
May be used for individual works, collections, or materials about war stories.
UF Anti-war stories
   Apocalyptic fantasies
   End-of-the-world fantasies
SA names of wars and battles with
   the subdivision *Fiction,* e.g.
   World War, 1939-1945—Fiction; to be added as needed
BT **Fiction**
   Historical fiction
War television programs 791.45
May be used for individual works, collections, or materials about war television programs.
BT **Television programs**
War use
USE subjects with the subdivision
   War use, e.g. **Dogs—War
   use;** to be added as needed
War use of animals
USE **Animals—War use**
War use of dogs
USE **Dogs—War use**
War veterans
USE **Veterans**
War work
USE names of wars with the subdivision *War work,* e.g. **World
   War, 1939-1945—War work;**
   to be added as needed
Warfare, Space
USE **Space warfare**
Warfare, Submarine
USE **Submarine warfare**
Warm air heating
USE **Hot air heating**
Wars
USE **Military history**

Naval history
War
Wars of the Roses, 1455-1485
USE **Great Britain—History—1455-
   1485, War of the Roses**
Warships 359.8; 623.8
UF Battle ships
   Battleships
   War ships
SA names of countries with the sub-
   head *Navy,* e.g. **United
   States. Navy;** and names of
   individual warships, to be
   added as needed
BT **Naval architecture**
   Naval art and science
   Sea power
   Ships
NT **Aircraft carriers**
   Submarines
   United States. Navy
RT **Navies**
Washing
USE **Laundry**
Wasps 595.79
UF Hymenoptera
BT **Insects**
Waste as fuel
USE **Waste products as fuel**
Waste disposal
USE **Refuse and refuse disposal**
   and types of waste disposal,
   e.g. **Radioactive waste dis-
   posal; Sewage disposal;** etc.,
   and types of industries, plants,
   and facilities with the subdivi-
   sion *Waste disposal,* e.g.
   **Chemical industry—Waste
   disposal;** to be added as
   needed
Waste (Economics) 339.4
BT **Economics**
Waste products 628.4
UF By-products
   Junk
   Trade waste
BT **Industrial chemistry**
   Manufactures
NT **Industrial wastes**
RT **Recycling**

BT = Broader Term   NT = Narrower Term   RT = Related Term   SA = See Also   UF = Used For

760

Waste products—*Continued*
    Refuse and refuse disposal
Waste products as fuel   333.793; 662
  UF   Energy conversion from waste
          Organic waste as fuel
          Waste as fuel
  BT   **Salvage**
  RT   **Biomass energy**
Waste products—Recycling
  USE   **Recycling**
Waste reclamation
  USE   **Recycling**
          Salvage
Wastes, Hazardous
  USE   **Hazardous wastes**
Wastes, Industrial
  USE   **Industrial wastes**
Wastes, Medical
  USE   **Medical wastes**
Watches
  USE   **Clocks and watches**
Water   551.4; 553.7
  UF   Hydrology
  BT   **Earth sciences**
          Hydraulics
  NT   **Drinking water**
          Floods
          Frost
          Geysers
          Hydrotherapy
          Ice
          Lakes
          Ocean
          Ponds
          Rain
          Rivers
          Sea water
          Snow
          Steam
  RT   **Hydraulic engineering**
          Water rights
Water—Analysis   546; 628.1
  BT   **Analytical chemistry**
  RT   **Water pollution**
Water animals
  USE   **Freshwater animals**
          Marine animals
Water ballet
  USE   **Synchronized swimming**

Water birds   598.176
  UF   Aquatic birds
          Water fowl
          Wild fowl
  SA   types of water birds, to be add-
          ed as needed
  BT   **Birds**
  NT   **Geese**
          Terns
Water color painting
  USE   **Watercolor painting**
Water colors
  USE   **Watercolor painting**
Water conduits
  USE   **Aqueducts**
Water conservation   333.91
  UF   Conservation of water
  BT   **Conservation of natural re-
          sources**
  RT   **Water supply**
Water cure
  USE   **Hydrotherapy**
Water farming
  USE   **Hydroponics**
Water flow
  USE   **Hydraulics**
Water—Fluoridation
  USE **Water fluoridation**
Water fluoridation   628.1
  UF   Fluoridation of water
          Water—Fluoridation *[Former
            heading]*
  BT   **Water supply**
  RT   **Teeth—Diseases**
Water fowl
  USE   **Water birds**
Water—Oil pollution
  USE   **Oil pollution of water**
Water plants
  USE   **Freshwater plants**
          Marine plants
Water pollution   363.739; 628.1
  UF   Detergent pollution of rivers,
          lakes, etc. *[Former heading]*
          Pollution of water
          River pollution
  SA   types of pollution, e.g. **Oil pol-
          lution of water;** to be added
          as needed
  BT   **Environmental health**

BT = Broader Term   NT = Narrower Term   RT = Related Term   SA = See Also   UF = Used For

Water pollution—*Continued*
    Pollution
    Public health
NT   Acid rain
    Marine pollution
    Oil pollution of water
RT   Industrial wastes
    Sewage disposal
    Water—Analysis
    Water supply

Water power   333.9; 621.2
UF   Hydroelectric power
BT   Energy resources
    Hydraulics
    Power (Mechanics)
    Renewable energy resources
    Rivers
    Water resources development
NT   Dams
    Hydraulic engineering
    Hydraulic machinery
    Hydroelectric power plants

Water—Purification
USE   Water purification

Water purification   628.1
UF   Purification of water
    Water—Purification *[Former heading]*
BT   Sanitation
    Water supply
NT   Sea water conversion

Water resources development   333.91
BT   Energy development
    Natural resources
NT   Hydroelectric power plants
    Inland navigation
    Irrigation
    Water power
    Water supply

Water rights   333.91; 346.04
BT   Law
RT   Water

Water safety   363.14; 797.028
UF   Aquatic sports—Safety measures
    Drowning prevention
    Water sports—Safety measures
BT   Accidents—Prevention

Water skiing   797.3
UF   Skiing, Water
BT   Water sports

Water sports   797
UF   Aquatic sports
SA   types of water sports, to be added as needed
BT   Sports
NT   Boats and boating
    Canoes and canoeing
    Deep diving
    Diving
    Fishing
    Rowing
    Sailing
    Surfing
    Swimming
    Water skiing
    Yachts and yachting

Water sports—Safety measures
USE   Water safety

Water supply (May subdiv. geog.)
    363.6; 628.1
UF   Waterworks
BT   Civil engineering
    Municipal engineering
    Public health
    Public utilities
    Sanitary engineering
    Sanitation
    Water resources development
NT   Aqueducts
    Dams
    Drinking water
    Forest influences
    Irrigation
    Water fluoridation
    Water purification
RT   Reservoirs
    Water conservation
    Water pollution
    Wells

Water supply engineering   628.1
BT   Civil engineering
    Engineering
NT   Boring
RT   Hydraulic engineering

Water transportation
USE   Shipping

Watercolor painting   751.42
UF   Water color painting
    Water colors
    Watercolors

BT = Broader Term   NT = Narrower Term   RT = Related Term   SA = See Also   UF = Used For

Watercolor painting—*Continued*
  BT Painting
Watercolors
  USE Watercolor painting
Watergate Affair, 1972-1974   973.924
  BT Misconduct in office
      Political corruption
      United States—History—1961-
        1974
Watering places
  USE Health resorts
Waterways   386
      Use for materials on rivers, lakes, and ca-
    nals used for transportation.
  BT Transportation
  NT Canals
      Lakes
      Rivers
  RT Inland navigation
Waterworks
  USE Water supply
Wave mechanics   530.12; 531
  BT Mechanics
      Quantum theory
      Waves
Waves   531
  BT Hydrodynamics
      Vibration
  NT Electric waves
      Ocean waves
      Radiation
      Sound waves
      Wave mechanics
Waves, Electromagnetic
  USE Electromagnetic waves
Waves, Ultrasonic
  USE Ultrasonic waves
Wealth   330.1
  UF Distribution of wealth
      Fortune
      Fortunes
      Riches
  BT Economics
      Finance
  NT Cost and standard of living
      Economic conditions
      Income
      Inheritance and succession
      Millionaires
      Profit
      Success

  RT Capital
      Money
      Property
Weaponry
  USE Weapons
Weapons   355.8; 623.4
  UF Arms and armor *[Former head-
        ing]*
      Weaponry
  BT Tools
  NT Bow and arrow
      Firearms
      Firearms industry
      Military weapons
  RT Armor
      Military art and science
Weapons, Atomic
  USE Nuclear weapons
Weapons, Enhanced radiation
  USE Neutron weapons
Weapons, Neutron
  USE Neutron weapons
Weapons, Nuclear
  USE Nuclear weapons
Weapons, Space
  USE Space weapons
Weariness
  USE Fatigue
Weather   551.6
      Use for materials on the state of the atmo-
    sphere at a given time and place with respect
    to heat or cold, wetness or dryness, calm or
    storm. Scientific materials on the atmosphere,
    especially weather factors, are entered under
    Meteorology. Materials on climate as it re-
    lates to humans and to plant and animal life,
    including the effects of changes of climate,
    are entered under **Climate.**
  SA names of countries, cities, etc.,
        with the subdivision *Climate,*
        e.g. **United States—Climate;**
        to be added as needed
  NT Humidity
      Rain
      Snow
      Storms
      Weather control
      Weather forecasting
      Winds
  RT Climate
      Meteorology
Weather control   551.68
  UF Artificial weather control

BT = Broader Term   NT = Narrower Term   RT = Related Term   SA = See Also   UF = Used For

Weather control—*Continued*
    Cloud seeding
    Rain making
    Weather modification
  BT Meteorology
      Weather
Weather—Folklore   398.26
  UF Weather lore
  BT Folklore
      Meteorology
      Weather forecasting
Weather forecasting   551.63
  UF Precipitation forecasting
  BT Forecasting
      Meteorology
      Weather
  NT Meteorology in aeronautics
      Weather—Folklore
Weather lore
  USE Weather—Folklore
Weather modification
  USE Weather control
Weather satellites
  USE Meteorological satellites
Weather stations
  USE Meteorological observatories
Weaving   677; 746.1; 746.41
  UF Hand weaving
  SA types of woven articles, e.g.
      Carpets; to be added as
      needed
  BT Handicraft
  NT Basket making
      Beadwork
      Lace and lace making
      Looms
  RT Carpets
      Textile industry
Web (Information retrieval system)
  USE World Wide Web
Web servers
  USE World Wide Web servers
Weddings   392.5; 395.2
  BT Marriage
  NT Marriage customs and rites
Weed killers
  USE Herbicides
Weeds   632
  BT Agricultural pests
      Economic botany

      Gardening
      Plants
Week   529
  BT Calendars
      Chronology
  RT Days
Weekly premium insurance
  USE Industrial life insurance
Weight control
  USE Weight loss
Weight lifting   796.41; 613.7
  UF Powerlifting
      Pumping iron
      Strength training
      Weight training
      Weightlifting
  BT Athletics
      Exercise
  RT Bodybuilding
Weight loss   613.2
  UF Body weight control
      Dieting
      Diets, Reducing
      Reducing *[Former heading]*
      Weight control
  BT Body weight
  RT Diet
      Exercise
Weight training
  USE Weight lifting
Weightlessness   531
  UF Free fall
      Gravity free state
      Subgravity state
      Zero gravity
  BT Environmental influence on
      humans
      Space medicine
Weightlifting
  USE Weight lifting
Weights and measures   389; 530.8
  UF Measures
      Metrology
  BT Physics
  NT Body weight
      Electric measurements
      Measuring instruments
      Volume (Cubic content)
  RT Measurement
      Metric system

BT = Broader Term   NT = Narrower Term   RT = Related Term   SA = See Also   UF = Used For

Welding 671.5
>
> UF   Oxyacetylene welding
> BT   **Blacksmithing**
>   **Forging**
>   **Ironwork**
>   **Metalwork**
> NT   **Electric welding**
> RT   **Soldering**

Welding, Electric
> USE   **Electric welding**

Welfare agencies
> USE   **Charities**

Welfare state (May subdiv. geog.)
    330.12; 361.6
> BT   **Economic policy**
>   **Public welfare**
>   **Social policy**
>   **State, The**

Welfare work
> USE   **Charities**
>   **Public welfare**
>   **Social work**

Welfare work in industry
> USE   **Industrial welfare**

Well boring
> USE   **Boring**

Well drilling, Oil
> USE   **Oil well drilling**

Wells 551.49; 628.1
> UF   Artesian wells
> BT   **Hydraulic engineering**
> RT   **Boring**
>   **Water supply**

West Africa 966
> Use for materials dealing collectively with the southern half of the western bulge of the African continent. The area is defined on the north by the Sahara and on the south and west by the Atlantic Ocean. The term is used loosely, but includes Benin, Burkina Faso, Cameroon, Gambia, Ghana, Guinea, Guinea-Bissau, Ivory Coast, Liberia, Nigeria, Senegal, Sierra Leone, and Togo. Sometimes, additional countries of the Sahel (Mali, Mauritania, and Niger) are also included.
> UF   Africa, West *[Former heading]*
> BT   **Africa**
> NT   **French-speaking West Africa**

West Germany
> USE   **Germany (West)**

West Indian literature (French) 840
> Use for collections and for materials on West Indian literature written originally in French.
> BT   **Literature**

West Indies, Indians of the
> USE   **Indians of the West Indies**

West Point (Military academy)
> USE   **United States Military Academy**

West (U.S.) 978
> Use for the region west of the Mississippi River.
> UF   Western States
> SA   names of individual states in this region, to be added as needed
> BT   **United States**
> NT   **Pacific Northwest**
>   **Pacific States**

West (U.S.)—Exploration 978
> BT   **United States—Exploration**
> RT   **Overland journeys to the Pacific**

West (U.S.)—History
> UF   Westward movement
> BT   **United States—History**

Western and country music
> USE   **Country music**

Western civilization 306.09; 909
> Use for materials on the culture and society stemming from the Greco-Roman traditions of the occident rather than those of Islam, India, or the Far East.
> UF   Civilization, Occidental *[Former heading]*
>   Civilization, Western
>   Occidental civilization
> BT   **Civilization**
>   **East and West**

Western comic books, strips, etc. 741.5
> May be used for individual works, collections, or materials about Western comics.
> BT   **Comic books, strips, etc.**

Western Europe
> USE   **Europe**

Western films 791.43
> May be used for individual works, collections, or materials about Western films.
> UF   Westerns
> SA   types of Western films, e.g. **Lone Ranger films;** to be added as needed
> BT   **Adventure films**
>   **Historical drama**
>   **Motion pictures**

BT = Broader Term   NT = Narrower Term   RT = Related Term   SA = See Also   UF = Used For

Western films—*Continued*
 NT Lone Ranger films
Western States
 USE West (U.S.)
Western stories   808.83; 813, etc.
   May be used for individual works, collections, or materials about post-19th-century fiction set in the 19th-century American West.
 UF Westerns
 BT **Adventure fiction**
    Fiction
    Historical fiction
Westerns
 USE **Western films**
    Western stories
    Westerns (Radio programs)
    Westerns (Television programs)
Westerns (Radio programs)   791.44
   May be used for individual works, collections, or materials about Westerns on the radio.
 UF Westerns
 BT **Radio programs**
Westerns (Television programs)   791.45
   May be used for individual works, collections, or materials about Western on television.
 UF Westerns
 BT **Television programs**
Westminster Abbey   726.5
 BT **Abbeys**
    Church buildings
Westward movement
 USE **Land settlement—United States**
    United States—Territorial expansion
    West (U.S.)—History
Wetlands
 UF Bogs
    Land
    Swamps
 SA types of wetlands, e.g. **Marshes;** to be added as needed
 BT **Land use**
 NT **Marshes**
 RT **Drainage**
    Reclamation of land
Whales   599.5
 BT **Mammals**
    Marine mammals
Whaling   639.2
 BT **Fisheries**

 Hunting
 Voyages and travels
Wheat   633.1
 UF Breadstuffs
 BT **Grain**
 RT **Flour**
Wheels   621.8; 629.2
 UF Car wheels
 BT **Simple machines**
 NT **Gearing**
    Tires
Which-way stories
 USE **Plot-your-own stories**
Whistle blowing   174; 342; 353.4
   Use for materials on the practice of calling public attention to corruption, mismanagement, or waste in government, business, the military, etc.
 UF Blowing the whistle
    Whistleblowing
 BT **Political corruption**
    Public interest
Whistleblowing
 USE **Whistle blowing**
White collar crimes   364.16
 UF Crimes, White collar
    Occupational crimes
 BT **Crime**
 NT **Fraud**
White supremacist movements
 USE **White supremacy movements**
White supremacy movements   320.5
 UF Skinheads
    White supremacist movements
 BT **Race relations**
    Racism
    Social movements
Whittling
 USE **Wood carving**
Whodunits
 USE **Mystery and detective plays**
    Mystery fiction
    Mystery films
    Mystery radio programs
    Mystery television programs
Whole language   372.62
   Use for materials on the integration of listening, speaking, writing, and reading skills in meaningful situations in which children participate actively.
 UF Integrated language arts (Holistic)

BT = Broader Term   NT = Narrower Term   RT = Related Term   SA = See Also   UF = Used For

Whole language—*Continued*

    Language arts (Holistic)

    Language experience approach in
      education

  BT Education—Experimental
      methods

      Language arts

      Reading

      Writing

Wholistic medicine

  USE **Holistic medicine**

Wica

  USE **Wicca**

Wicca 133.4

  UF Wica

  BT **Folklore**

      New Age movement

      Paganism

  RT **Witchcraft**

Wickedness

  USE **Good and evil**

Widowers 305.38; 306.88

  BT **Family**

      Husbands

      Men

      Single men

  RT **Single parent family**

Widows 305.48; 306.88

  BT **Family**

      Single women

      Wives

      Women

  RT **Single parent family**

Wife abuse 362.82

  UF Abuse of wives

      Battering of wives

      Wife battering

      Wife beating

  BT **Family violence**

  RT **Abused women**

Wife battering

  USE **Wife abuse**

Wife beating

  USE **Wife abuse**

Wigs 391.5

  BT **Costume**

      Hair

Wigwams

  USE **Indians of North America—
        Dwellings**

Wild animal dwellings

  USE **Animals—Habitations**

Wild animals

  USE **Animals**

      Wildlife

Wild cats 599.75; 636.8

    Use for materials on non-domesticated spe-
cies of cats or domestic cats living in a wild
state. Materials on domestic cats are entered
under **Cats.**

  UF Felidae

      Feral cats

      Wildcats

  SA types of wild cats, to be added
      as needed.

  BT **Mammals**

  RT **Cats**

Wild children 155.45

    Use for materials on children who have
been raised by animals or have lived their
formative years in the wild without contact
with human society

  UF Feral children *[Former heading]*

      Wolf children

  BT **Exceptional children**

Wild flowers 582.13

  UF Flowers, Wild

      Wildflowers

  BT **Flowers**

Wild flowers—Conservation

  USE **Plant conservation**

Wild fowl

  USE **Game and game birds**

      Water birds

Wildcats

  USE **Wild cats**

Wilderness areas 333.78

  UF Scenery

  BT **Forest reserves**

  RT **Conservation of natural re-
      sources**

      National parks and reserves

Wilderness survival 613.6; 796.5

  UF Bush survival

      Outdoor survival

  BT **Camping**

      Outdoor life

      Survival skills

  RT **Survival after airplane acci-
      dents, shipwrecks, etc.**

Wildflowers

  USE **Wild flowers**

BT = Broader Term   NT = Narrower Term   RT = Related Term   SA = See Also   UF = Used For

Wildlife (May subdiv. geog.) **333.95; 639**

Use for materials on wild animals in their natural environment, especially mammals, birds, and fishes that are hunted for sport or food.

UF   Feral animals

       Wild animals

SA   types of wildlife, e.g. **Desert animals;** to be added as needed

BT   **Animals**

NT   **Dangerous animals**

       Desert animals

       Forest animals

       Freshwater animals

       Furbearing animals

       Game and game birds

       Jungle animals

       Marine animals

       Mountain animals

       Rare animals

       Stream animals

       Swamp animals

Wildlife and pesticides

USE   **Pesticides and wildlife**

Wildlife conservation **639.9**

UF   Conservation of wildlife

       Preservation of wildlife

       Protection of wildlife

BT   **Conservation of natural resources**

       Economic zoology

       Endangered species

       Environmental protection

       Nature conservation

NT   **Birdbanding**

       Birds—Protection

       Game protection

       Game reserves

       Pesticides and wildlife

       Wildlife refuges

RT   **Rare animals**

Wildlife refuges **639.9**

UF   Refuges, Wildlife

       Sanctuaries, Wildlife

       Wildlife sanctuaries

SA   names of specific refuges, to be added as needed

BT   **Wildlife conservation**

Wildlife sanctuaries

USE   **Wildlife refuges**

Will

USE   **Brainwashing**

       Free will and determinism

Will power

USE   **Self-control**

Willpower

USE   **Self-control**

Wills **346.05**

UF   Bequests

       Legacies

BT   **Genealogy**

       Registers of births, etc.

NT   **Living wills**

RT   **Executors and administrators**

       Inheritance and succession

Wind

USE   **Winds**

Wind instruments **788**

UF   Brass instruments

       Woodwind instruments

SA   types of wind instruments, to be added as needed

BT   **Musical instruments**

NT   **Flutes**

RT   **Bands (Music)**

Wind power **333.9; 621.4**

BT   **Energy resources**

       Power (Mechanics)

       Renewable energy resources

RT   **Windmills**

Windbreaks **634.9**

UF   Shelterbelts

BT   **Tree planting**

Windmills **621.4**

BT   **Irrigation**

RT   **Wind power**

Window dressing

USE   **Show windows**

Window gardening **635.9**

UF   Greenhouses, Window

       Window greenhouses

       Windowbox gardening

       Windowsill gardening

BT   **Gardening**

       Indoor gardening

NT   **House plants**

RT   **Container gardening**

       Flower gardening

BT = Broader Term   NT = Narrower Term   RT = Related Term   SA = See Also   UF = Used For

Window greenhouses
USE **Window gardening**
Windowbox gardening
USE **Window gardening**
Windows 721
BT Architecture—Details
Building
Buildings
NT **Show windows**
RT **Glass**
Windows, Stained glass
USE **Glass painting and staining**
Windowsill gardening
USE **Window gardening**
Winds 551.51
UF Gales
Wind
BT **Meteorology**
Navigation
Physical geography
Weather
NT **Cyclones**
Hurricanes
Tornadoes
Typhoons
RT **Storms**
Windsurfing 797.3
UF Board sailing
Sailboarding
BT **Sailing**
Wine and wine making (May subdiv.
geog.) **641.2; 663**
UF Viticulture
BT **Alcoholic beverages**
RT **Fermentation**
Grapes
Vineyards
Winter resorts 796.9
BT **Resorts**
Winter sports 796.9
UF Ice sports
SA types of winter sports, to be
added as needed
BT **Sports**
NT **Hockey**
Ice skating
Skiing
Sledding
Wire agencies
USE **News agencies**

Wireless
USE **Radio**
Wiretapping 363.25
BT **Criminal investigation**
Right of privacy
RT **Eavesdropping**
Wiring, Electric
USE **Electric wiring**
Wishes 153.8
BT **Motivation (Psychology)**
Wit and humor 808.87; 817, etc.
May be used for individual works, collec-
tions, or materials about wit and humor.
UF Facetiae
Humor
SA wit and humor of particular
countries, e.g. **American wit
and humor;** and subjects
with the subdivision *Humor,*
e.g. **Music—Humor;** to be
added as needed
BT **Literature**
NT **American wit and humor**
Black humor (Literature)
Chapbooks
Comedies
Comedy
Comic books, strips, etc.
English wit and humor
Epigrams
Humorists
Humorous fiction
Humorous poetry
Jokes
Mock-heroic literature
Music—Humor
Nonsense verses
Parody
Practical jokes
Puns
Satire
Tall tales
**World War, 1939-1945—Hu-
mor**
RT **Anecdotes**
Witchcraft 133.4
UF Black art (Magic)
Black magic (Witchcraft)
Necromancy
Sorcery
Spirits

BT = Broader Term   NT = Narrower Term   RT = Related Term   SA = See Also   UF = Used For

Witchcraft—*Continued*
    Wizardry
  BT   **Folklore**
        Occultism
        Superstition
  NT   **Charms**
        Goddess religion
        Witches
  RT   **Demonology**
        Exorcism
        Magic
        Wicca
Witches 133.4
  UF   Covens
  BT   **Witchcraft**
Witnesses 345; 347
  UF   Cross-examination
  BT   **Litigation**
        Trials
Wives 306.872

    Use for materials on wives in general and for materials on the legal status of married women.

  UF   Married women *[Former heading]*
        Spouses
  BT   **Family**
        Marriage
        Married people
        Women
  NT   **Widows**
Wives of presidents—United States
  USE   **Presidents' spouses—United States**
Wives, Runaway
  USE   **Runaway adults**
Wizardry
  USE   **Witchcraft**
Wolf children
  USE   **Wild children**
Woman
  USE   **Women**
Women (May subdiv. geog.) **305.4**
  UF   Woman
  SA   women of particular racial or ethnic groups, e.g. **Mexican American women;** and women in various occupations and professions, e.g. **Women artists; Policewomen; Women**

in the motion picture industry; etc., to be added as needed
  NT   **Abused women**
        African American women
        Black women
        Businesswomen
        Indians of North America—Women
        Lesbians
        Mexican American women
        Mothers
        Nuns
        Policewomen
        Single women
        Widows
        Wives
        Women air pilots
        Women artists
        Women authors
        Women clergy
        Women in the motion picture industry
        Women judges
        Women physicians
        World War, 1939-1945—Women
        Young women
Women actors
  USE   **Actresses**
Women, African American
  USE   **African American women**
Women air pilots 629.13092; 920
  BT   **Air pilots**
        Women
Women artists 709.2; 920

    Use for materials on the attainments of several women in the area of art.

  BT   **Artists**
        Women
Women authors 809; 920

    Use for collections and for materials on the attainments of several women authors not limited to a single national literature or literary form.

  SA   literary forms and national literatures with the subdivision *Women authors,* e.g.
        American literature—Women authors; to be added as needed

---

Women authors—*Continued*
  BT   Authors
        Women
Women—Biography   920
  BT   Biography
Women—Biography—Dictionaries
    920.72
Women, Black
  USE   Black women
Women—Civil rights
  USE   Women's rights
Women clergy   200.92; 270.092
  BT   Clergy
        Women
  RT   Ordination of women
Women—Clothing
  USE   Women's clothing
Women—Clubs
  USE   Women—Societies
Women—Diseases   616.0082; 618.1
  UF   Diseases of women
        Gynecology
  BT   Diseases
  NT   Breast cancer
  RT   Women—Health and hygiene
Women—Dress
  USE   Women's clothing
Women—Education   371.822
  UF   Education of women
  BT   Education
  RT   Coeducation
Women—Emancipation
  USE   Women's rights
Women—Employment   331.4
  UF   Employment of women
        Girls—Employment
        Women—Occupations
        Working women
  SA   women in various occupations
        and professions, e.g. **Women
        artists; Policewomen; Wom-
        en in the motion picture in-
        dustry;** etc., to be added as
        needed
  BT   Employment
        Labor supply
  NT   Equal pay for equal work
        Self-employed women
  RT   Discrimination in employment

Women—Enfranchisement
  USE   Women—Suffrage
Women—Equal rights
  USE   Women's rights
Women—Health and hygiene   613
  UF   Gynecology
        Women—Hygiene
  BT   Health
        Hygiene
  NT   Women—Mental health
  RT   Women—Diseases
Women—History   305.409
    Use for comprehensive materials on the history of women, their socio-economic, political, and legal position, their participation in historical events, and their contributions to society. Materials dealing specifically with women's social condition and status, including historical discussions of the same, are entered under **Women—Social conditions.**
  BT   Feminism
        History
Women—Hygiene
  USE   Women—Health and hygiene
Women—Identity   305.4
  UF   Female identity
        Feminine identity
  BT   Identity (Psychology)
Women in art   704.9
    Use for materials on women depicted in works of art. Materials on the attainments of several women in the area of art are entered under **Women artists.**
  BT   Art
Women in business
  USE   Businesswomen
Women in literature   809
    Use for materials on the theme of women in works of literature. Collections and materials on several women authors not limited to a single national literature or literary form are entered under **Women authors.**
  BT   Characters and characteristics
        in literature
Women in motion pictures   791.43
    Use for materials discussing the portrayal of women in motion pictures. Materials discussing all aspects of women's involvement in motion pictures are entered under **Women in the motion picture industry.**
  BT   Motion pictures
Women in the Bible   220.8
  UF   Bible—Women
  BT   Bible—Biography

BT = Broader Term   NT = Narrower Term   RT = Related Term   SA = See Also   UF = Used For

Women in the motion picture industry
  791.43

Use for materials discussing all aspects of women's involvement in motion pictures. Materials discussing the portrayal of women in motion pictures are entered under **Women in motion pictures.**

BT   **Motion picture industry**
       Women

Women, Indian
USE   **Indians of North America—**
       Women

Women judges   347; 920
BT   **Judges**
       Women

Women—Mental health   362.2
BT   **Mental health**
       Women—Health and hygiene
RT   **Women—Psychology**

Women, Mexican American
USE   **Mexican American women**

Women—Occupations
USE   **Women—Employment**

Women—Ordination
USE   **Ordination of women**

Women physicians   610.69; 920
BT   **Physicians**
       Women

Women police officers
USE   **Policewomen**

Women—Political activity   324
BT   **Political participation**
NT   **Women politicians**

Women politicians   324.2092; 920
BT   **Politicians**
       Women—Political activity

Women—Psychology   155.3
UF   Feminine psychology
BT   **Psychology**
RT   **Women—Mental health**

Women—Religious life   248.4; 291.4
BT   **Religious life**
RT   **Goddess religion**

Women—Self-defense
USE   **Self-defense for women**

Women, Self-employed
USE   **Self-employed women**

Women, Single
USE   **Single women**

Women—Social conditions   305.42
Use for materials dealing specifically with women's social condition and status, including historical discussions of the same. Comprehensive materials on the history of women are entered under **Women—History.**

BT   **Social conditions**
NT   **Prostitution**
       Women's movement

Women—Societies   367
UF   Women—Clubs
       Women's clubs
       Women's organizations
BT   **Clubs**
       Societies
NT   **Girls' clubs**

Women—Suffrage   324.6
UF   Women—Enfranchisement
       Women's suffrage
BT   **Suffrage**
       Women's rights
RT   **Suffragists**

Women—United States   305.40973
UF   United States—Women

Women's clothing   646
UF   Women—Clothing
       Women—Dress
BT   **Clothing and dress**

Women's clubs
USE   **Women—Societies**

Women's liberation movement
USE   **Women's movement**

Women's movement   305.42; 323.3
Use for materials on activities aimed at obtaining equal rights and opportunities for women. Materials on the theory of the political and social equality of the sexes and women's perspectives on various subjects are entered under **Feminism.**

UF   Women's liberation movement
BT   **Women—Social conditions**
       Women's rights
RT   **Feminism**

Women's organizations
USE   **Women—Societies**

Women's rights   323.3; 342
UF   Emancipation of women
       Rights of women
       Women—Civil rights *[Former heading]*
       Women—Emancipation
       Women—Equal rights
BT   **Civil rights**
       Sex discrimination
NT   **Women—Suffrage**
       Women's movement

BT = Broader Term   NT = Narrower Term   RT = Related Term   SA = See Also   UF = Used For

Women's rights—*Continued*
RT   Feminism
      Pro-choice movement
      Pro-life movement
Women's self-defense
USE   Self-defense for women
Women's suffrage
USE   Women—Suffrage
Wonders
USE   Curiosities and wonders
Wood   620.1; 674

    Use for materials on the various types of wood, their chemical and physical properties, and how they are used.

UF   Timber
      Woods
SA   types of wood, e.g. **Oak;** to be added as needed
BT   **Building materials**
      Forest products
      Fuel
      Trees
NT   **Lumber and lumbering**
      Oak
      Plywood
      Woodwork
RT   **Forests and forestry**
Wood block printing
USE   **Wood engraving**
      Woodcuts
Wood carving   731.4; 736
UF   Carving, Wood
      Whittling
BT   **Carving (Decorative arts)**
      Decoration and ornament
      Woodwork
Wood engraving   761
UF   Block printing
      Wood block printing
BT   **Engraving**
Wood finishing   698
UF   Finishes and finishing
BT   **Industrial painting**
NT   **Furniture finishing**
      Lacquer and lacquering
      Varnish and varnishing
Wood—Preservation   674
UF   Preservation of wood
Wood turning
USE   **Turning**

Woodcuts   761
UF   Block printing
      Wood block printing
BT   **Prints**
Woods
USE   **Forests and forestry**
      Lumber and lumbering
      Wood
Woodwind instruments
USE   **Wind instruments**
Woodwork   684
BT   **Architecture—Details**
      Decorative arts
      Wood
NT   **Furniture making**
      Wood carving
RT   **Cabinetwork**
      Carpentry
      Turning
Woodworking machinery   621.9; 684
SA   types of woodworking machines, to be added as needed
BT   **Machinery**
NT   **Lathes**
Wool   677
BT   **Animal products**
      Fabrics
      Fibers
RT   **Yarn**
Word books
USE   **Picture dictionaries**
Word building
USE   **Word skills**
Word games   793.734
SA   types of word games, e.g. **Crossword puzzles;** to be added as needed
BT   **Games**
      Literary recreations
NT   **Crossword puzzles**
Word processing   652.5
BT   **Office management**
      Office practice
RT   **Desktop publishing**
Word processor keyboarding
USE   **Keyboarding (Electronics)**
Word processor keyboards
USE   **Keyboards (Electronics)**
Word skills   372.4; 418

    Use for educational materials on consonants, blends, vowels, prefixes and suffixes,

---

BT = Broader Term   NT = Narrower Term   RT = Related Term   SA = See Also   UF = Used For

Word skills—*Continued*
digraphs, syllables, root words, rhyming, and alphabet, etc.
  UF   Word building
          Words
  BT   **Reading**
  RT   **English language—Spelling**
Wordless stories
  USE   **Stories without words**
Words
  USE   **Vocabulary**
           Word skills
Words, New
  USE   **New words**
Work   158.7; 306.3
    Use for materials on the physical or mental exertion of individuals to produce or accomplish something. Materials on the collective human activities involved in the production and distribution of goods and services in an economy, as well as materials on the group of workers who render these services for wages, are entered under **Labor.**
  NT   **Employee morale**
          Job satisfaction
          Sex in the workplace
          Work and family
          Work environment
          Work ethic
  RT   **Labor**
          Occupations
Work addiction
  USE   **Workaholism**
Work and family   306.3; 306.87; 646.7
    Use for materials on the conflict or balance in people's lives between the demands of work and family.
  UF   Family and work
  BT   **Family**
          Work
  RT   **Dual career family**
Work at home
  USE   **Home business**
          Telecommuting
Work environment   658.2
  UF   Places of work
          Work places
          Working environment
          Workplace environment
          Worksite environment
  BT   **Environment**
          Work
  NT   **Machinery in the workplace**

Work ethic   174
  UF   Ethics, Work
          Protestant work ethic
          Work ethics *[Former heading]*
          Work, Ethics of
          Work ethos
  BT   **Ethics**
          Labor
          Work
Work ethics
  USE   **Work ethic**
Work, Ethics of
  USE   **Work ethic**
Work ethos
  USE   **Work ethic**
Work performance standards
  USE   **Performance standards**
Work places
  USE   **Work environment**
Work satisfaction
  USE   **Job satisfaction**
Work standards
  USE   **Production standards**
Work stoppages
  USE   **Strikes**
Work stress
  USE   **Job stress**
Workaholic syndrome
  USE   **Workaholism**
Workaholism   155.2; 616.85
  UF   Addiction to work
          Compulsive working
          Work addiction
          Workaholic syndrome
          Working, Compulsive
  BT   **Compulsive behavior**
Workers
  USE   **Employees**
          Labor
          Working class
Workers' compensation   368.4
  UF   Compensation
          Employers' liability
          Insurance, Workers' compensation
          Workmen's compensation
  BT   **Accident insurance**
          Health insurance
          Social security

BT = Broader Term   NT = Narrower Term   RT = Related Term   SA = See Also   UF = Used For

Workers' participation in management
  USE   **Participative management**
Working animals   636.088
  UF   Animals, Working
  SA   animals in specific working situ-
           ations, to be added as needed
  BT   **Animals**
         Domestic animals
         Economic zoology
  NT   **Animals in police work**
         Animals—War use
         Guide dogs
Working at home
  USE   **Home business**
         Telecommuting
Working children
  USE   **Children—Employment**
Working class   305.5
    Use for materials on the social class com-
    posed of persons who work for wages, usually
    in manual labor.
  UF   Blue collar workers
         Factory workers
         Industrial workers
         Labor and laboring classes *[For-*
           mer heading]
         Laborers
         Laboring class
         Laboring classes
         Manual workers
         Skilled workers
         Unskilled workers
         Workers
         Working classes
  BT   **Social classes**
  NT   **Proletariat**
  RT   **Labor**
Working classes
  USE   **Working class**
Working, Compulsive
  USE   **Workaholism**
Working couples
  USE   **Dual career family**
Working day
  USE   **Hours of labor**
Working environment
  USE   **Work environment**
Working hours
  USE   **Hours of labor**
Working parents, Children of
  USE   **Children of working parents**

Working robots
  USE   **Industrial robots**
Working women
  USE   **Women—Employment**
Workmen's compensation
  USE   **Workers' compensation**
Workplace environment
  USE   **Work environment**
Workshop councils
  USE   **Participative management**
Workshops, Teachers'
  USE   **Teachers' workshops**
Worksite environment
  USE   **Work environment**
World
  USE   **Earth**
World economics
  USE   **Commercial geography**
         Commercial policy
         Economic conditions
         Economic policy
         International competition
World, End of the
  USE   **End of the world**
World government
  USE   **International organization**
World history   909
  UF   History, Universal
         Universal history
  BT   **History**
  NT   **Ancient history**
         Geography
         Middle Ages
         Middle Ages—History
         Modern history
World language
  USE   **Universal language**
World order
  USE   **International relations**
World organization
  USE   **International organization**
World politics   909
    Use for historical accounts of international
    political affairs. Materials on the theory of in-
    ternational relations are entered under **Inter-**
    national relations.
  UF   International politics
  SA   names of countries with the sub-
           divisions *Foreign relations*
           and *Politics and government,*
           to be added as needed

BT = Broader Term   NT = Narrower Term   RT = Related Term   SA = See Also   UF = Used For

World politics—*Continued*
BT   Political science
NT   United States—Foreign rela-
         tions
      World War, 1914-1918
      World War, 1939-1945
      World War III
RT   Geopolitics
      International organization
      International relations
World politics—1945-   909.82
World politics—1945-1965   909.82
World politics—1945-1991   909.82
NT   Cold war
World politics—1965-   909.82
World politics—1991-   909.82
World records   030
UF   Human records
      Records of achievement
      Records, World
      World's records
BT   Curiosities and wonders
RT   Sports records
World War I
USE   **World War, 1914-1918**
World War II
USE   **World War, 1939-1945**
World War, 1914-1918 (May subdiv.
    geog.)   **940.3; 940.4**
    May be subdivided like **World War, 1939-**
    1945.
UF   European War, 1914-1918
      War of 1914
      World War I
BT   **Europe—History—1871-1918**
      Modern history—1900-1999
      (20th century)
      World politics
World War, 1914-1918—Chemical war-
    fare   940.4
UF   World War, 1914-1918—Gas
      warfare *[Former heading]*
BT   **Chemical warfare**
World War, 1914-1918—Economic as-
    pects   940.3
RT   **Reconstruction (1914-1939)**
World War, 1914-1918—Gas warfare
USE   **World War, 1914-1918—Chem-**
      ical warfare
World War, 1914-1918—Peace   940.3
BT   **Peace**

NT   **League of Nations**
World War, 1914-1918—Reconstruction
USE   **Reconstruction (1914-1939)**
World War, 1914-1918—Territorial ques-
    tions   940.3
NT   **Mandates**
World War, 1914-1918—United States
    940.3; 940.4; 973.91
UF   United States—European War,
      1914-1918
      United States—History—1914-
      1918, European War
      United States—History—1914-
      1918, World War
      United States—World War,
      1914-1918
World War, 1939-1945 (May subdiv.
    geog.)   **940.53; 940.54**
    Subdivisions used under this heading may
    be used under other wars.
UF   European War, 1939-1945
      War of 1939-1945
      World War II
SA   names of battles, campaigns,
      sieges, etc., e.g. **Ardennes,**
      Battle of the, 1944-1945;
      Pearl Harbor (Oahu, Ha-
      waii), Attack on, 1941; etc.,
      to be added as needed
BT   **Europe—History—1918-1945**
      Modern history—1900-1999
      (20th century)
      World politics
World War, 1939-1945—Aerial opera-
    tions   940.54
UF   World War, 1939-1945—Battles,
      sieges, etc.
BT   **Military aeronautics**
World War, 1939-1945—African Ameri-
    cans   940.53; 940.54
BT   **African Americans**
World War, 1939-1945—Amphibious op-
    erations   940.54
BT   **World War, 1939-1945—Naval**
      operations
World War, 1939-1945—Antiwar move-
    ments
USE   **World War, 1939-1945—Pro-**
      test movements
World War, 1939-1945—Armistices
    940.53

BT = Broader Term   NT = Narrower Term   RT = Related Term   SA = See Also   UF = Used For

World War, 1939-1945—Arms
USE World War, 1939-1945—
      Equipment and supplies
**World War, 1939-1945—Art and the
    war   940.53**
UF World War, 1939-1945—Iconog-
      raphy
      World War, 1939-1945, in art
BT **Art**
**World War, 1939-1945—Atrocities
    940.54**
SA names of specific atrocities and
      crimes, to be added as needed
BT **Atrocities**
**World War, 1939-1945—Battlefields
    940.54**
World War, 1939-1945—Battles, sieges,
    etc.
USE **World War, 1939-1945—Aerial
      operations
      World War, 1939-1945—Cam-
      paigns
      World War, 1939-1945—Naval
      operations**
**World War, 1939-1945—Biography
    920**
BT **Biography**
**World War, 1939-1945—Blockades
    940.54**
World War, 1939-1945—Campaigns
    (May subdiv. geog.)   **940.54**
UF World War, 1939-1945—Battles,
      sieges, etc.
SA names of battles, campaigns,
      sieges, etc., **Ardennes, Battle
      of the, 1944-1945;** to be add-
      ed as needed
NT **Ardennes, Battle of the, 1944-
      1945
      Normandy (France), Attack on,
      1944
      Pearl Harbor (Oahu, Hawaii),
      Attack on, 1941**
**World War, 1939-1945—Cartoons and
    caricatures   940.53**
UF World War, 1939-1945—Humor,
      caricatures, etc. *[Former
      heading]*
BT **Cartoons and caricatures**

World War, 1939-1945—Causes   940.53
NT **National socialism**
**World War, 1939-1945—Censorship
    940.54**
BT **Censorship**
World War, 1939-1945—Charities
USE **World War, 1939-1945—Civil-
      ian relief
      World War, 1939-1945—War
      work**
**World War, 1939-1945—Chemical war-
    fare   940.54**
BT **Chemical warfare**
**World War, 1939-1945—Children
    940.53**
BT **Children and war**
World War, 1939-1945—Civilian evacua-
    tion
USE **World War, 1939-1945—Evac-
      uation of civilians**
**World War, 1939-1945—Civilian relief
    940.54**
UF World War, 1939-1945—Chari-
      ties
BT **Charities
    Food relief
    Foreign aid
    Reconstruction (1939-1951)
    World War, 1939-1945—Food
    supply
    World War, 1939-1945—Medi-
    cal care
    World War, 1939-1945—War
    work**
RT **World War, 1939-1945—Refu-
    gees**
**World War, 1939-1945—Collaborationists
    940.53**
UF Fifth column
    Quislings
BT **World War, 1939-1945—Occu-
    pied territories**
**World War, 1939-1945—Congresses
    940.53**
BT **Congresses and conventions**
**World War, 1939-1945—Conscientious
    objectors   940.53**
BT **Conscientious objectors
    World War, 1939-1945—Pro-
    test movements**

BT = Broader Term   NT = Narrower Term   RT = Related Term   SA = See Also   UF = Used For

World War, 1939-1945—Conscientious objectors—*Continued*

NT   World War, 1939-1945—Draft resisters

World War, 1939-1945—Correspondents

USE   World War, 1939-1945—Journalists

World War, 1939-1945—Desertions 940.54

BT   Military desertion

World War, 1939-1945—Destruction and pillage   940.54

World War, 1939-1945—Diplomatic history   940.53

NT   World War, 1939-1945—Governments in exile

World War, 1939-1945—Displaced persons

USE   World War, 1939-1945—Refugees

World War, 1939-1945—Draft resisters 940.54

BT   Draft resisters

World War, 1939-1945—Conscientious objectors

World War, 1939-1945—Economic aspects   940.53

Use for materials on the economic causes of the war and the effect of the war on commerce and industry.

BT   War—Economic aspects

NT   World War, 1939-1945—Finance

World War, 1939-1945—Manpower

World War, 1939-1945—Reparations

RT   Reconstruction (1939-1951)

World War, 1939-1945—Education and the war   940.53

BT   Education

World War, 1939-1945—Engineering and construction   940.54

BT   Military engineering

World War, 1939-1945—Equipment and supplies   940.54

UF   World War, 1939-1945—Arms

World War, 1939-1945—Military supplies

World War, 1939-1945—Military weapons

World War, 1939-1945—Ordnance

World War, 1939-1945—Supplies

World War, 1939-1945—Weapons

BT   Military weapons

World War, 1939-1945—Ethical aspects 940.53

UF   World War, 1939-1945—Moral and religious aspects *[Former heading]*

BT   Ethics

World War, 1939-1945—Evacuation of civilians   940.54

UF   Civilian evacuation

World War, 1939-1945—Civilian evacuation

BT   Civil defense

World War, 1939-1945—Refugees

World War, 1939-1945—Fiction 808.83; 813, etc.

May be used for individual works, collections, or materials about fiction dealing with the Second World War.

World War, 1939-1945—Finance 940.53

Use for materials on the cost and financing of the war, including war debts, and the effect of the war on financial systems, including inflation.

BT   World War, 1939-1945—Economic aspects

World War, 1939-1945—Food question

USE   World War, 1939-1945—Food supply

World War, 1939-1945—Food supply 940.53

UF   World War, 1939-1945—Food question

BT   Food relief

NT   World War, 1939-1945—Civilian relief

World War, 1939-1945—Forced repatriation   940.53

BT   World War, 1939-1945—Prisoners and prisons

RT   World War, 1939-1945—Refugees

BT = Broader Term   NT = Narrower Term   RT = Related Term   SA = See Also   UF = Used For

World War, 1939-1945—Governments in
    exile   940.53
  UF   Governments in exile
  BT   World War, 1939-1945—Diplo-
         matic history
World War, 1939-1945—Guerrillas
  USE   World War, 1939-1945—Un-
          derground movements
World War, 1939-1945—Health aspects
    940.54
  BT   Armies—Medical care
       Military health
       Sanitation
World War, 1939-1945—Hospitals
  USE   World War, 1939-1945—Medi-
          cal care
World War, 1939-1945—Human resources
  USE   World War, 1939-1945—
          Manpower
World War, 1939-1945—Humor   940.53
  UF   World War, 1939-1945—Humor,
         caricatures, etc. *[Former
         heading]*
  BT   Wit and humor
World War, 1939-1945—Humor, carica-
    tures, etc.
  USE   World War, 1939-1945—Car-
          toons and caricatures
        World War, 1939-1945—Hu-
          mor
World War, 1939-1945—Iconography
  USE   World War, 1939-1945—Art
          and the war
World War, 1939-1945, in art
  USE   World War, 1939-1945—Art
          and the war
World War, 1939-1945, in literature
  USE   World War, 1939-1945—Liter-
          ature and the war
World War, 1939-1945, in motion pictures
  USE   World War, 1939-1945—Mo-
          tion pictures and the war
World War, 1939-1945—Influence
    940.53
World War, 1939-1945—Jews   940.53
  RT   Holocaust, 1933-1945
World War, 1939-1945—Jews—Rescue
    940.54
  UF   Rescue of Jews, 1939-1945
  BT   Jews—Persecutions

World War, 1939-1945—Journalists
    940.54
  UF   World War, 1939-1945—Corre-
         spondents
       World War, 1939-1945—War
         correspondents
  BT   Journalists
World War, 1939-1945—Literature and
    the war   809; 810, etc.; 940.53
  UF   World War, 1939-1945, in litera-
         ture
  BT   Literature
World War, 1939-1945—Manpower
    940.54
  UF   World War, 1939-1945—Human
         resources *[Former heading]*
  BT   World War, 1939-1945—Eco-
         nomic aspects
World War, 1939-1945—Maps   940.53
  BT   Maps
World War, 1939-1945—Medical care
    940.54
  UF   World War, 1939-1945—Hospi-
         tals
  BT   Armies—Medical care
       Military health
       Military hospitals
       Military medicine
  NT   World War, 1939-1945—Civil-
         ian relief
World War, 1939-1945—Military supplies
  USE   World War, 1939-1945—
          Equipment and supplies
World War, 1939-1945—Military weapons
  USE   World War, 1939-1945—
          Equipment and supplies
World War, 1939-1945—Missing in ac-
    tion   940.54
  BT   Missing in action
       World War, 1939-1945—Pris-
         oners and prisons
World War, 1939-1945—Monuments
    725
  BT   Monuments
World War, 1939-1945—Moral and reli-
    gious aspects
  USE   World War, 1939-1945—Ethi-
          cal aspects
        World War, 1939-1945—Reli-
          gious aspects

BT = Broader Term   NT = Narrower Term   RT = Related Term   SA = See Also   UF = Used For

World War, 1939-1945—Motion pictures and the war   791.43; 940.53

May be used for individual works, collections, or materials about films dealing with the Second World War.

UF   World War, 1939-1945, in motion pictures

BT   Motion pictures
      War films

World War, 1939-1945—Museums   940.53

BT   Museums

World War, 1939-1945—Naval operations   940.54

UF   World War, 1939-1945—Battles, sieges, etc.

NT   World War, 1939-1945—Amphibious operations

World War, 1939-1945—Naval operations—Submarine   940.54

UF   World War, 1939-1945—Submarine operations

BT   Submarine warfare

World War, 1939-1945—Occupied territories   940.54

Use for general treatment of the subject.

SA   names of countries with the subdivision *History—1940-1945, German occupation,* e.g. **Netherlands—History—1940-1945, German occupation;** or with the subdivision *History—1945- , Allied Occupation,* e.g. **Japan—History—1945-1952, Allied Occupation;** to be added as needed

BT   Military occupation
      World War, 1939-1945—Territorial questions

NT   Japan—History—1945-1952, Allied occupation
      Netherlands—History—1940-1945, German occupation
      World War, 1939-1945—Collaborationists
      World War, 1939-1945—Underground movements

World War, 1939-1945—Ordnance

USE   World War, 1939-1945—Equipment and supplies

World War, 1939-1945—Peace   940.53

BT   Peace

World War, 1939-1945—Personal narratives   940.53; 940.54

Use for collective or individual eyewitness reports or autobiographical accounts of the war in general. Accounts limited to a specific topic are entered under that topic.

BT   Autobiographies
      Biography

World War, 1939-1945—Pictorial works   940.53022

World War, 1939-1945—Poetry   808.81; 811, etc.; 811.008, etc.

May be used for individual works, collections, or materials about poetry dealing with the Second World War.

BT   Historical poetry
      War poetry

World War, 1939-1945—Prisoners and prisons   940.54

BT   Concentration camps
      Prisoners of war

NT   World War, 1939-1945—Forced repatriation
      World War, 1939-1945—Missing in action

World War, 1939-1945—Propaganda   940.54

BT   Propaganda

World War, 1939-1945—Protest movements   940.53

UF   World War, 1939-1945—Antiwar movements
      World War, 1939-1945—Protests, demonstrations, etc.
      [Former heading]

NT   World War, 1939-1945—Conscientious objectors

World War, 1939-1945—Protests, demonstrations, etc.

USE   World War, 1939-1945—Protest movements

World War, 1939-1945—Psychological aspects   940.53

BT   Psychological warfare

World War, 1939-1945—Public opinion   940.53

BT   Public opinion

World War, 1939-1945—Railroads

USE   World War, 1939-1945—Transportation

BT = Broader Term   NT = Narrower Term   RT = Related Term   SA = See Also   UF = Used For

World War, 1939-1945—Reconstruction
USE   Reconstruction (1939-1951)
World War, 1939-1945—Refugees
    940.53
  UF   World War, 1939-1945—Displaced persons
  BT   Political refugees
  NT   World War, 1939-1945—Evacuation of civilians
  RT   World War, 1939-1945—Civilian relief
      World War, 1939-1945—Forced repatriation
World War, 1939-1945—Regimental histories   940.54
World War, 1939-1945—Religious aspects   940.53
  UF   World War, 1939-1945—Moral and religious aspects *[Former heading]*
World War, 1939-1945—Reparations
    940.53
  UF   Reparations (World War, 1939-1945)
  BT   Reconstruction (1939-1951)
      World War, 1939-1945—Economic aspects
World War, 1939-1945—Resistance movements
USE   World War, 1939-1945—Underground movements
World War, 1939-1945—Secret service
    940.54
  BT   Secret service
World War, 1939-1945—Social aspects
    940.53
World War, 1939-1945—Social work
USE   World War, 1939-1945—War work
World War, 1939-1945—Songs   782.42
  UF   World War, 1939-1945—Songs and music *[Former heading]*
  BT   Military music
      War songs
World War, 1939-1945—Songs and music
USE   World War, 1939-1945—Songs
World War, 1939-1945—Sources
    940.53
  BT   History—Sources

World War, 1939-1945—Submarine operations
USE   World War, 1939-1945—Naval operations—Submarine
World War, 1939-1945—Supplies
USE   World War, 1939-1945—Equipment and supplies
World War, 1939-1945—Territorial questions   940.53
  BT   Boundaries
  NT   World War, 1939-1945—Occupied territories
World War, 1939-1945—Theater and the war   792; 940.53
  BT   Theater
World War, 1939-1945—Transportation
    940.54
  UF   World War, 1939-1945—Railroads
  BT   Transportation
World War, 1939-1945—Treaties
    940.53
  BT   Treaties
World War, 1939-1945—Underground movements   940.54
  UF   Anti-fascist movements
      Anti-Nazi movement
      Underground movements (World War, 1939-1945)
      World War, 1939-1945—Guerrillas
      World War, 1939-1945—Resistance movements
  BT   World War, 1939-1945—Occupied territories
World War, 1939-1945—United States
    940.53; 940.54; 973.917
  UF   United States—History—1939-1945, World War
      United States—World War, 1939-1945
World War, 1939-1945—War correspondents
USE   World War, 1939-1945—Journalists
World War, 1939-1945—War work
    940.53
  UF   World War, 1939-1945—Charities

BT = Broader Term   NT = Narrower Term   RT = Related Term   SA = See Also   UF = Used For

World War, 1939-1945—War work—*Con-tinued*

World War, 1939-1945—Social work

NT   **World War, 1939-1945—Civilian relief**

World War, 1939-1945—Weapons

USE   **World War, 1939-1945—Equipment and supplies**

World War, 1939-1945—Women 940.53; 940.54

BT   **Women**

World War III   355

UF   Third World War

BT   **War**

        World politics

World Wide Web   004.67

UF   Web (Information retrieval system)

        World Wide Web (Information retrieval system)

        WWW (Information retrieval system)

BT   **Internet**

NT   **World Wide Web servers**

World Wide Web (Information retrieval system)

USE   **World Wide Web**

World Wide Web servers   004.67

UF   Web servers

BT   **World Wide Web**

World's Fair (1992 : Seville, Spain)

USE   **Expo 92 (Seville, Spain)**

World's fairs

USE   **Exhibitions**

        Fairs

World's records

USE   **World records**

Worms   592

BT   **Invertebrates**

Worry   152.4

BT   **Emotions**

RT   **Anxiety**

Worship   248.3; 264; 291.3

UF   Devotion

BT   **Religion**

        Theology

NT   **Church year**

        Devotional exercises

        Prayer

        Public worship

        Sacrifice

Worship of the dead

USE   **Ancestor worship**

Worth

USE   **Values**

Wounded, First aid to

USE   **First aid**

Wounds and injuries   617.1

UF   Injuries

SA   classes of persons, animals, organs of the body, and plants and crops with the subdivision *Wounds and injuries,* e.g. **Horses—Wounds and injuries; Foot—Wounds and injuries;** etc., to be added as needed

BT   **Accidents**

NT   **Fractures**

Wrapping of gifts

USE   **Gift wrapping**

Wrecks

USE   **Accidents**

        Shipwrecks

Wrestling   796.812

BT   **Athletics**

NT   **Judo**

Writers

USE   **Authors**

Writing   411

Use for materials on the process or result of recording language in the form of conventionalized visible marks or signs on a surface. Materials limited to writing with a pen or pencil and practical or prescriptive guides to penmanship or the art of writing are entered under **Handwriting.** Materials on handwriting as an expression of the writer's character are entered under **Graphology.** Materials on the alphabet or writing of a particular language are entered under the name of the language with the subdivisions *Alphabet* and *Writing.*

BT   **Communication**

        Language and languages

        Language arts

NT   **Abbreviations**

        Alphabet

        Autographs

        Calligraphy

        Cryptography

        Graphology

        Handwriting

BT = Broader Term   NT = Narrower Term   RT = Related Term   SA = See Also   UF = Used For

Writing—*Continued*
       Hieroglyphics
       Picture writing
       Shorthand
       Typewriting
       Whole language
       Writing of numerals
  RT   Ciphers
Writing (Authorship)
  USE   Authorship
       Creative writing
Writing of numerals   513
  UF   Numeral formation
       Numeral writing
       Numerals, Writing of
  BT   **Handwriting**
       Numerals
       Writing
Writing—Patterning
  USE   **Language arts—Patterning**
Writing—Study and teaching
  USE   **Handwriting**
Writings of gay men
  USE   **Gay men's writings**
Writings of lesbians
  USE   **Lesbians' writings**
Wrought iron work
  USE   **Ironwork**
WWW (Information retrieval system)
  USE   **World Wide Web**
X-15 (Rocket aircraft)   629.133
  BT   **Rocket planes**
X-rays   539.7
  UF   Radiography
       Roentgen rays
       X rays *[Former heading]*
  BT   **Electromagnetic waves**
       Radiation
  NT   **Gamma rays**
       Tomography
       Vacuum tubes
  RT   **Radiotherapy**
X rays
  USE   **X-rays**
Xerographic art
  USE   **Copy art**
Xerography
  USE   **Photocopying**
YA literature
  USE   **Young adult literature**

Yacht basins
  USE   **Marinas**
Yachts and yachting   797.1
  UF   Regattas
  BT   **Boatbuilding**
       Boats and boating
       Ocean travel
       Ships
       Voyages and travels
       Water sports
  NT   **Marinas**
  RT   **Sailing**
Yard sales
  USE   **Garage sales**
Yarn   677
  BT   **Textile industry**
  NT   **Cotton**
       Flax
  RT   **Wool**
Yearbooks
  USE   **Periodicals**
       and subjects with the subdivision *Periodicals*, e.g. **Engineering—Periodicals**; to be added as needed
Yearbooks, Student
  USE   **School yearbooks**
Yeast   641.3
  BT   **Fermentation**
       Fungi
Yellow fever   616.9
  BT   **Tropical medicine**
Yeti   001.9
  UF   Abominable snowman
  BT   **Monsters**
       Mythical animals
Yiddish language   439
    May be subdivided like **English language.**
  UF   German Hebrew
       Jewish language
       Jews—Language
       Judaeo-German
  BT   **Language and languages**
Yiddish literature   839
    May use same subdivisions and names of literary forms as for **English literature.**
  BT   **Jewish literature**
Yippies
  USE   **Hippies**
Yoga   181; 613.7
  BT   **Hindu philosophy**

BT = Broader Term   NT = Narrower Term   RT = Related Term   SA = See Also   UF = Used For

Yoga—*Continued*
>>   Hinduism
>>   Theosophy
>   NT   Hatha yoga
Yoga exercises
>   USE   Hatha yoga
Yoga, Hatha
>   USE   Hatha yoga
Yom Kippur   296.4
>   UF   Atonement, Day of
>>   Day of Atonement
>   BT   Jewish holidays
Yom Kippur War, 1973
>   USE   Israel-Arab War, 1973
Yoruba (African people)   305.896
>   BT   Africans
>>   Native peoples
Yosemite National Park (Calif.)   719;
>   979.4
>   BT   National parks and reserves—
>>   United States
Yosemite National Park (Calif.)—Pictori-
>   al works   979.4
Young adult literature   808.8; 809;
>   810.8, etc.
>   Use for collections or materials about litera-
>   ture published for teenage readers. Materials
>   on the reading interests of teenagers and lists
>   of books for teenagers are entered under
>   **Teenagers—Books and reading.**
>   UF   Books for teenagers
>>   Teenage literature
>>   Teenagers—Literature
>>   YA literature
>>   Young adults' literature *[Former
>>   heading]*
>   BT   **Literature**
>   RT   **Young adults' library services**
Young adults
>   USE   **Teenagers**
>>   **Youth**
Young adults—Books and reading
>   USE   **Teenagers—Books and reading**
Young adults' library services   027.62
>   UF   Libraries and young adults
>>   Libraries, Young adults'
>>   Library services to teenagers
>>   Library services to young adults
>>   Teenagers' library services
>>   Young people's libraries
>   BT   **Library services**
>   RT   **Children's libraries**

>>   High school libraries
>>   **Young adult literature**
Young adults' literature
>   USE   **Young adult literature**
Young consumers   640.73; 658.8
>   UF   Children as consumers
>>   Teenage consumers
>>   Youth market
>   BT   **Consumers**
Young men   305.31
>   Use for materials on men in the general age
>   range of eighteen through twenty-five years.
>   Materials on the time of life between thirteen
>   and twenty-five, as well as on people in that
>   greater age range are entered under **Youth.**
>   BT   **Men**
>>   **Youth**
>   RT   **Boys**
Young people
>   USE   **Teenagers**
>>   **Youth**
Young people's libraries
>   USE   **Young adults' library services**
Young persons
>   USE   **Teenagers**
>>   **Youth**
Young women   305.4
>   Use for materials on women in the general
>   age range of eighteen through twenty-five
>   years. Materials on the time of life between
>   thirteen and twenty-five, as well as on people
>   in that greater age range are entered under
>   **Youth.**
>   BT   **Women**
>>   **Youth**
>   RT   **Girls**
Youngest child
>   USE   **Birth order**
Youth (May subdiv. geog.)   305.235
>   Use for materials on the time of life be-
>   tween thirteen and twenty-five years, as well
>   as on people in this general age range. Materi-
>   als limited to teen youth are entered under
>   **Teenagers.** Materials limited to people in the
>   general age range of eighteen through twenty-
>   five years of age are entered under **Young
>   men** or **Young women.** Materials on the pro-
>   cess or state of growing up are entered under
>   **Adolescence.**
>   UF   Young adults
>>   Young people
>>   Young persons
>   SA   youth of particular racial or eth-
>>   nic groups, to be added as
>>   needed

Youth—*Continued*
    BT   Age
    NT   African American youth
          Church work with youth
          Dropouts
          Teenagers
          Television and youth
          Young men
          Young women
Youth—Alcohol use   613.81; 616.86
    UF   Alcohol and youth
          Drinking and youth
    NT   **Drinking age**
Youth and drugs
    USE   **Youth—Drug use**
Youth and narcotics
    USE   **Youth—Drug use**
Youth and television
    USE   **Television and youth**
Youth—Drug use   613.8; 616.86
    UF   Drugs and youth
          Narcotics and youth
          Youth and drugs
          Youth and narcotics
    NT   **Teenagers—Drug use**
    RT   **Juvenile delinquency**
Youth—Employment   331.3
    UF   Child labor
          Employment of youth
    BT   **Age. and employment**
          Employment
          Labor
          Labor supply
    NT   **Teenagers—Employment**
    RT   **Summer employment**
Youth hostels   647.94
    UF   Hostels, Youth
          Tourist accommodations
    BT   **Community centers**
          Hotels and motels
Youth market
    USE   **Young consumers**
Youth movement (May subdiv. geog.)
    322.4
    UF   Student movement
          Student protests, demonstrations,
            etc.
          Student revolt
    BT   **Social movements**
    NT   **Students—Political activity**

Youth—Religious life   248.4; 291.4
    BT   **Religious life**
    NT   **Teenagers—Religious life**
Youth—United States   305.230973
    UF   American youth
          United States—Youth
    NT   **Teenagers—United States**
Zen Buddhism   294.3
    BT   **Buddhism**
Zeppelins
    USE   **Airships**
Zero gravity
    USE   **Weightlessness**
Zeus (Greek deity)   292.2
    BT   **Gods and goddesses**
Zinc   669
    BT   **Chemical elements**
          Metals
Zionism   320.5
    UF   Zionist movement
    RT   **Jews—Restoration**
Zionist movement
    USE   **Zionism**
Zip code (May subdiv. geog.)   383
    UF   Postal delivery code
    BT   **Postal service**
Zodiac   133.5; 523
    BT   **Astrology**
          Astronomy
Zoning   346.04; 354.3
    UF   City planning—Zone system
          Districting (in city planning)
    BT   **City planning**
Zoogeography
    USE   **Biogeography**
Zoological gardens
    USE   **Zoos**
Zoological specimens—Collection and
    preservation   590.75
    UF   Collections of natural specimens
          Preservation of zoological speci-
            mens
          Specimens, Preservation of
    SA   types of specimens with the sub-
          division *Collection and pres-*
          ervation, e.g. **Birds—Collec-**
          tion and preservation; to be
          added as needed
    BT   **Collectors and collecting**

BT = Broader Term   NT = Narrower Term   RT = Related Term   SA = See Also   UF = Used For

Zoological specimens—Collection and preservation—*Continued*
   NT   **Birds—Collection and preservation**
   RT   **Taxidermy**
Zoology   **590**

> Use for materials on the science of animals. Nonscientific materials on animals are entered under **Animals**.

   UF   Animal kingdom
           Animal physiology
           Fauna
   SA   names of divisions, classes, etc., of the animal kingdom, e.g. **Invertebrates; Vertebrates; Birds; Mammals;** etc.; and names of animals, to be added as needed
   BT   **Biology**
           Science
   NT   **Animal behavior**
           Animals—Anatomy
           Comparative anatomy
           Comparative psychology
           Economic zoology
           Embryology
   RT   **Animals**
           Natural history
           Zoos

Zoology—Anatomy
   USE   **Animals—Anatomy**
Zoology, Economic
   USE   **Economic zoology**
Zoology of the Bible
   USE   **Bible—Natural history**
Zoology—United States
   USE   **Animals—United States**
Zoos   **590.73**
   UF   Zoological gardens
   SA   names of individual zoos, to be added as needed
   BT   **Parks**
   NT   **Petting zoos**
   RT   **Animals**
           Zoology
